HARRIS'
Complete Guide to
NAICS

Acknowledgments

Creating a book of this scope doesn't happen without the hands-on support of many people. I want to express my profound appreciation to the following colleagues who comprised the team that made the vision of this book a reality—Diana Gardner, Colin Klein, Erin Murch, Carol Nuebler, Vicki Rees, Shelby Rosen, Paula Scroggy, and Robbie Zuchowsky. To Diana, none of this would have been possible without your expertise and guidance—cheers!

Additionally, I would like to express my deep appreciation to the senior management team at Harris, especially Dennis Abrahams, President, and David Wilkof, Vice President of Marketing, who had the vision and foresight to recognize the benefits and opportunities this book would provide our customers.

Also, a special thanks to John Murphy, Assistant Division Chief for Classification Activities at the Census Bureau, for never failing to have the answers to even the most mundane—yet important—questions.

Published by Harris InfoSource
2057 East Aurora Road
Twinsburg, OH 44087-1999
Phone: 1-800-888-5900
Fax: 1-800-643-5997

ISBN 1-55600-922-4
ISSN 1536-7436

www.harrisinfo.com
Copyright © 2001 by Harris InfoSource

First printing, September 2001

ISIC codes are the property of the United Nations and are published here by arrangement with:
United Nations
New York, NY 10017

Photographs provided by Cleveland, Ohio Public Library photograph collection, PhotoDisc™, DigitalVision and Dynamic Graphics, Inc.

A reference guide based on the *North American Industry Classification System* (NAICS), developed by the governments of the United States of America, Canada, and Mexico. Features complete NAICS titles and descriptions of industries as well as conversion tables to aid in the transition from the *Standard Industrial Classification* (SIC) coding system to NAICS—a changeover enacted in 1997 by the U.S. Office of Management and Budget. Also included are tables converting the *International Standard Industrial Classification* (ISIC) *Rev. 3* coding system to NAICS. Developed by the staff of Harris InfoSource.

Find us on the Internet at www.harrisinfo.com

HARRIS'
Complete Guide to
NAICS

Your ultimate reference to
NAICS, SIC & ISIC Codes

Edited by Scott M. Vogel

HARRIS INFOSOURCE™
Our Quality Enables Your Growth

Twinsburg, Ohio • www.harrisinfo.com

Foreword

TAKE THE KEYS, START THE CAR, AND LET'S GET UNDERWAY. Destination? The open highway of NAICS. In your hands is a valuable business tool—one that can steer your business in new directions and more closely focus your marketing initiatives.

Put the car in reverse and go back in time when a television was only capable of receiving three stations via an antenna. Now, we have the ability to receive over 500 stations that cater to almost every interest via fiber optic cable or satellite dish. You can even purchase a television set over the Internet.

The television is just one example of how industry has changed in manufacturing, design, retail, and function. The 60-year-old SIC code system was unable to adapt to these changes and in 1997 was replaced by the North American Industry Classification System (NAICS). NAICS is an exciting change that is more relevant, consistent, and flexible with today's ever-changing economy. This is a good change, as NAICS offers a new and more detailed view of the marketplace. That's a statement I can stand behind, following hundreds of hours of research and conversations with countless experts.

When I started this project, I thought I had a pretty good idea of how the switch to NAICS would positively impact the world of business statistics. Now that the book is complete, I've realized that NAICS affects much more than just facts and figures. Not only will NAICS make a positive impact today, it also paves the way for a clearer tomorrow.

Harris' Complete Guide to NAICS is designed to be an easy-to-use road map to classification codes. With that said, proceed to the NAICS highway and utilize the benefits of NAICS. Watch your organization grow and succeed.

—Scott M. Vogel

Table of Contents

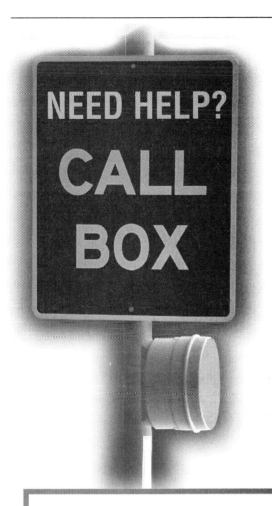

NEED HELP? CALL BOX

Harris' Complete Guide to NAICS

QUICK TIPS

To maximize your comprehension of NAICS in a minimal amount of time, we've created notes in the margins accompanied by the road signs below.

Use this guide as a kind of road map—enabling you to get the most out of the information contained within these pages.

You'll be on the road in no time.

Guide to Signs

ATTENTION
This icon highlights a significant tidbit of information which could impact the way you use/understand industry statistics.

GO TO
This sign acts as a link to other relevant areas of information or sections within the Guide. Think of these signs as a "hyperlink" within the book.

CONSTRUCTION
This symbol indicates that there has been work done to the sector, resulting in significant changes to the retired SIC structure.

NAICS Overview

NAICS Short Titles

SIC Short Titles

ISIC Short Titles

SIC to NAICS

NAICS to SIC

ISIC to NAICS

NAICS Titles & Descrip.

NAICS Alphabetical

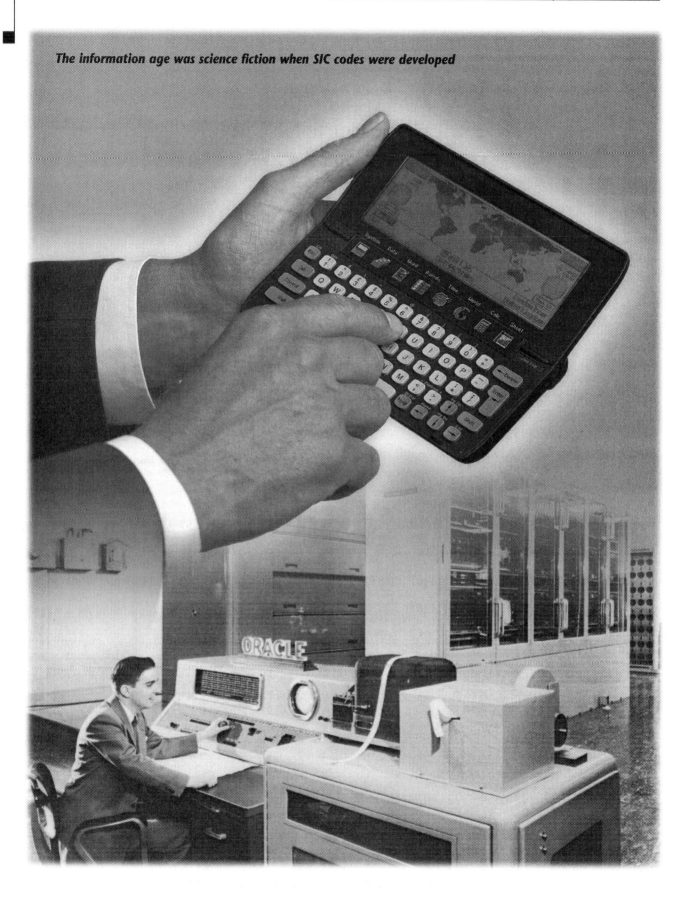

The information age was science fiction when SIC codes were developed

Who Should Use This Book?

MERGE: The Harris Interchange is your expressway to making the SIC to NAICS conversion and vice versa. See page 87 to get started.

NAICS is providing a relevant classification system for today's economy. For the first time you will be able to target specific businesses within the Information sector and Services economy. You will also have the ability to target the 358 new industries classified in NAICS. NAICS is the first global classification system allowing you to target businesses in Canada, Mexico, and the United States. The conversion tables—the Harris Interchange—provide you with all of the SIC and NAICS codes and allow you to find the NAICS codes for the businesses that you want to target. We designed this book to be used by anyone needing a better understanding of NAICS and the effect it will have on your business.

The NAICS codes can help anyone gain a clear perspective on target markets and classify customers according to new industries developed since the final SIC revision in 1987. Can you benefit from the new system? You bet.

Sales and Marketing

Today many of you use industry databases to target businesses for direct mailings, create prospect lists and sales territories, conduct market research, define competition, and analyze industries. Industry classification codes provide you an effective way to search the many private databases of business information in pursuit of your target audience. For the first time we have an industry classification system that focuses on an industry's process versus their product. The following example shows just how important this change can be. A manufacturer of industrial baking goods wanted to target bakeries for marketing purposes. Under SIC, the list of bakeries would include both bakeries that bake on the premises and retail only establishments.

Case Study: Learn how NAICS benefits sales & marketing professionals, see page 13.

Your list would include a large number of businesses that would not meet your market. Under NAICS you are able to distinguish between retail and wholesale establishments and create a list that will only target potential clients.

Recruiters

If you use industry databases to target companies for potential employees, the ability to search industry data via NAICS will be a great advantage. For the first time, you will have the opportunity to target the hot new industries within the economy. NAICS has specific sectors for businesses that provide information and provides greater granularity of the technology and services sectors of our economy. You will be able to create searches that target these businesses without having to spend lots of time sorting through lists of businesses that SIC classified under one broad Service division.

Professionals

If you identify yourself as a tax advisor, attorney, banker, accountant, or economist or are a part of any other profession that uses government

FACT
There are **358 new industries** that **SIC didn't identify**

data and forms, NAICS is a part of your everyday life. All federal forms now require NAICS. If you have used SIC codes in your federal filing of forms for your clients, you have already been required by the government to provide NAICS codes on these forms. The conversion tables provide you with a way to look up industries either by the old SIC code or the new NAICS code and find their counterparts.

The Harris Interchange: Your Reliable Reference Tool

Harris InfoSource provides accurate business information, since 1971. In the spirit of continuing to provide you with affordable ways to gain a competitive edge, Harris is publishing this NAICS classification reference book. Harris InfoSource understands how businesses use industry classifications and is dedicated to providing you with an easy-to-understand approach to implementing the use of NAICS in your organization.

Harris believes that the use of industry codes is essential to successful "best practice." Many of our customers currently use SIC codes to search industry databases. These searches provide them with ways to generate sales leads, create sales territories, target direct mailings, and focus on companies for recruitment purposes. SIC codes have been relied upon as a useful indexing method in Harris databases and across hundreds of U.S. databases from other information providers and online vendors. In 1997, the U.S. government replaced SIC codes with the North American Industry Classification System (NAICS). NAICS is more than a revision of SIC; it is a complete rewrite using a "fresh slate" approach.

Harris has stood alone as an information provider incorporating NAICS as a standard feature. To take full advantage of this enhancement to our products, you will need to understand how NAICS is different and how those differences will affect and improve your ability to target companies. For example, NAICS provides us with a classification system for the first time that provides users with a way to target businesses in the information sector. NAICS provides a focus on services and the new technology industries that have emerged in the last decade. These changes have resulted in the recoding of over five million business establishments to NAICS.

In the 30 years that Harris has been in business, we have witnessed the changes to the economy and the needs of our customers. We believe in the importance of providing in-depth, accurate information—including an up-to-date industry classification system. If you are doing business beyond North America, Harris InfoSource can also provide you with ISIC code information as an Official Licensee of United Nations ISIC classification codes.

NAICS Overview
All About NAICS

Curious about why the government decided to change its industrial code numbering system? Think that SIC doesn't need any improvements? How would you classify satellite communications?

Are you aware that NAICS has 10 more industrial sectors than SIC? Establishments are now classified and grouped based on similar processes versus end product. Are you in need of understanding and targeting industries from a global perspective versus just the United States? If you are looking for answers to these questions and others along those lines, take some time to read this section and gain an understanding of how NAICS is changing the way we classify industries.

FACT

NAICS has *10 more* industrial sectors than SIC

This section explores the following topics:

■ *Use of industrial codes today*

■ *Why NAICS is an improvement over SIC*

■ *New and improved Industry and Service Classifications*

■ *NAICS Hierarchy and Code structure*

■ *NAICS implementation and how the changes will affect your government and private vendor data*

Why do we have industrial codes?

The original purpose of industrial codes and the reason Standard Industrial Codes (SIC) were developed in the 1930s was to categorize the reporting of industrial activity data. This gave government agencies an effective way to perform their functions and provide better statistical economic analysis. Today this data is used in sales and marketing applications as a way to classify targeted organizations and potential prospects as well as measure their performance in the market.

SIC codes were developed during a time when our economy was manufacturing based—long before the development of a strong information and services economy. The United States of the 1930s had an internal focus compared to our current global view. Last updated in 1987 by the U.S. government, SIC codes no longer provide an effective way to classify our new and ever changing economy. Even with updates, it is impossible to effectively classify new e-commerce, telecommunications and computer industries in the 1930s framework that would have considered these ideas as far fetched as satellite communication and space travel.

NAICS Overview

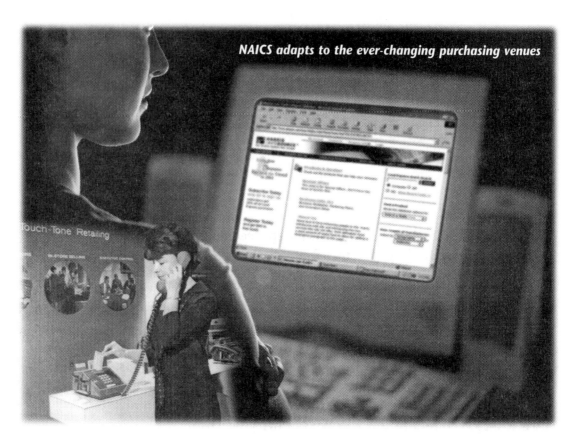

NAICS adapts to the ever-changing purchasing venues

How NAICS came about

In 1991 an international conference was held in Williamsburg, VA, to identify the issues to be considered when constructing a new classification system. Based on solicited feedback from appointed government specialists, the Economic Classification Policy Committee (ECPC), under the Office of Management and Budget (OMB), was formed and charged with taking a "fresh slate" approach to creating a new economic classification system. This new system would follow four principles:

1) Use a production-oriented conceptual framework
2) Pay special attention to
   - Emerging industries
   - Service industries
   - Advanced technology industries
3) Maintain time series continuity if possible
4) Increase compatibility with the United Nations International Standard Industrial Classification (ISIC)

By using these four guiding principles, NAICS moved away from the problems that constrain SIC toward a classification system that closely resembles the economy we work in today.

NAICS was developed in cooperation with Statistics Canada and Mexico's Instituto Nacional de Estadística, Geografía e Informática (INEGI), making it the first classification system that covers North America. This allows you to classify and compare information across North American countries, giving you a more global perspective. There is also an increased compatibility with the ISIC codes, providing you with a way to use NAICS to gather and compare industry data across the globe.

The Office of Management and Budget (OMB) adopted NAICS in 1997 as the industry classification system to be used by the statistical agencies of the United States. NAICS replaces the 1987 version of SIC.

A timeline for full government implementation is provided in the NAICS Implementation section of this document.

Go to page 24 and reference Figure 7 for the NAICS implementation plan.

Why is NAICS an improvement over SIC?

NAICS
Overview

By now it is probably evident that NAICS is a significant change from SIC. You may be asking "Why do I need to invest in a new classification system?" There are two reasons why it is vital: SIC has been replaced by NAICS and NAICS truly represents our present economy. This section outlines the benefits that come from using NAICS classifications and compares NAICS to SIC, showing why NAICS is superior to SIC.

Benefits of NAICS

For the first time, we have a classification system that recognizes the new industries in our economy and the importance of service based industries to our continuing growth. This is a great leap forward from SIC where in code 7389 Business Services Not Elsewhere Classified industries as wildly diverse as wig making, telemarketing and recording studios are grouped together. Many of us would be challenged to determine just what these industries have in common. There are a number of eight-digit systems that have attempted to fix this

problem, but remember they are based on SIC and still map back to this outdated division.

NAICS wiped the slate clean and brought together the following concepts:
- NAICS is based on a single conceptual framework: businesses that use similar production processes are grouped together. Keep in mind the example of code 7389 to understand the importance of this point.

This is a great leap forward from SIC where in code 7389 Business Services not elsewhere classified industries as wildly diverse as wig making, telemarketing and recording studios are grouped together.

SIC / NAICS
a comparison

SIC	NAICS
Use is being discontinued by all government agencies. For a complete implementation schedule see the Implementation section.	Used by all government agencies.
Published in 1941 – last updated 1987	Published in 1997 – updated every 5 years
Focus on manufacturing	Focus on Services and Emerging Technologies
US centric	Developed with Mexico and Canada Comparable to ISIC
Divisions grouped by major income derivation	Sectors grouped by similar production processes
10 divisions – 5 are service related 1004 defined industries – 416 are service related	20 sectors – 16 are service related 1170 defined industries – 565 are service related
4-digit system – not comparable to any other system*	6-digit system – comparable to 3 countries at 5-digit level

The following table outlines the significant differences between SIC and NAICS. The issues surrounding SIC also carry over to any proprietary code sets based on SIC.

Figure 1

*Private 8-digit systems based on SIC are also not comparable to any other system.

Overview

- NAICS was designed from its inception to include new and emerging industries. It recognizes new industries and provides a framework in which industries can be introduced in the future.
- NAICS was developed jointly with Canada and Mexico, enabling comparability of data among all three countries. Also compatible with the ISIC classification of the United Nations.

The advantages that NAICS will provide outweigh the short-term discomfort involved in changing your systems. NAICS provides the following principal advantages:

- **Relevant**—NAICS identifies new industries, revises concepts and reorganizes classifications.
- **Consistent**—NAICS classifies businesses into industries based on one principle instead of several. Businesses are classified together based upon similar production processes.
- **Comparable**—NAICS provides a North American industry classification system developed with Mexico and Canada.
- **Flexible**—Scheduled to be updated every five years. Regular updates will ensure that NAICS keeps pace with changes in our economy.

> *NAICS replaces or revises approximately 60 percent of the previously available SIC industries.*

What does it all mean?

NAICS provides 1,170 detailed United States industry classifications, a 15 percent increase in total classifications compared to those available under SIC. NAICS replaces or revises approximately 60 percent of the previously available SIC industries. It provides 358 new industries that SIC did not identify, 390 that are revised from their SIC definitions, and 422 that continue essentially the same.

So what does all this mean to you? Major shifts have occurred because of the "clean slate" approach used creating NAICS. This section explores the fundamental changes, including

- A list of new NAICS sectors compared to SIC divisions.
- A list of new sectors and major changes to existing sectors, including new definitions for Retail and Wholesale.
- An explanation of the new approach to classifying business.
- New Definitions for Establishment and Auxiliary Establishment.

NAICS Economic Sectors

Sectors are the highest classification in the NAICS system. It is similar to the familiar SIC Divisions. NAICS now has twice as many sectors as SIC divisions, increasing the number to 20 sectors. These new sectors reflect the new businesses that are now part of our changing economy.

Figure 2 lists each SIC division and shows it with the closest related NAICS sector. Note the new sectors that have no SIC counterpart. Also, keep in mind that even those that appear to have a good match at the sector/division level do not match at the lower levels. No NAICS sector has the same subsector classifications. Take the case of the Construction sector, one of the least changed sectors. It has three subsectors that are similar to the SIC; however three of the 28 detailed industries are new, and 14 are revised.

SIC Division / NAICS Sector *a comparison*

SIC Division title		NAICS Sector title	
A	Agriculture, Forestry, and Fishing	11	Agriculture, Forestry, and Hunting
B	Mining	21	Mining
C	Construction	23	Construction
D	Manufacturing	31-33	Manufacturing
E	Transportation, Communication and Public Utilities	22	Utilities
		48-49	Transportation and Warehousing
F	Wholesale Trade	42	Wholesale Trade
G	Retail Trade	44-45	Retail Trade
		72	Accommodation and Food Services
H	Finance, Insurance, and Real Estate	52	Finance and Insurance
		53	Real Estate and Rental and Leasing
I	Services	51	Information
		54	Professional, Scientific, and Technical Services
		56	Administrative and Support and Waste
		55	Management and Remediation Services
		61	Educational Services
		62	Health Care and Social Assistance
		71	Arts, Entertainment, and Recreation
		81	Other Services (except Public Administration)
J	Public Administration	92	Public Administration
K	None (previously, categories within each division)	55	Management of Companies and Enterprises

Figure 2

CASE STUDY:
Straight Facts Marketing, Inc.

The Company: Straight Facts Marketing, Inc. is a small consulting business that specializes in customer segmentation. In this case study we will explore how this consulting firm, using industry classification codes, identified and created customer segments for a leading manufacturer of specialized equipment for manufacturing waste cleanup.

Customer segments are defined by identifying groups with similar demographic characteristics. In the case of our manufacturer we will be looking at what is called

USER: LYNDA GORDON, PRINCIPAL

"firmographics"—characteristics applied to businesses versus consumers. The two most commonly used "firmographic" variables are size of customer and the industry classification for the targeted business. Industry classifications help to identify the nature of the business allowing you to group similar businesses. We will use two industry classifications in this case study: SIC and NAICS.

Problem: Straight Facts Marketing was hired by a manufacturing firm to help identify the types of businesses purchasing their products. The manufacturer has been in business for over 30 years and has a large customer base. Due to the specialization of their product line, they wanted to find out what types of manufacturing businesses used their equipment and create a targeted marketing plan.

Straight Facts Marketing linked the client's customer database to a private vendor's database of manufacturer information. For every customer record, they identified the SIC code and the number of employees listed in the vendor's database. Once this information was linked to all of the manufacturer's customers, the segmentation process began.

The data showed that 65 percent of the manufacturer's customers were included in SIC code 3599 —"Manufacturers of Industrial Machinery, Not Elsewhere Classified." Over 30,000 U.S. manufacturers are classified with this SIC code and their activities range from custom machining, sheet metal work manufacturing, precision turned product manufacturing and other miscellaneous manufacturing. This code covers exactly what its description reads

industrial machinery "not elsewhere classified." The one thing it didn't provide to our manufacturer was a clear understanding of how to target specific customer groups. Their problem was still unsolved.

Solution: Straight Facts Marketing, with the help of their private database vendor, discovered that NAICS codes could provide the manufacturer with the granularity they needed to properly segment their customers into meaningful markets. SIC 3599 is composed of 19 NAICS codes. When its client looked at its customers' NAICS classifications, it was discovered that of the 65 percent of its customers originally classified as SIC 3599, 25 percent were machine shops and the other 40 percent were distributed across 17 NAICS codes.

With this information, Straight Facts Marketing was able to build a schematic that provided detailed customer information including frequency of purchases, dollars spent, highest level of profit, and largest concentration of customers. This information allowed the client to develop a detailed targeted marketing plan including specific advertising programs in select trade journals and purchasing targeted prospect data.

The client feels confident about the data and, for the first time, believes that he understands more about his customers. Without NAICS this manufacturer would have been unable to gather enough detailed information about its customers to effectively target them. After all, how many trade journals are geared towards firms "not elsewhere classified."

Today, Straight Facts Marketing uses NAICS as a standard part of its segmentation work for clients. Lynda says she will never go back to just using SIC codes. NAICS allows her to produce meaningful customer segments for her clients.

Straight Facts Marketing, Inc., provides data analysis consulting services primarily to small- to mid-size manufacturing companies that market either to other manufacturers or directly to retail outlets. Lynda S. Gordon, the principal of Straight Facts Marketing, spent seventeen years as a market research director for such companies as PPG Industries, Sherwin-Williams and Revco Drug Stores and founded Straight Facts Marketing, Inc. in response to a perceived need among small- to mid-size companies that do not have full time research staff for cost-effective top quality market research and data analysis. Since 1996, Straight Facts Marketing, Inc., has helped companies identify target customer profiles, assess market position, and develop a prospecting/new business development strategy based on research information. For more information, contact Straight Facts Marketing at: SFMInc@adelphia.net.

NAICS
Overview

From telephone poles to satellites, a lot has changed in 60 years

Major Changes by Sector

Overview

If you have read this far and are feeling the overwhelming desire to run in the opposite direction and hope that NAICS will go away, we certainly understand. This next section outlines just how significant the NAICS changes really are and may take a couple of passes to fully sink in. But keep in mind that without NAICS you would have no way to effectively gather information about paging, cellular, HMO Medical Centers, and any of the other 355 new industries. After you have read through this section you will be prepared to meet the challenges of understanding how NAICS can give you a leg up in business.

The following provides a description of the new sectors that were added to NAICS. Seven of the new sectors reflect the service-providing businesses in the economy. For those looking for ways to target businesses within these sectors, you will need to take time to review these sectors in greater detail to gain understanding of how they are subdivided—enabling you to target only those industries that hold promise for you.

New **NAICS** United States Industries

Semiconductor machinery manufacturing
Fiber optic cable manufacturing
Software reproducing
Convenience stores
Gasoline station with convenience stores

Warehouse clubs and superstores
Food (health) supplement stores
Pet and pet supply stores
Pet care services
Cable networks

Satellite telecommunications
Paging
Cellular and other wireless telecommunications
Telecommunications resellers
Credit card issuing

Temporary help services
Telemarketing bureaus
Hazardous waste collection
HMO medical centers
Continuing care retirement communities
Casinos

Casino hotels
Bed-and breakfast inns
Limited-service restaurants
Automotive oil change lubricant shops
Diet and weight reducing centers

Figure 3

Major Changes by Sector

Accommodation and Food Service—Sector 72

This sector includes businesses that engage in lodging, food service, and lodging and food service combined. This sector recognizes that these services are often provided at the same location. The sector combines hotels and other lodging places, formerly included in the SIC Services division with eating and drinking places, formerly part of the SIC Retail Trade division. Highlights of this sector include

- 15 industries, 10 of which are new. Examples of new industries include limited-service restaurants and food service contractors.
- Eating and drinking establishments accounted for approximately 10 percent of reported SIC Retail Trade division sales. These establishments will now be reported as part of this service. This shows the huge potential of change you may encounter using economic statistics over the next couple of years as we all move to the NAICS classification system.

ATTENTION:
*Economic statistics
may be impacted.*

Arts, Entertainment and Recreation—Sector 71

This sector includes businesses engaged in meeting the cultural, entertainment, and recreational interests of their patrons. Highlights of this sector include

- 25 industries, 19 of which are new. Examples of new industries include golf courses, country clubs, casinos and sports teams.
- Two industries were moved to this sector from other SIC divisions.
- Most of these industries were included in the Services division of SIC.

*Visit page 587 for
greater detail on
this sector.*

Finance and Insurance—Sector 52

Today we can buy insurance from our banker and traditional banking services from our brokers with more changes on the horizon. This sector recognizes the changes occurring in the United States financial sector. Because of deregulation and the constantly changing structure of financial industries, this sector is not as comparable with Mexico and Canada as other sectors. Highlights of this sector include

- Real Estate was removed from this sector and included in the new sector Real Estate and Rental and Leasing.

*Visit page 517 for
greater detail on
this sector.*

Health Care and Social Assistance—Sector 62

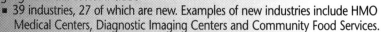

This sector recognizes the growing relationship between heath care and social assistance services. The industries in this sector are grouped in an order starting with those that provide intensive health care, moving to those providing some health care and social services, to those industries only providing social assistance services. Highlights of this sector include

- 39 industries, 27 of which are new. Examples of new industries include HMO Medical Centers, Diagnostic Imaging Centers and Community Food Services.
- One industry moved from the Transportation sector—Ambulance services

*Visit page 575 for
greater detail on
this sector.*

Major Changes by Sector

NAICS Overview

Information—Sector 51

This sector recognizes the emergence of businesses that create and disseminate products subject to copyright. This sector brings together businesses whose activities include the transformation of information into products and producing and distributing these products through means other than traditional wholesale/retail distribution channels. Highlights of this sector include

- 34 industries, 20 of which are new. Examples of new industries include paging, cellular and satellite telecommunications.
- Three industries moved from the Manufacturing sector including newspaper, book and periodical publishers.
- Four industries moved from the Services sector including software publishers, motion picture and sound recording industries information services and data processing services.
- One industry moved from Utilities and Transportation sector, broadcasting and telecommunications producers/distributors.

ATTENTION: New sector—20 new high tech industries.

Management of Companies and Enterprises—Sector 55

This sector is where all company headquarters are classified in NAICS. Headquarters were previously classified under the industry from which most of their income was derived. This change has the potential to reclassify a large number of employees out of manufacturing and retail sectors. There will be significant changes to employment statistics because of this change. An example of this is in 1997, Massachusetts had 455,951 manufacturing jobs in 10,076 establishments, according to County Business Patterns (using SIC codes). But the 1998 Country Business Patterns (using NAICS codes) shows only 409,938 jobs in 9,541 establishments, ten percent below the 1997 figure. However during this time the Bureau of Labor Statistics' Current Employment Statistics series (using the SIC code) shows Massachusetts manufacturing employment rising from 443,900 in March 1997 to 452,100 in March 1998. There is no way of knowing exactly how NAICS has caused these changes, but it does show us the difficulty we will experience until all government agencies have implemented NAICS. This will also affect anyone who wishes to compare management enterprises across targeted industries.

ATTENTION. Employment statistics will be impacted.

Manufacturing—Sector 31-33

This sector has been significantly restructured in NAICS. Classifications have been reorganized to recognize emerging industries and to increase comparability with Canada and Mexico. Significant changes to this sector include the addition of the Computer and Electronic Product Manufacturing sub-sector. This sub-sector includes establishments engaged in production of computers, computer peripherals, communications equipment and components for these industries. A number of important industries have been moved out of this sector, including publishing, logging, and on-site bakeries. An example of why this sector needed to be updated can be seen by looking at SIC 39 Miscellaneous Manufacturing Industries. This major group included businesses that ranged from the manufacturing of burial caskets to children's toys. Highlights of this sector include

- 79 new industries recognized
- 186 industries revised

Construction Ahead: 186 industries revised.

NAICS Overview

Major Changes by Sector

Retail and Wholesale Trade—Sector 42 and 44-45

These sectors have experienced a significant realignment of businesses under NAICS. Under SIC, businesses were classified as either Retail or Wholesale based on what type of customer they served. NAICS has changed the focus from the type of customer to how each business operates.

- Retailers typically have the following qualities: sell in small quantities using public oriented business methods like mass media advertising, high-traffic locations, and attractive displays.
- Wholesalers typically have the following qualities: sell in large quantities using business-oriented methods like specialized catalogs, customer contacts, and warehouse or office locations.

Construction Ahead: Complete overhaul of the retail & wholesale trade sectors.

This change has had a significant effect on the sector classification of many of the businesses in the Retail and Wholesale Sectors. If we take a look at a warehouse shopping club, under SIC this would have been classified under wholesale. Under NAICS we look at these establishments in a different light when we consider the fact that these businesses, advertise heavily, have large showrooms and count among their clientele regular consumers as well as businesses. These enterprises now are classified as Retail.

Professional, Scientific, and Technical Services—Sector 54

This sector includes businesses that use expert or skilled persons to provide specialized business and personal services. Highlights of this sector include

- 47 industries, 28 of which are new. Examples of new industries include interior design, environmental consulting and translation services.
- Seven industries were moved to this sector from other SIC divisions.

Visit page 539 for greater detail on this sector.

How do these changes affect you?

NAICS codes add dimension that has previously been lacking. Now you should see how significant the changes are and, indeed, why NAICS is superior to SIC. The greater your knowledge, the better prepared you will be to take advantage of what NAICS has to offer. Take a moment to consider the many significant changes between the SIC and NAICS systems, and the significant number of businesses reclassified.

NAICS changes are significant and, while two-thirds of the industries remain relatively the same, NAICS classifies a significant number of new industries never addressed by SIC and enacts changes to sector definitions that cause many similar industries to experience sector reclassification. Subsequent sections explore many of the implementation issues you will be facing with NAICS.

The following changes were identified as a result of the 1996 Refile Survey

- Approximately 16,000 merchant wholesalers were reclassified as retailers.
- Approximately 2,200 retailers were reclassified as wholesalers.
- Approximately 315 tire rebuilding and recaping establishments were moved from wholesale to manufacturing.
- Over 3,500 ambulance service establishments were moved to health services from transportation.

Production Based Classifications

As stated before, one of the significant differences between SIC and NAICS is the approach to how businesses are grouped in sectors. In SIC there was no standard classification approach. Some businesses were classified based upon their production processes; others were classified using different principles, such as type of customer. NAICS classifies each business into a detailed industry sector based on its production processes. Many of the identified businesses have been reclassified based on this; for examples,

NAICS codes are based on production process, not end product.

consider the movement of book publishing from the Manufacturing sector to the Information sector.

What is an Establishment/Auxiliary Establishment?

Auxiliary establishments produce services in support of other companies engaged in the enterprise. These services are intended to be used within an organization and can include services such as personnel or data processing. Under SIC these auxiliaries were classified in the same industry as their parent companies. NAICS chooses to classify auxiliaries based on the services they provide. This change provides better service activity information, but it will have a significant impact on employment statistics. Many employees previously classified under manufacturing and retail auxiliaries will now be reclassified into service industries.

> *Many employees previously classified under manufacturing and retail auxiliaries will now be reclassified into service industries.*

An establishment is generally a single physical location where business is conducted or where services or industrial operations are performed. There will be cases where records identify separate economic activities performed at one location; an example of this is a hotel with shops. The retailing activities of the gift shop are identified as separate establishments. So the hotel is classified individually as a hotel. Likewise, the gift shop is individually classified as a gift shop.

If this section demands a re-read, don't be alarmed. It's worth the extra attention.

NAICS Overview

Activities are treated as separate establishments provided:

1. No one industry description in the classification includes such combined activities
2. Separate reports can be prepared on the number of employees, their wages and salaries, sales or receipts, and expenses and
3. Employment and output are significant for both activities.

For industries with physically dispersed operations there are exceptions to the single location establishment. To determine the industrial code for an establishment engaged in multiple activities, you must first determine the primary activity of the establishment. The industry code assigned will be based on the establishment's principal product or services rendered. This will be determined by relative share of current production costs and capital investment at the establishment.

NAICS Numbering System

Even if your interest lies with industries that remain relatively unchanged from SIC to NAICS, you will still need to change. SIC is no longer the classification system for the United States. The numeric codes for NAICS are significantly different from SIC. NAICS was developed with a five-level hierarchy compared to four in SIC. See the NAICS Hierarchy table for a complete understanding of this concept. NAICS codes are made up of a maximum of six digits compared to the old four. For example, both NAICS and SIC include the detailed industry "Passenger Car Rental." However, in NAICS, it is code number 532111, and in SIC, it was code number 7514. The sixth digit is country specific. This digit is available for use by each of

NAICS Numbering System

Figure 5

the countries to recognize industries important to their economy as long as they fit within the framework of the five-digit system. These changes, along with the previous issues addressed in this document, will require you to make changes to your classification codes either for your personal company use or for your marketing/sales data searches. If you currently use SIC or a proprietary classification system based on SIC you will need to begin planning your implementation of NAICS.

NAICS has 725 codes at the five-digit level and 668 codes at the six-digit level, compared to 1,005 SIC codes at the four-digit level. There is agreement between the three countries at the following levels

- 2-digit level for Construction, Wholesale Trade, Retail Trade and Public Administration
- 3-digit level for Waste Management and Remediation Services, Finance, Utilities, Personal and Laundry Services and Religious, Grantmaking, Civic, Professional and Similar Organizations
- 4-digit level for Insurance and Real Estate
- 5-digit level for all remaining sectors and subsectors.

NAICS / SIC: Structure and Nomenclature

NAICS	
2-digit	Sector
3-digit	Subsector
4-digit	Industry Group
5-digit	NAICS Industry
6-digit	National Industry

SIC	
Division	Letter
Major Group	2-digit
Industry Group	3-digit
Industry	4-digit
—	—

Figure 4

NAICS United States Structure

Sector	Name	Sub-sectors	Industry groups	NAICS 5-digit industries	U.S. 6-digit industries	TOTAL U.S. industries	New industries
11	Agriculture, Forestry, Fishing and, Hunting	5	19	42	32	64	20
21	Mining	3	5	10	28	29	—
22	Utilities	1	3	6	6	10	6
23	Construction	3	14	28	—	28	3
31–33	Manufacturing	21	84	184	408	474	79
42	Wholesale Trade	2	18	69	—	69	—
44–45	Retail Trade	12	27	61	18	72	17
48-49	Transportation and Warehousing	11	29	42	25	57	28
51	Information	4	9	28	12	34	20
52	Finance and Insurance	5	11	32	15	42	23
53	Real Estate and Rental and Leasing	3	8	19	9	24	15
54	Professional, Scientific, and Technical Services	1	9	35	17	47	28
55	Management of Companies and Enterprises	1	1	1	3	3	1
56	Administrative and Support and Waste Management and Remediation Services	2	11	29	23	43	29
61	Educational Services	1	7	12	7	17	12
62	Health Care and Social Assistance	4	18	30	16	39	27
71	Arts, Entertainment, and Recreation	3	9	23	3	25	19
72	Accommodation and Food Services	2	7	11	7	15	10
81	Other Services (except Public Administration)	4	14	30	30	49	19
92	Public Administration	8	8	29	—	29	2
	TOTAL	96	311	721	659	1170	358

To learn more about the changes by sector go to pages 15-18.

Figure 6

NAICS
Overview

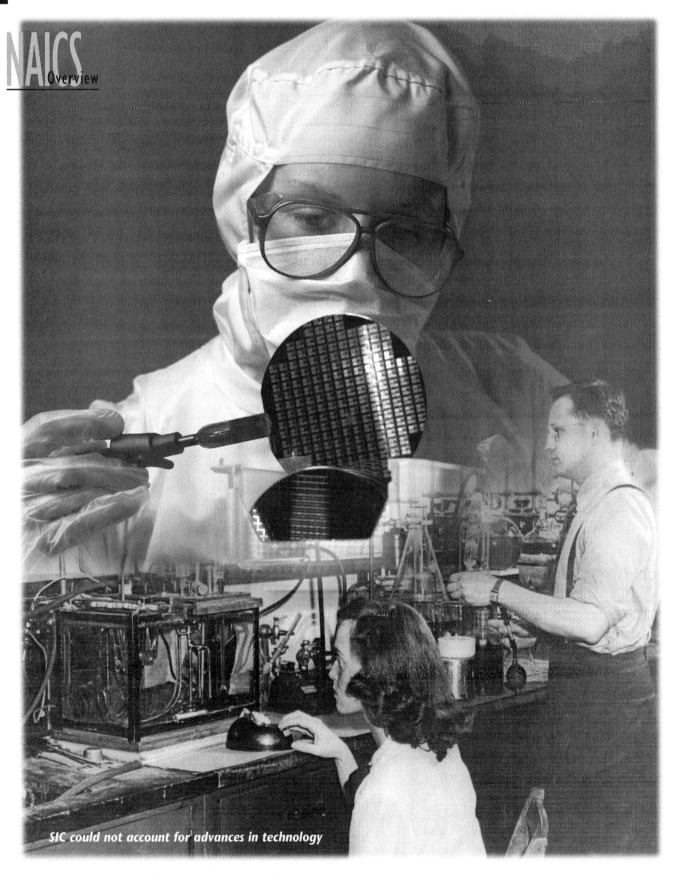

SIC could not account for advances in technology

Implementing NAICS

NAICS United States has been adopted for statistical use by all federal agencies. Implementation throughout all government agencies is currently underway and will continue at least through 2004 with the conversion of the Producer Price Index. Implementation plans and schedule dates differ with each government agency.

Wondering if you should care about how and when U.S. agencies implement NAICS? You might want to consider the following example of how Economic Census Data is used by companies. A soft drink bottler considered expanding into two related beverage manufacturing operations; milk and alcoholic beverages. Economic Census data shed light on industry specialization, company size, and the relationship of expenses to receipts—information that encouraged the bottler to diversify. If you use Economic Census Data to make sound business decisions, you need to understand NAICS today. The last available Economic Census was published using NAICS and future ones will not provide bridge information to SIC.

Bridge from SIC to NAICS

Government Sector Data: If you use government statistics, you will need to review and adjust your data sources, methods, analyses, and products. In previous sections we have outlined many of the differences between SIC and NAICS. NAICS continues 422 previous SIC industries with minimal changes. Data for these industries should remain comparable in both classification systems. However, even for these industries you will have to change classification code numbers and official titles. If you use the high level groupings, you will need to assess any changes in determining the comparability of statistics. For more detailed comparisons with past data you may require what the Census bureau calls "synthetic estimates"—applying the proportion of trends from details that make up one data set to the totals in a related data set or category.

If you use data for industries that are included in the 390 industries that have been redefined by NAICS

Convert SIC codes to NAICS codes. Turn to page 87.

and the 320 industries new to the classification system, there will be no directly comparable data.

Private Sector Data: Many of you have been using SIC codes to help you target customers, create direct mailing lists, and track down suppliers. The government retired SIC in 1997, but many businesses have continued using the system. 1987 was the last time SIC was updated? Do you remember what you were doing then? Chances are your life and your business have changed significantly since then. SIC is going away and you will need to move to NAICS to continue to grow your business. NAICS provides you with a classification system that is relevant to the economy of today and provides you with greater granularity of the growing services segment of our economy.

Case Study: Learn how NAICS benefits sales & marketing professionals, see page 13.

To take advantage of these changes you will need to spend time determining how you will convert to the use of NAICS. First, understand how your company currently uses SIC codes and what they are used for. This is required even if you are using a customized set of codes. Keep in mind that SIC is being phased out and all code sets based upon SIC have the same issues as the classification system they are built upon. Remember the example of 7389 Business Services, Not Elsewhere Classified, which contains a variety of businesses including wig making and recording studios. If you are using an eight-digit system based on SIC, you are still tied to the same 10 sectors that created this example. Next you must understand that implementing NAICS in your organization is significant. You will need to measure the scope of the conversion. Lastly, keep in mind that your information provider is there to help you make the transition to NAICS. Contact your information provider for information on their NAICS implementation plan.

FACT

SIC codes
no longer
provide an
effective way
to *classify* our
new and ever
changing
economy

Selected U.S. Agency Implementation Plans

	Availability
Bureau of the Census	
1997 Economic Census (every 5 years)	1999
1998 County Business Patterns (annual)	2000
1998 Annual Survey of Manufacturers	2000
2001 Manufacturers' Shipments, Inventories and Orders (monthly)	2001
1999 Annual Retail Trade	2001
Bureau of Economic Analysis	
1997 Foreign Direct Investment Benchmark (every 5 years)	1999
1998 Annual Foreign Direct Investment Survey	2000
1997 Benchmark Input-Output Accounts (every 5 years)	2002
2000 Annual U.S. Direct Investment Abroad Survey	2002
2001 Gross State Product by Industry (annual)	2003
Bureau of Labor Statistics	
2000 Employment and Wages Report (annual)	2001
2002 Current Employment Statistics Survey (monthly)	2003
2002 Occupational Employment Statistics (annual)	2003
2004 Producer Price Index (monthly)	2004
Internal Revenue Service	
1998 Income Tax Forms	1999

Figure 7

When does SIC go away?

With the 1997 publication of NAICS came the end of SIC as an industrial classification system in the United States. The conversion table for SIC to NAICS will be available for the upcoming 2002 NAICS update but will not be created for the 2007 NAICS update. The 1997 Economic Census is the last one to have data available for SIC industries. All government data, statistics, and forms will only be available using in NAICS. If you want to have relevant industry data, you need to implement NAICS within your organization. The government stopped maintaining SIC in 1987 and began the adoption of NAICS in 1997. NAICS takes a modern view of our economy and is equipped to deal with the industries that businesses will create in the future. Unlike metrics, a government initiative that never got off the ground, NAICS is already an integral part of government reporting and is here to stay.

> *The major changes coming with NAICS 2002 will be the increased definition of e-commerce.*

What's Next for NAICS

In 2002 a revised version of NAICS will be published as part of the regular update schedule. The major changes coming with NAICS 2002 will be the increased definition of e-commerce. For the first time the Information and Wholesale trade sectors will recognize Internet and Electronic Commerce industries in their own subsectors. The proposed major changes include the following:

ATTENTION: NAICS will be revised in 2002.

- New industries added to Wholesale Trade Sector creating a separate subsector for electronic markets formerly a part of subsector 25, Wholesale Electronic Markets and Agents and Brokers.
- New industries added to the Information Sector defining Internet activities such as Internet service providers, web search portals, and Internet publishing and broadcasting.
- New industries added to Construction distinguishing between erection of residential buildings and the erection of nonresidential buildings.
- A number of industries will be renamed.

Look for these changes and others in the republished NAICS 2002.

What does ISIC mean to you?

Over 100 countries currently use ISIC Revision 3. If you are doing business on a global basis, ISIC can provide you with a way to compare industry information and statistics across world economies. The advantage that using NAICS provides to you is the guiding principle of comparability at the 2-digit level between NAICS and ISIC. ISIC's purpose is not to replace national classifications, but to provide a framework for the international comparison of national statistics.

Harris is an official licensee of the United Nations ISIC classification codes.

Brief History of ISIC

The United Nations Statistical Commission held its first session two years after the end of World War II. The objective was to promote the development of key statistics worldwide and make them as comparable as possible. ISIC was designed to be an all purpose classification of economic activities to monitor reconstruction and the full use of resources. There have been three rounds of revisions of the ISIC system. Each revision has brought the classification system more in line with the ever changing world economies.

ISIC today provides a framework for comparability among various countries. It remains general allowing countries to create their own classification systems in greater detail to meet their national and specific concerns. ISIC is an international system that serves the needs of a diverse set of countries and economies. With each revision ISIC has been increasing the importance of service producing industries. Analysis of international trade in services is growing in importance.

ISIC is the only United Nations sanctioned all purpose classification system. The United Nations does not support the UN/SPSC. UN/SPSC codes are a privately held system based on SIC.

ATTENTION: *The United Nations does not support the UN/SPSC classification system.*

NAICS and ISIC can they be compared?

One of the principles that NAICS was founded on was comparability with the International Standard Industrial Classification (ISIC). NAICS is based upon a 5-level hierarchy and a 6-digit code. ISIC is based upon a 4-level hierarchy and a 4-digit code. Comparability was attempted at the 2-digit level of the ISIC code. The following table compares the structure of NAICS to ISIC.

Over 100 countries currently use ISIC Revision 3.

The **NAICS** Structure as compared to **ISIC**

NAICS		ISIC	
2-digit	Sector	Section	Letter
3-digit	Subsector	Division	2-digit
4-digit	Industry Group	Group	3-digit
5-digit	NAICS Industry	Class	4-digit
6-digit	National Industry	—	—

Figure 8

NAICS Overview

NAICS United States has 20 sectors, 97 subsectors, 311 industry groups and 1170 U.S. industries. ISIC has 17 sections, 60 divisions, 150 groups and 292 classes. The attempt was made to create 5-digit NAICS codes that did not cross a 2-digit ISIC boundary. NAICS is not always successful, but does provide greater comparability with ISIC Revision 3 than the 1987 revision of SIC.

Convert ISIC codes to NAICS codes. Turn to page 259.

Both systems classify at the establishment unit. Both organize industries into a hierarchical structure using similar terminology.

The major difference is the Information Sector that has been created in NAICS. Publishing is part of this sector along with software and database publishing. ISIC still classifies this under Manufacturing. Another difference is that the industries in ISIC classified in the Business Services division have been divided into two NAICS sectors, Professional, Scientific and Technical, and Administrative and Support. ■

a comparison

ISIC Divisions / NAICS Sectors

ISIC	
A	Agriculture, Hunting and Forestry
B	Fishing
C	Mining and Quarrying
D	Manufacturing
E	Electricity, Gas, Steam and Hot Water Supply
F	Construction
G	Wholesale and Retail Trade; Repair of Motor Vehicles, Motorcycles and Personal Household Goods
H	Hotels and Restaurants
I	Transport, Storage and Communications
J	Financial Intermediation
K	Real Estates, Renting and Business Activities
L	Public Administration and Defense; Compulsory Social Security
M	Education
N	Health and Social Work
O	Other Community, Social and Personal Services Activities

NAICS	
11	Agriculture, Forestry, Fishing and, Hunting
21	Mining
31–33	Manufacturing
22	Utilities
23	Construction
42	Wholesale Trade
44–45	Retail Trade
811	Repair and Maintenance (a subsector grouped with Sector 81, Other Services)
72	Accommodation and, Food Services
48-49	Transportation and, Warehousing
513	Broadcasting and Telecommunications (a subsector grouped with Sector 51, Information)
52	Finance and, Insurance
53	Real Estate and, Rental and, Leasing
54	Professional, Scientific, and, Technical Services
561	Administrative and Support (Waste Management and Remediation is part of Sector 56 in NAICS, but in ISIC is included in Division O and is shown below)
92	Public Administration
61	Educational Services
62	Health Care and Social Assistance
562	Waste Management and Remediation (see note above)
71	Arts, Entertainment, and, Recreation
81	Other Services (except NAICS subsector 811, Repair and Maintenance that is included in ISIC Division G)
51	Information
55	Management of Companies and Enterprises

Figure 9

HOW TO USE THIS SECTION:

This section supplies you with a comprehensive list of NAICS codes and their industry descriptions. The codes are divided by sector and are listed in descending order beginning with the two-digit sector title and ending with the six-digit national industry classification.

For a more detailed explanation of each code, turn to page 273.

NAICS Short Titles

SIC to NAICS
Interchange

51	**INFORMATION** ←	────────	**NAICS SECTOR TITLES (2-digit)**
513	**Broadcasting & Telecommunications** ←	────	**NAICS Subsector Titles (3-digit)**
	5132	Cable Networks & Program Distribution ←	NAICS Industry Group Titles (4-digit)
	51321	Cable Networks	
	51322	Cable & Other Program Distribution ←	NAICS Industry Titles (5-digit)
	5133	Telecommunications	
	51331	Wired Telecommunications Carriers	
	51332	Wireless Telecom Carriers (exc Satellite)	
	513321	Paging ←	NAICS U.S. Titles (6-digit)
	513322	Cellular & Other Wireless Telecommunications	

27

Abbreviations and Substitute Words

NAICS Short Titles

Access	Accessories
Activity	Activities
Admin	Administration
Ag	Agricultural
AC	Air-conditioning
Alloy	Alloying
Alum	Aluminum
&	and
Anodize	Anodizing
Arrange	Arrangement
Artf	Artificial
Audiology	Audiologists
Auto	Automotive
Aux	Auxiliary
Bookkeep	Bookkeeping
Broadcast	Broadcasting
Bldg	Building
Cabnt	Cabinet
Ctrs	Centers
Choc	Chocolate
Coin-op	Coin-operated
Comdty	Commodities
Comm	Communications
CD	Compact Disc
Compn	Component
Const	Construction
Contr	Contractor
Corp	Corporate
Devop	Development
Dist	Distribution
Draw	Drawing
Dryclean	Drycleaning
Elec	Electric; Electronic
Electropl	Electroplating
Embroid	Embroidery
Engrave	Engraving
Equip	Equipment
exc	except
Exec	Executive
Extrude	Extruding
Facil	Facilities
Farm	Farming
Figu	Figures
Fil	Filaments
Finishng	Finishing
Frgt	Freight
Gas	Gasoline
Gen	General
Gov	Government
Missile	Guided Missile
HH	Household
Htg	Heating
HVAC	Heating, Ventilation, Air-conditioning
Incl	Including
Ind	Industrial; Industries
Inspect	Inspection
Instrumnt	Instrument
Intermed	Intermediation
Ki	Kitchen
Lamnd	Laminated
Lease	Leasing
LTL	Less Than Truckload
License	Licensing
Log	Logistics
LDist	Long-distance

Mach	Machinery
Mgt	Management
Mfg	Manufacturing
Mil	Military
Misc	Miscellaneous
Movie	Motion Picture
MV	Motor Vehicle
Nav	Navigational
Nonres	Nonresidential
NEC	Not Elsewhere Classified
OT	Occupational Therapist
Oth	Other
Pkg	Packaging
Pt	Part
Perform	Performing
Photo	Photographic
Phys	Physical
PT	Physical Therapist
Plumb	Plumbing
Polish	Polishing
Postprod	Postproduction
Pol	Political
Pwr	Power
Prep	Preparation
Press	Pressing
Prim	Primary
Prod/Pro	Production
Prof	Professional
Prog	Program/Programs
Purch	Purchase; Purchased
RV	Recreational Vehicle
Refine	Refining
Refrig	Refrigeration
Reg	Regulation
R&M	Repair and Maintenance
R&D	Research and Development
Res	Resources
Roll	Rolling
Sci	Scientific
Security /Scrty	Securities
Shelv	Shelving
Shwcase	Showcase
/	Slash replaces comma
Smelt	Smelting
Spd	Speed
Sta	Stations
Subst	Substance
Supply /Supp	Supplies
Syn	Synthetic
Tech	Technical
Telecom	Telecommunications
TV	Television
Total	Totalizing
Transmsn	Transmission
Trans	Transportation
TL	Truckload
Turn	Turned
Util	Utility
Veg	Vegetable
Veh	Vehicle
HVAC	Ventilation, Heating, Air-conditioning
Whsle	Wholesalers
Wirless	Wireless
w/	with
w/o	without

Short Titles

North American Industry Classification System (NAICS)

11	**AGRICULTURE, FORESTRY, FISHING, AND HUNTING**

111	**Crop Production**
1111	Oilseed & Grain Farming
11111	Soybean Farming
11112	Oilseed (except Soybean) Farming
11113	Dry Pea & Bean Farming
11114	Wheat Farming
11115	Corn Farming
11116	Rice Farming
11119	Other Grain Farming
111191	Oilseed & Grain Combination Farming
111199	All Other Grain Farming
1112	Vegetable & Melon Farming
11121	Vegetable & Melon Farming
111211	Potato Farming
111219	Other Vegetable (except Potato) & Melon Farming
1113	Fruit & Tree Nut Farming
11131	Orange Groves
11132	Citrus (except Orange) Groves
11133	Noncitrus Fruit & Tree Nut Farming
111331	Apple Orchards
111332	Grape Vineyards
111333	Strawberry Farming
111334	Berry (except Strawberry) Farming
111335	Tree Nut Farming
111336	Fruit & Tree Nut Combination Farming
111339	Other Noncitrus Fruit Farming
1114	Greenhouse, Nursery & Floriculture Production
11141	Food Crops Grown Under Cover
111411	Mushroom Production
111419	Other Food Crops Grown Under Cover

11142	Nursery & Floriculture Production
111421	Nursery & Tree Production
111422	Floriculture Production
1119	Other Crop Farming
11191	Tobacco Farming
11192	Cotton Farming
11193	Sugarcane Farming
11194	Hay Farming
11199	All Other Crop Farming
111991	Sugar Beet Farming
111992	Peanut Farming
111998	All Other Miscellaneous Crop Farming

112	**Animal Production**
1121	Cattle Ranching & Farming
11211	Beef Cattle Ranching & Farming & Feedlots
112111	Beef Cattle Ranching & Farming
112112	Cattle Feedlots
11212	Dairy Cattle & Milk Production
11213	Dual Purpose Cattle Ranching & Farming
1122	Hog & Pig Farming
11221	Hog & Pig Farming
1123	Poultry & Egg Production
11231	Chicken Egg Production
11232	Broilers & Other Meat Type Chicken Production
11233	Turkey Production
11234	Poultry Hatcheries
11239	Other Poultry Production
1124	Sheep and Goat Farming
11241	Sheep Farming
11242	Goat Farming
1125	Animal Aquaculture
11251	Animal Aquaculture
112511	Finfish Farming & Fish Hatcheries
112512	Shellfish Farming
112519	Other Animal Aquaculture

Go to page 273 for in-depth NAICS code descriptions.

For a complete list of abbreviations and their definitions, see page 28

NAICS
Short Titles

1129	Other Animal Production
11291	Apiculture
11292	Horse & Other Equine Production
11293	Fur-bearing Animal & Rabbit Production
11299	All Other Animal Production

113   **Forestry and Logging**

1131	Timber Tract Operations
11311	Timber Tract Operations
1132	Forest Nurseries & Gathering Forest Products
11321	Forest Nurseries & Gathering Forest Products
1133	Logging
11331	Logging

114   **Fishing, Hunting, and Trapping**

1141	Fishing
11411	Fishing
114111	Finfish Fishing
114112	Shellfish Fishing
114119	Other Marine Fishing
1142	Hunting & Trapping
11421	Hunting & Trapping

115   **Agriculture, and Forestry Support Activities**

1151	Crop Production Support Activities
11511	Crop Production Support Activities
115111	Cotton Ginning
115112	Soil Preparation, Planting, & Cultivating
115113	Crop Harvesting, Primarily by Machine
115114	Postharvest Crop Activities (except Ginning)
115115	Farm Labor Contractors & Crew Leaders
115116	Farm Management Services
1152	Animal Production Support Activities
11521	Animal Production Support Activities
1153	Forestry Support Activities
11531	Forestry Support Activities

21   **MINING**

211   **Oil and Gas Extraction**

2111	Oil & Gas Extraction
21111	Oil & Gas Extraction
211111	Crude Petroleum & Natural Gas Extraction
211112	Natural Gas Liquid Extraction

212   **Mining, Except Oil and Gas**

2121	Coal Mining
21211	Coal Mining
212111	Bituminous Coal & Lignite Surface Mining
212112	Bituminous Coal Underground Mining
212113	Anthracite Mining
2122	Metal Ore Mining
21221	Iron Ore Mining
21222	Gold Ore & Silver Ore Mining
212221	Gold Ore Mining
212222	Silver Ore Mining
21223	Copper, Nickel, Lead & Zinc Mining
212231	Lead Ore & Zinc Ore Mining
212234	Copper Ore & Nickel Ore Mining
21229	Other Metal Ore Mining
212291	Uranium-Radium-Vanadium Ore Mining
212299	All Other Metal Ore Mining
2123	Nonmetallic Mineral Mining & Quarrying
21231	Stone Mining & Quarrying
212311	Dimension Stone Mining & Quarrying
212312	Crushed & Broken Limestone Mining & Quarrying
212313	Crushed & Broken Granite Mining & Quarrying
212319	Other Crushed & Broken Stone Mining & Quarrying
21232	Sand/Gravel/Clay/Refractory Minerals Mining
212321	Construction Sand & Gravel Mining
212322	Industrial Sand Mining
212324	Kaolin & Ball Clay Mining
212325	Clay & Ceramic & Refractory Minerals Mining
21239	Other Nonmetallic Mineral Mining & Quarrying
212391	Potash, Soda, & Borate Mineral Mining
212392	Phosphate Rock Mining
212393	Other Chemical & Fertilizer Mineral Mining
212399	All Other Nonmetallic Mineral Mining

213   **Mining Support Activities**

2131	Mining Support Activities
21311	Mining Support Activities
213111	Drilling Oil & Gas Wells
213112	Oil & Gas Operations Support Activities

213113	Support Activities for Coal Mining
213114	Support Activities for Metal Mining
213115	Nonmetallic Minerals Support Activity (except Fuels)

22   UTILITIES

221   Utilities

2211	Electric Power Generation, Transmsn & Distribution
22111	Electric Power Generation
221111	Hydroelectric Power Generation
221112	Fossil Fuel Electric Power Generation
221113	Nuclear Electric Power Generation
221119	Other Electric Power Generation
22112	Electric Power Transmsn, Control & Distribution
221121	Electric Bulk Power Transmission & Control
221122	Electric Power Distribution
2212	Natural Gas Distribution
22121	Natural Gas Distribution
2213	Water, Sewage & Other Systems
22131	Water Supply & Irrigation Systems
22132	Sewage Treatment Facilities
22133	Steam & Air-conditioning Supply

23   CONSTRUCTION

233   Building, Developing, and General Contracting

2331	Land Subdivision & Land Development
23311	Land Subdivision & Land Development
2332	Residential Building Construction
23321	Single-family Housing Construction
23322	Multifamily Housing Construction
2333	Nonresidential Building Construction
23331	Mfg & Industrial Building Construction
23332	Commercial & Institutional Bldg Construction

234   Heavy Construction

2341	Highway, Street, Bridge & Tunnel Construction
23411	Highway & Street Construction
23412	Bridge & Tunnel Construction
2349	Other Heavy Construction
23491	Water, Sewer & Pipeline Construction
23492	Pwr/Communication Transmsn Line Construction
23493	Industrial Nonbuilding Structure Construction
23499	All Other Heavy Construction

235   Special Trade Contractors

2351	Plumbing, Heating & AC Contractor
23511	Plumbing, Heating & AC Contractor
2352	Painting & Wall Covering Contractors
23521	Painting & Wall Covering Contractors
2353	Electrical Contractors
23531	Electrical Contractors
2354	Masonry/Drywall/Insulation/Tile Contractors
23541	Masonry & Stone Contractors
23542	Drywall, Acoustical & Insulation Contractors
23543	Tile, Marble, Terrazzo & Mosaic Contractors
2355	Carpentry & Floor Contractors
23551	Carpentry Contractors
23552	Floor Laying & Other Floor Contractors
2356	Roofing, Siding & Sheet Metal Contractors
23561	Roofing, Siding & Sheet Metal Contractors
2357	Concrete Contractors
23571	Concrete Contractors
2358	Water Well Drilling Contractors
23581	Water Well Drilling Contractors
2359	Other Special Trade Contractors
23591	Structural Steel Erection Contractors
23592	Glass & Glazing Contractors
23593	Excavation Contractors
23594	Wrecking & Demolition Contractors
23595	Bldg Equip & Other Mach Installation Contractor
23599	All Other Special Trade Contractors

NAICS
Short Titles

31-33	**MANUFACTURING**	
311	**Food Manufacturing**	
	3111	Animal Food Mfg
	31111	Animal Food Mfg
	311111	Dog & Cat Food Mfg
	311119	Other Animal Food Mfg
	3112	Grain & Oilseed Milling
	31121	Flour Milling & Malt Mfg
	311211	Flour Milling
	311212	Rice Milling
	311213	Malt Mfg
	31122	Starch & Vegetable Fats & Oils Mfg
	311221	Wet Corn Milling
	311222	Soybean Processing
	311223	Other Oilseed Processing
	311225	Fats & Oils Refining & Blending
	31123	Breakfast Cereal Mfg
	3113	Sugar & Confectionery Product Mfg
	31131	Sugar Mfg
	311311	Sugarcane Mills
	311312	Cane Sugar Refining
	311313	Beet Sugar Mfg
	31132	Choc & Confectionery Mfg from Cacao Beans
	31133	Confectionery Mfg from Purchased Chocolate
	31134	Nonchocolate Confectionery Mfg
	3114	Fruit & Veg Preserving & Specialty Food Mfg
	31141	Frozen Food Mfg
	311411	Frozen Fruit, Juice & Vegetable Mfg
	311412	Frozen Specialty Food Mfg
	31142	Fruit & Veg Canning, Pickling & Drying
	311421	Fruit & Vegetable Canning
	311422	Specialty Canning
	311423	Dried & Dehydrated Food Mfg
	3115	Dairy Product Mfg
	31151	Dairy Product (except Frozen) Mfg
	311511	Fluid Milk Mfg
	311512	Creamery Butter Mfg
	311513	Cheese Mfg
	311514	Dry/Condensed/Evaporated Dairy Product Mfg
	31152	Ice Cream & Frozen Dessert Mfg
	3116	Animal Slaughtering & Processing
	31161	Animal Slaughtering & Processing
	311611	Animal (except Poultry) Slaughtering
	311612	Meat Processed From Carcasses
	311613	Rendering & Meat Byproduct Processing
	311615	Poultry Processing
	3117	Seafood Product Preparation & Packaging
	31171	Seafood Product Preparation & Packaging
	311711	Seafood Canning
	311712	Fresh & Frozen Seafood Processing
	3118	Bakeries & Tortilla Mfg
	31181	Bread & Bakery Product Mfg
	311811	Retail Bakeries
	311812	Commercial Bakeries
	311813	Frozen Cakes, Pies & Other Pasteries Mfg
	31182	Cookie, Cracker & Pasta Mfg
	311821	Cookie & Cracker Mfg
	311822	Flour Mixes & Dough Mfg from Purchased Flour
	311823	Dry Pasta Mfg
	31183	Tortilla Mfg
	3119	Other Food Mfg
	31191	Snack Food Mfg
	311911	Roasted Nuts & Peanut Butter Mfg
	311919	Other Snack Food Mfg
	31192	Coffee & Tea Mfg
	31193	Flavoring Syrup & Concentrate Mfg
	31194	Seasoning & Dressing Mfg
	311941	Mayonnaise, Dressing & Other Prepared Sauce Mfg
	311942	Spice & Extract Mfg
	31199	All Other Food Mfg
	311991	Perishable Prepared Food Mfg
	311999	All Other Miscellaneous Food Mfg
312	**Beverage and Tobacco Product Manufacturing**	
	3121	Beverage Mfg
	31211	Soft Drink & Ice Mfg
	312111	Soft Drink Mfg
	312112	Bottled Water Mfg
	312113	Ice Mfg
	31212	Breweries
	31213	Wineries
	31214	Distilleries
	3122	Tobacco Mfg
	31221	Tobacco Stemming & Redrying
	31222	Tobacco Product Mfg

For a complete list of abbreviations and their definitions, see page 28

	312221	Cigarette Mfg
	312229	Other Tobacco Product Mfg
313		**Textile Mills**
	3131	Fiber, Yarn & Thread Mills
	31311	Fiber, Yarn & Thread Mills
	313111	Yarn Spinning Mills
	313112	Yarn Texturing, Throwing & Twisting Mills
	313113	Thread Mills
	3132	Fabric Mills
	31321	Broadwoven Fabric Mills
	31322	Narrow Fabric Mills & Schiffli Mach Embroid
	313221	Narrow Fabric Mills
	313222	Schiffli Machine Embroidery
	31323	Nonwoven Fabric Mills
	31324	Knit Fabric Mills
	313241	Weft Knit Fabric Mills
	313249	Other Knit Fabric & Lace Mills
	3133	Textile/Fabric Finishing/ Fabric Coating Mills
	31331	Textile & Fabric Finishing Mills
	313311	Broadwoven Fabric Finishing Mills
	313312	Textile/Fabric Finishing (except Broadwoven) Mill
	31332	Fabric Coating Mills
314		**Textile Product Mills**
	3141	Textile Furnishings Mills
	31411	Carpet & Rug Mills
	31412	Curtain & Linen Mills
	314121	Curtain & Drapery Mills
	314129	Other Household Textile Product Mills
	3149	Other Textile Product Mills
	31491	Textile Bag & Canvas Mills
	314911	Textile Bag Mills
	314912	Canvas & Related Product Mills
	31499	All Other Textile Product Mills
	314991	Rope, Cordage & Twine Mills
	314992	Tire Cord & Tire Fabric Mills
	314999	All Other Miscellaneous Textile Product Mills
315		**Apparel Manufacturing**
	3151	Apparel Knitting Mills
	31511	Hosiery & Sock Mills
	315111	Sheer Hosiery Mills
	315119	Other Hosiery & Sock Mills
	31519	Other Apparel Knitting Mills
	315191	Outerwear Knitting Mills

	315192	Underwear & Nightwear Knitting Mills
	3152	Cut & Sew Apparel Mfg
	31521	Cut & Sew Apparel Contractors
	315211	Men's/Boys' Cut & Sew Apparel Contractors
	315212	Women's/Girls'/Infants' Cut/Sew Apparel Contr
	31522	Men's/Boys' Cut & Sew Apparel Mfg
	315221	Men's/Boys' Cut & Sew Underwear/Nightwear Mfg
	315222	Men's/Boys' Cut & Sew Suit, Coat/Overcoat Mfg
	315223	Men's/Boys' Cut & Sew Shirt (except Work) Mfg
	315224	Men's/Boys' Cut & Sew Trouser/Slack/Jean Mfg
	315225	Men's/Boys' Cut & Sew Work Clothing Mfg
	315228	Men's/Boys' Cut & Sew Other Outerwear Mfg
	31523	Women's/Girls' Cut & Sew Apparel Mfg
	315231	Women's/Girls' Cut & Sew Lingerie Mfg
	315232	Women's/Girls' Cut & Sew Blouse Mfg
	315233	Women's/Girls' Cut & Sew Dress Mfg
	315234	Women's/Girls' Cut & Sew Suit/Coat/Skirt Mfg
	315239	Women's/Girls' Cut & Sew Other Outerwear Mfg
	31529	Other Cut & Sew Apparel Mfg
	315291	Infants' Cut & Sew Apparel Mfg
	315292	Fur & Leather Apparel Mfg
	315299	All Other Cut & Sew Apparel Mfg
	3159	Apparel Accessories & Other Apparel Mfg
	31599	Apparel Accessories & Other Apparel Mfg
	315991	Hat, Cap & Millinery Mfg
	315992	Glove & Mitten Mfg
	315993	Men's & Boys' Neckwear Mfg
	315999	Other Apparel Accessories & Other Apparel Mfg
316		**Leather and Allied Product Manufacturing**
	3161	Leather & Hide Tanning & Finishing
	31611	Leather & Hide Tanning & Finishing
	3162	Footwear Mfg
	31621	Footwear Mfg

Can't find what you're looking for? Go to the alphabetic section, starting on page 627.

316211	Rubber & Plastics Footwear Mfg
316212	House Slipper Mfg
316213	Men's Footwear (except Athletic) Mfg
316214	Women's Footwear (except Athletic) Mfg
316219	Other Footwear Mfg
3169	Other Leather & Allied Product Mfg
31699	Other Leather & Allied Product Mfg
316991	Luggage Mfg
316992	Women's Handbag & Purse Mfg
316993	Personal Leather Good (except Purse) Mfg
316999	All Other Leather Good Mfg

321 Wood Product Manufacturing

3211	Sawmills & Wood Preservation
32111	Sawmills & Wood Preservation
321113	Sawmills
321114	Wood Preservation
3212	Veneer, Plywood & Engineered Wood Product Mfg
32121	Veneer, Plywood & Engineered Wood Product Mfg
321211	Hardwood Veneer & Plywood Mfg
321212	Softwood Veneer & Plywood Mfg
321213	Engineered Wood Member (except Truss) Mfg
321214	Truss Mfg
321219	Reconstituted Wood Product Mfg
3219	Other Wood Product Mfg
32191	Millwork
321911	Wood Window & Door Mfg
321912	Cut Stock, Resawing Lumber & Planing
321918	Other Millwork (including Flooring)
32192	Wood Container & Pallet Mfg
32199	All Other Wood Product Mfg
321991	Manufactured Home (Mobile Home) Mfg
321992	Prefabricated Wood Building Mfg
321999	All Other Miscellaneous Wood Product Mfg

322 Paper Manufacturing

3221	Pulp, Paper & Paperboard Mills
32211	Pulp Mills
32212	Paper Mills
322121	Paper (except Newsprint) Mills
322122	Newsprint Mills
32213	Paperboard Mills
3222	Converted Paper Product Mfg
32221	Paperboard Container Mfg
322211	Corrugated & Solid Fiber Box Mfg
322212	Folding Paperboard Box Mfg
322213	Setup Paperboard Box Mfg
322214	Fiber Can, Tube, Drum & Similar Products Mfg
322215	Nonfolding Sanitary Food Container Mfg
32222	Paper Bag & Coated & Treated Paper Mfg
322221	Coated & Lamnd Pkg Paper & Plastics Film Mfg
322222	Coated & Laminated Paper Mfg
322223	Plastics, Foil, & Coated Paper Bag Mfg
322224	Uncoated Paper & Multiwall Bag Mfg
322225	Laminated Aluminum Foil Mfg for Flexible Pkg
322226	Surface-coated Paperboard Mfg
32223	Stationery Product Mfg
322231	Die-cut Paper & Paperboard Office Supply Mfg
322232	Envelope Mfg
322233	Stationery, Tablet & Related Product Mfg
32229	Other Converted Paper Product Mfg
322291	Sanitary Paper Product Mfg
322299	All Other Converted Paper Product Mfg

323 Printing and Related Support Activities

3231	Printing & Related Support Activities
32311	Printing
323110	Commercial Lithographic Printing
323111	Commercial Gravure Printing
323112	Commercial Flexographic Printing
323113	Commercial Screen Printing
323114	Quick Printing
323115	Digital Printing
323116	Manifold Business Form Printing
323117	Book Printing
323118	Blankbook, Looseleaf Binder & Device Mfg
323119	Other Commercial Printing
32312	Printing Support Activities
323121	Tradebinding & Related Work
323122	Prepress Services

For a complete list of abbreviations and their definitions, see page 28

324		**Petroleum and Coal Products Manufacturing**
	3241	Petroleum & Coal Products Mfg
	32411	Petroleum Refineries
	32412	Asphalt Paving, Roofing & Saturated Mat Mfg
	324121	Asphalt Paving Mixture & Block Mfg
	324122	Asphalt Shingle & Coating Materials Mfg
	32419	Other Petroleum & Coal Products Mfg
	324191	Petroleum Lubricating Oil & Grease Mfg
	324199	All Other Petroleum & Coal Products Mfg
325		**Chemical Manufacturing**
	3251	Basic Chemical Mfg
	32511	Petrochemical Mfg
	32512	Industrial Gas Mfg
	32513	Synthetic Dye & Pigment Mfg
	325131	Inorganic Dye & Pigment Mfg
	325132	Synthetic Organic Dye & Pigment Mfg
	32518	Other Basic Inorganic Chemical Mfg
	325181	Alkalies & Chlorine Mfg
	325182	Carbon Black Mfg
	325188	All Other Basic Inorganic Chemical Mfg
	32519	Other Basic Organic Chemical Mfg
	325191	Gum & Wood Chemical Mfg
	325192	Cyclic Crude & Intermediate Mfg
	325193	Ethyl Alcohol Mfg
	325199	All Other Basic Organic Chemical Mfg
	3252	Resin, Syn Rubber, Artf & Syn Fibers/Fil Mfg
	32521	Resin & Synthetic Rubber Mfg
	325211	Plastics Material & Resins Mfg
	325212	Synthetic Rubber Mfg
	32522	Artificial & Synthetic Fibers/Filaments Mfg
	325221	Cellulose Organic Fiber Mfg
	325222	Noncellulosic Organic Fiber Mfg
	3253	Pesticide, Fertilizer & Other Ag Chemical Mfg
	32531	Fertilizer Mfg
	325311	Nitrogenous Fertilizer Mfg
	325312	Phosphatic Fertilizer Mfg
	325314	Fertilizer (Mixing Only) Mfg
	32532	Pesticide & Other Agricultural Chemical Mfg

	3254	Pharmaceutical & Medicine Mfg
	32541	Pharmaceutical & Medicine Mfg
	325411	Medicinal & Botanical Mfg
	325412	Pharmaceutical Preparation Mfg
	325413	In vitro Diagnostic Substance Mfg
	325414	Biological Product (except Diagnostic) Mfg
	3255	Paint, Coating & Adhesive Mfg
	32551	Paint & Coating Mfg
	32552	Adhesive Mfg
	3256	Soap, Cleaners & Toilet Preparation Mfg
	32561	Soap & Cleaning Compound Mfg
	325611	Soap & Other Detergent Mfg
	325612	Polish & Other Sanitation Good Mfg
	325613	Surface Active Agent Mfg
	32562	Toilet Preparation Mfg
	3259	Other Chemical Product & Preparation Mfg
	32591	Printing Ink Mfg
	32592	Explosives Mfg
	32599	All Other Chemical Product & Preparation Mfg
	325991	Custom Compounding of Purchased Resin
	325992	Photo Film, Paper, Plate & Chemical Mfg
	325998	All Other Misc Chemical Product & Prep Mfg
326		**Plastics and Rubber Products Manufacturing**
	3261	Plastics Product Mfg
	32611	Unsupported Plastics Film, Sheet & Bag Mfg
	326111	Unsupported Plastics Bag Mfg
	326112	Unsupported Plastics Packaging Film/Sheet Mfg
	326113	Unsupported Plastics Film/Sheet (except Pkg) Mfg
	32612	Plastics Pipe/Fitting/ Unsupported Shapes Mfg
	326121	Unsupported Plastics Profile Shape Mfg
	326122	Plastics Pipe & Pipe Fitting Mfg
	32613	Laminated Plastics Plate, Sheet & Shape Mfg
	32614	Polystyrene Foam Product Mfg
	32615	Foam Product (except Polystyrene) Mfg
	32616	Plastics Bottle Mfg
	32619	Other Plastics Product Mfg
	326191	Plastics Plumbing Fixture Mfg
	326192	Resilient Floor Covering Mfg

NAICS
Short Titles

326199	All Other Plastics Product Mfg
3262	Rubber Product Mfg
32621	Tire Mfg
326211	Tire Mfg (except Retreading)
326212	Tire Retreading
32622	Rubber & Plastics Hoses & Belting Mfg
32629	Other Rubber Product Mfg
326291	Rubber Product Mfg for Mechanical Use
326299	All Other Rubber Product Mfg

327 Nonmetallic Mineral Product Manufacturing

3271	Clay Product & Refractory Mfg
32711	Pottery, Ceramics & Plumbing Fixture Mfg
327111	Vitreous Plumbing Fixtures/Access/Fitting Mfg
327112	Vitreous China & Other Pottery Product Mfg
327113	Porcelain Electrical Supply Mfg
32712	Clay Building Material & Refractories Mfg
327121	Brick & Structural Clay Tile Mfg
327122	Ceramic Wall & Floor Tile Mfg
327123	Other Structural Clay Product Mfg
327124	Clay Refractory Mfg
327125	Nonclay Refractory Mfg
3272	Glass & Glass Product Mfg
32721	Glass & Glass Product Mfg
327211	Flat Glass Mfg
327212	Other Pressed & Blown Glass & Glassware Mfg
327213	Glass Container Mfg
327215	Glass Product Mfg Made of Purchased Glass
3273	Cement & Concrete Product Mfg
32731	Cement Mfg
32732	Ready-mix Concrete Mfg
32733	Concrete Pipe, Brick & Block Mfg
327331	Concrete Block & Brick Mfg
327332	Concrete Pipe Mfg
32739	Other Concrete Product Mfg
3274	Lime & Gypsum Product Mfg
32741	Lime Mfg
32742	Gypsum Product Mfg
3279	Other Nonmetallic Mineral Product Mfg
32791	Abrasive Product Mfg
32799	All Other Nonmetallic Mineral Product Mfg
327991	Cut Stone & Stone Product Mfg
327992	Ground or Treated Mineral & Earth Mfg

327993	Mineral Wool Mfg
327999	All Other Misc Nonmetallic Mineral Product Mfg

331 Primary Metal Manufacturing

3311	Iron & Steel Mills & Ferroalloy Mfg
33111	Iron & Steel Mills & Ferroalloy Mfg
331111	Iron & Steel Mills
331112	Electrometallurgical Ferroalloy Product Mfg
3312	Steel Product Mfg from Purchased Steel
33121	Iron/Steel Pipe & Tube Mfg from Purch Steel
33122	Rolling & Drawing of Purchased Steel
331221	Rolled Steel Shape Mfg
331222	Steel Wire Drawing
3313	Alumina & Aluminum Production & Processing
33131	Alumina & Aluminum Production & Processing
331311	Alumina Refining
331312	Primary Aluminum Production
331314	Secondary Smelting & Alloying of Aluminum
331315	Aluminum Sheet, Plate & Foil Mfg
331316	Aluminum Extruded Product Mfg
331319	Other Aluminum Rolling & Drawing
3314	Nonferrous (except Alum) Production & Processing
33141	Nonferrous (except Aluminum) Smelting & Refining
331411	Primary Smelting & Refining of Copper
331419	Other Nonferrous Metal Prim Smelting/Refining
33142	Copper Rolling/Drawing/ Extruding & Alloying
331421	Copper Rolling, Drawing & Extruding
331422	Copper Wire (except Mechanical) Drawing
331423	Secondary Smelting/ Refining/Alloying of Copper
33149	Other Nonferrous Roll/Draw/ Extruding/Alloying
331491	Other Nonferrous Metal Roll/Draw/Extruding
331492	Other Nonferrous Secondary Smelt/Refine/Alloying
3315	Foundries
33151	Ferrous Metal Foundries
331511	Iron Foundries

331512	Steel Investment Foundries
331513	Steel Foundries (except Investment)
33152	Nonferrous Metal Foundries
331521	Aluminum Die-casting Foundries
331522	Nonferrous (except Alum) Die-casting Foundries
331524	Aluminum Foundries (except Die-casting)
331525	Copper Foundries (except Die-casting)
331528	Other Nonferrous Foundries (except Die-casting)

332 Fabricated Metal Product Manufacturing

3321	Forging & Stamping
33211	Forging & Stamping
332111	Iron & Steel Forging
332112	Nonferrous Forging
332114	Custom Roll Forming
332115	Crown & Closure Mfg
332116	Metal Stamping
332117	Powder Metallurgy Parts Mfg
3322	Cutlery & Handtool Mfg
33221	Cutlery & Handtool Mfg
332211	Cutlery & Flatware (except Precious) Mfg
332212	Hand & Edge Tool Mfg
332213	Saw Blade & Handsaw Mfg
332214	Kitchen Utensil, Pot & Pan Mfg
3323	Architectural & Structural Metals Mfg
33231	Plate Work & Fabricated Structural Production Mfg
332311	Prefab Metal Building & Component Mfg
332312	Fabricated Structural Metal Mfg
332313	Plate Work Mfg
33232	Ornamental & Architectural Metal Production Mfg
332321	Metal Window & Door Mfg
332322	Sheet Metal Work Mfg
332323	Ornamental & Architectural Metal Work Mfg
3324	Boiler, Tank & Shipping Container Mfg
33241	Power Boiler & Heat Exchanger Mfg
33242	Metal Tank (Heavy Gauge) Mfg
33243	Light Gauge Metal Container Mfg
332431	Metal Can Mfg
332439	Other Metal Container Mfg
3325	Hardware Mfg

33251	Hardware Mfg
3326	Spring & Wire Product Mfg
33261	Spring & Wire Product Mfg
332611	Spring (Heavy Gauge) Mfg
332612	Spring (Light Gauge) Mfg
332618	Other Fabricated Wire Product Mfg
3327	Mach Shops, Turn Production, Screw, Nut, Bolt Mfg
33271	Machine Shops
33272	Turned Product & Screw, Nut & Bolt Mfg
332721	Precision Turned Product Mfg
332722	Bolt, Nut, Screw, Rivet & Washer Mfg
3328	Coating/Engrave/Heat Treating & Other Activity
33281	Coating/Engrave/Heat Treating & Other Activity
332811	Metal Heat Treating
332812	Metal Coating, Engraving, & Allied Services
332813	Electropl/Plating/Polish/ Anodize/Coloring
3329	Other Fabricated Metal Product Mfg
33291	Metal Valve Mfg
332911	Industrial Valve Mfg
332912	Fluid Power Valve & Hose Fitting Mfg
332913	Plumbing Fixture Fitting & Trim Mfg
332919	Other Metal Valve & Pipe Fitting Mfg
33299	All Other Fabricated Metal Product Mfg
332991	Ball & Roller Bearing Mfg
332992	Small Arms Ammunition Mfg
332993	Ammunition (except Small Arms) Mfg
332994	Small Arms Mfg
332995	Other Ordnance & Accessories Mfg
332996	Fabricated Pipe & Pipe Fitting Mfg
332997	Industrial Pattern Mfg
332998	Enameled Iron & Metal Sanitary Ware Mfg
332999	All Other Misc Fabricated Metal Product Mfg

333 Machinery Manufacturing

3331	Ag, Construction & Mining Machinery Mfg
33311	Agricultural Implement Mfg
333111	Farm Machinery & Equipment Mfg

Convert NAICS codes to SIC codes. Turn to page 159.

Convert NAICS codes to SIC codes. Turn to page 159.

NAICS
Short Titles

333112	Lawn & Garden Equipment Mfg
33312	Construction Machinery Mfg
33313	Mining & Oil & Gas Field Machinery Mfg
333131	Mining Machinery & Equipment Mfg
333132	Oil & Gas Field Machinery & Equipment Mfg
3332	Industrial Machinery Mfg
33321	Sawmill & Woodworking Machinery Mfg
33322	Plastics & Rubber Industry Machinery Mfg
33329	Other Industrial Machinery Mfg
333291	Paper Industry Machinery Mfg
333292	Textile Machinery Mfg
333293	Printing Machinery & Equipment Mfg
333294	Food Product Machinery Mfg
333295	Semiconductor Machinery Mfg
333298	All Other Industrial Machinery Mfg
3333	Commercial & Service Industry Machinery Mfg
33331	Commercial & Service Industry Machinery Mfg
333311	Automatic Vending Machine Mfg
333312	Commercial Laundry, Dryclean & Press Mach Mfg
333313	Office Machinery Mfg
333314	Optical Instrument & Lens Mfg
333315	Photographic & Photocopying Equipment Mfg
333319	Other Commercial/Service Industry Machinery Mfg
3334	HVAC & Commercial Refrigeration Equipment Mfg
33341	HVAC & Commercial Refrigeration Equipment Mfg
333411	Air Purification Equipment Mfg
333412	Industrial & Commercial Fan & Blower Mfg
333414	Heating Equipment (except Warm Air Furnaces) Mfg
333415	AC/Warm Air Htg & Commercial Refrig Equip Mfg
3335	Metalworking Machinery Mfg
33351	Metalworking Machinery Mfg
333511	Industrial Mold Mfg
333512	Machine Tool (Metal Cutting Types) Mfg
333513	Machine Tool (Metal Forming Types) Mfg
333514	Special Die/Tool, Die Set, Jig & Fixture Mfg

333515	Cutting Tool & Machine Tool Accessory Mfg
333516	Rolling Mill Machinery & Equipment Mfg
333518	Other Metalworking Machinery Mfg
3336	Engine, Turbine & Power Transmsn Equip Mfg
33361	Engine, Turbine & Power Transmsn Equip Mfg
333611	Turbine & Turbine Generator Set Unit Mfg
333612	Spd Changer, Ind High-speed Drive & Gear Mfg
333613	Mechanical Power Transmission Equipment Mfg
333618	Other Engine Equipment Mfg
3339	Other General Purpose Machinery Mfg
33391	Pump & Compressor Mfg
333911	Pump & Pumping Equipment Mfg
333912	Air & Gas Compressor Mfg
333913	Measuring & Dispensing Pump Mfg
33392	Material Handling Equipment Mfg
333921	Elevator & Moving Stairway Mfg
333922	Conveyor & Conveying Equipment Mfg
333923	Overhead Crane, Hoist & Monorail System Mfg
333924	Ind Truck, Tractor, Trailer, Stacker Mach Mfg
33399	All Other General Purpose Machinery Mfg
333991	Power-driven Hand Tool Mfg
333992	Welding & Soldering Equipment Mfg
333993	Packaging Machinery Mfg
333994	Industrial Process Furnace & Oven Mfg
333995	Fluid Power Cylinder & Actuator Mfg
333996	Fluid Power Pump & Motor Mfg
333997	Scale & Balance (except Laboratory) Mfg
333999	All Other Misc General Purpose Machinery Mfg

334 Computer and Electronic Product Manufacturing

3341	Computer & Peripheral Equipment Mfg
33411	Computer & Peripheral Equipment Mfg
334111	Electronic Computer Mfg
334112	Computer Storage Device Mfg
334113	Computer Terminal Mfg

334119	Other Computer Peripheral Equipment Mfg
3342	Communications Equipment Mfg
33421	Telephone Apparatus Mfg
33422	Radio/TV Broadcast & Wireless Comm Equip Mfg
33429	Other Communications Equipment Mfg
3343	Audio & Video Equipment Mfg
33431	Audio & Video Equipment Mfg
3344	Semiconductor & Other Electronic Component Mfg
33441	Semiconductor & Other Electronic Component Mfg
334411	Electron Tube Mfg
334412	Bare Printed Circuit Board Mfg
334413	Semiconductor & Related Device Mfg
334414	Electronic Capacitor Mfg
334415	Electronic Resistor Mfg
334416	Electronic Coil/Transformer/ Other Inductor Mfg
334417	Electronic Connector Mfg
334418	Printed Circuit Assembly (Electronic Assembly) Mfg
334419	Other Electronic Component Mfg
3345	Nav/Measuring/Medical/ Control Instruments Mfg
33451	Nav/Measuring/Medical/ Control Instruments Mfg
334510	Electromedical Apparatus Mfg
334511	Search, Detection & Navigation Instrument Mfg
334512	Automatic Environmental Control Mfg
334513	Industrial Process Control Mfg
334514	Total Fluid Meter & Counting Device Mfg
334515	Electricity Measuring/Testing Instrument Mfg
334516	Analytical Laboratory Instrument Mfg
334517	Irradiation Apparatus Mfg
334518	Watch, Clock & Part Mfg
334519	Other Measuring & Controlling Device Mfg
3346	Mfg & Reproducing Magnetic & Optical Media
33461	Mfg & Reproducing Magnetic & Optical Media
334611	Software Reproducing
334612	Prerecorded CD/Tape/Record Reproducing
334613	Magnetic and Optical Recording Media Mfg

335 Electrical Equipment, Appliance, and Component Manufacturing

3351	Electric Lighting Equipment Mfg
33511	Electric Lamp Bulb & Part Mfg
33512	Lighting Fixture Mfg
335121	Residential Electric Lighting Fixture Mfg
335122	Commercial Electric Lighting Fixture Mfg
335129	Other Lighting Equipment Mfg
3352	Household Appliance Mfg
33521	Small Electrical Appliance Mfg
335211	Electric Housewares & Fan Mfg
335212	Household Vacuum Cleaner Mfg
33522	Major Appliance Mfg
335221	Household Cooking Appliance Mfg
335222	Household Refrigerator & Freezer Mfg
335224	Household Laundry Equipment Mfg
335228	Other Major Household Appliance Mfg
3353	Electrical Equipment Mfg
33531	Electrical Equipment Mfg
335311	Power/Distribution/Specialty Transformer Mfg
335312	Motor & Generator Mfg
335313	Switchgear & Switchboard Apparatus Mfg
335314	Relay & Industrial Control Mfg
3359	Other Electrical Equipment & Component Mfg
33591	Battery Mfg
335911	Storage Battery Mfg
335912	Primary Battery Mfg
33592	Communication & Energy Wire & Cable Mfg
335921	Fiber Optic Cable Mfg
335929	Other Communication & Energy Wire Mfg
33593	Wiring Device Mfg
335931	Current-carrying Wiring Device Mfg
335932	Noncurrent-carrying Wiring Device Mfg
33599	All Other Electrical Equipment & Component Mfg
335991	Carbon & Graphite Product Mfg
335999	All Other Misc Electrical Equip & Component Mfg

336 Transportation Equipment Manufacturing

3361	Motor Vehicle Mfg
33611	Automobile & Light Duty Motor Vehicle Mfg

NAICS
Short Titles

336111	Automobile Mfg
336112	Light Truck & Utility Vehicle Mfg
33612	Heavy Duty Truck Mfg
3362	Motor Vehicle Body & Trailer Mfg
33621	Motor Vehicle Body & Trailer Mfg
336211	Motor Vehicle Body Mfg
336212	Truck Trailer Mfg
336213	Motor Home Mfg
336214	Travel Trailer & Camper Mfg
3363	Motor Vehicle Parts Mfg
33631	Motor Vehicle Gas Engine & Engine Parts Mfg
336311	Carburetor, Piston, Piston Ring & Valve Mfg
336312	Gasoline Engine & Engine Parts Mfg
33632	MV Electrical & Electronic Equipment Mfg
336321	Vehicular Lighting Equipment Mfg
336322	Other MV Electrical & Electronic Equip Mfg
33633	Motor Vehicle Steering & Suspension Parts Mfg
33634	Motor Vehicle Brake System Mfg
33635	MV Transmission & Power Train Parts Mfg
33636	Motor Vehicle Seating & Interior Trim Mfg
33637	Motor Vehicle Metal Stamping
33639	Other Motor Vehicle Parts Mfg
336391	Motor Vehicle Air Conditioning Mfg
336399	All Other Motor Vehicle Parts Mfg
3364	Aerospace Product & Parts Mfg
33641	Aerospace Product & Parts Mfg
336411	Aircraft Mfg
336412	Aircraft Engine & Engine Parts Mfg
336413	Other Aircraft Part & Auxiliary Equipment Mfg
336414	Guided Missile & Space Vehicle Mfg
336415	Missile/Space Veh Propulsion Unit & Parts Mfg
336419	Other Missile/Space Veh Parts & Aux Equip Mfg
3365	Railroad Rolling Stock Mfg
33651	Railroad Rolling Stock Mfg
3366	Ship & Boat Building
33661	Ship & Boat Building
336611	Ship Building & Repairing
336612	Boat Building
3369	Other Transportation Equipment Mfg

33699	Other Transportation Equipment Mfg
336991	Motorcycle, Bicycle & Parts Mfg
336992	Mil Armored Vehicle, Tank & Tank Component Mfg
336999	All Other Transportation Equipment Mfg

337 Furniture and Related Product Manufacturing

3371	Household & Institutional Furniture & Kitchen Cabnt Mfg
33711	Wood Kitchen Cabinet & Countertop Mfg
33712	Household & Institutional Furniture Mfg
337121	Upholstered Household Furniture Mfg
337122	Nonupholstered Wood Household Furniture Mfg
337124	Metal Household Furniture Mfg
337125	Household Furniture (except Wood & Metal) Mfg
337127	Institutional Furniture Mfg
337129	Wood TV/Radio/Sewing Machine Cabinet Mfg
3372	Office Furniture (including Fixtures) Mfg
33721	Office Furniture (including Fixtures) Mfg
337211	Wood Office Furniture Mfg
337212	Custom Architectural Woodwork & Millwork Mfg
337214	Office Furniture (except Wood) Mfg
337215	Shwcase, Partition, Shelv & Locker Mfg
3379	Other Furniture Related Product Mfg
33791	Mattress Mfg
33792	Blind & Shade Mfg

339 Miscellaneous Manufacturing

3391	Medical Equipment & Supplies Mfg
33911	Medical Equipment & Supplies Mfg
339111	Laboratory Apparatus & Furniture Mfg
339112	Surgical & Medical Instrument Mfg
339113	Surgical Appliance & Supplies Mfg
339114	Dental Equipment & Supplies Mfg
339115	Ophthalmic Goods Mfg
339116	Dental Laboratories
3399	Other Miscellaneous Mfg
33991	Jewelry & Silverware Mfg

339911	Jewelry (except Costume) Mfg
339912	Silverware & Hollowware Mfg
339913	Jewelers' Material & Lapidary Work Mfg
339914	Costume Jewelry & Novelty Mfg
33992	Sporting & Athletic Goods Mfg
33993	Doll, Toy & Game Mfg
339931	Doll & Stuffed Toy Mfg
339932	Game, Toy & Children's Vehicle Mfg
33994	Office Supplies (except Paper) Mfg
339941	Pen & Mechanical Pencil Mfg
339942	Lead Pencil & Art Good Mfg
339943	Marking Device Mfg
339944	Carbon Paper & Inked Ribbon Mfg
33995	Sign Mfg
33999	All Other Misc Mfg
339991	Gasket, Packing & Sealing Device Mfg
339992	Musical Instrument Mfg
339993	Fastener, Button, Needle & Pin Mfg
339994	Broom, Brush & Mop Mfg
339995	Burial Casket Mfg
339999	All Other Miscellaneous Mfg

42 WHOLESALE TRADE

421 Wholesale Trade, Durable Goods

4211	Motor Vehicle/Motor Vehicle Pt & Supply Whsle
42111	Automobile & Other Motor Vehicle Whsle
42112	Motor Vehicle Supplies & New Parts Whsle
42113	Tire & Tube Whsle
42114	Motor Vehicle Parts (Used) Whsle
4212	Furniture & Home Furnishing Whsle
42121	Furniture Whsle
42122	Home Furnishing Whsle
4213	Lumber & Other Construction Materials Whsle
42131	Lumber, Plywood, Millwork & Wood Panel Whsle
42132	Brick & Related Construction Material Whsle
42133	Roofing, Siding & Insulation Material Whsle
42139	Other Construction Material Whsle
4214	Professional & Commercial Equip & Supp Whsle

42141	Photographic Equipment & Supplies Whsle
42142	Office Equipment Whsle
42143	Computer & Peripheral Equip & Software Whsle
42144	Other Commercial Equipment Whsle
42145	Medical/Dental/Hospital Equip & Supp Whsle
42146	Ophthalmic Goods Whsle
42149	Other Professional Equipment & Supplies Whsle
4215	Metal & Mineral (except Petroleum) Whsle
42151	Metal Service Centers & Offices
42152	Coal & Other Mineral & Ore Whsle
4216	Electrical Goods Whsle
42161	Elec Equip/Wiring Supp/Const Material Whsle
42162	Electric Appliance/TV/Radio Set Whsle
42169	Other Electronic Parts & Equipment Whsle
4217	Hardware, & Plumb & Heating Equip & Sup Whsle
42171	Hardware Whsle
42172	Plumbing & Heating Equipment & Supplies Whsle
42173	Warm Air Heating & AC Equip & Supplies Whsle
42174	Refrigeration Equipment & Supplies Whsle
4218	Machinery, Equipment & Supplies Whsle
42181	Const & Mining (except Petroleum) Equip Whsle
42182	Farm & Garden Machinery & Equipment Whsle
42183	Industrial Machinery & Equipment Whsle
42184	Industrial Supplies Whsle
42185	Service Establishment Equip & Supplies Whsle
42186	Transportation Equip/Supplies (except MV) Whsle
4219	Miscellaneous Durable Goods Whsle
42191	Sporting & Recreational Goods & Supply Whsle
42192	Toy & Hobby Goods & Supplies Whsle
42193	Recyclable Material Whsle
42194	Jewelry/Watch/Precious Stone & Metal Whsle
42199	Other Miscellaneous Durable Goods Whsle

Visit page 18 to learn about classification changes to the Wholesale Trade sector.

NAICS
Short Titles

422	**Wholesale Trade, Nondurable Goods**
4221	Paper & Paper Product Whsle
42211	Printing & Writing Paper Whsle
42212	Stationery & Office Supplies Whsle
42213	Industrial & Personal Service Paper Whsle
4222	Drugs & Druggists' Sundries Whsle
42221	Drugs & Druggists' Sundries Whsle
4223	Apparel, Piece Goods & Notions Whsle
42231	Piece Goods, Notions & Other Dry Goods Whsle
42232	Men's & Boys' Clothing & Furnishings Whsle
42233	Women's/Children's/Infants' Clothing Whsle
42234	Footwear Whsle
4224	Grocery & Related Product Whsle
42241	General Line Grocery Whsle
42242	Packaged Frozen Food Whsle
42243	Dairy Product (except Dried or Canned) Whsle
42244	Poultry & Poultry Product Whsle
42245	Confectionery Whsle
42246	Fish & Seafood Whsle
42247	Meat & Meat Product Whsle
42248	Fresh Fruit & Vegetable Whsle
42249	Other Grocery & Related Products Whsle
4225	Farm Product Raw Material Whsle
42251	Grain & Field Bean Whsle
42252	Livestock Whsle
42259	Other Farm Product Raw Material Whsle
4226	Chemical & Allied Products Whsle
42261	Plastics Materials & Basic Forms/Shapes Whsle
42269	Other Chemical & Allied Products Whsle
4227	Petroleum & Petroleum Products Whsle
42271	Petroleum Bulk Stations & Terminals
42272	Petroleum Production Whsle (except Bulk Stations & Terminals)
4228	Beer/Wine/Distilled Alcoholic Beverage Whsle
42281	Beer & Ale Whsle
42282	Wine & Distilled Alcoholic Beverage Whsle
4229	Miscellaneous Nondurable Goods Whsle

42291	Farm Supplies Whsle
42292	Book, Periodical & Newspaper Whsle
42293	Flower/Nursery Stock/Florists' Supplies Whsle
42294	Tobacco & Tobacco Product Whsle
42295	Paint, Varnish & Supplies Whsle
42299	Other Miscellaneous Nondurable Goods Whsle

44-45	**RETAIL TRADE**
441	**Motor Vehicle and Parts Dealers**
4411	Automobile Dealers
44111	New Car Dealers
44112	Used Car Dealers
4412	Other Motor Vehicle Dealers
44121	Recreational Vehicle Dealers
44122	Motorcycle & Boat & Other MV Dealers
441221	Motorcycle Dealers
441222	Boat Dealers
441229	All Other Motor Vehicle Dealers
4413	Automotive Parts, Accessories & Tire Stores
44131	Automotive Parts, Accessories & Tire Stores
44132	Tire Dealers
442	**Furniture and Home Furnishings Stores**
4421	Furniture Stores
44211	Furniture Stores
4422	Home Furnishings Stores
44221	Floor Covering Stores
44229	Other Home Furnishings Stores
442291	Window Treatment Stores
442299	All Other Home Furnishings Stores
443	**Electronics and Appliance Stores**
4431	Electronics & Appliance Stores
44311	Appliance, TV & Other Electronics Stores
443111	Household Appliance Stores
443112	Radio, Television & Other Electronics Stores
44312	Computer & Software Stores
44313	Camera & Photographic Supplies Stores
444	**Building Material and Garden Equipment and Supplies Dealers**
4441	Building Material & Supplies Dealers
44411	Home Centers

44412	Paint & Wallpaper Stores
44413	Hardware Stores
44419	Other Building Material Dealers
4442	Lawn & Garden Equip & Supplies Stores
44421	Outdoor Power Equipment Stores
44422	Nursery & Garden Centers

445 Food and Beverage Stores

4451	Grocery Stores
44511	Grocery (except Convenience) Stores
44512	Convenience Stores
4452	Specialty Food Stores
44521	Meat Markets
44522	Fish & Seafood Markets
44523	Fruit & Vegetable Markets
44529	Other Specialty Food Stores
445291	Baked Goods Stores
445292	Confectionery & Nut Stores
445299	All Other Specialty Food Stores
4453	Beer, Wine & Liquor Stores
44531	Beer, Wine & Liquor Stores

446 Health and Personal Care Stores

4461	Health & Personal Care Stores
44611	Pharmacies & Drug Stores
44612	Cosmetics, Beauty Supplies & Perfume Stores
44613	Optical Goods Stores
44619	Other Health & Personal Care Stores
446191	Food (Health) Supplement Stores
446199	All Other Health & Personal Care Stores

447 Gasoline Stations

4471	Gasoline Stations
44711	Gasoline Stations with Convenience Stores
44719	Other Gasoline Stations

448 Clothing and Clothing Accessories Stores

4481	Clothing Stores
44811	Men's Clothing Stores
44812	Women's Clothing Stores
44813	Children's & Infants' Clothing Stores
44814	Family Clothing Stores
44815	Clothing Accessories Stores
44819	Other Clothing Stores
4482	Shoe Stores

44821	Shoe Stores
4483	Jewelry, Luggage & Leather Goods Stores
44831	Jewelry Stores
44832	Luggage & Leather Goods Stores

451 Sporting Goods, Hobby, Book, and Music Stores

4511	Sporting Goods/Hobby/Musical Instrument Stores
45111	Sporting Goods Stores
45112	Hobby, Toy & Game Stores
45113	Sewing, Needlework & Piece Goods Stores
45114	Musical Instrument & Supplies Stores
4512	Book, Periodical & Music Stores
45121	Book Stores & News Dealers
451211	Book Stores
451212	News Dealers & Newsstands
45122	Prerecorded Tape, CD & Record Stores

452 General Merchandise Stores

4521	Department Stores
45211	Department Stores
4529	Other General Merchandise Stores
45291	Warehouse Clubs & Superstores
45299	All Other General Merchandise Stores

453 Miscellaneous Store Retailers

4531	Florists
45311	Florists
4532	Office Supplies, Stationery & Gift Stores
45321	Office Supplies & Stationery Stores
45322	Gift, Novelty & Souvenir Stores
4533	Used Merchandise Stores
45331	Used Merchandise Stores
4539	Other Miscellaneous Store Retailers
45391	Pet & Pet Supplies Stores
45392	Art Dealers
45393	Manufactured (Mobile) Home Dealers
45399	All Other Miscellaneous Store Retailers
453991	Tobacco Stores
453998	All Other Misc Store Retailers (except Tobacco)

Visit page 18 to learn about classification changes to the Retail Trade sector.

NAICS
Short Titles

454		**Nonstore Retailers**
	4541	Electronic Shopping & Mail-order Houses
	45411	Electronic Shopping & Mail-order Houses
	4542	Vending Machine Operators
	45421	Vending Machine Operators
	4543	Direct Selling Establishments
	45431	Fuel Dealers
	454311	Heating Oil Dealers
	454312	Liquefied Petroleum Gas (Bottled Gas) Dealers
	454319	Other Fuel Dealers
	45439	Other Direct Selling Establishments

48-49	**TRANSPORTATION AND WAREHOUSING**

481		**Air Transportation**
	4811	Scheduled Air Transportation
	48111	Scheduled Air Transportation
	481111	Scheduled Passenger Air Transportation
	481112	Scheduled Freight Air Transportation
	4812	Nonscheduled Air Transportation
	48121	Nonscheduled Air Transportation
	481211	Nonscheduled Chartered Passenger Air Trans
	481212	Nonscheduled Chartered Freight Air Trans
	481219	Other Nonscheduled Air Transportation

482		**Rail Transportation**
	4821	Rail Transportation
	48211	Rail Transportation
	482111	Line-haul Railroads
	482112	Short Line Railroads

483		**Water Transportation**
	4831	Deep Sea, Coastal & Great Lakes Water Transportation
	48311	Deep Sea, Coastal & Great Lakes Water Transportation
	483111	Deep Sea Freight Transportation
	483112	Deep Sea Passenger Transportation
	483113	Coastal & Great Lakes Freight Transportation
	483114	Coastal & Great Lakes Passenger Transportation
	4832	Inland Water Transportation
	48321	Inland Water Transportation
	483211	Inland Water Freight Transportation
	483212	Inland Water Passenger Transportation

484		**Truck Transportation**
	4841	General Freight Trucking
	48411	General Freight Trucking, Local
	48412	General Freight Trucking, Long-distance
	484121	General Freight Trucking, Long-distance, TL
	484122	General Freight Trucking, Long-distance, LTL
	4842	Specialized Freight Trucking
	48421	Used Household & Office Goods Moving
	48422	Specialized Frgt (except Used) Trucking, Local
	48423	Specialized Frgt (except Used) Trucking, Long-distance

485		**Transit and Ground Passenger Transportation**
	4851	Urban Transit Systems
	48511	Urban Transit Systems
	485111	Mixed Mode Transit Systems
	485112	Commuter Rail Systems
	485113	Bus & Other Motor Vehicle Transit Systems
	485119	Other Urban Transit Systems
	4852	Interurban & Rural Bus Transportation
	48521	Interurban & Rural Bus Transportation
	4853	Taxi & Limousine Service
	48531	Taxi Service
	48532	Limousine Service
	4854	School & Employee Bus Transportation
	48541	School & Employee Bus Transportation
	4855	Charter Bus Industry
	48551	Charter Bus Industry
	4859	Other Transit & Ground Passenger Transportation
	48599	Other Transit & Ground Passenger Transportation
	485991	Special Needs Transportation
	485999	All Other Transit & Ground Passenger Trans

486		**Pipeline Transportation**
	4861	Pipeline Transportation of Crude Oil
	48611	Pipeline Transportation of Crude Oil

4862	Pipeline Transportation of Natural Gas	
48621	Pipeline Transportation of Natural Gas	
4869	Other Pipeline Transportation	
48691	Pipeline Trans of Refined Petroleum Products	
48699	All Other Pipeline Transportation	

487 Scenic and Sightseeing Transportation

4871	Scenic & Sightseeing Transportation, Land
48711	Scenic & Sightseeing Transportation, Land
4872	Scenic & Sightseeing Transportation, Water
48721	Scenic & Sightseeing Transportation, Water
4879	Scenic & Sightseeing Transportation, Other
48799	Scenic & Sightseeing Transportation, Other

488 Transportation Support Activities

4881	Air Transportation Support Activities
48811	Airport Operations
488111	Air Traffic Control
488119	Other Airport Operations
48819	Other Air Transportation Support Activities
4882	Rail Transportation Support Activities
48821	Rail Transportation Support Activities
4883	Water Transportation Support Activities
48831	Port & Harbor Operations
48832	Marine Cargo Handling
48833	Navigational Services to Shipping
48839	Other Water Transportation Support Activities
4884	Road Transportation Support Activities
48841	Motor Vehicle Towing
48849	Other Road Transportation Support Activities
4885	Freight Transportation Arrangement
48851	Freight Transportation Arrangement
4889	Other Transportation Support Activities
48899	Other Transportation Support Activities

488991	Packing & Crating	
488999	All Other Transportation Support Activities	

491 Postal Service

4911	Postal Service
49111	Postal Service

492 Couriers and Messengers

4921	Couriers
49211	Couriers
4922	Local Messengers & Local Delivery
49221	Local Messengers & Local Delivery

493 Warehousing and Storage

4931	Warehousing & Storage
49311	General Warehousing & Storage
49312	Refrigerated Warehousing & Storage
49313	Farm Product Warehousing & Storage
49319	Other Warehousing & Storage

51 INFORMATION

511 Publishing Industries

5111	Newspaper/Periodical/ Book/Database Publishers
51111	Newspaper Publishers
51112	Periodical Publishers
51113	Book Publishers
51114	Database and Directory Publishers
51119	Other Publishers
511191	Greeting Card Publishers
511199	All Other Publishers
5112	Software Publishers
51121	Software Publishers

512 Motion Picture and Sound Recording Industries

5121	Motion Picture & Video Industries
51211	Motion Picture & Video Production
51212	Motion Picture & Video Distribution
51213	Motion Picture & Video Exhibition
512131	Motion Picture Theaters (except Drive-ins)
512132	Drive-in Motion Picture Theaters
51219	Postprod & Other Movie & Video Industries

Discover the highlights of the Information sector on page 17.

NAICS
Short Titles

	512191	Teleproduction & Other Postproduction Services
	512199	Other Motion Picture & Video Industries
	5122	Sound Recording Industries
	51221	Record Production
	51222	Integrated Record Production/Distribution
	51223	Music Publishers
	51224	Sound Recording Studios
	51229	Other Sound Recording Industries

513 **Broadcasting and Telecommunications**

	5131	Radio & Television Broadcasting
	51311	Radio Broadcasting
	513111	Radio Networks
	513112	Radio Stations
	51312	Television Broadcasting
	5132	Cable Networks & Program Distribution
	51321	Cable Networks
	51322	Cable & Other Program Distribution
	5133	Telecommunications
	51331	Wired Telecommunications Carriers
	51332	Wireless Telecom Carriers (except Satellite)
	513321	Paging
	513322	Cellular & Other Wireless Telecommunications
	51333	Telecommunications Resellers
	51334	Satellite Telecommunications
	51339	Other Telecommunications

514 **Information and Data Processing Services**

	5141	Information Services
	51411	News Syndicates
	51412	Libraries & Archives
	51419	Other Information Services
	514191	Online Information Services
	514199	All Other Information Services
	5142	Data Processing Services
	51421	Data Processing Services

52 **FINANCE AND INSURANCE**

521 **Monetary Authorities—Central Bank**

	5211	Monetary Authorities— Central Bank
	52111	Monetary Authorities— Central Bank

522 **Credit Intermediation and Related Activities**

	5221	Depository Credit Intermediation
	52211	Commercial Banking
	52212	Savings Institutions
	52213	Credit Unions
	52219	Other Depository Credit Intermediation
	5222	Nondepository Credit Intermediation
	52221	Credit Card Issuing
	52222	Sales Financing
	52229	Other Nondepository Credit Intermediation
	522291	Consumer Lending
	522292	Real Estate Credit
	522293	International Trade Financing
	522294	Secondary Market Financing
	522298	All Other Nondepository Credit Intermediation
	5223	Activities Related to Credit Intermediation
	52231	Mortgage & Nonmortgage Brokers
	52232	Financial Clearinghouse & Reserve Activities
	52239	Other Credit Intermediation Activities

523 **Security, Commodity Contracts, and Like Activity**

	5231	Security & Comdty Contracts Intermed & Brokerage
	52311	Investment Banking & Securities Dealing
	52312	Securities Brokerage
	52313	Commodity Contracts Dealing
	52314	Commodity Contracts Brokerage
	5232	Securities & Commodity Exchanges
	52321	Securities & Commodity Exchanges
	5239	Other Financial Investment Activities
	52391	Miscellaneous Intermediation
	52392	Portfolio Management
	52393	Investment Advice
	52399	All Other Financial Investment Activities
	523991	Trust, Fiduciary & Custody Activities
	523999	Miscellaneous Financial Investment Activities

For a complete list of abbreviations and their definitions, see page 28

524   **Insurance Carriers and Related Activities**

5241	Insurance Carriers
52411	Direct Life/Health/Medical Insurance Carriers
524113	Direct Life Insurance Carriers
524114	Direct Health & Medical Insurance Carriers
52412	Other Direct Insurance Carriers
524126	Direct Property & Casualty Insurance Carriers
524127	Direct Title Insurance Carriers
524128	All Other Direct Insurance Carriers
52413	Reinsurance Carriers
5242	Agencies & Other Insurance Related Activities
52421	Insurance Agencies & Brokerages
52429	Other Insurance Related Activities
524291	Claims Adjusting
524292	Insurance & Pension Funds, Third Party Admin
524298	All Other Insurance Related Activities

525   **Funds, Trusts, and Other Financial Vehicles**

5251	Insurance & Employee Benefit Funds
52511	Pension Funds
52512	Health & Welfare Funds
52519	Other Insurance Funds
5259	Other Investment Pools & Funds
52591	Open-end Investment Funds
52592	Trusts, Estates & Agency Accounts
52593	Real Estate Investment Trusts
52599	Other Financial Vehicles

53   **REAL ESTATE AND RENTAL AND LEASING**

531   **Real Estate**

5311	Lessors of Real Estate
53111	Lessors of Residential Buildings & Dwellings
53112	Lessors of Nonres Bldg (except Miniwarehouse)
53113	Lessors of Miniwarehouse & Self Storage Units
53119	Lessors of Other Real Estate Property
5312	Offices of Real Estate Agents & Brokers
53121	Offices of Real Estate Agents & Brokers
5313	Activities Related to Real Estate
53131	Real Estate Property Managers
531311	Residential Property Managers
531312	Nonresidential Property Managers
53132	Offices of Real Estate Appraisers
53139	Other Activities Related to Real Estate

532   **Rental and Leasing Services**

5321	Automotive Equipment Rental & Leasing
53211	Passenger Car Rental & Leasing
532111	Passenger Car Rental
532112	Passenger Car Leasing
53212	Truck, Utility Trailer & RV Rental & Leasing
5322	Consumer Goods Rental
53221	Consumer Electronics & Appliances Rental
53222	Formal Wear & Costume Rental
53223	Video Tape & Disk Rental
53229	Other Consumer Goods Rental
532291	Home Health Equipment Rental
532292	Recreational Goods Rental
532299	All Other Consumer Goods Rental
5323	General Rental Centers
53231	General Rental Centers
5324	Commercial/Industrial Equip Rental & Leasing
53241	Const/Trans/Mining Equip Rental & Leasing
532411	Commercial Trans Equip (except MV) Rental/Lease
532412	Const/Mining/Forestry Equip Rental & Leasing
53242	Office Machinery & Equipment Rental & Leasing
53249	Other Commercial/Industrial Equip Rental/Lease

533   **Lessors of Other Nonfinancial Intangible Asset**

5331	Lessors of Other Nonfinancial Intangible Asset
53311	Lessors of Other Nonfinancial Intangible Asset

NAICS
Short Titles

54	**PROFESSIONAL, SCIENTIFIC, AND TECHNICAL SERVICES**	
541	**Professional, Scientific, and Technical Services**	
	5411	Legal Services
	54111	Offices of Lawyers
	54112	Offices of Notaries
	54119	Other Legal Services
	541191	Title Abstract & Settlement Offices
	541199	All Other Legal Services
	5412	Accounting/Tax Prep/ Bookkeep/Payroll Services
	54121	Accounting/Tax Prep/ Bookkeep/Payroll Services
	541211	Offices of Certified Public Accountants
	541213	Tax Preparation Services
	541214	Payroll Services
	541219	Other Accounting Services
	5413	Architectural, Engineering & Related Services
	54131	Architectural Services
	54132	Landscape Architectural Services
	54133	Engineering Services
	54134	Drafting Services
	54135	Building Inspection Services
	54136	Geophysical Surveying & Mapping Services
	54137	Surveying/Mapping (except Geophysical) Services
	54138	Testing Laboratories
	5414	Specialized Design Services
	54141	Interior Design Services
	54142	Industrial Design Services
	54143	Graphic Design Services
	54149	Other Specialized Design Services
	5415	Computer Systems Design & Related Services
	54151	Computer Systems Design & Related Services
	541511	Custom Computer Programming Services
	541512	Computer Systems Design Services
	541513	Computer Facilities Management Services
	541519	Other Computer Related Services
	5416	Management, Sci & Tech Consulting Services
	54161	Management Consulting Services
	541611	Admin & Gen Management Consulting Services

	541612	Human Res & Exec Search Consulting Services
	541613	Marketing Consulting Services
	541614	Process, Phys Dist & Log Consulting Services
	541618	Other Management Consulting Services
	54162	Environmental Consulting Services
	54169	Other Scientific & Technical Consulting Services
	5417	Scientific R&D Services
	54171	R&D in Physical, Engineering & Life Sciences
	54172	R&D in Social Sciences & Humanities
	5418	Advertising & Related Services
	54181	Advertising Agencies
	54182	Public Relations Agencies
	54183	Media Buying Agencies
	54184	Media Representatives
	54185	Display Advertising
	54186	Direct Mail Advertising
	54187	Advertising Material Distribution Services
	54189	Other Services Related to Advertising
	5419	Other Professional/Scientific/ Technical Service
	54191	Marketing Research & Public Opinion Polling
	54192	Photographic Services
	541921	Photography Studios, Portrait
	541922	Commercial Photography
	54193	Translation & Interpretation Services
	54194	Veterinary Services
	54199	All Other Prof, Scientific & Technical Services
55	**MANAGEMENT OF COMPANIES AND ENTERPRISES**	
551	**Management of Companies and Enterprises**	
	5511	Management of Companies & Enterprises
	55111	Management of Companies & Enterprises
	551111	Offices of Bank Holding Companies
	551112	Offices of Other Holding Companies
	551114	Corp, Subsidiary & Regional Managing Offices

For a complete list of abbreviations and their definitions, see page 28

56	**ADMINISTRATIVE AND SUPPORT WASTE MANAGEMENT AND REMEDIATION SERVICES**

561	**Administrative and Support Services**
5611	Office Administrative Services
56111	Office Administrative Services
5612	Facilities Support Services
56121	Facilities Support Services
5613	Employment Services
56131	Employment Placement Agencies
56132	Temporary Help Services
56133	Employee Leasing Services
5614	Business Support Services
56141	Document Preparation Services
56142	Telephone Call Centers
561421	Telephone Answering Services
561422	Telemarketing Bureaus
56143	Business Service Centers
561431	Private Mail Centers
561439	Other Business Service Centers (incl Copy Shops)
56144	Collection Agencies
56145	Credit Bureaus
56149	Other Business Support Services
561491	Repossession Services
561492	Court Reporting & Stenotype Services
561499	All Other Business Support Services
5615	Travel Arrangement & Reservation Services
56151	Travel Agencies
56152	Tour Operators
56159	Other Travel Arrangement & Reservation Services
561591	Convention and Visitors Bureaus
561599	All Other Travel Arrange & Reservation Services
5616	Investigation & Security Services
56161	Investigation, Guard & Armored Car Services
561611	Investigation Services
561612	Security Guards & Patrol Services
561613	Armored Car Services
56162	Security Systems Services
561621	Security Systems Services, (except Locksmiths)
561622	Locksmiths
5617	Services to Buildings & Dwellings

56171	Exterminating & Pest Control Services
56172	Janitorial Services
56173	Landscaping Services
56174	Carpet & Upholstery Cleaning Services
56179	Other Services to Buildings & Dwellings
5619	Other Support Services
56191	Packaging & Labeling Services
56192	Convention & Trade Show Organizers
56199	All Other Support Services

562	**Waste Management and Remediation Services**
5621	Waste Collection
56211	Waste Collection
562111	Solid Waste Collection
562112	Hazardous Waste Collection
562119	Other Waste Collection
5622	Waste Treatment & Disposal
56221	Waste Treatment & Disposal
562211	Hazardous Waste Treatment & Disposal
562212	Solid Waste Landfill
562213	Solid Waste Combustors & Incinerators
562219	Other Nonhazardous Waste Treatment & Disposal
5629	Remediation & Other Waste Management Services
56291	Remediation Services
56292	Materials Recovery Facilities
56299	All Other Waste Management Services
562991	Septic Tank & Related Services
562998	All Other Miscellaneous Waste Management

61	**EDUCATIONAL SERVICES**

611	**Educational Services**
6111	Elementary & Secondary Schools
61111	Elementary & Secondary Schools
6112	Junior Colleges
61121	Junior Colleges
6113	Colleges, Universities & Professional Schools
61131	Colleges, Universities & Professional Schools
6114	Business Schools & Computer & Mgt Training
61141	Business & Secretarial Schools
61142	Computer Training

Convert NAICS codes to SIC codes. Turn to page 159.

For a complete list of abbreviations and their definitions, see page 28

NAICS
Short Titles

61143	Professional/Management Development Training
6115	Technical & Trade Schools
61151	Technical & Trade Schools
611511	Cosmetology & Barber Schools
611512	Flight Training
611513	Apprenticeship Training
611519	Other Technical & Trade Schools
6116	Other Schools & Instruction
61161	Fine Arts Schools
61162	Sports & Recreation Instruction
61163	Language Schools
61169	All Other Schools & Instruction
611691	Exam Preparation & Tutoring
611692	Automobile Driving Schools
611699	All Other Miscellaneous Schools & Instruction
6117	Educational Support Services
61171	Educational Support Services

62 HEALTH CARE AND SOCIAL ASSISTANCE

621 Ambulatory Health Care Services

6211	Offices of Physicians
62111	Offices of Physicians
621111	Offices of Physicians (except Mental Health)
621112	Offices of Physicians, Mental Health
6212	Offices of Dentists
62121	Offices of Dentists
6213	Offices of Other Health Practitioners
62131	Offices of Chiropractors
62132	Offices of Optometrists
62133	Offices of Other Mental Health Practitioners
62134	Offices of PT/OT/Speech Therapy & Audiology
62139	All Other Health Practitioners' Offices
621391	Offices of Podiatrists
621399	Offices of All Other Misc Health Practitioners
6214	Outpatient Care Centers
62141	Family Planning Centers
62142	Outpatient Mental Health/Substance Abuse Ctrs
62149	Other Outpatient Care Centers
621491	HMO Medical Centers
621492	Kidney Dialysis Centers
621493	Freestanding Ambulatory Surgery/Emergency Ctr
621498	All Other Outpatient Care Centers

6215	Medical & Diagnostic Laboratories
62151	Medical & Diagnostic Laboratories
621511	Medical Laboratories
621512	Diagnostic Imaging Centers
6216	Home Health Care Services
62161	Home Health Care Services
6219	Other Ambulatory Health Care Services
62191	Ambulance Services
62199	All Other Ambulatory Health Care Services
621991	Blood & Organ Banks
621999	All Other Misc Ambulatory Health Care Services

622 Hospitals

6221	General Medical & Surgical Hospitals
62211	General Medical & Surgical Hospitals
6222	Psychiatric & Substance Abuse Hospitals
62221	Psychiatric & Substance Abuse Hospitals
6223	Other Specialty Hospitals
62231	Other Specialty Hospitals

623 Nursing and Residential Care Facilities

6231	Nursing Care Facilities
62311	Nursing Care Facilities
6232	Residential Mental Retardation/Health Facilities
62321	Residential Mental Retardation Facilities
62322	Residential Mental Health/Subst Abuse Facilities
6233	Community Care Facilities for the Elderly
62331	Community Care Facilities for the Elderly
623311	Continuing Care Retirement Communities
623312	Homes for the Elderly
6239	Other Residential Care Facilities
62399	Other Residential Care Facilities

624 Social Assistance

6241	Individual & Family Services
62411	Child & Youth Services
62412	Services for Elderly & Disabled Persons
62419	Other Individual & Family Services
6242	Community/Emergency & Other Relief Services
62421	Community Food Services

	62422	Community Housing Services
	624221	Temporary Shelters
	624229	Other Community Housing Services
	62423	Emergency & Other Relief Services
	6243	Vocational Rehabilitation Services
	62431	Vocational Rehabilitation Services
	6244	Child Day Care Services
	62441	Child Day Care Services

71 ARTS, ENTERTAINMENT, AND RECREATION

711 Perform Arts, Spectator Sports, and Related Industries

	7111	Performing Arts Companies
	71111	Theater Companies & Dinner Theaters
	71112	Dance Companies
	71113	Musical Groups & Artists
	71119	Other Performing Arts Companies
	7112	Spectator Sports
	71121	Spectator Sports
	711211	Sports Teams and Clubs
	711212	Racetracks
	711219	Other Spectator Sports
	7113	Promoters of Entertainment Events
	71131	Promoters of Entertainment Events w/Facility
	71132	Promoters of Entertainment Events w/o Facility
	7114	Agents/Managers for Artists & Other Public Figu
	71141	Agents/Managers for Artists & Other Public Figu
	7115	Independent Artists, Writers & Performers
	71151	Independent Artists, Writers & Performers

712 Museums, Historical Sites, and Like Institutions

	7121	Museums, Historical Sites & Like Institutions
	71211	Museums
	71212	Historical Sites
	71213	Zoos & Botanical Gardens
	71219	Nature Parks & Other Similar Institutions

713 Amusement, Gambling & Recreation Industries

	7131	Amusement Parks & Arcades
	71311	Amusement & Theme Parks
	71312	Amusement Arcades
	7132	Gambling Industries
	71321	Casinos (except Hotel Casinos)
	71329	Other Gambling Industries
	7139	Other Amusement & Recreation Industries
	71391	Golf Courses & Country Clubs
	71392	Skiing Facilities
	71393	Marinas
	71394	Fitness & Recreational Sports Centers
	71395	Bowling Centers
	71399	All Other Amusement & Recreation Industries

72 ACCOMMODATION AND FOOD SERVICES

721 Accommodation

	7211	Traveler Accommodation
	72111	Hotels (except Casino Hotels) & Motels
	72112	Casino Hotels
	72119	Other Traveler Accommodation
	721191	Bed & Breakfast Inns
	721199	All Other Traveler Accommodation
	7212	RV Parks & Recreational Camps
	72121	RV Parks & Recreational Camps
	721211	RV Parks & Campgrounds
	721214	Recreational/Vacation Camps (except campgrounds)
	7213	Rooming & Boarding Houses
	72131	Rooming & Boarding Houses

722 Food Services and Drinking Places

	7221	Full-service Restaurants
	72211	Full-service Restaurants
	7222	Limited-service Eating Places
	72221	Limited-service Eating Places
	722211	Limited-service Restaurants
	722212	Cafeterias
	722213	Snack & Nonalcoholic Beverage Bars
	7223	Special Food Services
	72231	Food Service Contractors
	72232	Caterers
	72233	Mobile Food Services
	7224	Drinking Places (Alcoholic Beverages)
	72241	Drinking Places (Alcoholic Beverages)

Visit page 16 to learn about classification changes to the Accommodation & Food Service sector.

Convert NAICS codes to SIC codes. Turn to page 159.

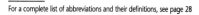

For a complete list of abbreviations and their definitions, see page 28

NAICS
Short Titles

81 OTHER SERVICES, EXCEPT PUBLIC ADMINISTRATION

811 Repair and Maintenance

8111	Automotive R&M
81111	Automotive Mechanical & Electrical R&M
811111	General Automotive Repair
811112	Automotive Exhaust System Repair
811113	Automotive Transmission Repair
811118	Other Automotive Mechanical & Electrical R&M
81112	Automotive Body/Paint/Interior & Glass Repair
811121	Automotive Body, Paint & Interior R&M
811122	Automotive Glass Replacement Shops
81119	Other Automotive R&M
811191	Automotive Oil Change & Lubrication Shops
811192	Carwashes
811198	All Other Automotive R&M
8112	Electronic & Precision Equipment R&M
81121	Electronic & Precision Equipment R&M
811211	Consumer Electronics R&M
811212	Computer & Office Machine R&M
811213	Communication Equipment R&M
811219	Other Electronic & Precision Equipment R&M
8113	Commercial Equipment (except Auto & Elec) R&M
81131	Commercial Equipment (except Auto & Elec) R&M
8114	Personal & Household Goods R&M
81141	Home/Garden Equipment & Appliance R&M
811411	Home & Garden Equipment R&M
811412	Appliance R&M
81142	Reupholstery & Furniture Repair
81143	Footwear & Leather Goods Repair
81149	Other Personal & Household Goods R&M

812 Personal and Laundry Services

8121	Personal Care Services
81211	Hair, Nail & Skin Care Services
812111	Barber Shops
812112	Beauty Salons
812113	Nail Salons
81219	Other Personal Care Services
812191	Diet & Weight Reducing Centers
812199	Other Personal Care Services
8122	Death Care Services
81221	Funeral Homes
81222	Cemeteries & Crematories
8123	Drycleaning & Laundry Services
81231	Coin-operated Laundries & Drycleaners
81232	Drycleaning & Laundry Services (except Coin-op)
81233	Linen & Uniform Supply
812331	Linen Supply
812332	Industrial Launderers
8129	Other Personal Services
81291	Pet Care (except Veterinary) Services
81292	Photofinishing
812921	Photofinishing Laboratories (except One-hour)
812922	One-hour Photofinishing
81293	Parking Lots & Garages
81299	All Other Personal Services

813 Religious, Grantmaking, Civic, Professional, and Similar Organizations

8131	Religious Organizations
81311	Religious Organizations
8132	Grantmaking & Giving Services
81321	Grantmaking & Giving Services
813211	Grantmaking Foundations
813212	Voluntary Health Organizations
813219	Other Grantmaking & Giving Services
8133	Social Advocacy Organizations
81331	Social Advocacy Organizations
813311	Human Rights Organizations
813312	Environment & Wildlife Organizations
813319	Other Social Advocacy Organizations
8134	Civic & Social Organizations
81341	Civic & Social Organizations
8139	Business/Labor/Political/Like Organizations
81391	Business Associations
81392	Professional Organizations
81393	Labor Unions & Similar Labor Organizations

	81394	Political Organizations
	81399	Other Similar Org (except Business/Prof/Labor/Pol)
814	**Private Households**	
	8141	Private Households
	81411	Private Households

92 PUBLIC ADMINISTRATION

921	**General Government Administration**	
	9211	General Government Administration
	92111	Executive Offices
	92112	Legislative Bodies
	92113	Public Finance Activities
	92114	Executive & Legislative Offices, Combined
	92115	American Indian & Alaska Native Tribal Gov
	92119	Other General Government Support
922	**Justice, Public Order, and Safety Activities**	
	9221	Justice, Public Order & Safety Activities
	92211	Courts
	92212	Police Protection
	92213	Legal Counsel & Prosecution
	92214	Correctional Institutions
	92215	Parole Offices & Probation Offices
	92216	Fire Protection
	92219	Other Justice/Public Order/Safety Activity
923	**Administration of Human Resource Programs**	
	9231	Administration of Human Resource Programs
	92311	Administration of Education Programs
	92312	Administration of Public Health Programs
	92313	Administration of Other Human Resource Programs
	92314	Administration of Veterans' Affairs

924	**Administration of Environmental Quality Programs**	
	9241	Administration of Environmental Quality Programs
	92411	Admin Air/Water Resource/Solid Waste Mgt Prog
	92412	Administration of Conservation Programs
925	**Administration of Housing Programs, Urban Planning, and Community Development**	
	9251	Admin Housing/Urban Planning/Community Devop
	92511	Administration of Housing Programs
	92512	Admin Urban Planning & Community/Rural Devop
926	**Administration of Economic Programs**	
	9261	Administration of Economic Programs
	92611	Administration of General Economic Programs
	92612	Regulation & Admin of Transportation Programs
	92613	Regulation & Administration of Utilities
	92614	Regulation Agricultural Marketing & Commodities
	92615	Reg/License/Inspect—Misc Commercial Sectors
927	**Space Research and Technology**	
	9271	Space Research & Technology
	92711	Space Research & Technology
928	**National Security and International Affairs**	
	9281	National Security & International Affairs
	92811	National Security
	92812	International Affairs

Can't find what you're looking for? Go to the alphabetic section, starting on page 627.

HOW TO USE THIS SECTION:

This section supplies you with a comprehensive list of SIC codes and their industry descriptions. The codes are separated by division and are listed in descending order beginning with the two-digit division title and ending with the four-digit industry classification.

To convert SIC codes to NAICS codes, turn to page 87.

SIC to NAICS Interchange

SIC Short Titles

C	CONSTRUCTION	←	SIC DIVISION TITLES (Letter)
15	BUILDING CONSTRUCTION, GENERAL CONTRACTORS	←	SIC MAJOR GROUP TITLES (2-digit)
	1521 General Contractors, Single Family Houses	←	SIC Industry Titles (4-digit)
	1522 General Contractors, Residential Other Than Single Family		

Short Titles

Standard Industrial Classification (SIC)

A AGRICULTURE, FORESTRY, AND FISHING

01 AGRICULTURAL PRODUCTION—CROPS

0111	Wheat Farm
0112	Rice Farm
0115	Corn Farm
0116	Soybean Farm
0119	Cash Grains, NEC
0131	Cotton Farms
0132	Tobacco Farm
0133	Sugarcane & Sugar Beet Farm
0134	Irish Potato Farm
0139	Field Crops, Except Cash Grains, NEC
0161	Vegetables & Melons
0171	Berry Crops
0172	Grape Vineyard
0173	Tree Nut Grove
0174	Citrus Fruit Grove
0175	Deciduous Tree Fruits
0179	Fruit & Tree Nuts, NEC
0181	Ornamental Floriculture & Nursery Products
0182	Food Crops Grown Under Cover
0191	General Farm, Primarily Crop

02 AGRICULTURAL PRODUCTION—LIVESTOCK

0211	Beef Cattle Feedlots
0212	Beef Cattle, Except Feedlots
0213	Hogs
0214	Sheep & Goats
0219	General Livestock, Except Dairy & Poultry
0241	Dairy Farm
0251	Broiler, Fryer & Roaster Chickens
0252	Chicken Eggs
0253	Turkeys & Turkey Eggs
0254	Poultry Hatcheries
0259	Poultry & Eggs, NEC
0271	Fur-bearing Animals & Rabbits
0272	Horse & Other Equine Production
0273	Animal Aquaculture
0279	Animal Specialties, NEC
0291	General Farms, Primarily Livestock & Animal Specialties

07 AGRICULTURAL SERVICES

0711	Soil Preparation Services
0721	Crop Planting, Cultivating & Protecting
0722	Crop Harvesting, Primarily by Machine
0723	Crop Preparation, Except Cotton Ginning
0724	Cotton Ginning
0741	Veterinary Services for Livestock
0742	Veterinary Animal Specialties
0751	Livestock Services, Except Veterinary
0752	Animal Specialty Services, Except Veterinary
0761	Farm Labor Contractors & Crew Leaders
0762	Farm Management Services
0781	Landscape Counseling & Planning
0782	Lawn & Garden Services
0783	Ornamental Shrub & Tree Services

08 FORESTRY

0811	Timber Tracts
0831	Forest Nurseries & Gathering of Forest Products
0851	Forestry Services

09 FISHING, HUNTING, AND TRAPPING

0912	Finfish
0913	Shellfish

Convert SIC codes to NAICS codes. Turn to page 87.

For a complete list of abbreviations and their definitions, see page 28

0919	Miscellaneous Marine Products	
0921	Fish Hatcheries & Preserves	
0971	Hunting & Trapping, & Game Propagation	

B MINING

10 METAL MINING

1011	Iron Ores
1021	Copper Ores
1031	Lead & Zinc Ores
1041	Gold Ores
1044	Silver Ores
1061	Ferroalloy Ores, Except Vanadium
1081	Metal Mining Services
1094	Uranium, Radium & Vanadium Ores
1099	Misc. Metal Ores, NEC

12 COAL MINING

1221	Bituminous Coal & Lignite: Surface Mining
1222	Bituminous Coal: Underground Mining
1231	Anthracite Mining
1241	Coal Mining Services

13 OIL AND GAS EXTRACTION

1311	Crude Petroleum & Natural Gas
1321	Natural Gas Liquids
1381	Drilling Oil & Gas Wells
1382	Oil & Gas Field Exploration Services
1389	Oil & Gas Field Services, NEC

14 MINING AND QUARRYING OF NONMETALLIC MINERALS, EXCEPT FUELS

1411	Dimension Stone
1422	Crushed & Broken Limestone
1423	Crushed & Broken Granite
1429	Crushed & Broken Stone, NEC
1442	Construction Sand & Gravel
1446	Industrial Sand
1455	Kaolin & Ball Clay
1459	Clay, Ceramic & Refractory Minerals, NEC
1474	Potash, Soda & Borate Minerals
1475	Phosphate Rock
1479	Chemical & Fertilizer Mining
1481	Nonmetalic Minerals Services, Except Fuels

1499	Misc. Nonmetallic Minerals, Except Fuels

C CONSTRUCTION

15 BUILDING CONSTRUCTION, GENERAL CONTRACTORS

1521	General Contractors, Single Family Houses
1522	General Contractors, Residential Other Than Single Family
1531	Operative Builders
1541	General Contractors, Industrial Buildings & Warehouses
1542	General Contractors, Nonresidential & Nonindustrial Buildings

16 HEAVY CONSTRUCTION OTHER THAN BUILDING

1611	Highway & Street Construction
1622	Bridge, Tunnel & Elevated Hwy Construction
1623	Water, Sewer & Utility Line Construction
1629	Heavy Construction, NEC

17 CONSTRUCTION—SPECIAL TRADE CONTRACTORS

1711	Plumbing, Heating & Air Conditioning Contractors
1721	Painting & Paper Hanging Contractors
1731	Electrical Work
1741	Masonry & Other Stonework
1742	Plastering, Drywall, Acoustical & Insulation Work
1743	Terrazzo, Tile, Marble & Mosaic Work
1751	Carpentry Work
1752	Floor Laying & Other Floor Work, NEC
1761	Roofing, Siding & Sheet Metal Work
1771	Concrete Work
1781	Water Well Drilling
1791	Structural Steel Erection
1793	Glass & Glazing Work
1794	Excavating & Grading Work
1795	Wrecking & Demolition Work
1796	Installation or Erection of Building Equipment & Machinery, NEC
1799	Special Trade Contractors, NEC

SIC Short Titles

For a complete list of abbreviations and their definitions, see page 28

D

MANUFACTURING

20		FOOD AND KINDRED PRODUCTS
	2011	Meat Packing Plants
	2013	Sausages & Meat Products
	2015	Poultry Slaughtering, Dressing & Processing
	2021	Butter
	2022	Cheese
	2023	Milk, Condensed & Evaporated
	2024	Ice Cream
	2026	Milk
	2032	Canned Specialties
	2033	Canned Fruits, Vegetables & Preserves
	2034	Dried Fruits, Vegetables & Soup
	2035	Pickled Fruits, Vegetables, Sauces & Dressings
	2037	Frozen Fruits, Juices & Vegetables
	2038	Frozen Specialties
	2041	Flour, Grain Milling
	2043	Cereal Breakfast Foods
	2044	Rice Milling
	2045	Flour, Blended & Prepared
	2046	Wet Corn Milling
	2047	Dog & Cat Food
	2048	Prepared Feeds For Animals & Fowls
	2051	Bread, Bakery Products Except Cookies & Crackers
	2052	Cookies & Crackers
	2053	Frozen Bakery Products
	2061	Sugar, Cane
	2062	Cane Sugar Refining
	2063	Beet Sugar
	2064	Candy & Confectionery Products
	2066	Chocolate & Cocoa Products
	2067	Chewing Gum
	2068	Salted & Roasted Nuts & Seeds
	2074	Cottonseed Oil Mills
	2075	Soybean Oil Mills
	2076	Vegetable Oil Mills, Except Corn, Cottonseed & Soybean
	2077	Animal, Marine Fats & Oils
	2079	Shortening, Table Oils, Margarine & Other Edible Fats & Oils, NEC

	2082	Malt Beverages
	2083	Malt
	2084	Wine & Brandy
	2085	Liquors, Distilled, Rectified & Blended
	2086	Soft Drinks
	2087	Flavoring Extracts & Syrups
	2091	Canned & Cured Fish & Seafoods
	2092	Fish & Seafoods, Fresh & Frozen
	2095	Coffee
	2096	Potato Chips & Similar Products
	2097	Manufactured Ice
	2098	Macaroni, Spaghetti & Noodles
	2099	Food Preparations, NEC

21		TOBACCO PRODUCTS
	2111	Cigarettes
	2121	Cigars
	2131	Chewing & Smoking Tobacco & Snuff
	2141	Tobacco Stemming & Redrying

22		TEXTILE MILL PRODUCTS
	2211	Cotton, Woven Fabric
	2221	Silk & Manmade Fiber
	2231	Wool, Woven Fabric
	2241	Fabric Mills, Cotton, Wool, Silk & Manmade
	2251	Women's Full-length & Knee-length Hosiery, Except Socks
	2252	Hosiery, NEC
	2253	Knit Outerwear Mills
	2254	Knit Underwear & Nightwear Mills
	2257	Circular Knit Fabric Mills
	2258	Lace & Warp Knit Fabric Mills
	2259	Knitting Mills, NEC
	2261	Finishers of Broadwoven Fabrics of Cotton
	2262	Silk & Manmade Fabric Finishers
	2269	Finishers of Textiles, NEC
	2273	Carpets & Rugs
	2281	Yarn Spinning Mills
	2282	Yarn Texturizing, Throwing, Twisting & Winding Mills
	2284	Thread Mills
	2295	Fabrics Coated Not Rubberized

SIC Short Titles

SIC Short Titles

2296	Tire Cord & Fabric	
2297	Fabrics, Nonwoven	
2298	Cordage & Twine	
2299	Textile Goods, NEC	

23 APPAREL AND OTHER FINISHED PRODUCTS MADE FROM FABRICS AND OTHER MATERIALS

2311	Men's & Boys' Suits, Coats & Overcoats
2321	Men's & Boys' Shirts
2322	Men's & Boys' Underwear & Nightwear
2323	Men's & Boys' Neckwear
2325	Men's & Boys' Separate Trousers & Casual Slacks
2326	Men's & Boys' Work Clothing
2329	Men's & Boys' Clothing, NEC
2331	Women's & Misses' & Juniors' Blouses & Shirts
2335	Women's & Misses' Dresses
2337	Women's & Misses' Suits, Coats & Skirts
2339	Women's & Misses' Outerwear, NEC
2341	Women's, Misses', Children's & Infants' Underwear & Nightwear
2342	Brassieres, Girdles & Allied Garments
2353	Hats, Caps & Millinery
2361	Children's & Infants' Dresses & Blouses
2369	Girls' & Infants' Outerwear, NEC
2371	Fur Goods
2381	Dress & Work Gloves
2384	Robes & Dressing Gowns
2385	Raincoats
2386	Leather & Sheep Lined Clothing
2387	Apparel Belts
2389	Apparel & Accessories, NEC
2391	Curtains & Draperies
2392	Housefurnishings: Textile
2393	Textile Bags
2394	Canvas Products
2395	Pleating & Stitching for the Trade
2396	Automotive Trimmings, Apparel Findings, Related Products
2397	Schiffli Machine Embroideries
2399	Fabricated Textile Products, NEC

24 LUMBER AND WOOD PRODUCTS—EXCEPT FURNITURE

2411	Logging
2421	Saw & Planing Mills
2426	Hardwood Dimension & Flooring Mills
2429	Special Product Sawmills, NEC
2431	Millwork
2434	Wood Kitchen Cabinets
2435	Hardwood Veneer & Plywood
2436	Softwood Veneer & Plywood
2439	Structural Wood Members, NEC
2441	Wood Boxes
2448	Wood Pallets & Skids
2449	Wood Containers, NEC
2451	Mobile Homes
2452	Prefabricated Wood Buildings & Components
2491	Wood Preserving
2493	Reconstituted Wood Products
2499	Wood Products, NEC

25 FURNITURE AND FIXTURES

2511	Wood Household Furniture
2512	Wood Household Furniture, Upholstered
2514	Metal Household Furniture
2515	Mattresses & Bedsprings
2517	Wood TV, Radio, Phonograph & Sewing Cabinets
2519	Household Furniture, NEC
2521	Wood Office Furniture
2522	Office Furniture, Except Wood
2531	Public Building & Related Furniture
2541	Wood, Office & Store Fixtures
2542	Partitions & Fixtures, Except Wood
2591	Drapery Hardware, Window Blinds & Shades
2599	Furniture & Fixtures, NEC

26 PAPER AND ALLIED PRODUCTS

2611	Pulp Mills
2621	Paper Mills
2631	Paperboard Mills
2652	Set-up Paperboard Boxes
2653	Corrugated & Solid Fiber Boxes
2655	Fiber Cans, Tubes & Drums
2656	Sanitary Food Containers
2657	Folding Paperboard Boxes
2671	Paper Coating & Laminating for Packaging

For a complete list of abbreviations and their definitions, see page 28

	2672	Paper Coating & Laminating, Except for Packaging		2841	Soap & Detergents
	2673	Bags: Plastics, Laminated & Coated		2842	Specialty Cleaning, Polishing & Sanitation Preparations
	2674	Bags: Uncoated Paper & Multiwall		2843	Surface Active & Finishing Agents, Sulfonated Oils
	2675	Die-cut Paper & Board		2844	Perfumes, Cosmetics & Toilet Preparations
	2676	Sanitary Paper Products		2851	Paints, Varnishes, Lacquers, & Enamels
	2677	Envelopes		2861	Gum & Wood Chemicals
	2678	Stationery Products		2865	Cyclic-crudes, Intermediates, Dyes & Org Pigments
	2679	Converted Paper Products, NEC		2869	Industrial Organic Chemicals, NEC

27 PRINTING, PUBLISHING, AND ALLIED INDUSTRIES

2711	Newspapers: Publishing & Printing
2721	Periodicals: Publishing & Printing
2731	Books: Publishing & Printing
2732	Book Printing, Not Publishing
2741	Misc Publishing
2752	Commercial Printing: Lithographic
2754	Commercial Printing: Gravure
2759	Commercial Printing
2761	Manifold Business Forms
2771	Greeting Card Publishing
2782	Blankbooks & Looseleaf Binders
2789	Bookbinding
2791	Typesetting
2796	Platemaking & Related Services

28 CHEMICALS AND ALLIED PRODUCTS

2812	Alkalies & Chlorine
2813	Industrial Gases
2816	Inorganic Pigments
2819	Industrial Inorganic Chemicals, NEC
2821	Plastics, Materials & Nonvulcanizable Elastomers
2822	Synthetic Rubber (Vulcanizable Elastomers)
2823	Cellulosic Man-made Fibers
2824	Man-made Organic Fibers, Except Cellulosic
2833	Medicinal Chemicals & Botanical Products
2834	Pharmaceuticals
2835	Diagnostic Substances
2836	Biological Products, Except Diagnostic Substances

2873	Nitrogenous Fertilizers
2874	Phosphatic Fertilizers
2875	Fertilizers, Mixing Only
2879	Pesticides & Agricultural Chemicals, NEC
2891	Adhesives & Sealants
2892	Explosives
2893	Printing Ink
2895	Carbon Black
2899	Chemical Preparations, NEC

29 PETROLEUM REFINING AND ALLIED INDUSTRIES

2911	Petroleum Refining
2951	Paving Mixtures & Blocks
2952	Asphalt Felts & Coatings
2992	Lubricating Oils & Greases
2999	Products of Petroleum & Coal, NEC

30 RUBBER AND MISCELLANEOUS PLASTIC PRODUCTS

3011	Tires & Inner Tubes
3021	Rubber & Plastics Footwear
3052	Rubber & Plastic Hose & Belting
3053	Gaskets, Packing & Sealing Devices
3061	Molded, Extruded & Lathecut Rubber Mechanical Goods
3069	Fabricated Rubber Products, NEC
3081	Plastic Unsupported Sheet & Film
3082	Plastic Unsupported Profile Shapes
3083	Plastic Laminated Plate & Sheet
3084	Plastic Pipe
3085	Plastic Bottles
3086	Plastic Foam Products
3087	Custom Compounding of Purchased Plastic Resins

Go to page 11 to learn more about the benefits of NAICS codes.

For a complete list of abbreviations and their definitions, see page 28

3088	Plastic Plumbing Fixtures
3089	Plastic Products, NEC

31 LEATHER AND LEATHER PRODUCTS

3111	Leather Tanning & Finishing
3131	Boot & Shoe Cut Stock & Findings
3142	House Slippers
3143	Men's Footwear, Except Athletic
3144	Women's Footwear, Except Athletic
3149	Footwear, NEC
3151	Leather Gloves & Mittens
3161	Luggage
3171	Handbags & Purses
3172	Personal Leather Goods
3199	Leather Goods, NEC

32 STONE, CLAY, GLASS, AND CONCRETE PRODUCTS

3211	Flat Glass
3221	Glass Containers
3229	Pressed & Blown Glassware, NEC
3231	Glass Products Made of Purchased Glass
3241	Cement, Hydraulic
3251	Brick & Structural Clay Tile
3253	Ceramic Wall & Floor Tile
3255	Clay Refractories
3259	Structural Clay Products, NEC
3261	China Plumbing Fixtures & Fittings
3262	China, Table & Kitchen Articles
3263	Earthenware, Whiteware, Table & Kitchen Articles
3264	Porcelain Electrical Supplies
3269	Pottery Products, NEC
3271	Concrete Block & Brick
3272	Concrete Products, NEC
3273	Ready-mixed Concrete
3274	Lime
3275	Gypsum Products
3281	Cut Stone Products
3291	Abrasive Products
3292	Asbestos Products
3295	Minerals & Earths: Ground or Treated
3296	Mineral Wool
3297	Nonclay Refractories
3299	Nonmetallic Mineral Products, NEC

33 PRIMARY METAL INDUSTRIES

3312	Blast Furnaces, Coke Ovens, Steel & Rolling Mills
3313	Electrometallurgical Products
3315	Steel Wire Drawing & Nails & Spikes
3316	Cold Rolled Steel Sheet, Strip & Bars
3317	Steel Pipe & Tubes
3321	Gray Iron Foundries
3322	Malleable Iron Foundries
3324	Steel Investment Foundries
3325	Steel Foundries, NEC
3331	Primary Smelting & Refining of Copper
3334	Primary Production of Aluminum
3339	Primary Nonferrous Metals, NEC
3341	Secondary Smelting & Refining of Nonferrous Metals
3351	Rolling, Drawing & Extruding of Copper
3353	Aluminum Sheet, Plate & Foil
3354	Aluminum Extruded Products
3355	Aluminum Rolling & Drawing, NEC
3356	Rolling, Drawing-extruding of Nonferrous Metals
3357	Nonferrous Wire Drawing
3363	Aluminum Die Castings
3364	Nonferrous Die Castings, Except Aluminum
3365	Aluminum Foundries
3366	Copper Foundries
3369	Nonferrous Foundries: Castings, NEC
3398	Metal Heat Treating
3399	Primary Metal Products, NEC

34 FABRICATED METAL PRODUCTS, EXCEPT MACHINERY, AND TRANSPORT EQUIPMENT

3411	Metal Cans
3412	Metal Barrels, Drums, Kegs & Pails
3421	Cutlery
3423	Hand & Edge Tools
3425	Hand Saws & Saw Blades
3429	Hardware, NEC
3431	Enameled Iron & Metal Sanitary Ware
3432	Plumbing Fixture Fittings & Trim, Brass
3433	Heating Equipment
3441	Fabricated Structural Steel

For a complete list of abbreviations and their definitions, see page 28

3442	Metal Doors, Sash, Frames, Molding & Trim
3443	Fabricated Plate Work
3444	Sheet Metal Work
3446	Architectural & Ornamental Metal Work
3448	Prefabricated Metal Buildings & Components
3449	Misc Metal Work
3451	Screw Machine Products
3452	Bolts, Nuts, Screws, Rivets & Washers
3462	Iron & Steel Forgings
3463	Nonferrous Forgings
3465	Automotive Stampings
3466	Crowns & Closures
3469	Metal Stampings, NEC
3471	Electroplating, Plating, Polishing, Anodizing & Coloring
3479	Coating & Engraving, NEC
3482	Small Arms Ammunition
3483	Ammunition, Large
3484	Small Arms
3489	Ordnance & Accessories, NEC
3491	Industrial Valves
3492	Fluid Power Valves & Hose Fittings
3493	Steel Springs, Except Wire
3494	Valves & Pipe Fittings, NEC
3495	Wire Springs
3496	Misc Fabricated Wire Products
3497	Metal Foil & Leaf
3498	Fabricated Pipe & Pipe Fittings
3499	Fabricated Metal Products, NEC

35 INDUSTRIAL AND COMMERCIAL MACHINERY AND COMPUTER EQUIPMENT

3511	Steam, Gas & Hydraulic Turbines & Engines
3519	Internal Combustion Engines, NEC
3523	Farm Machinery & Equipment
3524	Garden, Lawn Tractors & Equipment
3531	Construction Machinery & Equipment
3532	Mining Machinery & Equipment
3533	Oil Field Machinery & Equipment
3534	Elevators & Moving Stairways

3535	Conveyors & Equipment
3536	Hoists, Cranes & Monorails
3537	Industrial Trucks, Tractors, Trailers & Stackers
3541	Machine Tools: Cutting
3542	Machine Tools: Forming
3543	Industrial Patterns
3544	Dies, Tools, Jigs, Fixtures & Industrial Molds
3545	Machine Tool Accessories
3546	Power Hand Tools
3547	Rolling Mill Machinery & Equipment
3548	Welding Apparatus
3549	Metalworking Machinery, NEC
3552	Textile Machinery
3553	Woodworking Machinery
3554	Paper Industries Machinery
3555	Printing Trades Machinery & Equipment
3556	Food Products Machinery
3559	Special Industry Machinery, NEC
3561	Pumps & Pumping Equipment
3562	Ball & Roller Bearings
3563	Air & Gas Compressors
3564	Blowers & Fans
3565	Packaging Machinery
3566	Speed Changers, Drives & Gears
3567	Industrial Process Furnaces & Ovens
3568	Mechanical Power Transmission Equipment, NEC
3569	Industrial Machinery & Equipment, NEC
3571	Electronic Computers
3572	Computer Storage Devices
3575	Computer Terminals
3577	Computer Peripheral Equipment, NEC
3578	Calculating & Accounting Equipment
3579	Office Machines, NEC
3581	Automatic Vending Machines
3582	Commercial Laundry, Dry Clean & Pressing Machines
3585	Air Conditioning & Heating Equipment
3586	Measuring & Dispensing Pumps
3589	Service Industry Machines, NEC
3592	Carburetors, Pistons, Rings & Valves
3593	Fluid Power Cylinders & Actuators

SIC **Short Titles**

For a complete list of abbreviations and their definitions, see page 28

SIC Short Titles

3594	Fluid Power Pumps & Motors		3691	Storage Batteries	
3596	Scales & Balances, Except Laboratory		3692	Primary Batteries: Dry & Wet	
3599	Machinery & Equipment, Industrial & Commercial, NEC		3694	Electrical Equipment for Internal Combustion Engines	
			3695	Recording Media	
			3699	Electrical Machinery, Equipment & Supplies, NEC	

36 ELECTRONIC AND OTHER ELECTRONICAL EQUIPMENT AND COMPONENTS, EXCEPT COMPUTER EQUIPMENT

37 TRANSPORTATION EQUIPMENT

3612	Power, Distribution & Specialty Transformers	3711	Motor Vehicles & Car Bodies	
3613	Switchgear & Switchboard Apparatus	3713	Truck & Bus Bodies	
3621	Motors & Generators	3714	Motor Vehicle Parts & Access	
3624	Carbon & Graphite Products	3715	Truck Trailers	
3625	Relays & Industrial Controls	3716	Motor Homes	
3629	Electrical Industrial Apparatus, NEC	3721	Aircraft	
3631	Household Cooking Equipment	3724	Aircraft Engines & Engine Parts	
3632	Household Refrigerators & Freezers	3728	Aircraft Parts & Equipment, NEC	
3633	Household Laundry Equipment	3731	Shipbuilding & Repairing	
3634	Electric Household Appliances	3732	Boat Building & Repairing	
3635	Household Vacuum Cleaners	3743	Railroad Equipment	
3639	Household Appliances, NEC	3751	Motorcycles, Bicycles & Parts	
3641	Electric Lamps	3761	Guided Missiles & Space Vehicles	
3643	Current-carrying Wiring Devices	3764	Guided Missiles & Space Vehicle Propulsion Units & Propulsion Unit Parts	
3644	Noncurrent-carrying Wiring Devices	3769	Guided Missile/Space Vehicle Parts & Equipment, NEC	
3645	Residential Lighting Fixtures	3792	Travel Trailers & Campers	
3646	Commercial, Industrial & Institutional Lighting Fixtures	3795	Tanks & Tank Components	
3647	Vehicular Lighting Equipment	3799	Transportation Equipment, NEC	
3648	Lighting Equipment, NEC			

38 MEASURING, ANALYZING, AND CONTROLLING INSTRUMENTS

3651	Household Audio & Video Equipment	3812	Search, Detection, Navigation & Guidance Systs & Instruments	
3652	Phonograph Records & Magnetic Tape	3821	Laboratory Apparatus & Furniture	
3661	Telephone & Telegraph Apparatus	3822	Automatic Temperature Controls	
3663	Radio & TV Communications, Systs & Equipment, Broadcast/Studio	3823	Industrial Instruments For Measurement, Display & Control	
3669	Communications Equipment, NEC	3824	Fluid Meters & Counters	
3671	Radio & TV Receiving Electron Tubes	3825	Instruments For Measuring & Testing Electricity	
3672	Printed Circuit Boards	3826	Analytical Instruments	
3674	Semiconductors	3827	Optical Instruments	
3675	Electronic Capacitors	3829	Measuring & Controlling Devices, NEC	
3676	Electronic Resistors	3841	Surgical & Medical Instruments & Apparatus	
3677	Electronic Coils & Transformers	3842	Orthopedic, Prosthetic & Surgical Appliances/Supplies	
3678	Electronic Connectors	3843	Dental Equipment & Supplies	
3679	Electronic Components, NEC			

For a complete list of abbreviations and their definitions, see page 28

3844	X-ray Apparatus & Tubes
3845	Electromedical & Electrotherapeutic Apparatus
3851	Ophthalmic Goods
3861	Photographic Equipment & Supplies
3873	Watch & Clock Devices & Parts

39 MISCELLANEOUS MANUFACTURING INDUSTRIES

3911	Jewelry: Precious Metal
3914	Silverware, Plated & Stainless Steel Ware
3915	Jewelers' Findings & Lapidary Work
3931	Musical Instruments
3942	Dolls & Stuffed Toys
3944	Games, Toys & Children's Vehicles
3949	Sporting & Athletic Goods, NEC
3951	Pens & Mechanical Pencils
3952	Lead Pencils, Crayons & Artist's Materials
3953	Marking Devices
3955	Carbon Paper & Inked Ribbons
3961	Costume Jewelry & Novelties
3965	Fasteners, Buttons, Needles & Pins
3991	Brooms & Brushes
3993	Signs & Advertising Displays
3995	Burial Caskets
3996	Linoleum, Asphalted-felt-base & Other Hard Surface Floor Coverings, NEC
3999	Manufacturing Industries, NEC

E TRANSPORTATION AND PUBLIC UTILITIES

40 RAILROAD TRANSPORTATION

4011	Railroads, Line-hauling Operations
4013	Railroad Switching & Terminal Services

41 LOCAL AND SUBURBAN TRANSIT AND HIGHWAY TRANSPORTATION

4111	Local & Suburban Transit
4119	Local Passenger Transportation, NEC
4121	Taxicabs
4131	Interurban & Rural Bus Transportation
4141	Local Bus Charter Service
4142	Bus Charter Service, Except Local
4151	School Buses
4173	Terminal & Service Facilities for Motor Vehicle Passenger Transport

42 MOTOR FREIGHT TRANSPORTATION AND WAREHOUSING

4212	Local Trucking Without Storage
4213	Trucking, Except Local
4214	Local Trucking with Storage
4215	Courier Services, Except By Air
4221	Farm Product Warehousing & Storage
4222	Refrigerated Warehousing & Storage
4225	General Warehousing & Storage
4226	Special Warehousing & Storage, NEC
4231	Terminal & Joint Terminal Maintenance Facilities for Motor Freight Transport

43 U.S. POSTAL SERVICE

4311	U.S. Postal Service

44 WATER TRANSPORTATION

4412	Deep Sea Foreign Transportation of Freight
4424	Deep Sea Domestic Transportation of Freight
4432	Freight Transport. on Great Lakes—St. Lawrence Seaway
4449	Water Transportation of Freight, NEC
4481	Deep Sea Transportation of Passengers, Except by Ferry
4482	Ferries
4489	Water Transport of Passengers, NEC
4491	Marine Cargo Handling
4492	Towing & Tugboat Services
4493	Marinas
4499	Water Transportation Services, NEC

45 TRANSPORTATION BY AIR

4512	Air Transportation, Scheduled
4513	Air Courier Services
4522	Air Transportation, Nonscheduled

Convert SIC codes to NAICS codes. Turn to page 87.

For a complete list of abbreviations and their definitions, see page 28

SIC
Short Titles

	4581	Airports, Flying Fields & Terminal Services

46 PIPELINES, EXCEPT NATURAL GAS

	4612	Crude Petroleum Pipelines
	4613	Refined Petroleum Pipelines
	4619	Pipelines, NEC

47 TRANSPORTATION SERVICES

	4724	Travel Agencies
	4725	Tour Operators
	4729	Passenger Transportation Arrangement, NEC
	4731	Freight Forwarding & Arrangement
	4741	Rental of Railroad Cars
	4783	Packing & Crating Services
	4785	Fixed Facilities, Inspection, Weighing Services Transportation
	4789	Transportation Services, NEC

48 COMMUNICATIONS

	4812	Radiotelephone Communications
	4813	Telephone Communications, Except Radio
	4822	Telegraph & Other Message Communications
	4832	Radio Broadcasting Stations
	4833	Television Broadcasting Stations
	4841	Cable & Other Pay TV Services
	4899	Communication Services, NEC

49 ELECTRIC, GAS, AND SANITARY SERVICES

	4911	Electric Services
	4922	Natural Gas Transmission
	4923	Natural Gas Transmission & Distribution
	4924	Natural Gas Distribution
	4925	Mixed, Manufactured, or Liquefied Petroleum Gas Production and/or Distribution
	4931	Electric & Other Services Combined
	4932	Gas & Other Services Combined
	4939	Combination Utilities, NEC
	4941	Water Supply
	4952	Sewerage Systems
	4953	Refuse Systems
	4959	Sanitary Services, NEC

	4961	Steam & Air Conditioning Supply
	4971	Irrigation Systems

F WHOLESALE TRADE

50 WHOLESALE TRADE—DURABLE GOODS

	5012	Automobiles & Other Motor Vehicles Wholesale
	5013	Motor Vehicle Supplies & New Parts Wholesale
	5014	Tires & Tubes Wholesale
	5015	Motor Vehicle Parts, Used Wholesale
	5021	Furniture Wholesale
	5023	Home Furnishings Wholesale
	5031	Lumber, Plywood & Millwork Wholesale
	5032	Brick, Stone & Related Construction Materials Wholesale
	5033	Roofing, Siding & Insulation Materials Wholesale
	5039	Construction Materials, NEC Wholesale
	5043	Photographic Equipment & Supplies Wholesale
	5044	Office Equipment Wholesale
	5045	Computers & Peripheral Equipment & Software Wholesale
	5046	Commercial Equipment, NEC Wholesale
	5047	Medical, Dental & Hospital Equipment & Supplies Wholesale
	5048	Ophthalmic Goods Wholesale
	5049	Professional Equipment & Supplies, NEC Wholesale
	5051	Metals Service Centers
	5052	Coal & Other Minerals & Ores
	5063	Electrical Apparatus, Equipment, Wiring Supplies Wholesale
	5064	Electrical Appliances, TV & Radios Wholesale
	5065	Electronic Parts & Equipment Wholesale
	5072	Hardware Wholesale
	5074	Plumbing & Heating Supplies Wholesale
	5075	Heating & Air Conditioning Equipment & Supplies Wholesale
	5078	Refrigeration Equipment & Supplies Wholesale

For a complete list of abbreviations and their definitions, see page 28

5082	Construction & Mining Machinery & Equipment Wholesale		5153	Grain & Field Beans Wholesale
5083	Farm & Garden Machinery & Equipment Wholesale		5154	Livestock Wholesale
			5159	Farm-product Raw Materials, NEC Wholesale

5082 Construction & Mining Machinery & Equipment Wholesale

5083 Farm & Garden Machinery & Equipment Wholesale

5084 Industrial Machinery & Equipment Wholesale

5085 Industrial Supplies

5087 Service Establishment Equipment & Supplies Wholesale

5088 Transportation Equipment & Supplies, Except Motor Vehicles

5091 Sporting & Recreational Goods & Supplies Wholesale

5092 Toys & Hobby Goods & Supplies Wholesale

5093 Scrap & Waste Materials

5094 Jewelry, Watches, Precious Stones Wholesale

5099 Durable Goods, NEC Wholesale

51 WHOLESALE TRADE— NONDURABLE GOODS

5111 Printing & Writing Paper Wholesale

5112 Stationery & Office Supplies Wholesale

5113 Industrial & Personal Services Paper Wholesale

5122 Drugs, Drug Proprietaries & Sundries Wholesale

5131 Piece Goods, Notions & Dry Goods Wholesale

5136 Men's & Boys' Clothing & Furnishings Wholesale

5137 Women's, Children's & Infants Clothing Wholesale

5139 Footwear Wholesale

5141 Groceries, General Line Wholesale

5142 Packaged Frozen Foods Wholesale

5143 Dairy Products, Except Dried Or Canned Wholesale

5144 Poultry & Poultry Products Wholesale

5145 Confectionery Wholesale

5146 Fish & Seafood Wholesale

5147 Meats & Meat Products Wholesale

5148 Fresh Fruits & Vegetables Wholesale

5149 Groceries & Related Products, NEC Wholesale

5153 Grain & Field Beans Wholesale

5154 Livestock Wholesale

5159 Farm-product Raw Materials, NEC Wholesale

5162 Plastics Materials & Basic Shapes Wholesale

5169 Chemicals & Allied Products, NEC Wholesale

5171 Petroleum Bulk Stations & Terminals

5172 Petroleum & Petroleum Products Wholesalers, Except Bulk Stations & Terminals

5181 Beer & Ale Wholesale

5182 Wine & Distilled Alcoholic Beverages Wholesale

5191 Farm Supplies Wholesale

5192 Books, Periodicals & Newspapers Wholesale

5193 Flowers, Nursery Stock & Florists' Supplies Wholesale

5194 Tobacco & Tobacco Products Wholesale

5198 Paints, Varnishes & Supplies Wholesale

5199 Nondurable Goods, NEC Wholesale

G RETAIL TRADE

52 BUILDING MATERIALS, HARDWARE, GARDEN SUPPLIES, AND MOBILE HOME DEALERS

5211 Lumber & Other Building Material Dealers

5231 Paint, Glass, Wallpaper Stores

5251 Hardware Stores

5261 Retail Nurseries & Garden Stores

5271 Mobile Home Dealers

53 GENERAL MERCHANDISE STORES

5311 Department Stores

5331 Variety Stores

5399 General Merchandise Stores, Misc

54 FOOD STORES

5411 Grocery Stores

5421 Meat & Fish Markets, Including Freezer Provisioners

5431 Fruit & Vegetable Markets

5441 Candy, Nut & Confectionery Stores

5451 Dairy Products Stores

	5461	Retail Bakeries	5921	Liquor Stores
	5499	Food Stores, Misc	5932	Used Merchandise Stores

SIC Short Titles

55	**AUTOMOTIVE DEALERS AND SERVICES STATIONS**		5941	Sporting Goods & Bicycle Stores
	5511	Motor Vehicle Dealers (New & Used)	5942	Book Stores
	5521	Motor Vehicle Dealers (Used Only)	5943	Stationery Stores
	5531	Automotive & Home Supply Stores	5944	Jewelry Stores
	5541	Gasoline Service Stations	5945	Hobby, Toy & Game Store
	5551	Boat Dealers	5946	Camera & Photographic Supply Stores
	5561	Recreational Vehicle Dealers	5947	Gift, Novelty & Souvenir Stores
	5571	Motorcycle Dealers	5948	Luggage & Leather Goods Stores
	5599	Automotive Dealers, NEC	5949	Sewing, Needlework & Piece Goods Stores

55 AUTOMOTIVE DEALERS AND SERVICES STATIONS

5511	Motor Vehicle Dealers (New & Used)
5521	Motor Vehicle Dealers (Used Only)
5531	Automotive & Home Supply Stores
5541	Gasoline Service Stations
5551	Boat Dealers
5561	Recreational Vehicle Dealers
5571	Motorcycle Dealers
5599	Automotive Dealers, NEC

56 APPAREL AND ACCESSORY STORES

5611	Men's & Boys' Clothing & Access Stores
5621	Women's Clothing Stores
5632	Women's Access & Specialty Stores
5641	Children's & Infants' Clothing Stores
5651	Family Clothing Stores
5661	Shoe Stores
5699	Apparel & Accessory Stores, Misc

57 FUNITURE AND HOME FURNISHING STORES

5712	Furniture Stores
5713	Floor Covering Stores
5714	Drapery, Curtain & Upholstery Stores
5719	Home Furnishings Stores, Misc
5722	Household Appliance Stores
5731	Radio, TV & Consumer Electronics Stores
5734	Computer & Software Stores
5735	Record & Prerecorded Tape Stores
5736	Musical Instrument Stores

58 EATING AND DRINKING PLACES

5812	Eating Places
5813	Drinking Places (Alcoholic Beverages)

59 MISCELLANEOUS RETAIL

5912	Drug & Proprietary Stores

5921	Liquor Stores
5932	Used Merchandise Stores
5941	Sporting Goods & Bicycle Stores
5942	Book Stores
5943	Stationery Stores
5944	Jewelry Stores
5945	Hobby, Toy & Game Store
5946	Camera & Photographic Supply Stores
5947	Gift, Novelty & Souvenir Stores
5948	Luggage & Leather Goods Stores
5949	Sewing, Needlework & Piece Goods Stores
5961	Catalog & Mail-order Houses
5962	Automatic Merchandising Machine Operators
5963	Direct Selling Establishments
5983	Fuel Oil Dealers
5984	Liquefied Petroleum Gas Dealers
5989	Fuel Dealers, NEC
5992	Florists
5993	Tobacco Stores & Stands
5994	News Dealers & Newsstands
5995	Optical Goods Stores
5999	Misc Retail Stores, NEC

H FINANCE, INSURANCE, AND REAL ESTATE

60 DEPOSITORY INSTITUTIONS

6011	Federal Reserve Banks
6019	Central Reserve Depository Institutions, NEC
6021	National Commercial Banks
6022	State Commercial Banks
6029	Commercial Banks, NEC
6035	Federal Savings Institutions
6036	Savings Institutions, Except Federal
6061	Federal Credit Unions
6062	State Credit Unions
6081	Branches & Agencies of Foreign Banks
6082	Foreign Trade & International Banking Institutes
6091	Nondeposit Trust Facilities
6099	Functions Related to Deposit Banking, NEC

61 NONDEPOSITORY INSTITUTIONS

6111	Federal & Federally Sponsored Credit Agencies

For a complete list of abbreviations and their definitions, see page 28

6141	Personal Credit Institutions
6153	Credit Institutions, Short-term Business
6159	Credit Institutions, Misc Business
6162	Mortgage Bankers & Loan Correspondents
6163	Loan Brokers

62   SECURITY AND COMMODITY, BROKERS AND DEALERS

6211	Security Brokers & Dealers
6221	Commodity Contracts Brokers & Dealers
6231	Security & Commodity Exchanges
6282	Investment Advice
6289	Security & Commodity Services, NEC

63   INSURANCE CARRIERS

6311	Life Insurance Carriers
6321	Accident & Health Insurance
6324	Hospital & Medical Service Plans Carriers
6331	Fire, Marine & Casualty Insurance
6351	Surety Insurance Carriers
6361	Title Insurance
6371	Pension, Health & Welfare Funds
6399	Insurance Carriers, NEC

64   INSURANCE AGENTS, BROKERS, AND SERVICES

| 6411 | Insurance Agents, Brokers & Services |

65   REAL ESTATE

6512	Operators of Nonresidential Buildings
6513	Operators of Apartment Buildings
6514	Operators of Dwellings Other Than Apartment Buildings
6515	Operators of Residential Mobile Home Sites
6517	Lessors of Railroad Property
6519	Lessors of Real Estate, NEC
6531	Real Estate Agents & Managers
6541	Title Abstract Offices
6552	Land Subdividers & Developers
6553	Cemetery Subdividers & Developers, Except Cemeteries

67   HOLDING AND OTHER INVESTMENT OFFICES

6712	Offices of Bank Holding Companies
6719	Offices of Holding Companies, NEC
6722	Management Investment Offices, Open-ended
6726	Unit Investment Trusts, Face-amount Certificate Offices
6732	Education, Religious & Charitable Trusts
6733	Trust, Except Educational, Religious & Charitable
6792	Oil Royalty Traders
6794	Patent Owners & Lessors
6798	Real Estate Investment Trusts
6799	Investors, NEC

SERVICES

70   HOTELS AND OTHER LODGING PLACES

7011	Hotels, Motels & Tourist Courts
7021	Rooming & Boarding Houses
7032	Sporting & Recreational Camps
7033	Recreational Vehicle Parks & Camp Sites
7041	Membership-basis Hotels

72   PERSONAL SERVICES

7211	Power Laundries, Family & Commercial
7212	Garment Pressing & Agents for Laundries & Drycleaners
7213	Linen Supply
7215	Coin-operated Laundries & Cleaning
7216	Dry-cleaning Plants, Except Rug Cleaning
7217	Carpet & Upholstery Cleaning
7218	Industrial Launderers
7219	Laundry & Garment Services, NEC
7221	Photographic Studios, Portrait
7231	Beauty Shops
7241	Barber Shops
7251	Shoe Repair Shops & Shoeshine Parlors
7261	Funeral Services & Crematories
7291	Tax Return Preparation Services

Go to page 11 to learn more about the benefits of NAICS codes.

SIC
Short Titles

7299	Miscellaneous Personal Services, NEC

73 BUSINESS SERVICES

7311	Advertising Agencies
7312	Outdoor Advertising Services
7313	Radio, TV & Publishers Advertising Reps
7319	Advertising, NEC
7322	Adjustment & Collection Services
7323	Credit Reporting Services
7331	Direct Mail Advertising Services
7334	Photocopying & Duplicating Services
7335	Commercial Photography
7336	Commercial Art & Graphic Design
7338	Secretarial & Court Reporting Services
7342	Disinfecting & Pest Control Services
7349	Building Cleaning & Maintenance Services, NEC
7352	Medical Equipment Rental & Leasing
7353	Heavy Construction Equipment Rental & Leasing
7359	Equipment Rental & Leasing, NEC
7361	Employment Agencies
7363	Help Supply Services
7371	Custom Computer Programming Services
7372	Prepackaged Software
7373	Computer Integrated Systems Design
7374	Data & Computer Processing & Preparation
7375	Information Retrieval Services
7376	Computer Facilities Management Services
7377	Computer Rental & Leasing
7378	Computer Maintenance & Repair
7379	Computer Related Services, NEC
7381	Detective & Armored Car Services
7382	Security Systems Services
7383	News Syndicates
7384	Photofinishing Labs
7389	Business Services, NEC

75 AUTOMOTIVE REPAIR SERVICES AND PARKING

7513	Truck Rental & Leasing, Without Drivers
7514	Passenger Car Rental
7515	Passenger Car Leasing
7519	Utility Trailers & Recreational Vehicle Rental
7521	Automobile Parking Lots & Garages
7532	Top, Body & Upholstery Repair & Paint Shops
7533	Automotive Exhaust System Repair Shops
7534	Tire Retreading & Repair Shops
7536	Automotive Glass Replacement Shops
7537	Automotive Transmission Repair Shops
7538	General Automotive Repair Shop
7539	Automotive Repair Shops, NEC
7542	Car Washes
7549	Automotive Repair Services, NEC

76 MISCELLANEOUS REPAIR SERVICES

7622	Radio & TV Repair Shops
7623	Refrigeration & Air Conditioning Services & Repair Shop
7629	Electrical & Electronic Repair Shop, NEC
7631	Watch, Clock & Jewelry Repair
7641	Reupholstery & Furniture Repair
7692	Welding Repair
7694	Armature Rewinding Shops
7699	Repair Shop & Related Services, NEC

78 MOTION PICTURES

7812	Motion Picture & Video Tape Production
7819	Services Allied to Motion Picture Production
7822	Motion Picture & Video Tape Distribution
7829	Services Allied to Motion Picture Distribution
7832	Motion Picture Theaters, Except Drive-in
7833	Drive-in Motion Picture Theaters
7841	Video Tape Rental

For a complete list of abbreviations and their definitions, see page 28

79 AMUSEMENT AND RECREATION SERVICES

7911	Dance Studios, Schools & Halls
7922	Theatrical Producers (Except Motion Picture) & Misc Theatrical Services
7929	Bands, Orchestras, Actors & Entertainers & Entertainment Groups
7933	Bowling Centers
7941	Professional Sports Clubs & Promoters
7948	Racing & Track Operations
7991	Physical Fitness Facilities
7992	Public Golf Courses
7993	Coin-operated Amusement Devices & Arcades
7996	Amusement Parks
7997	Membership Sports & Recreation Clubs
7999	Amusement & Recreation Services, NEC

80 HEALTH SERVICES

8011	Offices & Clinics of Doctors of Medicine
8021	Offices & Clinics of Dentists
8031	Offices & Clinics of Doctors of Osteopathy
8041	Offices & Clinics of Chiropractors
8042	Offices & Clinics of Optometrists
8043	Offices & Clinics of Podiatrists
8049	Offices & Clinics of Health Practitioners, NEC
8051	Skilled Nursing Facilities
8052	Intermediate Care Facilities
8059	Nursing & Personal Care Facilities, NEC
8062	General Medical & Surgical Hospitals
8063	Psychiatric Hospitals
8069	Specialty Hospitals, Except Psychiatric
8071	Medical Laboratories
8072	Dental Laboratories
8082	Home Health Care Services
8092	Kidney Dialysis Centers
8093	Specialty Outpatient Facilities, NEC
8099	Health & Allied Services, NEC

81 LEGAL SERVICES

8111	Legal Services

82 EDUCATION SERVICES

8211	Elementary & Secondary Schools
8221	Colleges, Universities & Professional Schools
8222	Junior Colleges & Technical Institutes
8231	Libraries & Information Centers
8243	Data Processing Schools
8244	Business & Secretarial Schools
8249	Vocational Schools Except High Schools
8299	Schools & Educational Services, NEC

83 SOCIAL SERVICES

8322	Individual & Family Social Services
8331	Job Training & Vocational Rehabilitation Services
8351	Child Daycare Services
8361	Residential Care
8399	Social Services, NEC

84 MUSEUMS, BOTANICAL, AND ZOOLOGICAL GARDENS

8412	Museums & Art Galleries
8422	Arboreta, Botanical & Zoological Gardens

86 MEMBERSHIP ORGINIZATIONS

8611	Business Associations
8621	Professional Membership Organizations
8631	Labor Unions & Similar Organizations
8641	Civic, Social & Fraternal Associations
8651	Political Organizations
8661	Religious Organizations
8699	Membership Organizations, NEC

87 ENGINEERING, RESEARCH, MANAGEMENT, AND RELATED SERVICES

8711	Engineering Services
8712	Architectural Services
8713	Surveying Services
8721	Accounting, Auditing & Bookkeeping Services

For a complete list of abbreviations and their definitions, see page 28

8731	Commercial Physical & Biological Research
8732	Commercial Economic, Sociological & Educational Research
8733	Noncommercial Research Organization
8734	Testing Laboratories
8741	Management Services
8742	Management Consulting Services
8743	Public Relations Services
8744	Facilities Support Management Services
8748	Business Consulting Services, NEC

SIC
Short Titles

88 PRIVATE HOUSEHOLDS

8811	Private Households

89 SERVICES, NEC

8999	Services, NEC

J PUBLIC ADMINISTRATION

91 EXECUTIVE, LEGISLATIVE, AND GENERAL

9111	Executive Offices
9121	Legislative Bodies
9131	Executive & Legislative Combined
9199	General Government, NEC

92 JUSTICE, PUBLIC ORDER, AND SAFETY

9211	Courts
9221	Police Protection
9222	Legal Counsel & Prosecution
9223	Correctional Institutions
9224	Fire Protection
9229	Public Order & Safety, NEC

93 FINANCE, TAXATION, AND MONETARY POLICY

9311	Finance, Taxation & Monetary Policy

94 ADMINISTRATION OF HUMAN RESOURCES

9411	Admin of Educational Programs
9431	Admin of Public Health Programs
9441	Admin of Social & Man-power Programs
9451	Admin of Veterans' Affairs

95 ENVIRONMENTAL QUALITY AND HOUSING

9511	Air, Water & Solid Waste Management
9512	Land, Mineral, Wildlife Conservation
9531	Housing Programs
9532	Urban & Community Development

96 ADMINISTRATION OF ECONOMIC PROGRAMS

9611	Admin of General Economic Programs
9621	Regulation, Admin of Transportation
9631	Regulation, Admin of Utilities
9641	Regulation, Admin of Agricultural Marketing
9651	Regulation, Misc Commercial Sectors
9661	Space Research & Technology

97 NATIONAL SECURITY AND INTERNATIONAL AFFAIRS

9711	National Security
9721	International Affairs

K NONCLASSIFIABLE ESTABLISHMENTS

99 NONCLASSIFIABLE ESTABLISHMENTS

9999	Nonclassifiable Establishments

HOW TO USE THIS SECTION:

This section supplies you with a comprehensive list of ISIC codes and their industry descriptions. The codes are separated by section and are listed in descending order beginning with the section title and ending with the four-digit industry class description.

To convert ISIC codes to NAICS codes, turn to page 259.

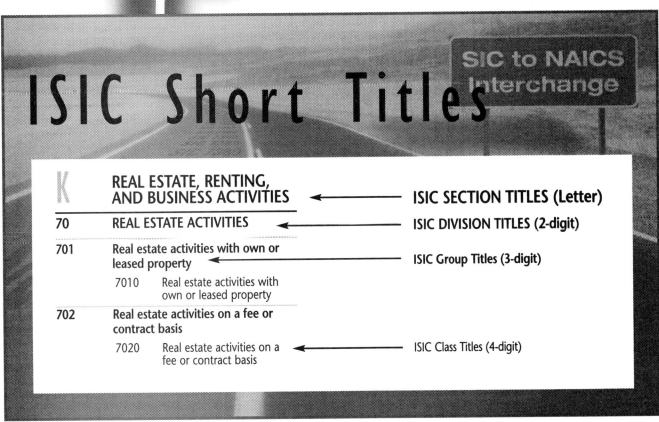

K	REAL ESTATE, RENTING, AND BUSINESS ACTIVITIES	← ISIC SECTION TITLES (Letter)
70	REAL ESTATE ACTIVITIES	← ISIC DIVISION TITLES (2-digit)
701	Real estate activities with own or leased property	← ISIC Group Titles (3-digit)
	7010 Real estate activities with own or leased property	
702	Real estate activities on a fee or contract basis	
	7020 Real estate activities on a fee or contract basis	← ISIC Class Titles (4-digit)

Harris is an official licensee of the United Nations ISIC classification codes.

Short Titles
International Standard
Industrial Classification (ISIC) Rev. 3

A AGRICULTURE, HUNTING, AND FORESTRY

01	**AGRICULTURE, HUNTING, AND RELATED SERVICE ACTIVITIES**
011	**Growing of crops; market gardening; horticulture**
0111	Growing of cereals and other crops, NEC
0112	Growing of vegetables, horticultural specialties and nursery products
0113	Growing of fruit, nuts, beverage and spice crops
012	**Farming of animals**
0121	Farming of cattle, sheep, goats, horses, asses, mules, and jennies; dairy farming
0122	Other animal farming; production of animal products NEC
013	**Growing of crops combined with farming of animals (mixed farming)**
0130	Growing of crops combined with farming of animals (mixed farming)
014	**Agricultural and animal husbandry service activities, except veterinary activities**
0140	Agricultural and animal husbandry service activities, except veterinary activities
015	**Hunting, trapping and game propagation including related service activities**
0150	Hunting, trapping, and game propagation including related service activities
02	**FORESTRY, LOGGING, AND RELATED SERVICE ACTIVITIES**
020	**Forestry, logging, and related service activities**
0200	Forestry, logging, and related service activities

B FISHING

05	**FISHING, OPERATION OF FISH HATCHERIES, AND FISH FARMS; SERVICE ACTIVITIES INCIDENTAL TO FISHING**
050	**Fishing, operation of fish hatcheries, and fish farms; service activities incidental to fishing**
0500	Fishing, operation of fish hatcheries, and fish farms; service activities incidental to fishing

C MINING AND QUARRYING

10	**MINING OF COAL AND LIGNITE; EXTRACTION OF PEAT**
101	**Mining and agglomeration of hard coal**
1010	Mining and agglomeration of hard coal
102	**Mining and agglomeration of lignite**
1020	Mining and agglomeration of lignite
103	**Extraction and agglomeration of peat**
1030	Extraction and agglomeration of peat
11	**EXTRACTION OF CRUDE PETROLEUM AND NATURAL GAS; SERVICE ACTIVITIES INCIDENTAL TO OIL AND GAS EXTRACTION (EXCEPT SURVEYING)**
111	**Extraction of crude petroleum and natural gas**
1110	Extraction of crude petroleum and natural gas
112	**Service activities incidental to oil and gas extraction (except surveying)**
1120	Service activities incidental to oil and gas extraction (except surveying)

ISIC
Short Titles

Convert ISIC codes to NAICS codes. Turn to page 259.

ISIC Short Titles

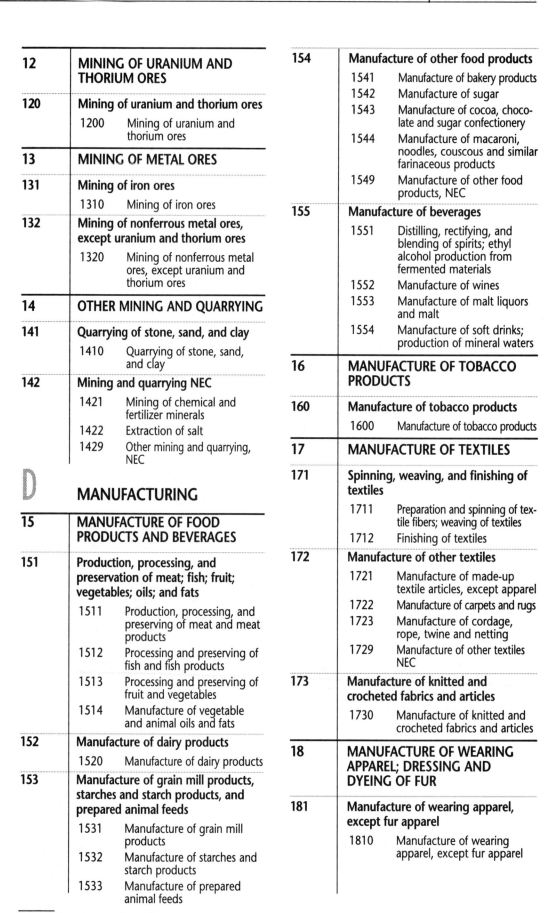

12	**MINING OF URANIUM AND THORIUM ORES**	
120	**Mining of uranium and thorium ores**	
	1200	Mining of uranium and thorium ores
13	**MINING OF METAL ORES**	
131	**Mining of iron ores**	
	1310	Mining of iron ores
132	**Mining of nonferrous metal ores, except uranium and thorium ores**	
	1320	Mining of nonferrous metal ores, except uranium and thorium ores
14	**OTHER MINING AND QUARRYING**	
141	**Quarrying of stone, sand, and clay**	
	1410	Quarrying of stone, sand, and clay
142	**Mining and quarrying NEC**	
	1421	Mining of chemical and fertilizer minerals
	1422	Extraction of salt
	1429	Other mining and quarrying, NEC

D MANUFACTURING

15	**MANUFACTURE OF FOOD PRODUCTS AND BEVERAGES**	
151	**Production, processing, and preservation of meat; fish; fruit; vegetables; oils; and fats**	
	1511	Production, processing, and preserving of meat and meat products
	1512	Processing and preserving of fish and fish products
	1513	Processing and preserving of fruit and vegetables
	1514	Manufacture of vegetable and animal oils and fats
152	**Manufacture of dairy products**	
	1520	Manufacture of dairy products
153	**Manufacture of grain mill products, starches and starch products, and prepared animal feeds**	
	1531	Manufacture of grain mill products
	1532	Manufacture of starches and starch products
	1533	Manufacture of prepared animal feeds

154	**Manufacture of other food products**	
	1541	Manufacture of bakery products
	1542	Manufacture of sugar
	1543	Manufacture of cocoa, chocolate and sugar confectionery
	1544	Manufacture of macaroni, noodles, couscous and similar farinaceous products
	1549	Manufacture of other food products, NEC
155	**Manufacture of beverages**	
	1551	Distilling, rectifying, and blending of spirits; ethyl alcohol production from fermented materials
	1552	Manufacture of wines
	1553	Manufacture of malt liquors and malt
	1554	Manufacture of soft drinks; production of mineral waters
16	**MANUFACTURE OF TOBACCO PRODUCTS**	
160	**Manufacture of tobacco products**	
	1600	Manufacture of tobacco products
17	**MANUFACTURE OF TEXTILES**	
171	**Spinning, weaving, and finishing of textiles**	
	1711	Preparation and spinning of textile fibers; weaving of textiles
	1712	Finishing of textiles
172	**Manufacture of other textiles**	
	1721	Manufacture of made-up textile articles, except apparel
	1722	Manufacture of carpets and rugs
	1723	Manufacture of cordage, rope, twine and netting
	1729	Manufacture of other textiles NEC
173	**Manufacture of knitted and crocheted fabrics and articles**	
	1730	Manufacture of knitted and crocheted fabrics and articles
18	**MANUFACTURE OF WEARING APPAREL; DRESSING AND DYEING OF FUR**	
181	**Manufacture of wearing apparel, except fur apparel**	
	1810	Manufacture of wearing apparel, except fur apparel

For a complete list of abbreviations and their definitions, see page 28

182	Dressing and dyeing of fur; manufacture of articles of fur
	1820 Dressing and dyeing of fur; manufacture of articles of fur

19	TANNING AND DRESSING OF LEATHER; MANUFACTURE OF LUGGAGE, HANDBAGS, SADDLERY, HARNESS, AND FOOTWEAR

191	Tanning and dressing of leather; manufacture of luggage, handbags, saddlery, and harness
	1911 Tanning and dressing of leather
	1912 Manufacture of luggage, handbags and the like, saddlery, and harness

192	Manufacture of footwear
	1920 Manufacture of footwear

20	MANUFACTURE OF WOOD AND OF PRODUCTS OF WOOD AND CORK, EXCEPT FURNITURE; MANUFACTURE OF ARTICLES OF STRAW AND PLAITING MATERIALS

201	Sawmilling and planing of wood
	2010 Sawmilling and planing of wood

202	Manufacture of products of wood, cork, straw, and plaiting materials
	2021 Manufacture of veneer sheets; manufacture of plywood, laminboard, particle board, and other panels and boards
	2022 Manufacture of builders' carpentry and joinery
	2023 Manufacture of wooden containers
	2029 Manufacture of other products of wood; manufacture of articles of cork, straw, and plaiting materials

21	MANUFACTURE OF PAPER AND PAPER PRODUCTS

210	Manufacture of paper and paper products
	2101 Manufacture of pulp, paper, and paperboard
	2102 Manufacture of corrugated paper and paperboard and of containers of paper and paperboard
	2109 Manufacture of other articles of paper and paperboard

22	PUBLISHING, PRINTING, AND REPRODUCTION OF RECORDED MEDIA

221	Publishing
	2211 Publishing of books, brochures, musical books and other publications
	2212 Publishing of newspapers, journals and periodicals
	2213 Publishing of recorded media
	2219 Other publishing

222	Printing and service activities related to printing
	2221 Printing
	2222 Service activities related to printing

223	Reproduction of recorded media
	2230 Reproduction of recorded media

23	MANUFACTURE OF COKE, REFINED PETROLEUM PRODUCTS, AND NUCLEAR FUEL

231	Manufacture of coke oven products
	2310 Manufacture of coke oven products

232	Manufacture of refined petroleum products
	2320 Manufacture of refined petroleum products

233	Processing of nuclear fuel
	2330 Processing of nuclear fuel

24	MANUFACTURE OF CHEMICALS AND CHEMICAL PRODUCTS

241	Manufacture of basic chemicals
	2411 Manufacture of basic chemicals, except fertilizers and nitrogen compounds
	2412 Manufacture of fertilizers and nitrogen compounds
	2413 Manufacture of plastics in primary forms and of synthetic rubber

242	Manufacture of other chemical products
	2421 Manufacture of pesticides and other agro-chemical products
	2422 Manufacture of paints, varnishes and similar coatings, printing ink, and mastics
	2423 Manufacture of pharmaceuticals, medicinal chemicals, and botanical products

ISIC Short Titles

Go to page 25 to learn more about ISIC codes.

2424	Manufacture of soap and detergents, cleaning and polishing preparations, perfumes, and toilet preparations
2429	Manufacture of other chemical products, NEC

243 Manufacture of man-made fibers

2430	Manufacture of man-made fibers

25 MANUFACTURE OF RUBBER AND PLASTICS PRODUCTS

251 Manufacture of rubber products

2511	Manufacture of rubber tires and tubes; retreading and rebuilding of rubber tires
2519	Manufacture of other rubber products

252 Manufacture of plastics products

2520	Manufacture of plastics products

26 MANUFACTURE OF OTHER NON-METALLIC MINERAL PRODUCTS

261 Manufacture of glass and glass products

2610	Manufacture of glass and glass products

269 Manufacture of nonmetallic mineral products, NEC

2691	Manufacture of nonstructural nonrefractory ceramic ware
2692	Manufacture of refractory ceramic products
2693	Manufacture of structural nonrefractory clay and ceramic products
2694	Manufacture of cement, lime, and plaster
2695	Manufacture of articles of concrete, cement, and plaster
2696	Cutting, shaping, and finishing of stone
2699	Manufacture of other non-metallic mineral products, NEC

27 MANUFACTURE OF BASIC METALS

271 Manufacture of basic iron and steel

2710	Manufacture of basic iron and steel

272 Manufacture of basic, precious, and nonferrous metals

2720	Manufacture of basic, precious, and nonferrous metals

273 Casting of metals

2731	Casting of iron and steel
2732	Casting of nonferrous metals

28 MANUFACTURE OF FABRICATED METAL PRODUCTS, EXCEPT MACHINERY AND EQUIPMENT

281 Manufacture of structural metal products, tanks, reservoirs, and steam generators

2811	Manufacture of structural metal products
2812	Manufacture of tanks, reservoirs, and containers of metal
2813	Manufacture of steam generators, except central heating hot water boilers

289 Manufacture of other fabricated metal products; metal working service activities

2891	Forging, pressing, stamping, and roll-forming of metal; powder metallurgy
2892	Treatment and coating of metals; general mechanical engineering on a fee or contract basis
2893	Manufacture of cutlery, hand tools, and general hardware
2899	Manufacture of other fabricated metal products, NEC

29 MANUFACTURE OF MACHINERY AND EQUIPMENT, NEC

291 Manufacture of general purpose machinery

2911	Manufacture of engines and turbines, except aircraft, vehicle, and cycle engines
2912	Manufacture of pumps, compressors, taps, and valves
2913	Manufacture of bearings, gears, gearing, and driving elements
2914	Manufacture of ovens, furnaces, and furnace burners
2915	Manufacture of lifting and handling equipment
2919	Manufacture of other general purpose machinery

292 Manufacture of special purpose machinery

2921	Manufacture of agricultural and forestry machinery
2922	Manufacture of machine-tools
2923	Manufacture of machinery for metallurgy
2924	Manufacture of machinery for mining, quarrying, and construction

ISIC Short Titles

	2925	Manufacture of machinery for food, beverage, and tobacco processing
	2926	Manufacture of machinery for textile, apparel, and leather production
	2927	Manufacture of weapons and ammunition
	2929	Manufacture of other special purpose machinery
293	**Manufacture of domestic appliances, NEC**	
	2930	Manufacture of domestic appliances, NEC

30 MANUFACTURE OF OFFICE, ACCOUNTING, AND COMPUTING MACHINERY

300 Manufacture of office, accounting, and computing machinery

  3000 Manufacture of office, accounting, and computing machinery

31 MANUFACTURE OF ELECTRICAL MACHINERY AND APPARATUS, NEC

311 Manufacture of electric motors, generators, and transformers

  3110 Manufacture of electric motors, generators, and transformers

312 Manufacture of electricity distribution and control apparatus

  3120 Manufacture of electricity distribution and control apparatus

313 Manufacture of insulated wire and cable

  3130 Manufacture of insulated wire and cable

314 Manufacture of accumulators, primary cells, and primary batteries

  3140 Manufacture of accumulators, primary cells, and primary batteries

315 Manufacture of electric lamps and lighting equipment

  3150 Manufacture of electric lamps and lighting equipment

319 Manufacture of other electrical equipment, NEC

  3190 Manufacture of other electrical equipment, NEC

32 MANUFACTURE OF RADIO, TELEVISION AND COMMUNICATION, EQUIPMENT, AND APPARATUS

321 Manufacture of electronic valves and tubes and other electronic components

  3210 Manufacture of electronic valves and tubes and other electronic components

322 Manufacture of television and radio transmitters and apparatus for line telephony and line telegraphy

  3220 Manufacture of television and radio transmitters and apparatus for line telephony and line telegraphy

323 Manufacture of television and radio receivers, sound or video recording or reproducing apparatus, and associated goods

  3230 Manufacture of television and radio receivers, sound or video recording or reproducing apparatus, and associated goods

33 MANUFACTURE OF MEDICAL, PRECISION AND OPTICAL INSTRUMENTS, WATCHES, AND CLOCKS

331 Manufacture of medical appliances and instruments and appliances for measuring, checking, testing, navigating, and other purposes, except optical instruments

  3311 Manufacture of medical and surgical equipment and orthopedic appliances

  3312 Manufacture of instruments and appliances for measuring, checking, testing, navigating, and other purposes; except industrial process control equipment

  3313 Manufacture of industrial process control equipment

332 Manufacture of optical instruments and photographic equipment

  3320 Manufacture of optical instruments and photographic equipment

333 Manufacture of watches and clocks

  3330 Manufacture of watches and clocks

Convert ISIC codes to NAICS codes. Turn to page 259.

For a complete list of abbreviations and their definitions, see page 28

ISIC Short Titles

34	**MANUFACTURE OF MOTOR VEHICLES, TRAILERS, AND SEMI-TRAILERS**
341	**Manufacture of motor vehicles**
3410	Manufacture of motor vehicles
342	**Manufacture of bodies (coachwork) for motor vehicles; manufacture of trailers and semi-trailers**
3420	Manufacture of bodies (coachwork) for motor vehicles; manufacture of trailers and semi-trailers
343	**Manufacture of parts and accessories for motor vehicles and their engines**
3430	Manufacture of parts and accessories for motor vehicles and their engines
35	**MANUFACTURE OF OTHER TRANSPORT EQUIPMENT**
351	**Building and repairing of ships and boats**
3511	Building and repairing of ships
3512	Building and repairing of pleasure and sporting boats
352	**Manufacture of railway and tramway locomotives and rolling stock**
3520	Manufacture of railway and tramway locomotives and rolling stock
353	**Manufacture of aircraft and spacecraft**
3530	Manufacture of aircraft and spacecraft
359	**Manufacture of transport equipment NEC**
3591	Manufacture of motorcycles
3592	Manufacture of bicycles and invalid carriages
3599	Manufacture of other transport equipment, NEC
36	**MANUFACTURE OF FURNITURE; MANUFACTURING, NEC**
361	**Manufacture of furniture**
3610	Manufacture of furniture
369	**Manufacturing, NEC**
3691	Manufacture of jewelry and related articles
3692	Manufacture of musical instruments
3693	Manufacture of sports goods

3694	Manufacture of games and toys
3699	Other manufacturing, NEC
37	**RECYCLING**
371	**Recycling of metal waste and scrap**
3710	Recycling of metal waste and scrap
372	**Recycling of nonmetal waste and scrap**
3720	Recycling of nonmetal waste and scrap

E ELECTRICITY, GAS, AND WATER SUPPLY

40	**ELECTRICITY, GAS, STEAM, AND HOT WATER SUPPLY**
401	**Production, collection, and distribution of electricity**
4010	Production, collection, and distribution of electricity of gas; distribution of gaseous fuels through mains
402	**Manufacture of gas; distribution of gaseous fuels through mains**
4020	Manufacture of gas; distribution of gaseous fuels through mains
403	**Steam and hot water supply**
4030	Steam and hot water supply
41	**COLLECTION, PURIFICATION, AND DISTRIBUTION OF WATER**
410	**Collection, purification, and distribution of water**
4100	Collection, purification, and distribution of water

F CONSTRUCTION

45	**CONSTRUCTION**
451	**Site preparation**
4510	Site preparation
452	**Building of complete constructions or parts thereof; civil engineering**
4520	Building of complete constructions or parts thereof; civil engineering
453	**Building installation**
4530	Building installation
454	**Building completion**
4540	Building completion

For a complete list of abbreviations and their definitions, see page 28

455	**Renting of construction or demolition equipment with operator**
	4550 Renting of construction or demolition equipment with operator

G WHOLESALE AND RETAIL TRADE; REPAIR OF MOTOR VEHICLES, MOTORCYCLES, AND PERSONAL AND HOUSEHOLD GOODS

50	**SALE, MAINTENANCE, AND REPAIR OF MOTOR VEHICLES AND MOTORCYCLES; RETAIL SALE OF AUTOMOTIVE FUEL**
501	**Sale of motor vehicles**
	5010 Sale of motor vehicles
502	**Maintenance and repair of motor vehicles**
	5020 Maintenance and repair of motor vehicles
503	**Sale of motor vehicle parts and accessories**
	5030 Sale of motor vehicle parts and accessories
504	**Sale, maintenance, and repair of motorcycles and related parts and accessories**
	5040 Sale, maintenance, and repair of motorcycles and related parts and accessories
505	**Retail sale of automotive fuel**
	5050 Retail sale of automotive fuel

51	**WHOLESALE TRADE AND COMMISSION TRADE, EXCEPT OF MOTOR VEHICLES AND MOTORCYCLES**
511	**Wholesale on a fee or contract basis**
	5110 Wholesale on a fee or contract basis
512	**Wholesale of agricultural raw materials, live animals, food, beverages, and tobacco**
	5121 Wholesale of agricultural raw materials and live animals
	5122 Wholesale of food, beverages, and tobacco
513	**Wholesale of household goods**
	5131 Wholesale of textiles, clothing, and footwear

	5139 Wholesale of other household goods
514	**Wholesale of nonagricultural intermediate products, waste, and scrap**
	5141 Wholesale of solid, liquid, and gaseous fuels and related products
	5142 Wholesale of metals and metal ores
	5143 Wholesale of construction materials, hardware, plumbing and heating equipment, and supplies
	5149 Wholesale of other intermediate products, waste, and scrap
515	**Wholesale of machinery, equipment, and supplies**
	5150 Wholesale of machinery, equipment, and supplies
519	**Other wholesale**
	5190 Other wholesale

52	**RETAIL TRADE, EXCEPT OF MOTOR VEHICLES AND MOTORCYCLES; REPAIR OF PERSONAL AND HOUSEHOLD GOODS**
521	**Nonspecialized retail trade in stores**
	5211 Retail sale in nonspecialized stores with food, beverages or tobacco predominating
	5219 Other retail sale in nonspecialized stores
522	**Retail sale of food, beverages, and tobacco in specialized stores**
	5220 Retail sale of food, beverages, and tobacco in specialized stores
523	**Other retail trade of new goods in specialized stores**
	5231 Retail sale of pharmaceutical and medical goods, cosmetic, and toilet articles
	5232 Retail sale of textiles, clothing, footwear, and leather goods
	5233 Retail sale of household appliances, articles, and equipment
	5234 Retail sale of hardware, paint, and glass
	5239 Other retail sale in specialized stores
524	**Retail sale of second-hand goods in stores**
	5240 Retail sale of second-hand goods in stores

Go to page 25 to learn more about ISIC codes.

ISIC Short Titles

525	Retail trade not in stores	
	5251	Retail sale via mail order houses
	5252	Retail sale via stalls and markets
	5259	Other nonstore retail sale
526	Repair of personal and household goods	
	5260	Repair of personal and household goods

H HOTELS AND RESTAURANTS

55	HOTELS AND RESTAURANTS	
551	Hotels, camping sites, and other provision of short-stay accommodation	
	5510	Hotels, camping sites, and other provision of short-stay accommodation
552	Restaurants, bars, and canteens	
	5520	Restaurants, bars, and canteens

I TRANSPORT, STORAGE, AND COMMUNICATIONS

60	LAND TRANSPORT; TRANSPORT VIA PIPELINES	
601	Transport via railways	
	6010	Transport via railways
602	Other land transport	
	6021	Other scheduled passenger land transport
	6022	Other nonscheduled passenger land transport
	6023	Freight transport by road
603	Transport via pipelines	
	6030	Transport via pipelines

61	WATER TRANSPORT	
611	Sea and coastal water transport	
	6110	Sea and coastal water transport
612	Inland water transport	
	6120	Inland water transport

62	AIR TRANSPORT	
621	Scheduled air transport	
	6210	Scheduled air transport

622	Nonscheduled air transport	
	6220	Nonscheduled air transport

63	SUPPORTING AND AUXILIARY TRANSPORT ACTIVITIES; ACTIVITIES OF TRAVEL AGENCIES	
630	Supporting and auxiliary transport activities; activities of travel agencies	
	6301	Cargo handling
	6302	Storage and warehousing
	6303	Other supporting transport activities
	6304	Activities of travel agencies and tour operators; tourist assistance activities, NEC
	6309	Activities of other transport agencies

64	POST AND TELECOMMUNICATIONS	
641	Post and courier activities	
	6411	National post activities
	6412	Courier activities other than national post activities
642	Telecommunications	
	6420	Telecommunications

J FINANCIAL INTERMEDIATION

65	FINANCIAL INTERMEDIATION, EXCEPT INSURANCE AND PENSION FUNDING	
651	Monetary intermediation	
	6511	Central banking
	6519	Other monetary intermediation
659	Other financial intermediation	
	6591	Financial leasing
	6592	Other credit granting
	6599	Other financial intermediation, NEC

66	INSURANCE AND PENSION FUNDING, EXCEPT COMPULSORY SOCIAL SECURITY	
660	Insurance and pension funding, except compulsory social security	
	6601	Life insurance
	6602	Pension funding
	6603	Nonlife insurance

ISIC
Short Titles

67	**ACTIVITIES AUXILIARY TO FINANCIAL INTERMEDIATION**
671	**Activities auxiliary to financial intermediation, except insurance and pension funding**
6711	Administration of financial markets
6712	Security dealing activities
6719	Activities auxiliary to financial intermediation, NEC
672	**Activities auxiliary to insurance and pension funding**
6720	Activities auxiliary to insurance and pension funding

K REAL ESTATE, RENTING, AND BUSINESS ACTIVITIES

70	**REAL ESTATE ACTIVITIES**
701	**Real estate activities with own or leased property**
7010	Real estate activities with own or leased property
702	**Real estate activities on a fee or contract basis**
7020	Real estate activities on a fee or contract basis

71	**RENTING OF MACHINERY AND EQUIPMENT WITHOUT OPERATOR AND OF PERSONAL AND HOUSEHOLD GOODS**
711	**Renting of transport equipment**
7111	Renting of land transport equipment
7112	Renting of water transport equipment
7113	Renting of air transport equipment
712	**Renting of other machinery and equipment**
7121	Renting of agricultural machinery and equipment
7122	Renting of construction and civil engineering machinery and equipment
7123	Renting of office machinery and equipment (including computers)
7129	Renting of other machinery and equipment, NEC

713	**Renting of personal and household goods, NEC**
7130	Renting of personal and household goods, NEC
72	**COMPUTER AND RELATED ACTIVITIES**
721	**Hardware consultancy**
7210	Hardware consultancy
722	**Software consultancy and supply**
7220	Software consultancy and supply
723	**Data processing**
7230	Data processing
724	**Data base activities**
7240	Data base activities
725	**Maintenance and repair of office, accounting, and computing machinery**
7250	Maintenance and repair of office, accounting, and computing machinery
729	**Other computer related activities**
7290	Other computer related activities
73	**RESEARCH AND DEVELOPMENT**
731	**Research and experimental development on natural sciences and engineering (NSE)**
7310	Research and experimental development on natural sciences and engineering (NSE)
732	**Research and experimental development on social sciences and humanities (SSH)**
7320	Research and experimental development on social sciences and humanities (SSH)
74	**OTHER BUSINESS ACTIVITIES**
741	**Legal, accounting, bookkeeping, and auditing activities; tax consultancy; market research and public opinion polling; business and management consultancy**
7411	Legal activities
7412	Accounting, book-keeping and auditing activities; tax consultancy
7413	Market research and public opinion polling
7414	Business and management consultancy activities

Convert ISIC codes to NAICS codes. Turn to page 259.

742 **Architectural, engineering, and other technical activities**

| 7421 | Architectural and engineering activities and related technical consultancy |
| 7422 | Technical testing and analysis |

743 **Advertising**

| 7430 | Advertising |

749 **Business activities, NEC**

7491	Labor recruitment and provision of personnel
7492	Investigation and security activities
7493	Building-cleaning activities
7494	Photographic activities
7495	Packaging activities
7499	Other business activities, NEC

ISIC
Short Titles

L

PUBLIC ADMINISTRATION AND DEFENSE; COMPULSORY SOCIAL SECURITY

75 **PUBLIC ADMINISTRATION AND DEFENSE; COMPULSORY SOCIAL SECURITY**

751 **Administration of the State and the economic and social policy of the community**

7511	General (over-all) public service activities
7512	Regulation of the activities of agencies that provide health care, education, cultural services, and other social services (except social security)
7513	Regulation of and contribution to more efficient operation of business
7514	Ancillary service activities for the government as a whole

752 **Provision of services to the community as a whole**

7521	Foreign affairs
7522	Defense activities
7523	Public order and safety activities

753 **Compulsory social security activities**

| 7530 | Compulsory social security activities |

M

EDUCATION

80 **EDUCATION**

801 **Primary education**

| 8010 | Primary education |

802 **Secondary education**

| 8021 | General secondary education |
| 8022 | Technical and vocational secondary education |

803 **Higher education**

| 8030 | Higher education |

809 **Adult and other education**

| 8090 | Adult and other education |

N

HEALTH AND SOCIAL WORK

85 **HEALTH AND SOCIAL WORK**

851 **Human health activities**

8511	Hospital activities
8512	Medical and dental practice activities
8519	Other human health activities

852 **Veterinary activities**

| 8520 | Veterinary activities |

853 **Social work activities**

| 8531 | Social work with accommodation |
| 8532 | Social work without accommodation |

O

OTHER COMMUNITY, SOCIAL, AND PERSONAL SERVICE ACTIVITIES

90 **SEWAGE AND REFUSE DISPOSAL, SANITATION, AND SIMILAR ACTIVITIES**

900 **Sewage and refuse disposal, sanitation, and similar activities**

| 9000 | Sewage and refuse disposal, sanitation, and similar activities |

91 **ACTIVITIES OF MEMBERSHIP ORGANIZATIONS, NEC**

911 **Activities of business, employers, and professional organizations**

| 9111 | Activities of business and employers organizations |
| 9112 | Activities of professional organizations |

912 **Activities of trade unions**

| 9120 | Activities of trade unions |

919 **Activities of other membership organizations**

| 9191 | Activities of religious organizations |

For a complete list of abbreviations and their definitions, see page 28

9192	Activities of political organizations
9199	Activities of other membership organizations, NEC

92 RECREATIONAL, CULTURAL, AND SPORTING ACTIVITIES

921 Motion picture, radio, television, and other entertainment activities

9211	Motion picture and video production and distribution
9212	Motion picture projection
9213	Radio and television activities
9214	Dramatic arts, music and other arts activities
9219	Other entertainment activities, NEC

922 News agency activities

9220	News agency activities

923 Library, archives, museums, and other cultural activities

9231	Library and archives activities
9232	Museums activities and preservation of historical sites and buildings
9233	Botanical and zoological gardens and nature reserves activities

924 Sporting and other recreational activities

9241	Sporting activities
9249	Other recreational activities

93 OTHER SERVICE ACTIVITIES

930 Other service activities

9301	Washing and (dry-) cleaning of textile and fur products
9302	Hairdressing and other beauty treatment
9303	Funeral and related activities
9309	Other service activities, NEC

P PRIVATE HOUSEHOLDS WITH EMPLOYED PERSONS

95 PRIVATE HOUSEHOLDS WITH EMPLOYED PERSONS

950 Private households with employed persons

9500	Private households with employed persons

Q EXTRATERRITORIAL ORGANIZATIONS AND BODIES

99 EXTRATERRITORIAL ORGANIZATIONS AND BODIES

990 Extraterritorial organizations and bodies

9900	Extraterritorial organizations and bodies

Go to page 25 to learn more about ISIC codes.

ISIC Short Titles

HOW TO USE THIS SECTION:

This section shows you all four-digit SIC codes and the NAICS or portions of NAICS that are comparable. The table is in numerical order by the SIC code. For each SIC industry you have the SIC code and description followed by the comparable NAICS code and description. If an **@** symbol is located in the SIC code column this indicates that this category cannot be reasonably approximated from NAICS based data. This will be an industry where you will experience a break in time series that is estimated to be greater than three percent of the 1992 value of output for the 1987 industry. If the abbreviation **(pt)** appears after the NAICS description this indicates that this industry contains components from other SIC codes.

Harris Interchange
SIC to NAICS Conversion

7389	Business Services, NEC			SIC Code
	• Sound Recording Studios	51224	Sound Recording Studios	
	• Audio Taping Services	51229	Other Sound Recording Industries (pt)	NAICS
	• Stock Photo Agencies and Press Clipping Services	514199	All Other Information Services (pt)	Corresponding Code
	• Process Services, Patent Agents, Notaries Public and Paralegal Services	541199	All Other Legal Services	
	• Bail Bonding	81299	All Other Personal Services (pt)	(pt) indicates that this industry
	• Mapmaking Services	54137	Surveying and Mapping (except Geophysical) Services (pt)	contains components from other SIC codes.
	• Interior Design	54141	Interior Design Services	
	• Industrial Design	54142	Industrial Design Services	
	• Drafting Service	54134	Drafting Services	
	• Fashion and Other Design Services	54149	Other Specialized Design Services	
	• Sign Painting and Lettering Shops, Showcard Painting, Mannequin Decorating	54189	Other Services Related to Advertising (pt) Services, and Other Advertising Related	

pt—Part of.

SIC to NAICS Conversion

SIC Code	1987 U.S. SIC Description	NAICS Code	1997 NAICS U.S. Description
01	**Agricultural Production—Crops**		
0111	Wheat	11114	Wheat Farming
0112	Rice	11116	Rice Farming
0115	Corn	11115	Corn Farming (pt)
0116	Soybeans	11111	Soybean Farming
0119	Cash Grains, NEC		
	• Dry Pea and Bean Farms	11113	Dry Pea and Bean Farming
	• Oilseed, except Soybean, Farms	11112	Oilseed (except Soybean) Farming
	• Popcorn Farms	11115	Corn Farming (pt)
	• Combination Oilseed and Grain Farms	111191	Oilseed and Grain Combination Farming
	• Other Farms	111199	All Other Grain Farming
0131	Cotton	11192	Cotton Farming
0132	Tobacco	11191	Tobacco Farming
0133	Sugarcane and Sugar Beets		
	• Sugar Beets	111991	Sugar Beet Farming
	• Sugarcane	11193	Sugarcane Farming
0134	Irish Potatoes	111211	Potato Farming
0139	Field Crops, except Cash Grains, NEC		
	• Hay Farms	11194	Hay Farming
	• Peanut Farming	111992	Peanut Farming
	• Sweet Potatoes and Yam Farms	111219	Other Vegetable (except Potato) and Melon Farming (pt)
	• Other Field Crop Farms	111998	All Other Miscellaneous Crop Farming (pt)
0161	Vegetables and Melons	111219	Other Vegetable (except Potato) and Melon Farming (pt)
0171	Berry Crops		
	• Strawberry Farms	111333	Strawberry Farming
	• Other Berry Farms	111334	Berry (except Strawberry) Farming
0172	Grapes	111332	Grape Vineyards
0173	Tree Nuts	111335	Tree Nut Farming
0174	Citrus Fruits		
	• Orange Groves and Farms	11131	Orange Groves
	• Other Citrus Groves and Farms	11132	Citrus (except Orange) Groves
0175	Deciduous Tree Fruits		
	• Apple Orchards and Farms	111331	Apple Orchards
	• Other Farms	111339	Other Noncitrus Fruit Farming (pt)
0179	Fruits and Tree Nuts, NEC		
	• Combination Fruit and Tree Nut Farms	111336	Fruit and Tree Nut Combination Farming
	• Other Farms	111339	Other Noncitrus Fruit Farming (pt)
0181	Ornamental Floriculture and Nursery Products		
	• Floriculture Farming	111422	Floriculture Production
	• Nursery Farming	111421	Nursery and Tree Production (pt)
0182	Food Crops Grown Under Cover		
	• Mushrooms, Growing of	111411	Mushroom Production
	• Other Food Crops Grown Under Cover	111419	Other Food Crops Grown Under Cover
0191	General Farms, Primarily Crop	111998	All Other Miscellaneous Crop Farming (pt)
02	**Agricultural Production—Livestock**		
0211	Beef Cattle Feedlots	112112	Cattle Feedlots
0212	Beef Cattle, except Feedlots	112111	Beef Cattle Ranching and Farming (pt)

pt—Part of.

Visit page 9 to learn more about NAICS codes.

SIC Code	1987 U.S. SIC Description	NAICS Code	1997 NAICS U.S. Description
0213	Hogs	11221	Hog and Pig Farming
0214	Sheep and Goats		
	• Sheep Farms	11241	Sheep Farming
	• Goat Farms	11242	Goat Farming
0219	General Livestock, except Dairy and Poultry	11299	All Other Animal Production (pt)
0241	Dairy Farms		
	• Dairy Heifer Replacement Farms	112111	Beef Cattle Ranching and Farming (pt)
	• Dairy Farms	11212	Dairy Cattle and Milk Production
0251	Broiler, Fryers, and Roaster Chickens	11232	Broilers and Other Meat-type Chicken Production
0252	Chicken Eggs	11231	Chicken Egg Production
0253	Turkey and Turkey Eggs	11233	Turkey Production
0254	Poultry Hatcheries	11234	Poultry Hatcheries
0259	Poultry and Eggs, NEC	11239	Other Poultry Production
0271	Fur-bearing Animals and Rabbits	11293	Fur-bearing Animal and Rabbit Production
0272	Horses and Other Equines	11292	Horse and Other Equine Production
0273	Animal Aquaculture		
	• Finfish Farms	112511	Finfish Farming and Fish Hatcheries (pt)
	• Shellfish Farms	112512	Shellfish Farming (pt)
	• Other Animal Aquaculture	112519	Other Animal Aquaculture (pt)
0279	Animal Specialties, NEC		
	• Alligator and Frog Production	112519	Other Animal Aquaculture (pt)
	• Bee Farms	11291	Apiculture
	• Other	11299	All Other Animal Production (pt)
0291	General Farms, Primarily Livestock and Animal Specialties	11299	All Other Animal Production (pt)
07	**Agricultural Services**		
0711	Soil Preparation Services	115112	Soil Preparation, Planting, and Cultivating (pt)
0721	Crop Planting, Cultivating, and Protecting	115112	Soil Preparation, Planting, and Cultivating (pt)
0722	Crop Harvesting, Primarily by Machine	115113	Crop Harvesting, Primarily by Machine
0723	Crop Preparation Services For Market, except Cotton Ginning		
	• Other	115114	Postharvest Crop Activities (except Cotton Ginning)
	• Custom Grain Grinding	311119	Other Animal Food Manufacturing (pt)
0724	Cotton Ginning	115111	Cotton Ginning
0741	Veterinary Services For Livestock	54194	Veterinary Services (pt)
0742	Veterinary Services for Animal Specialties	54194	Veterinary Services (pt)
0751	Livestock Services, except Veterinary		
	• Custom Slaughtering	311611	Animal (except Poultry) Slaughtering (pt)
	• Other Livestock Service, except Veterinary	11521	Support Activities for Animal Production (pt)
0752	Animal Specialty Services, except Veterinary		
	• Horses and Equines Services and Animal Production Breeding	11521	Support Activities for Animal Production (pt)
	• Pet Care Services	81291	Pet Care (except Veterinary) Services
0761	Farm Labor Contractors and Crew Leaders	115115	Farm Labor Contractors and Crew Leaders

pt—Part of.

SIC Code	1987 U.S. SIC Description	NAICS Code	1997 NAICS U.S. Description
0762	Farm Management Services	115116	Farm Management Services
0781	Landscape Counseling and Planning		
	• Horticulture Consulting	54169	Other Scientific and Technical Consulting Services (pt)
	• Landscape Architectural Services	54132	Landscape Architectural Services (pt)
0782	Lawn and Garden Services	56173	Landscaping Services (pt)
0783	Ornamental Shrub and Tree Services	56173	Landscaping Services (pt)
08	**Forestry**		
0811	Timber Tracts		
	• Short Rotation Woody Crops	111421	Nursery and Tree Production (pt)
	• Long Term Timber Farming	11311	Timber Tract Operations
0831	Forest Nurseries and Gathering of Forest Products		
	• Maple Sap	111998	All Other Miscellaneous Crop Farming (pt)
	• Other Forest Products	11321	Forest Nurseries and Gathering of Forest Products
0851	Forestry Services	11531	Support Activities for Forestry
09	**Fishing, Hunting, and Trapping**		
0912	Finfish	114111	Finfish Fishing
0913	Shellfish	114112	Shellfish Fishing
0919	Miscellaneous Marine Products		
	• Except Plant Aquaculture	114119	Other Marine Fishing
	• Plant Aquaculture	111998	All Other Miscellaneous Crop Farming (pt)
0921	Fish Hatcheries and Preserves		
	• Finfish Hatcheries	112511	Finfish Farming and Fish Hatcheries (pt)
	• Shellfish Hatcheries	112512	Shellfish Farming (pt)
0971	Hunting and Trapping and Game Propagation	11421	Hunting and Trapping
10	**Metal Mining**		
1011	Iron Ores	21221	Iron Ore Mining
1021	Copper Ores	212234	Copper Ore and Nickel Ore Mining (pt)
1031	Lead and Zinc Ores	212231	Lead Ore and Zinc Ore Mining
1041	Gold Ores	212221	Gold Ore Mining
1044	Silver Ores	212222	Silver Ore Mining
1061	Ferroalloy Ores, except Vanadium		
	• Nickel Ore Mining	212234	Copper Ore and Nickel Ore Mining (pt)
	• Other Ferroalloys (except nickel)	212299	Other Metal Ore Mining (pt)
1081	Metal Mining Services		
	• Metal Mining (except geophysical surveying)	213114	Support Activities for Metal Mining
	• Geophysical Surveying and Mapping	54136	Geophysical Surveying and Mapping Services (pt)
1094	Uranium-Radium-Vanadium Ores	212291	Uranium-Radium-Vanadium Ore Mining
1099	Miscellaneous Metal Ores, NEC	212299	Other Metal Ore Mining (pt)
12	**Coal Mining**		
1221	Bituminous Coal and Lignite Surface Mining	212111	Bituminous Coal and Lignite Surface Mining
1222	Bituminous Coal Underground Mining	212112	Bituminous Coal Underground Mining
1231	Anthracite Mining	212113	Anthracite Mining
1241	Coal Mining Services	213113	Support Activities for Coal Mining

pt—Part of.

SIC Code	1987 U.S. SIC Description	NAICS Code	1997 NAICS U.S. Description
13	**Oil and Gas Extraction**		
1311	Crude Petroleum and Natural Gas	211111	Crude Petroleum and Natural Gas Extraction
1321	Natural Gas Liquids	211112	Natural Gas Liquid Extraction (pt)
1381	Drilling Oil and Gas Wells	213111	Drilling Oil and Gas Wells
1382	Oil and Gas Field Exploration Services		
	• Geophysical Mapping and Surveying	54136	Geophysical Surveying and Mapping Services (pt)
	• Other Oil and Gas Field Exploration Services	213112	Support Activities for Oil and Gas Field Operations (pt)
1389	Oil and Gas Field Services, NEC	213112	Support Activities for Oil and Gas Field Operations (pt)
14	**Nonmetallic Minerals, except Fuels**		
1411	Dimension Stone	212311	Dimension Stone Mining and Quarrying
1422	Crushed and Broken Limestone	212312	Crushed and Broken Limestone Mining and Quarrying
1423	Crushed and Broken Granite	212313	Crushed and Broken Granite Mining and Quarrying
1429	Crushed and Broken Stone, NEC	212319	Other Crushed and Broken Stone Mining and Quarrying (pt)
1442	Construction Sand and Gravel	212321	Construction Sand and Gravel Mining
1446	Industrial Sand	212322	Industrial Sand Mining
1455	Kaolin and Ball Clay	212324	Kaolin and Ball Clay Mining
1459	Clay, Ceramic, and Refractory Minerals, NEC	212325	Clay and Ceramic and Refractory Minerals Mining
1474	Potash, Soda, and Borate Minerals	212391	Potash, Soda, and Borate Mineral Mining
1475	Phosphate Rock	212392	Phosphate Rock Mining
1479	Chemical and Fertilizer Mineral Mining, NEC	212393	Other Chemical and Fertilizer Mineral Mining
1481	Nonmetallic Minerals Services except Fuels		
	• Except Geophysical Mapping and Surveying	213115	Support Activities for Nonmetallic Minerals (except Fuels)
	• Geophysical Surveying and Mapping Services	54136	Geophysical Surveying and Mapping Services (pt)
1499	Miscellaneous Nonmetallic Minerals, except Fuels		
	• Bituminous Limestone and Bituminous Sandstone	212319	Other Crushed and Broken Stone Mining or Quarrying (pt)
	• Except Bituminous Limestone and Bituminous Sandstone	212399	All Other Nonmetallic Mineral Mining (pt)
15	**General Building Contractors**		
1521	General Contractors—Single-family Houses	23321	Single-family Housing Construction (pt)
1522	General Contractors—Residential Buildings, Other than Single-family		
	• Hotel and Motel Construction	23332	Commercial and Institutional Building Construction (pt)
	• Except Hotel and Motel Construction	23322	Multifamily Housing Construction (pt)
1531	Operative Builders		
	• Single-family Housing	23321	Single-family Housing Construction (pt)
	• Multifamily Housing	23322	Multifamily Housing Construction (pt)

pt—Part of.

SIC Code	1987 U.S. SIC Description	NAICS Code	1997 NAICS U.S. Description
	• Manufacturing and Light Industrial Buildings	23331	Manufacturing and Industrial Building Construction (pt)
	• Commercial and Institutional Buildings	23332	Commercial and Institutional Building Construction (pt)
1541	General Contractors—Industrial Buildings and Warehouses		
	• Public Warehouse Construction	23332	Commercial and Institutional Building Construction (pt)
	• Except Public Warehouse Construction	23331	Manufacturing and Industrial Building Construction (pt)
1542	General Contractors—Nonresidential Buildings, • Other than Industrial Buildings and Warehouses	23332	Commercial and Institutional Building Construction (pt)
16	**Heavy Construction Contractors**		
1611	Highway and Street Construction, except Elevated Highways	23411	Highway and Street Construction (pt)
1622	Bridge, Tunnel, and Elevated Highway Construction	23412	Bridge and Tunnel Construction (pt)
1623	Water, Sewer, Pipeline, and Communications and Power Line Construction		
	• Water, Sewer and Pipelines	23491	Water, Sewer, and Pipeline Construction (pt)
	• Power and Communication Transmission Lines	23492	Power and Communication Transmission Line Construction (pt)
1629	Heavy Construction, NEC		
	• Industrial Nonbuilding Structures Construction	23493	Industrial Nonbuilding Structure Construction (pt)
	• Nonbuilding Structures except Industrial Construction	23499	All Other Heavy Construction (pt)
17	**Special Trade Contractors**		
1711	Plumbing, Heating, and Air-conditioning	23511	Plumbing, Heating, and Air-conditioning Contractors (pt)
1721	Painting and Paper Hanging	23521	Painting and Wall Covering Contractors (pt)
1731	Electrical Work	23531	Electrical Contractors
1741	Masonry, Stone Setting, and Other Stone Work	23541	Masonry and Stone Contractors
1742	Plastering, Drywall, Acoustical, and Insulation Work	23542	Drywall, Plastering, Acoustical, and Insulation Contractors (pt)
1743	Terrazzo, Tile, Marble, and Mosaic Work		
	• Fresco Work	23542	Drywall, Plastering, Acoustical, and Insulation Contractors (pt)
	• Except Fresco Work	23543	Tile, Marble, Terrazzo, and Mosaic Contractor
1751	Carpentry Work	23551	Carpentry Contractors
1752	Floor Laying and Other Floor Work, NEC	23552	Floor Laying and Other Floor Contractors
1761	Roofing, Siding, and Sheet Metal Work	23561	Roofing, Siding, and Sheet Metal Contractors
1771	Concrete Work		
	• Stucco Construction	23542	Drywall, Plastering, Acoustical, and Insulation Contractors (pt)
	• Except Stucco Construction	23571	Concrete Contractors

SIC to NAICS

pt—Part of.

SIC Code	1987 U.S. SIC Description	NAICS Code	1997 NAICS U.S. Description
1781	Water Well Drilling	23581	Water Well Drilling Contractors
1791	Structural Steel Erection	23591	Structural Steel Erection Contractors
1793	Glass and Glazing Work	23592	Glass and Glazing Contractors (pt)
1794	Excavation Work	23593	Excavation Contractors
1795	Wrecking and Demolition Work	23594	Wrecking and Demolition Contractors
1796	Installation or Erection of Building Equipment, NEC	23595	Building Equipment and Other Machinery Installation Contractors
1799	Special Trade Contractors, NEC		
	• Paint and Wallpaper Stripping and Wallpaper Removal Contractors	23521	Painting and Wall Covering Contractors (pt)
	• Tinted Glass Work	23592	Glass and Glazing Contractors (pt)
	• Asbestos Abatement and Lead Paint Removal Contractors	56291	Remediation Services (pt)
	• All Other Special Trade Contractors	23599	All Other Special Trade Contractors
20	**Food and Kindred Products**		
2011	Meat Packing Plants	311611	Animal (except Poultry) Slaughtering (pt)
2013	Sausages and Other Prepared Meats		
	• Lard Made from Purchased Material	311613	Rendering and Meat Byproduct Processing (pt)
	• Except Lard Made from Purchased Material	311612	Meat Processed from Carcasses (pt)
2015	Poultry Slaughtering and Processing		
	• Poultry Processing	311615	Poultry Processing
	• Egg Processing	311999	All Other Miscellaneous Food Manufacturing (pt)
2021	Creamery Butter	311512	Creamery Butter Manufacturing
2022	Natural, Processed, and Imitation Cheese	311513	Cheese Manufacturing
2023	Dry, Condensed, and Evaporated Dairy Products	311514	Dry, Condensed, and Evaporated Dairy Product Manufacturing
2024	Ice Cream and Frozen Desserts	31152	Ice Cream and Frozen Dessert Manufacturing
2026	Fluid Milk		
	• Ultra-high Temperature	311514	Dry, Condensed, and Evaporated Dairy Product Manufacturing (pt)
	• Except Ultra-high Temperature	311511	Fluid Milk Manufacturing
2032	Canned Specialties		
	• Canned Specialties	311422	Specialty Canning
	• Canned Pudding	311999	All Other Miscellaneous Food Manufacturing (pt)
2033	Canned Fruits, Vegetables, Preserves, Jams, and Jellies	311421	Fruit and Vegetable Canning (pt)
2034	Dried and Dehydrated Fruits, Vegetables, and Soup Mixes		
	• Dried and Dehydrated Fruits and Vegetables	311423	Dried and Dehydrated Food Manufacturing (pt)
	• Soup Mixes Made from Purchased Dried and Dehydrated Vegetables	311999	All Other Miscellaneous Food Manufacturing (pt)
	• Vegetable Flours	311211	Flour Milling (pt)
2035	Pickled Fruits and Vegetables, Vegetable Sauces and Seasonings, and Salad Dressings		
	• Pickled Fruits and Vegetables	311421	Fruit and Vegetable Canning (pt)

SIC to NAICS

pt—Part of.

SIC Code	1987 U.S. SIC Description	NAICS Code	1997 NAICS U.S. Description
	• Sauces and Salad Dressings	311941	Mayonnaise, Dressing, and Other Prepared Sauce Manufacturing (pt)
2037	Frozen Fruits, Fruit Juices, and Vegetables	311411	Frozen Fruit, Juice, and Vegetable Processing
2038	Frozen Specialties, NEC	311412	Frozen Specialty Food Manufacturing
2041	Flour and Other Grain Mill Products	311211	Flour Milling (pt)
2043	Cereal Breakfast Foods		
	• Coffee Substitute	31192	Coffee and Tea Manufacturing (pt)
	• Breakfast Cereal	31123	Breakfast Cereal Manufacturing
2044	Rice Milling	311212	Rice Milling
2045	Prepared Flour Mixes and Doughs	311822	Flour Mixes and Dough Manufacturing from Purchased Flour
2046	Wet Corn Milling	311221	Wet Corn Milling
	• Refining Purchased Oil	311225	Fats and Oils Refining and Blending (pt)
	• Except Refining Purchased Oil	311221	Wet Corn Milling
2047	Dog and Cat Food	311111	Dog and Cat Food Manufacturing
2048	Prepared Feed and Feed Ingredients for Animals and Fowls, except Dogs and Cats		
	• Animal Slaughtering for Pet Food	311611	Animal (except Poultry) Slaughtering (pt)
	• Except Slaughtering Animals for Pet Food	311119	Other Animal Food Manufacturing (pt)
2051	Bread and Other Bakery Products, except Cookies and Crackers	311812	Commercial Bakeries (pt)
2052	Cookies and Crackers		
	• Cookie and Cracker	311821	Cookie and Cracker Manufacturing
	• Pretzels, except Soft	311919	Other Snack Food Manufacturing (pt)
	• Unleavened Bread and Soft Pretzels	311812	Commercial Bakeries (pt)
2053	Frozen Bakery Products, except Bread	311813	Frozen Cakes, Pies, and Other Pastries Manufacturing
2061	Cane Sugar, except Refining	311311	Sugarcane Mills
2062	Cane Sugar Refining	311312	Cane Sugar Refining
2063	Beet Sugar	311313	Beet Sugar Manufacturing
2064	Candy and Other Confectionery Products		
	• Chocolate Confectionery	31133	Confectionery Manufacturing from Purchased Chocolate (pt)
	• Nonchocolate Confectionery Manufacturing	31134	Nonchocolate Confectionery Manufacturing (pt)
2066	Chocolate and Cocoa Products		
	• Chocolate Products Made from Purchased Chocolate	31133	Confectionery Manufacturing from Purchased Chocolate (pt)
	• Chocolate and Confectionery Products Made from Cacao Beans	31132	Chocolate and Confectionery Manufacturing from Cacao Beans
2067	Chewing Gum	31134	Nonchocolate Confectionery Manufacturing (pt)
2068	Salted and Roasted Nuts and Seeds	311911	Roasted Nuts and Peanut Butter Manufacturing (pt)
2074	Cottonseed Oil Mills		
	• Cottonseed Processing	311223	Other Oilseed Processing (pt)
	• Processing Purchased Cottonseed Oil	311225	Fats and Oils Refining and Blending (pt)

Visit page 15 to learn more about major changes to NAICS sectors.

pt—Part of.

SIC Code	1987 U.S. SIC Description	NAICS Code	1997 NAICS U.S. Description
2075	Soybean Oil Mills		
	• Soybean Processing	311222	Soybean Processing (pt)
	• Processing Purchased Soybean Oil	311225	Fats and Oils Refining and Blending (pt)
2076	Vegetable Oil Mills, except Corn, Cottonseed, and Soybeans		
	• Vegetable Oilseed Processing, except Corn, Cottonseed, and Soybeans	311223	Other Oilseed Processing (pt)
	• Processing Purchased Vegetable Oils, except Corn, Cottonseed, and Soybeans	311225	Fats and Oils Refining and Blending (pt)
2077	Animal and Marine Fats and Oils		
	• Animal Fats and Oils	311613	Rendering and Meat Byproduct Processing
	• Canned Marine Fats and Oils	311711	Seafood Canning (pt)
	• Fresh and Frozen Marine Fats and Oils	311712	Fresh and Frozen Seafood Processing (pt)
2079	Shortening, Table Oils, Margarine, and Other Edible Fats and Oils, NEC		
	• Processing Fats and Oils from Purchased Fats and Oils	311225	Fats and Oils Refining and Blending (pt)
	• Processing Soybean Oil from Soybeans Crushed in the Same Establishment	311222	Soybean Processing (pt)
	• Processing Vegetable Oils, except Soybeans, from Oilseeds Crushed in the Same Establishment	311223	Other Oilseed Processing (pt)
2082	Malt Beverages		
	• Malt Extract	311942	Spice and Extract Manufacturing (pt)
	• Except Malt Extract	31212	Breweries
2083	Malt	311213	Malt Manufacturing
2084	Wines, Brandy, and Brandy Spirits	31213	Wineries (pt)
2085	Distilled and Blended Liquors		
	• Applejack	31213	Wineries (pt)
	• Except Applejack	31214	Distilleries
2086	Bottled and Canned Soft Drinks and Carbonated Waters		
	• Soft Drinks	312111	Soft Drink Manufacturing
	• Bottled Water	312112	Bottled Water Manufacturing (pt)
2087	Flavoring Extracts and Flavoring Syrups, NEC		
	• Coffee Flavoring and Syrups	31192	Coffee and Tea Manufacturing (pt)
	• Flavoring Syrup and Concentrate, except Coffee	31193	Flavoring Syrup and Concentrate Manufacturing
	• Flavoring Extracts, except Coffee, and Natural Food Colorings	311942	Spice and Extract Manufacturing (pt)
	• Powdered Drink Mix	311999	All Other Miscellaneous Food Manufacturing (pt)
2091	Canned and Cured Fish and Seafood	311711	Seafood Canning (pt)
2092	Prepared Fresh or Frozen Fish and Seafoods	311712	Fresh and Frozen Seafood Processing (pt)
2095	Roasted Coffee	31192	Coffee and Tea Manufacturing (pt)
2096	Potato Chips, Corn Chips, and Similar Snacks	311919	Other Snack Food Manufacturing (pt)
2097	Manufactured Ice	312113	Ice Manufacturing
2098	Macaroni, Spaghetti, Vermicelli, and Noodles	311823	Dry Pasta Manufacturing (pt)
2099	Food Preparations, NEC		
	• Reducing Maple Sap to Maple Syrup	111998	All Other Miscellaneous Crop Farming (pt)

SIC to NAICS

pt—Part of.

SIC Code	1987 U.S. SIC Description	NAICS Code	1997 NAICS U.S. Description
	• Marshmallow Creme	31134	Nonchocolate Confectionery Manufacturing (pt)
	• Peanut Butter	311911	Roasted Nuts and Peanut Butter Manufacturing (pt)
	• Potatoes, Dried and Packaged with Other Ingredients Made in Dehydration Plants, and Bouillon	311423	Dried and Dehydrated Food Manufacturing (pt)
	• Perishable Prepared Food	311991	Perishable Prepared Food Manufacturing
	• Rice, Uncooked and Packaged with Other Ingredients Made in Rice Mills	311212	Rice Milling (pt)
	• Tortillas	31183	Tortilla Manufacturing
	• Dry Pasta Packaged with Other Ingredients Made in Dry Pasta Plants	311823	Dry Pasta Manufacturing (pt)
	• Tea	31192	Coffee and Tea Manufacturing (pt)
	• Vinegar, Prepared Dips except Dairy and Cider	311941	Mayonnaise, Dressing, and Other Prepared Sauce Manufacturing (pt)
	• Spices and Extracts	311942	Spice and Extract Manufacturing (pt)
	• Other	311999	All Other Miscellaneous Food Manufacturing (pt)
21	**Tobacco Manufactures**		
2111	Cigarettes	312221	Cigarette Manufacturing
2121	Cigars	312229	Other Tobacco Product Manufacturing (pt)
2131	Chewing and Smoking Tobacco and Snuff	312229	Other Tobacco Product Manufacturing (pt)
2141	Tobacco Stemming and Redrying		
	• Reconstituted Tobacco	312229	Other Tobacco Product Manufacturing (pt)
	• Redrying and Stemming	31221	Tobacco Stemming and Redrying
22	**Textile Mill Products**		
2211	Broadwoven Fabric Mills, Cotton	31321	Broadwoven Fabric Mills (pt)
2221	Broadwoven Fabric Mills, Manmade Fiber and Silk	31321	Broadwoven Fabric Mills (pt)
2231	Broadwoven Fabric Mills, Wool (including Dyeing and Finishing)		
	• Except Wool Finishing only	31321	Broadwoven Fabric Mills (pt)
	• Wool Broadwoven Fabric Finishing only	313311	Broadwoven Fabric Finishing Mills (pt)
	• Wool Finishing only, except Broadwoven Fabric	313312	Textile and Fabric Finishing (except Broadwoven Fabric) Mills (pt)
2241	Narrow Fabric and Other Smallware Mills: Cotton, Wool, Silk, and Manmade Fiber	313221	Narrow Fabric Mills (pt)
2251	Women's Full-length and Knee-length Hosiery, except Socks		
	• Dyeing and Finishing Only	313312	Textile and Fabric Finishing (except Broadwoven Fabric) Mills (pt)
	• Except Dyeing and Finishing Only	315111	Sheer Hosiery Mills (pt)
2252	Hosiery, NEC		
	• Dyeing and Finishing Only	313312	Textile and Fabric Finishing (except Broadwoven Fabric) Mills (pt)
	• Girls' Hosiery, except Dyeing and Finishing Only	315111	Sheer Hosiery Mills (pt)
	• Socks, except Dyeing and Finishing Only	315119	Other Hosiery and Sock Mills

pt—Part of.

SIC Code	1987 U.S. SIC Description	NAICS Code	1997 NAICS U.S. Description
2253	Knit Outerwear Mills		
	• Dyeing and Finishing Only	313312	Textile and Fabric Finishing (except Broadwoven Fabric) Mills (pt)
	• Bathrobes and Lounging Robes Made in Knitting Mills except Dyeing and Finishing Only	315192	Underwear and Nightwear Knitting Mills (pt)
	• Except Dyeing and Finishing Only and Bathrobes and Lounging Robes	315191	Outerwear Knitting Mills (pt)
2254	Knit Underwear and Nightwear Mills		
	• Dyeing and Finishing Only	313312	Textile and Fabric Finishing (except Broadwoven Fabric) Mills (pt)
	• Except Dyeing and Finishing Only	315192	Underwear and Nightwear Knitting Mills (pt)
2257	Weft Knit Fabric Mills		
	• Except Finishing	313241	Weft Knit Fabric Mills (pt)
	• Finishing Only	313312	Textile and Fabric Finishing (except Broadwoven Fabric) Mills (pt)
2258	Lace and Warp Knit Fabric Mills		
	• Except Finishing	313249	Other Knit Fabric and Lace Mills (pt)
	• Finishing Only	313312	Textile and Fabric Finishing (except Broadwoven Fabric) Mills (pt)
2259	Knitting Mills, NEC		
	• Knit Gloves and Mittens	315191	Outerwear Knitting Mills (pt)
	• Girdles	315192	Underwear and Nightwear Knitting Mills (pt)
	• Finished Articles of Weft Knit Fabric	313241	Weft Knit Fabric Mills (pt)
	• Knit Gloves and Mittens, Dyeing and Finishing Only	313312	Textile and Fabric Finishing (except Broadwoven Fabric) Mills (pt)
	• Finished Articles of Warp Knit Fabric	313249	Other Knit Fabric and Lace Mills (pt)
2261	Finishers of Broadwoven Fabrics of Cotton	313311	Broadwoven Fabric Finishing Mills (pt)
2262	Finishers of Broadwoven Fabrics of Manmade Fiber and Silk	313311	Broadwoven Fabric Finishing Mills (pt)
2269	Finishers of Textiles, NEC	313312	Textile and Fabric Finishing (except Broadwoven Fabric) Mills (pt)
2273	Carpets and Rugs	31411	Carpet and Rug Mills
2281	Yarn Spinning Mills	313111	Yarn Spinning Mills (pt)
2282	Yarn Texturizing, Throwing, Twisting, and Winding Mills	313112	Yarn Texturing, Throwing, and Twisting Mills
2284	Thread Mills		
	• Except Finishing	313113	Thread Mills (pt)
	• Finishing	313312	Textile and Fabric Finishing (except Broadwoven Fabric) Mills (pt)
2295	Coated Fabrics, not Rubberized	31332	Fabric Coating Mills (pt)
2296	Tire Cord and Fabrics	314992	Tire Cord and Tire Fabric Mills
2297	Nonwoven Fabrics	31323	Nonwoven Fabric Mills (pt)
2298	Cordage and Twine	314991	Rope, Cordage, and Twine Mills
2299	Textile Goods, NEC		
	• Broadwoven Fabric of Jute, Linen, Hemp, and Ramie and Handwoven	31321	Broadwoven Fabric Mills (pt)
	• Nonwoven Felt	31323	Nonwoven Fabric Mills (pt)

pt—Part of.

SIC Code	1987 U.S. SIC Description	NAICS Code	1997 NAICS U.S. Description
	• Finishing Thread and Yarn of Flax, Hemp, Jute, Linen, and Ramie	313312	Textile and Fabric Finishing (except Broadwoven Fabrics) Mills (pt)
	• Narrow Woven Fabric of Jute, Linen, Hemp, and Ramie	313221	Narrow Fabric Mills (pt)
	• Thread of Hemp, Linen, and Ramie	313113	Thread Mills (pt)
	• Yarn of Flax, Hemp, Jute, and Ramie	313111	Yarn Spinning Mills (pt)
	• Recovery and Processing of Fibers and Waste	314999	All Other Miscellaneous Textile Product Mills (pt)
23	**Apparel and Other Textile Products**		
2311	Men's and Boys' Suits, Coats, and Overcoats		
	• Contractors	315211	Men's and Boys' Cut and Sew Apparel Contractors (pt)
	• Except Contractors	315222	Men's and Boys' Cut and Sew Suit, Coat, and Overcoat Manufacturing (pt)
2321	Men's and Boys' Shirts, except Work Shirts		
	• Contractors	315211	Men's and Boys' Cut and Sew Apparel Contractors (pt)
	• Except Contractors	315223	Men's and Boys' Cut and Sew Shirt, (except Work Shirt) Manufacturing (pt)
2322	Men's and Boys' Underwear and Nightwear		
	• Contractors	315211	Men's and Boys' Cut and Sew Apparel Contractors (pt)
	• Except Contractors	315221	Men's and Boys' Cut and Sew Underwear and Nightwear Manufacturing (pt)
2323	Men's and Boys' Neckwear		
	• Contractors	315211	Men's and Boys' Cut and Sew Apparel Contractors (pt)
	• Except Contractors	315993	Men's and Boys' Neckwear Manufacturing
2325	Men's and Boys' Trousers and Slacks		
	• Contractors	315211	Men's and Boys' Cut and Sew Apparel Contractors (pt)
	• Except Contractors	315224	Men's and Boys' Cut and Sew Trouser, Slack, and Jean Manufacturing (pt)
2326	Men's and Boys' Work Clothing		
	• Contractors	315211	Men's and Boys' Cut and Sew Apparel Contractors (pt)
	• Except Contractors	315225	Men's and Boys' Cut and Sew Work Clothing Manufacturing
2329	Men's and Boys' Clothing, NEC		
	• Contractors	315211	Men's and Boys' Cut and Sew Apparel Contractors (pt)
	• Except Contractors	315228	Men's and Boys' Cut and Sew Other Outerwear Manufacturing (pt)
	• Athletic Uniforms, except Contractors	315299	All Other Cut and Sew Apparel Manufacturing (pt)
2331	Women's, Misses', and Juniors' Blouses and Shirts		
	• Contractors	315212	Women's, Girls', and Infants' Cut and Sew Apparel Contractors (pt)
	• Except Contractors	315232	Women's and Girls' Cut and Sew Blouse and Shirt Manufacturing (pt)

Go to page 23 to learn about implementation of NAICS codes in the public and private sectors.

pt—Part of.

SIC Code	1987 U.S. SIC Description	NAICS Code	1997 NAICS U.S. Description
2335	Women's, Misses', and Juniors' Dresses		
	• Contractors	315212	Women's, Girls', and Infants' Cut and Sew Apparel Contractors (pt)
	• Except Contractors	315233	Women's and Girls' Cut and Sew Dress Manufacturing (pt)
2337	Women's, Misses' and Juniors' Suits, Skirts, and Coats		
	• Contractors	315212	Women's, Girls', and Infants' Cut and Sew Apparel Contractors (pt)
	• Except Contractors	315234	Women's and Girls' Cut and Sew Suit, Coat, Tailored Jacket, and Skirt Manufacturing (pt)
2339	Women's, Misses', and Juniors' Outerwear, NEC		
	• Scarves, except Contractors	315999	Other Apparel Accessories and Other Apparel Manufacturing (pt)
	• Contractors	315212	Women's, Girls', and Infants' Cut and Sew Apparel Contractors (pt)
	• Athletic Uniforms, except Contractors	315299	All Other Cut and Sew Apparel Manufacturing (pt)
	• All Other, except Contractors	315239	Women's and Girls' Cut and Sew Other Outerwear Manufacturing (pt)
2341	Women's, Misses', Children's, and Infants' Underwear and Nightwear		
	• Women's, Girls' and Infants' Contractors	315212	Women's, Girls', and Infants' Cut and Sew Apparel Contractors (pt)
	• Boys' Contractors	315211	Men's and Boys' Cut and Sew Apparel Contractors (pt)
	• Women's and Girls', except Contractors	315231	Women's and Girls' Cut and Sew Lingerie, Loungewear, and Nightwear Manufacturing (pt)
	• Boys', except Contractors	315221	Men's and Boys' Cut and Sew Underwear and Nightwear Manufacturing (pt)
	• Infants', except Contractors	315291	Infants' Cut and Sew Apparel Manufacturing (pt)
2342	Brassieres, Girdles, and Allied Garments		
	• Contractors	315212	Women's, Girls', and Infants' Cut and Sew Apparel Contractors (pt)
	• Except contractors	315231	Women's and Girls' Cut and Sew Lingerie, Loungewear, and Nightwear Manufacturing (pt)
2353	Hats, Caps, and Millinery		
	• Men's and Boys' Contractors	315211	Men's and Boys' Cut and Sew Apparel Contractors (pt)
	• Women's, Girls', and Infants' Contractors	315212	Women's, Girls', and Infants' Cut and Sew Apparel Contractors (pt)
	• Except Contractors	315991	Hat, Cap, and Millinery Manufacturing
2361	Girls', Children's, and Infants' Dresses, Blouses, and Shirts		
	• Infants' Dresses, Blouses, and Shirts, except Contractors	315291	Infants' Cut and Sew Apparel Manufacturing (pt)
	• Boys' Shirts, except Contractors	315223	Men's and Boys' Cut and Sew Shirt, (except Work Shirt) Manufacturing (pt)

pt—Part of.

SIC Code	1987 U.S. SIC Description	NAICS Code	1997 NAICS U.S. Description
	• Boys' Shirt Contractors	315211	Men's and Boys' Cut and Sew Apparel Contractors (pt)
	• Girls' Blouses and Shirts, except Contractors	315232	Women's and Girls' Cut and Sew Blouse and Shirt Manufacturing (pt)
	• Girls' Dresses, except Contractors	315233	Women's and Girls' Cut and Sew Dress Manufacturing (pt)
	• Girls' and Infants' Contractors	315212	Women's, Girls', and Infants' Cut and Sew Apparel Contractors (pt)
2369	Girls', Children's, and Infants' Outerwear NEC		
	• Infants' Outerwear, NEC, except Contractors	315291	Infants' Cut and Sew Apparel Manufacturing (pt)
	• Boys' Suits and Coats, except Contractors	315222	Men's and Boys' Cut and Sew Suit, Coat, and Overcoat Manufacturing (pt)
	• Boys' Trousers and Slacks, except Contractors	315224	Men's and Boys' Cut and Sew Trouser, Slack, and Jean Manufacturing (pt)
	• Boys' Outerwear, NEC, except Contractors	315228	Men's and Boys' Cut and Sew Other Outerwear Manufacturing (pt)
	• Boys' Robes, except Contractors	315221	Men's and Boys' Cut and Sew Underwear and Nightwear Manufacturing (pt)
	• Boys' Contractors	315211	Men's and Boys' Cut and Sew Apparel Contractors (pt)
	• Girls' Suits, Coats, Skirts, etc., except Contractors	315234	Women's and Girls' Cut and Sew Suit, Coat, Tailored Jacket, and Skirt Manufacturing (pt)
	• Girls' Outerwear, NEC, except Contractors	315239	Women's and Girls' Cut and Sew Other Outerwear Manufacturing (pt)
	• Girls' Robes, except Contractors	315231	Women's and Girls' Cut and Sew Lingerie, Loungewear, and Nightwear Manufacturing (pt)
	• Girls' Contractors	315212	Women's, Girls', and Infants' Cut and Sew Apparel Contractors (pt)
2371	Fur Goods		
	• Men's and Boys' Contractors	315211	Men's and Boys' Cut and Sew Apparel Contractors (pt)
	• Women's, Girls', and Infants' Contractors	315212	Women's, Girls', and Infants' Cut and Sew Apparel Contractors (pt)
	• Except Contractors	315292	Fur and Leather Apparel Manufacturing (pt)
2381	Dress and Work Gloves, except Knit and All-leather		
	• Men's and Boys' Contractors	315211	Men's and Boys' Cut and Sew Apparel Contractors (pt)
	• Women's, Girls', and Infants' Contractors	315212	Women's, Girls', and Infants' Cut and Sew Apparel Contractors (pt)
	• Except Contractors	315992	Glove and Mitten Manufacturing (pt)
2384	Robes and Dressing Gowns		
	• Women's except Contractors	315231	Women's and Girls' Cut and Sew Lingerie, Loungewear, and Nightwear Manufacturing (pt)
	• Men's except Contractors	315221	Men's and Boys' Cut and Sew Underwear and Nightwear Manufacturing (pt)
	• Men's and Boys' Contractors	315211	Men's and Boys' Cut and Sew Apparel Contractors (pt)

SIC to NAICS

pt—Part of.

SIC Code	1987 U.S. SIC Description	NAICS Code	1997 NAICS U.S. Description
	• Women's and Girls' Contractors	315212	Women's, Girls', and Infants' Cut and Sew Apparel Contractors (pt)
2385	Waterproof Outerwear		
	• Men's and Boys' Water Resistant or Water and Repellent Tailored Overcoats	315222	Men's and Boys' Cut and Sew Suit, Coat, Overcoat Manufacturing (pt)
	• Women's and Girls' Water Resistant or Water Repellent Tailored Coats	315234	Women's and Girls' Cut and Sew Suit, Coat, Tailored Jacket, and Skirt Manufacturing (pt)
	• Men's and Boys' Water Resistant or Water Repellent Nontailored Outerwear, except Rubber and Plastics and Contractors	315228	Men's and Boys' Cut and Sew Other Outerwear Manufacturing (pt)
	• Women's and Girls' Water Resistant or Water Repellent Nontailored Outerwear, except Rubber and Plastics and Contractors	315239	Women's and Girls' Cut and Sew Other Outerwear Manufacturing (pt)
	• Infants' Waterproof Outerwear except Contractors	315291	Infants' Cut and Sew Apparel Manufacturing (pt)
	• Waterproof Rubber and Plastic Outerwear, except Contractors	315299	All Other Cut and Sew Apparel Manufacturing (pt)
	• Accessories such as Aprons, Bibs, and Miscellaneous Waterproof Items, except Contractors	315999	Other Apparel Accessories and Other Apparel Manufacturing (pt)
	• Men's and Boys' Contractors	315211	Men's and Boys' Cut and Sew Apparel Contractors (pt)
	• Women's and Girls' Contractors	315212	Women's, Girls', and Infants' Cut and Sew Apparel Contractors (pt)
2386	Leather and Sheep-lined Clothing		
	• Men's and Boys' Contractors	315211	Men's and Boys' Cut and Sew Apparel Contractors (pt)
	• Women's, Girls', and Infants' Contractors	315212	Women's, Girls', and Infants' Cut and Sew Apparel Contractors (pt)
	• Except Contractors	315292	Fur and Leather Apparel Manufacturing (pt)
2387	Apparel Belts		
	• Men's and Boys' Contractors	315211	Men's and Boys' Cut and Sew Apparel Contractors (pt)
	• Women's, Girls', and Infants' Contractors	315212	Women's, Girls', and Infants' Cut and Sew Apparel Contractors (pt)
	• Except Contractors	315999	Other Apparel Accessories and Other Apparel Manufacturing (pt)
2389	Apparel and Accessories, NEC		
	• Handkerchiefs, Arm bands, etc.	315999	Other Apparel Accessories and Other Apparel Manufacturing (pt)
	• Academic and Clerical Outerwear	315299	All Other Cut and Sew Apparel Manufacturing (pt)
	• Garters and Garter Belts	315231	Women's and Girls' Cut and Sew Lingerie, Loungewear, and Nightwear Manufacturing (pt)
	• Women's Contractors	315212	Women's, Girls', and Infants' Cut and Sew Apparel Contractors (pt)
	• Men's Contractors	315211	Men's and Boys' Cut and Sew Apparel Contractors (pt)
2391	Curtains and Draperies	314121	Curtain and Drapery Mills (pt)

SIC to NAICS

SIC Code	1987 U.S. SIC Description	NAICS Code	1997 NAICS U.S. Description
2392	Housefurnishings, except Curtains and Draperies		
	• Blanket, Laundry, and Garment Storage Bags	314911	Textile Bag Mills (pt)
	• Dust Rags	314999	All Other Miscellaneous Textile Product Mills (pt)
	• Mops, Floor and Dust	339994	Broom, Brush, and Mop Manufacturing (pt)
	• Other Housefurnishings	314129	Other Household Textile Product Mills (pt)
2393	Textile Bags	314911	Textile Bag Mills (pt)
2394	Canvas and Related Products	314912	Canvas and Related Product Mills (pt)
2395	Pleating, Decorative and Novelty Stitching, and Tucking for the Trade		
	• Pleating and Stitching, except Apparel Contractors	314999	All Other Miscellaneous Textile Product Mills (pt)
	• Men's and Boys' Apparel Contractors	315211	Men's and Boys' Cut and Sew Apparel Contractors (pt)
	• Women's, Girls', and Infants' Apparel Contractors	315212	Women's, Girls', and Infants' Cut and Sew Apparel Contractors (pt)
2396	Automotive Trimmings, Apparel Findings, and Related Products		
	• Textile Automotive Trimmings	33636	Motor Vehicle Seating and Interior Trim Manufacturing (pt)
	• Apparel Findings and Trimmings	315999	Other Apparel Accessories and Other Apparel Manufacturing (pt)
	• Printing and Embossing on Fabric Articles	323113	Commercial Screen Printing (pt)
	• Other Apparel Products	314999	All Other Miscellaneous Textile Product Mills (pt)
2397	Schiffli Machine Embroideries	313222	Schiffli Machine Embroidery
2399	Fabricated Textile Products, NEC		
	• Seat Belts and Seat and Tire Covers	33636	Motor Vehicle Seating and Interior Trim Manufacturing (pt)
	• Apparel and Apparel Accessories	315999	Other Apparel Accessories and Other Apparel Manufacturing (pt)
	• Other Fabricated Textile Products	314999	All Other Miscellaneous Textile Product Mills (pt)
24	**Lumber and Wood Products**		
2411	Logging	11331	Logging
2421	Sawmills and Planing Mills, General		
	• Lumber Manufacturing from Purchased Lumber, Softwood Cut Stock, Wood Lath and Planing Mill Products	321912	Cut Stock, Resawing Lumber, and Planing (pt)
	• Sawmills	321113	Sawmills (pt)
	• Softwood Flooring	321918	Other Millwork (including Flooring) (pt)
	• Kiln Drying	321999	All Other Miscellaneous Wood Product Manufacturing (pt)
2426	Hardwood Dimension and Flooring Mills		
	• Hardwood Flooring	321918	Other Millwork (including Flooring) (pt)
	• Wood Furniture Frames	337215	Showcase, Partition, Shelving, and Locker Manufacturing (pt)
	• Other Hardwood Dimension Lumber Made from Logs and Bolts	321113	Sawmills (pt)
	• Other Hardwood Dimension except Flooring	321912	Cut Stock, Resawing Lumber, and Planing (pt)

pt—Part of.

Visit page 9 to learn more about NAICS codes.

SIC Code	1987 U.S. SIC Description	NAICS Code	1997 NAICS U.S. Description
2429	Special Product Sawmills, NEC		
	• Shingle Mills, Shakes	321113	Sawmills (pt)
	• Stave Manufacturing from Purchased Lumber	321912	Cut Stock, Resawing Lumber, and Planing (pt)
	• Cooperage Stock	32192	Wood Container and Pallet Manufacturing (pt)
	• Excelsior and Cooperage Headings	321999	All Other Miscellaneous Wood Product Manufacturing (pt)
2431	Millwork		
	• Wood Windows and Doors	321911	Wood Window and Door Manufacturing
	• Except Wood Windows and Doors	321918	Other Millwork (including Flooring) (pt)
2434	Wood Kitchen Cabinets	33711	Wood Kitchen Cabinet and Countertop Manufacturing (pt)
2435	Hardwood Veneer and Plywood	321211	Hardwood Veneer and Plywood Manufacturing
2436	Softwood Veneer and Plywood	321212	Softwood Veneer and Plywood Manufacturing
2439	Structural Wood Members, NEC		
	• Trusses	321214	Truss Manufacturing
	• Except Trusses	321213	Engineered Wood Member (except Truss) Manufacturing
2441	Nailed and Lock Corner Wood Boxes and Shook	32192	Wood Container and Pallet Manufacturing (pt)
2448	Wood Pallets and Skids	32192	Wood Container and Pallet Manufacturing (pt)
2449	Wood Containers, NEC	32192	Wood Container and Pallet Manufacturing (pt)
2451	Mobile Homes	321991	Manufactured Home (Mobile Home) Manufacturing
2452	Prefabricated Wood Buildings and Components	321992	Prefabricated Wood Building Manufacturing
2491	Wood Preserving	321114	Wood Preservation
2493	Reconstituted Wood Products	321219	Reconstituted Wood Product Manufacturing
2499	Wood Products, NEC		
	• Mirror and Picture Frames	339999	All Other Miscellaneous Manufacturing (pt)
	• Wood Cooling Towers	333414	Heating Equipment (except Warm Air Furnace) Manufacturing (pt)
	• Wood Tubs and Vats, Jewelry, Cigar Boxes, and Baskets, except Fruit, Fish, and Bait	32192	Wood Container and Pallet Manufacturing (pt)
	• Other Wood Products	321999	All Other Miscellaneous Wood Product Manufacturing (pt)
25	**Furniture and Fixtures**		
2511	Wood Household Furniture, except Upholstered		
	• Wood Box Spring Frames	337215	Showcase, Partition, Shelving, and Locker Manufacturing (pt)
	• Except Wood Box Spring Frames	337122	Wood Household Furniture (except Upholstered) Manufacturing (pt)
2512	Wood Household Furniture, Upholstered	337121	Upholstered Household Furniture Manufacturing (pt)

pt—Part of.

SIC Code	1987 U.S. SIC Description	NAICS Code	1997 NAICS U.S. Description
2514	Metal Household Furniture		
	• Except Upholstered and Metal Box Spring Frames	337124	Metal Household Furniture Manufacturing
	• Upholstered	337121	Upholstered Household Furniture Manufacturing (pt)
	• Metal Box Spring Frames	337215	Showcase, Partition, Shelving, and Locker Manufacturing (pt)
2515	Mattresses, Foundations, and Convertible Beds		
	• Mattresses and Foundations	33791	Mattress Manufacturing
	• Convertible Sofas	337121	Upholstered Household Furniture Manufacturing (pt)
2517	Wood Television, Radio, Phonograph and Sewing Machine Cabinets	337129	Wood Television, Radio, and Sewing Machine Cabinet Manufacturing
2519	Household Furniture, NEC	337125	Household Furniture (except Wood and Metal) Manufacturing
2521	Wood Office Furniture	337211	Wood Office Furniture Manufacturing
2522	Office Furniture, except Wood	337214	Office Furniture (except Wood) Manufacturing
2531	Public Building and Related Furniture		
	• Seats for Motor Vehicles	33636	Motor Vehicle Seating and Interior Trim Manufacturing (pt)
	• Furniture Made for Public Buildings	337127	Institutional Furniture Manufacturing (pt)
	• Blackboards	339942	Lead Pencil and Art Good Manufacturing (pt)
2541	Wood Office and Store Fixtures, Partitions, Shelving, and Lockers		
	• Wood Lunchroom Tables and Chairs	337127	Institutional Furniture Manufacturing (pt)
	• Custom Architectural Woodwork, Millwork and Fixtures	337212	Custom Architectural Woodwork and Millwork Manufacturing
	• Except Countertops, Custom Architectural Woodwork, Millwork, and Fixtures	337215	Showcase, Partition, Shelving, and Locker Manufacturing (pt)
2542	Office and Store Fixtures, Partitions, Shelving, and Lockers, except Wood		
	• Lunchroom Tables and Chairs (except wood)	337127	Institutional Furniture Manufacturing (pt)
	• Except Lunchroom Tables and Chairs (except wood)	337215	Showcase, Partition, Shelving, and Locker Manufacturing (pt)
2591	Drapery Hardware and Window Blinds and Shades	33792	Blind and Shade Manufacturing
2599	Furniture and Fixtures, NEC		
	• Hospital Beds	339111	Laboratory Apparatus and Furniture Manufacturing (pt)
	• Except Hospital Beds	337127	Institutional Furniture Manufacturing (pt)
26	**Paper and Allied Products**		
2611	Pulp Mills		
	• Pulp Producing Mills Only	32211	Pulp Mills
	• Pulp Mills Producing Paper	322121	Paper (except Newsprint) Mills (pt)
	• Pulp Mills Producing Newsprint	322122	Newsprint Mills (pt)
	• Pulp Mills Producing Paperboard	32213	Paperboard Mills (pt)
2621	Paper Mills		
	• Except Newsprint Mills	322121	Paper (except Newsprint) Mills (pt)
	• Newsprint Mills	322122	Newsprint Mills (pt)

pt—Part of.

SIC to NAICS

SIC Code	1987 U.S. SIC Description	NAICS Code	1997 NAICS U.S. Description
2631	Paperboard Mills	32213	Paperboard Mills (pt)
2652	Setup Paperboard Boxes	322213	Setup Paperboard Box Manufacturing
2653	Corrugated and Solid Fiber Boxes	322211	Corrugated and Solid Fiber Box Manufacturing (pt)
2655	Fiber Cans, Tubes, Drums, and Similar Products	322214	Fiber Can, Tube, Drum, and Similar Products Manufacturing
2656	Sanitary Food Containers, except Folding	322215	Nonfolding Sanitary Food Container Manufacturing
2657	Folding Paperboard Boxes, including Sanitary	322212	Folding Paperboard Box Manufacturing
2671	Packaging Paper and Plastics Film, Coated and Laminated		
	• Single-web Paper, Paper Multiweb Laminated Rolls and Sheets for Packaging Uses	322221	Coated and Laminated Packaging Paper and Plastics Film Manufacturing
	• Plastics Packaging Film and Sheet	326112	Unsupported Plastics Packaging Film and Sheet Manufacturing
2672	Coated and Laminated Paper, NEC	322222	Coated and Laminated Paper Manufacturing (pt)
2673	Plastics, Foil, and Coated Paper Bags		
	• Except All Plastics	322223	Plastics, Foil, and Coated Paper Bag Manufacturing
	• Plastics Bags	326111	Unsupported Plastics Bag Manufacturing
2674	Uncoated Paper and Multiwall Bags	322224	Uncoated Paper and Multiwall Bag Manufacturing
2675	Die-cut Paper and Paperboard and Cardboard		
	• File Folders, Tabulating Cards, and Other Paper and Paperboard Office Supplies	322231	Die-cut Paper and Paperboard Office Supplies Manufacturing (pt)
	• Pasted, Lined, Laminated, or Surface-coated Paperboard	322226	Surface-coated Paperboard Manufacturing
	• Die-cut Paper and Paperboard Products, except Office Supplies and Pasted, Lined, Laminated, or Surface-coated Paperboard	322299	All Other Converted Paper Product Manufacturing (pt)
2676	Sanitary Paper Products	322291	Sanitary Paper Product Manufacturing (pt)
2677	Envelopes	322232	Envelope Manufacturing
2678	Stationery, Tablets, and Related Products	322233	Stationery, Tablet, and Related Product Manufacturing
2679	Converted Paper and Paperboard Products, NEC		
	• Corrugated Paper	322211	Corrugated and Solid Fiber Box Manufacturing (pt)
	• Wallpaper and Gift Wrap Paper	322222	Coated and Laminated Paper Manufacturing (pt)
	• Paper Supplies for Business Machines and Other Paper Office Supplies	322231	Die-cut Paper and Paperboard Office Supplies Manufacturing (pt)
	• Other Converted Paper and Paperboard Products, such as Paper Filters, Crepe Paper, and Laminated and Tiled Wallboard	322299	All Other Converted Paper Product Manufacturing (pt)
27	**Printing and Publishing**		
2711	Newspapers: Publishing, or Publishing and Printing	51111	Newspaper Publishers
2721	Periodicals: Publishing, or Publishing and Printing	51112	Periodical Publishers (pt)

pt—Part of.

SIC Code	1987 U.S. SIC Description	NAICS Code	1997 NAICS U.S. Description
2731	Books: Publishing, or Publishing and Printing		
	• Music Book Publishing	51223	Music Publishers (pt)
	• All Other Book Publishers	51113	Book Publishers
2732	Book Printing	323117	Books Printing
2741	Miscellaneous Publishing		
	• Database Publishing	51114	Database and Directory Publishers (pt)
	• Shopping News	51112	Periodical Publishers (pt)
	• Technical Manuals and Books	51113	Book Publishers (pt)
	• Sheet Music Publishers	51223	Music Publishers (pt)
	• Miscellaneous Publishing, except Database, Shopping News, Technical Manuals and Books, and Sheet Music	511199	All Other Publishers
2752	Commercial Printing, Lithographic		
	• Quick Printing	323114	Quick Printing (pt)
	• Except Quick Printing	323110	Commercial Lithographic Printing (pt)
2754	Commercial Printing, Gravure	323111	Commercial Gravure Printing (pt)
2759	Commercial Printing, NEC		
	• Screen Printing	323113	Commercial Screen Printing (pt)
	• Flexographic Printing	323112	Commercial Flexographic Printing (pt)
	• Quick Printing	323114	Quick Printing (pt)
	• Digital Printing, except Quick Printing	323115	Digital Printing
	• Other Commercial Printing	323119	Other Commercial Printing (pt)
2761	Manifold Business Forms	323116	Manifold Business Form Printing (pt)
2771	Greeting Cards		
	• Lithographic Printing of Greeting Cards	323110	Commercial Lithographic Printing (pt)
	• Gravure Printing of Greeting Cards	323111	Commercial Gravure Printing (pt)
	• Flexographic Printing of Greeting Cards	323112	Commercial Flexographic Printing (pt)
	• Screen Printing of Greeting Cards	323113	Commercial Screen Printing (pt)
	• Other Printing of Greeting Cards	323119	Other Commercial Printing (pt)
	• Publishing Greeting Cards	511191	Greeting Card Publishers
2782	Blankbooks, Loose-leaf Binders and Devices		
	• Printing of Checkbooks	323116	Manifold Business Forms Printing (pt)
	• Blankbooks, Loose-leaf Binders and Devices	323118	Blankbook, Looseleaf Binders, and Devices Manufacturing
	• Bookbinding and Related Work	323121	Tradebinding and Related Work
2791	Typesetting	323122	Prepress Services (pt)
2796	Platemaking and Related Services	323122	Prepress Services (pt)
28	**Chemicals and Allied Products**		
2812	Alkalies and Chlorine	325181	Alkalies and Chlorine Manufacturing
2813	Industrial Gases	32512	Industrial Gas Manufacturing (pt)
2816	Inorganic Pigments		
	• Except Bone and Lamp Black	325131	Inorganic Dye and Pigment Manufacturing (pt)
	• Bone and Lamp Black	325182	Carbon Black Manufacturing (pt)
2819	Industrial Inorganic Chemicals, NEC		
	• Recovering Sulfur from Natural Gas	211112	Natural Gas Liquid Extraction (pt)
	• Activated Carbon and Charcoal	325998	All Other Miscellaneous Chemical Product and Preparation Manufacturing (pt)
	• Alumina	331311	Alumina Refining

Visit page 15 to learn more about major changes to NAICS sectors.

pt—Part of.

SIC Code	1987 U.S. SIC Description	NAICS Code	1997 NAICS U.S. Description
	• Inorganic Dyes	325131	Inorganic Dye and Pigment Manufacturing (pt)
	• Other	325188	All Other Basic Inorganic Chemical Manufacturing (pt)
2821	Plastics Material and Synthetic Resins, and Nonvulcanizable Elastomers	325211	Plastics Material and Resin Manufacturing
2822	Synthetic Rubber	325212	Synthetic Rubber Manufacturing
2823	Cellulosic Manmade Fibers	325221	Cellulosic Organic Fiber Manufacturing
2824	Manmade Organic Fibers, except Cellulosic	325222	Noncellulosic Organic Fiber Manufacturing
2833	Medicinal Chemicals and Botanical Products	325411	Medicinal and Botanical Manufacturing
2834	Pharmaceutical Preparations	325412	Pharmaceutical Preparation Manufacturing (pt)
2835	In Vitro and In Vivo Diagnostic Substances		
	• Except In Vitro Diagnostic	325412	Pharmaceutical Preparation Manufacturing (pt)
	• In Vitro Diagnostic Substances	325413	In Vitro Diagnostic Substance Manufacturing
2836	Biological Products, except Diagnostic Substances	325414	Biological Product (except Diagnostic) Manufacturing
2841	Soaps and Other Detergents, except Speciality Cleaners	325611	Soap and Other Detergent Manufacturing (pt)
2842	Speciality Cleaning, Polishing, and Sanitary Preparations	325612	Polish and Other Sanitation Good Manufacturing
2843	Surface Active Agents, Finishing Agents, Sulfonated Oils, and Assistants	325613	Surface Active Agent Manufacturing
2844	Perfumes, Cosmetics, and Other Toilet Preparations		
	• Toilet Preparations, except Toothpaste	32562	Toilet Preparation Manufacturing
	• Toothpaste	325611	Soap and Other Detergent Manufacturing (pt)
2851	Paints, Varnishes, Lacquers, Enamels, and Allied Products	32551	Paint and Coating Manufacturing (pt)
2861	Gum and Wood Chemicals	325191	Gum and Wood Chemical Manufacturing
2865	Cyclic Organic Crudes and Intermediates, and Organic Dyes and Pigments		
	• Aromatics	32511	Petrochemical Manufacturing (pt)
	• Organic Dyes and Pigments	325132	Synthetic Organic Dye and Pigment Manufacturing
	• Other	325192	Cyclic Crude and Intermediate Manufacturing
2869	Industrial Organic Chemicals, NEC		
	• Aliphatics	32511	Petrochemical Manufacturing (pt)
	• Carbon Bisulfide	325188	All Other Inorganic Chemical Manufacturing (pt)
	• Ethyl Alcohol	325193	Ethyl Alcohol Manufacturing
	• Fluorocarbon Gases	32512	Industrial Gas Manufacturing (pt)
	• Other	325199	All Other Basic Organic Chemical Manufacturing (pt)
2873	Nitrogenous Fertilizers	325311	Nitrogenous Fertilizer Manufacturing
2874	Phosphatic Fertilizers	325312	Phosphatic Fertilizer Manufacturing

pt—Part of.

SIC Code	1987 U.S. SIC Description	NAICS Code	1997 NAICS U.S. Description
2875	Fertilizers, Mixing Only	325314	Fertilizer (Mixing Only) Manufacturing
2879	Pesticides and Agricultural Chemicals, NEC	32532	Pesticide and Other Agricultural Chemical Manufacturing
2891	Adhesives and Sealants	32552	Adhesive Manufacturing
2892	Explosives	32592	Explosives Manufacturing
2893	Printing Ink	32591	Printing Ink Manufacturing
2895	Carbon Black	325182	Carbon Black Manufacturing (pt)
2899	Chemicals and Chemical Preparations, NEC		
	• Frit	32551	Paint and Coating Manufacturing (pt)
	• Table Salt	311942	Spice and Extract Manufacturing (pt)
	• Fatty Acids	325199	All Other Basic Organic Chemical Manufacturing (pt)
	• Other	325998	All Other Miscellaneous Chemical Product and Preparation Manufacturing (pt)

29 Petroleum and Coal Products

SIC Code	1987 U.S. SIC Description	NAICS Code	1997 NAICS U.S. Description
2911	Petroleum Refining	32411	Petroleum Refineries
2951	Asphalt Paving Mixtures and Blocks	324121	Asphalt Paving Mixture and Block Manufacturing
2952	Asphalt Felts and Coatings	324122	Asphalt Shingle and Coating Materials Manufacturing
2992	Lubricating Oils and Greases	324191	Petroleum Lubricating Oil and Grease Manufacturing
2999	Products of Petroleum and Coal, NEC	324199	All Other Petroleum and Coal Products Manufacturing (pt)

30 Rubber and Miscellaneous Plastics Products

SIC Code	1987 U.S. SIC Description	NAICS Code	1997 NAICS U.S. Description
3011	Tires and Inner Tubes	326211	Tire Manufacturing (except Retreading)
3021	Rubber and Plastics Footwear	316211	Rubber and Plastics Footwear Manufacturing
3052	Rubber and Plastics Hose and Belting	32622	Rubber and Plastics Hoses and Belting Manufacturing
3053	Gaskets, Packing, and Sealing Devices	339991	Gasket, Packing, and Sealing Device Manufacturing
3061	Molded, Extruded, and Lathe-cut Mechanical Rubber Goods	326291	Rubber Product Manufacturing for Mechanical Use
3069	Fabricated Rubber Products, NEC		
	• Rubberizing Fabric or Purchased Textile Products	31332	Fabric Coating Mills (pt)
	• Rubber Pants and Raincoats	315299	All Other Cut and Sew Apparel Manufacturing (pt)
	• Rubber Bibs, Aprons, and Bathing Caps	315999	Other Apparel Accessories and Other Apparel (pt)
	• Rubber Gloves and Life Jackets	339113	Surgical Appliance and Supplies Manufacturing (pt)
	• Rubber Wet Suits	33992	Sporting and Athletic Goods Manufacturing (pt)
	• Rubber Toys, except Dolls	339932	Game, Toy, and Children's Vehicle Manufacturing (pt)
	• Rubber Resilient Floor Covering	326192	Resilient Floor Covering Manufacturing (pt)
	• Other	326299	All Other Rubber Product Manufacturing

pt—Part of.

SIC to NAICS

SIC Code	1987 U.S. SIC Description	NAICS Code	1997 NAICS U.S. Description
3081	Unsupported Plastics Film and Sheet	326113	Unsupported Plastics Film and Sheet (except Packaging) Manufacturing
3082	Unsupported Plastics Profile Shapes	326121	Unsupported Plastics Profile Shape Manufacturing (pt)
3083	Laminated Plastics Plate, Sheet, and Profile Shapes	32613	Laminated Plastics Plate, Sheet, and Shape Manufacturing
3084	Plastics Pipe	326122	Plastics Pipe and Pipe Fitting Manufacturing (pt)
3085	Plastics Bottles	32616	Plastics Bottle Manufacturing
3086	Plastics Foam Products		
	• Urethane and Other Foam Products	32615	Urethane and Other Foam Product (except Polystyrene) Manufacturing
	• Polystyrene Foam Products	32614	Polystyrene Foam Product Manufacturing
3087	Custom Compounding of Purchased Plastics Resins	325991	Custom Compounding of Purchased Resin
3088	Plastics Plumbing Fixtures	326191	Plastics Plumbing Fixtures Manufacturing
3089	Plastics Products, NEC		
	• Pipe Fittings	326122	Plastics Pipe and Pipe Fitting Manufacturing (pt)
	• Plastics Sausage Casings	326121	Unsupported Plastics Profile Shape Manufacturing (pt)
	• Finished Plastics Furniture Parts	337215	Showcase, Partition, Shelving, and Locker Manufacturing (pt)
	• Other	326199	All Other Plastics Product Manufacturing (pt)
31	**Leather and Leather Products**		
3111	Leather Tanning and Finishing	31611	Leather and Hide Tanning and Finishing (pt)
3131	Boot and Shoe Cut Stock and Findings		
	• Wood Heels	321999	All Other Miscellaneous Wood Product Manufacturing (pt)
	• Metal Buckles	339993	Fastener, Button, Needle, and Pin Manufacturing (pt)
	• Except Wood Heels and Metal Buckles	316999	All Other Leather Good Manufacturing (pt)
3142	House Slippers	316212	House Slipper Manufacturing
3143	Men's Footwear, except Athletic	316213	Men's Footwear (except Athletic) Manufacturing
3144	Women's Footwear, except Athletic	316214	Women's Footwear (except Athletic) Manufacturing
3149	Footwear, except Rubber, NEC	316219	Other Footwear Manufacturing
3151	Leather Gloves and Mittens		
	• Men's and Boys' Contractors	315211	Men's and Boys' Cut and Sew Apparel Contractors (pt)
	• Women's, Girls', and Infants' Contractors	315212	Women's, Girls', and Infants' Cut and Sew Apparel Contractors (pt)
	• Except Contractors	315992	Glove and Mitten Manufacturing (pt)
3161	Luggage	316991	Luggage Manufacturing
3171	Women's Handbags and Purses	316992	Women's Handbag and Purse Manufacturing

pt—Part of.

SIC to NAICS

SIC Code	1987 U.S. SIC Description	NAICS Code	1997 NAICS U.S. Description
3172	Personal Leather Goods, except Women's Handbags and Purses	316993	Personal Leather Good (except Women's Handbag and Purse) Manufacturing
3199	Leather Goods, NEC	316999	All Other Leather Good Manufacturing (pt)
32	**Stone, Clay, Glass, and Concrete Products**		
3211	Flat Glass	327211	Flat Glass Manufacturing
3221	Glass Containers	327213	Glass Container Manufacturing
3229	Pressed and Blown Glass and Glassware, NEC	327212	Other Pressed and Blown Glass and Glassware Manufacturing
3231	Glass Products, Made of Purchased Glass	327215	Glass Product Manufacturing Made of Purchased Glass
3241	Cement, Hydraulic	32731	Cement Manufacturing
3251	Brick and Structural Clay Tile		
	• Slumped Brick	327331	Concrete Block and Brick Manufacturing (pt)
	• Except Slump Brick	327121	Brick and Structural Clay Tile Manufacturing
3253	Ceramic Wall and Floor Tile	327122	Ceramic Wall and Floor Tile Manufacturing
3255	Clay Refractories	327124	Clay Refractory Manufacturing
3259	Structural Clay Products, NEC	327123	Other Structural Clay Product Manufacturing
3261	Vitreous China Plumbing Fixtures and China and Earthenware Fittings and Bathroom Accessories	327111	Vitreous China Plumbing Fixture and China and Earthenware Bathroom Accessories Manufacturing
3262	Vitreous China Table and Kitchen Articles	327112	Vitreous China, Fine Earthenware, and Other Pottery Product Manufacturing (pt)
3263	Fine Earthenware (Whiteware) Table and Kitchen Articles	327112	Vitreous China, Fine Earthenware, and Other Pottery Product Manufacturing (pt)
3264	Porcelain Electrical Supplies	327113	Porcelain Electrical Supply Manufacturing
3269	Pottery Products, NEC	327112	Vitreous China, Fine Earthenware, and Other Pottery Product Manufacturing (pt)
3271	Concrete Block and Brick	327331	Concrete Block and Brick Manufacturing
3272	Concrete Products, except Block and Brick		
	• Dry Mixture Concrete	327999	All Other Miscellaneous Nonmetallic Mineral Product Manufacturing (pt)
	• Concrete Pipes	327332	Concrete Pipe Manufacturing
	• Other Concrete Products	32739	Other Concrete Product Manufacturing
3273	Ready-mixed Concrete	32732	Ready-mx Concrete Manufacturing
3274	Lime	32741	Lime Manufacturing
3275	Gypsum Products	32742	Gypsum Product Manufacturing (pt)
3281	Cut Stone and Stone Products	327991	Cut Stone and Stone Product Manufacturing
3291	Abrasive Products		
	• Steel Wool with or without Soap	332999	All Other Miscellaneous Fabricated Metal Product Manufacturing (pt)
	• Abrasive Products (except Steel Wool with or without Soap)	32791	Abrasive Product Manufacturing

SIC to NAICS

pt—Part of.

SIC Code	1987 U.S. SIC Description	NAICS Code	1997 NAICS U.S. Description
3292	Asbestos Products		
	• Asbestos Brake Linings and Pads	33634	Motor Vehicle Brake System Manufacturing (pt)
	• Other Asbestos Products	327999	All Other Miscellaneous Nonmetallic Mineral Product Manufacturing (pt)
3295	Minerals and Earths, Ground or Otherwise Treated		
	• Grinding, Washing, Separating, etc. of Minerals in SIC 1455	212324	Kaolin and Ball Clay Mining (pt)
	• Grinding, Washing, Separating, etc. of Minerals in SIC 1459	212325	Clay and Ceramic and Refractory Minerals Mining (pt)
	• Grinding, Washing, Separating, etc. of Minerals in SIC 1479	212393	Other Chemical and Fertilizer Mineral Mining (pt)
	• Grinding, Washing, Separating, etc. of Minerals in SIC 1499	212399	All Other Nonmetallic Mineral Mining (pt)
	• Except Grinding, Washing, Separating, etc.	327992	Ground or Treated Mineral and Earth Manufacturing
3296	Mineral Wool	327993	Mineral Wool Manufacturing
3297	Nonclay Refractories	327125	Nonclay Refractory Manufacturing
3299	Nonmetallic Mineral Products, NEC		
	• Clay Statuary	327112	Vitreous China, Fine Earthenware, and Other Pottery Product Manufacturing (pt)
	• Moldings, Ornamental and Architectural Plaster Work, and Gypsum Statuary	32742	Gypsum Product Manufacturing (pt)
	• Other Nonmetallic Mineral Products	327999	All Other Miscellaneous Nonmetallic Mineral Product Manufacturing (pt)

33 Primary Metal Industries

SIC Code	1987 U.S. SIC Description	NAICS Code	1997 NAICS U.S. Description
3312	Steel Works, Blast Furnaces (including Coke Ovens), and Rolling Mills		
	• Coke Ovens, not Integrated with Steel Mills	324199	All Other Petroleum and Coal Products Manufacturing (pt)
	• Hot Rolling Purchased Steel	331221	Rolled Steel Shape Manufacturing (pt)
	• Except Coke Ovens not Integrated with Steel Mills and Hot Rolling Purchased Steel	331111	Iron and Steel Mills (pt)
3313	Electrometallurgical Products, except Steel	331112	Electrometallurgical Ferroalloy Product Manufacturing
3315	Steel Wiredrawing and Steel Nails and Spikes		
	• Steel Wire Drawing	331222	Steel Wire Drawing
	• Nails, Spikes, Paper Clips, and Wire, not Made in Wire Drawing Plants	332618	Other Fabricated Wire Product Manufacturing (pt)
3316	Cold-rolled Steel Sheet, Strip, and Bars	331221	Rolled Steel Shape Manufacturing (pt)
3317	Steel Pipe and Tubes	33121	Iron and Steel Pipe and Tube Manufacturing from Purchased Steel
3321	Gray and Ductile Iron Foundries	331511	Iron Foundries (pt)
3322	Malleable Iron Foundries	331511	Iron Foundries (pt)
3324	Steel Investment Foundries	331512	Steel Investment Foundries
3325	Steel Foundries, NEC	331513	Steel Foundries (except Investment)
3331	Primary Smelting and Refining of Copper	331411	Primary Smelting and Refining of Copper
3334	Primary Production of Aluminum	331312	Primary Aluminum Production

pt—Part of.

SIC Code	1987 U.S. SIC Description	NAICS Code	1997 NAICS U.S. Description
3339	Primary Smelting and Refining of Nonferrous Metals, except Copper and Aluminum	331419	Primary Smelting and Refining of Nonferrous Metals (except Copper and Aluminum)
3341	Secondary Smelting and Refining of Nonferrous Metals		
	• Aluminum	331314	Secondary Smelting and Alloying of Aluminum (pt)
	• Copper	331423	Secondary Smelting, Refining, and Alloying of Copper (pt)
	• Except Aluminum and Copper	331492	Secondary Smelting, Refining, and Alloying of Nonferrous Metals (except Copper and Aluminum) (pt)
3351	Rolling, Drawing, and Extruding of Copper	331421	Copper Rolling, Drawing, and Extruding
3353	Aluminum Sheet, Plate, and Foil	331315	Aluminum Sheet, Plate, and Foil Manufacturing
3354	Aluminum Extruded Products	331316	Aluminum Extruded Product Manufacturing
3355	Aluminum Rolling and Drawing, NEC	331319	Other Aluminum Rolling and Drawing (pt)
3356	Rolling, Drawing, and Extruding of Nonferrous Metals, except Copper and Aluminum	331491	Nonferrous Metal (except Copper and Aluminum) Rolling, Drawing, and Extruding (pt)
3357	Drawing and Insulating of Nonferrous Wire		
	• Aluminum Wire Drawing	331319	Other Aluminum Rolling and Drawing (pt)
	• Copper Wire Drawing	331422	Copper Wire (except Mechanical) Drawing
	• Wire Drawing except Copper or Aluminum	331491	Nonferrous Metal (except Copper and Aluminum) Rolling, Drawing, and Extruding (pt)
	• Fiber Optic Cable - Insulating Only	335921	Fiber Optic Cable Manufacturing
	• All Other	335929	Other Communication and Energy Wire Manufacturing
3363	Aluminum Die-castings	331521	Aluminum Die-casting Foundries
3364	Nonferrous Die-castings, except Aluminum	331522	Nonferrous (except Aluminum) Die-casting Foundries
3365	Aluminum Foundries	331524	Aluminum Foundries (except Die-casting)
3366	Copper Foundries	331525	Copper Foundries (except Die-casting)
3369	Nonferrous Foundries, except Aluminum and Copper	331528	Other Nonferrous Foundries (except Die-casting)
3398	Metal Heat Treating	332811	Metal Heat Treating
3399	Primary Metal Products, NEC		
	• Aluminum Powder, Paste, Flakes, etc.	331314	Secondary Smelting and Alloying of Aluminum (pt)
	• Copper Powder, Flakes, Paste, etc.	331423	Secondary Smelting, Refining, and Alloying of Copper (pt)
	• Other Nonferrous Powder, Paste, Flakes, etc.	331492	Secondary Smelting, Refining, and Alloying of Nonferrous Metals (except Copper and Aluminum) (pt)
	• Making Ferrous Metal Powder, Paste, and Flake from Purchased Iron or Steel	331221	Rolled Steel Shape Manufacturing (pt)
	• Nonferrous Nails, Brads, Staples, etc.	332618	Other Fabricated Wire Product Manufacturing (pt)
	• Laminated Steel	332813	Electroplating, Plating, Polishing, Anodizing, and Coloring (pt)

pt—Part of.

Go to page 23 to learn about implementation of NAICS codes in the public and private sectors.

Visit page 9 to learn more about NAICS codes.

SIC Code	1987 U.S. SIC Description	NAICS Code	1997 NAICS U.S. Description
34	**Fabricated Metal Products**		
3411	Metal Cans	332431	Metal Can Manufacturing
3412	Metal Shipping Barrels, Drums, Kegs, and Pails	332439	Other Metal Container Manufacturing (pt)
3421	Cutlery		
	• except Tool-type Shears	332211	Cutlery and Flatware (except Precious) Manufacturing (pt)
	• Tool-type Shears	332212	Hand and Edge Tool Manufacturing (pt)
3423	Hand and Edge Tools, except Machine Tools and Handsaws	332212	Hand and Edge Tool Manufacturing (pt)
3425	Saw Blades and Handsaws	332213	Saw Blade and Handsaw Manufacturing
3429	Hardware, NEC		
	• Fireplace Fixtures, Traps, Handcuffs and Leg Irons, Ladder Jacks, and Other Like Metal Products	332999	All Other Miscellaneous Fabricated Metal Products Manufacturing (pt)
	• Vacuum and Insulated Bottles, Jugs, and Chests	332439	Other Metal Container Manufacturing (pt)
	• Turnbuckles and Hose Clamps	332722	Bolt, Nut, Screw, Rivet, and Washer Manufacturing (pt)
	• Luggage and Utility Racks	336399	All Other Motor Vehicle Parts Manufacturing (pt)
	• Fire Hose Nozzles and Couplings	332919	Other Metal Valve and Pipe Fitting Manufacturing (pt)
	• Convertible Bed Sleeper Mechanisms and Chair Glides	337215	Showcase, Partition, Shelving, and Locker Manufacturing (pt)
	• Other Hardware	33251	Hardware Manufacturing (pt)
3431	Enameled Iron and Metal Sanitary Ware	332998	Enameled Iron and Metal Sanitary Ware Manufacturing
3432	Plumbing Fixture Fittings and Trim		
	• Plumbing Fixture Fittings and Trim, except Metal Shower Rods and Lawn Hose Nozzles	332913	Plumbing Fixture Fitting and Trim Manufacturing
	• Lawn Hose Nozzles	332919	Other Metal Valve and Pipe Fitting Manufacturing (pt)
	• Metal Shower Rods	332999	All Other Miscellaneous Fabricated Metal Product Manufacturing (pt)
3433	Heating Equipment, except Electric and Warm Air Furnaces	333414	Heating Equipment Manufacturing, (except Warm Air Furnaces) (pt)
3441	Fabricated Structural Metal	332312	Fabricated Structural Metal Manufacturing (pt)
3442	Metal Doors, Sash, Frames, Molding, and Trim Manufacturing	332321	Metal Window and Door Manufacturing (pt)
3443	Fabricated Plate Work (Boiler Shops)		
	• Fabricated Plate Work and Metal Weldments	332313	Plate Work Manufacturing
	• Power Boilers and Heat Exchanges	33241	Power Boiler and Heat Exchanger Manufacturing (pt)
	• Heavy Gauge Tanks	33242	Metal Tank (Heavy Gauge) Manufacturing
	• Metal Cooling Towers	333414	Heating Equipment (except Warm Air Furnaces) Manufacturing (pt)
3444	Sheet Metal Work		
	• Ducts, Flumes, Flooring, Siding, Dampers, etc.	332322	Sheet Metal Work Manufacturing
	• Metal Bins and Vats	332439	Other Metal Container Manufacturing (pt)
	• Cooling Towers	333414	Heating Equipment (except Warm Air Furnaces) Manufacturing (pt)

pt—Part of.

SIC Code	1987 U.S. SIC Description	NAICS Code	1997 NAICS U.S. Description
3446	Architectural and Ornamental Metal Work	332323	Ornamental and Architectural Metal Work Manufacturing (pt)
3448	Prefabricated Metal Buildings and Components	332311	Prefabricated Metal Building and Component Manufacturing
3449	Miscellaneous Structural Metal Work		
	• Custom Roll Forming	332114	Custom Roll Forming
	• Fabricated Bar Joists and Concrete Reinforcing Bars	332312	Fabricated Structural Metal Manufacturing (pt)
	• Curtain Wall	332321	Metal Window and Door Manufacturing (pt)
	• Metal Plaster Bases	332323	Ornamental and Architectural Metal Work Manufacturing (pt)
3451	Screw Machine Products	332721	Precision Turned Product Manufacturing
3452	Bolts, Nuts, Screws, Rivets, and Washers	332722	Bolt, Nut, Screw, Rivet, and Washer Manufacturing (pt)
3462	Iron and Steel Forgings	332111	Iron and Steel Forging
3463	Nonferrous Forgings	332112	Nonferrous Forging
3465	Automotive Stamping	33637	Motor Vehicle Metal Stamping
3466	Crowns and Closures	332115	Crown and Closure Manufacturing
3469	Metal Stamping, NEC		
	• Metal Stamping, NEC (except Kitchen Utensils, Pots and Pans for Cooking, and Coins)	332116	Metal Stamping
	• Kitchen Utensils and Pots and Pans for Cooking	332214	Kitchen Utensil, Pot, and Pan Manufacturing
3471	Electroplating, Plating, Polishing, Anodizing, and Coloring	332813	Electroplating, Plating, Polishing, Anodizing, and Coloring (pt)
3479	Coating, Engraving, and Allied Services, NEC		
	• Jewelry Engraving and Etching, Costume Jewelry	339914	Costume Jewelry and Novelty Manufacturing (pt)
	• Jewelry Engraving and Etching, Precious Metal	339911	Jewelry (except Costume) Manufacturing (pt)
	• Silverware and Flatware Engraving and Etching	339912	Silverware and Hollowware Manufacturing (pt)
	• Other Coating, Engraving, and Allied Services	332812	Metal Coating, Engraving (except Jewelry and Silverware), and Allied Services to Manufacturers
3482	Small Arms Ammunition	332992	Small Arms Ammunition Manufacturing
3483	Ammunition, except for Small Arms	332993	Ammunition (except Small Arms) Manufacturing
3484	Small Arms	332994	Small Arms Manufacturing (pt)
3489	Ordnance and Accessories, NEC	332995	Other Ordnance and Accessories Manufacturing
3491	Industrial Valves	332911	Industrial Valve Manufacturing
3492	Fluid Power Valves and Hose Fittings	332912	Fluid Power Valve and Hose Fitting Manufacturing (pt)
3493	Steel Springs, except Wire	332611	Spring (Heavy Gauge) Manufacturing
3494	Valves and Pipe Fittings, NEC		
	• except Metal Pipe Hangers and Supports	332919	Other Metal Valve and Pipe Fitting Manufacturing (pt)
	• Metal Pipe Hangers and Supports	332999	All Other Miscellaneous Fabricated Metal Product Manufacturing (pt)

pt—Part of.

SIC Code	1987 U.S. SIC Description	NAICS Code	1997 NAICS U.S. Description
3495	Wire Springs		
	• Wire Springs (except Watch and Clock Springs)	332612	Spring (Light Gauge) Manufacturing
	• Watch and Clock Springs	334518	Watch, Clock, and Part Manufacturing (pt)
3496	Miscellaneous Fabricated Wire Products		
	• Grocery Carts	333924	Industrial Truck, Tractor, Trailer, and Stacker Machinery Manufacturing (pt)
	• except Grocery Carts	332618	Other Fabricated Wire Product Manufacturing (pt)
3497	Metal Foil and Leaf		
	• Laminated Aluminum Foil Rolls/Sheets for Flexible Packaging Uses	322225	Laminated Aluminum Foil Manufacturing for Flexible Packaging Uses
	• Foil and Foil Containers	332999	All Other Miscellaneous Fabricated Metal Product Manufacturing (pt)
3498	Fabricated Pipe and Pipe Fittings	332996	Fabricated Pipe and Pipe Fitting Manufacturing
3499	Fabricated Metal Products, NEC		
	• Metal Furniture Frames	337215	Showcase, Partition, Shelving, and Locker Manufacturing (pt)
	• Metal Motor Vehicle Seat Frames	33636	Motor Vehicle Seating and Interior Trim Manufacturing (pt)
	• Powder Metallurgy	332117	Powder Metallurgy Part Manufacturing
	• Metal Boxes	332439	Other Metal Container Manufacturing (pt)
	• Safe and Vault Locks	33251	Hardware Manufacturing (pt)
	• Metal Aerosol Valves	332919	Other Metal Valve and Pipe Fitting Manufacturing (pt)
	• Other Metal Products	332999	All Other Miscellaneous Fabricated Metal Product Manufacturing (pt)

35 Industrial Machinery and Equipment

SIC Code	1987 U.S. SIC Description	NAICS Code	1997 NAICS U.S. Description
3511	Steam, Gas, and Hydraulic Turbines, and Turbine Generator Set Units	333611	Turbine and Turbine Generator Set Unit Manufacturing
3519	Internal Combustion Engines, NEC		
	• Stationary Engine Radiators	336399	All Other Motor Vehicle Parts Manufacturing (pt)
	• except Stationary Engine Radiators	333618	Other Engine Equipment Manufacturing (pt)
3523	Farm Machinery and Equipment		
	• Farm Machinery and Equipment (except Corrals, Stalls, Holding Gates, Hand Hair Clippers for Animals, Farm Conveyors, and Elevators)	333111	Farm Machinery and Equipment Manufacturing
	• Corrals, Stalls, Holding Gates	332323	Ornamental and Architectural Metal Work Manufacturing (pt)
	• Hand Hair Clippers for Animals	332212	Hand and Edge Tool Manufacturing(pt)
	• Farm Conveyors and Farm Elevators, Stackers, and Bale Throwers	333922	Conveyor and Conveying Equipment Manufacturing (pt)
3524	Lawn and Garden Tractors and Home Lawn and Garden Equipment		
	• Lawn and Garden Tractors and Home Lawn and Garden Equipment (except Nonpowered Lawnmowers)	333112	Lawn and Garden Tractor and Home Lawn and Garden Equipment Manufacturing
	• Nonpowered Lawnmowers	332212	Hand and Edge Tool Manufacturing (pt)

pt—Part of.

SIC Code	1987 U.S. SIC Description	NAICS Code	1997 NAICS U.S. Description
3531	Construction Machinery and Equipment		
	• Railway Track Maintenance Equipment	33651	Railroad Rolling Stock Manufacturing (pt)
	• Winches, Aerial Work Platforms, and Automotive Wrecker Hoists	333923	Overhead Traveling Crane, Hoist, and Monorail System Manufacturing (pt)
	• Other Construction Machinery and Equipment	33312	Construction Machinery Manufacturing
3532	Mining Machinery and Equipment, except Oil and Gas Field Machinery and Equipment	333131	Mining Machinery and Equipment Manufacturing
3533	Oil and Gas Field Machinery and Equipment	333132	Oil and Gas Field Machinery and Equipment Manufacturing
3534	Elevators and Moving Stairways	333921	Elevator and Moving Stairway Manufacturing
3535	Conveyors and Conveying Equipment	333922	Conveyor and Conveying Equipment Manufacturing (pt)
3536	Overhead Traveling Cranes, Hoists, and Monorail Systems	333923	Overhead Traveling Crane, Hoist, and Monorail System Manufacturing (pt)
3537	Industrial Trucks, Tractors, Trailers, and Stackers		
	• Industrial Trucks, Tractors, Trailers, and Stackers (except Metal Pallets and Air Cargo Containers)	333924	Industrial Truck, Tractor, Trailer, and Stacker Machinery Manufacturing
	• Metal Pallets	332999	All Other Miscellaneous Fabricated Metal Product Manufacturing (pt)
	• Metal Air Cargo Containers	332439	Other Metal Container Manufacturing (pt)
3541	Machine Tools, Metal Cutting Type	333512	Machine Tool (Metal Cutting Types) Manufacturing
3542	Machine Tools, Metal Forming Type	333513	Machine Tool (Metal Forming Types) Manufacturing
3543	Industrial Patterns	332997	Industrial Pattern Manufacturing
3544	Special Dies and Tools, Die Sets, Jigs and Fixtures, and Industrial Molds		
	• Except Industrial Molds	333514	Special Die and Tool, Die Set, Jig, and Fixture Manufacturing
	• Industrial Molds	333511	Industrial Mold Manufacturing
3545	Cutting Tools, Machine Tool Accessories, and Machinists' Precision Measuring Devices		
	• Cutting Tools, Machine Tool Accessories, and Machinists' Precision Measuring Devices (except Precision Measuring Devices)	333515	Cutting Tool and Machine Tool Accessory Manufacturing
	• Precision Measuring Devices	332212	Hand and Edge Tool Manufacturing (pt)
3546	Power-driven Handtools	333991	Power-driven Handtool Manufacturing
3547	Rolling Mill Machinery and Equipment	333516	Rolling Mill Machinery and Equipment Manufacturing
3548	Electric and Gas Welding and Soldering Equipment		
	• Except Transformers for Arc-welding	333992	Welding and Soldering Equipment Manufacturing
	• Transformers for Arc-welding	335311	Power, Distribution, and Specialty Transformer Manufacturing (pt)
3549	Metalworking Machinery, NEC	333518	Other Metalworking Machinery Manufacturing
3552	Textile Machinery	333292	Textile Machinery Manufacturing

pt—Part of.

Visit page 15 to learn more about major changes to NAICS sectors.

SIC Code	1987 U.S. SIC Description	NAICS Code	1997 NAICS U.S. Description
3553	Woodworking Machinery	33321	Sawmill and Woodworking Machinery Manufacturing
3554	Paper Industries Machinery	333291	Paper Industry Machinery Manufacturing
3555	Printing Trades Machinery and Equipment	333293	Printing Machinery and Equipment Manufacturing
3556	Food Products Machinery	333294	Food Product Machinery Manufacturing
3559	Special Industry Machinery, NEC		
	• Rubber and Plastics Manufacturing Machinery	33322	Plastics and Rubber Industry Machinery Manufacturing
	• Nuclear Control Drive Mechanisms	33241	Power Boiler and Heat Exchanger Manufacturing (pt)
	• Automotive Maintenance Equipment	333319	Other Commercial and Service Industry Machinery Manufacturing (pt)
	• Semiconductor Machinery Manufacturing	333295	Semiconductor Manufacturing Machinery
	• Cotton Ginning Machinery	333111	Farm Machinery and Equipment Manufacturing (pt)
	• Except Rubber and Plastics Manufacturing Machinery, Semiconductor Manufacturing Machinery, Automotive Maintenance Equipment, Cotton Ginning Machinery, and Nuclear Control Device Mechanisms	333298	All Other Industrial Machinery Manufacturing (pt)
3561	Pumps and Pumping Equipment	333911	Pump and Pumping Equipment Manufacturing (pt)
3562	Ball and Roller Bearings	332991	Ball and Roller Bearing Manufacturing
3563	Air and Gas Compressors	333912	Air and Gas Compressor Manufacturing
3564	Industrial and Commercial Fans and Blowers and Air Purification Equipment		
	• Air Purification Equipment	333411	Air Purification Equipment Manufacturing
	• Fans and Blowers	333412	Industrial and Commercial Fan and Blower Manufacturing
3565	Packaging Machinery	333993	Packaging Machinery Manufacturing
3566	Speed Changers, Industrial High-speed Drives, and Gears	333612	Speed Changer, Industrial High-speed Drive, and Gear Manufacturing
3567	Industrial Process Furnaces and Ovens	333994	Industrial Process Furnace and Oven Manufacturing
3568	Mechanical Power Transmission Equipment, NEC	333613	Mechanical Power Transmission Equipment Manufacturing
3569	General Industrial Machinery and Equipment, NEC		
	• Electric Swimming Pool Heaters	333414	Heating Equipment (except Warm Air Furnace) Manufacturing (pt)
	• Textile Fire Hose	314999	All Other Miscellaneous Textile Product Mills (pt)
	• Except Electric Swimming Pool Heaters and Textile Fire Hoses	333999	All Other Miscellaneous General Purpose Machinery Manufacturing (pt)
3571	Electronic Computers	334111	Electronic Computer Manufacturing
3572	Computer Storage Devices	334112	Computer Storage Device Manufacturing
3575	Computer Terminals	334113	Computer Terminal Manufacturing

pt—Part of.

SIC Code	1987 U.S. SIC Description	NAICS Code	1997 NAICS U.S. Description
3577	Computer Peripheral Equipment, NEC		
	• Plotter Controllers	334418	Printed Circuit Assembly (Electronic Assembly) Manufacturing (pt)
	• Magnetic Tape Cleaner	334613	Magnetic Optical Recording Media Manufacturing (pt)
	• Except Plotter Controllers and Magnetic Tape Cleaners	334119	Other Computer Peripheral Equipment Manufacturing (pt)
3578	Calculating and Accounting Machines, except Electronic Computers		
	• Point of Sales Terminals and Fund Transfer Devices	334119	Other Computer Peripheral Equipment Manufacturing (pt)
	• Change Making Machines	333311	Automatic Vending Machine Manufacturing (pt)
	• Calculating and Accounting Machines, except Point of Sales Terminals and Fund Transfer Devices, and Change Making Machines	333313	Office Machinery Manufacturing (pt)
3579	Office Machines, NEC		
	• Pencil Sharpeners, Staplers, and Other Office Equipment	339942	Lead Pencil and Art Good Manufacturing (pt)
	• Time Clocks and Other Time Recording Devices	334518	Watch, Clock, and Part Manufacturing (pt)
	• Other Office Machines	333313	Office Machinery Manufacturing (pt)
3581	Automatic Vending Machines	333311	Automatic Vending Machine Manufacturing
3582	Commercial Laundry, Drycleaning, and Pressing Machines	333312	Commercial Laundry, Drycleaning, and Pressing Machine Manufacturing
3585	Air-conditioning and Warm Air Heating Equipment and Commercial and Industrial Refrigeration Equipment		
	• Motor Vehicle Air-conditioning	336391	Motor Vehicle Air-conditioning Manufacturing
	• Except Motor Vehicle Air-conditioning	333415	Air-conditioning and Warm Air Heating Equipment and Commercial and Industrial Refrigeration Equipment Manufacturing
3586	Measuring and Dispensing Pumps	333913	Measuring and Dispensing Pump Manufacturing
3589	Service Industry Machinery, NEC	333319	Other Commercial and Service Industry Machinery Manufacturing (pt)
3592	Carburetors, Pistons, Piston Rings, and Valves	336311	Carburetor, Piston, Piston Ring, and Valve Manufacturing
3593	Fluid Power Cylinders and Actuators	333995	Fluid Power Cylinder and Actuator Manufacturing
3594	Fluid Power Pumps and Motors	333996	Fluid Power Pump and Motor Manufacturing
3596	Scales and Balances, except Laboratory	333997	Scale and Balance (except Laboratory) Manufacturing
3599	Industrial and Commercial Machinery and Equipment, NEC		
	• Gasoline, Oil, and Intake Filters for Internal Combustion Engines, except Motor Vehicle	336399	All Other Motor Vehicle Part Manufacturing (pt)

SIC to NAICS

pt—Part of.

SIC Code	1987 U.S. SIC Description	NAICS Code	1997 NAICS U.S. Description
	• Flexible Metal Hose	332999	All Other Miscellaneous Fabricated Metal Product Manufacturing (pt)
	• Carnival Amusement Park Equipment	333319	Other Commercial and Service Industry Machinery Manufacturing (pt)
	• Machine Shops	33271	Machine Shops
	• Other Industrial and Commercial Machinery and Equipment	333999	All Other Miscellaneous General Purpose Machinery Manufacturing (pt)
36	**Electrical and Electronic Equipment**		
3612	Power, Distribution, and Specialty Transformers	335311	Power, Distribution, and Specialty Transformer Manufacturing (pt)
3613	Switchgear and Switchboard Apparatus	335313	Switchgear and Switchboard Apparatus Manufacturing
3621	Motors and Generators	335312	Motor and Generator Manufacturing (pt)
3624	Carbon and Graphite Products	335991	Carbon and Graphite Product Manufacturing
3625	Relays and Industrial Controls	335314	Relay and Industrial Control Manufacturing
3629	Electrical Industrial Apparatus, NEC	335999	All Other Miscellaneous Electrical Equipment and Component Manufacturing (pt)
3631	Household Cooking Equipment	335221	Household Cooking Appliance Manufacturing
3632	Household Refrigerators and Home and Farm Freezers	335222	Household Refrigerator and Home Freezer Manufacturing
3633	Household Laundry Equipment	335224	Household Laundry Equipment Manufacturing
3634	Electric Housewares and Fans		
	• Except Wall and Baseboard Heating Units for Permanent Installation, and Electronic Cigarette Lighters	335211	Electric Housewares and Household Fan Manufacturing
	• Electronic Cigarette Lighters	339999	All Other Miscellaneous Manufacturing (pt)
	• Wall and Baseboard Heating Units For Permanent Installation	333414	Heating Equipment (except Warm Air Furnaces) Manufacturing (pt)
3635	Household Vacuum Cleaners	335212	Household Vacuum Cleaner Manufacturing (pt)
3639	Household Appliances, NEC		
	• Floor Waxing and Floor Polishing Machines	335212	Household Vacuum Cleaner Manufacturing (pt)
	• Household Sewing Machines	333298	All Other Industrial Machinery Manufacturing (pt)
	• Other Household Appliances	335228	Other Major Household Appliance Manufacturing
3641	Electric Lamp Bulbs and Tubes	33511	Electric Lamp Bulb and Part Manufacturing
3643	Current-carrying Wiring Devices	335931	Current-carrying Wiring Device Manufacturing
3644	Noncurrent-carrying Wiring Devices		
	• Fish Wire, Electrical Wiring Tool	332212	Hand and Edge Tool Manufacturing (pt)
	• All Other Noncurrent-carrying Wiring Devices	335932	Noncurrent-carrying Wiring Device Manufacturing
3645	Residential Electric Lighting Fixtures	335121	Residential Electric Lighting Fixture Manufacturing (pt)

pt—Part of.

SIC Code	1987 U.S. SIC Description	NAICS Code	1997 NAICS U.S. Description
3646	Commercial, Industrial, and Institutional Electric Lighting Fixtures	335122	Commercial, Industrial, and Institutional Electric Lighting Fixture Manufacturing
3647	Vehicular Lighting Equipment	336321	Vehicular Lighting Equipment Manufacturing
3648	Lighting Equipment, NEC	335129	Other Lighting Equipment Manufacturing (pt)
3651	Household Audio and Video Equipment	33431	Audio and Video Equipment Manufacturing
3652	Phonograph Records and Prerecorded Audio Tapes and Disks		
	• Reproduction of Recording Media	334612	Prerecorded Compact Disc (except Software), Tape, and Record Reproducing (pt)
	• Integrated Record Companies, except Duplication Only	51222	Integrated Record Production/Distribution
3661	Telephone and Telegraph Apparatus		
	• Telephone and Telegraph Apparatus, except Consumer External Modems	33421	Telephone Apparatus Manufacturing
	• Consumer External Modems	334418	Printed Circuit Assembly (Electronic Assembly) Manufacturing (pt)
3663	Radio and Television Broadcasting and Communications Equipment	33422	Radio and Television Broadcasting and Wireless Communications Equipment Manufacturing (pt)
3669	Communications Equipment, NEC	33429	Other Communications Equipment Manufacturing
3671	Electron Tubes	334411	Electron Tube Manufacturing
3672	Printed Circuit Boards	334412	Bare Printed Circuit Board Manufacturing
3674	Semiconductors and Related Devices	334413	Semiconductor and Related Device Manufacturing
3675	Electronic Capacitors	334414	Electronic Capacitor Manufacturing
3676	Electronic Resistors	334415	Electronic Resistor Manufacturing
3677	Electronic Coils, Transformers, and Other Inductors	334416	Electronic Coil, Transformer, and Other Inductor Manufacturing (pt)
3678	Electronic Connectors	334417	Electronic Connector Manufacturing
3679	Electronic Components, NEC		
	• Antennas	33422	Radio and Television Broadcasting and Wireless Communications Equipment Manufacturing (pt)
	• Radio Headphones	33431	Audio and Video Equipment Manufacturing (pt)
	• Printed Circuit/Electronics Assembly	334418	Printed Circuit Assembly (Electronic Assembly) Manufacturing (pt)
	• Other Electronic Components	334419	Other Electronic Component Manufacturing
3691	Storage Batteries	335911	Storage Battery Manufacturing
3692	Primary Batteries, Dry and Wet	335912	Primary Battery Manufacturing
3694	Electrical Equipment for Internal Combustion Engines	336322	Other Motor Vehicle Electrical and Electronic Equipment Manufacturing (pt)
3695	Magnetic and Optical Recording Media	334613	Magnetic and Optical Recording Media Manufacturing

Visit page 9 to learn more about NAICS codes.

pt—Part of.

SIC Code	1987 U.S. SIC Description	NAICS Code	1997 NAICS U.S. Description
3699	Electrical Machinery, Equipment, and Supplies, NEC		
	• Electronic Teaching Machines and Flight Simulators	333319	Other Commercial and Service Industry Machinery Manufacturing (pt)
	• Outboard Electric Motors	333618	Other Engine Equipment Manufacturing (pt)
	• Laser Welding and Soldering Equipment	333992	Welding and Soldering Equipment Manufacturing (pt)
	• Other Lasers		*Classify According to Function*
	• Christmas Tree Lighting Sets, Electric Insect Lamps, Electric Fireplace Logs, and Trouble Lights	335129	Other Lighting Equipment Manufacturing (pt)
	• Other Electrical Machinery, Equipment, and Supplies	335999	All Other Miscellaneous Electrical Equipment and Component Manufacturing (pt)

37 Transportation Equipment

SIC Code	1987 U.S. SIC Description	NAICS Code	1997 NAICS U.S. Description
3711	Motor Vehicles and Passenger Car Bodies		
	• Automobiles	336111	Automobile Manufacturing
	• Light Truck and Utility Vehicles	336112	Light Truck and Utility Vehicle Manufacturing
	• Heavy Duty Trucks	33612	Heavy Duty Truck Manufacturing
	• Kit Car and Other Passenger Car Bodies	336211	Motor Vehicle Body Manufacturing (pt)
	• Military Armored Vehicles	336992	Military Armored Vehicle, Tank, and Tank Component Manufacturing (pt)
3713	Truck and Bus Bodies	336211	Motor Vehicle Body Manufacturing (pt)
3714	Motor Vehicle Parts and Accessories		
	• Dump-truck Lifting Mechanisms and Fifth Wheels	336211	Motor Vehicle Body Manufacturing (pt)
	• Gasoline Engines including Rebuilt and Engine Parts including Rebuilt for Motor Vehicles	336312	Gasoline Engine and Engine Parts Manufacturing
	• Wiring Harness Sets, Other than Ignition; Block Heaters and Battery Heaters; Instrument Board Assemblies; Permanent Defroster; Windshield Washer-wiper Mechanisms; Cruise Control Mechanisms; and Other Electrical Equipment for Internal Combustion Engine	336322	Other Motor Vehicle Electrical and Electronic Equipment Manufacturing (pt)
	• Steering and Suspension Parts	33633	Motor Vehicle Steering and Suspension Components (except Spring) Manufacturing
	• Brake and Brake Systems, including Assemblies	33634	Motor Vehicle Brake System Manufacturing (pt)
	• Transmissions and Power Train Parts, including Rebuilding	33635	Motor Vehicle Transmission and Power Train Parts Manufacturing
	• Other Motor Vehicle Parts	336399	All Other Motor Vehicle Parts Manufacturing (pt)
3715	Truck Trailers	336212	Truck Trailer Manufacturing
3716	Motor Homes	336213	Motor Home Manufacturing

SIC to NAICS

---

pt—Part of.

SIC Code	1987 U.S. SIC Description	NAICS Code	1997 NAICS U.S. Description
3721	Aircraft		
	• Research and Development	54171	Research and Development in the Physical, Engineering, and Life Sciences (pt)
	• Except Research and Development	336411	Aircraft Manufacturing
3724	Aircraft Engines and Engine Parts		
	• Except Research and Development	336412	Aircraft Engine and Engine Parts Manufacturing (pt)
	• Research and Development	54171	Research and Development in the Physical, Engineering, and Life Sciences (pt)
3728	Aircraft Parts and Auxiliary Equipment, NEC		
	• Fluid Power Aircraft Subassemblies	332912	Fluid Power Valve and Hose Fitting Manufacturing (pt)
	• Research and Development	54171	Research and Development in the Physical, Engineering, and Life Sciences (pt)
	• Target Drones	336411	Aircraft Manufacturing (pt)
	• Except Fluid Power Aircraft Subassemblies, Target Drones, and Research and Development	336413	Other Aircraft Parts and Auxiliary Equipment Manufacturing
3731	Ship Building and Repairing		
	• Floating Dry Docks not Associated with Shipyards	48839	Other Support Activities for Water Transportation (pt)
	• Ship Building and Repairing except Floating Dry Docks not Associated with Shipyards	336611	Ship Building and Repairing
3732	Boat Building and Repairing		
	• Boat Repair	81149	Other Personal and Household Goods Repair and Maintenance (pt)
	• Boat Building	336612	Boat Building
3743	Railroad Equipment		
	• Locomotive Fuel Lubricating or Cooling Medium Pumps	333911	Pump and Pumping Equipment Manufacturing (pt)
	• Other Railroad Equipment	33651	Railroad Rolling Stock Manufacturing (pt)
3751	Motorcycles, Bicycles, and Parts	336991	Motorcycle, Bicycle, and Parts Manufacturing (pt)
3761	Guided Missiles and Space Vehicles		
	• Except Research and Development	336414	Guided Missile and Space Vehicle Manufacturing
	• Research and Development	54171	Research and Development in the Physical, Engineering, and Life Sciences (pt)
3764	Guided Missile and Space Vehicle Propulsion Units and Propulsion Unit Parts		
	• Except Research and Development	336415	Guided Missile and Space Vehicle Propulsion Unit and Propulsion Unit Parts Manufacturing
	• Research and Development	54171	Research and Development in the Physical, Engineering, and Life Sciences (pt)
3769	Guided Missile Space Vehicle Parts and Auxiliary Equipment, NEC		
	• Except Research and Development	336419	Other Guided Missile and Space Vehicle Parts and Auxiliary Equipment Manufacturing
	• Research and Development	54171	Research and Development in the Physical, Engineering, and Life Sciences (pt)

pt—Part of.

SIC Code	1987 U.S. SIC Description	NAICS Code	1997 NAICS U.S. Description
3792	Travel Trailers and Campers	336214	Travel Trailer and Camper Manufacturing (pt)
3795	Tanks and Tank Components	336992	Military Armored Vehicle, Tank, and Tank Component Manufacturing (pt)
3799	Transportation Equipment, NEC		
	• Automobile, Boat, Utility, and Light Truck Trailers	336214	Travel Trailer and Camper Manufacturing (pt)
	• Trailer Hitches	336399	All Other Motor Vehicle Parts Manufacturing (pt)
	• Wheelbarrows	333924	Industrial Truck, Tractor, Trailer, and Stacker Machinery Manufacturing (pt)
	• Other Transportation Equipment	336999	All Other Transportation Equipment Manufacturing

38	**Instruments and Related Products**		
3812	Search, Detection, Navigation, Guidance, Aeronautical, and Nautical Systems and Instruments	334511	Search, Detection, Navigation, Guidance, Aeronautical, and Nautical System and Instrument Manufacturing
3821	Laboratory Apparatus and Furniture	339111	Laboratory Apparatus and Furniture Manufacturing (pt)
3822	Automatic Controls for Regulating Residential and Commercial Environments and Appliances	334512	Automatic Environmental Control Manufacturing for Regulating Residential, Commercial, and Appliance Use
3823	Industrial Instruments for Measurement, Display, and Control of Process Variables; and Related Products	334513	Instruments and Related Product Manufacturing for Measuring Displaying, and Controlling Industrial Process Variables
3824	Totalizing Fluid Meters and Counting Devices	334514	Totalizing Fluid Meter and Counting Device Manufacturing (pt)
3825	Instruments for Measuring and Testing of Electricity and Electrical Signals		
	• Automotive Ammeters and Voltmeters	334514	Totalizing Fluid Meters and Counting Device Manufacturing (pt)
	• Except Automotive Ammeters and Voltmeters	334515	Instrument Manufacturing for Measuring and Testing Electricity and Electrical Signals
3826	Laboratory Analytical Instruments	334516	Analytical Laboratory Instrument Manufacturing
3827	Optical Instruments and Lenses	333314	Optical Instrument and Lens Manufacturing
3829	Measuring and Controlling Devices, NEC		
	• Motor Vehicle Gauges	334514	Totalizing Fluid Meter and Counting Device Manufacturing (pt)
	• Medical Thermometers	339112	Surgical and Medical Instrument Manufacturing (pt)
	• Electronic Chronometers	334518	Watch, Clock, and Part Manufacturing
	• Except Medical Thermometers, Electronic Chronometers, and Motor Vehicle Gauges	334519	Other Measuring and Controlling Device Manufacturing
3841	Surgical and Medical Instruments and Apparatus		
	• Tranquilizer Guns	332994	Small Arms Manufacturing (pt)
	• Operating Tables	339111	Laboratory Apparatus and Furniture Manufacturing (pt)
	• Except Tranquilizer Guns and Operating Tables	339112	Surgical and Medical Instrument Manufacturing (pt)

pt—Part of.

SIC Code	1987 U.S. SIC Description	NAICS Code	1997 NAICS U.S. Description
3842	Orthopedic, Prosthetic, and Surgical Appliances and Supplies		
	• Incontinent and Bed Pads	322291	Sanitary Paper Product Manufacturing (pt)
	• Orthopedic, Prosthetic, and Surgical Appliances and Supplies, except Electronic Hearing Aids	339113	Surgical Appliance and Supplies Manufacturing
	• Electronic Hearing Aids	334510	Electromedical and Electrotherapeutic Apparatus Manufacturing (pt)
3843	Dental Equipment and Supplies	339114	Dental Equipment and Supplies Manufacturing
3844	X-Ray Apparatus and Tubes and Related Irradiation Apparatus	334517	Irradiation Apparatus Manufacturing (pt)
3845	Electromedical and Electrotherapeutic Apparatus		
	• CT and CAT Scanners	334517	Irradiation Apparatus Manufacturing (pt)
	• Other Electromedical and Electrotherapeutic Apparatus	334510	Electromedical and Electrotherapeutic Apparatus Manufacturing (pt)
3851	Ophthalmic Goods		
	• Intraocular Lenses	339113	Surgical and Medical Instrument Manufacturing (pt)
	• Except Intraocular Lenses	339115	Ophthalmic Goods Manufacturing (pt)
3861	Photographic Equipment and Supplies		
	• Photographic Equipment and Supplies (except Photographic Film, Paper, Plates, and Chemicals)	333315	Photographic and Photocopying Equipment Manufacturing
	• Photographic Film, Paper, Plates, and Chemicals	325992	Photographic Film, Paper, Plate, and Chemical Manufacturing
3873	Watches, Clocks, Clockwork Operated Devices, and Parts	334518	Watch, Clock, and Part Manufacturing (pt)
39	**Miscellaneous Manufacturing Industries**		
3911	Jewelry, Precious Metal	339911	Jewelry (except Costume) Manufacturing (pt)
3914	Silverware, Plated Ware, and Stainless Steel Ware		
	• Cutlery and Flatware Nonprecious and Precious Plated	332211	Cutlery and Flatware (except Precious) Manufacturing (pt)
	• Precious Plated Hollowware	332999	All Other Miscellaneous Fabricated Metal Product Manufacturing (pt)
	• Silverware, Plated Ware, and Stainless Steel Ware (except Nonprecious and Precious Plated Metal Cutlery and Flatware)	339912	Silverware and Hollowware Manufacturing (pt)
3915	Jewelers' Findings and Materials, and Lapidary Work		
	• Watch Jewels	334518	Watch, Clock, and Part Manufacturing (pt)
	• Except Watch Jewels	339913	Jewelers' Material and Lapidary Work Manufacturing
3931	Musical Instruments	339992	Musical Instrument Manufacturing
3942	Dolls and Stuffed Toys	339931	Doll and Stuffed Toy Manufacturing

Visit page 15 to learn more about major changes to NAICS sectors.

pt—Part of.

SIC Code	1987 U.S. SIC Description	NAICS Code	1997 NAICS U.S. Description
3944	Games, Toys, and Children's Vehicles, except Dolls and Bicycles		
	• Metal Tricycles	336991	Motorcycle, Bicycle, and Parts Manufacturing (pt)
	• Other Games, Toys, and Children's Vehicles	339932	Game, Toy, and Children's Vehicle Manufacturing
3949	Sporting and Athletic Goods, NEC	33992	Sporting and Athletic Good Manufacturing
3951	Pens, Mechanical Pencils, and Parts	339941	Pen and Mechanical Pencil Manufacturing
3952	Lead Pencils, Crayons, and Artist's Materials		
	• Drafting Tables and Boards	337127	Institutional Furniture Manufacturing (pt)
	• Drawing and India Ink	325998	All Other Miscellaneous Chemical and Preparation Manufacturing (pt)
	• Other	339942	Lead Pencil and Art Good Manufacturing (pt)
3953	Marking Devices	339943	Marking Device Manufacturing
3955	Carbon Paper and Inked Ribbons	339944	Carbon Paper and Inked Ribbon Manufacturing
3961	Costume Jewelry and Costume Novelties, except Precious Metals	339914	Costume Jewelry and Novelty Manufacturing (pt)
3965	Fasteners, Buttons, Needles, and Pins	339993	Fastener, Button, Needle, and Pin Manufacturing (pt)
3991	Brooms and Brushes	339994	Broom, Brush, and Mop Manufacturing (pt)
3993	Signs and Advertising Specialties		
	• Signs	33995	Sign Manufacturing
	• Advertising Specialties		*Classified According to the Product Produced*
3995	Burial Caskets	339995	Burial Casket Manufacturing
3996	Linoleum, Asphalted-felt-base, and Other Hard Surface Floor Coverings, NEC	326192	Resilient Floor Covering Manufacturing (pt)
3999	Manufacturing Industries, NEC		
	• Beauty and Barber Chairs	337127	Institutional Furniture Manufacturing (pt)
	• Other Beauty and Barber Shop Equipment	333319	Other Commercial and Service Industry Machinery Manufacturing (pt)
	• Fur Dressing and Bleaching	31611	Leather and Hide Tanning and Finishing (pt)
	• Lamp Shades of Paper or Textile	335121	Residential Electric Lighting Fixture Manufacturing (pt)
	• Matches	325998	All Other Miscellaneous Chemical Product and Preparation Manufacturing (pt)
	• Metal Products, such as Combs, Hair Curlers, etc.	332999	All Other Miscellaneous Fabricated Metal Product Manufacturing (pt)
	• Plastics Products, such as Combs, Hair Curlers, etc.	326199	All Other Plastics Product Manufacturing (pt)
	• Electric Hair Clippers for Humans	335211	Electric Housewares and Household Fan Manufacturing (pt)
	• Tape Measures	332212	Hand and Edge Tool Manufacturing (pt)
	• Human Hair Clippers, Hand Operated	332211	Cutlery and Flatware (except Precious) Manufacturing (pt)
	• Embroidery Kits	339932	Game, Toy, and Children's Vehicle Manufacturing (pt)
	• Other	339999	All Other Miscellaneous Manufacturing (pt)

pt—Part of.

SIC Code	1987 U.S. SIC Description	NAICS Code	1997 NAICS U.S. Description
40	**Railroad Transportation**		
4011	Railroads, Line-haul Operating	482111	Line-Haul Railroads
4013	Railroad Switching and Terminal Establishments		
	• Beltline and Logging Railroads	482112	Short Line Railroads
	• Other	48821	Support Activities for Rail Transportation (pt)
41	**Local and Interurban Passenger Transit**		
4111	Local and Suburban Transit		
	• Mixed Mode Transit Systems	485111	Mixed Mode Transit Systems
	• Commuter Rail Systems	485112	Commuter Rail Systems
	• Bus and Motor Vehicle Transit Systems	485113	Bus and Other Motor Vehicle Transit Systems
	• Other Urban Transit Systems	485119	Other Urban Transit Systems
	• Airport Limousine Transportation	485999	All Other Transit and Ground Passenger Transportation (pt)
4119	Local Passenger Transportation, NEC		
	• Ambulances	62191	Ambulance Service (pt)
	• Employee Transportation	48541	School and Employee Bus Transportation (pt)
	• Sightseeing Buses and Cable and Cog Railways, except Scenic	48711	Scenic and Sightseeing Transportation, Land (pt)
	• Special Needs Transportation	485991	Special Needs Transportation
	• Hearse Rental with Driver and Carpool and Vanpool Operations	485999	All Other Transit and Ground Passenger Transportation (pt)
	• Automobile Rental with Driver and Limousine Rental with Driver	48532	Limousine Service
4121	Taxicabs	48531	Taxi Service (pt)
4131	Inter-city and Rural Bus Transportation	48521	Interurban and Rural Bus Transportation
4141	Local Bus Charter Service	48551	Charter Bus Industry (pt)
4142	Bus Charter Service, except Local	48551	Charter Bus Industry (pt)
4151	School Buses	48541	School and Employee Bus Transportation (pt)
4173	Terminal and Service Facilities for Motor Vehicle Passenger Transportation	48849	Other Support Activities for Road Transportation (pt)
42	**Motor Freight Transportation and Warehousing**		
4212	Local Trucking without Storage		
	• Solid Waste Collection without Disposal	562111	Solid Waste Collection
	• Hazardous Waste Collection without Disposal	562112	Hazardous Waste Collection
	• Other Waste Collection without Disposal	562119	Other Waste Collection
	• Local General Freight Trucking without Storage	48411	General Freight Trucking, Local (pt)
	• Household Goods Moving without Storage	48421	Used Household and Office Goods Moving (pt)
	• Local Specialized Freight Trucking without Storage	48422	Specialized Freight (except Used Goods) Trucking, Local (pt)
4213	Trucking, except Local		
	• Long-distance Truckload General Freight Trucking	484121	General Freight Trucking, Long-distance, Truckload
	• Long-distance Less Than Truckload General Freight Trucking	484122	General Freight Trucking, Long-distance, Less Than Truckload

pt—Part of.

SIC Code	1987 U.S. SIC Description	NAICS Code	1997 NAICS U.S. Description
	• Long-distance Household Goods Moving	48421	Used Household and Office Goods Moving (pt)
	• Long-distance Specialized Freight Trucking	48423	Specialized Freight (except Used Goods) Trucking, Long-distance
4214	Local Trucking with Storage		
	• Local General Freight Trucking with Storage	48411	General Freight Trucking, Local (pt)
	• Local Household Goods Moving	48421	Used Household and Office Goods Moving (pt)
	• Local Specialized Freight Trucking with Storage	48422	Specialized Freight (except Used Goods) Trucking, Local (pt)
4215	Courier Services except by Air		
	• Hub and Spoke Intercity Delivery	49211	Couriers (pt)
	• Local Delivery	49221	Local Messengers and Local Delivery
4221	Farm Product Warehousing and Storage	49313	Farm Product Warehousing and Storage
4222	Refrigerated Warehousing and Storage	49312	Refrigerated Warehousing and Storage (pt)
4225	General Warehousing and Storage		
	• General Warehousing and Storage	49311	General Warehousing and Storage (pt)
	• Miniwarehouses and Self-storage Units	53113	Lessors of Miniwarehouses and Self-storage Units
4226	Special Warehousing and Storage, NEC		
	• Fur Storage	49312	Refrigerated Warehousing and Storage (pt)
	• General Warehousing in Foreign Trade Zones	49311	General Warehousing and Storage (pt)
	• Other	49319	Other Warehousing and Storage
4231	Terminal and Joint Terminal Maintenance Facilities for Motor Freight Transportation	48849	Other Support Activities for Road Transportation (pt)
43	**U.S. Postal Service**		
4311	United States Postal Service	49111	Postal Service (pt)
44	**Water Transportation**		
4412	Deep Sea Foreign Transportation of Freight	483111	Deep Sea Freight Transportation
4424	Deep Sea Domestic Transportation of Freight	483113	Coastal and Great Lakes Freight Transportation (pt)
4432	Freight Transportation on the Great Lakes - St. Lawrence Seaway	483113	Coastal and Great Lakes Freight Transportation (pt)
4449	Water Transportation of Freight, NEC	483211	Inland Water Freight Transportation
4481	Deep Sea Transportation of Passengers, except by Ferry		
	• Deep Sea Passenger Transportation	483112	Deep Sea Passenger Transportation
	• Coastal and Great Lakes Passenger Transportation	483114	Coastal and Great Lakes Passenger Transportation (pt)
4482	Ferries		
	• Coastal and Great Lakes Ferries	483114	Coastal and Great Lakes Passenger Transportation (pt)
	• Inland Water Ferries	483212	Inland Water Passenger Transportation (pt)
4489	Water Transportation of Passengers, NEC		
	• Water Taxis	483212	Inland Water Passenger Transportation (pt)
	• Airboats, Excursion Boats, and Sightseeing Boats	48721	Scenic and Sightseeing Transportation, Water (pt)
4491	Marine Cargo Handling		
	• Dock and Pier Operations	48831	Port and Harbor Operations (pt)

pt—Part of.

SIC Code	1987 U.S. SIC Description	NAICS Code	1997 NAICS U.S. Description
	• Except Dock and Pier Operations	48832	Marine Cargo Handling
4492	Towing and Tugboat Services	48833	Navigational Services to Shipping (pt)
4493	Marinas	71393	Marinas
4499	Water Transportation Services, NEC		
	• Boat and Ship Rental	532411	Commercial Air, Rail, and Water Transportation Equipment Rental and Leasing (pt)
	• Lighthouse and Canal Operations	48831	Port and Harbor Operations (pt)
	• Marine Salvage and Piloting Vessels In and Out of Harbors	48833	Navigational Services to Shipping (pt)
	• Other	48839	Other Support Activities for Water Transportation (pt)
45	**Transportation by Air**		
4512	Air Transportation, Scheduled		
	• Scheduled Passenger Air Transportation	481111	Scheduled Passenger Air Transportation
	• Scheduled Freight Air Transportation	481112	Scheduled Freight Air Transportation
4513	Air Courier Services	49211	Couriers (pt)
4522	Air Transportation, Nonscheduled		
	• Air Ambulance	62191	Ambulance Services (pt)
	• Nonscheduled Charter Freight Air Transportation	481212	Nonscheduled Chartered Freight Air Transportation
	• Nonscheduled Charter Passenger Air Transportation	481211	Nonscheduled Chartered Passenger Air Transportation
	• Sightseeing Aircraft	48799	Scenic and Sightseeing Transportation, Other (pt)
4581	Airports, Flying Fields, and Airport Terminal Services		
	• Air Traffic Control	488111	Air Traffic Control (pt)
	• Airfreight Handling at Airports, Hangar Operations, Airport Terminal Services, Aircraft Storage, Airports, and Flying Fields	488119	Other Airport Operations (pt)
	• Aircraft Cleaning and Janitorial Services	56172	Janitorial Services (pt)
	• Aircraft Servicing and Repairing	48819	Other Support Activities for Air Transportation
46	**Pipelines, except Natural Gas**		
4612	Crude Petroleum Pipelines	48611	Pipeline Transportation of Crude Oil
4613	Refined Petroleum Pipelines	48691	Pipeline Transportation of Refined Petroleum Products
4619	Pipelines, NEC	48699	All Other Pipeline Transportation
47	**Transportation Services**		
4724	Travel Agencies	56151	Travel Agencies
4725	Tour Operators	56152	Tour Operators
4729	Arrangement of Passenger Transportation, NEC		
	• Arrangement of Carpools and Vanpools	488999	All Other Support Activities for Transportation (pt)
	• Except Arrangement of Carpools and Vanpools	561599	All Other Travel Arrangement and Reservation Services (pt)

SIC to **NAICS**

pt—Part of.

SIC Code	1987 U.S. SIC Description	NAICS Code	1997 NAICS U.S. Description
4731	Arrangement of Transportation of Freight and Cargo		
	• Freight Rate Auditors and Tariff Consultants	541614	Process, Physical Distribution, and Logistics Consulting Services (pt)
	• Except Freight Rate Auditors and Tariff Consultants	48851	Freight Transportation Arrangement
4741	Rental of Railroad Cars		
	• Rental of Railroad Cars	532411	Commercial Air, Rail, and Water Transportation Equipment Rental and Leasing (pt)
	• Grain Leveling in Railroad Cars, Grain Trimming for Railroad Equipment, Precooling of Fruits and Vegetables in Connection with Transportation, and Railroad Car Cleaning, Icing, Ventilating and Heating	48821	Support Activities for Rail Transportation (pt)
4783	Packing and Crating	488991	Packing and Crating
4785	Fixed Facilities and Inspection and Weighing Services for Motor Vehicle Transportation		
	• Marine Cargo Checkers	48839	Other Support Activities for Water Transportation (pt)
	• Except Marine Cargo Checkers	48849	Other Support Activities for Road Transportation (pt)
4789	Transportation Services, NEC		
	• Pipeline Terminals and Stockyards for Transportation	488999	All Other Support Activities for Transportation (pt)
	• Horse-drawn Cabs and Carriages	48711	Scenic and Sightseeing Transportation, Land (pt)
	• Dining Car Operations on a Fee or Contract Basis	72231	Food Service Contractors
	• Other	48821	Support Activities for Rail Transportation (pt)
48	**Communications**		
4812	Radiotelephone Communications		
	• Paging Carriers	513321	Paging
	• Cellular Carriers	513322	Cellular and Other Wireless Telecommunications (pt)
	• Paging and Cellular Resellers	51333	Telecommunications Resellers (pt)
4813	Telephone Communications, except Radiotelephone		
	• Except Resellers	51331	Wired Telecommunications Carriers (pt)
	• Wired Resellers	51333	Telecommunications Resellers (pt)
	• Satellite Resellers	51334	Satellite Telecommunications (pt)
4822	Telegraph and Other Message Communications	51331	Wired Telecommunications Carriers (pt)
4832	Radio Broadcasting Stations		
	• Networks	513111	Radio Networks
	• Stations	513112	Radio Stations
4833	Television Broadcasting Stations	51312	Television Broadcasting
4841	Cable and Other Pay Television Services		
	• Cable Networks	51321	Cable Networks
	• Except Cable Networks	51322	Cable and Other Program Distribution

pt—Part of.

SIC Code	1987 U.S. SIC Description	NAICS Code	1997 NAICS U.S. Description
4899	Communications Services, NEC		
	• Taxi Cab Dispatch	48531	Taxi Service (pt)
	• Ship-to-shore Broadcasting Communications	513322	Cellular and Other Wireless Telecommunications (pt)
	• Satellite Communications	51334	Satellite Telecommunications (pt)
	• Except Taxi Cab Dispatch Ship-to-shore Communications and Satellite Communications	51339	Other Telecommunications
49	**Electric, Gas, and Sanitary Services**		
4911	Electric Services		
	• Hydroelectric Power Generation	221111	Hydroelectric Power Generation (pt)
	• Electric Power Generation by Fossil Fuels	221112	Fossil Fuel Electric Power Generation (pt)
	• Electric Power Generation by Nuclear Fuels	221113	Nuclear Electric Power Generation (pt)
	• Other Electric Power Generation	221119	Other Electric Power Generation (pt)
	• Electric Power Transmission and Control	221121	Electric Bulk Power Transmission and Control (pt)
	• Electric Power Distribution	221122	Electric Power Distribution (pt)
4922	Natural Gas Transmission	48621	Pipeline Transportation of Natural Gas (pt)
4923	Natural Gas Transmission and Distribution		
	• Distribution	22121	Natural Gas Distribution (pt)
	• Transmission	48621	Pipeline Transportation of Natural Gas (pt)
4924	Natural Gas Distribution	22121	Natural Gas Distribution (pt)
4925	Mixed, Manufactured, or Liquefied Petroleum Gas Production and/or Distribution	22121	Natural Gas Distribution (pt)
4931	Electric and Other Services Combined		
	• Hydroelectric Power Generation when Combined with Other Services	221111	Hydroelectric Power Generation (pt)
	• Electric Power Generation by Fossil Fuels when Combined with Other Services	221112	Fossil Fuel Electric Power Generation (pt)
	• Electric Power Generation by Nuclear Fuels when Combined with Other Services	221113	Nuclear Electric Power Generation (pt)
	• Other Electric Power Generation when Combined with Other Services	221119	Other Electric Power Generation (pt)
	• Electric Power Transmission when Combined with Other Services	221121	Electric Bulk Power Transmission and Control (pt)
	• Electric Power Distribution when Combined with Other Services	221122	Electric Power Distribution (pt)
	• Natural Gas when Combined with Electric Services	22121	Natural Gas Distribution (pt)
4932	Gas and Other Services Combined	22121	Natural Gas Distribution (pt)
4939	Combination Utilities, NEC		
	• Hydroelectric Power Generation when Combined with Other Services	221111	Hydroelectric Power Generation (pt)
	• Electric Power Generation by Fossil Fuels when Combined with Other Services	221112	Fossil Fuel Electric Power Generation (pt)
	• Electric Power Generation by Nuclear Fuels when Combined with Other Services	221113	Nuclear Electric Power Generation (pt)
	• Other Power Generation when Combined with Other Services	221119	Other Electric Power Generation (pt)
	• Electric Power Transmission when Combined with Other Services	221121	Electric Bulk Power Transmission and Control (pt)

SIC to NAICS

pt—Part of.

SIC Code	1987 U.S. SIC Description	NAICS Code	1997 NAICS U.S. Description
	• Electric Power Distribution when Combined with Other Services	221122	Electric Power Distribution (pt)
	• Natural Gas Distribution when Combined with Other Services	22121	Natural Gas Distribution (pt)
4941	Water Supply	22131	Water Supply and Irrigation Systems (pt)
4952	Sewerage Systems	22132	Sewage Treatment Facilities
4953	Refuse Systems		
	• Materials Recovery Facilities	56292	Materials Recovery Facilities
	• Hazardous Waste Treatment and Disposal	562211	Hazardous Waste Treatment and Disposal
	• Solid Waste Landfills	562212	Solid Waste Landfills
	• Solid Waste Combustors and Incinerators	562213	Solid Waste Combustors and Incinerators
	• Other Nonhazardous Waste Treatment and Disposal	562219	Other Nonhazardous Waste Treatment and Disposal
4959	Sanitary Services, NEC		
	• Vacuuming of Airport Runways	488119	Other Airport Operations (pt)
	• Remediation Services	56291	Remediation Services (pt)
	• Malaria Control and Mosquito Eradication	56171	Exterminating and Pest Control Services (pt)
	• Other	562998	All Other Miscellaneous Waste Management Services
4961	Steam and Air-conditioning Supply	22133	Steam and Air-conditioning Supply
4971	Irrigation Systems	22131	Water Supply and Irrigation Systems (pt)
50	**Wholesale Trade—Durable Goods**		
5012	Automobiles and Other Motor Vehicles	42111	Automobile and Other Motor Vehicle Wholesalers
5013	Motor Vehicle Supplies and New Parts		
	• Sold via Retail Method	44131	Automotive Parts and Accessories Stores (pt)
	• Sold via Wholesale Method	42112	Motor Vehicle Supplies and New Part Wholesalers
5014	Tires and Tubes		
	• Sold via Retail Method	44132	Tire Dealers (pt)—Retail
	• Sold via Wholesale Method	42113	Tire and Tube Wholesalers
5015	Motor Vehicle Parts, Used		
	• Sold via Retail Method	44131	Automotive Parts and Accessories (pt)
	• Sold via Wholesale Method	42114	Motor Vehicle Part (Used) Wholesalers
5021	Furniture		
	• Sold via Retail Method	44211	Furniture Stores (pt)
	• Sold via Wholesale Method	42121	Furniture Wholesalers
5023	Home Furnishings		
	• Sold via Retail Method	44221	Floor Covering Stores (pt)
	• Sold via Wholesale Method	42122	Home Furnishing Wholesalers
5031	Lumber, Plywood, Millwork, and Wood Panels	42131	Lumber, Plywood, Millwork, and Wood Panel Wholesalers
5032	Brick, Stone, and Related Construction Materials		
	• Sold via Retail Method	44419	Other Building Material Dealers (pt)
	• Sold via Wholesale Method	42132	Brick, Stone, and Related Construction Material Wholesalers
5033	Roofing, Siding, and Insulation Materials	42133	Roofing, Siding, and Insulation Material Wholesalers

SIC to NAICS

pt—Part of.

SIC Code	1987 U.S. SIC Description	NAICS Code	1997 NAICS U.S. Description
5039	Construction Materials, NEC		
	• Sold via Retail Method	44419	Other Building Material Dealers (pt)
	• Sold via Wholesale Method	42139	Other Construction Material Wholesalers
5043	Photographic Equipment and Supplies	42141	Photographic Equipment and Supplies Wholesalers
5044	Office Equipment		
	• Sold via Retail Method	45321	Office Supplies and Stationery Stores (pt)
	• Sold via Wholesale Method	42142	Office Equipment Wholesalers
5045	Computers and Computer Peripheral Equipment and Software		
	• Sold via Wholesale Method	42143	Computer and Computer Peripheral Equipment and Software Wholesalers
	• Sold via Retail Method	44312	Computer and Software Stores (pt)—Retail
5046	Commercial Equipment, NEC	42144	Other Commercial Equipment Wholesalers
5047	Medical, Dental, and Hospital Equipment and Supplies		
	• Sold via Wholesale Method	42145	Medical, Dental, and Hospital Equipment and Supplies Wholesalers
	• Sold via Retail Method	446199	All Other Health and Personal Care Stores (pt)—Retail
5048	Ophthalmic Goods	42146	Ophthalmic Goods Wholesalers
5049	Professional Equipment and Supplies, NEC		
	• Sold via Wholesale Method	42149	Other Professional Equipment and Supplies Wholesalers
	• Sold via Retail Method	45321	Office Supplies and Stationery Stores (pt)—Retail
5051	Metals Service Centers and Offices	42151	Metals Service Centers and Offices
5052	Coal and Other Minerals and Ores	42152	Coal and Other Mineral and Ore Wholesalers
5063	Electrical Apparatus and Equipment Wiring Supplies, and Construction Materials		
	• Sold via Retail Method	44419	Other Building Material Dealers (pt)
	• Sold via Wholesale Method	42161	Electrical Apparatus and Equipment, Wiring Supplies, and Construction Material Wholesalers
5064	Electrical Appliances, Television and Radio Sets	42162	Electrical Appliance, Television, and Radio Set Wholesalers
5065	Electronic Parts and Equipment, NEC	42169	Other Electronic Parts and Equipment Wholesalers
5072	Hardware		
	• Sold via Retail Method	44413	Hardware Stores (pt)—Retail
	• Sold via Wholesale Method	42171	Hardware Wholesalers
5074	Plumbing and Heating Equipment and Supplies (Hydronics)		
	• Sold via Retail Method	44419	Other Building Material Dealers (pt)
	• Sold via Wholesale Method	42172	Plumbing and Heating Equipment and Supplies (Hydronics) Wholesalers
5075	Warm Air Heating and Air-conditioning Equipment and Supplies	42173	Warm Air Heating and Air-conditioning Equipment and Supplies Wholesalers
5078	Refrigeration Equipment and Supplies	42174	Refrigeration Equipment and Supplies Wholesalers

Go to page 23 to learn about implementation of NAICS codes in the public and private sectors.

pt—Part of.

SIC Code	1987 U.S. SIC Description	NAICS Code	1997 NAICS U.S. Description
5082	Construction and Mining (except Petroleum) Machinery and Equipment	42181	Construction and Mining (except Petroleum) Machinery and Equipment Wholesalers
5083	Farm and Garden Machinery and Equipment		
	• Sold via Wholesale Method	42182	Farm and Garden Machinery and Equipment Wholesalers
	• Sold via Retail Method	44421	Outdoor Power Equipment Stores (pt)—Retail
5084	Industrial Machinery and Equipment	42183	Industrial Machinery and Equipment Wholesalers (pt)
5085	Industrial Supplies		
	• Fluid Power Accessories	42183	Industrial Machinery and Equipment Wholesalers (pt)
	• Except Fluid Power Accessories	42184	Industrial Supplies Wholesalers
5087	Service Establishment Equipment and Supplies		
	• Sold via Wholesale Method	42185	Service Establishment Equipment and Supplies Wholesalers
	• Sold via Retail Method Beauty and Barber Shop Equipment and Supplies	44612	Cosmetics, Beauty Supplies, and Perfume Stores (pt)
5088	Transportation Equipment and Supplies, except Motor Vehicles	42186	Transportation Equipment and Supplies (except Motor Vehicles) Wholesalers
5091	Sporting and Recreational Goods and Supplies	42191	Sporting and Recreational Goods and Supplies Wholesalers
5092	Toys and Hobby Goods and Supplies	42192	Toy and Hobby Goods and Supplies Wholesalers
5093	Scrap and Waste Materials	42193	Recyclable Material Wholesalers
5094	Jewelry, Watches, Precious Stones, and Precious Metals	42194	Jewelry, Watch, Precious Stone, and Precious Metal Wholesalers
5099	Durable Goods, NEC	42199	Other Miscellaneous Durable Goods Wholesalers (pt)
51	**Wholesale Trade—Nondurable Goods**		
5111	Printing and Writing Paper	42211	Printing and Writing Paper Wholesalers
5112	Stationery and Office Supplies		
	• Sold via Retail Method	45321	Office Supplies and Stationery Stores (pt)
	• Sold via Wholesale Method	42212	Stationery and Office Supplies Wholesalers
5113	Industrial and Personal Service Paper	42213	Industrial and Personal Service Paper Wholesalers
5122	Drugs, Drug Proprietaries, and Druggists' Sundries	42221	Drugs and Druggists' Sundries Wholesalers
5131	Piece Goods, Notions, and Other Dry Goods		
	• Converters, Broadwoven Piece Good Fabric	313311	Broadwoven Fabric Finishing Mills (pt)
	• Converters, except Broadwoven Fabric	313312	Textile and Fabric Finishing (except Broadwoven Fabric) Mills (pt)
	• Except Converters	42231	Piece Goods, Notions, and Other Dry Goods Wholesalers
5136	Men's and Boys' Clothing and Furnishings	42232	Men's and Boys' Clothing and Furnishings Wholesalers
5137	Women's, Children's, and Infants' Clothing and Accessories	42233	Women's, Children's, and Infants' Clothing and Accessories Wholesalers
5139	Footwear	42234	Footwear Wholesalers

pt—Part of.

SIC Code	1987 U.S. SIC Description	NAICS Code	1997 NAICS U.S. Description
5141	Groceries, General Line	42241	General Line Grocery Wholesalers
5142	Packaged Frozen Foods	42242	Packaged Frozen Food Wholesalers
5143	Dairy Products, except Dried or Canned	42243	Dairy Products (except Dried or Canned) Wholesalers
5144	Poultry and Poultry Products	42244	Poultry and Poultry Product Wholesalers
5145	Confectionery	42245	Confectionery Wholesalers
5146	Fish and Seafoods	42246	Fish and Seafood Wholesalers
5147	Meats and Meat Products		
	• Boxed Beef	311612	Meat Processed from Carcasses (pt)
	• Except Boxed Beef	42247	Meat and Meat Product Wholesalers
5148	Fresh Fruits and Vegetables	42248	Fresh Fruit and Vegetable Wholesalers
5149	Groceries and Related Products, NEC		
	• Bottling Mineral or Spring Water	312112	Bottled Water Manufacturing (pt)
	• Except Bottling Mineral or Spring Water	42249	Other Grocery and Related Product Wholesalers
5153	Grain and Field Beans	42251	Grain and Field Bean Wholesalers
5154	Livestock	42252	Livestock Wholesalers
5159	Farm-product Raw Materials, NEC	42259	Other Farm Product Raw Material Wholesalers
5162	Plastics Materials and Basic Forms and Shapes	42261	Plastics Materials and Basic Forms and Shapes Wholesalers
5169	Chemicals and Allied Products, NEC	42269	Other Chemical and Allied Products Wholesalers
5171	Petroleum Bulk Stations and Terminals		
	• Heating Oil Sold via Retail Method	454311	Heating Oil Dealers (pt)
	• LP Gas Sold via Retail Method	454312	Liquefied Petroleum Gas (Bottled Gas) Dealers (pt)
	• Sold via Wholesale Method	42271	Petroleum Bulk Stations and Terminals
5172	Petroleum and Petroleum Products Wholesalers, except Bulk Stations and Terminals	42272	Petroleum and Petroleum Products Wholesalers (except Bulk Stations and Terminals)
5181	Beer and Ale	42281	Beer and Ale Wholesalers
5182	Wine and Distilled Alcoholic Beverages	42282	Wine and Distilled Alcoholic Beverage Wholesalers
5191	Farm Supplies		
	• Lawn and Garden Supplies Sold via Retail Method	44422	Nursery and Garden Centers (pt)—Retail
	• Except Lawn and Garden Supplies Sold via Retail Method	42291	Farm Supplies Wholesalers
5192	Books, Periodicals, and Newspapers	42292	Book, Periodical, and Newspaper Wholesalers
5193	Flowers, Nursery Stock, and Florists' Supplies		
	• Sold via Wholesale Method	42293	Flower, Nursery Stock, and Florists' Supplies Wholesalers
	• Sold via Retail Method	44422	Nursery and Garden Centers (pt)—Retail
5194	Tobacco and Tobacco Products	42294	Tobacco and Tobacco Product Wholesalers
5198	Paint, Varnishes, and Supplies	42295	Paint, Varnish, and Supplies Wholesalers
5199	Nondurable Goods, NEC		
	• Advertising Specialties Goods Distributors	54189	Other Services Related to Advertising (pt)
	• Except Advertising Specialty	42299	Other Miscellaneous Nondurable Goods Wholesalers

pt—Part of.

SIC Code	1987 U.S. SIC Description	NAICS Code	1997 NAICS U.S. Description
52	**Building Materials, Hardware, Garden Supply, and Mobile Home**		
5211	Lumber and Other Building Materials Dealers		
	• Home Centers	44411	Home Centers
	• Except Home Centers	44419	Other Building Material Dealers (pt)
5231	Paint, Glass, and Wallpaper Stores		
	• Paint and Wallpaper	44412	Paint and Wallpaper Stores (pt)
	• Glass Stores	44419	Other Building Material Dealers (pt)
5251	Hardware Stores	44413	Hardware Stores (pt)
5261	Retail Nurseries, Lawn and Garden Supply Stores		
	• Except Outdoor Power Equipment	44422	Nursery and Garden Centers (pt)
	• Outdoor Power Equipment Stores	44421	Outdoor Power Equipment Stores (pt)
5271	Mobile Home Dealers	45393	Manufactured (Mobile) Home Dealers
53	**General Merchandise Stores**		
5311	Department Stores	45211	Department Stores
5331	Variety Stores	45299	All Other General Merchandise Stores (pt)
5399	Miscellaneous General Merchandise Stores		
	• Warehouse Clubs and General Merchandise Combination Stores	45291	Warehouse Clubs and Superstores (pt)
	• All Other General Merchandise Stores	45299	All Other General Merchandise Stores (pt)
54	**Food Stores**		
5411	Grocery Stores		
	• Convenience Stores with Gas	44711	Gasoline Stations with Convenience Stores (pt)
	• Supermarkets and Grocery Stores with Little General Merchandise	44511	Supermarkets and Other Grocery (except Convenience) Stores
	• Supermarkets and Grocery Stores with Substantial General Merchandise	45291	Warehouse Clubs and Superstores (pt)
	• Convenience Stores without Gas	44512	Convenience Stores
5421	Meat and Fish (Seafood) Markets, including Freezer Provisioners		
	• Freezer Provisioners	45439	Other Direct Selling Establishments (pt)
	• Meat Markets	44521	Meat Markets (pt)
	• Fish and Seafood Markets	44522	Fish and Seafood Markets
5431	Fruit and Vegetable Markets	44523	Fruit and Vegetable Markets
5441	Candy, Nut, and Confectionery Stores		
	• Confectionery and Nut Stores	445292	Confectionery and Nut Stores
	• Chocolate Candy Stores, Preparing Candy on Premises	31133	Confectionery Manufacturing from Purchased Chocolate (pt)
	• Nonchocolate Candy Stores, Preparing Candy on Premises	31134	Nonchocolate Confectionery Manufacturing (pt)
5451	Dairy Products Stores	445299	All Other Specialty Food Stores (pt)
5461	Retail Bakeries		
	• Doughnut Shops, Pretzel Shops, Cookie Shops, Bagel Shops, and Other Such Shops that Make and Sell for Immediate Consumption	722213	Snack and Nonalcoholic Beverage Bars (pt)
	• Bakeries That Make and Sell at the Same Location	311811	Retail Bakeries
	• Sales Only of All Other Baked Goods	445291	Baked Goods Stores

pt—Part of.

SIC Code	1987 U.S. SIC Description	NAICS Code	1997 NAICS U.S. Description
5499	Miscellaneous Food Stores		
	• Poultry and Poultry Products	44521	Meat Markets (pt)
	• Food Supplement Stores	446191	Food (Health) Supplement Stores
	• All Other Miscellaneous Food Stores	445299	All Other Specialty Food Stores (pt)
55	**Automotive Dealers and Gasoline Service Stations**		
5511	Motor Vehicle Dealers (New and Used)	44111	New Car Dealers
5521	Motor Vehicle Dealers (Used Only)	44112	Used Car Dealers
5531	Auto and Home Supply Stores		
	• Tire Dealers	44132	Tire Dealers (pt)
	• Auto Supply Stores	44131	Automotive Parts and Accessories Stores (pt)
	• Other Auto and Home Supply Stores	45299	All Other General Merchandise (pt)
5541	Gasoline Service Stations		
	• With Convenience Store	44711	Gasoline Stations with Convenience Store (pt)
	• Except with Convenience Stores	44719	Other Gasoline Stations
5551	Boat Dealers	441222	Boat Dealers
5561	Recreational Vehicle Dealers	44121	Recreational Vehicle Dealers
5571	Motorcycle Dealers	441221	Motorcycle Dealers
5599	Automotive Dealers, NEC	441229	All Other Motor Vehicle Dealers
56	**Apparel and Accessory Stores**		
5611	Men's and Boys' Clothing and Accessory Stores		
	• Men's Clothing Stores	44811	Men's Clothing Stores
	• Men's Accessory Stores	44815	Clothing Accessories Stores (pt)
5621	Women's Clothing Stores	44812	Women's Clothing Stores
5632	Women's Accessory and Specialty Stores		
	• Specialty Stores	44819	Other Clothing Stores (pt)
	• Accessory Stores	44815	Clothing Accessories Stores (pt)
5641	Children's and Infants' Wear Stores	44813	Children's and Infants' Clothing Stores
5651	Family Clothing Stores	44814	Family Clothing Stores
5661	Shoe Stores	44821	Shoe Stores
5699	Miscellaneous Apparel and Accessory Stores		
	• Custom Tailors and Seamstresses	*315*	*Included in Apparel Manufacturing Subsector Based on Type of Garment Produced*
	• Miscellaneous Apparel	44819	Other Clothing Stores (pt)
	• Miscellaneous Accessories	44815	Clothing Accessories Stores (pt)
57	**Furniture, Home Furnishings and Equipment Stores**		
5712	Furniture Stores		
	• Custom Made Wood Nonupholstered Furniture, except Cabinets and Upholstered	337122	Nonupholstered Wood Household Furniture Manufacturing (pt)
	• Custom Wood Cabinets	33711	Wood Kitchen Cabinet and Countertop Manufacturing (pt)
	• Upholstered Custom Made Furniture	337121	Upholstered Household Furniture Manufacturing (pt)
	• Except Custom Cabinet and Furniture Builders	44211	Furniture Stores (pt)
5713	Floor Covering Stores	44221	Floor Covering Stores (pt)

Visit page 9 to learn more about NAICS codes.

Visit page 15 to learn more about major changes to NAICS sectors.

pt—Part of.

SIC Code	1987 U.S. SIC Description	NAICS Code	1997 NAICS U.S. Description
5714	Drapery, Curtain, and Upholstery Stores		
	• Drapery and Curtain Stores	442291	Window Treatment Stores (pt)
	• Upholstery Stores	45113	Sewing, Needlework, and Piece Goods Stores (pt)
	• Custom Drapes	314121	Curtain and Drapery Mills (pt)
	• Custom Slipcovers	314129	Other Household Textile Product Mills (pt)
5719	Miscellaneous Homefurnishings Stores		
	• Blinds and Shades	442291	Window Treatment Stores (pt)
	Pottery and Crafts Made and Sold On-site		*Included in Manufacturing Sector Based on Article Produced*
	• except Blinds, Shades, and Pottery and Crafts Made and Sold On-site	442299	All Other Home Furnishings Stores (pt)
5722	Household Appliance Stores	443111	Household Appliance Stores
5731	Radio, Television, and Consumer Electronics Stores		
	• Except Auto Radio Stores	443112	Radio, Television, and Other Electronics Stores (pt)
	• Auto Radio Stores	44131	Automotive Parts and Accessories Stores (pt)
5734	Computer and Computer Software Stores	44312	Computer and Software Stores (pt)
5735	Record and Prerecorded Tape Stores	45122	Prerecorded Tape, Compact Disc, and Record Stores
5736	Musical Instrument Stores	45114	Musical Instrument and Supplies Stores
58	**Eating and Drinking Places**		
5812	Eating and Drinking Places		
	• Full-service Restaurants	72211	Full-service Restaurants
	• Limited Service Restaurants	722211	Limited-service Restaurants
	• Cafeterias	722212	Cafeterias
	• Snack and Nonalcoholic Beverage Bars	722213	Snack and Nonalcoholic Beverage Bars (pt)
	• Food Service Contractors	72231	Food Service Contractors
	• Caterers	72232	Caterers
	• Dinner Theaters	71111	Theater Companies and Dinner Theaters (pt)
5813	Drinking Places (Alcoholic Beverages)	72241	Drinking Places (Alcoholic Beverages)
59	**Miscellaneous Retail**		
5912	Drug Stores and Proprietary Stores	44611	Pharmacies and Drug Stores
5921	Liquor Stores	44531	Beer, Wine, and Liquor Stores
5932	Used Merchandise Stores		
	• Pawnshops	522298	All Other Nondepository Credit Intermediation
	• Except Pawn Shops	45331	Used Merchandise Stores
5941	Sporting Goods Stores and Bicycle Shops	45111	Sporting Goods Stores
5942	Book Stores	451211	Book Stores
5943	Stationery Stores	45321	Office Supplies and Stationery Stores (pt)
5944	Jewelry Stores	44831	Jewelry Stores
5945	Hobby, Toy, and Game Shops	45112	Hobby, Toy, and Game Stores
5946	Camera and Photographic Supply Stores	44313	Camera and Photographic Supplies Stores
5947	Gift, Novelty, and Souvenir Shops	45322	Gift, Novelty, and Souvenir Stores
5948	Luggage and Leather Goods Stores	44832	Luggage and Leather Goods Stores

SIC to NAICS

pt—Part of.

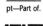

SIC Code	1987 U.S. SIC Description	NAICS Code	1997 NAICS U.S. Description
5949	Sewing, Needlework, and Piece Goods Stores	45113	Sewing, Needlework, and Piece Goods Stores (pt)
5961	Catalog and Mail-order Houses	45411	Electronic Shopping and Mail-order Houses
5962	Automatic Merchandising Machine Operator	45421	Vending Machine Operators
5963	Direct Selling Establishments		
	• Mobile Food Wagons	72233	Mobile Food Services
	• All Other Direct Selling Establishments	45439	Other Direct Selling Establishments (pt)
5983	Fuel Oil Dealers	454311	Heating Oil Dealers (pt)
5984	Liquefied Petroleum Gas (Bottled Gas) Dealers	454312	Liquefied Petroleum Gas (Bottled Gas) Dealers (pt)
5989	Fuel Dealers, NEC	454319	Other Fuel Dealers
5992	Florists	45311	Florists
5993	Tobacco Stores and Stands	453991	Tobacco Stores
5994	News Dealers and Newsstands	451212	News Dealers and Newsstands
5995	Optical Goods Stores		
	• Optical Stores Grinding Prescription Lenses, except One-hour Labs	339115	Ophthalmic Goods Manufacturing (pt)
	• Except Optical Laboratories Grinding Prescription Lenses	44613	Optical Goods Stores
5999	Miscellaneous Retail Stores, NEC		
	• Cosmetic Stores	44612	Cosmetics, Beauty Supplies, and Perfume Stores (pt)
	• Hearing Aid and Artificial Limb Stores	446199	All Other Health and Personal Care Stores (pt)
	• Pets and Pet Supply Stores	45391	Pet and Pet Supplies Stores
	• Art Dealers	45392	Art Dealers
	• Telephone and Typewriter Stores	443112	Radio, Television, and Other Electronics Stores (pt)
	• Other Miscellaneous Retail Stores	453998	All Other Miscellaneous Store Retailers (except Tobacco Stores) (pt)

60	Depository Institutions		
6011	Federal Reserve Banks	52111	Monetary Authorities—Central Banks
6019	Central Reserve Depository Institutions, NEC	522298	All Other Nondepository Credit Intermediation (pt)
6021	National Commercial Banks		
	• Commercial Banks	52211	Commercial Banking (pt)
	• Credit Card Issuing	52221	Credit Card Issuing (pt)
6022	State Commercial Banks		
	• Commercial Banks	52211	Commercial Banking (pt)
	• Credit Card Issuing	52221	Credit Card Issuing (pt)
	• Private and Industrial Banking	52219	Other Depository Intermediation
6029	Commercial Banks, NEC	52211	Commercial Banking (pt)
6035	Savings Institutions, Federally Chartered	52212	Savings Institutions (pt)
6036	Savings institutions, not Federally Chartered	52212	Savings Institutions (pt)
6061	Credit Unions, Federally Chartered	52213	Credit Unions (pt)
6062	Credit Unions, not Federally Chartered	52213	Credit Unions (pt)
6081	Branches and Agencies of Foreign Banks		
	• International Trade Financing	522293	International Trade Financing (pt)
	• Branches of Foreign Banks	52211	Commercial Banking (pt)
	• Agencies of Foreign Banks, except International Trade Financing	522298	All Other Nondepository Credit Intermediation (pt)

pt—Part of.

SIC Code	1987 U.S. SIC Description	NAICS Code	1997 NAICS U.S. Description
6082	Foreign Trade and International Banking Institutions		
	• International Trade Financing	522293	International Trade Financing (pt)
	• Except International Trade Financing	522298	All Other Nondepository Credit Intermediation (pt)
6091	Nondeposit Trust Facilities	523991	Trust, Fiduciary, and Custody Activities (pt)
6099	Functions Related to Deposit Banking, NEC		
	• Clearinghouses and Electronic Funds Transfer	52232	Financial Transactions Processing, Reserve, and Clearinghouse Activities (pt)
	• Foreign Currency Exchange	52313	Commodity Contracts Dealing (pt)
	• Escrow and Fiduciary Agencies	523991	Trust, Fiduciary, and Custody Activities (pt)
	• Other	52239	Other Activities Related to Credit Intermediation (pt)

61 Nondepository Credit Institutions

SIC Code	1987 U.S. SIC Description	NAICS Code	1997 NAICS U.S. Description
6111	Federal and Federally-sponsored Credit Agencies		
	• Federal Land Banks	522292	Real Estate Credit (pt)
	• Trade Banks	522293	International Trade Financing (pt)
	• Secondary Market Financing	522294	Secondary Market Financing
	• Other	522298	All Other Nondepository Credit Intermediation (pt)
6141	Personal Credit Institutions		
	• Credit Card Issuing	52221	Credit Card Issuing (pt)
	• Installment Sales Financing	52222	Sales Financing (pt)
	• Industrial Nondeposit Banks	522298	All Other Nondepository Credit Intermediation (pt)
	• Other	522291	Consumer Lending
6153	Short-term Business Credit Institutions, except Agricultural		
	• Credit Card Issuing	52221	Credit Card Issuing (pt)
	• Business Sales Finance	52222	Sales Financing (pt)
	• Credit Card Service	52232	Financial Transactions Processing, Reserve, and Clearinghouse Activities (pt)
	• Other	52391	Miscellaneous Intermediation (pt)
6159	Miscellaneous Business Credit Institutions		
	• Finance Leasing Combined with Loan Making	522	*Included in Credit Intermediation and Related Activities Subsector by Type of Credit*
	• Finance Leasing Combined with Sales Financing	52222	Sales Financing (pt)
	• Farm Mortgage Companies	522292	Real Estate Credit (pt)
	• Finance Leasing Without Loan Making	532	*Included in Rental and Leasing Services Subsector by Type of Equipment and Method of Operation*
	• Trade Banks	522293	International Trade Financing (pt)
	• Secondary Market Financing	522294	Secondary Market Financing (pt)
	• All Other	522298	All Other Nondepository Credit Intermediation (pt)
6162	Mortgage Bankers and Loan Correspondents		
	• Mortgage Bankers and Originators	522292	Real Estate Credit
	• Mortgage Servicing	52239	Other Activities Related to Credit Intermediation (pt)

pt—Part of.

SIC to NAICS

SIC Code	1987 U.S. SIC Description	NAICS Code	1997 NAICS U.S. Description
6163	Loan Brokers	52231	Mortgage and Nonmortgage Loan Brokers
62	**Security, Commodity Brokers, and Services**		
6211	Security Brokers, Dealers, and Flotation Companies		
	• Security Dealers and Underwriters	52311	Investment Banking and Securities Dealing
	• Security Brokers	52312	Securities Brokerage
	• Dealers and Brokers, except Securities Commodities, and Oil and Gas Lease	52391	Miscellaneous Intermediation (pt)
	• Oil and Gas Lease Brokers' Offices	523999	Miscellaneous Financial Investment Activities (pt)
6221	Commodity Contracts Brokers and Dealers		
	• Commodity Dealers	52313	Commodity Contracts Dealing (pt)
	• Commodity Brokers	52314	Commodity Contracts Brokerage
6231	Security and Commodity Exchanges	52321	Securities and Commodity Exchanges
6282	Investment Advice		
	• Portfolio Managers	52392	Portfolio Management (pt)
	• Other	52393	Investment Advice
6289	Services Allied with the Exchange of Securities or Commodities, NEC		
	• Securities Custodians	523991	Trust, Fiduciary, and Custody Activities (pt)
	• Other	523999	Miscellaneous Financial Investment Activities (pt)
63	**Insurance Carriers**		
6311	Life Insurance		
	• Life Insurers, Direct	524113	Direct Life Insurance Carriers
	• Reinsurance Carriers, Life	52413	Reinsurance Carriers (pt)
6321	Accident and Health Insurance		
	• Disability Insurers, Direct	524113	Direct Life Insurance Carriers (pt)
	• Accident and Health Insurers, Direct	524114	Direct Health and Medical Insurance Carriers (pt)
	• Self Insurers	52519	Other Insurance Funds (pt)
	• Reinsurance Carriers, Accident and Health	52413	Reinsurance Carriers (pt)
6324	Hospital and Medical Service Plans		
	• Health and Medical Insurers, Direct	524114	Direct Health and Medical Insurance Carriers (pt)
	• Self Insurers	52519	Other Insurance Funds (pt)
	• Reinsurance Carriers, Health and Medical	52413	Reinsurance Carriers (pt)
6331	Fire, Marine, and Casualty Insurance		
	• Fire, Marine, and Casualty Insurers, Direct	524126	Direct Property and Casualty Insurance Carriers (pt)
	• Contact Lens Insurance	524128	Other Direct Insurance (except Life, Health, and Medical) Carriers (pt)
	• Self Insurers	52519	Other Insurance Funds (pt)
	• Reinsurance Carriers, Fire, Marine, and Casualty	52413	Reinsurance Carriers (pt)
6351	Surety Insurance		
	• Financial Responsibility Insurers, Direct	524126	Direct Property and Casualty Insurance Carriers (pt)
	• Reinsurance Carriers, Financial Responsibility	52413	Reinsurance Carriers (pt)

Visit page 15 to learn more about major changes to NAICS sectors.

pt—Part of.

SIC Code	1987 U.S. SIC Description	NAICS Code	1997 NAICS U.S. Description
6361	Title Insurance		
	• Title Insurers, Direct	524127	Direct Title Insurance Carriers
	• Reinsurance Carriers, Title	52413	Reinsurance Carriers (pt)
6371	Pension, Health, and Welfare Funds		
	• Managers	52392	Portfolio Management (pt)
	• Administrators	524292	Third Party Administration of Insurance and Pension Funds (pt)
	• Pension Funds	52511	Pension Funds
	• Health and Welfare Funds	52512	Health and Welfare Funds
	• Profit Sharing Funds	52599	Other Financial Vehicles (pt)
6399	Insurance Carriers, NEC	524128	Other Direct Insurance (except Life, Health, and Medical) Carriers

64   Insurance Agents, Brokers, and Service

SIC Code	1987 U.S. SIC Description	NAICS Code	1997 NAICS U.S. Description
6411	Insurance Agents, Brokers, and Service		
	• Insurance Agents and Brokers	52421	Insurance Agencies and Brokerages
	• Claim Adjusters	524291	Claims Adjusting
	• Claim Processors	524292	Third Party Administrators of Insurance and Pension Funds (pt)
	• Other	524298	All Other Insurance Related Activities

65   Real Estate

SIC Code	1987 U.S. SIC Description	NAICS Code	1997 NAICS U.S. Description
6512	Operators of Nonresidential Buildings		
	• Stadium and Arena Owners	71131	Promoters of Performing Arts, Sports, and Similar Events with Facilities (pt)
	• Except Stadium and Arena Owners	53112	Lessors of Nonresidential Buildings (except Miniwarehouses)
6513	Operators of Apartment Buildings	53111	Lessors of Residential Buildings and Dwellings (pt)
6514	Operators of Dwellings Other Than Apartment Buildings	53111	Lessors of Residential Buildings and Dwellings (pt)
6515	Operators of Residential Mobile Home Sites	53119	Lessors of Other Real Estate Property(pt)
6517	Lessors of Railroad Property	53119	Lessors of Other Real Estate Property (pt)
6519	Lessors of Real Property, NEC	53119	Lessors of Other Real Estate Property (pt)
6531	Real Estate Agents and Managers		
	• Real Estate Agents and Brokers	53121	Offices of Real Estate Agents and Brokers
	• Condominium Associations	81399	Other Similar Organizations (except Business, Professional, Labor, and Political Organizations) (pt)
	• Residential Property Managers	531311	Residential Property Managers
	• Nonresidential Property Managers	531312	Nonresidential Property Managers
	• Real Estate Appraisers	53132	Offices of Real Estate Appraisers
	• Cemetery Management	81222	Cemeteries and Crematories (pt)
	• Other	53139	Other Activities Related to Real Estate
6541	Title Abstract Offices	541191	Title Abstract and Settlement Offices
6552	Land Subdividers and Developers, except Cemeteries	23311	Land Subdivision and Land Development
6553	Cemetery Subdividers and Developers	81222	Cemeteries and Crematories (pt)

67   Holding and Other Investment Offices

SIC Code	1987 U.S. SIC Description	NAICS Code	1997 NAICS U.S. Description
6712	Offices of Bank Holding Companies	551111	Offices of Bank Holding Companies
6719	Offices of Holding Companies, NEC	551112	Offices of Other Holding Companies
6722	Management Investment Offices, Open-end	52591	Open-end Investment Funds

pt—Part of.

SIC to NAICS

SIC Code	1987 U.S. SIC Description	NAICS Code	1997 NAICS U.S. Description
6726	Unit Investment Trusts, Face-amount Certificate Offices, and Closed-end Management Investment Offices	52599	Other Financial Vehicles
6732	Education, Religious, and Charitable Trusts	813211	Grantmaking Foundations
6733	Trusts, except Educational, Religious, and Charitable		
	• Managers	52392	Portfolio Management (pt)
	• Administrators of Private Estates	523991	Trust, Fiduciary, and Custody Services (pt)
	• Vacation Funds for Employees	52519	Other Insurance Funds (pt)
	• Personal Trusts, Estates, and Agency Accounts	52592	Trusts, Estates, and Agency Accounts
6792	Oil Royalty Traders		
	• Investing on Own Account	52391	Miscellaneous Intermediation (pt)
	• Oil Royalty Companies	53311	Lessors of Nonfinancial Intangible Assets (except Copyrighted Works) (pt)
6794	Patent Owners and Lessors	53311	Lessors of Nonfinancial Intangible Assets (except Copyrighted Works) (pt)
6798	Real Estate Investment Trusts	52593	Real Estate Investment Trusts
6799	Investors, NEC		
	• Venture Capital Companies, Investment Clubs, and Operators on Own Account	52391	Miscellaneous Intermediation (pt)
	• Commodity Contract Pool Operators	52392	Portfolio Management (pt)
	• Commodity Contract Trading Companies	52313	Commodity Contracts Dealing (pt)
70	**Hotels, Rooming Houses, Camps, and Other Lodging Places**		
7011	Hotels and Motels		
	• Hotels and Motels, except Casino Hotels	72111	Hotels (except Casino Hotels) and Motels (pt)
	• Casino Hotels	72112	Casino Hotels
	• Bed and Breakfast Inns	721191	Bed and Breakfast Inns
	• Other	721199	All Other Traveler Accommodation
7021	Rooming and Boarding Houses	72131	Rooming and Boarding Houses (pt)
7032	Sporting and Recreational Camps	721214	Recreational and Vacation Camps (except Campgrounds)
7033	Recreational Vehicle Parks and Campsites	721211	RV (Recreational Vehicle Parks) and Campgrounds
7041	Organization Hotels and Lodging Houses, on Membership Basis		
	• Organization Hotels	72111	Hotels (except Casino Hotels) and Motels (pt)
	• Other	72131	Rooming and Boarding Houses (pt)
72	**Personal Services**		
7211	Power Laundries, Family and Commercial	81232	Drycleaning and Laundry Services (except Coin-operated) (pt)
7212	Garment Pressing, and Agents for Laundries and Drycleaners	81232	Drycleaning and Laundry Services (except Coin-operated) (pt)
7213	Linen Supply	812331	Linen Supply (pt)
7215	Coin-operated Laundries and Drycleaning	81231	Coin-operated Laundries and Drycleaners
7216	Drycleaning Plants, except Rug Cleaning	81232	Drycleaning and Laundry Services (except Coin-operated) (pt)

pt—Part of.

SIC to NAICS

SIC Code	1987 U.S. SIC Description	NAICS Code	1997 NAICS U.S. Description
7217	Carpet and Upholstery Cleaning	56174	Carpet and Upholstery Cleaning Services
7218	Industrial Launderers	812332	Industrial Launderers
7219	Laundry and Garment Services, NEC		
	• Diaper Service	812331	Linen Supply (pt)
	• Clothing Alteration and Repair	81149	Other Personal and Household Goods Repair and Maintenance (pt)
	• Except Diaper Service and Clothing Alteration and Repair	81232	Drycleaning and Laundry Services (except Coin-operated)
7221	Photographic Studios, Portrait	541921	Photographic Studios, Portrait
7231	Beauty Shops		
	• Beauty Shops and Salons	812112	Beauty Salons
	• Manicure and Pedicure Salons	812113	Nail Salons
	• Beauty and Cosmetology Schools	611511	Cosmetology and Barber Schools (pt)
7241	Barber Shops		
	• Barber Shops	812111	Barber Shops
	• Barber Colleges	611511	Cosmetology and Barber Schools (pt)
7251	Shoe Repair Shops and Shoeshine Parlors		
	• Shoe Repair Shops	81143	Footwear and Leather Goods Repair (pt)
	• Shoeshine Parlors	81299	All Other Personal Services (pt)
7261	Funeral Services and Crematories		
	• Crematories	81222	Cemeteries and Crematories (pt)
	• Funeral Homes and Funeral Services	81221	Funeral Homes
7291	Tax Return Preparation Services	541213	Tax Preparation Services
7299	Miscellaneous Personal Services, NEC		
	• Babysitting Bureaus	56131	Employment Placement Agencies (pt)
	• Diet and Weight Reducing Services	812191	Diet and Weight Reducing Centers
	• Valet Parking Services	81293	Parking Lots and Garages (pt)
	• Formal Wear and Costume Rental	53222	Formal Wear and Costume Rental (pt)
	• Personal Care Services	812199	Other Personal Care Services
	• All Other Miscellaneous Personal Services, NEC	81299	All Other Personal Services (pt)
73	**Business Services**		
7311	Advertising Agencies	54181	Advertising Agencies
7312	Outdoor Advertising Services	54185	Display Advertising (pt)
7313	Radio, Television, and Publishers' Advertising Representatives	54184	Media Representatives
7319	Advertising, NEC		
	• Media Buying Services	54183	Media Buying Agencies
	• Display Advertising, except Outdoor	54185	Display Advertising (pt)
	• Advertising Materials Distributor Services	54187	Advertising Material Distribution Services
	• Other	54189	Other Services Related to Advertising (pt)
7322	Adjustment and Collection Services	56144	Collection Agencies
7323	Credit Reporting Services	56145	Credit Bureaus
7331	Direct Mail Advertising Services		
	• Mailing List Compilers	51114	Database and Directory Publishers (pt)
	• Other	54186	Direct Mail Advertising
7334	Photocopying and Duplicating Services		
	• Instant Printing	323114	Quick Printing (pt)
	• Photocopying and Duplicating Services, except Instant Printing	561439	Other Business Service Centers (including Copy Shops) (pt)

pt—Part of.

SIC Code	1987 U.S. SIC Description	NAICS Code	1997 NAICS U.S. Description
7335	Commercial Photography	541922	Commercial Photography (pt)
7336	Commercial Art and Graphic Design	54143	Graphic Design Services (pt)
7338	Secretarial and Court Reporting Services		
	• Secretarial Services	56141	Document Preparation Services
	• Court Reporting Services	561492	Court Reporting and Stenotype Services
7342	Disinfecting and Pest Control Services		
	• Disinfecting Services	56172	Janitorial Services (pt)
	• Exterminating and Pest Control Services	56171	Exterminating and Pest Control Services (pt)
7349	Building Cleaning and Maintenance Services, NEC		
	• Lighting Maintenance Services	56179	Other Services to Buildings and Dwellings (pt)
	• Except Lighting Maintenance Services	56172	Janitorial Services (pt)
7352	Medical Equipment Rental and Leasing		
	• Home Health Furniture and Equipment Rental and Leasing	532291	Home Health Equipment Rental
	• Medical Machinery Rental and Leasing	53249	Other Commercial and Industrial Machinery and Equipment Rental and Leasing (pt)
7353	Heavy Construction Equipment Rental and Leasing		
	• With Operator	23499	All Other Heavy Construction (pt)
	• Without Operator	532412	Construction, Mining, and Forestry Machinery and Equipment Rental and Leasing (pt)
7359	Equipment Rental and Leasing, NEC		
	• Consumer Electronics and Appliances Rental	53221	Consumer Electronics and Appliances Rental
	• General Rental Centers	53231	General Rental Centers
	• Residential Furniture, Party Supplies, and All Other Miscellaneous Consumer Goods Rental and Leasing	532299	All Other Consumer Goods Rental
	• Oilfield and Well Drilling Machinery and Equipment Rental and Leasing	532412	Construction, Mining, and Forestry Machinery and Equipment Rental and Leasing (pt)
	• Aircraft Rental and Leasing	532411	Commercial Air, Rail, and Water Transportation Equipment Rental and Leasing (pt)
	• Portable Toilet Rental	562991	Septic Tank and Related Services (pt)
	• Office Machinery and Equipment Rental and Leasing	53242	Office Machinery and Equipment Rental and Leasing (pt)
	• Industrial Trucks Rental and Leasing	53249	Other Commercial and Industrial Machinery and Equipment Rental and Leasing (pt)
7361	Employment Agencies		
	• Executive Placing Services	541612	Human Resources and Executive Search Consulting Services (pt)
	• Except Executive Placing Services	56131	Employment Placement Agencies (pt)
7363	Help Supply Services		
	• Temporary Help Supply	56132	Temporary Help Services
	• Employee Leasing Services	56133	Employee Leasing Services

pt—Part of.

SIC Code	1987 U.S. SIC Description	NAICS Code	1997 NAICS U.S. Description
7371	Computer Programming Services	541511	Custom Computer Programming Services
7372	Prepackaged Software		
	• Software Publishing	51121	Software Publishers
	• Reproduction of Software	334611	Software Reproducing
7373	Computer Integrated Systems Design	541512	Computer Systems Design Services (pt)
7374	Computer Processing and Data Preparation and Processing Services	51421	Data Processing Services
7375	Information Retrieval Services	514191	Online Information Services
7376	Computer Facilities Management Services	541513	Computer Facilities Management Services
7377	Computer Rental and Leasing	53242	Office Machinery and Equipment Rental and Leasing (pt)
7378	Computer Maintenance and Repair		
	• Retailing Computers from a Storefront and Repairing	44312	Computer and Software Stores (pt)
	• All Other Repair	811212	Computer and Office Machine Repair and Maintenance (pt)
7379	Computer Related Services, NEC		
	• Disk and Diskette Conversion and Recertification	51421	Data Processing Services (pt)
	• Computer Systems Consultants	541512	Computer Systems Design Services (pt)
	• Except Computer Systems Consultants and Disk and Diskette Conversion and Recertification	541519	Other Computer Related Services
7381	Detective, Guard, and Armored Car Services		
	• Detective Services	561611	Investigation Services
	• Guard Services	561612	Security Guards and Patrol Services
	• Armored Car Services	561613	Armored Car Services
7382	Security Systems Services	561621	Security Systems Services (except Locksmiths) (pt)
7383	News Syndicates		
	• Independent Correspondents	71151	Independent Artists, Writers, and Performers (pt)
	• Except Independent Correspondents	51411	News Syndicates
7384	Photofinishing Laboratories		
	• Photofinishing Laboratories (except One-hour)	812921	Photofinishing Laboratories (except One-hour)
	• One-hour Photofinishing	812922	One-hour Photo Finishing
7389	Business Services, NEC		
	• Sound Recording Studios	51224	Sound Recording Studios
	• Audio Taping Services	51229	Other Sound Recording Industries (pt)
	• Stock Photo Agencies and Press Clipping Services	514199	All Other Information Services (pt)
	• Process Services, Patent Agents, Notaries Public and Paralegal Services	541199	All Other Legal Services
	• Bail Bonding	81299	All Other Personal Services (pt)
	• Mapmaking Services	54137	Surveying and Mapping (except Geophysical) Services (pt)
	• Interior Design	54141	Interior Design Services
	• Industrial Design	54142	Industrial Design Services
	• Drafting Service	54134	Drafting Services
	• Fashion and Other Design Services	54149	Other Specialized Design Services

pt—Part of.

SIC Code	1987 U.S. SIC Description	NAICS Code	1997 NAICS U.S. Description
	• Sign Painting and Lettering Shops, Showcard Painting, Mannequin Decorating Services, and Other Advertising Related Business Services	54189	Other Services Related to Advertising (pt)
	• Translation and Interpretation Services	54193	Translation and Interpretation Services
	• Home and Building Inspection Services	54135	Building Inspection Services
	• Appraisers, except Insurance and Real Estate, and Miscellaneous Professional, Scientific, and Technical Services	54199	All Other Professional, Scientific, and Technical Services
	• Microfilm Services	51421	Data Processing Services (pt)
	• Agents and Brokers for Authors and Artists and Speaker Bureaus	71141	Agents and Managers for Artists, Athletes, Entertainers, and Other Public Figures (pt)
	• Yacht Brokers	42186	Transportation Equipment and Supplies (except Motor Vehicle) Wholesalers
	• Telephone Answering Services	561421	Telephone Answering Services
	• Aerosol Packaging	325998	All Other Miscellaneous Chemical Product and Preparation Manufacturing (pt)
	• Telemarketing Bureaus and Telephone Soliciting Services	561422	Telemarketing Bureaus
	• Private Mail Centers and Mail Box Rental	561431	Private Mail Centers
	• Business Service Centers, except Private Mail Centers and Mail Box Rental	561439	Other Business Service Centers (including Copy Shops)
	• Embroidery of Advertising on Shirts and Rug Binding for the Trade	314999	All Other Miscellaneous Textile Product Mills (pt)
	• Sponging Fabric for Tailors and Dressmakers	313311	Broadwoven Fabric Finishing Mills (pt)
	• Distribution of Telephone Directories on a Fee or Contract Basis	54187	Advertising Material Distribution Services
	• Post Office Contract Stations	49111	Postal Services (pt)
	• Apparel Pressing for the Trade	81232	Drycleaning and Laundry Services (except Coin-operated)
	• Recovery and Repossession	561491	Repossession Services (pt)
	• Packaging and Labeling Services	56191	Packaging and Labeling Services
	• Swimming Pool Cleaning and Maintenance	56179	Other Services to Buildings and Dwellings (pt)
	• Hotel and Restaurant Reservation Services and Time Share Condominium Exchange	561599	All Other Travel Arrangement and Reservation Services (pt)
	• Convention and Trade Show Services	56192	Convention and Trade Show Organizers
	• Convention and Visitors Bureaus and Tourist Information Service	561591	Convention and Visitors Bureaus
	• Credit Card and Check Validation Services	52232	Financial Transactions, Processing, Reserve, and Clearinghouse Activities (pt)
	• Business Support Services, except Telephone Answering, Telemarketing Bureaus, Private Mail Centers, and Repossession Services	561499	All Other Business Support Services
	• All Other Support Services	56199	All Other Support Services
75	**Automotive Repair, Services, and Parking**		
7513	Truck Rental and Leasing, without Drivers	53212	Truck, Utility Trailer, and RV (Recreational Vehicle) Rental and Leasing (pt)
7514	Passenger Car Rental	532111	Passenger Cars Rental

Visit page 9 to learn more about NAICS codes.

Visit page 15 to learn more about major changes to NAICS sectors.

pt—Part of.

SIC Code	1987 U.S. SIC Description	NAICS Code	1997 NAICS U.S. Description
7515	Passenger Car Leasing	532112	Passenger Cars Leasing
7519	Utility Trailer and Recreational Vehicle Rental	53212	Truck, Utility Trailer and RV (Recreational Vehicles) Rental and Leasing (pt)
7521	Automobile Parking	81293	Parking Lots and Garages (pt)
7532	Top, Body, and Upholstery Repair Shops and Paint Shops	811121	Automotive Body, Paint, and Interior Repair and Maintenance
7533	Automotive Exhaust System Repair Shops	811112	Automotive Exhaust System Repair
7534	Tire Retreading and Repair Shops		
	• Retreading	326212	Tire Retreading
	• Repair	811198	All Other Automotive Repair and Maintenance (pt)
7536	Automotive Glass Replacement Shops	811122	Automotive Glass Replacement Shops (pt)
7537	Automotive Transmission Repair Shops	811113	Automotive Transmission Repair
7538	General Automotive Repair Shops	811111	General Automotive Repair
7539	Automotive Repair Shops, NEC	811118	Other Automotive Mechanical and Electrical Repair and Maintenance
7542	Carwashes	811192	Carwashes
7549	Automotive Services, except Repair and Carwashes		
	• Automotive Window Tinting	811122	Automotive Glass Replacement Shops (pt)
	• Lubricating Services, Automotive	811191	Automotive Oil Change and Lubrication Shops
	• Towing	48841	Motor Vehicle Towing
	• Except Automotive Window Tinting, Lubricating Services, and Towing	811198	All Other Automotive Repair and Maintenance (pt)
76	**Miscellaneous Repair Services**		
7622	Radio and Television Repair Shops		
	• Retailing New Electronic Equipment from a Storefront and Repairing	443112	Radio, Television, and Other Electronics Stores (pt)
	• Other Stereo, TV, VCR, and Radio Repair	811211	Consumer Electronics Repair and Maintenance (pt)
	• Other Telecommunications Equipment Repair	811213	Communication Equipment Repair and Maintenance (pt)
7623	Refrigeration and Air-conditioning Services and Repair Shops		
	• Retailing New Refrigerators from a Storefront and Repairing Refrigerators	443111	Household Appliance Stores (pt)
	• Commercial Refrigerator Equipment Repair	81131	Commercial and Industrial Machinery and Equipment (except Automotive and Electronic) Repair and Maintenance (pt)
	• Except Commercial and Retailing New Refrigerators from a Storefront and Repairing Refrigerators	811412	Appliance Repair and Maintenance (pt)
7629	Electrical and Electronic Repair Shops, NEC		
	• Retailing New Electrical and Electronic Appliances from a Storefront and Repairing	443111	Household Appliance Stores (pt)
	• Business and Office Machine Repair, Electrical	811212	Computer and Office Machine Repair and Maintenance (pt)
	• Telephone Set Repair	811213	Communication Equipment Repair and Maintenance (pt)

pt—Part of.

SIC Code	1987 U.S. SIC Description	NAICS Code	1997 NAICS U.S. Description
	• Electrical Measuring Instrument Repair and Calibration, Medical Equipment Repair, Electrical	811219	Other Electronic and Precision Equipment Repair and Maintenance (pt)
	• Appliance Repair, Electrical; Washing Machine Repair; Electric Razor Repair (except Retailing New Appliances from a Storefront)	811412	Appliance Repair and Maintenance (pt)
	• Other Consumer Electronic Equipment Repair except Computer, Radio, Television, Stereo, and VCR	811211	Consumer Electronics Repair and Maintenance (pt)
7631	Watch, Clock, and Jewelry Repair	81149	Other Personal and Household Goods Repair and Maintenance (pt)
7641	Reupholstery and Furniture Repair		
	• Antique Furniture Restoration	71151	Independent Artists, Writers, and Performers (pt)
	• Except Antique Furniture Restoration	81142	Reupholstery and Furniture Repair
7692	Welding Repair	81131	Commercial and Industrial Machinery and Equipment (except Automotive and Electronic) Repair and Maintenance (pt)
7694	Armature Rewinding Shops		
	• Repair	81131	Commercial and Industrial Machinery and Equipment (except Automotive and Electronic) Repair and Maintenance (pt)
	• Remanufacturing	335312	Motor and Generator Manufacturing (pt)
7699	Repair Shops and Related Services, NEC		
	• Boiler Cleaning	23511	Plumbing, Heating, and Air-conditioning Contractors (pt)
	• Custom Picture Framing	442299	All Other Home Furnishings Stores (pt)
	• Locksmith Shops	561622	Locksmiths
	• Cesspool and Septic Tank Cleaning	562991	Septic Tank and Related Services (pt)
	• Furnace Ducts, Chimney, and Gutter Cleaning Services	56179	Other Services to Buildings and Dwellings (pt)
	• Sewer Cleaning and Rodding	562998	All Other Miscellaneous Waste Management Services (pt)
	• Ship Scaling	48839	Other Supporting Activities for Water Transportation (pt)
	• Other Non-automotive Transportation Equipment and Industrial Machinery and Equipment	81131	Commercial and Industrial Machinery and Equipment (except Automotive and Electronic) Repair and Maintenance (pt)
	• Retailing New Bicycles from a Storefront and Repairing Bicycles	45111	Sporting Goods Stores (pt)
	• Farriers	11521	Support Activities for Animal Production (pt)
	• Camera Repair	811211	Consumer Electronics Repair and Maintenance (pt)
	• Typewriter Repair	811212	Computer and Office Machine Repair and Maintenance (pt)
	• Dental Instrument Repair, Laboratory Instrument Repair, Medical Equipment and Other Electronic and Precision Equipment Repair, except Typewriters	811219	Other Electronic and Precision Equipment Repair and Maintenance (pt)

SIC to NAICS

pt—Part of.

SIC Code	1987 U.S. SIC Description	NAICS Code	1997 NAICS U.S. Description
	• Lawnmower Repair Shops, Sharpening and Repairing Knives, Saws, and Tools	811411	Home and Garden Equipment Repair and Maintenance
	• Taxidermists, and Antique Repair and Maintenance, except Antique Car Restoration	71151	Independent Artists, Writers, and Performers
	• Gas Appliance Repair Service, Sewing Machine Repair, Stove Repair Shops, and Other Non-Electrical Appliances	811412	Appliance Repair and Maintenance (pt)
	• Leather Goods Repair Shops, Luggage Repair Shops, Pocketbook Repair Shops	81143	Footwear and Leather Goods Repair (pt)
	• Except Industrial, Electronic, Home and Garden, Appliance, Locksmith, and Leather Goods	81149	Other Personal and Household Goods Repair and Maintenance (pt)

78 Motion Pictures

SIC Code	1987 U.S. SIC Description	NAICS Code	1997 NAICS U.S. Description
7812	Motion Picture and Video Tape Production	51211	Motion Picture and Video Production
7819	Services Allied to Motion Picture Production		
	• Teleproduction and Post-production Services	512191	Teleproduction and Other Post-production Services
	• Casting Bureaus	56131	Employment Placement Agencies (pt)
	• Wardrobe Rental (Motion Pictures)	53222	Formal Wear and Costumes Rental (pt)
	• Rental of Motion Picture Equipment	53249	Other Commercial and Industrial Machinery and Equipment Rental and Leasing (pt)
	• Talent Payment Services	541214	Payroll Services (pt)
	• Film Directors and Related Motion Picture Production Services, Independent	71151	Independent Artists, Writers, and Performers (pt)
	• Reproduction of Video	334612	Prerecorded Compact Disc (except Software), Tape, and Record Manufacturing (pt)
	• All Other Services	512199	Other Motion Picture and Video Industries (pt)
7822	Motion Picture and Video Tape Distribution		
	• Prerecorded Video Tapes (Wholesaling of)	42199	Other Miscellaneous Durable Goods Wholesalers (pt)
	• All Other	51212	Motion Picture and Video Distribution (pt)
7829	Services Allied to Motion Picture Distribution		
	• Booking Agencies	512199	Other Motion Picture and Video Industries (pt)
	• Film Archives	51412	Libraries and Archives (pt)
	• Commercial Distribution Film Libraries	51212	Motion Picture and Video Distribution (pt)
7832	Motion Picture Theaters, except Drive-in	512131	Motion Picture Theaters, except Drive-in
7833	Drive-in Motion Picture Theaters	512132	Drive-in Motion Picture Theaters
7841	Video Tape Rental	53223	Video Tapes and Disc Rental

79 Amusement and Recreational Services

SIC Code	1987 U.S. SIC Description	NAICS Code	1997 NAICS U.S. Description
7911	Dance Studios, Schools, and Halls		
	• Dance Studios and Halls	71399	All Other Amusement and Recreation Industries (pt)
	• Dance Schools	61161	Fine Arts Schools (pt)
7922	Theatrical Producers (except Motion Picture) and Miscellaneous Theatrical Services		
	• Casting Agencies	56131	Employment Placement Agencies (pt)
	• Theater and Opera Companies	71111	Theater Companies and Dinner Theaters (pt)

pt—Part of.

SIC to NAICS

SIC Code	1987 U.S. SIC Description	NAICS Code	1997 NAICS U.S. Description
	• Theatrical Agents	71141	Agents and Managers for Artists, Athletes, Entertainers, and Other Public Figures (pt)
	• Theatrical Ticket Agencies	561599	All Other Travel Arrangement and Reservation Services (pt)
	• Costume Design, Theatrical	71151	Independent Artists, Writers, and Performers (pt)
	• Ballet and Dance Companies	71112	Dance Companies
	• Theater Operators	71131	Promoters of Performing Arts, Sports, and Similar Events with Facilities (pt)
	• Theatrical Promoters	71132	Promoters of Performing Arts, Sports, and Similar Events without Facilities (pt)
	• Producers of Radio Programs	51229	Other Sound Recording Industries (pt)
	• Theatrical Equipment Rental	53249	Other Commercial and Industrial Machinery and Equipment Rental and Leasing (pt)
7929	Bands, Orchestras, Actors, and Other Entertainers and Entertainment Groups		
	• Musical Groups and Artists, Orchestras	71113	Musical Groups and Artists
	• Actors and Actresses	71151	Independent Artists, Writers, and Performers (pt)
	• Except Musical Groups and Artists, Actors and Actresses	71119	Other Performing Arts Companies (pt)
7933	Bowling Centers	71395	Bowling Centers
7941	Professional Sports Clubs and Promoters		
	• Professional Sports Clubs	711211	Sports Teams and Clubs
	• Sports Agents	71141	Agents and Managers for Artists, Athletes, Entertainers, and Other Public Figures (pt)
	• Sports Promoters	71132	Promoters of Arts, Sports, and Similar Events without Facilities (pt)
	• Stadium Operators	71131	Promoters of Arts, Sports, and Similar Events with Facilities (pt)
7948	Racing, including Track Operations		
	• Racetrack Operators	711212	Racetracks
	• Racing, except Track Operators	711219	Other Spectator Sports (pt)
7991	Physical Fitness Facilities	71394	Fitness and Recreational Sports Centers (pt)
7992	Public Golf Courses	71391	Golf Courses and Country Clubs (pt)
7993	Coin-operated Amusement Devices		
	• Amusement Arcades	71312	Amusement Arcades
	• Gambling (Slot Machine) Operators	71329	Other Gambling Industries (pt)
	• Except Amusement Arcades and Slot Machine Operators	71399	All Other Amusement and Recreation Industries (pt)
7996	Amusement Parks	71311	Amusement and Theme Parks
7997	Membership Sports and Recreation Clubs		
	• Golf Clubs	71391	Golf Courses and Country Clubs (pt)
	• Recreation Clubs with Facilities	71394	Fitness and Recreational Sports Centers (pt)
	• Recreation Clubs Without Facilities	71399	All Other Amusement and Recreation Industries (pt)
7999	Amusement and Recreation Services, NEC		
	• Ticket Agencies	561599	All Other Travel Arrangement and Reservation Services (pt)
	• Aerial Tramways, Scenic and Amusement	48799	Scenic and Sightseeing Transportation, Other (pt)

Go to page 23 to learn about implementation of NAICS codes in the public and private sectors.

pt—Part of.

SIC Code	1987 U.S. SIC Description	NAICS Code	1997 NAICS U.S. Description
	• Circus Companies and Traveling Carnival Shows	71119	Other Performing Arts Companies (pt)
	• Professional Athletes	711219	Other Spectator Sports (pt)
	• Skiing Facilities	71392	Skiing Facilities
	• Nonmembership Recreation Facilities	71394	Fitness and Recreational Sports Centers (pt)
	• Casinos, except Casino Hotels	71321	Casinos (except Casino Hotels)
	• Lottery, Bingo, Bookie, and Other Gaming Operations	71329	Other Gambling Industries (pt)
	• Caverns and Miscellaneous Commercial Parks	71219	Nature Parks and Other Similar Institutions (pt)
	• Sports Instruction	61162	Sports and Recreation Instruction
	• Nonathletic Recreational Instruction	611699	All Other Miscellaneous Schools and Instruction (pt)
	• State Fairs, Agriculture Fairs, and County Fairs with Facilities	71131	Promoters of Performing Arts, Sports, and Similar Events with Facilities (pt)
	• State Fairs, Agriculture Fairs, and County Fairs without Facilities	71132	Promoters of Performing Arts, Sports, and Similar Events without Facilities (pt)
	• Sports Equipment Rental	532292	Recreational Goods Rental
	• Scenic Transport Operations, Land	48711	Scenic and Sightseeing Transportation, Land (pt)
	• Charter Fishing	48721	Scenic and Sightseeing Transportation, Water (pt)
	• Amusement and Recreation Services, NEC (except Circuses, Professional Athletes, Caverns and Other Commercial Parks, Skiing Facilities, Casinos and Other Gambling Operations, Amusement and Recreation Facilities, Sports Instruction, Sports Equipment Rental, and Amusement or Scenic Transport Operations)	71399	All Other Amusement and Recreation Industries (pt)
80	**Health Services**		
8011	Offices and Clinics of Doctors of Medicine		
	• Surgical and Emergency Centers	621493	Freestanding Ambulatory Surgical and Emergency Centers
	• HMO Medical Centers	621491	HMO Medical Centers
	• Offices of Physicians, Mental Health Specialists	621112	Offices of Physicians, Mental Health Specialists (pt)
	• Offices of Physicians except Mental Health	621111	Offices of Physicians, (except Mental Health Specialists) (pt)
8021	Offices and Clinics of Dentists	62121	Offices of Dentists
8031	Offices and Clinics of Doctors of Osteopathy		
	• Offices of Doctors of Osteopathy, except Mental Health	621111	Offices of Physicians (except Mental Health Specialists) (pt)
	• Offices of Doctors of Osteopathy, Mental Health Specialists	621112	Offices of Physicians, Mental Health Specialists (pt)
8041	Offices and Clinics of Chiropractors	62131	Offices of Chiropractors
8042	Offices and Clinics of Optometrists	62132	Offices of Optometrists
8043	Offices and Clinics of Podiatrists	621391	Offices of Podiatrists
8049	Offices and Clinics of Health Practitioners, NEC		
	• Mental Health Practitioners, except Physicians	62133	Offices of Mental Health Practitioners (except Physicians)

pt—Part of.

SIC Code	1987 U.S. SIC Description	NAICS Code	1997 NAICS U.S. Description
	• Offices of Physical, Occupational, Recreational, and Speech Therapists and Audiologists	62134	Offices of Physical, Occupational, and Speech Therapists and Audiologists
	• Other Offices of Health Practitioners	621399	Offices of All Other Miscellaneous Health Practitioners
8051	Skilled Nursing Care Facilities		
	• Continuing Care Retirement Communities	623311	Continuing Care Retirement Communities (pt)
	• All Other Skilled Nursing Care Facilities	62311	Nursing Care Facilities (pt)
8052	Intermediate Care Facilities		
	• Continuing Care Retirement Communities	623311	Continuing Care Retirement Communities (pt)
	• Mental Retardation Facilities	62321	Residential Mental Retardation Facilities
	• Other Intermediate Care Facilities	62311	Nursing Care Facilities (pt)
8059	Nursing and Personal Care Facilities, NEC		
	• Continuing Care Retirement Communities	623311	Continuing Care Retirement Communities (pt)
	• Other Nursing and Personal Care Facilities	62311	Nursing Care Facilities (pt)
8062	General Medical and Surgical Hospitals	62211	General Medical and Surgical Hospitals (pt)
8063	Psychiatric Hospitals	62221	Psychiatric and Substance Abuse Hospitals (pt)
8069	Specialty Hospitals, except Psychiatric		
	• Children's Hospitals	62211	General Medical and Surgical Hospitals (pt)
	• Substance Abuse Hospitals	62221	Psychiatric and Substance Abuse Hospitals (pt)
	• Other Specialty Hospitals	62231	Specialty (except Psychiatric and Substance Abuse) Hospitals
8071	Medical Laboratories		
	• Diagnostic Imaging Centers	621512	Diagnostic Imaging Centers
	• Medical Laboratories, except Diagnostic Imaging Centers	621511	Medical Laboratories
8072	Dental Laboratories	339116	Dental Laboratories
8082	Home Health Care Services	62161	Home Health Care Services
8092	Kidney Dialysis Centers	621492	Kidney Dialysis Centers
8093	Specialty Outpatient Facilities, NEC		
	• Family Planning Centers	62141	Family Planning Centers (pt)
	• Outpatient Mental Health Facilities	62142	Outpatient Mental Health and Substance Abuse Centers
	• Other Specialty Outpatient Facilities	621498	All Other Outpatient Care Facilities
8099	Health and Allied Services, NEC		
	• Blood and Organ Banks	621991	Blood and Organ Banks
	• Medical Artists	54143	Graphic Design Services (pt)
	• Medical Photography	541922	Commercial Photography (pt)
	• Childbirth Preparation Classes	62141	Family Planning Centers (pt)
	• Other Health and Allied Services	621999	All Other Miscellaneous Ambulatory Health Care Services
81	**Legal Services**		
8111	Legal Services	54111	Offices of Lawyers
82	**Educational Services**		
8211	Elementary and Secondary Schools	61111	Elementary and Secondary Schools

pt—Part of.

SIC Code	1987 U.S. SIC Description	NAICS Code	1997 NAICS U.S. Description
8221	Colleges, Universities, and Professional Schools	61131	Colleges, Universities, and Professional Schools
8222	Junior Colleges and Technical Institutes	61121	Junior Colleges
8231	Libraries	51412	Libraries and Archive
8243	Data Processing Schools		
	• Computer Repair Training	611519	Other Technical and Trade Schools (pt)
	• Except Computer Repair Training	61142	Computer Training
8244	Business and Secretarial Schools	61141	Business and Secretarial Schools
8249	Vocational Schools, NEC		
	• Vocational Apprenticeship Training	611513	Apprenticeship Training
	• Aviation Schools	611512	Flight Training (pt)
	• Other Technical and Trade Schools	611519	Other Technical and Trade Schools (pt)
8299	Schools and Educational Services, NEC		
	• Flying Instruction	611512	Flight Training (pt)
	• Automobile Driving Instruction	611692	Automobile Driving Schools
	• Curriculum Development, Educational	61171	Educational Support Services (pt)
	• Exam Preparation and Tutoring	611691	Exam Preparation and Tutoring
	• Art Drama and Music Schools	61161	Fine Arts Schools (pt)
	• Language Schools	61163	Language Schools
	• Professional and Management Development Training	61143	Professional and Management Development Training Schools
	• Cooking and Modeling Schools	611519	Other Technical and Trade Schools (pt)
	• All Other Schools and Educational Services, NEC	611699	All Other Miscellaneous Schools and Instruction
83	**Social Services**		
8322	Individual and Family Social Services		
	• Child and Youth Services	62411	Child and Youth Services
	• Community Food Services	62421	Community Food Services
	• Community Housing Services, except Temporary Shelters	624229	Other Community Housing Services
	• Emergency and Other Relief Services	62423	Emergency and Other Relief Services
	• Services for the Elderly and Persons with Disabilities	62412	Services for the Elderly and Persons with Disabilities
	• Temporary Shelter	624221	Temporary Shelters
	• Parole Offices and Probation Offices	92215	Parole Offices and Probation Offices
	• Other Individual and Family Services	62419	Other Individual and Family Services
8331	Job Training and Vocational Rehabilitation Services	62431	Vocational Rehabilitation Services
8351	Child Day Care Services	62441	Child Day Care Services (pt)
8361	Residential Care		
	• Homes for the Elderly	623312	Homes for the Elderly
	• Mental Health and Substance Abuse Facilities	62322	Residential Mental Health and Substance Abuse Facilities
	• Other Residential Care	62399	Other Residential Care Facilities
8399	Social Services, NEC		
	• Voluntary Health Organizations	813212	Voluntary Health Organizations
	• Grantmaking and Giving	813219	Other Grantmaking and Giving Services
	• Human Rights Organizations	813311	Human Rights Organizations
	• Environment, Conservation, and Wildlife Organizations	813312	Environment, Conservation, and Wildlife Organizations (pt)
	• All Other Social Advocacy Organizations	813319	Other Social Advocacy Organizations

SIC to NAICS

pt—Part of.

SIC Code	1987 U.S. SIC Description	NAICS Code	1997 NAICS U.S. Description
84	**Museums, Art Galleries, Botanical and Zoological Gardens**		
8412	Museums and Art Galleries		
	• Museums	71211	Museums
	• Historical and Heritage Sites	71212	Historical Sites
8422	Arboreta and Botanical or Zoological Gardens		
	• Botanical and Zoological Gardens	71213	Zoos and Botanical Gardens
	• Nature Parks and Reserves	71219	Nature Parks and Other Similar Institutions (pt)
86	**Membership Organizations**		
8611	Business Associations	81391	Business Associations (pt)
8621	Professional Membership Organizations	81392	Professional Organizations
8631	Labor Unions and Similar Labor Organizations	81393	Labor Unions and Similar Labor Organizations
8641	Civic, Social, and Fraternal Associations		
	• Civic and Social Associations	81341	Civic and Social Organizations (except Business, Professional, Labor, and Political Organizations) (pt)
	• Homeowner and Condominium Associations	81399	Other Similar Organizations (pt)
	• American Indian and Alaska Native Tribal Governments	92115	American Indian and Alaska Native Tribal Governments
8651	Political Organizations	81394	Political Organizations
8661	Religious Organizations	81311	Religious Organizations
8699	Membership Organizations, NEC		
	• Except Humane Societies, Farm Business Organizations, Athletic Associations, and Travel Motor Clubs	81341	Civic and Social Organizations (pt)
	• Farm Business Organizations	81391	Business Associations (pt)
	• Humane Societies	813312	Environment, Conservation, and Wildlife Organizations (pt)
	• Travel Motor Clubs	561599	All Other Travel Arrangement and Reservation Services (pt)
	• Athletic Associations	81399	Other Similar Organizations (except Business, Professional, Labor, and Political Organizations) (pt)
87	**Engineering and Management Services**		
8711	Engineering Services	54133	Engineering Services (pt)
8712	Architectural Services	54131	Architectural Services
8713	Surveying Services		
	• Geophysical Surveying Services	54136	Geophysical Surveying and Mapping Services (pt)
	• Except Geophysical Surveying	54137	Surveying and Mapping (except Geophysical) Services (pt)
8721	Accounting, Auditing, and Bookkeeping Services		
	• Auditing Accountants	541211	Offices of Certified Public Accountants
	• Payroll Services	541214	Payroll Services (pt)
	• Other Accounting Services	541219	Other Accounting Services

pt—Part of.

SIC Code	1987 U.S. SIC Description	NAICS Code	1997 NAICS U.S. Description
8731	Commercial Physical and Biological Research	54171	Research and Development in the Physical, Engineering, and Life Sciences (pt)
8732	Commercial Economic, Sociological, and Educational Research		
	• Social Sciences and Humanities	54172	Research and Development in the Social Sciences and Humanities (pt)
	• Market Research and Opinion Research	54191	Marketing Research and Public Opinion Polling
8733	Noncommercial Research Organizations		
	• Physical, Engineering, and Life Services	54171	Research and Development in the Physical, Engineering, and Life Sciences (pt)
	• Social Sciences and Humanities	54172	Research and Development in the Social Sciences and Humanities (pt)
8734	Testing Laboratories		
	• Veterinary Testing Labs	54194	Veterinary Services (pt)
	• Except Veterinary Testing Labs	54138	Testing Laboratories
8741	Management Services		
	• Except Construction Management Services	56111	Office Administrative Services
	• Construction Management Services	23	*Included in Construction Sector by Type of Construction*
8742	Management Consulting Services		
	• Administrative and General Management Consulting	541611	Administrative Management and General Management Consulting Services
	• Human Resources and Personnel Management Consulting	541612	Human Resources and Executive Search Services (pt)
	• Marketing Consulting	541613	Marketing Consulting Services
	• Manufacturing Management, Physical Distribution, and Site Location Consulting	541614	Process, Physical Distribution, and Logistics Consulting Services (pt)
8743	Public Relations Services	54182	Public Relations Agencies
8744	Facilities Support Management Services	56121	Facilities Support Services
8748	Business Consulting Services, NEC		
	• Educational Test Development and Evaluation Services, Educational Testing, and Educational Consulting	61171	Educational Support Services (pt)
	• Safety Consulting and Security Consulting	54169	Other Scientific and Technical Consulting Services (pt)
	• Agriculture Consulting and Economic Consulting	54169	Other Scientific and Technical Consulting Services (pt)
	• Urban Planners and Industrial Development Organizations	54132	Landscape Architectural Services (pt)
	• Traffic Engineering Consulting	54133	Engineering Services (pt)
	• All Other Business Consulting Services	541618	Other Management Consulting Services
88	**Private Households**		
8811	Private Households	81411	Private Households
89	**Miscellaneous Services**		
8999	Services, NEC		
	• Authors, Artists, and Related Technical Services, Independent	71151	Independent Artists, Writers, and Performers (pt)
	• Record Production	51221	Record Production
	• Scientific and Related Consulting Services	54169	Other Scientific and Technical Consulting Services (pt)

pt—Part of.

SIC Code	1987 U.S. SIC Description	NAICS Code	1997 NAICS U.S. Description
	• Music Publishing	51223	Music Publishers (pt)
	• Actuarial Consulting	541612	Human Resources and Executive Search Consulting Services (pt)
	• All Other Information Providers	514199	All Other Information Services (pt)
	• Environmental Consultants	54162	Environmental Consulting Services
91	**Executive, Legislative, and General Government**		
9111	Executive Offices	92111	Executive Offices
9121	Legislative Bodies	92112	Legislative Bodies
9131	Executive and Legislative Offices, Combined	92114	Executive and Legislative Offices, Combined
9199	General Government, NEC	92119	Other General Government Support
92	**Justice, Public Order, and Safety**		
9211	Courts	92211	Courts
9221	Police Protection	92212	Police Protection
9222	Legal Counsel and Prosecution	92213	Legal Counsel and Prosecution
9223	Correctional Institutions	92214	Correctional Institutions
9224	Fire Protection	92216	Fire Protection
9229	Public Order and Safety, NEC	92219	Other Justice, Public Order, and Safety
93	**Finance, Taxation, and Monetary Policy**		
9311	Public Finance, Taxation, and Monetary Policy	92113	Public Finance Activities
94	**Administration of Human Resources**		
9411	Administration of Educational Programs	92311	Administration of Education Programs
9431	Administration of Public Health Programs	92312	Administration of Public Health Programs
9441	Administration of Social, Human Resource and Income Maintenance Programs	92313	Administration of Human Resource Programs (except Education, Public Health, and Veterans' Affairs Programs)
9451	Administration of Veterans' Affairs, except Health Insurance	92314	Administration of Veterans' Affairs
95	**Environmental Quality and Housing**		
9511	Air and Water Resource and Solid Waste Management	92411	Administration of Air and Water Resource and Solid Waste Management Programs
9512	Land, Mineral, Wildlife, and Forest Conservation	92412	Administration of Conservation Programs
9531	Administration of Housing Programs	92511	Administration of Housing Programs
9532	Administration of Urban Planning and Community and Rural Development	92512	Administration of Urban Planning and Community and Rural Development
96	**Administration of Economic Programs**		
9611	Administration of General Economic Programs	92611	Administration of General Economic Programs
9621	Regulation and Administration of Transportation Programs		
	• Air Traffic Control	488111	Air Traffic Control (pt)
	• Except Air Traffic Control	92612	Regulation and Administration of Transportation Programs
9631	Regulation and Administration of Communications, Electric, Gas, and Other Utilities	92613	Regulation and Administration of Communications, Electric, Gas, and Other Utilities

Visit page 9 to learn more about NAICS codes.

pt—Part of.

SIC Code	1987 U.S. SIC Description	NAICS Code	1997 NAICS U.S. Description
9641	Regulation of Agricultural Marketing and Commodities	92614	Regulation of Agricultural Marketing and Commodities
9651	Regulation, Licensing, and Inspection of Miscellaneous Commercial Sectors	92615	Regulation, Licensing, and Inspection of Miscellaneous Commercial Sectors
9661	Space Research and Technology	92711	Space Research and Technology
97	**National Security and International Affairs**		
9711	National Security	92811	National Security
9721	International Affairs	92812	International Affairs
99	**Nonclassifiable establishments**		
9999	Nonclassifiable Establishments	99999	Unclassified Establishments

pt—Part of.

HOW TO USE THIS SECTION:

This section shows you the full NAICS hierarchy and the 1987 SIC or portions of SIC that make up each NAICS Industry. The table is in numerical order by the NAICS code. For each line of the NAICS hierarchy you have the NAICS Code and Description followed by the comparable 1987 SIC Code and Description. There can be up to two additional columns of information for each line. One column shows a country code and the other shows a SIC comparability code.

Country: If there is no code in this column, the industry is comparable among Mexico, Canada and the United States. If there is a **c** in the column, the industry is comparable between Canada and the United States. If there is a **u** in the column, the industry is designated only for the United States. These codes enable you to determine the depth of comparability among the three countries.

SIC Comparability: Each NAICS industry is given a code explaining the extent of the change from the existing SIC code. If there is an **E** in the column, the industry is an existing industry without significant change. If there is an **R** in the column, the industry has been revised from the SIC definition. If there is an **N** in the column, the industry is a new industry and was not identified in SIC. If there is an **L** in the column, the industry is not applicable to the United States.

An asterisk (*) before a SIC code is an indication that only a portion of the SIC industry is comparable to the NAICS category. The portion will be described in parentheses as part of the 1987 SIC description.

Harris Interchange—
NAICS to SIC Conversion

SIC to NAICS Interchange

NAICS Code	1997 NAICS U.S. Description	Codes	SIC Code	1987 U.S. SIC Description
325992	Photographic Film, Paper, Plate, and Chemical Manufacturing	u N	*3861	Photographic Equipment and Supplies (photographic films, and paper, plates and chemicals)
325998	All Other Miscellaneous Chemical Product and Preparation Manufacturing	u R	*2819	Industrial Inorganic Chemicals, NEC (activated carbon and charcoal)
			*2899	Chemicals and Chemical Preparations, NEC (except frit and table salt)
			*3952	Lead Pencils and Art Goods (drawing inks and india ink)
			*3999	Manufacturing Industries, NEC (matches)
			*7389	Business Services, NEC (aerosol packaging)
326	Plastics and Rubber Products Manufacturing			
3261	Plastics Product Manufacturing			
32611	Unsupported Plastics Film, Sheet, and Bag Manufacturing			
326111	Unsupported Plastics Bag Manufacturing	c N	*2673	Plastics, Foil, and Coated Paper Bags

← Comparable SIC codes

Codes: u—unique to United States; c—common to U.S. and Canada; blank—common to 3 countries; E—existing industry; N—new industry; R—revised industry; * indicates part of a 1987 SIC; (cont'd)—continued; NEC—Not Elsewhere Classified

159

u = only for the U.S. c = comparable between Canada and the U.S. N = New industry and was not identified in SIC R = Revised from the SIC definition L = not applicable to the U.S.

NAICS to SIC Conversion

NAICS Code	1997 NAICS U.S. Description	Codes		SIC Code	1987 U.S. SIC Description
11	Agriculture, Forestry, Fishing, and Hunting				
111	Crop Production				
1111	Oilseed and Grain Farming				
11111	Soybean Farming		E	0116	Soybeans
11112	Oilseed (except Soybean) Farming		N	*0119	Cash Grains, NEC (oilseed, except soy bean farming)
11113	Dry Pea and Bean Farming		N	*0119	Cash Grains, NEC (dry pea and bean farms)
11114	Wheat Farming		E	0111	Wheat
11115	Corn Farming		R	0115	Corn
				*0119	Cash Grains, NEC (popcorn farming)
11116	Rice Farming		E	0112	Rice
11119	Other Grain Farming				
111191	Oilseed and Grain Combination	u	N	*0119	Cash Grains, NEC (oilseed and grain combination farms)
111199	All Other Grain Farming	u	R	*0119	Cash Grains, NEC (except popcorn, soy bean, and dry pea and bean, and oilseed and grain combination farms)
1112	Vegetable and Melon Farming				
11121	Vegetable and Melon Farming				
111211	Potato Farming	c	E	0134	Irish Potatoes
111219	Other Vegetable (except Potato) and Melon Farming	c	R	0161	Vegetables and Melons
				*0139	Field Crops Except Cash Grains (sweet potatoes and yams)
1113	Fruit and Tree Nut Farming				
11131	Orange Groves		N	*0174	Citrus Fruits (orange groves and farms)
11132	Citrus (except Orange) Groves		R	*0174	Citrus Fruits (except orange groves and farms)
11133	Noncitrus Fruit and Tree Nut				
111331	Apple Orchards	u	N	*0175	Deciduous Tree Fruits (apple orchards and farms)
111332	Grape Vineyards	u	E	0172	Grapes
111333	Strawberry Farming	u	N	*0171	Berry Crops (strawberry farms)
111334	Berry (except Strawberry) Farming	u	R	*0171	Berry Crops (except strawberry farms)
111335	Tree Nut Farming	u	E	0173	Tree Nuts
111336	Fruit and Tree Nut Combination	u	N	*0179	Fruits and Tree Nuts, NEC (combination farms)
111339	Other Noncitrus Fruit Farming	u	R	*0175	Deciduous Tree Fruits (except apple orchards and farms)
				*0179	Fruit and Tree Nuts, NEC (except combination farms)
1114	Greenhouse, Nursery, and Floriculture Production				
11141	Food Crops Grown Under Cover				
111411	Mushroom Production	c	N	*0182	Food Crops Grown Under Cover (mushrooms, growing of)
111419	Other Food Crops Grown Under Cover	c	R	*0182	Food Crops Grown Under Cover (except mushroom, growing of)

Visit page 9 to learn more about NAICS codes.

Codes: u—unique to United States; c—common to U.S. and Canada; blank—common to 3 countries; E—existing industry; N—new industry; R—revised industry;
* indicates part of a 1987 SIC; (cont'd)—continued; NEC—Not Elsewhere Classified

NAICS Code	1997 NAICS U.S. Description	Codes		SIC Code	1987 U.S. SIC Description
11142	Nursery and Floriculture Production				
111421	Nursery and Tree Production	c	N	*0181	Ornamental Floriculture and Nursery Products (nursery farming)
				*0811	Timber Tracts (short rotation woody crops)
111422	Floriculture Production	c	N	*0181	Ornamental Floriculture and Nursery Products (floriculture farming)
1119	Other Crop Farming				
11191	Tobacco Farming		E	0132	Tobacco
11192	Cotton Farming		E	0131	Cotton
11193	Sugarcane Farming		N	*0133	Sugarcane and Sugar Beets (sugarcane farms)
11194	Hay Farming		N	*0139	Field Crops, Except Cash Grains, NEC (hay farms)
11199	All Other Crop Farming				
111991	Sugar Beet Farming	u	N	*0133	Sugarcane and Sugar Beets (sugar beet farms)
111992	Peanut Farming	u	N	*0139	Field Crops, Except Cash Grains, NEC (peanut farms)
111998	All Other Miscellaneous Crop Farming	u	R	*0139	Field Crops, Except Cash Grains, NEC (except peanut, sweet potato, yam and hay farms)
				0191	General Farms, Primarily Crop
				*0831	Forest Products (maple sap, gathering of)
				*0919	Miscellaneous Marine Products (plant aquaculture)
				*2099	Food Preparations, NEC (reducing maple sap to maple syrup)
112	Animal Production				
1121	Cattle Ranching and Farming				
11211	Beef Cattle Ranching and Farming, including feedlots				
112111	Beef Cattle Ranching and Farming	u	R	0212	Beef Cattle, Except Feedlots
				*0241	Dairy Farms (dairy heifer replacement farms)
112112	Cattle Feedlots	u	E	0211	Beef Cattle Feedlots
11212	Dairy Cattle and Milk Production		R	*0241	Dairy Farms
11213	Dual Purpose Cattle Ranching and Farming		L		Null Set for U.S
1122	Hog and Pig Farming				
11221	Hog and Pig Farming		E	0213	Hogs
1123	Poultry and Egg Production				
11231	Chicken Egg Production		E	0252	Chicken Eggs
11232	Broilers and Other Meat Type		E	0251	Broiler, Fryers, and Roaster Chickens
11233	Turkey Production		E	0253	Turkey and Turkey Eggs
11234	Poultry Hatcheries		E	0254	Poultry Hatcheries
11239	Other Poultry Production		E	0259	Poultry and Eggs, NEC
1124	Sheep and Goat Farming				

Codes: u—unique to United States; c—common to U.S. and Canada; blank—common to 3 countries; E—existing industry; N—new industry; R—revised industry;
* indicates part of a 1987 SIC; (cont'd)—continued; NEC—Not Elsewhere Classified

NAICS Code	1997 NAICS U.S. Description	Codes		SIC Code	1987 U.S. SIC Description
11241	Sheep Farming		N	*0214	Sheep and Goats (sheep farms)
11242	Goat Farming		N	*0214	Sheep and Goats (goat farms)
1125	Animal Aquaculture				
11251	Animal Aquaculture				
112511	Finfish Farming and Fish Hatcheries	u	N	*0273	Animal Aquaculture (finfish farms)
				*0921	Fish Hatcheries and Preserves (finfish hatcheries)
112512	Shellfish Farming	u	N	*0273	Animal Aquaculture (shellfish farms)
				*0921	Fish Hatcheries and Preserves (shellfish hatcheries)
112519	Other Animal Aquaculture	u	R	*0273	Animal Aquaculture (except finfish and shellfish)
				*0279	Animal Specialties, NEC (alligator and frog production)
1129	Other Animal Production				
11291	Apiculture		N	*0279	Animal Specialties, NEC (apiculture)
11292	Horse and Other Equine Production		E	0272	Horses and Other Equines
11293	Fur-bearing Animal and Rabbit		E	0271	Fur-bearing Animals and Rabbits
11299	All Other Animal Production		R	0219	General Livestock, Except Dairy and Poultry
				*0279	Animal Specialties, NEC (except apiculture)
				0291	General Farms, Primarily Livestock and Animal Specialties
113	Forestry and Logging				
1131	Timber Tract Operations				
11311	Timber Tract Operations		R	*0811	Timber Tracts (long term timber farms)
1132	Forest Nurseries and Gathering of Forest Products				
11321	Forest Nurseries and Gathering of Forest Products		E	*0831	Forest Nurseries and Gathering of Forest Products (forest products, except gathering of maple sap)
1133	Logging				
11331	Logging		E	2411	Logging
114	Fishing, Hunting and Trapping				
1141	Fishing				
11411	Fishing				
114111	Finfish Fishing	u	E	0912	Finfish
114112	Shellfish Fishing	u	E	0913	Shellfish
114119	Other Marine Fishing	u	R	*0919	Miscellaneous Marine Products (except plant aquaculture)
1142	Hunting and Trapping				
11421	Hunting and Trapping		E	0971	Hunting and Trapping, and Game Propagation
115	Support Activities for Agriculture				
1151	Support Activities for Crop				
11511	Support Activities for Crop				
115111	Cotton Ginning	u	E	0724	Cotton Ginning

Codes: u—unique to United States; c—common to U.S. and Canada; blank—common to 3 countries; E—existing industry; N—new industry; R—revised industry;
* indicates part of a 1987 SIC; (cont'd)—continued; NEC—Not Elsewhere Classified

NAICS Code	1997 NAICS U.S. Description	Codes		SIC Code	1987 U.S. SIC Description
115112	Soil Preparation, Planting, and Cultivating	u	R	0711	Soil Preparation Services
				0721	Crop Planting, Cultivating, and Protecting
115113	Crop Harvesting, Primarily by Machine	u	E	0722	Crop Harvesting, Primarily by Machine
115114	Postharvest Crop Activities (except Cotton Ginning)	u	R	*0723	Crop Preparation Services For Market, Except Cotton Ginning (except custom grain grinding)
115115	Farm Labor Contractors and Crew Leaders	u	E	0761	Farm Labor Contractors and Crew
115116	Farm Management Services	u	E	0762	Farm Management Services
1152	Support Activities for Animal Production				
11521	Support Activities for Animal Production		N	*0751	Livestock Services, Except Veterinary (except custom slaughtering)
				*0752	Animal Specialty Services, Except Veterinary (horses and equines services and animal production breeding)
				*7699	Repair Services, NEC (farriers)
1153	Support Activities for Forestry				
11531	Support Activities for Forestry		E	0851	Forestry Services
21	**Mining**				
211	Oil and Gas Extraction				
2111	Oil and Gas Extraction				
21111	Oil and Gas Extraction				
211111	Crude Petroleum and Natural Gas	u	E	1311	Crude Petroleum and Natural Gas
211112	Natural Gas Liquid Extraction	u	R	1321	Natural Gas Liquids
				*2819	Industrial Inorganic Chemicals, NEC (recovering sulfur from natural gas)
212	Mining (except Oil and Gas)				
2121	Coal Mining				
21211	Coal Mining				
212111	Bituminous Coal and Lignite Surface Mining	u	E	1221	Bituminous Coal and Lignite Surface Mining
212112	Bituminous Coal Underground Mining	u	E	1222	Bituminous Coal Underground Mining
212113	Anthracite Mining	u	E	1231	Anthracite Mining
2122	Metal Ore Mining				
21221	Iron Ore Mining		E	1011	Iron Ores
21222	Gold Ore and Silver Ore Mining				
212221	Gold Ore Mining	u	E	1041	Gold Ores
212222	Silver Ore Mining	u	E	1044	Silver Ores
21223	Copper, Nickel, Lead, and Zinc				
212231	Lead Ore and Zinc Ore Mining	c	E	1031	Lead and Zinc Ores
212234	Copper Ore and Nickel Ore Mining	u	R	1021	Copper Ores
				*1061	Ferroalloy Ores, Except Vanadium (nickel)
21229	Other Metal Ore Mining				
212291	Uranium-Radium-Vanadium Ore Mining	u	E	1094	Uranium-Radium-Vanadium Ores
212299	All Other Metal Ore Mining	u	R	*1061	Ferroalloy Ores, Except Vanadium (other ferroalloys except nickel)

Codes: u—unique to United States; c—common to U.S. and Canada; blank—common to 3 countries; E—existing industry; N—new industry; R—revised industry; * indicates part of a 1987 SIC; (cont'd)—continued; NEC—Not Elsewhere Classified

NAICS Code	1997 NAICS U.S. Description	Codes		SIC Code	1987 U.S. SIC Description
212299	All Other Metal Ore Mining (cont'd)			1099	Miscellaneous Metal Ores, NEC
2123	Nonmetallic Mineral Mining and Quarrying				
21231	Stone Mining and Quarrying				
212311	Dimension Stone Mining and	u	E	1411	Dimension Stone
212312	Crushed and Broken Limestone Mining	u	E	1422	Crushed and Broken Limestone
212313	Crushed and Broken Granite Mining	u	E	1423	Crushed and Broken Granite
212319	Other Crushed and Broken Stone	u	R	1429	Crushed and Broken Stone, NEC
				*1499	Miscellaneous Nonmetallic Minerals, Except Fuels (bituminous limestone and bituminous sandstone)
21232	Sand, Gravel, Clay, and Ceramic and Ceramic and Refractory Minerals Mining and Quarrying				
212321	Construction Sand and Gravel Mining	u	E	1442	Construction Sand and Gravel
212322	Industrial Sand Mining	u	E	1446	Industrial Sand
212324	Kaolin and Ball Clay Mining	u	E	1455	Kaolin and Ball Clay
				*3295	Minerals and Earths, Ground or Otherwise Treated (grinding, washing, separating, etc., of minerals in SIC 1455)
212325	Clay and Ceramic and Refractory Minerals Mining	u	E	1459	Clay, Ceramic, and Refractory Minerals, NEC
				*3295	Minerals and Earths, Ground or Otherwise Treated (grinding, washing, separating, etc., of minerals in SIC 1459)
21239	Other Nonmetallic Mineral Mining				
212391	Potash, Soda, and Borate Mineral	u	E	1474	Potash, Soda, and Borate Minerals
212392	Phosphate Rock Mining	u	E	1475	Phosphate Rock
212393	Other Chemical and Fertilizer	u	E	1479	Chemical and Fertilizer Mineral Mining, NEC
				*3295	Minerals and Earths, Ground or Otherwise Treated (grinding, washing, separating, etc., of minerals in SIC 1479)
212399	All Other Nonmetallic Mineral Mining	u	R	*1499	Miscellaneous Nonmetallic Minerals, Except Fuels (excepting bituminous limestone and bituminous sandstone)
				*3295	Minerals and Earths, Ground or Otherwise Treated (grinding, washing, separating, etc., of minerals in SIC 1499)
213	Support Activities for Mining				
2131	Support Activities for Mining				
21311	Support Activities for Mining				
213111	Drilling Oil and Gas Wells	c	E	1381	Drilling Oil and Gas Wells
213112	Support Activities for Oil and Gas Operations	u	R	*1382	Oil and Gas Field Exploration Services (except geophysical mapping and surveying)
				1389	Oil and Gas Field Services, NEC
213113	Support Activities for Coal Mining	u	E	1241	Coal Mining Services

Visit page 15 to learn about major changes to NAICS sectors.

Codes: u—unique to United States; c—common to U.S. and Canada; blank—common to 3 countries; E—existing industry; N—new industry; R—revised industry; * indicates part of a 1987 SIC; (cont'd)—continued; NEC—Not Elsewhere Classified

NAICS Code	1997 NAICS U.S. Description	Codes		SIC Code	1987 U.S. SIC Description
213114	Support Activities for Metal Mining	u	R	*1081	Metal Mining Services (except geophysical surveying and mapping)
213115	Support Activities for Nonmetallic Minerals (except fuels)	u	R	*1481	Nonmetallic Minerals Services, Except Fuels (except geophysical surveying and mapping)
22	**Utilities**				
221	Utilities				
2211	Electric Power Generation, Transmission, and Distribution	c			
22111	Electric Power Generation	c			
221111	Hydroelectric Power Generation	c	N	*4911	Electric Services (hydroelectric power generation)
				*4931	Electric and Other Services Combined (hydroelectric power generation)
				*4939	Combination Utilities, NEC (hydroelectric power generation)
221112	Fossil Fuel Electric Power	c	N	*4911	Electric Services (fossil fuel power generation)
				*4931	Electric and Other Services Combined (fossil fuel power generation)
				*4939	Combination Utilities, NEC (fossil fuel power generation)
221113	Nuclear Electric Power Generation	c	N	*4911	Electric Services (nuclear electric power generation)
				*4931	Electric and Other Services Combined (nuclear power generation)
				*4939	Combination Utilities, NEC (nuclear power generation)
221119	Other Electric Power Generation	c	N	*4911	Electric Services (other electric power generation)
				*4931	Electric and Other Services Combined (other electric power generation)
				*4939	Combination Utilities, NEC (other electric power generation)
22112	Electric Power Transmission, Contol and Distribution	c			
221121	Electric Bulk Power Transmission, and Control	c	N	*4911	Electric Services (electric power transmission and control)
				*4931	Electric and Other Services Combined (electric power transmission and control)
				*4939	Combination Utilities, NEC (electric power transmission and control)
221122	Electric Power Distribution	c	N	*4911	Electric Services (electric power distribution)
				*4931	Electric and Other Services Combined (electric power distribution)
				*4939	Combination Utilities, NEC (electric power distribution)

Codes: u—unique to United States; c—common to U.S. and Canada; blank—common to 3 countries; E—existing industry; N—new industry; R—revised industry;
* indicates part of a 1987 SIC; (cont'd)—continued; NEC—Not Elsewhere Classified

NAICS Code	1997 NAICS U.S. Description	Codes		SIC Code	1987 U.S. SIC Description
2212	Natural Gas Distribution	c			
22121	Natural Gas Distribution	c	R	*4923	Natural Gas Transmission and Distribution (distribution)
				4924	Natural Gas Distribution
				4925	Mixed, Manufactured, or Liquefied Petroleum Gas Production and/or Distribution
				*4931	Electric and Other Services Combined (natural gas distribution)
				4932	Gas and Other Services Combined (natural gas distribution)
				*4939	Combination Utilities, NEC (natural gas distribution)
2213	Water, Sewage and Other Systems	c			
22131	Water Supply and Irrigation Systems	c	R	4941	Water Supply
				4971	Irrigation Systems
22132	Sewage Treatment Facilities	c	E	4952	Sewerage Systems
22133	Steam and Air-conditioning Supply	c	E	4961	Steam and Air-conditioning Supply
23	**Construction**				
233	Building, Developing, and General Contracting	u			
2331	Land Subdivision and Land Development	u			
23311	Land Subdivision and Land Development	u	E	6552	Land Subdividers and Developers, Except Cemeteries
2332	Residential Building Construction	u			
23321	Single Family Housing Construction	u	R	1521	General Contractors—Single-family Houses
				*1531	Operative Builders (single-family housing construction)
				*8741	Management Services (single-family housing construction management)
23322	Multi-family Housing Construction	u	R	*1522	General Contractors—Residential Building, Other Than Single-family (except hotel and motel construction)
				*1531	Operative Builders (multi-family housing construction)
				*8741	Management Services (multi-family housing construction management)
2333	Nonresidential Building Construction	u			
23331	Manufacturing and Industrial Building Construction	u	R	*1531	Operative Builders (manufacturing and light industrial building construction)
				*1541	General Contractors—Industrial Buildings and Warehouses (except public warehouse construction)
				*8741	Management Services (manufacturing and industrial building construction management)

Codes: u—unique to United States; c—common to U.S. and Canada; blank—common to 3 countries; E—existing industry; N—new industry; R—revised industry;
* indicates part of a 1987 SIC; (cont'd)—continued; NEC—Not Elsewhere Classified

NAICS Code	1997 NAICS U.S. Description	Codes		SIC Code	1987 U.S. SIC Description
23332	Commercial and Institutional Building Construction	u	R	*1522	General Contractors—Residential Building Other than Single-family (hotel and motel construction)
				*1531	Operative Builders (commercial and institutional building construction)
				*1541	General Contractors—Industrial Buildings and Warehouses (public warehouse construction)
				1542	General Contractors—Nonresidential Buildings, Other than Industrial Buildings and Warehouses
				*8741	Management Services (commercial and institutional building construction management)
234	Heavy Construction	u			
2341	Highway, Street, Bridge, and Tunnel Construction	u			
23411	Highway and Street Construction	u	R	1611	Highway and Street Construction, Except Elevated Highways
				*8741	Management Services (highway and street construction management)
23412	Bridge and Tunnel Construction	u	R	1622	Bridge, Tunnel, and Elevated Highway Construction
				*8741	Management Services (bridge and tunnel construction management)
2349	Other Heavy Construction	u			
23491	Water, Sewer, and Pipeline Construction	u	N	*1623	Water, Sewer, Pipeline, and Communications and Power Line Construction (water, sewer, and pipeline construction)
				*8741	Management Services (water, sewer, and pipeline construction management)
23492	Power and Communication Transmission Line Construction	u	N	*1623	Water, Sewer, Pipeline, and Communications and Power Line Construction (communications and power line construction)
				*8741	Management Services (power and communication transmission line construction management)
23493	Industrial Nonbuilding Structure Construction	u	N	*1629	Heavy Construction, NEC (industrial nonbuilding structures construction)
				*8741	Management Services (industrial nonbuilding structure construction management)
23499	All Other Heavy Construction	u	R	*1629	Heavy Construction, NEC (nonbuilding structures except industrial construction)
				*7353	Construction Equipment Rental and Leasing (construction equipment with operator)

Codes: u—unique to United States; c—common to U.S. and Canada; blank—common to 3 countries; E—existing industry; N—new industry; R—revised industry; * indicates part of a 1987 SIC; (cont'd)—continued; NEC—Not Elsewhere Classified

NAICS Code	1997 NAICS U.S. Description	Codes		SIC Code	1987 U.S. SIC Description
23499	All Other Heavy Construction (cont'd)			*8741	Management Services (other heavy construction management)
235	Special Trade Contractors	u			
2351	Plumbing, Heating, and Air-conditioning Contractors	u			
23511	Plumbing, Heating, and Air-conditioning Contractors	u	R	1711	Plumbing, Heating and Air-conditioning
				*7699	Repair Shops and Related Services (boiler cleaning)
2352	Painting and Wall Covering Contractors	u			
23521	Painting and Wall Covering Contractors	u	R	1721	Painting and Paper Hanging
				*1799	Special Trade Contractors, NEC (paint and wallpaper stripping and wallpaper removal contractors)
2353	Electrical Contractors	u			
23531	Electrical Contractors	u	E	1731	Electrical Work
2354	Masonry, Drywall, Insulation, and Tile Contractors	u			
23541	Masonry and Stone Contractors	u	E	1741	Masonry, Stone Setting, and Other Stone Work
23542	Drywall, Plastering, Acoustical, and Insulation Contractors	u	R	1742	Plastering, Drywall, Acoustical, and Insulation Work
				*1743	Terrazzo, Tile, Marble and Mosaic work (fresco work)
				*1771	Concrete Work (stucco construction)
23543	Tile, Marble, Terrazzo, and Mosaic Contractors	u	R	*1743	Terrazzo, Tile, Marble, and Mosaic Work (except fresco work)
2355	Carpentry and Floor Contractors	u			
23551	Carpentry Contractors	u	E	1751	Carpentry Work
23552	Floor Laying and Other Floor Contractors	u	E	1752	Floor Laying and Other Floor Work, NEC
2356	Roofing, Siding, and Sheet Metal Contractors	u			
23561	Roofing, Siding, and Sheet Metal Contractors	u	E	1761	Roofing, Siding, and Sheet Metal Work
2357	Concrete Contractors	u			
23571	Concrete Contractors	u	R	*1771	Concrete Work (except stucco construction)
2358	Water Well Drilling Contractors	u			
23581	Water Well Drilling Contractors	u	E	1781	Water Well Drilling
2359	Other Special Trade Contractors	u			
23591	Structural Steel Erection Contractors	u	E	1791	Structural Steel Erection
23592	Glass and Glazing Contractors	u	R	1793	Glass and Glazing Work
				*1799	Specialty Trade Contractors, NEC (tinting glass work)
23593	Excavation Contractors	u	E	1794	Excavation Work
23594	Wrecking and Demolition Contractors	u	E	1795	Wrecking and Demolition Work
23595	Building Equipment and Other Machinery	u	E	1796	Installation or Erection of Building Installation Contractors Equipment, NEC

Go to page 23 to learn about the implementation of NAICS codes in the public and private sectors.

Codes: u—unique to United States; c—common to U.S. and Canada; blank—common to 3 countries; E—existing industry; N—new industry; R—revised industry;
* indicates part of a 1987 SIC; (cont'd)—continued; NEC—Not Elsewhere Classified

NAICS Code	1997 NAICS U.S. Description	Codes		SIC Code	1987 U.S. SIC Description
23599	All Other Special Trade Contractors	u	R	*1799	Special Trade Contractors, NEC (except paint and wallpaper stripping, wall paper removal contractors, and tinting glass work)
31-33	**Manufacturing**				
311	Food Manufacturing				
3111	Animal Food Manufacturing				
31111	Animal Food Manufacturing				
311111	Dog and Cat Food Manufacturing	c	E	2047	Dog and Cat Food
311119	Other Animal Food Manufacturing	c	R	*2048	Prepared Feeds and Feed Ingredients for Animals and Fowls, Except Dogs and Cats (except slaughtering animals for pet food)
				*0723	Crop Production Services for Market, Except Cotton Ginning (custom grain grinding)
3112	Grain and Oilseed Milling				
31121	Flour Milling and Malt Manufacturing				
311211	Flour Milling	c	R	*2034	Dehydrated Fruits, Vegetables and Soup Mixes (vegetable flour)
				2041	Flour and Other Grain Mill Products
311212	Rice Milling	u	R	2044	Rice Milling
				*2099	Food Preparations, NEC (rice, uncooked and packaged with other ingredients made in rice mills)
311213	Malt Manufacturing	u	E	2083	Malt
31122	Starch and Vegetable Fats and Oils Manufacturing				
311221	Wet Corn Milling	c	R	*2046	Wet Corn Milling (except refining purchased oil)
311222	Soybean Processing	u	R	*2075	Soybean Oil Mills (soybean processing)
				*2079	Shortening, Table Oils, Margarine, and Other Edible Fats and Oils, NEC (processing soybean oil from soybeans crushed in the same establishment)
311223	Other Oilseed Processing	u	N	*2074	Cottonseed Oil Mills (cottonseed processing)
			R	*2079	Shortening, Table Oils, Margarine and Other Edible Fats and Oils, NEC (processing vegetable oils, except soy beans, from oilseeds crushed in the same establishment)
				*2076	Vegetable Oil Mills, Except Corn, Cottonseed, and Soybean (oilseed processing)
311225	Fats and Oils Refining and Blending	c	R	*2046	Wet Corn Milling (refining purchased oil)
				*2074	Cottonseed Oil Mills (processing purchased cottonseed oil)

Codes: u—unique to United States; c—common to U.S. and Canada; blank—common to 3 countries; E—existing industry; N—new industry; R—revised industry; * indicates part of a 1987 SIC; (cont'd)—continued; NEC—Not Elsewhere Classified

NAICS Code	1997 NAICS U.S. Description	Codes		SIC Code	1987 U.S. SIC Description
311225	Fats and Oils Refining and Blending (cont'd)			*2075	Soybean Oil Mills (processing purchased soybean oil)
				*2076	Vegetable Oil Mills, Except Corn, Cottonseed, and Soybean (processing purchased vegetable oils)
				*2079	Shortening, Table Oils, Margarine, and Other Edible Fats and Oils, NEC (processing fats and oils from purchased fats and oils)
31123	Breakfast Cereal Manufacturing		R	*2043	Cereal Breakfast Foods (breakfast cereal)
3113	Sugar and Confectionery Product Manufacturing				
31131	Sugar Manufacturing				
311311	Sugarcane Mills	u	E	2061	Cane Sugar, Except Refining
311312	Cane Sugar Refining	u	E	2062	Cane Sugar Refining
311313	Beet Sugar Manufacturing	u	E	2063	Beet Sugar
31132	Chocolate and Confectionery Manufacturing		R	*2066	Chocolate and Cocoa Products (except from Cacao Beans chocolate products, made from purchased chocolate)
31133	Confectionery Manufacturing from Purchased Chocolate		N	*2064	Candy and Other Confectionery Products (chocolate confectionery)
				*2066	Chocolate and Cocoa Products (chocolate products made from purchased chocolate)
				*5441	Candy, Nut, and Confectionery Stores (chocolate candy stores, preparing on premises)
31134	Nonchocolate Confectionery Manufacturing		N	*2064	Candy and Other Confectionery Products (nonchocolate confectionery)
				*5441	Candy, Nut, and Confectionery Stores (nonchocolate candy stores, preparing on premises)
				2067	Chewing Gum
				*2099	Food Preparations, NEC (marshmallow creme)
3114	Fruit and Vegetable Preserving, and Specialty Food Manufacturing				
31141	Frozen Food Manufacturing				
311411	Frozen Fruit, Juice, and Vegetable Manufacturing	u	E	2037	Frozen Fruits, Fruit Juices, and Vegetables
311412	Frozen Specialty Food Manufacturing	u	E	2038	Frozen Specialties, NEC
31142	Fruit and Vegetable Canning, Pickling, and Drying				
311421	Fruit and Vegetable Canning	u	R	2033	Canned Fruits, Vegetables, Preserves, Jams, and Jellies
				*2035	Pickled Fruits and Vegetables, Vegetable Sauces, and Seasonings and Salad Dressings (pickled fruits and vegetables)
311422	Specialty Canning	u	R	*2032	Canned Specialties (except canned puddings)

NAICS to SIC

Codes: u—unique to United States; c—common to U.S. and Canada; blank—common to 3 countries; E—existing industry; N—new industry; R—revised industry;
* indicates part of a 1987 SIC; (cont'd)—continued; NEC—Not Elsewhere Classified

NAICS Code	1997 NAICS U.S. Description	Codes		SIC Code	1987 U.S. SIC Description
311423	Dried and Dehydrated Food Manufacturing	u	R	*2034	Dried and Dehydrated Fruits, Vegetables and Soup Mixes Manufacturing (except vegetable flour and soup mixes made from purchased dried and dehydrated ingredients made in dehydration plants)
				*2099	Food Preparation, NEC (bouillon, and potatoes dried and packaged with other ingredients)
3115	Dairy Product Manufacturing				
31151	Dairy Product (except Frozen) Manufacturing				
311511	Fluid Milk Manufacturing	c	R	*2026	Fluid Milk (except ultra-high temperature)
311512	Creamery Butter Manufacturing	u	E	2021	Creamery Butter
311513	Cheese Manufacturing	u	E	2022	Natural, Processed, and Imitation Cheese
311514	Dry, Condensed, and Evaporated Dairy Product Manufacturing	u	R	2023	Dry, Condensed, and Evaporated Dairy Products
				*2026	Fluid Milk (ultra-high temperature)
31152	Ice Cream and Frozen Dessert Manufacturing		E	2024	Ice Cream and Frozen Desserts
3116	Animal Slaughtering and Processing				
31161	Animal Slaughtering and Processing				
311611	Animal (except Poultry) Slaughtering	c	R	*0751	Livestock Services, Except Veterinary (custom slaughtering)
				2011	Meat Packing Plants
				*2048	Prepared Feeds and Feed Ingredients for Animals and Fowls, Except Dogs and Cats (animal slaughtering for pet food)
311612	Meat Processed from Carcasses	u	R	*2013	Sausages and Other Prepared Meats (except lard made from purchased materials)
				*5147	Meat and Meat Products (boxed beef)
311613	Rendering and Meat Byproduct Processing	u	N	*2077	Animal and Marine Fats and Oils (animal fats and oils)
				*2013	Sausages and Other Prepared Meats (lard made from purchased materials)
311615	Poultry Processing	c	R	*2015	Poultry Slaughtering and Processing (poultry processing)
3117	Seafood Product Preparation and Packaging				
31171	Seafood Product Preparation and Packaging				
311711	Seafood Canning	u	R	*2077	Animal and Marine Fats and Oils (canned marine fats and oils)
				2091	Canned and Cured Fish and Seafood
311712	Fresh and Frozen Seafood Processing	u	R	*2077	Animal and Marine Fats and Oils (fresh and frozen marine fats and oils)
				2092	Prepared Fresh or Frozen Fish and Seafood

Codes: u—unique to United States; c—common to U.S. and Canada; blank—common to 3 countries; E—existing industry; N—new industry; R—revised industry; * indicates part of a 1987 SIC; (cont'd)—continued; NEC—Not Elsewhere Classified

NAICS Code	1997 NAICS U.S. Description	Codes		SIC Code	1987 U.S. SIC Description
3118	Bakeries and Tortilla Manufacturing				
31181	Bread and Bakery Product Manufacturing				
311811	Retail Bakeries	c	N	*5461	Retail Bakeries (bread, cake and related products baked and sold on premise)
311812	Commercial Bakeries	u	R	2051	Bread and Other Bakery Products, Except Cookies and Crackers
				*2052	Cookies and Crackers (unleavened bread and soft pretzels)
311813	Frozen Cakes, Pies, and Other Pastries Manufacturing	u	E	2053	Frozen Bakery Products, Except Bread
31182	Cookie, Cracker, and Pasta Manufacturing				
311821	Cookie and Cracker Manufacturing	c	R	*2052	Cookies and Crackers (except unleavened bread and pretzels)
311822	Flour Mixes and Dough Manufacturing	c	E	2045	Prepared Flour Mixes and Doughs
311823	Dry Pasta Manufacturing	c	R	2098	Macaroni, Spaghetti, Vermicelli, and Noodles
				*2099	Food Preparations, NEC (dry pasta packaged with other ingredients made in dry pasta plants)
31183	Tortilla Manufacturing		N	*2099	Food Preparations, NEC (tortillas)
3119	Other Food Manufacturing				
31191	Snack Food Manufacturing				
311911	Roasted Nuts and Peanut Butter Manufacturing	c	R	2068	Salted and Roasted Nuts and Seeds
				*2099	Food Preparations, NEC (peanut butter)
311919	Other Snack Food Manufacturing	c	R	*2052	Cookies and Crackers (pretzel, except soft)
				2096	Potato Chips, Corn Chips, and Similar Snacks
31192	Coffee and Tea Manufacturing		N	*2043	Cereal Breakfast Foods (coffee substitute)
				*2087	Flavoring Extracts and Flavoring Syrups, NEC (coffee flavoring and syrups)
				2095	Roasted Coffee
				*2099	Food Preparations, NEC (tea)
31193	Flavoring Syrup and Concentrate Manufacturing		R	*2087	Flavoring Extracts and Flavoring Syrups (flavoring syrup and concentrate, except coffee)
31194	Seasoning and Dressing Manufacturing				
311941	Mayonnaise, Dressing, and Other Prepared Sauce Manufacturing	u	N	*2035	Pickled Fruits and Vegetables, Vegetable Seasonings, and Sauces and Salad Dressings (sauces and salad dressing)
				*2099	Food Preparations, NEC—vinegar, prepared dips (except dairy) and cider
311942	Spice and Extract Manufacturing	u	N	*2082	Malt Beverages (malt extract)
				*2087	Flavoring Extracts and Flavoring Syrups (flavoring extracts and natural food colorings)

Visit page 9 to learn more about NAICS codes.

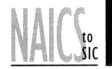

Codes: u—unique to United States; c—common to U.S. and Canada; blank—common to 3 countries; E—existing industry; N—new industry; R—revised industry;
* indicates part of a 1987 SIC; (cont'd)—continued; NEC—Not Elsewhere Classified

NAICS Code	1997 NAICS U.S. Description	Codes		SIC Code	1987 U.S. SIC Description
311942	Spice and Extract Manufacturing (cont'd)			*2099	Food Preparations, NEC (spices, dip mix, salad dressing mix, and seasoning mix)
				*2899	Chemical Preparations, NEC (table salt)
31199	All Other Food Manufacturing				
311991	Perishable Prepared Food Manufacturing	u	N	*2099	Food Preparations, NEC (perishable prepared food)
311999	All Other Miscellaneous Food Manufacturing	u	R	*2015	Poultry Slaughtering and Processing (egg processing)
				*2032	Canned Specialties (canned puddings)
				*2034	Dried and Dehydrated Fruits, Vegetables, and Soup Mixes (soup mixes made from purchased dehydrated ingredients)
				*2087	Flavoring Extracts and Flavoring Syrups (powered drink mix)
				*2099	Food Preparations, NEC (except bouillon, marshmallow creme, spices, extracts, peanut butter, perishable prepared foods, tortillas, tea, spices, dip mix, salad dressing mix, seasoning mix, and vinegar)
312	Beverage and Tobacco Product				
3121	Beverage Manufacturing				
31211	Soft Drink and Ice Manufacturing				
312111	Soft Drink Manufacturing	u	R	*2086	Bottled and Canned Soft Drinks and Carbonated Water (except bottled water)
312112	Bottled Water Manufacturing	u	N	*2086	Bottled and Canned Soft Drinks and Carbonated Water (bottled water)
				*5149	Groceries and Related Products, NEC (bottling mineral or spring water)
312113	Ice Manufacturing	u	E	2097	Manufactured Ice
31212	Breweries		R	*2082	Malt Beverages (except malt extract)
31213	Wineries		R	2084	Wines, Brandy, and Brandy Spirits
				*2085	Distilled and Blended Liquors (applejack)
31214	Distilleries		R	*2085	Distilled and Blended Liquors (except applejack)
3122	Tobacco Manufacturing				
31221	Tobacco Stemming and Redrying		R	*2141	Tobacco Stemming and Redrying (redrying and stemming)
31222	Tobacco Product Manufacturing				
312221	Cigarette Manufacturing	u	E	2111	Cigarettes
312229	Other Tobacco Product Manufacturing	u	N	2121	Cigars
				2131	Chewing and Smoking Tobacco and Snuff
				*2141	Tobacco Stemming and Redrying (reconstituted tobacco)
313	Textile Mills				

Codes: u—unique to United States; c—common to U.S. and Canada; blank—common to 3 countries; E—existing industry; N—new industry; R—revised industry; * indicates part of a 1987 SIC; (cont'd)—continued; NEC—Not Elsewhere Classified

NAICS Code	1997 NAICS U.S. Description	Codes		SIC Code	1987 U.S. SIC Description
3131	Fiber, Yarn, and Thread Mills				
31311	Fiber, Yarn, and Thread Mills				
313111	Yarn Spinning Mills	u	R	2281	Yarn Spinning Mills
				*2299	Textile Goods, NEC (yarn of flax, hemp, jute, and ramie)
313112	Yarn Texturizing, Throwing, and Twisting Mills	u	E	2282	Yarn Texturing, Throwing, Winding Mills
313113	Thread Mills	u	R	*2284	Thread Mills (except finishing)
				*2299	Textile Goods, NEC (thread of hemp, linen, and ramie)
3132	Fabric Mills				
31321	Broadwoven Fabric Mills		N	2211	Broadwoven Fabric Mills, Cotton
				2221	Broadwoven Fabric Mills, Man-made Fiber and Silk
				*2231	Broadwoven Fabric Mills, Wool (including Dyeing and Finishing) (except wool finishing only)
				*2299	Textile Goods, NEC (broadwoven fabrics of jute, linen, hemp, and ramie and handwoven)
31322	Narrow Fabric Mills and Schiffli Machine Embroidery				
313221	Narrow Fabric Mills	u	R	2241	Narrow Fabric and Other Smallware Mills: Cotton, Wool, Silk and Man-made Fiber
				*2299	Textile Goods, NEC (narrow woven fabric of jute, linen, hemp, and ramie)
313222	Schiffli Machine Embroidery	u	E	2397	Schiffli Machine Embroideries
313223	Nonwoven Fabric Mills		R	2297	Nonwoven Fabrics
				*2299	Textile Goods, NEC (nonwoven felt)
31324	Knit Fabric Mills				
313241	Weft Knit Fabric Mills	u	R	*2257	Weft Knit Fabric Mills (except finishing)
				*2259	Knitting Mills NEC (finished articles of weft knit fabric)
313249	Other Knit Fabric and Lace Mills	u	R	*2258	Lace and Warp Knit Fabric Mills (except finishing)
				*2259	Knitting Mills NEC (finished articles of warp knit fabric)
3133	Textile and Fabric Finishing and Fabric Coating Mills				
31331	Textile and Fabric Finishing Mills				
313311	Broadwoven Fabric Finishing Mills	u	N	*2231	Broadwoven Fabric Mills, Wool (wool broadwoven fabric finishing only)
				2261	Finishers of Broadwoven Fabrics of Cotton
				2262	Finishers of Broadwoven Fabrics of Man-made Fiber and Silk
				*5131	Piece Goods and Notions (broadwoven piece good converters)
				*7389	Business Services, NEC (sponging fabric for tailors and dressmakers)

Codes: u—unique to United States; c—common to U.S. and Canada; blank—common to 3 countries; E—existing industry; N—new industry; R—revised industry; * indicates part of a 1987 SIC; (cont'd)—continued; NEC—Not Elsewhere Classified

NAICS Code	1997 NAICS U.S. Description	Codes		SIC Code	1987 U.S. SIC Description
313312	Textile and Fabric Finishing (except Broadwoven Fabric) Mills	u	N	*2231	Broadwoven Fabric Mills, Wool (wool finishing only, except broadwoven fabric)
				*2251	Women's Full-length and Knee-length Hosiery, Except Socks (dyeing and finishing only)
				*2252	Hosiery, NEC (dyeing and finishing only)
				*2253	Knit Outerwear Mills (dyeing and finishing only)
				*2254	Knit Underwear and Nightwear Mills (dyeing and finishing only)
				*2257	Weft Knit Fabric Mills (finishing)
				*2258	Lace and Warp Knit Fabric Mills (finishing)
				*2259	Knitting Mills, NEC (dyeing and finishing knit gloves and mittens)
				2269	Finishers of Textiles, NEC
				*2284	Thread Mills (thread finishing)
				*2299	Textile Goods, NEC (finishing hard fiber thread and yarn)
				*5131	Piece Goods and Notions (converters, except broadwoven fabric)
31332	Fabric Coating Mills		R	2295	Coated Fabrics, Not Rubberized
				*3069	Fabricated Rubber Products, NEC (rubberizing fabric or purchased textile products)
314	Textile Product Mills				
3141	Textile Furnishings Mills				
31411	Carpet and Rug Mills		E	2273	Carpets and Rugs
31412	Curtain and Linen Mills				
314121	Curtain and Drapery Mills	u	R	2391	Curtains and Draperies
				*5714	Drapery, Curtain, and Upholstery Stores (custom drapes)
314129	Other Household Textile Product Mills	u	R	*2392	Housefurnishings, Except Curtains and Draperies (except mops and bags)
				*5714	Drapery, Curtain, and Upholstery Stores (custom slipcovers)
3149	Other Textile Product Mills				
31491	Textile Bag and Canvas Mills				
314911	Textile Bag Mills	u	R	*2392	Housefurnishings, Except Curtains and Draperies (blanket, laundry, and garment storage bags)
				2393	Textile Bags
314912	Canvas and Related Product Mills	u	E	2394	Canvas and Related Products
31499	All Other Textile Product Mills				
314991	Rope, Cordage, and Twine Mills	u	E	2298	Cordage and Twine
314992	Tire Cord and Tire Fabric Mills	u	E	2296	Tire Cord and Fabrics
314999	All Other Miscellaneous Textile Product Mills	u	R	*2299	Textile Goods, NEC (recovery and processing of fibers and waste)
				*2392	Housefurnishings, Except Curtains and Draperies (dust rags)

Codes: u—unique to United States; c—common to U.S. and Canada; blank—common to 3 countries; E—existing industry; N—new industry; R—revised industry;
* indicates part of a 1987 SIC; (cont'd)—continued; NEC—Not Elsewhere Classified

NAICS Code	1997 NAICS U.S. Description	Codes		SIC Code	1987 U.S. SIC Description
314999	All Other Miscellaneous Textile Product Mills (cont'd)			*2395	Pleating, Decorative and Novelty Stitching, and Tucking for the Trade (except apparel contractors)
				*3569	General Industrial Machinery and Equipment, NEC (textile fire hose)
				*7389	Business Services, NEC (embroidery of advertising on shirts and rug binding for the trade)
				*2396	Automotive Trimmings, Apparel Findings, and Related Products (textile products except automotive trimmings; apparel bindings and trimmings; and printing and embossing on fabric articles)
				*2399	Fabricated Textile Products, NEC (except apparel, automotive seat belts, and seat and tire covers)
315	Apparel Manufacturing				
3151	Apparel Knitting Mills				
31511	Hosiery and Sock Mills				
315111	Sheer Hosiery Mills	u	R	*2251	Women's Full-length and Knee-length Hosiery, (except dyeing and finishing only)
				*2252	Hosiery, NEC (girls' hosiery except dyeing and finishing only)
315119	Other Hosiery and Sock Mills	u	R	*2252	Hosiery, NEC (socks except dyeing and finishing only)
31519	Other Apparel Knitting Mills				
315191	Outerwear Knitting Mills	u	R	*2253	Knit Outerwear Mills (except dyeing and finishing only, and bath robes and lounge robes)
				*2259	Knitting Mills, NEC (gloves and mittens)
315192	Underwear and Nightwear Knitting Mills	u	R	*2254	Knit Underwear and Nightwear Mills (except dyeing and finishing only)
				*2259	Knitting Mills, NEC (girdles)
				*2253	Knit Outerwear Mills (bath robes and lounge robes made in knitting mills except dying and finishing only)
3152	Cut and Sew Apparel Manufacturing				
31521	Cut and Sew Apparel Contractors	c			
315211	Men's and Boys' Cut and Sew Apparel Contractors	u	N	*2311	Men's and Boys' Suits, Coats, and Overcoats (contractors)
				*2321	Men's and Boys' Shirts, Except Work Shirts (contractors)
				*2322	Men's and Boys' Underwear and Nightwear (contractors)
				*2323	Men's and Boys' Neckwear (contractors)
				*2325	Men's and Boys' Trousers and Slacks (contractors)

Visit page 15 to learn about major changes to NAICS sectors.

Codes: u—unique to United States; c—common to U.S. and Canada; blank—common to 3 countries; E—existing industry; N—new industry; R—revised industry; * indicates part of a 1987 SIC; (cont'd)—continued; NEC—Not Elsewhere Classified

NAICS Code	1997 NAICS U.S. Description	Codes	SIC Code	1987 U.S. SIC Description
315211	Men's and Boys' Cut and Sew Apparel (cont'd)		*2326	Men's and Boys' Work Clothing (contractors)
			*2329	Men's and Boys' Clothing, NEC (contractors)
			*2341	Women's, Misses', Children's, and Infants' Underwear and Nightwear (boys' contractors)
			*2353	Hats, Caps, and Millinery (men's and boys' contractors)
			*2361	Girls', Children's, and Infants' Dresses, Blouses, and Shirts (boys' contractors)
			*2369	Girls', Children's, and Infants' Outerwear, NEC (boys' contractors)
			*2371	Fur Goods (men's and boys' contractors)
			*2381	Dress and Work Gloves, Except Knit and All-leather (men's and boys' contractors)
			*2384	Robes and Dressing Gowns (men's and boys' contractors)
			*2385	Waterproof Outerwear (men's and boys' contractors)
			*2386	Leather and Sheep-lined Clothing (men's and boys' contractors)
			*2387	Apparel Belts (men's and boy's contractors)
			*2389	Apparel and Accessories, NEC (contractors)
			*2395	Pleating, Decorative and Novelty Stitching, and Tucking for the Trade (men's and boy's apparel contractors)
			*3151	Leather Gloves and Mittens (men's and boys' contractors)
315212	Women's, Girls', and Infants' Cut and Sew Apparel Contractors	u N	*2331	Women's, Misses', and Juniors' Blouses and Shirts (contractors)
			*2335	Women's, Misses' and Juniors' Dresses (contractors)
			*2337	Women's, Misses', and Juniors' Suits, Skirts, and Coats (contractors)
			*2339	Women's, Misses', and Juniors' Outerwear, NEC (contractors)
			*2341	Women's, Misses', Children's, and Infants' Underwear and Nightwear (contractors)
			*2342	Brassieres, Girdles, and Allied Garments (contractors)
			*2353	Hats, Caps, and Millinery (women's, girls', and infants' contractors)
			*2361	Girls', Children's, and Infants' Dresses, Blouses, and Shirts (girls' and infants' contractors)

NAICS Code	1997 NAICS U.S. Description	Codes		SIC Code	1987 U.S. SIC Description
315212	Women's, Girls', and Infants' Cut and Sew Apparel Contractors (cont'd)			*2369	Girls', Children's, and Infants' Outerwear, NEC (girls' and infants' contractors)
				*2371	Fur Goods (women's, girls' and infants' contractors)
				*2381	Dress and Work Gloves, Except Knit and All-leather (woman's, girls', and infants' contractors)
				*2384	Robes and Dressing Gowns (women's, girls', and infants' contractors)
				*2385	Waterproof Outerwear (women's, girls', and infants' contractors)
				*2386	Leather and Sheep-lined Clothing (women's, girls', and infants' contractors)
				*2387	Apparel Belts (women's, girls', and infants' contractors)
				*2389	Apparel and Accessories, NEC (contractors)
				*2395	Pleating, Decorative and Novelty Stitching, and Tucking for the Trade (women's, girls', and infants' apparel contractors)
			c	*3151	Leather Gloves and Mittens (women's, girls', and infants' contractors)
31522	Men's and Boys' Cut and Sew Apparel Manufacturing				
315221	Men's and Boys' Cut and Sew Underwear and Nightwear Manufacturing	c	R	*2322	Men's and Boys' Underwear and Nightwear (except contractors)
				*2341	Women's, Misses', Children's, and Infants' Underwear and Nightwear (boys' except contractors)
				*2369	Girls', Children's, and Infants' Outerwear, NEC (boys' robes except contractors)
				*2384	Robes and Dressing Gowns (men's except contractors)
315222	Men's and Boys' Cut and Sew Suit, Coat, and Overcoat Manufacturing	c	R	*2311	Men's and Boys' Suits, Coats, and Overcoats (except contractors)
				*2369	Girls', Children's, and Infants' Outerwear,NEC (boys' suits and coats except contractors)
				*2385	Waterproof Outerwear (men's and boys' water resistant or water repellent tailored overcoats, except contractors)
				*5699	Miscellaneous Apparel and Accessory Stores (custom tailors)
315223	Men's and Boys' Cut and Sew Shirt (except Work Shirt) Manufacturing	u	R	*2321	Men's and Boys' Shirts, Except Work Shirts (except contractors)
				*2361	Girls', Children's, and Infants' Dresses, Blouses, and Shirts (boys' shirts except contractors)
				*5699	Miscellaneous Apparel and Accessory Stores (custom tailors)

Codes: u—unique to United States; c—common to U.S. and Canada; blank—common to 3 countries; E—existing industry; N—new industry; R—revised industry;
* indicates part of a 1987 SIC; (cont'd)—continued; NEC—Not Elsewhere Classified

NAICS Code	1997 NAICS U.S. Description	Codes		SIC Code	1987 U.S. SIC Description
315224	Men's and Boys' Cut and Sew Trouser, Slack, and Jean Manufacturing	u	R	*2325	Men's and Boys' Trousers and Slacks (except contractors)
				*2369	Girls', Children's, and Infants' Outerwear, NEC (boys' trousers, slacks, and jeans except contractors)
315225	Men's and Boys' Cut and Sew Work Clothing Manufacturing	u	R	*2326	Men's and Boys' Work Clothing (except contractors)
315228	Men's and Boys' Cut and Sew Other Outerwear Manufacturing	u	R	*2329	Men's and Boys' Clothing, NEC (men's and boys' other outerwear except contractors)
				*2369	Girls', Children's, and Infants' Outerwear, NEC (boys' other outerwear except contractors)
				*2385	Waterproof Outerwear (men's and boys' water resistant or water repellent nontailored outerwear, except rubber and plastics and contractors)
31523	Women's and Girls' Cut and Sew Apparel Manufacturing				
315231	Women's and Girls' Cut and Sew Lingerie, Loungewear, and Nightwear Manufacturing	c	R	*2341	Women's, Misses', Children's, and Infants' Underwear and Nightwear (women and girls' except contractors)
				*2342	Brassieres, Girdles, and Allied Garments (except contractors)
				*2369	Girls', Children's, and Infants' Outerwear, NEC (girls' robes except contractors)
				*2384	Robes and Dressing Gowns (women's except contractors)
				*2389	Apparel and Accessories, NEC (garters and garter belts)
315232	Women's and Girls' Cut and Sew Blouse and Shirt Manufacturing	c	R	*2331	Women's, Misses', and Juniors' Blouses and Shirts (except contractors)
				*2361	Girls', Children's, and Infants' Dresses, Blouses and Shirts (girls' blouses and shirts except contractors)
315233	Women's and Girls' Cut and Sew Dress Manufacturing	c	R	*2335	Women's, Misses', and Juniors' Dresses (except contractors)
				*2361	Girls', Children's, and Infants' Dresses, Blouses and Shirts (girls' dresses except contractors)
				*5699	Miscellaneous Apparel and Accessory Stores (custom dressmakers)
315234	Women's and Girls' Cut and Sew Suit, Coat, Tailored Jacket, and Skirt Manufacturing	c	R	*2337	Women's, Misses', and Juniors' Suits, Skirts, and Coats (except contractors)
				*2369	Girls', Children's, and Infants' Outerwear, NEC (girls' suits, coats, jackets, and skirts except contractors)
				*2385	Waterproof Outerwear (women's and girls' water resistant or water repellent tailored coats, except contractors)

Codes: u—unique to United States; c—common to U.S. and Canada; blank—common to 3 countries; E—existing industry; N—new industry; R—revised industry; * indicates part of a 1987 SIC; (cont'd)—continued; NEC—Not Elsewhere Classified

NAICS Code	1997 NAICS U.S. Description	Codes		SIC Code	1987 U.S. SIC Description
315239	Women's and Girls' Cut and Sew Other Outerwear Manufacturing	c	R	*2339	Women's, Misses', and Juniors', Outerwear, NEC (except contractors)
				*2369	Girls', Children's, and Infants' Outerwear, NEC (girls' except contractors)
				*2385	Waterproof Outerwear (other women's and girls' water resistant or waterrepelent nontailored outerwear, except rubber and plastics and contractors)
31529	Other Cut and Sew Apparel Manufacturing	c			
315291	Infants' Cut and Sew Apparel Manufacturing	c	R	*2341	Women's, Misses', Children's, and Infants' Underwear and Nightwear (infants' except contractors)
				*2361	Girls', Children's, and Infants' Dresses, Blouses, and Shirts (infants' except contractors)
				*2369	Girls', Children's, and Infants' Outerwear, NEC (infants' except contractors)
				*2385	Waterproof Outerwear (infants' outerwear except contractors)
315292	Fur and Leather Apparel Manufacturing	c	R	*2371	Fur Goods (except contractors)
				*2386	Leather and Sheep-lined Clothing (except contractors)
315299	All Other Cut and Sew Apparel Manufacturing	c	R	2329	Men's and Boys' Outerwear, NEC (athletic uniforms except contractors)
				*2339	Women's, Misses', and Juniors' Outerwear, NEC (athletic uniforms except contractors)
				*2385	Waterproof Outerwear (waterproof rubber and plastics outerwear)
				*2389	Apparel and Accessories, NEC (academic and clerical outerwear, except contractors)
				*3069	Fabricated Rubber Products, NEC (rubber pants and raincoats)
3159	Apparel Accessories and Other Apparel Manufacturing				
31599	Apparel Accessories and Other Apparel Manufacturing				
315991	Hat, Cap, and Millinery Manufacturing	u	R	*2353	Hats, Caps, and Millinery (except contractors)
315992	Glove and Mitten Manufacturing	u	R	*2381	Dress and Work Gloves, Except Knit and All-leather (except contractors)
				*3151	Leather Gloves and Mittens (except contractors)
315993	Men's and Boys' Neckwear Manufacturing	u	R	*2323	Men's and Boys' Neckwear (except contractors)
315999	Other Apparel Accessories and Other Apparel Manufacturing	u	N	*2339	Women's, Misses', and Juniors' Outerwear, NEC (scarves)

Visit page 9 to learn more about NAICS codes.

Codes: u—unique to United States; c—common to U.S. and Canada; blank—common to 3 countries; E—existing industry; N—new industry; R—revised industry; * indicates part of a 1987 SIC; (cont'd)—continued; NEC—Not Elsewhere Classified

NAICS Code	1997 NAICS U.S. Description	Codes		SIC Code	1987 U.S. SIC Description
315999	Other Apparel Accessories and Other Apparel Manufacturing (cont'd)			*2385	Waterproof Outerwear (accessories such as aprons, bibs, and other miscellaneous waterproof items except contractors)
				*2387	Apparel Belts (except contractors)
				*2389	Apparel and Accessories, NEC (handkerchiefs, arm bands,etc.)
				*2396	Automotive Trimmings, Apparel Findings, and Related Products (apparel findings and trimming)
				*2399	Fabricated Textile Products, NEC (apparel and apparel accessories)
				*3069	Fabricated Rubber Products, NEC (rubber bibs, aprons and bathing caps)
316	Leather and Allied Product Manufacturing				
3161	Leather and Hide Tanning and Finishing				
31611	Leather and Hide Tanning and Finishing		R	3111	Leather Tanning and Finishing
				*3999	Manufacturing Industries, NEC (fur dressing and bleaching)
3162	Footwear Manufacturing				
31621	Footwear Manufacturing				
316211	Rubber and Plastics Footwear Manufacturing	u	E	3021	Rubber and Plastics Footwear
316212	House Slipper Manufacturing	u	E	3142	House Slippers
316213	Men's Footwear (except Athletic) Manufacturing	u	E	3143	Men's Footwear, except Athletic
316214	Women's Footwear (except Athletic) Manufacturing	u	E	3144	Women's Footwear, except Athletic
316219	Other Footwear Manufacturing	u	E	3149	Footwear Except Rubber, NEC
3169	Other Leather and Allied Product Manufacturing				
31699	Other Leather and Allied Product Manufacturing				
316991	Luggage Manufacturing	u	E	3161	Luggage
316992	Women's Handbag and Purse Manufacturing	u	E	3171	Women's Handbags and Purses
316993	Personal Leather Goods (except Women's Handbag and Purse) Manufacturing	u	E	3172	Personal Leather Goods, except Women's Handbags and Purses
316999	All Other Leather Goods Manufacturing	u	R	*3131	Boot and Shoe Cut Stock and Findings (except wood heels and metal buckles)
				3199	Leather Goods, NEC
321	Wood Product Manufacturing				
3211	Sawmills and Wood Preservation				
32111	Sawmills and Wood Preservation				
321113	Sawmills	u	R	*2421	Sawmills and Planing Mills, General (sawmills)

NAICS Code	1997 NAICS U.S. Description	Codes		SIC Code	1987 U.S. SIC Description
321113	Sawmills (cont'd)			*2426	Hardwood Dimension and Flooring Mills (hardwood dimension from logs and bolts)
				*2429	Special Product Sawmills, NEC (shingle mills, shakes)
321114	Wood Preservation	c	E	2491	Wood Preserving
3212	Veneer, Plywood, and Engineered Wood Product Manufacturing				
32121	Veneer, Plywood, and Engineered Wood Product Manufacturing				
321211	Hardwood Veneer and Plywood Manufacturing	c	E	2435	Hardwood Veneer and Plywood
321212	Softwood Veneer and Plywood Manufacturing	c	E	2436	Softwood Veneer and Plywood
321213	Engineered Wood Member (except Truss)	u	R	*2439	Structural Wood Members, NEC (except trusses)
321214	Truss Manufacturing	u	N	*2439	Structural Wood Members, NEC (trusses)
321219	Reconstituted Wood Product Manufacturing	u	E	2493	Reconstituted Wood Products
3219	Other Wood Product Manufacturing				
32191	Millwork				
321911	Wood Window and Door Manufacturing	c	N	*2431	Millwork (wood windows and doors)
321912	Cut Stock, Resawing Lumber, and Planing	u	N	*2421	Sawmills and Planing Mills, General (lumber manufacturing from purchased lumber, softwood cut stock, wood lath, fence pickets, and planing mill products)
				*2426	Hardwood Dimension and Flooring Mills (except flooring)
				*2429	Special Product Sawmills, NEC (stave manufacturing from purchased lumber)
321918	Other Millwork (including Flooring)	u	R	*2426	Hardwood Dimension and Flooring Mills (hardwood flooring)
				*2421	Sawmills and Planing Mills, General (soft wood flooring)
				*2431	Millwork (except wood doors and windows)
32192	Wood Container and Pallet Manufacturing			*2429	Special Product Sawmills, NEC (cooperage stock)
			N	2441	Nailed and Lock Corner Wood Boxes and Shook
				2448	Wood Pallets and Skids
				2449	Wood Containers, NEC
				*2499	Wood Products, NEC (wood tubs and vats, jewelry, cigar boxes, and baskets, except fruit, vegetable, fish and bait)
32199	All Other Wood Product				
321991	Manufactured Home (Mobile Home) Manufacturing	c	E	2451	Mobile Homes

NAICS to SIC

Codes: u—unique to United States; c—common to U.S. and Canada; blank—common to 3 countries; E—existing industry; N—new industry; R—revised industry; * indicates part of a 1987 SIC; (cont'd)—continued; NEC—Not Elsewhere Classified

NAICS Code	1997 NAICS U.S. Description	Codes		SIC Code	1987 U.S. SIC Description
321992	Prefabricated Wood Building Manufacturing	c	E	2452	Prefabricated Wood Buildings and Components
321999	All Other Miscellaneous Wood Product Manufacturing	c	R	*2421	Sawmills and Planing Mills, General (kiln drying)
				*2429	Special Product Sawmills, NEC (excelsior and cooperage headings)
				*2499	Wood Products, NEC (other wood products)
				*3131	Boot and Shoe Cut Stock and Findings (wood heels)
322	Paper Manufacturing				
3221	Pulp, Paper, and Paperboard Mills				
32211	Pulp Mills		R	*2611	Pulp Mills (pulp producing mills only)
32212	Paper Mills				
322121	Paper (except Newsprint) Mills	c	R	*2611	Pulp Mills (pulp mills producing paper)
				*2621	Paper Mills (except newsprint mills)
322122	Newsprint Mills	c	N	*2621	Paper Mills (newsprint mills)
				*2611	Pulp Mills (pulp mills producing newsprint)
32213	Paperboard Mills		R	*2611	Pulp Mills (pulp mills producing paperboard)
				2631	Paperboard Mills
3222	Converted Paper Product Manufacturing				
32221	Paperboard Container Manufacturing				
322211	Corrugated and Solid Fiber Box Manufacturing	c	R	2653	Corrugated and Solid Fiber Boxes
				*2679	Converted Paper and Paperboard Products, NEC (corrugated paper)
322212	Folding Paperboard Box Manufacturing	c	E	2657	Folding Paperboard Boxes, Including Sanitary
322213	Setup Paperboard Box Manufacturing	u	E	2652	Setup Paperboard Boxes
322214	Fiber Can, Tube, Drum, and Similar Products Manufacturing	u	E	2655	Fiber Cans, Tubes, Drums, and Similar Products
322215	Nonfolding Sanitary Food Container Manufacturing	u	E	2656	Sanitary Food Containers, except Folding
32222	Paper Bag and Coated and Treated Paper Manufacturing				
322221	Coated and Laminated Packaging Manufacturing	u	R	*2671	Packaging Paper and Plastics Film, Coated and Laminated Paper and Plastics Film (single-web paper, paper multi-web laminated rolls and sheets for packaging uses)
322222	Coated and Laminated Paper Manufacturing	u	R	2672	Coated and Laminated Paper, NEC
				*2679	Converted Paper and Paperboard Products, NEC (wallpaper and gift wrap paper)
322223	Plastics, Foil, and Coated Paper Bag Manufacturing	u	R	*2673	Plastics, Foil, and Coated Paper Bags (except all plastics)
322224	Uncoated Paper and Multi-wall Bag	u	E	2674	Uncoated Paper and Multiwall Bags

Codes: u—unique to United States; c—common to U.S. and Canada; blank—common to 3 countries; E—existing industry; N—new industry; R—revised industry;
    * indicates part of a 1987 SIC; (cont'd)—continued; NEC—Not Elsewhere Classified

NAICS Code	1997 NAICS U.S. Description	Codes		SIC Code	1987 U.S. SIC Description
322225	Laminated Aluminum Foil Manufacturing	u	N	*3497	Metal Foil and Leaf (laminated aluminum for Flexible Packaging Uses foil rolls and sheets for flexible packaging uses)
322226	Surface-coated Paperboard Manufacturing	u	N	*2675	Die-cut Paper and Paperboard and Cardboard (pasted, lined, laminated, or surface-coated paperboard)
32223	Stationery Product Manufacturing				
322231	Die-cut Paper and Paperboard Office Supplies Manufacturing	u	N	*2675	Die-cut Paper and Paperboard and Cardboard (file folders, tabulating cards, and other paper and paperboard office supplies)
				*2679	Converted Paper and Paperboard Products, NEC (paper supplies for business machines and other paper office supplies)
322232	Envelope Manufacturing	u	E	2677	Envelopes
322233	Stationery, Tablet, and Related Product Manufacturing	u	E	2678	Stationery, Tablets, and Related Products
32229	Other Converted Paper Product Manufacturing				
322291	Sanitary Paper Product Manufacturing	c	R	2676	Sanitary Paper Products
				*3842	Orthopedic, Prosthetic, and Surgical Appliances and Supplies (incontinent and bed pads)
322299	All Other Converted Paper Product Manufacturing	c	R	*2675	Die-cut Paper and Paperboard and Cardboard (Die-cut paper and paperboard products, except office supplies and pasted, lined, laminated, or surface-coated paperboard)
				*2679	Converted Paper and Paperboard Products, NEC (other converted paper and paperboard products, such as paper filters, crepe paper, and laminated and tiled wallboard)
323	Printing and Related Support Activities				
3231	Printing and Related Support Activities				
32311	Printing				
323110	Commercial Lithographic Printing	u	R	*2752	Commercial Printing, Lithographic (except quick printing)
				*2771	Greeting Cards (lithographic printing of greeting cards)
323111	Commercial Gravure Printing	u	R	2754	Commercial Printing, Gravure
				*2771	Greeting Cards (gravure printing of greeting cards)
323112	Commercial Flexographic Printing	u	N	*2759	Commercial Printing, NEC (flexographic printing)
				*2771	Greeting Cards (flexographic printing of greeting cards)

NAICS to SIC

Codes: u—unique to United States; c—common to U.S. and Canada; blank—common to 3 countries; E—existing industry; N—new industry; R—revised industry;
* indicates part of a 1987 SIC; (cont'd)—continued; NEC—Not Elsewhere Classified

NAICS Code	1997 NAICS U.S. Description	Codes		SIC Code	1987 U.S. SIC Description
323113	Commercial Screen Printing	c	N	*2396	Automotive Trimmings, Apparel Findings, and Related Products (printing and embossing on fabric articles)
				*2759	Commercial Printing, NEC (screen printing)
				*2771	Greeting Cards (screen printing of greeting cards)
323114	Quick Printing	c	N	*2752	Commercial Printing, Lithographic (quick printing)
				*2759	Commercial Printing, NEC (quick printing)
				*7334	Photocopying and Duplicating Services (instant printing)
323115	Digital Printing	c	N	*2759	Commercial Printing, NEC (digital printing, except quick printing)
323116	Manifold Business Forms Printing	c	R	2761	Manifold Business Forms
				*2782	Blankbooks, Looseleaf Binders, and Devices (checkbooks)
323117	Books Printing	u	E	2732	Book Printing
323118	Blankbook, Looseleaf Binders, and Devices Manufacturing	u	R	*2782	Blankbooks, Looseleaf Binders, and Devices (except checkbooks)
323119	Other Commercial Printing	u	R	*2759	Commercial Printing, NEC (other commercial printing except quick printing)
				*2771	Greeting Cards (other printing of greeting cards)
32312	Support Activities for Printing				
323121	Tradebinding and Related Work	u	E	2789	Bookbinding and Related Work
323122	Prepress Services	u	R	2791	Typesetting
				2796	Platemaking and Related Services
324	Petroleum and Coal Products Manufacturing				
3241	Petroleum and Coal Products Manufacturing				
32411	Petroleum Refineries		E	2911	Petroleum Refining
32412	Asphalt Paving, Roofing, and Saturated Materials Manufacturing				
324121	Asphalt Paving Mixture and Block Manufacturing	c	E	2951	Asphalt Paving Mixtures and Blocks
324122	Asphalt Shingle and Coating Materials Manufacturing	c	E	2952	Asphalt Felts and Coatings
32419	Other Petroleum and Coal Products Manufacturing				
324191	Petroleum Lubricating Oil and Grease Manufacturing	u	E	2992	Lubricating Oils and Greases
324199	All Other Petroleum and Coal Products Manufacturing	u	R	2999	Products of Petroleum and Coal, NEC
				*3312	Blast Furnaces and Steel Mills (coke ovens)
325	Chemical Manufacturing				
3251	Basic Chemical Manufacturing				

Codes: u—unique to United States; c—common to U.S. and Canada; blank—common to 3 countries; E—existing industry; N—new industry; R—revised industry; * indicates part of a 1987 SIC; (cont'd)—continued; NEC—Not Elsewhere Classified

186

Harris InfoSource

NAICS Code	1997 NAICS U.S. Description	Codes		SIC Code	1987 U.S. SIC Description
32511	Petrochemical Manufacturing		N	*2865	Cyclic Organic Crudes and Intermediates, and Organic Dyes and Pigments (aromatics)
				*2869	Industrial Organic Chemicals, NEC (aliphatics)
32512	Industrial Gas Manufacturing		R	2813	Industrial Gases
				*2869	Industrial Organic Chemicals, NEC (fluorocarbon gases)
32513	Synthetic Dye and Pigment Manufacturing				
325131	Inorganic Dye and Pigment Manufacturing	u	N	*2816	Inorganic Pigments (except bone and lamp black)
				*2819	Industrial Inorganic Chemicals, NEC (inorganic dyes)
325132	Synthetic Organic Dye and Pigment Manufacturing	u	N	*2865	Cyclic Organic Crudes and Intermediates, and Organic Dyes and Pigments (except aromatics and organic dyes and pigments)
32518	Other Basic Inorganic Chemical Manufacturing				
325181	Alkalies and Chlorine Manufacturing	c	E	2812	Alkalies and Chlorine
325182	Carbon Black Manufacturing	u	R	*2816	Inorganic pigments (bone and lamp black)
				2895	Carbon Black
325188	All Other Basic Inorganic Chemical Manufacturing	u	R	*2819	Industrial Inorganic Chemicals, NEC (except activated carbon and charcoal, alumina, and inorganic industrial dyes)
				*2869	Industrial Organic Chemicals, NEC (carbon bisulfide)
32519	Other Basic Organic Chemical				
325191	Gum and Wood Chemical Manufacturing	u	E	2861	Gum and Wood Chemicals
325192	Cyclic Crude and Intermediate Manufacturing	u	R	*2865	Cyclic Organic Crudes and Intermediates and Organic Dyes and Pigments (except aromatics and organic dyes and pigments)
325193	Ethyl Alcohol Manufacturing	u	N	*2869	Industrial Organic Chemicals (ethyl alcohol)
325199	All Other Basic Organic Chemical Manufacturing	u	R	*2869	Industrial Organic Chemicals, NEC (except aliphatics, carbon bisulfide, ethyl alcohol, and fluorocarbon gases)
				*2899	Chemical and Chemical Preparations, NEC (fatty acids)
3252	Resin, Synthetic Rubber, and Artificial and Synthetic Fibers and Filaments Manufacturing				
32521	Resin and Synthetic Rubber Manufacturing				
325211	Plastics Material and Resin Manufacturing	u	E	2821	Plastics Materials, Synthetic and Resins, and Nonvulcanizable Elastomers

Visit page 15 to learn about major changes to NAICS sectors.

Codes: u—unique to United States; c—common to U.S. and Canada; blank—common to 3 countries; E—existing industry; N—new industry; R—revised industry;
* indicates part of a 1987 SIC; (cont'd)—continued; NEC—Not Elsewhere Classified

NAICS Code	1997 NAICS U.S. Description	Codes		SIC Code	1987 U.S. SIC Description
325212	Synthetic Rubber Manufacturing	u	E	2822	Synthetic Rubber
32522	Artificial and Synthetic Fibers and Filaments Manufacturing				
325221	Cellulosic Organic Fiber Manufacturing	u	E	2823	Cellulosic Man-made Fibers
325222	Noncellulosic Organic Fiber Manufacturing	u	E	2824	Man-made Organic Fibers, except Cellulosic
3253	Pesticide, Fertilizer, and Other Agricultural Chemical Manufacturing				
32531	Fertilizer Manufacturing				
325311	Nitrogenous Fertilizer	u	E	2873	Nitrogenous Fertilizers
325312	Phosphatic Fertilizer Manufacturing	u	E	2874	Phosphatic Fertilizers
325314	Fertilizer (Mixing Only) Manufacturing	c	E	2875	Fertilizers, Mixing Only
32532	Pesticide and Other Agricultural Chemical Manufacturing		E	2879	Pesticides and Agricultural Chemicals, NEC
3254	Pharmaceutical and Medicine Manufacturing				
32541	Pharmaceutical and Medicine Manufacturing				
325411	Medicinal and Botanical Manufacturing	u	E	2833	Medicinal Chemicals and Botanical Products
325412	Pharmaceutical Preparation Manufacturing	u	R	2834 *2835	Pharmaceutical Preparations In Vitro and In Vivo Diagnostic Substances (except in vitro diagnostic)
325413	In Vitro Diagnostic Substance Manufacturing	u	N	*2835	In Vitro and In Vivo Diagnostic Substances (in vitro diagnostic substances)
325414	Biological Product (except Diagnostic) Manufacturing	u	E	2836	Biological Products, except Diagnostic Substance
3255	Paint, Coating, and Adhesive Manufacturing				
32551	Paint and Coating Manufacturing		R	2851 *2899	Paints, Varnishes, Lacquers, Enamels and Allied Products Chemicals and Chemical Preparations, NEC (frit)
32552	Adhesive Manufacturing		E	2891	Adhesives and Sealants
3256	Soap, Cleaning Compound, and Toilet Preparation Manufacturing				
32561	Soap and Cleaning Compound Manufacturing				
325611	Soap and Other Detergent Manufacturing	u	R	2841 *2844	Soaps and Other Detergents, except Specialty Cleaners Toilet Preparations (toothpaste)
325612	Polish and Other Sanitation Good Manufacturing	u	E	2842	Specialty Cleaning, Polishing, and Sanitary Preparations
325613	Surface Active Agent Manufacturing	u	E	2843	Surface Active Agents, Finishing Agents, Sulfonated Oils, and Assistants
32562	Toilet Preparation Manufacturing		R	*2844	Perfumes, Cosmetics, and Other Toilet Preparations (except toothpaste)

Codes: u—unique to United States; c—common to U.S. and Canada; blank—common to 3 countries; E—existing industry; N—new industry; R—revised industry; * indicates part of a 1987 SIC; (cont'd)—continued; NEC—Not Elsewhere Classified

NAICS Code	1997 NAICS U.S. Description	Codes		SIC Code	1987 U.S. SIC Description
3259	Other Chemical Product and Preparation Manufacturing				
32591	Printing Ink Manufacturing		E	2893	Printing Ink
32592	Explosives Manufacturing		E	2892	Explosives
32599	All Other Chemical Product and Preparation Manufacturing				
325991	Custom Compounding of Purchased Resins	c	E	3087	Custom Compounding of Purchased Plastics Resin
325992	Photographic Film, Paper, Plate, and Chemical Manufacturing	u	N	*3861	Photographic Equipment and Supplies (photographic films, and paper, plates and chemicals)
325998	All Other Miscellaneous Chemical Product and Preparation Manufacturing	u	R	*2819	Industrial Inorganic Chemicals, NEC (activated carbon and charcoal)
				*2899	Chemicals and Chemical Preparations, NEC (except frit and table salt)
				*3952	Lead Pencils and Art Goods (drawing inks and india ink)
				*3999	Manufacturing Industries, NEC (matches)
				*7389	Business Services, NEC (aerosol packaging)
326	Plastics and Rubber Products Manufacturing				
3261	Plastics Product Manufacturing				
32611	Unsupported Plastics Film, Sheet, and Bag Manufacturing				
326111	Unsupported Plastics Bag Manufacturing	c	N	*2673	Plastics, Foil, and Coated Paper Bags (plastics bags)
326112	Unsupported Plastics Packaging Film and Sheet Manufacturing	u	N	*2671	Packaging Paper and Plastics Film, Coated, and Laminated (plastics packaging film and sheet)
326113	Unsupported Plastics Film and Sheet (except Packaging) Manufacturing	u	E	3081	Unsupported Plastics Film and Sheets
32612	Plastics Pipe, Pipe Fitting, and Unsupported Profile Shapes Manufacturing				
326121	Unsupported Plastics Profile Shape Manufacturing	c	R	3082	Unsupported Plastics Profile Shapes
				*3089	Plastics Product, NEC (plastics sausage casings)
326122	Plastics Pipe and Pipe Fitting Manufacturing	c	R	3084	Plastics Pipe
				*3089	Plastics Products, NEC (pipe fittings)
32613	Laminated Plastics Plate, Sheet, and Shape Manufacturing		E	3083	Laminated Plastics Plate, Sheet, and Profile Shapes
32614	Polystyrene Foam Product Manufacturing		N	*3086	Plastics Foam Products (polystyrene foam products)
32615	Urethane and Other Foam Product (except Polystyrene) Manufacturing		N	*3086	Plastics Foam Products (urethane and other foam products)
32616	Plastics Bottle Manufacturing		E	3085	Plastics Bottles
32619	Other Plastics Product Manufacturing				
326191	Plastics Plumbing Fixture Manufacturing	c	E	3088	Plastics Plumbing Fixtures

Codes: u—unique to United States; c—common to U.S. and Canada; blank—common to 3 countries; E—existing industry; N—new industry; R—revised industry; * indicates part of a 1987 SIC; (cont'd)—continued; NEC—Not Elsewhere Classified

NAICS Code	1997 NAICS U.S. Description	Codes		SIC Code	1987 U.S. SIC Description
326192	Resilient Floor Covering Manufacturing	u	R	*3069	Fabricated Rubber Products, NEC (rubber resilient floor coverings)
				3996	Linoleum, Asphalted-felt-base, and Other Hard Surface Floor Coverings, NEC
326199	All Other Plastics Product Manufacturing	u	R	*3089	Plastics Products, NEC (except plastics pipe fittings and plastics sausage casings)
				*3999	Manufacturing Industries, NEC (plastics products such as combs, hair curlers, etc.)
3262	Rubber Product Manufacturing				
32621	Tire Manufacturing				
326211	Tire Manufacturing (except Retreading)	u	E	3011	Tires and Inner Tubes
326212	Tire Retreading	u	N	*7534	Tire Retreading and Repair Shops (rebuilding)
32622	Rubber and Plastics Hoses and Belting Manufacturing		E	3052	Rubber and Plastics Hose and Belting
32629	Other Rubber Product Manufacturing				
326291	Rubber Product Manufacturing for Mechanical Use	u	E	3061	Molded, Extruded, and Lathe-cut Mechanical Rubber Goods
326299	All Other Rubber Product Manufacturing	u	R	*3069	Fabricated Rubber Products, NEC (except rubberized fabric and rubber resilient floor covering)
327	Nonmetallic Mineral Product Manufacturing				
3271	Clay Product and Refractory Manufacturing				
32711	Pottery, Ceramics, and Plumbing Fixture Manufacturing				
327111	Vitreous China Plumbing Fixture and China and Earthenware Bathroom Accessories Manufacturing	u	E	3261	Vitreous China Plumbing Fixtures and China and Earthenware Fittings and Bathroom Accessories
327112	Vitreous China, Fine Earthenware, and Other Pottery Product Manufacturing	u	N	3262	Vitreous China Table and Kitchen Articles
				3263	Fine Earthenware (Whiteware) Table and Kitchen Articles
				3269	Pottery Products, NEC
				*3299	Nonmetallic Mineral Products, NEC (clay statuary)
327113	Porcelain Electrical Supply Manufacturing	u	E	3264	Porcelain Electrical Supplies
32712	Clay Building Material and Refractories Manufacturing				
327121	Brick and Structural Clay Tile Manufacturing	u	R	*3251	Brick and Structural Clay Tile (except slumped brick)
327122	Ceramic Wall and Floor Tile Manufacturing	u	E	3253	Ceramic Wall and Floor Tile
327123	Other Structural Clay Product Manufacturing	u	E	3259	Structural Clay Products, NEC
327124	Clay Refractory Manufacturing	u	E	3255	Clay Refractories

NAICS to SIC

Codes: u—unique to United States; c—common to U.S. and Canada; blank—common to 3 countries; E—existing industry; N—new industry; R—revised industry; * indicates part of a 1987 SIC; (cont'd)—continued; NEC—Not Elsewhere Classified

NAICS Code	1997 NAICS U.S. Description	Codes		SIC Code	1987 U.S. SIC Description
327125	Nonclay Refractory Manufacturing	u	E	3297	Nonclay Refractories
3272	Glass and Glass Product				
32721	Glass and Glass Product				
327211	Flat Glass Manufacturing	u	E	3211	Flat Glass
327212	Other Pressed and Blown Glass and Glassware Manufacturing	u	E	3229	Pressed and Blown Glass and Glassware, NEC
327213	Glass Container Manufacturing	u	E	3221	Glass Containers
327215	Glass Product Manufacturing Made of Purchased Glass	c	E	3231	Glass Products Made of Purchased Glass
3273	Cement and Concrete Product Manufacturing				
32731	Cement Manufacturing		E	3241	Cement, Hydraulic
32732	Ready-mix Concrete Manufacturing		E	3273	Ready-mixed Concrete
32733	Concrete Pipe, Brick, and Block Manufacturing				
327331	Concrete Block and Brick Manufacturing	u	R	*3251	Brick and Structural Clay Tile (slumped brick)
				3271	Concrete Block and Brick
327332	Concrete Pipe Manufacturing	u	N	*3272	Concrete Products, except Block and Brick (concrete pipe)
32739	Other Concrete Product Manufacturing		N	*3272	Concrete Products, except Block and Brick (concrete products, except dry mix concrete and pipe)
3274	Lime and Gypsum Product Manufacturing				
32741	Lime Manufacturing		E	3274	Lime
32742	Gypsum Product Manufacturing		R	3275	Gypsum Products
				*3299	Nonmetallic Mineral Products, NEC (moldings, ornamental and architectural plaster work and gypsum statuary)
3279	Other Nonmetallic Mineral Product Manufacturing				
32791	Abrasive Product Manufacturing		R	*3291	Abrasive Products (except steel wool with or without soap)
32799	All Other Nonmetallic Mineral Product Manufacturing				
327991	Cut Stone and Stone Product Manufacturing	u	L	3281	Cut Stone and Stone Products
327992	Ground or Treated Mineral and Earth Manufacturing	u	R	*3295	Minerals and Earths, Ground or Otherwise Treated (except grinding, washing, separating, etc., of nonmetallic minerals)
327993	Mineral Wool Manufacturing	u	E	3296	Mineral Wool
327999	All Other Miscellaneous Nonmetallic Mineral Product Manufacturing	u	R	*3272	Concrete Products, except Block and Brick (dry mixture concrete)
				*3292	Asbestos Products (except brake pads and linings)
				*3299	Nonmetallic Mineral Products, NEC (except moldings, ornamental and architectural plaster work, clay and gypsum statuary)

Codes: u—unique to United States; c—common to U.S. and Canada; blank—common to 3 countries; E—existing industry; N—new industry; R—revised industry; * indicates part of a 1987 SIC; (cont'd)—continued; NEC—Not Elsewhere Classified

NAICS Code	1997 NAICS U.S. Description	Codes		SIC Code	1987 U.S. SIC Description
331	Primary Metal Manufacturing				
3311	Iron and Steel Mills and Ferroalloy Manufacturing				
33111	Iron and Steel Mills and Ferroalloy Manufacturing				
331111	Iron and Steel Mills	u	N	*3312	Steel Works, Blast Furnaces (Including Coke Ovens), and Rolling Mills (except coke ovens not integrated with steel mills and hot-rolling purchased steel)
331112	Electrometallurgical Ferroalloy Product Manufacturing	u	E	3313	Electrometallurgical Products, except Steel
3312	Steel Product Manufacturing from Purchased Steel				
33121	Iron and Steel Pipe and Tube Manufacturing		E	3317	Steel Pipe and Tubes from Purchased Steel
33122	Rolling and Drawing of Purchased of Purchased Steel				
331221	Rolled Steel Shape Manufacturing	c	R	*3312	Steel Works, Blast Furnaces (including coke ovens), and Rolling Mills (hot-rolling purchased steel)
				3316	Cold-rolled Steel Sheet, Strip and Bars
				*3399	Primary Metal Products, NEC (making ferrous metal powder, paste, and flake from purchased iron or steel)
331222	Steel Wire Drawing	c	R	*3315	Steel Wire Drawing and Steel Nails and Spikes (steel, wire drawing)
3313	Alumina and Aluminum Production and Processing				
33131	Alumina and Aluminum Production and Processing				
331311	Alumina Refining	u	N	*2819	Industrial Inorganic Chemicals, NEC (alumina)
331312	Primary Aluminum Production	u	E	3334	Primary Production of Aluminum
331314	Secondary Smelting and Alloying of Aluminum	u	N	*3341	Secondary Smelting and Refining of Nonferrous Metals (aluminum)
				*3399	Primary Metal Products, NEC (aluminum powder, paste, flakes, etc.)
331315	Aluminum Sheet, Plate, and Foil Manufacturing	u	E	3353	Aluminum Sheet, Plate, and Foil
331316	Aluminum Extruded Product Manufacturing	u	E	3354	Aluminum Extruded Products
331319	Other Aluminum Rolling and Drawing	u	R	3355	Aluminum Rolling and Drawing, NEC
				*3357	Drawing and Insulating of Nonferrous Wire (aluminum wire drawing)
3314	Nonferrous Metal (except Aluminum) Production and Processing				
33141	Nonferrous Metal (except Aluminum) Smelting and Refining				
331411	Primary Smelting and Refining of Copper	u	E	3331	Primary Smelting and Refining of Copper

Codes: u—unique to United States; c—common to U.S. and Canada; blank—common to 3 countries; E—existing industry; N—new industry; R—revised industry; * indicates part of a 1987 SIC; (cont'd)—continued; NEC—Not Elsewhere Classified

192

Harris InfoSource

NAICS Code	1997 NAICS U.S. Description	Codes		SIC Code	1987 U.S. SIC Description
331419	Primary Smelting and Refining of Nonferrous Metal (except Copper and Aluminum)	u	E	3339	Primary Smelting and Refining of Nonferrous Metals, except Copper and Aluminum
33142	Copper Rolling, Drawing, Extruding, and Alloying				
331421	Copper Rolling, Drawing, and Extruding	u	E	3351	Rolling, Drawing, and Extruding of Copper
331422	Copper Wire (except Mechanical) Drawing	u	N	*3357	Drawing and Insulating of Nonferrous Wire (copper wire drawing)
331423	Secondary Smelting, Refining, and Alloying of Copper	u	R	*3341	Secondary Smelting and Refining of Nonferrous Metals (copper)
				*3399	Primary Metal Products, NEC (copper powders, flakes, paste, etc.)
33149	Nonferrous Metal (except Copper and Aluminum) Rolling, Drawing, Extruding, and Alloying				
331491	Nonferrous Metal (except Copper and Aluminum) Rolling, Drawing, and Extruding	u	R	3356	Rolling, Drawing, and Extruding of Nonferrous Metals, except Copper and Aluminum
				*3357	Drawing and Insulating of Nonferrous Wire (wire drawing except copper or aluminum)
331492	Secondary Smelting, Refining, and Alloying of Nonferrous Metal (except Copper and Aluminum)	u	N	*3341	Secondary Smelting and Refining of Nonferrous Metals (except copper and aluminum)
				*3399	Primary Metal Products, NEC (except copper and aluminum)
3315	Foundries				
33151	Ferrous Metal Foundries				
331511	Iron Foundries	c	R	3321	Gray and Ductile Iron Foundries
				3322	Malleable Iron Foundries
331512	Steel Investment Foundries	u	E	3324	Steel Investment Foundries
331513	Steel Foundries (except Investment)	u	E	3325	Steel Foundries, NEC
33152	Nonferrous Metal Foundries				
331521	Aluminum Die-casting Foundries	u	E	3363	Aluminum Die-castings
331522	Nonferrous (except Aluminum) Die-casting Foundries	u	E	3364	Nonferrous Die-castings, except Aluminum
331524	Aluminum Foundries (except Die-casting)	u	E	3365	Aluminum Foundries
331525	Copper Foundries (except Die-casting)	u	E	3366	Copper Foundries
331528	Other Nonferrous Foundries (except Die-casting)	u	E	3369	Nonferrous Foundries, except Aluminum and Copper
332	Fabricated Metal Product Manufacturing				
3321	Forging and Stamping				
33211	Forging and Stamping				
332111	Iron and Steel Forging	u	E	3462	Iron and Steel Forgings
332112	Nonferrous Forging	u	E	3463	Nonferrous Forgings
332114	Custom Roll Forming	u	N	*3449	Miscellaneous Structural Metal Work (custom roll forming)

Visit page 15 to learn about major changes to NAICS sectors.

Visit page 9 to learn more about NAICS codes.

Codes: u—unique to United States; c—common to U.S. and Canada; blank—common to 3 countries; E—existing industry; N—new industry; R—revised industry;
* indicates part of a 1987 SIC; (cont'd)—continued; NEC—Not Elsewhere Classified

NAICS Code	1997 NAICS U.S. Description	Codes		SIC Code	1987 U.S. SIC Description
332115	Crown and Closure Manufacturing	u	E	3466	Crowns and Closures
332116	Metal Stamping	u	N	*3469	Metal Stampings, NEC (except kitchen utensils, pots and pans for cooking, and coins)
332117	Powder Metallurgy Part	u	N	*3499	Fabricated Metal Products, NEC (powder metallurgy)
3322	Cutlery and Handtool Manufacturing				
33221	Cutlery and Handtool Manufacturing				
332211	Cutlery and Flatware (except Precious) Manufacturing	u	N	*3421	Cutlery (except tool-type shears)
				*3914	Silverware, Plated Ware, and Stainless Steel Ware (cutlery and flatware, non precious and precious plated)
				*3999	Manufacturing Industries, NEC (human hair clippers, hand operated)
332212	Hand and Edge Tool Manufacturing	u	R	*3421	Cutlery (tool-type shears)
				3423	Hand and Edge Tools, except Machine Tools and Handsaws
				*3523	Farm Machinery and Equipment (hand hair clippers for animals)
				*3524	Lawn and Garden Tractors and Home Lawn and Garden Equipment (nonpowered lawnmowers)
				*3545	Cutting Tools, Machine Tools Accessories, and Machinist Precision Measuring Devices (precision measuring devices)
				*3644	Noncurrent-carrying Wiring Devices (fish wire, electrical wiring tool)
				*3999	Manufacturing Industries, NEC (tape measures)
332213	Saw Blade and Handsaw Manufacturing	u	E	3425	Saw Blades and Handsaws
332214	Kitchen Utensil, Pot, and Pan Manufacturing	u	N	*3469	Metal Stampings, NEC (kitchen utensils, pots, and pans for cooking)
3323	Architectural and Structural Metals Manufacturing				
33231	Plate Work and Fabricated Structural Product				
332311	Prefabricated Metal Building and Component Manufacturing	c	E	3448	Prefabricated Metal Buildings and Components
332312	Fabricated Structural Metal Manufacturing	u	R	3441	Fabricated Structural Metal
				*3449	Miscellaneous Structural Metal Work (fabricated bar joists and concrete reinforcing bars)
332313	Plate Work Manufacturing	u	N	*3443	Fabricated Plate Work (Boiler Shops) (fabricated plate work and metal weldments)
33232	Ornamental and Architectural Metal Products Manufacturing				

NAICS Code	1997 NAICS U.S. Description	Codes		SIC Code	1987 U.S. SIC Description
332321	Metal Window and Door Manufacturing	c	R	3442	Metal Doors, Sash, Frames, Molding and Trim
				*3449	Miscellaneous Structural Metal Work (curtain wall)
332322	Sheet Metal Work Manufacturing	u	R	*3444	Sheet Metal Work (ducts, flumes, flooring, siding, dampers, etc.)
332323	Ornamental and Architectural Metal Manufacturing	u	R	3446	Architectural and Ornamental Metal Work
				*3449	Miscellaneous Structural Metal Work (metal plaster bases)
				*3523	Farm Machinery and Equipment (corrals, stalls, and holding gates)
3324	Boiler, Tank, and Shipping Container Manufacturing				
33241	Power Boiler and Heat Exchanger Manufacturing		N	*3443	Fabricated Plate Work (Boiler Shops) (power boilers and heat exchangers)
				*3559	Special Industry Machinery, NEC (nuclear control drive mechanisms)
33242	Metal Tank (Heavy Gauge) Manufacturing		N	*3443	Fabricated Plate Work (Boiler Shops) (heavy gauge tanks)
33243	Metal Can, Box, and Other Metal Container (Light Gauge) Manufacturing				
332431	Metal Can Manufacturing	c	E	3411	Metal Cans
332439	Other Metal Container Manufacturing	c	R	3412	Metal Shipping Barrels, Drums, Kegs, and Pails
				*3429	Hardware, NEC (vacuum and insulated bottles, jugs, and chests)
				*3444	Sheet Metal Work (metal bins and vats)
				*3499	Fabricated Metal Products, NEC (metal boxes)
				*3537	Industrial Trucks, Tractors, Trailers, and Stackers (metal air cargo containers)
3325	Hardware Manufacturing				
33251	Hardware Manufacturing		R	*3429	Hardware, NEC (other hardware)
				*3499	Fabricated Metal Products, NEC (safe and vault locks)
3326	Spring and Wire Product Manufacturing				
33261	Spring and Wire Product Manufacturing				
332611	Spring (Heavy Gauge) Manufacturing	c	E	3493	Steel Springs, except Wire
332612	Spring (Light Gauge) Manufacturing	u	R	*3495	Wire Springs (except watch and clock springs)
332618	Other Fabricated Wire Product Manufacturing	u	R	*3315	Steel Wiredrawing and Steel Nails and Spikes (nails, spikes, paper clips, and wire not made in wiredrawing plants)
				*3399	Primary Metal Products, NEC (nonferrous nails, brads, staples, etc.)
				*3496	Miscellaneous Fabricated Wire Products (except grocery carts)

Codes: u—unique to United States; c—common to U.S. and Canada; blank—common to 3 countries; E—existing industry; N—new industry; R—revised industry; * indicates part of a 1987 SIC; (cont'd)—continued; NEC—Not Elsewhere Classified

NAICS Code	1997 NAICS U.S. Description	Codes		SIC Code	1987 U.S. SIC Description
3327	Machine Shops; Turned Product; and Screw, Nut and Bolt Manufacturing				
33271	Machine Shops		N	*3599	Industrial and Commercial Machinery and Equipment, NEC (machine shops)
33272	Turned Product and Screw, Nut, and Bolt Manufacturing				
332721	Precision Turned Product Manufacturing	u	E	3451	Screw Machine Products
332722	Bolt, Nut, Screw, Rivet, and Washer Manufacturing	u	R	3452 *3429	Bolts, Nuts, Screws, Rivets, and Washers Hardware, NEC (turnbuckles and hose clamps)
3328	Coating, Engraving, Heat Treating, and Allied Activities				
33281	Coating, Engraving, Heat Treating, and Allied Activities				
332811	Metal Heat Treating	u	E	3398	Metal Heat Treating
332812	Metal Coating, Engraving (except Jewelry and Silverware), and Allied Services to Manufacturers	u	R	*3479	Coating, Engraving, and Allied Services, NEC (except jewelry, silverware, and flat ware engraving and etching)
332813	Electroplating, Plating, Polishing, Anodizing, and Coloring	u	R	*3399 3471	Primary Metal Products, NEC (laminating steel) Electroplating, Plating, Polishing, Anodizing, and Coloring
3329	Other Fabricated Metal Product Manufacturers				
33291	Metal Valve Manufacturing				
332911	Industrial Valve Manufacturing	u	E	3491	Industrial Valves
332912	Fluid Power Valve and Hose Fitting Manufacturing	u	R	3492 *3728	Fluid Power Valves and Hose Fittings Aircraft Parts and Auxiliary Equipment, NEC (fluid power aircraft subassemblies)
332913	Plumbing Fixture Fitting and Trim Manufacturing	u	R	*3432	Plumbing Fixture Fittings and Trim (except shower rods and lawn hose nozzles)
332919	Other Metal Valve and Pipe Fitting Manufacturing	u	R	*3429 *3494 *3499 *3432	Hardware, NEC (fire hose nozzles and couplings) Valves and Pipe Fittings, NEC (except metal pipe hangers and supports) Fabricated Metal Products, NEC (metal aerosol valves) Plumbing Fixture Fittings and Trim (lawn hose nozzles)
33299	All Other Fabricated Metal Product Manufacturing				
332991	Ball and Roller Bearing Manufacturing	c	E	3562	Ball and Roller Bearings
332992	Small Arms Ammunition Manufacturing	u	E	3482	Small Arms Ammunition
332993	Ammunition (except Small Arms)	u	E	3483	Ammunition, except for Small Arms Manufacturing
332994	Small Arms Manufacturing	u	R	3484 *3841	Small Arms Surgical and Medical Instruments and Apparatus (tranquilizer guns)

Codes: u—unique to United States; c—common to U.S. and Canada; blank—common to 3 countries; E—existing industry; N—new industry; R—revised industry;
* indicates part of a 1987 SIC; (cont'd)—continued; NEC—Not Elsewhere Classified

NAICS Code	1997 NAICS U.S. Description	Codes		SIC Code	1987 U.S. SIC Description
332995	Other Ordnance and Accessories Manufacturing	u	E	3489	Ordnance and Accessories, NEC
332996	Fabricated Pipe and Pipe Fitting Manufacturing	u	E	3498	Fabricated Pipe and Pipe Fittings
332997	Industrial Pattern Manufacturing	u	E	3543	Industrial Patterns
332998	Enameled Iron and Metal Sanitary Ware Manufacturing	u	E	3431	Enameled Iron and Metal Sanitary Ware
332999	All Other Miscellaneous Fabricated Metal Product Manufacturing	u	R	*3291	Abrasive Products (steel wool with or without soap)
				*3429	Hardware, NEC (fireplace fixtures, traps, handcuffs and leg irons, ladder jacks, and other like metal products)
				*3432	Plumbing Fixture Fittings and Trim (metal shower rods)
				*3494	Valves and Pipe Fittings, NEC (metal pipe hangers and supports)
				*3497	Metal Foil and Leaf (foil and foil containers)
				*3499	Fabricated Metal Products, NEC (other metal products)
				*3537	Industrial Trucks, Tractors, Trailers, and Stackers (metal pallets)
				*3599	Industrial and Commercial Machinery and Equipment, NEC (flexible metal hose)
				*3914	Silverware, Plated Ware, and Stainless Steel Ware (precious plated hollowware)
				*3999	Manufacturing Industries, NEC (other miscellaneous metal products, such as combs, hair curlers, etc.)
333	Machinery Manufacturing				
3331	Agriculture, Construction, and Mining Machinery Manufacturing				
33311	Agricultural Implement Manufacturing				
333111	Farm Machinery and Equipment Manufacturing	u	R	*3523	Farm Machinery and Equipment (except corrals, stalls, holding gates, hand clippers for animals, and farm conveyors/elevators)
				*3559	Industrial and Commercial Machinery and Equipment, NEC (cotton ginning machinery)
333112	Lawn and Garden Tractor and Home Lawn and Garden Equipment Manufacturing	u	R	*3524	Lawn and Garden Tractors and Home Lawn and Garden Equipment (except nonpowered lawnmowers)
33312	Construction Machinery Manufacturing		R	*3531	Construction Machinery and Equipment (except railway track maintenance equipment; winches, aerial work plat forms; and automotive wrecker hoists)
33313	Mining and Oil and Gas Field Machinery Manufacturing				

Codes: u—unique to United States; c—common to U.S. and Canada; blank—common to 3 countries; E—existing industry; N—new industry; R—revised industry;
* indicates part of a 1987 SIC; (cont'd)—continued; NEC—Not Elsewhere Classified

www.harrisinfo.com

197

NAICS Code	1997 NAICS U.S. Description	Codes		SIC Code	1987 U.S. SIC Description
333131	Mining Machinery and Equipment Manufacturing	u	E	3532	Mining Machinery and Equipment, except Oil and Gas Field Machinery and Equipment
333132	Oil and Gas Field Machinery and Equipment Manufacturing	u	E	3533	Oil and Gas Field Machinery and Equipment
3332	Industrial Machinery Manufacturing				
33321	Sawmill and Woodworking Machinery Manufacturing		E	3553	Woodworking Machinery
33322	Plastics and Rubber Industry Machinery		N	*3559	Special Industry Machinery, NEC (rubber and plastics manufacturing machinery)
33329	Other Industrial Machinery Manufacturing				
333291	Paper Industry Machinery Manufacturing	c	E	3554	Paper Industries Machinery
333292	Textile Machinery Manufacturing	u	E	3552	Textile Machinery
333293	Printing Machinery and Equipment Manufacturing	u	E	3555	Printing Trades Machinery and Equipment
333294	Food Product Machinery Manufacturing	u	E	3556	Food Products Machinery
333295	Semiconductor Machinery Manufacturing	u	N	*3559	Special Industry Machinery, NEC (semiconductor machinery manufacturing)
333298	All Other Industrial Machinery Manufacturing	u	R	*3559	Special Industry Machinery, NEC (except rubber and plastics manufacturing machinery, semiconductor manufacturing machinery, and automotive maintenance equipment)
				*3639	Household Appliances, NEC (household sewing machines)
3333	Commercial and Service Industry				
33331	Commercial and Service Industry				
333311	Automatic Vending Machine	u	R	3581	Automatic Vending Machines
				*3578	Calculating and Accounting Machines, Except Electronic Computers (change making machines)
333312	Commercial Laundry, Drycleaning, and Pressing Machine Manufacturing	u	E	3582	Commercial Laundry, Drycleaning and Pressing Machines
333313	Office Machinery Manufacturing	u	N	*3578	Calculating and Accounting Machinery, except Electronic Computers (except point of sales terminals, change making machines and funds transfer devices)
				*3579	Office Machines, NEC (except time clocks, time stamps, pencil sharpeners, stapling machines, etc.)
333314	Optical Instrument and Lens Manufacturing	u	E	3827	Optical Instruments and Lenses
333315	Photographic and Photocopying Equipment Manufacturing	u	N	*3861	Photographic Equipment and Supplies (except photographic film, paper, plates, and chemicals)

Codes: u—unique to United States; c—common to U.S. and Canada; blank—common to 3 countries; E—existing industry; N—new industry; R—revised industry;
* indicates part of a 1987 SIC; (cont'd)—continued; NEC—Not Elsewhere Classified

NAICS Code	1997 NAICS U.S. Description	Codes		SIC Code	1987 U.S. SIC Description
333319	Other Commercial and Service Industry Machinery Manufacturing	u	R	*3559	Special Industry Machinery, NEC (automotive maintenance equipment)
				3589	Service Industry Machinery, NEC
				*3599	Industrial and Commercial Machinery and Equipment, NEC (carnival amusement park equipment)
				*3699	Electrical Machinery, Equipment and Supplies, NEC (electronic teaching machines and flight simulators)
				*3999	Manufacturing Industries, NEC (beauty and barber shop equipment, except chairs)
3334	Ventilation, Heating, Air-conditioning, and Commercial Refrigeration Equipment Manufacturing				
33341	Ventilation, Heating, Air-conditioning, and Commercial Refrigeration Equipment Manufacturing				
333411	Air Purification Equipment	u	N	*3564	Industrial and Commercial Fans and Blowers and Air Purification Equipment (air purification equipment)
333412	Industrial and Commercial Fan and Blower Manufacturing	u	R	*3564	Industrial and Commercial Fans and Blowers and Air Purification Equipment (fans and blowers)
333414	Heating Equipment (except Warm Air Furnaces) Manufacturing	u	R	3433	Heating Equipment, except Electric and Warm Air Furnaces
				*3569	General Industrial Machinery and Equipment, NEC (electric swimming pool heaters)
				*3634	Electric Housewares and Fans (wall and baseboard heating units for permanent installation)
				*2499	Wood Products, NEC (wood cooling towers)
				*3443	Fabricated Plate Work (Boiler Shops) (metal cooling towers)
				*3444	Sheet Metal Work (sheet metal cooling towers)
333415	Air-conditioning and Warm Air Heating Equipment and Commercial and Industrial Refrigeration Equipment Manufacturing	u	R	*3585	Air-conditioning and Warm Air Heating Equipment and Commercial and Industrial Refrigeration Equipment (except motor vehicle Air-conditioning)
3335	Metalworking Machinery Manufacturing				
33351	Metalworking Machinery Manufacturing				
333511	Industrial Mold Manufacturing	c	R	*3544	Special Dies and Tools, Die Sets, Jigs and Fixtures, and Industrial Molds (industrial molds)
333512	Machine Tool (Metal Cutting Types) Manufacturing	u	E	3541	Machine Tools, Metal Cutting Type

NAICS Code	1997 NAICS U.S. Description	Codes		SIC Code	1987 U.S. SIC Description
333513	Machine Tool (Metal Forming Types) Manufacturing	u	E	3542	Machine Tools, Metal Forming Type
333514	Special Die and Tool, Die Set, Jig, and Fixture Manufacturing	u	R	*3544	Special Dies and Tools, Die Sets, Jigs and Fixtures, and Industrial Molds (except molds)
333515	Cutting Tool and Machine Tool Accessory Manufacturing	u	R	*3545	Cutting Tools, Machine Tool Accessories, and Machinists' Precision Measuring Devices (except precision measuring devices)
333516	Rolling Mill Machinery and Equipment Manufacturing	u	E	3547	Rolling Mill Machinery and Equipment
333518	Other Metalworking Machinery Manufacturing	u	E	3549	Metalworking Machinery, NEC
3336	Engine, Turbine, and Power Transmission Equipment Manufacturing				
33361	Engine, Turbine, and Power Transmission Equipment Manufacturing				
333611	Turbine and Turbine Generator Set Units Manufacturing	c	E	3511	Steam, Gas, and Hydraulic Turbines, and Turbine Generator Set Units
333612	Speed Changer, Industrial High-speed Drive, and Gear Manufacturing	u	E	3566	Speed Changers, Industrial High-speed Drives, and Gears
333613	Mechanical Power Transmission Equipment Manufacturing	u	E	3568	Mechanical Power Transmission Equipment, NEC
333618	Other Engine Equipment Manufacturing	u	R	*3519	Internal Combustion Engines, NEC (except stationary engine radiators)
				*3699	Electrical Machinery, Equipment and Supplies, NEC (outboard electric motors)
3339	Other General Purpose Machinery Manufacturing				
33391	Pump and Compressor Manufacturing				
333911	Pump and Pumping Equipment Manufacturing	u	R	3561	Pumps and Pumping Equipment
				*3743	Railroad Equipment (locomotive fuel lubricating or cooling medium pumps)
333912	Air and Gas Compressor Manufacturing	u	E	3563	Air and Gas Compressors
333913	Measuring and Dispensing Pump Manufacturing	u	E	3586	Measuring and Dispensing Pumps
33392	Material Handling Equipment Manufacturing				
333921	Elevator and Moving Stairway Manufacturing	u	E	3534	Elevators and Moving Stairways
333922	Conveyor and Conveying Equipment Manufacturing	u	R	*3523	Farm Machinery and Equipment (farm conveyors and elevators)
				3535	Conveyors and Conveying Equipment
333923	Overhead Traveling Crane, Hoist, and Monorail System Manufacturing	u	R	3536	Overhead Traveling Cranes, Hoists, and Monorail Systems
				*3531	Construction Machinery and Equipment (winches, aerial work platforms, and automobile wrecker hoists)

Codes: u—unique to United States; c—common to U.S. and Canada; blank—common to 3 countries; E—existing industry; N—new industry; R—revised industry;
* indicates part of a 1987 SIC; (cont'd)—continued; NEC—Not Elsewhere Classified

NAICS Code	1997 NAICS U.S. Description	Codes		SIC Code	1987 U.S. SIC Description
333924	Industrial Truck, Tractor, Trailer, and Stacker Machinery Manufacturing	u	R	*3496	Miscellaneous Fabricated Wire Products (grocery carts)
				*3537	Industrial Trucks, Tractors, Trailers, and Stackers (except metal pallets and metal air cargo containers)
				*3799	Transportation Equipment, NEC (wheelbarrows)
33399	All Other General Purpose Machinery Manufacturing				
333991	Power-driven Handtool Manufacturing	u	E	3546	Power-driven Handtools
333992	Welding and Soldering Equipment Manufacturing	u	R	*3548	Electric and Gas Welding and Soldering Equipment (except transformers for arc-welding)
				*3699	Electrical Machinery Equipment and Supplies, NEC (laser welding and soldering equipment)
333993	Packaging Machinery Manufacturing	u	E	3565	Packaging Machinery
333994	Industrial Process Furnace and Oven Manufacturing	u	E	3567	Industrial Process Furnaces and Ovens
333995	Fluid Power Cylinder and Actuator Manufacturing	u	E	3593	Fluid Power Cylinders and Actuators
333996	Fluid Power Pump and Motor Manufacturing	u	E	3594	Fluid Power Pumps and Motors
333997	Scale and Balance (except Laboratory) Manufacturing	u	E	3596	Scales and Balances, except Laboratory
333999	All Other Miscellaneous General Purpose Machinery Manufacturing	u	R	*3599	Industrial and Commercial Machinery and Equipment, NEC (other industrial and commercial machinery and equipment)
				*3569	General Industrial Machinery and Equipment, NEC (except fire hoses and electric swimming pool heaters)
334	Computer and Electronic Product Manufacturing				
3341	Computer and Peripheral Equipment Manufacturing				
33411	Computer and Peripheral Equipment Manufacturing				
334111	Electronic Computer Manufacturing	u	E	3571	Electronic Computers
334112	Computer Storage Device Manufacturing	u	E	3572	Computer Storage Devices
334113	Computer Terminal Manufacturing	u	E	3575	Computer Terminals
334119	Other Computer Peripheral Equipment Manufacturing	u	R	*3577	Computer Peripheral Equipment, NEC (except plotter controllers and magnetic tape cleaners)
				*3578	Calculating and Accounting Machines, Except Electronic Computers (point of sale terminals and fund transfer devices)
3342	Communications Equipment Manufacturing				

Go to page 23 to learn about the implementation of NAICS codes in the public and private sectors.

Codes: u—unique to United States; c—common to U.S. and Canada; blank—common to 3 countries; E—existing industry; N—new industry; R—revised industry;
* indicates part of a 1987 SIC; (cont'd)—continued; NEC—Not Elsewhere Classified

NAICS Code	1997 NAICS U.S. Description	Codes		SIC Code	1987 U.S. SIC Description
33421	Telephone Apparatus Manufacturing		R	*3661	Telephone and Telegraph Apparatus (except consumer external modems)
33422	Radio and Television Broadcasting and Wireless Communications Equipment Manufacturing		R	3663	Radio and Television Broadcasting and Communications Equipment
				*3679	Electronic Components, NEC (antennas)
33429	Other Communications Equipment Manufacturing		E	3669	Communications Equipment, NEC
3343	Audio and Video Equipment Manufacturing				
33431	Audio and Video Equipment Manufacturing		R	3651	Household Audio and Video Equipment
				*3679	Electronic Components, NEC (radio headphones)
3344	Semiconductor and Other Electronic Component Manufacturing				
33441	Semiconductor and Other Electronic Component Manufacturing				
334411	Electron Tube Manufacturing	u	E	3671	Electron Tubes
334412	Bare Printed Circuit Board Manufacturing	u	E	3672	Printed Circuit Boards
334413	Semiconductor and Related Device Manufacturing	u	E	3674	Semiconductors and Related Devices
334414	Electronic Capacitor Manufacturing	u	E	3675	Electronic Capacitors
334415	Electronic Resistor Manufacturing	u	E	3676	Electronic Resistors
334416	Electronic Coil, Transformer, and Other Inductor Manufacturing	u	E	3677	Electronic Coils, Transformers, and Other Inductors
334417	Electronic Connector Manufacturing	u	E	3678	Electronic Connectors
334418	Printed Circuit Assembly (Electronic Assembly) Manufacturing	u	N	*3577	Computer Peripheral Equipment, NEC (plotter controllers)
				*3679	Electronic Components, NEC (printed circuit/electronic assembly manufacturing)
				*3661	Telephone and Telegraph Apparatus (consumer external modems)
334419	Other Electronic Component Manufacturing	u	R	*3679	Electronic Components, NEC (other electronic components)
3345	Navigational, Measuring, Electromedical, and Control Instruments Manufacturing				
33451	Navigational, Measuring, Electromedical, and Control Instruments Manufacturing				
334510	Electromedical and Electrotherapeutic Apparatus Manufacturing	u	R	*3842	Orthopedic, Prosthetic and Surgical Appliances and Supplies (electronic hearing aids)
				*3845	Electromedical and Electrotherapeutic Apparatus (other electromedical and electrotherapeutic apparatus)
334511	Search, Detection, Navigation, Guidance, Aeronautical and Nautical System and Systems and Instrument Manufacturing	u	E	3812	Search, Detection, Navigation, Guidance, Aeronautical, and Nautical Instruments

Codes: u—unique to United States; c—common to U.S. and Canada; blank—common to 3 countries; E—existing industry; N—new industry; R—revised industry; * indicates part of a 1987 SIC; (cont'd)—continued; NEC—Not Elsewhere Classified

202

Harris InfoSource

NAICS Code	1997 NAICS U.S. Description	Codes		SIC Code	1987 U.S. SIC Description
334512	Automatic Environmental Control Manufacturing for Residential, Commercial, and Appliance Use	u	E	3822	Automatic Controls for Regulating Residential and Commercial Environments and Appliances
334513	Instruments and Related Products Manufacturing for Measuring, Displaying, and Controlling Industrial Process Variables	u	E	3823	Industrial Instruments for Measurement, Display, and Control of Process Variables; and Related Products
334514	Totalizing Fluid Meter and Counting Device Manufacturing	u	R	3824	Totalizing Fluid Meters and Counting Devices
				*3825	Instruments for Measuring and Testing of Electricity and Electrical Signals (auto motive ammeters and voltmeters)
				*3829	Measuring and Controlling Devices, NEC (motor vehicle gauges)
334515	Instrument Manufacturing for Measuring and Testing Electricity and Electrical Signals	u	R	*3825	Instruments for Measuring and Testing of Electricity and Electrical Signals (except automotive ammeters and voltmeters)
334516	Analytical Laboratory Instrument Manufacturing	u	F	3826	Laboratory Analytical Instruments
334517	Irradiation Apparatus Manufacturing	u	R	3844	X-ray Apparatus and Tubes and Related Irradiation Apparatus
				*3845	Electromedical and Electrotherapeutic Apparatus (CT and CAT Scanners)
334518	Watch, Clock, and Part Manufacturing	u	R	*3495	Wire Springs (clock and watch springs)
				*3579	Office Machines, NEC (time clocks and other time recording devices)
				*3829	Measuring and Controlling Devices, NEC (electronic chronometers)
				*3915	Jewelers Findings and Materials and Lapidary Work (watch jewels)
				3873	Watches, Clocks, Clockwork Operated Devices, and Parts
334519	Other Measuring and Controlling Device Manufacturing	u	R	*3829	Measuring and Controlling Devices, NEC (except medical thermometers, electronic chronometers and motor vehicle gauges)
3346	Manufacturing and Reproducing Magnetic and Optical Media				
33461	Manufacturing and Reproducing Magnetic and Optical Media				
334611	Software Reproducing	u	N	*7372	Prepackaged Software (reproduction of software)
334612	Prerecorded Compact Disc (except Software), Tape, and Record Producing	u	N	*3652	Phonograph Records and Prerecorded Audio Tapes and Disks (reproduction of all other media except video)
				*7819	Services Allied to Motion Picture Production (reproduction of video)
334613	Magnetic and Optical Recording	u	R	3695	Magnetic and Optical Recording Media

Codes: u—unique to United States; c—common to U.S. and Canada; blank—common to 3 countries; E—existing industry; N—new industry; R—revised industry;
* indicates part of a 1987 SIC; (cont'd)—continued; NEC—Not Elsewhere Classified

NAICS Code	1997 NAICS U.S. Description	Codes		SIC Code	1987 U.S. SIC Description
334613	Magnetic and Optical Recording (cont'd)			*3577	Computer Peripheral Equipment, NEC (magnetic tape cleaners)
335	Electrical Equipment, Appliance, and Component Manufacturing				
3351	Electric Lighting Equipment Manufacturing				
33511	Electric Lamp Bulb and Part Manufacturing		E	3641	Electric Lamp Bulbs and Tubes
33512	Lighting Fixture Manufacturing				
335121	Residential Electric Lighting Fixture Manufacturing	u	R	3645 *3999	Residential Electric Lighting Fixtures Manufacturing Industries, NEC (lamp shades of paper or textile)
335122	Commercial, Industrial, and Institutional Electric Lighting Fixture Manufacturing	u	E	3646	Commercial, Industrial, and Institutional Electric Lighting Fixtures
335129	Other Lighting Equipment Manufacturing	u	R	3648 *3699	Lighting Equipment, NEC Electrical Machinery, Equipment, and Supplies, NEC (Christmas tree lighting sets, electric insect lamps, electric fire place logs, and trouble lights)
3352	Household Appliance Manufacturing				
33521	Small Electrical Appliance Manufacturing				
335211	Electric Housewares and Household Fan Manufacturing	u	R	*3634 *3999	Electric Housewares and Fans (except wall and baseboard heating units for permanent installation and electronic cigarette lighters) Manufacturing Industries, NEC (electric hair clippers for humans)
335212	Household Vacuum Cleaner Manufacturing	u	R	3635 *3639	Household Vacuum Cleaners Household Appliances, NEC (floor waxing and floor polishing machines)
33522	Major Appliance Manufacturing				
335221	Household Cooking Appliance Manufacturing	u	E	3631	Household Cooking Equipment
335222	Household Refrigerator and Home Freezer Manufacturing	u	E	3632	Household Refrigerators and Home and Farm Freezers
335224	Household Laundry Equipment Manufacturing	u	E	3633	Household Laundry Equipment
335228	Other Major Household Appliance Manufacturing	u	R	*3639	Household Appliances, NEC (except floor waxing and floor polishing machines, and household sewing machines)
3353	Electrical Equipment Manufacturing				
33531	Electrical Equipment Manufacturing				
335311	Power, Distribution, and Specialty Transformer Manufacturing	c	R	*3548 3612	Electric and Gas Welding and Soldering Equipment (transformers for arc-welders) Power, Distribution, and Speciality Transformers

Codes: u—unique to United States; c—common to U.S. and Canada; blank—common to 3 countries; E—existing industry; N—new industry; R—revised industry; * indicates part of a 1987 SIC; (cont'd)—continued; NEC—Not Elsewhere Classified

NAICS Code	1997 NAICS U.S. Description	Codes		SIC Code	1987 U.S. SIC Description
335312	Motor and Generator Manufacturing	c	R	3621 *7694	Motors and Generators Armature Rewinding Shops (remanufacturing)
335313	Switchgear and Switchboard Apparatus Manufacturing	u	E	3613	Switchgear and Switchboard Apparatus
335314	Relay and Industrial Control Manufacturing	u	E	3625	Relays and Industrial Controls
3359	Other Electrical Equipment and Component Manufacturing				
33591	Battery Manufacturing				
335911	Storage Battery Manufacturing	u	E	3691	Storage Batteries
335912	Primary Battery Manufacturing	u	E	3692	Primary Batteries, Dry and Wet
33592	Communication and Energy Wire and Cable Manufacturing				
335921	Fiber Optic Cable Manufacturing	u	N	*3357	Drawing and Insulating of Nonferrous Wire (fiber optic cable-insulating only)
335929	Other Communication and Energy Wire Manufacturing	u	N	*3357	Drawing and Insulating of Nonferrous Wire (communication and energy wire, except fiber optic-insulating only)
33593	Wiring Device Manufacturing				
335931	Current-carrying Wiring Device Manufacturing	u	E	3643	Current-carrying Wiring Devices
335932	Noncurrent-carrying Wiring Device Manufacturing	u	R	*3644	Noncurrent-carrying Wiring Devices (except fishwire, electrical wiring tool)
33599	All Other Electrical Equipment and Component Manufacturing				
335991	Carbon and Graphite Product Manufacturing	u	E	3624	Carbon and Graphite Products
335999	All Other Miscellaneous Electrical Equipment and Component Manufacturing	u	R	3629 *3699	Electrical Industrial Apparatus, NEC Electrical Machinery, Equipment, and Supplies, NEC (other electrical industrial apparatus)
336	Transportation Equipment Manufacturing				
3361	Motor Vehicle Manufacturing				
33611	Automobile and Light Duty Motor Vehicle Manufacturing				
336111	Automobile Manufacturing	u	N	*3711	Motor Vehicles and Passenger Car Bodies (automobiles)
336112	Light Truck and Utility Vehicle Manufacturing	u	N	*3711	Motor Vehicles and Passenger Car Bodies (light trucks and utility vehicles)
33612	Heavy Duty Truck Manufacturing		N	*3711	Motor Vehicles and Passenger Car Bodies (heavy duty trucks)
3362	Motor Vehicle Body and Trailer Manufacturing				
33621	Motor Vehicle Body and Trailer Manufacturing				
336211	Motor Vehicle Body Manufacturing	c	R	*3711	Motor Vehicles and Passenger Car Bodies (kit car and other passenger car bodies)

Visit page 15 to learn about major changes to NAICS sectors.

 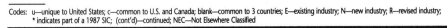

NAICS Code	1997 NAICS U.S. Description	Codes		SIC Code	1987 U.S. SIC Description
336211	Motor Vehicle Body Manufacturing (cont'd)			3713	Truck and Bus Bodies
				*3714	Motor Vehicle Parts and Accessories (dump truck lifting mechanisms and fifth wheels)
336212	Truck Trailer Manufacturing	c	E	3715	Truck Trailers
336213	Motor Home Manufacturing	u	E	3716	Motor Homes
336214	Travel Trailer and Camper Manufacturing	u	R	3792	Travel Trailers and Campers
				*3799	Transportation Equipment, NEC (automobile, boat, utility and light truck trailers)
3363	Motor Vehicle Parts Manufacturing				
33631	Motor Vehicle Gasoline Engine and Engine Parts Manufacturing				
336311	Carburetor, Piston, Piston Ring, and Valve Manufacturing	u	E	3592	Carburetors, Pistons, Piston Rings, and Valves
336312	Gasoline Engine and Engine Parts Manufacturing	u	N	*3714	Motor Vehicle Parts and Accessories (gasoline line engines and engine parts including rebuilt)
33632	Motor Vehicle Electrical and Electronic Equipment Manufacturing				
336321	Vehicular Lighting Equipment Manufacturing	u	E	3647	Vehicular Lighting Equipment
336322	Other Motor Vehicle Electrical and Electronic Equipment Manufacturing	u	R	3694	Electrical Equipment for Internal Combustion Engines
				*3714	Motor Vehicle Parts and Accessories (wiring harness sets, other than ignition; block heaters and battery heaters; instrument board assemblies; permanent defrosters; windshield washer-wiper mechanisms; cruise control mechanisms; and other electrical equipment for internal combustion engines
33633	Motor Vehicle Steering and Suspension Components (except Spring) Manufacturing		N	*3714	Motor Vehicle Parts and Accessories (steering and suspension parts)
33634	Motor Vehicle Brake System Manufacturing		N	*3292	Asbestos Products (asbestos brake linings and pads)
				*3714	Motor Vehicle Parts and Accessories (brake and brake systems, including assemblies)
33635	Motor Vehicle Transmission and Power Train Parts Manufacturing		N	*3714	Motor Vehicle Parts and Accessories (transmissions and power train parts, including rebuilding)
33636	Motor Vehicle Seating and Interior Trim Manufacturing		N	*2396	Automotive Trimmings, Apparel Findings, and Related Products (textile motor vehicle trimming)
				*2399	Fabricated Textile Products, NEC (seat belts, and seat and tire covers)

Codes: u—unique to United States; c—common to U.S. and Canada; blank—common to 3 countries; E—existing industry; N—new industry; R—revised industry;
* indicates part of a 1987 SIC; (cont'd)—continued; NEC—Not Elsewhere Classified

NAICS Code	1997 NAICS U.S. Description	Codes		SIC Code	1987 U.S. SIC Description
33636	Motor Vehicle Seating and Interior Trim Manufacturing (cont'd)			*2531	Public Building and Related Furniture (seats for motor vehicles)
				*3499	Fabricated Metal Products, NEC (metal motor vehicle seat frames)
33637	Motor Vehicle Metal Stamping		E	3465	Automotive Stampings
33639	Other Motor Vehicle Parts Manufacturing				
336391	Motor Vehicle Air-conditioning Manufacturing	u	N	*3585	Air-conditioning and Warm Air Heating Equipment and Commercial and Industrial Refrigeration Equipment (motor vehicle air-conditioning)
336399	All Other Motor Vehicle Parts Manufacturing	u	R	*3429	Hardware, NEC (luggage and utility racks)
				*3519	Internal Combustion Engines, NEC (stationary engine radiators)
				*3599	Industrial and Commercial Machinery and Equipment, NEC (gasoline, oil, and intake filters for internal combustion engines, except for motor vehicles)
				*3714	Motor Vehicle Parts and Accessories (except truck and bus bodies, trailers, engine and engine parts, motor vehicle electrical and electronic equipment, motor vehicle steering and suspension components, motor vehicle brake systems, and motor vehicle transmission and power train parts
				*3799	Transportation Equipment, NEC (trailer hitches)
3364	Aerospace Product and Parts Manufacturing				
33641	Aerospace Product and Parts Manufacturing				
336411	Aircraft Manufacturing	u	R	*3721	Aircraft (except research and development)
				*3728	Aircraft Parts and Auxiliary Equipment, NEC (target drones)
336412	Aircraft Engine and Engine Parts Manufacturing	u	R	*3724	Aircraft Engines and Engine Parts (except research and development)
336413	Other Aircraft Parts and Auxiliary Equipment Manufacturing	u	R	*3728	Guided Missiles and Space Vehicles (except research and development)
336414	Guided Missile and Space Vehicle Manufacturing	u	R	*3761	Guided Missiles and Space Vehicles (except research and development)
336415	Guided Missile and Space Vehicle Propulsion Unit and Propulsion Unit Parts Manufacturing	u	R	*3764	Guided Missile and Space Vehicle Propulsion Units and Propulsion Unit Parts (except research and development)
336419	Other Guided Missile and Space Vehicle Parts and Auxiliary Equipment Manufacturing	u	R	*3769	Guided Missile and Space Vehicle Parts and Auxiliary Equipment (except research and development)
3365	Railroad Rolling Stock Manufacturing				

Codes: u—unique to United States; c—common to U.S. and Canada; blank—common to 3 countries; E—existing industry; N—new industry; R—revised industry;
    * indicates part of a 1987 SIC; (cont'd)—continued; NEC—Not Elsewhere Classified

NAICS Code	1997 NAICS U.S. Description	Codes		SIC Code	1987 U.S. SIC Description
33651	Railroad Rolling Stock Manufacturing		R	*3531	Construction Machinery and Equipment (railway track maintenance equipment)
				*3743	Railroad Equipment (except locomotive fuel lubricating or cooling medium pumps)
3366	Ship and Boat Building				
33661	Ship and Boat Building				
336611	Ship Building and Repairing	c	R	*3731	Ship Building and Repairing (except floating dry docks not associated with shipyards)
336612	Boat Building	c	R	*3732	Boat Building and Repairing (boat building)
3369	Other Transportation Equipment Manufacturing				
33699	Other Transportation Equipment Manufacturing				
336991	Motorcycle, Bicycle, and Parts Manufacturing	u	R	*3944	Games, Toys, and Children's Vehicles, Except Dolls and Bicycles (metal tricycles)
				3751	Motorcycles, Bicycles and Parts
336992	Military Armored Vehicle, Tank, and Tank Component Manufacturing	u	R	*3711	Motor Vehicles and Passenger Car Bodies (military armored vehicles)
				3795	Tanks and Tank Components
336999	All Other Transportation Equipment Manufacturing	u	R	*3799	Transportation Equipment, NEC (except automobile, boat, utility light truck trailers, trailer hitches, and wheelbarrows)
337	Furniture and Related Product Manufacturing				
3371	Household and Institutional Furniture and Kitchen Cabinet Manufacturing				
33711	Wood Kitchen Cabinet and Countertop Manufacturing		R	2434	Wood Kitchen Cabinets
				*5712	Furniture Stores (custom wood cabinets)
33712	Household and Institutional Furniture Manufacturing				
337121	Upholstered Household Furniture Manufacturing	c	R	2512	Wood Household Furniture, Upholstered
				*2514	Metal Household Furniture (upholstered)
				*2515	Mattress, Foundations, and Convertible Beds (convertible sofas)
				*5712	Furniture (custom made upholstered household furniture except cabinets)
337122	Nonupholstered Wood Household Furniture Manufacturing	u	R	*2511	Wood Household Furniture, except Upholstered (except wood box spring frames)
				*5712	Furniture Stores (custom made wood nonupholstered household furniture except cabinets)
337124	Metal Household Furniture Manufacturing	u	R	*2514	Metal Household Furniture (except upholstered and metal box spring frames)

NAICS to SIC

Codes: u—unique to United States; c—common to U.S. and Canada; blank—common to 3 countries; E—existing industry; N—new industry; R—revised industry;
* indicates part of a 1987 SIC; (cont'd)—continued; NEC—Not Elsewhere Classified

NAICS Code	1997 NAICS U.S. Description	Codes		SIC Code	1987 U.S. SIC Description
337125	Household Furniture (except Wood and Metal) Manufacturing	u	E	2519	Household Furniture, NEC
337127	Institutional Furniture Manufacturing	c	R	*2531	Public Building and Related Furniture (furniture made for public buildings)
				*2541	Wood Office and Store Fixtures, Partitions, Shelving, and Lockers (wood lunchroom tables and chairs)
				*2542	Office and Store Fixtures, Partitions, Shelving, and Lockers, except Wood (lunchroom tables and chairs)
				*2599	Furniture and Fixtures, NEC (except hospital beds)
				*3952	Lead Pencils, Crayons, and Artist's Materials (drafting tables and boards)
				*3999	Manufacturing Industries, NEC (beauty and barber chairs)
337129	Wood Television, Radio, and Sewing Machine Cabinet Manufacturing	u	E	2517	Wood Television, Radio, Phonograph, and Sewing Machine Cabinets
3372	Office Furniture (including Fixtures) Manufacturing				
33721	Office Furniture (including Fixtures) Manufacturing				
337211	Wood Office Furniture Manufacturing	u	E	2521	Wood Office Furniture
337212	Custom Architectural Woodwork and Millwork Manufacturing	u	N	*2541	Wood Office and Store Fixtures, Partitions, Shelving, and Lockers (architectural woodwork, millwork, and fixtures)
337214	Office Furniture (except Wood) Manufacturing	c	E	2522	Office Furniture, except Wood
337215	Showcase, Partition, Shelving, and Locker Manufacturing	c	N	*2511	Wood Household Furniture, except Upholstered (wood box spring frames)
				*2514	Metal Household Furniture (metal box spring frames)
				*2542	Office and Store Fixtures, Partitions, Shelving and Lockers, except Wood (except lunchroom tables and chairs)
				*2541	Wood Office and Store Fixtures, Partitions, Shelving, and Lockers (except counter tops, custom architectural woodwork, millwork, lunchroom and other fixtures)
				*2426	Hardwood Dimension and Flooring Mills (wood furniture frames and finished furniture parts)
				*3089	Plastics Products, NEC (finished plastics furniture parts)
				*3429	Hardware, NEC (convertible bed sleeper mechanisms, chair glides)
				*3499	Fabricated Metal Products, NEC (metal furniture frames)

Visit page 9 to learn more about NAICS codes.

Codes: u—unique to United States; c—common to U.S. and Canada; blank—common to 3 countries; E—existing industry; N—new industry; R—revised industry; * indicates part of a 1987 SIC; (cont'd)—continued; NEC—Not Elsewhere Classified

www.harrisinfo.com

209

NAICS Code	1997 NAICS U.S. Description	Codes		SIC Code	1987 U.S. SIC Description
3379	Other Furniture Related Product Manufacturing				
33791	Mattress Manufacturing		R	*2515	Mattresses, Foundations, and Convertible Beds (mattresses and foundations)
33792	Blind and Shade Manufacturing		E	2591	Drapery Hardware and Window Blinds and Shades
339	Miscellaneous Manufacturing				
3391	Medical Equipment and Supplies Manufacturing				
33911	Medical Equipment and Supplies Manufacturing				
339111	Laboratory Apparatus and Furniture Manufacturing	u	R	*2599	Furniture and Fixtures, NEC (hospital beds)
				3821	Laboratory Apparatus and Furniture
				*3841	Surgical and Medical Instruments and Apparatus (operating tables)
339112	Surgical and Medical Instrument Manufacturing	u	R	*3841	Surgical and Medical Instruments and Apparatus (except tranquilizer guns and operating tables)
				*3829	Measuring and Controlling Devices, NEC (medical thermometers)
339113	Surgical Appliance and Supplies Manufacturing	u	R	*3069	Fabricated Rubber Products, NEC (rubber gloves and life jackets)
				*3842	Orthopedic, Prosthetic, and Surgical Appliances and Supplies (except electronic hearing aids)
				*3851	Ophthalmic Goods (intraocular lenses)
339114	Dental Equipment and Supplies Manufacturing	u	E	3843	Dental Equipment and Supplies
339115	Ophthalmic Goods Manufacturing	u	R	*3851	Ophthalmic Goods (except intraocular lenses)
				*5995	Optical Goods Stores (optical laboratories grinding of lenses to prescription)
339116	Dental Laboratories	u	E	8072	Dental Laboratories
3399	Other Miscellaneous Manufacturing				
33991	Jewelry and Silverware				
339911	Jewelry (except Costume) Manufacturing	u	R	*3479	Coating, Engraving, and Allied Services, NEC (jewelry engraving and etching, including precious metal)
				3911	Jewelry, Precious Metal
339912	Silverware and Hollowware Manufacturing	u	R	*3479	Coating, Engraving, and Allied Services, NEC (silver and plated ware engraving and etching)
				*3914	Silverware, Plated Ware, and Stainless Steel Ware (except nonprecious and precious plated metal cutlery and flatware)

Codes: u—unique to United States; c—common to U.S. and Canada; blank—common to 3 countries; E—existing industry; N—new industry; R—revised industry; * indicates part of a 1987 SIC; (cont'd)—continued; NEC—Not Elsewhere Classified

NAICS Code	1997 NAICS U.S. Description	Codes		SIC Code	1987 U.S. SIC Description
339913	Jewelers' Material and Lapidary Work Manufacturing	u	R	*3915	Jewelers' Findings and Materials, and Lapidary Work (except watch jewels)
339914	Costume Jewelry and Novelty Manufacturing	u	R	*3479	Coating, Engraving, and Allied Services, NEC (costume jewelry engraving and etching)
				3961	Costume Jewelry and Costume Novelties, Except Precious Metal
33992	Sporting and Athletic Goods Manufacturing		E	3949	Sporting and Athletic Goods, NEC
				*3069	Fabricated Rubber Products, NEC (wet suits)
33993	Doll, Toy, and Game Manufacturing				
339931	Doll and Stuffed Toy Manufacturing	u	E	3942	Dolls and Stuffed Toys
339932	Game, Toy, and Children's Vehicle Manufacturing	u	R	*3069	Fabricated Rubber Products, NEC (rubber toys, except dolls)
				*3944	Games, Toys, and Children's Vehicles, Except Dolls and Bicycles (except metal tricycles)
				*3999	Manufacturing Industries, NEC (embroidery kits)
33994	Office Supplies (except Paper) Manufacturing				
339941	Pen and Mechanical Pencil Manufacturing	u	E	3951	Pens, Mechanical Pencils, and Parts
339942	Lead Pencil and Art Good Manufacturing	u	R	*2531	Public Buildings and Related Furniture (blackboards)
				*3579	Office Machines, NEC (pencil sharpeners, staplers and other office equipment)
				*3952	Lead Pencils, Crayons, and Artists' Materials (except drawing and india ink, and drafting tables and boards)
339943	Marking Device Manufacturing	u	E	3953	Marking Devices
339944	Carbon Paper and Inked Ribbon Manufacturing	u	E	3955	Carbon Paper and Inked Ribbons
33995	Sign Manufacturing		R	*3993	Signs and Advertising Specialties (signs)
33999	All Other Miscellaneous Manufacturing				
339991	Gasket, Packing, and Sealing Device Manufacturing	u	E	3053	Gaskets, Packing, and Sealing Devices
339992	Musical Instrument Manufacturing	u	E	3931	Musical Instruments
339993	Fastener, Button, Needle, and Pin Manufacturing	u	R	3965	Fasteners, Buttons, Needles, and Pins
				*3131	Boat and Shoe Cut Stock and Findings (metal buckles)
339994	Broom, Brush, and Mop Manufacturing	u	R	3991	Brooms and Brushes
				*2392	Housefurnishings, except Curtains and Draperies (mops, floor and dust)
339995	Burial Casket Manufacturing	u	E	3995	Burial Caskets
339999	All Other Miscellaneous Manufacturing	u	R	*2499	Wood Products, NEC (mirror and picture frames)
				*3634	Electric Housewares and Fans (electronic cigarette lighters)

NAICS to SIC

Codes: u—unique to United States; c—common to U.S. and Canada; blank—common to 3 countries; E—existing industry; N—new industry; R—revised industry; * indicates part of a 1987 SIC; (cont'd)—continued; NEC—Not Elsewhere Classified

NAICS Code	1997 NAICS U.S. Description	Codes		SIC Code	1987 U.S. SIC Description
339999	All Other Miscellaneous Manufacturing (cont'd)			*3999	Manufacturing Industries, NEC (other miscellaneous products not specially provided for previously)
42	**Wholesale Trade**				
421	Wholesale Trade, Durable Goods	u			
4211	Motor Vehicle and Motor Vehicle Parts and Supplies Wholesalers	u			
42111	Automobile and Other Motor Vehicle Wholesalers	u	E	5012	Automobiles and Other Motor Vehicles
42112	Motor Vehicle Supplies and New Parts Wholesalers	u	R	*5013	Motor Vehicle Supplies and New Parts (except parts sold via retail methods)
42113	Tire and Tube Wholesalers Wholesalers	u	R	*5014	Tires and Tubes (except tires sold via retail method)
42114	Motor Vehicle Parts (Used) Wholesalers	u	R	*5015	Motor Vehicle Parts, Used (except sold via retail method)
4212	Furniture and Home Furnishing Wholesalers	u			
42121	Furniture Wholesalers	u	R	*5021	Furniture (except furniture sold via retail method)
42122	Home Furnishing Wholesalers	u	R	*5023	Homefurnishings (except homefurnishings sold via retail method)
4213	Lumber and Other Construction Materials Wholesalers	u			
42131	Lumber, Plywood, Millwork, and Wood Panel Wholesalers	u	E	5031	Lumber, Plywood, Millwork, and Wood Panels
42132	Brick, Stone, and Related Construction Material Wholesalers	u	R	5032	Brick, Stone, and Related Construction Materials (except construction materials sold via retail method)
42133	Roofing, Siding, and Insulation Material Wholesalers	u	E	5033	Roofing, Siding, and Insulation Materials
42139	Other Construction Material Wholesalers	u	R	*5039	Construction Materials, NEC (sold via wholesale method)
4214	Professional and Commercial Equipment and Supplies Wholesalers	u			
42141	Photographic Equipment and Supplies Wholesalers	u	E	5043	Photographic Equipment and Supplies
42142	Office Equipment Wholesalers	u	R	*5044	Office Equipment (except sold via retail method)
42143	Computer and Computer Peripheral Equipment and Software Wholesalers	u	R	*5045	Computers and Computer Peripherals Equipment and Software (except computers, equipment, and software sold via retail method)
42144	Other Commercial Equipment Wholesalers	u	E	5046	Commercial Equipment, NEC
42145	Medical, Dental, and Hospital Equipment and Supplies Wholesalers	u	R	*5047	Medical, Dental and Hospital Equipment and Supplies (except medical, dental, and hospital equipment and supplies sold via retail method)

Codes: u—unique to United States; c—common to U.S. and Canada; blank—common to 3 countries; E—existing industry; N—new industry; R—revised industry; * indicates part of a 1987 SIC; (cont'd)—continued; NEC—Not Elsewhere Classified

NAICS Code	1997 NAICS U.S. Description	Codes		SIC Code	1987 U.S. SIC Description
42146	Ophthalmic Goods Wholesalers	u	E	5048	Ophthalmic Goods
42149	Other Professional Equipment and Supplies Wholesalers	u	R	*5049	Professional Equipment and Supplies, NEC (except religious and school supplies sold via retail method)
4215	Metal and Mineral (except Petroleum) Wholesalers	u			
42151	Metal Service Centers and Offices	u	E	5051	Metals Service Centers and Offices
42152	Coal and Other Mineral and Ore Wholesalers	u	E	5052	Coal and Other Mineral and Ores
4216	Electrical Goods Wholesalers	u			
42161	Electrical Apparatus and Equipment, Wiring Supplies, and Construction Material Wholesalers	u	R	*5063	Electrical Apparatus and Equipment, Wiring Supplies and Construction Materials (exceptelectrical supplies sold via retail method)
42162	Electrical Appliance, Television, and Radio Set Wholesalers	u	E	5064	Electrical Appliances, Television and Radio Sets
42169	Other Electronic Parts and Equipment Wholesalers	u	E	5065	Electronic Parts and Equipment, NEC
4217	Hardware, and Plumbing and Heating Equipment and Supplies Wholesalers	u			
42171	Hardware Wholesalers	u	R	*5072	Hardware (except sold via retail method)
42172	Plumbing and Heating Equipment and Supplies (Hydronics) Wholesalers	u	R	*5074	Plumbing and Heating Equipment and Supplies (Hydronics) (except plumbing equipment sold via retail method)
42173	Warm Air Heating and Air-conditioning Equipment and Supplies Wholesalers	u	E	5075	Warm Air Heating and Air-conditioning Equipment and Supplies
42174	Refrigeration Equipment and Supplies Wholesalers	u	E	5078	Refrigeration Equipment and Supplies
4218	Machinery, Equipment, and Supplies Wholesalers	u			
42181	Construction and Mining (except Oil Well) Machinery and Equipment Wholesalers	u	E	5082	Construction and Mining (Except Petroleum) Machinery and Equipment
42182	Farm and Garden Machinery and Equipment Wholesalers	u	R	*5083	Farm and Garden Machinery and Equipment (except lawn and garden equipment sold via retail method)
42183	Industrial Machinery and Equipment Wholesalers	u	R	5084 *5085	Industrial Machinery and Equipment Industrial Supplies (fluid power accessories)
42184	Industrial Supplies Wholesalers	u	R	*5085	Industrial Supplies (except fluid power accessories)
42185	Service Establishment Equipment and Supplies Wholesalers	u	R	*5087	Service Establishment Equipment and Supplies (except sales of the service establishment equipment and supplies sold via retail method)
42186	Transportation Equipment and Supplies (except Motor Vehicle) Wholesalers	u	R	5088 *7389	Transportation Equipment and Supplies, Except Motor Vehicles Business Services, NEC (yacht brokers)

Codes: u—unique to United States; c—common to U.S. and Canada; blank—common to 3 countries; E—existing industry; N—new industry; R—revised industry;
  * indicates part of a 1987 SIC; (cont'd)—continued; NEC—Not Elsewhere Classified

NAICS Code	1997 NAICS U.S. Description	Codes		SIC Code	1987 U.S. SIC Description
4219	Miscellaneous Durable Goods Wholesalers	u			
42191	Sporting and Recreational Goods and Supplies Wholesalers	u	E	5091	Sporting and Recreational Goods and Supplies
42192	Toy and Hobby Goods and Supplies Wholesalers	u	E	5092	Toys and Hobby Goods and Supplies
42193	Recyclable Material Wholesalers	u	E	5093	Scrap and Waste Materials
42194	Jewelry, Watch, Precious Stone, and Precious Metal Wholesalers	u	E	5094	Jewelry, Watches, Precious Stones, and Precious Metals
42199	Other Miscellaneous Durable Goods Wholesalers	u	R	5099 *7822	Durable Goods, NEC Motion Picture and Video Tape Distribution (prerecorded video tapes—distribution)
422	Wholesale Trade, Nondurable Goods	u			
4221	Paper and Paper Product Wholesalers	u			
42211	Printing and Writing Paper Wholesalers	u	E	5111	Printing and Writing Paper
42212	Stationery and Office Supplies Wholesalers	u	R	*5112	Stationery and Office Supplies (except stationery and office supplies sold via retail method)
42213	Industrial and Personal Service Paper Wholesalers	u	E	5113	Industrial and Personal Service Paper
4222	Drugs and Druggists' Sundries Wholesalers	u			
42221	Drugs and Druggists' Sundries Wholesalers	u	E	5122	Drugs, Drug Proprietaries, and Druggists' Sundries
4223	Apparel, Piece Goods, and Notions Wholesalers	u			
42231	Piece Goods, Notions, and Other Dry Goods Wholesalers	u	R	*5131	Piece Goods, Notions, and Other Dry Goods (except piece goods converters)
42232	Men's and Boys' Clothing and Furnishings Wholesalers	u	E	5136	Men's and Boys' Clothing and Furnishings
42233	Women's, Children's, and Infants' Clothing Accessories Wholesalers	u	E	5137	Women's, Children's, and Infants' and Clothing and Accessories
42234	Footwear Wholesalers	u	E	5139	Footwear
4224	Grocery and Related Product Wholesalers	u			
42241	General Line Grocery Wholesalers	u	E	5141	Groceries, General Line
42242	Packaged Frozen Food Wholesalers	u	E	5142	Packaged Frozen Foods
42243	Dairy Product (except Dried or Canned) Wholesalers	u	E	5143	Dairy Products, except Dried or Canned
42244	Poultry and Poultry Product Wholesalers	u	E	5144	Poultry and Poultry Products
42245	Confectionery Wholesalers	u	E	5145	Confectionery
42246	Fish and Seafood Wholesalers	u	E	5146	Fish and Seafoods
42247	Meat and Meat Product Wholesalers	u	R	*5147	Meats and Meat Products (except boxed beef)
42248	Fresh Fruit and Vegetable Wholesalers	u	E	5148	Fresh Fruits and Vegetables
42249	Other Grocery and Related Products Wholesalers	u	R	*5149	Groceries and Related Products, NEC (except bottling mineral or spring water)

Codes: u—unique to United States; c—common to U.S. and Canada; blank—common to 3 countries; E—existing industry; N—new industry; R—revised industry; * indicates part of a 1987 SIC; (cont'd)—continued; NEC—Not Elsewhere Classified

NAICS Code	1997 NAICS U.S. Description	Codes		SIC Code	1987 U.S. SIC Description
4225	Farm Product Raw Material Wholesalers	u			
42251	Grain and Field Bean Wholesalers	u	E	5153	Grain and Field Beans
42252	Livestock Wholesalers	u	E	5154	Livestock
42259	Other Farm Product Raw Material Wholesalers	u	E	5159	Farm-product Raw Materials, NEC
4226	Chemical and Allied Products Wholesalers	u			
42261	Plastics Materials and Basic Forms and Shapes Wholesalers	u	E	5162	Plastics Materials and Basic Forms and Shapes
42269	Other Chemical and Allied Products Wholesalers	u	E	5169	Chemicals and Allied Products, NEC
4227	Petroleum and Petroleum Products Wholesalers	u			
42271	Petroleum Bulk Stations and Terminals	u	R	*5171	Petroleum Bulk Stations and Terminals (except petroleum sold via retail method)
42272	Petroleum and Petroleum Products Wholesalers (except Bulk Stations and Terminals)	u	E	5172	Petroleum and Petroleum Products Wholesalers, except Bulk Stations and Terminals
4228	Beer, Wine, and Distilled Alcoholic Beverage Wholesalers	u			
42281	Beer and Ale Wholesalers	u	E	5181	Beer and Ale
42282	Wine and Distilled Alcoholic Beverage	u	E	5182	Wine and Distilled Alcoholic Beverages Wholesalers
4229	Miscellaneous Nondurable Goods Wholesalers	u			
42291	Farm Supplies Wholesalers	u	R	*5191	Farm Supplies (except lawn and garden supplies sold via retail method)
42292	Book, Periodical, and Newspaper Wholesalers	u	E	5192	Books, Periodicals, and Newspapers
42293	Flower, Nursery Stock, and Florists' Supplies Wholesalers	u	E	*5193	Flowers, Nursery Stock, and Florists' Supplies (except nursery stock sold via retail method)
42294	Tobacco and Tobacco Product Wholesalers	u	E	5194	Tobacco and Tobacco Products
42295	Paint, Varnish, and Supplies Wholesalers	u	E	5198	Paints, Varnishes, and Supplies
42299	Other Miscellaneous Nondurable Goods Wholesalers	u	R	*5199	Nondurable Goods, NEC (except specialty advertising)
44-45	**Retail Trade**				
441	Motor Vehicle and Parts Dealers	c			
4411	Automobile Dealers	c			
44111	New Car Dealers	c	E	5511	Motor Vehicle Dealers (New and Used)
44112	Used Car Dealers	c	E	5521	Motor Vehicle Dealers (Used Only)
4412	Other Motor Vehicle Dealers	c			
44121	Recreational Vehicle Dealers	c	E	5561	Recreational Vehicle Dealers
44122	Motorcycle, Boat, and Other Motor Vehicle Dealers	c			
441221	Motorcycle Dealers	u	E	5571	Motorcycle Dealers

Codes: u—unique to United States; c—common to U.S. and Canada; blank—common to 3 countries; E—existing industry; N—new industry; R—revised industry;
  * indicates part of a 1987 SIC; (cont'd)—continued; NEC—Not Elsewhere Classified

NAICS Code	1997 NAICS U.S. Description	Codes		SIC Code	1987 U.S. SIC Description
441222	Boat Dealers	u	E	5551	Boat Dealers
441229	All Other Motor Vehicle Dealers	u	E	5599	Automotive Dealers, NEC
4413	Automotive Parts, Accessories, and Tire Stores	c			
44131	Automotive Parts and Accessories Stores	c	N	*5013	Motor Vehicle Supplies and New Parts (Wholesale) (auto parts sold via retail method)
				*5731	Radio, Television, and Consumer Electronics Stores (automobile radios)
				*5015	Motor Vehicle Parts, Used (sold via retail method)
				*5531	Auto and Home Supply Stores (auto supply stores)
44132	Tire Dealers	c	N	*5014	Tires and Tubes (Wholesale) (tires and tubes sold via retail method)
				*5531	Auto and Home Supply Stores (tires and tubes)
442	Furniture and Home Furnishings Stores	c			
4421	Furniture Stores	c			
44211	Furniture Stores	c	R	*5021	Furniture (Wholesale) (sold via the retail method)
				*5712	Furniture Stores (except custom furniture and cabinets)
4422	Home Furnishings Stores	c			
44221	Floor Covering Stores	c	R	*5023	Homefurnishings (Wholesale) (floor covering sold via retail method)
				5713	Floor Coverings Stores
44229	Other Home Furnishings Stores	c			
442291	Window Treatment Stores	c	N	*5714	Drapery, Curtain, and Upholstery Stores (drapery and curtain stores)
				*5719	Miscellaneous Homefurnishings Stores (blinds and shades)
442299	All Other Home Furnishings Stores	u	R	*5719	Miscellaneous Homefurnishings Stores (except pottery and crafts made and sold on site and window furnishings)
				*7699	Repair Shops and Related Services, NEC (custom picture framing)
443	Electronics and Appliance Stores	c			
4431	Electronics and Appliance Stores	c			
44311	Appliance, Television, and Other Electronics Stores	c			
443111	Household Appliance Stores	u	R	5722	Household Appliance Stores
				*7623	Refrigeration and Air-conditioning Service and Repair Shops (retailing new refrigerators from a storefront and repairing refrigerators)
				*7629	Electrical and Electronic Repair Shops, NEC (retailing new electrical and electronic appliances from a storefront and repairing appliances)

Codes: u—unique to United States; c—common to U.S. and Canada; blank—common to 3 countries; E—existing industry; N—new industry; R—revised industry;
* indicates part of a 1987 SIC; (cont'd)—continued; NEC—Not Elsewhere Classified

NAICS Code	1997 NAICS U.S. Description	Codes		SIC Code	1987 U.S. SIC Description
443112	Radio, Television, and Other Electronics Stores	u	R	*5731	Radio, Television, and Consumer Electronics Stores (except auto radios)
				*5999	Miscellaneous Retail Stores, NEC (typewriters and telephones)
				*7622	Radio and Television Repair Shops (retailing new radios and TVs from a storefront and repairing radios and TVs)
44312	Computer and Software Stores	c	R	*5045	Computers and Computer Peripheral Equipment and Software (sold via retail method)
				5734	Computer and Computer Software Stores
				*7378	Computer Maintenance and Repair (retailing new computers from a store front and repairing computers)
44313	Camera and Photographic Supplies Stores	c	E	5946	Camera and Photographic Supply Stores
444	Building Material and Garden Equipment and Supplies Dealers	c			
4441	Building Material and Supplies Dealers	c			
44411	Home Centers	c	N	*5211	Lumber and Other Building Materials Dealers (home center stores)
44412	Paint and Wallpaper Stores	c	R	*5231	Paint, Glass, and Wallpaper Stores (paint and wallpaper)
44413	Hardware Stores	c	R	*5072	Hardware (sold via retail method)
				5251	Hardware Stores
44419	Other Building Material Dealers	c	R	*5032	Brick, Stone, and Related Construction Materials (Wholesale) (sold via retail method)
				*5039	Construction Materials, NEC (Wholesale) (glass, sold via retail method)
				*5063	Electrical Apparatus and Equipment, Wiring Supplies, and Construction Materials (Wholesale) (sold via retail method)
				*5074	Plumbing and Heating Equipment and Supplies (Hydronics, sold via retail method)
				*5211	Lumber and Other Building Materials Dealers (except home centers)
				*5231	Paint, Glass, and Wallpaper Stores (glass)
4442	Lawn and Garden Equipment and Supplies Stores	c			
44421	Outdoor Power Equipment Stores	c	N	*5083	Farm and Garden Machinery and Equipment (Wholesale) (sold via retail method)
				*5261	Retail Nurseries, Lawn and Garden Supply Stores (outdoor power equipment)

Visit page 9 to learn more about NAICS codes.

Codes: u—unique to United States; c—common to U.S. and Canada; blank—common to 3 countries; E—existing industry; N—new industry; R—revised industry;
* indicates part of a 1987 SIC; (cont'd)—continued; NEC—Not Elsewhere Classified

NAICS Code	1997 NAICS U.S. Description	Codes		SIC Code	1987 U.S. SIC Description
44422	Nursery and Garden Centers	c	R	*5191	Farm Supplies (sold via retail method)
				*5193	Flowers, Nursery Stock, and Florists' Supplies (sold via retail method)
				*5261	Retail Nurseries, Lawn and Garden Supply Stores (except outdoor power equipment)
445	Food and Beverage Stores	c			
4451	Grocery Stores	c			
44511	Supermarkets and Other Grocery (except Convenience) Stores	c	N	*5411	Grocery Stores (except convenience stores and grocery stores with substantial general merchandise)
44512	Convenience Stores	c	N	*5411	Grocery Stores (convenience stores without gas)
4452	Specialty Food Stores	c			
44521	Meat Markets	c	R	*5421	Meat and Fish (Seafood) Markets, Including Freezer Provisioners (meat except freezer provisioners)
				*5499	Miscellaneous Food Stores (poultry and poultry products)
44522	Fish and Seafood Markets	c	N	*5421	Meat and Fish (Seafood) Markets, Including Freezer Provisioners (seafood)
44523	Fruit and Vegetable Markets	c	E	5431	Fruit and Vegetable Markets
44529	Other Specialty Food Stores	c			
445291	Baked Goods Stores	c	R	*5461	Retail Bakeries (selling only)
445292	Confectionery and Nut Stores	c	E	5441	Candy, Nut and Confectionery Stores
445299	All Other Specialty Food Stores	c	R	*5499	Miscellaneous Food Stores (except food supplements, poultry stores, and stores with food for immediate consumption)
				5451	Dairy Products Stores
4453	Beer, Wine, and Liquor Stores	c			
44531	Beer, Wine, and Liquor Stores	c	E	5921	Liquor Stores
446	Health and Personal Care Stores	c			
4461	Health and Personal Care Stores	c			
44611	Pharmacies and Drug Stores	c	E	5912	Drug Stores and Proprietary Stores
44612	Cosmetics, Beauty Supplies, and Perfume Stores	c	N	*5087	Service Establishment Equipment and Supplies (beauty and barber shop equipment and supplies sold via retail method)
				*5999	Miscellaneous Retail Stores, NEC (cosmetics and perfumes)
44613	Optical Goods Stores	c	R	*5995	Optical Goods Stores (except labs grinding prescription lenses)
44619	Other Health and Personal Care Stores	c			
446191	Food (Health) Supplement Stores	c	N	*5499	Miscellaneous Food Stores (food supplements)
446199	All Other Health and Personal Care Stores	c	N	*5047	Medical, Dental, and Hospital Equipment and Supplies (sold via retail method)
				*5999	Miscellaneous Retail Stores, NEC (hearing aids and artificial limbs)

NAICS to SIC

Codes: u—unique to United States; c—common to U.S. and Canada; blank—common to 3 countries; E—existing industry; N—new industry; R—revised industry;
* indicates part of a 1987 SIC; (cont'd)—continued; NEC—Not Elsewhere Classified

218 Harris InfoSource

NAICS Code	1997 NAICS U.S. Description	Codes		SIC Code	1987 U.S. SIC Description
447	Gasoline Stations	c			
4471	Gasoline Stations	c			
44711	Gasoline Stations with Convenience Stores	c	N	*5541	Gasoline Service Station (gasoline station with convenience store)
				*5411	Grocery Stores (convenience store with gas)
44719	Other Gasoline Stations	c	N	*5541	Gasoline Service Station (gasoline station without convenience store)
448	Clothing and Clothing Accessories Stores	c			
4481	Clothing Stores	c			
44811	Men's Clothing Stores	c	R	*5611	Men's and Boys' Clothing and Accessory Stores (clothing stores)
44812	Women's Clothing Stores	c	E	5621	Women's Clothing Stores
44813	Children's and Infants' Clothing Stores	c	E	5641	Children's and Infants' Wear Stores
44814	Family Clothing Stores	c	E	5651	Family Clothing Stores
44815	Clothing Accessories Stores	c	N	*5611	Men's and Boys' Clothing and Accessory Stores (accessories)
				*5632	Women's Accessory and Specialty Stores (accessories)
				*5699	Miscellaneous Apparel and Accessory Stores (accessories)
44819	Other Clothing Stores	c	R	*5699	Miscellaneous Apparel and Accessory Stores (miscellaneous apparel)
				*5632	Women's Accessory and Specialty Stores (specialty stores)
4482	Shoe Stores	c			
44821	Shoe Stores	c	E	5661	Shoe Stores
4483	Jewelry, Luggage, and Leather Goods Stores	c			
44831	Jewelry Stores	c	R	5944	Jewelry Stores
44832	Luggage and Leather Goods Stores	c	E	5948	Luggage and Leather Goods Stores
451	Sporting Goods, Hobby, Book, and Music Stores	c			
4511	Sporting Goods, Hobby, and Musical Instrument Stores	c			
45111	Sporting Goods Stores	c	R	5941	Sporting Goods Stores and Bicycle Shops
				*7699	Repair Shops and Related Services, NEC (retailing new bicycles from a storefront and repairing bicycles)
45112	Hobby, Toy, and Game Stores	c	E	5945	Hobby, Toy, and Game Stores
45113	Sewing, Needlework, and Piece Goods Stores	c	R	*5714	Drapery, Curtain, and Upholstery Stores (upholstery materials)
				5949	Sewing, Needlework, and Piece Goods Stores
45114	Musical Instrument and Supplies Stores	c	E	5736	Musical Instruments Stores
4512	Book, Periodical, and Music Stores	c			
45121	Book Stores and News Dealers	c			
451211	Book Stores	u	E	5942	Book Stores
451212	News Dealers and Newsstands	u	E	5994	News Dealers and Newsstands

Go to page 23 to learn about the implementation of NAICS codes in the public and private sectors.

Codes: u—unique to United States; c—common to U.S. and Canada; blank—common to 3 countries; E—existing industry; N—new industry; R—revised industry;
   * indicates part of a 1987 SIC; (cont'd)—continued; NEC—Not Elsewhere Classified

NAICS Code	1997 NAICS U.S. Description	Codes		SIC Code	1987 U.S. SIC Description
45122	Prerecorded Tape, Compact Disc, and Record Stores	c	E	5735	Record and Prerecorded Tape Stores
452	General Merchandise Stores	c			
4521	Department Stores	c			
45211	Department Stores	c	E	5311	Department Stores
4529	Other General Merchandise Stores	c			
45291	Warehouse Clubs and Superstores	c	N	*5399	Miscellaneous General Merchandise Stores (warehouse clubs and supermarket/general merchandise combination)
				*5411	Grocery Stores (grocery stores and supermarkets selling substantial amounts of nonfood items)
45299	All Other General Merchandise Stores	c	R	*5399	Miscellaneous General Merchandise Stores (except warehouse club and supermarket/general merchandise combination)
				5331	Variety Stores
				*5531	Auto and Home Supply Stores (other auto and home supply stores)
453	Miscellaneous Store Retailers	c			
4531	Florists	c			
45311	Florists	c	E	5992	Florists
4532	Office Supplies, Stationery, and Gift Stores	c			
45321	Office Supplies and Stationery Stores	c	R	*5044	Office Equipment (sold via retail method)
				*5049	Professional Equipment and Supplies, NEC (school supplies sold via retail method)
				*5112	Stationery and Office Supplies (sold via retail method)
45321	Office Supplies and Stationery Stores			5943	Stationery Stores
45322	Gift, Novelty, and Souvenir Stores	c	E	5947	Gift, Novelty, and Souvenir Shops
4533	Used Merchandise Stores	c			
45331	Used Merchandise Stores	c	R	*5932	Used Merchandise Stores (except pawn shops)
4539	Other Miscellaneous Store Retailers	c			
45391	Pet and Pet Supplies Stores	c	N	*5999	Miscellaneous Retail Stores, NEC (pet and pet supplies)
45392	Art Dealers	c	N	*5999	Miscellaneous Retail Stores, NEC (art dealer)
45393	Manufactured (Mobile) Home Dealers	c	E	5271	Mobile Home Dealers
45399	All Other Miscellaneous Store Retailers	c			
453991	Tobacco Stores	u	E	5993	Tobacco Stores and Stands
453998	All Other Miscellaneous Store Retailers (except Tobacco Stores)	u	R	*5999	Miscellaneous Retail Stores, NEC (except art, pet and pet supplies, hearing aids, artificial limbs, cosmetics, telephones, typewriters, personal appliances, and rough gems)

Codes: u—unique to United States; c—common to U.S. and Canada; blank—common to 3 countries; E—existing industry; N—new industry; R—revised industry; * indicates part of a 1987 SIC; (cont'd)—continued; NEC—Not Elsewhere Classified

220

Harris InfoSource

NAICS Code	1997 NAICS U.S. Description	Codes		SIC Code	1987 U.S. SIC Description
454	Nonstore Retailers	c			
4541	Electronic Shopping and Mail-order Houses	c			
45411	Electronic Shopping and Mail-order Houses	c	E	5961	Catalog and Mail-order Houses
4542	Vending Machine Operators	c			
45421	Vending Machine Operators	c	E	5962	Automatic Merchandise Machine Operators
4543	Direct Selling Establishments	c			
45431	Fuel Dealers	c			
454311	Heating Oil Dealers	u	R	*5171	Petroleum Bulk Stations and Terminals (heating oil sold to final consumer)
				5983	Fuel Oil Dealers
454312	Liquefied Petroleum Gas (Bottled Gas) Dealers	u	R	*5171	Petroleum Bulk Stations and Terminals (LP gas sold to final consumer)
				5984	Liquefied Petroleum Gas (Bottled Gas) Dealers
454319	Other Fuel Dealers	u	E	5989	Fuel Dealers, NEC
45439	Other Direct Selling Establishments	c	R	*5421	Meat and Fish (Seafood) Markets, Including Freezer Provisioners (freezer provisioners)
				*5963	Direct Selling Establishments (except mobile food services)
48-49	**Transportation and Warehousing**				
481	Air Transportation				
4811	Scheduled Air Transportation				
48111	Scheduled Air Transportation				
481111	Scheduled Passenger Air Transportation	u	N	*4512	Air Transportation, Scheduled (passenger)
481112	Scheduled Freight Air Transportation	u	N	*4512	Air Transportation, Scheduled (freight)
4812	Nonscheduled Air Transportation				
48121	Nonscheduled Air Transportation				
481211	Nonscheduled Chartered Passenger Air Transportation	u	N	*4522	Air Transportation, Nonscheduled (passenger)
481212	Nonscheduled Chartered Freight Air Transportation	u	N	*4522	Air Transportation, Nonscheduled (freight)
481219	Other Nonscheduled Air Transportation				Establishments that use general purpose aircraft to provide a variety of specialized flying services
482	Rail Transportation				
4821	Rail Transportation				
48211	Rail Transportation				
482111	Line-haul Railroads	u	E	4011	Railroads, Line-haul Operating
482112	Short Line Railroads	c	N	*4013	Railroad Switching and Terminal Establishments (belt line and logging railroads)
483	Water Transportation				

Codes: u—unique to United States; c—common to U.S. and Canada; blank—common to 3 countries; E—existing industry; N—new industry; R—revised industry;
* indicates part of a 1987 SIC; (cont'd)—continued; NEC—Not Elsewhere Classified

NAICS to SIC

NAICS Code	1997 NAICS U.S. Description	Codes		SIC Code	1987 U.S. SIC Description
4831	Deep Sea, Coastal, and Great Lakes Water Transportation				
48311	Deep Sea, Coastal, and Great Lakes Water Transportation				
483111	Deep Sea Freight Transportation	u	E	4412	Deep Sea Foreign Transportation of Freight
483112	Deep Sea Passenger Transportation	u	R	*4481	Deep Sea Transportation of Passengers, Except by Ferry (deep sea activities)
483113	Coastal and Great Lakes Freight Transportation	u	R	4424	Deep Sea Domestic Transportation of Freight
				4432	Freight Transportation on the Great Lakes—St. Lawrence Seaway
483114	Coastal and Great Lakes Passenger Transportation	u	R	*4481	Deep Sea Transportation of Passengers, Except by Ferry (coastal activities)
				*4482	Ferries (coastal and Great Lakes)
4832	Inland Water Transportation				
48321	Inland Water Transportation				
483211	Inland Water Freight Transportation	u	E	4449	Water Transportation of Freight, NEC
483212	Inland Water Passenger Transportation	u	R	*4482	Ferries (inland)
				*4489	Water Transportation of Passengers, NEC (water taxi)
484	Truck Transportation				
4841	General Freight Trucking				
48411	General Freight Trucking, Local		N	*4212	Local Trucking without Storage (general freight)
				*4214	Local Trucking with Storage (general freight)
48412	General Freight Trucking, Long-distance				
484121	General Freight Trucking, Long-distance, Truckload	c	N	*4213	Trucking, except Local (general freight, truckload)
484122	General Freight Trucking, Long-distance, Less Than Truckload	c	N	*4213	Trucking, except Local (general freight, less than truckload)
4842	Specialized Freight Trucking				
48421	Used Household and Office Goods Moving		N	*4212	Local Trucking Without Storage (house hold goods moving)
				*4213	Trucking, except Local (household goods moving)
				*4214	Local Trucking With Storage (household goods moving)
48422	Specialized Freight (except Used Goods) Trucking, Local		N	*4212	Local Trucking without Storage (specialized freight)
				*4214	Local Trucking with Storage (specialized freight)
48423	Specialized Freight (except Used Goods)		N	*4213	Trucking, except Local Trucking, Long-distance (specialized freight)
485	Transit and Ground Passenger Transportation				
4851	Urban Transit Systems				
48511	Urban Transit Systems				

Codes: u—unique to United States; c—common to U.S. and Canada; blank—common to 3 countries; E—existing industry; N—new industry; R—revised industry;
       * indicates part of a 1987 SIC; (cont'd)—continued; NEC—Not Elsewhere Classified

NAICS Code	1997 NAICS U.S. Description	Codes		SIC Code	1987 U.S. SIC Description
485111	Mixed Mode Transit Systems	u	N	*4111	Local and Suburban Transit (mixed mode)
485112	Commuter Rail Systems	u	N	*4111	Local and Suburban Transit (commuter rail)
485113	Bus and Other Motor Vehicle Transit Systems	u	N	*4111	Local and Suburban Transit (bus and motor vehicle)
485119	Other Urban Transit Systems	u	N	*4111	Local and Suburban Transit (other than mixed mode, commuter rail, and bus and motor vehicle)
4852	Interurban and Rural Bus Transportation				
48521	Interurban and Rural Bus Transportation		E	4131	Inter-city and Rural Bus Transportation
4853	Taxi and Limousine Service				
48531	Taxi Service		R	4121	Taxicabs
				*4899	Communications Services, NEC (taxi cab dispatch services)
48532	Limousine Service		N	*4119	Local Passenger Transportation, NEC (limousine rental with driver and automobile rental with driver)
4854	School and Employee Bus Transportation				
48541	School and Employee Bus Transportation		R	4151	School Buses
				*4119	Local Passenger Transportation, NEC (employee transportation)
4855	Charter Bus Industry				
48551	Charter Bus Industry		R	4141	Local Charter Bus Service
				4142	Bus Charter Services, except Local
4859	Other Transit and Ground Passenger Transportation				
48599	Other Transit and Ground Passenger Transportation				
485991	Special Needs Transportation	u	N	*4119	Local Passenger Transportation, NEC (special needs transportation)
485999	All Other Transit and Ground Passenger Transportation	u	R	*4111	Local and Suburban Transit (airport transportation service)
				*4119	Local Passenger Transportation, NEC (hearse rental with driver and carpool and vanpool operation)
486	Pipeline Transportation				
4861	Pipeline Transportation of Crude Oil				
48611	Pipeline Transportation of Crude Oil		E	4612	Crude Petroleum Pipelines
4862	Pipeline Transportation of Natural Gas				
48621	Pipeline Transportation of Natural Gas		R	4922	Natural Gas Transmission
				*4923	Natural Gas Transmission and Distribution (transmission)
4869	Other Pipeline Transportation				
48691	Pipeline Transportation of Refined		E	4613	Refined Petroleum Pipelines
48699	All Other Pipeline Transportation		E	4619	Pipelines, NEC
487	Scenic and Sightseeing Transportation				

Visit page 15 to learn about major changes to NAICS sectors.

Codes: u—unique to United States; c—common to U.S. and Canada; blank—common to 3 countries; E—existing industry; N—new industry; R—revised industry; * indicates part of a 1987 SIC; (cont'd)—continued; NEC—Not Elsewhere Classified

NAICS Code	1997 NAICS U.S. Description	Codes	SIC Code	1987 U.S. SIC Description
4871	Scenic and Sightseeing Transportation, Land			
48711	Scenic and Sightseeing Transportation, Land	N	*4119	Local Passenger Transportation, NEC (sight seeing buses and cable and cog railways, except scenic)
			*4789	Transportation Services, NEC (horse-drawn cabs and carriages)
			*7999	Amusement and Recreation Services, NEC (scenic transport operations, land)
4872	Scenic and Sightseeing Transportation, Water			
48721	Scenic and Sightseeing Transportation, Water	N	*4489	Water Transportation of Passengers, NEC (airboats, excursion boats, and sightseeing boats)
			*7999	Amusement and Recreation Services, NEC (charter fishing)
4879	Scenic and Sightseeing Transportation, Other			
48799	Scenic and Sightseeing Transportation, Other	N	*4522	Air Transportation, Nonscheduled (sightseeing planes)
			*7999	Amusement and Recreation Services, NEC (aerial tramways, scenic and amusement)
488	Support Activities for Transportation			
4881	Support Activities for Air Transportation			
48811	Airport Operations			
488111	Air Traffic Control	c N	*4581	Airports, Flying Fields, and Airport Terminal Services (private air traffic control)
			*9621	Regulation and Administration of Transportation Programs (government air traffic control)
488119	Other Airport Operations	c N	*4581	Airports, Flying Fields, and Airport Terminal Services (airfreight handling at airports, hangar operations, airport terminal services, aircraft storage, airports, and flying fields)
			*4959	Sanitary Services, NEC (vacuuming of runways)
48819	Other Support Activities for Air Transportation	N	*4581	Airports, Flying Fields, and Airport Terminal Services (aircraft servicing and repairing)
4882	Support Activities for Rail Transportation			
48821	Support Activities for Rail Transportation	R	*4013	Railroad Switching and Terminal Establishments (all but short line railroads)
			*4741	Rental of Railroad Cars (grain leveling in railroad cars, grain trimming for railroad equipment, precooling of fruits and vegetables in connection with transportation, and railroad car cleaning, icing, ventilating, and heating)

Codes: u—unique to United States; c—common to U.S. and Canada; blank—common to 3 countries; E—existing industry; N—new industry; R—revised industry;
* indicates part of a 1987 SIC; (cont'd)—continued; NEC—Not Elsewhere Classified

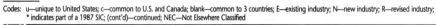

NAICS Code	1997 NAICS U.S. Description	Codes	SIC Code	1987 U.S. SIC Description
48821	Support Activities for Rail Transportation (cont'd)		*4789	Transportation Services, NEC (car loading and unloading; cleaning of rail road ballasts; dining, parlor, sleeping, and other car operations; and railroad maintenance)
4883	Support Activities for Water Transportation			
48831	Port and Harbor Operations	N	*4491	Marine Cargo Handling (dock and pier operations)
			*4499	Water Transportation Services, NEC (lighthouse and canal operations)
48832	Marine Cargo Handling	R	*4491	Marine Cargo Handling (all but dock and pier operations)
48833	Navigational Services to Shipping	N	*4492	Towing and Tugboat Services
			*4499	Water Transportation Services, NEC (piloting vessels in and out of harbors and marine salvage)
48839	Other Support Activities for Water Transportation	R	*3731	Ship Building and Repairing (floating dry docks not associated with a shipyard)
			*4499	Water Transportation Services, NEC (all but lighthouse operations, piloting vessels in and out of harbors, boat and ship rental, marine salvage, and canal operations)
			*4785	Fixed Facilities and Inspection and Weighing Services for Motor Vehicle Transportation (marine cargo checkers)
			*7699	Repair Shops and Related Services, NEC (ship scaling)
4884	Support Activities for Road Transportation			
48841	Motor Vehicle Towing	N	*7549	Automotive Services, except Repair and Carwashes (towing)
48849	Other Support Activities for Road Transportation	R	4173	Terminal and Service Facilities for Motor Vehicle Passenger Transportation
			4231	Terminal and Joint Terminal Maintenance Facilities for Motor Freight Transportation
			*4785	Fixed Facilities and Inspection and Weighing Services for Motor Vehicle Transportation (all but marine cargo checkers)
4885	Freight Transportation Arrangement			
48851	Freight Transportation Arrangement	R	*4731	Arrangement of Transportation of Freight and Cargo (except freight rate auditors and tariff consultants)
4889	Other Support Activities for Transportation			
48899	Other Support Activities for Transportation			

Codes: u—unique to United States; c—common to U.S. and Canada; blank—common to 3 countries; E—existing industry; N—new industry; R—revised industry;
     * indicates part of a 1987 SIC; (cont'd)—continued; NEC—Not Elsewhere Classified

NAICS Code	1997 NAICS U.S. Description	Codes		SIC Code	1987 U.S. SIC Description
488991	Packing and Crating	u	E	4783	Packing and Crating
488999	All Other Support Activities for Transportation	u	R	*4729	Arrangement of Passenger Transportation, NEC (arrangement of carpools and van pools)
				*4789	Transportation Services, NEC (pipeline terminals and stockyards for transportation)
491	Postal Service				
4911	Postal Service				
49111	Postal Service		R	4311	United States Postal Service
				*7389	Business Services, NEC (post office contract stations)
492	Couriers and Messengers				
4921	Couriers				
49211	Couriers		R	*4215	Courier Services, except by Air (hub and spoke inter-city delivery)
				4513	Air Courier Services
4922	Local Messengers and Local Delivery				
49221	Local Messengers and Local Delivery		N	*4215	Courier Services, except by Air (local delivery)
493	Warehousing and Storage				
4931	Warehousing and Storage				
49311	General Warehousing and Storage		R	*4225	General Warehousing and Storage (all but self-storage miniwarehouse warehousing)
				*4226	Special Warehousing and Storage, NEC (warehousing in foreign trade zones)
49312	Refrigerated Warehousing and Storage		R	4222	Refrigerated Warehousing and Storage
				*4226	Special Warehousing and Storage, NEC (fur storage)
49313	Farm Product Warehousing and Storage		E	4221	Farm Product Warehousing and Storage
49319	Other Warehousing and Storage		R	*4226	Special Warehousing and Storage, NEC (all but fur storage and warehousing in foreign trade zones)
51	**Information**				
511	Publishing Industries				
5111	Newspaper, Periodical, Book, and Database Publishers				
51111	Newspaper Publishers		E	2711	Newspapers: Publishing, or Publishing and Printing
51112	Periodical Publishers		R	2721	Periodicals: Publishing, or Publishing and Printing
				*2741	Miscellaneous Publishing (shopping news)
51113	Book Publishers		R	*2731	Books: Publishing, or Publishing and Printing (except music books)
				*2741	Miscellaneous Publishing (technical manuals and books)

Codes: u—unique to United States; c—common to U.S. and Canada; blank—common to 3 countries; E—existing industry; N—new industry; R—revised industry; * indicates part of a 1987 SIC; (cont'd)—continued; NEC—Not Elsewhere Classified

NAICS Code	1997 NAICS U.S. Description	Codes		SIC Code	1987 U.S. SIC Description
51114	Database and Directory Publishers		N	*2741	Miscellaneous Publishing (database publishers)
				*7331	Direct Mail Advertising Services (mailing list compilers)
51119	Other Publishers				
511191	Greeting Card Publishers	u	R	*2771	Greeting Cards (publishing greeting cards)
511199	All Other Publishers	u	R	*2741	Miscellaneous Publishing (except database, sheet music, shopping news, and technical manuals and book publishing)
5112	Software Publishers				
51121	Software Publishers		R	*7372	Prepackaged Software (software publishing)
512	Motion Picture and Sound Recording Industries				
5121	Motion Picture and Video Industries				
51211	Motion Picture and Video Production		E	7812	Motion Picture and Video Tape Production
51212	Motion Picture and Video Distribution		R	*7822	Motion Picture and Video Tape Distribution (except video tape and cassette wholesalers)
				*7829	Services Allied to Motion Picture Distribution (commercial distribution film libraries)
51213	Motion Picture and Video Exhibition				
512131	Motion Picture Theaters (except Drive-ins)	u	E	7832	Motion Picture Theaters, except Drive-in
512132	Drive-in Motion Picture Theaters	u	E	7833	Drive-in Motion Picture Theaters
51219	Postproduction and Other Motion Picture and Video Industries				
512191	Teleproduction and Other Postproduction	u	N	*7819	Services Allied to Motion Picture Production Services (teleproduction and postproduction services)
512199	Other Motion Picture and Video Industries	u	N	*7819	Services Allied to Motion Picture Production (except casting bureaus, wardrobe and equipment rental, talent payment services, teleproduction and other postproduction services, reproduction of videos, and film distributors and other related motion picture production services)
512199	Other Motion Picture and Video Industries			*7829	Services Allied to Motion Picture Distribution (booking agencies)
5122	Sound Recording Industries				
51221	Record Production		N	*8999	Services, NEC (record production)
51222	Integrated Record Production/ Distribution		N	*3652	Phonograph Records and Prerecorded Audio Tapes and Disks (integrated record companies, except duplication only)

Go to page 23 to learn about the implementation of NAICS codes in the public and private sectors.

Codes: u—unique to United States; c—common to U.S. and Canada; blank—common to 3 countries; E—existing industry; N—new industry; R—revised industry;
        * indicates part of a 1987 SIC; (cont'd)—continued; NEC—Not Elsewhere Classified

NAICS Code	1997 NAICS U.S. Description	Codes		SIC Code	1987 U.S. SIC Description
51223	Music Publishers		N	*2731	Books: Publishing, or Publishing and Printing (music books)
				*2741	Miscellaneous Publishing (sheet music publishing)
				*8999	Services, NEC (music publishing)
51224	Sound Recording Studios		N	*7389	Business Services, NEC (recording studios)
51229	Other Sound Recording Industries		N	*7389	Business Services, NEC (audio taping services)
				*7922	Theatrical Producers (Except Motion Picture) and Miscellaneous Theatrical Services (producers of radio programs)
513	Broadcasting and Telecommunications				
5131	Radio and Television Broadcasting				
51311	Radio Broadcasting				
513111	Radio Networks	u	N	*4832	Radio Broadcasting Stations (networks)
513112	Radio Stations	u	N	*4832	Radio Broadcasting Stations (except networks)
51312	Television Broadcasting		N	4833	Television Broadcasting Stations
5132	Cable Networks and Program Distribution				
51321	Cable Networks		N	*4841	Cable and Other Pay Television Services (cable networks)
51322	Cable and Other Program Distribution		N	*4841	Cable and Other Pay Television Services (except cable networks)
5133	Telecommunications				
51331	Wired Telecommunications Carriers		N	*4813	Telephone Communications, except Radiotelephone (except resellers)
				4822	Telegraph and Other Message Communications
51332	Wireless Telecommunications Carriers (except Satellite)				
513321	Paging	u	N	*4812	Radiotelephone Communications (paging carriers)
513322	Cellular and Other Wireless Telecommunications	u	N	*4812	Radiotelephone Communications (cellular carriers)
				*4899	Communications Services, NEC (ship-to-shore broadcasting)
51333	Telecommunications Resellers		N	*4812	Radio Communications (paging and cellular resellers)
				*4813	Telephone Communications, except Radiotelephone (wired resellers)
51334	Satellite Telecommunications		N	*4899	Communications Services, NEC (satellite communications)
				*4813	Telephone Communications, except Radiotelephone (satellite resellers)
51339	Other Telecommunications		N	*4899	Communications Services, NEC (except radio dispatch, ship-to-shore, and satellite communications)

Codes: u—unique to United States; c—common to U.S. and Canada; blank—common to 3 countries; E—existing industry; N—new industry; R—revised industry; * indicates part of a 1987 SIC; (cont'd)—continued; NEC—Not Elsewhere Classified

NAICS Code	1997 NAICS U.S. Description	Codes		SIC Code	1987 U.S. SIC Description
514	Information Services and Data Processing Services				
5141	Information Services				
51411	News Syndicates		R	*7383	News Syndicates (except independent news correspondents)
51412	Libraries and Archives		R	8231	Libraries
				*7829	Services Allied to Motion Picture Distribution (film archives)
51419	Other Information Services				
514191	Online Information Services	c	E	7375	Information Retrieval Services
514199	All Other Information Services	c	N	*8999	Services, NEC (miscellaneous information providers)
				*7389	Business Services, NEC (stock photo agencies, press clipping services)
5142	Data Processing Services				
51421	Data Processing Services		R	7374	Computer Processing and Data Preparation and Processing Services
				*7379	Computer Related Services, NEC (disk and diskette conversion and recertification)
				*7389	Business Services, NEC (microfilm services)
52	**Finance and Insurance**				
521	Monetary Authorities—Central Bank				
5211	Monetary Authorities—Central Bank				
52111	Monetary Authorities—Central Bank	c	E	6011	Federal Reserve Banks
522	Credit Intermediation and Related Activities				
5221	Depository Credit Intermediation	c			
52211	Commercial Banking	c	R	*6021	National Commercial Banks (banking)
				*6022	State Commercial Banks (commercial banking)
				6029	Commercial Banks, NEC
				*6081	Branches and Agencies of Foreign Banks (branches)
52212	Savings Institutions	u	R	6035	Savings Institutions, Federally Chartered
				6036	Savings Institutions, Not Federally Chartered
52213	Credit Unions	c	R	6061	Credit Unions, Federally Chartered
				6062	Credit Unions, Not Federally Chartered
52219	Other Depository Credit Intermediation	c	N	*6022	State Commercial Banks (private and industrial banking)
5222	Nondepository Credit Intermediation	c			
52221	Credit Card Issuing	c	N	*6021	National Commercial Banks (credit card issuing)
				*6022	State Commercial Banks (credit card issuing)

NAICS to SIC

Codes: u—unique to United States; c—common to U.S. and Canada; blank—common to 3 countries; E—existing industry; N—new industry; R—revised industry;
* indicates part of a 1987 SIC; (cont'd)—continued; NEC—Not Elsewhere Classified

NAICS Code	1997 NAICS U.S. Description	Codes		SIC Code	1987 U.S. SIC Description
52221	Credit Card Issuing (cont'd)			*6141	Personal Credit Institutions (credit card issuing)
				*6153	Short-term Business Credit Institutions, Except Agricultural (credit card issuing)
52222	Sales Financing	c	N	*6141	Personal Credit Institutions (installment sales finance)
				*6153	Short-term Business Credit Institutions, Except Agricultural (business sales finance)
				*6159	Miscellaneous Business Credit Institutions (finance leasing combined with sales financing)
52229	Other Nondepository Credit Intermediation	c			
522291	Consumer Lending	c	R	*6141	Personal Credit Institutions (except installment sales finance and credit card issuing)
522292	Real Estate Credit	u	R	*6111	Foreign Trade and International Banking Institutions (Federal Land Banks)
				*6162	Mortgage Bankers and Loan Correspondents (mortgage bankers and originators)
				*6159	Miscellaneous Business Credit Institutions (farm mortgage companies)
522293	International Trade Financing Institutions	u	N	*6081	Branches and Agencies of Foreign Banks (international trade financing)
				*6082	Foreign Trade and International Banking Institutions (international trade financing)
				*6111	Federal and Federally Sponsored Credit Agencies (trade banks)
				*6159	Miscellaneous Business Credit (trade banks)
522294	Secondary Market Financing	u	N	*6111	Federal and Federally Sponsored Credit Agencies (secondary market financing)
				*6159	Miscellaneous Business Credit Institutions (secondary market financing)
522298	All Other Nondepository Credit	u	N	*5932	Used Merchandise Stores (pawnshops) Intermediation
				6019	Central Reserve Depository Institutions, NEC
				*6081	Branches and Agencies of Foreign Banks (agencies, except international trade financing)
				*6082	Foreign Trade and International Banking Institutions (except international trade financing)
				*6111	Federal and Federally Sponsored Credit Agencies (except trade banks, secondary market financing and Federal Land Banks)

Codes: u—unique to United States; c—common to U.S. and Canada; blank—common to 3 countries; E—existing industry; N—new industry; R—revised industry; * indicates part of a 1987 SIC; (cont'd)—continued; NEC—Not Elsewhere Classified

230

Harris InfoSource

NAICS Code	1997 NAICS U.S. Description	Codes		SIC Code	1987 U.S. SIC Description
522298	All Other Nondepository Credit (cont'd)			*6141	Personal Credit Institutions (industrial nondeposit banks)
				*6159	Miscellaneous Business Credit Institutions (except trade banks, farm mortgage companies, secondary market, financing, and finance leasing)
5223	Activities Related to Credit Intermediation	c			
52231	Mortgage and Nonmortgage Loan Brokers	c	E	6163	Loan Brokers
52232	Financial Transactions Processing, Reserve, and Clearinghouse Activities	c	N	*6099	Functions Related to Depository Banking, NEC (electronic funds transfer networks and clearinghouse associations)
				*6153	Short-term Business Credit Institutions, except Agricultural (credit card service)
				*7389	Business Services, NEC (credit card and validation service)
52239	Other Activities Related to Credit Intermediation	c	N	*6099	Functions Related to Depository Banking, NEC (except electronic funds transfer networks and clearinghouses, foreign currency exchanges, escrow and fiduciary agencies and deposit brokers)
				*6162	Mortgage Bankers and Loan Correspondents (mortgage servicing)
523	Securities, Commodity Contracts, and Other Financial Investments and Related Activities				
5231	Securities and Commodity Contracts Intermediation and Brokerage				
52311	Investment Banking and Securities Dealing	c	N	*6211	Security Brokers, Dealers, and Flotation Companies (security dealers and underwriters)
52312	Securities Brokerage	c	N	*6211	Security Brokers, Dealers, and Flotation Companies (security brokers)
52313	Commodity Contracts Dealing	c	N	*6099	Functions Related to Depository Banking, NEC (foreign currency exchange)
				*6799	Investors, NEC (commodity contract trading companies)
				*6221	Commodity Contracts Brokers and Dealers (commodity dealers)
52314	Commodity Contracts Brokerage	c	N	*6221	Commodity Contracts Brokers and Dealers (commodity brokers)
5232	Securities and Commodity Exchanges				
52321	Securities and Commodity Exchanges		E	6231	Security and Commodity Exchanges
5239	Other Financial Investment Activities				
52391	Miscellaneous Intermediation	c	N	*6211	Security Brokers, Dealers, and Flotation Companies (except security and commodity dealers, security brokers and oil and gas lease brokers)

Codes: u—unique to United States; c—common to U.S. and Canada; blank—common to 3 countries; E—existing industry; N—new industry; R—revised industry;
* indicates part of a 1987 SIC; (cont'd)—continued; NEC—Not Elsewhere Classified

NAICS Code	1997 NAICS U.S. Description	Codes		SIC Code	1987 U.S. SIC Description
52391	Miscellaneous Intermediation (cont'd)			*6153	Short-term Business Credit Institutions, Except Agricultural (except credit card service and issuing and business sales finance)
				*6792	Oil Royalty Traders (investing on own account)
				*6799	Investors, NEC (venture capital companies, investment clubs, and speculators for own account)
52392	Portfolio Management	c	N	*6282	Investment Advice (portfolio managers)
				*6371	Pension, Health, and Welfare Funds (managers)
				*6733	Trust, except Educational, Religious, and Charitable (managers)
				*6799	Investors, NEC (commodity contract pool operators)
52393	Investment Advice	c	R	*6282	Investment Advice (except portfolio managers)
52399	All Other Financial Investment Activities	c			
523991	Trust, Fiduciary, and Custody Activities	u	N	6091	Nondeposit Trust Facilities
				*6099	Functions Related to Depository Banking, NEC (escrow and fiduciary agencies)
				*6289	Services Allied With the Exchange of Securities or Commodities, NEC (security custodians)
				*6733	Trusts, except Educational, Religious, and Charitable (administrators of private estates)
523999	Miscellaneous Financial Investment Activities	u	R	*6211	Security Brokers, Dealers, and Flotation Companies (oil and gas lease brokers' officers)
				*6289	Services Allied With the Exchange of Securities or Commodities, NEC (except securities custodians)
524	Insurance Carriers and Related Activities				
5241	Insurance Carriers				
52411	Direct Life, Health, and Medical Insurance Carriers	c			
524113	Direct Life Insurance Carriers	u	R	*6311	Life Insurance (life insurers—direct)
				*6321	Accident and Health Insurance (disability insurers—direct)
524114	Direct Health and Medical Insurance Carriers	u	R	*6324	Hospital and Medical Service Plans (health and medical insurers—direct)
				*6321	Accident and Health Insurance (health and medical insurers—direct)
52412	Direct Insurance (except Life, Health, and Medical) Carriers	c			
524126	Direct Property and Casualty Insurance Carriers	u	R	*6331	Fire, Marine, and Casualty Insurance (fire, marine, and casualty insurers—direct, except contact lens insurance)

Codes: u—unique to United States; c—common to U.S. and Canada; blank—common to 3 countries; E—existing industry; N—new industry; R—revised industry; * indicates part of a 1987 SIC; (cont'd)—continued; NEC—Not Elsewhere Classified

232

Harris InfoSource

NAICS Code	1997 NAICS U.S. Description	Codes		SIC Code	1987 U.S. SIC Description
524126	Direct Property and Casualty Insurance Carriers (cont'd)			*6351	Surety Insurance (financial responsibility insurers—direct)
524127	Direct Title Insurance Carriers	u	R	*6361	Title Insurance (title insurers—direct)
524128	Other Direct Insurance (except Life, Health, and Medical) Carriers	u	R	*6331	Fire, Marine, and Casualty Insurance (contact lens insurance)
				6399	Insurance Carriers, NEC
52413	Reinsurance Carriers	c	N	*6311	Life Insurance (reinsurers)
				*6321	Accident and Health Insurance (reinsurers)
				*6324	Hospital and Medical Service Plans (reinsurers)
				*6331	Fire, Marine, and Casualty Insurance (reinsurers)
				*6351	Surety Insurance (reinsurers)
				*6361	Title Insurance (reinsurers)
5242	Agencies, Brokerages, and Other Insurance Related Activities				
52421	Insurance Agencies and Brokerages	c	R	*6411	Insurance Agents, Brokers, and Service (insurance agents and brokers)
52429	Other Insurance Related Activities	c			
524291	Claims Adjusting	c	N	*6411	Insurance Agents, Brokers, and Service (insurance claims adjusters)
524292	Third Party Administration of Insurance and Pension Funds	u	N	*6371	Pension, Health, and Welfare Funds (administrators)
				*6411	Insurance Agents, Brokers, and Service (processors)
524298	All Other Insurance Related Activities	u	N	*6411	Insurance Agents, Brokers, and Service (except processors, agents and brokers, and claims adjusters)
525	Funds, Trusts, and Other Financial Vehicles	u			
5251	Insurance and Employee Benefit Funds	u			
52511	Pension Funds	u	N	*6371	Pension, Health, and Welfare Funds (pension funds)
52512	Health and Welfare Funds	u	N	*6371	Pension, Health, and Welfare Funds (health and welfare funds)
52519	Other Insurance Funds	u	N	*6321	Accident and Health Insurance (self insurers)
				*6324	Hospital and Medical Service Plans (self insurers)
				*6331	Fire, Marine, and Casualty Insurance (self insurers)
				*6733	Trusts, except Educational, Religious, and Charitable (vacation funds for employees)
5259	Other Investment Pools and Funds	u			
52591	Open-end Investment Funds	u	E	6722	Management Investment Offices, Open-end
52592	Trusts, Estates, and Agency Accounts	u	N	*6733	Trusts, except Educational, Religious, and Charitable (personal trusts, estates, and agency accounts)

Codes: u—unique to United States; c—common to U.S. and Canada; blank—common to 3 countries; E—existing industry; N—new industry; R—revised industry;
* indicates part of a 1987 SIC; (cont'd)—continued; NEC—Not Elsewhere Classified

NAICS Code	1997 NAICS U.S. Description	Codes		SIC Code	1987 U.S. SIC Description
52593	Real Estate Investment Trusts	u	E	6798	Real Estate Investment Trusts
52599	Other Financial Vehicles	u	R	*6371	Pension, Health, and Welfare Funds (profit sharing funds)
				6726	Unit Investment Trusts, Face-amount Certificate Offices, and Closed-end Management Investment Offices
53	**Real Estate and Rental and Leasing**				
531	Real Estate				
5311	Lessors of Real Estate				
53111	Lessors of Residential Buildings and Dwellings	c	R	6513	Operators of Apartment Buildings
				6514	Operators of Dwellings Other Than Apartment
53112	Lessors of Nonresidential Buildings (except Miniwarehouses)	c	N	*6512	Operators of Nonresidential Buildings (other except stadium and arena owners)
53113	Lessors of Miniwarehouses and Self-storage	c	N	*4225	General Warehousing and Storage Units (miniwarehouses and self-storage units)
53119	Lessors of Other Real Estate Property	c	R	6515	Operators of Residential Mobile Home Sites
				6517	Lessors of Railroad Property
				6519	Lessors of Real Property, NEC
5312	Offices of Real Estate Agents and Brokers				
53121	Offices of Real Estate Agents and Brokers		N	*6531	Real Estate Agents Managers (agents and brokers)
5313	Activities Related to Real Estate				
53131	Real Estate Property Managers	c			
531311	Residential Property Managers	u	N	*6531	Real Estate Agents and Managers (managers—esidential, real estate)
531312	Nonresidential Property Managers	u	N	*6531	Real Estate Agents and Managers (managers—nonresidential, real estate)
53132	Offices of Real Estate Appraisers	c	N	*6531	Real Estate Agents and Managers (appraisers)
53139	Other Activities Related to Real Estate	c	N	*6531	Real Estate Agents and Managers (except real estate managers, condominium management, cemetery management, agents and brokers, and appraisers)
532	Rental and Leasing Services				
5321	Automotive Equipment Rental and Leasing				
53211	Passenger Car Rental and Leasing				
532111	Passenger Car Rental	c	E	7514	Passenger Car Rental
532112	Passenger Car Leasing	c	E	7515	Passenger Car Leasing
53212	Truck, Utility Trailer, and RV (Recreational Vehicle) Rental and Leasing		N	7513	Truck Rental and Leasing Without Drivers
				7519	Utility Trailers and Recreational Vehicle Rental

Codes: u—unique to United States; c—common to U.S. and Canada; blank—common to 3 countries; E—existing industry; N—new industry; R—revised industry; * indicates part of a 1987 SIC; (cont'd)—continued; NEC—Not Elsewhere Classified

234

Harris InfoSource

NAICS Code	1997 NAICS U.S. Description	Codes		SIC Code	1987 U.S. SIC Description
5322	Consumer Goods Rental				
53221	Consumer Electronics and Appliances Rental		N	*7359	Equipment Rental and Leasing, NEC (appliances, TV, VCR, and electronic equipment rental)
53222	Formal Wear and Costume Rental		N	*7299	Miscellaneous Personal Services, NEC (formal wear and costume rental)
				*7819	Services Allied to Motion Picture Production (wardrobe rental for motion picture film production)
53223	Video Tape and Disc Rental		E	7841	Video Tape Rental
53229	Other Consumer Goods Rental				
532291	Home Health Equipment Rental	u	N	*7352	Medical Equipment Rental and Leasing (home health furniture and equipment rental and leasing)
532292	Recreational Goods Rental	u	N	*7999	Amusement and Recreation Services, NEC (rental of canoes, pleasure boats, bicycles, motorcycles, mopeds, go carts, etc.)
532299	All Other Consumer Goods Rental	u	R	*7359	Equipment Rental and Leasing, NEC (except transportation equipment, industrial equipment, and consumer electronics, appliances, and home and garden equipment)
5323	General Rental Centers				
53231	General Rental Centers		N	*7359	Equipment Rental and Leasing, NEC (general rental centers)
5324	Commercial and Industrial Machinery and Equipment Rental and Leasing				
53241	Construction, Transportation, Mining, and Forestry Machinery and Equipment Rental and Leasing				
532411	Commercial Air, Rail, and Water Transportation Equipment Rental and Leasing	u	N	*4499	Water Transportation Services, NEC (boat and ship rental, commercial)
				*4741	Rental of Railroad Cars (rental of railroad cars)
				*7359	Equipment Rental and Leasing, NEC (aircraft rental and leasing)
532412	Construction, Mining, and Forestry Machinery and Equipment Rental and Leasing	u	R	*7353	Heavy Construction Equipment Rental and Leasing (without operators)
				*7359	Equipment Rental and Leasing, NEC (oil field and well drilling equipment)
53242	Office Machinery and Equipment Rental and Leasing		N	*7359	Equipment Rental and Leasing (office machine rental and leasing)
				7377	Computer Rental and Leasing
53249	Other Commercial and Industrial Machinery and Equipment Rental and Leasing		N	*7352	Medical Equipment Rental and Leasing (medical machinery and equipment)
				*7359	Equipment Rental and Leasing, NEC (industrial truck and equipment rental and leasing)

Go to page 23 to learn about the implementation of NAICS codes in the public and private sectors.

Codes: u—unique to United States; c—common to U.S. and Canada; blank—common to 3 countries; E—existing industry; N—new industry; R—revised industry;
* indicates part of a 1987 SIC; (cont'd)—continued; NEC—Not Elsewhere Classified

NAICS Code	1997 NAICS U.S. Description	Codes		SIC Code	1987 U.S. SIC Description
53249	Other Commercial and Industrial Machinery and Equipment Rental and Leasing (cont'd)			*7819	Services Allied to Motion Picture Production (motion picture equipment rental)
				*7922	Theatrical Producers (Except Motion Picture) and Miscellaneous Theatrical Services (theatrical equipment rental)
533	Lessors of Nonfinancial Intangible Assets (except Copyrighted Works)				
5331	Lessors of Nonfinancial Intangible Assets (except Copyrighted Works)				
53311	Lessors of Nonfinancial Intangible Assets (except Copyrighted Works)		R	*6792	Oil Royalty Traders (except investors on own account)
				6794	Patent Owners and Lessors
54	**Professional, Scientific, and Technical Services**				
541	Professional, Scientific, and Technical Services				
5411	Legal Services				
54111	Offices of Lawyers		E	8111	Legal Services
54112	Offices of Notaries		L		Null Set for U.S.
54119	Other Legal Services				
541191	Title Abstract and Settlement Offices	u	E	6541	Title Abstract Offices
541199	All Other Legal Services	u	N	*7389	Business Services, NEC (process services, patent agents, notaries public, paralegal services)
5412	Accounting, Tax Preparation, Bookkeeping, and Payroll Services				
54121	Accounting, Tax Preparation, Bookkeeping, and Payroll Services				
541211	Offices of Certified Public Accountants	u	N	*8721	Accounting, Auditing, and Bookkeeping Services (auditing accountants)
541213	Tax Preparation Services	c	E	7291	Tax Return Preparation Services
541214	Payroll Services	u	N	*7819	Services Allied to Motion Picture Production (talent payment services)
				*8721	Accounting, Auditing, and Bookkeeping Services (payroll services)
541219	Other Accounting Services	u	N	*8721	Accounting, Auditing, and Bookkeeping Services (other accounting services)
5413	Architectural, Engineering, and Related Services				
54131	Architectural Services		E	8712	Architectural Services
54132	Landscape Architectural Services		R	*0781	Landscape Counseling and Planning (except horticultural consulting)
				*8748	Business Consulting Services, NEC (urban planners and industrial development organizations)
54133	Engineering Services		R	8711	Engineering Services
				*8748	Business Consulting Services, NEC (traffic engineering consulting)

Codes: u—unique to United States; c—common to U.S. and Canada; blank—common to 3 countries; E—existing industry; N—new industry; R—revised industry;
* indicates part of a 1987 SIC; (cont'd)—continued; NEC—Not Elsewhere Classified

NAICS Code	1997 NAICS U.S. Description	Codes		SIC Code	1987 U.S. SIC Description
54134	Drafting Services		N	*7389	Business Services, NEC (drafting service)
54135	Building Inspection Services		N	*7389	Business Services, NEC (home and building inspection services)
54136	Geophysical Surveying and Mapping Services		N	*8713	Surveying Services (geophysical surveying)
				*1081	Metal Mining Services (geophysical surveying and mapping)
				*1382	Oil and Gas Field Exploration Services (geophysical surveying and mapping)
				*1481	Nonmetallic Minerals Services, except Fuels (geophysical surveying and mapping)
54137	Surveying and Mapping (except Geophysical) Services		N	*7389	Business Services, NEC (map making services)
				*8713	Surveying Services (except geophysical surveying)
54138	Testing Laboratories		R	*8734	Testing Laboratories (except veterinary testing laboratories)
5414	Specialized Design Services				
54141	Interior Design Services		N	*7389	Business Services, NEC (interior design)
54142	Industrial Design Services		N	*7389	Business Services, NEC (industrial design)
54143	Graphic Design Services		R	7336	Commercial Art and Graphic Design
				*8099	Health and Allied Services, NEC (medical artists)
54149	Other Specialized Design Services		N	*7389	Business Services, NEC (fashion and other design services)
5415	Computer Systems Design and Related Services				
54151	Computer Systems Design and Related Services				
541511	Custom Computer Programming Services	u	E	7371	Computer Programming Services
541512	Computer Systems Design Services	u	N	7373	Computer Integrated Systems Design
				*7379	Computer Related Services, NEC (computer systems consultants)
541513	Computer Facilities Management Services	u	E	7376	Computer Facilities Management Services
541519	Other Computer Related Services	u	R	*7379	Computer Related Services, NEC (except computer systems consultants and disk and diskette conversion and recertification)
5416	Management, Scientific, and Technical Consulting Services				
54161	Management Consulting Services				
541611	Administrative Management and General Management Consulting Services	c	N	*8742	Management Consulting Services (administrative management and general management consulting)
541612	Human Resources and Executive Search Consulting Services	c	N	*8742	Management Consulting Services (human resources and personnel management consulting)

Codes: u—unique to United States; c—common to U.S. and Canada; blank—common to 3 countries; E—existing industry; N—new industry; R—revised industry;
* indicates part of a 1987 SIC; (cont'd)—continued; NEC—Not Elsewhere Classified

NAICS Code	1997 NAICS U.S. Description	Codes		SIC Code	1987 U.S. SIC Description
541612	Human Resources and Executive Search Consulting Services (cont'd)			*7361	Employment Agencies (executive placement services)
				*8999	Services, NEC (actuarial consulting)
541613	Marketing Consulting Services	u	N	*8742	Management Consulting Services (marketing consulting)
541614	Process, Physical Distribution, and Logistics Consulting Services	u	N	*8742	Management Consulting Services (manufacturing management, physical distribution, and site location consulting)
				*4731	Arrangement of Transportation of Freight and Cargo (freight rate-auditors and tariff consulting)
541618	Other Management Consulting Services	u	N	*8748	Business Consulting Services, NEC (except educational testing and consulting, economic consulting, safety and security, agriculture consulting, urban planning and industrial development organizations)
54162	Environmental Consulting Services		N	*8999	Services, NEC (environmental consultants)
54169	Other Scientific and Technical Consulting Services		N	*0781	Landscape Counseling and Planning (horticulture consulting)
				*8748	Business Consulting Services, NEC (safety, security, agriculture, and economic consultants)
				*8999	Services, NEC (scientific and related consulting services)
5417	Scientific Research and Development Services				
54171	Research and Development in the Physical, Engineering, and Life Sciences		N	*3721	Aircraft (research and development)
				*3724	Aircraft Engines and Engine Parts (research and development)
				*3728	Aircraft Parts and Auxiliary Equipment, NEC (research and development)
				*3761	Guided Missiles and Space Vehicles (research and development)
				*3764	Guided Missile and Space Vehicle Propulsion Units and Propulsion Unit Parts (research and development)
				*3769	Guided Missile Space Vehicle Parts and Auxiliary Equipment, NEC (research and development)
				8731	Commercial Physical and Biological Research
				*8733	Noncommercial Research Organizations (physical, engineering, and life sciences)
54172	Research and Development in the Social Sciences and Humanities		N	*8732	Commercial Economic, Sociological, and Educational Research (social sciences and humanities)
				*8733	Noncommercial Research Organizations (social sciences and humanities)

NAICS Code	1997 NAICS U.S. Description	Codes		SIC Code	1987 U.S. SIC Description
5418	Advertising and Related Services				
54181	Advertising Agencies		E	7311	Advertising Agencies
54182	Public Relations Agencies		E	8743	Public Relations Services
54183	Media Buying Agencies		N	*7319	Advertising, NEC (media buying services)
54184	Media Representatives		E	7313	Radio, Television, and Publishers' Advertising Representatives
54185	Display Advertising		N	7312	Outdoor Advertising Services
				*7319	Advertising, NEC (display advertising, except outdoor)
54186	Direct Mail Advertising		R	*7331	Direct Mail Advertising Services (except mailing list compilers)
54187	Advertising Material Distribution Services		N	*7319	Advertising, NEC (advertising materials distributor)
				*7389	Business Services, NEC (distribution of telephone directories on a fee or contract basis)
54189	Other Services Related to Advertising		N	*7319	Advertising, NEC (except media buying, display advertising, except outdoor; and advertising material distributors)
				*5199	Nondurable Goods, NEC (advertising specialities goods distributors)
				*7389	Business Services, NEC (sign painting and lettering, showcard painting, mannequin decorating service, and other advertising related business services)
5419	Other Professional, Scientific, and Technical Services				
54191	Marketing Research and Public Opinion Polling		N	*8732	Commercial Economic, Sociological, and Educational Research (market research and opinion research)
54192	Photographic Services				
541921	Photography Studios, Portrait	u	E	7221	Photographic Studios, Portrait
541922	Commercial Photography	u	R	*7335	Commercial Photography (except when combined with a variety of aircraft-based services)
				*8099	Health and Allied Services, NEC (medical photography)
54193	Translation and Interpretation Services		N	*7389	Business Services, NEC (translation and interpretation services)
54194	Veterinary Services		R	0741	Veterinary Services for Livestock
54194	Veterinary Services			0742	Veterinary Services for Animal Specialties
54194	Veterinary Services			*8734	Testing Laboratories (veterinary testing laboratories)
54199	All Other Professional, Scientific, and Technical Services		N	*7389	Business Services (appraisers, except insurance and real estate, and miscellaneous professional, scientific, and technical services)
55	**Management of Companies and Enterprises**				

Codes: u—unique to United States; c—common to U.S. and Canada; blank—common to 3 countries; E—existing industry; N—new industry; R—revised industry;
    * indicates part of a 1987 SIC; (cont'd)—continued; NEC—Not Elsewhere Classified

NAICS Code	1997 NAICS U.S. Description	Codes		SIC Code	1987 U.S. SIC Description
551	Management of Companies and Enterprises				
5511	Management of Companies and Enterprises				
55111	Management of Companies and Enterprises				
551111	Offices of Bank Holding Companies	u	E	6712	Offices of Bank Holding Companies
551112	Offices of Other Holding Companies	u	E	6719	Offices of Holding Companies, NEC
551114	Corporate, Subsidiary, and Regional Managing Offices	c	N		These establishments were included as auxiliaries in the 1987 Standard Industrial Classification
56	**Administrative and Support and Waste Management and Remediation Services**				
561	Administrative and Support Services				
5611	Office Administrative Services				
56111	Office Administrative Services		R	*8741	Management Services (except construction management)
5612	Facilities Support Services				
56121	Facilities Support Services		E	8744	Facilities Support Management Services
5613	Employment Services				
56131	Employment Placement Agencies		R	*7299	Miscellaneous Personal Services, NEC (babysitting bureaus)
				*7361	Employment Agencies (except executive placing services)
				*7819	Services Allied to Motion Picture Production (casting bureaus)
				*7922	Theatrical Producers and Miscellaneous Theatrical Services (casting agencies)
56132	Temporary Help Services		N	*7363	Help Supply Services (except employee leasing service)
56133	Employee Leasing Services		N	*7363	Help Supply Services (except temporary help service)
5614	Business Support Services				
56141	Document Preparation Services		N	*7338	Secretarlal and Court Reporting (except court reporting)
56142	Telephone Call Centers				
561421	Telephone Answering Services	u	N	*7389	Business Services, NEC (telephone answering)
561422	Telemarketing Bureaus	u	N	*7389	Business Services, NEC (telemarketing bureaus and telephone soliciting)
56143	Business Service Centers				
561431	Private Mail Centers	u	N	*7389	Business Services, NEC (private mail centers and mailbox rental)
561439	Other Business Service Centers (including Copy Shops)	u	R	*7334	Photocopying and Duplicating Services (except instant printing)
				*7389	Business Services, NEC (other business service centers, except private mail centers and mailbox rental)

Codes: u—unique to United States; c—common to U.S. and Canada; blank—common to 3 countries; E—existing industry; N—new industry; R—revised industry; * indicates part of a 1987 SIC; (cont'd)—continued; NEC—Not Elsewhere Classified

NAICS Code	1997 NAICS U.S. Description	Codes		SIC Code	1987 U.S. SIC Description
56144	Collection Agencies		E	7322	Adjustment and Collection Services
56145	Credit Bureaus		E	7323	Credit Reporting Services
56149	Other Business Support Services				
561491	Repossession Services	u	N	*7389	Business Services, NEC (recovery and repossession services)
561492	Court Reporting and Stenotype Services	u	N	*7338	Secretarial and Court Reporting (except secretarial)
561499	All Other Business Support Services	u	N	*7389	Business Services, NEC (business support services except telephone answering, telemarketing bureaus, private mail centers and repossession services)
5615	Travel Arrangement and Reservation Services				
56151	Travel Agencies		E	4724	Travel Agencies
56152	Tour Operators		E	4725	Tour Operators
56159	Other Travel Arrangement and Reservation Services				
561591	Convention and Visitors Bureaus	u	N	*7389	Business Services, NEC (convention and visitors bureaus, tourist information bureaus)
561599	All Other Travel Arrangement and Reservation Services	u	N	*4729	Arrangement of Passenger Transportation, NEC (except arrangement of vanpools and carpools)
				*7389	Business Services, NEC (reservation systems: hotel and restaurants and time-share condominium exchange)
				*7999	Amusement and Recreation Services, NEC (ticket agencies)
				*8699	Membership Organizations, NEC (travel motor clubs)
				*7922	Theatrical Producers (except motion pictures) and Miscellaneous Theatrical Services (theatrical ticket agencies)
5616	Investigation and Security Services				
56161	Investigation, Guard, and Armored Car Services				
561611	Investigation Services Services	c	N	*7381	Detective, Guard, and Armored Car (detective services)
561612	Security Guards and Patrol Services	c	N	*7381	Detective, Guard, and Armored Car Services (guard services)
561613	Armored Car Services Services	c	N	*7381	Detective, Guard, and Armored Car (armored car services)
56162	Security Systems Services				
561621	Security Systems Services (except Locksmiths)	c	E	7382	Security Systems Services
561622	Locksmiths	c	N	*7699	Repair Shops and Related Services, NEC (locksmith shops)
5617	Services to Buildings and Dwellings				
56171	Exterminating and Pest Control Services		R	*4959	Sanitary Services, NEC (mosquito eradication)

Codes: u—unique to United States; c—common to U.S. and Canada; blank—common to 3 countries; E—existing industry; N—new industry; R—revised industry;
* indicates part of a 1987 SIC; (cont'd)—continued; NEC—Not Elsewhere Classified

NAICS Code	1997 NAICS U.S. Description	Codes		SIC Code	1987 U.S. SIC Description
56171	Exterminating and Pest Control Services (cont'd)			*7342	Disinfecting and Pest Control Services (exterminating and pest control)
56172	Janitorial Services	R		*7342	Disinfecting and Pest Control Services (except exterminating)
				*7349	Building Cleaning and Maintenance Services, NEC (except lighting maintenance services)
				*4581	Airports, Flying Fields, and Airport Terminal Services (airplane cleaning and janitorial services)
56173	Landscaping Services	R		0782	Lawn and Garden Services
				0783	Ornamental Shrub and Tree Services
56174	Carpet and Upholstery Cleaning Services	E		7217	Carpet and Upholstery Cleaning
56179	Other Services to Buildings and Dwellings	N		*7389	Business Services, NEC (swimming pool cleaning and maintenance)
				*7349	Building Cleaning and Maintenance Services, NEC (lighting maintenance service)
				*7699	Repair Shops and Related Services, NEC (furnace, duct, chimney, gutter, and drain cleaning services)
5619	Other Support Services				
56191	Packaging and Labeling Services	N		*7389	Business Services, NEC (packaging and labeling services)
56192	Convention and Trade Show Organizers	N		*7389	Business Services, NEC (convention and trade show services)
56199	All Other Support Services	N		*7389	Business Services, NEC (other support services except packaging and labeling, convention and trade shows services, convention and visitor bureaus, tourist information bureaus)
562	Waste Management and Remediation Services				
5621	Waste Collection	c			
56211	Waste Collection	c			
562111	Solid Waste Collection	u	N	*4212	Local Trucking Without Storage (solid waste collection without disposal)
562112	Hazardous Waste Collection	u	N	*4212	Local Trucking Without Storage (haz ardous waste collection without disposal)
562119	Other Waste Collection	u	N	*4212	Local Trucking Without Storage (other waste collection without disposal)
5622	Waste Treatment and Disposal	c			
56221	Waste Treatment and Disposal	c			
562211	Hazardous Waste Treatment and Disposal	u	N	*4953	Refuse Systems (hazardous waste treatment and disposal)
562212	Solid Waste Landfill	u	N	*4953	Refuse Systems (solid waste landfills)
562213	Solid Waste Combustors and Incinerators	u	N	*4953	Refuse Systems (solid waste combustors and incinerators)
562219	Other Nonhazardous Waste Treatment and Disposal	u	N	*4953	Refuse Systems (other nonhazardous waste treatment and disposal)

Codes: u—unique to United States; c—common to U.S. and Canada; blank—common to 3 countries; E—existing industry; N—new industry; R—revised industry; * indicates part of a 1987 SIC; (cont'd)—continued; NEC—Not Elsewhere Classified

NAICS Code	1997 NAICS U.S. Description	Codes		SIC Code	1987 U.S. SIC Description
5629	Remediation and Other Waste Management Services	c			
56291	Remediation Services	c	N	*1799	Special Trade Contractors, NEC (asbestos abatement and lead paint removal contractors)
				*4959	Sanitary Services, NEC (remediation services)
56292	Materials Recovery Facilities	c	N	*4953	Refuse Systems (materials recovery facilities)
56299	All Other Waste Management Services	c			
562991	Septic Tank and Related Services	u	N	*7359	Equipment Rental and Leasing, NEC (portable toilet rental)
				*7699	Repair Shops and Related Services, NEC (cesspool and septic tank cleaning)
562998	All Other Miscellaneous Waste Management Services	u	R	*4959	Sanitary Services, NEC (all but remediation services, malaria control, mosquito eradication, snowplowing, street sweeping, and airport runway vacuuming)
				*7699	Repair Shops and Related Services, NEC (sewer cleaning and rodding)
61	**Educational Services**				
611	Educational Services				
6111	Elementary and Secondary Schools				
61111	Elementary and Secondary Schools	c	E	8211	Elementary and Secondary Schools
6112	Junior Colleges				
61121	Junior Colleges		E	8222	Junior Colleges and Technical Institutes
6113	Colleges, Universities, and Professional Schools				
61131	Colleges, Universities, and Professional Schools		E	8221	Colleges, Universities, and Professional Schools
6114	Business Schools and Computer and Management Training				
61141	Business and Secretarial Schools		E	8244	Business and Secretarial Schools
61142	Computer Training		R	*8243	Data Processing Schools (except computer repair training)
61143	Professional and Management Development Training		N	*8299	Schools and Educational Services, NEC (professional and management development training)
6115	Technical and Trade Schools				
61151	Technical and Trade Schools				
611511	Cosmetology and Barber Schools	u	N	*7231	Beauty Shops (beauty and cosmetology schools)
				*7241	Barber Shops (barber colleges)
611512	Flight Training	u	N	*8249	Vocational Schools, NEC (aviation schools, excluding flying instruction)
				*8299	Schools and Educational Services, NEC (flying instruction)

Codes: u—unique to United States; c—common to U.S. and Canada; blank—common to 3 countries; E—existing industry; N—new industry; R—revised industry;
* indicates part of a 1987 SIC; (cont'd)—continued; NEC—Not Elsewhere Classified

NAICS Code	1997 NAICS U.S. Description	Codes		SIC Code	1987 U.S. SIC Description
611513	Apprenticeship Training	u	N	*8249	Vocational Schools, NEC (vocational apprenticeship training)
611519	Other Technical and Trade Schools	u	N	*8249	Vocational Schools, NEC (except aviation and flight training and apprenticeship training)
				*8243	Data Processing Schools (computer repair training)
				*8299	Schools and Educational Services, NEC (modeling and cooking schools)
6116	Other Schools and Instruction				
61161	Fine Arts Schools		N	*8299	Schools and Educational Services, NEC (art, drama, and music schools)
				*7911	Dance Studios, Schools, and Halls (dance instructors, and professional and other dance schools)
61162	Sports and Recreation Instruction		N	*7999	Amusement and Recreation Services, NEC (baseball, basketball, bowling, gymnastic, judo, karate, parachute, scuba and skin diving, skating, ski, swimming, tennis, and other sports instruction; and sports instructional schools and camps)
61163	Language Schools		N	*8299	Schools and Educational Services, NEC (language schools)
61169	All Other Schools and Instruction				
611691	Exam Preparation and Tutoring	u	N	*8299	Schools and Educational Services, NEC (exam preparation and tutoring)
611692	Automobile Driving Schools	u	N	*8299	Schools and Educational Services, NEC (automobile driving instruction)
611699	All Other Miscellaneous Schools and Instruction	u	N	*7999	Amusement and Recreation Services, NEC (nonathletic recreational instruction)
				*8299	Schools and Educational Services, NEC (except professional and management training, aviation and flight training, fine arts schools, language schools, exam preparation and tutoring, automobile driving schools, and educational support services)
6117	Educational Support Services				
61171	Educational Support Services		N	*8299	Schools and Educational Services NEC (except instruction)
				*8748	Business Consulting Services, NEC (educational test development and evaluation services, educational testing services, and educational consultants)
62	**Health Care and Social Assistance**				
621	Ambulatory Health Care Services				
6211	Offices of Physicians				

Codes: u—unique to United States; c—common to U.S. and Canada; blank—common to 3 countries; E—existing industry; N—new industry; R—revised industry; * indicates part of a 1987 SIC; (cont'd)—continued; NEC—Not Elsewhere Classified

244 Harris InfoSource

NAICS Code	1997 NAICS U.S. Description	Codes		SIC Code	1987 U.S. SIC Description
62111	Offices of Physicians				
621111	Offices of Physicians (except Mental Health Specialists)	u	N	*8011	Offices and Clinics of Doctors of Medicine (except mental health specialists)
				*8031	Offices and Clinics of Doctors of Osteopathy (except mental health specialists)
621112	Offices of Physicians, Mental Health Specialists	u	N	*8011	Offices and Clinics of Doctors of Medicine (mental health specialists)
				*8031	Offices and Clinics of Doctors of Osteopathy (mental health specialists)
6212	Offices of Dentists				
62121	Offices of Dentists		E	8021	Offices and Clinics of Dentists
6213	Offices of Other Health Practitioners				
62131	Offices of Chiropractors		E	8041	Offices and Clinics of Chiropractors
62132	Offices of Optometrists		E	8042	Offices and Clinics of Optometrists
62133	Offices of Mental Health Practitioners (except Physicians)		N	*8049	Offices and Clinics of Health Practitioners, NEC (mental health practitioners except physicians)
62134	Offices of Physical, Occupational and Speech Therapists, and Audiologists		N	*8049	Offices and Clinics of Health Practitioners, NEC (physical, occupational, recreational and speech therapists, and audiologists)
62139	Offices of All Other Health Practitioners				
621391	Offices of Podiatrists	u	E	8043	Offices and Clinics of Podiatrists
621399	Offices of All Other Miscellaneous Health Practitioners	u	N	*8049	Offices and Clinics of Health Practitioners, NEC (except mental health practitioners, physical, occupational, speech therapists, and audiologists)
6214	Outpatient Care Centers				
62141	Family Planning Centers		N	*8093	Speciality Outpatient Facilities, NEC (family planning centers)
				*8099	Health and Allied Services, NEC (child birth preparation)
62142	Outpatient Mental Health and Substance Abuse Centers		N	*8093	Specialty Outpatient Facilities, NEC (mental health facilities)
62149	Other Outpatient Care Centers				
621491	HMO Medical Centers	u	N	*8011	Offices and Clinics of Doctors of Medicine (HMO Medical Centers)
621492	Kidney Dialysis Centers	u	E	8092	Kidney Dialysis Centers
621493	Freestanding Ambulatory Surgical and Emergency Centers	u	N	*8011	Offices and Clinics of Doctors of Medicine (surgical and emergency centers)
621498	All Other Outpatient Care Centers	u	N	*8093	Specialty Outpatient Facilities, NEC (except family planning and mental health centers)
6215	Medical and Diagnostic Laboratories				
62151	Medical and Diagnostic Laboratories				

Visit page 15 to learn about major changes to NAICS sectors.

Codes: u—unique to United States; c—common to U.S. and Canada; blank—common to 3 countries; E—existing industry; N—new industry; R—revised industry; * indicates part of a 1987 SIC; (cont'd)—continued; NEC—Not Elsewhere Classified

NAICS Code	1997 NAICS U.S. Description	Codes		SIC Code	1987 U.S. SIC Description
621511	Medical Laboratories	u	R	*8071	Medical Laboratories (except diagnostic imaging centers)
621512	Diagnostic Imaging Centers	u	N	*8071	Medical Laboratories (diagnostic imaging centers)
6216	Home Health Care Services				
62161	Home Health Care Services		E	8082	Home Health Care Services
6219	Other Ambulatory Health Care Services				
62191	Ambulance Services		N	*4119	Local Passenger Transportation, NEC (land ambulance)
				*4522	Air Transportation, Nonscheduled (air ambulance)
62199	All Other Ambulatory Health Care Services				
621991	Blood and Organ Banks	u	N	*8099	Health and Allied Services, NEC (blood and organ banks)
621999	All Other Miscellaneous Ambulatory Health Care Services	u	N	*8099	Health and Allied Services, NEC (except blood and organ banks, medical artists, medical photography, and childbirth preparation classes)
622	Hospitals				
6221	General Medical and Surgical Hospitals				
62211	General Medical and Surgical Hospitals		R	8062	General Medical and Surgical Hospitals
				*8069	Specialty Hospitals, except Psychiatric (children's hospitals)
6222	Psychiatric and Substance Abuse Hospitals				
62221	Psychiatric and Substance Abuse Hospitals		R	8063	Psychiatric Hospitals
				*8069	Specialty Hospitals, except Psychiatric (substance abuse hospitals)
6223	Specialty (except Psychiatric and Substance Abuse) Hospitals				
62231	Specialty (except Psychiatric and Substance Abuse) Hospitals		R	*8069	Specialty Hospitals, except Psychiatric (except children's and substance abuse hospitals)
623	Nursing and Residential Care Facilities				
6231	Nursing Care Facilities				
62311	Nursing Care Facilities		N	*8051	Skilled Nursing Care Facilities (except continuing care retirement communities)
				*8052	Intermediate Care Facilities (except continuing care retirement communities and mental retardation facilities)
				*8059	Nursing and Personal Care Facilities, NEC (except continuing care retirement communities)
				6232	Residential Mental Retardation, Mental Health and Substance Abuse Facilities
62321	Residential Mental Retardation Facilities		N	*8052	Intermediate Care Facilities (mental retardation facilities)

Codes: u—unique to United States; c—common to U.S. and Canada; blank—common to 3 countries; E—existing industry; N—new industry; R—revised industry; * indicates part of a 1987 SIC; (cont'd)—continued; NEC—Not Elsewhere Classified

NAICS Code	1997 NAICS U.S. Description	Codes		SIC Code	1987 U.S. SIC Description
62322	Residential Mental Health and Substance Abuse Facilities		N	*8361	Residential Care (mental health and substance abuse facilities)
6233	Community Care Facilities for the Elderly				
62331	Community Care Facilities for the Elderly				
623311	Continuing Care Retirement Communities	u	N	*8051	Skilled Nursing Care Facilities (continuing care retirement communities)
				*8052	Intermediate Care Facilities (continuing care retirement communities)
				*8059	Nursing and Personal Care Facilities, NEC (continuing care retirement communities)
623312	Homes for the Elderly	u	N	*8361	Residential Care (homes for the elderly)
6239	Other Residential Care Facilities				
62399	Other Residential Care Facilities		N	*8361	Residential Care (except mental health and substance abuse facilities, homes for the elderly)
624	Social Assistance				
6241	Individual and Family Services				
62411	Child and Youth Services		N	*8322	Individual and Family Social Services (child and youth services)
62412	Services for the Elderly and Persons with Disabilities		N	*8322	Individual and Family Social Services (services for the elderly and disabled)
62419	Other Individual and Family Services		N	*8322	Individual and Family Social Services (except services for children, youth, elderly, disabled; food, housing, emergency and relief)
6242	Community Food and Housing, and Emergency and Other Relief Services				
62421	Community Food Services		N	*8322	Individual and Family Social Services (food services)
62422	Community Housing Services				
624221	Temporary Shelters	u	N	*8322	Individual and Family Social Services (temporary shelter)
624229	Other Community Housing Services	u	N	*8322	Individual and Family Social Services (housing services except temporary shelter)
62423	Emergency and Other Relief Services		N	*8322	Individual and Family Social Services (emergency and relief services)
6243	Vocational Rehabilitation Services				
62431	Vocational Rehabilitation Services		E	8331	Job Training and Vocational Rehabilitation Services
6244	Child Day Care Services				
62441	Child Day Care Services		E	8351	Child Day Care Services
71	**Arts, Entertainment, and Recreation**				
711	Performing Arts, Spectator Sports, and Related Industries				

Codes: u—unique to United States; c—common to U.S. and Canada; blank—common to 3 countries; E—existing industry; N—new industry; R—revised industry;
* indicates part of a 1987 SIC; (cont'd)—continued; NEC—Not Elsewhere Classified

NAICS Code	1997 NAICS U.S. Description	Codes		SIC Code	1987 U.S. SIC Description
7111	Performing Arts Companies				
71111	Theater Companies and Dinner Theaters		N	*5812	Eating Places (dinner theaters)
				*7922	Theatrical Producers (Except Motion Pictures) and Miscellaneous Theatrical Services (theater companies, opera companies)
71112	Dance Companies		N	*7922	Theatrical Producers (Except Motion Pictures) and Miscellaneous Theatrical Services (ballet and dance companies)
71113	Musical Groups and Artists		N	*7929	Bands, Orchestras, Actors, and Entertainment Groups (musical groups and artists and orchestras)
			N	*7929	Bands, Orchestras, Actors, and Entertainment Groups, (except musical groups, artists, actors, and actresses)
				*7999	Amusement and Recreation Services, NEC (circus companies and traveling carnival shows)
7112	Spectator Sports				
71121	Spectator Sports				
711211	Sports Teams and Clubs	c	N	*7941	Professional Sports Clubs and Promoters (professional sports clubs)
711212	Racetracks	u	N	*7948	Racing, Including Track Operations (track operations)
711219	Other Spectator Sports	u	N	*7948	Racing, Including Track Operations (except track operators)
				*7999	Amusement and Recreation Services, NEC (professional athletes)
7113	Promoters of Performing Arts, Sports, and Similar Events				
71131	Promoters of Performing Arts, Sports, and Similar Events with Facilities		N	*6512	Operators of Nonresidential Buildings (stadium and arena owners)
				*7922	Theatrical Producers (Except Motion Picture) and Miscellaneous Theatrical Services (theater operators)
				*7941	Professional Sports Clubs and Promoters (stadium operators)
				*7999	Amusement and Recreation Services, NEC (state fairs, agriculture fairs and county fairs with facilities)
71132	Promoters of Performing Arts, Sports, and Similar Events without Facilities		N	*7922	Theatrical Producers (Except Motion Picture) and Miscellaneous Theatrical Services (theatrical promoters)
				*7941	Professional Sports Clubs and Promoters (sports promoters)
				*7999	Amusement and Recreation Services, NEC (state fairs, agriculture fairs and county fairs without facilities)
7114	Agents and Managers for Artists, Athletes, Entertainers, and Other Public Figures				

Codes: u—unique to United States; c—common to U.S. and Canada; blank—common to 3 countries; E—existing industry; N—new industry; R—revised industry; * indicates part of a 1987 SIC; (cont'd)—continued; NEC—Not Elsewhere Classified

NAICS Code	1997 NAICS U.S. Description	Codes	SIC Code	1987 U.S. SIC Description
71141	Agents and Managers for Artists, Athletes, Entertainers, and Other Public Figures	N	*7389	Business Services, NEC (agents and brokers for authors and artists and speaker bureaus)
			*7922	Theatrical Producers (Except Motion Picture) and Miscellaneous Theatrical Services (theatrical agents)
			*7941	Professional Sports Clubs and Promoters (sports agents)
7115	Independent Artists, Writers, and Performers			
71151	Independent Artists, Writers, and Performers	N	*7819	Services Allied to Motion Picture Production (film directors and related motion picture production services, independent)
			*7699	Repair Shops and Related Services, NEC (taxidermists and antique repair and restoration, except antique car restoration)
			*7929	Bands, Orchestras, Actors, and Other Entertainers and Entertainment Groups (actors and actresses)
			*7383	News Syndicates (independent news correspondents)
			*7641	Reupholstery and Furniture Repair (antique furniture restoration)
			*7922	Theatrical Producers (Except Motion Picture) and Miscellaneous Theatrical Services (costume design, theatrical)
			*8999	Services, NEC (authors, artists, and related technical services, independent)
712	Museums, Historical Sites, and Similar Institutions			
7121	Museums, Historical Sites, and Similar Institutions			
71211	Museums	R	*8412	Museums and Art Galleries (except historic and heritage sites)
71212	Historical Sites	N	*8412	Museums and Art Galleries (historic and heritage sites)
71213	Zoos and Botanical Gardens	R	*8422	Arboreta and Botanical or Zoological Gardens (except nature parks and reserves)
71219	Nature Parks and Other Similar Institutions	N	*7999	Amusement and Recreation Services, NEC (caverns and miscellaneous commercial parks)
			*8422	Arboreta and Botanical or Zoological Gardens (nature parks and reserves)
713	Amusement, Gambling, and Recreation Industries			
7131	Amusement Parks and Arcades			
71311	Amusement and Theme Parks	E	7996	Amusement Parks

Codes: u—unique to United States; c—common to U.S. and Canada; blank—common to 3 countries; E—existing industry; N—new industry; R—revised industry;
* indicates part of a 1987 SIC; (cont'd)—continued; NEC—Not Elsewhere Classified

NAICS Code	1997 NAICS U.S. Description	Codes	SIC Code	1987 U.S. SIC Description
71312	Amusement Arcades	R	*7993	Coin-operated Amusement Devices (amusement arcades)
7132	Gambling Industries			
71321	Casinos (except Casino Hotels)	N	*7999	Amusement and Recreation Services, NEC (casinos, except hotel casinos)
71329	Other Gambling Industries	N	*7993	Coin-operated Amusement Devices (slot machine operators)
			*7999	Amusement and Recreation Services, NEC (lottery, bingo, bookie, and other gambling operations)
7139	Other Amusement and Recreation Industries			
71391	Golf Courses and Country Clubs	N	7992	Public Golf Courses
			*7997	Membership Sports and Recreation Clubs (golf clubs)
71392	Skiing Facilities	N	*7999	Amusement and Recreation Services, NEC (skiing facilities)
71393	Marinas	E	4493	Marinas
71394	Fitness and Recreational Sports Centers	N	7991	Physical Fitness Facilities
			*7997	Membership Sports and Recreation Clubs (recreation clubs with facilities)
			*7999	Amusement and Recreation Services, NEC (nonmembership recreation facilities)
71395	Bowling Centers	E	7933	Bowling Centers
71399	All Other Amusement and Recreation Industries	N	*7911	Dance Studios, Schools, and Halls (except instruction)
			*7993	Amusement and Recreation Services, NEC (except amusement arcades and slot machine operators)
			*7997	Membership Sports and Recreation Clubs (recreation clubs without facilities)
			*7999	Amusement and Recreation Services, NEC (except circuses, professional athletes, caverns and other commercial parks, skiing facilities, casinos and other gambling operations, amusement and recreation facilities, sports instruction, sports equipment rental, ticket agencies, and amusement or scenic transport operations)
72	**Accommodation and Food Services**			
721	Accommodation			
7211	Traveler Accommodation			
72111	Hotels (except Casino Hotels) and Motels	R	*7011	Hotels and Motels (hotels and motels, except casino hotels)
			*7041	Organization Hotels and Lodging Houses, on Membership Basis (hotels)
72112	Casino Hotels	N	*7011	Hotels and Motels (casino hotels)

Codes: u—unique to United States; c—common to U.S. and Canada; blank—common to 3 countries; E—existing industry; N—new industry; R—revised industry; * indicates part of a 1987 SIC; (cont'd)—continued; NEC—Not Elsewhere Classified

250

Harris InfoSource

NAICS Code	1997 NAICS U.S. Description	Codes		SIC Code	1987 U.S. SIC Description
72119	Other Traveler Accommodation				
721191	Bed-and-breakfast Inns	c	N	*7011	Hotels and Motels (bed and breakfast inns)
721199	All Other Traveler Accommodation	u	N	*7011	Hotels and Motels (except hotels, motels, and bed and breakfast inns)
7212	RV (Recreational Vehicle) Parks and Recreational Camps				
72121	RV (Recreational Vehicle) Parks and Recreational Camps				
721211	RV (Recreational Vehicle) Parks and Campgrounds	c	E	7033	Recreational Vehicle Parks and Campgrounds
721214	Recreational and Vacation Camps (except Campgrounds)	u	E	7032	Sporting and Recreational Camps
7213	Rooming and Boarding Houses				
72131	Rooming and Boarding Houses		R	7021	Rooming and Boarding Houses
				*7041	Organization Hotels and Lodging Houses, on Membership Basis (except hotels)
722	Food Services and Drinking Places				
7221	Full-service Restaurants				
72211	Full-service Restaurants		N	*5812	Eating Places (full-service restaurants)
7222	Limited-service Eating Places				
72221	Limited-service Eating Places				
722211	Limited-service Restaurants	u	N	*5812	Eating Places (limited-service restaurants)
722212	Cafeterias	u	N	*5812	Eating Places (cafeterias)
722213	Snack and Nonalcoholic Beverage Bars	u	N	*5812	Eating Places (snack and nonalcoholic beverage bars)
				*5461	Retail Bakeries (snacks)
7223	Special Food Services				
72231	Food Service Contractors		N	*4789	Transportation Services, NEC (dining car operations on a fee or contract basis)
				*5812	Eating Places (food service contractors)
72232	Caterers		N	*5812	Eating Places (caterers)
72233	Mobile Food Services		N	*5963	Direct Selling Establishments (mobile food wagons)
7224	Drinking Places (Alcoholic Beverages)				
72241	Drinking Places (Alcoholic Beverages)		E	5813	Drinking Places (alcoholic beverages)
81	**Other Services (except Public Administration)**				
811	Repair and Maintenance				
8111	Automotive Repair and Maintenance				
81111	Automotive Mechanical and Electrical Repair and Maintenance				
811111	General Automotive Repair	c	E	7538	General Automotive Repair Shops
811112	Automotive Exhaust System Repair	c	E	7533	Automotive Exhaust System Repair Shops

Codes: u—unique to United States; c—common to U.S. and Canada; blank—common to 3 countries; E—existing industry; N—new industry; R—revised industry;
* indicates part of a 1987 SIC; (cont'd)—continued; NEC—Not Elsewhere Classified

www.harrisinfo.com 251

NAICS Code	1997 NAICS U.S. Description	Codes		SIC Code	1987 U.S. SIC Description
811113	Automotive Transmission Repair	u	E	7537	Automotive Transmission Repair Shops
811118	Other Automotive Mechanical and Electrical Repair and Maintenance	u	E	7539	Automotive Repair Shops, NEC
81112	Automotive Body, Paint, Interior, and Glass Repair				
811121	Automotive Body, Paint, and Interior Repair and Maintenance	c	E	7532	Top, Body, and Upholstery Repair Shops and Paint Shops
811122	Automotive Glass Replacement Shops	c	R	7536	Automotive Glass Replacement Shops
				*7549	Automotive Services, except Repair and Carwashes (automotive window tinting)
81119	Other Automotive Repair and Maintenance				
811191	Automotive Oil Change and Lubrication Shops	u	N	*7549	Automotive Services, except Repair and Carwashes (lubricating service, automotive)
811192	Car Washes	c	E	7542	Carwashes
811198	All Other Automotive Repair and Maintenance	u	R	*7534	Tire Retreading and Repair Shops (repair)
				*7549	Automotive Services, except Repair and Carwashes (except automotive window tinting, lubricating, and towing)
8112	Electronic and Precision Equipment Repair and Maintenance				
81121	Electronic and Precision Equipment Repair and Maintenance				
811211	Consumer Electronics Repair and Maintenance	u	N	*7622	Radio and Television Repair Shops (other stereo, TV, VCR, and radio)
				*7629	Electrical and Electronic Repair Shops, NEC (other consumer equipment except computer, TV, stereo, VCR, and radio)
				*7699	Repair Shops and Related Services, NEC (camera repair)
811212	Computer and Office Machine Repair and Maintenance	u	N	7378	Computer Maintenance and Repair (except retailing new computers from a storefront and repairing)
				*7629	Electrical and Electronic Repair Shops, NEC (business and office machine repair, electrical)
				*7699	Repair Shops and Related Services, NEC (typewriter repair)
811213	Communication Equipment Repair and Maintenance	u	N	*7622	Radio and Television Repair Shops (other telecommunication equipment repair)
				*7629	Electrical and Electronic Repair Shops, NEC (telephone set repair)
811219	Other Electronic and Precision Equipment Repair and Maintenance	u	N	*7629	Electrical and Electronic Repair Shops, NEC (electrical measuring instrument repair and calibration, medical electrical equipment repair)

Codes: u—unique to United States; c—common to U.S. and Canada; blank—common to 3 countries; E—existing industry; N—new industry; R—revised industry; * indicates part of a 1987 SIC; (cont'd)—continued; NEC—Not Elsewhere Classified

252 Harris InfoSource

NAICS Code	1997 NAICS U.S. Description	Codes		SIC Code	1987 U.S. SIC Description
811219	Other Electronic and Precision Equipment Repair and Maintenance (cont'd)			*7699	Repair Shops and Related Services, NEC (dental instrument repair, laboratory instrument repair, medical equipment and other electronic and precision equipment repair, except typewriters)
8113	Commercial and Industrial Machinery and Equipment (except Automotive and Electronic) Repair and Maintenance				
81131	Commercial and Industrial Machinery and Equipment (except Automotive and Electronic) Repair and Maintenance		R	*7699	Repair Shops and Related Services, NEC (other non-automotive transportation equipment and industrial machines and equipment)
				*7623	Refrigeration and Air-conditioning Services and Repair Shops (commercial refrigerator equipment repair)
				7692	Welding Repair
				*7694	Armature Rewinding Shops (repair)
8114	Personal and Household Goods Repair and Maintenance				
81141	Home and Garden Equipment and Appliance Repair and Maintenance				
811411	Home and Garden Equipment Repair and Maintenance	c	N	*7699	Repair Shops and Related Services, NEC (lawnmower repair shops, sharpening and repairing knives, saws and tools)
811412	Appliance Repair and Maintenance	c	N	*7623	Refrigeration and Air-conditioning Service and Repair Shops (except commercial and retailing new refrigerators from a storefront and repairing)
				*7629	Electrical and Electronic Repair Shops, NEC—appliance repair, electrical; washing machine repair; electric razor repair (except retailing new appliances from a storefront and repairing)
				*7699	Repair Shops and Related Services, NEC (gas appliance repair service, sewing machine repair, stove repair shops, and other non-electrical appliance)
81142	Reupholstery and Furniture Repair		R	*7641	Reupholstery and Furniture Repair (except antique furniture restoration)
81143	Footwear and Leather Goods Repair		R	*7251	Shoe Repair and Shoeshine Parlors (shoe repair shops)
81143	Footwear and Leather Goods Repair			*7699	Repair Shops and Related Services (leather goods repair shops, luggage repair shops, pocketbook repair shops)
81149	Other Personal and Household Goods Repair and Maintenance		N	*3732	Boat Building and Repairing (pleasure boat repair)
				*7219	Laundry and Garment Services, NEC (alteration and repair)
				7631	Watch, Clock, and Jewelry Repair

Codes: u—unique to United States; c—common to U.S. and Canada; blank—common to 3 countries; E—existing industry; N—new industry; R—revised industry; * indicates part of a 1987 SIC; (cont'd)—continued; NEC—Not Elsewhere Classified

NAICS Code	1997 NAICS U.S. Description	Codes		SIC Code	1987 U.S. SIC Description
81149	Other Personal and Household Goods Repair and Maintenance (cont'd)			*7699	Repair Shops and Related Services, NEC (except industrial, electronic, home and garden, appliance, and leather goods)
812	Personal and Laundry Services				
8121	Personal Care Services	c			
81211	Hair, Nail, and Skin Care Services	c			
812111	Barber Shops	u	R	*7241	Barber Shops (except barber colleges)
812112	Beauty Salons	u	R	*7231	Beauty Shops (except beauty and cosmetology schools and manicure and pedicure salons)
812113	Nail Salons	u	N	*7231	Beauty Shops (manicure and pedicure salons)
81219	Other Personal Care Services	c			
812191	Diet and Weight Reducing Centers	u	N	*7299	Miscellaneous Personal Services, NEC (diet and weight reducing services)
812199	Other Personal Care Services	u	N	*7299	Miscellaneous Personal Services, NEC (personal care services)
8122	Death Care Services	c			
81221	Funeral Homes and Funeral Services	c	R	*7261	Funeral Services and Crematories (funeral homes and services)
81222	Cemeteries and Crematories	c	R	*6531	Real Estate Agents and Managers (cemetery management)
				6553	Cemetery Subdividers and Developers
				*7261	Funeral Services and Crematories (crematories)
8123	Drycleaning and Laundry Services	c			
81231	Coin-operated Laundries and Drycleaners	c	E	7215	Coin-operated Laundry and Drycleaning
81232	Drycleaning and Laundry Services (except Coin-operated)	c	R	7211	Power Laundries, Family and Commercial
				*7389	Business Services, NEC (apparel pressing service for the trade)
				7216	Drycleaning Plants, except Rug Cleaning
				7212	Garment Pressing, and Agents for Laundries and Drycleaners
				*7219	Laundry and Garment Services, NEC (except diaper service and clothing alteration and repair)
81233	Linen and Uniform Supply	c			
812331	Linen Supply	u	R	7213	Linen Supply
812331	Linen Supply			*7219	Laundry and Garment Services, NEC (diaper service)
812332	Industrial Launderers	u	E	7218	Industrial Launderers
8129	Other Personal Services	c			
81291	Pet Care (except Veterinary) Services	c	R	*0752	Animal Speciality Services, except Veterinary (pet care services, except veterinary)
81292	Photofinishing	c			

Codes: u—unique to United States; c—common to U.S. and Canada; blank—common to 3 countries; E—existing industry; N—new industry; R—revised industry;
* indicates part of a 1987 SIC; (cont'd)—continued; NEC—Not Elsewhere Classified

NAICS Code	1997 NAICS U.S. Description	Codes		SIC Code	1987 U.S. SIC Description
812921	Photofinishing Laboratories (except One-hour)	c	N	*7384	Photofinishing Laboratories (except One-hour)
812922	One-hour Photofinishing	c	N	*7384	Photofinishing Laboratories (One-hour)
81293	Parking Lots and Garages	c	R	7521	Automobile Parking
				*7299	Miscellaneous Personal Services, NEC (valet parking services)
81299	All Other Personal Services	c	R	*7299	Miscellaneous Personal Services, NEC (except diet and weight reducing services, personal care services, valet parking services, and formal wear and costume rental service)
				*7251	Shoe Repair Shops and Shoeshine Parlors (shoeshine parlors)
				*7389	Miscellaneous Business Services (bail bonding)
813	Religious, Grantmaking, Civic, Professional, and Similar Organizations				
8131	Religious Organizations	c			
81311	Religious Organizations	c	E	8661	Religious Organizations
8132	Grantmaking and Giving Services	c			
81321	Grantmaking and Giving Services	c			
813211	Grantmaking Foundations Trusts	u	E	6732	Educational, Religious, and Charitable
813212	Voluntary Health Organizations	u	N	*8399	Social Services, NEC (voluntary health organizations)
813219	Other Grantmaking and Giving Services	u	N	*8399	Social Services, NEC (grantmaking and giving)
8133	Social Advocacy Organizations	c			
81331	Social Advocacy Organizations	c			
813311	Human Rights Organizations	u	N	*8399	Social Services, NEC (human rights organizations)
813312	Environment, Conservation and Wildlife Organizations	u	N	*8399	Social Services, NEC (environment, conservation, and wildlife advocacy)
				*8699	Membership Organizations, NEC (humane societies)
813319	Other Social Advocacy Organizations	u	N	*8399	Social Services, NEC (except human rights, environment, conservation and wildlife organizations, grantmaking and giving, and voluntary health organizations)
8134	Civic and Social Organizations	c			
81341	Civic and Social Organizations	c	N	*8641	Civic, Social, and Fraternal Organizations (except condominium and homeowner associations)
				*8699	Membership Organizations, NEC (except humane societies, farm business organizations, athletic associations, and travel motor clubs)
8139	Business, Professional, Labor, Political, and Similar Organizations	c			

Go to page 23 to learn about the implementation of NAICS codes in the public and private sectors.

Codes: u—unique to United States; c—common to U.S. and Canada; blank—common to 3 countries; E—existing industry; N—new industry; R—revised industry; * indicates part of a 1987 SIC; (cont'd)—continued; NEC—Not Elsewhere Classified

NAICS Code	1997 NAICS U.S. Description	Codes		SIC Code	1987 U.S. SIC Description
81391	Business Associations	c	R	8611	Business Associations
				*8699	Membership Organizations, NEC (farm business organizations)
81392	Professional Organizations	c	E	8621	Professional Membership Organizations
81393	Labor Unions and Similar Labor Organizations	c	E	8631	Labor Unions and Similar Labor Organizations
81394	Political Organizations	c	E	8651	Political Organizations
81399	Other Similar Organizations (except Business, Professional, Labor, and Political Organizations)	c	R	*6531	Real Estate Agents and Managers (condominium associations)
				*8641	Civic, Social, and Fraternal Organizations (condominium and homeowner associations)
				*8699	Membership Organizations, NEC (athletic associations)
814	Private Households				
8141	Private Households				
81411	Private Households		E	8811	Private Households
92	**Public Administration**				
921	Executive, Legislative, and Other General Government Support	u			
9211	Executive, Legislative, and Other General Government Support	u			
92111	Executive Offices	u	E	9111	Executive Offices
92112	Legislative Bodies	u	E	9121	Legislative Bodies
92113	Public Finance Activities	u	E	9311	Public Finance, Taxation, and Monetary Policy
92114	Executive and Legislative Offices, Combined	u	E	9131	Executive and Legislative Office, Combined
92115	American Indian and Alaska Native Tribal Governments	u	N	*8641	Civic, Social, and Fraternal Organizations (Indian Tribal Councils)
92119	Other General Government Support	u	E	9199	General Government, NEC
922	Justice, Public Order, and Safety Activities	u			
9221	Justice, Public Order, and Safety Activities	u			
92211	Courts	u	E	9211	Courts
92212	Police Protection	u	E	9221	Police Protection
92213	Legal Counsel and Prosecution	u	E	9222	Legal Counsel and Prosecution
92214	Correctional Institutions	u	E	9223	Correctional Institutions
92215	Parole Offices and Probation Offices	u	N	*8322	Individual and Family Social Services (parole and probation offices)
92216	Fire Protection	u	E	9224	Fire Protection
92219	Other Justice, Public Order, and Safety Activities	u	E	9229	Public Order and Safety, NEC
923	Administration of Human Resource Programs	u			
9231	Administration of Human Resource Programs	u			

Codes: u—unique to United States; c—common to U.S. and Canada; blank—common to 3 countries; E—existing industry; N—new industry; R—revised industry;
* indicates part of a 1987 SIC; (cont'd)—continued; NEC—Not Elsewhere Classified

NAICS Code	1997 NAICS U.S. Description	Codes		SIC Code	1987 U.S. SIC Description
92311	Administration of Education Programs	u	E	9411	Administration of Educational Programs
92312	Administration of Public Health Programs	u	E	9431	Administration of Public Health Programs
92313	Administration of Human Resource	u	E	9441	Administration of Social, Human Resource Programs (except Education, Public Health, and Income Maintenance Programs and Veterans' Affairs Programs)
92314	Administration of Veterans' Affairs	u	E	9451	Administration of Veterans' Affairs, except Health and Insurance
924	Administration of Environmental Quality Programs	u			
9241	Administration of Environmental Quality Programs	u			
92411	Administration of Air and Water Resource and Solid Waste Management Programs	u	E	9511	Air and Water Resource and Solid Waste Management
92412	Administration of Conservation Programs	u	E	9512	Land, Mineral, Wildlife, and Forest Conservation
925	Administration of Housing Programs, Urban Planning, and Community Development	u			
9251	Administration of Housing Programs, Urban Planning, and Community Development	u			
92511	Administration of Housing Programs	u	E	9531	Administration of Housing Programs
92512	Administration of Urban Planning and Community and Rural Development	u	E	9532	Administration of Urban Planning and Community and Rural Development
926	Administration of Economic Programs	u			
9261	Administration of Economic Programs	u			
92611	Administration of General Economic Programs	u	E	9611	Administration of General Economic Programs
92612	Regulation and Administration of Transportation Programs	u	R	*9621	Regulation and Administration of Transportation Programs (except air traffic control)
92613	Regulation and Administration of Communications, Electric, Gas, and Other Utilities	u	E	9631	Regulation and Administration of Communications, Electric, Gas, and Other Utilities
92614	Regulation of Agricultural Marketing and Commodities	u	E	9641	Regulation of Agricultural Marketing and Commodities
92615	Regulation, Licensing, and Inspection of Miscellaneous Commercial Sectors	u	E	9651	Regulation, Licensing, and Inspection of Miscellaneous Commercial Sectors
927	Space Research and Technology	u			
9271	Space Research and Technology	u			
92711	Space Research and Technology	u	E	9661	Space Research and Technology
928	National Security and International Affairs	u			
9281	National Security and International Affairs	u			
92811	National Security	u	E	9711	National Security
92812	International Affairs	u	E	9721	International Affairs
99999	Unclassified establishments	u	R	9999	Nonclassifiable establishments

Codes: u—unique to United States; c—common to U.S. and Canada; blank—common to 3 countries; E—existing industry; N—new industry; R—revised industry;
  * indicates part of a 1987 SIC; (cont'd)—continued; NEC—Not Elsewhere Classified

HOW TO USE THIS SECTION:

This section shows you all ISIC sections and the NAICS or portions of NAICS sectors and subsectors that are comparable. The table is in alphabetical order by the ISIC section. For each ISIC section you have the ISIC code and title followed by the comparable NAICS code and description of conversion. The ISIC Manufacturing section has been taken down to the division level for comparison to NAICS. Keep in mind that only the portion in the NAICS conversion description is comparable to the ISIC section or division.

Harris Interchange—
ISIC to NAICS Conversion

ISIC Code	ISIC Title	NAICS Code	NAICS Title	Description of Conversion
K	Real Estate, Renting, and Business Activities	11	Agriculture, Forestry, Fishing, and Hunting	Farm management services
		21	Mining and Oil and Gas Extraction	Mineral exploration services, except geophysical
		23	Construction	Real property developers and sub-dividers; construction management; building exhibits
		325	Chemical Manufacturing	Aerosol packaging services
		51	Information and Cultural Industries	Software publishers; data processing services; data base publishing
		53	Real Estate and Rental and Leasing	Buying, selling, renting and operating real estate; rental of machinery and equipment, transportation equipment, and personal and household equipment

ISIC Rev. 3 to NAICS conversion table is an excerpt from the United Nations Dept. of Economic and Social Affairs Statistics Division paper, "NAICS and ISIC—Now and the Future," by Carole A. Amber, Bureau of Census, USA. Developed by Statistics Canada.
Harris is an official licensee of the United Nations ISIC classification codes.

ISIC to NAICS Conversion

ISIC Code	ISIC Title	NAICS Code	NAICS Title	Description of Link
A	Agriculture, Hunting, and Forestry	11	Agriculture, Forestry, Fishing, and Hunting	Agriculture, forestry, and hunting
		22	Utilities	Water distribution for irrigation
		312	Beverage and Tobacco Product Manufacturing	Integrated grape growing and wine manufacturing
		56	Administrative and Support, Waste Management, and Remediation Services	Landscape maintenance services; tree services
		81	Other Services	Pet care and boarding services; animal training; animal humane societies
B	Fishing	11	Agriculture, Forestry, Fishing, and Hunting	Fish hatcheries; fish farming; and fishing
		311	Food Manufacturing	Fish factory ships
C	Mining and Quarrying	21	Mining and Oil and Gas Extraction	Oil and gas extraction; mineral extraction; quarrying; beneficiation of ores; support services for oil and gas extraction
		324	Petroleum and Coal Products Manufacturing	Coal fuel briquettes, agglomerating
D	Manufacturing	81	Other Services (except Public Administration)	Repair and maintenance of industrial, commercial, and similar machinery and equipment, except office and computing equipment; blacksmiths; and welding shops
D15	Manufacture of Food Products and Beverages	11	Agriculture, Forestry, Fishing, and Hunting	Maple syrup and sugar produced in central facilities
		311	Food Manufacturing	Human and animal food product manufacturing, except milling malt and producing maple syrup and sugar in central facilities
		312	Beverage and Tobacco Product Manufacturing	Beverage manufacturing; milling malt
		325	Chemical Manufacturing	Industrial alcohol, manufacturing
D16	Manufacture of Tobacco Products	312	Beverage and Tobacco Product Manufacturing	Tobacco product manufacturing
D17	Manufacture of Textiles	313	Textile Mills	Fiber, yarn, and thread mills; woven, nonwoven, knitted, and coated fabric mills; fabric and clothing finishing mills
		314	Textile Product Mills	Carpets, curtains, linens, textile bags, canvas products, and other textile end products, manufacturing
		315	Clothing Manufacturing	Clothing knitting mills, trimmings for clothing, manufacturing
		322	Paper Manufacturing	Textile material disposable sanitary napkins and towels, manufacturing
		323	Printing and Related Support Activities	Silk-screening on made-up textile articles
		336	Transportation Equipment Manufacturing	Automobile fabric accessories, manufacturing

ISIC Code	ISIC Title	NAICS Code	NAICS Title	Description of Link
		337	Furniture and Related Product Manufacturing	Textile fabric window shades and blinds, manufacturing
		339	Miscellaneous Manufacturing	Textile material surgical drapes; life preservers, except inflatable, manufacturing
		56	Administrative and Support, Waste Management and Remediation Services	Textile cutting and folding services
D18	Manufacture of Wearing Apparel; Dressing and Dyeing of Fur	313	Textile Mills	Finishing clothing
		314	Textile Product Mills	Diaper manufacturing; embroidering on clothing
		315	Clothing Manufacturing	Cut and sew clothing manufacturing and contracting
		316	Leather and Allied Product Manufacturing	Fur dressing and dyeing; leather welders' sleeves, leggings and aprons, manufacturing
		323	Printing and Related Support Activities	Printing on clothing
		339	Miscellaneous Manufacturing	Bulletproof and fireproof clothing, manufacturing
D19	Tanning and Dressing of Leather; Manufacture of Luggage, Handbags, Saddlery, Harness, and Footwear	316	Leather and Allied Product Manufacturing	Tanning and dressing of leather; footwear (except wood, plastic and rubber parts) manufacturing; luggage, handbag, saddlery, and harness manufacturing
		321	Wood Product Manufacturing	Wood footwear parts, manufacturing
		326	Plastics and Rubber Products Manufacturing	Plastic and rubber footwear parts, manufacturing
		339	Miscellaneous Manufacturing	Leather gaskets and seals, manufacturing
D20	Manufacture of Wood and of Products of Wood and Cork, except Furniture; Manufacture of Articles of Straw and Plaiting Materials	11	Agriculture, Forestry, Fishing, and Hunting	Barking and chipping in the forest
		314	Textile Product Mills	Woven straw mats, manufacturing
		321	Wood Product Manufacturing	Sawmills; shingle, veneer, and plywood mills; millworking; manufacturing particle board, fiberboard, and waferboard; manufacturing wood structural products, containers, prefabricated buildings, and miscellaneous wood products; wood preservation
		337	Furniture and Related Product Manufacturing	Window shades and blinds, except textile fabric; wood drapery hardware; wood furniture frames and parts, manufacturing
		339	Miscellaneous Manufacturing	Wood signs; wood picture and mirror frames; cork gaskets, manufacturing

ISIC Code	ISIC Title	NAICS Code	NAICS Title	Description of Link
D21	Manufacture of Paper and Paper Product	322	Paper Manufacturing	Manufacturing pulp, paper, and converted paper products, made wholly or partly of paper
		323	Printing and Related Support Activities	Printing paper labels and tags
		339	Miscellaneous Manufacturing	Carbon paper, manufacturing
D22	Publishing, Printing, and Reproduction of Recorded Media	323	Printing and Related Support Activities	Printing on paper; printing support services (prepress and bindery)
		334	Computer and Electronic Product Manufacturing	Mass reproduction of recordings on optical and magnetic media
		51	Information and Cultural Industries	Publishing and combined publishing and printing
D23	Manufacture of Coke, Refined Petroleum Products, and Nuclear Fuel	324	Petroleum and Coal Products Manufacturing	Petroleum refineries; coke ovens; manufacturing petroleum oils and greases
		325	Chemical Manufacturing	Nuclear fuel, manufacturing
		331	Primary Metal Manufacturing	Uranium refining
D24	Manufacture of Chemicals and Chemical Products	311	Food Manufacturing	Table salt manufacturing
		325	Chemical Manufacturing	Manufacturing basic chemicals; synthetic rubber and plastics resins; and chemical preparations, including fertilizers, pesticides, pharmaceuticals, paints, adhesives, soap and cleaning compounds, toiletries, inks, explosives, and photographic chemicals
		332	Fabricated Metal Product Manufacturing	Percussion caps and primers, soap-impregnated scouring pads, manufacturing
		334	Computer and Electronic Product Manufacturing	Blank optical and magnetic media, manufacturing
		339	Miscellaneous Manufacturing	Artists' paints and colors; absorbent cotton; dressings, bandages, and sutures; dental compounds, cement, and filling materials, manufacturing
D25	Manufacture of Rubber and Plastics Products	314	Textile Product Mills	Plastic shower curtains and tablecloths; woven plastic bags
		315	Clothing Manufacturing	Heat sealed plastic clothing (e.g. waterproof clothing), manufacturing
		322	Paper Manufacturing	Cellophane adhesive tape
		325	Chemical Manufacturing	Cellophane film and sheet, manufacturing
		326	Plastics and Rubber Products Manufacturing	Plastic and rubber basic shapes (e.g. film, sheet, pipe, and laminates); plastic foam products; plastic bags, bottles, and other containers; miscellaneous plastic products (e.g. hardware, combs, and kitchenware), manufacturing

ISIC Code	ISIC Title	NAICS Code	NAICS Title	Description of Link
		332	Fabricated Metal Product Manufacturing	Fluid power hose assemblies, manufacturing
		337	Furniture and Related Product Manufacturing	Plastic furniture frames and parts, manufacturing
		339	Miscellaneous Manufacturing	Rubber seals and gaskets; plastic safety helmets; noise protectors; ear and nose plugs; fiberglass burial vaults, manufacturing
D26	Manufacture of Other Non-metallic Mineral Products	324	Petroleum and Coal Products Manufacturing	Tar and asphalt and asphalt products (e.g. saturated felts and shingles), manufacturing
		327	Non-metallic Mineral Product Manufacturing	Glass, cement, concrete, and lime; refractories, abrasives, and other products of clay, glass, cement, concrete, gypsum, stone, and other non-metallic minerals, manufacturing
		335	Electrical Equipment, Appliance, and Component Manufacturing	Carbon and graphite fiber and blocks, manufacturing
D27	Manufacture of Basic Metals	322	Paper Manufacturing	Foil laminates, manufacturing
		331	Primary Metal Manufacturing	Iron and steel mills; non-ferrous smelters and refiners; rolling, drawing, casting, extruding, and alloying metals
		332	Fabricated Metal Product Manufacturing	Metal foil, made from purchased metal, except aluminum; armor plate; reinforcing bars; galvanized and plastic-coated steel wire
D28	Manufacture of Fabricated Metal Products, except Machinery and Equipment	11	Agriculture, Forestry, Fishing, and Hunting	Farriers
		332	Paper Manufacturing	Foil bags, manufacturing
		331	Primary Metal Manufacturing	Cast iron cooking utensils, cast iron manhole covers, and cast metal ship propellers, manufacturing
		332	Fabricated Metal Product Manufacturing	Forging and stamping; machine shops; coating, engraving, heat treating, and other metal services; cutlery and non-powered hand tools; architectural and structural metal products; boilers, tanks, and metal containers, except cargo; springs; except precision; wire products, except insulated; metal hardware; metal turned products; screws, nuts, and bolts; miscellaneous fabricated metal products, manufacturing
		333	Machinery Manufacturing	Welding electrodes; metal-cutting dies; poultry incubators; heating boilers and radiators, manufacturing
		334	Computer and Electronic Product Manufacturing	Precision springs, manufacturing

ISIC Code	ISIC Title	NAICS Code	NAICS Title	Description of Link
		337	Furniture and Related Product Manufacturing	Metal drapery hardware, manufacturing
		339	Miscellaneous Manufacturing	Jewelry engraving and polishing; domestic sewing needles; safety pins; clothing fasteners; metal safety helmets; pewter and plated ware; metal grave vaults; metal signs and name plates, manufacturing
D29	Manufacture of Machinery and Equipment, NEC	332	Fabricated Metal Product Manufacturing	Apparatus for metallurgy (e.g. melting pots); weapons and ammunition; metal valves; roller and ball bearings; block and tackle; metal pallets and skids; heat exchangers; industrial autoclaves; gas absorbers and fractioning columns, manufacturing
		333	Machinery Manufacturing	Machinery specialized for use in the agricultural, construction, forestry, mining, manufacturing (except metallurgy), and service industries; ventilation, air conditioning and commercial refrigeration machinery; metalworking machinery; engine, turbine, and power transmission equipment, except generator sets and motor vehicle engines; pumps and compressors, except motor vehicle and laboratory; powered materials handling equipment; miscellaneous general purpose machinery; industrial molds; machine tool attachments, manufacturing
		335	Electrical Equipment, Appliance, and Component Manufacturing	Household appliances, electric and non-electric; ultrasonic cleaning equipment, manufacturing
		336	Transportation Equipment Manufacturing	Motor vehicle and aircraft engine pumps; hydraulic hoists and tailgate loaders; air, oil, and gas filters; rail laying and tamping equipment, manufacturing
		339	Miscellaneous Manufacturing	Laboratory equipment; artists' air brushes; fire extinguishers; metal gaskets; industrial sewing machines needles, manufacturing
D30	Manufacture of Office, Accounting, and Computing Machinery	333	Machinery Manufacturing	Store and office machines (except computers), manufacturing
		334	Computer and Electronic Product Manufacturing	Computers, peripheral equipment, and memory modules, manufacturing
		339	Miscellaneous Manufacturing	Pencil sharpeners, staplers, and similar office equipment, manufacturing
D31	Manufacture of Electrical Machinery and Apparatus, NEC	326	Plastics and Rubber Products Manufacturing	Battery boxes and separators, manufacturing
		333	Machinery Manufacturing	Generator sets and arc welding generators; electric outboard motors, manufacturing

ISIC Code	ISIC Title	NAICS Code	NAICS Title	Description of Link
		334	Computer and Electronic Product Manufacturing	Electronic transformers, coils, chokes, inductors, switches and connectors, and other electronic components; harness assemblies for electronic use; alarm and signaling equipment, manufacturing
		335	Electrical Equipment, Appliance, and Component Manufacturing	Electric lighting equipment, except motor vehicle lighting fixtures; equipment for generating and distributing electrical power; batteries; electric and communications wire and cable, and wiring devices; miscellaneous electrical equipment and components, manufacturing
		336	Transportation Equipment Manufacturing	Transportation equipment lighting fixtures; automobile electrical equipment, manufacturing
		339	Miscellaneous Manufacturing	Electric signs and scoreboards, manufacturing
D32	Manufacture of Radio, Television, and Communication Equipment and Apparatus	334	Computer and Electronic Product Manufacturing	Communications equipment and apparatus; audio and video equipment, manufacturing
		335	Electrical Equipment, Appliance and Component Manufacturing	Electric condensers and capacitors, manufacturing
D33	Manufacture of Medical, Precision and Optical Instruments, Watches, and Clocks	327	Non-metallic Mineral Product Manufacturing	Optical fibers and cables (not individually sheathed), manufacturing
		332	Fabricated Metal Product	Measuring tools for use in the hand, manufacturing
		333	Machinery Manufacturing	Sterilizer equipment, barber and beauty shop, massage equipment; automotive testing equipment, optical measuring, testing and inspecting equipment, manufacturing
		334	Computer and Electronic Product Manufacturing	Navigational and guidance instruments; electronic measuring, medical, and controlling devices; electronic medical equipment; photographic and other optical equipment; watches, clocks, and other timing devices, manufacturing
		337	Furniture and Related Product Manufacturing	Barber and beauty shop furniture, manufacturing
		339	Miscellaneous Manufacturing	Medical equipment and supplies, except electronic; orthopedic and prosthetic devices and appliances; spectacles; metal watch bands, manufacturing
D34	Manufacturing of Motor Vehicle, Trailers and Semi-trailers	321	Wood Product Manufacturing	Mobile homes and buildings, manufacturing
		326	Plastics and Rubber Products Manufacturing	Plastic air freight container, manufacturing
		332	Fabricated Metal Product Manufacturing	Metal cargo container, manufacturing
		333	Machinery Manufacturing	Motor vehicle diesel engines (including rebuilding), manufacturing

ISIC Code	ISIC Title	NAICS Code	NAICS Title	Description of Link
		336	Transportation Equipment Manufacturing	Motor vehicle, trailers and semi-trailers, and their parts, manufacturing
D35	Manufacture of Other Transport Equipment	326	Plastics and Rubber Products Manufacturing	Inflatable rubber or plastic boats and life rafts, manufacturing
		332	Fabricated Metal Product Manufacturing	Prefabricated ship sections; fabricated metal parts for railway locomotives and rolling stock; aircraft fluid power assemblies, manufacturing
		333	Machinery Manufacturing	Non-powered materials handling equipment; flight simulators, electronic, manufacturing
		334	Computer and Electronic Product Manufacturing	Communication satellites; mechanical signaling and traffic control equipment for railways and highways, manufacturing
		336	Transportation Equipment Manufacturing	Aerospace equipment and parts; railway locomotives and rolling stock; ships and boats; motorcycles and bicycles; recreational vehicles; military armored vehicles; animal-drawn vehicles, manufacturing
		339	Miscellaneous Manufacturing	Wheelchairs, manufacturing
		41	Wholesale Trade	Dismantling ships
		48-49	Transportation and Warehousing	Ship repair, not in shipyards; repair of locomotive and rolling stock
D36	Manufacturing of Furniture; Manufacturing, NEC	324	Petroleum and Coal Products Manufacturing	Asphalt floor tile, manufacturing
		325	Chemical Manufacturing	Matches and packaged lighter fluid, manufacturing
		326	Plastics and Rubber Products Manufacturing	Resilient floor coverings; rubber balls, plastic vacuum bottles, plastic smokers' pipes, plastic identification tags, manufacturing
		332	Fabricated Metal Product Manufacturing	Thermoses; wire sieves; metal badges, manufacturing
		333	Machinery Manufacturing	Amusement park rides, manufacturing
		336	Transportation Equipment Manufacturing	Transportation equipment seating, manufacturing
		337	Furniture and Related Product Manufacturing	Furniture, NEC Manufacturing
		339	Miscellaneous Manufacturing	Musical instruments; laboratory furniture; blackboards; jewelry; sporting goods, games and toys; cigarette lighters; candles; umbrellas; pens and pencils; brooms, brushes and mops; miscellaneous products, NEC, manufacturing
		71	Arts, Entertainment, and Recreation	Taxidermy services
D37	Recycling	314	Textile Products Mills	Recovering textiles fibers from waste

ISIC Code	ISIC Title	NAICS Code	NAICS Title	Description of Link
		325	Chemical Manufacturing	Recovery of cellulosic fibers and fiber mixtures from waste
		326	Plastics and Rubber Products Manufacturing	Reclaimed rubber (reworked by manufacturing processes)
		331	Primary Metal Manufacturing	Recovery of metal from waste and scrap
		41	Wholesale Trade	Shredding tires for rubber and metal content; grinding plastic into flakes
E	Electricity, Gas, and Water Supply	22	Utilities	Electric power generation, transmission and distribution; natural gas distributing; water collection, treatment, and distribution systems
F	Construction	21	Mining and Oil and Gas Extraction	Support services (including drilling for mining, except oil and gas
		23	Construction	Construction, repairing and renovating buildings and engineering works
		48-49	Transportation and Warehousing	Maintenance of railway rights-of-ways and structures
		56	Administrative and Support, Waste Management, and Remediation Services	Cleaning building exteriors
G	Wholesale and Retail Trade; Repair of Motor Vehicle, Motorcycles, and Personal and Household Goods	313	Textile Mills	Fabric converters
		41	Wholesale Trade	Wholesale trade
		44-45	Retail Trade	Retail trade
		48-49	Transportation and Warehousing	Motor vehicle towing services
		51	Information and Cultural Industries	Distribution of musical recordings from masters
		52	Finance and Insurance	Pawnbrokers
		56	Administrative and Support, Waste Management, and Remediation Services	Locksmith services; bottle depots
		81	Other Services (except Public Administration)	Repair and maintenance of motor vehicles; repair and maintenance of personal and household goods
H	Hotel and Restaurants	71	Arts, Entertainment, and Recreation	Dinner theatres
		72	Accommodation and Food Services	Accommodation and food services
I	Transport, Storage, and Communication	48-49	Transportation and Warehousing	Transportation, warehousing, and storage
		51	Information and Cultural Industries	Post office, couriers and telecommunications (including cable and pay-TV); transportation rate services
		53	Real Estate and Rental and Leasing	Self-storage

ISIC Code	ISIC Title	NAICS Code	NAICS Title	Description of Link
		54	Professional, Scientific, and Technical Services	Freight rate information services
		56	Administrative and Support, Waste Management and Remediation Services	Travel agencies; ticket offices; tour operators; accommodation and car rental reservation services
		71	Arts, Entertainment, and Recreation	Pleasure boat docking services; tourist guide services
		81	Other Services (except Public Administration)	Automobile parking services
J	Financial Intermediation	51	Information and Cultural Industries	Buying and licensing artistic and literary works (e.g. music, software, books)
		52	Finance and Insurance	Central banking; banks and other deposit-accepting and credit-granting intermediaries; security and commodity brokerages and exchanges; portfolio management; insurance, except government-operated; financial leasing services, when combined with sales financing services
		53	Real Estate and Rental and Leasing	Financial leasing services, not combined with sales financing services; franchises, selling or licensing; buying and leasing oil royalties; patent buying and licensing
		54	Professional, Scientific, and Technical Services	Actuarial consulting services
		55	Management of Companies and Enterprises	Management holding companies, of financial institutions
K	Real Estate, Renting, and Business Activities	11	Agriculture, Forestry, Fishing, and Hunting	Farm management services
		21	Mining and Oil and Gas Extraction	Mineral exploration services, except geophysical
		23	Construction	Real property developers and sub-dividers; construction management; building exhibits
		325	Chemical Manufacturing	Aerosol packaging services
		51	Information and Cultural Industries	Software publishers; data processing services; data base publishing
		53	Real Estate and Rental and Leasing	Buying, selling, renting and operating real estate; rental of machinery and equipment, transportation equipment, and personal and household equipment
		54	Professional, Scientific, and Technical Services	Legal services; architectural services; engineering services; computer systems design and related services; accounting and bookkeeping services; advertising services; business management consulting; research and development services; geophysical exploration; surveying and mapping services; technical testing and analysis services, except medical; photo graphic services

ISIC Code	ISIC Title	NAICS Code	NAICS Title	Description of Link
		55	Management of Companies and Enterprises	Management holding companies, of nonfinancial institutions
		56	Administrative and Support, Waste Management and Remediation Services	Security and investigation services; janitorial services; employment services, except theatrical; copy shops; portable toilet services; other business support services, such as private mailing services, collection agencies, computer word processing, and telephone call centers
		61	Educational Services	Educational consulting services
		71	Arts, Entertainment, and Recreation	Independent models; agents and brokers for artists and entertainers; costume design services
		81	Other Services (except Public Administration)	Repair and maintenance of office, accounting, and computing equipment; photofinishing; cleaning industrial filters; cleaning tanks and boilers; bail bonding; condominium; corporation management
L	Pubic Administration and Defense; Compulsory Social Security	52	Finance and Insurance	Government-operated automobile insurance
		91	Public Administration	Public administration; defense service; compulsory social security activities, except direct provision of welfare services.
M	Education	61	Educational Services	Education, except that associated with recreational activities
N	Health and Social Work	54	Professional, Scientific, and Technical Services	Consumer credit counseling service; veterinary services, including animal hospitals
		61	Educational Services	Child guidance centers, educational; vocational guidance centers
		62	Health Care and Social Assistance	Human health care; social assistance services, such as welfare and child protection
		81	Other Services (except Public Administration)	Grantmaking and giving services
O	Other Community, Social, and Personal Service Activities	22	Utilities	Sewage treatment and disposal
		41	Wholesale Trade	Recorded video tapes, wholesaling
		48-49	Transportation and Warehousing	Highway, street, bridge, and runway cleaning and snow removal
		51	Information and Cultural Industries	Radio and television broadcasting; motion picture and sound recording services; libraries; news reporting services; betting information services; inventors
		53	Real Estate and Rental and Leasing	Recreational equipment rental services; carpet and rug rental services; locker (except food) rental services
		54	Professional, Scientific, and Technical Services	Motion picture consulting services

ISIC Code	ISIC Title	NAICS Code	NAICS Title	Description of Link
		56	Administrative and Support, Waste Management and Remediation Services	Waste management and remediation services, except portable toilet services; parking lot cleaning; theatrical ticket agencies; film and theatre employment services; license bureaus
		61	Educational Services	Education, associated with recreational activities
		71	Arts, Entertainment, and Recreation	Performing arts facilities and promoters; museums and historical sites; sports teams, sporting facilities and sports promoters; recreational facilities; physical fitness facilities; coin-operated machine operations and arcades; lotteries and other gambling operations
		81	Other Services (except Public Administration)	Membership organizations; religious organizations; laundry and dry cleaning services; hair care and other esthetic services; funeral services; special occasion greeting services; miscellaneous personal services
P	Private Households with Employed Persons	81	Other Services (except Public Administration)	Private households employing domestic personnel (including chauffeurs, nannies, babysitters)
Q	Extra-territorial Organizations and Bodies	91	Public Administration	Foreign and international missions
	Not Defined	56	Administrative and Support, Waste Management and Remediation Services	Facilities management services

HOW TO USE THIS SECTION:

This section supplies you with detailed descriptions of each of the 20 sectors designated within the NAICS coding system. Each "chapter" begins with a narrative overview of the sector as a whole and then breaks down the industries and services, beginning with the two-digit sector designation up through the six-digit national industry classification. Keep in mind that at the six-digit level, individual classifications may or may not be designated with a "US" or a "CAN" notation indicating comparability between industries throughout Canada, Mexico and the United States.

NAICS Titles
and Descriptions of Industries

SIC to NAICS Interchange

▶**513 BROADCASTING AND TELECOMMUNICATIONS** ◀——————— NAICS Sector Titles and Descriptions (3-Digit)
Industries in the Broadcasting and Telecommunications subsector include establishments providing point-to-point communications. . .

5133 Telecommunications ◀——————— NAICS Industry Group Titles and Descriptions (4-Digit)
This industry group comprises establishments primarily engaged in operating, maintaining or providing access to facilities for the transmission of . . .

51331 Wired Telecommunications Carriers ◀——————— NAICS Industry Titles and Descriptions (5-Digit)
See industry description for 513310 below.

513310 Wired Telecommunications Carriers ◀——————— NAICS U.S. Industry Titles and Descriptions (6-Digit)
This industry comprises establishments engaged in (1) operating and maintaining switching and transmission facilities . . .

■ Broadcasting scheduled television programs via cable or satellite facilities on . . . ◀——————— Cross-Reference Section

Cross-Reference Section
NAICS 6-Digit
NAICS 5-Digit
NAICS 4-Digit
NAICS 3-Digit

Sector ‖

Agriculture, Forestry,
Fishing, and Hunting

The Sector as a Whole

THE AGRICULTURE, FORESTRY, FISHING, AND HUNTING sector comprises establishments primarily engaged in growing crops, raising animals, harvesting timber, and harvesting fish and other animals from a farm, ranch, or their natural habitats.

The establishments in this sector are often described as farms, ranches, dairies, greenhouses, nurseries, orchards, or hatcheries. A farm may consist of a single tract of land or a number of separate tracts that may be held under different tenures. For example, the farm operator may own one tract and rent another. The operator may operate it alone or with the assistance of members of the household or hired employees, or it may be operated by a partnership, corporation, or other type of organization. When a landowner has one or more tenants, renters, croppers, or managers, the land operated by each is considered a farm.

The sector distinguishes two basic activities: agricultural production and agricultural support activities. Agricultural production includes establishments performing the complete farm or ranch operation, such as farm owner-operators, tenant farm operators, and sharecroppers. Agricultural support activities include establishments that perform one or more activities associated with farm operation, such as soil preparation, planting, harvesting, and management, on a contract or fee basis.

Excluded from the Agriculture, Forestry, Hunting and Fishing sector are establishments primarily engaged in agricultural research and establishments primarily engaged in administering programs for regulating and conserving land, mineral, wildlife, and forest use. These establishments are classified in Industry 54171, Research and Development in the Physical, Engineering, and Life Sciences; and Industry 92412, Administration of Conservation Programs, respectively.

➡111 CROP PRODUCTION

Industries in the Crop Production subsector grow crops mainly for food and fiber. The subsector comprises establishments, such as farms, orchards, groves, greenhouses, and nurseries, primarily engaged in growing crops, plants, vines, or trees and their seeds.

The industries in this subsector are grouped by similarity of production activity, including biological and physiological characteristics and economic requirements, the length of growing season, degree of crop rotation, extent of input specialization, labor requirements, and capital demands. The production process is typically completed when the raw product or commodity grown reaches the "farm gate" for market, that is, at the point of first sale or price determination.

Establishments are classified to the crop production subsector when crop production (i.e., value of crops for market) accounts for one-half or more of the establishment's total agricultural production. Within the subsector, establishments are classified to a specific industry when a product or industry family of products (i.e., oilseed and grain farming, vegetable and melon farming, fruit and tree nut farming) account for one-half or more of the establishment's agricultural production. Establishments with one-half or more crop production with no one product or family of products of an industry accounting for one-half of the establishment's agricultural production are treated as general combination crop farming and are classified in Industry 11199, All Other Crop Farming.

Sector ‖

Agriculture, Forestry,
Fishing, and Hunting

Industries in the Crop Production subsector include establishments that own, operate, and manage and those that operate and manage. Those that manage only are classified in Subsector 115, Support Activities for Agriculture and Forestry.

1111 Oilseed and Grain Farming

This industry group comprises establishments primarily engaged in (1) growing oilseed and/or grain crops and/or (2) producing oilseed and grain seeds. These crops have an annual life cycle and are typically grown in open fields.

11111 Soybean Farming

See industry description for 111110 below.

111110 Soybean Farming

This industry comprises establishments primarily engaged in growing soybeans and/or producing soybean seeds.

■ Establishments engaged in growing soybeans in combination with grain(s) with the soybeans or grain(s) not accounting for one-half of the establishment's agricultural production (value of crops for market) are classified in U.S. Industry 111191, Oilseed and Grain Combination Farming.

11112 Oilseed (except Soybean) Farming

See industry description for 111120 below.

111120 Oilseed (except Soybean) Farming

This industry comprises establishments primarily engaged in growing fibrous oilseed producing plants and/or producing oilseed seeds, such as sunflower, safflower, flax, rape, canola, and sesame.

■ Growing soybeans are classified in Industry 111110, Soybean Farming; and
■ Growing oilseed(s) in combination with grain(s) with no one oilseed (or family of oilseeds) or grain(s) (or family of grains) accounting for one-half of the establishment's agricultural production (value of crops for market) are classified in U.S. Industry 111191, Oilseed and Grain Combination Farming.

11113 Dry Pea and Bean Farming

See industry description for 111130 below.

111130 Dry Pea and Bean Farming

This industry comprises establishments primarily engaged in growing dried peas, beans, and/or lentils.

■ Establishments primarily engaged in growing fresh green beans and peas are classified in U.S. Industry 111219, Other Vegetable (except Potato) and Melon Farming.

11114 Wheat Farming

See industry description for 111140 below.

111140 Wheat Farming

This industry comprises establishments primarily engaged in growing wheat and/or producing wheat seeds.

■ Establishments growing wheat in combination with oilseed(s) with the wheat or oilseed(s) not accounting for one-half of the establishment's agricultural production (value of crops for market) are classified in U.S. Industry 111191, Oilseed and Grain Combination Farming.

11115 Corn Farming

See industry description for 111150 below.

111150 Corn Farming

This industry comprises establishments primarily engaged in growing corn (except sweet corn) and/or producing corn seeds.

■ Growing sweet corn are classified in U.S. Industry 111219, Other Vegetable (except Potato) and Melon Farming; and
■ Growing corn in combination with oilseed(s) with the corn or oilseed(s) not accounting for one-half of the establishment's production (value of crops for market) are classified in U.S. Industry 111191, Oilseed and Grain Combination Farming.

Sector 11

Agriculture, Forestry, Fishing, and Hunting

■ = Cross-References

US—United States industry only. CAN—United States and Canadian industries are comparable. When neither US nor CAN appears, Canadian, Mexican, and United States industries are comparable.

276

Harris InfoSource

11116 Rice Farming
See industry description for 111160 below.

111160 Rice Farming
This industry comprises establishments primarily engaged in growing rice (except wild rice) and/or producing rice seeds.

- Growing wild rice are classified in U.S. Industry 111199, All Other Grain Farming; and
- Engaged in growing rice in combination with oilseed(s) with the rice or oilseed(s) not accounting for one-half of the establishment's agricultural production (value of crops for market) are classified in U.S. Industry 111191, Oilseed and Grain Combination Farming.

11119 Other Grain Farming
This industry comprises establishments primarily engaged in (1) growing grain(s) and/or producing grain seeds (except wheat, corn, and rice) or (2) growing a combination of grain(s) and oilseed(s) with no one grain (or family of grains) or oilseed (or family of oilseeds) accounting for one-half of the establishment's agriculture production (value of crops for market). Combination grain(s) and oilseed(s) establishments may produce oilseed(s) and grain(s) seeds and/or grow oilseed(s) and grain(s).

- Growing wheat are classified in U.S. Industry 11114, Wheat Farming;
- Growing corn (except sweet corn) are classified in U.S. Industry 11115, Corn Farming;
- Growing sweet corn are classified in U.S. Industry 11121, Vegetable and Melon Farming; and
- Growing rice (except wild rice) are classified in U.S. Industry 11116, Rice Farming.

111191 Oilseed and Grain Combination Farming ^{US}
This U.S. industry comprises establishments engaged in growing a combination of oilseed(s) and grain(s) with no one oilseed (or family of oilseeds) or grain (or family of grains) accounting for one-half of the establishment's agricultural production (value of crops for market). These establishments may produce oilseed(s) and grain(s) seeds and/or grow oilseed(s) and grain(s).

- Establishments engaged in growing one grain (or family of grains) or oilseed (or family of oilseeds) accounting for one-half of the establishment's agriculture production (value of crops for market) are classified in Industry Group 1111, Oilseed and Grain Farming accordingly by the prominent grain(s) or oilseed(s) grown.

111199 All Other Grain Farming ^{US}
This U.S. industry comprises establishments primarily engaged in growing grains and/or producing grain(s) seeds (except wheat, corn, rice, and oilseed(s) and grain(s) combinations).

- Growing wheat are classified in Industry 111140, Wheat Farming;
- Growing corn are classified in Industry 111150, Corn Farming;
- Growing rice (except wild rice) are classified in Industry 111160, Rice Farming;
- Growing sweet corn are classified in U.S. Industry 111219, Other Vegetable (except Potato) and Melon Farming; and
- Growing a combination of grain(s) and oilseed(s) with no one grain (or family of grains) or oilseed (or family of oilseeds) accounting for one-half of the establishment's agricultural production (value of crops for market) are classified in U.S. Industry 111191, Oilseed and Grain Combination Farming.

1112 Vegetable and Melon Farming
This industry group comprises establishments primarily engaged in growing root and tuber crops (except sugar beets and peanuts) or edible plants and/or producing root and tuber or edible plant seeds. The crops included in this group have an annual growth cycle and are grown in open fields. Climate and cultural practices limit producing areas but often permit the growing of a combination of crops in a year.

11121 Vegetable and Melon Farming
This industry comprises establishments primarily engaged in one or more of the following: (1) growing vegetable and/or melon crops; (2) producing vegetable and melon seeds; and (3) growing vegetable and/or melon bedding plants.

- Growing sugar beets are classified in Industry 11199, All Other Crop Farming;
- Growing vegetables and melons under glass or protective cover are classified in Industry 11141, Food Crops Grown Under Cover;
- Growing dry peas and beans are classified in Industry 11113, Dry Pea and Bean Farming;
- Growing corn (except sweet corn) are classified in Industry 11115, Corn Farming;

Sector II

Agriculture, Forestry, Fishing, and Hunting

■ = Cross-References

US—United States industry only. CAN—United States and Canadian industries are comparable. When neither US nor CAN appears, Canadian, Mexican, and United States industries are comparable.

■ Canning, pickling, and/or drying (artificially) vegetables are classified in Industry 31142, Fruit and Vegetable Canning, Pickling and Drying; and
■ Growing fruit on trees and other fruit-bearing plants (except melons) are classified in Industry Group 1113, Fruit and Tree Nut Farming.

111211 Potato Farming ^{CAN}
This U.S. industry comprises establishments primarily engaged in growing potatoes and/or producing seed potatoes (except sweet potatoes).

■ Growing sweet potatoes, cassava, and yams are classified in U.S. Industry 111219, Other Vegetable (except Potato) and Melon Farming; and
■ Canning or drying potatoes are classified in Industry 31142, Fruit and Vegetable Canning, Pickling and Drying.

111219 Other Vegetable (except Potato) and Melon Farming ^{CAN}
This U.S. industry comprises establishments primarily engaged in one or more of the following: (1) growing melons and/or vegetables (except potatoes; dry peas; dry beans; field, silage, or seed corn; and sugar beets); (2) producing vegetable and/or melon seeds; and (3) growing vegetable and/or melon bedding plants.

■ Growing potatoes are classified in U.S. Industry 111211, Potato Farming;
■ Growing sugar beets are classified in U.S. Industry 111991, Sugar Beet Farming;
■ Growing vegetables and melons under glass or protective cover are classified in U.S. Industry 111419, Other Food Crops Grown Under Cover;
■ Growing dry peas and beans are classified in Industry 111130, Dry Pea and Bean Farming;
■ Growing corn (except sweet corn) are classified in Industry 111150, Corn Farming;
■ Canning, pickling, and/or drying (artificially) vegetables are classified in Industry 31142, Fruit and Vegetable Canning, Pickling and Drying; and
■ Growing fruit on trees and other fruit-bearing plants (except melons) are classified in Industry Group 1113, Fruit and Tree Nut Farming.

1113 Fruit and Tree Nut Farming
This industry group comprises establishments primarily engaged in growing fruit and/or tree nutcrops. The crops included in this industry group are generally not grown from seeds and have a perennial life cycle.

11131 Orange Groves
See industry description for 111310 below.

111310 Orange Groves
This industry comprises establishments primarily engaged in growing oranges.

11132 Citrus (except Orange) Groves
See industry description for 111320 below.

111320 Citrus (except Orange) Groves
This industry comprises establishments primarily engaged in growing citrus fruits (except oranges).

■ Establishments primarily engaged in growing oranges are classified in Industry 111310, Orange Groves.

11133 Noncitrus Fruit and Tree Nut Farming
This industry comprises establishments primarily engaged in one or more of the following: (1) growing noncitrus fruits (e.g., apples, grapes, berries, peaches); (2) growing tree nuts (e.g., pecans, almonds, pistachios); or (3) growing a combination of fruit(s) and tree nut(s) with no one fruit (or family of fruit) or family of tree nuts accounting for one-half of the establishment's agriculture production (value of crops for market).

■ Harvesting berries or nuts from native and noncultivated plants are classified in Industry 11321, Forest Nurseries and Gathering of Forest Products; and
■ Canning and/or drying (artificially) fruit are classified in Industry 31142, Fruit and Vegetable Canning, Pickling and Drying.

■ = Cross-References

Sector **11**
Agriculture, Forestry, Fishing, and Hunting

US—United States industry only. CAN—United States and Canadian industries are comparable. When neither US nor CAN appears, Canadian, Mexican, and United States industries are comparable.

278

Harris InfoSource

111331 Apple Orchards ᵁˢ
This U.S. industry comprises establishments primarily engaged in growing apples.

- Establishments engaged in growing apples in combination with tree nut(s) with the apples or family of tree nuts not accounting for one-half of the establishment's agriculture production (i.e., value of crops for market) are classified in U.S. Industry 111336, Fruit and Tree Nut Combination Farming.

111332 Grape Vineyards ᵁˢ
This U.S. industry comprises establishments primarily engaged in growing grapes and/or growing grapes to sun dry into raisins.

- Drying grapes artificially are classified in U.S. Industry 311423, Dried and Dehydrated Food Manufacturing; and
- Growing grapes in combination with tree nut(s) with the grapes or family of tree nuts not accounting for one-half of the establishment's agriculture production (i.e., value of crops for market) are classified in U.S. Industry 111336, Fruit and Tree Nut Combination Farming.

111333 Strawberry Farming ᵁˢ
This U.S. industry comprises establishments primarily engaged in growing strawberries.

- Establishments engaged in growing strawberries in combination with tree nut(s) with the strawberries or family of tree nuts not accounting for one-half of the establishment's agriculture production (i.e., value of crops for market) are classified in U.S. Industry 111336, Fruit and Tree Nut Combination Farming.

111334 Berry (except Strawberry) Farming ᵁˢ
This U.S. industry comprises establishments primarily engaged in growing berries.

- Growing strawberries are classified in U.S. Industry 111333, Strawberry Farming;
- Harvesting berries from native and noncultivated bushes or vines are classified in Industry 113210, Forest Nurseries and Gathering of Forest Products; and
- Growing berries in combination with tree nut(s) with the berries or family of tree nuts not accounting for one-half of the establishment's agriculture production (i.e., value of crops for market) are classified in U.S. Industry 111336, Fruit and Tree Nut Combination Farming.

111335 Tree Nut Farming ᵁˢ
This U.S. industry comprises establishments primarily engaged in growing tree nuts.

- Growing coconut and coffee are classified in U.S. Industry 111339, Other Noncitrus Fruit Farming; and
- Growing tree nut(s) in combination with fruit(s) with no one fruit (or family of fruit or of tree nuts) accounting for one-half of the establishment's agriculture production (i.e., value of crops for market) are classified in U.S. Industry 111336, Fruit and Tree Nut Combination Farming.

111336 Fruit and Tree Nut Combination Farming ᵁˢ
This U.S. industry comprises establishments primarily engaged in growing a combination of fruit(s) and tree nut(s) with no one fruit (or family of fruit) or family of tree nuts accounting for one-half of the establishment's agriculture production (i.e., value of crops for market).

- Establishments engaged in growing fruit(s) or the family of tree nut(s) accounting for one-half of the establishment's agriculture production (i.e., value of crops for market) are classified in Industry Group 1113, Fruit and Tree Nut Farming accordingly by the prominent fruit(s) or tree nut(s) grown.

111339 Other Noncitrus Fruit Farming ᵁˢ
This U.S. industry comprises establishments primarily engaged in growing noncitrus fruits—except apples, grapes, berries, and fruit(s) and tree nut(s) combinations.

- Growing apples are classified in U.S. Industry 111331, Apple Orchards;
- Growing grapes including sun drying of grapes into raisins are classified in U.S. Industry 111332, Grape Vineyards;
- Growing strawberries are classified in U.S. Industry 111333, Strawberry Farming;
- Growing berries (except strawberries) are classified in U.S. Industry 111334, Berry (except Strawberry) Farming;
- Drying fruit artificially are classified in U.S. Industry 311423, Dried and Dehydrated Food Manufacturing; and
- Growing noncitrus fruit(s) in combination with tree nut(s) with no one fruit (or family of fruits) or family of tree nuts accounting for one-half of the establishment's agriculture production (i.e., value of crops for market) are classified in U.S. Industry 111336, Fruit and Tree Nut Combination Farming.

1114 Greenhouse, Nursery, and Floriculture Production
This industry group comprises establishments primarily engaged in growing crops of any kind under cover and/or growing nursery stock and flowers. "Under cover" is generally defined as greenhouses, cold frames, cloth

Sector 11

Agriculture, Forestry, Fishing, and Hunting

■ = Cross-References

houses, and lath houses. The crops grown are removed at various stages of maturity and have annual and perennial life cycles. The nursery stock includes short rotation woody crops that have growth cycles of 10 years or less.

11141 Food Crops Grown Under Cover
This industry comprises establishments primarily engaged in growing food crops (e.g., fruits, melons, tomatoes) under glass or protective cover.

- Establishments primarily engaged in growing vegetable and melon bedding plants are classified in Industry 11121, Vegetable and Melon Farming.

111411 Mushroom Production ^{CAN}
This U.S. industry comprises establishments primarily engaged in growing mushrooms under cover in mines underground, or in other controlled environments.

111419 Other Food Crops Grown Under Cover ^{CAN}
This U.S. industry comprises establishments primarily engaged in growing food crops (except mushrooms) under glass or protective cover.

- Establishments primarily engaged in growing mushrooms under cover are classified in U.S. Industry 111411, Mushroom Production.

11142 Nursery and Floriculture Production
This industry comprises establishments primarily engaged in (1) growing nursery and floriculture products (e.g., nursery stock, shrubbery, cut flowers, flower seeds, foliage plants) under cover or in open fields and/or (2) growing short rotation woody trees with a growing and harvesting cycle of 10 years or less for pulp or tree stock (e.g., cut Christmas trees, cottonwoods).

- Growing vegetable and melon bedding plants are classified in Industry 11121, Vegetable and Melon Farming;
- Operating timber tracts (i.e., growing cycle greater than 10 years) are classified in Industry 11311, Timber Tract Operations; and
- Retailing nursery, tree stock, and floriculture products primarily purchased from others are classified in Industry 44422, Nursery and Garden Centers.

111421 Nursery and Tree Production ^{CAN}
This U.S. industry comprises establishments primarily engaged in (1) growing nursery products, nursery stock, shrubbery, bulbs, fruit stock, sod, and so forth, under cover or in open fields and/or (2) growing short rotation woody trees with a growth and harvest cycle of 10 years or less for pulp or tree stock.

- Growing vegetable and melon bedding plants are classified in Industry 11121, Vegetable and Melon Farming;
- Operating timber tracts (i.e., growing cycle greater than 10 years) are classified in Industry 113110, Timber Tract Operations; and
- Retailing nursery, tree stock, and floriculture products primarily purchased from others are classified in Industry 444220, Nursery and Garden Centers.

111422 Floriculture Production ^{CAN}
This U.S. industry comprises establishments primarily engaged in growing and/or producing floriculture products (e.g., cut flowers and roses, cut cultivated greens, potted flowering and foliage plants, and flower seeds) under cover and in open fields.

- Establishments primarily engaged in retailing floriculture products primarily purchased from others are classified in Industry 444220, Nursery and Garden Centers.

1119 Other Crop Farming
This industry group comprises establishments primarily engaged in (1) growing crops (except oilseed and/or grain; vegetable and/or melon; fruit and tree nut; and greenhouse, nursery, and/or floriculture products). These establishments grow crops, such as tobacco, cotton, sugarcane, hay, sugar beets, peanuts, agave, herbs and spices, and hay and grass seeds; or (2) growing a combination of crops—except a combination of oilseed(s) and grain(s) and a combination of fruit(s) and tree nut(s).

11191 Tobacco Farming
See industry description for 111910 below.

Sector 11

Agriculture, Forestry, Fishing, and Hunting

■ = Cross-References

US—United States industry only. CAN—United States and Canadian industries are comparable. When neither US nor CAN appears, Canadian, Mexican, and United States industries are comparable.

280

Harris InfoSource

111910 Tobacco Farming
This industry comprises establishments primarily engaged in growing tobacco.

11192 Cotton Farming
See industry description for 111920 below.

111920 Cotton Farming
This industry comprises establishments primarily engaged in growing cotton.

- Establishments primarily engaged in ginning cotton are classified in U.S. Industry 115111, Cotton Ginning.

11193 Sugarcane Farming
See industry description for 111930 below.

111930 Sugarcane Farming
This industry comprises establishments primarily engaged in growing sugarcane.

11194 Hay Farming
See industry description for 111940 below.

111940 Hay Farming
This industry comprises establishments primarily engaged in growing hay, alfalfa, clover, and/or mixed hay.

- Growing grain hay are classified in Industry Group 1111, Oilseed and Grain Farming; and
- Growing grass and hay seeds are classified in U.S. Industry 111998, All Other Miscellaneous Crop Farming.

11199 All Other Crop Farming
This industry comprises establishments primarily engaged in (1) growing crops (except oilseeds and/or grains; vegetables and/or melons; fruits and/or tree nuts; greenhouse, nursery and/or floriculture products; tobacco; cotton; sugarcane; or hay) or (2) growing a combination of crops (except a combination of oilseed(s) and grain(s); and a combination of fruit(s) and tree nut(s)) with no one crop or family of crops accounting for one-half of the establishment's agricultural production (i.e., value of crops for market).

- Growing oilseeds and/or wheat, corn, rice, or other grains are classified in Industry Group 1111, Oilseed and Grain Farming;
- Growing vegetables and/or melons are classified in Industry Group 1112, Vegetable and Melon Farming;
- Growing fruits and/or tree nuts are classified in Industry Group 1113, Fruit and Tree Nut Farming;
- Growing greenhouse, nursery, and/or floriculture products are classified in Industry Group 1114, Greenhouse, Nursery, and Floriculture Production;
- Growing tobacco are classified in Industry 11191, Tobacco Farming;
- Growing cotton are classified in Industry 11192, Cotton Farming;
- Growing sugarcane are classified in Industry 11193, Sugarcane Farming; and
- Growing hay are classified in Industry 11194, Hay Farming.

111991 Sugar Beet Farming [US]
This U.S. industry comprises establishments primarily engaged in growing sugar beets.

- Establishments primarily engaged in growing beets (except sugar beets) are classified in U.S. Industry 111219, Other Vegetable (except Potato) and Melon Farming.

111992 Peanut Farming [US]
This U.S. industry comprises establishments primarily engaged in growing peanuts.

111998 All Other Miscellaneous Crop Farming [US]
This U.S. industry comprises establishments primarily engaged in one of the following: (1) growing crops (except oilseeds and/or grains; vegetables and/or melons; fruits and/or tree nuts; greenhouse, nursery and/or floriculture products; tobacco; cotton; sugarcane; hay; sugar beets; or peanuts); (2) growing a combination of crops (except a combination of oilseed(s) and grain(s); and a combination of fruit(s) and tree nut(s)) with no one crop or family of crop(s) accounting for one-half of the establishment's agricultural production (i.e., value of crops for market); or (3) gathering tea or maple sap.

Sector 11

Agriculture, Forestry, Fishing, and Hunting

■ = Cross-References

US—United States industry only. CAN—United States and Canadian industries are comparable. When neither US nor CAN appears, Canadian, Mexican, and United States industries are comparable.

- Growing oilseeds and/or wheat, corn, rice, or other grains are classified in Industry Group 1111, Oilseed and Grain Farming;
- Growing vegetables and/or melons are classified in Industry Group 1112, Vegetable and Melon Farming;
- Growing fruits and/or tree nuts are classified in Industry Group 1113, Fruit and Tree Nut Farming;
- Growing greenhouse, nursery and/or floriculture products are classified in Industry Group 1114, Greenhouse, Nursery, and Floriculture Production;
- Growing tobacco are classified in Industry 111910, Tobacco Farming;
- Growing cotton are classified in Industry 111920, Cotton Farming;
- Growing sugarcane are classified in Industry 111930, Sugarcane Farming;
- Growing hay are classified in Industry 111940, Hay Farming;
- Growing sugar beets are classified in U.S. Industry 111991, Sugar Beet Farming; and
- Growing peanuts are classified in U.S. Industry 111992, Peanut Farming.

➡ 112 ANIMAL PRODUCTION

Industries in the Animal Production subsector raise or fatten animals for the sale of animals or animal products. The subsector comprises establishments, such as ranches, farms, and feedlots primarily engaged in keeping, grazing, breeding, or feeding animals. These animals are kept for the products they produce or for eventual sale. The animals are generally raised in various environments, from total confinement or captivity to feeding on an open range pasture.

The industries in this subsector are grouped by important factors, such as suitable grazing or pasture-land, specialized buildings, type of equipment, and the amount and types of labor required. Establishments are classified to the Animal Production subsector when animal production (i.e., value of animals for market) accounts for one-half or more of the establishment's total agricultural production. Establishments with one-half or more animal production with no one animal product or family of animal products of an industry accounting for one-half of the establishment's agricultural production are treated as combination animal farming classified to Industry 11299, All Other Animal Production.

1121 Cattle Ranching and Farming

This industry group comprises establishments primarily engaged in raising cattle, milking dairy cattle, or feeding cattle for fattening.

11211 Beef Cattle Ranching and Farming, including Feedlots

This industry comprises establishments primarily engaged in raising cattle (including cattle for dairy herd replacements), or feeding cattle for fattening.

- Milking dairy cattle are classified in Industry 11212, Dairy Cattle and Milk Production; and
- Operating stockyards for transportation and not buying, selling, or auctioning livestock are classified in Industry 48899, Other Support Activities for Transportation.

112111 Beef Cattle Ranching and Farming ᵁˢ

This U.S. industry comprises establishments primarily engaged in raising cattle (including cattle for dairy herd replacements).

- Establishments primarily engaged in milking dairy cattle are classified in Industry 112120, Dairy Cattle and Milk Production.

112112 Cattle Feedlots ᵁˢ

This U.S. industry comprises establishments primarily engaged in feeding cattle for fattening.

- Establishments primarily engaged in operating stockyards for transportation and not buying, selling, or auctioning livestock are classified in U.S. Industry 488999, All Other Support Activities for Transportation.

11212 Dairy Cattle and Milk Production

See industry description for 112120 below.

112120 Dairy Cattle and Milk Production

This industry comprises establishments primarily engaged in milking dairy cattle.

- Raising dairy herd replacements are classified in U.S. Industry 112111, Beef Cattle Ranching and Farming; and
- Milking goats are classified in Industry 112420, Goat Farming.

■ = Cross-References

Sector 11

Agriculture, Forestry, Fishing, and Hunting

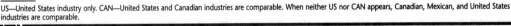

US—United States industry only. CAN—United States and Canadian industries are comparable. When neither US nor CAN appears, Canadian, Mexican, and United States industries are comparable.

282

Harris InfoSource

11213 Dual-purpose Cattle Ranching and Farming
See industry description for 112130 below.

112130 Dual-purpose Cattle Ranching and Farming
This industry comprises establishments primarily engaged in raising cattle for both milking and meat production.

- ■ Milking dairy cattle are classified in Industry 11212, Dairy Cattle and Milk Production;
- ■ Raising cattle or feeding cattle for fattening are classified in Industry 11211, Beef Cattle Ranching and Farming, including Feedlots; and
- ■ Operating stockyards for transportation and not buying, selling, or auctioning livestock are classified in U.S. Industry 48899, All Other Support Activities for Transportation.

1122 Hog and Pig Farming

11221 Hog and Pig Farming
See industry description for 112210 below.

112210 Hog and Pig Farming
This industry comprises establishments primarily engaged in raising hogs and pigs. These establishments may include farming activities, such as breeding, farrowing, and the raising of weanling pigs, feeder pigs, or market size hogs.

- ■ Establishments primarily engaged in operating stockyards for transportation and not buying, selling, or auctioning livestock are classified in U.S. Industry 488999, All Other Support Activities for Transportation.

1123 Poultry and Egg Production
This industry group comprises establishments primarily engaged in breeding, hatching, and raising poultry for meat or egg production.

11231 Chicken Egg Production
See industry description for 112310 below.

112310 Chicken Egg Production
This industry comprises establishments primarily engaged in raising chickens for egg production. The eggs produced may be for use as table eggs or hatching eggs.

- ■ Establishments primarily engaged in raising chickens for the production of meat are classified in Industry 112320, Broilers and Other Meat-type Chicken Production.

11232 Broilers and Other Meat Type Chicken Production
See industry description for 112320 below.

112320 Broilers and Other Meat Type Chicken Production
This industry comprises establishments primarily engaged in raising broilers, fryers, roasters, and other meat type chickens.

- ■ Establishments primarily engaged in raising chickens for egg production are classified in Industry 112310, Chicken Egg Production.

11233 Turkey Production
See industry description for 112330 below.

112330 Turkey Production
This industry comprises establishments primarily engaged in raising turkeys for meat or egg production.

11234 Poultry Hatcheries
See industry description for 112340 below.

Sector 11

Agriculture, Forestry, Fishing, and Hunting

■ = Cross-References

US—United States industry only. CAN—United States and Canadian industries are comparable. When neither US nor CAN appears, Canadian, Mexican, and United States industries are comparable.

www.harrisinfo.com

283

112340 Poultry Hatcheries
This industry comprises establishments primarily engaged in hatching poultry of any kind.

11239 Other Poultry Production
See industry description for 112390 below.

112390 Other Poultry Production
This industry comprises establishments primarily engaged in raising poultry (except chickens for meat or egg production and turkeys).

- Establishments primarily engaged in raising aviary birds, such as parakeets, canaries, and lovebirds, are classified in Industry 112990, All Other Animal Production;
- Raising chickens for egg production are classified in Industry 112310, Chicken Egg Production;
- Raising broilers and other meat type chickens are classified in Industry 112320, Broilers and Other Meat-type Chicken Production;
- Raising turkeys are classified in Industry 112330, Turkey Production; and
- Raising swans, peacocks, flamingos or other "adornment birds" are classified in Industry 112990, All Other Animal Production.

1124 Sheep and Goat Farming
This industry group comprises establishments primarily engaged in raising sheep, lambs, and goats, or feeding lambs for fattening.

11241 Sheep Farming
See industry description for 112410 below.

112410 Sheep Farming
This industry comprises establishments primarily engaged in raising sheep and lambs, or feeding lambs for fattening. The sheep or lambs may be raised for sale or wool production.

- Establishments primarily engaged in operating stockyards for transportation and not buying, selling, or auctioning livestock are classified in U.S. Industry 488999, All Other Support Activities for Transportation.

11242 Goat Farming
See industry description for 112420 below.

112420 Goat Farming
This industry comprises establishments primarily engaged in raising goats.

1125 Animal Aquaculture

11251 Animal Aquaculture
This industry comprises establishments primarily engaged in the farm raising of finfish, shellfish, or any other kind of animal aquaculture. These establishments use some form of intervention in the rearing process to enhance production, such as holding in captivity, regular stocking, feeding, and protecting from predators.

- Establishments primarily engaged in the catching or taking of fish and other aquatic animals from their natural habitat are classified in Industry 11411, Fishing.

112511 Finfish Farming and Fish Hatcheries US
This U.S. industry comprises establishments primarily engaged in (1) farm raising finfish (e.g., catfish, trout, goldfish, tropical fish, minnows) and/or (2) hatching fish of any kind.

- Establishments primarily engaged in the catching or taking of finfish from their natural habitat are classified in U.S. Industry 114111, Finfish Fishing.

■ = Cross-References

Sector 11

Agriculture, Forestry, Fishing, and Hunting

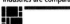

US—United States industry only. CAN—United States and Canadian industries are comparable. When neither US nor CAN appears, Canadian, Mexican, and United States industries are comparable.

284

Harris InfoSource

112512 Shellfish Farming ᵁˢ

This U.S. industry comprises establishments primarily engaged in farm raising shellfish (e.g., crayfish, shrimp, oysters, clams, mollusks).

■ Establishments primarily engaged in the catching or taking of shellfish from their natural habitat are classified in U.S. Industry 114112, Shellfish Fishing.

112519 Other Animal Aquaculture ᵁˢ

This U.S. industry comprises establishments primarily engaged in farm raising animal aquaculture (except finfish and shellfish). Alligator, frog, or turtle production is included in this industry.

■ Miscellaneous fishing activities, such as catching or taking of terrapins, turtles, and frogs in their natural habitat, are classified in U.S. Industry 114119, Other Marine Fishing;
■ Farm raising finfish are classified in U.S. Industry 112511, Finfish Farming and Fish Hatcheries; and
■ Farm raising shellfish are classified in U.S. Industry 112512, Shellfish Farming.

1129 Other Animal Production

This industry group comprises establishments primarily engaged in raising animals and insects (except cattle, hogs and pigs, poultry, sheep and goats, animal aquaculture) for sale or product production. These establishments are primarily engaged in raising one of the following: bees, horses and other equines, rabbits and other fur-bearing animals, and so forth, and producing products, such as honey and other bee products. Establishments primarily engaged in raising a combination of animals with no one animal or family of animals accounting for one-half of the establishment's agricultural production (i.e., value of animals for market) are included in this industry group.

11291 Apiculture

See industry description for 112910 below.

112910 Apiculture

This industry comprises establishments primarily engaged in raising bees. These establishments may collect and gather honey; and/or sell queen bees, packages of bees, royal jelly, bees' wax, propolis, venom, and/or other bee products.

11292 Horses and Other Equine Production

See industry description for 112920 below.

112920 Horses and Other Equine Production

This industry comprises establishments primarily engaged in raising horses, mules, donkeys, and other equines.

■ Establishments primarily engaged in equine boarding are classified in Industry 115210, Support Activities for Animal Production; and
■ Equine owners entering horses in racing or other spectator sporting events are classified in U.S. Industry 711219, Other Spectator Sports.

11293 Fur-bearing Animal and Rabbit Production

See industry description for 112930 below.

112930 Fur-bearing Animal and Rabbit Production

This industry comprises establishments primarily engaged in raising fur-bearing animals including rabbits. These animals may be raised for sale or for their pelt production.

■ Establishments primarily engaged in the trapping or hunting of wild fur-bearing animals are classified in Industry 114210, Hunting and Trapping.

11299 All Other Animal Production

See industry description for 112990 below.

Sector 11

Agriculture, Forestry, Fishing, and Hunting

■ = Cross-References

US—United States industry only. CAN—United States and Canadian industries are comparable. When neither US nor CAN appears, Canadian, Mexican, and United States industries are comparable.

www.harrisinfo.com

285

112990 All Other Animal Production

This industry comprises establishments primarily engaged in: (1) raising animals (except cattle, hogs and pigs, poultry, sheep and goats, animal aquaculture, apiculture, horses and other equines; and fur-bearing animals including rabbits) or (2) raising a combination of animals, with no one animal or family of animals accounting for one-half of the establishment's agricultural production (i.e., value of animals for market) are included in this industry.

- Raising cattle, dairy cattle or feeding cattle for fattening are classified in Industry Group 1121, Cattle Ranching and Farming;
- Raising hogs and pigs are classified in Industry Group 1122, Hog and Pig Farming;
- Raising poultry and raising poultry for egg production are classified in Industry Group 1123, Poultry and Egg Production;
- Raising sheep and goats are classified in Industry Group 1124, Sheep and Goat Farming;
- Raising animal aquaculture are classified in Industry Group 1125, Animal Aquaculture;
- Raising bees are classified in Industry 112910, Apiculture;
- Raising horses and other equines are classified in Industry 112920, Horses and Other Equine Production; and
- Raising fur-bearing animals including rabbits are classified in Industry 112930, Fur-Bearing Animals and Rabbit Production.

▶113 FORESTRY AND LOGGING

Industries in the Forestry and Logging subsector grow and harvest timber on a long production cycle (i.e., of 10 years or more). Long production cycles use different production processes than short production cycles, which require more horticultural interventions prior to harvest, resulting in processes more similar to those found in the Crop Production subsector. Consequently, Christmas tree production and other production involving production cycles of less than 10 years, are classified in the Crop Production subsector.

Industries in this subsector specialize in different stages of the production cycle. Reforestation requires production of seedlings in specialized nurseries. Timber production requires natural forest or suitable areas of land that are available for a long duration. The maturation time for timber depends upon the species of tree, the climatic conditions of the region, and the intended purpose of the timber. The harvesting of timber (except when done on an extremely small scale) requires specialized machinery unique to the industry. Establishments gathering forest products, such as gums, barks, balsam needles, rhizomes, fibers, Spanish moss, and ginseng and truffles, are also included in this subsector.

1131 Timber Tract Operations

11311 Timber Tract Operations

See industry description for 113110 below.

113110 Timber Tract Operations

This industry comprises establishments primarily engaged in the operation of timber tracts for the purpose of selling standing timber.

- Acting as lessors of land with trees as real estate property are classified in Industry 53119, Lessors of Other Real Estate Property;
- Growing short rotation woody trees (i.e., growing and harvesting cycle is 10 years or less) are classified in U.S. Industry 111421, Nursery and Tree Production; and
- Cutting timber are classified in Industry 113310, Logging.

1132 Forest Nurseries and Gathering of Forest Products

11321 Forest Nurseries and Gathering of Forest Products

See industry description for 113210 below.

113210 Forest Nurseries and Gathering of Forest Products

This industry comprises establishments primarily engaged in (1) growing trees for reforestation and/or (2) gathering forest products, such as gums, barks, balsam needles, rhizomes, fibers, Spanish moss, ginseng, and truffles.

- Gathering tea and maple sap are classified in U.S. Industry 111998, All Other Miscellaneous Crop Farming; and
- Processing maple syrup into other products are classified in Industry 31199, All Other Food Manufacturing.
1133 Logging

Sector 11

Agriculture, Forestry, Fishing, and Hunting

US—United States industry only. CAN—United States and Canadian industries are comparable. When neither US nor CAN appears, Canadian, Mexican, and United States industries are comparable.

11331 Logging
See industry description for 113310 below.

113310 Logging
This industry comprises establishments primarily engaged in one or more of the following: (1) cutting timber; (2) cutting and transporting timber; and (3) producing wood chips in the field.

- Establishments primarily engaged in trucking timber are classified in Industry 484220, Specialized Freight (except Used Goods) Trucking, Local.

▶114 FISHING, HUNTING AND TRAPPING

Industries in the Fishing, Hunting, and Trapping subsector harvest fish and other wild animals from their natural habitats and are dependent upon a continued supply of the natural resource. The harvesting of fish is the predominant economic activity of this subsector and it usually requires specialized vessels that, by the nature of their size, configuration and equipment, are not suitable for any other type of production, such as transportation.

Hunting and trapping activities utilize a wide variety of production processes and are classified in the same subsector as fishing because the availability of resources and the constraints imposed, such as conservation requirements and proper habitat maintenance, are similar.

1141 Fishing

11411 Fishing
This industry comprises establishments primarily engaged in the commercial catching or taking of finfish, shellfish, or miscellaneous marine products from a natural habitat, such as the catching of bluefish, eels, salmon, tuna, clams, crabs, lobsters, mussels, oysters, shrimp, frogs, sea urchins, and turtles.

- Farm raising finfish, shellfish or other marine animals are classified in Industry 11251, Animal Aquaculture; and
- Gathering and processing (known as "floating factory ships") seafood into canned seafood products are classified in Industry 31171, Seafood Product Preparation and Packaging.

114111 Finfish Fishing US
This U.S. industry comprises establishments primarily engaged in the commercial catching or taking of finfish (e.g., bluefish, salmon, trout, tuna) from their natural habitat.

- Farm raising finfish are classified in U.S. Industry 112511, Finfish Farming and Fish Hatcheries; and
- Gathering and processing (known as "floating factory ships") seafood into canned seafood products are classified in U.S. Industry 311711, Seafood Canning.

114112 Shellfish Fishing US
This U.S. industry comprises establishments primarily engaged in the commercial catching or taking of shellfish (e.g., clams, crabs, lobsters, mussels, oysters, sea urchins, shrimp) from their natural habitat.

- Establishments primarily engaged in farm raising shellfish are classified in U.S. Industry 112512, Shellfish Farming.

114119 Other Marine Fishing US
This U.S. industry comprises establishments primarily engaged in the commercial catching or taking of marine animals (except finfish and shellfish).

- Raising animal aquaculture (except finfish and shellfish) are classified in U.S. Industry 112519, Other Animal Aquaculture;
- The commercial catching or taking of finfish from their natural habitat are classified in U.S. Industry 114111, Finfish Fishing; and
- The commercial catching or taking of shellfish from their natural habitat are classified in U.S. Industry 114112, Shellfish Fishing.

1142 Hunting and Trapping

11421 Hunting and Trapping
See industry description for 114210 below.

Sector **11**

Agriculture, Forestry,
Fishing, and Hunting

■ = Cross-References

US—United States industry only. CAN—United States and Canadian industries are comparable. When neither US nor CAN appears, Canadian, Mexican, and United States industries are comparable.

114210 Hunting and Trapping

This industry comprises establishments primarily engaged in one or more of the following: (1) commercial hunting and trapping; (2) operating commercial game preserves, such as game retreats; and (3) operating hunting preserves.

- Operating nature preserves are classified in Industry 712190, Nature Parks and Other Similar Institutions; and
- Farm raising rabbits and other fur-bearing animals are classified in Industry 112930, Fur-bearing Animal and Rabbit Production.

▶115 SUPPORT ACTIVITIES FOR AGRICULTURE AND FORESTRY

Industries in the Support Activities for Agriculture and Forestry subsector provide support services that are an essential part of agricultural and forestry production. These support activities may be performed by the agriculture or forestry producing establishment or conducted independently as an alternative source of inputs required for the production process for a given crop, animal, or forestry industry. Establishments that primarily perform these activities independent of the agriculture or forestry-producing establishment are in this subsector.

1151 Support Activities for Crop Production

11511 Support Activities for Crop Production

This industry comprises establishments primarily engaged in providing support activities for growing crops.

- Performing crop production that are generally known as farms, orchards, groves, or vineyards (including sharecroppers and tenant farms), are classified in the appropriate crop industry within Subsector 111, Crop Production;
- Providing support activities for forestry are classified in Industry 11531, Support Activities for Forestry;
- Landscaping and horticultural services, such as lawn and maintenance care and ornamental shrub and tree services, are classified in Industry 56173, Landscaping Services;
- Land clearing, land leveling, and earth moving for terracing, ponds, and irrigation are classified in Industry 23499, All Other Heavy Construction;
- Artificially drying and dehydrating fruits and vegetables are classified in Industry 31142, Fruit and Vegetable Canning, Pickling and Drying;
- Stemming and redrying tobacco are classified in Industry 31221, Tobacco Stemming and Redrying;
- Providing water for irrigation are classified in Industry 22131, Water Supply and Irrigation Systems; and
- Buying farm products, such as fruits or vegetables, for resale to other wholesalers or retailers, and preparing them for market or further processing are classified in Industry 42248, Fresh Fruit and Vegetable Wholesalers.

115111 Cotton Ginning ᵁˢ

This U.S. industry comprises establishments primarily engaged in ginning cotton.

115112 Soil Preparation, Planting, and Cultivating ᵁˢ

This U.S. industry comprises establishments primarily engaged in performing a soil preparation activity or crop production service, such as plowing, fertilizing, seedbed preparation, planting, cultivating, and crop protecting services.

- Land clearing, land leveling, and earth moving for terracing, ponds, and irrigation are classified in Industry 234990, All Other Heavy Construction; and
- Providing water for irrigation are classified in Industry 221310, Water Supply and Irrigation Systems.

115113 Crop Harvesting, Primarily by Machine ᵁˢ

This U.S. industry comprises establishments primarily engaged in mechanical harvesting, picking, and combining of crops, and related activities. The servicing establishment provides the machinery used.

- Providing personnel for manual harvesting are classified in U.S. Industry 115115, Farm Labor Contractors and Crew Leaders; and
- Providing farm management services (i.e., a contract or fee basis) and arranging or contracting crop mechanical or manual harvesting operations for the farm(s) it manages are classified in U.S. Industry 115116, Farm Management Services.

115114 Post-harvest Crop Activities (except Cotton Ginning) ᵁˢ

This U.S. industry comprises establishments primarily engaged in performing services on crops, subsequent to their harvest, with the intent of preparing them for market or further processing. These establishments provide post-harvest activities, such as crop cleaning, sun drying, shelling, fumigating, curing, sorting, grading, packing, and cooling.

Sector 11

Agriculture, Forestry, Fishing, and Hunting

US—United States industry only. CAN—United States and Canadian industries are comparable. When neither US nor CAN appears, Canadian, Mexican, and United States industries are comparable.

- Ginning cotton are classified in U.S. Industry 115111, Cotton Ginning;
- Artificially drying and dehydrating fruits and vegetables are classified in U.S. Industry 311423, Dried and Dehydrated Food Manufacturing;
- Stemming and re drying tobacco are classified in Industry 312210, Tobacco Stemming and Redrying,
- Buying farm products for resale to other wholesalers or retailers and preparing them for market or further processing are classified in Industry 422480, Fresh Fruit and Vegetable Wholesalers; and
- Providing farm management services (i.e., a contract or fee basis) and arranging or contracting post-harvesting crop activities for the farm(s) it manages are classified in U.S. Industry 115116, Farm Management Services.

115115 Farm Labor Contractors and Crew Leaders US

This U.S. industry comprises establishments primarily engaged in supplying labor for agricultural production or harvesting.

- Providing machine harvesting are classified in U.S. Industry 115113, Crop Harvesting, Primarily by Machine; and
- Providing farm management services (i.e., a contract or fee basis) and arranging or contracting farm labor for the farm(s) it manages are classified in U.S. Industry 115116, Farm Management Services.

115116 Farm Management Services US

This U.S. industry comprises establishments primarily engaged in providing farm management services on a contract or fee basis usually to citrus groves, orchards, or vineyards. These establishments always provide management and may arrange or contract for the partial or the complete operations of the farm establishment(s) it manages. Operational activities may include cultivating, harvesting, and/or other specialized agricultural support activities.

- Establishments primarily engaged in crop production that are generally known as farms, orchards, groves, or vineyards (including share croppers and tenant farms), are classified in the appropriate crop industry within Subsector 111, Crop Production.

1152 Support Activities for Animal Production

11521 Support Activities for Animal Production
See industry description for 115210 below.

115210 Support Activities for Animal Production
This industry comprises establishments primarily engaged in performing support activities related to raising livestock (e.g., cattle, goats, hogs, horses, poultry, sheep). These establishments may perform one or more of the following: (1) breeding services for animals, including companion animals (e.g., cats, dogs, pet birds); (2) pedigree record services; (3) boarding horses; (4) dairy herd improvement activities; (5) livestock spraying; and (6) sheep dipping and shearing.

1153 Support Activities for Forestry

11531 Support Activities for Forestry
See industry description for 115310 below.

115310 Support Activities for Forestry
This industry comprises establishments primarily engaged in performing particular support activities related to timber production, wood technology, forestry economics and marketing, and forest protection. These establishments may provide support activities for forestry, such as estimating timber, forest fire fighting, forest pest control, and consulting on wood attributes and reforestation.

- Establishments primarily engaged in the public administration and conservation of forestlands are classified in Industry 924120, Administration of Conservation Programs.

Sector 11

Agriculture, Forestry, Fishing, and Hunting

■ = Cross-References

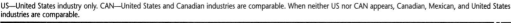
US—United States industry only. CAN—United States and Canadian industries are comparable. When neither US nor CAN appears, Canadian, Mexican, and United States industries are comparable.

www.harrisinfo.com 289

NAICS United States Structure

Sector	Name	Sub-sectors	Industry groups	NAICS 5-digit industries	U.S. 6-digit industries	TOTAL U.S. industries	New industries
11	Agriculture, Forestry, Fishing and, Hunting	5	19	42	32	64	20
21	Mining	3	5	10	28	29	—
22	Utilities	1	3	6	6	10	6
23	Construction	3	14	28	—	28	3
31–33	Manufacturing	21	84	184	408	474	79
42	Wholesale Trade	2	18	69	—	69	—
44–45	Retail Trade	12	27	61	18	72	17
48-49	Transportation and Warehousing	11	29	42	25	57	28
51	Information	4	9	28	12	34	20
52	Finance and Insurance	5	11	32	15	42	23
53	Real Estate and Rental and Leasing	3	8	19	9	24	15
54	Professional, Scientific, and Technical Services	1	9	35	17	47	28
55	Management of Companies and Enterprises	1	1	1	3	3	1
56	Administrative and Support and Waste Management and Remediation Services	2	11	29	23	43	29
61	Educational Services	1	7	12	7	17	12
62	Health Care and Social Assistance	4	18	30	16	39	27
71	Arts, Entertainment, and Recreation	3	9	23	3	25	19
72	Accommodation and Food Services	2	7	11	7	15	10
81	Other Services (except Public Administration)	4	14	30	30	49	19
92	Public Administration	8	8	29	—	29	2
	TOTAL	96	311	721	659	1170	358

To learn more about the changes by sector go to pages 15-18.

Sector 11

Agriculture, Forestry, Fishing, and Hunting

Sector 21 Mining

The Sector as a Whole

THE MINING sector comprises establishments that extract naturally occurring mineral solids, such as coal and ores; liquid minerals, such as crude petroleum; and gases, such as natural gas. The term mining is used in the broad sense to include quarrying, well operations, beneficiating (e.g., crushing, screening, washing, and flotation), and other preparation customarily performed at the mine site, or as a part of mining activity.

The Mining sector distinguishes two basic activities: mine operation and mining support activities. Mine operation includes establishments operating mines, quarries, or oil and gas wells on their own account or for others on a contract or fee basis. Mining support activities include establishments that perform exploration (except geophysical surveying) and/or other mining services on a contract or fee basis.

Establishments in the Mining sector are grouped and classified according to the natural resource mined or to be mined. Industries include establishments that develop the mine site, extract the natural resources, and/or those that beneficiate (i.e., prepare) the mineral mined. Beneficiation is the process whereby the extracted material is reduced to particles that can be separated into mineral and waste, the former suitable for further processing or direct use. The operations that take place in beneficiation are primarily mechanical, such as grinding, washing, magnetic separation, and centrifugal separation. In contrast, manufacturing operations primarily use chemical and electrochemical processes, such as electrolysis and distillation. However some treatments, such as heat treatments, take place in both the beneficiation and the manufacturing (i.e., smelting/refining) stages. The range of preparation activities varies by mineral and the purity of any given ore deposit. While some minerals, such as petroleum and natural gas, require little or no preparation, others are washed and screened, while yet others, such as gold and silver, can be transformed into bullion before leaving the mine site.

Mining, beneficiating, and manufacturing activities often occur in a single location. Separate receipts will be collected for these activities whenever possible. When receipts cannot be broken out between mining and manufacturing, establishments that mine or quarry nonmetallic minerals, beneficiate the nonmetallic minerals into more finished manufactured products are classified based on the primary activity of the establishment. A mine that manufactures a small amount of finished products will be classified in Sector 21, Mining. An establishment that mines whose primary output is a more finished manufactured product will be classified in Sector 31-33, Manufacturing.

▶211 OIL AND GAS EXTRACTION

Industries in the Oil and Gas Extraction subsector operate and/or develop oil and gas field properties. Such activities may include exploration for crude petroleum and natural gas; drilling, completing, and equipping wells; operating separators, emulsion breakers, desilting equipment, and field gathering lines for crude petroleum; and all other activities in the preparation of oil and gas up to the point of shipment from the producing property. This subsector includes the production of crude petroleum, the mining and extraction of oil from oil shale and oil sands, and the production of natural gas and recovery of hydrocarbon liquids.

Establishments in this subsector include those that operate oil and gas wells on their own account or for others on a contract or fee basis. Establishments primarily engaged in providing support services, on a fee or contract basis, required for the drilling or operation of oil and gas wells (except geophysical surveying and mapping) are classified in Subsector 213, Support Activities for Mining.

2111 Oil and Gas Extraction

21111 Oil and Gas Extraction

This industry comprises establishments primarily engaged in operating and/or developing oil and gas field properties and establishments primarily engaged in recovering liquid hydrocarbons from oil and gas field gases. Such activities may include exploration for crude petroleum and natural gas; drilling, completing, and equipping wells; operation of separators, emulsion breakers, desilting equipment, and field gathering lines for crude petroleum; and all other activities in the preparation of oil and gas up to the point of shipment from the producing property. This industry includes the production of crude petroleum, the mining and extraction of oil from oil shale and oil sands, the production of natural gas and the recovery of hydrocarbon liquids from oil and gas field gases. Establishments in this industry operate oil and gas wells on their own account or for others on a contract or fee basis.

- Performing oil field services for operators on a contract or fee basis are classified in Industry 21311, Support Activities for Mining;
- Manufacturing acyclic and cyclic aromatic hydrocarbons from refined petroleum or liquid hydrocarbons are classified in Industry 32511, Petrochemical Manufacturing;
- Refining crude petroleum into refined petroleum and liquid hydrocarbons are classified in Industry 32411, Petroleum Refineries; and
- Recovering helium from natural gas are classified in Industry 32512, Industrial Gas Manufacturing.

211111 Crude Petroleum and Natural Gas Extraction US

This U.S. industry comprises establishments primarily engaged in (1) the exploration, development and/or the production of petroleum or natural gas from wells in which the hydrocarbons will initially flow or can be produced using normal pumping techniques, or (2) the production of crude petroleum from surface shales or tar sands or from reservoirs in which the hydrocarbons are semi-solids. Establishments in this industry operate oil and gas wells on their own account or for others on a contract or fee basis.

- Performing oil field services for operators on a contract or fee basis are classified in Industry 21311, Support Activities for Mining;
- Refining crude petroleum into refined petroleum and liquid hydrocarbons are classified in Industry 324110, Petroleum Refineries; and
- Recovering helium from natural gas are classified in Industry 325120, Industrial Gas Manufacturing.

211112 Natural Gas Liquid Extraction US

This U.S. industry comprises establishments primarily engaged in the recovery of liquid hydrocarbons from oil and gas field gases. Establishments primarily engaged in sulfur recovery from natural gas are included in this industry.

- Establishments primarily engaged in manufacturing acyclic and cyclic aromatic hydrocarbons from refined petroleum or converting refined petroleum into liquid hydrocarbons (petrochemicals) and/or recovering liquid hydrocarbons are classified in Industry 325110, Petrochemical Manufacturing;
- Refining crude petroleum into refined petroleum and liquid hydrocarbons are classified in Industry 324110, Petroleum Refineries; and
- Recovering helium from natural gas are classified in Industry 325120, Industrial Gas Manufacturing.

➤212 MINING (EXCEPT OIL AND GAS)

Industries in the Mining (except Oil and Gas) subsector primarily engage in mining, mine site development, and beneficiating (i.e, preparing) metallic minerals and nonmetallic minerals, including coal. The term "mining" is used in the broad sense to include ore extraction, quarrying, and beneficiating (e.g., crushing, screening, washing, sizing, concentrating, and flotation), customarily done at the mine site.

Beneficiation is the process whereby the extracted material is reduced to particles which can be separated into mineral and waste, the former suitable for further processing or direct use. The operations that take place in beneficiation are primarily mechanical, such as grinding, washing, magnetic separation, centrifugal separation, and so on. In contrast, manufacturing operations primarily use chemical and electrochemical processes, such as electrolysis, distillation, and so on. However some treatments, such as heat treatments, take place in both stages: the beneficiation and the manufacturing (i.e., smelting/refining) stages. The range of preparation activities varies by mineral and the purity of any given ore deposit. While some minerals, such as petroleum and natural gas, require little or no preparation, others are washed and screened, while yet others, such as gold and silver, can be transformed into bullion before leaving the mine site.

Sector**21**

Mining

■ = Cross-References

US—United States industry only. CAN—United States and Canadian industries are comparable. When neither US nor CAN appears, Canadian, Mexican, and United States industries are comparable.

292

Harris InfoSource

Establishments in the Mining (except Oil and Gas) subsector include those that have complete responsibility for operating mines and quarries (except oil and gas wells) and those that operate mines and quarries (except oil and gas wells) for others on a contract or fee basis. Establishments primarily engaged in providing support services, on a contract or fee basis, required for the mining and quarrying of minerals are classified in Subsector 213, Support Activities for Mining.

2121 Coal Mining

21211 Coal Mining
This industry comprises establishments primarily engaged in one or more of the following: (1) mining bituminous coal, anthracite, and lignite by underground mining, auger mining, strip mining, culm bank mining, and other surface mining; (2) developing coal mine sites; and (3) beneficiating (i.e., preparing) coal (e.g., cleaning, washing, screening, and sizing coal).

- Establishments primarily engaged in manufacturing code oven products in coke oven establishments are classified in Industry 32419, Other Petroleum and Coal Products Manufacturing; and
- Manufacturing coal products in steel mills are classified in Industry 33111, Iron and Steel Mills and Ferroalloy Manufacturing.

212111 Bituminous Coal and Lignite Surface Mining ᵁˢ
This U.S. industry comprises establishments primarily engaged in one or more of the following: (1) surface mining or development of bituminous coal and lignite; (2) developing bituminous coal and lignite surface mine sites; and (3) beneficiating bituminous coal (e.g., cleaning, washing, screening, and sizing coal) whether mined on surface or underground.

- Establishments primarily engaged in manufacturing coke oven products in coke oven establishments are classified in U.S. Industry 324199, All Other Petroleum and Coal Products Manufacturing;
- Underground mining of bituminous coal are classified in U.S. Industry 212112, Bitumi-nous Coal Underground Mining; and
- Mining and/or beneficiating anthracite coal are classified in U.S. Industry 212113, Anthracite Mining.

212112 Bituminous Coal Underground Mining ᵁˢ
This U.S. industry comprises establishments primarily engaged in one or more of the following: (1) the underground mining of bituminous coal; (2) developing bituminous coal underground mine sites; and (3) the underground mining and beneficiating bituminous coal (e.g, cleaning, washing, screening, and sizing coal).

- Manufacturing coke oven products in coke oven establishments are classified in U.S. Industry 324199, All Other Petroleum and Coal Products Manufacturing;
- Surface mining and/or beneficiating of bituminous coal or lignite are classified in U.S. Industry 212111, Bituminous Coal and Lignite Surface Mining; and
- Mining and/or beneficiating anthracite coal are classified in U.S. Industry 212113, Anthracite Mining.

212113 Anthracite Mining ᵁˢ
This U.S. industry comprises establishments primarily engaged in one or more of the following: (1) mining anthracite coal; (2) developing anthracite coal mining sites; and (3) beneficiating anthracite coal (e.g., cleaning, washing, screening, and sizing coal).

- Manufacturing coke oven products in coke oven establishments are classified in U.S. Industry 324199, All Other Petroleum and Coal Products Manufacturing;
- Surface mining and/or beneficiating bituminous coal or lignite are classified in U.S. Industry 212111, Bituminous Coal and Lignite Surface Mining; and
- Underground mining of bituminous coal are classified in U.S. Industry 212112, Bituminous Coal Underground Mining.

2122 Metal Ore Mining
This industry group comprises establishments primarily engaged in developing mine sites or mining metallic minerals, and establishments primarily engaged in ore dressing and beneficiating (i.e., preparing) operations, such as crushing, grinding, washing, drying, sintering, concentrating, calcining, and leaching. Beneficiating may be performed at mills operated in conjunction with the mines served or at mills, such as custom mills, operated separately.

21221 Iron Ore Mining
See industry description for 212210 below.

Sector **21**

Mining

■ = Cross-References

US—United States industry only. CAN—United States and Canadian industries are comparable. When neither US nor CAN appears, Canadian, Mexican, and United States industries are comparable.

www.harrisinfo.com

293

212210 Iron Ore Mining

This industry comprises establishments primarily engaged in (1) developing mine sites, mining, and/or beneficiating (i.e., preparing) iron ores and manganiferous ores valued chiefly for their iron content and/or (2) producing sinter iron ore (except iron ore produced in iron and steel mills) and other iron ore agglomerates.

■ Establishments primarily engaged in manufacturing pig iron ore are classified in U.S. Industry331111, Iron and Steel Mills

21222 Gold Ore and Silver Ore Mining

This industry comprises establishments primarily engaged in developing the mine site, mining, and/or beneficiating (i.e., preparing) ores valued chiefly for their gold and or silver content. Establishments primarily engaged in the transformation of the gold and silver into bullion or dore bar in combination with mining activities are included in this industry.

■ Establishments primarily engaged in manufacturing gold or silver bullion or dore bar without mining are classified in Industry 33141, Nonferrous Metal (except Aluminum) Smelting and Refining.

212221 Gold Ore Mining ᵁˢ

This U.S. industry comprises establishments primarily engaged in developing the mine site, mining, and/or beneficiating (i.e., preparing) ores valued chiefly for their gold content. Establishments primarily engaged in transformation of the gold into bullion or dore bar in combination with mining activities are included in this industry.

■ Establishments primarily engaged in manufacturing gold bullion or dore bar without mining are classified in U.S. Industry 331419, Primary Smelting and Refining of Nonferrous Metal (except Copper and Aluminum).

212222 Silver Ore Mining ᵁˢ

This U.S. industry comprises establishments primarily engaged in developing the mine site, mining, and/or beneficiating (i.e, preparing) ores valued chiefly for their silver content. Establishments primarily engaged in transformation of the silver into bullion or dore bar in combination with mining activities are included in this industry.

■ Establishments primarily engaged in manufacturing silver bullion or dore bar without mining are classified in U.S. Industry 331419, Primary Smelting and Refining of Nonferrous Metal (except Copper and Aluminum).

21223 Copper, Nickel, Lead, and Zinc Mining

This industry comprises establishments primarily engaged in developing the mine site, mining, and/or beneficiating (i.e., preparing) ores valued chiefly for their copper, nickel, lead, or zinc content. Beneficiating includes the transformation of ores into concentrates.

■ Refining copper concentrates are classified in Industry 33141, Nonferrous Metal (except Aluminum) Smelting and Refining; and
■ Developing the mine site, mining, and/or beneficiating iron and manganiferous ores valued for their iron content are classified in Industry 21221, Iron Ore Mining.

212231 Lead Ore and Zinc Ore Mining ᶜᴬᴺ

This U.S. industry comprises establishments primarily engaged in developing the mine site, mining, and/or beneficiating (i.e., preparing) lead ores, zinc ores, or lead-zinc ores.

212234 Copper Ore and Nickel Ore Mining ᵁˢ

This U.S. industry comprises establishments primarily engaged in (1) developing the mine site, mining, and/or beneficiating (i.e, preparing) copper and/or nickel ores, and (2) recovering copper concentrates by the precipitation, leaching, or electrowinning of copper ore.

■ Establishments primarily engaged in refining copper concentrates are classified in U.S. Industry 331411, Primary Smelting and Refining of Copper.

21229 Other Metal Ore Mining

This industry comprises establishments primarily engaged in developing the mine site, mining, and/or beneficiating (i.e., preparing) metal ores (except iron and manganiferous ores valued for their iron content, gold ore, silver ore, copper, nickel, lead, and zinc ore).

■ Developing the mine site, mining, and/or beneficiating iron and manganiferous ores valued chiefly for their iron content are classified in Industry 21221, Iron Ore Mining;

Sector **21**

Mining

■ = Cross-References

US—United States industry only. CAN—United States and Canadian industries are comparable. When neither US nor CAN appears, Canadian, Mexican, and United States industries are comparable.

294

Harris InfoSource

■ Developing the mine site, mining, and/or beneficiating ores valued chiefly for their gold or silver content are classified in Industry 21222, Gold Ore and Silver Ore Mining;
■ Developing the mine site, mining, and/or beneficiating ores valued chiefly for their copper, nickel, lead, or zinc content are classified in Industry 21223, Copper, Nickel, Lead, and Zinc Mining; and Enriching uranium are classified in Industry 32518, Other Basic Inorganic Chemical Manufacturing.

212291 Uranium-Radium-Vanadium Ore Mining ᵁˢ

This U.S. industry comprises establishments primarily engaged in developing the mine site, mining, and/or beneficiating (i.e., preparing) uranium-radium-vanadium ores.

■ Establishments primarily engaged in enriching uranium are classified in U.S. Industry 325188, All Other Basic Inorganic Chemical Manufacturing.

212299 All Other Metal Ore Mining ᵁˢ

This U.S. industry comprises establishments primarily engaged in developing the mine site, mining, and/or beneficiating (i.e., preparing) metal ores (except iron and manganiferous ores valued for their iron content, gold ore, silver ore, copper, nickel, lead, zinc, and uranium-radium-vanadium ore).

■ Developing the mine site, mining, and/or beneficiating iron and manganiferous ores valued for their iron content are classified in Industry 212210, Iron Ore Mining;
■ Developing the mine site, mining, and/or beneficiating ores valued chiefly for their gold or silver content are classified in Industry 21222, Gold Ore and Silver Ore Mining;
■ Developing the mine site, mining, and/or beneficiating ores valued chiefly for their copper, nickel, lead, or zinc content are classified in Industry 21223, Copper, Nickel, Lead, and Zinc Mining; and
■ Developing the mine site, mining, and/or beneficiating uranium-radium-vanadium ores are classified in U.S. Industry 212291, Uranium-Radium-Vanadium Ore Mining.

2123 Nonmetallic Mineral Mining and Quarrying

This industry group comprises establishments primarily engaged in developing mine sites, or in mining or quarrying nonmetallic minerals (except fuels). Also included are certain well and brine operations, and preparation plants primarily engaged in beneficiating (e.g., crushing, grinding, washing, and concentrating) nonmetallic minerals.

Beneficiation is the process whereby the extracted material is reduced to particles which can be separated into mineral and waste, the former suitable for further processing or direct use. The operations that take place in beneficiation are primarily mechanical, such as grinding, washing, magnetic separation, and centrifugal separation. In contrast, manufacturing operations primarily use chemical and electrochemical processes, such as electrolysis and distillation. However some treatments, such as heat treatments, take place in both the beneficiation and the manufacturing (i.e., smelting/refining) stages. The range of preparation activities varies by mineral and the purity of any given ore deposit. While some minerals, such as petroleum and natural gas, require little or no preparation, others are washed and screened, while yet others, such as gold and silver, can be transformed into bullion before leaving the mine site.

21231 Stone Mining and Quarrying

This industry comprises (1) establishments primarily engaged in developing the mine site, mining or quarrying dimension stone (i.e., rough blocks and/or slabs of stone), or mining and quarrying crushed and broken stone and/or (2) preparation plants primarily engaged in beneficiating stone (e.g., crushing, grinding, washing, screening, pulverizing, and sizing).

■ Producing lime are classified in Industry 32741, Lime Manufacturing; and
■ Quarrying and dressing dimension stone are classified Industry 32799, All Other Nonmetallic Mineral Product Manufacturing.

212311 Dimension Stone Mining and Quarrying ᵁˢ

This U.S. industry comprises establishments primarily engaged in developing the mine site and/or mining or quarrying dimension stone (i.e., rough blocks and/or slabs of stone).

■ Establishments primarily engaged in dressing dimension stone and manufacturing stone products are classified in U.S. Industry 327991, Cut Stone and Stone Product Manufacturing.

212312 Crushed and Broken Limestone Mining and Quarrying ᵁˢ

This U.S. industry comprises (1) establishments primarily engaged in developing the mine site,

Sector **21**

Mining

■ = Cross-References

US—United States industry only. CAN—United States and Canadian industries are comparable. When neither US nor CAN appears, Canadian, Mexican, and United States industries are comparable.

www.harrisinfo.com

295

mining or quarrying crushed and broken limestone (including related rocks, such as dolomite, cement rock, marl, travertine, and calcareous tufa), and (2) preparation plants primarily engaged in beneficiating limestone (e.g., grinding or pulverizing).

■ Producing lime are classified in Industry 327410, Lime Manufacturing; and Mining or quarrying bituminous limestone are classified U.S. Industry 212319, Other Crushed and Broken Stone Mining and Quarrying.

212313 Crushed and Broken Granite Mining and Quarrying US

This U.S. industry comprises (1) establishments primarily engaged in developing the mine site, and/or mining or quarrying crushed and broken granite (including related rocks, such as gneiss, syenite, and diorite) and (2) preparation plants primarily engaged in beneficiating granite (e.g. grinding or pulverizing).

212319 Other Crushed and Broken Stone Mining and Quarrying US

This U.S. industry comprises (1) establishments primarily engaged in developing the mine site and/or mining or quarrying crushed and broken stone (except limestone and granite), (2) preparation plants primarily engaged in beneficiating (e.g., grinding and pulverizing) stone (except limestone and granite), and (3) establishments primarily engaged in mining or quarrying bituminous limestone and bituminous sandstone.

■ Mining or quarrying crushed and broken limestone are classified in U.S. Industry 212312, Crushed and Broken Limestone Mining and Quarrying; and
■ Mining or quarrying crushed and broken granite are classified in U.S. Industry 212313, Crushed and Broken Granite Mining and Quarrying.

21232 Sand, Gravel, Clay, and Ceramic and Refractory Minerals Mining and Quarrying

This industry comprises (1) establishments primarily engaged in developing the mine site and/or mining, quarrying, dredging for sand and gravel, or mining clay, (e.g., china clay, paper clay and slip clay) and (2) preparation plants primarily engaged in beneficiating (e.g., washing, screening, and grinding) sand and gravel, clay, and ceramic and refractory minerals.

■ Calcining, dead burning, or otherwise processing (i.e., beyond basic preparation) clay or refractory minerals are classified in Industry 32799, All Other Nonmetallic Mineral Product Manufacturing;
■ Shaping, molding, baking, burning, or hardening nonclay ceramics, clay and nonclay refractories, and structural clay products are classified in Industry 32712, Clay Building Material and Refractories Manufacturing; and
■ Shaping, molding, glazing, and firing pottery, ceramics, and plumbing fixtures are classified in Industry 32711, Pottery, Ceramics and Plumbing Fixture Manufacturing.

212321 Construction Sand and Gravel Mining US

This U.S. industry comprises establishments primarily engaged in one or more of the following: (1) operating commercial grade (i.e., construction) sand and gravel pits; (2) dredging for commercial grade sand and gravel; and (3) washing, screening, or otherwise preparing commercial grade sand and gravel.

■ Establishments primarily engaged in mining industrial grade sand are classified in U.S. Industry 212322, Industrial Sand Mining.

212322 Industrial Sand Mining US

This U.S. industry comprises establishments primarily engaged in one or more of the following: (1) operating industrial grade sand pits; (2) dredging for industrial grade sand; and (3) washing, screening, or otherwise preparing industrial grade sand.

■ Establishments primarily engaged in mining commercial (i.e., construction) grade gravel are classified in U.S. Industry 212321, Construction Sand and Gravel Mining.

212324 Kaolin and Ball Clay Mining US

This U.S. industry comprises (1) establishments primarily engaged in developing the mine site and/or mining kaolin or ball clay (e.g., china clay, paper clay, and slip clay) and (2) establishments primarily engaged in beneficiating (i.e., preparing) kaolin or ball clay.

■ Establishments primarily engaged in calcining, dead burning, or otherwise processing (i.e., beyond basic preparation) kaolin and ball clay are classified in U.S. Industry 327992, Ground or Treated Mineral and Earth Manufacturing.

212325 Clay and Ceramic and Refractory Minerals Mining US

This U.S. industry comprises establishments primarily engaged in one or more of the following: (1) mining clay (except kaolin and ball), ceramic, or refractory minerals; (2) developing the mine site

Sector **21**

Mining

■ = Cross-References

US—United States industry only. CAN—United States and Canadian industries are comparable. When neither US nor CAN appears, Canadian, Mexican, and United States industries are comparable.

296

Harris InfoSource

for clay, ceramic, or refractory minerals; and (3) beneficiating (i.e., preparing) clay (except kaolin and ball), ceramic, or refractory minerals.

- Shaping, molding, baking, burning, or hardening clay and nonclay refractories, and structural clay products are classified in Industry 32712, Clay Building Material and Refractories Manufacturing;
- Developing the mine site, mining, and/or beneficiating kaolin or ball clay are classified in U.S. Industry 212324, Kaolin and Ball Clay Mining; and
- Shaping, molding, glazing, and firing pottery, ceramics, and plumbing fixtures are classified in Industry 32711, Pottery, Ceramics and Plumbing Fixture Manufacturing.

21239 Other Nonmetallic Mineral Mining and Quarrying

This industry comprises establishments primarily engaged in developing the mine site, mining, and/or milling or otherwise beneficiating (i.e., preparing) nonmetallic minerals (except coal, stone, sand, gravel, clay, ceramic, and refractory minerals).

- Mining or quarrying dimension stone are classified in Industry 21231, Stone Mining and Quarrying;
- Mining or quarrying sand, gravel, clay and ceramic and refractory minerals are classified in Industry 21232, Sand, Gravel, Clay, and Ceramic and Refractory Minerals Mining and Quarrying;
- Calcining, dead burning, or otherwise processing (i.e., beyond basic preparation) minerals, such as talc, mica, feldspar, barite, and soapstone, are classified in Industry 32799, All Other Nonmetallic Mineral Product Manufacturing;
- Manufacturing boron compounds and potassium salts are classified in Industry 32518, Other Basic Inorganic Chemical Manufacturing;
- Manufacturing table salt are classified in Industry 31194, Seasoning and Dressing Manufacturing; Manufacturing salt (except table salt) are classified in Industry 32599, All Other Chemical Product and Preparation Manufacturing; and
- Manufacturing phosphoric acid, superphosphates, or other phosphatic fertilizer materials are classified in Industry 32531, Fertilizer Manufacturing.

212391 Potash, Soda, and Borate Mineral Mining US

This U.S. industry comprises establishments primarily engaged in developing the mine site, mining and/or milling, or otherwise beneficiating (i.e., preparing) natural potassium, sodium, or boron compounds. Drylake brine operations are included in this industry, as well as establishments engaged in producing the specified minerals from underground and open pit mines.

- Manufacturing boron compounds and potassium salts are classified in U.S. Industry 325188, All Other Basic Inorganic Chemical Manufacturing;
- Manufacturing sodium carbonate are classified in U.S. Industry 325181, Alkalies and Chlorine Manufacturing; and
- Manufacturing table salt are classified in U.S. Industry 311942, Spice and Extract Manufacturing.

212392 Phosphate Rock Mining US

This U.S. industry comprises establishments primarily engaged in developing the mine site, mining, milling, and/or drying or otherwise beneficiating (i.e., preparing) phosphate rock.

- Establishments primarily engaged in manufacturing phosphoric acid, superphosphates, or other phosphatic fertilizer materials are classified in U.S. Industry 325312, Phosphatic Fertilizer Manufacturing.

212393 Other Chemical and Fertilizer Mineral Mining US

This U.S. industry comprises establishments primarily engaged in developing the mine site, mining, milling, and/or drying or otherwise beneficiating (i.e., preparing) chemical or fertilizer mineral raw materials (except potash, soda, boron, and phosphate rock).

- Mining and/or milling or otherwise beneficiating natural potassium, sodium, or boron compounds are classified in U.S. Industry 212391, Potash, Soda, and Borate Mineral Mining;
- Manufacturing industrial salt are classified in U.S. Industry 325998, All Other Miscellaneous Chemical Product and Preparation Manufacturing;
- Mining, milling, drying, and/or sintering or otherwise beneficiating phosphate rock are classified in U.S. Industry 212392, Phosphate Rock Mining; and
- Manufacturing table salt are classified in U.S. Industry 311942, Spice and Extract Manufacturing.

212399 All Other Nonmetallic Mineral Mining US

This U.S. industry comprises establishments primarily engaged in developing the mine site, mining and/or milling or otherwise beneficiating (i.e., preparing) nonmetallic minerals (except stone, sand, gravel, clay, ceramic, refractory minerals, chemical and fertilizer minerals).

- Mining or quarrying dimension stone are classified in Industry 21231, Stone Mining and Quarrying;
- Mining, quarrying, or beneficiating sand, gravel, clay, and ceramic and refractory minerals are classified in Industry 21232, Sand, Gravel, Clay, and Ceramic and Refractory Minerals Mining and Quarrying;

Sector **21**

Mining

■ = Cross-References

US—United States industry only. CAN—United States and Canadian industries are comparable. When neither US nor CAN appears, Canadian, Mexican, and United States industries are comparable.

www.harrisinfo.com

297

- Mining, quarrying or beneficiating natural potash, soda, and borate are classified in U.S. Industry 212391, Potash, Soda, and Borate Mineral Mining; and
- Mining and/or milling or otherwise beneficiating phosphate rock are classified in U.S. Industry 212392, Phosphate Rock Mining.

▶213 SUPPORT ACTIVITIES FOR MINING

Industries in the Support Activities for Mining subsector group establishments primarily providing support services, on a fee or contract basis, required for the mining and quarrying of minerals and for the extraction of oil and gas. Establishments performing exploration (except geophysical surveying and mapping) for minerals, on a contract or fee basis, are included in this subsector. Exploration includes traditional prospecting methods, such as taking core samples and making geological observations at prospective sites.

The activities performed on a fee or contract basis by establishments in the Support Activities for Mining subsector are also often performed in-house by mining operators. These activities include: taking core samples, making geological observations at prospective sites, and such oil and gas operations as spudding in, drilling in, redrilling, directional drilling, excavating slush pits and cellars; grading and building foundations at well locations; well surveying; running, cutting, and pulling casings, tubes and rods; cementing wells; shooting wells; perforating well casings; acidizing and chemically treating wells; and cleaning out, bailing, and swabbing wells.

2131 Support Activities for Mining

21311 Support Activities for Mining

This industry comprises establishments primarily engaged in providing support services, on a fee or contract basis, required for the mining and quarrying of minerals and for the extraction of oil and gas. Drilling, taking core samples, and making geological observations at prospective sites (except geophysical surveying and mapping) for minerals, on a fee or contract basis, is included in this industry.

- Performing geophysical surveying services for minerals (i.e., coal, metal ores, oil and gas, and nonmetallic minerals) on a contract or fee basis are classified in Industry 54136, Geophysical Surveying and Mapping Services;
- Mining, quarrying, and/or beneficiating on a contract or fee basis are classified in Subsector 212, Mining (except Oil and Gas) based on the mineral mined; and
- Operating oil and gas field properties on a contract or fee basis are classified in Subsector 211, Oil and Gas Extraction based on the activity.

213111 Drilling Oil and Gas Wells CAN

This U.S. industry comprises establishments primarily engaged in drilling oil and gas wells for others on a contract or fee basis. This industry includes contractors that specialize in spudding in, drilling in, redrilling, and directional drilling.

- Performing exploration (except geophysical surveying and mapping) services for oil and gas on a contract or fee basis are classified in U.S. Industry 213112, Support Activities for Oil and Gas Operations; and
- Performing geophysical surveying and mapping services for oil and gas on a contract or fee basis are classified in Industry 541360, Geophysical Surveying and Mapping Services.

213112 Support Activities for Oil and Gas Operations US

This U.S. industry comprises establishments primarily engaged in performing oil and gas field services (except contract drilling) for others, on a contract or fee basis. Services included are exploration (except geophysical surveying and mapping); excavating slush pits and cellars; grading and building foundations at well locations; well surveying; running, cutting, and pulling casings, tubes, and rods; cementing wells; shooting wells; perforating well casings; acidizing and chemically treating wells; and cleaning out, bailing, and swabbing wells.

- Contract drilling for oil and gas are classified in U.S. Industry 213111, Drilling Oil and Gas Wells;
- Operating oil and gas field properties on a contract or fee basis are classified in Subsector 211, Oil and Gas Extraction, based on the activity; and
- Performing geophysical surveying and mapping services for oil and gas on a contract or fee basis are classified in Industry 541360, Geophysical Surveying and Mapping Services.

Sector **21**

Mining

■ = Cross-References

US—United States industry only. CAN—United States and Canadian industries are comparable. When neither US nor CAN appears, Canadian, Mexican, and United States industries are comparable.

298

Harris InfoSource

213113 Support Activities for Coal Mining ᵁˢ

This U.S. industry comprises establishments primarily engaged in providing support services, on a fee or contract basis, required for coal mining. Exploration for coal is included in this industry. Exploration includes traditional prospecting methods, such as taking core samples and making geological observations at prospective sites.

- Performing geophysical surveying services for coal on a contract or fee basis are classified in Industry 541360, Geophysical Surveying and Mapping Services; and
- Operating coal mines or quarries on a contract or fee basis are classified in Industry Group 2121, Coal Mining, based on the type of coal mined.

213114 Support Activities for Metal Mining ᵁˢ

This U.S. industry comprises establishments primarily engaged in providing support services, on a fee or contract basis, required for the mining and quarrying of metallic minerals and for the extraction of metal ores. Exploration for minerals is included in this industry. Exploration (except geophysical surveying and mapping services) includes traditional prospecting methods, such as taking core samples and making geological observations at prospective sites.

- Performing geophysical surveying services for metallic minerals on a contract or fee basis are classified in Industry 541360, Geophysical Surveying and Mapping Services; and
- Operating metallic mineral mines or quarries on a contract or fee basis are classified in Industry Group 2122, Metal Ore Mining, based on the type of ore mined.

213115 Support Activities for Nonmetallic Minerals (except Fuels)ᵁˢ

This U.S. industry comprises establishments primarily engaged in providing support services, on a fee or contract basis, required for the mining and quarrying of nonmetallic minerals and for the extraction of nonmetallic minerals. Exploration for minerals is included in this industry. Exploration (except geophysical surveying and mapping services) includes traditional prospecting methods, such as taking core samples and making geological observations at prospective sites.

- Performing geophysical survey services for nonmetallic minerals on a contract or fee basis are classified in Industry 541360, Geophysical Surveying and Mapping Services; and
- Operating nonmetallic mineral mines or quarries on a contract or fee basis are classified in Industry Group 2123, Nonmetallic Mineral Mining and Quarrying, based on the type of mineral mined or quarried.

Sector **21**

Mining

■ = Cross-References

US—United States industry only. CAN—United States and Canadian industries are comparable. When neither US nor CAN appears, Canadian, Mexican, and United States industries are comparable.

www.harrisinfo.com

299

NAICS United States Structure

Sector	Name	Sub-sectors	Industry groups	NAICS 5-digit industries	U.S. 6-digit industries	TOTAL U.S. industries	New industries
11	Agriculture, Forestry, Fishing and, Hunting	5	19	42	32	64	20
21	Mining	3	5	10	28	29	—
22	Utilities	1	3	6	6	10	6
23	Construction	3	14	28	—	28	3
31–33	Manufacturing	21	84	184	408	474	79
42	Wholesale Trade	2	18	69	—	69	—
44–45	Retail Trade	12	27	61	18	72	17
48-49	Transportation and Warehousing	11	29	42	25	57	28
51	Information	4	9	28	12	34	20
52	Finance and Insurance	5	11	32	15	42	23
53	Real Estate and Rental and Leasing	3	8	19	9	24	15
54	Professional, Scientific, and Technical Services	1	9	35	17	47	28
55	Management of Companies and Enterprises	1	1	1	3	3	1
56	Administrative and Support and Waste Management and Remediation Services	2	11	29	23	43	29
61	Educational Services	1	7	12	7	17	12
62	Health Care and Social Assistance	4	18	30	16	39	27
71	Arts, Entertainment, and Recreation	3	9	23	3	25	19
72	Accommodation and Food Services	2	7	11	7	15	10
81	Other Services (except Public Administration)	4	14	30	30	49	19
92	Public Administration	8	8	29	—	29	2
	TOTAL	96	311	721	659	1170	358

To learn more about the changes by sector go to pages 15-18.

Sector 21

Mining

Sector 22 Utilities

The Sector as a Whole

THE UTILITIES sector comprises establishments engaged in the provision of the following utility services: electric power, natural gas, steam supply, water supply, and sewage removal. Within this sector, the specific activities associated with the utility services provided vary by utility: electric power includes generation, transmission, and distribution; natural gas includes distribution; steam supply includes provision and/or distribution; water supply includes treatment and distribution; and sewage removal includes collection, treatment, and disposal of waste through sewer systems and sewage treatment facilities.

Excluded from this sector are establishments primarily engaged in waste management services classified in Subsector 562, Waste Management and Remediation Services. These establishments also collect, treat, and dispose of waste materials; however, they do not use sewer systems or sewage treatment facilities.

➡ 221 UTILITIES

Industries in the Utilities subsector provide electric power, natural gas, steam supply, water supply, and sewage removal through a permanent infrastructure of lines, mains, and pipes. Establishments are grouped together based on the utility service provided and the particular system or facilities required to perform the service.

2211 Electric Power Generation, Transmission and Distribution ᶜᴬᴺ

This industry group comprises establishments primarily engaged in generating, transmitting, and/or distributing electric power. Establishments in this industry group may perform one or more of the following activities: (1) operate generation facilities that produce electric energy; (2) operate transmission systems that convey the electricity from the generation facility to the distribution system; and (3) operate distribution systems that convey electric power received from the generation facility or the transmission system to the final consumer.

22111 Electric Power Generation ᶜᴬᴺ

This industry comprises establishments primarily engaged in operating electric power generation facilities. These facilities convert other forms of energy, such as water power (i.e., hydroelectric), fossil fuels, nuclear power, and solar power, into electrical energy. The establishments in this industry produce electric energy and provide electricity to transmission systems or to electric power distribution systems.

■ Establishments primarily engaged in operating trash incinerators that also generate electricity are classified in Industry 56221, Waste Treatment and Disposal.

221111 Hydroelectric Power Generation ᶜᴬᴺ

This U.S. industry comprises establishments primarily engaged in operating hydroelectric power generation facilities. These facilities use water power to drive a turbine and produce electric energy. The electric energy produced in these establishment is provided to electric power transmission systems or to electric power distribution systems.

Sector 22
Utilities

■ = Cross-References

US—United States industry only. CAN—United States and Canadian industries are comparable. When neither US nor CAN appears, Canadian, Mexican, and United States industries are comparable.

www.harrisinfo.com

301

221112 Fossil Fuel Electric Power Generation ^{CAN}

This U.S. industry comprises establishments primarily engaged in operating fossil fuel powered electric power generation facilities. These facilities use fossil fuels, such as coal, oil, or gas, in internal combustion or combustion turbine conventional steam process to produce electric energy. The electric energy produced in these establishments are provided to electric power transmission systems or to electric power distribution systems.

221113 Nuclear Electric Power Generation ^{CAN}

This U.S. industry comprises establishments primarily engaged in operating nuclear electric power generation facilities. These facilities use nuclear power to produce electric energy. The electric energy produced in these establishments are provided to electric power transmission systems or to electric power distribution systems.

221119 Other Electric Power Generation ^{CAN}

This U.S. industry comprises establishments primarily engaged in operating electric power generation facilities (except hydroelectric, fossil fuel, nuclear). These facilities convert other forms of energy, such as solar, wind, or tidal power, into electrical energy. The electric energy produced in these establishment is provided to electric power transmission systems or to electric power distribution systems.

- Operating trash disposal incinerators that also generate electricity are classified in U.S. Industry 562213, Solid Waste Combustors and Incinerators;
- Operating hydroelectric power generation facilities are classified in U.S. Industry 221111, Hydroelectric Power Generation;
- Operating fossil fuel powered electric power generation facilities are classified in U.S. Industry 221112, Fossil Fuel Electric Power Generation; and
- Operating nuclear electric power generation facilities are classified in U.S. Industry 221113, Nuclear Electric Power Generation.

22112 Electric Power Transmission, Control, and Distribution ^{CAN}

This industry comprises establishments primarily engaged in operating electric power transmission systems, controlling (i.e., regulating voltages) the transmission of electricity, and/or distributing electricity. The transmission system includes lines and transformer stations. These establishments arrange, facilitate, or coordinate the transmission of electricity from the generating source to the distribution centers, other electric utilities, or final consumers. The distribution system consists of lines, poles, meters, and wiring that deliver the electricity to final consumers.

- Establishments primarily engaged in generating electric energy are classified in Industry 22111, Electric Power Generation.

221121 Electric Bulk Power Transmission and Control ^{CAN}

This U.S. industry comprises establishments primarily engaged in operating electric power transmission systems and/or controlling (i.e., regulatory voltage) the transmission of electricity from the generating source to distribution centers or other electric utilities. The transmission system includes lines and transformer stations.

- Generating electric energy are classified in Industry 22111, Electric Power Generation; and
- Distributing electricity to final consumers are classified in U.S. Industry 221122, Electric Power Distribution.

221122 Electric Power Distribution ^{CAN}

This U.S. industry comprises electric power establishments primarily engaged in (1) operating electric power distribution systems (i.e., consisting of lines, poles, meters, and wiring) or (2) operating as electric power brokers or agents that arrange the sale of electricity via power distribution systems operated by others.

- Generating electric energy are classified in Industry 22111, Electric Power Generation; and
- Transmitting electricity between generating sources or distribution centers are classified in U.S. Industry 221121, Electric Bulk Power Transmission and Control.

2212 Natural Gas Distribution ^{CAN}

22121 Natural Gas Distribution ^{CAN}

See industry description for 221210 below.

Sector **22**

Utilities

■ = Cross-References

US—United States industry only. CAN—United States and Canadian industries are comparable. When neither US nor CAN appears, Canadian, Mexican, and United States industries are comparable.

302

Harris InfoSource

221210 Natural Gas Distribution ^{CAN}

This industry comprises: (1) establishments primarily engaged in operating gas distribution systems (e.g., mains, meters); (2) establishments known as gas marketers that buy gas from the well and sell it to a distribution system; (3) establishments known as gas brokers or agents that arrange the sale of gas over gas distribution systems operated by others; and (4) establishments primarily engaged in transmitting and distributing gas to final consumers.

■ Pipeline transportation of natural gas from process plants to local distribution systems are classified in Industry 486210, Pipeline Transportation of Natural Gas; and
■ Retailing liquified petroleum (LP) gas via direct selling are classified in U.S. Industry 454312, Liquefied Petroleum Gas (Bottled Gas) Dealers.

2213 Water, Sewage, and Other Systems ^{CAN}

22131 Water Supply and Irrigation Systems ^{CAN}

See industry description for 221310 below.

221310 Water Supply and Irrigation Systems ^{CAN}

This industry comprises establishments primarily engaged in operating water treatment plants and/or operating water supply systems. The water supply system may include pumping stations, aqueducts, and/or distribution mains. The water may be used for drinking, irrigation, or other uses.

22132 Sewage Treatment Facilities ^{CAN}

See industry description for 221320 below.

221320 Sewage Treatment Facilities ^{CAN}

This industry comprises establishments primarily engaged in operating sewer systems or sewage treatment facilities that collect, treat, and dispose of waste.

■ Operating waste treatment or disposal facilities (except sewer systems or sewage treatment facilities) are classified in Industry 56221, Waste Treatment and Disposal;
■ Pumping (i.e., cleaning) septic tanks and cesspools are classified in U.S. Industry 562991, Septic Tank and Related Services; and
■ Cleaning and rodding sewers and catch basins are classified in U.S. Industry 562998, All Other Miscellaneous Waste Management Services.

22133 Steam and Air-conditioning Supply ^{CAN}

See industry description for 221330 below.

221330 Steam and Air-conditioning Supply ^{CAN}

This industry comprises establishments primarily engaged in providing steam, heated air, or cooled air. The steam distribution may be through mains.

Sector **22**

Utilities

■ = Cross-References

US—United States industry only. CAN—United States and Canadian industries are comparable. When neither US nor CAN appears, Canadian, Mexican, and United States industries are comparable.

www.harrisinfo.com 303

NAICS United States Structure

Sector	Name	Sub-sectors	Industry groups	NAICS 5-digit industries	U.S. 6-digit industries	TOTAL U.S. industries	New industries
11	Agriculture, Forestry, Fishing and, Hunting	5	19	42	32	64	20
21	Mining	3	5	10	28	29	—
22	Utilities	1	3	6	6	10	6
23	Construction	3	14	28	—	28	3
31–33	Manufacturing	21	84	184	408	474	79
42	Wholesale Trade	2	18	69	—	69	—
44-45	Retail Trade	12	27	61	18	72	17
48-49	Transportation and Warehousing	11	29	42	25	57	28
51	Information	4	9	28	12	34	20
52	Finance and Insurance	5	11	32	15	42	23
53	Real Estate and Rental and Leasing	3	8	19	9	24	15
54	Professional, Scientific, and Technical Services	1	9	35	17	47	28
55	Management of Companies and Enterprises	1	1	1	3	3	1
56	Administrative and Support and Waste Management and Remediation Services	2	11	29	23	43	29
61	Educational Services	1	7	12	7	17	12
62	Health Care and Social Assistance	4	18	30	16	39	27
71	Arts, Entertainment, and Recreation	3	9	23	3	25	19
72	Accommodation and Food Services	2	7	11	7	15	10
81	Other Services (except Public Administration)	4	14	30	30	49	19
92	Public Administration	8	8	29	—	29	2
	TOTAL	96	311	721	659	1170	358

To learn more about the changes by sector go to pages 15-18.

Sector **22**

Utilities

Sector 23 Construction

The Sector as a Whole

The Construction sector comprises establishments primarily engaged in the construction of buildings and other structures, heavy construction (except buildings), additions, alterations, reconstruction, installation, and maintenance and repairs. Establishments engaged in demolition or wrecking of buildings and other structures, clearing of building sites, and sale of materials from demolished structures are also included. This sector also includes those establishments engaged in blasting, test drilling, landfill, leveling, earth-moving, excavating, land drainage, and other land preparation. The industries within this sector have been defined on the basis of their unique production processes. As with all industries, the production processes are distinguished by their use of specialized human resources and specialized physical capital. Construction activities are generally administered or managed at a relatively fixed place of business, but the actual construction work is performed at one or more different project sites.

This sector is divided into three subsectors of construction activities: (1) building construction and land subdivision and land development; (2) heavy construction (except buildings), such as highways, power plants, and pipelines; and (3) construction activity by special trade contractors.

Establishments classified in Subsector 233, Building, Developing, and General Contracting and Subsector 234, Heavy Construction, usually assume responsibility for an entire construction project, and may subcontract some or all of the actual construction work. Operative builders who build on their own account for sale, and land subdividers and land developers, who engage in subdividing real property into lots for sale, are included in Subsector 233, Building, Developing, and General Contracting. (Special trade contractors are included in Subsector 234, Heavy Construction, if they are engaged in activities primarily relating to heavy construction, such as grading for highways.) Establishments included in these subsectors operate as general contractors, design-builders, engineer-constructors, joint-venture contractors, and turnkey construction contractors. Establishments identified as construction management firms are also included.

Establishments classified in Subsector 235, Special Trade Contractors, are primarily engaged in specialized construction activities, such as plumbing, painting, and electrical work, and work for builders and general contractors under subcontract or directly for project owners. Establishments engaged in demolition or wrecking of buildings and other structures, dismantling of machinery, excavating, shoring and underpinning, anchored earth retention activities, foundation drilling, and grading for buildings are also included in this subsector.

"Force account" construction is construction work performed by an establishment primarily engaged in some business other than construction, for its own account and use, and by employees of the establishment. This activity is not included in this industry sector unless the construction work performed is the primary activity of a separate establishment of the enterprise.

Sector 23 Construction

The installation of prefabricated building equipment and materials, such as elevators and revolving doors, is classified in the Construction sector. Installation work incidental to sales by employees of a manufacturing or retail establishment is classified as an activity of those establishments.

➡233 BUILDING, DEVELOPING, AND GENERAL CONTRACTING ᵁˢ

Industries in the Building, Developing, and General Contracting subsector comprises establishments primarily responsible for the entire construction (i.e., new work, additions, alterations, and repair) of building projects. Builders, developers, and general contractors, as well as land subdividers and land developers are included in this subsector. Establishments identified as construction management firms for building projects are also included. The construction work may be for others and performed by custom builders, general contractors, design builders, engineer-constructors, joint-venture contractors, and turnkey contractors, or may be on their own account for sale and performed by speculative or operative builders.

2331 Land Subdivision and Land Development ᵁˢ

23311 Land Subdivision and Land Development ᵁˢ
See industry description for 233110 below.

233110 Land Subdivision and Land Development ᵁˢ
This industry comprises establishments primarily engaged in subdividing real property into lots and/or developing building lots for sale.

■ Establishments primarily engaged in constructing buildings on lots they subdivide or develop are classified in Industry Group 2332, Residential Building Construction, or Industry Group 2333, Nonresidential Building Construction, based on the type of construction project.

2332 Residential Building Construction ᵁˢ

23321 Single Family Housing Construction ᵁˢ
See industry description for 233210 below.

233210 Single Family Housing Construction ᵁˢ
This industry comprises establishments primarily responsible for the entire construction (i.e., new work, additions, alterations, and repairs) of single family residential housing units (e.g., single family detached houses, town houses, or row houses where each housing unit is separated by a ground-to-roof wall and where no housing units are constructed above or below). This industry includes establishments responsible for additions and alterations to mobile homes and on-site assembly of modular and prefabricated houses. Establishments identified as single family construction management firms are also included in this industry. Establishments in this industry may perform work for others or on their own account for sale as speculative or operative builders. Kinds of establishments include single family housing custom builders, general contractors, design builders, engineer-constructors, joint-venture contractors, and turnkey contractors.

■ Establishments primarily engaged in performing mobile home site setup and tie-down work are classified in Industry 235990, All Other Special Trade Contractors; and
■ Performing specialized construction work on single family housing units generally on a subcontract basis are classified in Subsector 235, Special Trade Contractors.

23322 Multifamily Housing Construction ᵁˢ
See industry description for 233220 below.

233220 Multifamily Housing Construction ᵁˢ
This industry comprises establishments primarily responsible for the entire construction (i.e., new work, additions, alterations, and repairs) of multifamily residential housing units (e.g., highrise, garden, and town house apartments where each unit is not separated by a ground-to-roof wall). The units may be constructed for sale as condominiums or cooperatives, or for rental as apartments. Establishments identified as multifamily construction management firms are also included in this industry. Establishments in this industry may perform work for others or on their own account for sale as speculative or operative builders. Kinds of establishments include multifamily housing general contractors, design builders, engineer-constructors, joint-venture contractors, and turnkey contractors.

Sector **23**

Construction

■ = Cross-References

US—United States industry only. CAN—United States and Canadian industries are comparable. When neither US nor CAN appears, Canadian, Mexican, and United States industries are comparable.

306

Harris InfoSource

■ Establishments primarily engaged in performing specialized construction work on multifamily housing units generally on a subcontract basis are classified in Subsector 235, Special Trade Contractors; and
■ Developing, constructing, and operating residential buildings on their own account for investment purposes are classified in Industry 531110, Lessors of Residential Buildings and Dwellings

2333 Nonresidential Building Construction US

23331 Manufacturing and Industrial Building Construction US
See industry description for 233310 below.

233310 Manufacturing and Industrial Building Construction US
This industry comprises establishments primarily responsible for the entire construction (i.e., new work, additions, alterations, and repairs) of manufacturing and industrial buildings (e.g., plants, mills, factories). Establishments identified as manufacturing and industrial building construction management firms are also included in this industry. Kinds of establishments include manufacturing and industrial building general contractors, design builders, engineer-constructors, joint-venture contractors, and turnkey contractors.

■ Establishments primarily engaged in constructing commercial and institutional buildings are classified in Industry 233320, Commercial and Institutional Building Construction;
■ Constructing heavy, nonbuilding industrial structures are classified in Industry 234930, Industrial Nonbuilding Structure Construction; and
■ Performing specialized construction work on manufacturing and industrial buildings generally on a subcontract basis are classified in Subsector 235, Special Trade Contractors.

23332 Commercial and Institutional Building Construction US
See industry description for 233320 below.

233320 Commercial and Institutional Building Construction US
This industry comprises establishments primarily responsible for the entire construction (i.e., new work, additions, alterations, and repairs) of commercial and institutional buildings (e.g., stores, schools, hospitals office buildings, public warehouses). Establishments identified as commercial and institutional building construction management firms are also included in this industry. Kinds of establishments include commercial and institutional building general contractors, design builders, engineer-constructors, joint-venture contractors, and turnkey contractors.

■ Establishments primarily engaged in performing specialized construction work on commercial and institutional buildings generally on a subcontract basis are classified in Subsector 235, Special Trade Contractors; and
■ Constructing manufacturing and industrial buildings are classified in Industry 233310, Manufacturing and Industrial Building Construction.

▶234 HEAVY CONSTRUCTION US
Industries in the Heavy Construction subsector group establishments that engage in the construction of heavy engineering and industrial projects (except buildings), for example, highways, power plants, and pipelines. The construction work performed may include new work, reconstruction, or repairs. Establishments identified as heavy construction management firms are also included. Establishments in this subsector usually assume responsibility for entire nonbuilding projects but may subcontract some or all of the actual construction work. Special trade contractors are included in this group if they are engaged in activities primarily related to heavy construction, for example, grading for highways. Kinds of establishments include heavy construction general contractors, design builders, engineer-constructors, and joint-venture contractors.

2341 Highway, Street, Bridge, and Tunnel Construction US

23411 Highway and Street Construction US
See industry description for 234110 below.

Sector 23

Construction

■ = Cross-References

234110 Highway and Street Construction us

This industry comprises: (1) establishments primarily responsible for the entire construction (i.e., new work, reconstruction, or repairs) of highways (except elevated), streets, roads, or airport runways; (2) establishments identified as highway and street construction management firms; and (3) establishments identified as special trade contractors engaged in performing subcontract work primarily related to highway and street construction (e.g., grading for highways, installing guardrails, public sidewalk construction). Establishments in this industry may subcontract some or all of the actual construction work. Kinds of establishments include highway and street general contractors, design builders, engineer-constructors, and joint-venture contractors.

- Establishments primarily engaged in constructing elevated highways are classified in Industry 234120, Bridge and Tunnel Construction;
- Constructing private driveways and private sidewalks are classified in Industry 235710, Concrete Contractors; and
- Traffic lane painting are classified in Industry 235210, Painting and Wall Covering Contractors.

23412 Bridge and Tunnel Construction us

See industry description for 234120 below.

234120 Bridge and Tunnel Construction us

This industry comprises: (1) establishments primarily responsible for the entire construction (i.e., new work, reconstruction, or repairs) of bridges, viaducts, elevated highways, and tunnels; (2) establishments identified as bridge and tunnel construction management firms; and (3) establishments identified as special trade contractors primarily engaged in performing subcontract work related to bridge and tunnel construction. Establishments in this industry may subcontract some or all of the actual construction work. Kinds of establishments include bridge and tunnel general contractors, design builders, engineer-constructors, and joint-venture contractors.

- Establishments primarily engaged in and responsible for entire subway construction projects as general contractors, design-builders, engineer-constructors, or joint-venture contractors are classified in Industry 234990, All Other Heavy Construction; and
- Establishments primarily engaged in bridge painting are classified in Industry 235210, Painting and Wall Covering Contractors.

2349 Other Heavy Construction us

This industry group comprises establishments primarily engaged in heavy nonbuilding construction (except highway, street, bridge, and tunnel construction).

23491 Water, Sewer, and Pipeline Construction us

See industry description for 234910 below.

234910 Water, Sewer, and Pipeline Construction us

This industry comprises: (1) establishments primarily responsible for the entire construction (i.e., new work, reconstruction, rehabilitation, or repairs) of water mains, sewers, drains, gas mains, natural gas pumping stations, and gas and oil pipelines; (2) establishments identified as water, sewer, and pipeline construction management firms; and (3) establishments identified as special trade contractors engaged in activities primarily related to water, sewer, and pipeline construction. Establishments in this industry may subcontract some or all of the actual construction work. Kinds of establishments include water, sewer, and pipeline general contractors, design builders, engineer-constructors, and joint-venture contractors.

- Establishments primarily engaged in the construction of water and sewer treatment plants are classified in Industry 234990, All Other Heavy Construction.

23492 Power and Communication Transmission Line Construction us

See industry description for 234920 below.

234920 Power and Communication Transmission Line Construction us

This industry comprises: (1) establishments primarily responsible for the entire construction (i.e., new work, reconstruction, or repairs) of electric power and communication transmission lines and towers, radio and television transmitting/receiving towers, cable laying, and cable television lines;

Sector 23

Construction

■ = Cross-References

US—United States industry only. CAN—United States and Canadian industries are comparable. When neither US nor CAN appears, Canadian, Mexican, and United States industries are comparable.

308

Harris InfoSource

(2) establishments identified as power and communication transmission line construction management firms; and (3) establishments identified as special trade contractors engaged in activities primarily related to power and communication transmission line construction. Establishments in this industry may subcontract some or all of the actual construction work. Kinds of establishments include power and communication transmission line general contractors, design builders, engineer-constructors, and joint-venture contractors.

- Establishments primarily engaged in performing electrical work within buildings are classified in Industry 235310, Electrical Contractors; and
- Installation and maintenance of power and communication transmission lines performed by broadcasting and telecommunications companies are classified in Subsector 513, Broadcasting and Telecommunications.

23493 Industrial Nonbuilding Structure Construction US
See industry description for 234930 below.

234930 Industrial Nonbuilding Structure Construction US
This industry comprises: (1) establishments primarily responsible for the entire construction (i.e., new work, reconstruction, or repairs) of heavy industrial nonbuilding structures, such as chemical complexes or facilities, cement plants, petroleum refineries, industrial incinerators, ovens, kilns, power plants (except hydroelectric plants), and nuclear reactor containment structures; (2) establishments identified as industrial nonbuilding construction management firms; and (3) establishments identified as special trade contractors engaged in activities primarily related to industrial nonbuilding construction. Establishments in this industry may subcontract some or all of the actual construction work. Kinds of establishments include industrial nonbuilding general contractors, design builders, engineer-constructors, and joint-venture contractors.

- Establishments primarily engaged in constructing manufacturing and industrial buildings are classified in Industry 233310, Manufacturing and Industrial Building Construction; and
- Constructing hydroelectric plants are classified in Industry 234990, All Other Heavy Construction.

23499 All Other Heavy Construction US
See industry description for 234990 below.

234990 All Other Heavy Construction US
This industry comprises: (1) establishments primarily responsible for the entire construction (i.e., new work, reconstruction, or repairs) of heavy nonbuilding construction projects (except highway, street, bridge, tunnel, water lines, sewer lines, pipelines, power and communication transmission lines, and industrial nonbuilding structures); (2) establishments identified as all other heavy construction management firms; (3) establishments primarily engaged in construction equipment rental with an operator; and (4) establishments identified as special trade contractors engaged in activities related primarily to all other heavy construction. Typical projects constructed by establishments in this industry include athletic fields, dams, dikes, docks, drainage projects, golf courses, harbors, parks, reservoirs, canals, sewage treatment plants, water treatment plants, hydroelectric plants, subways, and other mass transit projects. Establishments in this industry may subcontract some or all of the actual construction work. Kinds of establishments include heavy construction general contractors, design builders, engineer-constructors, and joint-venture contractors.

- Establishments primarily engaged in constructing highways (except elevated) and streets are classified in Industry 234110, Highway and Street Construction;
- Constructing bridges via ducts, elevated highways, and tunnels are classified in Industry 234120, Bridge and Tunnel Construction;
- Constructing water mains, sewers, and pipelines are classified in Industry 234910, Water, Sewer, and Pipeline Construction;
- Constructing communication transmission lines are classified in Industry 234920, Power and Communication Transmission Line Construction;
- Constructing industrial nonbuilding structures are classified in Industry 234930, Industrial Nonbuilding Structure Construction; and
- Heavy equipment rental without an operator are classified in U.S. Industry 532412, Construction, Mining and Forestry Machinery and Equipment Rental and Leasing.

Sector 23

Construction

■ = Cross-References

US—United States industry only. CAN—United States and Canadian industries are comparable. When neither US nor CAN appears, Canadian, Mexican, and United States industries are comparable.

www.harrisinfo.com 309

▶235 SPECIAL TRADE CONTRACTORS ᵁˢ

Industries in the Special Trade Contractors subsector engage in specialized construction activities, such as plumbing, painting, and electrical work. Those establishments that engage in activities primarily related to heavy construction, such as grading for highways, are classified in Subsector 234, Heavy Construction. The activities of this subsector may be subcontracted from builders or general contractors or it may be performed directly for project owners. The construction work performed may include new work, additions, alterations, or maintenance and repairs. Special trade contractors usually perform most of their work at the job site, although they may have shops where they perform prefabrication and other work.

2351 Plumbing, Heating, and Air-conditioning Contractors ᵁˢ

23511 Plumbing, Heating, and Air-conditioning Contractors ᵁˢ
See industry description for 235110 below.

235110 Plumbing, Heating, and Air-conditioning Contractors ᵁˢ
This industry comprises establishments primarily engaged in one or more of the following: (1) installing plumbing, heating, and air-conditioning equipment; (2) servicing plumbing, heating, and air-conditioning equipment; and (3) the combined activity of selling and installing plumbing, heating, and air-conditioning equipment. The plumbing, heating, and air-conditioning work performed includes new work, additions, alterations, and maintenance and repairs. The activities performed by these establishments range from duct fabrication and installation at the site to installation of refrigeration equipment, installation of sprinkler systems, and installation of environmental controls.

2352 Painting and Wall Covering Contractors ᵁˢ

23521 Painting and Wall Covering Contractors ᵁˢ
See industry description for 235210 below.

235210 Painting and Wall Covering Contractors ᵁˢ
This industry comprises establishments primarily engaged in interior or exterior painting and interior wall covering. The painting and wall covering work performed includes new work, additions, alterations, and maintenance and repairs. Activities performed by these establishments range from bridge, ship, and traffic lane painting to paint and wall covering removal.

- ■ Establishments primarily engaged in roof painting are classified in Industry 235610, Roofing, Siding, and Sheet Metal Contractors; and
- ■ Installing wood paneling are classified in Industry 235510, Carpentry Contractors.

2353 Electrical Contractors ᵁˢ

23531 Electrical Contractors ᵁˢ
See industry description for 235310 below.

235310 Electrical Contractors ᵁˢ
This industry comprises establishments primarily engaged in one or more of the following: (1) performing electrical work at the site (e.g., installing wiring); (2) servicing electrical equipment at the site; and (3) the combined activity of selling and installing electrical equipment. The electrical work performed includes new work, additions, alterations, and maintenance and repairs.

- ■ Establishments primarily engaged in constructing power and communication transmission lines are classified in Industry 234920, Power and Communication Transmission Line Construction; and
- ■ Installing burglar and fire alarms are classified in U.S. Industry 561621, Security Systems Services (except Locksmiths).

Sector **23**

Construction

■ = Cross-References

US—United States industry only. CAN—United States and Canadian industries are comparable. When neither US nor CAN appears, Canadian, Mexican, and United States industries are comparable.

310   Harris InfoSource

2354 Masonry, Drywall, Insulation, and Tile Contractors US

23541 Masonry and Stone Contractors US
See industry description for 235410 below.

235410 Masonry and Stone Contractors US
This industry comprises establishments primarily engaged in masonry work, stone setting, and other stone work. The masonry work, stone setting, and other stone work performed includes new work, additions, alterations, and maintenance and repairs. Activities performed by establishments in this industry range from the construction of foundations made of block, stone, or brick to glass block laying; exterior marble, granite and slate work; and tuck pointing.

- Establishments primarily engaged in installing concrete parking areas, foundations, retaining walls, and private driveways and walks are classified in Industry 235710, Concrete Contractors.

23542 Drywall, Plastering, Acoustical, and Insulation Contractors US
See industry description for 235420 below.

235420 Drywall, Plastering, Acoustical, and Insulation Contractors US
This industry comprises establishments primarily engaged in drywall, plaster work, acoustical, and building insulation work. The drywall, plaster work, acoustical, and insulation work performed includes new work, additions, alterations, and maintenance and repairs. Plaster work includes applying plain or ornamental plaster, including installation of lathing to receive plaster.

- Establishments primarily engaged in insulating pipes and boilers are classified in Industry 235990, All Other Special Trade Contractors.

23543 Tile, Marble, Terrazzo, and Mosaic Contractors US
See industry description for 235430 below.

235430 Tile, Marble, Terrazzo, and Mosaic Contractors US
This industry comprises establishments primarily engaged in (1) setting and installing ceramic tile, marble (interior only), terrazzo, and mosaic and/or (2) mixing marble particles and cement to make terrazzo at the job site. The tile, marble, terrazzo, and mosaic work performed includes new work, additions, alterations, and maintenance and repairs.

- Establishments primarily engaged in manufacturing precast terrazzo products are classified in Industry 327390, Other Concrete Product Manufacturing; and
- Exterior marble work are classified in Industry 235410, Masonry and Stone Contractors.

2355 Carpentry and Floor Contractors US

23551 Carpentry Contractors US
See industry description for 235510 below.

235510 Carpentry Contractors US
This industry comprises establishments primarily engaged in framing, carpentry, and finishing work. The carpentry work performed includes new work, additions, alterations, and maintenance and repairs. Activities performed by establishments in this industry range from the installation of doors and windows to paneling, steel framing work, and ship joinery.

- Establishments primarily engaged in building custom kitchen cabinets in a shop are classified in Industry 337110, Wood Kitchen Cabinet and Countertop Manufacturing.

23552 Floor Laying and Other Floor Contractors US
See industry description for 235520 below.

Sector 23

Construction

■ = Cross-References

US—United States industry only. CAN—United States and Canadian industries are comparable. When neither US nor CAN appears, Canadian, Mexican, and United States industries are comparable.

235520 Floor Laying and Other Floor Contractors US

This industry comprises establishments primarily engaged in the installation of resilient floor tile, carpeting, linoleum, and wood or resilient flooring. The floor laying and other floor work performed includes new work, additions, alterations, and maintenance and repairs.

- Establishments primarily engaged in installing stone or ceramic floor tile are classified in Industry 235430, Tile, Marble, Terrazzo, and Mosaic Contractors;
- Establishments primarily engaged in laying concrete flooring are classified in Industry 235710, Concrete Contractors; and
- Stores selling and installing carpet and other flooring products as retail establishments are classified in Sector 44-45, Retail Trade.

2356 Roofing, Siding, and Sheet Metal Contractors US

23561 Roofing, Siding, and Sheet Metal Contractors US

See industry description for 235610 below.

235610 Roofing, Siding, and Sheet Metal Contractors US

This industry comprises establishments primarily engaged in the installation of roofing, siding, sheet metal work, and roof drainage-related work, such as downspouts and gutters. Activities performed by these establishments also include treating roofs (i.e., by spraying, painting, or coating), copper smithing, tin smithing, installing skylights, installing metal ceilings, flashing, duct work, and capping. The roofing, siding, and sheet metal work performed includes new work, additions, alterations, and maintenance and repairs.

2357 Concrete Contractors US

23571 Concrete Contractors US

See industry description for 235710 below.

235710 Concrete Contractors US

This industry comprises establishments primarily engaged in the use of concrete and asphalt to produce parking areas, building foundations, structures, and retaining walls, and in the use of all materials to produce patios, private driveways, and private walks. Activities performed by these establishments include grout and shotcrete work. The concrete work performed includes new work, additions, alterations, and maintenance and repairs.

- Establishments primarily engaged in constructing or paving streets, highways, and public sidewalks are classified in Industry 234110, Highway and Street Construction; and
- Constructing swimming pools are classified in Industry 235990, All Other Special Trade Contractors.

2358 Water Well Drilling Contractors US

23581 Water Well Drilling Contractors US

See industry description for 235810 below.

235810 Water Well Drilling Contractors US

This industry comprises establishments primarily engaged in drilling, tapping, and capping of water wells, and geothermal drilling. The water well drilling work performed includes new work, servicing, and maintenance and repairs.

- Establishments primarily engaged in drilling oil and gas field water intake wells are classified in Industry 21311, Support Activities for Mining.

2359 Other Special Trade Contractors US

This industry group comprises establishments primarily engaged in specialized construction activities (except plumbing, painting, electrical, masonry, drywall, insulation, tile, carpentry, flooring work, roofing, siding, sheet metal, concrete, and water well drilling).

■ = Cross-References

Sector **23**

Construction

US—United States industry only. CAN—United States and Canadian industries are comparable. When neither US nor CAN appears, Canadian, Mexican, and United States industries are comparable.

23591 Structural Steel Erection Contractors US
See industry description for 235910 below.

235910 Structural Steel Erection Contractors US
This industry comprises establishments primarily engaged in one or more of the following: (1) erecting metal, structural steel, and similar products of prestressed or precast concrete to produce structural elements, building exteriors, and elevator fronts; (2) setting rods, bars, rebar, mesh, and cages, to reinforce poured-in-place concrete; and (3) erecting cooling towers and metal storage tanks. The structural steel erection work performed includes new work, additions, alterations, reconstruction, and maintenance and repairs.

- Establishments primarily engaged in structural work for nonbuilding projects are classified in Subsector 234, Heavy Construction.

23592 Glass and Glazing Contractors US
See industry description for 235920 below.

235920 Glass and Glazing Contractors US
This industry comprises establishments primarily engaged in installing glass (i.e., glazing work) and/or tinting glass. The glass work performed includes new work, additions, alterations, and maintenance and repairs.

- Establishments primarily engaged in the replacement, repair, and/or tinting of automotive glass are classified in U.S. Industry 811122, Automotive Glass Replacement Shops.

23593 Excavation Contractors US
See industry description for 235930 below.

235930 Excavation Contractors US
This industry comprises establishments primarily engaged in preparing land for building construction. Activities performed by these establishments are drilling shafts, foundation digging, foundation drilling, and grading. The excavation work performed includes new work, additions, alterations, and repairs.

- Establishments primarily engaged in concrete work are classified in Industry 235710, Concrete Contractors;
- Trenching, earthmoving and land clearing not related to building construction are classified in Subsector 234, Heavy Construction; or in Sector 21, Mining; and
- Earth retention or shoring are classified in Industry 235990, All Other Special Trade Contractors.

23594 Wrecking and Demolition Contractors US
See industry description for 235940 below.

235940 Wrecking and Demolition Contractors US
This industry comprises establishments primarily engaged in the wrecking and demolition of buildings and other structures, including underground tank removal and the dismantling of steel oil tanks, except those for hazardous materials. The establishments engaged in wrecking and demolition work may or may not sell materials derived from demolishing operations.

- Establishments primarily engaged in demolition of tanks in oil fields are classified in U.S. Industry 213112, Support Activities for Oil and Gas Operations; and
- Environmental remediation work, such as the removal of underground steel tanks for hazardous materials, are classified in Industry 562910, Remediation Services.

23595 Building Equipment and Other Machinery Installation Contractors US
See industry description for 235950 below.

Sector 23

Construction

■ = Cross-References

US—United States industry only. CAN—United States and Canadian industries are comparable. When neither US nor CAN appears, Canadian, Mexican, and United States industries are comparable.

235950 Building Equipment and Other Machinery Installation Contractors [US]

This industry comprises establishments primarily engaged in one or more of the following: (1) the installation or dismantling of building equipment, machinery or other industrial equipment (except plumbing, heating, air conditioning or electrical equipment); (2) machine rigging; and 3) millwriting. Types of equipment installed include automated and revolving doors, conveyor systems, dumbwaiters, dust collecting equipment, elevators, small incinerators, pneumatic tubes systems, and built-in vacuum cleaning systems. The building equipment and other machinery installation work performed includes new work, additions, alterations, and maintenance and repairs.

- Establishments primarily engaged in installing plumbing, heating, or air-conditioning equipment are classified in Industry 235110, Plumbing, Heating, and Air-conditioning Contractors;
- Installing electrical equipment are classified in Industry 235310, Electrical Contractors;
- Constructing of industrial incinerator, furnace, and oven structures are classified in Industry 234930, Industrial Nonbuilding Structure Construction; and
- Manufacturing of industrial equipment with incidental installation are classified in Sector 31-33, Manufacturing.

23599 All Other Special Trade Contractors [US]

See industry description for 235990 below.

235990 All Other Special Trade Contractors [US]

This industry comprises establishments primarily engaged in specialized construction work, (except plumbing, painting, electrical, masonry, drywall, insulation, tile, carpentry, flooring, roofing, siding, sheet metal work, concrete work, glass and glazing, structural steel erection, excavation, wrecking and demolition, and building equipment installation work). Activities undertaken by these establishments include constructing swimming pools and fences, house moving, waterproofing, dewatering, dampproofing, fireproofing, and sandblasting; installing antennas, artificial turf, awnings, countertops, fire escapes, forms for poured concrete, gasoline pumps, lightning conductors, ornamental metal, shoring systems, and signs (on buildings); and specialized activities, such as bathtub refinishing, coating and glazing of concrete surfaces, gas leakage detection, insulation of pipes and boilers, mobile home site setup and tie-down, posthole digging, radon remediation, scaffolding work, and on-site welding. The other special trade work performed includes new work, additions, alterations, and maintenance and repairs.

- Establishments primarily engaged in installing plumbing, heating, and air-conditioning equipment are classified in Industry 235110, Plumbing, Heating, and Air-conditioning Contractors;
- Painting and interior wall covering are classified in Industry 235210, Painting and Wall Covering Contractors;
- Installing electrical equipment are classified in Industry 235310, Electrical Contractors;
- Masonry work, drywall work, insulation work, and tile work are classified in Industry Group 2354, Masonry, Drywall, Insulation, and Tile Contractors; Carpentry work are classified in Industry 235510, Carpentry Contractors;
- Installing flooring are classified in Industry 235520, Floor Laying and Other Floor Contractors;
- Installing roofing, siding, and sheet metal are classified in Industry 235610, Roofing, Siding, and Sheet Metal Contractors;
- The use of concrete and asphalt in their work are classified in Industry 235710, Concrete Contractors;
- Erecting structural steel are classified in Industry 235910, Structural Steel Erection Contractors;
- Installing or tinting glass are classified in Industry 235920, Glass and Glazing Contractors;
- Preparing land for building construction are classified in Industry 235930, Excavation Contractors;
- Wrecking and demolitions are classified in Industry 235940, Wrecking and Demolition Contractors;
- Environmental remediation work, such as asbestos abatement, are classified in Industry 562910, Remediation Services;
- Installing or dismantling building equipment, machinery, and other industrial equipment are classified in Industry 235950, Building Equipment and Other Machinery Installation Contractors;
- Equipment rental without an operator are classified in U.S. Industry 532412, Construction, Mining, and Forestry Machinery and Equipment Rental and Leasing; and
- Construction equipment rental with an operator are classified in Industry 234990, All Other Heavy Construction.

Sector **23**

Construction

■ = Cross-References

US—United States industry only. CAN—United States and Canadian industries are comparable. When neither US nor CAN appears, Canadian, Mexican, and United States industries are comparable.

Sector 31-33 Manufacturing

The Sector as a Whole

THE MANUFACTURING sector comprises establishments engaged in the mechanical, physical, or chemical transformation of materials, substances, or components into new products. The assembling of component parts of manufactured products is considered manufacturing, except in cases where the activity is appropriately classified in Sector 23, Construction.

Establishments in the Manufacturing sector are often described as plants, factories, or mills and characteristically use power-driven machines and materials-handling equipment. However, establishments that transform materials or substances into new products by hand or in the worker's home and those engaged in selling to the general public products made on the same premises from which they are sold, such as bakeries, candy stores, and custom tailors, may also be included in this sector. Manufacturing establishments may process materials or may contract with other establishments to process their materials for them. Both types of establishments are included in manufacturing.

The materials, substances, or components transformed by manufacturing establishments are raw materials that are products of agriculture, forestry, fishing, mining, or quarrying as well as products of other manufacturing establishments. The materials used may be purchased directly from producers, obtained through customary trade channels, or secured without recourse to the market by transferring the product from one establishment to another, under the same ownership.

The new product of a manufacturing establishment may be finished in the sense that it is ready for utilization or consumption, or it may be semifinished to become an input for an establishment engaged in further manufacturing. For example, the product of the alumina refinery is the input used in the primary production of aluminum; primary aluminum is the input to an aluminum wire drawing plant; and aluminum wire is the input for a fabricated wire product manufacturing establishment.

The subsectors in the Manufacturing sector generally reflect distinct production processes related to material inputs, production equipment, and employee skills. In the machinery area, where assembling is a key activity, parts and accessories for manufactured products are classified in the industry of the finished manufactured item when they are made for separate sale. For example, a replacement refrigerator door would be classified with refrigerators and an attachment for a piece of metal working machinery would be classified with metal working machinery. However, components—input from other manufacturing establishments—are classified based on the production function of the component manufacturer. For example, electronic components are classified in Subsector 334, Computer and Electronic Product Manufacturing and stampings are classified in Subsector 332, Fabricated Metal Product Manufacturing.

Manufacturing establishments often perform one or more activities that are classified outside the Manufacturing sector of NAICS. For instance, almost all manufacturing has some captive research and development or administrative operations, such as accounting, payroll, or management. These captive services are treated the same as captive manufacturing activities. When the services are provided by separate establishments, they are classified to the NAICS sector where such services are primary, not in manufacturing.

The boundaries of manufacturing and the other sectors of the classification system can be somewhat blurry. The establishments in the manufacturing sector are engaged in the transformation 93 of materials into new products. Their output is a new product. However, the definition of what constitutes a new product can

Visit page 17 to learn about classifi-cation changes to this sector.

Sector 31-33
Manufacturing

315

be somewhat subjective. As clarification, the following activities are considered manufacturing in NAICS:

Milk bottling and pasteurizing;
Water bottling and processing;
Fresh fish packaging (oyster shucking, fish filleting);
Apparel jobbing (assigning of materials to contract factories or shops for fabrication or other contract operations) as well as contracting on materials owned by others;
Printing and related activities;
Ready-mixed concrete production;
Leather converting;

Grinding of lenses to prescription;
Wood preserving
Electroplating, plating, metal heat treating, and polishing for the trade;
Lapidary work for the trade;
Fabricating signs and advertising displays;
Rebuilding or remanufacturing machinery (i.e., automotive parts);
Ship repair and renovation;
Machine shops; and
Tire retreading

They include:

1. Logging, classified in Sector 11, Agriculture, Forestry, Fishing and Hunting is considered a harvesting operation;

2. The beneficiating of ores and other minerals, classified in Sector 21, Mining, is considered part of the activity of mining;

3. The construction of structures and fabricating operations performed at the site of construction by contractors, is classified in Sector 23, Construction;

4. Establishments engaged in breaking of bulk and redistribution in smaller lots, including packaging, repackaging, or bottling products, such as liquors or chemicals; the customized assembly of computers; sorting of scrap; mixing paints to customer order; and cutting metals to customer order, classified in Sector 42, Wholesale Trade or Sector 44-45, Retail Trade, produce a modified version of the same product, not a new product; and

5. Publishing and the combined activity of publishing and printing, classified in Sector 51, Information, perform the transformation of information into a product where as the value of the product to the consumer lies in the information content, not in the format in which it is distributed (i.e., the book or software diskette).

▶311 FOOD MANUFACTURING

Industries in the Food Manufacturing subsector transform livestock and agricultural products into products for intermediate or final consumption. The industry groups are distinguished by the raw materials (generally of animal or vegetable origin) processed into food products. The food products manufactured in these establishments are typically sold to wholesalers or retailers for distribution to consumers, but establishments primarily engaged in retailing bakery and candy products made on the premises not for immediate consumption are included. Establishments primarily engaged in manufacturing beverages are classified in Subsector 312, Beverage and Tobacco Product Manufacturing.

3111 Animal Food Manufacturing

31111 Animal Food Manufacturing
This industry comprises establishments primarily engaged in manufacturing food and feed for animals from ingredients, such as grains, oilseed mill products, and meat products.

- ■ Slaughtering animals for feed are classified in Industry 31161, Animal Slaughtering and Processing; and
- ■ Manufacturing vitamins and minerals for animals are classified in Industry 32541, Pharmaceutical and Medicine Manufacturing.

Sector 31-33 Manufacturing

■ = Cross-References

US—United States industry only. CAN—United States and Canadian industries are comparable. When neither US nor CAN appears, Canadian, Mexican, and United States industries are comparable.

316

Harris InfoSource

311111 Dog and Cat Food Manufacturing ^{CAN}

This U.S. industry comprises establishments primarily engaged in manufacturing dog and cat food from ingredients, such as grains, oilseed mill products, and meat products.

- Manufacturing food for animals (except dog and cat) are classified in U.S. Industry 311119, Other Animal Food Manufacturing;
- Slaughtering animals for feed are classified in Industry 31161, Animal Slaughtering and Processing; and
- Manufacturing vitamins and minerals for dogs and cats are classified in Industry 32541, Pharmaceutical and Medicine Manufacturing.

311119 Other Animal Food Manufacturing ^{CAN}

This U.S. industry comprises establishments primarily engaged in manufacturing animal food (except dog and cat) from ingredients, such as grains, oilseed mill products, and meat products. .

- Manufacturing dog and cat foods are classified in U.S. Industry 311111, Dog and Cat Food Manufacturing;
- Slaughtering animals for feed are classified in Industry 31161, Animal Slaughtering and Processing; and
- Manufacturing vitamins and minerals for animals are classified in Industry 32541, Pharmaceutical and Medicine Manufacturing.

3112 Grain and Oilseed Milling

31121 Flour Milling and Malt Manufacturing

This industry comprises establishments primarily engaged in one or more of the following: (1) milling flour or meal from grains or vegetables; (2) preparing flour mixes or doughs from flour milled in the same establishment; (3) milling, cleaning, and polishing rice; and (4) manufacturing malt from barley, rye, or other grains.

- Preparing breakfast cereals from flour milled in the same establishment are classified in Industry 31123, Breakfast Cereal Manufacturing;
- Crushing soybeans or wet milling corn and vegetables are classified in Industry 31122, Starch and Vegetable Fats and Oils Manufacturing;
- Manufacturing prepared flour mixes or doughs from flour ground elsewhere are classified in Industry 31182, Cookie, Cracker, and Pasta Manufacturing;
- Brewing malt beverages are classified in Industry 31212, Breweries;
- Mixing purchased dried and dehydrated ingredients with purchased rice are classified in Industry 31199, All Other Food Manufacturing;
- Drying and/or dehydrating ingredients and packaging them with purchased rice are classified in Industry 31142, Fruit and Vegetable Canning, Pickling and Drying; and
- Manufacturing malt extract and syrups are classified in Industry 31194, Seasoning and Dressing Manufacturing.

311211 Flour Milling ^{CAN}

This U.S. industry comprises establishments primarily engaged in (1) milling flour or meal from grains (except rice) or vegetables and/or (2) milling flour and preparing flour mixes or doughs.

- Preparing breakfast cereals from flour milled in the same establishment are classified in Industry 311230, Breakfast Cereal Manufacturing;
- Manufacturing prepared flour mixes or doughs from flour ground elsewhere are classified in U.S. Industry 311822, Flour Mixes and Dough Manufacturing from Purchased Flour;
- Milling rice or cleaning and polishing rice are classified in U.S. Industry 311212, Rice Milling;
- Wet milling corn and vegetables are classified in U.S. Industry 311221, Wet Corn Milling; and Crushing soybean and extracting soybean oil are classified in U.S. Industry 311222, Soybean Processing.

311212 Rice Milling ^{US}

This U.S. industry comprises establishments primarily engaged in one of the following: (1) milling rice; (2) cleaning and polishing rice; or (3) milling, cleaning, and polishing rice. The establishments in this industry may package the rice they mill with other ingredients.

- Drying and/or dehydrating ingredients and packaging them with purchased rice are classified in U.S. Industry 311423, Dried and Dehydrated Food Manufacturing; and
- Mixing purchased dried and/or dehydrated ingredients with purchased rice are classified in U.S. Industry 311999, All Other Miscellaneous Food Manufacturing.

311213 Malt Manufacturing ^{US}

This U.S. industry comprises establishments primarily engaged in manufacturing malt from barley, rye, or other grains.

Visit page 17 to learn about classification changes to this sector.

Sector

31-33

Manufacturing

■ = Cross-References

US—United States industry only. CAN—United States and Canadian industries are comparable. When neither US nor CAN appears, Canadian, Mexican, and United States industries are comparable.

www.harrisinfo.com 317

- Brewing malt beverages are classified in Industry 312120, Breweries; and
- Manufacturing malt extract and syrups are classified in U.S. Industry 311942, Spice and Extract Manufacturing.

31122 Starch and Vegetable Fats and Oils Manufacturing

This industry comprises establishments primarily engaged in one or more of the following: (1) wet milling corn and vegetables; (2) crushing oilseeds and tree nuts; (3) refining and/or blending vegetable oils; (4) manufacturing shortening and margarine; and (5) blending purchased animal fats with vegetable fats.

- Manufacturing table syrups from corn syrup and starch base dessert powders are classified in Industry 31199, All Other Food Manufacturing;
- Reducing maple sap to maple syrup are classified in Industry 11199, All Other Crop Farming;
- Milling flour or meal from grains and vegetables are classified in Industry 31121, Flour Milling and Malt Manufacturing;
- Wet milling corn to produce nonpotable ethyl alcohol are classified in Industry 32519, Other Basic Organic Chemical Manufacturing; Rendering or refining animal fats and oils are classified in Industry 31161, Animal Slaughtering and Processing; and
- Manufacturing laundry starches are classified in Industry 32561, Soap and Cleaning Compound Manufacturing.

311221 Wet Corn Milling CAN

This U.S. industry comprises establishments primarily engaged in wet milling corn and other vegetables (except to make ethyl alcohol). Examples of products made in these establishments are corn sweeteners, such as glucose, dextrose, and fructose; corn oil; and starches (except laundry).

- Refining and/or blending corn oil from purchased oils are classified in U.S. Industry 311225, Fats and Oils Refining and Blending;
- Manufacturing sweetening syrups from corn syrup and starch base dessert powders are classified in U.S. Industry 311999, All Other Miscellaneous Food Manufacturing;
- Reducing maple sap to maple syrup are classified in U.S. Industry 111998, All Other Miscellaneous Crop Farming;
- Milling corn are classified in U.S. Industry 311211, Flour Milling;
- Wet milling corn to produce nonpotable ethyl alcohol are classified in U.S. Industry 325193, Ethyl Alcohol Manufacturing; and
- Manufacturing laundry starches are classified in U.S. Industry 325612, Polish and Other Sanitation Good Manufacturing.

311222 Soybean Processing US

This U.S. industry comprises establishments engaged in crushing soybeans. Examples of products produced in these establishments are soybean oil, soybean cake and meal, and soybean protein isolates and concentrates.

- Refining and/or blending soybean oil from purchased oil are classified in U.S. Industry 311225, Fats and Oils Refining and Blending;
- Wet milling corn and other vegetables are classified in U.S. Industry 311221, Wet Corn Milling; and
- Crushing oilseeds (except soybeans) and tree nuts are classified in U.S. Industry 311223, Other Oilseed Processing.

311223 Other Oilseed Processing US

This U.S. industry comprises establishments engaged in crushing oilseeds (except soybeans) and tree nuts, such as cottonseeds, linseeds, peanuts, and sunflower seeds.

- Wet milling corn and other vegetables are classified in U.S. Industry 311221, Wet Corn Milling;
- Crushing soybeans are classified in U.S. Industry 311222, Soybean Processing; and
- Refining and/or blending vegetable, oilseed, and tree nut oils from purchased oils are classified in U.S. Industry 311225, Fats and Oils Refining and Blending.

Sector
31-33
Manufacturing

311225 Fats and Oils Refining and Blending CAN

This U.S. industry comprises establishments primarily engaged in one or more of the following: (1) manufacturing shortening and margarine from purchased fats and oils; (2) refining and/or blending vegetable, oilseed, and tree nut oils from purchased oils; and (3) blending purchased animal fats with purchased vegetable fats.

- Refining and/or blending soybean oil in soybean crushing mills are classified in U.S. Industry 311222, Soybean Processing;
- Refining and/or blending corn oil made by wet corn milling are classified in U.S. Industry 311221, Wet Corn Milling;
- Refining and/or blending oilseeds (except soybeans) and tree nuts in crushing mills are classified in U.S. Industry 311223, Other Oilseed Processing; and
- Rendering or refining animal fats and oils are classified in Industry 31161, Animal Slaughtering and Processing.

31123 Breakfast Cereal Manufacturing

See industry description for 311230 below.

■ = Cross-References

US—United States industry only. CAN—United States and Canadian industries are comparable. When neither US nor CAN appears, Canadian, Mexican, and United States industries are comparable.

311230 Breakfast Cereal Manufacturing

This industry comprises establishments primarily engaged in manufacturing breakfast cereal foods.

- Manufacturing nonchocolate-coated granola bars and other types of breakfast bars are classified in Industry 311340, Nonchocolate Confectionery Manufacturing; Manufacturing chocolate-coated granola bars from purchased chocolate are classified in Industry 311330, Confectionery Manufacturing from Purchased Chocolate;

- Manufacturing chocolate-coated granola bars from cacao beans are classified in Industry 311320, Chocolate and Confectionery Manufacturing from Cacao Beans; and
- Manufacturing coffee substitutes from grain are classified in Industry 311920, Coffee and Tea Manufacturing.

3113 Sugar and Confectionery Product Manufacturing

This industry group comprises (1) establishments that process agricultural inputs, such as sugarcane, beet, and cacao, to give rise to a new product (sugar or chocolate) and (2) those that begin with sugar and chocolate and process these further.

31131 Sugar Manufacturing

This industry comprises establishments primarily engaged in manufacturing raw sugar, liquid sugar, and refined sugar from sugarcane, raw cane sugar and sugarbeets.

- Manufacturing corn sweeteners by wet milling corn are classified in Industry 31122, Starch and Vegetable Fats and Oils Manufacturing;
- Manufacturing table syrups from corn syrup and starch base dessert powders are classified in Industry 31199, All Other Food Manufacturing;
- Reducing maple sap to maple syrup are classified in Industry 11199, All Other Crop Farming; and
- Manufacturing synthetic sweeteners (i.e., sweetening agents), such as saccharin and sugar substitutes (i.e., synthetic sweetener blended with other ingredients), are classified in Subsector 325, Chemical Manufacturing.

311311 Sugarcane Mills US

This U.S. industry comprises establishments primarily engaged in processing sugarcane.

- Manufacturing refined cane sugar from raw cane sugar are classified in U.S. Industry 311312, Cane Sugar Refining;
- Manufacturing beet sugar are classified in U.S. Industry 311313, Beet Sugar Manufacturing;
- Manufacturing corn sweetener by wet milling corn are classified in U.S. Industry 311221, Wet Corn Milling; Manufacturing table syrups from corn syrup are classified in U.S. Industry 311999, All Other Miscellaneous Food Manufacturing; and
- Manufacturing synthetic sweeteners (i.e., sweetening agents), such as saccharin and sugar substitutes (i.e., synthetic sweetener blended with other ingredients), are classified in Subsector 325, Chemical Manufacturing.

311312 Cane Sugar Refining US

This U.S. industry comprises establishments primarily engaged in refining cane sugar from raw cane sugar.

- Processing and refining sugarcane are classified in U.S. Industry 311311, Sugarcane Mills;
- Manufacturing beet sugar are classified in U.S. Industry 311313, Beet Sugar Manufacturing;
- Manufacturing corn sweetener by wet milling corn are classified in U.S. Industry 311221, Wet Corn Milling;
- Reducing maple sap to maple syrup are classified in U.S. Industry 111998, All Other Miscellaneous Crop Farming;
- Manufacturing table syrups from corn syrup are classified in U.S. Industry 311999, All Other Miscellaneous Food Manufacturing; and
- Manufacturing synthetic sweeteners (i.e., sweetening agents), such as saccharin and sugar substitutes (i.e., synthetic sweetener blended with other ingredients), are classified in Subsector 325, Chemical Manufacturing.

311313 Beet Sugar Manufacturing US

This U.S. industry comprises establishments primarily engaged in manufacturing refined beet sugar from sugarbeets.

- Manufacturing raw cane sugar and/or refined cane sugar from sugarcane are classified in U.S. Industry 311311, Sugarcane Mills;
- Manufacturing refined cane sugar from raw cane sugar are classified in U.S. Industry 311312, Cane Sugar Refining;
- Manufacturing corn sweeteners by wet milling corn are classified in U.S. Industry 311221, Wet Corn Milling; Manufacturing table syrups from corn syrup are classified in U.S. Industry 311999, All Other Miscellaneous Food Manufacturing;
- Reducing maple sap to maple syrup are classified in U.S. Industry 111998, All Other Miscellaneous Crop Farming; and
- Manufacturing synthetic sweeteners (i.e., sweetening agents), such as saccharin and sugar substitutes (i.e., synthetic sweetener blended with other ingredients), are classified in Subsector 325, Chemical Manufacturing.

31132 Chocolate and Confectionery Manufacturing from Cacao Beans

See industry description for 311320 below.

Visit page 17 to learn about classification changes to this sector.

Sector
31-33

Manufacturing

■ = Cross-References

US—United States industry only. CAN—United States and Canadian industries are comparable. When neither US nor CAN appears, Canadian, Mexican, and United States industries are comparable.

www.harrisinfo.com

319

311320 Chocolate and Confectionery Manufacturing from Cacao Beans

This industry comprises establishments primarily engaged in shelling, roasting, and grinding cacao beans and making chocolate cacao products and chocolate confectioneries.

- Manufacturing, not for immediate consumption, chocolate confectioneries from chocolate made elsewhere are classified in Industry 311330, Confectionery Manufacturing from Purchased Chocolate;
- Manufacturing, not for immediate consumption, nonchocolate candies are classified in Industry 311340, Nonchocolate Confectionery Manufacturing;
- Preparing and selling confectioneries for immediate consumption are classified in U.S. Industry 722213, Snack and Nonalcoholic Beverage Bars; and
- Retailing confectioneries not for immediate consumption made elsewhere are classified in U.S. Industry 445292, Confectionery and Nut Stores.

31133 Confectionery Manufacturing from Purchased Chocolate

See industry description for 311330 below.

311330 Confectionery Manufacturing from Purchased Chocolate

This industry comprises establishments primarily engaged in manufacturing chocolate confectioneries from chocolate produced elsewhere. Included in this industry are establishments primarily engaged in retailing chocolate confectionery products not for immediate consumption made on the premises from chocolate made elsewhere.

- Manufacturing chocolate confectioneries from cacao beans are classified in Industry 311320, Chocolate and Confectionery Manufacturing from Cacao Beans; Manufacturing nonchocolate confectioneries are classified in Industry 311340, Nonchocolate Confectionery Manufacturing;
- Retailing confectioneries not for immediate consumption made elsewhere are classified in U.S. Industry 445292, Confectionery and Nut Stores; and
- Preparing and selling confectioneries for immediate consumption are classified in U.S. Industry 722213, Snack and Nonalcoholic Beverage Bars.

31134 Nonchocolate Confectionery Manufacturing

See industry description for 311340 below.

311340 Nonchocolate Confectionery Manufacturing

This industry comprises establishments primarily engaged in manufacturing nonchocolate confectioneries. Included in this industry are establishments primary engaged in retailing nonchocolate confectionery products not for immediate consumption made on the premises.

- Manufacturing chocolate confectioneries from cacao beans are classified in Industry 311320, Chocolate and Confectionery Manufacturing from Cacao Beans;
- Manufacturing chocolate confectioneries from chocolate made elsewhere are classified in Industry 311330, Confectionery Manufacturing from Purchased Chocolate;
- Retailing confectioneries not for immediate consumption made elsewhere are classified in U.S. Industry 445292, Confectionery and Nut Stores;
- Preparing and selling confectioneries for immediate consumption are classified in U.S. Industry 722213, Snack and Nonalcoholic Beverage Bars; and
- Roasting, salting, drying, cooking, or canning nuts and seeds are classified in U.S. Industry 311911, Roasted Nuts and Peanut Butter Manufacturing.

3114 Fruit and Vegetable Preserving and Specialty Food Manufacturing

This industry group includes (1) establishments that freeze food and (2) those that use preservation processes, such as pickling, canning, and dehydrating. Both types begin their production process with inputs of vegetable or animal origin.

31141 Frozen Food Manufacturing

This industry comprises establishments primarily engaged in manufacturing frozen fruit, frozen juices, frozen vegetables, and frozen specialty foods (except seafood), such as frozen dinners, entrees, and side dishes; frozen pizza; frozen whipped toppings; and frozen waffles, pancakes, and french toast.

- Manufacturing frozen dairy specialties are classified in Industry 31152, Ice Cream and Frozen Dessert Manufacturing;
- Manufacturing frozen bakery products are classified in Industry 31181, Bread and Bakery Product Manufacturing;
- Manufacturing frozen seafood products are classified in Industry 31171, Seafood Product Preparation and Packaging; and
- Manufacturing frozen meat products are classified in Industry 31161, Animal Slaughtering and Processing.

■ = Cross-References

Sector
31-33
Manufacturing

US—United States industry only. CAN—United States and Canadian industries are comparable. When neither US nor CAN appears, Canadian, Mexican, and United States industries are comparable.

320   Harris InfoSource

311411 Frozen Fruit, Juice, and Vegetable Manufacturing ᵁˢ
This U.S. industry comprises establishments primarily engaged in manufacturing frozen fruits; frozen vegetables; and frozen fruit juices, –ades, drinks, cocktail mixes and concentrates.

- Establishments primarily engaged in manufacturing frozen specialty foods are classified in U.S. Industry 311412, Frozen Specialty Food Manufacturing.

311412 Frozen Specialty Food Manufacturing ᵁˢ
This U.S. industry comprises establishments primarily engaged in manufacturing frozen specialty foods (except seafood), such as frozen dinners, entrees, and side dishes; frozen pizza; frozen whipped topping; and frozen waffles, pancakes, and french toast.

- Manufacturing frozen dairy specialties are classified in Industry 311520, Ice Cream and Frozen Dessert Manufacturing;
- Manufacturing frozen bakery products are classified in U.S. Industry 311813, Frozen Cakes, Pies, and Other Pastries Manufacturing;
- Manufacturing frozen fruits, frozen fruit juices, and frozen vegetables are classified in U.S. Industry 311411, Frozen Fruit, Juice, and Vegetable Manufacturing;
- Manufacturing frozen meat products are classified in Industry 31161, Animal Slaughtering and Processing; and
- Manufacturing frozen seafood products are classified in U.S. Industry 311712, Fresh and Frozen Seafood Processing.

31142 Fruit and Vegetable Canning, Pickling, and Drying
This industry comprises establishments primarily engaged in manufacturing canned, pickled, and dried fruits, vegetables, and specialty foods. Establishments in this industry may package the dried or dehydrated ingredients they make with other purchased ingredients. Examples of products made by these establishments are canned juices; canned baby foods; canned soups (except seafood); canned dry beans; canned tomato-based sauces, such as catsup, salsa, chili, spaghetti, barbeque, and tomato paste; pickles, relishes, jams and jellies, dried soup mixes and bullions, and sauerkraut.

- Manufacturing canned dairy products are classified in Industry 31151, Dairy Product (except Frozen) Manufacturing;
- Manufacturing canned seafood soups and seafood products are classified in Industry 31171, Seafood Product Preparation and Packaging;
- Manufacturing canned meat products are classified in Industry 31161, Animal Slaughtering and Processing;
- Milling rice and packaging it with other ingredients or manufacturing vegetable flours and meals are classified in Industry 31121, Flour Milling and Malt Manufacturing;
- Manufacturing dry pasta and packaging it with other ingredients are classified in Industry 31182, Cookie, Cracker, and Pasta Manufacturing;
- Mixing purchased dried and/or dehydrated potatoes, rice, and pasta and packaging them with other purchased ingredients; mixing purchased dried and/or dehydrated ingredients for soup mixes and bouillon; and manufacturing canned puddings are classified in Industry 31199, All Other Food Manufacturing;
- Manufacturing dry salad dressing and dry sauce mixes are classified in Industry 31194, Seasoning and Dressing Manufacturing; and
- Manufacturing canned fruit and vegetable drinks, cocktails, and –ades are classified in Industry 31211, Soft Drink and Ice Manufacturing.

311421 Fruit and Vegetable Canning ᵁˢ
This U.S. industry comprises establishments primarily engaged in manufacturing canned, pickled, and brined fruits and vegetables. Examples of products made in these establishments are canned juices; canned jams and jellies; canned tomato-based sauces, such as catsup, salsa, chili, spaghetti, barbeque, and tomato paste; pickles, relishes, and sauerkraut.

- Manufacturing canned baby foods, canned soups (except seafood), and canned specialty foods (except seafood) are classified in U.S. Industry 311422, Specialty Canning;
- Manufacturing canned seafood soups and canned seafood products are classified in U.S. Industry 311711, Seafood Canning;
- Manufacturing canned meat products are classified in Industry 31161, Animal Slaughtering and Processing; and
- Manufacturing canned fruit and canned vegetable drinks, –ades, and cocktails are classified in U.S. Industry 312111, Soft Drink Manufacturing.

311422 Specialty Canning ᵁˢ
This U.S. industry comprises establishments primarily engaged in manufacturing canned specialty foods. Examples of products made in these establishments are canned baby food, canned baked beans, canned soups (except seafood), canned spaghetti, and other canned nationality foods.

- Manufacturing canned dairy products are classified in U.S. Industry 311514, Dry, Condensed, and Evaporated Dairy Product Manufacturing;
- Manufacturing canned fruits, canned vegetables, and canned juices are classified in U.S. Industry 311421, Fruit and Vegetable Canning;

Visit page 17 to learn about classification changes to this sector.

Sector
31-33
Manufacturing

■ = Cross-References

US—United States industry only. CAN—United States and Canadian industries are comparable. When neither US nor CAN appears, Canadian, Mexican, and United States industries are comparable.

www.harrisinfo.com

321

■ Manufacturing canned seafood soups and canned seafood products are classified in U.S. Industry 311711, Seafood Canning;

■ Manufacturing canned meat products are classified in Industry 31161, Animal Slaughtering and Processing; and

■ Manufacturing canned puddings are classified in U.S. Industry 311999, All Other Miscellaneous Food Manufacturing.

311423 Dried and Dehydrated Food Manufacturing ᵁˢ

This U.S. industry comprises establishments primarily engaged in (1) drying (including freeze-dried) and/or dehydrating fruits, vegetables, and soup mixes and bouillon and/or (2) drying and/or dehydrating ingredients and packaging them with other purchased ingredients, such as rice and dry pasta.

■ Milling rice and packaging it with other ingredients are classified in U.S. Industry 311212, Rice Milling;

■ Manufacturing dry pasta and packaging it with other ingredients are classified in U.S. Industry 311823, Dry Pasta Manufacturing;

■ Manufacturing vegetable flours and meals are classified in U.S. Industry 311211, Flour Milling; Mixing purchased dried and/or dehydrated potatoes, rice, and dry pasta, and packaging them with other purchased ingredients, and mixing purchased dried and/or dehydrated ingredients for soup mixes and bouillon are classified in U.S. Industry 311999, All Other Miscellaneous Food Manufacturing; and

■ Manufacturing dry salad dressing and dry sauce mixes are classified in U.S. Industry 311942, Spice and Extract Manufacturing.

3115 Dairy Product Manufacturing

This industry group comprises establishments that manufacture dairy products from raw milk, processed milk, and dairy substitutes.

31151 Dairy Product (except Frozen) Manufacturing

This industry comprises establishments primarily engaged in one or more of the following: (1) manufacturing dairy products (except frozen) from raw milk and/or processed milk products; (2) manufacturing dairy substitutes (except frozen) from soybeans and other nondairy substances; and (3) manufacturing dry, condensed, concentrated, and evaporated dairy and dairy substitute products.

■ Manufacturing cheese-based salad dressings are classified in Industry 31194, Seasoning and Dressing Manufacturing;

■ Manufacturing margarine or margarine-butter blends are classified in Industry 31122, Starch and Vegetable Fats and Oils Manufacturing;

■ Manufacturing frozen whipped toppings are classified in Industry 31141, Frozen Food Manufacturing; and

■ Manufacturing ice cream, frozen yogurt, and other frozen dairy desserts are classified in Industry 31152, Ice Cream and Frozen Dessert Manufacturing.

311511 Fluid Milk Manufacturing ᶜᴬᴺ

This U.S. industry comprises establishments primarily engaged in (1) manufacturing processed milk products, such as pasteurized milk or cream and sour cream and/or (2) manufacturing fluid milk dairy substitutes from soybeans and other nondairy substances.

■ Manufacturing dry mix whipped toppings, canned milk, and ultra high temperature milk are classified in U.S. Industry 311514, Dry, Condensed, and Evaporated Dairy Product Manufacturing;

■ Manufacturing frozen whipped toppings are classified in U.S. Industry 311412, Frozen Specialty Food Manufacturing; and

■ Manufacturing ice cream and frozen yogurt and other frozen desserts are classified in Industry 311520, Ice Cream and Frozen Dessert Manufacturing.

311512 Creamery Butter Manufacturing ᵁˢ

This U.S. industry comprises establishments primarily engaged in manufacturing creamery butter from milk and/or processed milk products.

■ Establishments primarily engaged in manufacturing margarine or margarine-butter blends are classified in U.S. Industry 311225, Fats and Oils Refining and Blending.

311513 Cheese Manufacturing ᵁˢ

This U.S. industry comprises establishments primarily engaged in (1) manufacturing cheese products (except cottage cheese) from raw milk and/or processed milk products and/or (2) manufacturing cheese substitutes from soybean and other nondairy substances.

■ Manufacturing cheese-based salad dressings are classified in U.S. Industry 311941, Mayonnaise, Dressing, and Other Prepared Sauce Manufacturing; and

■ Manufacturing cottage cheese are classified in U.S. Industry 311511, Fluid Milk Manufacturing.

Sector

31-33

Manufacturing

■ = Cross-References

US—United States industry only. CAN—United States and Canadian industries are comparable. When neither US nor CAN appears, Canadian, Mexican, and United States industries are comparable.

322

Harris InfoSource

311514 Dry, Condensed, and Evaporated Dairy Product Manufacturing ᵁˢ
This U.S. industry comprises establishments primarily engaged in manufacturing dry, condensed, and evaporated milk and dairy substitute products.

- Manufacturing fluid milk products are classified in U.S. Industry 311511, Fluid Milk Manufacturing;
- Manufacturing creamery butter are classified in U.S. Industry 311512, Creamery Butter Manufacturing; and
- Manufacturing cheese products are classified in U.S. Industry 311513, Cheese Manufacturing.

31152 Ice Cream and Frozen Dessert Manufacturing
See industry description for 311520 below.

311520 Ice Cream and Frozen Dessert Manufacturing
This industry comprises establishments primarily engaged in manufacturing ice cream, frozen yogurts, frozen ices, sherbets, frozen tofu, and other frozen desserts (except bakery products).

- Manufacturing frozen bakery products are classified in U.S. Industry 311813, Frozen Cakes, Pies, and Other Pastries Manufacturing; and
- Manufacturing ice cream and ice milk mixes are classified in U.S. Industry 311514, Dry, Condensed, and Evaporated Dairy Product Manufacturing.

3116 Animal Slaughtering and Processing

31161 Animal Slaughtering and Processing
This industry comprises establishments primarily engaged in one or more of the following: (1) slaughtering animals; (2) preparing processed meats and meat byproducts; and (3) rendering and/or refining animal fat, bones, and meat scraps. This industry includes establishments primarily engaged in assembly cutting and packing of meats (i.e., boxed meats) from purchased carcasses.

- Manufacturing canned meat for baby food are classified in Industry 31142, Fruit and Vegetable Canning, Pickling and Drying;
- Manufacturing meat-based animal feeds from carcasses are classified in Industry 31111, Animal Food Manufacturing;
- Blending purchased animal fats with vegetable fats are classified in Industry 31122, Starch and Vegetable Fats and Oils Manufacturing;
- Manufacturing canned and frozen specialty foods containing meat, such as nationality foods (e.g., enchiladas, pizza, egg rolls) and frozen dinners, are classified in Industry Group 3114, Fruit and Vegetable Preserving and Specialty Food Manufacturing;
- Drying, freezing, or breaking eggs are classified in Industry 31199, All Other Food Manufacturing; and
- Cutting meat (except box meat) are classified in Industry 42247, Meat and Meat Product Wholesalers.

311611 Animal (except Poultry) Slaughtering ᶜᴬᴺ
This U.S. industry comprises establishments primarily engaged in slaughtering animals (except poultry and small game). Establishments that slaughter and prepare meats are included in this industry.

- Processing meat and meat byproducts (except poultry and small game) from purchased meats are classified in U.S. Industry 311612, Meat Processed from Carcasses;
- Slaughtering and/or processing poultry and small game are classified in U.S. Industry 311615, Poultry Processing;
- Rendering lard and other animal fats and oils, animal fat, bones, and meat scraps are classified in U.S. Industry 3116133, Rendering and Meat Byproduct Processing; and
- Manufacturing canned and frozen specialty foods containing meat, such as nationality foods (e.g., enchiladas, egg rolls, pizza) and frozen dinners, are classified in Industry Group 3114, Fruit and Vegetable Preserving and Specialty Food Manufacturing.

311612 Meat Processed from Carcasses ᵁˢ
This U.S. industry comprises establishments primarily engaged in processing or preserving meat and meat byproducts (except poultry and small game) from purchased meats. This industry includes establishments primarily engaged in assembly cutting and packing of meats (i.e., boxed meats) from purchased meats.

- Slaughtering animals (except poultry and small game) are classified in U.S. Industry 311611, Animal (except Poultry) Slaughtering;
- Slaughtering poultry and small game are classified in U.S. Industry 311615, Poultry Processing;
- Rendering animal fat, bones, and meat scraps are classified in U.S. Industry 311613, Rendering and Meat Byproduct Processing;
- Manufacturing canned meats for baby food are classified in U.S. Industry 311422, Specialty Canning;
- Manufacturing meat-based animal feeds from carcasses are classified in Industry 31111, Animal Food Manufacturing;
- Manufacturing canned and frozen specialty foods containing meat, such as nationality foods (e.g., enchiladas, egg rolls, pizza) and frozen dinners, are classified in Industry Group 3114, Fruit and Vegetable Preserving and Specialty Food Manufacturing; and
- Cutting meat (except boxed meat) are classified in U.S. Industry 422470, Meat and Meat Product Wholesalers.

Visit page 17 to learn about classification changes to this sector.

Sector
31-33
Manufacturing

■ = Cross-References

US—United States industry only. CAN—United States and Canadian industries are comparable. When neither US nor CAN appears, Canadian, Mexican, and United States industries are comparable.

311613 Rendering and Meat Byproduct Processing ᵁˢ

This U.S. industry comprises establishments primarily engaged in rendering animal fat, bones, and meat scraps.

- Establishments primarily engaged in blending purchased animal fats with vegetable fats are classified in U.S. Industry 311225, Fats and Oils Refining and Blending.

311615 Poultry Processing ᶜᴬᴺ

This U.S. industry comprises establishments primarily engaged in (1) slaughtering poultry and small game and/or (2) preparing processed poultry and small game meat and meat byproducts.

- Slaughtering animals (except poultry and small game) and/or preparing meats are classified in U.S. Industry 311611, Animal (except Poultry) Slaughtering;
- Preparing meat and meat byproducts (except poultry and small game) from purchased meats are classified in U.S. Industry 311612, Meat Processed from Carcasses;
- Rendering animal fat, bones, and meat scraps are classified in U.S. Industry 311613, Rendering and Meat Byproduct Processing;
- Canning poultry and small game for baby food are classified in U.S. Industry 311422, Specialty Canning;
- Producing meat-based animal feeds from carcasses are classified in Industry 31111, Animal Food Manufacturing;
- Manufacturing canned and frozen meat products, such as nationality foods (e.g., enchiladas, egg rolls, pizza) and frozen dinners, are classified in Industry Group 3114, Fruit and Vegetable Preserving and Specialty Food Manufacturing; and
- Drying, freezing, and breaking eggs are classified in U.S. Industry 311999, All Other Miscellaneous Food Manufacturing.

3117 Seafood Product Preparation and Packaging

31171 Seafood Product Preparation and Packaging

This industry comprises establishments primarily engaged in one or more of the following: (1) canning seafood (including soup); (2) smoking, salting, and drying seafoods; (3) eviscerating fresh fish by removing heads, fins, scales, bones, and entrails; (4) shucking and packing fresh shellfish; (5) processing marine fats and oils; and (6) freezing seafood. Establishments known as "floating factory ships" that are engaged in the gathering and processing of seafood into canned seafood products are included in this industry.

311711 Seafood Canning ᵁˢ

This U.S. industry comprises establishments primarily engaged in (1) canning seafood (including soup) and marine fats and oils and/or (2) smoking, salting, and drying seafoods. Establishments known as "floating factory ships" that are engaged in the gathering and processing of seafood into canned seafood products are included in this industry.

- Establishments primarily engaged in preparing fresh and frozen seafood and marine fats and oils are classified in U.S. Industry 311712, Fresh and Frozen Seafood Processing.

311712 Fresh and Frozen Seafood Processing ᵁˢ

This U.S. industry comprises establishments primarily engaged in one or more of the following: (1) eviscerating fresh fish by removing heads, fins, scales, bones, and entrails; (2) shucking and packing fresh shellfish; (3) manufacturing frozen seafood; and (4) processing fresh and frozen marine fats and oils.

- Establishments primarily engaged in canning and curing seafood are classified in U.S. Industry 311711, Seafood Canning.

3118 Bakeries and Tortilla Manufacturing

31181 Bread and Bakery Product Manufacturing

This industry comprises establishments primarily engaged in manufacturing fresh and frozen bread and other bakery products.

- Manufacturing cookies and crackers are classified in Industry 31182, Cookie, Cracker, and Pasta Manufacturing;
- Preparing and selling bakery products (e.g., cookies, pretzels) for immediate consumption are classified in Industry 72221, Limited-service Eating Places;
- Retailing bakery products not for immediate consumption made elsewhere are classified in Industry 44529, Other Specialty Food Stores; and
- Manufacturing pretzels (except soft) are classified in Industry 31191, Snack Food Manufacturing.

311811 Retail Bakeries ᶜᴬᴺ

This U.S. industry comprises establishments primarily engaged in retailing bread and other bakery products not for immediate consumption made on the premises from flour, not from prepared dough.

Sector
31-33
Manufacturing

■ = Cross-References

US—United States industry only. CAN—United States and Canadian industries are comparable. When neither US nor CAN appears, Canadian, Mexican, and United States industries are comparable.

324

Harris InfoSource

- Retailing bakery products not for immediate consumption made elsewhere are classified in U.S. Industry 445291, Baked Goods Stores;
- Preparing and selling bakery products (e.g., cookies, pretzels) for immediate consumption are classified in U.S. Industry 722213, Snack and Nonalcoholic Beverage Bars;
- Manufacturing fresh or frozen breads and other fresh bakery (except cookies and crackers) products are classified in U.S. Industry 311812, Commercial Bakeries; and
- Manufacturing cookies and crackers are classified in U.S. Industry 311821, Cookie and Cracker Manufacturing.

311812 Commercial Bakeries US

This U.S. industry comprises establishments primarily engaged in manufacturing fresh and frozen bread and bread-type rolls and other fresh bakery (except cookies and crackers) products.

- Retailing bread and other bakery products not for immediate consumption made on the premises from flour, not from prepared dough are classified in U.S. Industry 311811, Retail Bakeries;
- Manufacturing frozen bakery products (except bread) are classified in U.S. Industry 311813, Frozen Cakes, Pies, and Other Pastries Manufacturing;
- Preparing and selling bakery products (e.g., cookies, pretzels) for immediate consumption are classified in U.S. Industry 722213, Snack and Nonalcoholic Beverage Bars;
- Retailing bakery products not for immediate consumption made elsewhere are classified in U.S. Industry 445291, Baked Goods Stores;
- Manufacturing cookies and crackers are classified in U.S. Industry 311821, Cookie and Cracker Manufacturing; and
- Manufacturing pretzels (except soft) are classified in U.S. Industry 311919, Other Snack Food Manufacturing.

311813 Frozen Cakes, Pies, and Other Pastries Manufacturing US

This U.S. industry comprises establishments primarily engaged in manufacturing frozen bakery products (except bread), such as cakes, pies, and doughnuts.

- Manufacturing frozen breads are classified in U.S. Industry 311812, Commercial Bakeries;
- Retailing bakery products not for immediate consumption made on the premises from flour, not from prepared dough are classified in U.S. Industry 311811, Retail Bakeries;
- Preparing and selling bakery products (e.g., cookies, pretzels) for immediate consumption are classified in U.S. Industry 722213, Snack and Nonalcoholic Beverage Bars;
- Manufacturing cookies and crackers are classified in U.S. Industry 311821, Cookie and Cracker Manufacturing; and
- Retailing bakery products not for immediate consumption made elsewhere are classified in U.S. Industry 445291, Baked Goods Stores.

31182 Cookie, Cracker, and Pasta Manufacturing

This industry comprises establishments primarily engaged in one of the following: (1) manufacturing cookies and crackers; (2) preparing flour and dough mixes and dough from flour ground elsewhere; and (3) manufacturing dry pasta. The establishments in this industry may package the dry pasta they manufacture with other ingredients.

- Preparing and selling bakery products (eg., cookies, pretzels) for immediate consumption are classified in Industry 72221, Limited-service Eating Places;
- Retailing bakery products not for immediate consumption made elsewhere are classified in Industry 44529, Other Specialty Food Stores;
- Manufacturing bakery products (e.g., bread, cookies, pies) are classified in Industry 31181, Bread and Bakery Product Manufacturing;
- Milling flour and preparing flour mixes or doughs are classified in Industry 31121, Flour Milling and Malt Manufacturing;
- Manufacturing canned pasta specialties are classified in Industry 31142, Fruit and Vegetable Canning, Pickling and Drying;
- Manufacturing fresh pasta are classified in Industry 31199, All Other Food Manufacturing;
- Manufacturing pretzels (except soft) are classified in Industry 31191, Snack Food Manufacturing;
- Mixing purchased dried and/or dehydrated ingredients with purchased dry pasta are classified in Industry 31199, All Other Food Manufacturing; and
- Drying and/or dehydrating ingredients and packaging them with purchased dry pasta are classified in Industry 31142, Fruit and Vegetable Canning, Pickling, and Drying.

311821 Cookie and Cracker Manufacturing CAN

This U.S. industry comprises establishments primarily engaged in manufacturing cookies, crackers, and other products, such as ice cream cones.

- Preparing and selling bakery products (e.g., cookies, pretzels) for immediate consumption are classified in U.S. Industry 722213, Snack and Nonalcoholic Beverage Bars;
- Retailing bakery products not for immediate consumption made elsewhere are classified in U.S. Industry 445291, Baked Goods Stores;
- Manufacturing bakery products (e.g., breads, cookies, pies) are classified in Industry 31181, Bread and Bakery Product Manufacturing; and
- Manufacturing pretzels (except soft) are classified in U.S. Industry 311919, Other Snack Food Manufacturing.

Visit page 17 to learn about classification changes to this sector.

Sector 31-33

Manufacturing

■ = Cross-References

311822 Flour Mixes and Dough Manufacturing from Purchased Flour CAN

This U.S. industry comprises establishments primarily engaged in manufacturing prepared flour mixes or dough mixes from flour ground elsewhere.

- Establishments primarily engaged in milling flour and preparing flour mixes or doughs are classified in U.S. Industry 311211, Flour Milling.

311823 Dry Pasta Manufacturing CAN

This U.S. industry comprises establishments primarily engaged in manufacturing dry pasta. The establishments in this industry may package the dry pasta they manufacture with other ingredients.

- Manufacturing fresh pasta are classified in U.S. Industry 311991, Perishable Prepared Food Manufacturing;
- Manufacturing pasta specialties are classified in Industry Group 3114, Fruit and Vegetable Preserving and Specialty Food Manufacturing;
- Mixing purchased dried and/or dehydrated ingredients with purchased dry pasta are classified in U.S. Industry 311999, All Other Miscellaneous Food Manufacturing; and
- Drying and/or dehydrating ingredients packaged with purchased dry pasta are classified in U.S. Industry 311423, Dried and Dehydrated Food Manufacturing.

31183 Tortilla Manufacturing

See industry description for 311830 below.

311830 Tortilla Manufacturing

This industry comprises establishments primarily engaged in manufacturing tortillas.

- Manufacturing canned nationality foods using tortillas are classified in U.S. Industry 311422, Specialty Canning;
- Manufacturing frozen nationality foods using tortillas are classified in U.S. Industry 311412, Frozen Specialty Food Manufacturing; and
- Manufacturing tortilla chips are classified in U.S. Industry 311919, Other Snack Food Manufacturing.

3119 Other Food Manufacturing

This industry group comprises establishments primarily engaged in manufacturing food (except animal food; grain and oilseed milling; sugar and confectionery products; preserved fruit, vegetable, and specialty foods; dairy products; meat products; seafood products; and bakeries and tortillas). The industry group includes industries with different productive processes, such as snack food manufacturing; coffee and tea manufacturing; concentrate, syrup, condiment, and spice manufacturing; and, in general, an entire range of other miscellaneous food product manufacturing.

31191 Snack Food Manufacturing

This industry comprises establishments primarily engaged in one or more of the following: (1) salting, roasting, drying, cooking, or canning nuts; (2) processing grains or seeds into snacks; (3) manufacturing peanut butter; and (4) manufacturing potato chips, corn chips, popped popcorn, pretzels (except soft), pork rinds, and similar snacks.

- Manufacturing crackers are classified in Industry 31182, Cookie, Cracker, and Pasta Manufacturing;
- Manufacturing unpopped popcorn are classified in Industry 31199, All Other Food Manufacturing;
- Manufacturing chocolate or candy-coated nuts and candy-covered popcorn are classified in Industry Group 3113, Sugar and Confectionery Product Manufacturing; and
- Manufacturing soft pretzels are classified in Industry 31181, Bread and Bakery Product Manufacturing.

311911 Roasted Nuts and Peanut Butter Manufacturing CAN

This U.S. industry comprises establishments primarily engaged in one or more of the following: (1) salting, roasting, drying, cooking, or canning nuts; (2) processing grains or seeds into snacks; and (3) manufacturing peanut butter.

- Establishments primarily engaged in manufacturing chocolate or candy-coated nuts and candy-covered popcorn are classified in Industry Group 3113, Sugar and Confectionery Product Manufacturing.

311919 Other Snack Food Manufacturing CAN

This U.S. industry comprises establishments primarily engaged in manufacturing snack foods (except roasted nuts and peanut butter).

- Manufacturing cookies and crackers are classified in U.S. Industry 311821, Cookie and Cracker Manufacturing;
- Manufacturing candy covered popcorn and nonchocolate granola bars are classified in Industry 311340, Nonchocolate Confectionery Manufacturing;

Sector
31-33

Manufacturing

■ = Cross-References

US—United States industry only. CAN—United States and Canadian industries are comparable. When neither US nor CAN appears, Canadian, Mexican, and United States industries are comparable.

326

Harris InfoSource

- Salting, roasting, drying, cooking, or canning nuts and seeds are classified in U.S. Industry 311911, Roasted Nuts and Peanut Butter Manufacturing;
- Manufacturing unpopped popcorn are classified in U.S. Industry 311999, All Other Miscellaneous Food Manufacturing; and
- Manufacturing soft pretzels are classified in U.S. Industry 311812, Commercial Bakeries.

31192 Coffee and Tea Manufacturing
See industry description for 311920 below.

311920 Coffee and Tea Manufacturing
This industry comprises establishments primarily engaged in one or more of the following: (1) roasting coffee; (2) manufacturing coffee and tea concentrates (including instant and freeze-dried); (3) blending tea; (4) manufacturing herbal tea; and (5) manufacturing coffee extracts, flavorings, and syrups.

- Establishments primarily engaged in bottling and canning ice tea are classified in U.S. Industry 312111, Soft Drink Manufacturing.

31193 Flavoring Syrup and Concentrate Manufacturing
See industry description for 311930 below.

311930 Flavoring Syrup and Concentrate Manufacturing
This industry comprises establishments primarily engaged in manufacturing flavoring syrup drink concentrates and related products for soda fountain use or for the manufacture of soft drinks.

- Manufacturing chocolate syrup are classified in Industry 311320, Chocolate and Confectionery Manufacturing from Cacao Beans;
- Manufacturing flavoring extracts (except coffee and meat) and natural food colorings are classified in U.S. Industry 311942, Spice and Extract Manufacturing;
- Manufacturing coffee extracts are classified in Industry 311920, Coffee and Tea Manufacturing;
- Manufacturing meat extracts are classified in Industry 31161, Animal Slaughtering and Processing;
- Manufacturing powdered drink mixes (except coffee, tea, chocolate, or milk-based) and table syrup from corn syrup are classified in U.S. Industry 311999, All Other Miscellaneous Food Manufacturing;
- Reducing maple sap to maple syrup are classified in U.S. Industry 111998, All Other Miscellaneous Crop Farming; and
- Manufacturing natural nonfood colorings are classified in U.S. Industry 325199, All Other Basic Organic Chemical Manufacturing.

Visit page 17 to learn about classification changes to this sector.

31194 Seasoning and Dressing Manufacturing
This industry comprises establishments primarily engaged in one or more of the following: (1) manufacturing dressings and sauces, such as mayonnaise, salad dressing, vinegar, mustard, horseradish, soy sauce, tarter sauce, Worcestershire sauce, and other prepared sauces (except tomato-based and gravies); (2) manufacturing spices, table salt, seasoning, and flavoring extracts (except coffee and meat), and natural food colorings; and (3) manufacturing dry mix food preparations, such as salad dressing mixes, gravy and sauce mixes, frosting mixes, and other dry mix preparations.

- Manufacturing catsup and other tomato-based sauces are classified in Industry 31142, Fruit and Vegetable Canning, Pickling and Drying;
- Mixing purchased dried and/or dehydrated potato, rice, and pasta and packaging them with other purchased ingredients, and manufacturing prepared frosting are classified in Industry 31199, All Other Food Manufacturing;
- Drying and/or dehydrating ingredients for dry soup mixes and bouillon are classified in Industry 31142, Fruit and Vegetable Canning, Pickling and Drying;

- Mixing purchased dried and/or dehydrated ingredients for dry soup mixes and bouillon are classified in Industry 31199, All Other Food Manufacturing;
- Manufacturing industrial salts are classified in Industry 32599, Other Chemical Product and Preparation Manufacturing;
- Manufacturing flavoring syrups (except coffee) are classified in Industry 31193, Flavoring Syrup and Concentrate Manufacturing;
- Manufacturing synthetic food colorings are classified in Industry 32513, Synthetic Dye and Pigment Manufacturing;
- Manufacturing natural organic colorings for nonfood uses are classified in Industry 32519, Other Basic Organic Chemical Manufacturing;
- Manufacturing coffee extracts are classified in Industry 31192, Coffee and Tea Manufacturing;
- Manufacturing meat extracts are classified in Industry 31161, Animal Slaughtering and Processing; and
- Manufacturing gravies are classified in Industry 31199, All Other Food Manufacturing.

311941 Mayonnaise, Dressing, and Other Prepared Sauce Manufacturing [US]
This U.S. industry comprises establishments primarily engaged in manufacturing mayonnaise, salad dressing, vinegar, mustard, horseradish, soy sauce, tarter sauce, Worcestershire sauce, and other prepared sauces (except tomato-based and gravy).

Sector
31-33
Manufacturing

■ = Cross-References

US—United States industry only. CAN—United States and Canadian industries are comparable. When neither US nor CAN appears, Canadian, Mexican, and United States industries are comparable.

www.harrisinfo.com

327

- Manufacturing catsup and similar tomato-based sauces are classified in U.S. Industry 311421, Fruit and Vegetable Canning;
- Manufacturing dry salad dressing and dry sauce mixes are classified in U.S. Industry 311942, Spice and Extract Manufacturing; and
- Manufacturing gravies are classified in U.S. Industry 311999, All Other Miscellaneous Food Manufacturing.

311942 Spice and Extract Manufacturing US

This U.S. industry comprises establishments primarily engaged in (1) manufacturing spices, table salt, seasonings, flavoring extracts (except coffee and meat), and natural food colorings and/or (2) manufacturing dry mix food preparations, such as salad dressing mixes, gravy and sauce mixes, frosting mixes, and other dry mix preparations.

- Manufacturing catsup and other tomato-based sauces are classified in U.S. Industry 311421, Fruit and Vegetable Canning;
- Manufacturing mayonnaise, dressings, and prepared nontomato-based sauces are classified in U.S. Industry 311941, Mayonnaise, Dressing, and Other Prepared Sauce Manufacturing;
- Manufacturing industrial salts are classified in U.S. Industry 325998, All Other Miscellaneous Chemical Product and Preparation Manufacturing;
- Drying and/or dehydrating ingredients for dry soup mixes and bouillon are classified in U.S. Industry 311423, Dried and Dehydrated Food Manufacturing;
- Mixing purchased dried and/or dehydrated ingredients for dry soup mixes and bouillon are classified in U.S. Industry 311999, All Other Miscellaneous Food Manufacturing;
- Manufacturing flavoring syrups are classified in Industry 311930, Flavoring Syrup and Concentrate Manufacturing;
- Manufacturing dried and dehydrated potato, rice, or dry pasta packaged with other ingredients, and prepared frostings are classified in U.S. Industry 311999, All Other Miscellaneous Food Manufacturing;
- Manufacturing coffee extracts are classified in Industry 311920, Coffee and Tea Manufacturing;
- Manufacturing meat extracts are classified in Industry 31161, Animal Slaughtering and Processing;
- Manufacturing synthetic food colorings are classified in U.S. Industry 325132, Synthetic Organic Dye and Pigment Manufacturing; and
- Manufacturing natural organic colorings for nonfood uses are classified in U.S. Industry 325199, All Other Basic Organic Chemical Manufacturing.

31199 All Other Food Manufacturing

This industry comprises establishments primarily engaged in manufacturing food (except animal food; grain and oilseed milling; sugar and confectionery products; preserved fruits, vegetables, and specialties; dairy products; meat products; seafood products; bakeries and tortillas; snack foods; coffee and tea; flavoring syrups and concentrates; seasonings; and dressings). Included in this industry are establishments primarily engaged in mixing purchased dried and/or dehydrated ingredients including those mixing purchased dried and/or dehydrated ingredients for soup mixes and bouillon.

- Manufacturing animal foods are classified in Industry Group 3111, Animal Food Manufacturing;
- Milling grain and oilseed are classified in Industry Group 3112, Grain and Oilseed Milling;
- Manufacturing sugar and confectionery products are classified in Industry Group 3113, Sugar and Confectionery Product Manufacturing;
- Preserving fruit, vegetables, and specialty foods are classified in Industry Group 3114, Fruit and Vegetable Preserving and Specialty Food Manufacturing;
- Manufacturing dairy products are classified in Industry Group 3115, Dairy Product Manufacturing;
- Manufacturing meat products are classified in Industry Group 3116, Animal Slaughtering and Processing;
- Manufacturing seafood products are classified in Industry Group 3117, Seafood Product Preparation and Packaging;
- Manufacturing bakery and tortilla products are classified in Industry Group 3118, Bakeries and Tortilla Manufacturing;
- Manufacturing snack foods are classified in Industry 31191, Snack Food Manufacturing;
- Manufacturing coffee and tea are classified in Industry 31192, Coffee and Tea Manufacturing;
- Manufacturing flavoring syrups and concentrates are classified in Industry 31193, Flavoring Syrup and Concentrate Manufacturing;
- Manufacturing seasonings and dressings are classified in Industry 31194, Seasoning and Dressing Manufacturing;
- Milling rice and packaging it with other ingredients are classified in Industry 31121, Flour Milling and Malt Manufacturing;
- Manufacturing dry pasta and packaging it with other ingredients are classified in Industry 31182, Cookie, Cracker, and Pasta Manufacturing; and Drying and/or dehydrating ingredients and packaging them with other purchased ingredients are classified in Industry 31142, Fruit and Vegetable Canning, Pickling and Drying.

311991 Perishable Prepared Food Manufacturing US

This U.S. industry comprises establishments primarily engaged in manufacturing perishable prepared foods, such as salads, sandwiches, prepared meals, fresh pizza, fresh pasta, and peeled or cut vegetables.

311999 All Other Miscellaneous Food Manufacturing US

This U.S. industry comprises establishments primarily engaged in manufacturing food (except animal food; grain and oilseed milling; sugar and confectionery products; preserved fruits, vegetables, and specialties; dairy products; meat products; seafood products; bakeries and tortillas; snack foods; coffee

Sector
31-33
Manufacturing

■ = Cross-References

US—United States industry only. CAN—United States and Canadian industries are comparable. When neither US nor CAN appears, Canadian, Mexican, and United States industries are comparable.

328

Harris InfoSource

and tea; flavoring syrups and concentrates; seasonings and dressings; and perishable prepared food). Included in this industry are establishments primarily engaged in mixing purchased dried and/or dehydrated ingredients including those mixing purchased dried and/or dehydrated ingredients for soup mixes and bouillon.

- Manufacturing animal foods are classified in Industry Group 3111, Animal Food Manufacturing;
- Milling grain and oilseed are classified in Industry Group 3112, Grain and Oilseed Milling;
- Manufacturing sugar and confectionery products are classified in Industry Group 3113, Sugar and Confectionery Product Manufacturing;
- Preserving fruit, vegetable, and specialty foods are classified in Industry Group 3114, Fruit and Vegetable Preserving and Specialty Food Manufacturing;
- Manufacturing dairy products are classified in Industry Group 3115, Dairy Product Manufacturing;
- Manufacturing meat products are classified in Industry Group 3116, Meat Product Manufacturing;
- Manufacturing seafood products are classified in Industry Group 3117, Seafood Product Preparation and Packaging;
- Manufacturing bakery and tortilla products are classified in Industry Group 3118, Bakeries and Tortilla Manufacturing;
- Manufacturing snack foods are classified in Industry 31191, Snack Food Manufacturing;
- Manufacturing coffee and tea are classified in Industry 31192, Coffee and Tea Manufacturing;
- Manufacturing flavoring syrups and concentrates are classified in Industry 31193, Flavoring Syrup and Concentrate Manufacturing;
- Manufacturing seasonings and dressings are classified in Industry 31194, Seasoning and Dressing Manufacturing;
- Manufacturing perishable prepared foods are classified in U.S. Industry 311991, Perishable Prepared Food Manufacturing;
- Milling rice and packaging it with other ingredients are classified in U.S. Industry 311212, Rice Milling;
- Manufacturing dry pasta and packaging it with ingredients are classified in U.S. Industry 311823, Dry Pasta Manufacturing; and
- Drying and/or dehydrating ingredients and packaging them with other purchased ingredients are classified in U.S. Industry 311423, Dried and Dehydrated Food Manufacturing.

▶312 BEVERAGE AND TOBACCO PRODUCT MANUFACTURING

Industries in the Beverage and Tobacco Product Manufacturing subsector manufacture beverages and tobacco products. The industry group, Beverage Manufacturing, includes three types of establishments: (1) those that manufacture nonalcoholic beverages; (2) those that manufacture alcoholic beverages through the fermentation process; and (3) those that produce distilled alcoholic beverages. Ice manufacturing, while not a beverage, is included with nonalcoholic beverage manufacturing because it uses the same production process as water purification.

In the case of activities related to the manufacture of beverages, the structure follows the defined productive processes. Brandy, a distilled beverage, was not placed under distillery product manufacturing, but rather under the NAICS class for winery product manufacturing since the productive process used in the manufacturing of alcoholic grape-based beverages produces both wines (fermented beverage) and brandies (distilled beverage).

The industry group, Tobacco Manufacturing, includes two types of establishments: (1) those engaged in redrying and stemming tobacco and (2) those that manufacture tobacco products, such as cigarettes and cigars.

Visit page 17 to learn about classification changes to this sector.

3121 Beverage Manufacturing

31211 Soft Drink and Ice Manufacturing
This industry comprises establishments primarily engaged in one or more of the following: (1) manufacturing soft drinks; (2) manufacturing ice; and (3) purifying and bottling water.

- Canning fruit and vegetable juices are classified in Industry 31142, Fruit and Vegetable Canning, Pickling and Drying;
- Manufacturing soft drink bases are classified in Industry 31193, Flavoring Syrup and Concentrate Manufacturing;
- Manufacturing nonalcoholic cider are classified in Industry 31199, All Other Food Manufacturing;
- Manufacturing dry ice are classified in Industry 32512, Industrial Gas Manufacturing;
- Manufacturing milk-based drinks are classified in Industry 31151, Dairy Product (except Frozen) Manufacturing;
- Manufacturing nonalcoholic beers are classified in Industry 31212, Breweries;
- Manufacturing nonalcoholic wines are classified in Industry 31213, Wineries; and
- Bottling purchased purified water are classified in Industry 42249, Other Grocery and Related Products Wholesalers.

312111 Soft Drink Manufacturing US
This U.S. industry comprises establishments primarily engaged in manufacturing soft drinks and artificially carbonated waters.

Sector 31-33

Manufacturing

■ = Cross-References

US—United States industry only. CAN—United States and Canadian industries are comparable. When neither US nor CAN appears, Canadian, Mexican, and United States industries are comparable.

www.harrisinfo.com

329

- Canning fruit and vegetable juices are classified in U.S. Industry 311421, Fruit and Vegetable Canning;
- Manufacturing fruit syrups for flavoring are classified in Industry 31193, Flavoring Syrup and Concentrate Manufacturing;
- Manufacturing nonalcoholic cider are classified in U.S. Industry 311999, All Other Miscellaneous Food Manufacturing;
- Purifying and bottling water (except artificially carbonated and flavored water) are classified in U.S. Industry 312112, Bottled Water Manufacturing;
- Manufacturing milk-based drinks are classified in U.S. Industry 311511, Fluid Milk Manufacturing;
- Manufacturing nonalcoholic beers are classified in Industry 312120, Breweries; and
- Manufacturing nonalcoholic wines are classified in Industry 312130, Wineries.

312112 Bottled Water Manufacturing ᵁˢ

This U.S. industry comprises establishments primarily engaged in purifying and bottling water (including naturally carbonated).

- Manufacturing artificially carbonated waters are classified in U.S. Industry 312111, Soft Drink Manufacturing; and
- Bottling purchased purified water are classified in Industry 422490, Other Grocery and Related Products Wholesalers.

312113 Ice Manufacturing ᵁˢ

This U.S. industry comprises establishments primarily engaged in manufacturing ice.

- Establishments primarily engaged in manufacturing dry ice are classified in Industry 325120, Industrial Gas Manufacturing.

31212 Breweries

See industry description for 312120 below.

312120 Breweries

This industry comprises establishments primarily engaged in brewing beer, ale, malt liquors, and non-alcoholic beer.

- Bottling purchased malt beverages are classified in Industry 422810, Beer and Ale Wholesalers; and
- Manufacturing malt are classified in U.S. Industry 311213, Malt Manufacturing.

31213 Wineries

See industry description for 312130 below.

312130 Wineries

This industry comprises establishments primarily engaged in one or more of the following: (1) growing grapes and manufacturing wine and brandies; (2) manufacturing wine and brandies from grapes and other fruits grown elsewhere; and (3) blending wines and brandies.

- Establishments primarily engaged in bottling wines made elsewhere are classified in Industry 422820, Wine and Distilled Alcoholic Beverage Wholesalers.

31214 Distilleries

See industry description for 312140 below.

312140 Distilleries

This industry comprises establishments primarily engaged in one or more of the following: (1) distilling potable liquors (except brandies); (2) distilling and blending liquors; and (3) blending and mixing liquors and other ingredients.

- Manufacturing nonpotable ethyl alcohol are classified in U.S. Industry 325193, Ethyl Alcohol Manufacturing;
- Bottling liquors made elsewhere are classified in Industry 422820, Wine and Distilled Alcoholic Beverage Wholesalers; and
- Manufacturing brandies are classified in Industry 312130, Wineries.

3122 Tobacco Manufacturing

31221 Tobacco Stemming and Redrying

See industry description for 312210 below.

312210 Tobacco Stemming and Redrying

This industry comprises establishments primarily engaged in the stemming and redrying of tobacco.

- Reconstituting tobacco are classified in U.S. Industry 312229, Other Tobacco Product Manufacturing; and
- Selling leaf tobacco as merchant wholesalers, agents, or brokers, and that also engage in stemming tobacco are classified in Industry 422940, Tobacco and Tobacco Product Wholesalers.

Sector 31-33

Manufacturing

■ = Cross-References

US—United States industry only. CAN—United States and Canadian industries are comparable. When neither US nor CAN appears, Canadian, Mexican, and United States industries are comparable.

330

Harris InfoSource

31222 Tobacco Product Manufacturing

This industry comprises establishments primarily engaged in manufacturing cigarettes, cigars, smoking and chewing tobacco, and reconstituted tobacco.

- Establishments primarily engaged in stemming and redrying tobacco are classified in Industry 31221 Tobacco Stemming and Redrying.

312221 Cigarette Manufacturing ᵁˢ

This U.S. industry comprises establishments primarily engaged in manufacturing cigarettes.

- Establishments primarily engaged in manufacturing cigars, smoking tobacco, chewing tobacco, and reconstituted tobacco are classified in U.S. Industry 312229, Other Tobacco Product Manufacturing.

312229 Other Tobacco Product Manufacturing ᵁˢ

This U.S. industry comprises establishments primarily engaged in manufacturing tobacco products (except cigarettes).

- Manufacturing cigarettes are classified in U.S. Industry 312221, Cigarette Manufacturing; and
- Stemming and redrying tobacco are classified in Industry 312210, Tobacco Stemming and Redrying.

➡ 313 TEXTILE MILLS

Industries in the Textile Mills subsector group establishments that transform a basic fiber (natural or synthetic) into a product, such as yarn or fabric, that is further manufactured into usable items, such as apparel, sheets towels, and textile bags for individual or industrial consumption. The further manufacturing may be performed in the same establishment and classified in this subsector, or it may be performed at a separate establishment and be classified elsewhere in manufacturing.

The main processes in this subsector include preparation and spinning of fiber, knitting or weaving of fabric, and the finishing of the textile. The NAICS structure follows and captures this process flow. Major industries in this flow, such as preparation of fibers, weaving of fabric, knitting of fabric, and fiber and fabric finishing, are uniquely identified. Texturizing, throwing, twisting, and winding of yarn contains aspects of both fiber preparation and fiber finishing and is classified with preparation of fibers rather than with finishing of fiber.

NAICS separates the manufacturing of primary textiles and the manufacturing of textile products (except apparel) when the textile product is produced from purchased primary textiles, such as fabric. The manufacturing of textile products (except apparel) from purchased fabric is classified in Subsector 314, Textile Product Mills, and apparel from purchased fabric is classified in Subsector 315, Apparel Manufacturing.

Excluded from this subsector are establishments that weave or knit fabric and make garments. These establishments are included in Subsector 315, Apparel Manufacturing.

3131 Fiber, Yarn, and Thread Mills

31311 Fiber, Yarn, and Thread Mills

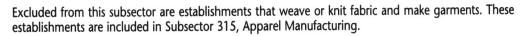

This Industry comprises establishments primarily engaged in one or more of the following: (1) spinning yarn; (2) manufacturing thread of any fiber; (3) texturizing, throwing, twisting, and winding purchased yarn or manmade fiber filaments; and (4) producing hemp yarn and further processing into rope or bags.

- Establishments primarily engaged in manufacturing artificial and synthetic fibers and filaments and texturizing these filaments are classified in Industry 32522, Artificial and Synthetic Fibers and Filaments Manufacturing.

313111 Yarn Spinning Mills ᵁˢ

This U.S. industry comprises establishments primarily engaged in spinning yarn from any fiber and/or producing hemp yarn and further processing into rope or bags.

313112 Yarn Texturizing, Throwing, and Twisting Mills ᵁˢ

This U.S. industry comprises establishments primarily engaged in texturizing, throwing, twisting, spooling, or winding purchased yarns or manmade fiber filaments.

- Establishments primarily engaged in manufacturing artificial and synthetic fiber and filament and texturizing these fibers and filaments are classified in Industry 32522, Artificial and Synthetic Fibers and Filament Manufacturing.

Visit page 17 to learn about classification changes to this sector.

Sector
31-33
Manufacturing

■ = Cross-References

US—United States industry only. CAN—United States and Canadian industries are comparable. When neither US nor CAN appears, Canadian, Mexican, and United States industries are comparable.

www.harrisinfo.com

331

313113 Thread Mills [US]

This U.S. industry comprises establishments primarily engaged in manufacturing thread (e.g., sewing, hand-knitting, crochet) of all fibers.

3132 Fabric Mills

31321 Broadwoven Fabric Mills

See industry description for 313210 below.

313210 Broadwoven Fabric Mills

This industry comprises establishments primarily engaged in weaving broadwoven fabrics and felts (except tire fabrics and rugs). Establishments in this industry may weave only, weave and finish, or weave, finish, and further fabricate fabric products.

- Weaving widths specifically constructed for cutting to narrow widths are classified in U.S. Industry 313221, Narrow Fabric Mills;
- Weaving or tufting carpet and rugs are classified in Industry 314110, Carpet and Rug Mills; and
- Making tire cord and fabrics are classified in Industry 31499, All Other Textile Product Mills.

31322 Narrow Fabric Mills and Schiffli Machine Embroidery

This industry comprises establishments primarily engaged in one or more of the following: (1) weaving or braiding narrow fabrics; (2) manufacturing Schiffli machine embroideries; and (3) making fabric-covered elastic yarn and thread.

313221 Narrow Fabric Mills [US]

This U.S. industry comprises establishments primarily engaged in (1) weaving or braiding narrow fabrics in their final form or initially made in wider widths that are specially constructed for narrower widths and/or (2) making fabric-covered elastic yarn and thread. Establishments in this industry may weave only; weave and finish; or weave, finish, and further fabricate fabric products.

313222 Schiffli Machine Embroidery [US]

This U.S. industry comprises establishments primarily engaged in manufacturing Schiffli machine embroideries.

31323 Nonwoven Fabric Mills

See industry description for 313230 below.

313230 Nonwoven Fabric Mills

This industry comprises establishments primarily engaged in manufacturing nonwoven fabrics and felts. Processes used include bonding and/or interlocking fibers by mechanical, chemical, thermal, or solvent means, or by combinations thereof.

31324 Knit Fabric Mills

This industry comprises establishments primarily engaged in one of the following: (1) knitting weft (i.e., circular) and warp (i.e., flat) fabric; (2) knitting and finishing weft and warp fabric; (3) manufacturing lace; or (4) manufacturing, dyeing, and finishing lace and lace goods. Establishments in this industry may knit only; knit and finish; or knit, finish, and further fabricate fabric products (except apparel).

- Establishments primarily engaged in knitting apparel as classified in Industry Group 3151, Apparel Knitting Mills.

313241 Weft Knit Fabric Mills [US]

This U.S. industry comprises establishments primarily engaged in knitting weft (i.e., circular) fabric or knitting and finishing weft fabric. Establishments in this industry may knit only; knit and finish; or knit, finish, and further fabricate fabric products (except apparel).

- Establishments primarily engaged in knitting apparel as classified in Industry Group 3151, Apparel Knitting Mills.

313249 Other Knit Fabric and Lace Mills [US]

This U.S. industry comprises establishments primarily engaged in one of the following: (1) knitting warp (i.e., flat) fabric; (2) knitting and finishing warp fabric; (3) manufacturing lace; or (4) manufacturing,

Sector

31-33

Manufacturing

■ = Cross-References

US—United States industry only. CAN—United States and Canadian industries are comparable. When neither US nor CAN appears, Canadian, Mexican, and United States industries are comparable.

dyeing, or finishing lace and lace goods. Establishments in this industry may knit only; knit and finish; or knit, finish, and further fabricate fabric products (except apparel).

- Establishments primarily engaged in knitting apparel as classified in Industry Group 3151, Apparel Knitting Mills.

3133 Textile and Fabric Finishing and Fabric Coating Mills

31331 Textile and Fabric Finishing Mills

This industry comprises (1) establishments primarily engaged in finishing of textiles, fabrics, and apparel, and (2) establishments of converters who buy fabric goods in the grey, have them finished on contract, and sell at wholesale. Finishing operations include: bleaching, dyeing, printing (e.g., roller, screen, flock, plisse), stonewashing, and other mechanical finishing, such as preshrinking, shrinking, sponging, calendering, mercerizing, and napping; as well as cleaning, scouring, and the preparation of natural fibers and raw stock.

- Coating or impregnating fabrics are classified in Industry 31332, Fabric Coating Mills;
- Knitting or knitting and finishing fabric are classified in Industry 31324, Knit Fabric Mills;
- Manufacturing and finishing apparel are classified in Subsector 315, Apparel Manufacturing;
- Weaving and finishing fabrics are classified in Industry Group 3132, Fabric Mills;
- Manufacturing and finishing rugs and carpets are classified in Industry 31411, Carpet and Rug Mills; and
- Printing on apparel are classified in Industry 32311, Printing.

313311 Broadwoven Fabric Finishing Mills US

This U.S. industry comprises (1) establishments primarily engaged in finishing broadwoven fabrics and (2) establishments of converters who buy broadwoven fabrics in the grey, have them finished on contract, and sell at wholesale. Finishing operations include bleaching, dyeing, printing (roller, screen, flock, plisse), and other mechanical finishing, such as preshrinking, shrinking, sponging, calendering, mercerizing and napping.

- Coating or impregnating fabrics are classified in Industry 313320, Fabric Coating Mills; and
- Weaving and finishing broadwoven fabrics are classified in Industry 313210, Broad-woven Fabric Mills.

313312 Textile and Fabric Finishing (except Broadwoven Fabric) Mills US

This U.S. industry comprises (1) establishments primarily engaged in dyeing, bleaching, printing, and other finishing of textiles, apparel, and fabrics (except broadwoven) and (2) establishments of converters who buy fabrics (except broadwoven) in the grey, have them finished on contract, and sell at wholesale. Finishing operations include bleaching, dyeing, printing (e.g., roller, screen, flock, plisse), stonewashing, and other mechanical finishing, such as preshrinking, shrinking, sponging, calendering, mercerizing and napping; as well as cleaning, scouring, and the preparation of natural fibers and raw stock.

- Knitting and finishing fabric are classified in Industry 31324, Knit Fabric Mills;
- Finishing broadwoven fabric are classified in U.S. Industry 313311, Broadwoven Fabric Finishing Mills;
- Weaving and finishing narrow woven fabric are classified in U.S. Industry 313221, Narrow Fabric Mills;
- Manufacturing and finishing apparel are classified in Subsector 315, Apparel Manufacturing;
- Coating or impregnating fabrics are classified in Industry 313320, Fabric Coating Mills; and
- Printing on apparel are classified in Industry 32311, Printing.

31332 Fabric Coating Mills

See industry description for 313320 below.

313320 Fabric Coating Mills

This industry comprises establishments primarily engaged in coating, laminating, varnishing, waxing, and rubberizing textiles and apparel.

- Establishments primarily engaged in dyeing and finishing textiles are classified in Industry 31331, Textile and Fabric Finishing Mills.

➡314 TEXTILE PRODUCT MILLS

Industries in the Textile Product Mills subsector group establishments that made textile products (except apparel). With a few exceptions, processes used in these industries are generally cut and sew (i.e., purchasing fabric and cutting and sewing to make nonapparel textile products, such as sheets and towels).

Visit page 17 to learn about classification changes to this sector.

Sector
31-33

Manufacturing

■ = Cross-References

US—United States industry only. CAN—United States and Canadian industries are comparable. When neither US nor CAN appears, Canadian, Mexican, and United States industries are comparable.

www.harrisinfo.com

 333

3141 Textile Furnishings Mills

31411 Carpet and Rug Mills
See industry description for 314110 below.

314110 Carpet and Rug Mills
This industry comprises establishments primarily engaged in (1) manufacturing woven, tufted, and other carpets and rugs, such as art squares, floor mattings, needlepunch carpeting, and door mats and mattings, from textile materials or from twisted paper, grasses, reeds, sisal, jute, or rags and/or (2) finishing carpets and rugs.

31412 Curtain and Linen Mills
This industry comprises establishments primarily engaged in manufacturing household textile products, such as curtains, draperies, linens, bedspreads, sheets, tablecloths, towels, and shower curtains, from purchased materials.

- Weaving fabrics are classified in Industry 31321, Broadwoven Fabric Mills;
- Manufacturing lace curtains on lace machines are classified in Industry 31324, Knit Fabric Mills;
- Manufacturing textile blanket, wardrobe, and laundry bags are classified in Industry 31491, Textile Bag and Canvas Mills; and
- Manufacturing mops are classified in Industry 33999, All Other Miscellaneous Manufacturing.

314121 Curtain and Drapery Mills US
This U.S. industry comprises establishments primarily engaged in manufacturing window curtains and draperies from purchased fabrics or sheet goods. The curtains and draperies may be made on a stock or custom basis for sale to individual retail customers.

- Establishments primarily engaged in manufacturing lace curtains on lace machines are classified in Industry 313249, Other Knit Fabric and Lace Mills.

314129 Other Household Textile Product Mills US
This U.S. industry comprises establishments primarily engaged in manufacturing household textile products (except window curtains and draperies), such as bedspreads, sheets, tablecloths, towels, and shower curtains, from purchased materials.

- Weaving fabrics are classified in Industry 313210, Broadwoven Fabric Mills;
- Manufacturing blanket, laundry, and wardrobe bags are classified in U.S. Industry 314911, Textile Bag Mills;
- Manufacturing mops are classified in U.S. Industry 339994, Broom, Brush, and Mop Manufacturing; and
- Manufacturing window curtains and draperies are classified in U.S. Industry 314121, Curtain and Drapery Mills.

3149 Other Textile Product Mills
This industry group comprises establishments primarily engaged in making textile products, (except carpets and rugs, curtains and draperies, and other household textile products) from purchased materials.

31491 Textile Bag and Canvas Mills
This industry comprises establishments primarily engaged in manufacturing textile bags, awnings, tents, and related products from purchased textile fabrics.

- Manufacturing plastic bags are classified in Industry 32611, Unsupported Plastics Film, Sheet, and Bag Manufacturing;
- Manufacturing canvas blinds and shades are classified in Industry 33792, Blind and Shade Manufacturing;
- Manufacturing luggage are classified in Industry 31699, Other Leather and Allied Product Manufacturing; and
- Manufacturing women's handbags and purses of leather or other material (except precious metal) are classified in Industry 31699, Other Leather and Allied Product Manufacturing.

314911 Textile Bag Mills US
This U.S. industry comprises establishments primarily engaged in manufacturing bags from purchased textile fabrics or yarns.

- Manufacturing plastics bags are classified in U.S. Industry 326111, Unsupported Plastics Bag Manufacturing;
- Manufacturing luggage are classified in U.S. Industry 316991, Luggage Manufacturing; and
- Manufacturing women's handbags and purses of leather or other material, except precious metal are classified in U.S. Industry 316992, Women's Handbag and Purse Manufacturing.

Sector
31-33
Manufacturing

■ = Cross-References

US—United States industry only. CAN—United States and Canadian industries are comparable. When neither US nor CAN appears, Canadian, Mexican, and United States industries are comparable.

334

Harris InfoSource

314912 Canvas and Related Product Mills ^{US}

This U.S. industry comprises establishments primarily engaged in manufacturing canvas and canvas-like products, such as awnings, sails, tarpaulins, and tents, from purchased fabrics.

- Manufacturing canvas blinds and shades are classified in Industry 337920, Blind and Shade Manufacturing; and
- Manufacturing canvas bags are classified in U.S. Industry 314911, Textile Bag Mills.

31499 All Other Textile Product Mills

This industry comprises establishments primarily engaged in manufacturing nonapparel textile products (except carpet, rugs, curtains, linens, bags, and canvas products) from purchased materials.

- Manufacturing yarns and thread are classified in Industry 31311, Fiber, Yarn, and Thread Mills;
- Manufacturing carpets and rugs are classified in Industry 31411, Carpet and Rug Mills;
- Manufacturing apparel are classified in Subsector 315, Apparel Manufacturing;
- Manufacturing curtains and linens are classified in Industry 31412, Curtain and Linen Mills; and
- Manufacturing textile bags and canvas products are classified in Industry 31491, Textile Bag and Canvas Mills.

314991 Rope, Cordage, and Twine Mills ^{US}

This U.S. industry comprises establishments primarily engaged in manufacturing rope, cable, cordage, twine, and related products from all materials (e.g., abaca, sisal, henequen, hemp, cotton, paper, jute, flax, manmade fibers including glass).

- Establishments primarily engaged in manufacturing yarns and filaments are classified in U.S. Industry 313111, Yarn Spinning Mills.

314992 Tire Cord and Tire Fabric Mills ^{US}

This U.S. industry comprises establishments primarily engaged in manufacturing cord and fabric of polyester, rayon, cotton, glass, steel, or other materials for use in reinforcing rubber tires, industrial belting, and similar uses.

314999 All Other Miscellaneous Textile Product Mills ^{US}

This U.S. industry comprises establishments primarily engaged in manufacturing textile products (except carpets and rugs; curtains and linens; textile bags and canvas products; rope, cordage, and twine; and tire cords and tire fabrics) from purchased materials.

- Manufacturing yarns and thread are classified in Industry 31311, Fiber, Yarn, and Thread Mills;
- Manufacturing carpets and rugs are classified in Industry 314110, Carpet and Rug Mills;
- Manufacturing curtains and linens are classified in Industry 31412, Curtain and Linen Mills;
- Manufacturing textile bags and canvas products are classified in Industry 31491, Textile Bag and Canvas Mills;
- Manufacturing rope, cordage, and twine are classified in U.S. Industry 314991, Rope, Cordage, and Twine Mills; and
- Manufacturing tire cords and tire fabrics are classified in U.S. Industry 314992, Tire Cord and Tire Fabric Mills.

➡315 APPAREL MANUFACTURING

Industries in the Apparel Manufacturing subsector group establishments with two distinct manufacturing processes: (1) cut and sew (i.e., purchasing fabric and cutting and sewing to make a garment) and (2) the manufacture of garments in establishments that first knit fabric and then cut and sew the fabric into a garment. The Apparel Manufacturing subsector includes a diverse range of establishments manufacturing full lines of ready-to-wear apparel and custom apparel: apparel contractors, performing cutting or sewing operations on materials owned by others; jobbers performing entrepreneurial functions involved in apparel manufacture; and tailors, manufacturing custom garments for individual clients are all included. Knitting, when done alone, is classified in the Textile Mills subsector, but when knitting is combined with the production of complete garments, the activity is classified in Apparel Manufacturing.

3151 Apparel Knitting Mills

This industry group comprises establishments primarily engaged in knitting apparel or knitting fabric and then manufacturing apparel. This industry group includes jobbers performing entrepreneurial functions involved in knitting apparel and accessories. Knitting fabric, without manufacturing apparel, is classified in Subsector 313, Textile Mills.

31511 Hosiery and Sock Mills

This industry comprises establishments primarily engaged in knitting or knitting and finishing hosiery and socks.

Visit page 17 to learn about classification changes to this sector.

Sector
31-33
Manufacturing

 = Cross-References

US—United States industry only. CAN—United States and Canadian industries are comparable. When neither US nor CAN appears, Canadian, Mexican, and United States industries are comparable.

www.harrisinfo.com

335

■ Manufacturing orthopedic hosiery are classified in Industry 33911, Medical Equipment and Supplies Manufacturing;
■ Manufacturing slipper socks from purchased socks are classified in Industry 31621, Footwear Manufacturing; and
■ Finishing apparel products only are classified in Industry 31331, Textile and Fabric Finishing Mills.

315111 Sheer Hosiery Mills ᵁˢ

This U.S. industry comprises establishments primarily engaged in knitting or knitting and finishing women's, misses', and girls' full-length and knee-length sheer hosiery (except socks).

■ Knitting or knitting and finishing socks are classified in U.S. Industry 315119, Other Hosiery and Sock Mills;
■ Finishing apparel products only are classified in U.S. Industry 313312, Textile and Fabric Finishing (except Broadwoven Fabric) Mills; and
■ Manufacturing orthopedic hosiery are classified in U.S. Industry 339113, Surgical Appliance and Supplies Manufacturing.

315119 Other Hosiery and Sock Mills ᵁˢ

This U.S. industry comprises establishments primarily engaged in knitting or knitting and finishing hosiery (except women's, misses', and girls' sheer hosiery).

■ Knitting or knitting and finishing women's, misses', and girls' full-length and knee-length sheer hosiery are classified in U.S. Industry 315111, Sheer Hosiery Mills;
■ Manufacturing orthopedic hosiery are classified in U.S. Industry 339113, Surgical Appliance and Supplies Manufacturing;
■ Finishing apparel products only are classified in U.S. Industry 313312, Textile and Fabric Finishing (except Broadwoven Fabric) Mills; and
■ Manufacturing slipper socks from purchased socks are classified in U.S. Industry 316212 House Slipper Manufacturing.

31519 Other Apparel Knitting Mills

This industry comprises establishments primarily engaged in one of the following: (1) knitting underwear, outerwear, and/or nightwear; (2) knitting fabric and manufacturing underwear, outerwear, and/or nightwear; or (3) knitting, manufacturing, and finishing knit underwear, outerwear, and/or nightwear.

■ Manufacturing outerwear, underwear, and nightwear from purchased fabric are classified in Industry Group 3152, Cut and Sew Apparel Manufacturing; and
■ Finishing apparel products only are classified in Industry 31331, Textile and Fabric Finishing Mills.

315191 Outerwear Knitting Mills ᵁˢ

This U.S. industry comprises establishments primarily engaged in one or more of the following: (1) knitting outerwear; (2) knitting fabric and manufacturing outerwear; and (3) knitting, manufacturing, and finishing knit outerwear. Examples of products made in knit outerwear mills are shirts, shorts, sweat suits, sweaters, gloves, and pants.

■ Manufacturing outerwear from purchased fabric are classified in Industry Group 3152, Cut and Sew Apparel Manufacturing;
■ Finishing apparel products only are classified in U.S. Industry 313312, Textile and Fabric Finishing (except Broadwoven Fabric) Mills; and
■ Knitting underwear and nightwear, knitting fabric and manufacturing underwear and nightwear, or knitting, manufacturing, and finishing knit underwear and nightwear are classified in U.S. Industry 315192, Underwear and Nightwear Knitting Mills.

315192 Underwear and Nightwear Knitting Mills ᵁˢ

This U.S. industry comprises establishments primarily engaged in one of the following: (1) knitting underwear and nightwear; (2) knitting fabric and manufacturing underwear and nightwear; or (3) knitting, manufacturing, and finishing knit underwear and nightwear. Examples of products produced in underwear and nightwear knitting mills are briefs, underwear T-shirts, pajamas, nightshirts, foundation garments, and panties.

■ Manufacturing underwear and nightwear from purchased fabric are classified in Industry Group 3152, Cut and Sew Apparel Manufacturing; and
■ Finishing apparel products only are classified in U.S. Industry 313312, Textile and Fabric Finishing (except Broadwoven Fabric) Mills.

Sector
31-33
Manufacturing

3152 Cut and Sew Apparel Manufacturing

This industry group comprises establishments primarily engaged in manufacturing cut and sew apparel from woven fabric or purchased knit fabric. Included in this industry group is a diverse range of establishments manufacturing full lines of ready-to-wear apparel and custom apparel: apparel contractors, performing cutting or sewing operations on materials owned by others; jobbers performing entrepreneurial functions involved in apparel manufacture; and tailors, manufacturing custom garments for individual clients. Establishments weaving or knitting fabric, without manufacturing apparel, are classified in Subsector 313, Textile Mills.

■ = Cross-References

US—United States industry only. CAN—United States and Canadian industries are comparable. When neither US nor CAN appears, Canadian, Mexican, and United States industries are comparable.

336   Harris InfoSource

31521 Cut and Sew Apparel Contractors ^{CAN}

This industry comprises establishments commonly referred to as contractors primarily engaged in (1) cutting materials owned by others for apparel and accessories and/or (2) sewing materials owned by others for apparel and accessories.

- Manufacturing men's and boys' apparel from purchased fabric are classified in Industry 31522, Men's and Boys' Cut and Sew Apparel Manufacturing;
- Manufacturing women's and girls' apparel from purchased fabric are classified in Industry 31523, Women's and Girls' Cut and Sew Apparel Manufacturing;
- Manufacturing infants' apparel and all other cut and sew apparel from purchased fabric are classified in Industry 31529, Other Cut and Sew Apparel Manufacturing; and
- Manufacturing apparel accessories from purchased fabric are classified in Industry 31599, Apparel Accessories and Other Apparel Manufacturing.

315211 Men's and Boys' Cut and Sew Apparel Contractors ^{US}

This U.S. industry comprises establishments commonly referred to as contractors primarily engaged in (1) cutting materials owned by others for men's and boys' apparel and/or (2) sewing materials owned by others for men's and boys' apparel.

- Manufacturing men's and boys' apparel from purchased fabric are classified in Industry 31522, Men's and Boys' Cut and Sew Apparel Manufacturing;
- Manufacturing infants' apparel from purchased fabric are classified in U.S. Industry 315291, Infants' Cut and Sew Apparel Manufacturing; and
- Manufacturing men's and boys' apparel accessories from purchased fabric are classified in Industry 31599, Apparel Accessories and Other Apparel Manufacturing.

315212 Women's, Girls', and Infants' Cut and Sew Apparel Contractors ^{US}

This U.S. industry comprises establishments commonly referred to as contractors primarily engaged in (1) cutting materials owned by others for women's, girls', and infants' apparel and accessories and/or (2) sewing materials owned by others for women's, girls', and infants' apparel and accessories.

- Manufacturing women's and girls' apparel from purchased fabric are classified in Industry 31523, Women's and Girls' Cut and Sew Apparel Manufacturing;
- Manufacturing infants' apparel from purchased fabric are classified in U.S. Industry 315291, Infants' Cut and Sew Apparel Manufacturing; and
- Manufacturing women's, girls', and infants' apparel accessories from purchased fabric are classified in Industry 31599, Apparel Accessories and Other Apparel Manufacturing.

31522 Men's and Boys' Cut and Sew Apparel Manufacturing ^{CAN}

This industry comprises establishments primarily engaged in manufacturing men's and boys' cut and sew apparel from purchased fabric. Men's and boys' clothing jobbers, who perform entrepreneurial functions involved in apparel manufacture, including buying raw materials, designing and preparing samples, arranging for apparel to be made from their materials, and marketing finished apparel, are included.

- Cutting and/or sewing materials owned by others for men's and boys' apparel are classified in Industry 31521, Cut and Sew Apparel Contractors;
- Knitting men's and boys' apparel or knitting fabric and manufacturing men's and boys' apparel are classified in Industry Group 3151, Apparel Knitting Mills; and
- Manufacturing fur or leather apparel and team athletic uniforms are classified in Industry 31529, Other Cut and Sew Apparel Manufacturing.

315221 Men's and Boys' Cut and Sew Underwear and Nightwear Manufacturing ^{CAN}

This U.S. industry comprises establishments primarily engaged in manufacturing men's and boys' underwear and nightwear from purchased fabric. Men's and boys' underwear and nightwear jobbers, who perform entrepreneurial functions involved in apparel manufacture, including buying raw materials, designing and preparing samples, arranging for apparel to be made from their materials, and marketing finished apparel, are included. Examples of products made by these establishments are briefs, bathrobes, underwear T-shirts and shorts, nightshirts, and pajamas.

- Knitting men's and boys' underwear and nightwear and/or knitting and manufacturing men's and boys' underwear and nightwear are classified in U.S. Industry 315192, Underwear and Nightwear Knitting Mills; and
- Cutting and/or sewing materials owned by others for men's and boys' underwear and nightwear are classified in U.S. Industry 315211, Men's and Boys' Cut and Sew Apparel Contractors.

Visit page 17 to learn about classification changes to this sector.

Manufacturing

■ = Cross-References

315222 Men's and Boys' Cut and Sew Suit, Coat, and Overcoat Manufacturing ^{CAN}

This U.S. industry comprises establishments primarily engaged in manufacturing men's and boys' suits, overcoats, sport coats, tuxedoes, dress uniforms, and other tailored apparel (except fur and leather) from purchased fabric. Men's and boys' suit, coat, and overcoat jobbers, who perform entrepreneurial functions involved in apparel manufacture, including buying raw materials, designing and preparing samples, arranging for apparel to be made from their materials, and marketing finished apparel, are included.

- Manufacturing men's and boys' nontailored coats and jackets such as down coats and windbreakers made from purchased fabric are classified in U.S. Industry 315228, Men's and Boys' Cut and Sew Other Outerwear Manufacturing;
- Manufacturing fur and leather apparel are classified in U.S. Industry 315292, Fur and Leather Apparel Manufacturing; Manufacturing men's and boys' washable service apparel from purchased fabric are classified in U.S. Industry 315225, Men's and Boys' Cut and Sew Work Clothing Manufacturing;
- Manufacturing men's and boys' team athletic uniforms from purchased fabric are classified in U.S. Industry 315299, All Other Cut and Sew Apparel Manufacturing; and
- Cutting and/or sewing materials owned by others for men's and boys' suits, coats, and overcoats are classified in U.S. Industry 315211, Men's and Boys' Cut and Sew Apparel Contractors.

315223 Men's and Boys' Cut and Sew Shirt (except Work Shirt) Manufacturing ^{US}

This U.S. industry comprises establishments primarily engaged in manufacturing men's and boys' outerwear shirts from purchased fabric. Men's and boys' shirt (except work shirt) jobbers, who perform entrepreneurial functions involved in apparel manufacture, including buying raw materials, designing and preparing samples, arranging for apparel to be made from their materials, and marketing finished apparel, are included. Unisex outerwear shirts, such as T-shirts and sweatshirts that are sized without specific reference to gender (i.e., adult S, M, L, XL) are included in this industry.

- Manufacturing men's and boys' work shirts from purchased fabric are classified in U.S. Industry 315225, Men's and Boys' Cut and Sew Work Clothing Manufacturing;
- Manufacturing men's and boys' underwear T-shirts and underwear tank tops from purchased fabric are classified in U.S. Industry 315221, Men's and Boys' Cut and Sew Underwear and Nightwear Manufacturing;
- Cutting and/or sewing materials owned by others for men's and boys' shirts are classified in U.S. Industry 315211, Men's and Boys' Cut and Sew Apparel Contractors; and
- Knitting men's and boys' outerwear shirts or knitting fabric and manufacturing men's and boys' outerwear shirts are classified in U.S. Industry 315191, Outerwear Knitting Mills.

315224 Men's and Boys' Cut and Sew Trouser, Slack, and Jean Manufacturing ^{US}

This U.S. industry comprises establishments primarily engaged in manufacturing men's and boys' jeans, dungarees, and other separate trousers and slacks (except work pants) from purchased fabric. Men's and boys' trouser, slack, and jean jobbers, who perform entrepreneurial functions involved in apparel manufacture, including buying raw materials, designing and preparing samples, arranging for apparel to be made from their materials, and marketing finished apparel, are included.

- Manufacturing men's and boys' work pants from purchased fabric are classified in U.S. Industry 315225, Men's and Boys' Cut and Sew Work Clothing Manufacturing; Manufacturing men's and boys' washable service apparel from purchased fabric are classified in U.S. Industry 315225, Men's and Boys' Cut and Sew Work Clothing Manufacturing;
- Manufacturing men's and boys' team athletic uniforms from purchased fabric are classified in U.S. Industry 315299, All Other Cut and Sew Apparel Manufacturing; and
- Cutting and/or sewing materials owned by others for men's and boys' suits, coats, and overcoats are classified in U.S. Industry 315211, Men's and Boys' Cut and Sew Apparel Contractors.

315223 Men's and Boys' Cut and Sew Shirt (except Work Shirt) Manufacturing ^{US}

This U.S. industry comprises establishments primarily engaged in manufacturing men's and boys' outerwear shirts from purchased fabric. Men's and boys' shirt (except work shirt) jobbers, who perform entrepreneurial functions involved in apparel manufacture, including buying raw materials, designing and preparing samples, arranging for apparel to be made from their materials, and marketing finished apparel, are included. Unisex outerwear shirts, such as T-shirts and sweatshirts that are sized without specific reference to gender (i.e., adult S, M, L, XL) are included in this industry.

- Manufacturing men's and boys' work shirts from purchased fabric are classified in U.S. Industry 315225, Men's and Boys' Cut and Sew Work Clothing Manufacturing;
- Manufacturing men's and boys' underwear T-shirts and underwear tank tops from purchased fabric are classified in U.S. Industry 315221, Men's and Boys' Cut and Sew Underwear and Nightwear Manufacturing;
- Cutting and/or sewing materials owned by others for men's and boys' shirts are classified in U.S. Industry 315211, Men's and Boys' Cut and Sew Apparel Contractors; and

Sector

31-33

Manufacturing

■ = Cross-References

US—United States industry only. CAN—United States and Canadian industries are comparable. When neither US nor CAN appears, Canadian, Mexican, and United States industries are comparable.

338

Harris InfoSource

■ Knitting men's and boys' outerwear shirts or knitting fabric and manufacturing men's and boys' outerwear shirts are classified in U.S. Industry 315191, Outerwear Knitting Mills.

315224 Men's and Boys' Cut and Sew Trouser, Slack, and Jean Manufacturing US

This U.S. industry comprises establishments primarily engaged in manufacturing men's and boys' jeans, dungarees, and other separate trousers and slacks (except work pants) from purchased fabric. Men's and boys' trouser, slack, and jean jobbers, who perform entrepreneurial functions involved in apparel manufacture, including buying raw materials, designing and preparing samples, arranging for apparel to be made from their materials, and marketing finished apparel, are included.

■ Manufacturing men's and boys' work pants from purchased fabric are classified in U.S. Industry 315225, Men's and Boys' Cut and Sew Work Clothing Manufacturing; Manufacturing fur and leather apparel are classified in U.S. Industry 315292, Fur and Leather Apparel Manufacturing;
■ Manufacturing men's and boys' sweatpants and shorts from purchased fabric are classified in U.S. Industry 315228, Men's and Boys' Cut and Sew Other Outerwear Manufacturing; and
■ Cutting and/or sewing materials owned by others for men's and boys' separate trousers, slacks, and jeans are classified in U.S. Industry 315211, Men's and Boys' Cut and Sew Apparel Contractors.

315225 Men's and Boys' Cut and Sew Work Clothing Manufacturing US

This U.S. industry comprises establishments primarily engaged in manufacturing men's and boys' work shirts, work pants (excluding jeans and dungarees), other work clothing, and washable service apparel from purchased fabric. Men's and boys' work clothing jobbers, who perform entrepreneurial functions involved in apparel manufacture, including buying raw materials, designing and preparing samples, arranging for apparel to be made from their materials, and marketing finished apparel, are included. Examples of products made by these establishments are washable service apparel, laboratory coats, work shirts, work pants (except jeans and dungarees), and hospital apparel.

■ Manufacturing men's and boys' separate trousers, slacks, and pants, including jeans and dungarees from purchased fabric are classified in U.S. Industry 315224, Men's and Boys' Cut and Sew Trouser, Slack, and Jean Manufacturing; and
■ Cutting and/or sewing materials owned by others for men's and boys' work clothing are classified in U.S. Industry 315211, Men's and Boys' Cut and Sew Apparel Contractors.

315228 Men's and Boys' Cut and Sew Other Outerwear Manufacturing US

This U.S. industry comprises establishments primarily engaged in manufacturing men's and boys' cut and sew outerwear from purchased fabric (except underwear, nightwear, shirts, suits, overcoats and tailored coats, separate trousers and slacks, and work clothing). Men's and boys' other outerwear jobbers, who perform entrepreneurial functions involved in apparel manufacture, including buying raw materials, designing and preparing samples, arranging for apparel to be made from their materials, and marketing finished apparel, are included. Unisex sweatpants and similar garments that are sized without specific reference to gender (i.e., adult S, M, L, XL) are also included in this industry. Examples of products made by these establishments are athletic clothing (except athletic uniforms), bathing suits, down coats, outerwear shorts, windbreakers and jackets, and jogging suits.

■ Manufacturing men's and boys' athletic uniforms from purchased fabric are classified in U.S. Industry 315299, All Other Cut and Sew Apparel Manufacturing; Manufacturing leather and fur apparel are classified in U.S. Industry 315292, Fur and Leather Apparel Manufacturing;
■ Knitting men's and boys' apparel or knitting fabric and manufacturing men's and boys' apparel are classified in Industry Group 3151, Apparel Knitting Mills;
■ Cutting and/or sewing materials owned by others for men's and boys' apparel are classified in U.S. Industry 315211, Men's and Boys' Cut and Sew Apparel Contractors;
■ Manufacturing men's and boys' underwear and nightwear from purchased fabric are classified in U.S. Industry 315221, Men's and Boys' Cut and Sew Underwear and Nightwear Manufacturing;
■ Manufacturing men's and boys' tailored suits, coats, and overcoats from purchased fabric are classified in U.S. Industry 315222, Men's and Boys' Cut and Sew Suit, Coat and Overcoat Manufacturing;
■ Manufacturing men's and boys' outerwear shirts (except work shirts) from purchased fabric are classified in U.S. Industry 315223, Men's and Boys' Cut and Sew Shirt (except Work Shirt) Manufacturing;
■ Manufacturing men's and boys' separate pants, trousers, and slacks from purchased fabric are classified in U.S. Industry 315224, Men's and Boys' Cut and Sew Trouser, Slack, and Jean Manufacturing; and
■ Manufacturing men's and boys' work clothing from purchased fabric are classified in U.S. Industry 315225, Men's and Boys' Cut and Sew Work Clothing Manufacturing.

31523 Women's and Girls' Cut and Sew Apparel Manufacturing CAN

This industry comprises establishments primarily engaged in manufacturing women's and girls' apparel from purchased fabric. Women's and girls' clothing jobbers, who perform entrepreneurial functions

Visit page 17 to learn about classification changes to this sector.

Sector
31-33

Manufacturing

■ = Cross-References

US—United States industry only. CAN—United States and Canadian industries are comparable. When neither US nor CAN appears, Canadian, Mexican, and United States industries are comparable.

www.harrisinfo.com 339

involved in apparel manufacture, including buying raw materials, designing and preparing samples, arranging for apparel to be made from their materials, and marketing finished apparel, are included.

- Knitting women's and girls' apparel or knitting fabric and manufacturing women's and girls' apparel are classified in Industry Group 3151, Apparel Knitting Mills;
- Manufacturing unisex outerwear garments, such as T-shirts, sweatshirts, and sweatpants that are sized without reference to specific gender (i.e., adult S, M, L, XL), are classified in Industry 31522, Men's and Boys' Cut and Sew Apparel Manufacturing;
- Cutting and/or sewing materials owned by others for women's and girls' apparel are classified in Industry 31521, Cut and Sew Apparel Contractors; and
- Manufacturing fur or leather apparel and team athletic uniforms are classified in Industry 31529, Other Cut and Sew Apparel Manufacturing.

315231 Women's and Girls' Cut and Sew Lingerie, Loungewear, and Nightwear Manufacturing ^{CAN}

This U.S. industry comprises establishments primarily engaged in manufacturing women's and girls' bras, girdles, and other underwear; lingerie; loungewear; and nightwear from purchased fabric. Women's and girls' lingerie, loungewear, and nightwear jobbers, who perform entrepreneurial functions involved in apparel manufacture, including buying raw materials, designing and preparing samples, arranging for apparel to be made from their materials, and marketing finished apparel, are included. Examples of products made by these establishments are bathrobes, foundation garments, nightgowns, pajamas, panties, and slips.

- Knitting women's and girls' underwear, nightwear, and lingerie or knitting fabric and manufacturing women's and girls' underwear, nightwear, and lingerie are classified in U.S. Industry 315192, Underwear and Nightwear Knitting Mills; and
- Cutting and/or sewing materials owned by others for women's and girls' underwear, nightwear, and lingerie are classified in U.S. Industry 315212, Women's, Girls', and Infants' Cut and Sew Apparel Contractors.

315232 Women's and Girls' Cut and Sew Blouse and Shirt Manufacturing ^{CAN}

This U.S. industry comprises establishments primarily engaged in manufacturing women's and girls' blouses and shirts from purchased fabric. Women's and girls' blouse and shirt jobbers, who perform entrepreneurial functions involved in apparel manufacture, including buying raw materials, designing and preparing samples, arranging for apparel to be made from their materials, and marketing finished apparel, are included.

- Knitting women's and girls' blouses, shirts, and tops or knitting fabric and manufacturing women's and girls' blouses, shirts, and tops are classified in U.S. Industry 315191, Outerwear Knitting Mills;
- Manufacturing unisex outerwear shirts, such as T-shirts and sweatshirts that are sized without specific reference to gender (i.e., adult S, M, L, XL), are classified in U.S. Industry 315223, Men's and Boys' Cut and Sew Shirt (except Work Shirt) Manufacturing; and
- Cutting and/or sewing materials owned by others for women's and girls' shirts and blouses are classified in U.S. Industry 315212, Women's, Girls', and Infants' Cut and Sew Apparel Contractors.

315233 Women's and Girls' Cut and Sew Dress Manufacturing ^{CAN}

This U.S. industry comprises establishments primarily engaged in manufacturing women's and girls' dresses from purchased fabric. Women's and girls' dress jobbers, who perform entrepreneurial functions involved in apparel manufacture, including buying raw materials, designing and preparing samples, arranging for apparel to be made from their materials, and marketing finished apparel, are included.

- Knitting women's and girls' dresses or knitting fabric and manufacturing women's and girls' dresses are classified in U.S. Industry 315191, Outerwear Knitting Mills; and
- Cutting and/or sewing materials owned by others for women's and girls' dresses are classified in U.S. Industry 315212, Women's, Girls', and Infants' Cut and Sew Apparel Contractors.

315234 Women's and Girls' Cut and Sew Suit, Coat, Tailored Jacket, and Skirt Manufacturing ^{CAN}

This U.S. industry comprises establishments primarily engaged in manufacturing women's and girls' suits, pantsuits, skirts, tailored jackets, vests, raincoats, and other tailored coats, (except fur and leather coats) from purchased fabric. Women's and girls' suit, coat, tailored jacket, and skirt jobbers, who perform entrepreneurial functions involved in apparel manufacture, including buying raw materials, designing and preparing samples, arranging for apparel to be made from their materials, and marketing finished apparel, are included.

- Manufacturing women's and girls' team athletic uniforms from purchased fabric are classified in U.S. Industry 315299, All Other Cut and Sew Apparel Manufacturing;

Sector
31-33
Manufacturing

■ = Cross-References

US—United States industry only. CAN—United States and Canadian industries are comparable. When neither US nor CAN appears, Canadian, Mexican, and United States industries are comparable.

340

Harris InfoSource

■ Manufacturing women's and girls' separate slacks, jeans, pants, and nontailored coats and jackets, such as down coats and windbreakers from purchased fabric, are classified in U.S. Industry 315239, Women's and Girls' Cut and Sew Other Outerwear Manufacturing;
■ Manufacturing fur and leather apparel are classified in U.S. Industry 315292, Fur and Leather Apparel Manufacturing;
■ Knitting women's and girls' tailored skirts, suits, vests, and coats or knitting fabric and manufacturing women's and girls' tailored skirts, suits, vests, and coats are classified in U.S. Industry 315191, Outerwear Knitting Mills; and
■ Cutting and/or sewing materials owned by others for women's and girls' suits, coats, tailored jackets, and skirts are classified in U.S. Industry 315212, Women's, Girls', and Infants' Cut and Sew Apparel Contractors.

315239 Women's and Girls' Cut and Sew Other Outerwear Manufacturing CAN

This U.S. industry comprises establishments primarily engaged in manufacturing women's and girls' cut and sew apparel from purchased fabric (except underwear, lingerie, nightwear, blouses, shirts, dresses, suits, tailored coats, tailored jackets, and skirts). Women's and girls' other outerwear clothing jobbers, who perform entrepreneurial functions involved in apparel manufacture, including buying raw materials, designing and preparing samples, arranging for apparel to be made from their materials, and marketing finished apparel, are included. Examples of products made by these establishments are bathing suits, down coats, sweaters, jogging suits, outerwear pants and shorts, and windbreakers.

■ Manufacturing women's and girls' team athletic uniforms from purchased fabric are classified in U.S. Industry 315299, All Other Cut and Sew Apparel Manufacturing;
■ Knitting women's and girls' apparel or knitting fabric and manufacturing women's and girls' apparel are classified in U.S. Industry 315191, Outerwear Knitting Mills;
■ Manufacturing women's and girls' fur and leather apparel are classified in U.S. Industry 315292, Fur and Leather Apparel Manufacturing;
■ Cutting and/or sewing materials owned by others for women's and girls' apparel are classified in U.S. Industry 315212, Women's, Girls', and Infants' Cut and Sew Apparel Contractors;
■ Manufacturing women's and girls' lingerie, loungewear, and nightwear from purchased fabric are classified in U.S. Industry 315231, Women's and Girls' Cut and Sew Lingerie, Loungewear, and Nightwear Manufacturing;
■ Manufacturing women's and girls' blouses and outerwear shirts from purchased fabric are classified in U.S. Industry 315232, Women's and Girls' Cut and Sew Blouse and Shirt Manufacturing;
■ Manufacturing unisex sweatpants and similar outerwear garments that are sized without specific reference to gender (i.e., adult S, M, L, XL) are classified in U.S. Industry 315228, Men's and Boys' Cut and Sew Other Outerwear Manufacturing;
■ Manufacturing women's and girls' dresses from purchased fabric are classified in U.S. Industry 315233, Women's and Girls' Cut and Sew Dress Manufacturing; and
■ Manufacturing women's and girls' suits, skirts, and tailored coats and jackets from purchased fabric are classified in U.S. Industry 315234, Women's and Girls' Cut and Sew Suit, Coat, Tailored Jacket, and Skirt Manufacturing.

31529 Other Cut and Sew Apparel Manufacturing CAN

This industry comprises establishments primarily engaged in manufacturing cut and sew apparel from purchased fabric (except men's, boys', women's, and girls' apparel). This industry includes establishments manufacturing apparel, such as fur apparel, leather apparel, infants' apparel, costumes, and clerical vestments.

■ Manufacturing men's and boys' apparel from purchased fabric are classified in Industry 31522, Men's and Boys' Cut and Sew Apparel Manufacturing;
■ Manufacturing women's and girls' apparel from purchased fabric are classified in Industry 31523, Women's and Girls' Cut and Sew Apparel Manufacturing;
■ Knitting apparel or knitting fabric and manufacturing apparel are classified in Industry Group 3151, Apparel Knitting Mills;
■ Cutting and/or sewing materials owned by others for apparel are classified in Industry 31521, Cut and Sew Apparel Contractors;
■ Manufacturing fur and leather mittens and gloves are classified in Industry 31599, Apparel Accessories and Other Apparel Manufacturing; and
■ Dyeing and dressing furs are classified in Industry 31611, Leather and Hide Tanning and Finishing.

315291 Infants' Cut and Sew Apparel Manufacturing CAN

This U.S. industry comprises establishments primarily engaged in manufacturing infants' dresses, blouses, shirts, and all other infants' wear from purchased fabric. Infants' clothing jobbers, who perform entrepreneurial functions involved in apparel manufacture, including buying raw materials, designing and preparing samples, arranging for apparel to be made from their materials, and marketing finished apparel, are included. For the purposes of classification, the term "infants' apparel" includes apparel for young children of an age not exceeding 24 months.

■ Knitting infants' apparel or knitting fabric and manufacturing infants' apparel are classified in U.S. Industry 315191, Outerwear Knitting Mills; and

Visit page 17 to learn about classification changes to this sector.

Sector

31-33

Manufacturing

■ = Cross-References

US—United States industry only. CAN—United States and Canadian industries are comparable. When neither US nor CAN appears, Canadian, Mexican, and United States industries are comparable.

www.harrisinfo.com

341

■ Cutting and/or sewing materials owned by others for infants' apparel are classified in U.S. Industry 315212, Women's, Girls', and Infants' Cut and Sew Apparel Contractors.

315292 Fur and Leather Apparel Manufacturing ^{CAN}

This U.S. industry comprises establishments primarily engaged in manufacturing cut and sew fur and leather apparel, and sheep-lined clothing. Fur and leather apparel jobbers, who perform entrepreneurial functions involved in apparel manufacture, including buying raw materials, designing and preparing samples, arranging for apparel to be made from their materials, and marketing finished apparel, are included.

■ Cutting and/or sewing materials owned by others for apparel are classified in Industry 31521, Cut and Sew Apparel Contractors;
■ Dyeing and dressing furs are classified in Industry 316110, Leather and Hide Tanning and Finishing; and Manufacturing fur and leather mittens and gloves are classified in U.S. Industry 315992, Glove and Mitten Manufacturing.

315299 All Other Cut and Sew Apparel Manufacturing ^{CAN}

This U.S. industry comprises establishments primarily engaged in manufacturing cut and sew apparel form purchased fabric (except cut and sew apparel contractors; men's and boys' cut and sew underwear, nightwear, suits, coats, shirts, trousers, work clothing, and other outerwear; women's and girls' lingerie, blouses, shirts, dresses, suits, coats, and other outerwear; infants' apparel; and fur and leather apparel). Clothing jobbers for these products, who perform entrepreneurial functions involved in apparel manufacture, including buying raw materials, designing and preparing samples, arranging for apparel to be made from their materials, and marketing finished apparel, are included. Examples of products made by these establishments are team athletic uniforms, band uniforms, academic caps and gowns, clerical vestments, and costumes.

■ Cutting and/or sewing materials owned by others for apparel are classified in Industry 31521, Cut and Sew Apparel Contractors;
■ Knitting apparel or knitting fabric and manufacturing apparel are classified in Industry Group 3151, Apparel Knitting Mills;
■ Manufacturing men's and boys' underwear and nightwear from purchased fabric are classified in U.S. Industry 315221, Men's and Boys' Cut and Sew Underwear and Nightwear Manufacturing;
■ Manufacturing men's and boys' suits, coats, and overcoats from purchased fabric are classified in U.S. Industry 315222, Men's and Boys' Cut and Sew Suit, Coat and Overcoat Manufacturing;
■ Manufacturing men's and boys' shirts (except work shirts) from purchased fabric are classified in U.S. Industry 315223, Men's and Boys' Cut and Sew Shirt (except Work Shirt) Manufacturing;
■ Manufacturing men's and boys' pants, slacks, trousers, and jeans from purchased fabric are classified in U.S. Industry 315224, Men's and Boys' Cut and Sew Trouser, Slack, and Jean Manufacturing;
■ Manufacturing men's and boys' work clothing from purchased fabric are classified in U.S. Industry 315225, Men's and Boys' Cut and Sew Work Clothing Manufacturing;
■ Manufacturing other men's and boys' outerwear from purchased fabric are classified in U.S. Industry 315228, Men's and Boys' Cut and Sew Other Outerwear Manufacturing;
■ Manufacturing women's and girls' lingerie and nightwear from purchased fabric are classified in U.S. Industry 315231, Women's and Girls' Cut and Sew Lingerie, Loungewear, and Nightwear Manufacturing;
■ Manufacturing women's and girls' blouses and shirts from purchased fabric are classified in U.S. Industry 315232, Women's and Girls' Cut and Sew Blouse and Shirt Manufacturing;
■ Manufacturing women's and girls' dresses from purchased fabric are classified in U.S. Industry 315233, Women's and Girls' Cut and Sew Dress Manufacturing;
■ Manufacturing women's and girls' suits, tailored coats and jackets, and skirts from purchased fabric are classified in U.S. Industry 315234, Women's and Girls' Cut and Sew Suit, Coat, Tailored Jacket, and Skirt Manufacturing;
■ Manufacturing other women's and girls' outerwear from purchased fabric are classified in U.S. Industry 315239, Women's and Girls' Cut and Sew Other Outerwear Manufacturing;
■ Manufacturing infants' apparel from purchased fabric are classified in U.S. Industry 315291, Infants' Cut and Sew Apparel Manufacturing; and
■ Manufacturing fur and leather apparel are classified in U.S. Industry 315292, Fur and Leather Apparel Manufacturing.

3159 Apparel Accessories and Other Apparel Manufacturing

This industry group comprises establishments primarily engaged in manufacturing apparel accessories and other apparel (except apparel knitting mills, apparel contractors, men's and boys' cut and sew apparel, women's and girls' cut and sew apparel, infants' cut and sew apparel, fur and leather apparel, and all other cut and sew apparel). This industry group includes jobbers performing entrepreneurial functions involved in manufacturing apparel accessories.

■ = Cross-References

US—United States industry only. CAN—United States and Canadian industries are comparable. When neither US nor CAN appears, Canadian, Mexican, and United States industries are comparable.

Sector
31-33

Manufacturing

31599 Apparel Accessories and Other Apparel Manufacturing

This industry comprises establishments primarily engaged in manufacturing apparel and accessories (except apparel knitting mills, cut and sew apparel contractors, men's and boys' cut and sew apparel, women's and girls' cut and sew apparel, and other cut and sew apparel). Jobbers, who perform entrepreneurial functions involved in apparel accessories manufacture, including buying raw materials, designing and preparing samples, arranging for apparel accessories to be made from their materials, and marketing finished apparel accessories, are included. Examples of products made by these establishments are belts, caps, gloves (except medical, sporting, safety), hats, and neckties.

- Cutting and/or sewing materials owned by others for apparel accessories are classified in Industry 31521, Cut and Sew Apparel Contractors;
- Manufacturing paper hats and caps are classified in Industry 32229, Other Converted Paper Product Manufacturing; Manufacturing plastics or rubber hats and caps (except bathing caps) are classified in Subsector 326, Plastics and Rubber Products Manufacturing;
- Manufacturing athletic gloves, such as boxing gloves, baseball gloves, golf gloves, batting gloves, and racquetball gloves, are classified in Industry 33992, Sporting and Athletic Goods Manufacturing;
- Manufacturing metal fabric, metal mesh, or rubber gloves are classified in Industry 33911, Medical Equipment and Supplies Manufacturing;
- Knitting apparel, mittens, gloves, hats, and caps or knitting fabric and manufacturing apparel, mittens, gloves, hats, and caps are classified in Industry Group 3151, Apparel Knitting Mills;
- Cutting and/or sewing materials owned by others for apparel are classified in Industry 31521, Cut and Sew Apparel Contractors;
- Manufacturing men's and boys' underwear and outerwear from purchased fabric are classified in Industry 31522, Men's and Boys' Cut and Sew Apparel Manufacturing;
- Manufacturing women's and girls' underwear and outerwear from purchased fabric are classified in Industry 31523, Women's and Girls' Cut and Sew Apparel Manufacturing; and
- Manufacturing other apparel from purchased fabric and manufacturing fur and leather apparel, hats, and caps are classified in Industry 31529, Other Cut and Sew Apparel Manufacturing.

315991 Hat, Cap, and Millinery Manufacturing ᵁˢ

This U.S. industry comprises establishments primarily engaged in manufacturing cut and sew hats, caps, millinery, and hat bodies from purchased fabric. Jobbers, who perform entrepreneurial functions involved in hat, cap, and millinery manufacture, including buying raw materials, designing and preparing samples, arranging for hats, caps, and millinery to be made from their materials, and marketing finished hats, caps, and millinery, are included.

- Cutting and/or sewing materials owned by others for hats, caps, and millinery are classified in Industry 31521, Cut and Sew Apparel Contractors;
- Manufacturing paper hats and caps are classified in U.S. Industry 322299, All Other Converted Paper Product Manufacturing;
- Manufacturing plastics or rubber hats and caps (except bathing caps) are classified in Subsector 326, Plastics and Rubber Products Manufacturing; and
- Manufacturing fur and leather hats and caps are classified in U.S. Industry 315292, Fur and Leather Apparel Manufacturing.

Visit page 17 to learn about classification changes to this sector.

315992 Glove and Mitten Manufacturing ᵁˢ

This U.S. industry comprises establishments primarily engaged in manufacturing cut and sew gloves (except rubber, metal, and athletic gloves) and mittens from purchased fabric, fur, leather, or from combinations of fabric, fur, or leather. Jobbers, who perform entrepreneurial functions involved in glove and mitten manufacture, including buying raw materials, designing and preparing samples, arranging for gloves and mittens to be made from their materials, and marketing finished gloves and mittens, are included.

- Cutting and/or sewing materials owned by others for gloves and mittens are classified in Industry 31521, Cut and Sew Apparel Contractors;
- Knitting mittens and gloves or knitting fabric and manufacturing mittens and gloves are classified in U.S. Industry 315191, Outerwear Knitting Mills;
- Manufacturing athletic gloves, such as boxing gloves, baseball gloves, golf gloves, batting gloves, and racquetball gloves are classified in Industry 339920, Sporting and Athletic Goods Manufacturing; and
- Manufacturing metal fabric, metal mesh, or rubber gloves are classified in U.S. Industry 339113, Surgical Appliance and Supplies Manufacturing.

Sector
31-33

Manufacturing

315993 Men's and Boys' Neckwear Manufacturing ᵁˢ

This U.S. industry comprises establishments primarily engaged in manufacturing men's and boys' cut and sew neckties, scarves, and mufflers from purchased fabric, leather, or from combinations of leather and fabric. Men's and boys' neckwear jobbers, who perform entrepreneurial functions involved in

■ = Cross-References

US—United States industry only. CAN—United States and Canadian industries are comparable. When neither US nor CAN appears, Canadian, Mexican, and United States industries are comparable.

neckwear manufacture, including buying raw materials, designing and preparing samples, arranging for neckwear to be made from their materials, and marketing finished neckwear, are included.

■ Establishments primarily engaged in cutting and/or sewing materials owned by others for men's and boys' neckwear are classified in U.S. Industry 315211, Men's and Boys' Cut and Sew Apparel Contractors.

315999 Other Apparel Accessories and Other Apparel Manufacturing ᵁˢ
This U.S. industry comprises establishments primarily engaged in manufacturing apparel and apparel accessories (except apparel knitting mills; cut and sew apparel contractors; cut and sew apparel; hats and caps; mittens and gloves; and men's and boys' neckwear). Jobbers for these products, who perform entrepreneurial functions involved in other apparel and accessory manufacture, including buying raw materials, designing and preparing samples, arranging for other apparel and accessories to be made from their materials, and marketing finished other apparel and accessories, are included. Examples of products made by these establishments are apparel trimmings and findings, belts, women's scarves, suspenders, and waterproof outerwear.

■ Knitting apparel or knitting fabric and manufacturing apparel are classified in Industry Group 3151, Apparel Knitting Mills;
■ Cutting and/or sewing materials owned by others for apparel are classified in Industry 31521, Cut and Sew Apparel Contractors;
■ Manufacturing men's and boys' cut and sew underwear and outerwear from purchased fabric are classified in Industry 31522, Men's and Boys' Cut and Sew Apparel Manufacturing;
■ Manufacturing women's and girls' cut and sew underwear and outerwear from purchased fabric are classified in Industry 31523, Women's and Girls' Cut and Sew Apparel Manufacturing;
■ Manufacturing infants' cut and sew apparel from purchased fabric are classified in U.S. Industry 315291, Infants' Cut and Sew Apparel Manufacturing;
■ Manufacturing fur and leather apparel are classified in U.S. Industry 315292, Fur and Leather Apparel Manufacturing;
■ Manufacturing hats, caps, and millinery are classified in U.S. Industry 315991, Hat, Cap, and Millinery Manufacturing;
■ Manufacturing gloves and mittens are classified in U.S. Industry 315992, Glove and Mitten Manufacturing; and
■ Manufacturing men's and boys' neckwear are classified in U.S. Industry 315993, Men's and Boys' Neckwear Manufacturing.

▶316 LEATHER AND ALLIED PRODUCT MANUFACTURING
Establishments in the Leather and Allied Product Manufacturing subsector transform hides into leather by tanning or curing and fabricating the leather into products for final consumption. It also includes the manufacture of similar products from other materials, including products (except apparel) made from "leather substitutes," such as rubber, plastics, or textiles. Rubber footwear, textile luggage, and plastics purses or wallets are examples of "leather substitute" products included in this group. The products made from leather substitutes are included in this subsector because they are made in similar ways leather products are made (e.g., luggage). They are made in the same establishments, so it is not practical to separate them.

The inclusion of leather making in this subsector is partly because leather tanning is a relatively small industry that has few close neighbors as a production process, partly because leather is an input to some of the other products classified in this subsector and partly for historical reasons.

3161 Leather and Hide Tanning and Finishing

31611 Leather and Hide Tanning and Finishing
See industry description for 316110 below

316110 Leather and Hide Tanning and Finishing
This industry comprises establishments primarily engaged in one or more of the following: (1) tanning, currying, and finishing hides and skins; (2) having others process hides and skins on a contract basis; and (3) dyeing or dressing furs.

3162 Footwear Manufacturing

31621 Footwear Manufacturing
This industry comprises establishments primarily engaged in manufacturing footwear (except orthopedic extension footwear).

■ Establishments primarily engaged in manufacturing orthopedic extension footwear are classified in Industry 33911, Medical Equipment and Supplies Manufacturing.

Sector
31-33
Manufacturing

■ = Cross-References

US—United States industry only. CAN—United States and Canadian industries are comparable. When neither US nor CAN appears, Canadian, Mexican, and United States industries are comparable.

316211 Rubber and Plastics Footwear Manufacturing ᵁˢ

This U.S. industry comprises establishments primarily engaged in manufacturing rubber and plastics footwear with vulcanized rubber or plastics soles, molded or cemented to rubber, plastics, or fabric uppers, and rubber and plastics protective footwear.

- Manufacturing house slippers with fabric uppers and rubber or plastics soles are classified in U.S. Industry 316212, House Slipper Manufacturing;
- Manufacturing men's footwear (except athletic) with leather or vinyl uppers, regardless of sole material are classified in U.S. Industry 316213, Men's Footwear (except Athletic) Manufacturing;
- Manufacturing women's footwear (except athletic) with leather or vinyl uppers, regardless of sole material are classified in U.S. Industry 316214, Women's Footwear (except Athletic) Manufacturing; and
- Manufacturing youths' children's and infants' footwear and athletic footwear with leather or vinyl uppers, regardless of sole material are classified in U.S. Industry 316219, Other Footwear Manufacturing.

316212 House Slipper Manufacturing ᵁˢ

This U.S. industry comprises establishments primarily engaged in manufacturing house slippers and slipper socks, regardless of material.

316213 Men's Footwear (except Athletic) Manufacturing ᵁˢ

This U.S. industry comprises establishments primarily engaged in manufacturing men's footwear designed primarily for dress, street, and work. This industry includes men's shoes with rubber or plastics soles and leather or vinyl uppers.

- Manufacturing men's footwear with fabric uppers and rubber or plastics soles are classified in U.S. Industry 316211, Rubber and Plastics Footwear Manufacturing;
- Manufacturing orthopedic extension footwear are classified in U.S. Industry 339113, Surgical Appliance and Supplies Manufacturing; and
- Manufacturing men's leather or vinyl upper athletic footwear and youths' and boys' footwear are classified in U.S. Industry 316219, Other Footwear Manufacturing.

316214 Women's Footwear (except Athletic) Manufacturing ᵁˢ

This U.S. industry comprises establishments primarily engaged in manufacturing women's footwear designed for dress, street, and work. This industry includes women's shoes with rubber or plastics soles and leather or vinyl uppers.

- Manufacturing women's footwear with fabric uppers and rubber or plastics soles and rubber or plastics sandals are classified in U.S. Industry 316211, Rubber and Plastics Footwear Manufacturing;
- Manufacturing orthopedic extension footwear are classified in U.S. Industry 339113, Surgical Appliance and Supplies Manufacturing; and
- Manufacturing women's leather or vinyl upper athletic footwear and youths' and girls' footwear are classified in U.S. Industry 316219, Other Footwear Manufacturing.

316219 Other Footwear Manufacturing ᵁˢ

This U.S. industry comprises establishments primarily engaged in manufacturing other footwear–except rubber and plastics footwear; house slippers; men's footwear (except athletic); and women's footwear (except athletic).

- Manufacturing rubber and plastics footwear with fabric uppers are classified in U.S. Industry 316211, Rubber and Plastics Footwear Manufacturing;
- Manufacturing house slippers are classified in U.S. Industry 316212, House Slipper Manufacturing;
- Manufacturing men's footwear (except athletic) are classified in U.S. Industry 316213, Men's Footwear (except Athletic) Manufacturing;
- Manufacturing orthopedic extension footwear are classified in Industry 339113, Surgical Appliance and Supplies Manufacturing; and
- Manufacturing women's footwear (except athletic) are classified in U.S. Industry 316214, Women's Footwear (except Athletic) Manufacturing.

3169 Other Leather and Allied Product Manufacturing

31699 Other Leather and Allied Product Manufacturing

This industry comprises establishments primarily engaged in manufacturing leather products (except footwear and apparel) from purchased leather or leather substitutes (e.g., fabric, plastics).

- Manufacturing leather apparel are classified in Industry 31529, Other Cut and Sew Apparel Manufacturing;

Visit page 17 to learn about classification changes to this sector.

Sector
31-33
Manufacturing

■ = Cross-References

US—United States industry only. CAN—United States and Canadian industries are comparable. When neither US nor CAN appears, Canadian, Mexican, and United States industries are comparable.

www.harrisinfo.com

345

■ Manufacturing leather gloves, mittens, belts, and apparel accessories are classified in Industry 31599, Apparel Accessories and Other Apparel Manufacturing;

■ Manufacturing footwear are classified in Industry 31621, Footwear Manufacturing;

■ Manufacturing nonleather soles are classified elsewhere based on the primary input material;

■ Manufacturing small articles made of metal carried on or about the person made of metal are classified in Industry 33991, Jewelry and Silverware Manufacturing; and

■ Manufacturing leather gaskets are classified in Industry 33999, All Other Miscellaneous Manufacturing.

316991 Luggage Manufacturing ᵁˢ

This U.S. industry comprises establishments primarily engaged in manufacturing luggage of any material.

316992 Women's Handbag and Purse Manufacturing ᵁˢ

This U.S. industry comprises establishments primarily engaged in manufacturing women's handbags and purses of any material (except precious metal).

■ Establishments primarily engaged in manufacturing precious metal handbags and purses are classified in U.S. Industry 339911, Jewelry (except Costume) Manufacturing.

316993 Personal Leather Good (except Women's Handbag and Purse) Manufacturing ᵁˢ

This U.S. industry comprises establishments primarily engaged in manufacturing personal leather goods (i.e., small articles of any material (except metal) normally carried on or about the person or in a handbag). Examples of personal leather goods made by these establishments are billfolds, coin purses, key cases, toilet kits, and watchbands (except metal).

■ Manufacturing personal goods of precious metal are classified in U.S. Industry 339911, Jewelry (except Costume) Manufacturing; and

■ Manufacturing personal goods of metal (except precious) are classified in U.S. Industry 339914, Costume Jewelry and Novelty Manufacturing.

316999 All Other Leather Good Manufacturing ᵁˢ

This U.S. industry comprises establishments primarily engaged in manufacturing leather goods (except footwear, luggage, handbags, purses, and personal leather goods).

■ Manufacturing leather gloves or mittens are classified in U.S. Industry 315992, Glove and Mitten Manufacturing;

■ Manufacturing leather apparel belts are classified in U.S. Industry 315999, Other Apparel Accessories and Other Apparel Manufacturing;

■ Manufacturing footwear are classified in Industry 31621, Footwear Manufacturing;

■ Manufacturing luggage of any material are classified in U.S. Industry 316991, Luggage Manufacturing;

■ Manufacturing handbags and purses are classified in U.S. Industry 316992, Women's Handbag and Purse Manufacturing;

■ Manufacturing personal leather goods, such as wallets and key cases, of all materials (except metal) are classified in U.S. Industry 316993, Personal Leather Good (except Women's Handbag and Purse) Manufacturing;

■ Manufacturing nonleather soles are classified elsewhere based on the primary input material;

■ Manufacturing leather apparel are classified in U.S. Industry 315292, Fur and Leather Apparel Manufacturing; and

■ Manufacturing leather gaskets are classified in U.S. Industry 339991, Gasket, Packing, and Sealing Device Manufacturing.

▶321 WOOD PRODUCT MANUFACTURING

Industries in the Wood Product Manufacturing subsector manufacture wood products, such as lumber, plywood, veneers, wood containers, wood flooring, wood trusses, manufactured homes (i.e., mobile home), and prefabricated wood buildings. The production processes of the Wood Product Manufacturing subsector include sawing, planing, shaping, laminating, and assembling of wood products starting from logs that are cut into bolts, or lumber that then may be further cut, or shaped by lathes or other shaping tools. The lumber or other transformed wood shapes may also be subsequently planed or smoothed, and assembled into finished products, such as wood containers.

The Wood Product Manufacturing subsector includes establishments that make wood products from logs and bolts that are sawed and shaped, and establishments that purchase sawed lumber and make wood products. With the exception of sawmills and wood preservation establishments, the establishments are grouped into industries mainly based on the specific products manufactured.

3211 Sawmills and Wood Preservation

This industry group comprises establishments whose primary production process begins with logs or bolts that are transformed into boards, dimension lumber, beams, timbers, poles, ties, shingles, shakes, siding,

Sector

31-33

Manufacturing

■ = Cross-References

US—United States industry only. CAN—United States and Canadian industries are comparable. When neither US nor CAN appears, Canadian, Mexican, and United States industries are comparable.

346

Harris InfoSource

and wood chips. Establishments that cut and treat round wood and/or treat wood products made in other establishments to prevent rotting by impregnation with creosote or other chemical compounds are also included in this industry group.

32111 Sawmills and Wood Preservation

This industry comprises establishments primarily engaged in one or more of the following: (1) sawing dimension lumber, boards, beams, timber, poles, ties, shingles, shakes, siding, and wood chips from logs or bolts; (2) sawing round wood poles, pilings, and posts and treating them with preservative; and (3) treating wood sawed, planed, or shaped in other establishments with creosote or other preservative to prevent decay and to protect against fire and insects. Sawmills may plane the rough lumber that they make with a planing machine to achieve smoothness and uniformity of size.

- Operating portable chipper mills in the field are classified in Industry 11331, Logging;
- Manufacturing wood products (except round wood poles, pilings, and posts) and treating them with preservative are classified elsewhere in Subsector 321, Wood Product Manufacturing, based on the related production process;
- Manufacturing veneer from logs and bolts or manufacturing engineered lumber and structural members other than solid wood are classified in Industry 32121, Veneer, Plywood, and Engineered Wood Product Manufacturing; and
- Planing purchased lumber or manufacturing cut stock or dimension stock (i.e., shapes) from logs or bolts are classified in Industry 32191, Millwork.

321113 Sawmills ^{US}

This U.S. industry comprises establishments primarily engaged in sawing dimension lumber, boards, beams, timbers, poles, ties, shingles, shakes, siding, and wood chips from logs or bolts. Sawmills may plane the rough lumber that they make with a planing machine to achieve smoothness and uniformity of size.

- Planing purchased lumber or manufacturing cut stock or dimension stock (i.e., shapes) from logs or bolts are classified in Industry 32191, Millwork;
- Manufacturing veneer from logs or bolts are classified in Industry 32121, Veneer, Plywood, and Engineered Wood Product Manufacturing; and
- Operating portable chipper mills in the field are classified in Industry 113310, Logging.

321114 Wood Preservation ^{CAN}

This U.S. industry comprises establishments primarily engaged in (1) treating wood sawed, planed, or shaped in other establishments with creosote or other preservative, such as chromated copper arsenate, to prevent decay and to protect against fire and insects and/or (2) sawing round wood poles, pilings, and posts and treating them with preservative.

- Establishments primarily engaged in manufacturing wood products (except round wood poles, pilings, and posts) and treating them with preservative are classified elsewhere in Subsector 321, Wood Product Manufacturing, based on the related production process.

3212 Veneer, Plywood, and Engineered Wood Product Manufacturing

32121 Veneer, Plywood, and Engineered Wood Product Manufacturing

This industry comprises establishments primarily engaged in one or more of the following: (1) manufacturing veneer and/or plywood; (2) manufacturing engineered wood members; and (3) manufacturing reconstituted wood products. This industry includes manufacturing plywood from veneer made in the same establishment or from veneer made in other establishments, and manufacturing plywood faced with nonwood materials, such as plastics or metal.

- Manufacturing veneer and further processing that veneer into wood containers or wood container parts in the same establishment are classified in Industry 32192, Wood Container and Pallet Manufacturing;
- Manufacturing prefabricated wood buildings or wood sections, and panels for buildings are classified in Industry 32199, All Other Wood Product Manufacturing; and
- Manufacturing solid wood structural members, such as dimension lumber and timber from logs or bolts in sawmills are classified in Industry 32111, Sawmills and Wood Preservation.

321211 Hardwood Veneer and Plywood Manufacturing ^{CAN}

This U.S. industry comprises establishments primarily engaged in manufacturing hardwood veneer and/or hardwood plywood.

- Manufacturing veneer and further processing that veneer into wood containers or wood container parts are classified in Industry 321920, Wood Container and Pallet Manufacturing;

Visit page 17 to learn about classification changes to this sector.

Sector

31-33

Manufacturing

■ = Cross-References

US—United States industry only. CAN—United States and Canadian industries are comparable. When neither US nor CAN appears, Canadian, Mexican, and United States industries are comparable.

■ Manufacturing softwood veneer and softwood plywood are classified in U.S. Industry 321212, Softwood Veneer and Plywood Manufacturing; and

■ Manufacturing reconstituted wood sheets and boards are classified in U.S. Industry 321219, Reconstituted Wood Product Manufacturing.

321212 Softwood Veneer and Plywood Manufacturing ^{CAN}

This U.S. industry comprises establishments primarily engaged in manufacturing softwood veneer and/or softwood plywood.

■ Manufacturing veneer and further processing that veneer into wood containers or wood container parts are classified in Industry 321920, Wood Container and Pallet Manufacturing;

■ Manufacturing hardwood veneer and hardwood plywood are classified in U.S. Industry 321211, Hardwood Veneer and Plywood Manufacturing; and

■ Manufacturing reconstituted wood sheets and boards are classified in U.S. Industry 321219, Reconstituted Wood Product Manufacturing.

321213 Engineered Wood Member (except Truss) Manufacturing ^{US}

This U.S. industry comprises establishments primarily engaged in manufacturing fabricated or laminated wood arches and/or other fabricated or laminated wood structural members.

■ Manufacturing prefabricated wood buildings, or wood sections, and panels for buildings are classified in U.S. Industry 321992, Prefabricated Wood Building Manufacturing;

■ Manufacturing wood trusses are classified in U.S. Industry 321214, Truss Manufacturing; and

■ Manufacturing solid wood structural members, such as dimension lumber and timber from logs or bolts, are classified in U.S. Industry 321113, Sawmills.

321214 Truss Manufacturing ^{US}

This U.S. industry comprises establishments primarily engaged in manufacturing laminated or fabricated wood roof and floor trusses.

■ Establishments primarily engaged in manufacturing wood I-joists are classified in U.S. Industry 321213, Engineered Wood Member (except Truss) Manufacturing.

321219 Reconstituted Wood Product Manufacturing ^{US}

This U.S. industry comprises establishments primarily engaged in manufacturing reconstituted wood sheets and boards.

■ Manufacturing softwood plywood are classified in U.S. Industry 321212, Softwood Veneer and Plywood Manufacturing; and

■ Manufacturing hardwood plywood are classified in U.S. Industry 321211, Hardwood Veneer and Plywood Manufacturing.

3219 Other Wood Product Manufacturing

This industry group comprises establishments primarily engaged in manufacturing wood products (except establishments operating sawmills and wood preservation facilities; and establishments manufacturing veneer, plywood, or engineered wood products).

Sector
31-33
Manufacturing

32191 Millwork

This industry comprises establishments primarily engaged in manufacturing hardwood and softwood cut stock and dimension stock (i.e., shapes); wood windows and wood doors; and other millwork including wood flooring. Dimension stock or cut stock is defined as lumber and worked wood products cut or shaped to specialized sizes. These establishments generally use woodworking machinery, such as jointers, planers, lathes, and routers to shape wood.

■ Manufacturing dimension lumber, boards, beams, timbers, poles, ties, shingles, shakes, siding, and wood chips from logs and bolts are classified in Industry 32111, Sawmills and Wood Preservation;

■ Fabricating millwork at the construction site are classified in Sector 23, Construction; and

■ Manufacturing wood furniture frames and finished wood furniture parts are classified in Industry 33721, Office Furniture (including Fixtures) Manufacturing.

321911 Wood Window and Door Manufacturing ^{CAN}

This U.S. industry comprises establishments primarily engaged in manufacturing window and door units, sash, window and door frames, and doors from wood or wood clad with metal or plastics.

■ Establishments primarily engaged in fabricating wood windows or wood doors at the construction site are classified in Sector 23, Construction.

■ = Cross-References

US—United States industry only. CAN—United States and Canadian industries are comparable. When neither US nor CAN appears, Canadian, Mexican, and United States industries are comparable.

321912 Cut Stock, Resawing Lumber, and Planing [US]

This U.S. industry comprises establishments primarily engaged in one or more of the following: (1) manufacturing dimension lumber from purchased lumber; (2) manufacturing dimension stock (i.e., shapes) or cut stock; (3) resawing the output of sawmills; and (4) planing purchased lumber. These establishments generally use woodworking machinery, such as jointers, planers, lathes, and routers to shape wood.

- Manufacturing dimension lumber, boards, beams, timbers, poles, ties, shingles, shakes, siding, and wood chips from logs or bolts are classified in U.S. Industry 321113, Sawmills;
- Manufacturing wood stairwork, wood molding, wood trim, and other millwork are classified in U.S. Industry 321918, Other Millwork (including Flooring); and
- Manufacturing wood furniture frames and finished wood furniture parts are classified in U.S. Industry 337215, Showcase, Partition, Shelving, and Locker Manufacturing.

321918 Other Millwork (including Flooring) [US]

This U.S. industry comprises establishments primarily engaged in manufacturing millwork (except wood windows, wood doors, and cut stock).

- Manufacturing wood windows and doors are classified in U.S. Industry 321911, Wood Window and Door Manufacturing; and
- Manufacturing cut stock, resawing lumber, and/or planing purchased lumber are classified in U.S. Industry 321912, Cut Stock, Resawing Lumber, and Planing.

32192 Wood Container and Pallet Manufacturing

See industry description for 321920 below

321920 Wood Container and Pallet Manufacturing

This industry comprises establishments primarily engaged in manufacturing wood pallets, wood box shook, wood boxes, other wood containers, and wood parts for pallets and containers.

- Establishments primarily engaged in manufacturing wood burial caskets are classified in U.S. Industry 339995, Burial Casket Manufacturing.

32199 All Other Wood Product Manufacturing

This industry comprises establishments primarily engaged in manufacturing wood products (except establishments operating sawmills and wood preservation facilities; and establishments manufacturing veneer, plywood, engineered wood products, millwork, wood containers, or pallets).

- Operating sawmills or preserving wood are classified in Industry 32111, Sawmills and Wood Preservation;
- Manufacturing veneer, plywood, and engineered wood products are classified in Industry 32121, Veneer, Plywood, and Engineered Wood Product Manufacturing;
- Manufacturing millwork are classified in Industry 32191, Millwork;
- Manufacturing wood containers, pallets, and wood container parts are classified in Industry 32192, Wood Container and Pallet Manufacturing;
- Manufacturing travel trailers with self-contained facilities for storage of water and waste are classified in Industry 33621, Motor Vehicle Body and Trailer Manufacturing; and
- Fabricating of wood buildings or wood sections and panels for buildings at the construction site are classified in Sector 23, Construction.

321991 Manufactured Home (Mobile Home) Manufacturing [US]

This U.S. industry comprises establishments primarily engaged in making manufactured homes (i.e., mobile homes) and nonresidential mobile buildings. Manufactured homes are designed to accept permanent water, sewer, and utility connections and although equipped with wheels, they are not intended for regular highway movement.

- Manufacturing prefabricated wood buildings not equipped with wheels are classified in U.S. Industry 321992, Prefabricated Wood Building Manufacturing; and
- Manufacturing travel trailers with self-contained facilities for storage of water and waste are classified in U.S. Industry 336214, Travel Trailer and Camper Manufacturing.

321992 Prefabricated Wood Building Manufacturing [CAN]

This U.S. industry comprises establishments primarily engaged in manufacturing prefabricated wood buildings and wood sections and panels for prefabricated wood buildings.

- Fabricating wood buildings or wood sections and panels for buildings at the construction site are classified in Sector 23, Construction; and

Visit page 17 to learn about classification changes to this sector.

Manufacturing

■ = Cross-References

US—United States industry only. CAN—United States and Canadian industries are comparable. When neither US nor CAN appears, Canadian, Mexican, and United States industries are comparable.

■ Making manufactured homes (i.e., mobile homes) are classified in U.S. Industry 321991, Manufactured Home (Mobile Home) Manufacturing.

321999 All Other Miscellaneous Wood Product Manufacturing ^{CAN}
This U.S. industry comprises establishments primarily engaged in manufacturing wood products (except establishments operating sawmills and preservation facilities; establishments manufacturing veneer, engineered wood products, millwork, wood containers, pallets, and wood container parts; and establishments making manufactured homes (i.e., mobile homes) and prefabricated buildings and components).

■ Operating sawmills and preserving wood are classified in Industry 32111, Sawmills and Wood Preservation;
■ Manufacturing veneer and engineered wood products are classified in Industry 32121, Veneer, Plywood, and Engineered Wood Product Manufacturing;
■ Manufacturing millwork are classified in Industry 32191, Millwork;
■ Manufacturing boxes, box shook, wood containers, pallets, and wood parts for containers are classified in Industry 321920, Wood Container and Pallet Manufacturing;
■ Making manufactured homes (i.e., mobile homes) are classified in U.S. Industry 321991, Manufactured Home (Mobile Home) Manufacturing; and
■ Manufacturing prefabricated wood buildings or wood sections and panels for buildings are classified in U.S. Industry 321992, Prefabricated Wood Building Manufacturing.

▶322 PAPER MANUFACTURING

Industries in the Paper Manufacturing subsector make pulp, paper, or converted paper products. The manufacturing of these products is grouped together because they constitute a series of vertically connected processes. More than one is often carried out in a single establishment. There are essentially three activities. The manufacturing of pulp involves separating the cellulose fibers from other impurities in wood or used paper. The manufacturing of paper involves matting these fibers into a sheet. Converted paper products are made from paper and other materials by various cutting and shaping techniques and includes coating and laminating activities.

The Paper Manufacturing subsector is subdivided into two industry groups, the first for the manufacturing of pulp and paper and the second for the manufacturing of converted paper products. Paper making is treated as the core activity of the subsector. Therefore, any establishment that makes paper (including paperboard), either alone or in combination with pulp manufacturing or paper converting, is classified as a paper or paperboard mill. Establishments that make pulp without making paper are classified as pulp mills. Pulp mills, paper mills and paperboard mills comprise the first industry group.

Establishments that make products from purchased paper and other materials make up the second industry group, Converted Paper Product Manufacturing. This general activity is then subdivided based, for the most part, on process distinctions. Paperboard container manufacturing uses corrugating, cutting, and shaping machinery to form paperboard into containers. Paper bag and coated and treated paper manufacturing establishments cut and coat paper and foil. Stationery product manufacturing establishments make a variety of paper products used for writing, filing, and similar applications. Other converted paper product manufacturing includes, in particular, the conversion of sanitary paper stock into such things as tissue paper and disposable diapers.

An important process used in the Paper Bag and Coated and Treated Paper Manufacturing industry is lamination, often combined with coating. Lamination and coating makes a composite material with improved properties of strength, impermeability, and so on. The laminated materials may be paper, metal foil, or plastics film. While paper is often one of the components, it is not always. Lamination of plastics film to plastics film is classified in the NAICS Subsector 326, Plastics and Rubber Products Manufacturing, because establishments that do this often first make the film.

The same situation holds with respect to bags. The manufacturing of bags from plastics only, whether or not laminated, is classified in Subsector 326, Plastics and Rubber Products Manufacturing, but all other bag manufacturing is classified in this subsector.

Excluded from this subsector are photosensitive papers. These papers are chemically treated and are classified in Industry 32599, All Other Chemical Product and Preparation Manufacturing.

Sector
31-33
Manufacturing

■ = Cross-References

US—United States industry only. CAN—United States and Canadian industries are comparable. When neither US nor CAN appears, Canadian, Mexican, and United States industries are comparable.

350

Harris InfoSource

3221 Pulp, Paper, and Paperboard Mills
This industry group comprises establishments primarily engaged in manufacturing pulp, paper, or paperboard.

32211 Pulp Mills
See industry description for 322110 below.

322110 Pulp Mills
This industry comprises establishments primarily engaged in manufacturing pulp without manufacturing paper or paperboard. The pulp is made by separating the cellulose fibers from the other impurities in wood or other materials, such as used or recycled rags, linters, scrap paper, and straw.

- Manufacturing both pulp and paper are classified in Industry 32212, Paper Mills; and
- Manufacturing both pulp and paperboard are classified in Industry 322130, Paperboard Mills.

32212 Paper Mills
This industry comprises establishments primarily engaged in manufacturing paper from pulp. These establishments may manufacture or purchase pulp. In addition, the establishments may convert the paper they make. The activity of making paper classifies an establishment into this industry regardless of the output.

- Manufacturing pulp without manufacturing paper are classified in Industry 32211, Pulp Mills;
- Manufacturing paperboard are classified in Industry 32213, Paperboard Mills;
- Converting paper without manufacturing paper are classified in Industry Group 3222, Converted Paper Product Manufacturing; and
- Manufacturing photographic sensitized paper are classified in Industry 32599, All Other Chemical Product and Preparation Manufacturing.

322121 Paper (except Newsprint) Mills ^{CAN}
This U.S. industry comprises establishments primarily engaged in manufacturing paper (except newsprint and uncoated groundwood paper) from pulp. These establishments may manufacture or purchase pulp. In addition, the establishments may also convert the paper they make.

- Manufacturing newsprint and uncoated groundwood paper are classified in U.S. Industry 322122, Newsprint Mills;
- Converting paper without manufacturing paper are classified in Industry Group 3222, Converted Paper Product Manufacturing;
- Manufacturing paperboard are classified in Industry 322130, Paperboard Mills;
- Manufacturing pulp without manufacturing paper are classified in Industry 322110, Pulp Mills; and
- Manufacturing photographic sensitized paper from purchased paper are classified in U.S. Industry 325992, Photographic Film, Paper, Plate, and Chemical Manufacturing.

322122 Newsprint Mills ^{CAN}
This U.S. industry comprises establishments primarily engaged in manufacturing newsprint and uncoated groundwood paper from pulp. These establishments may manufacture or purchase pulp. In addition, the establishments may also convert the paper they make.

- Manufacturing paper (except newsprint and uncoated groundwood) are classified in U.S. Industry 322121, Paper (except Newsprint) Mills;
- Converting paper without manufacturing paper are classified in Industry Group 3222, Converted Paper Product Manufacturing;
- Manufacturing paperboard are classified in Industry 322130, Paperboard Mills; and
- Manufacturing pulp without manufacturing paper are classified in Industry 322110, Pulp Mills.

32213 Paperboard Mills
See industry description for 322130 below.

322130 Paperboard Mills
This industry comprises establishments primarily engaged in manufacturing paperboard from pulp. These establishments may manufacture or purchase pulp. In addition, the establishments may also convert the paperboard they make.

- Manufacturing pulp without manufacturing paperboard are classified in Industry 322110, Pulp Mills;
- Converting paperboard without manufacturing paperboard are classified in Industry Group 3222, Converted Paper Product Manufacturing; and
- Manufacturing insulation board and other reconstituted wood fiberboard are classified in U.S. Industry 321219, Reconstituted Wood Product Manufacturing.

Visit page 17 to learn about classification changes to this sector.

Sector

31-33

Manufacturing

■ = Cross-References

US—United States industry only. CAN—United States and Canadian industries are comparable. When neither US nor CAN appears, Canadian, Mexican, and United States industries are comparable.

www.harrisinfo.com

351

3222 Converted Paper Product Manufacturing

This industry group comprises establishments primarily engaged in converting paper or paperboard without manufacturing paper or paperboard.

32221 Paperboard Container Manufacturing

This industry comprises establishments primarily engaged in converting paperboard into containers without manufacturing paperboard. These establishments use corrugating, cutting, and shaping machinery to form paperboard into containers. Products made by these establishments include boxes; corrugated sheets, pads, and pallets; paper dishes; and fiber drums and reels.

- Manufacturing similar items of plastics materials are classified in Industry Group 3261, Plastics Product Manufacturing;
- Manufacturing paperboard and converting paperboard into containers are classified in Industry 32213, Paperboard Mills;
- Manufacturing egg cartons, food trays, and other food containers from molded pulp are classified in Industry 32229, Other Converted Paper Product Manufacturing;
- Manufacturing paper and converting paper into containers are classified in Industry 32212, Paper Mills; and
- Manufacturing paperbags without manufacturing paper are classified in Industry 32222, Paper Bag and Coated and Treated Paper Manufacturing.

322211 Corrugated and Solid Fiber Box Manufacturing CAN

This U.S. industry comprises establishments primarily engaged in laminating purchased paper or paperboard into corrugated or solid fiber boxes and related products, such as pads, partitions, pallets, and corrugated paper without manufacturing paperboard. These boxes are generally used for shipping.

- Manufacturing setup paperboard boxes (except corrugated or laminated solid fiber boxes) are classified in U.S. Industry 322213, Setup Paperboard Box Manufacturing;
- Manufacturing folding paperboard boxes (except corrugated or laminated solid fiber boxes) are classified in U.S. Industry 322212, Folding Paperboard Box Manufacturing; and
- Manufacturing paperboard and converting paperboard into boxes are classified in Industry 322130, Paperboard Mills.

322212 Folding Paperboard Box Manufacturing CAN

This U.S. industry comprises establishments primarily engaged in converting paperboard (except corrugated) into folding paperboard boxes without manufacturing paper and paperboard.

- Manufacturing setup paperboard boxes (except corrugated) are classified in U.S. Industry 322213, Setup Paperboard Box Manufacturing;
- Manufacturing corrugated and solid fiber boxes are classified in U.S. Industry 322211, Corrugated and Solid Fiber Box Manufacturing;
- Manufacturing paperboard and converting paperboard into containers are classified in Industry 322130, Paperboard Mills;
- Manufacturing paper and converting paper into containers are classified in Industry 32212, Paper Mills;
- Manufacturing milk cartons are classified in U.S. Industry 322215, Nonfolding Sanitary Food Container Manufacturing; and
- Manufacturing paper bags are classified in Industry 32222, Paper Bag and Coated and Treated Paper Manufacturing.

322213 Setup Paperboard Box Manufacturing US

This U.S. industry comprises establishments primarily engaged in converting paperboard into setup paperboard boxes (i.e., rigid-sided boxes not shipped flat) without manufacturing paperboard.

- Manufacturing folding paperboard boxes (except corrugated) are classified in U.S. Industry 322212, Folding Paperboard Box Manufacturing;
- Manufacturing corrugated and solid fiber boxes are classified in U.S. Industry 322211, Corrugated and Solid Fiber Box Manufacturing; and
- Manufacturing paperboard and converting paperboard into containers are classified in Industry 322130, Paperboard Mills.

322214 Fiber Can, Tube, Drum, and Similar Products Manufacturing US

This U.S. industry comprises establishments primarily engaged in converting paperboard into fiber cans, tubes, drums, and similar products without manufacturing paperboard.

- Establishments engaged in manufacturing paperboard and converting paperboard into containers are classified in Industry 322130, Paperboard Mills.

322215 Nonfolding Sanitary Food Container Manufacturing US

This U.S. industry comprises establishments primarily engaged in converting sanitary foodboard into food containers (except folding).

- Manufacturing sanitary food containers of solely plastics materials are classified in Industry Group 3261, Plastics Product Manufacturing;

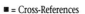

■ = Cross-References

Sector

31-33

Manufacturing

US—United States industry only. CAN—United States and Canadian industries are comparable. When neither US nor CAN appears, Canadian, Mexican, and United States industries are comparable.

352

Harris InfoSource

- Manufacturing egg cartons, food trays, and other food containers from molded pulp are classified in U.S. Industry 322299, All Other Converted Paper Product Manufacturing; and
- Manufacturing folding sanitary cartons are classified in U.S. Industry 322212, Folding Paperboard Box Manufacturing.

32222 Paper Bag and Coated and Treated Paper Manufacturing

This industry comprises establishments primarily engaged in one or more of the following: (1) cutting and coating paper and paperboard; (2) cutting and laminating paper and paperboard and other flexible materials (except plastics film to plastics film); (3) manufacturing bags or multiwall bags or sacks of paper, metal foil, coated paper, or laminates or coated combinations of paper and foil with plastics film; (4) manufacturing laminated aluminum and other converted metal foils from purchased foils; and (5) surface coating paper or paperboard.

- Manufacturing paper from pulp are classified in Industry 32212, Paper Mills;
- Manufacturing photographic sensitized paper are classified in Industry 32599, All Other Chemical Product and Preparation Manufacturing;
- Manufacturing textile bags are classified in Industry 31491, Textile Bag and Canvas Mills;
- Manufacturing single and multiwall plastics bags or plastics laminated bags are classified in Industry 32611, Unsupported Plastics Film, Sheet, and Bag Manufacturing;
- Making aluminum and aluminum foil are classified in Industry 33131, Alumina and Aluminum Production and Processing; and
- Cutting purchased aluminum foil into smaller lengths and widths are classified in Industry 33299, All Other Fabricated Metal Product Manufacturing.

322221 Coated and Laminated Packaging Paper and Plastics Film Manufacturing [US]

This U.S. industry comprises establishments primarily engaged in performing one or more of the following activities associated with the manufacturing of packaging materials: (1) cutting and coating paper; and (2) cutting and laminating paper with other flexible materials (except plastics to plastics or foil to paper laminates). The products made in this industry are made from purchased sheet materials and may be printed in the same establishment.

- Manufacturing coated or laminated paper for nonpackaging purposes are classified in U.S. Industry 322222, Coated and Laminated Paper Manufacturing;
- Manufacturing unsupported plastics film are classified in U.S. Industry 326113, Unsupported Plastics Film and Sheet (except Packaging) Manufacturing;
- Manufacturing laminated aluminum foil for flexible packaging uses are classified in U.S. Industry 322225, Laminated Aluminum Foil Manufacturing for Flexible Packaging Uses;
- Making aluminum and aluminum foil are classified in Industry 33131, Alumina and Aluminum Production and Processing;
- Cutting purchased aluminum foil into smaller lengths and widths are classified in U.S. Industry 332999, All Other Miscellaneous Fabricated Metal Product Manufacturing; and
- Manufacturing paper from pulp are classified in Industry 32212, Paper Mills.

322222 Coated and Laminated Paper Manufacturing [US]

This U.S. industry comprises establishments primarily engaged in performing one or more of the following activities associated with making products designed for purposes other than packaging: (1) cutting and coating paper; (2) cutting and laminating paper and other flexible materials (except plastics film to plastics film); and (3) manufacturing converted aluminum and other metal foils for nonpackaging uses from purchased foils. The products made in this industry are made from purchased sheet materials and may be printed in the same establishment.

- Manufacturing coated and laminated paper for packaging uses are classified in U.S. Industry 322221, Coated and Laminated Packaging Paper and Plastics Film Manufacturing;
- Manufacturing photographic sensitized paper are classified in U.S. Industry 325992, Photographic Film, Paper, Plate, and Chemical Manufacturing;
- Making aluminum and aluminum foil are classified in Industry 33131, Alumina and Aluminum Production and Processing;
- Cutting purchased aluminum foil into smaller lengths and widths are classified in U.S. Industry 332999, All Other Miscellaneous Fabricated Metal Product Manufacturing; and
- Manufacturing laminated aluminum foil for flexible packaging uses are classified in U.S. Industry 322225, Laminated Aluminum Foil Manufacturing for Flexible Packaging Uses.

322223 Plastics, Foil, and Coated Paper Bag Manufacturing [US]

This U.S. industry comprises establishments primarily engaged in manufacturing bags of coated paper, of metal foil, or of laminated or coated combinations of plastics, foil, and paper, whether or not printed.

- Manufacturing uncoated paper bags and multiwall bags and sacks are classified in U.S. Industry 322224, Uncoated Paper and Multiwall Bag Manufacturing;
- Manufacturing textile bags are classified in U.S. Industry 314911, Textile Bag Mills; and

Visit page 17 to learn about classification changes to this sector.

Sector
31-33
Manufacturing

■ = Cross-References

US—United States industry only. CAN—United States and Canadian industries are comparable. When neither US nor CAN appears, Canadian, Mexican, and United States industries are comparable.

www.harrisinfo.com

353

■ Manufacturing single and multiwall plastics bags are classified in U.S. Industry 326111, Unsupported Plastics Bag Manufacturing.

322224 Uncoated Paper and Multiwall Bag Manufacturing US
This U.S. industry comprises establishments primarily engaged in manufacturing uncoated paper bags or multiwall bags and sacks.

■ Manufacturing single wall and multiwall bags from plastics unsupported film are classified in U.S. Industry 326111, Unsupported Plastics Bag Manufacturing;
■ Manufacturing bags of coated paper, of metal foil, or of laminated or coated combinations of plastics, foil, and paper bags are classified in U.S. Industry 322223, Plastics, Foil, and Coated Paper Bag Manufacturing; and
■ Manufacturing textile bags are classified in U.S. Industry 314911, Textile Bag Mills.

322225 Laminated Aluminum Foil Manufacturing for Flexible Packaging Uses US
This U.S. industry comprises establishments primarily engaged in laminating aluminum and other metal foil into products with flexible packaging uses or gift wrap and other packaging wrap applications.

■ Manufacturing plain aluminum foil are classified in U.S. Industry 331315, Aluminum Sheet, Plate, and Foil Manufacturing;
■ Manufacturing laminated aluminum bags and liners are classified in U.S. Industry 322223, Plastics, Foil, and Coated Paper Bag Manufacturing;
■ Manufacturing converted aluminum and other metal foils for nonpackaging uses from purchased foils are classified in U.S. Industry 322222, Coated and Laminated Paper Manufacturing; and
■ Manufacturing cookware, dinnerware, and other semirigid metal containers are classified in U.S. Industry 332999, All Other Miscellaneous Fabricated Metal Product Manufacturing.

322226 Surface-coated Paperboard Manufacturing US
This U.S. industry comprises establishments primarily engaged in laminating, lining, or surface coating purchased paperboard to make other paperboard products.

32223 Stationery Product Manufacturing
This industry comprises establishments primarily engaged in converting paper or paperboard into products used for writing, filing, art work, and similar applications.

■ Establishments primarily engaged in manufacturing die-cut paper and paperboard products other than office supplies are classified in U.S. Industry 322299, All Other Converted Paper Product Manufacturing.

322231 Die-cut Paper and Paperboard Office Supplies Manufacturing US
This U.S. industry comprises establishments primarily engaged in converting paper rollstock or paperboard into die-cut paper or paperboard office supplies. For the purpose of this industry, office supplies are defined as office products, such as filing folders, index cards, rolls for adding machines, file separators and dividers, tabulating cards, and other paper and paperboard office supplies.

■ Manufacturing die-cut paper and paperboard products (except office supplies) are classified in U.S. Industry 322299, All Other Converted Paper Product Manufacturing; and
■ Manufacturing paper and paperboard products used for writing and similar applications (e.g., looseleaf fillers, notebooks, pads, stationery, tablets) are classified in U.S. Industry 322233, Stationery, Tablet, and Related Product Manufacturing.

322232 Envelope Manufacturing US
This U.S. industry comprises establishments primarily engaged in manufacturing envelopes for mailing or stationery of any material including combinations.

■ Establishments primarily engaged in manufacturing stationery are classified in U.S. Industry 322233, Stationery, Tablet, and Related Product Manufacturing.

322233 Stationery, Tablet, and Related Product Manufacturing US
This U.S. industry comprises establishments primarily engaged in converting paper and paperboard into products used for writing and similar applications (e.g., looseleaf fillers, notebooks, pads, stationery, tablets).

■ Manufacturing envelopes are classified in U.S. Industry 322232, Envelope Manufacturing; and
■ Manufacturing die-cut paper and paperboard office supplies are classified in U.S. Industry 322231, Die-cut Paper and Paperboard Office Supplies Manufacturing.

■ = Cross-References

Sector

31-33

Manufacturing

US—United States industry only. CAN—United States and Canadian industries are comparable. When neither US nor CAN appears, Canadian, Mexican, and United States industries are comparable.

354

Harris InfoSource

32229 Other Converted Paper Product Manufacturing

This industry comprises establishments primarily engaged in (1) converting paper and paperboard into products (except containers, bags, coated and treated paper and paperboard, and stationery products), or (2) converting pulp into pulp products, such as disposable diapers, or molded pulp egg cartons, food trays, and dishes. Processes used include laminating or lining purchased paper or paperboard.

- Manufacturing pulp from wood or from other materials are classified in Industry 32211, Pulp Mills;
- Manufacturing paper from pulp or making pulp and manufacturing paper are classified in Industry 32212, Paper Mills;
- Manufacturing paperboard from pulp or making pulp and manufacturing paperboard are classified in Industry 32213, Paperboard Mills;
- Manufacturing paperboard containers are classified in Industry 32221, Paperboard Container Manufacturing;
- Manufacturing bags of coated, laminated, or uncoated paper, of metal foil, or combinations thereof are classified in Industry 32222, Paper Bag and Coated and Treated Paper Manufacturing; and
- Manufacturing stationery and other related office supplies are classified in Industry 32223, Stationery Product Manufacturing.

322291 Sanitary Paper Product Manufacturing ^{CAN}

This U.S. industry comprises establishments primarily engaged in converting purchased sanitary paper stock or wadding into sanitary paper products, such as facial tissues and handkerchiefs, table napkins, toilet paper, towels, disposable diapers, sanitary napkins, and tampons.

322299 All Other Converted Paper Product Manufacturing ^{CAN}

This U.S. industry comprises establishments primarily engaged in converting paper or paperboard into products (except containers, bags, coated and treated paper, stationery products, and sanitary paper products) or converting pulp into pulp products, such as egg cartons, food trays, and other food containers from molded pulp.

- Manufacturing pulp from wood or from other materials are classified in Industry 322110, Pulp Mills;
- Manufacturing paper from pulp or making pulp and manufacturing paper are classified in Industry 32212, Paper Mills;
- Manufacturing paperboard from pulp or making pulp and manufacturing paperboard are classified in Industry 322130, Paperboard Mills;
- Manufacturing paperboard containers are classified in Industry 32221, Paperboard Container Manufacturing;
- Manufacturing bags of coated, laminated, or uncoated paper, of metal foil, or combinations thereof are classified in Industry 32222, Paper Bag and Coated and Treated Paper Manufacturing; and
- Manufacturing stationery and other related office supplies are classified in Industry 32223, Stationery Product Manufacturing.

▶ 323 PRINTING AND RELATED SUPPORT ACTIVITIES

Industries in the Printing and Related Support Activities subsector print products, such as newspapers, books, periodicals, business forms, greeting cards, and other materials, and perform support activities, such as bookbinding, platemaking services, and data imaging. The support activities included here are an integral part of the printing industry, and a product (a printing plate, a bound book, or a computer disk or file) that is an integral part of the printing industry is almost always provided by these operations.

Processes used in printing include a variety of methods used to transfer an image from a plate, screen, or computer file to some medium, such as paper, plastics, metal, textile articles, or wood. The most prominent of these methods is to transfer the image from a plate or screen to the medium (lithographic, gravure, screen, and flexographic printing). A rapidly growing new technology uses a computer file to directly "drive" the printing mechanism to create the image and new electrostatic and other types of equipment (digital or nonimpact printing).

In contrast to many other classification systems that locate publishing of printed materials in manufacturing, NAICS classifies the publishing of printed products in Subsector 511, Publishing Industries. Though printing and publishing are often carried out by the same enterprise (a newspaper, for example), it is less and less the case that these distinct activities are carried out in the same establishment. When publishing and printing are done in the same establishment, the establishment is classified in Sector 51, Information, in the appropriate NAICS industry even if the receipts for printing exceed those for publishing.

This subsector includes printing on clothing because the production process for that activity is printing, not clothing manufacturing. For instance, the printing of T-shirts is included in this subsector. In contrast, printing on fabric (or grey goods) is not included. This activity is part of the process of finishing the fabric and is included in the NAICS Textile Mills subsector in Industry 31331, Textile and Fabric Finishing Mills.

Visit page 17 to learn about classification changes to this sector.

Sector 31-33

Manufacturing

■ = Cross-References

US—United States industry only. CAN—United States and Canadian industries are comparable. When neither US nor CAN appears, Canadian, Mexican, and United States industries are comparable.

3231 Printing and Related Support Activities

32311 Printing

This industry comprises establishments primarily engaged in printing on apparel and textile products, paper, metal, glass, plastics, and other materials, except fabric (grey goods). The printing processes employed include, but are not limited to, lithographic, gravure, screen, flexographic, digital, and letterpress. Establishments in this industry do not manufacture the stock that they print but may perform postprinting activities, such as bending, cutting, or laminating the materials they print, and mailing.

- Providing photocopying service on nondigital photocopy equipment without performing traditional printing activities are classified in Industry 56143, Business Service Centers;
- Printing on grey goods are classified in Industry 31331, Textile and Fabric Finishing Mills;
- Printing and publishing, known as publishers, are classified in Subsector 511, Publishing Industries; and
- Performing prepress or postpress services without performing traditional printing activities are classified in Industry 32312, Support Services for Printing.

323110 Commercial Lithographic Printing US

This U.S. industry comprises establishments primarily engaged in lithographic (i.e., offset) printing without publishing (except books, grey goods, and manifold business forms). This industry includes establishments engaged in lithographic printing on purchased stock materials, such as stationery, letterhead, invitations, labels, and similar items, on a job order basis.

- Quick printing are classified in U.S. Industry 323114, Quick Printing;
- Printing on grey goods are classified in Industry 31331, Textile and Fabric Finishing Mills;
- Printing books and pamphlets are classified in U.S. Industry 323117, Books Printing;
- Printing manifold business forms including checkbooks are classified in U.S. Industry 323116, Manifold Business Forms Printing;
- Manufacturing printed stationery, invitations, labels, and similar items are classified in Subsector 322, Paper Manufacturing; and
- Printing and publishing, known as publishers, are classified in Subsector 511, Publishing Industries.

323111 Commercial Gravure Printing US

This U.S. industry comprises establishments primarily engaged in gravure printing without publishing (except books, grey goods, and manifold business forms). This industry includes establishments engaged in gravure printing on purchased stock materials, such as stationery, letterhead, invitations, labels, and similar items, on a job order basis.

- Printing on grey goods are classified in Industry 31331, Textile and Fabric Finishing Mills;
- Printing books and pamphlets are classified in U.S. Industry 323117, Book Printing;
- Printing manifold business forms including checkbooks are classified in U.S. Industry 323116, Manifold Business Form Printing;
- Manufacturing printed stationery, invitations, labels, and similar items are classified in Subsector 322, Paper Manufacturing; and
- Printing and publishing, known as publishers, are classified in Subsector 511, Publishing Industries.

323112 Commercial Flexographic Printing US

This U.S. industry comprises establishments primarily engaged in flexographic printing without publishing (except books, grey goods, and manifold business forms). This industry includes establishments engaged in flexographic printing on purchased stock materials, such as stationery, invitations, labels, and similar items, on a job order basis.

- Printing on grey goods are classified in Industry 31331, Textile and Fabric Finishing Mills;
- Printing books and pamphlets are classified in U.S. Industry 323117, Books Printing;
- Printing manifold business forms including checkbooks are classified in U.S. Industry 323116, Manifold Business Forms Printing;
- Manufacturing printed stationery, invitations, labels, and similar items are classified elsewhere in Subsector 322, Manufacturing; and
- Printing and publishing, known as publishers, are classified in Subsector 511, Publishing Industries.

323113 Commercial Screen Printing CAN

This U.S. industry comprises establishments primarily engaged in screen printing without publishing (except books, grey goods, and manifold business forms). This industry includes establishments engaged in screen printing on purchased stock materials, such as stationery, invitations, labels, and

Sector
31-33

Manufacturing

■ = Cross-References

US—United States industry only. CAN—United States and Canadian industries are comparable. When neither US nor CAN appears, Canadian, Mexican, and United States industries are comparable.

356

Harris InfoSource

similar items, on a job order basis. Establishments primarily engaged in printing on apparel and textile products, such as T-shirts, caps, jackets, towels, and napkins, are included in this industry.

- Printing on grey goods are classified in Industry 31331, Textile and Fabric Finishing Mills;
- Printing books and pamphlets are classified in U.S. Industry 323117, Books Printing;
- Printing manifold business forms including checkbooks are classified in U.S. Industry 323116, Manifold Business Forms Printing;
- Manufacturing printed stationery, invitations, labels, and similar items are classified in Subsector 322, Paper Manufacturing; and
- Printing and publishing, known as publishers, are classified in Subsector 511, Publishing Industries.

323114 Quick Printing ^{CAN}

This U.S. industry comprises establishments primarily engaged in traditional printing activities, such as short-run offset printing or prepress services, in combination with providing document photocopying service. Prepress services include receiving documents in electronic format and directly duplicating from the electronic file and formatting, colorizing, and otherwise modifying the original document to improve presentation. These establishments, known as quick printers, generally provide short-run printing and copying with fast turnaround times.

- Providing photocopying service on nondigital photocopy equipment without performing traditional printing activities are classified in U.S. Industry 561439, Other Business Service Centers (including Copy Shops);
- Printing on lithographic equipment known as commercial lithographic printers are classified in U.S. Industry 323110, Commercial Lithographic Printing; and
- Digital printing on graphical material are classified in U.S. Industry 323115, Digital Printing.

323115 Digital Printing ^{CAN}

This U.S. industry comprises establishments primarily engaged in printing graphical materials using digital printing equipment. Establishments known as digital printers typically provide sophisticated prepress services including using scanners to input images and computers to manipulate and format the graphic images prior to printing.

- Establishments primarily engaged in printing with "up front" computer files on conventional-type printing equipment are classified based on the type of printing equipment (e.g., lithographic, flexographic, screen) being used.

323116 Manifold Business Forms Printing ^{CAN}

This U.S. industry comprises establishments primarily engaged in printing special forms, including checkbooks, for use in the operation of a business. The forms may be in single and multiple sets, including carbonized, interleaved with carbon, or otherwise processed for multiple reproduction.

- Establishments primarily engaged in manufacturing single layered continuous computer paper and similar products are classified in U.S. Industry 322231, Die-cut Paper and Paperboard Office Supplies Manufacturing.

323117 Books Printing ^{US}

This U.S. industry comprises establishments primarily engaged in printing or printing and binding books and pamphlets without publishing.

- Printing and publishing, known as book publishers, are classified in Subsector 511, Publishing Industries; and
- Binding books without printing in the same establishment are classified in U.S. Industry 323121, Tradebinding and Related Work.

323118 Blankbook, Looseleaf Binders, and Devices Manufacturing ^{US}

This U.S. industry comprises establishments primarily engaged in manufacturing blankbooks, looseleaf devices, and binders. Establishments in this industry may print or print and bind.

- Checkbook printing are classified in U.S. Industry 323116, Manifold Business Form Printing; and
- Binding books without printing in the same establishment are classified in U.S. Industry 323121, Tradebinding and Related Work.

323119 Other Commercial Printing ^{US}

This U.S. industry comprises establishments primarily engaged in commercial printing (except lithographic, gravure, screen, or flexographic printing) without publishing (except books, grey goods, and manifold business forms). Printing processes included in this industry are letterpress printing and engraving printing. This industry includes establishments engaged in commercial printing on purchased stock materials, such as stationery, invitations, labels, and similar items, on a job order basis.

Visit page 17 to learn about classification changes to this sector.

Sector
31-33

Manufacturing

■ = Cross-References

US—United States industry only. CAN—United States and Canadian industries are comparable. When neither US nor CAN appears, Canadian, Mexican, and United States industries are comparable.

- Lithographic, gravure, screen, or flexographic printing on purchased stock materials (except books, grey goods, and manifold business forms) are classified in Industry 32311, Printing, by printing process employed;
- Printing on grey goods are classified in Industry 31331, Textile and Fabric Finishing Mills;
- Quick printing are classified in U.S. Industry 323114, Quick Printing;
- Digital printing on graphical materials are classified in U.S. Industry 323115, Digital Printing;
- Printing books and pamphlets are classified in U.S. Industry 323117, Books Printing;
- Printing manifold business forms including checkbooks are classified in U.S. Industry 323116, Manifold Business Forms Printing;
- Manufacturing printed stationery, invitations, labels, and similar items are classified in Subsector 322, Paper Manufacturing; and
- Printing and publishing, known as book publishers, are classified in Subsector 511, Publishing Industries.

32312 Support Activities for Printing

This industry comprises establishments primarily engaged in performing prepress (e.g., platemaking, typesetting) and postpress services (e.g., book binding) in support of printing activities.

- Engraving of the type done on metal are classified in Industry 33281, Coating, Engraving, Heat Treating, and Allied Activities;
- Manufacturing photosensitive plates for printing are classified in Industry 32599, All Other Chemical Product and Preparation Manufacturing;
- Manufacturing blank plates for printing are classified in Industry 33329, Other Industrial Machinery Manufacturing; and
- Printing books or printing and binding books are classified in Industry 32311, Printing.

323121 Tradebinding and Related Work ᵁˢ

This U.S. industry comprises establishments primarily engaged in one or more of the following: (1) tradebinding; (2) sample mounting; and (3) postpress services (e.g., book or paper bronzing, die-cutting, edging, embossing, folding, gilding, gluing, indexing).

- Establishments primarily engaged in printing books or printing and binding books are classified in U.S. Industry 323117, Books Printing.

323122 Prepress Services ᵁˢ

This U.S. industry comprises (1) establishments primarily engaged in prepress services, such as imagesetting or typesetting, for printers and (2) establishments primarily engaged in preparing film or plates for printing purposes.

- Engraving of the type done on metal are classified in U.S. Industry 332812, Metal Coating, Engraving (except jewelry and silverware), and Allied Services to Manufacturers;
- Manufacturing blank plates (except photosensitive plates) for printing are classified in U.S. Industry 333293, Printing Machinery and Equipment Manufacturing; and
- Manufacturing photosensitive plates for printing are classified in U.S. Industry 325992, Photographic Film, Paper, Plate, and Chemical Manufacturing.

▶324 PETROLEUM AND COAL PRODUCTS MANUFACTURING

The Petroleum and Coal Products Manufacturing subsector is based on the transformation of crude petroleum and coal into usable products. The dominant process is petroleum refining that involves the separation of crude petroleum into component products through such techniques as cracking and distillation.

In addition, this subsector includes establishments that primarily further process refined petroleum and coal products and produce products, such as asphalt coatings and petroleum lubricating oils. However, establishments that manufacture petrochemicals from refined petroleum are classified in Industry 32511, Petrochemical Manufacturing.

3241 Petroleum and Coal Products Manufacturing

32411 Petroleum Refineries
See industry description for 324110 below.

324110 Petroleum Refineries
This industry comprises establishments primarily engaged in refining crude petroleum into refined petroleum. Petroleum refining involves one or more of the following activities: (1) fractionation; (2) straight distillation of crude oil; and (3) cracking.

Sector 31-33

Manufacturing

■ = Cross-References

US—United States industry only. CAN—United States and Canadian industries are comparable. When neither US nor CAN appears, Canadian, Mexican, and United States industries are comparable.

- Manufacturing asphalt paving, roofing, and saturated materials from refined petroleum are classified in Industry 32412, Asphalt Paving, Roofing, and Saturated Materials Manufacturing;
- Manufacturing paper mats and felts and saturating them with asphalt or tar into rolls and sheets are classified in U.S. Industry 322121, Paper (except Newsprint) Mills;
- Blending or compounding refined petroleum to make lubricating oils and greases and/or re-refining used petroleum lubricating oils are classified in U.S. Industry 324191, Petroleum Lubricating Oil and Grease Manufacturing;
- Manufacturing synthetic lubricating oils and greases are classified in U.S. Industry 325998, All Other Miscellaneous Chemical Product and Preparation Manufacturing; Recovering natural gasoline and/or liquid hydrocarbons from oil and gas field gases are classified in Industry 21111, Oil and Gas Extraction;
- Manufacturing acyclic and cyclic aromatic hydrocarbons (i.e., petrochemicals) from refined petroleum or liquid hydrocarbons are classified in Industry 325110, Petrochemical Manufacturing;
- Manufacturing cyclic and acyclic chemicals (except petrochemicals) are classified in Industry 32519, Other Basic Organic Chemical Manufacturing;
- Manufacturing coke oven products in steel mills are classified in U.S. Industry 331111, Iron and Steel Mills; and
- Manufacturing coke oven products in coke oven establishments are classified in U.S. Industry, 324199, All Other Petroleum and Coal Products Manufacturing.

32412 Asphalt Paving, Roofing, and Saturated Materials Manufacturing
This industry comprises establishments primarily engaged in (1) manufacturing asphalt and tar paving mixtures and blocks and roofing cements and coatings from purchased asphaltic materials and/or (2) saturating purchased mats and felts with asphalt or tar from purchased asphaltic materials.

- Refining crude petroleum and manufacturing asphalt and tar paving, roofing, and saturated materials are classified in Industry 324110, Petroleum Refineries; and
- Manufacturing paper mats and felts and saturating them with asphalt or tar are classified in Industry 32212, Paper Mills.

324121 Asphalt Paving Mixture and Block Manufacturing CAN
This U.S. industry comprises establishments primarily engaged in manufacturing asphalt and tar paving mixtures and blocks from purchased asphaltic materials.

- Establishments primarily engaged in refining crude petroleum and manufacturing asphalt and tar paving mixtures and blocks are classified in Industry 324110, Petroleum Refineries.

324122 Asphalt Shingle and Coating Materials Manufacturing CAN
This U.S. industry comprises establishments primarily engaged in (1) saturating purchased mats and felts with asphalt or tar from purchased asphaltic materials and (2) manufacturing asphalt and tar and roofing cements and coatings from purchased asphaltic materials.

- Refining crude petroleum and saturating purchased mats and felts with asphalt or tar into rolls and sheets and/or refining crude petroleum and manufacturing asphalt and tar roofing cements and coatings are classified in Industry 324110, Petroleum Refineries; and
- Manufacturing paper mats and felts and saturating them with asphalt or tar into rolls and sheets are classified in U.S. Industry 322121, Paper (except Newsprint) Mills.

32419 Other Petroleum and Coal Products Manufacturing
This industry comprises establishments primarily engaged in manufacturing petroleum products (except asphalt paving, roofing and saturated materials) from refined petroleum or coal products made in coke ovens not integrated with a steel mill.

- Manufacturing petroleum products by refining crude petroleum are classified in Industry 32411, Petroleum Refineries;
- Manufacturing asphalt and tar paving, roofing, and saturated materials from refined petroleum are classified in Industry 32412, Asphalt Paving, Roofing, and Saturated Materials Manufacturing;
- Manufacturing coke oven products in steel mills are classified in Industry 33111, Iron and Steel Mills and Ferroalloy Manufacturing;
- Manufacturing acyclic and cyclic aromatic hydrocarbons (i.e., petrochemicals) from refined petroleum or liquid hydrocarbons are classified in Industry 32511, Petrochemical Manufacturing;
- Manufacturing cyclic and acyclic organic chemicals (except petrochemicals) are classified in Industry 32519, Other Basic Organic Chemical Manufacturing; and
- Manufacturing synthetic lubricating oils and greases are classified in Industry 32599, All Other Chemical Product and Preparation Manufacturing.

324191 Petroleum Lubricating Oil and Grease Manufacturing US
This U.S. industry comprises establishments primarily engaged in blending or compounding refined petroleum to make lubricating oils and greases and/or re-refining used petroleum lubricating oils.

- Refining crude petroleum and manufacturing lubricating oils and greases are classified in Industry 324110, Petroleum Refineries; and

Visit page 17 to learn about classification changes to this sector.

Sector
31-33

Manufacturing

■ = Cross-References

US—United States industry only. CAN—United States and Canadian industries are comparable. When neither US nor CAN appears, Canadian, Mexican, and United States industries are comparable.

www.harrisinfo.com

359

■ Manufacturing synthetic lubricating oils and greases are classified in U.S. Industry 325998, All Other Miscellaneous Chemical Product and Preparation Manufacturing.

324199 All Other Petroleum and Coal Products Manufacturing US

This U.S. industry comprises establishments primarily engaged in manufacturing petroleum products (except asphalt paving, roofing, and saturated materials and lubricating oils and greases) from refined petroleum and coal products made in coke ovens not integrated with a steel mill.

■ Manufacturing petroleum products by refining crude petroleum are classified in Industry 324110, Petroleum Refining;
■ Manufacturing asphalt paving and roofing materials from refined petroleum are classified in Industry 32412, Asphalt Paving, Roofing, and Saturated Materials Manufacturing;
■ Blending and compounding petroleum lubricating oils and greases and/or re-refining used petroleum lubrication oils and greases are classified in U.S. Industry 324191, Petroleum Lubricating Oil and Grease Manufacturing;
■ Manufacturing coke oven products in steel mills are classified in U.S. Industry 331111, Iron and Steel Mills;
■ Manufacturing acyclic and cyclic aromatic hydrocarbons (i.e., petrochemicals) from refined petroleum or liquid hydrocarbons are classified in Industry 325110, Petrochemical Manufacturing; and
■ Manufacturing cyclic and acyclic organic chemicals (except petrochemicals) are classified in Industry 32519, Other Basic Organic Chemical Manufacturing.

➡325 CHEMICAL MANUFACTURING

The Chemical Manufacturing subsector is based on the transformation of organic and inorganic raw materials by a chemical process and the formulation of products. This subsector distinguishes the production of basic chemicals that comprise the first industry group from the production of intermediate and end products produced by further processing of basic chemicals that make up the remaining industry groups.

This subsector does not include all industries transforming raw materials by a chemical process. It is common for some chemical processing to occur during mining operations. These beneficiating operations, such as copper concentrating, are classified in Sector 21, Mining. Furthermore, the refining of crude petroleum is included in Subsector 324, Petroleum and Coal Products Manufacturing. In addition, the manufacturing of aluminum oxide is included in Subsector 331, Primary Metal Manufacturing; and beverage distilleries are classified in Subsector 312, Beverage and Tobacco Product Manufacturing. As in the case of these two activities, the grouping of industries into sub-sectors may take into account the association of the activities performed with other activities in the subsector.

3251 Basic Chemical Manufacturing

This industry group comprises establishments primarily engaged in manufacturing chemicals using basic processes, such as thermal cracking and distillation. Chemicals manufactured in this industry group are usually separate chemical elements or separate chemically-defined compounds.

32511 Petrochemical Manufacturing
See industry description for 325110 below.

325110 Petrochemical Manufacturing
This industry comprises establishments primarily engaged in (1) manufacturing acyclic (i.e., aliphatic) hydrocarbons such as ethylene, propylene, and butylene made from refined petroleum or liquid hydrocarbon and/or (2) manufacturing cyclic aromatic hydrocarbons such as benzene, toluene, styrene, xylene, ethyl benzene, and cumene made from refined petroleum or liquid hydrocarbons.

■ Manufacturing petrochemicals by refining crude petroleum are classified in Industry 324110, Petroleum Refineries;
■ Manufacturing acetylene are classified in Industry 325120, Industrial Gas Manufacturing;
■ Manufacturing basic organic chemicals (except petrochemicals) are classified in Industry 325190, Other Basic Organic Chemical Manufacturing; and
■ Recovering liquid hydrocarbons from oil and gas field gases are classified in Industry 211110, Oil and Gas Extraction.

32512 Industrial Gas Manufacturing
See industry description for 325120 below.

325120 Industrial Gas Manufacturing
This industry comprises establishments primarily engaged in manufacturing industrial organic and inorganic gases in compressed, liquid, and solid forms.

Sector
31-33

Manufacturing

■ = Cross-References

US—United States industry only. CAN—United States and Canadian industries are comparable. When neither US nor CAN appears, Canadian, Mexican, and United States industries are comparable.

360

Harris InfoSource

■ Manufacturing chlorine gas are classified in U.S. Industry 325181, Alkalies and Chlorine Manufacturing; and
■ Manufacturing ethane and butane gases made from refined petroleum or liquid hydrocarbons are classified in Industry 325110, Petrochemical Manufacturing.

32513 Synthetic Dye and Pigment Manufacturing

This industry comprises establishments primarily engaged in manufacturing synthetic organic and inorganic dyes and pigments, such as lakes and toners (except electrostatic and photographic).

■ Manufacturing wood byproducts used as dying materials are classified in Industry 32519, Other Basic Organic Chemical Manufacturing;
■ Manufacturing carbon, bone, and lamp black are classified in Industry 32518, Other Basic Inorganic Chemical Manufacturing;
■ Manufacturing electrostatic and photographic toners are classified in Industry 32599, All Other Chemical Product Manufacturing;
■ Manufacturing natural food colorings are classified in Industry 31193, Flavoring Syrup and Concentrate Manufacturing; and
■ Manufacturing natural organic colorings for nonfood uses are classified in Industry 32519, Other Basic Organic Chemical Manufacturing.

325131 Inorganic Dye and Pigment Manufacturing US

This U.S. industry comprises establishments primarily engaged in manufacturing inorganic dyes and pigments.

■ Manufacturing wood byproducts used as dyeing materials are classified in U.S. Industry 325191, Gum and Wood Chemical Manufacturing;
■ Manufacturing organic synthetic dyes and pigments are classified in U.S. Industry 325132, Organic Dye and Pigment Manufacturing;
■ Manufacturing carbon, bone, and lamp black are classified in U.S. Industry 325182, Carbon Black Manufacturing; and
■ Manufacturing natural food colorings are classified in Industry 311930, Flavoring Syrup and Concentrate Manufacturing.

325132 Synthetic Organic Dye and Pigment Manufacturing US

This U.S. industry comprises establishments primarily engaged in manufacturing synthetic organic dyes and pigments, such as lakes and toners (except electrostatic and photographic).

■ Manufacturing wood byproducts used as dyeing materials are classified in U.S. Industry 325191, Gum and Wood Chemical Manufacturing;
■ Manufacturing inorganic dyes and pigments are classified in U.S. Industry 325131, Inorganic Dye and Pigment Manufacturing;
■ Manufacturing electrostatic and photographic toners are classified in U.S. Industry 325992, Photographic Film, Paper, Plate, and Chemical Manufacturing;
■ Manufacturing natural food colorings are classified in Industry 311930, Flavoring Syrup and Concentrate Manufacturing; and
■ Manufacturing natural organic colorings for nonfood uses (except wood byproducts) are classified in U.S. Industry 325199, All Other Basic Organic Chemical Manufacturing.

Visit page 17 to learn about classification changes to this sector.

32518 Other Basic Inorganic Chemical Manufacturing

This industry comprises establishments primarily engaged in manufacturing basic inorganic chemicals (except industrial gases and synthetic dyes and pigments).

■ Manufacturing industrial gases are classified in Industry 32512, Industrial Gas Manufacturing;
■ Manufacturing inorganic dyes and pigments are classified in Industry 32513, Dye and Pigment Manufacturing;
■ Manufacturing household bleaches are classified in Industry 32561, Soap and Cleaning Compound Manufacturing;
■ Mining and/or beneficiating alkalies are classified in Industry 21239, Other Nonmetallic Mineral Mining and Quarrying;
■ Manufacturing chlorine preparations (e.g., for swimming pools) are classified in Industry 32599, All Other Chemical Product and Preparation Manufacturing;
■ Manufacturing nitrogenous and phosphoric fertilizers and fertilizer materials are classified in Industry 32531, Fertilizer Manufacturing;
■ Manufacturing aluminum oxide (alumina) are classified in Industry 33131, Alumina and Aluminum Production and Processing;
■ Manufacturing inorganic insecticidal, herbicidal, fungicidal and pesticidal preparations are classified in Industry 32532, Pesticide and Other Agricultural Chemical Manufacturing; and
■ Manufacturing photographic chemicals are classified in Industry 32599, All Other Chemical Product Manufacturing.

Sector
31-33
Manufacturing

325181 Alkalies and Chlorine Manufacturing CAN

This U.S. industry comprises establishments primarily engaged in manufacturing chlorine, sodium hydroxide (i.e., caustic soda), and other alkalies often using an electrolysis process.

■ Mining and beneficiating alkalies are classified in U.S. Industry 212391, Potash, Soda, and Borate Mineral Mining;
■ Manufacturing chlorine preparations (e.g., for swimming pools) are classified in U.S. Industry 325998, All Other Miscellaneous Chemical Product and Preparation Manufacturing;

■ = Cross-References

US—United States industry only. CAN—United States and Canadian industries are comparable. When neither US nor CAN appears, Canadian, Mexican, and United States industries are comparable.

www.harrisinfo.com

 361

■ Manufacturing industrial bleaches are classified in U.S. Industry 325188, All Other Basic Inorganic Chemical Manufacturing; and
■ Manufacturing household bleaches are classified in U.S. Industry 325611, Soap and Other Detergent Manufacturing.

325182 Carbon Black Manufacturing US

This U.S. industry comprises establishments primarily engaged in manufacturing carbon black, bone black, and lamp black.

■ Establishments primarily engaged in manufacturing pigments are classified in Industry 32513, Synthetic Dye and Pigment Manufacturing.

325188 All Other Basic Inorganic Chemical Manufacturing US

This U.S. industry comprises establishments primarily engaged in manufacturing basic inorganic chemicals (except industrial gases, inorganic dyes and pigments, alkalies and chlorine, and carbon black).

■ Manufacturing industrial gases are classified in Industry 325120, Industrial Gas Manufacturing;
■ Manufacturing inorganic dyes and pigments are classified in U.S. Industry 325131, Inorganic Dye and Pigment Manufacturing;
■ Manufacturing alkalies and chlorine are classified in U.S. Industry 325181, Alkalies and Chlorine Manufacturing;
■ Manufacturing carbon black are classified in U.S. Industry 325182, Carbon Black Manufacturing;
■ Manufacturing household bleaches are classified in U.S. Industry 325612, Polish and Other Sanitation Good Manufacturing;
■ Manufacturing nitrogenous and phosphoric fertilizers and fertilizer material are classified in Industry 32531, Fertilizer Manufacturing;
■ Manufacturing aluminum oxide (i.e., alumina) are classified in U.S. Industry 331311, Alumina Refining;
■ Manufacturing inorganic insecticidal, herbicidal, fungicidal, and pesticidal preparations are classified in Industry 325320, Pesticide and Other Agriculture Chemical Manufacturing; and
■ Manufacturing photographic chemicals are classified in U.S. Industry 325992, Photographic Film, Paper, Plate, and Chemical Manufacturing

32519 Other Basic Organic Chemical Manufacturing

This industry comprises establishments primarily engaged in manufacturing basic organic chemicals (except petrochemicals, industrial gases, and synthetic dyes and pigments).

■ Manufacturing petrochemicals from refined petroleum or liquid hydrocarbons are classified in Industry 32511, Petrochemical Manufacturing;
■ Manufacturing petrochemicals by refining crude petroleum are classified in Industry 32411, Petroleum Refineries;
■ Manufacturing organic industrial gases are classified in Industry 32512, Industrial Gas Manufacturing;
■ Manufacturing synthetic organic dyes and pigments are classified in Industry 32513, Synthetic Dye and Pigment Manufacturing;
■ Manufacturing natural glycerin are classified in Industry 32561, Soap and Cleaning Compound Manufacturing;
■ Manufacturing activated charcoal are classified in Industry 32599, All Other Chemical Product and Preparation Manufacturing;
■ Manufacturing organic insecticidal, herbicidal, fungicidal, and pesticidal preparations are classified in Industry 32532, Pesticide and Other Agriculture Chemical Manufacturing;
■ Manufacturing elastomers are classified in Industry 32521, Resin and Synthetic Rubber Manufacturing;
■ Manufacturing urea are classified in Industry 32531, Fertilizer Manufacturing;
■ Manufacturing coal tar crudes in integrated steel mills with coke ovens are classified in Industry 33111, Iron and Steel Mills and Ferroalloy Manufacturing;
■ Manufacturing coal tar crudes in coke ovens not intergrated with steel mills and fuel briquettes from refined petroleum are classified in Industry 32419, Other Petroleum and Coal Products Manufacturing; and
■ Manufacturing natural food colorings are classified in Industry 31194, Seasoning and Dressing Manufacturing.

325191 Gum and Wood Chemical Manufacturing US

This U.S. industry comprises establishments primarily engaged in (1) distilling wood or gum into products, such as tall oil and wood distillates, and (2) manufacturing wood or gum chemicals, such as naval stores, natural tanning materials, charcoal briquettes, and charcoal (except activated).

■ Manufacturing activated charcoal are classified in U.S. Industry 325998, All Other Miscellaneous Chemical Product and Preparation Manufacturing; and
■ Manufacturing fuel briquettes from refined petroleum are classified in U.S. Industry 324199, All Other Petroleum and Coal Products Manufacturing.

325192 Cyclic Crude and Intermediate Manufacturing US

This U.S. industry comprises establishments primarily engaged in (1) distilling coal tars and/or (2) manufacturing cyclic crudes or, cyclic intermediates (i.e., hydrocarbons, except aromatic petrochemicals) from refined petroleum or natural gas.

Sector
31-33
Manufacturing

■ = Cross-References

US—United States industry only. CAN—United States and Canadian industries are comparable. When neither US nor CAN appears, Canadian, Mexican, and United States industries are comparable.

362

Harris InfoSource

- Manufacturing cyclic chemicals (except aromatic and intermediates) are classified in U.S. Industry 325199, All Other Basic Organic Chemical Manufacturing;
- Manufacturing aromatic petrochemicals from refined petroleum or natural gas are classified in Industry 325110, Petrochemical Manufacturing;
- Manufacturing aromatic petrochemicals by refining crude petroleum are classified in Industry 324110, Petroleum Refineries;
- Distilling wood products are classified in U.S. Industry 325191, Gum and Wood Chemical Manufacturing;
- Manufacturing coal tar crudes in steel mills with coke ovens are classified in U.S. Industry 331111, Iron and Steel Mills; and
- Manufacturing coal tar crudes in coke oven establishments and fuel briquettes from refined petroleum are classified in U.S. Industry 324199, All Other Petroleum and Coal Products Manufacturing.

325193 Ethyl Alcohol Manufacturing ᵁˢ

This U.S. industry comprises establishments primarily engaged in manufacturing nonpotable ethyl alcohol.

- Distilling liquors (except brandy) are classified in Industry 312140, Distilleries; and
- Manufacturing brandies are classified in Industry 312130, Wineries.

325199 All Other Basic Organic Chemical Manufacturing ᵁˢ

This U.S. industry comprises establishments primarily engaged in manufacturing basic organic chemical products (except aromatic petrochemicals, industrial gases, synthetic organic dyes and pigments, gum and wood chemicals, cyclic crudes and intermediates, and ethyl alcohol).

- Manufacturing aromatic petrochemicals from refined petroleum or natural gas are classified in Industry 325110, Petrochemical Manufacturing;
- Manufacturing aromatic petrochemicals by refining crude petroleum are classified in Industry 324110, Petroleum Refineries;
- Manufacturing organic industrial gases are classified in Industry 325120, Industrial Gas Manufacturing;
- Manufacturing synthetic organic dyes and pigments are classified in U.S. Industry 325132, Synthetic Organic Dye and Pigment Manufacturing;
- Manufacturing ethyl alcohol are classified in U.S. Industry 325193, Ethyl Alcohol Manufacturing;
- Manufacturing organic insecticidal, herbicidal, fungicidal, and pesticidal preparations are classified in Industry 325320, Pesticide and Other Agriculture Chemical Manufacturing;
- Manufacturing elastomers are classified in Industry 325210, Resin and Synthetic Rubber Manufacturing;
- Manufacturing urea are classified in U.S. Industry 325311, Nitrogenous Fertilizer Manufacturing;
- Manufacturing natural glycerin are classified in U.S. Industry 325611, Soap and Other Detergent Manufacturing; and
- Manufacturing natural food colorings are classified in U.S. Industry 311942, Spice and Extract Manufacturing.

3252 Resin, Synthetic Rubber, and Artificial Synthetic Fibers and Filaments Manufacturing

32521 Resin and Synthetic Rubber Manufacturing

This industry comprises establishments primarily engaged in one or more of the following: (1) manufacturing synthetic resins, plastics materials, and nonvulcanizable elastomers and mixing and blending resins on a custom basis; (2) manufacturing noncustomized synthetic resins; and (3) manufacturing synthetic rubber.

- Manufacturing plastics resins and converting resins into plastics products are classified in Industry Group 3261, Plastics Product Manufacturing;
- Processing natural, synthetic, or reclaimed rubber into intermediate or final products are classified in Industry Group 3262, Rubber Product Manufacturing;
- Custom compounding resins made elsewhere are classified in Industry 32599, All Other Chemical Product and Preparation Manufacturing; and
- Manufacturing resin adhesives are classified in Industry 32552, Adhesive Manufacturing.

325211 Plastics Material and Resin Manufacturing ᵁˢ

This U.S. industry comprises establishments primarily engaged in (1) manufacturing resins, plastics materials, and nonvulcanizable thermoplastic elastomers and mixing and blending resins on a custom basis and/or (2) manufacturing noncustomized synthetic resins.

- Manufacturing plastics resins and converting the resins into plastics products are classified in 3261, Plastics Product Manufacturing;
- Custom compounding resins made elsewhere are classified in U.S. Industry 325991, Custom Compounding of Purchased Resin; and
- Manufacturing plastics adhesives are classified in Industry 325520, Adhesive Manufacturing.

325212 Synthetic Rubber Manufacturing ᵁˢ

This U.S. industry consists of establishments primarily engaged in manufacturing synthetic rubber.

Visit page 17 to learn about classification changes to this sector.

Sector
31-33

Manufacturing

■ = Cross-References

US—United States industry only. CAN—United States and Canadian industries are comparable. When neither US nor CAN appears, Canadian, Mexican, and United States industries are comparable.

www.harrisinfo.com

363

- Processing natural, synthetic, or reclaimed rubber into intermediate or final products (except adhesives) are classified in Industry Group 3262, Rubber Product Manufacturing; and
- Manufacturing rubber adhesives are classified Industry 325520, Adhesive Manufacturing.

32522 Artificial and Synthetic Fibers and Filaments Manufacturing US

This industry comprises establishments primarily engaged in (1) manufacturing cellulosic (i.e., rayon and acetate) and noncellulosic (i.e., nylon, polyolefin, and polyester) fibers and filaments in the form of monofilament, filament yarn, staple, or tow or (2) manufacturing and texturing cellulosic and noncellulosic fibers and filaments.

- Texturizing cellulosic and noncellulosic fiber and filament made elsewhere are classified in Industry 31311, Fiber, Yarn, and Thread Mills; and
- Manufacturing textile glass fibers are classified in Industry 32721, Glass and Glass Product Manufacturing.

325221 Cellulosic Organic Fiber Manufacturing US

This U.S. industry comprises establishments primarily engaged in (1) manufacturing cellulosic (i.e., rayon and acetate) fibers and filaments in the form of monofilament, filament yarn, staple, or tow or (2) manufacturing and texturizing cellulosic fibers and filaments.

- Texturizing cellulosic fibers and filaments made elsewhere are classified in U.S. Industry 313112, Yarn Texturing, Throwing, and Twisting Mills; and
- Manufacturing noncellulosic fibers and filaments are classified in U.S. Industry 325222, Noncellulosic Organic Fiber Manufacturing.

325222 Noncellulosic Organic Fiber Manufacturing US

This U.S. industry consists of establishments primarily engaged in (1) manufacturing noncellulosic (i.e., nylon, polyolefin, and polyester) fibers and filaments in the form of monofilament, filament yarn, staple, or tow or (2) manufacturing and texturizing noncellulosic fibers and filaments.

- Texturizing noncellulosic fibers are classified in U.S. Industry 313112, Yarn Texturing, Throwing, and Twisting Mills;
- Manufacturing cellulose fibers are classified in U.S. Industry 325221, Cellulosic Organic Fiber Manufacturing; and
- Manufacturing textile glass fibers are classified in U.S. Industry 327212, Other Pressed and Blown Glass and Glassware Manufacturing.

3253 Pesticide, Fertilizer, and Other Agricultural Chemical Manufacturing

32531 Fertilizer Manufacturing

This industry comprises establishments primarily engaged in one or more of the following: (1) manufacturing nitrogenous or phosphatic fertilizer materials; (2) manufacturing fertilizers from sewage or animal waste; (3) manufacturing nitrogenous or phosphatic materials and mixing with other ingredients into fertilizers; and (4) mixing ingredients made elsewhere into fertilizers.

325311 Nitrogenous Fertilizer Manufacturing US

This U.S. industry comprises establishments primarily engaged in one or more of the following: (1) manufacturing nitrogenous fertilizer materials and mixing ingredients into fertilizers; (2) manufacturing fertilizers from sewage or animal waste; and (3) manufacturing nitrogenous materials and mixing them into fertilizers.

- Establishments primarily engaged in mixing ingredients made elsewhere into nitrogenous fertilizers are classified in U.S. Industry 325314, Fertilizer (Mixing Only) Manufacturing.

325312 Phosphatic Fertilizer Manufacturing US

This U.S. industry comprises establishments primarily engaged in (1) manufacturing phosphatic fertilizer materials or (2) manufacturing phosphatic materials and mixing them into fertilizers.

- Establishments primarily engaged in mixing ingredients made elsewhere into phosphatic fertilizers are classified in U.S. Industry 325314, Fertilizer (Mixing Only) Manufacturing.

325314 Fertilizer (Mixing Only) Manufacturing CAN

This U.S. industry comprises establishments primarily engaged in mixing ingredients made elsewhere into fertilizers.

- Manufacturing nitrogenous fertilizer materials or fertilizer materials from sewage or animal waste and mixing these ingredients into nitrogenous fertilizers are classified in U.S. Industry 325311, Nitrogenous Fertilizer Manufacturing; and

---

Sector

31-33

Manufacturing

■ = Cross-References

US—United States industry only. CAN—United States and Canadian industries are comparable. When neither US nor CAN appears, Canadian, Mexican, and United States industries are comparable.

364

Harris InfoSource

■ Manufacturing phosphatic fertilizer materials and mixing ingredients into fertilizers are classified in U.S. Industry 325312, Phosphatic Fertilizer Manufacturing.

32532 Pesticide and Other Agricultural Chemical Manufacturing
See industry description for 325320 below.

325320 Pesticide and Other Agricultural Chemical Manufacturing
This industry comprises establishments primarily engaged in the formulation and preparation of agricultural and household pest control chemicals (except fertilizers).

■ Manufacturing basic chemicals requiring further processing before use as agriculture chemicals are classified in Industry Group 3251, Basic Chemical Manufacturing;
■ Manufacturing fertilizers are classified in Industry 325310, Fertilizer Manufacturing; and
■ Manufacturing agricultural lime products are classified in Industry 327410, Lime Manufacturing.

3254 Pharmaceutical and Medicine Manufacturing

32541 Pharmaceutical and Medicine Manufacturing
This industry comprises establishments primarily engaged in one or more of the following: (1) manufacturing biological and medicinal products; (2) processing (i.e., grading, grinding, and milling) botanical drugs and herbs; (3) isolating active medicinal principals from botanical drugs and herbs; and (4) manufacturing pharmaceutical products intended for internal and external consumption in such forms as ampoules, tablets, capsules, vials, ointments, powders, solutions, and suspensions.

325411 Medicinal and Botanical Manufacturing ᵁˢ
This U.S. industry comprises establishments primarily engaged in (1) manufacturing uncompounded medicinal chemicals and their derivatives (i.e., generally for use by pharmaceutical preparation manufacturers) and/or (2) grading, grinding, and milling uncompounded botanicals.

■ Manufacturing packaged compounded medicinals and botanicals are classified in U.S. Industry 325412, Pharmaceutical Preparation Manufacturing; and
■ Manufacturing vaccines, toxoids, blood fractions, and culture media of plant or animal origin (except for diagnostic use) are classified in U.S. Industry 325414, Biological Product (except Diagnostic) Manufacturing.

325412 Pharmaceutical Preparation Manufacturing ᵁˢ
This U.S. industry comprises establishments primarily engaged in manufacturing invivo diagnostic substances and pharmaceutical preparations (except biological) intended for internal and external consumption in dose forms, such as ampoules, tablets, capsules, vials, ointments, powders, solutions, and suspensions.

■ Manufacturing uncompounded medicinal chemicals and their derivatives are classified in U.S. Industry 325411, Medicinal and Botanical Manufacturing;
■ Manufacturing in vitro diagnostic substances are classified in U.S. Industry 325413; In Vitro Diagnostic Substance Manufacturing; and
■ Manufacturing vaccines, toxoids, blood fractions, and culture media of plant or animal origin (except for diagnostic use) are classified in U.S. Industry 325414, Biological Product (except Diagnostic) Manufacturing.

325413 In Vitro Diagnostic Substance Manufacturing ᵁˢ
This U.S. industry comprises establishments primarily engaged in manufacturing in vitro (i.e., not taken internally) diagnostic substances, such as chemical, biological, or radioactive substances. The substances are used for diagnostic tests that are performed in test tubes, petri dishes, machines, and other diagnostic test-type devices.

■ Establishments primarily engaged in manufacturing in vivo diagnostic substances are classified in U.S. Industry 325412, Pharmaceutical Preparation Manufacturing.

325414 Biological Product (except Diagnostic) Manufacturing ᵁˢ
This U.S. industry comprises establishments primarily engaged in manufacturing vaccines, toxoids, blood fractions, and culture media of plant or animal origin (except diagnostic).

■ Manufacturing in vitro diagnostic substances are classified in U.S. Industry 325413, In Vitro Diagnostic Substance Manufacturing; and

Visit page 17 to learn about classification changes to this sector.

Manufacturing

■ = Cross-References

US—United States industry only. CAN—United States and Canadian industries are comparable. When neither US nor CAN appears, Canadian, Mexican, and United States industries are comparable.

■ Manufacturing pharmaceutical preparations, (except biological and in vivo diagnostic substances) are classified in U.S. Industry 325412, Pharmaceutical Preparation Manufacturing.

3255 Paint, Coating, and Adhesive Manufacturing

32551 Paint and Coating Manufacturing
See industry description for 325510 below.

325510 Paint and Coating Manufacturing
This industry comprises establishments primarily engaged in (1) mixing pigments, solvents, and binders into paints and other coatings, such as stains, varnishes, lacquers, enamels, shellacs, and water repellant coatings for concrete and masonry, and/or (2) manufacturing allied paint products, such as putties, paint and varnish removers, paint brush cleaners, and frit.

■ Manufacturing creosote are classified in Industry 32519, Other Basic Organic Chemical Manufacturing;
■ Manufacturing caulking compounds and sealants are classified in Industry 325520, Adhesive Manufacturing;
■ Manufacturing artists' paints are classified in U.S. Industry 339942, Lead Pencil and Art Good Manufacturing; and
■ Manufacturing turpentine are classified in U.S. Industry 325191, Gum and Wood Chemical Manufacturing.

32552 Adhesive Manufacturing
See industry description for 325520 below.

325520 Adhesive Manufacturing
This industry comprises establishments primarily engaged in manufacturing adhesives, glues, and caulking compounds.

■ Manufacturing asphalt and tar roofing cements from purchased asphaltic materials are classified in Industry 324122, Asphalt Shingle and Coating Materials Manufacturing; and
■ Manufacturing gypsum based caulking compounds are classified in Industry 327420, Gypsum and Gypsum Product Manufacturing.

3256 Soap, Cleaning Compound, and Toilet Preparation Manufacturing

32561 Soap and Cleaning Compound Manufacturing
This industry comprises establishments primarily engaged in manufacturing and packaging soap and other cleaning compounds, surface active agents, and textile and leather finishing agents used to reduce tension or speed the drying process.

■ Manufacturing synthetic glycerin are classified in Industry 32519, Other Basic Organic Chemical Manufacturing;
■ Manufacturing industrial bleaches are classified in Industry 32518 Other Basic Inorganic Chemical Manufacturing; and
■ Manufacturing shampoos and shaving preparations are classified in Industry 32562, Toilet Preparation Manufacturing.

325611 Soap and Other Detergent Manufacturing US
This U.S. industry comprises establishments primarily engaged in manufacturing and packaging soaps and other detergents, such as laundry detergents; dishwashing detergents; toothpaste gels, and tooth powders; and natural glycerin.

■ Manufacturing synthetic glycerin are classified in U.S. Industry 325199, All Other Basic Organic Chemical Manufacturing; and
■ Manufacturing shampoos and shaving preparations are classified in Industry 325620, Toilet Preparation Manufacturing.

325612 Polish and Other Sanitation Good Manufacturing US
This U.S. industry comprises establishments primarily engaged in manufacturing and packaging polishes and specialty cleaning preparations.

■ Establishments primarily engaged in manufacturing chlorine dioxide (i.e., industrial bleaching agent) are classified in U.S. Industry 325188, All Other Basic Inorganic Chemical Manufacturing.

325613 Surface Active Agent Manufacturing US
This U.S. industry comprises establishments primarily engaged in (1) manufacturing bulk surface active agents for use as wetting agents, emulsifiers, and penetrants, and/or (2) manufacturing textiles and leather finishing agents used to reduce tension or speed the drying process.

Sector
31-33

Manufacturing

■ = Cross-References

US—United States industry only. CAN—United States and Canadian industries are comparable. When neither US nor CAN appears, Canadian, Mexican, and United States industries are comparable.

366

Harris InfoSource

32562 Toilet Preparation Manufacturing
See industry description for 325620 below.

325620 Toilet Preparation Manufacturing
This industry comprises establishments primarily engaged in preparing, blending, compounding, and packaging toilet preparations, such as perfumes, shaving preparations, hair preparations, face creams, lotions (including sunscreens), and other cosmetic preparations.

- Establishments primarily engaged in manufacturing toothpaste are classified in U.S. Industry 325611, Soap and Other Detergent Manufacturing.

3259 Other Chemical Product and Preparation Manufacturing
This industry group comprises establishments primarily engaged in manufacturing chemical products (except basic chemicals; resins, synthetic rubber, cellulosic and noncellulosic fibers and filaments; pesticides, fertilizers, and other agricultural chemicals; pharmaceuticals and medicines; paints, coatings, and adhesives; soaps and cleaning compounds; and toilet preparations).

32591 Printing Ink Manufacturing
See industry description for 325910 below.

325910 Printing Ink Manufacturing
This industry comprises establishments primarily engaged in manufacturing printing and inkjet inks and inkjet cartridges.

- Recycling inkjet cartridges are classified in U.S. Industry 811212, Computer and Office Machine Repair and Maintenance;
- Manufacturing writing, drawing, and stamping ink are classified in U.S. Industry 325998, All Other Miscellaneous Chemical Product and Preparation Manufacturing;
- Manufacturing toners and toner cartridges for photocopiers, fax machines, computer printers and similar office machines are classified in U.S. Industry 325992, Photographic Film, Paper, Plate, and Chemical Manufacturing; and
- Manufacturing inkjet cartridges are classified in U.S. Industry 334119, Other Computer Peripheral Equipment Manufacturing.

32592 Explosives Manufacturing
See industry description for 325920 below.

325920 Explosives Manufacturing
This industry comprises establishments primarily engaged in manufacturing explosives.

- Manufacturing ammunition, ammunition detonators, and percussion caps are classified in U.S. Industry 332992, Small Arms Ammunition Manufacturing; and
- Manufacturing pyrotechnics are classified in U.S. Industry 325998, All Other Miscellaneous Chemical Product and Preparation Manufacturing.

32599 All Other Chemical Product and Preparation Manufacturing
This industry comprises establishments primarily engaged in manufacturing chemical products (except basic chemicals, resins, and synthetic rubber; cellulosic and noncellulosic fibers and filaments; pesticides, fertilizers, and other agricultural chemicals; pharmaceuticals and medicines; paints, coatings, and adhesives; and soaps, cleaning compounds, and toilet preparations; printing inks; and explosives).

- Manufacturing basic chemicals are classified in Industry Group 3251, Basic Chemical Manufacturing;
- Manufacturing resins, synthetic rubber, and artificial synthetic fibers and filaments are classified in Industry Group 3252, Resin, Synthetic Rubber, and Artificial and Synthetic Fibers and Filaments Manufacturing;
- Manufacturing pesticides, fertilizers, and other agricultural chemicals are classified in Industry Group 3253, Pesticide, Fertilizer, and Other Agriculture Chemical Manufacturing;
- Manufacturing pharmaceuticals and medicine including medicinal vegetable gelatin (i.e., agar-agar) are classified in Industry Group 3254, Pharmaceutical and Medicine Manufacturing;
- Manufacturing paints, coatings, and adhesives are classified in Industry Group 3255, Paint, Coating, and Adhesive Manufacturing;
- Manufacturing soaps and cleaning compounds are classified in Industry Group 3256, Soap, Cleaning Compound, and Toilet Preparation Manufacturing;
- Manufacturing printing and inkjet inks are classified in Industry 32591, Printing Ink Manufacturing;
- Manufacturing explosives are classified in Industry 32592, Explosives Manufacturing; Manufacturing photographic toner cartridges are classified in Industry 33331, Commercial and Service Industry Machinery Manufacturing;
- Manufacturing computer printer toner cartridges are classified in Industry 33411, Computer and Peripheral Equipment Manufacturing;

Visit page 17 to learn about classification changes to this sector.

Sector

31-33

Manufacturing

■ = Cross-References

US—United States industry only. CAN—United States and Canadian industries are comparable. When neither US nor CAN appears, Canadian, Mexican, and United States industries are comparable.

www.harrisinfo.com

367

- Manufacturing facsimile toner cartridges are classified in Industry 33429, Other Communications Equipment Manufacturing;
- Manufacturing photographic paper stock (i.e., unsensitized) and paper mats, mounts, easels, and folders for photographic use are classified in Subsector 322, Paper Manufacturing;
- Manufacturing dessert gelatins are classified in Industry 31199, All Other Miscellaneous Food Manufacturing; and
- Manufacturing medicinal gelatins are classified in Industry 32541, Pharmaceutical and Medicine Manufacturing.

325991 Custom Compounding of Purchased Resins ᶜᴬᴺ

This industry comprises establishments primarily engaged in (1) custom mixing and blending plastics resins made elsewhere or (2) reformulating plastics resins from recycled plastics products.

- Establishments primarily engaged in manufacturing synthetic resins and custom mixing and blending resins are classified in U.S. Industry 325211, Plastics Material and Resin Manufacturing.

325992 Photographic Film, Paper, Plate, and Chemical Manufacturing ᵁˢ

This U.S. industry comprises establishments primarily engaged in manufacturing sensitized film, sensitized paper, sensitized cloth, sensitized plates, toners (i.e., for photocopiers, laser printers, and similar electrostatic printing devices), toner cartridges, and photographic chemicals.

- Establishments primarily engaged in manufacturing photographic paper stock (i.e., unsensitized) and paper mats, mounts, easels, and folders for photographic use are classified in Subsector 322, Paper Manufacturing.

325998 All Other Miscellaneous Chemical Product and Preparation Manufacturing ᵁˢ

This U.S. industry comprises establishments primarily engaged in manufacturing chemical products (except basic chemicals, resins, synthetic rubber; cellulosic and noncellulosic fiber and filaments; pesticides, fertilizers, and other agricultural chemicals; pharmaceuticals and medicines; paints, coatings and adhesives; soap, cleaning compounds, and toilet preparations; printing inks; explosives; custom compounding of purchased resins; and photographic films, papers, plates, and chemicals).

- Manufacturing basic chemicals are classified in Industry Group 3251, Basic Chemical Manufacturing;
- Manufacturing resins, synthetic rubber, and artificial synthetic fibers and filaments are classified in Industry Group 3252, Resin, Synthetic Rubber, and Artificial and Synthetic Fibers and Filaments Manufacturing;
- Manufacturing pesticides, fertilizers, and other agricultural chemicals are classified in Industry Group 3253, Pesticide, Fertilizer, and Other Agriculture Chemical Manufacturing;
- Manufacturing pharmaceuticals and medicines including medicinal vegetable gelatin (i.e., agar-agar) are classified in Industry Group 3254, Pharmaceutical and Medicine Manufacturing;
- Manufacturing paints, coatings, and adhesives are classified in Industry Group 3255, Paint, Coating, and Adhesive Manufacturing;
- Manufacturing soaps and cleaning compounds are classified in Industry Group 3256, Soap, Cleaning Compound, and Toilet Preparation Manufacturing;
- Manufacturing printing and inkjet inks are classified in Industry 325910, Printing Ink Manufacturing;
- Manufacturing explosives are classified in Industry 325920, Explosives Manufacturing;
- Custom compounding purchased plastics resins are classified in U.S. Industry 325991, Custom Compounding of Purchased Resin;
- Manufacturing photographic films, papers, plates, and chemicals are classified in U.S. Industry 325992, Photographic Film, Paper, Plate, and Chemical Manufacturing; and
- Manufacturing dessert gelatin are classified in U.S. Industry 311999, All Other Miscellaneous Food Manufacturing.

▶326 PLASTICS AND RUBBER PRODUCTS MANUFACTURING

Industries in the Plastics and Rubber Products Manufacturing subsector make goods by processing plastics materials and raw rubber. The core technology employed by establishments in this subsector is that of plastics or rubber product production. Plastics and rubber are combined in the same subsector because plastics are increasingly being used as a substitute for rubber; however the subsector is generally restricted to the production of products made of just one material, either solely plastics or rubber.

Many manufacturing activities use plastics or rubber, for example the manufacture of footwear, or furniture. Typically, the production process of these products involves more than one material. In these cases, technologies that allow disparate materials to be formed and combined are of central importance in describing the manufacturing activity. In NAICS, such activities (the footwear and furniture manufacturing) are not classified in the Plastics and Rubber Products Manufacturing subsector because the core technologies for these activities are diverse and involve multiple materials.

Within the Plastics and Rubber Products Manufacturing subsector, a distinction is made between plastics and rubber products at the industry group level, although it is not a rigid distinction, as can be seen from

■ = Cross-References

US—United States industry only. CAN—United States and Canadian industries are comparable. When neither US nor CAN appears, Canadian, Mexican, and United States industries are comparable.

368

Harris InfoSource

the definition of Industry 32622, Rubber and Plastics Hose and Belting Manufacturing. As materials technology progresses, plastics are increasingly being used as a substitute for rubber; and eventually, the distinction may disappear as a basis for establishment classification.

In keeping with the core technology focus of plastics, lamination of plastics film to plastics film as well as the production of bags from plastics only is classified in this subsector. Lamination and bag production involving plastics and materials other than plastics are classified in the NAICS Subsector 322, Paper Manufacturing.

3261 Plastics Product Manufacturing

This industry group comprises establishments primarily engaged in processing new or spent (i.e., recycled) plastics resins into intermediate or final products, using such processes as compression molding; extrusion molding; injection molding; blow molding; and casting. Within most of these industries, the production process is such that a wide variety of products can be made.

32611 Unsupported Plastics Film, Sheet, and Bag Manufacturing

This industry comprises establishments primarily engaged in (1) converting plastics resins into unsupported plastics film and sheet and/or (2) forming, coating or laminating plastics film and sheet into plastics bags.

- Laminating plastics sheet (except for packaging) are classified in Industry 32613, Laminated Plastics Plate, Sheet, and Shapes Manufacturing;
- Manufacturing plastics blister and bubble packaging are classified in Industry 32619, Other Plastics Product Manufacturing; and
- Coating or laminating combinations of plastics, foils and paper (except plastics film to plastics film) into film, sheet or bags are classified in Industry 32222, Paper Bag and Coated and Treated Paper Manufacturing.

326111 Unsupported Plastics Bag Manufacturing ^{CAN}

This U.S. industry comprises establishments primarily engaged in (1) converting plastics resins into plastics bags or (2) forming, coating or laminating plastics film and sheet into single wall or multiwall plastics bags. Establishments in this industry may print on the bags they manufacture.

- Manufacturing laminated or coated combinations of plastics, foils and paper (except plastics film to plastics film) materials into single wall bags are classified in U.S. Industry 322223, Plastics, Foil, and Coated Paper Bag Manufacturing; and
- Manufacturing laminated or coated combinations of plastics, foils and paper (except plastics film to plastics film) into multiwalled bags are classified in U.S. Industry 322224, Uncoated Paper and Multiwall Bag Manufacturing.

326112 Unsupported Plastics Packaging Film and Sheet Manufacturing ^{US}

This U.S. industry comprises establishments primarily engaged in converting plastics resins into plastics packaging (flexible) film and packaging sheet.

- Converting plastics resins into plastics film and unlaminated sheet (except packaging) are classified in U.S. Industry 326113, Unsupported Plastics Film and Sheet (except Packaging) Manufacturing;
- Laminating or coating packaging combinations of plastics, foils and paper (except plastics film to plastics film) film and sheet are classified in U.S. Industry 322221, Coated and Laminated Packaging Paper and Plastics Film Manufacturing;
- Laminating or coating combinations of plastics, foils, and paper (except plastics film to plastics film) nonpackaging film and sheet are classified in U.S. Industry 322222, Coated and Laminated Paper Manufacturing;
- Laminating plastics sheet (except for packaging) are classified in Industry 326130, Laminated Plastics Plate, Sheet, and Shapes Manufacturing, and
- Manufacturing plastics bags are classified in U.S. Industry 326111, Unsupported Plastics Bag Manufacturing.

326113 Unsupported Plastics Film and Sheet (except Packaging) Manufacturing ^{US}

This U.S. industry comprises establishments primarily engaged in converting plastics resins into plastics film and unlaminated sheet (except packaging).

- Converting plastics resins into plastics packaging film and unlaminated packaging sheet are classified in U.S. Industry 326112, Unsupported Plastics Packaging Film and Sheet Manufacturing;
- Laminating plastics sheet (except for packaging) are classified in Industry 326130, Laminated Plastics Plate, Sheet, and Shapes Manufacturing; Laminating or coating a combination of plastics, foils, and paper (except plastics film to plastics film) nonpackaging film and sheet are classified in U.S. Industry 322222, Coated and Laminated Paper Manufacturing; and
- Manufacturing plastics bags are classified in U.S. Industry 326111, Unsupported Plastics Bag Manufacturing.

32612 Plastics Pipe, Pipe Fitting, and Unsupported Profile Shape Manufacturing

This industry comprises establishments primarily engaged in manufacturing plastics pipes and pipe fittings, and plastics profile shapes such as rod, tube, and sausage casings.

Visit page 17 to learn about classification changes to this sector.

Sector

31-33

Manufacturing

■ = Cross-References

- Manufacturing plastics hose are classified in Industry 32622, Rubber and Plastics Hoses and Belting Manufacturing;
- Manufacturing noncurrent carrying plastics conduit are classified in Industry 33593, Wiring Device Manufacturing;
- Manufacturing plastics plumbing fixtures are classified in Industry 32619, Other Plastics Product Manufacturing; and
- Manufacturing plastics film, plastics unlaminated sheet, and plastics bags are classified in Industry 32611, Unsupported Plastics Film, Sheet, and Bag Manufacturing.

326121 Unsupported Plastics Profile Shapes Manufacturing ^{CAN}

This U.S. industry comprises establishments primarily engaged in converting plastics resins into nonrigid plastics profile shapes (except film, sheet and bags), such as rod, tube, and sausage casings.

- Manufacturing plastics film, plastics unlaminated sheet, and plastics bags are classified in Industry 32611, Unsupported Plastics Film, Sheet, and Bag Manufacturing; and
- Manufacturing plastics hoses are classified in Industry 326220, Rubber and Plastics Hoses and Belting Manufacturing.

326122 Plastics Pipe and Pipe Fitting Manufacturing ^{CAN}

This U.S. industry comprises establishments primarily engaged in converting plastics resins into rigid plastics pipes and pipe fittings.

- Manufacturing plastics hose are classified in Industry 326220, Rubber and Plastics Hoses and Belting Manufacturing;
- Manufacturing noncurrent-carrying plastics conduit are classified in U.S. Industry 335932, Noncurrent-carrying Wiring Device Manufacturing; and
- Manufacturing plastics plumbing fixtures are classified in U.S. Industry 326191, Plastics Plumbing Fixture Manufacturing.

32613 Laminated Plastics Plate, Sheet, and Shape Manufacturing

See industry description for 326130 below.

326130 Laminated Plastics Plate, Sheet, and Shape Manufacturing

This industry comprises establishments primarily engaged in laminating plastics profile shapes such as plate, sheet (except packaging), and rod. The lamination process generally involves bonding or impregnating profiles with plastics resins and compressing them under heat.

- Manufacturing plastics film, plastics unlaminated sheet, and plastics bags are classified in Industry 32611, Unsupported Plastics Film, Sheet, and Bag Manufacturing;
- Coating or laminating nonplastics film, sheet, or bags with plastics are classified in Industry 32222, Paper Bag and Coated and Treated Paper Manufacturing; and
- Manufacturing plastics bags are classified in U.S. Industry 326111, Unsupported Plastics Bag Manufacturing.

32614 Polystyrene Foam Product Manufacturing

See industry description for 326140 below.

326140 Polystyrene Foam Product Manufacturing

This industry comprises establishments primarily engaged in manufacturing polystyrene foam products.

- Establishments primarily engaged in manufacturing plastics foam products (except polystyrene) are classified in Industry 326150, Urethane and Other Foam Product (except Polystyrene) Manufacturing.

32615 Urethane and Other Foam Product (except Polystyrene) Manufacturing

See industry description for 326150 below.

326150 Urethane and Other Foam Product (except Polystyrene) Manufacturing

This industry comprises establishments primarily engaged in manufacturing plastics foam products (except polystyrene).

- Establishments primarily engaged in manufacturing polystyrene foam products are classified in Industry 326140, Polystyrene Foam Product Manufacturing.

32616 Plastics Bottle Manufacturing

See industry description for 32616 below.

326160 Plastics Bottle Manufacturing

This industry comprises establishments primarily engaged in manufacturing plastics bottles.

- Establishments primarily engaged in manufacturing plastics containers (except bottles) are classified in U.S. Industry 326199, All Other Plastics Product Manufacturing.

Sector

31-33

Manufacturing

■ = Cross-References

US—United States industry only. CAN—United States and Canadian industries are comparable. When neither US nor CAN appears, Canadian, Mexican, and United States industries are comparable.

370

Harris InfoSource

32619 Other Plastics Product Manufacturing

This industry comprises establishments primarily engaged in manufacturing resilient floor covering and other plastics products (except film, sheet, bags, profile shapes, pipes, pipe fittings, laminates, foam products, and bottles).

- Manufacturing plastics film, plastics unlaminated sheet, and plastics bags are classified in Industry 32611, Unsupported Plastics Film, Sheet, and Bag Manufacturing;
- Manufacturing plastics pipes, pipe fittings and plastics profile shapes (except films, sheet, bags) are classified in Industry 32612, Plastic Pipe, Pipe Fitting, and Unsupported Profile Shapes Manufacturing;
- Laminating plastics profile shapes, such as plate, sheet and rod, are classified in Industry 32613, Laminated Plastics Plate, Sheets and Shapes Manufacturing;
- Manufacturing polystyrene foam products are classified in Industry 32614, Polystyrene Foam Product Manufacturing;
- Manufacturing foam products (except polystyrene) are classified in Industry 32615 Urethane and Other Foam Product (except Polystyrene) Manufacturing;
- Manufacturing plastics bottles are classified in Industry 32616, Plastics Bottle Manufacturing;
- Manufacturing plastics furniture parts are classified in Industry 33721, Office Furniture (including Fixtures) Manufacturing;
- Assembling plastics components into plumbing fixture fittings, such as faucets, are classified in Industry 33291, Metal Valve Manufacturing; and
- Manufacturing rubber floor mats and rubber treads are classified in Industry 32629, Office Rubber Product Manufacturing.

326191 Plastics Plumbing Fixture Manufacturing CAN

This U.S. industry comprises establishments primarily engaged in manufacturing plastics or fiberglass plumbing fixtures. Examples of products made by these establishments are plastics or fiberglass bathtubs, hot tubs, portable toilets, and shower stalls.

- Assembling plastics components into plumbing fixture fittings, such as faucets, are classified in U.S. Industry 332913, Plumbing Fixture Fitting and Trim Manufacturing; and
- Manufacturing plastics pipe and pipe fittings are classified in U.S. Industry 326122, Plastics Pipe and Pipe Fitting Manufacturing.

326192 Resilient Floor Covering Manufacturing US

This U.S. industry comprises establishments primarily engaged in manufacturing resilient floor coverings for permanent installation.

- Establishments primarily engaged in manufacturing rubber floor mats and rubber treads are classified in U.S. Industry 326299, All Other Rubber Product Manufacturing.

Visit page 17 to learn about classification changes to this sector.

326199 All Other Plastics Product Manufacturing US

This U.S. industry comprises establishments primarily engaged in manufacturing plastics products (except film, sheet, bags, profile shapes, pipes, pipe fittings, laminates, foam products, bottles, plumbing fixtures, and resilient floor coverings).

- Manufacturing plastics film, plastics unlaminated sheet, and plastics bags are classified in Industry 32611 Unsupported Plastics Film, Sheet, and Bag Manufacturing;
- Manufacturing plastics pipes, pipe fittings, and plastics profile shapes (except film, sheet, bags) are classified in Industry 32612, Plastics Pipe, Pipe Fittings, and Unsupported Plastics Profile Shapes Manufacturing;
- Manufacturing plastic pipes and pipe fittings are classified in U.S. Industry 326122, Plastics Pipe and Pipe Fitting Manufacturing;
- Laminating plastics profile shapes, such as plate, sheet, and rod, are classified in Industry 326130, Laminated Plastics Plate, Sheet, and Shapes Manufacturing;
- Manufacturing polystyrene foam products are classified in Industry 326140, Polystyrene Foam Product Manufacturing;
- Manufacturing foam (except polystyrene) products are classified in Industry 326150, Urethane and Other Foam Product (except Polystyrene) Manufacturing;
- Manufacturing plastics bottles are classified in Industry 326160, Plastics Bottle Manufacturing;
- Manufacturing plastics furniture parts and components are classified in U.S. Industry 337215, Showcase, Partition, Shelving, and Locker Manufacturing;
- Manufacturing plastics plumbing fixtures are classified in U.S. Industry 326191, Plastics Plumbing Fixture Manufacturing;
- Manufacturing resilient floor coverings are classified in U.S. Industry 326192, Resilient Floor Covering Manufacturing; and
- Assembling plastics components into plumbing fixtures fittings such as faucets are classified in U.S. Industry 332913, Plumbing Fixture Fitting and Trim Manufacturing.

Sector

31-33

Manufacturing

3262 Rubber Product Manufacturing

This industry group comprises establishments primarily engaged in processing natural, and synthetic or reclaimed rubber materials into intermediate or final products using processes such as vulcanizing, cementing, molding, extruding, and lathe-cutting.

■ = Cross-References

US—United States industry only. CAN—United States and Canadian industries are comparable. When neither US nor CAN appears, Canadian, Mexican, and United States industries are comparable.

32621 Tire Manufacturing

This industry comprises establishments primarily engaged in manufacturing tires and inner tubes from natural and synthetic rubber and retreading or rebuilding tires.

- Repairing tires, such as plugging, are classified in Industry 81119, Other Automotive Repair and Maintenance; and
- Retailing tires are classified in the Industry 44132, Tire Dealers.

326211 Tire Manufacturing (except Retreading)ᵘˢ

This U.S. industry comprises establishments primarily engaged in manufacturing tires and inner tubes from natural and synthetic rubber.

- Establishments primarily engaged in retreading or rebuilding tires are classified in U.S. Industry 326212, Tire Retreading.

326212 Tire Retreading ᵘˢ

This U.S. industry comprises establishments primarily engaged in retreading, or rebuilding tires.

- Repairing tires, such as pluggings are classified in U.S. Industry 811198, All Other Automotive Repair and Maintenance;
- Retailing tires are classified in Industry 441320, Tire Dealers; and
- Manufacturing tires and inner tubes from natural and synthetic rubber are classified in U.S. Industry 326211, Tire Manufacturing (except Retreading).

32622 Rubber and Plastics Hoses and Belting Manufacturing

See industry description for 326220 below.

326220 Rubber and Plastics Hoses and Belting Manufacturing

This industry comprises establishments primarily engaged in manufacturing rubber hose and/or plastics (reinforced) hose and belting from natural and synthetic rubber and/or plastics resins. Establishments manufacturing garden hoses from purchased hose are included in this industry.

- Manufacturing rubber tubing are classified in U.S. Industry 326299, All Other Rubber Product Manufacturing;
- Manufacturing plastics tubing are classified in U.S. Industry 326121, Unsupported Plastics Profile Shapes Manufacturing; and
- Manufacturing fluid power hose assemblies are classified in U.S. Industry 332912, Fluid Power Valve and Hose Fitting Manufacturing.

32629 Other Rubber Product Manufacturing

This industry comprises establishments primarily engaged in manufacturing rubber products (except tires, hoses, and belting) from natural and synthetic rubber.

- Manufacturing tires and inner tubes are classified in Industry 32621, Tire Manufacturing;
- Manufacturing rubber hoses and belting are classified in Industry 32622, Rubber and Plastics Hoses and Belting Manufacturing;
- Rubberizing fabric are classified in Industry 31332, Fabric Coating Mills;
- Manufacturing rubber gaskets, packing and sealing devices are classified in Industry 33999, All Other Miscellaneous Manufacturing;
- Manufacturing rubber gloves are classified in Industry 33911, Medical Equipment and Supplies Manufacturing;
- Manufacturing rubber clothing accessories (e.g., bathing caps) are classified in Industry 31599, Apparel Accessories and Other Apparel Manufacturing; and
- Manufacturing rubber toys are classified in Industry 33993, Doll, Toy, and Game Manufacturing.

326291 Rubber Product Manufacturing for Mechanical Use ᵘˢ

This U.S. industry comprises establishments primarily engaged in molding, extruding or lathe-cutting rubber to manufacture rubber goods (except tubing) for mechanical applications. Products of this industry are generally parts for motor vehicles, machinery, and equipment.

- Establishments primarily engaged in manufacturing rubber tubing from natural and synthetic rubber and manufacturing rubber products for mechanical applications using a process other than molding, extruding or lathe-cutting are classified in U.S. Industry 326299, All Other Rubber Product Manufacturing.

326299 All Other Rubber Product Manufacturing ᵘˢ

This U.S. industry comprises establishments primarily engaged in manufacturing rubber products (except tires; hoses and belting; and molded, extruded, and lathe-cut rubber goods for mechanical applications) from natural and synthetic rubber.

- Manufacturing tires and inner tubes and tire rebuilding are classified in Industry 32621, Tire Manufacturing;
- Manufacturing rubber hoses and belting are classified in Industry 326220, Rubber and Plastics Hoses and Belting Manufacturing;
- Molding, extruding, and lathe-cutting rubber to manufacture rubber goods (except tubing) for mechanical applications are classified in Industry 326291, Rubber Product Manufacturing for Mechanical Use;

Sector

31-33

Manufacturing

■ = Cross-References

US—United States industry only. CAN—United States and Canadian industries are comparable. When neither US nor CAN appears, Canadian, Mexican, and United States industries are comparable.

■ Rubberizing fabrics are classified in Industry 313320, Fabric Coating Mills;
■ Manufacturing rubber gaskets, packing and sealing devices are classified in U.S. Industry 339991, Gasket, Packing, and Sealing Device Manufacturing;
■ Manufacturing rubber toys are classified in Industry 33993, Doll, Toy, and Game Manufacturing;
■ Manufacturing rubber gloves are classified in U.S. Industry 339113, Surgical Appliance and Supplies Manufacturing; and
■ Manufacturing rubber clothing accessories (e.g., bathing caps) are classified in U.S. Industry 315999, Other Apparel Accessories and Other Apparel Manufacturing.

➡327 NONMETALLIC MINERAL PRODUCT MANUFACTURING

The Nonmetallic Mineral Product Manufacturing subsector transforms mined or quarried nonmetallic minerals, such as sand, gravel, stone, clay, and refractory materials, into products for intermediate or final consumption. Processes used include grinding, mixing, cutting, shaping, and honing. Heat often is used in the process and chemicals are frequently mixed to change the composition, purity, and chemical properties for the intended product. For example, glass is produced by heating silica sand to the melting point (sometimes combined with cullet or recycled glass) and then drawn, floated, or blow molded to the desired shape or thickness. Refractory materials are heated and then formed into bricks or other shapes for use in industrial applications.

The Nonmetallic Mineral Product Manufacturing subsector includes establishments that manufacture products, such as bricks, refractories, ceramic products, and glass and glass products, such as plate glass and containers. Also included are cement and concrete products, lime, gypsum and other nonmetallic mineral products including abrasive products, ceramic plumbing fixtures, statuary, cut stone products, and mineral wool. The products are used in a wide range of activities from construction and heavy and light manufacturing to articles for personal use.

Mining, beneficiating, and manufacturing activities often occur in a single location. Separate receipts will be collected for these activities whenever possible. When receipts cannot be broken out between mining and manufacturing, establishments that mine or quarry nonmetallic minerals, beneficiate the nonmetallic minerals and further process the nonmetallic minerals into a more finished manufactured product are classified based on the primary activity of the establishment. A mine that manufactures a small amount of finished products will be classified in Sector 21, Mining. An establishment that mines whose primary output is a more-finished manufactured product will be classified in the Manufacturing Sector.

Excluded from the Nonmetallic Mineral Product Manufacturing subsector are establishments that primarily beneficiate mined nonmetallic minerals. Beneficiation is the process whereby the extracted material is reduced to particles that can be separated into mineral and waste, the former suitable for further processing or direct use. Beneficiation establishments are included in Sector 21, Mining.

3271 Clay Product and Refractory Manufacturing

32711 Pottery, Ceramics, and Plumbing Fixture Manufacturing
This industry comprises establishments primarily engaged in shaping, molding, glazing, and firing pottery, ceramics, and plumbing fixtures made entirely or partly of clay or other ceramic materials.

■ Manufacturing ferrite microwave devices and electronic components are classified in Subsector 334, Computer and Electronic Product Manufacturing;
■ Manufacturing enameled iron and steel plumbing fixtures are classified in Industry 33299, All Other Fabricated Metal Product Manufacturing;
■ Manufacturing metal bathroom accessories are classified in Subsector 332, Fabricated Metal Product Manufacturing;
■ Manufacturing plastic bathroom accessories, cultured marble, and other plastic plumbing fixtures are classified in Industry 32619, Other Plastics Product Manufacturing; and
■ Manufacturing clay building materials, such as ceramic tile, bricks, and clay roofing tiles, and refractories are classified in Industry 32712, Clay Building Material and Refractories Manufacturing.

327111 Vitreous China Plumbing Fixture and China and Earthenware Bathroom Accessories Manufacturing US
This U.S. industry comprises establishments primarily engaged in manufacturing vitreous china plumbing fixtures and china and earthenware bathroom accessories, such as faucet handles, towel bars, and soap dishes.

Visit page 17 to learn about classification changes to this sector.

Sector
31-33

Manufacturing

■ = Cross-References

US—United States industry only. CAN—United States and Canadian industries are comparable. When neither US nor CAN appears, Canadian, Mexican, and United States industries are comparable.

www.harrisinfo.com 373

■ Manufacturing enameled iron and steel plumbing fixtures are classified in U.S. Industry 332998, Enameled Iron and Metal Sanitary Ware Manufacturing;

■ Manufacturing metal bathroom accessories are classified in Subsector 332, Fabricated Metal Product Manufacturing;

■ Manufacturing plastic bathroom accessories are classified in U.S. Industry 326199, All Other Plastics Product Manufacturing;

■ Manufacturing cultured marble and other plastic plumbing fixtures are classified in U.S. Industry 326191, Plastics Plumbing Fixture Manufacturing; and

■ Manufacturing china and earthenware products (except bathroom fixtures and accessories) are classified in U.S. Industry 327112, Vitreous China, Fine Earthenware, and Other Pottery Product Manufacturing.

327112 Vitreous China, Fine Earthenware, and Other Pottery Product Manufacturing ^{US}

This U.S. industry comprises establishments primarily engaged in manufacturing table and kitchen articles, art and ornamental items, and similar vitreous china, fine earthenware, stoneware, coarse earthenware, and pottery products.

■ Manufacturing vitreous china plumbing fixtures are classified in U.S. Industry 327111, Vitreous China Plumbing Fixture and China and Earthenware Bathroom Accessories Manufacturing;

■ Manufacturing porcelain and ceramic electrical products, such as insulators, are classified in U.S. Industry 327113, Porcelain Electrical Supply Manufacturing; and

■ Manufacturing clay building materials, such as ceramic tile, bricks, and clay roofing tiles, and refractories, are classified in Industry 32712, Clay Building Material and Refractories Manufacturing.

327113 Porcelain Electrical Supply Manufacturing ^{US}

This U.S. industry comprises establishments primarily engaged in manufacturing porcelain electrical insulators, molded porcelain parts for electrical devices, ferrite or ceramic magnets, and electronic and electrical supplies from nonmetallic minerals, such as clay and ceramic materials.

■ Establishments primarily engaged in manufacturing ferrite microwave devices and electronic components are classified in Subsector 334, Computer and Electronic Product Manufacturing.

32712 Clay Building Material and Refractories Manufacturing

This industry comprises establishments primarily engaged in shaping, molding, baking, burning, or hardening clay refractories, nonclay refractories, ceramic tile, structural clay tile, brick, and other structural clay building materials.

■ Manufacturing glass blocks are classified in Industry 32721, Glass and Glass Product Manufacturing;

■ Manufacturing concrete brick and block are classified in Industry 32733, Concrete Pipe, Brick, and Block Manufacturing; and

■ Manufacturing resilient flooring are classified in Industry 32619, Other Plastics Product Manufacturing.

327121 Brick and Structural Clay Tile Manufacturing ^{US}

This U.S. industry comprises establishments primarily engaged in manufacturing brick and structural clay tiles.

■ Manufacturing clay fire brick (i.e., refractories) are classified in U.S. Industry 327124, Clay Refractory Manufacturing;

■ Manufacturing nonclay fire brick (i.e., refractories) are classified in U.S. Industry 327125, Nonclay Refractory Manufacturing;

■ Manufacturing glass brick are classified in Industry 32721, Glass and Glass Product Manufacturing;

■ Manufacturing concrete bricks are classified in U.S. Industry 327331, Concrete Block and Brick Manufacturing; and

■ Manufacturing adobe bricks or clay roofing tiles are classified in U.S. Industry 327123, Other Structural Clay Product Manufacturing.

327122 Ceramic Wall and Floor Tile Manufacturing ^{US}

This U.S. industry comprises establishments primarily engaged in manufacturing ceramic wall and floor tiles.

■ Manufacturing structural clay tiles are classified in U.S. Industry 327121, Brick and Structural Clay Tile Manufacturing;

■ Manufacturing clay drain tiles are classified in U.S. Industry 327123, Other Structural Clay Product Manufacturing; and

■ Manufacturing resilient flooring and asphalt floor tiles are classified in U.S. Industry 326192, Resilient Floor Covering Manufacturing.

327123 Other Structural Clay Product Manufacturing ^{US}

This U.S. industry comprises establishments primarily engaged in manufacturing clay sewer pipe, drain tile, flue lining tile, architectural terracotta, and other structural clay products.

■ Manufacturing bricks and structural clay tiles are classified in U.S. Industry 327121, Brick and Structural Clay Tile Manufacturing;

■ Manufacturing ceramic floor and wall tiles are classified in U.S. Industry 327122, Ceramic Wall and Floor Tile Manufacturing;

Sector

31-33

Manufacturing

■ = Cross-References

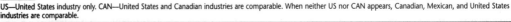

US—United States industry only. CAN—United States and Canadian industries are comparable. When neither US nor CAN appears, Canadian, Mexican, and United States industries are comparable.

374

Harris InfoSource

■ Manufacturing clay refractories are classified in U.S. Industry 327124, Clay Refractory Manufacturing; and
■ Manufacturing nonclay refractories are classified in U.S. Industry 327125, Nonclay Refractory Manufacturing.

327124 Clay Refractory Manufacturing US

This U.S. industry comprises establishments primarily engaged in manufacturing clay refratory, mortar, brick, block, tile, and fabricated clay refractories, such as melting pots. A refractory is a material that will retain its shape and chemical identity when subjected to high temperatures and is used in applications that require extreme resistance to heat, such as furnace linings.

■ Establishments primarily engaged in manufacturing nonclay refractories are classified in U.S. Industry 327125, Nonclay Refractory Manufacturing.

327125 Nonclay Refractory Manufacturing US

This U.S. industry comprises establishments primarily engaged in manufacturing nonclay refractory, mortar, brick, block, tile, and fabricated nonclay refractories such as graphite, magnesite, silica, or alumina crucibles. Arefractory is a material that will retain its shape and chemical identity when subjected to high temperatures and is used in applications that require extreme resistance to heat, such as furnace linings.

■ Establishments primarily engaged in manufacturing clay refractories are classified in U.S. Industry 327124, Clay Refractory Manufacturing.

3272 Glass and Glass Product Manufacturing

32721 Glass and Glass Product Manufacturing

This industry comprises establishments primarily engaged in manufacturing glass and/or glass products. Establishments in this industry may manufacture glass and/or glass products by melting silica sand or cullet, or purchasing glass.

■ Manufacturing glass wool (i.e., fiberglass) insulation products are classified in Industry 32799, All Other Nonmetallic Mineral Product Manufacturing;
■ Manufacturing optical lenses (except ophthalmic), such as magnifying, photographic, and projection lenses, are classified in Industry 33331, Commercial and Service Industry Machinery Manufacturing;
■ Grinding ophthalmic (i.e., eyeglass) lenses for the trade are classified in Industry 33911, Medical Equipment and Supplies Manufacturing; and
■ Manufacturing fiber optic cable from purchased fiber optic strand are classified in Industry 33592, Communication and Energy Wire and Cable Manufacturing.

Visit page 17 to learn about classification changes to this sector.

327211 Flat Glass Manufacturing US

This U.S. industry comprises establishments primarily engaged in (1) manufacturing flat glass by melting silica sand or cullet or (2) manufacturing both flat glass and laminated glass by melting silica sand or cullet.

■ Establishments primarily engaged in manufacturing laminated glass from purchased flat glass are classified in U.S. Industry 327215, Glass Product Manufacturing Made of Purchased Glass.

327212 Other Pressed and Blown Glass and Glassware Manufacturing US

This U.S. industry comprises establishments primarily engaged in manufacturing glass by melting silica sand or cullet and making pressed, blown, or shaped glass or glassware (except glass packaging containers).

■ Manufacturing flat glass are classified in U.S. Industry 327211, Flat Glass Manufacturing;
■ Manufacturing glass packaging containers in glassmaking operations are classified in U.S. Industry 327213, Glass Container Manufacturing;
■ Manufacturing glass wool (i.e., fiberglass) insulation are classified in U.S. Industry 327993, Mineral Wool Manufacturing;
■ Manufacturing glassware from purchased glass are classified in U.S. Industry 327215, Glass Product Manufacturing Made of Purchased Glass; and
■ Manufacturing fiber optic cable are classified in U.S. Industry 335921, Fiber Optic Cable Manufacturing.

Sector

31-33

Manufacturing

327213 Glass Container Manufacturing US

This U.S. industry comprises establishments primarily engaged in manufacturing glass packaging containers.

■ = Cross-References

US—United States industry only. CAN—United States and Canadian industries are comparable. When neither US nor CAN appears, Canadian, Mexican, and United States industries are comparable.

www.harrisinfo.com

 375

327215 Glass Product Manufacturing Made Of Purchased Glass ^{CAN}

This U.S. industry comprises establishments primarily engaged in remelting, pressing, blowing, or shaping purchased glass.

- Manufacturing optical lenses (except ophthalmic), such as magnifying, photographic and projection lenses, are classified in U.S. Industry 333314, Optical Instrument and Lens Manufacturing;
- Manufacturing ophthalmic (i.e., eyeglass) lenses are classified in U.S. Industry 339115, Ophthalmic Goods Manufacturing; and
- Manufacturing fiber optic cable from purchased fiber optic strand are classified in U.S. Industry 335921, Fiber Optic Cable Manufacturing.

3273 Cement and Concrete Product Manufacturing

32731 Cement Manufacturing
See industry description for 327310 below.

327310 Cement Manufacturing
This industry comprises establishments primarily engaged in manufacturing portland, natural, masonry, pozzalanic, and other hydraulic cements. Cement manufacturing establishments may calcine earths or mine, quarry, manufacture, or purchase lime.

- Mining or quarrying limestone are classified in U.S. Industry 212312, Crushed and Broken Limestone Mining and Quarrying;
- Manufacturing lime are classified in Industry 327410, Lime Manufacturing;
- Manufacturing ready-mix concrete are classified in Industry 327320, Ready-mix Concrete Manufacturing; and
- Manufacturing dry mix concrete are classified in U.S. Industry 327999, All Other Miscellaneous Nonmetallic Mineral Product Manufacturing.

32732 Ready-mix Concrete Manufacturing
See industry description for 327320 below.

327320 Ready-mix Concrete Manufacturing
This industry comprises establishments, such as batch plants or mix plants, primarily engaged in manufacturing concrete delivered to a purchaser in a plastic and unhardened state. Ready-mix concrete manufacturing establishments may mine, quarry, or purchase sand and gravel.

- Operating sand or gravel pits are classified in U.S. Industry 212321, Construction Sand and Gravel Mining; and
- Manufacturing dry mix concrete are classified in U.S. Industry 327999, All Other Miscellaneous Nonmetallic Mineral Product Manufacturing.

32733 Concrete Pipe, Brick, and Block Manufacturing
This industry comprises establishments primarily engaged in manufacturing concrete pipe, brick, and block.

- Establishments primarily engaged in manufacturing concrete products (except brick, block, and pipe) are classified in Industry 32739, Other Concrete Product Manufacturing.

327331 Concrete Block and Brick Manufacturing ^{US}
This U.S. industry comprises establishments primarily engaged in manufacturing concrete block and brick.

327332 Concrete Pipe Manufacturing ^{US}
This U.S. industry comprises establishments primarily engaged in manufacturing concrete pipe.

32739 Other Concrete Product Manufacturing
See industry description for 327390 below.

327390 Other Concrete Product Manufacturing
This industry comprises establishments primarily engaged in manufacturing concrete products (except block, brick, and pipe).

- Manufacturing concrete brick and block are classified in U.S. Industry 327331, Concrete Block and Brick Manufacturing; and
- Manufacturing concrete pipe are classified in U.S. Industry 327332, Concrete Pipe Manufacturing.

3274 Lime and Gypsum Product Manufacturing

32741 Lime Manufacturing
See industry description for 327410 below.

Sector
31-33

Manufacturing

■ = Cross-References

US—United States industry only. CAN—United States and Canadian industries are comparable. When neither US nor CAN appears, Canadian, Mexican, and United States industries are comparable.

376

Harris InfoSource

327410 Lime Manufacturing

This industry comprises establishments primarily engaged in manufacturing lime from calcitic limestone, dolomitic limestone, or other calcareous materials, such as coral, chalk, and shells. Lime manufacturing establishments may mine, quarry, collect, or purchase the sources of calcium carbonate.

- Establishments primarily engaged in manufacturing dolomite refractories are classified in U.S. Industry 327125, Nonclay Refractory Manufacturing.

32742 Gypsum Product Manufacturing

See industry description for 327420 below.

327420 Gypsum Product Manufacturing

This industry comprises establishments primarily engaged in manufacturing gypsum products such as wallboard, plaster, plasterboard, molding, ornamental moldings, statuary, and architectural plaster work. Gypsum product manufacturing establishments may mine, quarry, or purchase gypsum.

- Establishments primarily engaged in operating gypsum mines or quarries are classified in U.S. Industry 212399, All Other Nonmetallic Mineral Mining.

3279 Other Nonmetallic Mineral Product Manufacturing

The Other Nonmetallic Mineral Product Manufacturing industry group comprises establishments manufacturing nonmetallic mineral products (except clay products, refractory products, glass products, cement and concrete products, lime, and gypsum products).

32791 Abrasive Product Manufacturing

See industry description for 327910 below.

327910 Abrasive Product Manufacturing

This industry comprises establishments primarily engaged in manufacturing abrasive grinding wheels of natural or synthetic materials, abrasive-coated products, and other abrasive products.

- Mining and cutting grindstones, pulpstones, and whetstones are classified in U.S. Industry 212399, All Other Nonmetallic Mineral Mining;
- Manufacturing plastic scouring pads are classified in U.S. Industry 326199, All Other Plastics Product Manufacturing; and
- Manufacturing metallic scouring sponges and soap impregnated scouring pads are classified in U.S. Industry 332999, All Other Miscellaneous Fabricated Metal Product Manufacturing.

32799 All Other Nonmetallic Mineral Product Manufacturing

This industry comprises establishments primarily engaged in manufacturing nonmetallic mineral products (except pottery, ceramics, and plumbing fixtures; clay building materials and refractories; glass and glass products; cement; ready-mix concrete; concrete products; lime; gypsum products; and abrasive products).

- Manufacturing pottery, ceramics, and plumbing fixtures are classified in Industry 32711, Pottery, Ceramics, and Plumbing Fixture Manufacturing;
- Mining or quarrying stone, earth, or other nonmetallic minerals are classified in Industry Group 2123, Nonmetallic Mineral Mining and Quarrying
- Buying and selling semifinished monuments and tombstones with no work other than polishing, lettering, or shaping to custom order are classified in Sector 42, Wholesale Trade or Sector 44-45, Retail Trade;
- Manufacturing clay building materials and refractories are classified in Industry 32712, Clay Building Material and Refractories Manufacturing;
- Manufacturing glass and glass products are classified in Industry 32721, Glass and Glass Product Manufacturing;
- Manufacturing cement are classified in Industry 32731, Cement Manufacturing;
- Mixing and delivering ready-mix concrete are classified in Industry 32732, Ready-mix Concrete Manufacturing;
- Manufacturing concrete pipe, brick, and block are classified in Industry 32733, Concrete Pipe, Brick, and Block Manufacturing;
- Manufacturing concrete products (except pipe, brick, and block) are classified in Industry 32739, Other Concrete Product Manufacturing;
- Manufacturing lime are classified in Industry 32741, Lime Manufacturing;
- Manufacturing gypsum products are classified in Industry 32742, Gypsum Product Manufacturing;
- Manufacturing abrasive products are classified in Industry 32791, Abrasive Product Manufacturing; and
- Manufacturing metallic scouring pads and steel wool are classified in Industry 33299, All Other Fabricated Metal Product Manufacturing.

Visit page 17 to learn about classification changes to this sector.

Sector
31-33
Manufacturing

■ = Cross-References

US—United States industry only. CAN—United States and Canadian industries are comparable. When neither US nor CAN appears, Canadian, Mexican, and United States industries are comparable.

www.harrisinfo.com 377

327991 Cut Stone and Stone Product Manufacturing ᵁˢ

This U.S. industry comprises establishments primarily engaged in cutting, shaping, and finishing granite, marble, limestone, slate, and other stone for building and miscellaneous uses. Stone product manufacturing establishments may mine, quarry, or purchase stone.

- Mining or quarrying stone are classified in Industry Group 2123, Nonmetallic Mineral Mining and Quarrying; and
- Buying and selling semifinished monuments and tombstones with no work other than polishing, lettering, or shaping to custom order are classified in Sector 42, Wholesale Trade or Sector 44-45, Retail Trade.

327992 Ground or Treated Mineral and Earth Manufacturing ᵁˢ

This U.S. industry comprises establishments primarily engaged in calcining, dead burning, or otherwise processing beyond beneficiation, clays, ceramic and refractory minerals, barite, and miscellaneous nonmetallic minerals.

- Establishments primarily engaged in crushing, grinding, pulverizing, washing, screening, sizing, or otherwise beneficiating mined clays, ceramics and refractory, and other miscellaneous nonmetallic minerals are classified in Industry Group 2123, Nonmetallic Mineral Mining and Quarrying.

327993 Mineral Wool Manufacturing ᵁˢ

This U.S. industry comprises establishments primarily engaged in manufacturing mineral wool and mineral wool (i.e., fiberglass) insulation products made of such siliceous materials as rock, slag, and glass or combinations thereof.

- Establishments primarily engaged in manufacturing metallic scouring pads and steel wool are classified in U.S. Industry 332999, All Other Miscellaneous Fabricated Metal Product Manufacturing.

327999 All Other Miscellaneous Nonmetallic Mineral Product Manufacturing ᵁˢ

This U.S. industry comprises establishments primarily engaged in manufacturing nonmetallic mineral products (except pottery, ceramics, and plumbing fixtures; clay building materials and refractories; glass and glass products; cement; ready-mix concrete; concrete products; lime; gypsum products; abrasive products; cut stone and stone products; ground and treated minerals and earth; and mineral wool).

- Manufacturing pottery, ceramics, and plumbing fixtures are classified in Industry 32711, Pottery, Ceramics, and Plumbing Fixture Manufacturing;
- Manufacturing clay building materials and refractories are classified in Industry 32712, Clay Building Material and Refractories Manufacturing;
- Manufacturing glass and glass products are classified in Industry 32721, Glass and Glass Product Manufacturing;
- Manufacturing cement are classified in Industry 327310, Cement Manufacturing;
- Mixing and delivering ready-mix concrete are classified in Industry 327320, Ready-mix Concrete Manufacturing;
- Manufacturing concrete pipe, brick, and block are classified in Industry 32733, Concrete Pipe, Brick, and Block Manufacturing;
- Manufacturing concrete products (except pipe, brick, and block) are classified in Industry 327390, Other Concrete Product Manufacturing;
- Manufacturing lime are classified in Industry 327410, Lime Manufacturing;
- Manufacturing gypsum products are classified in Industry 327420, Gypsum Product Manufacturing;
- Manufacturing abrasives and abrasive products are classified in Industry 327910, Abrasive Product Manufacturing;
- Manufacturing cut stone and stone products are classified in U.S. Industry 327991, Cut Stone and Stone Product Manufacturing;
- Manufacturing ground and treated minerals and earth (i.e., not at the mine site) are classified in U.S. Industry 327992, Ground or Treated Mineral and Earth Manufacturing; and
- Manufacturing mineral wool and fiberglass insulation products are classified in U.S. Industry 327993, Mineral Wool Manufacturing.

▶331 PRIMARY METAL MANUFACTURING

Industries in the Primary Metal Manufacturing subsector smelt and/or refine ferrous and nonferrous metals from ore, pig or scrap, using electrometallurgical and other process metallurgical techniques. Establishments in this subsector also manufacture metal alloys and superalloys by introducing other chemical elements to pure metals. The output of smelting and refining, usually in ingot form, is used in rolling, drawing, and extruding operations to make sheet, strip, bar, rod, or wire, and in molten form to make castings and other basic metal products.

Primary manufacturing of ferrous and nonferrous metals begins with ore or concentrate as the primary input. Establishments manufacturing primary metals from ore and/or concentrate remain classified in the primary smelting, primary refining, or iron and steel mill, industries regardless of the form of their output.

Sector
31-33

Manufacturing

■ = Cross-References

US—United States industry only. CAN—United States and Canadian industries are comparable. When neither US nor CAN appears, Canadian, Mexican, and United States industries are comparable.

378

Harris InfoSource

Establishments primarily engaged in secondary smelting and/or secondary refining recover ferrous and nonferrous metals from scrap and/or dross. The output of the secondary smelting and/or secondary refining industries is limited to shapes, such as ingot or billet, that will be further processed. Recovery of metals from scrap often occurs in establishments that are primarily engaged in activities, such as rolling, drawing, extruding, or similar processes.

Excluded from the Primary Metal Manufacturing subsector are establishments primarily engaged in manufacturing ferrous and nonferrous forgings (except ferrous forgings made in steel mills) and stampings. Although forging, stamping, and casting are all methods used to make metal shapes, forging and stamping do not use molten metals and are included in Subsector 332, Fabricated Metal Product Manufacturing. Establishments primarily engaged in operating coke ovens are classified in Industry 32419, Other Petroleum and Coal Products Manufacturing.

3311 Iron and Steel Mills and Ferroalloy Manufacturing

33111 Iron and Steel Mills and Ferroalloy Manufacturing
This industry comprises establishments primarily engaged in one or more of the following: (1) direct reduction of iron ore; (2) manufacturing pig iron in molten or solid form; (3) converting pig iron into steel; (4) manufacturing ferroalloys; (5) making steel; (6) making steel and manufacturing shapes (e.g., bar, plate, rod, sheet, strip, wire); and (7) making steel and forming pipe and tube.

- Manufacturing nonferrous superalloys, such as cobalt or nickel-based superalloys, are classified in Industry 33149, Nonferrous Metal (except Copper and Aluminum) Rolling, Drawing, Extruding, and Alloying; and
- Operating coke ovens are classified in Industry 32419, Other Petroleum and Coal Products Manufacturing.

331111 Iron and Steel Mills ^{US}
This U.S. industry comprises establishments primarily engaged in one or more of the following: (1) direct reduction of iron ore; (2) manufacturing pig iron in molten or solid form; (3) converting pig iron into steel; (4) making steel; (5) making steel and manufacturing shapes (e.g., bar, plate, rod, sheet, strip, wire); and (6) making steel and forming tube and pipe.

- Manufacturing ferroalloys (i.e., alloying elements used to improve, strengthen, or otherwise alter the characteristics of steel) are classified in U.S. Industry 331112, Electrometallurgical Ferroalloy Product Manufacturing; and
- Operating coke ovens are classified in U.S. Industry 324199, All Other Petroleum and Coal Products Manufacturing.

Visit page 17 to learn about classification changes to this sector.

331112 Electrometallurgical Ferroalloy Product Manufacturing ^{US}
This U.S. industry comprises establishments primarily engaged in manufacturing electro-metallurgical ferroalloys. Ferroalloys add critical elements, such as silicon and manganese for carbon steel and chromium, vanadium, tungsten, titanium, and molybdenum for low- and high-alloy metals. Ferroalloys include iron-rich alloys and more pure forms of elements added during the steel manufacturing process that alter or improve the characteristics of the metal being made.

- Manufacturing electrometallurgical steel and iron-based superalloys are classified in U.S. Industry 331111, Iron and Steel Mills; and
- Manufacturing nonferrous superalloys, such as cobalt or nickel-based superalloys, are classified in U.S. Industry 331492, Secondary Smelting, Refining, and Alloying of Nonferrous Metal (except Copper and Aluminum)

3312 Steel Product Manufacturing from Purchased Steel
This industry group comprises establishments primarily engaged in manufacturing iron and steel tube and pipe, drawing steel wire, and rolling or drawing shapes from purchased iron or steel.

Sector
31-33
Manufacturing

33121 Iron and Steel Pipe and Tube Manufacturing from Purchased Steel
See industry description for 331210 below.

331210 Iron and Steel Pipe and Tube Manufacturing from Purchased Steel
This industry comprises establishments primarily engaged in manufacturing welded, riveted, or seamless pipe and tube from purchased iron or steel.

- Establishments primarily engaged in making steel and further processing the steel into steel pipe and tube are classified in U.S. Industry 331111, Iron and Steel Mills.

■ = Cross-References

US—United States industry only. CAN—United States and Canadian industries are comparable. When neither US nor CAN appears, Canadian, Mexican, and United States industries are comparable.

www.harrisinfo.com

379

33122 Rolling and Drawing of Purchased Steel

This industry comprises establishments primarily engaged in rolling and/or drawing steel shapes, such as plate, sheet, strip, rod, and bar, from purchased steel.

- Making steel and rolling and/or drawing steel are classified in Industry 33111, Iron and Steel Mills and Ferroalloy Manufacturing; and
- Manufacturing wire products from purchased wire are classified in Industry 33261, Spring and Wire Product Manufacturing.

331221 Rolled Steel Shape Manufacturing ^{CAN}

This U.S. industry comprises establishments primarily engaged in rolling or drawing shapes (except wire), such as plate, sheet, strip, rod, and bar, from purchased steel.

- Making steel and rolling or drawing steel shapes are classified in U.S. Industry 331111, Iron and Steel Mills; and
- Drawing wire from purchased steel are classified in U.S. Industry 331222, Steel Wire Drawing.

331222 Steel Wire Drawing ^{CAN}

This U.S. industry comprises establishments primarily engaged in drawing wire from purchased steel.

- Making steel and drawing steel wire are classified in U.S. Industry 331111, Iron and Steel Mills; and
- Manufacturing wire products, such as nails, spikes, and paper clips, from purchased steel wire are classified in Industry 33261, Spring and Wire Product Manufacturing.

3313 Alumina and Aluminum Production and Processing

33131 Alumina and Aluminum Production and Processing

This industry comprises establishments primarily engaged in one or more of the following: (1) refining alumina; (2) making (i.e., the primary production) aluminum from alumina; (3) recovering aluminum from scrap or dross; (4) alloying purchased aluminum; and (5) manufacturing aluminum primary forms (e.g., bar, foil, pipe, plate, rod, sheet, tube, wire).

- Manufacturing aluminum oxide abrasives and refractories are classified in Subsector 327, Nonmetallic Mineral Product Manufacturing;
- Sorting and breaking up scrap aluminum metal without also smelting or refining are classified in Sector 42, Wholesale Trade; and
- Operating facilities where commingled recyclable materials, such as paper, plastics, used beverage cans, and metals are sorted into distinct categories without also smelting or refining are classified in Industry 56292, Materials Recovery Facilities.

331311 Alumina Refining ^{US}

This U.S. industry comprises establishments primarily engaged in refining alumina (i.e., aluminum oxide) generally from bauxite.

- Manufacturing aluminum oxide abrasives and refractories are classified in Subsector 327, Nonmetallic Mineral Product Manufacturing; and
- Making aluminum from alumina are classified in U.S. Industry 331312, Primary Aluminum Production.

331312 Primary Aluminum Production ^{US}

This U.S. industry comprises establishments primarily engaged in (1) making aluminum from alumina and/or (2) making aluminum from alumina and rolling, drawing, extruding, or casting the aluminum they make into primary forms (e.g., bar, billet, ingot, plate, rod, sheet, strip). Establishments in this industry may make primary aluminum or aluminum-based alloys from alumina.

- Refining alumina are classified in U.S. Industry 331311, Alumina Refining; and
- Recovering aluminum from scrap or alloying purchased aluminum are classified in U.S. Industry 331314, Secondary Smelting and Alloying of Aluminum.

331314 Secondary Smelting and Alloying of Aluminum ^{US}

This U.S. industry comprises establishments primarily engaged in (1) recovering aluminum and aluminum alloys from scrap and/or dross (i.e., secondary smelting) and making billet or ingot (except by rolling) and/or (2) manufacturing alloys, powder, paste, or flake from purchased aluminum.

- Making aluminum and/or aluminum alloys from alumina are classified in U.S. Industry 331312, Primary Aluminum Production;
- Refining alumina are classified in U.S. Industry 331311, Alumina Refining; Manufacturing aluminum sheet, plate, and foil from purchased aluminum or by recovering aluminum from scrap and flat rolling or continuous casting are classified in U.S. Industry 331315, Aluminum Sheet, Plate, and Foil Manufacturing;

US—United States industry only. CAN—United States and Canadian industries are comparable. When neither US nor CAN appears, Canadian, Mexican, and United States industries are comparable.

- Manufacturing aluminum extruded products from purchased aluminum or by recovering aluminum from scrap and extruding are classified in U.S. Industry 331316, Aluminum Extruded Product Manufacturing;
- Manufacturing rolled ingot, billet from purchased aluminum or by recovering aluminum from scrap and rolling or drawing are classified in U.S. Industry 331319, Other Aluminum Rolling and Drawing;
- Sorting and breaking up scrap metal without also smelting or refining are classified in Industry 421930, Recyclable Material Wholesalers; and
- Operating facilities where commingled recyclable materials, such as paper, plastics, used beverage cans, and metals, are sorted into distinct categories without also smelting or refining are classified in Industry 562920, Materials Recovery Facilities.

331315 Aluminum Sheet, Plate, and Foil Manufacturing US

This U.S. industry comprises establishments primarily engaged in (1) flat rolling or continuous casting sheet, plate, foil and welded tube from purchased aluminum and/or (2) recovering aluminum from scrap and flat rolling or continuous casting sheet, plate, foil, and welded tube in integrated mills.

- Establishments primarily engaged in making aluminum from alumina and flat rolling or continuous casting aluminum sheet, plate, foil, and welded tube are classified in U.S. Industry 331312, Primary Aluminum Production.

331316 Aluminum Extruded Product Manufacturing US

This U.S. industry comprises establishments primarily engaged in (1) extruding aluminum bar, pipe, and tube blooms or extruding or drawing tube from purchased aluminum; and/or (2) recovering aluminum from scrap and extruding bar, pipe, and tube blooms or drawing tube in integrated mills.

- Establishments primarily engaged in making aluminum from alumina and extruding aluminum bar, pipe, tube or tube blooms are classified in U.S. Industry 331312, Primary Aluminum Production.

331319 Other Aluminum Rolling and Drawing US

This U.S. Industry comprises establishments primarily engaged in (1) rolling, drawing, or extruding shapes (except flat rolled sheet, plate, foil, and welded tube; extruded rod, bar, pipe, and tube blooms; and drawn or extruded tube) from purchased aluminum and/or (2) recovering aluminum from scrap and rolling, drawing or extruding shapes (except flat rolled sheet, plate, foil, and welded tube; extruded rod, bar, pipe, and tube blooms; and drawn or extruded tube) in integrated mills.

- Flat rolling sheet, plate, foil, and welded tube from either purchased aluminum or by recovering aluminum from scrap and flat rolling or continuous casting are classified in U.S. Industry 331315, Aluminum Sheet, Plate, and Foil Manufacturing;
- Extruding rod, bar, pipe, tube and tube blooms or drawing tube from purchased aluminum or by recovering aluminum from scrap and extruding are classified in U.S. Industry 331316, Aluminum Extruded Product Manufacturing; and
- Making aluminum from alumina and making aluminum shapes are classified in U.S. Industry 331312, Primary Aluminum Production.

Visit page 17 to learn about classification changes to this sector.

3314 Nonferrous Metal (except Aluminum) Production and Processing

33141 Nonferrous Metal (except Aluminum) Smelting and Refining

This industry comprises establishments primarily engaged in (1) smelting ores into nonferrous metals and/or (2) the primary refining of nonferrous metals (except aluminum) using electrolytic or other processes.

- Making aluminum from alumina or recovery of aluminum from scrap are classified in Industry 33131, Alumina and Aluminum Production and Processing;
- Recovering copper or copper alloys from scrap or dross and/or alloying, rolling, drawing, and extruding purchased copper are classified in Industry 33142, Copper Rolling, Drawing, Extruding, and Alloying;
- Recovering nonferrous metals (except copper and aluminum) from scrap and/or alloying, rolling, drawing, and extruding purchased nonferrous metals (except copper and aluminum) are classified in Industry 33149, Nonferrous Metal (except Copper and Aluminum) Rolling, Drawing, Extruding, and Alloying;
- Mining and making copper and other nonferrous concentrates (including gold and silver bullion) using processes, such as solvent extraction or electrowinning, are classified in Industry Group 2122, Metal Ore Mining; Sorting and breaking up scrap metal without also smelting or refining are classified in Sector 42, Wholesale Trade; and
- Operating facilities where commingled recyclable materials, such as paper, plastics, used beverage cans, and metals, are sorted into distinct categories without also smelting or refining are classified in Industry 56292, Materials Recovery Facilities.

331411 Primary Smelting and Refining of Copper US

This U.S. industry comprises establishments primarily engaged in (1) smelting copper ore and/or (2) the primary refining of copper by electrolytic methods or other processes. Establishments in this industry make primary copper and copper-based alloys, such as brass and bronze, from ore or concentrates.

Sector
31-33

Manufacturing

■ = Cross-References

US—United States industry only. CAN—United States and Canadian industries are comparable. When neither US nor CAN appears, Canadian, Mexican, and United States industries are comparable.

www.harrisinfo.com

 381

■ Recovering copper or copper alloys from scrap and making primary forms; and/or alloying purchased copper are classified in U.S. Industry 331423, Secondary Smelting, Refining, and Alloying of Copper;

■ Mining and making copper concentrates by processes, such as solvent extraction or electrowinning, are classified in U.S. Industry 212234, Copper Ore and Nickel Ore Mining;

■ Drawing copper wire (except mechanical) from purchased copper or recovering copper from scrap and drawing wire (except mechanical) are classified in U.S. Industry 331422, Copper Wire (except Mechanical) Drawing; and

■ Rolling, drawing, or extruding copper shapes (except communication and energy wire) from purchased copper or recovering copper from scrap and rolling, drawing, and extruding copper shapes are classified in U.S. Industry 331421, Copper Rolling, Drawing, and Extruding.

331419 Primary Smelting and Refining of Nonferrous Metal (except Copper and Aluminum)[US]

This U.S. industry comprises establishments primarily engaged in (1) making (i.e., the primary production) nonferrous metals by smelting ore and/or (2) the primary refining of nonferrous metals by electrolytic methods or other processes.

■ Recovering nonferrous metals (except copper and aluminum) from scrap and making primary forms and/or alloying purchased nonferrous metals (except copper and aluminum) are classified in U.S. Industry 331492, Secondary Smelting, Refining, and Alloying of Nonferrous Metal (except Copper and Aluminum);

■ Making aluminum from alumina are classified in U.S. Industry 331312, Primary Aluminum Production;

■ Primary smelting and primary refining of copper are classified in U.S. Industry 331411, Primary Smelting and Refining of Copper;

■ Mining and making copper and other nonferrous concentrates (including gold and silver bullion), by processes, such as solvent extraction or electrowinning, are classified in Industry Group 2122, Metal Ore Mining; and

■ Rolling, drawing, and/or extruding nonferrous metal shapes (except copper and aluminum) from purchased nonferrous metals (except copper and aluminum) or by recovering nonferrous metals (except copper and aluminum) and rolling, drawing, or extruding are classified in U.S. Industry 331491, Nonferrous Metal (except Copper and Aluminum) Rolling, Drawing, and Extruding.

33142 Copper Rolling, Drawing, Extruding, and Alloying

This industry comprises establishments primarily engaged in one or more of the following: (1) recovering copper or copper alloys from scraps; (2) alloying purchased copper; (3) rolling, drawing, or extruding shapes, (e.g., bar, plate, sheet, strip, tube, and wire) from purchased copper; and (4) recovering copper or copper alloys from scrap and rolling drawing, or extruding shapes (e.g., bar, plate, sheet, strip, tube, and wire).

■ Smelting copper ore, primary copper refining, and/or rolling, drawing or extruding primary copper made in the same establishment are classified in Industry 33141, Nonferrous Metal (except Aluminum) Smelting and Refining;

■ Manufacturing wire products from purchased wire are classified in Industry 33261, Spring and Wire Product Manufacturing;

■ Insulating purchased copper wire are classified in Industry 33592, Communication and Energy Wire and Cable Manufacturing;

■ Sorting and breaking up scrap metal without also smelting or refining are classified in Sector 42, Wholesale Trade;

■ Operating facilities where commingled recyclable materials, such as paper, plastics, used beverage cans, and metals, are sorted into distinct categories without also smelting or refining are classified in Industry 56292, Materials Recovery Facilities;

■ Die-casting purchased copper are classified in Industry 33152, Nonferrous Metal Foundries; and

■ Recovering nonferrous metals (except copper and aluminum) from scrap, and/or rolling, drawing, extruding, or alloying purchased nonferrous metals (except copper and aluminum) are classified in Industry 33149, Nonferrous Metal (except Copper and Aluminum) Rolling, Drawing, Extruding, and Alloying.

331421 Copper Rolling, Drawing, and Extruding [US]

This U.S. industry comprises establishments primarily engaged in (1) rolling, drawing, and/or extruding shapes (e.g., bar, plate, sheet, strip, tube (except bare or insulated copper communication or energy wire) from purchased copper; and/or (2) recovering copper from scrap and rolling, drawing, and/or extruding shapes (e.g., bar, plate, sheet, strip, tube (except bare or insulated copper communication or energy wire in integrated mills.)

■ Recovering copper or copper alloys from scrap and making primary forms and/or alloying purchased copper are classified in U.S. Industry 331423, Secondary Smelting, Refining, and Alloying of Copper;

■ Drawing copper wire (except mechanical) from purchased copper or recovering copper from scrap and drawing copper wire (except mechanical) are classified in U.S. Industry 331422, Copper Wire (except Mechanical) Drawing;

■ Die-casting purchased copper are classified in U.S. Industry 331522, Nonferrous (except Aluminum) Die-casting Foundries;

■ Making primary copper and rolling, drawing, and/or extruding copper shapes (e.g., bar, plate, rod, sheet, strip) are classified in U.S. Industry 331411, Primary Smelting and Refining of Copper; and

■ Rolling, drawing, or extruding shapes from purchased nonferrous metal (except copper and aluminum) or recovering nonferrous metals from scrap and rolling, drawing or extruding are classified in U.S. Industry 331491, Nonferrous Metal (except Copper and Aluminum) Rolling, Drawing, and Extruding.

Sector
31-33
Manufacturing

■ = Cross-References

US—United States industry only. CAN—United States and Canadian industries are comparable. When neither US nor CAN appears, Canadian, Mexican, and United States industries are comparable.

382

Harris InfoSource

331422 Copper Wire (except Mechanical) Drawing US

This U.S. industry comprises establishments primarily engaged in drawing or drawing and insulating communication and energy wire and cable from purchased copper or in integrated secondary smelting and wire drawing plants.

- Manufacturing copper mechanical wire from purchased copper or by recovering copper from scrap and drawing or extruding are classified in U.S. Industry 331421, Copper Rolling, Drawing, and Extruding;
- Insulating purchased copper wire are classified in U.S. Industry 335929, Other Communication and Energy Wire Manufacturing;
- Making primary copper and drawing copper wire are classified in U.S. Industry 331411, Primary Smelting and Refining of Copper; and
- Manufacturing wire products from purchased copper wire are classified in Industry 33261, Spring and Wire Product Manufacturing.

331423 Secondary Smelting, Refining, and Alloying of Copper US

This U.S. industry comprises establishments primarily engaged in (1) recovering copper and copper alloys from scrap and/or (2) alloying purchased copper. Establishments in this industry make primary forms, such as ingot, wire bar, cake, and slab from copper or copper alloys, such as brass and bronze.

- Sorting and breaking up scrap metal without also smelting or refining are classified in Industry 421930, Recyclable Material Wholesalers;
- Operating facilities where commingled recyclable materials, such as paper, plastics, used beverage cans, and metals, are sorted into distinct categories without also smelting or refining are classified in Industry 562920, Materials Recovery Facilities;
- Smelting copper ore and/or the primary refining of copper are classified in U.S. Industry 331411, Primary Smelting and Refining of Copper;
- Recovering copper and copper alloys from scrap and rolling, drawing, or extruding shapes are classified in U.S. Industry 331421, Copper Rolling, Drawing, and Extruding;
- Recovering copper and copper alloys from scrap and drawing wire (except mechanical) are classified in U.S. Industry 331422, Copper Wire (except Mechanical) Drawing; and
- Recovering nonferrous metals (except copper, aluminum) from scrap and making primary forms and/or alloying purchased nonferrous metals (except copper and aluminum) are classified in U.S. Industry 331492, Secondary Smelting, Refining, and Alloying of Nonferrous Metal (except Copper and Aluminum).

33149 Nonferrous Metal (except Copper and Aluminum) Rolling, Drawing, Extruding, and Alloying

This industry comprises establishments primarily engaged in one or more of the following: (1) recovering nonferrous metals (except copper and aluminum) and nonferrous metal alloys from scrap; (2) alloying purchased nonferrous metals (except copper and aluminum); (3) rolling, drawing, and extruding shapes from purchased nonferrous metals (except copper and aluminum); and (4) recovering nonferrous metals from scrap (except copper and aluminum) and rolling, drawing, or extruding shapes in integrated facilities.

Visit page 17 to learn about classification changes to this sector.

- Rolling, drawing, and/or extruding aluminum or secondary smelting and alloying of aluminum are classified in Industry 33131, Alumina and Aluminum Production and Processing;
- Recovering copper and copper alloys from scrap, alloying purchased copper, rolling, drawing, or extruding shapes from purchased copper, and recovering copper or copper alloys from scrap and rolling, drawing, or extruding shapes in integrated mills are classified in Industry 33142, Copper Rolling, Drawing, Extruding, and Alloying;
- Insulating purchased nonferrous wire are classified in Industry 33592, Communication and Energy Wire and Cable Manufacturing;
- Making primary nonferrous metals and rolling, drawing, or extruding nonferrous metal shapes are classified in Industry 33141, Nonferrous Metal (except Aluminum) Smelting and Refining;
- Manufacturing products from purchased wire are classified in Industry 33261, Spring and Wire Product Manufacturing;
- Sorting and breaking up scrap metal without also smelting or refining are classified in Sector 42, Wholesale Trade; and
- Operating facilities where commingled recyclable materials, such as paper, plastics, used beverage cans, and metals, are sorted into distinct categories without also smelting or refining are classified in Industry 56292, Materials Recovery Facilities.

331491 Nonferrous Metal (except Copper and Aluminum) Rolling, Drawing, and Extruding US

This U.S. industry comprises establishments primarily engaged in (1) rolling, drawing, or extruding shapes (e.g., bar, plate, sheet, strip, tube) from purchased nonferrous metals) and/or (2) recovering nonferrous metals from scrap and rolling, drawing, and/or extruding shapes (e.g., bar, plate, sheet, strip, tube) in integrated mills.

- Rolling, drawing, and/or extruding shapes from purchased copper or recovering copper from scrap and rolling, drawing, or extruding shapes are classified in U.S. Industry 331421, Copper Rolling, Drawing, and Extruding;

Manufacturing

■ = Cross-References

US—United States industry only. CAN—United States and Canadian industries are comparable. When neither US nor CAN appears, Canadian, Mexican, and United States industries are comparable.

- Recovering nonferrous metals (except copper and aluminum) from scrap and making primary forms and/or alloying purchased nonferrous metals are classified in U.S. Industry 331492, Secondary Smelting, Refining, and Alloying of Nonferrous Metal (except Copper and Aluminum);
- Rolling, drawing, and/or extruding aluminum are classified in Industry 33131, Alumina and Aluminum Production and Processing;
- Making primary nonferrous metals and rolling, drawing, or extruding nonferrous metal shapes are classified in U.S. Industry 331419, Primary Smelting and Refining of Nonferrous Metal (except Copper and Aluminum); and
- Insulating purchased nonferrous wire are classified in U.S. Industry 335929, Other Communication and Energy Wire Manufacturing.

331492 Secondary Smelting, Refining, and Alloying of Nonferrous Metal (except Copper and Aluminum)^{US}

This U.S. industry comprises establishments primarily engaged in (1) alloying purchased nonferrous metals and/or (2) recovering nonferrous metals from scrap. Establishments in this industry make primary forms (e.g., bar, billet, bloom, cake, ingot, slab, slug, wire) using smelting or refining processes.

- Recovering aluminum and aluminum alloys from scrap and/or alloying purchased aluminum are classified in U.S. Industry 331314, Secondary Smelting and Alloying of Aluminum;
- Sorting and breaking up scrap metal without also smelting or refining are classified in Industry 421930, Recyclable Material Wholesalers;
- Recovering nonferrous metals from scrap and rolling, drawing, or extruding shapes in integrated facilities are classified in U.S. Industry 331491, Nonferrous Metal (except Copper and Aluminum) Rolling, Drawing, and Extruding;
- Operating facilities where commingled recyclable materials, such as paper, plastics, used beverage cans, and metals, are sorted into distinct categories without also smelting or refining are classified in Industry 562920, Materials Recovery Facilities; and
- Recovering copper and copper alloys from scrap and making primary forms; and/or alloying purchased copper are classified in U.S. Industry 331423, Secondary Smelting, Refining, and Alloying of Copper.

3315 Foundries

This industry group comprises establishments primarily engaged in pouring molten metal into molds or dies to form castings. Establishments making castings and further manufacturing, such as machining or assembling, a specific manufactured product are classified in the industry of the finished product. Foundries may perform operations, such as cleaning and deburring, on the castings they manufacture. More involved processes, such as tapping, threading, milling, or machining to tight tolerances, that transform castings into more finished products are classified elsewhere in the manufacturing sector based on the product being made.

Establishments in this industry group make castings from purchased metals or in integrated secondary smelting and casting facilities. When the production of primary metals is combined with making castings, the establishment is classified in 331 with the primary metal being made.

33151 Ferrous Metal Foundries
This industry comprises establishments primarily engaged in pouring molten iron and steel into molds of a desired shape to made castings. Establishments in this industry purchase iron and steel made in other establishments.

- Establishments primarily engaged in manufacturing iron or steel castings and further manufacturing them into finished products are classified based on the specific finished product.

331511 Iron Foundries ^{CAN}

This U.S. industry comprises establishments primarily engaged in pouring molten pig iron or iron alloys into molds to manufacture castings, (e.g., cast iron man-hole covers, cast iron pipe, cast iron skillets). Establishments in this industry purchase iron made in other establishments.

- Establishments primarily engaged in manufacturing iron castings and further manufacturing them into finished products are classified based on the specific finished product.

331512 Steel Investment Foundries ^{US}

This U.S. industry comprises establishments primarily engaged in manufacturing steel investment castings. Investment molds are formed by covering a wax shape with a refractory slurry. After the refractory slurry hardens, the wax is melted, leaving a seamless mold. Investment molds provide highly detailed, consistent castings. Establishments in this industry purchase steel made in other establishments.

- Manufacturing steel castings (except steel investment castings) are classified in U.S. Industry 331513, Steel Foundries (except Investment); and

Sector
31-33

Manufacturing

■ = Cross-References

US—United States industry only. CAN—United States and Canadian industries are comparable. When neither US nor CAN appears, Canadian, Mexican, and United States industries are comparable.

384

Harris InfoSource

■ Manufacturing steel investment castings and further manufacturing them into finished products are classified based on the specific finished product.

331513 Steel Foundries (except Investment)[US]

This U.S. industry comprises establishments primarily engaged in manufacturing steel castings (except steel investment castings). Establishments in this industry purchase steel made in other establishments.

■ Manufacturing steel investment castings are classified in U.S. Industry 331512, Steel Investment Foundries; and
■ Manufacturing steel castings and further manufacturing them into finished products are classified based on the specific finished product.

33152 Nonferrous Metal Foundries

This industry comprises establishments primarily engaged in pouring and/or introducing molten nonferrous metal, under high pressure, into metal molds or dies to manufacture castings. Establishments in this industry purchase nonferrous metals made in other establishments.

■ Manufacturing iron or steel castings are classified in Industry 33151, Ferrous Metal Foundries; and
■ Manufacturing nonferrous metal castings and further manufacturing them into finished products are classified based on the specific finished product.

331521 Aluminum Die-casting Foundries [US]

This U.S. industry comprises establishments primarily engaged in introducing molten aluminum, under high pressure, into molds or dies to make aluminum die-castings. Establishments in this industry purchase aluminum made in other establishments.

■ Pouring molten aluminum into molds to manufacture aluminum castings are classified in U.S. Industry 331524, Aluminum Foundries (except Die-casting); and
■ Manufacturing aluminum die-castings and further manufacturing them into finished products are classified based on the specific finished product.

331522 Nonferrous (except Aluminum) Die-casting Foundries [US]

This U.S. industry comprises establishments primarily engaged in introducing molten nonferrous metal (except aluminum), under high pressure, into molds to make nonferrous metal die-castings. Establishments in this industry purchase nonferrous metals made in other establishments.

■ Manufacturing aluminum die-castings are classified in U.S. Industry 331521, Aluminum Die-casting Foundries;
■ Pouring molten aluminum into molds to manufacture aluminum castings are classified in U.S. Industry 331524, Aluminum Foundries (except Die-casting);
■ Pouring molten copper into molds to manufacture copper castings are classified in U.S. Industry 331525, Copper Foundries (except Die-casting);
■ Pouring molten nonferrous metal (except copper and aluminum) into molds to manufacture nonferrous (except copper and aluminum) castings are classified in U.S. Industry 331528, Other Nonferrous Foundries (except Die-casting); and
■ Manufacturing nonferrous die-castings and further manufacturing them into finished products are classified based on the specific finished product.

331524 Aluminum Foundries (except Die-casting)[US]

This U.S. industry comprises establishments primarily engaged in pouring molten aluminum into molds to manufacture aluminum castings. Establishments in this industry purchase aluminum made in other establishments.

■ Manufacturing aluminum die-castings are classified in U.S. Industry 331521, Aluminum Die-casting Foundries; and
■ Manufacturing aluminum or aluminum alloy castings and further manufacturing them into finished products are classified based on the specific finished product.

331525 Copper Foundries (except Die-casting)[US]

This U.S. industry comprises establishments primarily engaged in pouring molten copper into molds to manufacture copper castings. Establishments in this industry purchase copper made in other establishments.

■ Manufacturing copper die-castings are classified in U.S. Industry 331522, Nonferrous (except Aluminum) Die-casting Foundries; and
■ Manufacturing copper castings and further manufacturing them into finished products are classified based on the specific finished product.

Visit page 17 to learn about classification changes to this sector.

Sector
31-33

Manufacturing

■ = Cross-References

US—United States industry only. CAN—United States and Canadian industries are comparable. When neither US nor CAN appears, Canadian, Mexican, and United States industries are comparable.

www.harrisinfo.com

385

331528 Other Nonferrous Foundries (except Die-casting)ᵁˢ

This U.S. industry comprises establishments primarily engaged in pouring molten nonferrous metals (except aluminum and copper) into molds to manufacture nonferrous castings (except aluminum die-castings, nonferrous (except aluminum) die-castings, aluminum castings, and copper castings). Establishments in this industry purchase nonferrous metals, such as nickel, lead, and zinc, made in other establishments.

- Manufacturing aluminum die-castings are classified in U.S. Industry 331521, Aluminum Die-casting Foundries;
- Manufacturing nonferrous (except aluminum) die-castings are classified in U.S. Industry 331522, Nonferrous (except Aluminum) Die-casting Foundries; Pouring molten aluminum into molds to manufacture aluminum castings are classified in U.S. Industry 331524, Aluminum Foundries (except Die-casting);
- Manufacturing copper castings are classified in U.S. Industry 331525, Copper Foundries (except Die-casting); and
- Manufacturing nonferrous castings and further manufacturing them into finished products are classified based on the specific finished product.

▶332 FABRICATED METAL PRODUCT MANUFACTURING

Industries in the Fabricated Metal Product Manufacturing subsector transform metal into intermediate or end products, other than machinery, computers and electronics, and metal furniture or treating metals and metal formed products fabricated elsewhere. Important fabricated metal processes are forging, stamping, bending, forming, and machining, used to shape individual pieces of metal; and other processes, such as welding and assembling, used to join separate parts together. Establishments in this subsector may use one of these processes or a combination of these processes.

The NAICS structure for this subsector distinguishes the forging and stamping processes in a single industry. The remaining industries, in the subsector, group establishments based on similar combinations of processes used to make products.

The manufacturing performed in the Fabricated Metal Product Manufacturing subsector begins with manufactured metal shapes. The establishments in this sector further fabricate the purchased metal shapes into a product. For instance, the Spring and Wire Product Manufacturing industry starts with wire and fabricates such items.

Within manufacturing there are other establishments that make the same products made by this subsector; only these establishments begin production further back in the production process. These establishments have a more integrated operation. For instance, one establishment may manufacture steel, draw it into wire, and make wire products in the same establishment. Such operations are classified in the Primary Metal Manufacturing subsector.

3321 Forging and Stamping

33211 Forging and Stamping

This industry comprises establishments primarily engaged in one or more of the following: (1) manufacturing forgings from purchased metals; (2) manufacturing metal custom roll forming products; (3) manufacturing metal stamped and spun products (except automotive, cans, coins); and (4) manufacturing powder metallurgy products. Establishments making metal forgings, metal stampings, and metal spun products and further manufacturing (e.g., machining, assembling) a specific manufactured product are classified in the industry of the finished product. Metal forging, metal stamping, and metal spun products establishments may perform surface finishing operations, such as cleaning and deburring, on the products they manufacture.

- Manufacturing metal forgings in integrated primary metal establishments are classified in Subsector 331, Primary Metal Manufacturing; Stamping automotive stampings are classified in Industry 33637, Motor Vehicle Metal Stamping;
- Manufacturing and installing rolled formed seamless gutters at construction sites are classified in Industry 23561, Roofing, Siding, and Sheet Meal Contractors; and
- Stamping coins are classified in Industry 33991, Jewelry and Silverware Manufacturing.

332111 Iron and Steel Forging ᵁˢ

This U.S. industry comprises establishments primarily engaged in manufacturing iron and steel forgings from purchased iron and steel by hammering mill shapes. Establishments making iron and steel forgings

Sector
31-33

Manufacturing

■ = Cross-References

US—United States industry only. CAN—United States and Canadian industries are comparable. When neither US nor CAN appears, Canadian, Mexican, and United States industries are comparable.

386

Harris InfoSource

and further manufacturing (e.g., machining, assembling) a specific manufactured product are classified in the industry of the finished product. Iron and steel forging establishments may perform surface finishing operations, such as cleaning and deburring, on the forgings they manufacture.

- Manufacturing iron and steel forgings in integrated iron and steel mills are classified in U.S. Industry 331111, Iron and Steel Mills; and
- Manufacturing nonferrous forgings are classified in U.S. Industry 332112, Nonferrous Forging.

332112 Nonferrous Forging US

This U.S. industry comprises establishments primarily engaged in manufacturing nonferrous forgings from purchased nonferrous metals by hammering mill shapes. Establishments making nonferrous forgings and further manufacturing (e.g., machining, assembling) a specific manufactured product are classified in the industry of the finished product. Nonferrous forging establishments may perform surface finishing operations, such as cleaning and deburring, on the forgings they manufacture.

- Manufacturing iron and steel forgings are classified in U.S. Industry 332111, Iron and Steel Forging; and
- Manufacturing nonferrous forgings in integrated primary or secondary nonferrous metal production facilities are classified in Subsector 331, Primary Metal Manufacturing.

332114 Custom Roll Forming US

This U.S. industry comprises establishments primarily engaged in custom roll forming metal products by use of rotary motion of rolls with various contours to bend or shape the products.

- Establishments primarily engaged in manufacturing and installing rolled formed seamless gutters at construction sites are classified in Industry 235610, Roofing, Siding, and Sheet Metal Contractors.

332115 Crown and Closure Manufacturing US

This U.S. industry comprises establishments primarily engaged in stamping metal crowns and closures, such as bottle caps and home canning lids and rings.

332116 Metal Stamping US

This U.S. industry comprises establishments primarily engaged in manufacturing unfinished metal stampings and spinning unfinished metal products (except crowns, cans, closures, automotive, and coins). Establishments making metal stampings and metal spun products and further manufacturing (e.g., machining, assembling) a specific product are classified in the industry of the finished product. Metal stamping and metal spun products establishments may perform surface finishing operations, such as cleaning and deburring, on the products they manufacture.

- Stamping automotive stampings are classified in Industry 336370, Motor Vehicle Metal Stamping;
- Stamping metal crowns and closures are classified in U.S. Industry 332115, Crown and Closure Manufacturing;
- Manufacturing metal cans are classified in U.S. Industry 332431, Metal Can Manufacturing; and
- Stamping coins are classified in U.S. Industry 339911, Jewelry (except Costume) Manufacturing.

332117 Powder Metallurgy Part Manufacturing US

This U.S. industry comprises establishments primarily engaged in manufacturing powder metallurgy products by compacting them in a shaped die and sintering. Establishments in this industry generally make a wide range of parts on a job or order basis.

3322 Cutlery and Handtool Manufacturing

33221 Cutlery and Handtool Manufacturing

This industry comprises establishments primarily engaged in one or more of the following: (1) manufacturing nonprecious and precious plated metal cutlery and flatware; (2) manufacturing nonpowered hand and edge tools, (3) manufacturing nonpowered handsaws; (4) manufacturing saw blades, all types (including those for sawing machines); and (5) manufacturing metal kitchen utensils (except cutting-type) and pots and pans (except those manufactured by casting (e.g., cast iron skillets) or stamped without further fabrication).

- Manufacturing precious (except precious plated) metal cutlery and flatware are classified in Industry 33991, Jewelry and Silverware Manufacturing;
- Manufacturing electric razors and hair clippers for use on humans are classified in Industry 33521, Small Electrical Appliance Manufacturing;

Visit page 17 to learn about classification changes to this sector.

Manufacturing

■ = Cross-References

US—United States industry only. CAN—United States and Canadian industries are comparable. When neither US nor CAN appears, Canadian, Mexican, and United States industries are comparable.

www.harrisinfo.com

 387

■ Manufacturing power hedge shears and trimmers and electric hair clippers for use on animals are classified in Industry 33311, Agricultural Implement Manufacturing;

■ Manufacturing metal cutting dies, attachments, and accessories for machine tools are classified in Industry 33351, Metalworking Machinery Manufacturing;

■ Manufacturing handheld power-driven handtools are classified in Industry 33399, All Other General Purpose Machinery Manufacturing; and

■ Manufacturing finished cast iron kitchen utensils (i.e., cast iron skillets) and castings for kitchen utensils, pots, and pans are classified in Industry Group 3315, Foundries.

332211 Cutlery and Flatware (except Precious) Manufacturing ᵘˢ

This U.S. industry comprises establishments primarily engaged in manufacturing nonprecious and precious plated metal cutlery and flatware.

■ Manufacturing precious (except precious plated) metal cutlery and flatware are classified in U.S. Industry 339912, Silverware and Hollowware Manufacturing;

■ Manufacturing electric razors and hair clippers for use on humans and housewares are classified in U.S. Industry 335211, Electric Housewares and Household Fan Manufacturing;

■ Manufacturing power hedge shears and trimmers and electric hair clippers for animal use are classified in U.S. Industry 333112, Lawn and Garden Tractor and Home Lawn and Garden Equipment Manufacturing; and

■ Manufacturing nonelectric hair clippers for use on animals are classified in U.S. Industry 332212, Hand and Edge Tool Manufacturing.

332212 Hand and Edge Tool Manufacturing ᵘˢ

This industry comprises establishments primarily engaged in manufacturing nonpowered hand and edge tools (except saws).

■ Manufacturing saw blades and handsaws are classified in U.S. Industry 332213, Saw Blade and Handsaw Manufacturing;

■ Manufacturing metal cutting dies, attachments, and accessories for machine tools are classified in Industry 33351, Metalworking Machinery Manufacturing;

■ Manufacturing handheld power-driven handtools are classified in U.S. Industry 333991, Power-driven Handtool Manufacturing;

■ Manufacturing electric razors and hair clippers for use on humans are classified in U.S. Industry 335211, Electric Housewares and Household Fan Manufacturing;

■ Manufacturing electric hair clippers for use on animals are classified in U.S. Industry 333111, Farm Machinery and Equipment Manufacturing; and

■ Manufacturing nonelectric household-type scissors and shears are classified in U.S. Industry 332211, Cutlery and Flatware (except Precious) Manufacturing.

332213 Saw Blade and Handsaw Manufacturing ᵘˢ

This U.S. industry comprises establishments primarily engaged in (1) manufacturing nonpowered handsaws and/or (2) manufacturing saw blades, all types (including those for power sawing machines).

■ Establishments primarily engaged in manufacturing handheld powered saws are classified in U.S. Industry 333991, Power-driven Handtool Manufacturing.

332214 Kitchen Utensil, Pot, and Pan Manufacturing ᵘˢ

This U.S. industry comprises establishments primarily engaged in manufacturing metal kitchen utensils (except cutting-type), pots, and pans (except those manufactured by casting (e.g., cast iron skillets) or stamped without further fabrication).

■ Manufacturing finished cast metal kitchen utensils or castings for kitchen utensils are classified in Industry Group 3315, Foundries;

■ Manufacturing stampings for kitchen utensils, pots, and pans are classified in U.S. Industry 332116, Metal Stamping; and

■ Manufacturing metal cutting-type kitchen utensils are classified in U.S. Industry 332211, Cutlery and Flatware (except Precious) Manufacturing.

3323 Architectural and Structural Metals Manufacturing

33231 Plate Work and Fabricated Structural Product Manufacturing

This industry comprises establishments primarily engaged in manufacturing one or more of the following: (1) prefabricated metal buildings, panels and sections; (2) structural metal products; and (3) metal plate work products.

■ Making manufactured homes (i.e., mobile homes) and prefabricated wood buildings are classified in Industry 32199, All Other Wood Product Manufacturing;

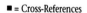 = Cross-References

Sector
31-33
Manufacturing

US—United States industry only. CAN—United States and Canadian industries are comparable. When neither US nor CAN appears, Canadian, Mexican, and United States industries are comparable.

388

Harris InfoSource

- Constructing buildings, bridges, and other heavy construction projects on site are classified in Sector 23, Construction;
- Building ships, boats and barges are classified in Industry 33661, Ship and Boat Building;
- Manufacturing power boilers and heat exchangers are classified in Industry 33241, Power Boiler and Heat Exchanger Manufacturing;
- Manufacturing heavy gauge tanks are classified in Industry 33242, Metal Tank (Heavy Gauge) Manufacturing;
- Manufacturing metal plate cooling towers are classified in Industry 33341, Ventilation, Heating, Air-conditioning, and Commercial Refrigeration Equipment Manufacturing; and
- Manufacturing metal windows, doors and studs are classified in Industry 33232, Ornamental and Architectural Metal Products Manufacturing.

332311 Prefabricated Metal Building and Component Manufacturing CAN

This U.S. industry comprises establishments primarily engaged in manufacturing prefabricated metal buildings, panels and sections.

- Making manufactured homes (i.e., mobile homes) and prefabricated wood buildings are classified in Industry 32199, All Other Wood Product Manufacturing;
- Constructing prefabricated buildings on site are classified in Industry Group 233, Building, Developing, and General Contracting; and
- Manufacturing metal windows and doors are classified in U.S. Industry 332321, Metal Window and Door Manufacturing.

332312 Fabricated Structural Metal Manufacturing US

This U.S. industry comprises establishments primarily engaged in fabricating structural metal products, such as concrete reinforcing bars and fabricated bar joists.

- Manufacturing metal windows and doors are classified in U.S. Industry 332321, Metal Window and Door Manufacturing;
- Manufacturing metal studs are classified in U.S. Industry 332322, Sheet Metal Work Manufacturing;
- Constructing buildings, bridges and other heavy construction projects on site are classified in Sector 23, Construction;
- Building ships, boats and barges are classified in Industry 33661, Ship and Boat Building; and
- Prefabricating metal buildings, panels and sections are classified in U.S. Industry 332311, Prefabricated Metal Building and Component Manufacturing.

332313 Plate Work Manufacturing US

This industry comprises establishments primarily engaged in manufacturing fabricated metal plate work by cutting, punching, bending, shaping, and welding purchased metal plate.

- Manufacturing power boilers and heat exchangers are classified in Industry 332410, Power Boiler and Heat Exchanger Manufacturing;
- Manufacturing heavy gauge tanks are classified in Industry 332420, Metal Tank (Heavy Gauge) Manufacturing; and
- Manufacturing metal plate cooling towers are classified in U.S. Industry 333415, Air-conditioning and Warm Air Heating Equipment and Commercial and Industrial Refrigeration Equipment Manufacturing.

33232 Ornamental and Architectural Metal Products Manufacturing

This industry comprises establishments primarily engaged in manufacturing one or more of the following: (1) metal framed windows (i.e., typically using purchased glass) and metal doors; (2) sheet metal work; and (3) ornamental and architectural metal products.

- Manufacturing metal covered (i.e., clad) wood windows and doors are classified in Industry 32191, Millwork;
- Manufacturing bins, cans, vats, and light tanks of sheet metal are classified in Industry 33243, Metal Can, Box, and Other Metal Container (Light Gauge) Manufacturing;
- Manufacturing prefabricated metal buildings, panels, and sections are classified in Industry 33231, Plate Work and Fabricated Structural Product Manufacturing;
- Fabricating sheet metal work on site are classified in Sector 23, Construction;
- Manufacturing metal stampings (except automotive, coins) and custom roll forming products are classified in Industry 33211, Forging and Stamping;
- Manufacturing automotive stampings are classified in Industry 33637, Motor Vechile Metal Stamping; and
- Stamping coins are classified in Industry 33991, Jewelry and Silverware Manufacturing.

332321 Metal Window and Door Manufacturing CAN

This U.S. industry comprises establishments primarily engaged in manufacturing metal framed windows (i.e., typically using purchased glass) and metal doors. Examples of products made by these establishments are metal door frames; metal framed window and door screens; metal molding and trim (except automotive); and metal curtain walls.

- Manufacturing wood or metal covered (i.e., clad) wood framed windows and doors are classified in U.S. Industry 321911, Wood Window and Door Manufacturing; and
- Manufacturing metal automotive molding and trim are classified in Industry 336370, Motor Vehicle Metal Stamping.

Visit page 17 to learn about classification changes to this sector.

Sector 31-33

Manufacturing

■ = Cross-References

US—United States industry only. CAN—United States and Canadian industries are comparable. When neither US nor CAN appears, Canadian, Mexican, and United States industries are comparable.

332322 Sheet Metal Work Manufacturing ^{US}

This U.S. industry comprises establishments primarily engaged in manufacturing sheet metal work (except stampings).

- Manufacturing sheet metal bins, vats and light tanks of sheet metal are classified in U.S. Industry 332439, Other Metal Container Manufacturing;
- Manufacturing metal cans, lids, and ends are classified in U.S. Industry 332431, Metal Can Manufacturing;
- Fabricating sheet metal work on site are classified in Sector 23, Construction;
- Manufacturing metal stampings (except automotive, coins) and custom roll forming products are classified in Industry 33211, Forging and Stamping;
- Manufacturing automotive stampings are classified in Industry 336370, Motor Vehicle Metal Stamping; and
- Stamping coins are classified in U.S. Industry 339911, Jewelry (except Costume) Manufacturing.

332323 Ornamental and Architectural Metal Work Manufacturing ^{US}

This U.S. industry comprises establishments primarily engaged in manufacturing ornamental and architectural metal work, such as staircases, metal open steel flooring, fire escapes, railings, and scaffolding.

- Establishments primarily engaged in manufacturing prefabricated metal buildings, panels, and sections are classified in U.S. Industry 332311, Prefabricated Metal Building and Component Manufacturing.

3324 Boiler, Tank, and Shipping Container Manufacturing

33241 Power Boiler and Heat Exchanger Manufacturing

See industry description for 332410 below.

332410 Power Boiler and Heat Exchanger Manufacturing

This industry comprises establishments primarily engaged in manufacturing power boilers and heat exchangers. Establishments in this industry may perform installation in addition to manufacturing power boilers and heat exchangers.

- Manufacturing heavy gauge metal tanks are classified in Industry 332420, Metal Tank (Heavy Gauge) Manufacturing;
- Manufacturing stream or hot water low pressure heating boilers are classified in U.S. Industry 333414, Heating Equipment (except Warm Air Furnaces) Manufacturing; and
- Installing power boilers and heat exchanges without manufacturing are classified in Industry 235110, Plumbing, Heating, and Air-conditioning Contractors.

33242 Metal Tank (Heavy Gauge) Manufacturing

See industry description for 332420 below.

332420 Metal Tank (Heavy Gauge) Manufacturing

This industry comprises establishments primarily engaged in cutting, forming, and joining heavy gauge metal to manufacture tanks, vessels, and other containers.

- Manufacturing power boilers are classified in Industry 332410, Power Boiler and Heat Exchanger Manufacturing;
- Manufacturing light gauge metal containers are classified in Industry 33243, Metal Can, Box, and Other Metal Container (Light Gauge) Manufacturing; and
- Installing heavy gauge metal tanks without manufacturing are classified in Sector 23, Construction.

33243 Metal Can, Box, and Other Metal Container (Light Gauge) Manufacturing

This industry comprises establishments primarily engaged in forming light gauge metal containers.

- Manufacturing foil containers are classified in Industry 33299, All Other Fabricated Metal Product Manufacturing;
- Reconditioning barrels and drums are classified in Industry 81131, Commercial and Industrial Machinery and Equipment (except Automotive and Electronic) Repair and Maintenance; and
- Manufacturing heavy gauge metal containers are classified in Industry 33242, Metal Tank (Heavy Gauge) Manufacturing.

332431 Metal Can Manufacturing ^{CAN}

This U.S. industry comprises establishments primarily engaged in manufacturing metal cans, lids, and ends.

- Manufacturing foil containers are classified in U.S. Industry 332999, All Other Miscellaneous-laneous Fabricated Metal Product Manufacturing; and
- Manufacturing light gauge metal containers (except cans) are classified in U.S. Industry 332439, Other Metal Container Manufacturing.

■ = Cross-References

Sector
31-33
Manufacturing

US—United States industry only. CAN—United States and Canadian industries are comparable. When neither US nor CAN appears, Canadian, Mexican, and United States industries are comparable.

390   Harris InfoSource

332439 Other Metal Container Manufacturing CAN

This U.S. industry comprises establishments primarily engaged in manufacturing metal (light gauge) containers (except cans).

- Manufacturing foil containers are classified in U.S. Industry 332999, All Other Miscellaneous-laneous Fabricated Metal Product Manufacturing;
- Manufacturing metal cans are classified in U.S. Industry 332431, Metal Can Manufacturing;
- Reconditioning barrels and drums are classified in Industry 811310, Commercial and Industrial Machinery and Equipment (except Automotive and Electronic) Repair and Maintenance; and
- Manufacturing heavy gauge metal containers are classified in Industry 332420, Metal Tank (Heavy Gauge) Manufacturing.

3325 Hardware Manufacturing

33251 Hardware Manufacturing
See industry description for 332510 below.

332510 Hardware Manufacturing

This industry comprises establishments primarily engaged in manufacturing metal hardware, such as metal hinges, metal handles, keys, and locks (except coin-operated, time locks).

- Manufacturing bolts, nuts, screws, rivets, washers, hose clamps, and turn buckles are classified in U.S. Industry 332722, Bolt, Nut, Screw, Rivet, and Washer Manufacturing;
- Manufacturing nails and spikes from wire drawn elsewhere are classified in U.S. Industry 332618, Other Fabricated Wire Product Manufacturing;
- Manufacturing metal furniture parts (except hardware) are classified in U.S. Industry 337215, Showcase, Partition, Shelving, and Locker Manufacturing;
- Drawing wire and manufacturing nails and spikes are classified in Subsector 331, Primary Metal Manufacturing;
- Manufacturing pole line and transmission hardware are classified in U.S. Industry 335932, Noncurrent-carrying Wiring Device Manufacturing;
- Manufacturing coin-operated locking mechanisms are classified in U.S. Industry 333311, Automatic Vending Machine Manufacturing;
- Manufacturing time locks are classified in U.S. Industry 334518, Watch, Clock, and Part Manufacturing;
- Manufacturing fireplace fixtures and equipment, traps, handcuffs and leg irons, ladder jacks, and other like metal products are classified in U.S. Industry 332999, All Other Miscellaneous Fabricated Metal Product Manufacturing;
- Manufacturing fire hose nozzles and couplings are classified in U.S. Industry 332919, Other Metal Valve and Pipe Fitting Manufacturing; and
- Manufacturing luggage and utility racks are classified in U.S. Industry 336399, All Other Motor Vehicle Parts Manufacturing.

3326 Spring and Wire Product Manufacturing

33261 Spring and Wire Product Manufacturing

This industry comprises establishments primarily engaged in (1) manufacturing steel springs by forming, such as cutting, bending, and heat winding metal rod or strip stock and/or (2) manufacturing wire springs and fabricated wire products from wire drawn elsewhere (except watch and clock springs).

- Manufacturing watch and clock springs from purchased wire are classified in Industry 33451, Navigational, Measuring, Electromedical, and Control Instruments Manufacturing;
- Drawing wire and manufacturing wire products are classified in Subsector 331, Primary Metal Manufacturing; and
- Manufacturing nonferrous insulated wire from wire drawn elsewhere are classified in Industry 33592, Communication and Energy Wire and Cable Manufacturing.

332611 Spring (Heavy Gauge) Manufacturing CAN

This U.S. industry comprises establishments primarily engaged in manufacturing heavy gauge springs by forming, such as cutting, bending, and heat winding rod or strip stock.

- Manufacturing light gauge springs from purchased wire or strip are classified in U.S. Industry 332612, Spring (Light Gauge) Manufacturing; and
- Drawing wire and manufacturing wire spring are classified in Subsector 331, Primary Metal Manufacturing.

332612 Spring (Light Gauge) Manufacturing US

This U.S. industry comprises establishments primarily engaged in manufacturing light gauge springs from purchased wire or strip.

- Manufacturing watch and clock springs are classified in U.S. Industry 334518, Watch, Clock, and Part Manufacturing;
- Manufacturing heavy gauge springs are classified in U.S. Industry 332611, Spring (Heavy Gauge) Manufacturing; and
- Drawing wire and manufacturing wire spring are classified in Subsector 331, Primary Metal Manufacturing.

Visit page 17 to learn about classification changes to this sector.

Sector
31-33
Manufacturing

■ = Cross-References

US—United States industry only. CAN—United States and Canadian industries are comparable. When neither US nor CAN appears, Canadian, Mexican, and United States industries are comparable.

www.harrisinfo.com 391

332618 Other Fabricated Wire Product Manufacturing ᵁˢ

This industry comprises establishments primarily engaged in manufacturing fabricated wire products (except springs) made from purchased wire.

- Drawing wire and manufacturing wire products are classified in Sector 331, Primary Metal Manufacturing;
- Manufacturing heavy gauge springs are classified in U.S. Industry 332611, Spring (Heavy Gauge) Manufacturing;
- Manufacturing light gauge springs from purchased wire or strip are classified in U.S. Industry 332612, Spring (Light Gauge) Manufacturing; and
- Insulating nonferrous wire from wire drawn elsewhere are classified in Industry 33592, Communication and Energy Wire and Cable Manufacturing.

3327 Machine Shops; Turned Product; and Screw, Nut, and Bolt Manufacturing

33271 Machine Shops
See industry description for 332710 below.

332710 Machine Shops

This industry comprises establishments known as machine shops primarily engaged in machining metal parts on a job or order basis. Generally machine shop jobs are low volume using machine tools, such as lathes (including computer numerically controlled); automatic screw machines; and machines for boring, grinding, and milling.

- Repairing industrial machinery and equipment are classified in Industry 81131, Commercial and Industrial Machinery and Equipment (except Automotive and Electronic) Repair and Maintenance; and
- Manufacturing parts (except on a job or order basis) for machinery and equipment are generally classified in the same manufacturing industry that makes complete machinery and equipment.

33272 Turned Product and Screw, Nut, and Bolt Manufacturing

This industry comprises establishments primarily engaged in (1) machining precision turned products or (2) manufacturing metal bolts, nuts, screws, rivets, and other industrial fasteners. Included in this industry are establishments primarily engaged manufacturing parts for machinery and equipment on a customized basis.

- Establishments primarily engaged in manufacturing plastics fasteners are classified in Industry 32619, Other Plastics Product Manufacturing.

332721 Precision Turned Product Manufacturing ᵁˢ

This U.S. industry comprises establishments known as precision turned manufacturers primarily engaged in machining precision products of all materials on a job or order basis. Generally precision turned product jobs are large volume using machines, such as automatic screw machines, rotary transfer machines, computer numerically controlled (CNC) lathes, or turning centers.

- Establishments primarily engaged in manufacturing metal bolts, nuts, screws, rivets, washers, and other industrial fasteners on machines, such as headers, threaders, and nut forming machines, are classified in U.S. Industry 332722, Bolt, Nut, Screw, Rivet, and Washer Manufacturing.

332722 Bolt, Nut, Screw, Rivet, and Washer Manufacturing ᵁˢ

This U.S. industry comprises establishments primarily engaged in manufacturing metal bolts, nuts, screws, rivets, and washers, and other industrial fasteners using machines, such as headers, threaders, and nut forming machines.

- Manufacturing precision turned products are classified in U.S. Industry 332721, Precision Turned Product Manufacturing; and
- Plastics fasteners are classified in U.S. Industry 326199, All Other Plastics Product Manufacturing.

3328 Coating, Engraving, Heat Treating, and Allied Activities

33281 Coating, Engraving, Heat Treating, and Allied Activities

This industry comprises establishments primarily engaged in one or more of the following: (1) heat treating metals and metal products; (2) enameling, lacquering, varnishing metals and metal products; (3) hot dip galvanizing metals and metal products; (4) engraving, chasing, or etching metals and metal products (except jewelry; personal goods carried on or about the person, such as compacts and cigarette cases; precious metal products (except precious plated flatware and other plated ware); and printing plates); (5) powder coating metals and metal products; (6) electroplating, plating, anodizing, coloring,

Sector
31-33

Manufacturing

■ = Cross-References

US—United States industry only. CAN—United States and Canadian industries are comparable. When neither US nor CAN appears, Canadian, Mexican, and United States industries are comparable.

392

Harris InfoSource

and finishing metals and metal products; and (7) providing other metal surfacing services for the trade. Establishments in this industry coat engravings and heat treat metals and metal formed products fabricated elsewhere.

- Engraving, chasing or etching jewelry, metal personal goods, or precious (except precious plated) metal flatware and other plated ware are classified in Industry 33991, Jewelry and Silverware Manufacturing;
- Engraving, chasing or etching printing plates are classified in Industry 32312, Support Activities for Printing; and
- Both fabricating and coating, engraving, and heat treating metals and metal products are classified in manufacturing according to the product made.

332811 Metal Heat Treating [US]
This U.S. industry comprises establishments primarily engaged in heat treating, such as annealing, tempering, and brazing, metals and metal products for the trade.

- Establishments primarily engaged in both fabricating and heat treating metal products are classified in the Manufacturing sector according to the product made.

332812 Metal Coating, Engraving (except Jewelry and Silverware), and Allied Services to Manufacturers [US]
This U.S. industry comprises establishments primarily engaged in one or more of the following: (1) enameling, lacquering, and varnishing metals and metal products; (2) hot dip galvanizing metals and metal products; (3) engraving, chasing, or etching metals and metal products (except jewelry; personal goods carried on or about the person, such as compacts and cigarette cases; precious metal products (except precious plated flatware and other plated ware); and printing plates); (4) powder coating metals and metal products; and (5) providing other metal surfacing services for the trade.

- Both fabricating and coating and engraving products are classified in the Manufacturing sector according to the product made;
- Engraving, chasing or etching jewelry, metal personal goods, or precious metal products (except precious plated metal flatware and other plated ware) are classified in Industry 33991, Jewelry and Silverware Manufacturing; and
- Engraving, chasing or etching printing plates are classified in U.S. Industry 323122, Prepress Services.

332813 Electroplating, Plating, Polishing, Anodizing, and Coloring [US]
This U.S. industry comprises establishments primarily engaged in electroplating, plating, anodizing, coloring, buffing, polishing, cleaning, and sandblasting metals and metal products for the trade.

- Establishments primarily engaged in both fabricating and electroplating, plating, polishing, anodizing, and coloring products are classified in the Manufacturing sector according to the product made.

Visit page 17 to learn about classification changes to this sector.

3329 Other Fabricated Metal Product Manufacturing
This industry group comprises establishments primarily engaged in manufacturing fabricated metal products (except forgings and stampings, cutlery and handtools, architectural and structural metals, boilers, tanks, shipping containers, hardware, spring and wire products, machine shop products, turned products, screws, and nuts and bolts).

33291 Metal Valve Manufacturing
This industry comprises establishments primarily engaged in manufacturing one or more of the following metal valves: (1) industrial valves; (2) fluid power valves and hose fittings, (3) plumbing fixture fittings and trim; and (4) other metal valves and pipe fittings.

- Manufacturing fluid power cylinder and pumps are classified in Industry 33399, All Other General Purpose Machinery Manufacturing;
- Manufacturing intake and exhaust valves for internal combustion engines are classified in Industry 33631, Motor Vehicle Gasoline Engine and Engine Parts Manufacturing;
- Manufacturing metal shower rods and metal couplings from purchased metal pipe are classified in Industry 33299, All Other Fabricated Metal Product Manufacturing;
- Manufacturing plastics aerosol spray nozzles are classified in Industry 32619, Other Plastics Product Manufacturing;
- Casting iron pipe fittings and couplings without machining are classified in Industry 33151, Ferrous Metal Foundries; and
- Manufacturing plastics pipe fittings and couplings are classified in Industry 32612, Plastics Pipe, Pipe Fitting, and Unsupported Profile Shape Manufacturing.

332911 Industrial Valve Manufacturing [US]
This U.S. industry comprises establishments primarily engaged in manufacturing industrial valves and valves for water works and municipal water systems.

Sector
31-33
Manufacturing

■ = Cross-References

US—United States industry only. CAN—United States and Canadian industries are comparable. When neither US nor CAN appears, Canadian, Mexican, and United States industries are comparable.

www.harrisinfo.com

393

■ Manufacturing fluid power valves are classified in U.S. Industry 332912, Fluid Power Valve and Hose Fitting Manufacturing; and
■ Manufacturing plumbing and heating valves are classified in U.S. Industry 332919, Other Metal Valve and Pipe Fitting Manufacturing.

332912 Fluid Power Valve and Hose Fitting Manufacturing ᵁˢ

This U.S. industry comprises establishments primarily engaged in manufacturing fluid power valves and hose fittings.

■ Manufacturing fluid power cylinders are classified in U.S. Industry 333995, Fluid Power Cylinder and Actuator Manufacturing;
■ Manufacturing fluid power pumps are classified in U.S. Industry 333996, Fluid Power Pump and Motor Manufacturing;
■ Manufacturing intake and exhaust valves for internal combustion engines are classified in U.S. Industry 336311, Carburetor, Piston, Piston Ring, and Valve Manufacturing;
■ Manufacturing industrial-type valves are classified in U.S. Industry 332911, Industrial Valve Manufacturing; and
■ Manufacturing plumbing and heating valves are classified in U.S. Industry 332919, Other Metal Valve and Pipe Fitting Manufacturing.

332913 Plumbing Fixture Fitting and Trim Manufacturing ᵁˢ

This U.S. industry comprises establishments primarily engaged in manufacturing metal and plastics plumbing fixture fittings and trim, such as faucets, flush valves, and shower heads.

■ Manufacturing metal shower rods are classified in U.S. Industry 332999, All Other Miscellaneous Fabricated Metal Product Manufacturing; and
■ Manufacturing fire hose nozzles, lawn hose nozzles, water traps, and couplings are classified in U.S. Industry 332919, Other Metal Valve and Pipe Fitting Manufacturing.

332919 Other Metal Valve and Pipe Fitting Manufacturing ᵁˢ

This U.S. industry comprises establishments primarily engaged in manufacturing metal valves (except industrial valves, fluid power valves, fluid power hose fittings, and plumbing fixture fittings and trim).

■ Manufacturing fluid power valves and hose fittings are classified in U.S. Industry 332912, Fluid Power Valve and Hose Fitting Manufacturing;
■ Manufacturing industrial valves are classified in U.S. Industry 332911, Industrial Valve Manufacturing;
■ Manufacturing plastics aerosol spray nozzles are classified in U.S. Industry 326199, All Other Plastics Product Manufacturing;
■ Casting iron pipe fittings and couplings without machining are classified in U.S. Industry 331511, Iron Foundries;
■ Manufacturing metal couplings from purchased metal pipe are classified in U.S. Industry 332996, Fabricated Pipe and Pipe Fitting Manufacturing; and
■ Manufacturing plastics pipe fittings and couplings are classified in U.S. Industry 326122, Plastics Pipe and Pipe Fitting Manufacturing.

33299 All Other Fabricated Metal Product Manufacturing

This industry comprises establishments primarily engaged in manufacturing fabricated metal products (except forgings and stampings, cutlery and handtools, architectural and structural metal products, boilers, tanks, shipping containers, hardware, spring and wire products, machine shop products, turned products, screws, nuts and bolts, and metal valves).

■ Manufacturing forging and stamping and powder metallurgy parts are classified in Industry 33211, Forging and Stamping;
■ Manufacturing cutlery and handtools are classified in Industry 33221, Cutlery and Handtool Manufacturing;
■ Manufacturing architectural and structural metals are classified in Industry Group 3323, Architectural and Structural Metals Manufacturing;
■ Manufacturing boilers, tanks, and shipping containers are classified in Industry Group 3324, Boiler, Tank, and Shipping Container Manufacturing;
■ Manufacturing hardware and safe and vault locks are classified in Industry 33251, Hardware Manufacturing;
■ Manufacturing spring and wire products are classified in Industry 33261, Spring and Wire Product Manufacturing;
■ Manufacturing machine shop products, turned products, screws, and nuts and bolts are classified in Industry Group 3327, Machine Shops; Turned Product; and Screw, Nut, and Bolt Manufacturing;
■ Coating, engraving, heat treating and allied activities are classified in Industry 33281, Coating, Engraving, Heat Treating, and Allied Activities;
■ Manufacturing plain bearings are classified in Industry 33361, Engine, Turbine, and Power Transmission Equipment Manufacturing;
■ Manufacturing military tanks are classified in Industry 33699, Other Transportation Equipment Manufacturing;
■ Manufacturing guided missiles are classified in Industry 33641, Aerospace Product and Parts Manufacturing;
■ Manufacturing cast iron pipe and fittings are classified in Industry 33151, Ferrous Metal Foundries;
■ Manufacturing pipe system fittings (except cast iron couplings and couplings made from purchased pipe) and metal aerosol spray nozzles are classified in Industry 33291, Metal Valve Manufacturing;
■ Manufacturing welded and seamless steel pipes from purchased steel are classified in Industry 33121, Iron and Steel Pipe and Tube Manufacturing from Purchased Steel;
■ Manufacturing plastics plumbing fixtures and plastics portable chemical toilets are classified in Industry 32619, Other Plastics Product Manufacturing;

Sector 31-33

Manufacturing

■ = Cross-References

US—United States industry only. CAN—United States and Canadian industries are comparable. When neither US nor CAN appears, Canadian, Mexican, and United States industries are comparable.

394

Harris InfoSource

- Manufacturing vitreous and semivitreous pottery sanitary ware are classified in Industry 32711, Pottery, Ceramics, and Plumbing Fixture Manufacturing;
- Manufacturing blasting caps, detonating caps, and safety fuses are classified in Industry 32592, Explosives Manufacturing;
- Manufacturing fireworks are classified in Industry 32599, All Other Chemical Product and Preparation Manufacturing;
- Manufacturing metal furniture frames are classified in Industry 33721, Office Furniture (including Fixtures) Manufacturing;
- Manufacturing nonprecious metal trophies are classified in Industry 33991, Jewelry and Silverware Manufacturing;
- Manufacturing metal mechanically refrigerated drinking fountains are classified in Industry 33341, Ventilation, Heating, Air-conditioning, and Commercial Refrigeration Equipment Manufacturing;
- Manufacturing metal foil bags are classified in Industry 32222, Paper Bag and Coated and Treated Paper Manufacturing;
- Manufacturing aluminum foil are classified in Industry 33131, Alumina and Aluminum Production and Processing;
- Manufacturing metal foil (except aluminum) are classified in Industry Group 3314, Nonferrous Metal (except Aluminum) Production and Process; and
- Manufacturing metal burial vaults are classified in Industry 33999, All Other Miscellaneous Manufacturing.

332991 Ball and Roller Bearing Manufacturing CAN

This U.S. industry comprises establishments primarily engaged in manufacturing ball and roller bearings of all materials.

- Establishments primarily engaged in manufacturing plain bearings are classified in U.S. Industry 333613, Mechanical Power Transmission Equipment Manufacturing.

332992 Small Arms Ammunition Manufacturing US

This U.S. industry comprises establishments primarily engaged in manufacturing small arms ammunition.

- Manufacturing ammunition (except small arms) are classified in U.S. Industry 332993, Ammunition (except Small Arms) Manufacturing;
- Manufacturing blasting and detonating caps and safety fuses are classified in Industry 325920, Explosives Manufacturing; and
- Manufacturing fireworks are classified in U.S. Industry 325998, All Other Miscellaneous Chemical Product and Preparation Manufacturing.

332993 Ammunition (except Small Arms) Manufacturing US

This U.S. industry comprises establishments primarily engaged in manufacturing ammunition (except small arms). Examples of products made by these establishments are bombs, depth charges, rockets (except guided missiles), grenades, mines, and torpedoes.

- Manufacturing small arms ammunition are classified in U.S. Industry 332992, Small Arms Ammunition Manufacturing;
- Manufacturing blasting and detonating caps and safety fuses are classified in Industry 325920, Explosives Manufacturing;
- Manufacturing fireworks are classified in U.S. Industry 325998, All Other Miscellaneous Chemical Product and Preparation Manufacturing; and
- Manufacturing guided missiles are classified in U.S. Industry 336414, Guided Missile and Space Vehicle Manufacturing.

332994 Small Arms Manufacturing US

This U.S. industry comprises establishments primarily engaged in manufacturing small firearms that are carried and fired by the individual.

- Establishments primarily engaged in manufacturing firearms (except small) are classified in U.S. Industry 332995, Other Ordnance and Accessories Manufacturing.

332995 Other Ordnance and Accessories Manufacturing US

This U.S. industry comprises establishments primarily engaged in manufacturing ordnance (except small arms) and accessories.

- Manufacturing small arms are classified in U.S. Industry 332994, Small Arms Manufacturing;
- Manufacturing military tanks are classified in U.S. Industry 336992, Military Armored Vehicle, Tank, and Tank Component Manufacturing; and
- Manufacturing guided missiles are classified in U.S. Industry 336414, Guided Missile and Space Vehicle Manufacturing.

332996 Fabricated Pipe and Pipe Fitting Manufacturing US

This U.S. industry comprises establishments primarily engaged in fabricating (such as cutting, threading and bending) metal pipes and pipe fittings made from purchased metal pipe.

- Manufacturing cast iron pipe and fittings are classified in U.S. Industry 331511, Iron Foundries;
- Manufacturing pipe system fittings (except cast iron couplings) are classified in U.S. Industry 332919, Other Metal Valve and Pipe Fitting Manufacturing; and
- Manufacturing welded and seamless steel pipes from purchased steel are classified in Industry 331210, Iron and Steel Pipe and Tube Manufacturing from Purchased Steel.

Visit page 17 to learn about classification changes to this sector.

Sector 31-33

Manufacturing

■ = Cross-References

US—United States industry only. CAN—United States and Canadian industries are comparable. When neither US nor CAN appears, Canadian, Mexican, and United States industries are comparable.

332997 Industrial Pattern Manufacturing ᵁˢ

This U.S. industry comprises establishments primarily engaged in manufacturing industrial patterns.

332998 Enameled Iron and Metal Sanitary Ware Manufacturing ᵁˢ

This U.S. industry comprises establishments primarily engaged in manufacturing enameled iron and metal sanitary ware.

- Manufacturing plastics plumbing fixtures are classified in U.S. Industry 326191, Plastics Plumbing Fixture Manufacturing;
- Manufacturing vitreous and semivitreous pottery sanitary ware are classified in U.S. Industry 327111, Vitreous China Plumbing Fixture and China and Earthenware Bathroom Accessories Manufacturing;
- Manufacturing plastics portable chemical toilets are classified in U.S. Industry 326199, All Other Plastics Product Manufacturing; and
- Manufacturing metal mechanically refrigerated drinking fountains are classified in U.S. Industry 333415, Air-conditioning and Warm Air Heating Equipment and Commercial and Industrial Refrigeration Equipment Manufacturing.

332999 All Other Miscellaneous Fabricated Metal Product Manufacturing ᵁˢ

This U.S. industry comprises establishments primarily engaged in manufacturing fabricated metal products (except forgings and stampings, cutlery and handtools, architectural and structural metals, boilers, tanks, shipping containers, hardware, spring and wire products, machine shop products, turned products, screws, nuts and bolts, metal valves, ball and roller bearings, ammunition, small arms and other ordnances, fabricated pipes and pipe fittings, industrial patterns, and enameled iron and metal sanitary ware).

- Manufacturing forgings and stampings are classified in Industry 33211, Forgings and Stampings;
- Manufacturing cutlery and handtools are classified in Industry 33221, Cutlery and Handtool Manufacturing;
- Manufacturing architectural and structural metals are classified in Industry Group 3323, Architectural and Structural Metals Manufacturing;
- Manufacturing boilers, tanks, and shipping containers are classified in Industry Group 3324, Boiler, Tank, and Shipping Container Manufacturing;
- Manufacturing hardware and safe and vault locks are classified in Industry 332510, Hardware Manufacturing;
- Manufacturing spring and wire products are classified in Industry 33261, Spring and Wire Product Manufacturing;
- Manufacturing machine shop products, turned products, screws, and nut and bolt are classified in Industry Group 3327, Machine Shops; Turned Product; and Screw Nut, and Bolt Manufacturing;
- Coating, engraving, heat treating and allied activities are classified in Industry 33281, Coating, Engraving, Heat Treating, and Allied Activities;
- Manufacturing ball and roller bearings are classified in U.S. Industry 332991, Ball and Roller Bearing Manufacturing;
- Manufacturing small arms ammunition are classified in U.S. Industry 332992, Small Arms Ammunition Manufacturing;
- Manufacturing ammunition (except small arms) are classified in U.S. Industry 332993, Ammunition (except Small Arms) Manufacturing;
- Manufacturing small firearms that are carried and fired by the individual are classified in U.S. Industry 332994, Small Arms Manufacturing;
- Manufacturing ordnances (except small) and accessories are classified in U.S. Industry 332995, Other Ordnance and Accessories Manufacturing;
- Manufacturing metal pipes and pipe fittings from metal pipe produced elsewhere are classified in U.S. Industry 332996, Fabricated Pipe and Pipe Fitting Manufacturing;
- Manufacturing cast iron pipe and fittings are classified in U.S. Industry 331511, Iron Foundries;
- Manufacturing welded and seamless steel pipes from purchased steel are classified in Industry 331210, Iron and Steel Pipe and Tube Manufacturing form Purchased Steel;
- Manufacturing metal furniture frames are classified in U.S. 337215, Showcase, Partition, Shelving, and Locker Manufacturing;
- Manufacturing powder metallurgy parts are classified in U.S. Industry 332117, Powder Metallurgy Part Manufacturing;
- Manufacturing metal boxes are classified in U.S. Industry 332439, Other Metal Container Manufacturing;
- Manufacturing metal nozzles, hose couplings, and aerosol valves are classified in U.S. Industry 332919, Other Metal Valve and Pipe Fitting Manufacturing;
- Manufacturing nonprecious metal trophies are classified in U.S. Industry 339914, Costume Jewelry and Novelty Manufacturing;
- Manufacturing metal foil bags are classified in U.S Industry 322223, Plastics, Foil, and Coated Paper Bag Manufacturing;
- Manufacturing aluminum foil are classified in Industry 33131, Alumina and Aluminum Production and Processing;
- Manufacturing metal foil (except aluminum) are classified in Industry Group 3314, Nonferrous Metal (except Aluminum) Production and Processing; and
- Manufacturing metal burial vaults are classified in U.S. Industry 339995, Burial Casket Manufacturing.

▶333 MACHINERY MANUFACTURING

Industries in the Machinery Manufacturing subsector create end products that apply mechanical force, for example, the application of gears and levers, to perform work. Some important processes for the manufacture of machinery are forging, stamping, bending, forming, and machining that are used to shape

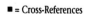

Sector
31-33
Manufacturing

■ = Cross-References

US—United States industry only. CAN—United States and Canadian industries are comparable. When neither US nor CAN appears, Canadian, Mexican, and United States industries are comparable.

396

Harris InfoSource

individual pieces of metal. Processes, such as welding and assembling are used to join separate parts together. Although these processes are similar to those used in metal fabricating establishments, machinery manufacturing is different because it typically employs multiple metal forming processes in manufacturing the various parts of the machine. Moreover, complex assembly operations are an inherent part of the production process.

In general, design considerations are very important in machinery production. Establishments specialize in making machinery designed for particular applications. Thus, design is considered to be part of the production process for the purpose of implementing NAICS. The NAICS structure reflects this by defining industries and industry groups that make machinery for different applications. A broad distinction exists between machinery that is generally used in a variety of industrial applications (i.e., general purpose machinery) and machinery that is designed to be used in a particular industry (i.e., special purpose machinery). Three industry groups consist of special purpose machinery—Agricultural, Construction, and Mining Machinery Manufacturing; Industrial Machinery Manufacturing; and Commercial and Service Industry Machinery Manufacturing. The other industry groups make general-purpose machinery: Ventilation, Heating, Air Conditioning, and Commercial Refrigeration Equipment Manufacturing; Metalworking Machinery Manufacturing; Engine, Turbine, and Power Transmission Equipment Manufacturing; and Other General Purpose Machinery Manufacturing.

3331 Agriculture, Construction, and Mining Machinery Manufacturing

33311 Agricultural Implement Manufacturing
This industry comprises establishments primarily engaged in manufacturing farm machinery and equipment, powered mowing equipment and other powered home lawn and garden equipment.

- Manufacturing agricultural handtools and nonpowered lawnmowers are classified in Industry 33221, Cutlery and Handtool Manufacturing;
- Manufacturing farm conveyors are classified in Industry 33392, Material Handling Equipment Manufacturing; and
- Manufacturing forestry machinery and equipment such as brush, limb and log chippers; log splitters; and equipment are classified in Industry 33312, Construction Machinery Manufacturing.

333111 Farm Machinery and Equipment Manufacturing US
This U.S. industry comprises establishments primarily engaged in manufacturing agricultural and farm machinery and equipment, and other turf and grounds care equipment, including planting, harvesting, and grass mowing equipment (except lawn and garden-type).

- Manufacturing farm conveyors are classified in U.S. Industry 333922, Conveyor and Conveying Equipment Manufacturing;
- Manufacturing tractors and lawnmowers for home lawn and garden care are classified in U.S. Industry 333112, Lawn and Garden Tractor and Home Lawn and Garden Equipment Manufacturing; and
- Manufacturing construction-type tractors are classified in Industry 333120, Construction Machinery Manufacturing.

333112 Lawn and Garden Tractor and Home Lawn and Garden Equipment Manufacturing US
This U.S. industry comprises establishments primarily engaged in manufacturing powered lawnmowers, lawn and garden tractors, and other home lawn and garden equipment, such as tillers, shredders, and yard vacuums and blowers.

- Manufacturing commercial mowing and other turf and grounds care equipment are classified in U.S. Industry 333111, Farm Machinery and Equipment Manufacturing; and
- Manufacturing nonpowered lawn and garden shears, edgers, pruners, and lawnmowers are classified in Industry 33221, Cutlery and Handtool Manufacturing.

33312 Construction Machinery Manufacturing
See industry description for 333120 below.

333120 Construction Machinery Manufacturing
This industry comprises establishments primarily engaged in manufacturing construction machinery, surface mining machinery, and logging equipment.

- Manufacturing drilling and underground mining machinery and equipment are classified in Industry 33313, Mining and Oil and Gas Field Machinery Manufacturing;

Visit page 17 to learn about classification changes to this sector.

Manufacturing

= Cross-References

US—United States industry only. CAN—United States and Canadian industries are comparable. When neither US nor CAN appears, Canadian, Mexican, and United States industries are comparable.

■ Manufacturing industrial plant overhead traveling cranes, hoists, truck-type cranes and hoists, winches, aerial work platforms, and automotive wrecker hoists are classified in Industry 33392, Material Handling Equipment Manufacturing; and
■ Manufacturing rail layers, ballast distributors and other railroad track-laying equipment are classified in Industry 336510, Railroad Rolling Stock Manufacturing.

33313 Mining and Oil and Gas Field Machinery Manufacturing

This industry comprises establishments primarily engaged in manufacturing oil and gas field and underground mining machinery and equipment.

■ Manufacturing offshore oil and gas well drilling and production floating platforms are classified in Industry 33661, Ship and Boat Building;
■ Manufacturing surface mining machinery and equipment are classified in Industry 33312, Construction Machinery Manufacturing;
■ Manufacturing coal and ore conveyors are classified in Industry 33392, Material Handling Equipment Manufacturing;
■ Manufacturing underground mining locomotives are classified in Industry 33651, Railroad Rolling Stock Manufacturing; and
■ Manufacturing pumps and pumping equipment are classified in Industry 33391, Pump and Compressor Manufacturing.

333131 Mining Machinery and Equipment Manufacturing ᵁˢ

This U.S. industry comprises establishments primarily engaged in (1) manufacturing underground mining machinery and equipment, such as coal breakers, mining cars, core drills, coal cutters, rock drills and (2) manufacturing mineral beneficiating machinery and equipment used in surface or underground mines.

■ Manufacturing surface mining machinery and equipment are classified in Industry 333120, Construction Machinery Manufacturing;
■ Manufacturing well-drilling machinery are classified in U.S. Industry 333132, Oil and Gas Field Machinery and Equipment Manufacturing;
■ Manufacturing coal and ore conveyors are classified in U.S. Industry 333922, Conveyor and Conveying Equipment Manufacturing; and
■ Manufacturing underground mining locomotives are classified in Industry 336510, Railroad Rolling Stock Manufacturing.

333132 Oil and Gas Field Machinery and Equipment Manufacturing ᵁˢ

This U.S. industry comprises establishments primarily engaged in (1) manufacturing oil and gas field machinery and equipment, such as oil and gas field drilling machinery and equipment; oil and gas field production machinery and equipment; and oil and gas field derricks and (2) manufacturing water well drilling machinery.

■ Manufacturing offshore oil and gas well drilling and production floating platforms are classified in U.S. Industry 336611, Ship Building and Repairing;
■ Manufacturing underground mining drills are classified in U.S. Industry 333131, Mining Machinery and Equipment Manufacturing; and
■ Manufacturing pumps and pumping equipment are classified in U.S. Industry 333911, Pump and Pumping Equipment Manufacturing.

3332 Industrial Machinery Manufacturing

33321 Sawmill and Woodworking Machinery Manufacturing
See industry description for 333210 below.

333210 Sawmill and Woodworking Machinery Manufacturing

This industry comprises establishments primarily engaged in manufacturing sawmill and woodworking machinery (except handheld), such as circular and band sawing equipment, planing machinery, and sanding machinery.

■ Manufacturing planes, axes, drawknives, and handsaws are classified in Industry 33221, Cutlery and Handtool Manufacturing; and
■ Manufacturing power-driven handtools are classified in U.S. Industry 333991, Power-driven Handtool Manufacturing.

33322 Plastics and Rubber Industry Machinery Manufacturing
See industry description for 333220 below.

333220 Plastics and Rubber Industry Machinery Manufacturing
This industry comprises establishments primarily engaged in manufacturing plastics and rubber products making machinery, such as plastics compression, extrusion and injection molding machinery

Sector
31-33
Manufacturing

■ = Cross-References

US—United States industry only. CAN—United States and Canadian industries are comparable. When neither US nor CAN appears, Canadian, Mexican, and United States industries are comparable.

and equipment, and tire building and recapping machinery and equipment.

- Establishments primarily engaged in manufacturing industrial metal molds for plastics and rubber products making machinery are classified in U.S. Industry 333511, Industrial Mold Manufacturing.

33329 Other Industrial Machinery Manufacturing

This industry comprises establishments primarily engaged in manufacturing industrial machinery (except agricultural and farm-type, construction, mining, sawmill and woodworking, and plastics and rubber products making machinery).

- Manufacturing agricultural and farm-type, construction, and mining machinery are classified in Industry Group 3331, Agriculture, Construction, and Mining Machinery Manufacturing;
- Manufacturing sawmill and woodworking machinery are classified in Industry 33321, Sawmill and Woodworking Machinery Manufacturing;
- Manufacturing plastics and rubber products making machinery are classified in Industry 33322, Plastics and Rubber Industry Machinery Manufacturing;
- Manufacturing food and beverage packaging machinery are classified in Industry 33399, All Other General Purpose Machinery Manufacturing;
- Manufacturing commercial and industrial refrigeration and freezer equipment are classified in Industry 33341, Ventilation, Heating, Air-conditioning, and Commercial Refrigeration Equipment Manufacturing;
- Manufacturing commercial-type cooking and food warming equipment, automotive maintenance equipment (except mechanics' handtools) and photocopiers are classified in Industry 33331, Commercial and Service Industry Machinery Manufacturing; and
- Manufacturing mechanics' handtools are classified in Industry 33221, Cutlery and Handtool Manufacturing.

333291 Paper Industry Machinery Manufacturing CAN

This U.S. industry comprises establishments primarily engaged in manufacturing paper industry machinery for making paper and paper products, such as pulp making machinery, paper and paperboard making machinery, and paper and paperboard converting machinery.

- Establishments primarily engaged in manufacturing printing machinery are classified in U.S. Industry 333293, Printing Machinery and Equipment Manufacturing.

333292 Textile Machinery Manufacturing US

This U.S. industry comprises establishments primarily engaged in manufacturing textile machinery for making thread, yarn, and fiber.

- Establishments primarily engaged in manufacturing sewing machines are classified in U.S. Industry 333298, All Other Industrial Machinery Manufacturing.

333293 Printing Machinery and Equipment Manufacturing US

This U.S. industry comprises establishments primarily engaged in manufacturing printing and bookbinding machinery and equipment, such as printing presses, typesetting machinery, and bindery machinery.

- Manufacturing textile printing machinery are classified in U.S. Industry 333292, Textile Machinery Manufacturing; and
- Manufacturing photocopiers are classified in U.S. Industry 333315, Photographic and Photocopying Equipment Manufacturing.

333294 Food Product Machinery Manufacturing US

This U.S. industry comprises establishments primarily engaged in manufacturing food and beverage manufacturing-type machinery and equipment, such as dairy product plant machinery and equipment (e.g., homogenizers, pasteurizers, ice cream freezers), bakery machinery and equipment (e.g., dough mixers, bake ovens, pastry rolling machines), meat and poultry processing and preparation machinery, and other commercial food products machinery (e.g., slicers, choppers, and mixers).

- Manufacturing food and beverage packaging machinery are classified in U.S. Industry 333993, Packaging Machinery Manufacturing;
- Manufacturing commercial and industrial refrigeration and freezer equipment are classified in U.S. Industry 333415, Air Conditioning and Warm Air Heating Equipment and Commercial and Industrial Refrigeration Equipment Manufacturing; and
- Manufacturing commercial-type cooking and food warming equipment are classified in U.S. Industry 333319, Other Commercial and Service Industry Machinery Manufacturing.

333295 Semiconductor Machinery Manufacturing US

This U.S. industry comprises establishments primarily engaged in manufacturing wafer processing equipment, semiconductor assembly and packaging equipment, and other semiconductor making machinery.

Visit page 17 to learn about classification changes to this sector.

Sector
31-33

Manufacturing

■ = Cross-References

US—United States industry only. CAN—United States and Canadian industries are comparable. When neither US nor CAN appears, Canadian, Mexican, and United States industries are comparable.

■ Manufacturing printed circuit board manufacturing machinery are classified in U.S. Industry 333298, All Other Industrial Machinery Manufacturing; and
■ Manufacturing semiconductor testing instruments are classified in U.S. Industry 334515, Instrument Manufacturing for Measuring and Testing Electricity and Electrical Signals.

333298 All Other Industrial Machinery Manufacturing US

This U.S. industry comprises establishments primarily engaged in manufacturing industrial machinery (except agricultural and farm-type, construction and mining machinery, sawmill and woodworking machinery, plastics and rubber making machinery, paper and paperboard making machinery, textile machinery, printing machinery and equipment, food manufacturing-type machinery, and semiconductor making machinery).

■ Manufacturing agricultural and farm-type, construction, and mining machinery are classified in Industry Group 3331, Agriculture, Construction, and Mining Machinery Manufacturing;
■ Manufacturing sawmill and woodworking machinery are classified in Industry 333210, Sawmill and Woodworking Machinery Manufacturing;
■ Manufacturing plastics and rubber products making machinery are classified in Industry 333220, Plastics and Rubber Industry Machinery Manufacturing;
■ Manufacturing paper and paperboard making machinery are classified in U.S. Industry 333291, Paper Industry Machinery Manufacturing;
■ Manufacturing textile machinery are classified in U.S. Industry 333292, Textile Machinery Manufacturing;
■ Manufacturing printing and bookbinding machinery and equipment are classified in U.S. Industry 333293, Printing Machinery and Equipment Manufacturing;
■ Manufacturing food and beverage manufacturing-type machinery are classified in U.S. Industry 333294, Food Product Machinery Manufacturing;
■ Manufacturing semiconductor making machinery are classified in U.S. Industry 333295, Semiconductor Machinery Manufacturing;
■ Manufacturing automotive maintenance equipment (except mechanics' handtools) are classified in U.S. Industry 333319, Other Commercial and Service Industry Machinery Manufacturing; and
■ Manufacturing mechanics' handtools are classified in U.S. Industry 332212, Hand and Edge Tool Manufacturing.

3333 Commercial and Service Industry Machinery Manufacturing

33331 Commercial and Service Industry Machinery Manufacturing

This industry comprises establishments primarily engaged in manufacturing commercial and service machinery, such as automatic vending machinery, commercial laundry and dry-cleaning machinery, office machinery, photographic and photocopying machinery, optical instruments and machinery, automotive maintenance equipment (except mechanic's handtools), industrial vacuum cleaners, and commercial-type cooking equipment.

■ Manufacturing household-type appliances are classified in Industry Group 3352, House-hold Appliance Manufacturing;
■ Manufacturing computer and peripheral equipment (including point-of-sale terminals and funds transfer devices (ATMs)) are classified in Industry 33411, Computer and Peripheral Equipment Manufacturing;
■ Manufacturing facsimile equipment are classified in Industry 33421, Telephone Apparatus Manufacturing;
■ Manufacturing timeclocks, timestamps, and electron and proton microscopes are classified in Industry 33451, Navigational, Measuring, Electromedical, and Control Instruments Manufacturing;
■ Manufacturing pencil sharpeners and staplers are classified in Industry 33994, Office Supplies (except Paper) Manufacturing;
■ Manufacturing sensitized film, paper, cloth, and plates, and prepared photographic chemicals are classified in Industry 32599, All Other Chemical Product and Preparation Manufacturing;
■ Manufacturing ophthalmic focus lenses are classified in Industry 33911, Medical Equipment and Supplies Manufacturing;
■ Manufacturing television, video, and digital cameras are classified in Subsector 334, Computer and Electronic Product Manufacturing;
■ Manufacturing coin-operated arcade games are classified in Industry 33999, All Other Miscellaneous Manufacturing;
■ Manufacturing mechanics' handtools are classified in Industry 33221, Cutlery and Handtool Manufacturing;
■ Manufacturing molded plastics lens blanks are classified in Industry 32619, Other Plastics Product Manufacturing; and
■ Manufacturing molded glass lens blanks are classified in Industry 32721, Glass and Glass Product Manufacturing.

333311 Automatic Vending Machine Manufacturing US

This U.S. industry comprises establishments primarily engaged in (1) manufacturing coin, token, currency or magnetic card operated vending machines and/or (2) manufacturing coin operated mechanism for machines, such as vending machines, lockers, and laundry machines.

■ Establishments primarily engaged in manufacturing coin-operated arcade games are classified in U.S. Industry 339999, All Other Miscellaneous Manufacturing.

■ = Cross-References

Sector
31-33
Manufacturing

US—United States industry only. CAN—United States and Canadian industries are comparable. When neither US nor CAN appears, Canadian, Mexican, and United States industries are comparable.

400

Harris InfoSource

333312 Commercial Laundry, Drycleaning, and Pressing Machine Manufacturing [US]

This U.S. industry comprises establishments primarily engaged in manufacturing commercial and industrial laundry and drycleaning equipment and pressing machines.

- Establishments primarily engaged in manufacturing household-type laundry equipment are classified in U.S. Industry 335224, Household Laundry Equipment Manufacturing.

333313 Office Machinery Manufacturing [US]

This U.S. industry comprises establishments primarily engaged in manufacturing office machinery (except computers and photocopying equipment), such as mailhandling machinery and equipment, calculators, typewriters, and dedicated word processing equipment.

- Manufacturing computers and peripheral (including point-of-sale terminals and automatic teller machines (ATMs)) equipment are classified in Industry 33411, Computer and Peripheral Equipment Manufacturing;
- Manufacturing photocopy equipment are classified in U.S. Industry 333315, Photographic and Photocopying Equipment Manufacturing;
- Manufacturing facsimile equipment are classified in Industry 334210, Telephone Apparatus Manufacturing;
- Manufacturing timeclocks and timestamps are classified in U.S. Industry 334518, Watch, Clock, and Part Manufacturing; and
- Manufacturing pencil sharpeners, staplers, staple removers, hand paper punches, cutters, trimmers, and other hand office equipment are classified in U.S. Industry 339942, Lead Pencil and Art Good Manufacturing.

333314 Optical Instrument and Lens Manufacturing [US]

This U.S. industry comprises establishments primarily engaged in one or more of the following: (1) manufacturing optical instruments and lens, such as binoculars, microscopes (except electron, proton), telescopes, prisms, and lenses (except ophthalmic); (2) coating or polishing lenses (except ophthalmic); and (3) mounting lenses (except ophthalmic).

- Manufacturing ophthalmic focus lenses are classified in U.S. Industry 339115, Ophthalmic Goods Manufacturing;
- Manufacturing electron and proton microscopes are classified in U.S. Industry 334516, Analytical Laboratory Instrument Manufacturing;
- Manufacturing molded plastics lens blanks are classified in U.S. Industry 326199, All Other Plastics Product Manufacturing; and
- Manufacturing molded glass lens blanks are classified in U.S. Industry 327212, Other Pressed and Blown Glass and Glassware Manufacturing.

333315 Photographic and Photocopying Equipment Manufacturing [US]

This U.S. industry comprises establishments primarily engaged in manufacturing photographic and photocopying equipment, such as cameras (except television, video, digital projectors, film developing equipment, photocopying equipment, and microfilm equipment).

- Manufacturing sensitized film, paper, cloth, and plates, and prepared photographic chemicals are classified in U.S. Industry 325992, Photographic Film, Paper, Plate, and Chemical Manufacturing;
- Manufacturing photographic lenses are classified in U.S. Industry 333314, Optical Instrument and Lens Manufacturing; and
- Manufacturing television, video, and digital cameras are classified in Subsector 334, Computer and Electronic Product Manufacturing.

333319 Other Commercial and Service Industry Machinery Manufacturing [US]

This U.S. industry comprises establishments primarily engaged in manufacturing commercial and service industry equipment (except automatic vending machines, commercial laundry, drycleaning and pressing machines, office machinery, optical instruments and lenses, and photographic and photocopying equipment).

- Manufacturing automatic vending machines are classified in U.S. Industry 333311, Automatic Vending Machine Manufacturing;
- Manufacturing commercial laundry drycleaning and pressing machines are classified in U.S. Industry 333312, Commercial Laundry, Drycleaning, and Pressing Machine Manufacturing;
- Manufacturing office machinery are classified in U.S. Industry 333313, Office Machinery Manufacturing;
- Manufacturing optical instruments and lenses are classified in U.S. Industry 333314, Optical Instrument and Lens Manufacturing;
- Manufacturing photographic and photocopying equipment are classified in U.S. Industry 333315, Photographic and Photocopying Equipment Manufacturing;
- Manufacturing household-type appliances are classified in Industry Group 3352, Household Appliance Manufacturing; and
- Manufacturing mechanics' handtools are classified in U.S. Industry 332212, Hand and Edge Tool Manufacturing.

Visit page 17 to learn about classification changes to this sector.

Sector

31-33

Manufacturing

■ = Cross-References

US—United States industry only. CAN—United States and Canadian industries are comparable. When neither US nor CAN appears, Canadian, Mexican, and United States industries are comparable.

www.harrisinfo.com

401

3334 Ventilation, Heating, Air-conditioning, and Commercial Refrigeration Equipment Manufacturing

33341 Ventilation, Heating, Air-conditioning, and Commercial Refrigeration Equipment Manufacturing

This industry comprises establishments primarily engaged in manufacturing ventilating, heating, air-conditioning, and commercial and industrial refrigeration and freezer equipment.

- Manufacturing household-type fans (except attic), portable electric space heaters, humidifiers, dehumidifiers, and air purification equipment are classified in Industry 33521, Small Electrical Appliance Manufacturing;
- Manufacturing household-type appliances, such as cooking stoves, ranges, refrigerators, and freezers are classified in Industry 33522, Major Appliance Manufacturing;
- Manufacturing commercial-type cooking equipment are classified in Industry 33329, Other Industrial Machinery Manufacturing;
- Manufacturing industrial, power, and marine boilers are classified in Industry 33241, Power Boiler and Heat Exchanger Manufacturing;
- Manufacturing industrial process furnaces and ovens are classified in Industry 33399, All Other General Purpose Machinery Manufacturing; and
- Manufacturing motor vehicle air-conditioning systems and compressors are classified in Industry 33639, Other Motor Vehicle Parts Manufacturing.

333411 Air Purification Equipment Manufacturing ᵁˢ

This U.S. industry comprises establishments primarily engaged in manufacturing stationary air purification equipment, such as industrial dust and fume collection equipment, electrostatic precipitation equipment, warm air furnace filters, air washers, and other dust collection equipment.

- Manufacturing air-conditioning units (except motor vehicle) are classified in U.S. Industry 333415, Air-conditioning and Warm Air Heating Equipment and Commercial and Industrial Refrigeration Equipment Manufacturing;
- Manufacturing motor vehicle air-conditioning systems and compressors are classified in U.S. Industry 336391, Motor Vehicle Air-conditioning Manufacturing;
- Manufacturing household-type fans (except attic) and portable air purification equipment are classified in U.S. Industry 335211, Electric Housewares and Household Fan Manufacturing; and
- Manufacturing industrial and commercial blowers, industrial and commercial exhaust and ventilating fans, and attic fans are classified in U.S. Industry 333412, Industrial and Commercial Fan and Blower Manufacturing.

333412 Industrial and Commercial Fan and Blower Manufacturing ᵁˢ

This U.S. industry comprises establishments primarily engaged in manufacturing attic fans and industrial and commercial fans and blowers, such as commercial exhaust fans and commercial ventilating fans.

- Manufacturing air-conditioning units (except motor vehicle) are classified in U.S. Industry 333415, Air-conditioning and Warm Air Heating Equipment and Commercial and Industrial Refrigeration Equipment Manufacturing;
- Manufacturing motor vehicle air-conditioning systems and compressors are classified in U.S. Industry 336391, Motor Vehicle Air-conditioning Manufacturing;
- Manufacturing household-type fans (except attic) and portable air purification equipment are classified in U.S. Industry 335211, Electric Housewares and Household Fan Manufacturing; and
- Manufacturing stationary air purification equipment are classified in U.S. Industry 333411, Air Purification Equipment Manufacturing.

333414 Heating Equipment (except Warm Air Furnaces) Manufacturing ᵁˢ

This U.S. industry comprises establishments primarily engaged in manufacturing heating equipment (except electric and warm air furnaces), such as heating boilers, heating stoves, floor and wall furnaces, and wall and baseboard heating units.

- Manufacturing warm air furnaces are classified in U.S. Industry 333415, Air-conditioning and Warm Air Heating Equipment and Commercial and Industrial Refrigeration Equipment Manufacturing;
- Manufacturing electric space heaters are classified in U.S. Industry 335211, Electric Housewares and Household Fan Manufacturing;
- Manufacturing household-type cooking stoves and ranges are classified in U.S. Industry 335221, Household Cooking Appliance Manufacturing;
- Manufacturing industrial, power, and marine boilers are classified in Industry 332410, Power Boiler and Heat Exchanger Manufacturing;
- Manufacturing industrial process furnaces and ovens are classified in U.S. Industry 333994, Industrial Process Furnace and Oven Manufacturing; and
- Manufacturing commercial-type cooking equipment are classified in U.S. Industry 333319, Other Commercial and Service Industry Machinery Manufacturing.

Sector

31-33

Manufacturing

■ = Cross-References

US—United States industry only. CAN—United States and Canadian industries are comparable. When neither US nor CAN appears, Canadian, Mexican, and United States industries are comparable.

402

Harris InfoSource

333415 Air-conditioning and Warm Air Heating Equipment and Commercial and Industrial Refrigeration Equipment Manufacturing ᵘˢ

This U.S. industry comprises establishments primarily engaged in (1) manufacturing air-conditioning (except motor vehicle) and warm air furnace equipment and/or (2) manufacturing commercial and industrial refrigeration and freezer equipment.

- Manufacturing motor vehicle air-conditioning systems and compressors are classified in U.S. Industry 336391, Motor Vehicle Air-conditioning Manufacturing;
- Manufacturing household-type refrigerators and freezers are classified in U.S. Industry 335222, Household Refrigerator and Home Freezer Manufacturing;
- Manufacturing portable electric space heaters, humidifiers, and dehumidifiers are classified in U.S. Industry 335211, Electric Housewares and Household Fan Manufacturing;
- Manufacturing heating boilers, heating stoves, floor and wall mount furnaces, and electric wall and baseboard heating units are classified in U.S. Industry 333414, Heating Equipment (except Warm Air Furnaces) Manufacturing; and
- Manufacturing furnace air filters are classified in U.S. Industry 333411, Air Purification Equipment Manufacturing.

3335 Metalworking Machinery Manufacturing

33351 Metalworking Machinery Manufacturing

This industry comprises establishments primarily engaged in manufacturing metalworking machinery, such as metal cutting and metal forming machine tools; cutting tools; and accessories for metalworking machinery; special dies, tools, jigs, and fixtures; industrial molds; rolling mill machinery; assembly machinery; coil handling, conversion, or straightening equipment; and wire drawing and fabricating machines.

- Manufacturing handtools (except power-driven), cutting dies (except metal cutting), sawblades, and handsaws are classified in Industry 33221, Cutlery and Handtool Manufacturing;
- Manufacturing casting molds for heavy steel ingots are classified in Industry 33151, Ferrous Metal Foundries; and
- Manufacturing power-driven handtools and welding and soldering equipment are classified in Industry 33399, All Other General Purpose Machinery Manufacturing.

333511 Industrial Mold Manufacturing ᶜᴬᴺ

This U.S. industry comprises establishments primarily engaged in manufacturing industrial molds for casting metals or forming other materials, such as plastics, glass, or rubber.

- Establishments primarily engaged in manufacturing casting molds for steel ingots are classified in U.S. Industry 331511, Iron Foundries.

333512 Machine Tool (Metal Cutting Types) Manufacturing ᵘˢ

This U.S. industry comprises establishments primarily engaged in manufacturing metal cutting machine tools (except handtools).

- Manufacturing welding and soldering equipment are classified in U.S. Industry 333992, Welding and Soldering Equipment Manufacturing;
- Manufacturing metal-forming machine tools are classified in U.S. Industry 333513, Machine Tool (Metal Forming Types) Manufacturing;
- Manufacturing power-driven metal cutting handtools are classified in U.S. Industry 333991, Power-driven Handtool Manufacturing; and
- Manufacturing accessories and attachments for metal cutting machine tools are classified in U.S. Industry 333515, Cutting Tool and Machine Tool Accessory Manufacturing.

333513 Machine Tool (Metal Forming Types) Manufacturing ᵘˢ

This U.S. industry comprises establishments primarily engaged in manufacturing metal forming machine tools (except handtools), such as punching, sheering, bending, forming, pressing, forging and die-casting machines.

- Manufacturing welding and soldering equipment are classified in U.S. Industry 333992, Welding and Soldering Equipment Manufacturing;
- Manufacturing metal-cutting machine tools are classified in U.S. Industry 333512, Machine Tool (Metal Cutting Types) Manufacturing;
- Manufacturing power-driven handtools are classified in U.S. Industry 333991, Power-driven Handtool Manufacturing;
- Manufacturing rolling mill machinery and equipment are classified in U.S. Industry 333516, Rolling Mill Machinery and Equipment Manufacturing; and
- Manufacturing accessories and attachments for metal forming machine tools are classified in U.S. Industry 333515, Cutting Tool and Machine Tool Accessory Manufacturing.

Visit page 17 to learn about classification changes to this sector.

Manufacturing

■ = Cross-References

US—United States industry only. CAN—United States and Canadian industries are comparable. When neither US nor CAN appears, Canadian, Mexican, and United States industries are comparable.

333514 Special Die and Tool, Die Set, Jig, and Fixture Manufacturing ^{US}

This U.S. industry comprises establishments, known as tool and die shops, primarily engaged in manufacturing special tools and fixtures, such as cutting dies and jigs.

- Manufacturing molds for die-casting and foundry casting; and metal molds for plaster working, rubber working, plastics working, and glass working machinery are classified in U.S. Industry 333511, Industrial Mold Manufacturing;
- Manufacturing molds for heavy steel ingots are classified in U.S. Industry 331511, Iron Foundries; and
- Manufacturing cutting dies for materials other than metal are classified in U.S. Industry 332212, Hand and Edge Tool Manufacturing.

333515 Cutting Tool and Machine Tool Accessory Manufacturing ^{US}

This U.S. industry comprises establishments primarily engaged in manufacturing accessories and attachments for metal cutting and metal forming machine tools.

- Manufacturing accessories and attachments for cutting and forming machines (except metal cutting, metal forming machinery) are classified in U.S. Industry 332212, Hand and Edge Tool Manufacturing; and
- Manufacturing saw blades and handsaws are classified in U.S. Industry 332213, Saw Blade and Handsaw Manufacturing.

333516 Rolling Mill Machinery and Equipment Manufacturing ^{US}

This U.S. industry comprises establishments primarily engaged in manufacturing rolling mill machinery and equipment for metal production.

333518 Other Metalworking Machinery Manufacturing ^{US}

This U.S. industry comprises establishments primarily engaged in manufacturing metal working machinery (except industrial molds; metal cutting machine tools; metal forming machine tools; special dies and tools, die sets, jigs, and fixtures; cutting tools and machine tool accessories; and rolling mill machinery and equipment).

- Manufacturing industrial molds are classified in U.S. Industry 333511, Industrial Mold Manufacturing;
- Manufacturing metal cutting machinery are classified in U.S. Industry 333512, Machine Tool (Metal Cutting Types) Manufacturing;
- Manufacturing metal forming machinery are classified in U.S. Industry 333513, Machine Tool (Metal Forming Types) Manufacturing;
- Manufacturing special dies and tools, die sets, jigs, and fixtures are classified in U.S. Industry 333514, Special Die and Tool, Die Set, Jig, and Fixture Manufacturing;
- Manufacturing cutting tools and machine tool accessories are classified in U.S. Industry 333515, Cutting Tool and Machine Tool Accessory Manufacturing; and
- Manufacturing rolling mill machinery are classified in U.S. Industry 333516, Rolling Mill Machinery and Equipment Manufacturing.

3336 Engine, Turbine, and Power Transmission Equipment Manufacturing

33361 Engine, Turbine, and Power Transmission Equipment Manufacturing

This industry comprises establishments primarily engaged in manufacturing turbines, power transmission equipment, and internal combustion engines (except automotive gasoline and aircraft).

- Manufacturing motor vehicle power transmission equipment are classified in Industry 33635, Motor Vehicle Transmission and Power Train Parts Manufacturing;
- Manufacturing aircraft engines and aircraft power transmission equipment are classified in Industry 33641, Aerospace Product and Parts Manufacturing;
- Manufacturing ball and roller bearings are classified in Industry 33299, All Other Fabricated Metal Product Manufacturing;
- Manufacturing automotive engines (except diesel) are classified in Industry 33631, Motor Vehicle Gasoline Engine and Engine Parts Manufacturing; and
- Manufacturing electric power transmission, electric power distribution equipment, generators, or prime mover generator sets (except turbines) are classified in Industry 33531, Electrical Equipment Manufacturing.

333611 Turbine and Turbine Generator Set Units Manufacturing ^{CAN}

This U.S. industry comprises establishments primarily engaged in manufacturing turbines (except aircraft); and complete turbine generator set units, such as steam, hydraulic, gas, and wind.

- Manufacturing aircraft turbines are classified in U.S. Industry 336412, Aircraft Engine and Engine Parts Manufacturing; and
- Manufacturing generators or prime mover generator sets (except turbines) are classified in U.S. Industry 335312, Motor and Generator Manufacturing.

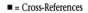 = Cross-References

Sector
31-33
Manufacturing

US—United States industry only. CAN—United States and Canadian industries are comparable. When neither US nor CAN appears, Canadian, Mexican, and United States industries are comparable.

404 Harris InfoSource

333612 Speed Changer, Industrial High-speed Drive, and Gear Manufacturing ᵁˢ

This U.S. industry comprises establishments primarily engaged in manufacturing gears, speed changers, and industrial high-speed drives (except hydrostatic).

- Manufacturing motor vehicle power transmission equipment are classified in Industry 336350, Motor Vehicle Transmission and Power Train Parts Manufacturing;
- Manufacturing aircraft power transmission equipment are classified in U.S. Industry 336413, Other Aircraft Parts and Auxiliary Equipment Manufacturing; and
- Manufacturing industrial hydrostatic transmissions are classified in U.S. Industry 333613, Mechanical Power Transmission Equipment Manufacturing.

333613 Mechanical Power Transmission Equipment Manufacturing ᵁˢ

This U.S. industry comprises establishments primarily engaged in manufacturing mechanical power transmission equipment (except motor vehicle and aircraft), such as plain bearings, brakes and clutches (except motor vehicle and electromagnetic industrial control), couplings, joints, and drive chains.

- Manufacturing motor vehicle power transmission equipment are classified in Industry 336350, Motor Vehicle Transmission and Power Train Parts Manufacturing;
- Manufacturing aircraft power transmission equipment are classified in U.S. Industry 336413, Other Aircraft Parts and Auxiliary Equipment Manufacturing;
- Manufacturing ball and roller bearings are classified in U.S. Industry 332991, Ball and Roller Bearing Manufacturing; and
- Manufacturing gears, speed changers, and industrial high-speed drives (except hydrostatic) are classified in U.S. Industry 333612, Speed Changer, Industrial High-speed Drive, and Gear Manufacturing.

333618 Other Engine Equipment Manufacturing ᵁˢ

This U.S. industry comprises establishments primarily engaged in manufacturing internal combustion engines (except automotive gasoline and aircraft).

- Manufacturing gasoline motor vehicle engines and motor vehicle transmissions are classified in Industry Group 3363, Motor Vehicle Parts Manufacturing;
- Manufacturing gasoline aircraft engines and aircraft transmissions are classified in Industry 33641, Aerospace Product and Parts Manufacturing;
- Manufacturing turbine and turbine generator sets units are classified in U.S. Industry 333611, Turbine and Turbine Generator Set Units Manufacturing;
- Manufacturing speed changers and industrial high-speed drivers and gears are classified in U.S. Industry 333612, Speed Changer, Industrial High-speed Drive, and Gear Manufacturing; and
- Manufacturing mechanical power transmission equipment (except motor vehicle and aircraft) are classified in U.S. Industry 333613, Mechanical Power Transmission Equipment Manufacturing.

Visit page 17 to learn about classification changes to this sector.

3339 Other General Purpose Machinery Manufacturing

33391 Pump and Compressor Manufacturing

This industry comprises establishments primarily engaged in manufacturing pumps and compressors, such as general purpose air and gas compressors, nonagricultural spraying and dusting equipment, general purpose pumps and pumping equipment (except fluid power pumps and motors), and measuring and dispensing pumps.

- Manufacturing fluid power pumps and motors and handheld pneumatic spraying equipment are classified in Industry 33399, All Other General Purpose Machinery Manufacturing;
- Manufacturing agricultural spraying and dusting equipment are classified in Industry 33311, Agricultural Implement Manufacturing;
- Manufacturing laboratory vacuum pumps are classified in Industry 33911, Medical Equipment and Supplies Manufacturing;
- Manufacturing pumps and air-conditioning systems and compressors for motor vehicles are classified in Industry Group 3363, Motor Vehicle Parts Manufacturing; and
- Manufacturing air-conditioning systems and compressors (except motor vehicle) are classified in Industry 33341, Ventilation, Heating, Air-conditioning, and Commercial Refrigeration Equipment Manufacturing.

333911 Pump and Pumping Equipment Manufacturing ᵁˢ

This U.S. industry comprises establishments primarily engaged in manufacturing general purpose pumps and pumping equipment (except fluid power pumps and motors), such as reciprocating pumps, turbine pumps, centrifugal pumps, rotary pumps, diaphragm pumps, domestic water system pumps, oil well and oil field pumps and sump pumps.

Sector
31-33
Manufacturing

■ = Cross-References

US—United States industry only. CAN—United States and Canadian industries are comparable. When neither US nor CAN appears, Canadian, Mexican, and United States industries are comparable.

■ Manufacturing fluid power pumps and motors are classified in U.S. Industry 333996, Fluid Power Pump and Motor Manufacturing;
■ Manufacturing measuring and dispensing pumps are classified in U.S. Industry 333913, Measuring and Dispensing Pump Manufacturing;
■ Manufacturing vacuum pumps (except laboratory) are classified in U.S. Industry 333912, Air and Gas Compressor Manufacturing;
■ Manufacturing laboratory vacuum pumps are classified in U.S. Industry 339111, Laboratory Apparatus and Furniture Manufacturing; and
■ Manufacturing fluid pumps for motor vehicles, such as oil pumps, water pumps, and power steering pumps, are classified in Industry Group 3363, Motor Vehicle Parts Manufacturing.

333912 Air and Gas Compressor Manufacturing US
This U.S. industry comprises establishments primarily engaged in manufacturing general purpose air and gas compressors, such as reciprocating compressors, centrifugal compressors, vacuum pumps (except laboratory), and nonagricultural spraying and dusting compressors and spray gun units.

■ Manufacturing refrigeration and air-conditioning (except motor vehicle) systems and compressors are classified in U.S. Industry 333415, Air-conditioning and Warm Air Heating Equipment and Commercial and Industrial Refrigeration Equipment Manufacturing;
■ Manufacturing motor vehicle air-conditioning systems and compressors are classified in U.S. Industry 336391, Motor Vehicle Air-conditioning Manufacturing;
■ Manufacturing fluid power pumps and motors are classified in U.S. Industry 333996, Fluid Power Pump and Motor Manufacturing;
■ Manufacturing agricultural spraying and dusting equipment are classified in U.S. Industry 333111, Farm Machinery and Equipment Manufacturing;
■ Manufacturing laboratory vacuum pumps are classified in U.S. Industry 339111, Laboratory Apparatus and Furniture Manufacturing; and
■ Manufacturing handheld pneumatic spray guns are classified in U.S. Industry 333991, Power-driven Handtool Manufacturing

333913 Measuring and Dispensing Pump Manufacturing US
This U.S. industry comprises establishments primarily engaged in manufacturing measuring and dispensing pumps, such as gasoline pumps and lubricating oil measuring and dispensing pumps.

■ Establishments primarily engaged in manufacturing pumps and pumping equipment for general industrial use are classified in U.S. Industry 333911, Pump and Pumping Equipment Manufacturing.

33392 Material Handling Equipment Manufacturing
This industry comprises establishments primarily engaged in manufacturing material handling equipment, such as elevators and moving stairs; conveyors and conveying equipment; overhead traveling cranes, hoists, and monorail systems; and industrial trucks, tractors, trailers, and stacker machinery.

■ Manufacturing motor vehicle-type trailers are classified in Industry 33621, Motor Vehicle Body and Trailer Manufacturing;
■ Manufacturing farm-type tractors are classified in Industry 33311, Agricultural Implement Manufacturing;
■ Manufacturing construction-type tractors and cranes are classified in Industry 33312, Construction Machinery Manufacturing; and
■ Manufacturing power transmission pulleys are classified in Industry 33361, Engine, Turbine, and Power Transmission Equipment Manufacturing.

333921 Elevator and Moving Stairway Manufacturing US
This U.S. industry comprises establishments primarily engaged in manufacturing elevators and moving stairways.

■ Establishments primarily engaged in manufacturing commercial conveyor systems and equipment are classified in U.S. Industry 333922, Conveyor and Conveying Equipment Manufacturing.

333922 Conveyor and Conveying Equipment Manufacturing US
This U.S. industry comprises establishments primarily engaged in manufacturing conveyors and conveying equipment, such as gravity conveyors, trolley conveyors, tow conveyors, pneumatic tube conveyors, carousel conveyors, farm conveyors, and belt conveyors.

■ Manufacturing passenger or freight elevators, dumbwaiters, and moving stairways are classified in U.S. Industry 333921, Elevator and Moving Stairway Manufacturing; and
■ Manufacturing overhead traveling cranes and monorail systems are classified in U.S. Industry 333923, Overhead Traveling Crane, Hoist, and Monorail System Manufacturing.

Sector
31-33
Manufacturing

■ = Cross-References

US—United States industry only. CAN—United States and Canadian industries are comparable. When neither US nor CAN appears, Canadian, Mexican, and United States industries are comparable.

406

Harris InfoSource

333923 Overhead Traveling Crane, Hoist, and Monorail System Manufacturing US

This U.S. industry comprises establishments primarily engaged in manufacturing overhead traveling cranes, hoists, and monorail systems.

- Manufacturing construction-type cranes are classified in Industry 333120, Construction Machinery Manufacturing;
- Manufacturing aircraft loading hoists are classified in U.S. Industry 333924, Industrial Truck, Tractor, Trailer, and Stacker Machinery Manufacturing; and
- Manufacturing power transmission pulleys are classified in U.S. Industry 333613, Mechanical Power Transmission Equipment Manufacturing.

333924 Industrial Truck, Tractor, Trailer, and Stacker Machinery Manufacturing US

This U.S. industry comprises establishments primarily engaged in manufacturing industrial trucks, tractors, trailers, and stackers (i.e., truck-type) such as forklifts, pallet loaders and unloaders, and portable loading docks.

- Manufacturing motor vehicle-type trailers are classified in U.S. Industry 336212, Truck Trailer Manufacturing;
- Manufacturing farm-type tractors are classified in U.S. Industry 333111, Farm Machinery and Equipment Manufacturing; and
- Manufacturing construction-type tractors are classified in Industry 333120, Construction Machinery Manufacturing.

33399 All Other General Purpose Machinery Manufacturing

This industry comprises establishments primarily engaged in manufacturing general purpose machinery (except ventilation, heating, air-conditioning, and commercial refrigeration equipment; metal working machinery; engines, turbines, and power transmission equipment; pumps and compressors; and material handling equipment).

- Manufacturing ventilating, heating, air-conditioning (except motor vehicle), commercial refrigeration, and furnace filters are classified in Industry 33341, Ventilation, Heating, Air-conditioning, and Commercial Refrigeration Equipment Manufacturing;
- Manufacturing metalworking machinery are classified in Industry Group 3335, Metal-working Machinery Manufacturing;
- Manufacturing engine, turbine and power transmission equipment are classified in Industry Group 3336, Engine, Turbine, and Power Transmission Equipment Manufacturing;
- Manufacturing pumps and compressors are classified in Industry 33391, Pump and Compressor Manufacturing;
- Manufacturing material handling equipment are classified in Industry 33392, Material Handling Equipment Manufacturing;
- Manufacturing motor vehicle air-conditioning systems and compressors, engine filters, and pumps are classified in Industry Group 3363, Motor Vehicle Parts Manufacturing;
- Manufacturing laboratory scales, balances, ovens, and furnaces are classified in Industry 33911, Medical Equipment and Supplies Manufacturing;
- Manufacturing metal cutting and metal forming machinery are classified in Industry 33351, Metalworking Machinery Manufacturing;
- Manufacturing power driven heavy construction and milling hand operated tools, such as tampers and augers, are classified in Industries 33312, Construction Machinery Manufacturing and 33313, Mining and Oil and Gas Field Machinery Manufacturing;
- Manufacturing bakery ovens and industrial kilns, such as cement, wood, and chemical, are classified in Industry 33329, Other Industrial Machinery Manufacturing;
- Manufacturing mechanical jacks, handheld soldering irons, countersink bits, drill bits, router bits, milling cutters, and other machine tools for woodcutting are classified in Industry 33221, Cutlery and Handtool Manufacturing;
- Manufacturing carnival amusement park equipment, automotive maintenance equipment, and coin-operated vending machines are classified in Industry 33331, Commercial and Service Industry Machinery Manufacturing; and
- Manufacturing transformers for arc-welding are classified in Industry 33531, Electrical Equipment Manufacturing.

333991 Power-driven Handtool Manufacturing US

This U.S. industry comprises establishments primarily engaged in manufacturing power driven (e.g., battery, corded, pneumatic) handtools, such as drills, screwguns, circular saws, chain saws, staplers, and nailers.

- Manufacturing metal cutting-type and metal forming-type machines (including home workshop) are classified in Industry 33351, Metalworking Machinery Manufacturing;
- Manufacturing countersink bits, drill bits, router bits, milling cutters, and other machine tools for woodcutting are classified in U.S. Industry 332212, Hand and Edge Tool Manufacturing;
- Manufacturing power-driven heavy construction or mining hand operated tools, such as tampers, jackhammers, and augers, are classified in Industries 333120, Construction Machinery Manufacturing and 333130, Mining and Oil and Gas Field Machinery Manufacturing; and
- Manufacturing powered home lawn and garden equipment are classified in U.S. Industry 333112, Lawn and Garden Tractor and Home Lawn and Garden Equipment Manufacturing.

333992 Welding and Soldering Equipment Manufacturing US

This U.S. industry comprises establishments primarily engaged in manufacturing welding and soldering equipment and accessories (except transformers), such as arc, resistance, gas, plasma, laser,

Visit page 17 to learn about classification changes to this sector.

Sector
31-33

Manufacturing

■ = Cross-References

US—United States industry only. CAN—United States and Canadian industries are comparable. When neither US nor CAN appears, Canadian, Mexican, and United States industries are comparable.

www.harrisinfo.com 407

electron beam, and ultrasonic welding equipment; welding electrodes; coated or cored welding wire; and soldering equipment (except handheld).

- Manufacturing handheld soldering irons are classified in U.S. Industry 332212, Hand and Edge Tool Manufacturing; and
- Manufacturing transformers for arc-welding are classified in U.S. Industry 335311, Power, Distribution, and Specialty Transformer Manufacturing.

333993 Packaging Machinery Manufacturing US
This U.S. industry comprises establishments primarily engaged in manufacturing packaging machinery, such as wrapping, bottling, canning, and labeling machinery.

333994 Industrial Process Furnace and Oven Manufacturing US
This U.S. Industry comprises establishments primarily engaged in manufacturing industrial process furnaces, ovens, induction and dielectric heating equipment, and kilns (except cement, chemical, wood).

- Manufacturing bakery ovens are classified in U.S. Industry 333294, Food Product Machinery Manufacturing;
- Manufacturing cement, wood, and chemical kilns are classified in U.S. Industry 333298, All Other Industrial Machinery Manufacturing;
- Manufacturing cremating ovens are classified in U.S. Industry 333999, All Other Miscellaneous General Purpose Machinery Manufacturing; and
- Manufacturing laboratory furnaces and ovens are classified in U.S. Industry 339111, Laboratory Apparatus and Furniture Manufacturing.

333995 Fluid Power Cylinder and Actuator Manufacturing US
This U.S. industry comprises establishments primarily engaged in manufacturing fluid power (i.e., hydraulic and pneumatic) cylinders and actuators.

333996 Fluid Power Pump and Motor Manufacturing US
This U.S. industry comprises establishments primarily engaged in manufacturing fluid power (i.e., hydraulic and pneumatic) pumps and motors.

- Manufacturing fluid pumps for motor vehicles, such as oil pumps, water pumps, and power steering pumps are classified in Industry Group 3363, Motor Vehicle Parts Manufacturing;
- Manufacturing general purpose pumps (except fluid power) are classified in U.S. Industry 333911, Pump and Pumping Equipment Manufacturing; and
- Manufacturing air compressors are classified in U.S. Industry 333912, Air and Gas Compressor Manufacturing.

333997 Scale and Balance (except Laboratory) Manufacturing US
This U.S. industry comprises establishments primarily engaged in manufacturing scales and balances (except laboratory).

- Establishments primarily engaged in manufacturing laboratory scales and balances are classified in U.S. Industry 339111, Laboratory Apparatus and Furniture Manufacturing.

333999 All Other Miscellaneous General Purpose Machinery Manufacturing US
This U.S. industry comprises establishments primarily engaged in manufacturing general purpose machinery (except ventilating, heating, air-conditioning, and commercial refrigeration equipment; metal working machinery; engines, turbines, and power transmission equipment; pumps and compressors; material handling equipment; power-driven handtools; welding and soldering equipment; packaging machinery; industrial process furnaces and ovens; fluid power cylinders and actuators; fluid power pumps and motors; and scales and balances).

- Manufacturing ventilating, heating, air-conditioning (except motor vehicle), and commercial refrigeration are classified in Industry 33341, Ventilation, Heating, Air-conditioning, and Commercial Refrigeration Manufacturing;
- Manufacturing motor vehicle air-conditioning systems and compressors are classified in U.S. Industry 336391, Motor Vehicle Air-conditioning Manufacturing;
- Manufacturing metalworking machinery are classified in Industry Group 3335, Metal-working Machinery Manufacturing;
- Manufacturing engine, turbine, and power transmission equipment are classified in Industry Group 3336, Engine, Turbine, and Power Transmission Equipment Manufacturing;
- Manufacturing pumps and compressors are classified in Industry 33391, Pump and Compressor Manufacturing;
- Manufacturing material handling equipment are classified in Industry 33392, Material Handling Equipment Manufacturing;
- Manufacturing power-driven handtools are classified in U.S. Industry 333991, Power-driven Handtool Manufacturing;
- Manufacturing welding and soldering equipment (except handheld soldering irons) are classified in U.S. Industry 333992, Welding and Soldering Equipment Manufacturing;
- Manufacturing packaging machinery are classified in U.S. Industry 333993, Packaging Machinery Manufacturing;

Sector
31-33
Manufacturing

■ = Cross-References

US—United States industry only. CAN—United States and Canadian industries are comparable. When neither US nor CAN appears, Canadian, Mexican, and United States industries are comparable.

408

Harris InfoSource

■ Manufacturing bakery ovens and cement, wood, and chemical kilns are classified in U.S. Industry 333298, All Other Industrial Machinery Manufacturing;

■ Manufacturing industrial process furnaces and ovens (except bakery) are classified in U.S. Industry 333994, Industrial Process Furnace and Oven Manufacturing;

■ Manufacturing fluid power cylinders and actuators are classified in U.S. Industry 333995, Fluid Power Cylinder and Actuator Manufacturing;

■ Manufacturing fluid power pumps and motors are classified in U.S. Industry 333996, Fluid Power Pump and Motor Manufacturing;

■ Manufacturing scales and balances (except laboratory) are classified in U.S. Industry 333997, Scale and Balance (except Laboratory) Manufacturing (except Laboratory);

■ Manufacturing carnival and amusement park equipment, automotive maintenance equipment and coin-operated vending machines are classified in Industry 33331, Commercial and Service Industry Machinery Manufacturing;

■ Manufacturing motor vehicle engine filters and pumps are classified in Industry Group 3363, Motor Vehicle Parts Manufacturing; and

■ Manufacturing mechanical jacks are classified in U.S. Industry 332212, Hand and Edge Tool Manufacturing.

▶334 COMPUTER AND ELECTRONIC PRODUCT MANUFACTURING

Industries in the Computer and Electronic Product Manufacturing subsector group establishments that manufacture computers, computer peripherals, communications equipment, and similar electronic products, and establishments that manufacture components for such products. The Computer and Electronic Product Manufacturing industries have been combined in the hierarchy of NAICS because of the economic significance they have attained. Their rapid growth suggests that they will become even more important to the economies of all three North American countries in the future, and in addition their manufacturing processes are fundamentally different from the manufacturing processes of other machinery and equipment. The design and use of integrated circuits and the application of highly specialized miniaturization technologies are common elements in the production technologies of the computer and electronic subsector. Convergence of technology motivates this NAICS subsector. Digitalization of sound recording, for example, causes both the medium (the compact disc) and the equipment to resemble the technologies for recording, storing, transmitting, and manipulating data. Communications technology and equipment have been converging with computer technology. When technologically-related components are in the same sector, it makes it easier to adjust the classification for future changes, without needing to redefine its basic structure. The creation of the Computer and Electronic Product Manufacturing subsector will assist in delineating new and emerging industries because the activities that will serve as the probable sources of new industries, such as computer manufacturing and communications equipment manufacturing, or computers and audio equipment are brought together. As new activities emerge, they are less likely therefore, to cross the subsector boundaries of the classification.

Visit page 17 to learn about classification changes to this sector.

3341 Computer and Peripheral Equipment Manufacturing

33411 Computer and Peripheral Equipment Manufacturing

This industry comprises establishments primarily engaged in manufacturing and/or assembling electronic computers, such as mainframes, personal computers, workstations, laptops, and computer servers; and computer peripheral equipment, such as storage devices, printers, monitors, input/output devices and terminals. Computers can be analog, digital, or hybrid. Digital computers, the most common type, are devices that do all of the following: (1) store the processing program or programs and the data immediately necessary for the execution of the program; (2) can be freely programmed in accordance with the requirements of the user; (3) perform arithmetical computations specified by the user; and (4) execute, without human intervention, a processing program that requires the computer to modify its execution by logical decision during the processing run. Analog computers are capable of simulating mathematical models and comprise at least analog, control, and programming elements.

■ Manufacturing digital telecommunications switches, local area network and wide area network communications equipment, such as bridges, routers, and gateways, are classified in Industry 33421, Telephone Apparatus Manufacturing;

■ Manufacturing blank magnetic and optical recording media are classified in Industry 33461, Manufacturing and Reproducing Magnetic and Optical Media;

■ Manufacturing machinery or equipment that incorporate electronic computers for operation or control purposes and embedded control applications are classified in the Manufacturing sector based on the classification of the complete machinery or equipment;

■ Manufacturing external audio speakers for computer use are classified in Industry 33431, Audio and Video Equipment Manufacturing;

■ = Cross-References

US—United States industry only. CAN—United States and Canadian industries are comparable. When neither US nor CAN appears, Canadian, Mexican, and United States industries are comparable.

www.harrisinfo.com 409

- Manufacturing internal loaded printed circuit board devices, such as sound, video, controller, and network interface cards; internal and external computer modems; and semiconductor storage devices, are classified in Industry 33441, Semiconductor and Other Electronic Component Manufacturing; and
- Manufacturing other parts, such as casings, stampings, cable sets, and switches, for computers, storage devices and other peripheral equipment, are classified in the Manufacturing sector based on their associated production processes.

334111 Electronic Computer Manufacturing ᵁˢ

This U.S. industry comprises establishments primarily engaged in manufacturing and/or assembling electronic computers, such as mainframes, personal computers, workstations, laptops, and computer servers. Computers can be analog, digital, or hybrid. Digital computers, the most common type, are devices that do all of the following: (1) store the processing program or programs and the data immediately necessary for the execution of the program; (2) can be freely programmed in accordance with the requirements of the user; (3) perform arithmetical computations specified by the user; and (4) execute, without human intervention, a processing program that requires the computer to modify its execution by logical decision during the processing run. Analog computers are capable of simulating mathematical models and contain at least analog, control, and programming elements. The manufacture of computers includes the assembly or integration of processors, coprocessors, memory, storage, and input/output devices into a user-programmable final product.

- Manufacturing digital telecommunications switches, local area network and wide area network communication equipment, such as bridges, routers, and gateways, are classified in Industry 334210, Telephone Apparatus Manufacturing;
- Manufacturing blank magnetic and optical recording media are classified in U.S. Industry 334613, Magnetic and Optical Recording Media Manufacturing;
- Manufacturing machinery or equipment that incorporates electronic computers for operation or control purposes and embedded control applications are classified in the Manufacturing sector based on the classification of the complete machinery or equipment;
- Manufacturing internal, loaded, printed circuit board devices, such as sound, video, controller, and network interface cards; internal and external computer modems; and solid state storage devices for computers, are classified in Industry 33441, Semiconductor and Other Electronic Component Manufacturing; and
- Manufacturing other parts, such as casings, stampings, cable sets, and switches, for computers, are classified in the Manufacturing sector based on their associated production processes.

334112 Computer Storage Device Manufacturing ᵁˢ

This U.S. industry comprises establishments primarily engaged in manufacturing computer storage devices that allow the storage and retrieval of data from a phase change, magnetic, optical, or magnetic/optical media. Examples of products made by these establishments are CD-ROM drives, floppy disk drives, hard disk drives, and tape storage and backup units.

- Manufacturing blank magnetic and optical recording media are classified in U.S. Industry 334613, Magnetic and Optical Recording Media Manufacturing;
- Manufacturing semiconductor storage devices, such as memory chips, are classified in U.S. Industry 334413, Semiconductor and Related Device Manufacturing;
- Manufacturing drive controller cards, internal or external to the storage device are classified in U.S. Industry 334418, Printed Circuit Assembly (Electronic Assembly) Manufacturing; and
- Manufacturing other parts, such as casings, stampings, cable sets, and switches, for computer storage devices, are classified in the Manufacturing sector based on their associated production processes.

334113 Computer Terminal Manufacturing ᵁˢ

This U.S. industry comprises establishments primarily engaged in manufacturing computer terminals. Computer terminals are input/output devices that connect with a central computer for processing.

- Manufacturing point-of-sale terminals, funds transfer, automatic teller machines, and monitors are classified in U.S. Industry 334119, Other Computer Peripheral Equipment Manufacturing;
- Manufacturing internal loaded printed circuit board devices, such as sound, video, controller, and network interface cards for computer terminals, are classified in U.S. Industry 334418, Printed Circuit Assembly (Electronic Assembly) Manufacturing; and
- Manufacturing other parts, such as casings, stampings, cable sets, and switches, for computer terminals, are classified in the Manufacturing sector based on their associated production processes.

334119 Other Computer Peripheral Equipment Manufacturing ᵁˢ

This U.S. industry comprises establishments primarily engaged in manufacturing computer peripheral equipment (except storage devices and computer terminals).

- Manufacturing local area network and wide area network communications equipment, such as bridges, routers, and gateways, are classified in Industry 334210, Telephone Apparatus Manufacturing;
- Manufacturing computer storage devices are classified in U.S. Industry 334112, Computer Storage Device Manufacturing;

Sector

31-33

Manufacturing

■ = Cross-References

US—United States industry only. CAN—United States and Canadian industries are comparable. When neither US nor CAN appears, Canadian, Mexican, and United States industries are comparable.

410 Harris InfoSource

■ Manufacturing computer terminals are classified in U.S. Industry 334113, Computer Terminal Manufacturing;
■ Manufacturing external audio speakers for computer use are classified in Industry 334310, Audio and Video Equipment Manufacturing;
■ Manufacturing internal, loaded, printed circuit board devices, such as sound, video, controller, and network interface cards; and internal and external computer modems used as computer peripherals, are classified in U.S. Industry 334418, Printed Circuit Assembly (Electronic Assembly) Manufacturing; and
■ Manufacturing other parts, such as casings, stampings, cable sets, and switches, for computer peripheral equipment, are classified in the Manufacturing sector based on their associated production processes.

3342 Communications Equipment Manufacturing

33421 Telephone Apparatus Manufacturing
See industry description for 334210 below.

334210 Telephone Apparatus Manufacturing
This industry comprises establishments primarily engaged in manufacturing wire telephone and data communications equipment. These products may be standalone or board-level components of a larger system. Examples of products made by these establishments are central office switching equipment, cordless telephones (except cellular), PBX equipment, telephones, telephone answering machines, and data communications equipment, such as bridges, routers, and gateways.

■ Manufacturing internal and external computer modems, fax/modems and electronic components used in telephone apparatus are classified in Industry 33441, Semiconductor and Other Electronic Component Manufacturing; and
■ Manufacturing cellular telephones are classified in Industry 334220, Radio and Television Broadcasting and Wireless Communications Equipment Manufacturing.

33422 Radio and Television Broadcasting and Wireless Communications Equipment Manufacturing
See industry description for 334220 below.

334220 Radio and Television Broadcasting and Wireless Communications Equipment Manufacturing
This industry comprises establishments primarily engaged in manufacturing radio and television broadcast and wireless communications equipment. Examples of products made by these establishments are: transmitting and receiving antennas, cable television equipment, GPS equipment, pagers, cellular phones, mobile communications equipment, and radio and television studio and broadcasting equipment.

■ Manufacturing household-type audio and video equipment, such as televisions and radio sets, are classified in Industry 334310, Audio and Video Equipment Manufacturing; and
■ Manufacturing wired and nonwired intercommunications equipment (i.e., intercoms) are classified in Industry 334290, Other Communications Equipment Manufacturing.

33429 Other Communications Equipment Manufacturing
See industry description for 334290 below.

334290 Other Communications Equipment Manufacturing
This industry comprises establishments primarily engaged in manufacturing communications equipment (except telephone apparatus, and radio and television broadcast, and wireless communications equipment).

■ Manufacturing telephone apparatus are classified in Industry 334210, Telephone Apparatus Manufacturing;
■ Manufacturing radio and television broadcast and wireless communication equipment are classified in Industry 334220, Radio and Television Broadcasting and Wireless Communications Equipment Manufacturing; and
■ Manufacturing automobile audio and related equipment are classified in Industry 334310, Audio and Video Equipment Manufacturing.

3343 Audio and Video Equipment Manufacturing

33431 Audio and Video Equipment Manufacturing
See industry description for 334310 below.

Visit page 17 to learn about classification changes to this sector.

Sector
31-33
Manufacturing

■ = Cross-References

US—United States industry only. CAN—United States and Canadian industries are comparable. When neither US nor CAN appears, Canadian, Mexican, and United States industries are comparable.

334310 Audio and Video Equipment Manufacturing

This industry comprises establishments primarily engaged in manufacturing electronic audio and video equipment for home entertainment, motor vehicle, public address and musical instrument amplifications. Examples of products made by these establishments are video cassette recorders, televisions, stereo equipment, speaker systems, household-type video cameras, jukeboxes, and amplifiers for musical instruments and public address systems.

- Manufacturing telephone answering machines are classified in Industry 334210, Telephone Apparatus Manufacturing;
- Manufacturing photographic (i.e., still and motion picture) equipment are classified in U.S. Industry 333315, Photographic and Photocopying Equipment Manufacturing;
- Manufacturing phonograph needles and cartridges are classified in Industry 33441, Semiconductor and Other Electronic Component Manufacturing;
- Manufacturing auto theft alarms are classified in Industry 334290, Other Communications Equipment Manufacturing; and
- Manufacturing mobile radios, such as citizens band and FM transceivers for household or motor vehicle uses; studio and broadcast video cameras; and cable decoders and satellite television equipment, are classified in Industry 334220, Radio and Television Broadcasting and Wireless Communications Equipment Manufacturing.

3344 Semiconductor and Other Electronic Component Manufacturing

33441 Semiconductor and Other Electronic Component Manufacturing

This industry comprises establishments primarily engaged in manufacturing semiconductors and other components for electronic applications. Examples of products made by these establishments are capacitors, resistors, microprocessors, bare and loaded printed circuit boards, electron tubes, electronic connectors, and computer modems.

- Manufacturing X-ray tubes are classified in Industry 33451, Navigational, Measuring, Electromedical, and Control Instruments Manufacturing;
- Manufacturing glass blanks for electron tubes are classified in Industry 32721, Glass and Glass Product Manufacturing;
- Manufacturing telephone system components or modules are classified in Industry 33421, Telephone Apparatus Manufacturing;
- Manufacturing finished products that incorporate loaded printed circuit boards are classified in the Manufacturing sector based on the production process of making the final product;
- Manufacturing communications antennas are classified in Industry 33422, Radio and Television Broadcasting and Wireless Communications Equipment Manufacturing; and
- Manufacturing coils, switches, transformers, connectors, capacitors, rheostats, and similar devices for electrical applications are classified in Subsector 335, Electrical Equipment, Appliance, and Component Manufacturing.

334411 Electron Tube Manufacturing US

This U.S. industry comprises establishments primarily engaged in manufacturing electron tubes and parts (except glass blanks). Examples of products made by these establishments are cathode ray tubes (i.e., picture tubes), klystron tubes, magnetron tubes, and traveling wave tubes.

- Manufacturing X-ray tubes are classified in U.S. Industry 334517, Irradiation Apparatus Manufacturing; and
- Manufacturing glass blanks for electron tubes are classified in Industry 32721, Glass and Glass Product Manufacturing.

334412 Bare Printed Circuit Board Manufacturing US

This U.S. industry comprises establishments primarily engaged in manufacturing bare (i.e., rigid or flexible) printed circuit boards without mounted electronic components. These establishments print, perforate, plate, screen, etch, or photoprint interconnecting pathways for electric current on laminates.

- Loading components onto printed circuit boards, or whose output is loaded printed circuit boards are classified in U.S. Industry 334418, Printed Circuit Assembly (Electronic Assembly) Manufacturing; and
- Manufacturing printed circuit laminates are classified in U.S. Industry 334419, Other Electronic Component Manufacturing.

334413 Semiconductor and Related Device Manufacturing US

This U.S. industry comprises establishments primarily engaged in manufacturing semiconductors and related solid state devices. Examples of products made by these establishments are integrated circuits, memory chips, microprocessors, diodes, transistors, solar cells and other optoelectronic devices.

334414 Electronic Capacitor Manufacturing US

This U.S. industry comprises establishments primarily engaged in manufacturing electronic fixed and variable capacitors and condensers.

■ = Cross-References

Sector

31-33

Manufacturing

US—United States industry only. CAN—United States and Canadian industries are comparable. When neither US nor CAN appears, Canadian, Mexican, and United States industries are comparable.

412

Harris InfoSource

■ Establishments primarily engaged in manufacturing electrical capacitors for power generation and distribution, heavy industrial equipment, induction heating and melting, and similar industrial applications are classified in U.S. Industry 335999, All Other Miscellaneous Electrical Equipment and Component Manufacturing.

334415 Electronic Resistor Manufacturing ^{US}

This U.S. industry comprises establishments primarily engaged in manufacturing electronic resistors, such as fixed and variable resistors, resistor networks, thermistors, and varistors.

■ Establishments primarily engaged in manufacturing electronic rheostats are classified in U.S. Industry 334419, Other Electronic Component Manufacturing.

334416 Electronic Coil, Transformer, and Other Inductor Manufacturing ^{US}

This U.S. industry comprises establishments primarily engaged in manufacturing electronic inductors, such as coils and transformers.

■ Establishments primarily engaged in manufacturing electrical transformers used in the generation, storage, transmission, transformation, distribution, and utilization of electrical energy are classified in U.S. Industry 335311, Power, Distribution, and Specialty Transformer Manufacturing.

334417 Electronic Connector Manufacturing ^{US}

This U.S. industry comprises establishments primarily engaged in manufacturing electronic connectors, such as coaxial, cylindrical, rack and panel, pin and sleeve, printed circuit and fiber optic.

■ Establishments primarily engaged in manufacturing electrical connectors, such as plugs, bus bars, twist on wire connectors and terminals, are classified in U.S. Industry 335931, Current-carrying Wiring Device Manufacturing.

334418 Printed Circuit Assembly (Electronic Assembly) Manufacturing ^{US}

This U.S. industry comprises establishments primarily engaged in loading components onto printed circuit boards or who manufacture and ship loaded printed circuit boards. Also known as printed circuit assemblies, electronics assemblies, or modules, these products are printed circuit boards that have some or all of the semiconductor and electronic components inserted or mounted and are inputs to a wide variety of electronic systems and devices.

■ Manufacturing printed circuit laminates are classified in U.S. Industry 334419, Other Electronic Component Manufacturing;
■ Manufacturing bare printed circuit boards are classified in U.S. Industry 334412, Bare Printed Circuit Board Manufacturing;
■ Manufacturing telephone system components or modules are classified in Industry 334210, Telephone Apparatus Manufacturing; and
■ Manufacturing finished products that incorporate loaded printed circuit boards are classified in the Manufacturing sector based on the production process of making the final product.

Visit page 17 to learn about classification changes to this sector.

334419 Other Electronic Component Manufacturing ^{US}

This U.S. industry comprises establishments primarily engaged in manufacturing electronic components (except electron tubes; bare printed circuit boards; semiconductors and related devices; electronic capacitors; electronic resistors; coils, transformers and other inductors; connectors; and loaded printed circuit boards).

■ Manufacturing electron tubes are classified in U.S. Industry 334411, Electron Tube Manufacturing;
■ Manufacturing bare printed circuit boards are classified in U.S. Industry 334412, Bare Printed Circuit Board Manufacturing;
■ Manufacturing semiconductors and related devices are classified in U.S. Industry 334413, Semiconductor and Related Device Manufacturing;
■ Manufacturing electronic capacitors are classified in U.S. Industry 334414, Electronic Capacitor Manufacturing;
■ Manufacturing electronic resistors are classified in U.S. Industry 334415, Electronic Resistor Manufacturing;
■ Manufacturing electronic inductors are classified in U.S. Industry 334416, Electronic Coil, Transformer, and Other Inductor Manufacturing;
■ Manufacturing electronic connectors are classified in U.S. Industry 334417, Electronic Connector Manufacturing;
■ Loading components onto printed circuit boards or whose output is loaded printed circuit boards are classified in U.S. Industry 334418, Printed Circuit Assembly (Electronic Assembly) Manufacturing; and
■ Manufacturing communications antennas are classified in Industry 334220, Radio and Television Broadcasting and Wireless Communications Equipment Manufacturing.

3345 Navigational, Measuring, Electromedical, and Control Instruments Manufacturing

33451 Navigational, Measuring, Electromedical, and Control Instruments Manufacturing

This industry comprises establishments primarily engaged in manufacturing navigational, measuring,

Manufacturing

■ = Cross-References

US—United States industry only. CAN—United States and Canadian industries are comparable. When neither US nor CAN appears, Canadian, Mexican, and United States industries are comparable.

www.harrisinfo.com 413

electromedical, and control instruments. Examples of products made by these establishments are aeronautical instruments, appliance regulators and controls (except switches), laboratory analytical instruments, navigation and guidance systems, and physical properties testing equipment.

- Manufacturing global positioning system (GPS) equipment are classified in Industry 33422, Radio and Television Broadcasting and Wireless Communications Equipment Manufacturing;
- Manufacturing motor control switches and relays (including timing relays) are classified in Industry 33531, Electrical Equipment Manufacturing;
- Manufacturing switches for appliances are classified in Industry 33593, Wiring Device Manufacturing;
- Manufacturing optical instruments are classified in Industry 33331, Commercial and Service Industry Machinery Manufacturing;
- Manufacturing equipment for measuring and testing communications signals are classified in Industry Group 3342, Communications Equipment Manufacturing;
- Manufacturing glass watch and clock crystals are classified in Industry 32721, Glass and Glass Product Manufacturing;
- Manufacturing plastics watch and clock crystals are classified in Industry 32619, Other Plastics Product Manufacturing; and
- Manufacturing medical thermometers and other nonelectrical medical apparatus are classified in Industry Group 3391, Medical Equipment and Supplies Manufacturing.

334510 Electromedical and Electrotherapeutic Apparatus Manufacturing ᵁˢ

This U.S. industry comprises establishments primarily engaged in manufacturing electromedical and electrotherapeutic apparatus, such as magnetic resonance imaging equipment, medical ultrasound equipment, pacemakers, hearing aids, electrocardiographs, and electromedical endoscopic equipment.

- Manufacturing medical irradiation apparatus are classified in U.S. Industry 334517, Irradiation Apparatus Manufacturing; and
- Manufacturing nonelectrical medical and therapeutic apparatus are classified in Industry Group 3391, Medical Equipment and Supplies Manufacturing.

334511 Search, Detection, Navigation, Guidance, Aeronautical, and Nautical System and Instrument Manufacturing ᵁˢ

This U.S. industry comprises establishments primarily engaged in manufacturing search, detection, navigation, guidance, aeronautical, and nautical systems and instruments. Examples of products made by these establishments are aircraft instruments (except engine), flight recorders, navigational instruments and systems, radar systems and equipment, and sonar systems and equipment.

- Manufacturing global positioning system (GPS) equipment are classified in Industry 334220, Radio and Television Broadcasting and Wireless Communications Equipment Manufacturing; and
- Manufacturing aircraft engine instruments and meteorological systems and equipment are classified in U.S. Industry 334519, Other Measuring and Controlling Device Manufacturing.

334512 Automatic Environmental Control Manufacturing for Residential, Commercial, and Appliance Use ᵁˢ

This U.S. industry comprises establishments primarily engaged in manufacturing automatic controls and regulators for applications, such as heating, air-conditioning, refrigeration and appliances.

- Manufacturing industrial process controls are classified in U.S. Industry 334513, Instruments and Related Products Manufacturing for Measuring, Displaying, and Controlling Industrial Process Variables;
- Manufacturing motor control switches and relays are classified in U.S. Industry 335314, Relay and Industrial Control Manufacturing;
- Manufacturing switches for appliances are classified in U.S. Industry 335931, Current-carrying Wiring Device Manufacturing; and
- Manufacturing appliance timers are classified in U.S. Industry 334518, Watch, Clock, and Part Manufacturing.

334513 Instruments and Related Products Manufacturing for Measuring, Displaying, and Controlling Industrial Process Variables ᵁˢ

This U.S. industry comprises establishments primarily engaged in manufacturing instruments and related devices for measuring, displaying, indicating, recording, transmitting, and controlling industrial process variables. These instruments measure, display or control (monitor, analyze, and so forth) industrial process variables, such as temperature, humidity, pressure, vacuum, combustion, flow, level, viscosity, density, acidity, concentration, and rotation.

- Manufacturing instruments for measuring or testing of electricity and electrical signals are classified in U.S. Industry 334515, Instrument Manufacturing for Measuring and Testing Electricity and Electrical Signals;
- Manufacturing medical thermometers are classified in U.S. Industry 339112, Surgical and Medical Instruments Manufacturing;
- Manufacturing glass hydrometers and thermometers for other nonmedical uses are classified in U.S. Industry 334519, Other Measuring and Controlling Device Manufacturing;

Sector

31-33

Manufacturing

■ = Cross-References

US—United States industry only. CAN—United States and Canadian industries are comparable. When neither US nor CAN appears, Canadian, Mexican, and United States industries are comparable.

414

Harris InfoSource

- Manufacturing instruments and instrumentation systems for laboratory analysis of samples are classified in U.S. Industry 334516, Analytical Laboratory Instrument Manufacturing; and
- Manufacturing optical alignment and display instruments, optical comparators, and optical test and inspection equipment are classified in U.S. Industry 333314, Optical Instrument and Lens Manufacturing.

334514 Totalizing Fluid Meter and Counting Device Manufacturing US

This U.S. industry comprises establishments primarily engaged in manufacturing totalizing (i.e., registering) fluid meters and counting devices. Examples of products made by these establishments are gas consumption meters, water consumption meters, parking meters, taxi meters, motor vehicle gauges, and fare collection equipment.

- Manufacturing integrating meters and counters for measuring the characteristics of electricity and electrical signals are classified in U.S. Industry 334515, Instrument Manufacturing for Measuring and Testing Electricity and Electrical Signals; and
- Manufacturing instruments and devices that measure, display, or control (i.e., monitor or analyze) related industrial process variables are classified in U.S. Industry 334513, Instruments and Related Products Manufacturing for Measuring, Displaying, and Controlling Industrial Process Variables.

334515 Instrument Manufacturing for Measuring and Testing Electricity and Electrical Signals US

This U.S. industry comprises establishments primarily engaged in manufacturing instruments for measuring and testing the characteristics of electricity and electrical signals. Examples of products made by these establishments are circuit and continuity testers, volt meters, ohm meters, wattmeters, multimeters, and semiconductor test equipment.

- Manufacturing electronic monitoring, evaluating, and other electronic support equipment for navigational, radar, and sonar systems are classified in U.S. Industry 334511, Search, Detection, Navigation, Guidance, Aeronautical, and Nautical System and Instrument Manufacturing; and
- Manufacturing equipment for measuring and testing communications signals are classified in Industry Group 3342, Communications Equipment Manufacturing.

334516 Analytical Laboratory Instrument Manufacturing US

This U.S. industry comprises establishments primarily engaged in manufacturing instruments and instrumentation systems for laboratory analysis of the chemical or physical composition or concentration of samples of solid, fluid, gaseous, or composite material.

- Manufacturing instruments for monitoring and analyzing continuous samples from medical patients are classified in U.S. Industry 334510, Electromedical and Electrotherapeutic Apparatus Manufacturing; and
- Manufacturing instruments and related devices that measure, display, or control (i.e., monitor or analyze) industrial process variables are classified in U.S. Industry 334513, Instruments and Related Products Manufacturing for Measuring, Displaying, and Controlling Industrial Process Variables.

334517 Irradiation Apparatus Manufacturing US

This U.S. industry comprises establishments primarily engaged in manufacturing irradiation apparatus and tubes for applications, such as medical diagnostic, medical therapeutic, industrial, research and scientific evaluation. Irradiation can take the form of beta-rays, gamma-rays, X-rays, or other ionizing radiation.

334518 Watch, Clock, and Part Manufacturing US

This U.S. industry comprises establishments primarily engaged in manufacturing and/or assembling: clocks; watches; timing mechanisms for clockwork operated devices; time clocks; time and date recording devices; and clock and watch parts (except crystals), such as springs, jewels, and modules.

- Manufacturing glass watch and clock crystals are classified in Industry 32721, Glass and Glass Product Manufacturing;
- Manufacturing plastics watch and clock crystals are classified in U.S. Industry 326199, All Other Plastics Product Manufacturing; and
- Manufacturing timing relays are classified in U.S. Industry 335314, Relay and Industrial Control Manufacturing.

334519 Other Measuring and Controlling Device Manufacturing US

This U.S. industry comprises establishments primarily engaged in manufacturing measuring and controlling devices (except search, detection, navigation, guidance, aeronautical, and nautical instruments and systems; automatic environmental controls for residential, commercial, and appliance use; instruments for measurement, display, and control of industrial process variables; totalizing fluid

Visit page 17 to learn about classification changes to this sector.

Manufacturing

■ = Cross-References

US—United States industry only. CAN—United States and Canadian industries are comparable. When neither US nor CAN appears, Canadian, Mexican, and United States industries are comparable.

www.harrisinfo.com

415

meters and counting devices; instruments for measuring and testing electricity and electrical signals; analytical laboratory instruments; watches, clocks, and parts; irradiation equipment; and electromedical and electrotherapeutic apparatus).

- Manufacturing medical thermometers are classified in U.S. Industry 339112, Surgical and Medical Instrument Manufacturing;
- Manufacturing search, detection, navigation, guidance, aeronautical, and nautical systems and instruments are classified in U.S. Industry 334511, Search, Detection, Navigation, Guidance, Aeronautical, and Nautical System and Instrument Manufacturing;
- Manufacturing automatic controls and regulators for applications, such as heating, air-conditioning, refrigeration and appliances, are classified in U.S. Industry 334512, Automatic Environmental Control Manufacturing for Residential, Commercial, and Appliance Use;
- Manufacturing instruments and related devices that measure, display, or control (i.e., monitor or analyze) industrial process variables are classified in U.S. Industry 334513, Instruments and Related Products Manufacturing for Measuring, Displaying, and Controlling Industrial Process Variables;
- Manufacturing totalizing (i.e., registering) fluid meters and counting devices, including motor vehicle gauges are classified in U.S. Industry 334514, Totalizing Fluid Meter and Counting Device Manufacturing;
- Manufacturing instruments for measuring and testing the characteristics of electricity and electrical signals are classified in U.S. Industry 334515, Instrument Manufacturing for Measuring and Testing Electricity and Electrical Signals;
- Manufacturing instruments for laboratory analysis of the physical composition or concentration of samples of solid, fluid, gaseous, or composite materials are classified in U.S. Industry 334516, Analytical Laboratory Instrument Manufacturing;
- Manufacturing and/or assembling watches, clocks, or parts are classified in U.S. Industry 334518, Watch, Clock, and Part Manufacturing;
- Manufacturing X-ray apparatus, tubes, or related irradiation apparatus are classified in U.S. Industry 334517, Irradiation Apparatus Manufacturing; and
- Manufacturing electromedical and electrotherapeutic apparatus are classified in U.S. Industry 334510, Electromedical and Electrotherapeutic Apparatus Manufacturing.

3346 Manufacturing and Reproducing Magnetic and Optical Media

33461 Manufacturing and Reproducing Magnetic and Optical Media
This industry comprises establishments primarily engaged in (1) manufacturing optical and magnetic media, such as blank audio tape, blank video tape, and blank diskettes and/or (2) mass duplicating (i.e., making copies) audio, video, software, and other data on magnetic, optical, and similar media.

- Designing, developing, and publishing prepackaged software are classified in Industry 51121, Software Publishers; and
- Audio, motion picture and/or video production and/or distribution are classified in Subsector 512, Motion Picture and Sound Recording Industries.

334611 Software Reproducing ᵁˢ
This U.S. industry comprises establishments primarily engaged in mass reproducing computer software. These establishments do not generally develop any software, they mass reproduce data and programs on magnetic media, such as diskettes, tapes, or cartridges. Establishments in this industry mass reproduce products, such as CD-ROMs and game cartridges.

- Establishments primarily engaged in designing, developing, and publishing prepackaged software are classified in Industry 511210, Software Publishers.

334612 Prerecorded Compact Disc (except Software), Tape, and Record Reproducing ᵁˢ
This U.S. industry comprises establishments primarily engaged in mass reproducing audio and video material on magnetic or optical media. Examples of products mass reproduced by these establishments are audio compact discs, prerecorded audio and video cassettes, and laser discs.

- Designing, developing, and publishing prepackaged software are classified in Industry 511210, Software Publishers;
- Audio, motion picture and/or video production and/or distribution are classified in Subsector 512, Motion Picture and Sound Recording Industries; and
- Manufacturing blank audio and video tape, blank diskettes, and blank optical discs are classified in U.S. Industry 334613, Magnetic and Optical Recording Media Manufacturing.

334613 Magnetic and Optical Recording Media Manufacturing ᵁˢ
This U.S. industry comprises establishments primarily engaged in manufacturing magnetic and optical recording media, such as blank magnetic tape, blank diskettes, blank optical discs, hard drive media, and blank magnetic tape cassettes.

- Mass reproducing computer software are classified in U.S. Industry 334611, Software Reproducing; and
- Mass reproducing audio and video material are classified in U.S. Industry 334612, Prerecorded Compact Disc (Except Software), Tape, and Record Reproducing.

Sector
31-33
Manufacturing

■ = Cross-References

US—United States industry only. CAN—United States and Canadian industries are comparable. When neither US nor CAN appears, Canadian, Mexican, and United States industries are comparable.

416

Harris InfoSource

➡335 ELECTRICAL EQUIPMENT, APPLIANCE, AND COMPONENT MANUFACTURING

Industries in the Electrical Equipment, Appliance, and Component Manufacturing subsector manufacture products that generate, distribute and use electrical power. Electric Lighting Equipment Manufacturing establishments produce electric lamp bulbs, lighting fixtures, and parts. Household Appliance Manufacturing establishments make both small and major electrical appliances and parts. Electrical Equipment Manufacturing establishments make goods, such as electric motors, generators, transformers, and switchgear apparatus. Other Electrical Equipment and Component Manufacturing establishments make devices for storing electrical power (e.g., batteries), for transmitting electricity (e.g., insulated wire), and wiring devices (e.g., electrical outlets, fuse boxes, and light switches).

3351 Electric Lighting Equipment Manufacturing

33511 Electric Lamp Bulb and Part Manufacturing
See industry description for 335110 below.

335110 Electric Lamp Bulb and Part Manufacturing
This industry comprises establishments primarily engaged in manufacturing electric light bulbs and tubes, and parts and components (except glass blanks for electric light bulbs).

- Manufacturing glass blanks for electric light bulbs are classified in U.S. Industry 327212, Other Pressed and Blown Glass and Glassware Manufacturing;
- Manufacturing vehicular lighting fixtures are classified in U.S. Industry 336321, Vehicular Lighting Equipment Manufacturing;
- Manufacturing light emitting diodes (LEDs) are classified in U.S. Industry 334413, Semiconductor and Related Device Manufacturing; and
- Manufacturing other lighting fixtures (except vehicular) are classified in Industry 33512, Lighting Fixture Manufacturing.

33512 Lighting Fixture Manufacturing
This industry comprises establishments primarily engaged in manufacturing electric lighting fixtures (except vehicular), nonelectric lighting equipment, lamp shades (except glass and plastics) and lighting fixture components (except current-carrying wiring devices).

- Manufacturing vehicular lighting fixtures are classified in Industry 33632, Motor Vehicle Electrical and Electronic Equipment Manufacturing;
- Manufacturing electric light bulbs, tubes, and parts are classified in Industry 33511, Electric Lamp Bulb and Part Manufacturing;
- Manufacturing current-carrying wiring devices for lighting fixtures are classified in Industry 33593, Wiring Devices Manufacturing;
- Manufacturing ceiling fans or bath fans with integrated lighting fixtures are classified in Industry 33521, Small Electrical Appliance Manufacturing;
- Manufacturing plastics lamp shades are classified in Industry 32619, Other Plastics Product Manufacturing;
- Manufacturing glassware and glass parts for lighting fixtures are classified in Industry 32721, Glass and Glass Product Manufacturing; and
- Manufacturing signaling devices that incorporate electric light bulbs, such as traffic and railway signals, are classified in Industry 33429, Other Communications Equipment Manufacturing.

335121 Residential Electric Lighting Fixture Manufacturing ᵁˢ
This U.S. industry comprises establishments primarily engaged in manufacturing fixed or portable residential electric lighting fixtures and lamp shades of metal, paper, or textiles. Residential electric lighting fixtures include those for use both inside and outside the residence.

- Manufacturing glassware for residential lighting fixtures are classified in Industry 32721, Glass and Glass Product Manufacturing;
- Manufacturing plastics lamp shades are classified in U.S. Industry 326199, All Other Plastics Product Manufacturing;
- Manufacturing electric light bulbs, tubes, and parts are classified in Industry 335110, Electric Lamp Bulb and Part Manufacturing;
- Manufacturing ceiling fans or bath fans with integrated lighting fixtures are classified in U.S. Industry 335211, Electric Housewares and Household Fan Manufacturing;
- Manufacturing current-carrying wiring devices for lighting fixtures are classified in U.S. Industry 335931, Current-carrying Wiring Device Manufacturing;
- Manufacturing commercial, industrial, and institutional electric lighting fixtures are classified in U.S. Industry 335122, Commercial, Industrial, and Institutional Electric Lighting Fixture Manufacturing; and
- Manufacturing other lighting fixtures, such as street lights, flashlights, and nonelectric lighting fixtures, are classified in U.S. Industry 335129, Other Lighting Equipment Manufacturing.

Visit page 17 to learn about classification changes to this sector.

Sector

31-33

Manufacturing

■ = Cross-References

US—United States industry only. CAN—United States and Canadian industries are comparable. When neither US nor CAN appears, Canadian, Mexican, and United States industries are comparable.

www.harrisinfo.com

417

335122 Commercial, Industrial, and Institutional Electric Lighting Fixture Manufacturing ᵁˢ

This U.S. industry comprises establishments primarily engaged in manufacturing commercial, industrial, and institutional electric lighting fixtures.

- Manufacturing glassware for commercial, industrial, and institutional electric lighting fixtures are classified in Industry 32721, Glass and Glass Product Manufacturing;
- Manufacturing residential electric lighting fixtures are classified in U.S. Industry 335121, Residential Electric Lighting Fixture Manufacturing;
- Manufacturing current-carrying wiring devices for lighting fixtures are classified in U.S. Industry 335931, Current-carrying Wiring Device Manufacturing;
- Manufacturing vehicular lighting fixtures are classified in U.S. Industry 336321, Vehicular Lighting Equipment Manufacturing;
- Manufacturing electric light bulbs, tubes, and parts are classified in Industry 335110, Electric Lamp Bulb and Part Manufacturing; and
- Manufacturing other lighting fixtures, such as street lights, flashlights, and nonelectric lighting equipment, are classified in U.S. Industry 335129, Other Lighting Equipment Manufacturing.

335129 Other Lighting Equipment Manufacturing ᵁˢ

This U.S. industry comprises establishments primarily engaged in manufacturing electric lighting fixtures (except residential, commercial, industrial, institutional, and vehicular electric lighting fixtures) and nonelectric lighting equipment.

- Manufacturing glassware for lighting fixtures are classified in Industry 32721, Glass and Glass Product Manufacturing;
- Manufacturing electric light bulbs, tubes, and parts are classified in Industry 335110, Electric Lamp Bulb and Part Manufacturing;
- Manufacturing current-carrying wiring devices for lighting fixtures are classified in U.S. Industry 335931, Current-carrying Wiring Device Manufacturing;
- Manufacturing residential electric lighting fixtures are classified in U.S. Industry 335121, Residential Electric Lighting Fixture Manufacturing;
- Manufacturing commercial, industrial, and institutional electric lighting fixtures are classified in U.S. Industry 335122, Commercial, Industrial, and Institutional Electric Lighting Fixture Manufacturing;
- Manufacturing vehicular lighting fixtures are classified in U.S. Industry 336321, Vehicular Lighting Equipment Manufacturing; and
- Manufacturing signaling devices that incorporate electric light bulbs, such as traffic and railway signals, are classified in Industry 334290, Other Communications Equipment Manufacturing.

3352 Household Appliance Manufacturing

33521 Small Electrical Appliance Manufacturing

This industry comprises establishments primarily engaged in manufacturing small electric appliances and electric housewares, household-type fans, household-type vacuum cleaners, and other electric household-type floor care machines.

- Manufacturing room air-conditioners, attic fans, wall and baseboard heating units for permanent installation, and commercial ventilation and exhaust fans are classified in Industry 33341, Ventilation, Heating, Air-conditioning, and Commercial Refrigeration Equipment Manufacturing;
- Manufacturing commercial, industrial, and institutional vacuum cleaners, and mechanical carpet sweepers are classified in Industry 33331, Commercial and Service Industry Machinery Manufacturing;
- Manufacturing major household-type appliances, such as washing machines, dryers, stoves, and hot water heaters, are classified in Industry 33522, Major Appliance Manufacturing; and
- Installing central vacuum cleaning systems are classified in Sector 23, Construction.

335211 Electric Housewares and Household Fan Manufacturing ᵁˢ

This U.S. industry comprises establishments primarily engaged in manufacturing small electric appliances and electric housewares for heating, cooking, and other purposes, and electric household-type fans (except attic fans).

- Manufacturing attic fans are classified in U.S. Industry 333412, Industrial and Commercial Fan and Blower Manufacturing;
- Manufacturing wall and baseboard heating units for permanent installation are classified in U.S. Industry 333414, Heating Equipment (except Warm Air Furnaces) Manufacturing;
- Manufacturing room air-conditioners are classified in U.S. Industry 333415, Air-conditioning and Warm Air Heating Equipment and Commercial and Industrial Refrigeration Equipment Manufacturing; and
- Manufacturing microwave and convection ovens are classified in U.S. Industry 335221, Household Cooking Appliance Manufacturing.

Sector
31-33
Manufacturing

■ = Cross-References

US—United States industry only. CAN—United States and Canadian industries are comparable. When neither US nor CAN appears, Canadian, Mexican, and United States industries are comparable.

418

Harris InfoSource

335212 Household Vacuum Cleaner Manufacturing [US]
This U.S. industry comprises establishments primarily engaged in manufacturing electric vacuum cleaners, electric floor waxing machines, and other electric floor care machines typically for household use.

- Manufacturing electric vacuum cleaners for commercial, industrial, and institutional uses, and mechanical carpet sweepers are classified in U.S. Industry 333319, Other Commercial and Service Industry Machinery Manufacturing; and
- Installing central vacuum cleaning systems are classified in Industry 235950, Building Equipment and Other Machinery Installation Contractors.

33522 Major Appliance Manufacturing
This industry comprises establishments primarily engaged in manufacturing household-type cooking appliances, household-type laundry equipment, household-type refrigerators, upright and chest freezers, and other electrical and nonelectrical major household-type appliances, such as dishwashers, water heaters, and garbage disposal units.

- Manufacturing small electric appliances and electric housewares, such as hot plates, griddles, toasters, and electric irons, are classified in Industry 33521, Small Electrical Appliance Manufacturing;
- Manufacturing commercial and industrial refrigerators and freezers are classified in Industry 33341, Ventilation, Heating, Air-conditioning, and Commercial Refrigeration Equipment Manufacturing;
- Manufacturing commercial-type cooking equipment and commercial-type laundry, drycleaning, and pressing equipment are classified in Industry 33331, Commercial and Service Industry Machinery Manufacturing; and
- Manufacturing household-type sewing machines are classified in Industry 33329, Other Industrial Machinery Manufacturing.

335221 Household Cooking Appliance Manufacturing [US]
This U.S. industry comprises establishments primarily engaged in manufacturing household-type electric and nonelectric cooking equipment (except small electric appliances and electric housewares).

- Manufacturing small electric appliances and electric housewares used for cooking, such as electric skillets, electric hot plates, electric griddles, toasters, and percolators, are classified in U.S. Industry 335211, Electric Housewares and Household Fan Manufacturing; and
- Manufacturing commercial-type cooking equipment are classified in U.S. Industry 333319, Other Commercial and Service Industry Machinery Manufacturing.

335222 Household Refrigerator and Home Freezer Manufacturing [US]
This U.S. industry comprises establishments primarily engaged in manufacturing household-type refrigerators and upright and chest freezers.

- Establishments primarily engaged in manufacturing commercial and industrial refrigeration equipment, such as refrigerators and freezers, are classified in U.S. Industry 333415, Air-conditioning and Warm Air Heating Equipment and Commercial and Industrial Refrigeration Equipment Manufacturing.

335224 Household Laundry Equipment Manufacturing [US]
This U.S. industry comprises establishments primarily engaged in manufacturing household-type laundry equipment.

- Manufacturing portable electric irons are classified in U.S. Industry 335211, Electric Housewares and Household Fan Manufacturing; and
- Manufacturing commercial-type laundry and drycleaning equipment are classified in U.S. Industry 333312, Commercial Laundry, Drycleaning, and Pressing Machine Manufacturing.

335228 Other Major Household Appliance Manufacturing [US]
This U.S. industry comprises establishments primarily engaged in manufacturing electric and nonelectric major household-type appliances (except cooking equipment, refrigerators, upright and chest freezers, and household-type laundry equipment).

- Manufacturing household-type cooking equipment are classified in U.S. Industry 335221, Household Cooking Appliance Manufacturing;
- Manufacturing household-type sewing machines are classified in U.S. Industry 333298, All Other Industrial Machinery Manufacturing;
- Manufacturing household-type refrigerators and upright and chest freezers are classified in U.S. Industry 335222, Household Refrigerator and Home Freezer Manufacturing; and
- Manufacturing small electric appliances are classified in U.S. Industry 335211, Electric Housewares and Household Fan Manufacturing.

Visit page 17 to learn about classification changes to this sector.

Sector
31-33
Manufacturing

■ = Cross-References

US—United States industry only. CAN—United States and Canadian industries are comparable. When neither US nor CAN appears, Canadian, Mexican, and United States industries are comparable.

www.harrisinfo.com

 419

3353 Electrical Equipment Manufacturing

33531 Electrical Equipment Manufacturing
This industry comprises establishments primarily engaged in manufacturing power, distribution, and specialty transformers; electric motors, generators, and motor generator sets; switchgear and switchboard apparatus; relays; and industrial controls.

- Manufacturing turbine generator set units and electric outboard motors are classified in Industry 33361, Engine, Turbine, and Power Transmission Equipment Manufacturing;
- Manufacturing electronic component-type transformers and switches are classified in Industry 33441, Semiconductor and Other Electronic Component Manufacturing;
- Manufacturing environmental controls and industrial process control instruments are classified in Industry 33451, Navigational, Measuring, Electromedical, and Control Instruments Manufacturing;
- Manufacturing switches for electrical circuits, such as pushbutton and snap switches, are classified in Industry 33593, Wiring Device Manufacturing;
- Manufacturing complete for welding and soldering equipment are classified in Industry 33399, All Other General Purpose Machinery Manufacturing; and
- Manufacturing starting motors and generators for internal combustion engines are classified in Industry 33632, Motor Vehicle Electrical and Electronic Equipment Manufacturing.

335311 Power, Distribution, and Specialty Transformer Manufacturing CAN
This U.S. industry comprises establishments primarily engaged in manufacturing power, distribution, and specialty transformers (except electronic components). Industrial-type and consumer-type transformers in this industry vary (e.g., step up or step down) voltage but do not convert alternating to direct or direct to alternating current.

- Establishments primarily engaged in manufacturing electronic component-type transformers are classified in U.S. Industry 334416, Electronic Coil, Transformers, and Other Inductor Manufacturing.

335312 Motor and Generator Manufacturing CAN
This U.S. industry comprises establishments primarily engaged in manufacturing electric motors (except internal combustion engine starting motors), power generators (except battery charging alternators for internal combustion engines), and motor generator sets (except turbine generator set units). This industry includes establishments rewinding armatures on a factory basis.

- Manufacturing electric outboard motors are classified in U.S. Industry 333618, Other Engine Equipment Manufacturing;
- Manufacturing gas, steam, or hydraulic turbine generator set units are classified in U.S. Industry 333611, Turbine and Turbine Generator Set Units Manufacturing;
- Manufacturing starting motors and battery charging alternators for internal combustion engines are classified in U.S. Industry 336322, Other Motor Vehicle Electrical and Electronic Equipment Manufacturing;
- Rewinding armatures, not on a factory basis, are classified in Industry 811310, Commercial and Industrial Machinery and Equipment (except Automotive and Electronic) Repair and Maintenance; and
- Manufacturing complete welding and soldering equipment are classified in U.S. Industry 333992, Welding and Soldering Equipment Manufacturing.

335313 Switchgear and Switchboard Apparatus Manufacturing US
This U.S. industry comprises establishments primarily engaged in manufacturing switchgear and switchboard apparatus.

- Manufacturing relays are classified in U.S. Industry 335314, Relay and Industrial Control Manufacturing;
- Manufacturing switches for electronic applications are classified in U.S. Industry 334419, Other Electronic Component Manufacturing; and
- Manufacturing snap, pushbutton, and similar switches for electrical circuits are classified in U.S. Industry 335931, Current-carrying Wiring Device Manufacturing.

335314 Relay and Industrial Control Manufacturing US
This U.S. industry comprises establishments primarily engaged in manufacturing relays, motor starters and controllers, and other industrial controls and control accessories.

- Manufacturing environmental and appliance control equipment are classified in U.S. Industry 334512, Automatic Environmental Control Manufacturing for Residential, Commercial, and Appliance Use; and
- Manufacturing instruments for controlling industrial process variables are classified in U.S. Industry 334513, Instruments and Related Products Manufacturing for Measuring, Displaying, and Controlling Industrial Process Variables.

■ = Cross-References

Sector
31-33
Manufacturing

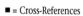

US—United States industry only. CAN—United States and Canadian industries are comparable. When neither US nor CAN appears, Canadian, Mexican, and United States industries are comparable.

420

Harris InfoSource

3359 Other Electrical Equipment and Component Manufacturing

This industry group comprises establishments manufacturing electrical equipment and components (except electric lighting equipment, household-type appliances, transformers, switchgear, relays, motors, and generators).

33591 Battery Manufacturing

This industry comprises establishments primarily engaged in manufacturing primary and storage batteries.

335911 Storage Battery Manufacturing ᵁˢ

This U.S. industry comprises establishments primarily engaged in manufacturing storage batteries.

- Establishments primarily engaged in manufacturing primary batteries are classified in U.S. Industry 335912, Primary Battery Manufacturing.

335912 Primary Battery Manufacturing ᵁˢ

This U.S. industry comprises establishments primarily engaged in manufacturing wet or dry primary batteries.

- Establishments primarily engaged in manufacturing storage batteries are classified in U.S. Industry 335911, Storage Battery Manufacturing.

33592 Communication and Energy Wire and Cable Manufacturing

This industry comprises establishments insulating fiber-optic cable, and manufacturing insulated nonferrous wire and cable from nonferrous wire drawn in other establishments.

- Drawing nonferrous wire are classified in Subsector 331, Primary Metal Manufacturing;
- Manufacturing cable sets consisting of insulated wire and various connectors for electronic applications are classified in Industry 33441, Semiconductor and Other Electronic Component Manufacturing;
- Manufacturing extension cords, appliance cords, and similar electrical cord sets from purchased, insulated wire or cable are classified in Industry 33599, All Other Electrical Equipment and Component Manufacturing; and
- Manufacturing unsheathed fiber-optic materials are classified in Industry 32721, Glass and Glass Product Manufacturing.

335921 Fiber Optic Cable Manufacturing ᵁˢ

This U.S. industry comprises establishments primarily engaged in manufacturing insulated fiber-optic cable from purchased fiber-optic strand.

- Manufacturing unsheathed fiber-optic materials are classified in Industry 32721, Glass and Glass Product Manufacturing; and
- Manufacturing insulated nonferrous wire and cable from purchased wire are classified in U.S. Industry 335929, Other Communication and Energy Wire Manufacturing.

335929 Other Communication and Energy Wire Manufacturing ᵁˢ

This U.S. industry comprises establishments primarily engaged in manufacturing insulated wire and cable of nonferrous metals from purchased wire.

- Manufacturing cable sets consisting of insulated wire and various connectors for electronic applications are classified in U.S. Industry 334419, Other Electronic Component Manufacturing;
- Manufacturing extension cords, appliance cords, and similar electrical cord sets from purchased insulated wire are classified in U.S. Industry 335999, All Other Miscellaneous Electrical Equipment and Component Manufacturing;
- Drawing and insulating copper wire in the same establishment are classified in U.S. Industry 331422, Copper Wire (except Mechanical) Drawing;
- Drawing and insulating aluminum wire in the same establishment are classified in U.S. Industry 331319, Other Aluminum Rolling and Drawing; and
- Drawing nonferrous wire (except copper and aluminum) are classified in U.S. Industry 331491, Nonferrous Metal (except Copper and Aluminum) Rolling, Drawing, and Extruding.

33593 Wiring Device Manufacturing

This industry comprises establishments primarily engaged in manufacturing current-carrying wiring devices and noncurrent-carrying wiring devices for wiring electrical circuits.

- Manufacturing ceramic and glass insulators are classified in Subsector 327, Nonmetallic Mineral Product Manufacturing; and
- Manufacturing electronic component-type connectors, sockets, and switches are classified in Industry 33441, Semiconductor and Other Electronic Component Manufacturing.

335931 Current-carrying Wiring Device Manufacturing ᵁˢ

This U.S. industry comprises establishments primarily engaged in manufacturing current-carrying wiring devices.

- Manufacturing electronic component-type connectors are classified in U.S. Industry 334417, Electronic Connector Manufacturing;

Visit page 17 to learn about classification changes to this sector.

Sector
31-33

Manufacturing

■ = Cross-References

US—United States industry only. CAN—United States and Canadian industries are comparable. When neither US nor CAN appears, Canadian, Mexican, and United States industries are comparable.

www.harrisinfo.com

421

■ Manufacturing noncurrent-carrying wiring devices are classified in U.S. Industry 335932, Noncurrent-carrying Wiring Device Manufacturing; and
■ Manufacturing electronic component-type sockets and switches are classified in U.S. Industry 334419, Other Electronic Component Manufacturing.

335932 Noncurrent-carrying Wiring Device Manufacturing US
This U.S. industry comprises establishments primarily engaged in manufacturing noncurrent-carrying wiring devices.

■ Manufacturing porcelain and ceramic insulators are classified in U.S. Industry 327113, Porcelain Electrical Supply Manufacturing;
■ Manufacturing current-carrying wiring devices are classified in U.S. Industry 335931, Current-carrying Wiring Device Manufacturing; and
■ Manufacturing glass insulators are classified in Industry 32721, Glass and Glass Product Manufacturing.

33599 All Other Electrical Equipment and Component Manufacturing
This industry comprises establishments primarily engaged in manufacturing electrical equipment (except electric lighting equipment, household-type appliances, transformers, motors, generators, switchgear, relays, industrial controls, batteries, communication and energy wire and cable, and wiring devices).

■ Manufacturing lighting equipment are classified in Industry Group 3351, Electric Lighting Equipment Manufacturing;
■ Manufacturing household-type appliances are classified in Industry Group 3352, Household Appliance Manufacturing;
■ Manufacturing transformers, motors, generators, switchgear, relays, and industrial controls are classified in Industry 33531, Electrical Equipment Manufacturing;
■ Manufacturing batteries are classified in Industry 33591, Battery Manufacturing;
■ Manufacturing communication and energy wire are classified in Industry 33592, Communication and Energy Wire and Cable Manufacturing;
■ Manufacturing current-carrying and noncurrent-carrying wiring devices are classified in Industry 33593, Wiring Device Manufacturing;
■ Manufacturing carbon or graphite gaskets are classified in Industry 33999, All Other Miscellaneous Manufacturing;
■ Manufacturing electronic component-type rectifiers, voltage regulating integrated circuits, power converting integrated circuits, electronic capacitors, electronic resistors, and similar devices are classified in Industry 33441, Semiconductor and Other Electronic Component Manufacturing; and
■ Manufacturing equipment incorporating lasers are classified in various subsectors of manufacturing based on the associated production process of the finished equipment.

335991 Carbon and Graphite Product Manufacturing US
This U.S. industry comprises establishments primarily engaged in manufacturing carbon, graphite, and metal-graphite brushes and brush stock; carbon or graphite electrodes for thermal and electrolytic uses; carbon and graphite fibers; and other carbon, graphite, and metal-graphite products.

■ Establishments primarily engaged in manufacturing carbon or graphite gaskets are classified in U.S. Industry 339991, Gasket, Packing, and Sealing Device Manufacturing.

335999 All Other Miscellaneous Electrical Equipment and Component Manufacturing US
This U.S. industry comprises establishments primarily engaged in manufacturing industrial and commercial electric apparatus and other equipment (except lighting equipment, household appliances, transformers, motors, generators, switchgear, relays, industrial controls, batteries, communication and energy wire and cable, wiring devices, and carbon and graphite products). This industry includes power converters (i.e., AC to DC and DC to AC), power supplies, surge suppressors, and similar equipment for industrial-type and consumer-type equipment.

■ Manufacturing lighting equipment are classified in Industry Group 3351, Electric Lighting Equipment Manufacturing;
■ Manufacturing household-type appliances are classified in Industry Group 3352, Household Appliance Manufacturing;
■ Manufacturing transformers, motors, generators, switchgear, relays, and industrial controls are classified in Industry 33531, Electrical Equipment Manufacturing;
■ Manufacturing primary and storage batteries are classified in Industry 33591, Battery Manufacturing;
■ Manufacturing communication and energy wire and cable from purchased wire are classified in Industry 33592, Communication and Energy Wire and Cable Manufacturing;
■ Manufacturing current-carrying and noncurrent-carrying wiring devices are classified in Industry 33593, Wiring Device Manufacturing;
■ Manufacturing electronic component-type rectifiers (except semiconductor) are classified in U.S. Industry 334419, Other Electronic Component Manufacturing;
■ Manufacturing semiconductor rectifiers, voltage regulating integrated circuits, power converting integrated circuits, and similar semiconductor devices are classified in U.S. Industry 334413, Semiconductor and Related Device Manufacturing;

Sector 31-33

Manufacturing

■ = Cross-References

US—United States industry only. CAN—United States and Canadian industries are comparable. When neither US nor CAN appears, Canadian, Mexican, and United States industries are comparable.

422

Harris InfoSource

■ Manufacturing electronic component-type capacitors and condensers are classified in U.S. Industry 334414, Electronic Capacitor Manufacturing;
■ Manufacturing carbon and graphite products are classified in U.S. Industry 335991, Carbon and Graphite Product Manufacturing; and
■ Manufacturing equipment incorporating lasers are classified in various manufacturing subsectors based on the associated production process of the finished equipment.

⇒ 336 TRANSPORTATION EQUIPMENT MANUFACTURING

Industries in the Transportation Equipment Manufacturing subsector produce equipment for transporting people and goods. Transportation equipment is a type of machinery. An entire subsector is devoted to this activity because of the significance of its economic size in all three North American countries.

Establishments in this subsector utilize production processes similar to those of other machinery manufacturing establishments—bending, forming, welding, machining, and assembling metal or plastic parts into components and finished products. However, the assembly of components and subassemblies and their further assembly into finished vehicles tends to be a more common production process in this subsector than in the Machinery Manufacturing subsector.

NAICS has industry groups for the manufacture of equipment for each mode of transport—road, rail, air and water. Parts for motor vehicles warrant a separate industry group because of their importance and because parts manufacture requires less assembly, and the establishments that manufacture only parts are not as vertically integrated as those that make complete vehicles.

Land use motor vehicle equipment not designed for highway operation (e.g., agricultural equipment, construction equipment, and materials handling equipment) is classified in the appropriate NAICS subsector based on the type and use of the equipment.

3361 Motor Vehicle Manufacturing

33611 Automobile and Light Duty Motor Vehicle Manufacturing
This industry comprises establishments primarily engaged in (1) manufacturing complete automobile and light duty motor vehicles (i.e., body and chassis or unibody) or (2) manufacturing chassis only.

■ Establishments primarily engaged in manufacturing car, truck, and bus bodies and assembling vehicles on a purchased chassis and manufacturing kit cars for highway use are classified in Industry 33621, Motor Vehicle Body and Trailer Manufacturing.

336111 Automobile Manufacturing ᵁˢ
This U.S. industry comprises establishments primarily engaged in (1) manufacturing complete automobiles (i.e., body and chassis or unibody) or (2) manufacturing automobile chassis only.

■ Establishments primarily engaged in manufacturing car bodies and assembling vehicles on a purchased chassis and manufacturing kit cars for highway use are classified in U.S. Industry 336211, Motor Vehicle Body Manufacturing.

336112 Light Truck and Utility Vehicle Manufacturing ᵁˢ
This U.S. industry comprises establishments primarily engaged in (1) manufacturing complete light trucks and utility vehicles (i.e., body and chassis) or (2) manufacturing light truck and utility vehicle chassis only. Vehicles made include light duty vans, pick-up trucks, minivans, and sport utility vehicles.

■ Establishments primarily engaged in manufacturing truck and bus bodies and assembling vehicles on a purchased chassis are classified in U.S. Industry 336211, Motor Vehicle Body Manufacturing.

33612 Heavy Duty Truck Manufacturing
See industry description for 336120 below.

336120 Heavy Duty Truck Manufacturing
This industry comprises establishments primarily engaged in (1) manufacturing heavy duty truck chassis and assembling complete heavy duty trucks, buses, heavy duty motor homes, and other special purpose heavy duty motor vehicles for highway use or (2) manufacturing heavy duty truck chassis only.

■ Manufacturing truck and bus bodies and assembling vehicles on a purchased chassis are classified in U.S. Industry 336211, Motor Vehicle Body Manufacturing;

Visit page 17 to learn about classification changes to this sector.

Manufacturing

■ = Cross-References

US—United States industry only. CAN—United States and Canadian industries are comparable. When neither US nor CAN appears, Canadian, Mexican, and United States industries are comparable.

www.harrisinfo.com 423

- Manufacturing motor homes on purchased chassis are classified in U.S. Industry 336213, Motor Home Manufacturing;
- Manufacturing vans, minivans, and light trucks are classified in Industry 336112, Light Truck and Utility Vehicle Manufacturing;
- Manufacturing military armored vehicles are classified in U.S. Industry 336992, Military Armored Vehicle, Tank, and Tank Component Manufacturing; and
- Manufacturing off highway construction equipment are classified in Industry 333120, Construction Machinery Manufacturing.

3362 Motor Vehicle Body and Trailer Manufacturing

33621 Motor Vehicle Body and Trailer Manufacturing

This industry comprises establishments primarily engaged in (1) manufacturing motor vehicle bodies and cabs or (2) manufacturing truck, automobile and utility trailers, truck trailer chassis, detachable trailer bodies and detachable trailer chassis. The products made may be sold separately or may be assembled on purchased chassis and sold as complete vehicles. Motor homes are units where the motor and the living quarters are contained in the same integrated unit, while travel trailers are designed to be towed by a motor unit, such as an automobile or a light truck.

- Making manufactured homes (i.e., mobile homes) are classified in Industry 32199, All Other Wood Product Manufacturing;
- Customizing automotive vehicle and trailer interiors (i.e. van conversions) on an individual basis are classified in Industry 81112, Automotive Body, Paint, Interior, and Glass Repair;
- Manufacturing light duty motor home chassis and assembling complete motor homes are classified in Industry 33611, Automobile and Light Duty Motor Vehicle Manufacturing; and
- Manufacturing heavy duty truck chassis and assembling heavy duty trucks, buses, motor homes, and other special purpose heavy duty motor vehicles for highway use are classified in Industry 33612, Heavy Duty Truck Manufacturing.

336211 Motor Vehicle Body Manufacturing CAN

This U.S. industry comprises establishments primarily engaged in manufacturing truck and bus bodies and cabs and automobile bodies. The products made may be sold separately or may be assembled on purchased chassis and sold as complete vehicles.

- Establishments primarily engaged in manufacturing heavy duty chassis and assembling heavy duty trucks, buses, motor homes, and other special purpose heavy duty motor vehicles for highway use are classified in Industry 336120, Heavy Duty Truck Manufacturing.

336212 Truck Trailer Manufacturing CAN

This U.S. industry comprises establishments primarily engaged in manufacturing truck trailers, truck trailer chassis, cargo container chassis, detachable trailer bodies, and detachable trailer chassis for sale separately.

- Establishments primarily engaged in manufacturing utility trailers, light-truck trailers, and travel trailers are classified in U.S. Industry 336214, Travel Trailer and Camper Manufacturing.

336213 Motor Home Manufacturing US

This U.S. industry comprises establishments primarily engaged in (1) manufacturing motor homes on purchased chassis and/or (2) manufacturing conversion vans on an assembly line basis. Motor homes are units where the motor and the living quarters are integrated in the same unit.

- Manufacturing light duty motor homes chassis and assembling complete motor homes are classified in U.S. Industry 336112, Light Truck and Utility Vehicle Manufacturing;
- Customizing automotive vehicle and trailer interiors (i.e. van conversions) on an individual basis are classified in U.S. Industry 811121, Automotive Body, Paint, and Interior Repair and Maintenance; and
- Producing manufactured homes (i.e., mobile homes) are classified in U.S. Industry 321991, Manufactured Home (Mobile Home) Manufacturing.

336214 Travel Trailer and Camper Manufacturing US

This U.S. industry comprises establishments primarily engaged in one or more of the following: (1) manufacturing travel trailers and campers designed to attach to motor vehicles; (2) manufacturing pickup coaches (i.e., campers) and caps (i.e., covers) for mounting on pickup trucks; and (3) manufacturing automobile, utility and light-truck trailers. Travel trailers do not have their own motor but are designed to be towed by a motor unit, such as an automobile or a light truck.

- Establishments primarily engaged in making manufactured homes (i.e., mobile homes) designed to accept permanent water, sewer, and utility connections and equipped with wheels, but not intended for regular highway use, are classified in U.S. Industry 321991, Manufactured Home (Mobile Home) Manufacturing.

Sector
31-33

Manufacturing

■ = Cross-References

US—United States industry only. CAN—United States and Canadian industries are comparable. When neither US nor CAN appears, Canadian, Mexican, and United States industries are comparable.

424

Harris InfoSource

3363 Motor Vehicle Parts Manufacturing

33631 Motor Vehicle Gasoline Engine and Engine Parts Manufacturing

This industry comprises establishments primarily engaged in manufacturing and/or rebuilding motor vehicle gasoline engines, and engine parts, whether or not for vehicular use.

- Manufacturing wiring harnesses and other vehicular electrical and electronic equipment are classified in Industry 33632, Motor Vehicle Electrical and Electronic Equipment Manufacturing;
- Manufacturing transmission and power train equipment are classified in Industry 33635, Motor Vehicle Transmission and Power Train Parts Manufacturing;
- Manufacturing radiators are classified in Industry 33639, Other Motor Vehicle Parts Manufacturing;
- Manufacturing steering and suspension components are classified in Industry 33633, Motor Vehicle Steering and Suspension Components (except Spring) Manufacturing;
- Manufacturing parts for machine repair and equipment parts (except electric) on a job or shop basis are classified in Industry 33271, Machine Shops;
- Manufacturing rubber and plastic belts and hoses without fittings are classified in Industry 32622, Rubber and Plastics Hoses and Belting Manufacturing; and
- Manufacturing stationary and diesel engines are classified in Industry 33361, Engine, Turbine, and Power Transmission Equipment Manufacturing.

336311 Carburetor, Piston, Piston Ring, and Valve Manufacturing US

This U.S. industry comprises establishments primarily engaged in manufacturing and/or rebuilding carburetors, pistons, piston rings, and engine intake and exhaust valves.

- Establishments primarily engaged in manufacturing parts for machine repair and equipment parts (except electric) on a job or shop basis are classified in Industry 332710, Machine Shops.

336312 Gasoline Engine and Engine Parts Manufacturing US

This U.S. industry comprises establishments primarily engaged in manufacturing and/or rebuilding gasoline motor vehicle engines and gasoline motor vehicle engine parts, excluding carburetors, pistons, piston rings, and valves.

- Manufacturing carburetors, pistons, piston rings, and valves are classified in U.S. Industry 336311, Carburetor, Piston, Piston Ring, and Valve Manufacturing;
- Manufacturing wiring harnesses and other vehicular electrical and electronic equipment are classified in U.S. Industry 336322, Other Motor Vehicle Electrical and Electronic Equipment Manufacturing;
- Manufacturing transmission and power train equipment are classified in Industry 336350, Motor Vehicle Transmission and Power Train Parts Manufacturing;
- Manufacturing radiators are classified in U.S. Industry 336399, All Other Motor Vehicle Parts Manufacturing;
- Manufacturing steering and suspension components are classified in Industry 336330, Motor Vehicle Steering and Suspension Components (except Spring) Manufacturing;
- Manufacturing rubber and plastic belts and hoses without fittings are classified in Industry 326220, Rubber and Plastics Hoses and Belting Manufacturing; and
- Manufacturing stationary and diesel engines are classified in U.S. Industry 333618, Other Engine Equipment Manufacturing.

33632 Motor Vehicle Electrical and Electronic Equipment Manufacturing

This industry comprises establishments primarily engaged in (1) manufacturing vehicular lighting and/or (2) manufacturing and/or rebuilding motor vehicle electrical and electronic equipment. The products made can be used for all types of transportation equipment (i.e., aircraft, automobiles, trains, ships).

- Manufacturing automotive lamps are classified in Industry 33511, Electric Lamp Bulb and Part Manufacturing;
- Manufacturing batteries are classified in Industry 33591, Battery Manufacturing;
- Manufacturing electric motors for motor vehicles (including electric vehicles) are classified in Industry 33531, Electrical Equipment Manufacturing;
- Manufacturing railway traffic control signals and passenger car alarms are classified in Industry 33429, Other Communications Equipment Manufacturing; and
- Manufacturing car stereos are classified in Industry 33431, Audio and Video Equipment Manufacturing.

336321 Vehicular Lighting Equipment Manufacturing US

This U.S. industry comprises establishments primarily engaged in manufacturing vehicular lighting fixtures.

- Establishments primarily engaged in manufacturing automotive lamps (i.e., bulbs) are classified in Industry 335110, Electric Lamp Bulb and Part Manufacturing.

336322 Other Motor Vehicle Electrical and Electronic Equipment Manufacturing US

This U.S. industry comprises establishments primarily engaged in manufacturing and/or rebuilding electrical and electronic equipment for motor vehicles and internal combustion engines.

Visit page 17 to learn about classification changes to this sector.

Sector
31-33
Manufacturing

■ = Cross-References

US—United States industry only. CAN—United States and Canadian industries are comparable. When neither US nor CAN appears, Canadian, Mexican, and United States industries are comparable.

www.harrisinfo.com

425

- Manufacturing vehicular lighting equipment are classified in U.S. Industry 336321, Vehicular Lighting Equipment Manufacturing;
- Manufacturing automotive lamps are classified in Industry 335110, Electric Lamp Bulb and Part Manufacturing;
- Manufacturing batteries are classified in U.S. Industry 335911, Storage Battery Manufacturing;
- Manufacturing electric motors for electric vehicles are classified in U.S. Industry 335312, Motor and Generator Manufacturing;
- Manufacturing railway traffic control signals and passenger car alarms are classified in Industry 334290, Other Communications Equipment Manufacturing; and
- Manufacturing car stereos are classified in Industry 334310, Audio and Video Equipment Manufacturing.

33633 Motor Vehicle Steering and Suspension Components (except Spring) Manufacturing

See industry description for 336330 below.

336330 Motor Vehicle Steering and Suspension Components (except Spring) Manufacturing

This industry comprises establishments primarily engaged in manufacturing and/or rebuilding motor vehicle steering mechanisms and suspension components (except springs).

- Establishments primarily engaged in manufacturing springs are classified in Industry 33261, Spring and Wire Product Manufacturing.

33634 Motor Vehicle Brake System Manufacturing

See industry description for 336340 below.

336340 Motor Vehicle Brake System Manufacturing

This industry comprises establishments primarily engaged in manufacturing and/or rebuilding motor vehicle brake systems and related components.

- Establishments primarily engaged in manufacturing rubber and plastics belts and hoses without fittings are classified in Industry 326220, Rubber and Plastics Hoses and Belting Manufacturing.

33635 Motor Vehicle Transmission and Power Train Parts Manufacturing

See industry description for 336350 below.

336350 Motor Vehicle Transmission and Power Train Parts Manufacturing

This industry comprises establishments primarily engaged in manufacturing and/or rebuilding motor vehicle transmission and power train parts.

33636 Motor Vehicle Seating and Interior Trim Manufacturing

See industry description for 336360 below.

336360 Motor Vehicle Seating and Interior Trim Manufacturing

This industry comprises establishments primarily engaged in manufacturing motor vehicle seating, seats, seat frames, seat belts, and interior trimmings.

- Establishments primarily engaged in manufacturing convertible tops for vehicles and those manufacturing air bags are classified in U.S. Industry 336399, All Other Motor Vehicle Parts Manufacturing.

33637 Motor Vehicle Metal Stamping

See industry description for 336370 below.

336370 Motor Vehicle Metal Stamping

This industry comprises establishments primarily engaged in manufacturing motor vehicle stampings, such as fenders, tops, body parts, trim, and molding.

- Manufacturing stampings and further processing the stampings are classified according to the process of the specific product made; and
- Manufacturing stampings (except motor vehicle) are classified in U.S. Industry 332116 Metal Stamping.

33639 Other Motor Vehicle Parts Manufacturing

This industry comprises establishments primarily engaged in manufacturing and/or rebuilding motor vehicle parts and accessories (except motor vehicle gasoline engines and engine parts, motor vehicle

Sector
31-33

Manufacturing

US—United States industry only. CAN—United States and Canadian industries are comparable. When neither US nor CAN appears, Canadian, Mexican, and United States industries are comparable.

426

Harris InfoSource

electrical and electronic equipment, motor vehicle steering and suspension components, motor vehicle brake systems, motor vehicle transmission and power train parts, motor vehicle seating and interior trim, and motor vehicle stampings).

- Manufacturing motor vehicle gasoline engines and engine parts are classified in Industry 33631, Motor Vehicle Gasoline Engine and Engine Parts Manufacturing;
- Manufacturing motor vehicle electrical and electronic equipment are classified in Industry 33632, Motor Vehicle Electrical and Electronic Equipment Manufacturing;
- Manufacturing motor vehicle steering and suspension components are classified in Industry 33633, Motor Vehicle Steering and Suspension Components (except Spring) Manufacturing;
- Manufacturing motor vehicle brake systems are classified in Industry 33634, Motor Vehicle Brake System Manufacturing;
- Manufacturing motor vehicle transmission and power train parts are classified in Industry 33635, Motor Vehicle Transmission and Power Train Parts Manufacturing;
- Manufacturing motor vehicle seating and interior trim are classified in Industry 33636, Motor Vehicle Seating and Interior Trim Manufacturing;
- Manufacturing motor vehicle stampings are classified in Industry 33637, Motor Vehicle Metal Stamping; and
- Manufacturing air-conditioning systems and compressors (except motor vehicle air-conditioning systems) are classified in Industry 33341, Ventilation, Heating, Air-conditioning, and Commercial Refrigeration Equipment Manufacturing.

336391 Motor Vehicle Air-conditioning Manufacturing US

This U.S. industry comprises establishments primarily engaged in manufacturing air-conditioning systems and compressors for motor vehicles, such as automobiles, trucks, buses, aircraft, farm machinery, construction machinery, and other related vehicles.

- Establishments primarily engaged in manufacturing air-conditioning systems and compressors (except motor vehicle air-conditioning systems) are classified in U.S. Industry 333415, Air-conditioning and Warm Air Heating Equipment and Commercial and Industrial Refrigeration Equipment Manufacturing.

336399 All Other Motor Vehicle Parts Manufacturing US

This U.S. industry comprises establishments primarily engaged in manufacturing and/or rebuilding motor vehicle parts and accessories (except motor vehicle gasoline engines and engine parts, motor vehicle electrical and electronic equipment, motor vehicle steering and suspension components, motor vehicle brake systems, motor vehicle transmission and power train parts, motor vehicle seating and interior trim, motor vehicle stampings, and motor vehicle air-conditioning systems and compressors).

- Manufacturing motor vehicle gasoline engines and engine parts are classified in Industry 33631, Motor Vehicle Gasoline Engine and Engine Parts Manufacturing;
- Manufacturing motor vehicle electrical and electronic equipment are classified in Industry 33632, Motor Vehicle Electrical and Electronic Equipment Manufacturing;
- Manufacturing motor vehicle steering and suspension components are classified in Industry 336330, Motor Vehicle Steering and Suspension Components (except Spring) Manufacturing;
- Manufacturing motor vehicle brake systems are classified in Industry 336340, Motor Vehicle Brake System Manufacturing;
- Manufacturing motor vehicle transmission and power train parts are classified in Industry 336350, Motor Vehicle Transmission and Power Train Parts Manufacturing;
- Manufacturing motor vehicle seating and interior trim are classified in Industry 336360, Motor Vehicle Seating and Interior Trim Manufacturing;
- Manufacturing motor vehicle stampings are classified in Industry 336370, Motor Vehicle Metal Stamping; and
- Manufacturing motor vehicle air-conditioning systems and compressors are classified in U.S. Industry 336391, Motor Vehicle Air-conditioning Manufacturing.

3364 Aerospace Product and Parts Manufacturing

33641 Aerospace Product and Parts Manufacturing

This industry comprises establishments primarily engaged in one or more of the following: (1) manufacturing complete aircraft, missiles, or space vehicles; (2) manufacturing aerospace engines, propulsion units, auxiliary equipment or parts; (3) developing and making prototypes of aerospace products; (4) aircraft conversion (i.e., major modifications to systems); and (5) complete aircraft or propulsion systems overhaul and rebuilding (i.e., periodic restoration of aircraft to original design specifications).

- Establishments primarily engaged in manufacturing space satellites are classified in Industry 33422, Radio and Television Broadcasting and Wireless Communications Equipment Manufacturing;
- Establishments primarily engaged in the repair of aircraft or aircraft engines (except overhauling, conversion, and rebuilding) are classified in Industry 48819, Other Support Activities for Air Transportation;
- Research and development establishments primarily engaged in aerospace R&D (except prototype production) are classified in Industry 54171, Research and Development in the Physical, Engineering, and Life Sciences;
- Establishments primarily engaged in manufacturing aircraft engine intake and exhaust valves, pistons, or engine filters are classified in Industry 33631, Motor Vehicle Gasoline Engine and Engine Parts Manufacturing;

Visit page 17 to learn about classification changes to this sector.

Manufacturing

■ = Cross-References

US—United States industry only. CAN—United States and Canadian industries are comparable. When neither US nor CAN appears, Canadian, Mexican, and United States industries are comparable.

www.harrisinfo.com

427

- Establishments primarily engaged in manufacturing of aircraft seating are classified in Industry 33636, Motor Vehicle Seating and Interior Trim Manufacturing;
- Establishments primarily engaged in manufacturing aeronautical, navigational, and guidance systems and instruments are classified in Industry 33451, Navigational, Measuring, Electromedical, and Control Instruments Manufacturing;
- Establishment primarily engaged in manufacturing aircraft engine electrical (aeronautical electrical) equipment or aircraft lighting fixtures are classified in Industry 33632, Motor Vehicle Electrical and Electronic Equipment Manufacturing; and
- Establishments primarily engaged in manufacturing of aircraft fluid power subassemblies are classified in Industry 33291, Metal Valve Manufacturing.

336411 Aircraft Manufacturing US

This U.S. industry comprises establishments primarily engaged in one or more of the following: (1) manufacturing or assembling complete aircraft; (2) developing and making aircraft prototypes; (3) aircraft conversion (i.e., major modifications to systems); and (4) complete aircraft overhaul and rebuilding (i.e., periodic restoration of aircraft to original design specifications).

- Establishments primarily engaged in manufacturing guided missiles and space vehicles are classified in U.S. Industry 336414, Guided Missile and Space Vehicle Manufacturing;
- Establishments primarily engaged in the repair of aircraft (except overhauling, conversion, and rebuilding) are classified in Industry 488190, Other Support Activities for Air Transportation; and
- Research and development establishments primarily engaged in aircraft R&D (except prototype production) are classified in Industry 541710, Research and Development in the Physical, Engineering, and Life Sciences.

336412 Aircraft Engine and Engine Parts Manufacturing US

This U.S. industry comprises establishments primarily engaged in one or more of the following: (1) manufacturing aircraft engines and engine parts; (2) developing and making prototypes of aircraft engines and engine parts; (3) aircraft propulsion system conversion (i.e., major modifications to systems); and (4) aircraft propulsion systems overhaul and rebuilding (i.e., periodic restoration of aircraft propulsion system to original design specifications).

- Establishments primarily engaged in manufacturing guided missile and space vehicle propulsion units and parts are classified in U.S. Industry 336415, Guided Missile and Space Vehicle Propulsion Unit and Propulsion Unit Parts Manufacturing;
- Establishments primarily engaged in manufacturing aircraft intake and exhaust valves and pistons are classified in U.S. Industry 336311, Carburetor, Piston, Piston Ring, and Valve Manufacturing;
- Establishments primarily engaged in manufacturing aircraft internal combustion engine filters are classified in U.S. Industry 336312, Gasoline Engine and Engine Parts Manufacturing;
- Establishments primarily engaged in the repair of aircraft engines (except overhauling, conversion, and rebuilding) are classified in Industry 488190, Other Support Activities for Air Transportation;
- Research and development establishments primarily engaged in aircraft engine and engine parts R&D (except prototype production) are classified in Industry 541710, Research and Development in the Physical, Engineering, and Life Sciences; and
- Establishments primarily engaged in manufacturing aeronautical instruments are classified in U.S. Industry 334511, Search, Detection, Navigation, Guidance, Aeronautical, and Nautical System and Instrument Manufacturing.

336413 Other Aircraft Parts and Auxiliary Equipment Manufacturing US

This U.S. industry comprises establishment primarily engaged in (1) manufacturing aircraft parts or auxiliary equipment (except engines and aircraft fluid power subassemblies) and/or (2) developing and making prototypes of aircraft parts and auxiliary equipment. Auxiliary equipment includes such items as crop dusting apparatus, armament racks, inflight refueling equipment, and external fuel tanks.

- Establishments primarily engaged in manufacturing aircraft engines and engine parts are classified in U.S. Industry 336412, Aircraft Engine and Engine Parts Manufacturing;
- Establishments primarily engaged in manufacturing aeronautical instruments are classified in U.S. Industry 334511, Search, Detection, Navigation, Guidance, Aeronautical, and Nautical System and Instrument Manufacturing;
- Establishments primarily engaged in manufacturing aircraft lighting fixtures are classified in U.S. Industry 336321, Vehicular Lighting Equipment Manufacturing;
- Establishments primarily engaged in manufacturing aircraft engine electrical (aeronautical electrical) equipment are classified in U.S. Industry 336322, Other Motor Vehicle Electrical and Electronic Equipment Manufacturing;
- Establishments primarily engaged in manufacturing guided missile and space vehicle parts and auxiliary equipment are classified in U.S. Industry 336419, Other Guided Missile and Space Vehicle Parts and Auxiliary Equipment Manufacturing;
- Establishments primarily engaged in manufacturing of aircraft fluid power subassemblies are classified in U.S. Industry 332912, Fluid Power Valve and Hose Fitting Manufacturing;
- Establishments primarily engaged in manufacturing of aircraft seating are classified in Industry 336360, Motor Vehicle Seating and Interior Trim Manufacturing; and
- Research and development establishments primarily engaged in aircraft parts and auxiliary equipment R&D (except prototype production) are classified in Industry 541710, Research and Development in the Physical, Engineering, and Life Sciences.

336414 Guided Missile and Space Vehicle Manufacturing US

This U.S. industry comprises establishments primarily engaged in (1) manufacturing complete

Sector
31-33

Manufacturing

■ = Cross-References

guided missiles and space vehicles and/or (2) developing and making prototypes of guided missile or space vehicles.

- Establishments primarily engaged in manufacturing space satellites are classified in Industry 334220, Radio and Television Broadcasting and Wireless Communications Equipment Manufacturing; and
- Research and development establishments primarily engaged in guided missile and space vehicle R&D (except prototype production) are classified in Industry 541710, Research and Development in the Physical, Engineering, and Life Sciences.

336415 Guided Missile and Space Vehicle Propulsion Unit and Propulsion Unit Parts Manufacturing US

This U.S. industry comprises establishments primarily engaged in (1) manufacturing guided missile and/or space vehicle propulsion units and propulsion unit parts and/or (2) developing and making prototypes of guided missile and space vehicle propulsion units and propulsion unit parts.

- Research and development establishments primarily engaged in guided missile and space propulsion unit and propulsion unit parts R&D (except prototype production) are classified in Industry 541710, Research and Development in the Physical, Engineering, and Life Sciences.

336419 Other Guided Missile and Space Vehicle Parts and Auxiliary Equipment Manufacturing US

This U.S. Industry comprises establishments primarily engaged in (1) manufacturing guided missile and space vehicle parts and auxiliary equipment (except guided missile and space vehicle propulsion units and propulsion unit parts) and/or (2) developing and making prototypes of guided missile and space vehicle parts and auxiliary equipment.

- Establishments primarily engaged in manufacturing navigational and guidance systems are classified in U.S. Industry 334511, Search, Detection, Navigation, Guidance, Aeronautical, and Nautical System and Instrument Manufacturing;
- Establishments primarily engaged in manufacturing guided missile and space vehicle propulsion units and propulsion unit parts are classified in U.S. Industry 336415, Guided Missile and Space Vehicle Propulsion Unit and Propulsion Unit Parts Manufacturing; and
- Research and development establishments primarily engaged in guided missile and space vehicle parts and auxiliary equipment R&D (except prototype production) are classified in Industry 541710, Research and Development in the Physical, Engineering, and Life Sciences.

3365 Railroad Rolling Stock Manufacturing

33651 Railroad Rolling Stock Manufacturing
See industry description for 336510 below.

336510 Railroad Rolling Stock Manufacturing
This industry comprises establishments primarily engaged in one or more of the following: (1) manufacturing and/or rebuilding locomotives, locomotive frames and parts; (2) manufacturing railroad, street, and rapid transit cars and car equipment for operation on rails for freight and passenger service; and (3) manufacturing rail layers, ballast distributors, rail tamping equipment and other railway track maintenance equipment.

- Establishments primarily engaged in manufacturing mining rail cars are classified in U.S. Industry 333131, Mining Machinery and Equipment Manufacturing;
- Establishments primarily engaged in manufacturing locomotive fuel lubricating or cooling medium pumps are classified in U.S. Industry 333911, Pump and Pumping Equipment Manufacturing;
- Repair establishments of railroad and local transit companies primarily engaged in repairing railroad and transit cars are classified in Industry 488210, Support Activities for Rail Transportation; and
- Establishments not owned by railroad or local transit companies primarily engaged in repairing railroad cars and locomotive engines are classified in Industry 811310, Commercial and Industrial Machinery and Equipment (except Automotive and Electronic) Repair and Maintenance.

3366 Ship and Boat Building

33661 Ship and Boat Building
This industry comprises establishments primarily engaged in operating shipyards or boat yards (i.e., ship or boat manufacturing facilities). Shipyards are fixed facilities with drydocks and fabrication equipment capable of building a ship, defined as watercraft typically suitable or intended for other than personal or

Visit page 17 to learn about classification changes to this sector.

Sector
31-33
Manufacturing

■ = Cross-References

US—United States industry only. CAN—United States and Canadian industries are comparable. When neither US nor CAN appears, Canadian, Mexican, and United States industries are comparable.

www.harrisinfo.com

 429

recreational use. Boats are defined as watercraft typically suitable or intended for personal use. Activities of shipyards include the construction of ships, their repair, conversion and alteration, the production of prefabricated ship and barge sections, and specialized services, such as ship scaling.

- Manufacturing rubber boats are classified in Industry 32629, Other Rubber Product Manufacturing;
- Manufacturing nonrigid (i.e., inflatable) plastics boats are classified in Industry 32619, Other Plastics Product Manufacturing;
- Fabricating structural assemblies or components for ships, or subcontractors engaged in ship painting, joinery, carpentry work, and electrical wiring installation, are classified based on the production process used; and
- Ship repairs performed in floating drydocks are classified in Industry 48839, Other Support Activities for Water Transportation.

336611 Ship Building and Repairing ^{CAN}

This U.S. industry comprises establishments primarily engaged in operating a shipyard. Shipyards are fixed facilities with drydocks and fabrication equipment capable of building a ship, defined as watercraft typically suitable or intended for other than personal or recreational use. Activities of shipyards include the construction of ships, their repair, conversion and alteration, the production of prefabricated ship and barge sections, and specialized services, such as ship scaling.

- Fabricating structural assemblies or components for ships, or subcontractors engaged in ship painting, joinery, carpentry work, and electrical wiring installation are classified based on the production process used; and
- Ship repairs performed in floating drydocks are classified in Industry 488390, Other Support Activities for Water Transportation.

336612 Boat Building ^{CAN}

This U.S. industry comprises establishments primarily engaged in building boats. Boats are defined as watercraft not built in shipyards and typically of the type suitable or intended for personal use.

- Ship building or ship repairs performed in a shipyard are classified in U.S. Industry 336611, Ship Building and Repairing;
- Manufacturing rubber boats and life rafts are classified in U.S. Industry 326299, All Other Rubber Product Manufacturing; and
- Manufacturing nonrigid (i.e., inflatable) plastics boats are classified in U.S. Industry 326199, All Other Plastics Product Manufacturing.

3369 Other Transportation Equipment Manufacturing

This industry group comprises establishments primarily engaged in manufacturing transportation equipment (except motor vehicles and parts, aerospace products and parts, railroad rolling stock, ship building, and boat manufacturing).

33699 Other Transportation Equipment Manufacturing

This industry comprises establishments primarily engaged in manufacturing motorcycles, bicycles, metal tricycles, complete military armored vehicles, tanks, self-propelled weapons, vehicles pulled by draft animals, and other transportation equipment (except motor vehicles, boats, ships, railroad rolling stock, and aerospace products), including parts thereof.

- Manufacturing ships and boats are classified in Industry 33661, Ship and Boat Building;
- Manufacturing aerospace products and parts are classified in Industry 33641, Aerospace Product and Parts Manufacturing;
- Manufacturing motor vehicle parts are classified in Industry Group 3363, Motor Vehicle Parts Manufacturing;
- Manufacturing children's vehicles (except bicycles and metal tricycles) are classified in Industry 33993, Doll, Toy, and Game Manufacturing; and
- Manufacturing railroad rolling stock are classified in Industry 33651, Railroad Rolling Stock Manufacturing; and
- Manufacturing motor vehicles are classified in Industry Group 3361, Motor Vehicle Manufacturing.

336991 Motorcycle, Bicycle, and Parts Manufacturing ^{US}

This U.S. industry comprises establishments primarily engaged in manufacturing motorcycles, bicycles, tricycles and similar equipment, and parts.

- Manufacturing children's vehicles (except bicycles and metal tricycles) are classified in U.S. Industry 339932, Game, Toy, and Children's Vehicle Manufacturing; and
- Manufacturing golf carts and other similar personnel carriers are classified in U.S. Industry 336999, All Other Transportation Equipment Manufacturing.

336992 Military Armored Vehicle, Tank, and Tank Component Manufacturing ^{US}

This U.S. industry comprises establishments primarily engaged in manufacturing complete military armored vehicles, combat tanks, specialized components for combat tanks, and self-propelled weapons.

US—United States industry only. CAN—United States and Canadian industries are comparable. When neither US nor CAN appears, Canadian, Mexican, and United States industries are comparable.

Sector 31-33 Manufacturing

■ Establishments primarily engaged in manufacturing nonarmored military universal carriers are classified in U.S. Industry 336112, Light Truck and Utility Vehicle Manufacturing.

336999 All Other Transportation Equipment Manufacturing [US]

This U.S. industry comprises establishments primarily engaged in manufacturing transportation equipment (except motor vehicles, motor vehicle parts, boats, ships, railroad rolling stock, aerospace products, motorcycles, bicycles, armored vehicles and tanks).

■ Manufacturing motorcycles, bicycles and parts are classified in U.S. Industry 336991, Motorcycle, Bicycle, and Parts Manufacturing;
■ Manufacturing military armored vehicles, tanks, and tank components are classified in U.S. Industry 336992, Military Armored Vehicle, Tank, and Tank Component Manufacturing;
■ Manufacturing ships and boats are classified in Industry 33661, Ship and Boat Building;
■ Manufacturing aerospace products and parts are classified in Industry 33641, Aerospace Product and Parts Manufacturing;
■ Manufacturing motor vehicle parts are classified in Industry Group 3363, Motor Vehicle Parts Manufacturing;
■ Manufacturing railroad rolling stock are classified in Industry 336510, Railroad Rolling Stock Manufacturing; and
■ Manufacturing motor vehicles are classified in Industry Group 3361, Motor Vehicle Manufacturing.

▶337 FURNITURE AND RELATED PRODUCT MANUFACTURING

Industries in the Furniture and Related Product Manufacturing subsector make furniture and related articles, such as mattresses, window blinds, cabinets, and fixtures. The processes used in the manufacture of furniture include the cutting, bending, molding, laminating, and assembly of such materials as wood, metal, glass, plastics, and rattan. However, the production process for furniture is not solely bending metal, cutting and shaping wood, or extruding and molding plastics. Design and fashion trends play an important part in the production of furniture. The integrated design of the article for both esthetic and functional qualities is also a major part of the process of manufacturing furniture. Design services may be performed by the furniture establishment's work force or may be purchased from industrial designers.

Furniture may be made of any material, but the most common ones used in North America are metal and wood. Furniture manufacturing establishments may specialize in making articles primarily from one material. Some of the equipment required to make a wooden table, for example, is different from that used to make a metal one. However, furniture is usually made from several materials. A wooden table might have metal brackets, and a wooden chair a fabric or plastics seat. Therefore, in NAICS, furniture initially is classified based on the type of furniture (application for which it is designed) rather than the material used. For example, an upholstered sofa is treated as household furniture, although it may also be used in hotels or offices.

When classifying furniture according to the component material from which it is made, furniture made from more than one material is classified based on the material used in the frame, or if there is no frame, the predominant component material. Upholstered household furniture (excluding kitchen and dining room chairs with upholstered seats) is classified without regard to the frame material. Kitchen or dining room chairs with upholstered seats are classified according to the frame material.

Furniture may be made on a stock or custom basis and may be shipped assembled or unassembled (i.e., knockdown). The manufacture of furniture parts and frames is included in this subsector.

Some of the processes used in furniture manufacturing are similar to processes that are used in other segments of manufacturing. For example, cutting and assembly occurs in the production of wood trusses that are classified in Subsector 321, Wood Product Manufacturing. However, the multiple processes that distinguish wood furniture manufacturing from wood product manufacturing warrant inclusion of wooden furniture manufacturing in the Furniture and Related Product Manufacturing subsector. Metal furniture manufacturing uses techniques that are also employed in the manufacturing of roll-formed products classified in Subsector 332, Fabricated Metal Product Manufacturing. The molding process for plastics furniture is similar to the molding of other plastics products. However, plastics furniture producing establishments tend to specialize in furniture.

NAICS attempts to keep furniture manufacturing together, but there are two notable exceptions: seating for transportation equipment and laboratory and hospital furniture. These exceptions are related to that fact that some of the aspects of the production process for these products, primarily the design, are highly integrated with that of other manufactured goods, namely motor vehicles and health equipment.

Visit page 17 to learn about classification changes to this sector.

Sector
31-33
Manufacturing

■ = Cross-References

US—United States industry only. CAN—United States and Canadian industries are comparable. When neither US nor CAN appears, Canadian, Mexican, and United States industries are comparable.

3371 Household and Institutional Furniture and Kitchen Cabinet Manufacturing

This industry group comprises establishments manufacturing household-type furniture, such as living room, kitchen and bedroom furniture and institutional (i.e., public building) furniture, such as furniture for schools, theaters, and churches.

33711 Wood Kitchen Cabinet and Countertop Manufacturing

See industry description for 337110 below.

337110 Wood Kitchen Cabinet and Countertop Manufacturing

This industry comprises establishments primarily engaged in manufacturing wood or plastics laminated on wood kitchen cabinets, bathroom vanities, and countertops (except freestanding). The cabinets and counters may be made on a stock or custom basis.

- Manufacturing metal kitchen and bathroom cabinets (except freestanding) are classified in U.S. Industry 337124, Metal Household Furniture Manufacturing;
- Manufacturing plastics countertops are classified in U.S. Industry 326199, All Other Plastics Product Manufacturing;
- Manufacturing stone countertops are classified in U.S. Industry 327991, Cut Stone and Stone Product Manufacturing; and
- Manufacturing wood or plastics laminated on wood countertops (except kitchen and bathroom) are classified in U.S. Industry 337215, Showcase, Partition, Shelving, and Locker Manufacturing.

33712 Household and Institutional Furniture Manufacturing

This industry comprises establishments primarily engaged in manufacturing household-type and public building furniture (i.e., library, school, theater, and church furniture). The furniture may be made on a stock or custom basis and may be assembled or unassembled (i.e., knockdown).

- Manufacturing laboratory and hospital furniture are classified in Industry 33911, Medical Equipment and Supplies Manufacturing;
- Manufacturing wood or plastics laminated on wood kitchen cabinets, bathroom vanities, and countertops (except freestanding) are classified in Industry 33711, Wood Kitchen Cabinet and Countertop Manufacturing;
- Manufacturing office-type furniture and/or office or store fixtures are classified in Industry 33721, Office Furniture (including Fixtures) Manufacturing; and
- Repairing or refinishing furniture are classified in Industry 81142, Reupholstery and Furniture Repair.

337121 Upholstered Household Furniture Manufacturing CAN

This U.S. industry comprises establishments primarily engaged in manufacturing upholstered household-type furniture. The furniture may be made on a stock or custom basis.

- Reupholstering furniture or upholstering frames to individual order are classified in Industry 811420, Reupholstery and Furniture Repair;
- Wood kitchen and dining room chairs with upholstered seats or backs are classified in U. S. Industry 337122, Nonupholstered Wood Household Furniture Manufacturing;
- Metal kitchen and dining room chairs with upholstered seats or backs are classified in U.S. Industry 337124, Metal Household Furniture Manufacturing; and
- Kitchen and dining room chairs (except wood and metal) with upholstered seats or backs are classified in U.S. Industry 337125, Household Furniture (except Wood and Metal) Manufacturing.

337122 Nonupholstered Wood Household Furniture Manufacturing US

This U.S. industry comprises establishments primarily engaged in manufacturing nonupholstered wood household-type furniture and freestanding cabinets (except television, radio, and sewing machine cabinets). The furniture may be made on a stock or custom basis and may be assembled or unassembled (i.e., knockdown).

- Manufacturing reed, rattan, plastics and similar furniture are classified in U.S. Industry 337125, Household Furniture (except Wood and Metal) Manufacturing;
- Manufacturing wood or plastics laminated on wood kitchen cabinets, bathroom vanities, and countertops (except freestanding) are classified in Industry 337110, Wood Kitchen Cabinet and Countertop Manufacturing;
- Manufacturing wood television, stereo, loudspeaker, and sewing machine cabinets (i.e., housings) are classified in U.S. Industry 337129, Wood Television, Radio, and Sewing Machine Cabinet Manufacturing; and
- Repairing or refinishing furniture are classified in Industry 811420, Reupholstery and Furniture Repair.

337124 Metal Household Furniture Manufacturing US

This U.S. industry comprises establishments primarily engaged in manufacturing metal household-type furniture and freestanding cabinets. The furniture may be made on a stock or custom basis and may be assembled or unassembled (i.e., knockdown).

Sector
31-33
Manufacturing

■ = Cross-References

US—United States industry only. CAN—United States and Canadian industries are comparable. When neither US nor CAN appears, Canadian, Mexican, and United States industries are comparable.

432

Harris InfoSource

■ Establishments primarily engaged in manufacturing metal laboratory and hospital furniture including beds are classified in Industry 33911, Medical Equipment and Supplies Manufacturing.

337125 Household Furniture (except Wood and Metal) Manufacturing ᵁˢ

This U.S. industry comprises establishments primarily engaged in manufacturing household-type furniture of materials other than wood or metal, such as plastics, reed, rattan, wicker, and fiberglass. The furniture may be made on a stock or custom basis and may be assembled or unassembled (i.e., knockdown).

■ Manufacturing concrete, ceramic, or stone furniture are classified in Subsector 327, Nonmetallic Mineral Product Manufacturing, according to the materials used;
■ Manufacturing upholstered household-type furniture are classified in U.S. Industry 337121, Upholstered Household Furniture Manufacturing;
■ Manufacturing metal household-type furniture are classified in U.S. Industry 337124, Metal Household Furniture Manufacturing; and
■ Manufacturing nonupholstered wood household-type furniture are classified in U.S. Industry 337122, Nonupholstered Wood Household Furniture Manufacturing.

337127 Institutional Furniture Manufacturing ᶜᴬᴺ

This U.S. industry comprises establishments primarily engaged in manufacturing institutional-type furniture (e.g., library, school, theater, and church furniture). The furniture may be made on a stock or custom basis and may be assembled or unassembled (i.e., knockdown).

■ Manufacturing laboratory and hospital furniture are classified in Industry 33911, Medical Equipment and Supplies Manufacturing;
■ Manufacturing wood kitchen cabinets, wood bathroom vanities, and countertops designed for permanent installation are classified in Industry 337110, Wood Kitchen Cabinet and Countertop Manufacturing;
■ Manufacturing office-type furniture and/or office or store fixtures are classified in Industry 33721, Office Furniture (including Fixtures) Manufacturing; and
■ Repairing or refinishing furniture are classified in Industry 811420, Reupholstery and Furniture Repair.

337129 Wood Television, Radio, and Sewing Machine Cabinet Manufacturing ᵁˢ

This industry comprises establishments primarily engaged in manufacturing wood cabinets used as housings by television, stereo, loudspeaker, and sewing machine manufacturers.

■ Manufacturing plastics housings used by television, stereo, loudspeaker, and sewing machine manufacturers are classified in U.S. Industry 326199, All Other Plastics Product Manufacturing;
■ Manufacturing metal housings used by television, stereo, loudspeaker, and sewing machine manufacturers are classified in U.S. Industry 332322, Sheet Metal Work Manufacturing;
■ Manufacturing freestanding wood household-type cabinets (e.g., entertainment centers, stands) for consumer electronics are classified in U.S. Industry 337122, Nonupholstered Wood Household Furniture Manufacturing;
■ Manufacturing freestanding metal household-type cabinets (e.g., entertainment centers, stands) for consumer electronics are classified in U.S. Industry 337124, Metal Household Furniture Manufacturing; and
■ Manufacturing freestanding household-type cabinets (e.g., entertainment centers, stands) (except wood and metal) for consumer electronics are classified in U.S. Industry 337125, Household Furniture (except Wood and Metal) Manufacturing.

3372 Office Furniture (including Fixtures) Manufacturing

33721 Office Furniture (including Fixtures) Manufacturing

This industry comprises establishments primarily engaged in manufacturing office furniture and/or office and store fixtures. The furniture may be made on a stock or custom basis and may be assembled or unassembled (i.e., knockdown).

■ Manufacturing millwork on a factory basis are classified in Industry 32191, Millwork;
■ Manufacturing household-type and institutional-type furniture are classified in Industry 33712, Household and Institutional Furniture Manufacturing;
■ Manufacturing refrigerated cabinets, showcases, and display cases are classified in Industry 33341, Ventilation, Heating, Air-conditioning, and Commercial Refrigeration Equipment Manufacturing; and
■ Manufacturing metal safes and vaults are classified in Industry 33299, All Other Fabricated Metal Product Manufacturing.

337211 Wood Office Furniture Manufacturing ᵁˢ

This U.S. industry comprises establishments primarily engaged in manufacturing wood office-type furniture. The furniture may be made on a stock or custom basis and may be assembled or unassembled (i.e., knockdown).

Visit page 17 to learn about classification changes to this sector.

Sector

31-33

Manufacturing

■ = Cross-References

US—United States industry only. CAN—United States and Canadian industries are comparable. When neither US nor CAN appears, Canadian, Mexican, and United States industries are comparable.

337212 Custom Architectural Woodwork and Millwork Manufacturing ᵁˢ

This U.S. industry comprises establishments primarily engaged in manufacturing custom designed interiors consisting of architectural woodwork and fixtures utilizing wood, wood products, and plastics laminates. All of the industry output is made to individual order on a job shop basis and requires skilled craftsmen as a labor input. A job might include custom manufacturing of display fixtures, gondolas, wall shelving units, entrance and window architectural detail, sales and reception counters, wall paneling, and matching furniture.

- Manufacturing millwork on a factory basis are classified in U.S. Industry 321918, Other Millwork (including Flooring);
- Manufacturing wood office-type furniture on a stock or custom basis are classified in U.S. Industry 337211, Wood Office Furniture Manufacturing; and
- Manufacturing wood office-type furniture and store fixtures on a stock basis are classified in U.S. Industry 337215, Showcase, Partition, Shelving, and Locker Manufacturing.

337214 Office Furniture (except Wood) Manufacturing ᶜᴬᴺ

This U.S. industry comprises establishments primarily engaged in manufacturing nonwood office-type furniture. The furniture may be made on a stock or custom basis and may be assembled or unassembled (i.e., knockdown).

337215 Showcase, Partition, Shelving, and Locker Manufacturing ᶜᴬᴺ

This U.S. industry comprises establishments primarily engaged in manufacturing wood and nonwood office and store fixtures, shelving, lockers, frames, partitions, and related fabricated products of wood and nonwood materials, including plastics laminated fixture tops. The products are made on a stock basis and may be assembled or unassembled (i.e., knockdown). Establishments exclusively making furniture parts (e.g., frames) are included in this industry.

- Manufacturing refrigerated cabinets, showcases, and display cases are classified in U.S. Industry 333415, Air-conditioning and Warm Air Heating Equipment and Commercial and Industrial Refrigeration Equipment Manufacturing;
- Manufacturing metal safes and vaults are classified in U.S. Industry 332999, All Other Miscellaneous Fabricated Metal Product Manufacturing; and
- Manufacturing wood or plastics laminated kitchen and bathroom countertops are classified in Industry 337110, Wood Kitchen Cabinet and Countertop Manufacturing.

3379 Other Furniture Related Product Manufacturing

This industry group comprises establishments manufacturing furniture related products, such as mattresses, blinds, and shades.

33791 Mattress Manufacturing

See industry description for 337910 below.

337910 Mattress Manufacturing

This industry comprises establishments primarily engaged in manufacturing innerspring, box spring, and non-innerspring mattresses, including mattresses for waterbeds.

- Manufacturing individual wire springs are classified in Industry 33261, Spring and Wire Product Manufacturing; and
- Manufacturing inflatable mattresses are classified in Subsector 326, Plastics and Rubber Products Manufacturing.

33792 Blind and Shade Manufacturing

See industry description for 337920 below.

337920 Blind and Shade Manufacturing

This industry comprises establishments primarily engaged in manufacturing one or more of the following: venetian blinds, other window blinds, shades; curtain and drapery rods, poles; and/or curtain and drapery fixtures. The blinds, and shades may be made on a stock or custom basis and may be made of any material.

- Manufacturing canvas awnings are classified in U.S. Industry 314912, Canvas and Related Product Mills; and
- Manufacturing curtains and draperies are classified in U.S. Industry 314121, Curtain and Drapery Mills.

▶339 MISCELLANEOUS MANUFACTURING

Industries in the Miscellaneous Manufacturing subsector make a wide range of products that cannot readily be classified in specific NAICS subsectors in manufacturing. Processes used by these establishments vary

Sector

31-33

Manufacturing

■ = Cross-References

US—United States industry only. CAN—United States and Canadian industries are comparable. When neither US nor CAN appears, Canadian, Mexican, and United States industries are comparable.

434

Harris InfoSource

significantly, both among and within industries. For example, a variety of manufacturing processes are used in manufacturing sporting and athletic goods that include products, such as tennis racquets and golf balls. The processes for these products differ from each other, and the processes differ significantly from the fabrication processes used in making dolls or toys, the melting and shaping of precious metals to make jewelry, and the bending, forming, and assembly used in making medical products.

The industries in this subsector are defined by what is made rather than how it is made. Although individual establishments might be appropriately classified elsewhere in the NAICS structure, for historical continuity, these product-based industries were maintained. In most cases, no one process or material predominates for an industry.

Establishments in this subsector manufacture products as diverse as medical equipment and supplies, jewelry, sporting goods, toys, and office supplies.

3391 Medical Equipment and Supplies Manufacturing

33911 Medical Equipment and Supplies Manufacturing

This industry comprises establishments primarily engaged in manufacturing medical equipment and supplies. Examples of products made by these establishments are laboratory apparatus and furniture, surgical and medical instruments, surgical appliances and supplies, dental equipment and supplies, orthodontic goods, dentures, and orthodontic appliances.

- Manufacturing laboratory instruments, X-ray apparatus, electromedical apparatus (including electronic hearing aids), and thermometers (except medical) are classified in Industry 33451, Navigational, Measuring, Electromedical, and Control Instruments Manufacturing;
- Manufacturing molded glass lens blanks are classified in Industry 32721, Glass and Glass Product Manufacturing;
- Manufacturing molded plastics lens blanks are classified in Industry 32619, Other Plastics Product Manufacturing;
- Retailing and grinding prescription eyeglasses are classified in Industry 44613, Optical Goods Stores; and
- Manufacturing sporting goods helmets and protective equipment are classified in Industry, 33992 Sporting and Athletic Goods Manufacturing.

339111 Laboratory Apparatus and Furniture Manufacturing [US]

This U.S. industry comprises establishments primarily engaged in manufacturing laboratory apparatus and laboratory and hospital furniture (except dental). Examples of products made by these establishments are hospital beds, operating room tables, laboratory balances and scales, furnaces, ovens, centrifuges, cabinets, cases, benches, tables, and stools.

- Manufacturing dental laboratory apparatus and furniture are classified in U.S. Industry 339114, Dental Equipment and Supplies Manufacturing; and
- Manufacturing laboratory instruments are classified in U.S. Industry 334516, Analytical Laboratory Instrument Manufacturing.

339112 Surgical and Medical Instrument Manufacturing [US]

This U.S. industry comprises establishments primarily engaged in manufacturing medical, surgical, ophthalmic, and veterinary instruments and apparatus (except electrotherapeutic, electromedical and irradiation apparatus). Examples of products made by these establishments are syringes, hypodermic needles, anesthesia apparatus, blood transfusion equipment, catheters, surgical clamps, and medical thermometers.

- Manufacturing electromedical and electrotherapeutic apparatus are classified in U.S. Industry 334510, Electromedical and Electrotherapeutic Apparatus Manufacturing;
- Manufacturing irradiation apparatus are classified in U.S. Industry 334517, Irradiation Apparatus Manufacturing;
- Manufacturing surgical and orthopedic appliances are classified in U.S. Industry 339113 Surgical Appliance and Supplies Manufacturing;
- Manufacturing dental equipment, dental supplies, dental laboratory apparatus, and dental laboratory furniture are classified in U.S. Industry 339114, Dental Equipment and Supplies Manufacturing;
- Manufacturing laboratory apparatus and laboratory and hospital furniture (except dental) are classified in U.S. Industry 339111, Laboratory Apparatus and Furniture Manufacturing; and
- Manufacturing thermometers (except medical) are classified in U.S. Industry 334519, Other Measuring and Controlling Device Manufacturing.

339113 Surgical Appliance and Supplies Manufacturing [US]

This U.S. industry comprises establishments primarily engaged in manufacturing surgical appliances

Visit page 17 to learn about classification changes to this sector.

Sector

31-33

Manufacturing

■ = Cross-References

US—United States industry only. CAN—United States and Canadian industries are comparable. When neither US nor CAN appears, Canadian, Mexican, and United States industries are comparable.

www.harrisinfo.com

435

and supplies. Examples of products made by these establishments are orthopedic devices, prosthetic appliances, surgical dressings, crutches, surgical sutures, and personal industrial safety devices (except protective eyeware).

■ Manufacturing dental equipment, dental supplies, dental laboratory apparatus, and dental laboratory furniture are classified in U.S. Industry 339114, Dental Equipment and Supplies Manufacturing;
■ Manufacturing laboratory apparatus and laboratory and hospital furniture (except dental) are classified in U.S. Industry 339111, Laboratory Apparatus and Furniture Manufacturing;
■ Manufacturing electronic hearing aids are classified in U.S. Industry 334510, Electromedical and Electrotherapeutic Apparatus Manufacturing;
■ Manufacturing industrial protective eyeware are classified in U.S. Industry 339115, Ophthalmic Goods Manufacturing; and
■ Manufacturing sporting goods helmets and protective equipment are classified in Industry 339920, Sporting and Athletic Goods Manufacturing.

339114 Dental Equipment and Supplies Manufacturing ᵁˢ
This U.S. industry comprises establishments primarily engaged in manufacturing dental equipment and supplies used by dental laboratories and offices of dentists, such as dental chairs, dental instrument delivery systems, dental hand instruments, and dental impression material.

■ Manufacturing dentures, crowns, bridges, and orthodontic appliances customized for individual application are classified in U.S. Industry 339116, Dental Laboratories; and
■ Manufacturing laboratory apparatus and laboratory and hospital furniture (except dental) are classified in U.S. Industry 339111, Laboratory Apparatus and Furniture Manufacturing.

339115 Ophthalmic Goods Manufacturing ᵁˢ
This U.S. industry comprises establishments primarily engaged in manufacturing ophthalmic goods. Examples of products made by these establishments are prescription eyeglasses (except manufactured in a retail setting), contact lenses, sunglasses, eyeglass frames, and reading glasses made to standard powers.

■ Manufacturing molded glass lens blanks are classified in U.S. Industry 327212, Other Pressed and Blown Glass and Glassware Manufacturing;
■ Manufacturing molded plastics lens blanks are classified in U.S. Industry 326199, All Other Plastics Product Manufacturing; and
■ Retailing and grinding prescription eyeglasses are classified in Industry 446130, Optical Goods Stores.

339116 Dental Laboratories ᵁˢ
This U.S. industry comprises establishments primarily engaged in manufacturing dentures, crowns, bridges, and orthodontic appliances customized for individual application.

■ Establishments primarily engaged in manufacturing dental equipment and supplies are classified in U.S. Industry 339114, Dental Equipment and Supplies Manufacturing.

3399 Other Miscellaneous Manufacturing

33991 Jewelry and Silverware Manufacturing
This industry comprises establishments primarily engaged in one or more of the following: (1) manufacturing, engraving, chasing, or etching jewelry; (2) manufacturing metal personal goods (i.e., small articles carried on or about the person, such as compacts or cigarette cases); (3) manufacturing, engraving, chasing, or etching precious metal solid, precious metal clad, or pewter cutlery and flatware; (4) manufacturing, engraving, chasing, or etching personal metal goods (i.e., small articles carried on or about the person, such as compacts or cigarette cases); (5) stamping coins; (6) manufacturing unassembled jewelry parts and stock shop products, such as sheet, wire, and tubing; (7) cutting, slabbing, tumbling, carving, engraving, polishing, or faceting precious or semiprecious stones and gems; (8) recutting, repolishing, and setting gem stones; and (9) drilling, sawing, and peeling cultured and costume pearls.

■ Manufacturing nonprecious and precious plated metal cutlery and flatware are classified in Industry 33221, Cutlery and Handtool Manufacturing;
■ Manufacturing nonprecious plated ware (except cutlery, flatware) are classified in Industry 33299, All Other Fabricated Metal Product Manufacturing;
■ Engraving, chasing, or etching nonprecious and precious plated metal flatware and other plated ware and plated jewelry are classified in Industry 33281, Coating, Engraving, Heat Treating, and Allied Activities;
■ Manufacturing synthetic stones or gem stones are classified in Industry 32799, All Other Nonmetallic Mineral Product Manufacturing; and

Sector
31-33

Manufacturing

■ = Cross-References

US—United States industry only. CAN—United States and Canadian industries are comparable. When neither US nor CAN appears, Canadian, Mexican, and United States industries are comparable.

436

Harris InfoSource

■ Manufacturing personal goods (except metal) carried on or about the person, such as compacts and cigarette cases, are classified in Industry 31699, Other Leather and Allied Product Manufacturing.

339911 Jewelry (except Costume) Manufacturing US

This U.S. industry comprises establishments primarily engaged in one or more of the following: (1) manufacturing, engraving, chasing, or etching precious metal solid or precious metal clad jewelry; (2) manufacturing, engraving, chasing, or etching personal goods (i.e., small articles carried on or about the person, such as compacts or cigarette cases) made of precious solid or clad metal; and (3) stamping coins.

■ Manufacturing, engraving, chasing, or etching costume jewelry and nonprecious metal personal goods are classified in U.S. Industry 339914, Costume Jewelry and Novelty Manufacturing;
■ Manufacturing jewelers' materials or performing lapidary work are classified in U.S. Industry 339913, Jewelers' Material and Lapidary Work Manufacturing; and
■ Plating jewelry are classified in U.S. Industry 332813, Electroplating, Plating, Polishing, Anodizing and Coloring.

339912 Silverware and Hollowware Manufacturing US

This U.S. industry comprises establishments primarily engaged in manufacturing, engraving, chasing, or etching precious metal solid, precious metal clad, or pewter flatware and other plated ware.

■ Manufacturing nonprecious and precious plated metal cutlery and flatware are classified in U.S. Industry 332211, Cutlery and Flatware (except Precious) Manufacturing;
■ Manufacturing nonprecious metal plated ware (except cutlery and flatware) are classified in U.S. Industry 332999, All Other Miscellaneous Fabricated Metal Product Manufacturing;
■ Engraving, chasing, or etching nonprecious and precious plated metal cutlery, flatware and other plated ware are classified in U.S. Industry 332812, Metal Coating, Engraving (except Jewelry and Silverware), and Allied Services to Manufactures; and
■ Manufacturing, engraving, chasing, or etching precious (except precious plated) metal jewelry and personal goods are classified in U.S. Industry 339911, Jewelry (excluding Costume) Manufacturing.

339913 Jewelers' Material and Lapidary Work Manufacturing US

This U.S. industry comprises establishments primarily engaged in one or more of the following: (1) manufacturing unassembled jewelry parts and stock shop products, such as sheet, wire, and tubing; (2) cutting, slabbing, tumbling, carving, engraving, polishing or faceting precious or semiprecious stones and gems; (3) recutting, repolishing, and setting gem stones; and (4) drilling, sawing, and peeling cultured pearls.

■ Manufacturing synthetic stones are classified in Industry U.S. 327999, All Other Miscellaneous Nonmetallic Mineral Product Manufacturing; and
■ Manufacturing costume pearls are classified in U.S. Industry 339914, Costume Jewelry and Novelty Manufacturing.

Visit page 17 to learn about classification changes to this sector.

339914 Costume Jewelry and Novelty Manufacturing US

This U.S. industry comprises establishments primarily engaged in (1) manufacturing, engraving, chasing, and etching costume jewelry; and/or (2) manufacturing, engraving, chasing, or etching nonprecious metal personal goods (i.e., small articles carried on or about the person, such as compacts or cigarette cases). This industry includes establishments primarily engaged in manufacturing precious plated jewelry and precious plated personal goods.

■ Manufacturing, engraving, chasing, or etching precious (except precious plated) metal jewelry and novelties are classified in U.S. Industry 339911, Jewelry (excluding Costume) Manufacturing;
■ Manufacturing personal goods (except metal) carried on or about the person, such as compacts and cigarette cases, are classified in U.S. Industry 316993, Personal Leather Goods (except Women's Handbag and Purse) Manufacturing; and
■ Manufacturing synthetic stones are classified in U.S. Industry 327999, All Other Miscellaneous Nonmetallic Mineral Product Manufacturing.

33992 Sporting and Athletic Goods Manufacturing

See industry description for 339920 below.

339920 Sporting and Athletic Goods Manufacturing

This industry comprises establishments primarily engaged in manufacturing sporting and athletic goods (except apparel and footwear).

■ Manufacturing athletic apparel are classified in Subsector 315, Apparel Manufacturing;
■ Manufacturing athletic footwear are classified in U.S. Industry 316219, Other Footwear Manufacturing; and
■ Manufacturing small arms and small arms ammunition are classified in Industry 33299, All Other Fabricated Metal Product Manufacturing.

Manufacturing

■ = Cross-References

33993 Doll, Toy, and Game Manufacturing

This industry comprises establishments primarily engaged in manufacturing dolls, toys, and games, such as complete dolls, doll parts, doll clothes, action figures, toys, games (including electronic), hobby kits, and children's vehicles (except metal bicycles and tricycles).

- Manufacturing bicycles and metal tricycles are classified in Industry 33699, Other Transportation Equipment Manufacturing;
- Manufacturing sporting and athletic goods are classified in Industry 33992, Sporting and Athletic Goods Manufacturing;
- Manufacturing coin-operated game machines are classified in Industry 33999, All Other Miscellaneous Manufacturing; and
- Manufacturing electronic video game cartridges and reproducing video game software are classified in Industry 33461, Manufacturing and Reproducing Magnetic and Optical Media.

339931 Doll and Stuffed Toy Manufacturing ᵁˢ

This U.S. industry comprises establishments primarily engaged in manufacturing complete dolls, doll parts, and doll clothes, action figures, and stuffed toys.

- Establishments primarily engaged in manufacturing toys (except stuffed) are classified in U.S. Industry 339932, Game, Toy, and Children's Vehicle Manufacturing.

339932 Game, Toy, and Children's Vehicle Manufacturing ᵁˢ

This U.S. industry comprises establishments primarily engaged in manufacturing games (including electronic), toys, and children's vehicles (except bicycles and metal tricycles).

- Manufacturing dolls and stuffed toys are classified in U.S. Industry 339931, Doll and Stuffed Toy Manufacturing;
- Manufacturing metal tricycles and bicycles are classified in U.S. Industry 336991, Motorcycle, Bicycle, and Parts Manufacturing;
- Manufacturing sporting and athletic goods are classified in Industry 339920, Sporting and Athletic Goods Manufacturing;
- Manufacturing coin-operated game machines are classified in U.S. Industry 339999, All Other Miscellaneous Manufacturing; and
- Mass reproducing electronic video game cartridges are classified in U.S. Industry 334611, Software Reproducing.

33994 Office Supplies (except Paper) Manufacturing

This industry comprises establishments primarily engaged in manufacturing office supplies. Examples of products made by these establishments are pens, pencils, felt tip markers, crayons, chalk, pencil sharpeners, staplers, hand operated stamps, modeling clay, and inked ribbons.

- Manufacturing writing, drawing, and india inks are classified in Industry 32599, All Other Chemical Product and Preparation Manufacturing;
- Manufacturing drafting tables and boards are classified in Industry 33712, Household and Institutional Furniture Manufacturing;
- Manufacturing rubber erasers are classified in Industry 32629, Other Rubber Product Manufacturing;
- Manufacturing paper office supplies are classified in Subsector 322, Paper Manufacturing;
- Manufacturing manifold business forms, blankbooks, and looseleaf binders are classified in Industry 32311, Printing; and
- Manufacturing inkjet cartridges are classified in Industry 32591, Printing Ink Manufacturing.

339941 Pen and Mechanical Pencil Manufacturing ᵁˢ

This U.S. industry comprises establishments primarily engaged in manufacturing pens, ballpoint pen refills and cartridges, mechanical pencils, and felt tipped markers.

- Manufacturing nonmechanical pencils and pencil leads are classified in U.S. Industry 339942, Lead Pencil and Art Good Manufacturing;
- Manufacturing writing, drawing, and india inks are classified in U.S. Industry 325998, All Other Miscellaneous Chemical Product and Preparation Manufacturing; and
- Manufacturing rubber erasers are classified in U.S. Industry 326299, All Other Rubber Product Manufacturing.

339942 Lead Pencil and Art Good Manufacturing ᵁˢ

This U.S. industry comprises establishments primarily engaged in manufacturing nonmechanical pencils, and art goods. Examples of products made by these establishments are pencil leads, crayons, chalk, framed blackboards, pencil sharpeners, staplers, artists' palettes and paints, and modeling clay.

- Manufacturing mechanical pencils are classified in U.S. Industry 339941, Pen and Mechanical Pencil Manufacturing;
- Manufacturing writing, drawing, and india inks are classified in U.S. Industry 325998, All Other Miscellaneous Chemical Product and Preparation Manufacturing;
- Manufacturing rubber erasers are classified in U.S. Industry 326299, All Other Rubber Product Manufacturing;
- Manufacturing paper office supplies are classified in Subsector 322, Paper Manufacturing;
- Printing manifold business forms and manufacturing blankbooks and looseleaf binders and devices are classified in Industry 32311, Printing; and
- Manufacturing drafting tables and boards are classified in U.S. Industry 337127, Institutional Furniture Manufacturing.

Sector

31-33

Manufacturing

■ = Cross-References

US—United States industry only. CAN—United States and Canadian industries are comparable. When neither US nor CAN appears, Canadian, Mexican, and United States industries are comparable.

339943 Marking Device Manufacturing US

This U.S. industry comprises establishments primarily engaged in manufacturing marking devices, such as hand operated stamps, embossing stamps, stamp pads, and stencils.

- Establishments primarily engaged in manufacturing felt tipped markers are classified in U.S. Industry 339941, Pen and Mechanical Pencil Manufacturing.

339944 Carbon Paper and Inked Ribbon Manufacturing US

This U.S. industry comprises establishments primarily engaged in manufacturing carbon paper and inked ribbons.

- Establishments primarily engaged in manufacturing inkjet cartridges are classified in Industry 325910, Printing Ink Manufacturing.

33995 Sign Manufacturing

See industry description for 39950 below.

339950 Sign Manufacturing

This industry comprises establishments primarily engaged in manufacturing signs and related displays of all materials (except printing paper and paperboard signs, notices, displays).

- Printing advertising specialties or printing paper and paperboard signs, notices, and displays are classified in Industry 32311, Printing;
- Manufacturing and printing advertising specialties are classified in the manufacturing sector according to products manufactured;
- Manufacturing die-cut paperboard displays are classified in U.S. Industry 322299, All Other Converted Paper Product Manufacturing; and
- Sign lettering and painting are classified in Industry 541890, Other Services Related to Advertising.

33999 All Other Miscellaneous Manufacturing.

This industry comprises establishments primarily engaged in miscellaneous manufacturing (except medical equipment and supplies, jewelry and flatware, sporting and athletic goods, dolls, toys, games, office supplies (except paper), and signs).

- Manufacturing medical equipment and supplies are classified in Industry Group 3391; Medical Equipment and Supplies Manufacturing
- Manufacturing jewelry and flatware are classified in Industry 33991, Jewelry and Silverware Manufacturing;
- Manufacturing sporting and athletic goods are classified in Industry 33992, Sporting and Athletic Goods Manufacturing;
- Manufacturing dolls, toys, and games are classified in Industry 33993, Doll, Toy, and Game Manufacturing;
- Manufacturing office supplies (except paper) are classified in Industry 39994, Office Supplies (except Paper) Manufacturing;
- Manufacturing signs are classified in Industry 33995, Sign Manufacturing;
- Manufacturing concrete burial vaults are classified in Industry 32739, Other Concrete Product Manufacturing;
- Manufacturing Christmas tree glass ornaments and glass lamp shades are classified in Industry 32721, Glass and Glass Product Manufacturing;
- Manufacturing Christmas tree lighting sets are classified in Industry 33512, Lighting Fixture Manufacturing;
- Manufacturing beauty and barber chairs are classified in Industry 33712, Household and Institutional Furniture Manufacturing;
- Manufacturing burnt wood articles are classified in Industry 32199, All Other Wood Product Manufacturing;
- Dressing and bleaching furs are classified in Industry 31611, Leather and Hide Tanning and Finishing;
- Manufacturing paper, textile, and metal lamp shades are classified in Industry 33512, Lighting Fixture Manufacturing;
- Manufacturing plastics lamp shades are classified in Industry 32619, Other Plastics Product Manufacturing;
- Manufacturing matches are classified in Industry 32599, All Other Chemical Product and Preparation Manufacturing;
- Manufacturing metal products, such as metal combs and hair curlers, are classified in Industry 33299, All Other Fabricated Metal Product Manufacturing;
- Manufacturing plastics products, such as plastics combs and hair curlers, are classified in Industry 32619, Other Plastics Product Manufacturing; and
- Manufacturing electric hair clippers for use on humans are classified in Industry 33521, Small Electrical Appliance Manufacturing.

339991 Gasket, Packing, and Sealing Device Manufacturing US

This industry comprises establishments primarily engaged in manufacturing gaskets, packing, and sealing devices of all materials.

339992 Musical Instrument Manufacturing US

This U.S. industry comprises establishments primarily engaged in manufacturing musical instruments (except toys).

Visit page 17 to learn about classification changes to this sector.

Sector
31-33

Manufacturing

■ = Cross-References

■ Establishments primarily engaged in manufacturing toy musical instruments are classified in U.S. Industry 339932, Game, Toy, and Children's Vehicle Manufacturing.

339993 Fastener, Button, Needle, and Pin Manufacturing ᵁˢ

This U.S. industry comprises establishments primarily engaged in manufacturing fasteners, buttons, needles, pins, and buckles (except precious metals or precious and semiprecious stones and gems).

■ Manufacturing buttons, pins, and buckles made of precious metals or precious and semiprecious stones and gems are classified in U.S. Industry 339911, Jewelry (except Costume) Manufacturing;
■ Manufacturing hypodermic and suture needles are classified in U.S. Industry 339112, Surgical and Medical Instrument Manufacturing; and
■ Manufacturing phonograph and styli needles are classified in U.S. Industry 334419, Other Electronic Component Manufacturing.

339994 Broom, Brush, and Mop Manufacturing ᵁˢ

This U.S. industry comprises establishments primarily engaged in manufacturing brooms, mops, and brushes.

339995 Burial Casket Manufacturing ᵁˢ

This U.S. industry comprises establishments primarily engaged in manufacturing burial caskets, cases, and vaults (except concrete).

■ Establishments primarily engaged in manufacturing concrete burial vaults are classified in Industry 327390, Other Concrete Product Manufacturing.

339999 All Other Miscellaneous Manufacturing ᵁˢ

This U.S. industry comprises establishments primarily engaged in miscellaneous manufacturing (except medical equipment and supplies, jewelry and flatware, sporting and athletic goods, dolls, toys, games, office supplies (except paper), musical instruments, fasteners, buttons, needles, pins, brooms, brushes, mops, and burial caskets).

■ Manufacturing medical equipment and supplies are classified in Industry Group 3391, Medical Equipment and Supplies Manufacturing;
■ Manufacturing jewelry and flatware are classified in Industry 33991, Jewelry and Silverware Manufacturing;
■ Manufacturing sporting and athletic goods are classified in Industry 339920, Sporting and Athletic Goods Manufacturing;
■ Manufacturing dolls, toys, and games are classified in Industry 33993, Doll, Toy, and Game Manufacturing;
■ Manufacturing office supplies (except paper) are classified in Industry 39994, Office Supplies (except Paper) Manufacturing;
■ Manufacturing signs are classified in Industry 33995, Sign Manufacturing;
■ Manufacturing gasket, packing, and sealing devices are classified in U.S. Industry 339991, Gasket, Packing, and Sealing Device Manufacturing;
■ Manufacturing musical instruments are classified in U.S. Industry 339992, Musical Instrument Manufacturing;
■ Manufacturing fasteners, buttons, needles, and pins are classified in U.S. Industry 339993, Fastener, Button, Needle, and Pin Manufacturing;
■ Manufacturing brooms, brushes, and mops are classified in U.S. Industry 339994, Broom, Brush, and Mop Manufacturing;
■ Manufacturing burial caskets are classified in U.S. Industry 339995, Burial Casket Manufacturing;
■ Manufacturing Christmas tree glass ornaments and glass lamp shades are classified in U.S. Industry 327215, Glass Product Manufacturing Made of Purchased Glass;
■ Manufacturing Christmas tree lighting sets are classified in U.S. Industry 335129, Other Lighting Equipment Manufacturing;
■ Manufacturing beauty and barber chairs are classified in U.S. Industry 337127, Institutional Furniture Manufacturing;
■ Manufacturing burnt wood articles are classified in U.S. Industry 321999, All Other Miscellaneous Wood Product Manufacturing;
■ Dressing and bleaching furs are classified in Industry 316110, Leather and Hide Tanning and Finishing;
■ Manufacturing paper, textile, and metal lamp shades are classified in U.S. Industry 335121, Residential Electric Lighting Fixture Manufacturing;
■ Manufacturing plastics lamp shades are classified in U.S. Industry 326199, All Other Plastics Product Manufacturing;
■ Manufacturing matches are classified in U.S. Industry 325998, All Other Miscellaneous Chemical Product and Preparation Manufacturing;
■ Manufacturing metal products, such as metal combs and hair curlers, are classified in U.S. Industry 332999, All Other Miscellaneous Fabricated Metal Product Manufacturing;
■ Manufacturing plastics products, such as plastics combs and hair curlers, are classified in U.S. Industry 326199, All Other Plastics Product Manufacturing; and
■ Manufacturing electric hair clippers for use on humans are classified in U.S. Industry 335211, Electric Housewares and Household Fan Manufacturing.

Sector
31-33
Manufacturing

■ = Cross-References

US—United States industry only. CAN—United States and Canadian industries are comparable. When neither US nor CAN appears, Canadian, Mexican, and United States industries are comparable.

440

Harris InfoSource

Sector 42

Wholesale Trade

The Sector as a Whole

THE WHOLESALE TRADE sector comprises establishments engaged in wholesaling merchandise, generally without transformation, and rendering services incidental to the sale of merchandise.

The wholesaling process is an intermediate step in the distribution of merchandise. Wholesalers are organized to sell or arrange the purchase or sale of (a) goods for resale (i.e., goods sold to other wholesalers or retailers), (b) capital or durable nonconsumer goods, and (c) raw and intermediate materials and supplies used in production.

Wholesalers sell merchandise to other businesses and normally operate from a warehouse or office. These warehouses and offices are characterized by having little or no display of merchandise. In addition, neither the design nor the location of the premises is intended to solicit walk-in traffic. Wholesalers do not normally use advertising directed to the general public. Customers are generally reached initially via telephone, in-person marketing, or by specialized advertising that may include Internet and other electronic means. Follow-up orders are either vendor-initiated or client-initiated, generally based on previous sales, and typically exhibit strong ties between sellers and buyers. In fact, transactions are often conducted between wholesalers and clients that have long-standing business relationships.

This sector comprises two main types of wholesalers: those that sell goods on their own account and those that arrange sales and purchases for others for a commission or fee.

(1) Establishments that sell goods on their own account are known as wholesale merchants, distributors, jobbers, drop shippers, import/export merchants, and sales branches. These establishments typically maintain their own warehouse, where they receive and handle goods for their customers. Goods are generally sold without transformation, but may include integral functions, such as sorting, packaging, labeling, and other marketing services.

(2) Establishments arranging for the purchase or sale of goods owned by others or purchasing goods on a commission basis are known as agents and brokers, commission merchants, import/export agents and brokers, auction companies, and manufacturers' representatives. These establishments operate from offices and generally do not own or handle the goods they sell.

Some wholesale establishments may be connected with a single manufacturer and promote and sell the particular manufacturers' products to a wide range of other wholesalers or retailers. Other wholesalers may be connected to a retail chain or a limited number of retail chains and only provide a variety of products needed by that particular retail operation(s). These wholesalers may obtain the products from a wide range of manufacturers. Still other wholesalers may not take title to the goods, but act as agents and brokers for a commission.

Although, in general, wholesaling normally denotes sales in large volumes, durable nonconsumer goods may be sold in single units. Sales of capital or durable nonconsumer good used in the production of goods and services, such as farm machinery, medium and heavy duty trucks, and industrial machinery, are always included in wholesale trade.

Visit page 18 to learn about classification changes to this sector.

Sector 42
Wholesale Trade

US—United States industry only. CAN—United States and Canadian industries are comparable. When neither US nor CAN appears, Canadian, Mexican, and United States industries are comparable.

▶421 WHOLESALE TRADE, DURABLE GOODS ᵁˢ

Industries in the Wholesale Trade, Durable Goods subsector sell or arrange the purchase or sale of capital or durable goods to other businesses. Durable goods are new or used items generally with a normal life expectancy of three years or more. Durable goods wholesale trade establishments are engaged in wholesaling products, such as motor vehicles, furniture, construction materials, machinery and equipment (including household-type appliances), metals and minerals (except petroleum), sporting goods, toys and hobby goods, recyclable materials, and parts.

The detailed industries within the subsector are organized in the classification structure based on the products sold. Within an industry, the types of establishments may vary, including wholesale merchants and/or agents and brokers.

4211 Motor Vehicle and Motor Vehicle Parts and Supplies Wholesalers ᵁˢ

This industry group comprises establishments primarily engaged in wholesaling automobiles and other motor vehicles, motor vehicle supplies, tires, and new and used parts.

42111 Automobile and Other Motor Vehicle Wholesalers ᵁˢ

See industry description for 421110 below.

421110 Automobile and Other Motor Vehicle Wholesalers ᵁˢ

This industry comprises establishments primarily engaged in wholesaling new and used passenger automobiles, trucks, trailers, and other motor vehicles, such as motorcycles, motor homes, and snowmobiles.

42112 Motor Vehicle Supplies and New Parts Wholesalers ᵁˢ

See industry description for 421120 below.

421120 Motor Vehicle Supplies and New Parts Wholesalers ᵁˢ

This industry comprises establishments primarily engaged in wholesaling motor vehicle supplies, accessories, tools, and equipment; and new motor vehicle parts (except new tires and tubes).

- ■ Wholesaling new and/or used tires and tubes are classified in Industry 421130, Tire and Tube Wholesalers;
- ■ Wholesaling automotive chemicals (except lubricating oils and greases) are classified in Industry 422690, Other Chemical and Allied Products Wholesalers;
- ■ Wholesaling lubricating oils and greases are classified in Industry 422720, Petroleum and Petroleum Products Wholesalers (except Bulk Stations and Terminals); and
- ■ Wholesaling used motor vehicle parts are classified in Industry 421140, Motor Vehicle Parts (Used) Wholesalers.

42113 Tire and Tube Wholesalers ᵁˢ

See industry description for 421130 below.

421130 Tire and Tube Wholesalers ᵁˢ

This industry comprises establishments primarily engaged in wholesaling new and/or used tires and tubes for passenger and commercial vehicles.

42114 Motor Vehicle Parts (Used) Wholesalers ᵁˢ

See industry description for 421140 below.

421140 Motor Vehicle Parts (Used) Wholesalers ᵁˢ

This industry comprises establishments primarily engaged in wholesaling used motor vehicle parts (excepted tires and tubes) and establishments primarily engaged in dismantling motor vehicles for the purpose of selling the parts.

- ■ Dismantling motor vehicles for the purpose of selling scrap are classified in Industry 421930, Recyclable Material Wholesalers; and
- ■ Wholesaling new and/or used tires and tubes are classified in Industry 421130, Tire and Tube Wholesalers.

■ = Cross-References

Sector 42

Wholesale Trade

US—United States industry only. CAN—United States and Canadian industries are comparable. When neither US nor CAN appears, Canadian, Mexican, and United States industries are comparable.

442

Harris InfoSource

4212 Furniture and Home Furnishing Wholesalers ᵁˢ

42121 Furniture Wholesalers ᵁˢ
See industry description for 421210 below.

421210 Furniture Wholesalers ᵁˢ
This industry comprises establishments primarily engaged in wholesaling furniture (except hospital beds, medical furniture, and drafting tables).

- Wholesaling partitions, shelving, lockers, and store fixtures are classified in Industry 421440, Other Commercial Equipment Wholesalers;
- Wholesaling hospital beds and medical furniture are classified in Industry 421450, Medical, Dental, and Hospital Equipment and Supplies Wholesalers; and
- Wholesaling drafting tables are classified in Industry 421490, Other Professional Equipment and Supplies Wholesalers.

42122 Home Furnishing Wholesalers ᵁˢ
See industry description for 421220 below.

421220 Home Furnishing Wholesalers ᵁˢ
This industry comprises establishments primarily engaged in wholesaling home furnishings and/or housewares.

- Wholesaling electrical household-type goods are classified in Industry 421620, Electrical Appliance, Television, and Radio Set Wholesalers; and
- Wholesaling precious metal flatware are classified in Industry 421940, Jewelry, Watch, Precious Stone, and Precious Metal Wholesalers.

4213 Lumber and Other Construction Materials Wholesalers ᵁˢ

42131 Lumber, Plywood, Millwork, and Wood Panel Wholesalers ᵁˢ
See industry description for 421310 below.

421310 Lumber, Plywood, Millwork, and Wood Panel Wholesalers ᵁˢ
This industry comprises establishments primarily engaged in wholesaling lumber; plywood; reconstituted wood fiber products; wood fencing; doors and windows and their frames (all materials); wood roofing and siding; and/or other wood or metal millwork.

- Establishments primarily engaged in wholesaling timber and timber products, such as railroad ties, logs, firewood, and pulpwood, are classified in Industry 421990, Other Miscellaneous Durable Goods Wholesalers.

42132 Brick, Stone, and Related Construction Material Wholesalers ᵁˢ
See industry description for 421320 below.

421320 Brick, Stone, and Related Construction Material Wholesalers ᵁˢ
This industry comprises establishments primarily engaged in wholesaling stone, cement, lime, construction sand, and gravel; brick; asphalt and concrete mixtures; and/or concrete, stone, and structural clay products.

- Wholesaling refractory brick and other refractory products are classified in Industry 421840, Industrial Supplies Wholesalers; and
- Selling ready-mixed concrete are classified in Industry 327320, Ready-mix Concrete Manufacturing.

42133 Roofing, Siding, and Insulation Material Wholesalers ᵁˢ
See industry description for 421330 below.

421330 Roofing, Siding, and Insulation Material Wholesalers ᵁˢ
This industry comprises establishments primarily engaged in wholesaling nonwood roofing and nonwood siding and insulation materials.

- Establishments primarily engaged in wholesaling wood roofing and wood siding are classified in Industry 421310, Lumber, Plywood, Millwork, and Wood Panel Wholesalers.

Visit page 18 to learn about classification changes to this sector.

Sector **42**

Wholesale Trade

■ = Cross-References

US—United States industry only. CAN—United States and Canadian industries are comparable. When neither US nor CAN appears, Canadian, Mexican, and United States industries are comparable.

42139 Other Construction Material Wholesalers ^{US}
See industry description for 421390 below.

421390 Other Construction Material Wholesalers ^{US}
This industry comprises (1) establishments primarily engaged in wholesaling manufactured homes (i.e., mobile homes) and/or prefabricated buildings and (2) establishments primarily engaged in wholesaling construction materials (except lumber, plywood, millwood, wood panel, brick, stone, roofing, siding, and insulation material).

- Wholesaling products of the primary metals industries are classified in Industry 421510, Metal Service Centers and Offices;
- Wholesaling lumber; plywood; reconstituted wood fiber products; wood fencing; doors, windows, and their frames; wood roofing and wood siding; and other wood or metal millwork are classified in Industry 421310, Lumber, Plywood, Millwork, and Wood Panel Wholesalers;
- Wholesaling stone, cement, lime, construction sand and gravel, brick, asphalt and concrete mixtures (except ready-mix concrete); and/or concrete, stone, and structural clay products are classified in Industry 421320, Brick, Stone, and Related Construction Material Wholesalers;
- Wholesaling nonwood roofing and nonwood siding and insulation materials are classified in Industry 421330, Roofing, Siding, and Insulation Material Wholesalers; and
- Selling ready-mix concrete are classified in Industry 327320, Ready-mix Concrete Manufacturing.

4214 Professional and Commercial Equipment and Supplies Wholesalers ^{US}
This industry group comprises establishments primarily engaged in wholesaling photographic equipment and supplies; office, computer, and computer peripheral equipment; and medical, dental, hospital, ophthalmic, and other commercial and professional equipment and supplies.

42141 Photographic Equipment and Supplies Wholesalers ^{US}
See industry description for 421410 below.

421410 Photographic Equipment and Supplies Wholesalers ^{US}
This industry comprises establishments primarily engaged in wholesaling photographic equipment and supplies (except office equipment).

- Wholesaling household-type video cameras are classified in Industry 421620, Electrical Appliance, Television, and Radio Set Wholesalers; and
- Wholesaling office equipment, such as photocopy and microfilm equipment are classified in Industry 421420, Office Equipment Wholesalers.

42142 Office Equipment Wholesalers ^{US}
See industry description for 421420 below.

421420 Office Equipment Wholesalers ^{US}
This industry comprises establishments primarily engaged in wholesaling office machines and related equipment (except computers and computer peripheral equipment).

- Wholesaling office furniture are classified in Industry 421210, Furniture Wholesalers;
- Wholesaling computers and computer peripheral equipment are classified in Industry 421430, Computer and Computer Peripheral Equipment and Software Wholesalers; and
- Wholesaling office supplies are classified in Industry 422120, Stationery and Office Supplies Wholesalers.

42143 Computer and Computer Peripheral Equipment and Software Wholesalers ^{US}
See industry description for 421430 below.

421430 Computer and Computer Peripheral Equipment and Software Wholesalers ^{US}
This industry comprises establishments primarily engaged in wholesaling computers, computer peripheral equipment, loaded computer boards, and/or computer software.

- Wholesaling modems and other electronic communications equipment are classified in Industry 421690, Other Electronic Parts and Equipment Wholesalers; and
- Selling, planning, and designing computer systems that integrate computer hardware, software, and communication technologies are classified in U.S. Industry 541512, Computer Systems Design Services.

Sector **42**
Wholesale Trade

■ = Cross-References

US—United States industry only. CAN—United States and Canadian industries are comparable. When neither US nor CAN appears, Canadian, Mexican, and United States industries are comparable.

444

Harris InfoSource

42144 Other Commercial Equipment Wholesalers US
See industry description for 421440 below.

421440 Other Commercial Equipment Wholesalers US
This industry comprises establishments primarily engaged in wholesaling commercial and related machines and equipment (except photographic equipment and supplies; office equipment; and computers and computer peripheral equipment and software) generally used in restaurants and stores.

- Wholesaling photographic equipment and supplies are classified in Industry 421410, Photographic Equipment and Supplies Wholesalers;
- Wholesaling office machines and related equipment are classified in Industry 421420, Office Equipment Wholesalers;
- Wholesaling computers, computer peripheral equipment, and computer software are classified in Industry 421430, Computer and Computer Peripheral Equipment and Software Wholesalers;
- Wholesaling laboratory scales and balances are classified in Industry 421490, Other Professional Equipment and Supplies Wholesalers; and
- Wholesaling refrigerated store fixtures are classified in Industry 421740, Refrigeration Equipment and Supplies Wholesalers.

42145 Medical, Dental, and Hospital Equipment and Supplies Wholesalers US
See industry description for 421450 below.

421450 Medical, Dental, and Hospital Equipment and Supplies Wholesalers US
This industry comprises establishments primarily engaged in wholesaling medical professional equipment, instruments, and supplies (except ophthalmic equipment, instruments and goods used by ophthalmologists, optometrists, and opticians).

- Establishments primarily engaged in wholesaling professional equipment, instruments and/or goods sold, prescribed, or used by ophthalmologists, optometrists, and opticians are classified in Industry 421460, Ophthalmic Goods Wholesalers.

42146 Ophthalmic Goods Wholesalers US
See industry description for 421460 below.

421460 Ophthalmic Goods Wholesalers US
This industry comprises establishments primarily engaged in wholesaling professional equipment, instruments, and/or goods sold, prescribed, or used by ophthalmologists, optometrists, and opticians.

42149 Other Professional Equipment and Supplies Wholesalers US
See industry description for 421490 below.

421490 Other Professional Equipment and Supplies Wholesalers US
This industry comprises establishments primarily engaged in wholesaling professional equipment and supplies (except ophthalmic goods and medical, dental, and hospital equipment and supplies).

- Wholesaling professional equipment, instruments, and/or goods sold, prescribed, or used by ophthalmologists, optometrists, and opticians, such as ophthalmic frames and lenses, and sunglasses, are classified in Industry 421460, Ophthalmic Goods Wholesalers;
- Wholesaling medical professional equipment, instruments, and supplies used by medical and dental practitioners (except ophthalmic equipment, instruments, and goods used by ophthalmologists, optometrists, and opticians) and medical facilities are classified in Industry 421450, Medical, Dental, and Hospital Equipment and Supplies Wholesalers;
- Wholesaling silverware and plated flatware are classified in Industry 421940, Jewelry, Watch, Precious Stone, and Precious Metal Wholesalers;
- Wholesaling books are classified in Industry 422920, Book, Periodical, and Newspaper Wholesalers; and
- Wholesaling school furniture are classified in Industry 421210, Furniture Wholesalers.

4215 Metal and Mineral (except Petroleum) Wholesalers US

42151 Metal Service Centers and Offices
See industry description for 421510 below.

421510 Metal Service Centers and Offices
This industry comprises establishments primarily engaged in wholesaling products of the primary metals industries. Service centers maintain inventory and may perform functions, such as sawing, shearing,

Visit page 18 to learn about classification changes to this sector.

Sector **42**
Wholesale Trade

■ = Cross-References

US—United States industry only. CAN—United States and Canadian industries are comparable. When neither US nor CAN appears, Canadian, Mexican, and United States industries are comparable.

www.harrisinfo.com

445

bending, leveling, cleaning, or edging, on a custom basis as part of sales transactions. Sales offices are usually affiliated or owned by a particular manufacturer and take orders but have no inventory.

- Wholesaling gold, silver, and platinum are classified in Industry 421940, Jewelry, Watch, Precious Stone, and Precious Metal Wholesalers;
- Wholesaling automotive, industrial, and other recyclable metal scrap are classified in Industry 421930, Recyclable Material Wholesalers; and
- Wholesaling insulated wire are classified in Industry 421610, Electrical Apparatus and Equipment, Wiring Supplies, and Construction Material Wholesalers.

42152 Coal and Other Mineral and Ore Wholesalers US
See industry description for 421520 below.

421520 Coal and Other Mineral and Ore Wholesalers US
This industry comprises establishments primarily engaged in wholesaling coal, coke, metal ores, and/or nonmetallic minerals (except precious and semiprecious stones and minerals used in construction, such as sand and gravel).

- Wholesaling nonmetallic minerals used in construction, such as sand and gravel, are classified in Industry 421320, Brick, Stone, and Related Construction Material Wholesalers;
- Wholesaling crude petroleum are classified in Industry Group 4227, Petroleum and Petroleum Products Wholesalers; and
- Wholesaling precious and semiprecious stones and metals are classified in Industry 421940, Jewelry, Watch, Precious Stone, and Precious Metal Wholesalers.

4216 Electrical Goods Wholesalers US

42161 Electrical Apparatus and Equipment, Wiring Supplies, and Construction Material Wholesalers US
See industry description for 421610 below.

421610 Electrical Apparatus and Equipment, Wiring Supplies, and Construction Material Wholesalers US
This industry comprises establishments primarily engaged in wholesaling electrical construction materials; wiring supplies; electric light fixtures; light bulbs; and/or electrical power equipment for the generation, transmission, distribution, or control of electric energy.

42162 Electrical Appliance, Television, and Radio Set Wholesalers US
See industry description for 421620 below.

421620 Electrical Appliance, Television, and Radio Set Wholesalers US
This industry comprises establishments primarily engaged in wholesaling household-type electrical appliances, room air-conditioners, gas clothes dryers, and/or household-type audio or video equipment.

- Wholesaling gas household-type appliances (except gas clothes dryers) are classified in Industry 421720, Plumbing and Heating Equipment and Supplies (Hydronics) Wholesalers; and
- Wholesaling nonhousehold-type video cameras are classified in Industry 421410, Photographic Equipment and Supplies Wholesalers.

42169 Other Electronic Parts and Equipment Wholesalers US
See industry description for 421690 below.

421690 Other Electronic Parts and Equipment Wholesalers US
This industry comprises establishments primarily engaged in wholesaling electronic parts and equipment (except electrical apparatus and equipment, wiring supplies and construction material; and electrical appliances, television and radio sets).

- Wholesaling household-type electrical appliances, televisions, and radio sets are classified in Industry 421620, Electrical Appliance, Television, and Radio Set Wholesalers;

Sector **42**

Wholesale Trade

■ = Cross-References

US—United States industry only. CAN—United States and Canadian industries are comparable. When neither US nor CAN appears, Canadian, Mexican, and United States industries are comparable.

446

Harris InfoSource

- Wholesaling computers, computer peripheral equipment, and loaded computer boards are classified in Industry 421430, Computer and Computer Peripheral Equipment and Software Wholesalers; and
- Wholesaling electrical construction materials, wiring supplies, electric light fixtures, light bulbs; and/or electrical power equipment for generation, transmission, distribution, or control of electric energy are classified in Industry 421610, Electrical Apparatus and Equipment, Wiring Supplies, and Construction Material Wholesalers.

4217 Hardware and Plumbing and Heating Equipment and Supplies Wholesalers ᵁˢ

42171 Hardware Wholesalers ᵁˢ
See industry description for 421710 below.

421710 Hardware Wholesalers ᵁˢ
This industry comprises establishments primarily engaged in wholesaling hardware, knives, or hand tools.

- Wholesaling nails, noninsulated wire, and screening are classified in Industry 421510, Metal Service Centers and Offices;
- Wholesaling motor vehicle hand tools and equipment are classified in Industry 421120, Motor Vehicle Supplies and New Parts Wholesalers;
- Wholesaling machinists' precision hand tools are classified in Industry 421830, Industrial Machinery and Equipment Wholesalers; and
- Wholesaling disposable plastics knives and eating utensils are classified in Industry 422130, Industrial and Personal Service Paper Wholesalers.

42172 Plumbing and Heating Equipment and Supplies (Hydronics) Wholesalers ᵁˢ
See industry description for 421720 below.

421720 Plumbing and Heating Equipment and Supplies (Hydronics) Wholesalers ᵁˢ
This industry comprises establishments primarily engaged in wholesaling plumbing equipment, hydronic heating equipment, household-type gas appliances (except gas clothes dryers), and/or supplies.

- Selling and installing plumbing, heating and air conditioning equipment are classified in Industry 235110, Plumbing, Heating, and Air-conditioning Contractors;
- Wholesaling warm air heating and air-conditioning equipment are classified in Industry 421730, Warm Air Heating and Air-conditioning Equipment and Supplies Wholesalers; and
- Wholesaling household-type electrical appliances, room air conditioners, gas clothes dryers, and/or household-type audio or video equipment are classified in Industry 421620, Electrical Appliance, Television, and Radio Set Wholesalers.

42173 Warm Air Heating and Air-conditioning Equipment and Supplies Wholesalers ᵁˢ
See industry description for 421730 below.

421730 Warm Air Heating and Air-conditioning Equipment and Supplies Wholesalers ᵁˢ
This industry comprises establishments primarily engaged in wholesaling warm air heating and air-conditioning equipment and supplies.

- Wholesaling household-type electrical appliances and room air-conditioners are classified in Industry 421620, Electrical Appliance, Television, and Radio Set Wholesalers;
- Wholesaling hydronic heating equipment are classified in Industry 421720, Plumbing, and Heating Equipment and Supplies (Hydronics) Wholesalers; and
- Selling and installing warm air heating and air-conditioning equipment are classified in Industry 235110, Plumbing, Heating, and Air-conditioning Contractors.

42174 Refrigeration Equipment and Supplies Wholesalers ᵁˢ
See industry description for 421740 below.

421740 Refrigeration Equipment and Supplies Wholesalers ᵁˢ
This industry comprises establishments primarily engaged in wholesaling refrigeration equipment (except household-type refrigerators, freezers, and air-conditioners).

- Wholesaling household-type refrigerators, freezers, and room air-conditioners are classified in Industry 421620, Electrical Appliance, Television, and Radio Set Wholesalers; and
- Wholesaling air-conditioning equipment (except room units) are classified Industry 421730, Warm Air Heating and Air-conditioning Equipment and Supplies Wholesalers.

Visit page 18 to learn about classification changes to this sector.

Sector 42

Wholesale Trade

■ = Cross-References

US—United States industry only. CAN—United States and Canadian industries are comparable. When neither US nor CAN appears, Canadian, Mexican, and United States industries are comparable.

www.harrisinfo.com

447

4218 Machinery, Equipment, and Supplies Wholesalers US

This industry group comprises establishments primarily engaged in wholesaling construction, mining, farm, garden, industrial, service establishment, and transportation machinery, equipment and supplies.

42181 Construction and Mining (except Oil Well) Machinery and Equipment Wholesalers US

See industry description for 421810 below.

421810 Construction and Mining (except Oil Well) Machinery and Equipment Wholesalers US

This industry comprises establishments primarily engaged in wholesaling specialized machinery, equipment, and related parts generally used in construction, mining (except oil well) and logging activities.

- Establishments primarily engaged in wholesaling oil well machinery and equipment are classified in Industry 421830, Industrial Machinery and Equipment Wholesalers.

42182 Farm and Garden Machinery and Equipment Wholesalers US

See industry description for 421820 below.

421820 Farm and Garden Machinery and Equipment Wholesalers US

This industry comprises establishments primarily engaged in wholesaling specialized machinery, equipment, and related parts generally used in agricultural, farm, and lawn and garden activities.

42183 Industrial Machinery and Equipment Wholesalers US

See industry description for 421830 below.

421830 Industrial Machinery and Equipment Wholesalers US

This industry comprises establishments primarily engaged in wholesaling specialized machinery, equipment, and related parts generally used in manufacturing, oil well, and warehousing activities.

- Wholesaling specialized machinery, equipment, and related parts generally used in construction, mining (except oil well), and logging activities are classified in Industry 421810, Construction and Mining (except Oil Well) Machinery and Equipment Wholesalers; and
- Wholesaling supplies used in machinery and equipment generally used in manufacturing, oil well, and warehousing activities are classified in Industry 421840, Industrial Supplies Wholesalers.

42184 Industrial Supplies Wholesalers US

See industry description for 421840 below.

421840 Industrial Supplies Wholesalers US

This industry comprises establishments primarily engaged in wholesaling supplies used in machinery and equipment generally used in manufacturing, oil well, and warehousing activities.

- Wholesaling hydraulic and pneumatic (fluid-power) pumps, motors, pistons, and valves are classified in Industry 421830, Industrial Machinery and Equipment Wholesalers; and
- Wholesaling welding gases are classified in Industry 422690, Other Chemical and Allied Products Wholesalers.

42185 Service Establishment Equipment and Supplies Wholesalers US

See industry description for 421850 below.

421850 Service Establishment Equipment and Supplies Wholesalers US

This industry comprises establishments primarily engaged in wholesaling specialized equipment and supplies of the type used by service establishments (except specialized equipment and supplies used in offices, stores, hotels, restaurants, schools, health and medical facilities, photographic facilities, as well as specialized equipment used in transportation and construction activities).

- Wholesaling janitorial and automotive chemicals are classified in Industry 422690, Other Chemical and Allied Products Wholesalers; and

■ = Cross-References

Sector **42**
Wholesale Trade

■ Wholesaling piece goods, fabrics, yarns, thread and other notions are classified in Industry 422310, Piece Goods, Notions, and Other Dry Goods Wholesalers.

42186 Transportation Equipment and Supplies (except Motor Vehicle) Wholesalers US
See industry description for 421860 below.

421860 Transportation Equipment and Supplies (except Motor Vehicle) Wholesalers US
This industry comprises establishments primarily engaged in wholesaling transportation equipment and supplies (except marine pleasure craft and motor vehicles).

■ Wholesaling motor vehicles and motor vehicle parts are classified in Industry Group 4211, Motor Vehicle and Motor Vehicle Parts and Supplies Wholesalers; and
■ Wholesaling marine pleasure craft are classified in Industry 421910, Sporting and Recreational Goods and Supplies Wholesalers.

4219 Miscellaneous Durable Goods Wholesalers US
This industry group comprises establishments primarily engaged in wholesaling sporting, recreational, toy, hobby, and jewelry goods and supplies, and precious stones and metals.

42191 Sporting and Recreational Goods and Supplies Wholesalers US
See industry description for 421910 below.

421910 Sporting and Recreational Goods and Supplies Wholesalers US
This industry comprises establishments primarily engaged in wholesaling sporting goods and accessories; billiard and pool supplies; sporting firearms and ammunition; and/or marine pleasure craft, equipment, and supplies.

■ Wholesaling motor vehicles and trailers are classified in Industry 421110, Automobile and Other Motor Vehicle Wholesalers;
■ Wholesaling motorized passenger golf carts are classified in Industry 421860, Transportation Equipment and Supplies (except Motor Vehicle) Wholesalers;
■ Wholesaling athletic apparel are classified in Industry Group 4223, Apparel, Piece Goods, and Notions Wholesalers; and
■ Wholesaling athletic footwear are classified in Industry 422340, Footwear Wholesalers.

42192 Toy and Hobby Goods and Supplies Wholesalers US
See industry description for 421920 below.

421920 Toy and Hobby Goods and Supplies Wholesalers US
This industry comprises establishments primarily engaged in wholesaling games, toys, fireworks, playing cards, hobby goods and supplies, and/or related goods.

42193 Recyclable Material Wholesalers US
See industry description for 421930 below.

421930 Recyclable Material Wholesalers US
This industry comprises establishments primarily engaged in wholesaling scrap from automotive, industrial, and other recyclable materials. Included in this industry are auto wreckers primarily engaged in dismantling motor vehicles for the purpose of wholesaling scrap.

■ Dismantling motor vehicles for the purpose of selling used parts are classified in Industry 421140, Motor Vehicle Parts (Used) Wholesalers; and
■ Operating facilities for separating and sorting recyclable materials are classified in Industry 562920, Materials Recovery Facilities.

42194 Jewelry, Watch, Precious Stone, and Precious Metal Wholesalers US
See industry description for 421940 below.

421940 Jewelry, Watch, Precious Stone, and Precious Metal Wholesalers US
This industry comprises establishments primarily engaged in wholesaling jewelry, precious and

Visit page 18 to learn about classification changes to this sector.

Sector 42
Wholesale Trade

■ = Cross-References

US—United States industry only. CAN—United States and Canadian industries are comparable. When neither US nor CAN appears, Canadian, Mexican, and United States industries are comparable.

www.harrisinfo.com

449

semiprecious stones, precious metals and metal flatware, costume jewelry, watches, clocks, silverware, and/or jewelers' findings.

- Wholesaling precious metal ores or concentrates are classified in Industry 421520, Coal and Other Mineral and Ore Wholesalers; and
- Wholesaling nonprecious flatware are classified in Industry 421220, Home Furnishing Wholesalers.

42199 Other Miscellaneous Durable Goods Wholesalers US
See industry description for 421990 below.

421990 Other Miscellaneous Durable Goods Wholesalers US
This industry comprises establishments primarily engaged in wholesaling durable goods (except motor vehicle and motor vehicle parts and supplies; furniture and home furnishings; lumber and other construction materials; professional and commercial equipment and supplies; metals and minerals (except petroleum); electrical goods; hardware, and plumbing and heating equipment and supplies; machinery, equipment and supplies; sporting and recreational goods and supplies; toy and hobby goods and supplies; recyclable materials; and jewelry, watches, precious stones and precious metals).

- Wholesaling automobiles and other motor vehicles, motor vehicle supplies, tires, and new and used parts are classified in Industry Group 4211, Motor Vehicle and Motor Vehicle Parts and Supplies Wholesalers;
- Wholesaling furniture and home furnishings are classified in Industry Group 4212, Furniture and Home Furnishing Wholesalers;
- Wholesaling lumber, plywood, millwork, wood panels, brick, stone, roofing, siding, and other nonelectrical construction materials are classified in Industry Group 4213, Lumber and Other Construction Materials Wholesalers;
- Wholesaling photographic; office; computer and computer peripheral; medical, dental, hospital, ophthalmic; and other commercial and professional equipment and supplies are classified in Industry Group 4214, Professional and Commercial Equipment and Supplies Wholesalers;
- Wholesaling coal and other minerals and ores and semi-finished metal products are classified in Industry Group 4215, Metal and Mineral (except Petroleum) Wholesalers;
- Wholesaling electrical goods are classified in Industry Group 4216, Electrical Goods Wholesalers;
- Wholesaling hardware, and plumbing, heating, air conditioning, and refrigeration equipment and supplies are classified in Industry Group 4217, Hardware, and Plumbing and Heating Equipment and Supplies Wholesalers;
- Wholesaling construction, mining, farm, garden, industrial, service establishment, and transportation machinery, equipment and supplies are classified in Industry Group 4218, Machinery, Equipment, and Supplies Wholesalers;
- Wholesaling sporting goods and accessories; billiard and pool supplies; sporting firearms and ammunition; and/or marine pleasure craft, equipment, and supplies are classified in Industry 421910, Sporting and Recreational Goods and Supplies Wholesalers;
- Wholesaling toys, fireworks, playing cards, hobby goods and supplies and/or related goods are classified in Industry 421920, Toy and Hobby Goods and Supplies Wholesalers;
- Wholesaling automotive, industrial, and other recyclable materials are classified in Industry 421930, Recyclable Material Wholesalers; and
- Wholesaling jewelry, precious and semiprecious stones, precious metals and metal flatware, costume jewelry, watches, clocks, silverware, and/or jewelers' findings are classified in Industry 421940, Jewelry, Watch, Precious Stone, and Precious Metal Wholesalers.

▶422 WHOLESALE TRADE, NONDURABLE GOODS US
Industries in the Wholesale Trade, Nondurable Goods subsector sell or arrange the purchase or sale of nondurable goods to other businesses. Nondurable goods are items generally with a normal life expectancy of less than three years. Nondurable goods wholesale trade establishments are engaged in wholesaling products, such as paper and paper products, chemicals and chemical products, drugs, textiles and textile products, apparel, footwear, groceries, farm products, petroleum and petroleum products, alcoholic beverages, books, magazines, newspapers, flowers and nursery stock, and tobacco products.

The detailed industries within the subsector are organized in the classification structure based on the products sold. Within an industry, the types of establishments may vary, including wholesale merchants and/or agents and brokers.

4221 Paper and Paper Product Wholesalers US

42211 Printing and Writing Paper Wholesalers US
See industry description for 422110 below.

Sector 42

Wholesale Trade

■ = Cross-References

US—United States industry only. CAN—United States and Canadian industries are comparable. When neither US nor CAN appears, Canadian, Mexican, and United States industries are comparable.

450

Harris InfoSource

422110 Printing and Writing Paper Wholesalers [US]

This industry comprises establishments primarily engaged in wholesaling bulk printing and/or writing paper generally on rolls for further processing.

- Establishments primarily engaged in wholesaling stationery are classified in Industry 422120, Stationery and Office Supplies Wholesalers.

42212 Stationery and Office Supplies Wholesalers [US]

See industry description for 422120 below.

422120 Stationery and Office Supplies Wholesalers [US]

This industry comprises establishments primarily engaged in wholesaling stationery, office supplies and/or gift-wrap.

- Establishments primarily engaged in wholesaling bulk printing and/or writing paper are classified in Industry 422110, Printing and Writing Paper Wholesalers.

42213 Industrial and Personal Service Paper Wholesalers [US]

See industry description for 422130 below.

422130 Industrial and Personal Service Paper Wholesalers [US]

This industry comprises establishments primarily engaged in wholesaling wrapping and other coarse paper, paperboard, converted paper (except stationery and office supplies), and/or related disposable plastics products.

- Establishments primarily engaged in stationery, office supplies, and/or gift-wrap are classified in Industry 422120, Stationery and Office Supplies Wholesalers.

4222 Drugs and Druggists' Sundries Wholesalers [US]

42221 Drugs and Druggists' Sundries Wholesalers [US]

See industry description for 422210 below.

Visit page 18 to learn about classification changes to this sector.

422210 Drugs and Druggists' Sundries Wholesalers [US]

This industry comprises establishments primarily engaged in wholesaling biological and medical products; botanical drugs and herbs; and pharmaceutical products intended for internal and external consumption in such forms as ampoules, tablets, capsules, vials, ointments, powders, solutions, and suspensions.

- Establishments primarily engaged in wholesaling surgical, dental, and hospital equipment are classified in Industry 421450, Medical, Dental, and Hospital Equipment and Supplies Wholesalers.

4223 Apparel, Piece Goods, and Notions Wholesalers [US]

42231 Piece Goods, Notions, and Other Dry Goods Wholesalers [US]

See industry description for 422310 below.

Sector 42

Wholesale Trade

422310 Piece Goods, Notions, and Other Dry Goods Wholesalers [US]

This industry comprises establishments primarily engaged in wholesaling piece goods, fabrics, yarns, thread and other notions, and/or hair accessories.

- Establishments primarily engaged as converters who buy fabric goods in the grey, have them finished on a contract basis, and sell at wholesale are classified in Industry 31331, Textile and Fabric Finishing Mills.

42232 Men's and Boys' Clothing and Furnishings Wholesalers [US]

See industry description for 422320 below.

■ = Cross-References

US—United States industry only. CAN—United States and Canadian industries are comparable. When neither US nor CAN appears, Canadian, Mexican, and United States industries are comparable.

www.harrisinfo.com

451

422320 Men's and Boys' Clothing and Furnishings Wholesalers ᵁˢ

This industry comprises establishments primarily engaged in wholesaling men's and/or boys' clothing and furnishings.

- ■ Establishments primarily engaged in wholesaling unisex clothing and men's fur clothing are classified in Industry 422330, Women's, Children's, and Infants' Clothing and Accessories Wholesalers.

42233 Women's, Children's, and Infants' Clothing and Accessories Wholesalers ᵁˢ

See industry description for 422330 below.

422330 Women's, Children's, and Infants' Clothing and Accessories Wholesalers ᵁˢ

This industry comprises establishments primarily engaged in wholesaling (1) women's, children's, infants', and/or unisex clothing and accessories and/or (2) fur clothing.

42234 Footwear Wholesalers ᵁˢ

See industry description for 422340 below.

422340 Footwear Wholesalers ᵁˢ

This industry comprises establishments primarily engaged in wholesaling footwear (including athletic) of leather, rubber, and other materials.

4224 Grocery and Related Product Wholesalers ᵁˢ

42241 General Line Grocery Wholesalers ᵁˢ

See industry description for 422410 below.

422410 General Line Grocery Wholesalers ᵁˢ

This industry comprises establishments primarily engaged in wholesaling a general line (wide range) of groceries.

- ■ Establishments primarily engaged in wholesaling a specialized line of groceries are classified according to the product sold.

42242 Packaged Frozen Food Wholesalers ᵁˢ

See industry description for 422420 below.

422420 Packaged Frozen Food Wholesalers ᵁˢ

This industry comprises establishments primarily engaged in wholesaling packaged frozen foods (except dairy products).

- ■ Establishments primarily engaged in wholesaling frozen dairy products are classified in Industry 422430, Dairy Product (except Dried or Canned) Wholesalers.

42243 Dairy Product (except Dried or Canned) Wholesalers ᵁˢ

See industry description for 422430 below.

422430 Dairy Product (except Dried or Canned) Wholesalers ᵁˢ

This industry comprises establishments primarily engaged in wholesaling dairy products (except dried or canned).

- ■ Wholesaling dried or canned dairy products and dairy substitutes are classified in Industry 422490, Other Grocery and Related Products Wholesalers; and
- ■ Pasteurizing and bottling milk are classified in U.S. Industry 311511, Fluid Milk Manufacturing.

42244 Poultry and Poultry Product Wholesalers ᵁˢ

See industry description for 422440 below.

Sector 42

Wholesale Trade

■ = Cross-References

US—United States industry only. CAN—United States and Canadian industries are comparable. When neither US nor CAN appears, Canadian, Mexican, and United States industries are comparable.

452

Harris InfoSource

422440 Poultry and Poultry Product Wholesalers US

This industry comprises establishments primarily engaged in wholesaling poultry and/or poultry products (except canned and packaged frozen).

- Wholesaling packaged frozen poultry are classified in Industry 422420, Packaged Frozen Food Wholesalers;
- Wholesaling canned poultry are classified in Industry 422490, Other Grocery and Related Products Wholesalers; and
- Slaughtering and dressing poultry are classified in U.S. Industry 311615, Poultry Processing.

42245 Confectionery Wholesalers US

See industry description for 422450 below.

422450 Confectionery Wholesalers US

This industry comprises establishments primarily engaged in wholesaling confectioneries; salted or roasted nuts; popcorn; potato, corn, and similar chips; and/or fountain fruits and syrups.

- Wholesaling frozen pretzels are classified in Industry 422420, Packaged Frozen Food Wholesalers; and
- Wholesaling pretzels (except frozen) are classified in Industry 422490, Other Grocery and Related Products Wholesalers.

42246 Fish and Seafood Wholesalers US

See industry description for 422460 below.

422460 Fish and Seafood Wholesalers US

This industry comprises establishments primarily engaged in wholesaling fish and seafood (except canned or packaged frozen).

- Wholesaling packaged frozen fish and seafood are classified in Industry 422420, Packaged Frozen Food Wholesalers;
- Wholesaling canned fish and seafood are classified in Industry 422490, Other Grocery and Related Products Wholesalers; and
- Canning, smoking, salting, drying, or freezing seafood and shucking and packing fresh shellfish are classified in Industry 31171, Seafood Product Preparation and Packaging.

42247 Meat and Meat Product Wholesalers US

See industry description for 422470 below.

422470 Meat and Meat Product Wholesalers US

This industry comprises establishments primarily engaged in wholesaling meats and meat products (except canned and packaged frozen) and/or lard.

- Wholesaling packaged frozen meats are classified in Industry 422420, Packaged Frozen Food Wholesalers;
- Wholesaling canned meats are classified in Industry 422490, Other Grocery and Related Products Wholesalers; and
- Preparing boxed beef are classified in U.S. Industry 311612, Meat Processed from Carcasses.

42248 Fresh Fruit and Vegetable Wholesalers US

See industry description for 422480 below.

422480 Fresh Fruit and Vegetable Wholesalers US

This industry comprises establishments primarily engaged in wholesaling fresh fruits and vegetables.

42249 Other Grocery and Related Products Wholesalers US

See industry description for 422490 below.

422490 Other Grocery and Related Products Wholesalers US

This industry comprises establishments primarily engaged in wholesaling groceries and related products (except a general line of groceries; packaged frozen food; dairy products (except dried and canned); poultry products (except canned); confectioneries; fish and seafood (except canned); meat products (except canned); and fresh fruits and vegetables). Included in this industry are establishments primarily engaged in bottling and wholesaling spring and mineral waters processed by others.

- Wholesaling grains, field beans, livestock, and other farm product raw materials are classified in Industry Group 4225, Farm Product Raw Material Wholesalers;

Visit page 18 to learn about classification changes to this sector.

Sector **42**

Wholesale Trade

■ = Cross-References

US—United States industry only. CAN—United States and Canadian industries are comparable. When neither US nor CAN appears, Canadian, Mexican, and United States industries are comparable.

- Wholesaling beer, wine, and distilled alcoholic beverages are classified in Industry Group 4228, Beer, Wine, and Distilled Alcoholic Beverage Wholesalers;
- Bottling soft drinks are classified in Industry 31211, Soft Drink and Ice Manufacturing;
- Wholesaling a general line of groceries are classified in Industry 422410, General Line Grocery Wholesalers;
- Wholesaling packaged frozen foods (except dairy) are classified in Industry 422420, Packaged Frozen Food Wholesalers;
- Wholesaling dairy products are classified in Industry 422430, Dairy Products (except Dried or Canned) Wholesalers;
- Wholesaling poultry and poultry products (except canned and packaged frozen) are classified in Industry 422440, Poultry and Poultry Product Wholesalers;
- Wholesaling confectioneries; salted or roasted nuts; popcorn; potato, corn, and similar chips; and/or fountain fruits and syrups are classified in Industry 422450, Confectionery Wholesalers;
- Wholesaling fish and seafood (except canned and packaged frozen) are classified in Industry 422460, Fish and Seafood Wholesalers;
- Wholesaling meats (except canned and packaged frozen) are classified in Industry 422470, Meat and Meat Product Wholesalers;
- Wholesaling fresh fruits and vegetables are classified in Industry 422480, Fresh Fruit and Vegetable Wholesalers; and
- Roasting coffee are classified in Industry 311920, Coffee and Tea Manufacturing.

4225 Farm Product Raw Material Wholesalers US

This industry group comprises establishments primarily engaged in wholesaling agricultural products (except raw milk, live poultry, and fresh fruit and vegetables), such as grains, field beans, livestock, and other farm product raw materials (excluding seeds).

42251 Grain and Field Bean Wholesalers US

See industry description for 422510 below.

422510 Grain and Field Bean Wholesalers US

This industry comprises establishments primarily engaged in wholesaling grains, such as corn, wheat, oats, barley, and unpolished rice; dry beans; and soybeans and other inedible beans. Included in this industry are establishments primarily engaged in operating country or terminal grain elevators primarily for the purpose of wholesaling.

- Wholesaling field and garden seeds are classified in Industry 422910, Farm Supplies Wholesalers; and
- Operating grain elevators for storage only are classified in Industry 493130, Farm Product Warehousing and Storage.

42252 Livestock Wholesalers US

See industry description for 422520 below.

422520 Livestock Wholesalers US

This industry comprises establishments primarily engaged in wholesaling livestock (except horses and mules).

- Establishments primarily engaged in wholesaling horses and mules are classified in Industry 422590, Other Farm Product Raw Material Wholesalers.

42259 Other Farm Product Raw Material Wholesalers US

See industry description for 422590 below.

422590 Other Farm Product Raw Material Wholesalers US

This industry comprises establishments primarily engaged in wholesaling farm products (except grain and field beans, livestock, raw milk, live poultry, and fresh fruits and vegetables).

- Wholesaling raw milk are classified in Industry 422430, Dairy Product (except Dried or Canned) Wholesalers;
- Wholesaling live poultry (except chicks) are classified in Industry 422440, Poultry and Poultry Product Wholesalers;
- Wholesaling grain, dry beans, and soybeans and other inedible beans are classified in Industry 422510, Grain and Field Bean Wholesalers;
- Wholesaling livestock (except horses and mules), such as cattle, hogs, sheep, and goats are classified in Industry 422520, Livestock Wholesalers; and
- Wholesaling fresh fruits and vegetables are classified in Industry 422480, Fresh Fruit and Vegetable Wholesalers.

4226 Chemical and Allied Products Wholesalers US

This industry group comprises establishments primarily engaged in wholesaling chemicals; plastics materials and basic forms and shapes; and allied products.

Sector **42**

Wholesale Trade

■ = Cross-References

US—United States industry only. CAN—United States and Canadian industries are comparable. When neither US nor CAN appears, Canadian, Mexican, and United States industries are comparable.

454

Harris InfoSource

42261 Plastics Materials and Basic Forms and Shapes Wholesalers [US]
See industry description for 422610 below.

422610 Plastics Materials and Basic Forms and Shapes Wholesalers [US]
This industry comprises establishments primarily engaged in wholesaling plastics materials and resins, and unsupported plastics film, sheet, sheeting, rod, tube, and other basic forms and shapes.

42269 Other Chemical and Allied Products Wholesalers [US]
See industry description for 422690 below.

422690 Other Chemical and Allied Products Wholesalers [US]
This industry comprises establishments primarily engaged in wholesaling chemicals and allied products (except agricultural and medicinal chemicals, paints and varnishes, fireworks, and plastics materials and basic forms and shapes).

Visit page 18 to learn about classification changes to this sector.

- Wholesaling ammunition are classified in Industry Group 4219, Miscellaneous Durable Goods Wholesalers;
- Wholesaling biological and medical products; botanical drugs and herbs; and pharmaceutical products intended for internal and external consumption in such forms as ampoules, tablets, capsules, vials, ointments, powders, solutions, and suspensions are classified in Industry 422210, Drugs and Druggists' Sundries Wholesalers;
- Wholesaling farm supplies, such as animal feeds, fertilizers, agricultural chemicals, pesticides, seeds and plant bulbs, are classified in Industry 422910, Farm Supplies Wholesalers;
- Wholesaling paints, and varnishes and similar coatings, pigments, wallpaper, and supplies, such as paint brushes and rollers, are classified in Industry 422950, Paint, Varnish and Supplies Wholesalers;
- Wholesaling lubricating oils and greases are classified in Industry 422720, Petroleum and Petroleum Products Wholesalers (except Bulk Stations and Terminals);
- Wholesaling fireworks are classified in Industry 421920, Toy and Hobby Goods and Supplies Wholesalers; and
- Wholesaling plastics materials and resins, and unsupported plastics film, sheet, sheeting, rod, tube, and other basic forms and shapes are classified in Industry 422610, Plastics Materials and Basic Forms and Shapes Wholesalers.

4227 Petroleum and Petroleum Products Wholesalers [US]

42271 Petroleum Bulk Stations and Terminals
See industry description for 422710 below.

422710 Petroleum Bulk Stations and Terminals
This industry comprises establishments with bulk liquid storage facilities primarily engaged in wholesaling crude petroleum and petroleum products, including liquefied petroleum gas.

- Establishments primarily engaged in bulk storage of petroleum are classified in Industry 493190, Other Warehousing and Storage.

42272 Petroleum and Petroleum Products Wholesalers [US]
(except Bulk Stations and Terminals)
See industry description for 422720 below.

422720 Petroleum and Petroleum Products Wholesalers [US]
(except Bulk Stations and Terminals)
This industry comprises establishments primarily engaged in wholesaling petroleum and petroleum products (except from bulk liquid storage facilities).

- Establishments primarily engaged in wholesaling crude petroleum and petroleum products from bulk liquid storage facilities are classified in Industry 422710, Petroleum Bulk Stations and Terminals.

4228 Beer, Wine, and Distilled Alcoholic Beverage Wholesalers [US]

42281 Beer and Ale Wholesalers [US]
See industry description for 422810 below.

Sector 42
Wholesale Trade

■ = Cross-References

US—United States industry only. CAN—United States and Canadian industries are comparable. When neither US nor CAN appears, Canadian, Mexican, and United States industries are comparable.

www.harrisinfo.com

455

422810 Beer and Ale Wholesalers US

This industry comprises establishments primarily engaged in wholesaling beer, ale, porter, and other fermented malt beverages.

42282 Wine and Distilled Alcoholic Beverage Wholesalers US

See industry description for 422820 below.

422820 Wine and Distilled Alcoholic Beverage Wholesalers US

This industry comprises establishments primarily engaged in wholesaling wine, distilled alcoholic beverages, and/or neutral spirits and ethyl alcohol used in blended wines and distilled liquors.

4229 Miscellaneous Nondurable Goods Wholesalers US

This industry group comprises establishments primarily engaged in wholesaling nondurable goods, such as farm supplies; books, periodicals and newspapers; flowers; nursery stock; paints; varnishes; tobacco and tobacco products; and other miscellaneous nondurable goods, such as cut Christmas trees and pet supplies.

42291 Farm Supplies Wholesalers US

See industry description for 422910 below.

422910 Farm Supplies Wholesalers US

This industry comprises establishments primarily engaged in wholesaling farm supplies, such as animal feeds, fertilizers, agricultural chemicals, pesticides, plant seeds, and plant bulbs.

- ■ Wholesaling pet food are classified in Industry 422490, Other Grocery and Related Products Wholesalers;
- ■ Wholesaling grains are classified in Industry 422510, Grain and Field Bean Wholesalers;
- ■ Wholesaling pet supplies are classified in Industry 422990, Other Miscellaneous Nondurable Goods Wholesalers; and
- ■ Wholesaling nursery stock (except seeds and plant bulbs) are classified in Industry 422930, Flower, Nursery Stock, and Florists' Supplies Wholesalers.

42292 Book, Periodical, and Newspaper Wholesalers US

See industry description for 422920 below.

422920 Book, Periodical, and Newspaper Wholesalers US

This industry comprises establishments primarily engaged in wholesaling books, periodicals, and newspapers.

42293 Flower, Nursery Stock, and Florists' Supplies Wholesalers US

See industry description for 422930 below.

422930 Flower, Nursery Stock, and Florists' Supplies Wholesalers US

This industry comprises establishments primarily engaged in wholesaling flowers, florists' supplies, and/or nursery stock (except seeds and plant bulbs).

- ■ Wholesaling cut Christmas trees are classified in Industry 422990, Other Miscellaneous Nondurable Goods Wholesalers; and
- ■ Wholesaling plant seeds and plant bulbs are classified in Industry 422910, Farm Supplies Wholesalers.

42294 Tobacco and Tobacco Product Wholesalers US

See industry description for 422940 below.

422940 Tobacco and Tobacco Product Wholesalers US

This industry comprises establishments primarily engaged in wholesaling tobacco products, such as cigarettes, snuff, cigars, and pipe tobacco.

- ■ Establishments primarily engaged in wholesaling leaf tobacco are classified in Industry 422590, Other Farm Product Raw Material Wholesalers.

Sector **42**

Wholesale Trade

■ = Cross-References

US—United States industry only. CAN—United States and Canadian industries are comparable. When neither US nor CAN appears, Canadian, Mexican, and United States industries are comparable.

456

Harris InfoSource

42295 Paint, Varnish, and Supplies Wholesalers ^{US}
See industry description for 422950 below.

422950 Paint, Varnish, and Supplies Wholesalers ^{US}
This industry comprises establishments primarily engaged in wholesaling paints, varnishes, and similar coatings; pigments; wallpaper; and supplies, such as paint brushes and rollers.

- Establishments primarily engaged in wholesaling artists' paints are classified in Industry 422990, Other Miscellaneous Nondurable Goods Wholesalers.

42299 Other Miscellaneous Nondurable Goods Wholesalers ^{US}
See industry description for 422990 below.

422990 Other Miscellaneous Nondurable Goods Wholesalers ^{US}
This industry comprises establishments primarily engaged in wholesaling nondurable goods (except printing and writing paper; stationery and office supplies; industrial and personal service paper; drugs and druggists' sundries; apparel, piece goods, and notions; grocery and related products; farm product raw materials; chemical and allied products; petroleum and petroleum products; beer, wine, and distilled alcoholic beverages; farm supplies; books, periodicals and newspapers; flower, nursery stock and florists' supplies; tobacco and tobacco products; and paint, varnishes, wallpaper, and supplies).

Visit page 18 to learn about classification changes to this sector.

- Wholesaling advertising specialties are classified in Industry 541870, Advertising Material Distribution Services;
- Wholesaling farm supplies are classified in Industry 422910, Farm Supplies Wholesalers;
- Wholesaling books, periodicals, and newspapers are classified in Industry 422920, Book, Periodical, and Newspaper Wholesalers;
- Wholesaling flowers, nursery stock, and florists' supplies are classified in Industry 422930, Flower, Nursery Stock, and Florists' Supplies Wholesalers;
- Wholesaling tobacco and its products are classified in Industry 422940, Tobacco and Tobacco Product Wholesalers;
- Wholesaling paints, varnishes, and similar coatings; pigments; wallpaper; and supplies are classified in Industry 422950, Paint, Varnish, and Supplies Wholesalers;
- Wholesaling bulk printing and/or writing paper are classified in Industry 422110, Printing and Writing Paper Wholesalers;
- Wholesaling stationery, office supplies, and/or gift wrap are classified in Industry 422120, Stationery and Office Supplies Wholesalers;
- Wholesaling wrapping and other coarse paper, paperboard, converted paper (except stationery and office supplies), and related disposable plastics products are classified in Industry 422130, Industrial and Personal Service Paper Wholesalers;
- Wholesaling biological and medical products; botanical drugs and herbs; and pharmaceutical products intended for internal and external consumption are classified in Industry 422210, Drugs and Druggists' Sundries Wholesalers;
- Wholesaling clothing and accessories, footwear, piece goods, yard goods, notions, and/or hair accessories are classified in Industry Group 4223, Apparel, Piece Goods, and Notions Wholesalers;
- Wholesaling meat, poultry, seafood, confectioneries, fruits and vegetables; and other groceries are related products are classified in Industry Group 4224, Grocery and Related Product Wholesalers;
- Wholesaling grains, field beans, livestock, and other farm product raw materials are classified in Industry Group 4225, Farm Product Raw Material Wholesalers;
- Wholesaling chemicals; plastics materials and basic forms and shapes; and allied products are classified in Industry Group 4226, Chemical and Allied Products Wholesalers;
- Wholesaling petroleum and petroleum products are classified in Industry Group 4227, Petroleum and Petroleum Products Wholesalers;
- Wholesaling beer, ale, wine, and distilled alcoholic beverages are classified Industry Group 4228, Beer, Wine, and Distilled Alcoholic Beverage Wholesalers;
- Wholesaling pet foods are classified in Industry 422490, Other Grocery and Related Products Wholesalers; and
- Wholesaling religious statuaries are classified in Industry 421990, Other Miscellaneous Durable Goods Wholesalers.

Sector **42**

Wholesale Trade

■ = Cross-References

US—United States industry only. CAN—United States and Canadian industries are comparable. When neither US nor CAN appears, Canadian, Mexican, and United States industries are comparable.

www.harrisinfo.com

457

NAICS United States Structure

Sector	Name	Sub-sectors	Industry groups	NAICS 5-digit industries	U.S. 6-digit industries	TOTAL U.S. industries	New industries
11	Agriculture, Forestry, Fishing and, Hunting	5	19	42	32	64	20
21	Mining	3	5	10	28	29	—
22	Utilities	1	3	6	6	10	6
23	Construction	3	14	28	—	28	3
31–33	Manufacturing	21	84	184	408	474	79
42	Wholesale Trade	2	18	69	—	69	—
44–45	Retail Trade	12	27	61	18	72	17
48-49	Transportation and Warehousing	11	29	42	25	57	28
51	Information	4	9	28	12	34	20
52	Finance and Insurance	5	11	32	15	42	23
53	Real Estate and Rental and Leasing	3	8	19	9	24	15
54	Professional, Scientific, and Technical Services	1	9	35	17	47	28
55	Management of Companies and Enterprises	1	1	1	3	3	1
56	Administrative and Support and Waste Management and Remediation Services	2	11	29	23	43	29
61	Educational Services	1	7	12	7	17	12
62	Health Care and Social Assistance	4	18	30	16	39	27
71	Arts, Entertainment, and Recreation	3	9	23	3	25	19
72	Accommodation and Food Services	2	7	11	7	15	10
81	Other Services (except Public Administration)	4	14	30	30	49	19
92	Public Administration	8	8	29	—	29	2
	TOTAL	96	311	721	659	1170	358

To learn more about the changes by sector go to pages 15-18.

Sector 42

Wholesale Trade

Sector 44-45 Retail Trade

The Sector as a Whole

THE RETAIL TRADE sector comprises establishments engaged in retailing merchandise, generally without transformation, and rendering services incidental to the sale of merchandise.

The retailing process is the final step in the distribution of merchandise; retailers are, therefore, organized to sell merchandise in small quantities to the general public. This sector comprises two main types of retailers: store and nonstore retailers.

1. Store retailers operate fixed point-of-sale locations, located and designed to attract a high volume of walk-in customers. In general, retail stores have extensive displays of merchandise and use mass-media advertising to attract customers. They typically sell merchandise to the general public for personal or household consumption, but some also serve business and institutional clients. These include establishments, such as office supply stores, computer and software stores, building materials dealers, plumbing supply stores, and electrical supply stores. Catalog showrooms, gasoline services stations, automotive dealers, and mobile home dealers are treated as store retailers.

In addition to retailing merchandise, some types of store retailers are also engaged in the provision of after-sales services, such as repair and installation. For example, new automobile dealers, electronic and appliance stores, and musical instrument and supply stores often provide repair services. As a general rule, establishments engaged in retailing merchandise and providing after-sales services are classified in this sector.

The first eleven subsectors of retail trade are store retailers. The establishments are grouped into industries and industry groups typically based on one or more of the following criteria:

(a) The merchandise line or lines carried by the store; for example, specialty stores are distinguished from general-line stores.

(b) The usual trade designation of the establishments. This criterion applies in cases where a store type is well recognized by the industry and the public, but difficult to define strictly in terms of commodity lines carried; for example, pharmacies, hardware stores, and department stores.

(c) Capital requirements in terms of display equipment; for example, food stores have equipment requirements not found in other retail industries.

(d) Human resource requirements in terms of expertise; for example, the staff of an automobile dealer requires knowledge in financing, registering, and licensing issues that are not necessary in other retail industries.

2. Nonstore retailers, like store retailers, are organized to serve the general public, but their retailing methods differ. The establishments of this subsector reach customers and market merchandise with methods, such as the broadcasting of "infomercials," the broadcasting and publishing of direct-response advertising, the publishing of paper and electronic catalogs, door-to-door solicitation, in-home demonstration, selling from portable stalls (street vendors, except food), and distribution through vending machines. Establishments engaged in the direct sale (nonstore) of products, such as home heating oil dealers and home delivery newspaper routes.

Visit page 18 to learn about classification changes to this sector.

Sector 44-45

Retail Trade

US—United States industry only. CAN—United States and Canadian industries are comparable. When neither US nor CAN appears, Canadian, Mexican, and United States industries are comparable.

The buying of goods for resale is a characteristic of retail trade establishments that particularly distinguishes them from establishments in the agriculture, manufacturing, and construction industries. For example, farms that sell their products at or from the point of production are not classified in retail, but rather in agriculture. Similarly, establishments that both manufacture and sell their products to the general public are not classified in retail, but rather in manufacturing. However, establishments that engage in processing activities incidental to retailing are classified in retail. This includes establishments, such as optical goods stores that do in-store grinding of lenses, and meat and seafood markets.

Wholesalers also engage in the buying of goods for resale, but they are not usually organized to serve the general public. They typically operate from a warehouse or office and neither the design nor the location of these premises is intended to solicit a high volume of walk-in traffic. Wholesalers supply institutional, industrial, wholesale, and retail clients; their operations are, therefore, generally organized to purchase, sell, and deliver merchandise in larger quantities. However, dealers of durable nonconsumer goods, such as farm machinery and heavy-duty trucks, are included in wholesale trade even if they often sell these products in single units.

▶441 MOTOR VEHICLE AND PARTS DEALERS ^{CAN}

Industries in the Motor Vehicle and Parts Dealers subsector retail motor vehicle and parts merchandise from fixed point-of-sale locations. Establishments in this subsector typically operate from a showroom and/or an open lot where the vehicles are on display. The display of vehicles and the related parts require little by way of display equipment. The personnel generally include both the sales and sales support staff familiar with the requirements for registering and financing a vehicle as well as a staff of parts experts and mechanics trained to provide repair and maintenance services for the vehicles. Specific industries have been included in this subsector to identify the type of vehicle being retailed.

Sales of capital or durable nonconsumer goods, such as medium and heavy-duty trucks, are always included in wholesale trade. These goods are virtually never sold through retail methods.

4411 Automobile Dealers ^{CAN}
This industry group comprises establishments primarily engaged in retailing new and used automobiles and light trucks, such as sport utility vehicles, and passenger and cargo vans.

44111 New Car Dealers ^{CAN}
See industry description for 441110 below.

441110 New Car Dealers ^{CAN}
This industry comprises establishments primarily engaged in retailing new automobiles and light trucks, such as sport utility vehicles, and passenger and cargo vans, or retailing these new vehicles in combination with activities, such as repair services, retailing used cars, and selling replacement parts and accessories.

- Retailing used automobiles and light trucks without retailing new automobiles and light trucks are classified in Industry 441120, Used Car Dealers.
- Providing automotive repair services without retailing new automotive vehicles are classified in Industry Group 8111, Automotive Repair and Maintenance.

44112 Used Car Dealers ^{CAN}
See industry description for 441120 below.

441120 Used Car Dealers ^{CAN}
This industry comprises establishments primarily engaged in retailing used automobiles and light trucks, such as sport utility vehicles, and passenger and cargo vans.

- Establishments primarily engaged in retailing new automobiles and light trucks are classified in Industry 441110, New Car Dealers.

 = Cross-References

Sector
44-45
Retail Trade

US—United States industry only. CAN—United States and Canadian industries are comparable. When neither US nor CAN appears, Canadian, Mexican, and United States industries are comparable.

460

Harris InfoSource

4412 Other Motor Vehicle Dealers ^{CAN}

This industry group comprises establishments primarily engaged in retailing new and used vehicles (except automobiles, light trucks, such as sport utility vehicles, and passenger and cargo vans).

44121 Recreational Vehicle Dealers ^{CAN}

See industry description for 441210 below.

441210 Recreational Vehicle Dealers ^{CAN}

This industry comprises establishments primarily engaged in retailing new and/or used recreational vehicles—commonly referred to as RVs—or retailing these new vehicles in combination with activities, such as repair services and selling replacement parts and accessories.

- Retailing new or used boat trailers and utility trailers are classified in Industry 44122, Motorcycle, Boat, and Other Motor Vehicle Dealers; and
- Retailing manufactured homes (i.e., mobile homes), parts, and equipment are classified in Industry 453930, Manufactured (Mobile) Home Dealers.

44122 Motorcycle, Boat, and Other Motor Vehicle Dealers ^{CAN}

This industry comprises establishments primarily engaged in retailing new and used motorcycles, boats, and other vehicles (except automobiles, light trucks, and recreational vehicles), or retailing these new vehicles in combination with activities, such as repair services and selling replacement parts and accessories.

- Retailing new nonmotorized bicycles, surfboards, or wind sail boards are classified in Industry 45111, Sporting Goods Stores;
- Retailing used nonmotorized bicycles, surfboards, or wind sail boards are classified in Industry 45331, Used Merchandise Stores;
- Retailing new or used automobiles and light trucks are classified in Industry Group 4411, Automotive Dealers;
- Retailing new or used recreational vehicles, such as travel trailers, are classified in Industry 44121, Recreational Vehicle Dealers;
- Providing repair services for vehicles without retailing new vehicles are classified in the appropriate industry for the repair services; and
- Retailing fuel and marine supplies at a marina are classified in Industry 71393, Marinas

441221 Motorcycle Dealers ^{US}

This U.S. industry comprises establishments primarily engaged in retailing new and/or used motorcycles, motor scooters, motor bikes, mopeds, off-road all-terrain vehicles, and personal watercraft, or retailing these new vehicles in combination with repair services and selling replacement parts and accessories.

- Providing motorcycle repair services without retailing new motorcycles are classified in Industry 811490, Other Personal and Household Goods Repair and Maintenance;
- Retailing new nonmotorized bicycles are classified in Industry 451110, Sporting Goods Stores;
- Retailing used nonmotorized bicycles are classified in Industry 453310, Used Merchandise Stores; and
- Retailing new or used boats are classified in U.S. Industry 441222, Boat Dealers.

441222 Boat Dealers ^{US}

This U.S. industry comprises establishments primarily engaged in (1) retailing new and/or used boats or retailing new boats in combination with activities, such as repair services and selling replacement parts and accessories, and/or (2) retailing new and/or used outboard motors, boat trailers, marine supplies, parts, and accessories.

- Retailing new surfboards or wind sail boards are classified in Industry 451110, Sporting Goods Stores;
- Retailing used surfboards or wind sail boards are classified in Industry 453310, Used Merchandise Stores;
- Providing boat repair services without retailing new boats are classified in Industry 811490, Other Personal or Household Goods Repair and Maintenance;
- Retailing new or used personal watercraft are classified in U.S. Industry 441221, Motorcycle Dealers; and
- Operating docking and/or storage facilities for pleasure craft owners are classified in Industry 713930, Marinas.

441229 All Other Motor Vehicle Dealers ^{US}

This U.S. industry comprises establishments primarily engaged in retailing new and/or used utility trailers and vehicles (except automobiles, light trucks, recreational vehicles, motorcycles, boats, motor scooters, motorbikes, off-road all-terrain vehicles, and personal watercraft) or retailing these new vehicles in combination with activities, such as repair services and selling replacement parts and accessories.

Visit page 18 to learn about classification changes to this sector.

Sector
44-45

Retail Trade

■ = Cross-References

US—United States industry only. CAN—United States and Canadian industries are comparable. When neither US nor CAN appears, Canadian, Mexican, and United States industries are comparable.

www.harrisinfo.com

461

- Retailing new automobiles and light trucks are classified in Industry 441110, New Car Dealers;
- Retailing used automobiles and light trucks are classified in Industry 441120, Used Car Dealers;
- Retailing new or used recreational vehicles, such as travel trailers, are classified in Industry 441210, Recreational Vehicle Dealers;
- Retailing new or used motorcycles, motor scooters, motorbikes, off-road all-terrain vehicles, and personal watercraft are classified in U.S. Industry 441221, Motorcycle Dealers;
- Retailing new or used boats, outboard motors, boat trailers, and marine supplies are classified in U.S. Industry 441222, Boat Dealers; and
- Providing vehicle repair services without retailing new vehicles are classified in the appropriate industry for the repair services.

4413 Automotive Parts, Accessories, and Tire Stores ^{CAN}

44131 Automotive Parts and Accessories Stores ^{CAN}
See industry description for 441310 below.

441310 Automotive Parts and Accessories Stores ^{CAN}
This industry comprises one or more of the following: (1) establishments known as automotive supply stores primarily engaged in retailing new, used, and/or rebuilt automotive parts and accessories; (2) automotive supply stores that are primarily engaged in both retailing automotive parts and accessories and repairing automobiles; and (3) establishments primarily engaged in retailing and installing automotive accessories.

- Retailing automotive parts and accessories via electronic home shopping, mail-order, or direct sale are classified in Subsector 454, Nonstore Retailers;
- Retailing new or used tires are classified in Industry 441320, Tire Dealers; and
- Repairing and replacing automotive parts, such as transmissions, mufflers, brake linings, and glass (except establishments known as automotive supply stores), are classified in Industry 81111, Automotive Mechanical and Electrical Repair and Maintenance.

44132 Tire Dealers ^{CAN}
See industry description for 441320 below.

441320 Tire Dealers ^{CAN}
This industry comprises establishments primarily engaged in retailing new and/or used tires and tubes or retailing new tires in combination with automotive repair services.

- Retailing tires via electronic home shopping, mail-order, or direct sale are classified in Subsector 454, Nonstore Retailers; and
- Providing automotive repair services without retailing new tires are classified in U.S. Industry 811198, All Other Automotive Repair and Maintenance.

▶442 FURNITURE AND HOME FURNISHINGS STORES ^{CAN}
Industries in the Furniture and Home Furnishings Stores subsector retail new furniture and home furnishings merchandise from fixed point-of-sale locations. Establishments in this subsector usually operate from showrooms and have substantial areas for the presentation of their products. Many offer interior decorating services in addition to the sale of products.

4421 Furniture Stores ^{CAN}

44211 Furniture Stores ^{CAN}
See industry description for 442110 below.

442110 Furniture Stores ^{CAN}
This industry comprises establishments primarily engaged in retailing new furniture, such as household furniture (e.g., baby furniture box springs and mattresses) and outdoor furniture; office furniture (except those sold in combination with office supplies and equipment); and/or furniture sold in combination with major appliances, home electronics, home furnishings, and/or floor covering.

- Retailing furniture via electronic home shopping, mail order, or direct sale are classified in Subsector 454, Nonstore Retailers;
- Retailing used furniture are classified in Industry 453310, Used Merchandise Stores;
- Retailing custom furniture made on premises are classified in Subsector 337, Furniture and Related Product Manufacturing; and

■ = Cross-References

Sector
44-45
Retail Trade

US—United States industry only. CAN—United States and Canadian industries are comparable. When neither US nor CAN appears, Canadian, Mexican, and United States industries are comparable.

462

Harris InfoSource

■ Retailing new office furniture and a range of new office equipment and supplies are classified in Industry 453210, Office Supplies and Stationery Stores.

4422 Home Furnishings Stores ^{CAN}

This industry group comprises establishments primarily engaged in retailing new home furnishings (except furniture).

44221 Floor Covering Stores ^{CAN}

See industry descriptions for 442210 below.

442210 Floor Covering Stores ^{CAN}

This industry comprises establishments primarily engaged in retailing new floor coverings, such as rugs and carpets, vinyl floor coverings, and floor tile (except ceramic or wood only); or retailing new floor coverings in combination with installation and repair services.

■ Retailing floor coverings via electronic home shopping, mail-order, or direct sale are classified in Subsector 454, Nonstore Retailers;
■ Installing floor coverings without retailing new floor coverings are classified in Industry 235520, Floor Laying and Other Floor Contractors;
■ Retailing ceramic floor tile or wood floor coverings only are classified in Industry 444190, Other Building Material Dealers; and
■ Retailing used rugs and carpets are classified in Industry 453310, Used Merchandise Stores.

44229 Other Home Furnishings Stores ^{CAN}

This industry comprises establishments primarily engaged in retailing new home furnishings (except furniture and floor coverings).

■ Retailing home furnishings via electronic home shopping, mail-order, or direct sale are classified in Subsector 454, Nonstore Retailers;
■ Retailing custom curtains and draperies made on premises are classified in Industry 31412, Curtain and Linen Mills;
■ Retailing new mirrored glass, lighting fixtures, and new ceramic floor tile or wood floor coverings only are classified in Industry 44419, Other Building Material Dealers;
■ Retailing new furniture are classified in Industry 44211, Furniture Stores;
■ Retailing new floor coverings (except ceramic or wood only) are classified in Industry 44221, Floor Covering Stores; and
■ Retailing used home furnishings are classified in Industry 45331, Used Merchandise Stores.

442291 Window Treatment Stores ^{CAN}

This U.S. industry comprises establishments primarily engaged in retailing new window treatments, such as curtains, drapes, blinds, and shades.

■ Retailing window treatments via electronic home shopping, mail-order, or direct sale are classified in Subsector 454, Nonstore Retailers; and
■ Retailing custom curtains and draperies made on premises are classified in U.S. Industry 314121, Curtain and Drapery Mills.

442299 All Other Home Furnishings Stores ^{US}

This U.S. industry comprises establishments primarily engaged in retailing new home furnishings (except floor coverings, furniture, and window treatments).

■ Selling home furnishings via electronic home shopping, mail order, or direct sale are classified in Subsector 454, Nonstore Retailers;
■ Retailing new mirrored glass lighting fixtures are classified in Industry 444190, Other Building Material Dealers;
■ Retailing new furniture are classified in Industry 442110, Furniture Stores;
■ Retailing new floor coverings are classified in Industry 442210, Floor Covering Stores;
■ Retailing new window treatments are classified in U.S. Industry 442291, Window Treatment Stores; and
■ Retailing used home furnishings are classified in Industry 453310, Used Merchandise Stores.

➡443 ELECTRONICS AND APPLIANCE STORES ^{CAN}

Industries in the Electronics and Appliance Stores subsector retail new electronics and appliance merchandise from point-of-sale locations. Establishments in this subsector often operate from locations that have special provisions for floor displays requiring special electrical capacity to accommodate the proper demonstration of the products. The staff includes sales personnel knowledgeable in the characteristics and warranties of the line of goods retailed and may also include trained repairpersons to handle the maintenance and repair of the electronic equipment and appliances. The classifications within this subsector are made principally on the type of product and knowledge required to operate each type of store.

Visit page 18 to learn about classification changes to this sector.

Sector
44-45

Retail Trade

■ = Cross-References

US—United States industry only. CAN—United States and Canadian industries are comparable. When neither US nor CAN appears, Canadian, Mexican, and United States industries are comparable.

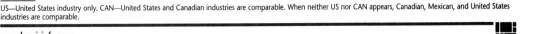

4431 Electronics and Appliance Stores ^{CAN}

This industry group comprises establishments primarily engaged in retailing the following new products: household-type appliances, cameras, computers, and other electronic goods.

44311 Appliance, Television, and Other Electronics Stores ^{CAN}

This industry comprises establishments primarily engaged in retailing one of the following: (1) retailing an array of new household-type appliances and consumer-type electronic products, such as radios, televisions, and computers; (2) specializing in retailing a single line of new consumer-type electronic products (except computers); and (3) retailing these new products in combination with repair services.

- Retailing new electronic products via electronic home shopping, mail-order, or direct sale are classified in Subsector 454, Nonstore Retailers;
- Retailing new computers, computer peripherals, and prepackaged computer software without retailing other consumer-type electronic products or office equipment, office furniture, and office supplies; or retailing these products in combination with repair services are classified in Industry 44312, Computer and Software Stores;
- Retailing new computers, computer peripherals, and prepackaged software in combination with retailing new office equipment, office furniture, and office supplies are classified in Industry 45321, Office Supplies and Stationery Stores;
- Retailing new sewing machines in combination with selling new sewing supplies, fabrics, patterns, yarns, and other needlework accessories are classified in Industry 45113, Sewing, Needlework, and Piece Goods Stores;
- Retailing new electronic toys are classified in Industry 45112, Hobby, Toy, and Game Stores;
- Providing television or other electronic products repair services without retailing new televisions or electronic products are classified in Industry 81121, Electronic and Precision Equipment Repair and Maintenance;
- Providing appliance repair services without retailing new appliances are classified in Industry 81141, Home and Garden Equipment and Appliance Repair and Maintenance;
- Retailing used appliance and electronic products are classified in Industry 45331, Used Merchandise Stores;
- Retailing new still and motion picture cameras are classified in Industry 44313, Camera and Photographic Supplies Stores; and
- Retailing automotive electronic sound systems are classified in Industry 44131, Automotive Parts and Accessories Stores.

443111 Household Appliance Stores ^{US}

This U.S. industry comprises establishments known as appliance stores primarily engaged in retailing an array of new household appliances, such as refrigerators, dishwashers, ovens, irons, coffeemakers, hair dryers, electric razors, room air-conditioners, microwave ovens, sewing machines, and vacuum cleaners, or retailing new appliances in combination with appliance repair services.

- Retailing household appliances via electronic home shopping, mail-order, or direct sale are classified in Subsector 454, Nonstore Retailers;
- Retailing new sewing machines in combination with selling new sewing supplies, fabrics, patterns, yarns, and other needlework accessories are classified in Industry 451130, Sewing, Needlework, and Piece Goods Stores;
- Providing appliance repair services without retailing new appliances are classified in U.S. Industry 811412, Appliance Repair and Maintenance; and
- Retailing used appliances are classified in Industry 453310, Used Merchandise Stores.

443112 Radio, Television, and Other Electronics Stores ^{US}

This U.S. industry comprises: (1) establishments known as consumer electronics stores primarily engaged in retailing a general line of new consumer-type electronic products; (2) establishments specializing in retailing a single line of consumer-type electronic products (except computers); or (3) establishments primarily engaged in retailing these new electronic products in combination with repair services.

- Retailing electronic goods via electronic home shopping, mail-order, or direct sale are classified in Subsector 454, Nonstore Retailers;
- Retailing automotive electronic sound systems are classified in Industry 441310, Automotive Parts and Accessories Stores;
- Retailing new computers, computer peripherals, and prepackaged computer software without retailing other consumer-type electronic products or office equipment, office furniture and office supplies; or retailing these new computer products in combination with repair services are classified in Industry 443120, Computer and Software Stores;
- Retailing new computers, computer peripherals, and prepackaged software in combination with retailing new office equipment, office furniture, and office supplies are classified in Industry 453210, Office Supplies and Stationery Stores;
- Retailing new still and motion picture cameras are classified in Industry 443130, Camera and Photographic Supplies Stores;
- Providing television or other electronic equipment repair services without retailing new televisions or electronic products are classified in Industry 81121, Electronic and Precision Equipment Repair and Maintenance;
- Retailing new electronic toys are classified in Industry 451120, Hobby, Toy, and Game Stores; and
- Retailing used electronics are classified in Industry 453310, Used Merchandise Stores.

■ = Cross-References

44312 Computer and Software Stores ^{CAN}

See industry description for 443120 below.

Sector
44-45
Retail Trade

US—United States industry only. CAN—United States and Canadian industries are comparable. When neither US nor CAN appears, Canadian, Mexican, and United States industries are comparable.

464

Harris InfoSource

443120 Computer and Software Stores ^{CAN}

This industry comprises establishments primarily engaged in retailing new computers, computer peripherals, and prepackaged computer software without retailing other consumer-type electronic products or office equipment, office furniture and office supplies; or retailing these new products in combination with repair and support services.

- Retailing computers and software via electronic home shopping, mail-order, or direct sale are classified in Subsector 454, Nonstore Retailers;
- Retailing new electronic toys, such as video games and handheld electronic games, are classified in Industry 451120, Hobby, Toy, and Game Stores;
- Providing computer repair services without retailing new computers are classified in U.S. Industry 811212, Computer and Office Machine Repair and Maintenance;
- Retailing new computers, computer peripherals, and prepackaged software in combination with retailing new office equipment, office furniture, and office supplies are classified in Industry 453210, Office Supplies and Stationery Stores;
- Retailing a general line of new electronic products or specializing in retailing a single line of consumer-type electronic products (except computers) are classified in U.S. Industry 443112, Radio, Television, and Other Electronics Stores; and
- Retailing used computers, computer software, video games, and handheld electronic games are classified in Industry 453310, Used Merchandise Stores.

44313 Camera and Photographic Supplies Stores ^{CAN}

See industry description for 443130 below.

443130 Camera and Photographic Supplies Stores ^{CAN}

This industry comprises establishments primarily engaged in either retailing new cameras, photographic equipment, and photographic supplies or retailing new cameras and photographic equipment in combination with activities, such as repair services and film developing.

- Retailing camera and photographic supplies via electronic home shopping, mail-order, or direct sale are classified in Subsector 454, Nonstore Retailers;
- Retailing new video cameras are classified in U.S. Industry 443112, Radio, Television, and Other Electronics Stores;
- One-hour film developing without retailing a range of new photographic equipment and supplies are classified in U.S. Industry 812922, One-hour Photofinishing;
- Providing repair services for photographic equipment without retailing new photographic equipment are classified in U.S. Industry 811211, Consumer Electronics Repair and Maintenance;
- Developing film and/or producing photographic prints, slides, and enlargements (except one-hour photofinishing labs) are classified in U.S. Industry 812921, Photofinishing Laboratories (except One-hour); and
- Retailing used cameras and photographic equipment are classified in Industry 453310, Used Merchandise Stores.

▶444 BUILDING MATERIAL AND GARDEN EQUIPMENT AND SUPPLIES DEALERS ^{CAN}

Industries in the Building Material and Garden Equipment and Supplies Dealers subsector retail new building material and garden equipment and supplies merchandise from fixed point-of-sale locations. Establishments in this subsector have display equipment designed to handle lumber and related products and garden equipment and supplies that may be kept either indoors or outdoors under covered areas. The staff is usually knowledgeable in the use of the specific products being retailed in the construction, repair, and maintenance of the home and associated grounds.

4441 Building Material and Supplies Dealers ^{CAN}

This industry group comprises establishments primarily engaged in retailing new building materials and supplies.

44411 Home Centers ^{CAN}

See industry description for 444110 below.

444110 Home Centers ^{CAN}

This industry comprises establishments known as home centers primarily engaged in retailing a general line of new home repair and improvement materials and supplies, such as lumber, plumbing goods, electrical goods, tools, housewares, hardware, and lawn and garden supplies, with no one merchandise line predominating. The merchandise lines are normally arranged in separate departments.

44412 Paint and Wallpaper Stores ^{CAN}

See industry description for 444120 below.

Visit page 18 to learn about classification changes to this sector.

Sector
44-45

Retail Trade

■ = Cross-References

US—United States industry only. CAN—United States and Canadian industries are comparable. When neither US nor CAN appears, Canadian, Mexican, and United States industries are comparable.

www.harrisinfo.com

465

444120 Paint and Wallpaper Stores CAN

This industry comprises establishments known as paint and wallpaper stores primarily engaged in retailing paint, wallpaper, and related supplies.

44413 Hardware Stores CAN

See industry description for 444130 below.

444130 Hardware Stores CAN

This industry comprises establishments known as hardware stores primarily engaged in retailing a general line of new hardware items, such as tools and builders' hardware.

- Retailing hardware items via electronic home shopping, mail order, or direct sale are classified in Subsector 454, Nonstore Retailers;
- Retailing a general line of home repair and improvement materials and supplies known as home centers are classified in Industry 444110, Home Centers; and
- Retailing used hardware items are classified in Industry 453310, Used Merchandise Stores.

44419 Other Building Material Dealers CAN

See industry description for 444190 below.

444190 Other Building Material Dealers CAN

This industry comprises establishments (except those known as home centers, paint and wallpaper stores, and hardware stores) primarily engaged in retailing specialized lines of new building materials, such as lumber, fencing, glass, doors, plumbing fixtures and supplies, electrical supplies, prefabricated buildings and kits, and kitchen and bath cabinets and countertops to be installed.

- Retailing building materials via electronic home shopping, mail-order, or direct sale are classified in Subsector 454, Nonstore Retailers
- Retailing used building materials are classified in Industry 453310, Used Merchandise Stores;
- Providing carpentry/installation services for products are classified in Industry 235510, Carpentry Contractors;
- Installing plumbing fixtures and supplies are classified in Industry 235110, Plumbing, Heating, and Air-conditioning Contractors;
- Installing electrical supplies, such as lighting fixtures and ceiling fans, are classified in Industry 235310, Electrical Contractors; and
- Making custom furniture (e.g. kitchen cabinets) are classified in Subsector 337, Furniture and Related Product Manufacturing.
- Retailing a general line of new hardware items, known as hardware stores, are classified in Industry 444130, Hardware Stores;
- Retailing paint and wallpaper, known as paint and wallpaper stores, are classified in Industry 444120, Paint and Wallpaper Stores; and
- Retailing a general line of home repair and improvement materials and supplies, known as home centers, are classified in Industry 444110, Home Centers.

4442 Lawn and Garden Equipment and Supplies Stores CAN

This industry group comprises establishments primarily engaged in retailing new lawn and garden equipment and supplies.

44421 Outdoor Power Equipment Stores CAN

See industry description for 444210 below.

444210 Outdoor Power Equipment Stores CAN

This industry comprises establishments primarily engaged in retailing new outdoor power equipment or retailing new outdoor power equipment in combination with activities, such as repair services and selling replacement parts.

- Retailing outdoor power equipment via electronic home shopping, mail-order, or direct sale are classified in Subsector 454, Nonstore Retailers;
- Providing outdoor power equipment repair services without retailing new outdoor power equipment are classified in U.S. Industry 811411, Home and Garden Equipment Repair and Maintenance; and
- Retailing used outdoor power equipment are classified in Industry 453310, Used Merchandise Stores.

44422 Nursery and Garden Centers CAN

See industry description for 444220 below.

Sector **44-45**

Retail Trade

■ = Cross-References

US—United States industry only. CAN—United States and Canadian industries are comparable. When neither US nor CAN appears, Canadian, Mexican, and United States industries are comparable.

466

Harris InfoSource

444220 Nursery and Garden Centers ^{CAN}

This industry comprises establishments primarily engaged in retailing nursery and garden products, such as trees, shrubs, plants, seeds, bulbs, and sod, that are predominantly grown elsewhere. These establishments may sell a limited amount of a product they grow themselves.

- Retailing nursery and garden products via electronic home shopping, mail-order, or direct sale are classified in Subsector 454, Nonstore Retailers;
- Providing landscaping services are classified in Industry 561730, Landscaping Services; and
- Growing and retailing nursery stock are classified in U.S. Industry 111421, Nursery and Tree Production.

▶445 FOOD AND BEVERAGE STORES ^{CAN}

Industries in the Food and Beverage Stores subsector usually retail food and beverage merchandise from fixed point-of-sale locations. Establishments in this subsector have special equipment (e.g., freezers, refrigerated display cases, refrigerators) for displaying food and beverage goods. They have staff trained in the processing of food products to guarantee the proper storage and sanitary conditions required by regulatory authority.

4451 Grocery Stores ^{CAN}

This industry group comprises establishments primarily engaged in retailing a general line of food products.

44511 Supermarkets and Other Grocery (except Convenience) Stores ^{CAN}

See industry description for 445110 below.

445110 Supermarkets and Other Grocery (except Convenience) Stores ^{CAN}

This industry comprises establishments generally known as supermarkets and grocery stores primarily engaged in retailing a general line of food, such as canned and frozen foods; fresh fruits and vegetables; and fresh and prepared meats, fish, and poultry. Included in this industry are delicatessen-type establishments primarily engaged in retailing a general line of food.

- Retailing automotive fuels in combination with a convenience store or food mart are classified in Industry 447110, Gasoline Stations with Convenience Stores;
- Retailing a limited line of goods, known as convenience stores or food marts (except those with fuel pumps), are classified in Industry 445120, Convenience Stores;
- Retailing frozen food and freezer plans via direct sales to residential customers are classified in Industry 454390, Other Direct Selling Establishments;
- Providing food services in delicatessen-type establishments are classified in U.S. Industry 722211, Limited-service Restaurants; and
- Retailing fresh meat in delicatessen-type establishments are classified in Industry 445210, Meat Markets.

44512 Convenience Stores ^{CAN}

See industry description for 445120 below.

445120 Convenience Stores ^{CAN}

This industry comprises establishments known as convenience stores or food marts (except those with fuel pumps) primarily engaged in retailing a limited line of goods that generally includes milk, bread, soda, and snacks.

- Retailing a general line of food, known as supermarkets and grocery stores, are classified in Industry 445110, Supermarkets and Other Grocery (except Convenience) Stores; and
- Retailing automotive fuels in combination with a convenience store or food mart are classified in Industry 447110, Gasoline Stations with Convenience Stores.

4452 Specialty Food Stores ^{CAN}

This industry group comprises establishments primarily engaged in retailing specialized lines of food.

44521 Meat Markets ^{CAN}

See industry description for 445210 below.

Visit page 18 to learn about classification changes to this sector.

Retail Trade

■ = Cross-References

445210 Meat Markets ^{CAN}

This industry comprises establishments primarily engaged in retailing fresh, frozen, or cured meats and poultry. Delicatessen-type establishments primarily engaged in retailing fresh meat are included in this industry.

- Retailing meat and poultry via electronic home shopping, mail-order, or direct sale are classified in Subsector 454, Nonstore Retailers;
- Retailing a general line of food, known as supermarkets and grocery stores, are classified in Industry 445110, Supermarkets and Other Grocery (except Convenience) Stores; and
- Providing food services in delicatessen-type establishments are classified in U.S. Industry 722211, Limited-service Restaurants.

44522 Fish and Seafood Markets ^{CAN}

See industry description for 445220 below.

445220 Fish and Seafood Markets ^{CAN}

This industry comprises establishments primarily engaged in retailing fresh, frozen, or cured fish and seafood products.

- Establishments primarily engaged in retailing fish and seafood products via electronic home shopping, mail-order, or direct sale are classified in Subsector 454, Nonstore Retailers.

44523 Fruit and Vegetable Markets ^{CAN}

See industry descriptions for 445230 below.

445230 Fruit and Vegetable Markets ^{CAN}

This industry comprises establishments primarily engaged in retailing fresh fruits and vegetables.

- Retailing fruits and vegetables via electronic home shopping, mail-order, or direct sale are classified in Subsector 454, Nonstore Retailers; and
- Growing and selling vegetables and/or fruits at roadside stands are classified in Subsector 111, Crop Production.

44529 Other Specialty Food Stores ^{CAN}

This industry comprises establishments primarily engaged in retailing specialty foods (except meat, fish, seafood, and fruits and vegetables) not for immediate consumption and not made on premises.

- Retailing specialty foods via electronic home shopping, mail-order, or direct sale are classified in Subsector 454, Nonstore Retailers;
- Retailing baked goods made on the premises, but not for immediate consumption are classified in Industry 31181, Bread and Bakery Product Manufacturing;
- Retailing fresh, frozen, or cured meats and poultry are classified in Industry 44521, Meat Markets;
- Retailing fresh, frozen, or cured fish and seafood products are classified in Industry 44522, Fish and Seafood Markets;
- Retailing fresh fruits and vegetables are classified in Industry 44523, Fruit and Vegetable Markets;
- Retailing candy and confectionery products not for immediate consumption and not made on premises are classified in Industry Group 3113, Sugar and Confectionery Product Manufacturing; and
- Selling snack foods (e.g., doughnuts, bagels, ice cream, popcorn) for immediate consumption are classified in Subsector 722, Food Services and Drinking Places.

445291 Baked Goods Stores ^{CAN}

This U.S. industry comprises establishments primarily engaged in retailing baked goods not for immediate consumption and not made on the premises.

- Retailing baked goods via electronic home shopping, mail-order, or direct sale are classified in Subsector 454, Nonstore Retailers;
- Selling snack foods (e.g., doughnuts, bagels, ice cream, popcorn) for immediate consumption are classified in U.S. Industry 722213, Snack and Nonalcoholic Beverage Bars; and
- Retailing baked goods made on the premises but not for immediate consumption are classified in Industry 311811, Retail Bakeries.

445292 Confectionery and Nut Stores ^{CAN}

This U.S. industry comprises establishments primarily engaged in retailing candy and other confections, nuts, and popcorn not for immediate consumption and not made on the premises.

- Retailing confectionery goods and nuts via electronic home shopping, mail-order, or direct sale are classified in Subsector 454, Nonstore Retailers;
- Retailing confectionery goods and nuts made on premises and not packaged for immediate consumption are classified in Industry Group 3113, Sugar and Confectionery Product Manufacturing;

Sector
44-45

Retail Trade

■ = Cross-References

US—United States industry only. CAN—United States and Canadian industries are comparable. When neither US nor CAN appears, Canadian, Mexican, and United States industries are comparable.

468

Harris InfoSource

- Selling snack foods (e.g., doughnuts, bagels, ice cream, popcorn) for immediate consumption are classified in U.S. Industry 722213, Snack and Nonalcoholic Beverage Bars; and
- Retailing baked goods made on the premises but not for immediate consumption are classified in Industry 311811, Retail Bakeries.

445299 All Other Specialty Food Stores ^{CAN}

This U.S. industry comprises establishments primarily engaged in retailing miscellaneous specialty foods (except meat, fish, seafood, fruit and vegetables, confections, nuts, popcorn, and baked goods) not for immediate consumption and not made on the premises.

- Retailing specialty foods via electronic home shopping, mail-order, or direct sale are classified in Subsector 454, Nonstore Retailers;
- Selling snack foods (e.g., doughnuts, bagels, ice cream, popcorn) for immediate consumption are classified in U.S. Industry 722213, Snack and Nonalcoholic Beverage Bars;
- Retailing fresh, frozen, or cured meats and poultry are classified in Industry 445210, Meat Markets;
- Retailing fresh, frozen, or cured fish and seafood products are classified in Industry 445220, Fish and Seafood Markets;
- Retailing fresh fruits and vegetables are classified in Industry 445230, Fruit and Vegetable Markets;
- Retailing candy and other confections, nuts, and popcorn not for immediate consumption and not made on the premises are classified in U.S. Industry 445292, Confectionery and Nut Stores; and
- Retailing baked goods not for immediate consumption and not made on the premises are classified in U.S. Industry 445291, Baked Goods Stores.

4453 Beer, Wine, and Liquor Stores ^{CAN}

44531 Beer, Wine, and Liquor Stores ^{CAN}
See industry description for 445310 below.

445310 Beer, Wine, and Liquor Stores ^{CAN}

This industry comprises establishments primarily engaged in retailing packaged alcoholic beverages, such as ale, beer, wine, and liquor.

- Establishments primarily engaged in retailing packaged liquor in combination with providing prepared drinks for immediate consumption on the premises are classified in Industry 722410, Drinking Places (Alcoholic Beverages).

➡446 HEALTH AND PERSONAL CARE STORES ^{CAN}

Industries in the Health and Personal Care Stores subsector retail health and personal care merchandise from fixed point-of-sale locations. Establishments in this subsector are characterized principally by the products they retail, and some health and personal care stores may have specialized staff trained in dealing with the products. Staff may include pharmacists, opticians, and other professionals engaged in retailing, advising customers, and/or fitting the product sold to the customer's needs.

4461 Health and Personal Care Stores ^{CAN}

This industry group comprises establishments primarily engaged in retailing health and personal care products.

44611 Pharmacies and Drug Stores ^{CAN}
See industry descriptions for 446110 below.

446110 Pharmacies and Drug Stores ^{CAN}

This industry comprises establishments known as pharmacies and drug stores engaged in retailing prescription or nonprescription drugs and medicines.

- Retailing food supplement products, such as vitamins, nutrition supplements, and body enhancing supplements, are classified in U.S. Industry 446191, Food (Health) Supplement Stores; and
- Retailing prescription and nonprescription drugs via electronic home shopping, mail-order, or direct sale are classified in Subsector 454, Nonstore Retailers.

44612 Cosmetics, Beauty Supplies, and Perfume Stores ^{CAN}
See industry descriptions for 446120 below.

Visit page 18 to learn about classification changes to this sector.

Sector
44-45
Retail Trade

■ = Cross-References

446120 Cosmetics, Beauty Supplies, and Perfume Stores ^{CAN}

This industry comprises establishments known as a cosmetic or perfume stores or beauty supply shops primarily engaged in retailing cosmetics, perfumes, toiletries, and personal grooming products.

- Providing beauty parlor services are classified in U.S. Industry 812112, Beauty Salons; and
- Retailing perfumes, cosmetics, and beauty supplies via electronic home shopping, mail-order, or direct sale are classified in Subsector 454, Nonstore Retailers.

44613 Optical Goods Stores ^{CAN}

See industry descriptions for 446130 below.

446130 Optical Goods Stores ^{CAN}

This industry comprises establishments primarily engaged in one or more of the following: (1) retailing and fitting prescription eyeglasses and contact lenses; (2) retailing prescription eyeglasses in combination with the grinding of lenses to order on the premises; and (3) selling nonprescription eyeglasses.

- Grinding lenses without retailing lenses are classified in U.S. Industry 339115, Ophthalmic Goods Manufacturing;
- The private or group practice of optometry, even though glasses and contact lenses are sold at these establishments are classified Industry 621320, Offices of Optometrists; and
- Retailing eyeglasses and contact lenses via mail-order are classified in Industry 454110, Electronic Shopping and Mail-order Houses.

44619 Other Health and Personal Care Stores ^{CAN}

This industry comprises establishments primarily engaged in retailing health and personal care items (except drugs, medicines, optical goods, perfumes, cosmetics, and beauty supplies).

- Retailing health and personal care items via electronic home shopping, mail-order, or direct sale are classified in Subsector 454, Nonstore Retailers;
- Retailing orthopedic shoes are classified in Industry 44821, Shoe Stores;
- Retailing orthopedic and prosthetic appliances that are made on premises are classified in Industry 33911, Medical Equipment and Supplies Manufacturing;
- Retailing prescription and nonprescription drugs and medicines are classified in Industry 44611, Pharmacies and Drug Stores;
- Retailing eyeglasses and contact lenses are classified in Industry 44613, Optical Goods Stores;
- Retailing perfumes, cosmetics, and beauty supplies are classified in Industry 44612, Cosmetics, Beauty Supplies, and Perfume Stores; and
- Retailing naturally organic foods, such as fruits and vegetables, dairy products, and cereals and grains, are classified in Subsector 445, Food and Beverage Stores.

446191 Food (Health) Supplement Stores ^{CAN}

This U.S. industry comprises establishments primarily engaged in retailing food supplement products, such as vitamins, nutrition supplements, and body enhancing supplements.

- Retailing food supplement products via electronic home shopping, mail-order, or direct sale are classified in Subsector 454, Nonstore Retailers;
- Retailing prescription and nonprescription drugs and medicines are classified in Industry 446110, Pharmacies and Drug Stores; and
- Retailing naturally organic foods, such as fruits and vegetables, dairy products, and cereals and grains, are classified in Subsector 445, Food and Beverage Stores.

446199 All Other Health and Personal Care Stores ^{CAN}

This U.S. industry comprises establishments primarily engaged in retailing specialized lines of health and personal care merchandise (except drugs, medicines, optical goods, cosmetics, beauty supplies, perfume, and food supplement products).

- Retailing specialized health and personal care merchandise via electronic home shopping, mail-order, or direct sale are classified in Subsector 454, Nonstore Retailers;
- Retailing food supplement products are classified in U.S. Industry 446191, Food (Health) Supplement Stores;
- Retailing prescription or nonprescription drugs and medicines are classified in Industry 446110, Pharmacies and Drug Stores;
- Retailing eyeglasses and contact lenses are classified in Industry 446130, Optical Goods Stores;
- Retailing perfumes, cosmetics, and beauty supplies are classified in Industry 446120, Cosmetics, Beauty Supplies, and Perfume Stores;
- Retailing orthopedic shoes are classified in Industry 448210, Shoe Stores; and
- Retailing orthopedic and prosthetic appliances that are made on premises are classified in U.S. Industry 339113, Surgical Appliance and Supplies Manufacturing.

Sector
44-45

Retail Trade

■ = Cross-References

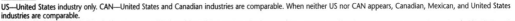
US—United States industry only. CAN—United States and Canadian industries are comparable. When neither US nor CAN appears, Canadian, Mexican, and United States industries are comparable.

470

Harris InfoSource

➡447 GASOLINE STATIONS ^{CAN} CAN

Industries in the Gasoline Stations subsector group establishments retailing automotive fuels (e.g., gasoline, diesel fuel, gasohol) and automotive oils and retailing these products in combination with convenience store items. These establishments have specialized equipment for the storage and dispensing of automotive fuels.

4471 Gasoline Stations CAN

44711 Gasoline Stations with Convenience Stores CAN
See industry descriptions for 447110 below.

447110 Gasoline Stations with Convenience Stores CAN
This industry comprises establishments engaged in retailing automotive fuels (e.g., diesel fuel, gasohol, gasoline) in combination with convenience store or food mart items. These establishments can either be in a convenience store (i.e., food mart) setting or a gasoline station setting. These establishments may also provide automotive repair services.

- Retailing automotive fuels without a convenience store are classified in Industry 447190, Other Gasoline Stations; and
- Retailing a limited line of goods, known as convenience stores or food marts (except those with fuel pumps), are classified in Industry 445120, Convenience Stores.

44719 Other Gasoline Stations CAN
See industry descriptions for 447190 below.

447190 Other Gasoline Stations CAN
This industry comprises establishments known as gasoline stations (except those with convenience stores) primarily engaged in one of the following: (1) retailing automotive fuels (e.g., diesel fuel, gasohol, gasoline) or (2) retailing these fuels in combination with activities, such as repair services, selling automotive oils, replacement parts, and accessories, and/or with restaurants.

- Repairing motor vehicles without retailing automotive fuels are classified in Industry 81111, Automotive Mechanical and Electrical Repair and Maintenance; and
- Retailing automotive fuels in combination with a convenience store or food mart are classified in Industry 447110, Gasoline Stations with Convenience Stores.

➡448 CLOTHING AND CLOTHING ACCESSORIES STORES ^{CAN}

Industries in the Clothing and Clothing Accessories Stores subsector retailing new clothing and clothing accessories merchandise from fixed point-of-sale locations. Establishments in this subsector have similar display equipment and staff that is knowledgeable regarding fashion trends and the proper match of styles, colors, and combinations of clothing and accessories to the characteristics and tastes of the customer.

4481 Clothing Stores CAN
This industry group comprises establishments primarily engaged in retailing new clothing.

44811 Men's Clothing Stores CAN
See industry descriptions for 448110 below.

448110 Men's Clothing Stores CAN
This industry comprises establishments primarily engaged in retailing a general line of new men's and boys' clothing. These establishments may provide basic alterations, such as hemming, taking in or letting out seams, or lengthening or shortening sleeves.

- Retailing men's and boys' clothing via electronic home shopping, mail-order, or direct sale are classified in Subsector 454, Nonstore Retailers;
- Retailing custom men's clothing made on the premises are classified in Industry Group 3152, Cut and Sew Apparel Manufacturing;
- Retailing new men's and boys' accessories are classified in Industry 448150, Clothing Accessories Stores;
- Retailing specialized new apparel, such as raincoats, leather coats, fur apparel, and swimwear, are classified in Industry 448190, Other Clothing Stores;

Visit page 18 to learn about classification changes to this sector.

Retail Trade

■ = Cross-References

US—United States industry only. CAN—United States and Canadian industries are comparable. When neither US nor CAN appears, Canadian, Mexican, and United States industries are comparable.

■ Retailing new clothing for all genders and age groups are classified in Industry 448140, Family Clothing Stores;

■ Retailing secondhand clothes are classified in Industry 453310, Used Merchandise Stores; and

■ Providing clothing alterations and repair are classified in Industry 811490, Other Personal and Household Goods Repair and Maintenance.

44812 Women's Clothing Stores CAN

See industry description for 448120 below.

448120 Women's Clothing Stores CAN

This industry comprises establishments primarily engaged in retailing a general line of new women's, misses' and juniors' clothing, including maternity wear. These establishments may provide basic alterations, such as hemming, taking in or letting out seams, or lengthening or shortening sleeves.

■ Retailing women's clothing via electronic home shopping, mail-order, or direct sale are classified in Subsector 454, Nonstore Retailers;

■ Retailing custom women's clothing made on premises are classified in Industry Group 3152, Cut and Sew Apparel Manufacturing;

■ Retailing new women's accessories are classified in Industry 448150, Clothing Accessories Stores;

■ Retailing new clothing for all genders and age groups are classified in Industry 448140, Family Clothing Stores;

■ Retailing specialized new apparel, such as bridal gowns, raincoats, leather coats, fur apparel, and swimwear, are classified in Industry 448190, Other Clothing Stores;

■ Retailing secondhand clothes are classified in Industry 453310, Used Merchandise Stores; and

■ Providing clothing alterations and repair are classified in Industry 811490, Other Personal and Household Goods Repair and Maintenance.

44813 Children's and Infants' Clothing Stores CAN

See industry description for 448130 below.

448130 Children's and Infants' Clothing Stores CAN

This industry comprises establishments primarily engaged in retailing a general line of new children's and infants' clothing. These establishments may provide basic alterations, such as hemming, taking in or letting out seams, or lengthening or shortening sleeves.

■ Retailing children's and infants' clothing via electronic home shopping, mail-order, or direct sale are classified in Subsector 454, Nonstore Retailers;

■ Retailing new children's and infants' accessories are classified in Industry 448150, Clothing Accessories Stores;

■ Retailing new clothing for all genders or age groups are classified in Industry 448140, Family Clothing Stores;

■ Retailing secondhand clothes are classified in Industry 453310, Used Merchandise Stores; and

■ Providing clothing alterations and repair are classified in Industry 811490, Other Personal and Household Goods Repair and Maintenance.

44814 Family Clothing Stores CAN

See industry description for 448140 below.

Retail Trade

448140 Family Clothing Stores CAN

This industry comprises establishments primarily engaged in retailing a general line of new clothing for men, women, and children, without specializing in sales for an individual gender or age group. These establishments may provide basic alterations, such as hemming, taking in or letting out seams, or lengthening or shortening sleeves.

■ Retailing clothing for all genders via electronic home shopping, mail-order, or direct sale are classified in Subsector 454, Nonstore Retailers;

■ Retailing new men's and boys' clothing are classified in Industry 448110, Men's Clothing Stores;

■ Retailing new children's and infants' clothing are classified in Industry 448130, Children's and Infants' Clothing Stores;

■ Retailing new women's, misses', and juniors' clothing are classified in Industry 448120, Women's Clothing Stores;

■ Retailing specialized new apparel, such as raincoats, bridal gowns, leather coats, fur apparel, and swimwear, are classified in Industry 448190, Other Clothing Stores;

■ Retailing secondhand clothes are classified in Industry 453310, Used Merchandise Stores; and

■ Providing clothing alterations and repair are classified in Industry 811490, Other Personal and Household Goods Repair and Maintenance.

44815 Clothing Accessories Stores CAN

■ = Cross-References

See industry descriptions for 448150 below.

US—United States industry only. CAN—United States and Canadian industries are comparable. When neither US nor CAN appears, Canadian, Mexican, and United States industries are comparable.

448150 Clothing Accessories Stores ^{CAN}

This industry comprises establishments primarily engaged in retailing single or combination lines of new clothing accessories, such as hats and caps, costume jewelry, gloves, handbags, ties, wigs, toupees, and belts.

- Retailing specialized lines of clothing via electronic home shopping, mail-order, or direct sale are classified in Subsector 454, Nonstore Retailers;
- Retailing precious jewelry and watches are classified in Industry 448310, Jewelry Stores;
- Retailing used clothing accessories are classified in Industry 453310, Used Merchandise Stores;
- Retailing luggage, briefcases, trunks, or these products in combination with a general line of leather items (except leather apparel), known as luggage and leather goods stores, are classified in Industry 448320, Luggage and Leather Goods Stores; and
- Retailing leather apparel are classified in Industry 448190, Other Clothing Stores.

44819 Other Clothing Stores ^{CAN}

See industry description for 448190 below.

448190 Other Clothing Stores ^{CAN}

This industry comprises establishments primarily engaged in retailing specialized lines of new clothing (except general lines of men's, women's, children's, infants', and family clothing). These establishments may provide basic alterations, such as hemming, taking in or letting out seams, or lengthening or shortening sleeves.

- Retailing specialized apparel via electronic home shopping, mail-order, or direct sale are classified in Subsector 454, Nonstore Retailers;
- Retailing custom apparel and accessories made on the premises are classified in Subsector 315, Apparel Manufacturing;
- Retailing new women's, misses', and juniors' clothing, including maternity wear are classified in Industry 448120, Women's Clothing Stores;
- Retailing new men's and boys' clothing are classified in Industry 448110, Men's Clothing Stores;
- Retailing new children's and infants' clothing are classified in Industry 448130, Children's and Infants' Clothing Stores;
- Retailing new clothing for all genders or age groups are classified in Industry 448140, Family Clothing Stores;
- Retailing athletic uniforms are classified in Industry 451110, Sporting Goods Stores;
- Retailing secondhand clothes are classified in Industry 453310, Used Merchandise Stores;
- Retailing luggage, briefcases, trunks, or these products in combination with a general line of leather items (except leather apparel), known as luggage and leather good stores, are classified in Industry 448320, Luggage and Leather Goods Stores; and
- Providing clothing alterations and repair are classified in Industry 811490, Other Personal Household Goods Repair and Maintenance.

4482 Shoe Stores ^{CAN}

44821 Shoe Stores ^{CAN}

See industry description for 448210 below.

448210 Shoe Stores ^{CAN}

This industry comprises establishments primarily engaged in retailing all types of new footwear (except hosiery and specialty sports footwear, such as golf shoes, bowling shoes, and spiked shoes). Establishments primarily engaged in retailing new tennis shoes or sneakers are included in this industry.

- Retailing footwear via electronic home shopping, mail-order, or direct sale are classified in Subsector 454, Nonstore Retailers;
- Retailing hosiery are classified in Industry 448190, Other Clothing Stores;
- Retailing new specialty sports footwear (e.g., bowling shoes, golf shoes, spiked shoes) are classified in Industry 451110, Sporting Goods Stores; and
- Retailing used footwear are classified in Industry 453310, Used Merchandise Stores.

4483 Jewelry, Luggage, and Leather Goods Stores ^{CAN}

This industry group comprises establishments primarily engaged in retailing new jewelry (except costume jewelry); new silver and plated silverware; new watches and clocks; and new luggage with or without a general line of new leather goods and accessories, such as hats, gloves, handbags, ties, and belts.

44831 Jewelry Stores ^{CAN}

See industry descriptions for 448310 below.

Visit page 18 to learn about classification changes to this sector.

Sector

44-45

Retail Trade

■ = Cross-References

US—United States industry only. CAN—United States and Canadian industries are comparable. When neither US nor CAN appears, Canadian, Mexican, and United States industries are comparable.

www.harrisinfo.com

473

448310 Jewelry Stores ^{CAN}

This industry comprises establishments primarily engaged in retailing one or more of the following items: (1) new jewelry (except costume jewelry); (2) new sterling and plated silverware; and (3) new watches and clocks. Also included are establishments retailing these new products in combination with lapidary work and/or repair services.

- Retailing new costume jewelry are classified in Industry 448150, Clothing Accessories Stores;
- Retailing jewelry via electronic home shopping, mail-order, or direct sale are classified in Subsector 454, Nonstore Retailers;
- Retailing antiques or used jewelry, silverware, and watches and clocks are classified in Industry 453310, Used Merchandise Stores;
- Providing jewelry or watch and clock repair without retailing new jewelry or watches and clocks are classified in Industry 811490, Other Personal and Household Goods Repair and Maintenance; and
- Cutting and setting gem stones are classified in U.S. Industry 339913, Jewelers' Material and Lapidary Work Manufacturing.

44832 Luggage and Leather Goods Stores ^{CAN}

See industry descriptions for 448320 below.

448320 Luggage and Leather Goods Stores ^{CAN}

This industry comprises establishments known as luggage and leather goods stores primarily engaged in retailing new luggage, briefcases, trunks, or these new products in combination with a general line of leather items (except leather apparel), such as belts, gloves, and handbags.

- Retailing luggage and leather goods via electronic home shopping, mail-order, or direct sale are classified in Subsector 454, Nonstore Retailers;
- Retailing used luggage and leather goods are classified in Industry 453310, Used Merchandise Stores;
- Retailing single or combination lines of new clothing accessories (e.g., gloves, handbags, or leather belts) are classified in Industry 448150, Clothing Accessories Stores; and
- Retailing new leather coats are classified in Industry 448190, Other Clothing Stores.

▶451 SPORTING GOODS, HOBBY, BOOK, AND MUSIC STORES ^{CAN}

Industries in the Sporting Goods, Hobby, Book, and Music Stores subsector are engaged in retailing and providing expertise on use of sporting equipment or other specific leisure activities, such as needlework and musical instruments. Bookstores are also included in this subsector.

4511 Sporting Goods, Hobby, and Musical Instrument Stores ^{CAN}

This industry group comprises establishments primarily engaged in retailing new sporting goods, games and toys, and musical instruments.

45111 Sporting Goods Stores ^{CAN}

See industry description for 451110 below.

451110 Sporting Goods Stores ^{CAN}

This industry comprises establishments primarily engaged in retailing new sporting goods, such as bicycles and bicycle parts; camping equipment; exercise and fitness equipment; athletic uniforms; specialty sports footwear; and sporting goods, equipment, and accessories.

- Retailing sporting goods via electronic home shopping, mail order, or direct sale are classified in Subsector 454, Nonstore Retailers;
- Retailing new or used campers (pickup coaches) and camping trailers are classified in Industry 441210, Recreational Vehicle Dealers;
- Retailing new or used snowmobiles, motorized bicycles, and motorized golf carts are classified in Industry 44122, Motorcycle, Boat, and Other Motor Vehicle Dealers;
- Retailing new shoes (except specialty sports footwear, such as golf shoes, bowling shoes, and spiked shoes) are classified in Industry 448210, Shoe Stores;
- Repairing or servicing sporting goods, without retailing new sporting goods are classified in Industry 811490, Other Personal and Household Goods Repair and Maintenance; and
- Retailing used sporting goods and used bicycles are classified in Industry 453310, Used Merchandise Stores.

45112 Hobby, Toy, and Game Stores ^{CAN}

See industry description for 451120 below.

Sector
44-45
Retail Trade

■ = Cross-References

451120 Hobby, Toy, and Game Stores ^{CAN}
This industry comprises establishments primarily engaged in retailing new toys, games, and hobby and craft supplies (except needlecraft).

- Retailing toys, games, and hobby and craft supplies via electronic home shopping, mail-order, or direct sale are classified in Subsector 454, Nonstore Retailers;
- Retailing artists' supplies or collectors' items, such as coins, stamps, autographs, and cards are classified in U.S. Industry 453998, All Other Miscellaneous Store Retailers (except Tobacco Stores);
- Retailing new computer software (e.g., game software) are classified in Industry 443120, Computer and Software Stores;
- Retailing used toys, games, and hobby supplies are classified in Industry 453310, Used Merchandise Stores; and
- Retailing new sewing supplies, fabrics, and needlework accessories are classified in Industry 451130, Sewing, Needlework, and Piece Goods Stores.

45113 Sewing, Needlework, and Piece Goods Stores ^{CAN}
See industry description for 451130 below.

451130 Sewing, Needlework, and Piece Goods Stores ^{CAN}
This industry comprises establishments primarily engaged in retailing new sewing supplies, fabrics, patterns, yarns, and other needlework accessories or retailing these products in combination with selling new sewing machines.

- Retailing sewing supplies via electronic home shopping, mail-order, or direct sale are classified in Subsector 454, Nonstore Retailers;
- Retailing new sewing machines only and in combination with retailing other new appliances are classified in U.S. Industry 443111, Household Appliance Stores; and
- Retailing used sewing, needlework, and piece goods are classified in Industry 453310, Used Merchandise Stores.

45114 Musical Instrument and Supplies Stores ^{CAN}
See industry description for 451140 below.

451140 Musical Instrument and Supplies Stores ^{CAN}
This industry comprises establishments primarily engaged in retailing new musical instruments, sheet music, and related supplies; or retailing these new products in combination with musical instrument repair, rental, or music instruction.

- Retailing musical instruments, sheet music, and related supplies via electronic home shopping, mail-order, or direct sale are classified in Subsector 454, Nonstore Retailers;
- Retailing new musical recordings are classified in Industry 451220, Prerecorded Tape, Compact Disc, and Record Stores; and
- Retailing used musical instruments, sheet music, and related supplies are classified in Industry 453310, Used Merchandise Stores.

4512 Book, Periodical, and Music Stores ^{CAN}
This industry group comprises establishments primarily engaged in retailing new books, newspapers, magazines, and prerecorded audio and video media.

45121 Book Stores and News Dealers ^{CAN}
This industry comprises establishments primarily engaged in retailing new books, newspapers, magazines, and other periodicals.

- Retailing newspapers, magazines, and other periodicals via electronic home shopping, mail-order, or direct sale are classified in Subsector 454, Nonstore Retailers;
- Home delivery of newspapers are classified in Industry 45439, Other Direct Selling Establishments; and
- Retailing used books, newspapers, magazines, and other periodicals are classified in Industry 45331, Used Merchandise Stores.

451211 Book Stores ^{US}
This U.S. industry comprises establishments primarily engaged in retailing new books.

- Retailing books via electronic home shopping, mail-order, or direct sale are classified in Subsector 454, Nonstore Retailers; and
- Retailing used books are classified in Industry 453310, Used Merchandise Stores.

Visit page 18 to learn about classification changes to this sector.

Sector
44-45
Retail Trade

■ = Cross-References

US—United States industry only. CAN—United States and Canadian industries are comparable. When neither US nor CAN appears, Canadian, Mexican, and United States industries are comparable.

451212 News Dealers and Newsstands ^{US}

This U.S. industry comprises establishments primarily engaged in retailing current newspapers, magazines, and other periodicals.

- Home delivery of newspapers are classified in Industry 454390, Other Direct Selling Establishments;
- Retailing newspapers and periodicals by mail-order are classified in Industry 454110, Electronic Shopping and Mail-order Houses; and
- Retailing used newspapers, magazines, and other periodicals are classified in Industry 453310, Used Merchandise Stores.

45122 Prerecorded Tape, Compact Disc, and Record Stores ^{CAN}

See industry description for 451220 below.

451220 Prerecorded Tape, Compact Disc, and Record Stores ^{CAN}

This industry comprises establishments primarily engaged in retailing new prerecorded audio and video tapes, compact discs (CDs), and phonograph records.

- Retailing new computer software are classified in Industry 443120, Computer and Software Stores;
- Retailing prerecorded tapes, compact discs, and records by mail-order are classified in Industry 454110, Electronic Shopping and Mail-order Houses;
- Retailing used phonograph records and prerecorded audio and video tapes and discs are classified in Industry 453310, Used Merchandise Stores; and
- Retailing new audio sound equipment (except automotive) are classified in U.S. Industry 443112, Radio, Television, and Other Electronics Stores.

▶452 GENERAL MERCHANDISE STORES ^{CAN}

Industries in the General Merchandise Stores subsector retail new general merchandise from fixed point-of-sale locations. Establishments in this subsector are unique in that they have the equipment and staff capable of retailing a large variety of goods from a single location. This includes a variety of display equipment and staff trained to provide information on many lines of products.

4521 Department Stores ^{CAN}

45211 Department Stores ^{CAN}

See industry description for 452110 below.

452110 Department Stores ^{CAN}

This industry comprises establishments known as department stores primarily engaged in retailing a wide range of the following new products with no one merchandise line predominating: apparel, furniture, appliances and home furnishings; and selected additional items, such as paint, hardware, toiletries, cosmetics, photographic equipment, jewelry, toys, and sporting goods. Merchandise lines are normally arranged in separate departments.

- Retailing prepackaged grocery items in combination with general lines of merchandise with no one merchandise line predominating are classified in Industry 452910, Warehouse Clubs and Superstores;
- Retailing general lines of merchandise via electronic home shopping, mail-order, or direct sale are classified in Subsector 454, Nonstore Retailers; and
- Retailing used merchandise are classified in Industry 453310, Used Merchandise Stores.

4529 Other General Merchandise Stores ^{CAN}

This industry group comprises establishments primarily engaged in retailing new goods in general merchandise stores (except department stores).

45291 Warehouse Clubs and Superstores ^{CAN}

See industry description for 452910 below.

452910 Warehouse Clubs and Superstores ^{CAN}

This industry comprises establishments known as warehouse clubs, superstores or supercenters primarily engaged in retailing a general line of groceries in combination with general lines of new merchandise, such as apparel, furniture, and appliances.

Sector
44-45

Retail Trade

■ = Cross-References

US—United States industry only. CAN—United States and Canadian industries are comparable. When neither US nor CAN appears, Canadian, Mexican, and United States industries are comparable.

■ Retailing general lines of merchandise via electronic home shopping, mail-order, or direct sale are classified in Subsector 454, Nonstore Retailers;
■ Retailing a general line of food, generally known as supermarkets and grocery stores, are classified in Industry 445110, Supermarkets and Other Grocery (except Convenience) Stores;
■ Retailing general lines of new merchandise with little grocery item sales are classified in Industry 452990, All Other General Merchandise Stores;
■ Retailing new merchandise in department stores are classified in Industry 452110, Department Stores; and
■ Retailing used merchandise are classified in Industry 453310, Used Merchandise Stores.

45299 All Other General Merchandise Stores CAN
See industry description for 452990 below.

452990 All Other General Merchandise Stores CAN
This industry comprises establishments primarily engaged in retailing new goods in general merchandise stores (except department stores, warehouse clubs, superstores, and supercenters). These establishments retail a general line of new merchandise, such as apparel, automotive parts, dry goods, hardware, groceries, housewares or home furnishings, and other lines in limited amounts, with none of the lines predominating.

■ Retailing general lines of merchandise via electronic home shopping, mail-order, or direct sale are classified in Subsector 454, Nonstore Retailers;
■ Retailing automotive parts are classified in Industry 441310, Automotive Parts and Accessories Stores;
■ Retailing merchandise in department stores are classified in Industry 452110, Department Stores;
■ Retailing merchandise in warehouse clubs, superstores, or supercenters are classified in Industry 452910, Warehouse Clubs and Superstores;
■ Retailing merchandise in catalogue showrooms of mail-order houses are classified in Industry 454110, Electronic Shopping and Mail-order Houses;
■ Retailing a general line of new hardware items, known as hardware stores, are classified in Industry 444130, Hardware Stores;
■ Retailing a general line of new home repair and improvement materials and supplies, known as home centers, are classified in Industry 444110, Home Centers; and
■ Retailing used merchandise are classified in Industry 453310, Used Merchandise Stores.

▶453 MISCELLANEOUS STORE RETAILERS CAN
Industries in the Miscellaneous Store Retailers subsector retail merchandise from fixed point-of-sale locations (except new or used motor vehicles and parts; new furniture and house furnishings; new appliances and electronic products; new building materials; and garden equipment and supplies; food and beverages; health and personal care goods; gasoline; new clothing and accessories; and new sporting goods, hobby goods, books, and music). Establishments in this subsector include stores with unique characteristics like florists, used merchandise stores, and pet and pet supply stores as well as other store retailers.

4531 Florists CAN

45311 Florists CAN
See industry description for 453110 below.

453110 Florists CAN
This industry comprises establishments known as florists primarily engaged in retailing cut flowers, floral arrangements, and potted plants purchased from others. These establishments usually prepare the arrangements they sell.

■ Retailing flowers or nursery stock grown on premises are classified in Industry 11142, Nursery and Floriculture Production;
■ Retailing trees, shrubs, plants, seeds, bulbs, and sod grown elsewhere are classified in Industry 444220, Nursery and Garden Centers; and
■ Retailing flowers via electronic home shopping, mail-order, or direct sale are classified in Subsector 454, Nonstore Retailers.

4532 Office Supplies, Stationery, and Gift Stores CAN

45321 Office Supplies and Stationery Stores CAN
See industry description for 453210 below.

Visit page 18 to learn about classification changes to this sector.

Sector
44-45
Retail Trade

■ = Cross-References

US—United States industry only. CAN—United States and Canadian industries are comparable. When neither US nor CAN appears, Canadian, Mexican, and United States industries are comparable.

www.harrisinfo.com

 477

453210 Office Supplies and Stationery Stores ^{CAN}

This industry comprises establishments primarily engaged in one or more of the following: (1) retailing new stationery, school supplies, and office supplies; (2) selling a combination of new office equipment, furniture, and supplies; and (3) selling new office equipment, furniture, and supplies in combination with selling new computers.

- Retailing stationery, school supplies, and office supplies via electronic shopping, mail-order, or direct sale are classified in Subsector 454, Nonstore Retailers;
- Retailing greeting cards are classified in Industry 453220, Gift, Novelty, and Souvenir Stores;
- Retailing new typewriters are classified in U.S. Industry 443112, Radio, Television, and Other Electronics Stores;
- Retailing new computers without retailing other consumer-type electronic products or office equipment, furniture, and supplies are classified in Industry 443120, Computer and Software Stores;
- Printing business forms are classified in Industry 32311, Printing;
- Retailing new office furniture are classified in Industry 442110, Furniture Stores; and
- Retailing used office supplies are classified in Industry 453310, Used Merchandise Stores.

45322 Gift, Novelty, and Souvenir Stores ^{CAN}

See industry description for 453220 below.

453220 Gift, Novelty, and Souvenir Stores ^{CAN}

This industry comprises establishments primarily engaged in retailing new gifts, novelty merchandise, souvenirs, greeting cards, seasonal and holiday decorations, and curios.

- Retailing gifts and novelties via electronic home shopping, mail-order, or direct sale are classified in Subsector 454, Nonstore Retailers;
- Retailing stationery are classified in Industry 453210, Office Supplies and Stationery Stores; and
- Retailing used curios and novelties are classified in Industry 453310, Used Merchandise Stores.

4533 Used Merchandise Stores ^{CAN}

45331 Used Merchandise Stores ^{CAN}

See industry description for 453310 below.

453310 Used Merchandise Stores ^{CAN}

This industry comprises establishments primarily engaged in retailing used merchandise, antiques, and secondhand goods (except motor vehicles, such as automobiles, RVs, motorcycles, and boats; motor vehicle parts; tires; and mobile homes).

- Retailing used merchandise via electronic home shopping, mail-order, or direct sale are classified in Subsector 454, Nonstore Retailers;
- Operating pawnshops are classified in U.S. Industry 522298, All Other Nondepository Credit Intermediation;
- Retailing used automobiles are classified in Industry 441120, Used Car Dealers;
- Retailing used automobile parts (except tires and tubes) are classified in Industry 441310, Automotive Parts and Accessories Stores;
- Retailing used tires are classified in Industry 441320, Tire Dealers;
- Retailing used mobile homes are classified in Industry 453930, Manufactured (Mobile) Home Dealers;
- Retailing used motorcycles are classified in U.S. Industry 441221, Motorcycle Dealers;
- Retailing used recreational vehicles are classified in Industry 441210, Recreation Vehicle Dealers;
- Retailing used boats are classified in U.S. Industry 441222, Boat Dealers;
- Retailing used aircraft, snowmobiles, and utility trailers are classified in U.S. Industry 441229, All Other Motor Vehicle Dealers; and
- Retailing a general line of used merchandise on an auction basis (not for others) are classified in U.S. Industry 453998, All Other Miscellaneous Store Retailers (except Tobacco Stores).

4539 Other Miscellaneous Store Retailers ^{CAN}

This industry group comprises establishments primarily engaged in retailing new miscellaneous specialty store merchandise (except motor vehicle and parts dealers; furniture and home furnishings stores; consumer-type electronics and appliance stores; building material and garden equipment and supplies dealers; food and beverage stores; health and personal care stores; gasoline stations; clothing and clothing accessories stores; sporting goods, hobby, book, and music stores; general merchandise stores; florists; office supplies, stationery, and gift stores; and used merchandise stores).

■ = Cross-References

Sector 44-45 Retail Trade

US—United States industry only. CAN—United States and Canadian industries are comparable. When neither US nor CAN appears, Canadian, Mexican, and United States industries are comparable.

478

Harris InfoSource

45391 Pet and Pet Supplies Stores CAN
See industry descriptions for 453910 below.

453910 Pet and Pet Supplies Stores CAN
This industry comprises establishments primarily engaged in retailing pets, pet foods, and pet supplies.

- Retailing pets, pet foods, and pet supplies via electronic home shopping, mail-order, or direct sale are classified in Subsector 454, Nonstore Retailers;
- Providing pet grooming and boarding services are classified in Industry 812910, Pet Care (except Veterinary) Services; and
- Providing veterinary services are classified in Industry 541940, Veterinary Services.

45392 Art Dealers CAN
See industry descriptions for 453920 below.

453920 Art Dealers CAN
This industry comprises establishments primarily engaged in retailing original and limited edition art works. Included in this industry are establishments primarily engaged in displaying works of art for retail sale in art galleries.

- Retailing original and limited edition art works via electronic home shopping, mail-order, or direct sale are classified in Subsector 454, Nonstore Retailers;
- Retailing art reproductions (except limited editions) are classified in U.S. Industry 442299, All Other Home Furnishings Stores;
- Retailing artists' supplies are classified in U.S. Industry 453998, All Other Miscellaneous Store Retailers (except Tobacco Stores); and
- Displaying works of art not for retail sale in art galleries are classified in Industry 712110, Museums.

45393 Manufactured (Mobile) Home Dealers CAN
See industry description for 453930 below.

453930 Manufactured (Mobile) Home Dealers CAN
This industry comprises establishments primarily engaged in retailing new and/or used manufactured homes (i.e., mobile homes), parts, and equipment.

- Retailing new or used motor homes, campers, and travel trailers are classified in Industry 441210, Recreational Vehicle Dealers; and
- Retailing prefabricated buildings and kits without construction are classified in Industry 444190, Other Building Material Dealers.

45399 All Other Miscellaneous Store Retailers CAN
This industry comprises establishments primarily engaged in retailing specialized lines of merchandise (except motor vehicle and parts dealers; furniture and home furnishings stores; electronic and appliance stores; building material and garden equipment and supplies dealers; food and beverage stores; health and personal care stores; gasoline stations; clothing and clothing accessories stores; sporting goods, hobby, book, and music stores; general merchandise stores; florists; office supplies, stationery and gift stores; used merchandise stores; pet and pet supplies; art dealers; and manufactured home (i.e., mobile home) dealers. This industry also includes establishments primarily engaged in retailing a general line of new and used merchandise on an auction basis.

- Retailing merchandise via electronic home shopping, mail-order, or direct sale are classified in Subsector 454, Nonstore Retailers;
- Auctioning on the location of others as independent auctioneers are classified in Industry 56199, All Other Support Services;
- Retailing pets and pet supplies are classified in Industry 45391, Pet and Pet Supplies Stores;
- Retailing original and limited edition art works are classified in Industry 45392, Art Dealers;
- Retailing manufactured homes (i.e., mobile homes) are classified in Industry 45393, Manufactured (Mobile) Home Dealers;
- Retailing new books are classified in Industry 45121, Book Stores and News Dealers;
- Retailing new jewelry (except costume jewelry) are classified in Industry 44831, Jewelry Stores;
- Retailing new costume jewelry are classified in Industry 44815, Clothing Accessories Stores; and
- Retailing used merchandise (except automobiles, RVs, mobile homes, motorcycles, boats, motor vehicle parts, and tires) are classified in Industry 453310, Used Merchandise Stores.

453991 Tobacco Stores US
This U.S. industry comprises establishments primarily engaged in retailing cigarettes, cigars, tobacco, pipes, and other smokers' supplies.

- Establishments primarily engaged in retailing tobacco products and supplies via electronic home shopping, mail-order, or direct sale are classified in Subsector 454, Nonstore Retailers.

Visit page 18 to learn about classification changes to this sector.

Sector
44-45

Retail Trade

■ = Cross-References

US—United States industry only. CAN—United States and Canadian industries are comparable. When neither US nor CAN appears, Canadian, Mexican, and United States industries are comparable.

www.harrisinfo.com

479

453998 All Other Miscellaneous Store Retailers (except Tobacco Stores)^{us}

This U.S. industry comprises establishments primarily engaged in retailing specialized lines of merchandise (except motor vehicle and parts dealers; furniture and home furnishings stores; electronic and appliance stores; building material and garden equipment and supplies dealers; food and beverage stores; health and personal care stores; gasoline stations; clothing and clothing accessories stores; sporting goods, hobby, book and music stores; general merchandise stores; florists; office supplies, stationery and gift stores; used merchandise stores; pet and pet supplies stores; art dealers; manufactured home (i.e., mobile homes) dealers; and tobacco stores). This industry also includes establishments primarily engaged in retailing a general line of new and used merchandise on an auction basis.

■ Retailing specialized lines of merchandise via electronic home shopping, mail-order, of direct sale are classified in Subsector 454, Nonstore Retailers;
■ Auctioning (i.e., on the location of others as independent auctioneers) are classified in Industry 561990, All Other Support Services;
■ Retailing pets and pet supplies are classified in Industry 453910, Pet and Pet Supplies Stores;
■ Retailing original and limited edition art works are classified in Industry 453920, Art Dealers;
■ Retailing manufactured homes (i.e., mobile homes) are classified in Industry 453930, Manufactured (Mobile) Home Dealers;
■ Retailing cigarettes, cigars, tobacco, pipes, and other smokers' supplies are classified in U.S. Industry 453991, Tobacco Stores;
■ Retailing antiques are classified in Industry 453310, Used Merchandise Stores;
■ Retailing new books are classified in U.S. Industry 451211, Book Stores;
■ Retailing new jewelry (except costume jewelry) are classified in Industry 448310, Jewelry Stores; and
■ Retailing new costume jewelry are classified in Industry 448150, Clothing Accessories Stores.

▶454 NONSTORE RETAILERS ^{CAN}

Industries in the Nonstore Retailers subsector retail merchandise using methods, such as the broadcasting of infomercials, the broadcasting and publishing of direct-response advertising, the publishing of paper and electronic catalogues, door-to-door solicitation, in-home demonstration, selling from portable stalls and distribution through vending machines. Establishments in this subsector include mail-order houses, vending machine operators, home delivery sales, door-to-door sales, party plan sales, electronic shopping, and sales through portable stalls (e.g., street vendors, except food). Establishments engaged in the direct sale (i.e., nonstore) of products, such as home heating oil dealers, newspaper delivery are included in this subsector.

4541 Electronic Shopping and Mail-order Houses ^{CAN}

45411 Electronic Shopping and Mail-order Houses ^{CAN}
See industry description for 454110 below.

454110 Electronic Shopping and Mail-order Houses ^{CAN}
This industry comprises establishments primarily engaged in retailing all types of merchandise by means of mail or by electronic media, such as interactive television or computer. Included in this industry are establishments primarily engaged in retailing from catalogue showrooms of mail-order houses.

■ Establishments primarily engaged in providing telemarketing (e.g., telephone marketing) services for others are classified in U.S. Industry 561422, Telemarketing Bureaus.

4542 Vending Machine Operators ^{CAN}

45421 Vending Machine Operators ^{CAN}
See industry description for 454210 below.

454210 Vending Machine Operators ^{CAN}
This industry comprises establishments primarily engaged in retailing merchandise through vending machines that they service.

■ Selling insurance policies through vending machines are classified in Subsector 524, Insurance Carriers and Related Activities;
■ Supplying and servicing coin-operated photobooths, restrooms, and lockers are classified in Industry 812990, All Other Personal Services; and
■ Supplying and servicing coin-operated amusement and gambling devices in places of business operated by others are classified in Subsector 713, Amusement, Gambling, and Recreation Industries.

Sector
44-45

Retail Trade

■ = Cross-References

US—United States industry only. CAN—United States and Canadian industries are comparable. When neither US nor CAN appears, Canadian, Mexican, and United States industries are comparable.

480

Harris InfoSource

4543 Direct Selling Establishments ^{CAN}

This industry group comprises establishments primarily engaged in nonstore retailing (except electronic, mail-order, or vending machine sales). These establishments typically go to the customers' location rather than the customer coming to them (e.g., door-to-door sales, home parties). Examples of establishments in this industry are home delivery newspaper routes; home delivery of heating oil, liquefied petroleum (LP) gas, and other fuels; locker meat provisioners; frozen food and freezer plan providers; coffee break services providers; and bottled water or water softener services.

45431 Fuel Dealers ^{CAN}

This industry comprises establishments primarily engaged in retailing heating oil, liquefied petroleum (LP) gas, and other fuels via direct selling.

- Providing oil burner repair services are classified in Industry 81141, Home and Garden Equipment and Appliance Repair and Maintenance; and
- Installing oil burners are classified in Industry 23511, Plumbing, Heating, and Air-conditioning Contractors.

454311 Heating Oil Dealers ^{US}

This U.S. industry comprises establishments primarily engaged in retailing heating oil via direct selling.

- Providing oil burner repair services are classified in U.S. Industry 811411, Home and Garden Equipment Repair and Maintenance; and
- Installing oil burners are classified in Industry 235110, Plumbing, Heating, and Air-conditioning Contractors.

454312 Liquefied Petroleum Gas (Bottled Gas) Dealers ^{US}

This U.S. industry comprises establishments primarily engaged in retailing liquefied petroleum (LP) gas via direct selling.

454319 Other Fuel Dealers ^{US}

This U.S. industry comprises establishments primarily engaged in retailing fuels (except liquefied petroleum gas and heating oil) via direct selling.

45439 Other Direct Selling Establishments ^{CAN}

See industry description for 454390 below.

454390 Other Direct Selling Establishments ^{CAN}

This industry comprises establishments primarily engaged in retailing merchandise (except food for immediate consumption and fuel) via direct sale to the customer by means, such as in-house sales (i.e., party plan merchandising), truck or wagon sales, and portable stalls (i.e., street vendors).

- Preparing and selling meals and snacks for immediate consumption from motorized vehicles or nonmotorized carts catering a route are classified in Industry 722330, Mobile Food Services;
- Retailing heating oil via direct sale are classified in U.S. Industry 454311, Heating Oil Dealers;
- Retailing liquefied petroleum (LP) gas via direct sale are classified in U.S. Industry 454312, Liquefied Petroleum Gas (Bottled Gas) Dealers; and
- Retailing other fuels, such as coal or wood, via direct sale are classified in U.S. Industry 454319, Other Fuel Dealers.

Visit page 18 to learn about classification changes to this sector.

Sector
44-45

Retail Trade

■ = Cross-References

US—United States industry only. CAN—United States and Canadian industries are comparable. When neither US nor CAN appears, Canadian, Mexican, and United States industries are comparable.

NAICS United States Structure

Sector	Name	Sub-sectors	Industry groups	NAICS 5-digit industries	U.S. 6-digit industries	TOTAL U.S. industries	New industries
11	Agriculture, Forestry, Fishing and, Hunting	5	19	42	32	64	20
21	Mining	3	5	10	28	29	—
22	Utilities	1	3	6	6	10	6
23	Construction	3	14	28	—	28	3
31–33	Manufacturing	21	84	184	408	474	79
42	Wholesale Trade	2	18	69	—	69	—
44–45	Retail Trade	12	27	61	18	72	17
48-49	Transportation and Warehousing	11	29	42	25	57	28
51	Information	4	9	28	12	34	20
52	Finance and Insurance	5	11	32	15	42	23
53	Real Estate and Rental and Leasing	3	8	19	9	24	15
54	Professional, Scientific, and Technical Services	1	9	35	17	47	28
55	Management of Companies and Enterprises	1	1	1	3	3	1
56	Administrative and Support and Waste Management and Remediation Services	2	11	29	23	43	29
61	Educational Services	1	7	12	7	17	12
62	Health Care and Social Assistance	4	18	30	16	39	27
71	Arts, Entertainment, and Recreation	3	9	23	3	25	19
72	Accommodation and Food Services	2	7	11	7	15	10
81	Other Services (except Public Administration)	4	14	30	30	49	19
92	Public Administration	8	8	29	—	29	2
	TOTAL	96	311	721	659	1170	358

To learn more about the changes by sector go to pages 15-18.

Sector
44-45
Retail Trade

Sector 48-49
Transportation and Warehousing

The Sector as a Whole

THE TRANSPORTATION AND WAREHOUSING sector includes industries providing transportation of passengers and cargo, warehousing and storage for goods, scenic and sightseeing transportation, and support activities related to modes of transportation. Establishments in these industries use transportation equipment or transportation related facilities as a productive asset. The type of equipment depends on the mode of transportation. The modes of transportation are air, rail, water, road, and pipeline.

The Transportation and Warehousing sector distinguishes three basic types of activities: subsectors for each mode of transportation, a subsector for warehousing and storage, and a subsector for establishments providing support activities for transportation. In addition, there are subsectors for establishments that provide passenger transportation for scenic and sightseeing purposes, postal services, and courier services.

A separate subsector for support activities is established in the sector because, first, support activities for transportation are inherently multimodal, such as freight transportation arrangement, or have multimodal aspects. Secondly, there are production process similarities among the support activity industries.

One of the support activities identified in the support activity subsector is the routine repair and maintenance of transportation equipment (e.g., aircraft at an airport, railroad rolling stock at a railroad terminal, or ships at a harbor or port facility). Such establishments do not perform complete overhauling or rebuilding of transportation equipment (i.e., periodic restoration of transportation equipment to original design specifications) or transportation equipment conversion (i.e., major modification to systems). An establishment that primarily performs factory (or shipyard) overhauls, rebuilding, or conversions of aircraft, railroad rolling stock, or a ship is classified in Subsector 336, Transportation Equipment Manufacturing according to the type of equipment.

Many of the establishments in this sector often operate on networks, with physical facilities, labor forces, and equipment spread over an extensive geographic area.

Warehousing establishments in this sector are distinguished from merchant wholesaling in that the warehouse establishments do not sell the goods.

Excluded from this sector are establishments primarily engaged in providing travel agent services that support transportation and other establishments, such as hotels, businesses, and government agencies. These establishments are classified in Sector 56, Administrative and Support, Waste Management, and Remediation Services. Also, establishments primarily engaged in providing rental and leasing of transportation equipment without operator are classified in Subsector 532, Rental and Leasing Services.

Sector 48-49
Transportation and Warehousing

▶481 AIR TRANSPORTATION

Industries in the Air Transportation subsector provide air transportation of passengers and/or cargo using aircraft, such as airplanes and helicopters. The subsector distinguishes scheduled from nonscheduled air transportation. Scheduled air carriers fly regular routes on regular schedules and operate even if flights are

US—United States industry only. CAN—United States and Canadian industries are comparable. When neither US nor CAN appears, Canadian, Mexican, and United States industries are comparable.

www.harrisinfo.com

483

only partially loaded. Nonscheduled carriers often operate during nonpeak time slots at busy airports. These establishments have more flexibility with respect to choice of airport, hours of operation, load factors, and similar operational characteristics. Nonscheduled carriers provide chartered air transportation of passengers, cargo, or specialty flying services. Specialty flying services establishments use general purpose aircraft to provide a variety of specialized flying services.

Scenic and sightseeing air transportation and air courier services are not included in this subsector but are included in Subsector 487, Scenic and Sightseeing Transportation and in Subsector 492, Couriers and Messengers. Although these activities may use aircraft, they are different from the activities included in air transportation. Air sightseeing does not usually involve place-to-place transportation; the passenger's flight (e.g., balloon ride, aerial sightseeing) typically starts and ends at the same location. Courier services (individual package or cargo delivery) includes more than air transportation; road transportation is usually required to deliver the cargo to the intended recipient.

4811 Scheduled Air Transportation

48111 Scheduled Air Transportation
This industry comprises establishments primarily engaged in providing air transportation of passengers and/or cargo over regular routes and on regular schedules. Establishments in this industry operate flights, even if partially loaded. Establishments primarily engaged in providing scheduled air transportation of mail on a contract basis are included in this industry.

- Providing air courier services are classified in Industry 49211, Couriers;
- Providing air transportation of passengers, cargo, or specialty flying services with no regular routes and regular schedules are classified in Industry 48121, Nonscheduled Air Transportation; and
- Providing helicopter rides for scenic and sightseeing transportation are classified in Industry 48799, Scenic and Sightseeing Transportation, Other.

481111 Scheduled Passenger Air Transportation
This U.S. industry comprises establishments primarily engaged in providing air transportation of passengers or passengers and freight over regular routes and on regular schedules. Establishments in this industry operate flights even if partially loaded. Scheduled air passenger carriers including commuter and helicopter carriers (except scenic and sightseeing) are included in this industry.

- Providing air transportation of passengers or passengers and cargo with no regular routes and regular schedules are classified in U.S. Industry 481211; Nonscheduled Chartered Passenger Air Transportation;
- Providing helicopter rides for scenic and sightseeing transportation are classified in Industry 487990, Scenic and Sightseeing Transportation, Other; and
- Providing air transportation of cargo (without transporting passengers) over regular routes and on regular schedules are classified in U.S. Industry 481112, Scheduled Freight Air Transportation.

481112 Scheduled Freight Air Transportation us
This U.S. industry comprises establishments primarily engaged in providing air transportation of cargo without transporting passengers over regular routes and on regular schedules. Establishments in this industry operate flights even if partially loaded. Establishments primarily engaged in providing scheduled air transportation of mail on a contract basis are included in this industry.

- Providing air courier services are classified in Industry 492110, Couriers;
- Providing air transportation of cargo with no regular routes and regular schedules are classified in U.S. Industry 481212, Nonscheduled Chartered Freight Air Transportation; and
- Providing air transportation of passengers or passengers and cargo over regular routes and on regular schedules are classified in U.S. Industry 481112, Scheduled Passenger Air Transportation.

4812 Nonscheduled Air Transportation

48121 Nonscheduled Air Transportation
This industry comprises establishments primarily engaged in (1) providing air transportation of passengers and/or cargo with no regular routes and regular schedules or (2) providing specialty flying services with no regular routes and regular schedules using general purpose aircraft. These establishments have more flexibility with respect to choice of airports, hours of operation, load factors, and similar operational characteristics.

Sector 48-49

Transportation and Warehousing

■ = Cross-References

US—United States industry only. CAN—United States and Canadian industries are comparable. When neither US nor CAN appears, Canadian, Mexican, and United States industries are comparable.

- Crop dusting using specialized aircraft are classified in Industry 11511, Support Activities for Crop Production;
- Fighting forest fires using specialized water bombers are classified in Industry 11531, Support Activities for Forestry;
- Providing air transportation of passengers and/or cargo over regular routes and on regular schedules are classified in Industry 48111, Scheduled Air Transportation;
- Providing specialized air sightseeing services are classified in Industry 48799, Scenic and Sightseeing Transportation, Other;
- Aerial gathering of geophysical data are classified in Industry 54136, Geophysical Surveying and Mapping Services;
- Providing aerial and/or other surveying and mapping services are classified in Industry 54137, Surveying and Mapping (except Geophysical) Services;
- Providing air ambulance services using specialized equipment are classified in Industry 62191, Ambulance Services;
- Operating specialized flying schools, including all training for commercial pilots are classified in Industry 61151, Technical and Trade Schools;
- Operating recreation aviation clubs are classified in Industry 71399, All Other Amusement and Recreation Industries;
- Operating advocacy aviation clubs are classified in U.S. Industry 81331, Social Advocacy Organizations; and
- Providing air courier services are classified in Industry 49211, Couriers.

481211 Nonscheduled Chartered Passenger Air Transportation US

This U.S. industry comprises establishments primarily engaged in providing air transportation of passengers or passengers and cargo with no regular routes and regular schedules.

- Providing specialty air transportation or flying services with no regular routes and regular schedules using general purpose aircraft are classified in U.S. Industry 481219, Other Nonscheduled Air Transportation;
- Providing specialized air sightseeing services are classified in Industry 487990, Scenic and Sightseeing Transportation, Other;
- Providing air transportation of passengers or passengers and cargo over regular routes and on regular schedules are classified in U.S. Industry 481111, Scheduled Passenger Air Transportation; and
- Providing air transportation of cargo (without transporting passengers) with no regular routes and schedules are classified in U.S. Industry 481212, Nonscheduled Chartered Freight Air Transportation.

481212 Nonscheduled Chartered Freight Air Transportation US

This U.S. industry comprises establishments primarily engaged in providing air transportation of cargo without transporting passengers with no regular routes and regular schedules.

- Providing specialty air transportation or flying services with no regular routes and regular schedules using general purpose aircraft are classified in U.S. Industry 481219, Other Nonscheduled Air Transportation;
- Providing air courier services are classified in Industry 492110, Couriers;
- Providing air transportation of cargo without transporting passengers over regular routes and on regular schedules are classified in U.S. Industry 481112, Scheduled Freight Air Transportation; and
- Providing air transportation of cargo and passengers with no regular routes and schedules are classified in U.S. Industry 481211, Nonscheduled Chartered Passenger Air Transportation.

481219 Other Nonscheduled Air Transportation US

This U.S. industry comprises establishments primarily engaged in providing air transportation with no regular routes and regular schedules (except nonscheduled chartered passenger and/or cargo air transportation). These establishments provide a variety of specialty air transportation or flying services based on individual customer needs using general purpose aircraft.

- Providing air transportation of passengers or passengers and cargo with no regular routes and regular schedules are classified in U.S. Industry 481211, Nonscheduled Chartered Passenger Air Transportation;
- Providing air transportation of cargo without transporting passengers with no regular routes and regular schedules are classified in U.S. Industry 481212, Nonscheduled Chartered Freight Air Transportation;
- Crop dusting using specialized aircraft are classified in U.S. Industry 115112, Soil Preparation, Planting, and Cultivating;
- Fighting forest fires using specialized water bombers are classified in Industry 115310, Support Activities for Forestry;
- Providing specialized air sightseeing services are classified in Industry 487990, Scenic and Sightseeing Transportation, Other;
- Operating specialized flying schools, including all training for commercial pilots are classified in U.S. Industry 611512, Flight Training;
- Providing specialized air ambulance services using specialized equipment are classified in U.S. Industry 621999, All Other Miscellaneous Ambulatory Health Care Services;
- Operating recreation aviation clubs are classified in Industry 713990, All Other Amusement and Recreation Industries;
- Operating advocacy aviation clubs are classified in U.S. Industry 813319, Other Social Advocacy Organizations;
- Aerial gathering of geophysical data for surveying and mapping are classified in Industry 541360, Geophysical Surveying and Mapping Services; and
- Providing aerial and/or other surveying and mapping services are classified in Industry 541370, Surveying and Mapping (except Geophysical) Services.

➡ 482 RAIL TRANSPORTATION

Industries in the Rail Transportation subsector provide rail transportation of passengers and/or cargo using railroad rolling stock. The railroads in this subsector primarily either operate on networks, with physical

Sector
48-49

Transportation and Warehousing

■ = Cross-References

US—United States industry only. CAN—United States and Canadian industries are comparable. When neither US nor CAN appears, Canadian, Mexican, and United States industries are comparable.

facilities, labor force, and equipment spread over an extensive geographic area, or operate over a short distance on a local rail line.

Scenic and sightseeing rail transportation and street railroads, commuter rail, and rapid transit are not included in this subsector but are included in Subsector 487, Scenic and Sightseeing Transportation, and Subsector 485, Transit and Ground Passenger Transportation, respectively. Although these activities use railroad rolling stock, they are different from the activities included in rail transportation. Sightseeing and scenic railroads do not usually involve place-to-place transportation; the passenger's trip typically starts and ends at the same location. Commuter railroads operate in a manner more consistent with local and urban transit and are often part of integrated transit systems.

4821 Rail Transportation

48211 Rail Transportation
This industry comprises establishments primarily engaged in operating railroads (except street railroads, commuter rail, urban rapid transit, and scenic and sightseeing trains). Line-haul railroads and short line railroads are included in this industry.

- Operating street railroads, commuter rail, and urban rapid transit systems are classified in Industry Group 4851, Urban Transit Systems;
- Operating scenic and sightseeing trains are classified in Industry 48711, Scenic and Sightseeing Transportation, Land; and
- Operating switching and terminal facilities as separate establishments are classified in Industry 48821, Support Activities for Rail Transportation.

482111 Line-haul Railroads ᵁˢ
This U.S. industry comprises establishments known as line-haul railroads primarily engaged in operating railroads for the transport of passengers and/or cargo over a long distance within a rail network. These establishments provide for the inner-city movement of trains between the terminals and stations on main and branch lines of a line-haul rail network (except for local switching services).

- Operating switching and terminal facilities as separate establishments are classified in Industry 488210, Support Activities for Rail Transportation;
- Operating railroads over a short distance on local rail lines are classified in U.S. Industry 482112, Short Line Railroads; and
- Operating commuter rail systems are classified in U.S. Industry 485112, Commuter Rail Systems.

482112 Short Line Railroads ᶜᴬᴺ
This U.S. industry comprises establishments known as short line railroads primarily engaged in operating railroads for the transport of cargo over a short distance on local rail lines not part of a rail network.

- Operating street railroads, commuter rail, and urban rapid transit systems are classified in Industry Group 4851, Urban Transit Systems;
- Operating scenic and sightseeing trains are classified in Industry 487110, Scenic and Sightseeing Transportation, Land;
- Operating switching and terminal facilities as separate establishments are classified in Industry 488210, Support Activities for Rail Transportation; and
- Operating railroads for the transport of passengers and/or cargo over a long distance are classified in U.S. Industry 482111, Line-haul Railroads.

▶483 WATER TRANSPORTATION
Industries in the Water Transportation subsector provide water transportation of passengers and cargo using watercraft, such as ships, barges, and boats.

The subsector is composed of two industry groups: (1) one for deep sea, coastal, and Great Lakes; and (2) one for inland water transportation. This split typically reflects the difference in equipment used.

Scenic and sightseeing water transportation services are not included in this subsector but are included in Subsector 487, Scenic and Sightseeing Transportation. Although these activities use watercraft, they are different from the activities included in water transportation. Water sightseeing does not usually involve place-to-place transportation; the passenger's trip starts and ends at the same location.

4831 Deep Sea, Coastal, and Great Lakes Water Transportation

■ = Cross-References

Sector 48-49
Transportation and Warehousing

US—United States industry only. CAN—United States and Canadian industries are comparable. When neither US nor CAN appears, Canadian, Mexican, and United States industries are comparable.

48311 Deep Sea, Coastal, and Great Lakes Water Transportation

This industry comprises establishments primarily engaged in providing deep sea, coastal, Great Lakes, and St. Lawrence Seaway water transportation. Marine transportation establishments using the facilities of the St. Lawrence Seaway Authority Commission are considered to be using the Great Lakes Water Transportation System.

- Providing inland water transportation on lakes, rivers, or intracoastal waterways (except on the Great Lakes System) are classified in Industry 48321, Inland Water Transportation;
- Providing scenic and sightseeing water transportation, such as harbor cruises, are classified in Industry 48721, Scenic and Sightseeing Transportation, Water; and
- Operating floating casinos (i.e., gambling cruises, riverboat gambling casinos) are classified in Industry 71321, Casinos (except Casino Hotels).

483111 Deep Sea Freight Transportation US

This U.S. industry comprises establishments primarily engaged in providing deep sea transportation of cargo to or from foreign ports.

- Establishments primarily engaged in providing deep sea transportation of cargo to and from domestic ports are classified in U.S. Industry 483113, Coastal and Great Lakes Freight Transportation.

483112 Deep Sea Passenger Transportation US

This U.S. industry comprises establishments primarily engaged in providing deep sea transportation of passengers to or from foreign ports.

- Providing deep sea transportation of passengers to and from domestic ports are classified in U.S. Industry 483114, Coastal and Great Lakes Passenger Transportation; and
- Operating floating casinos (i.e., gambling cruises) are classified in Industry 713210, Casinos (except Casino Hotels).

483113 Coastal and Great Lakes Freight Transportation US

This U.S. industry comprises establishments primarily engaged in providing water transportation of cargo in coastal waters, on the Great Lakes System, or deep seas between ports of the United States, Puerto Rico, and United States island possessions or protectorates. Marine transportation establishments using the facilities of the St. Lawrence Seaway Authority Commission are considered to be using the Great Lakes Water Transportation System. Establishments primarily engaged in providing coastal and/or Great Lakes barge transportation services are included in this industry.

- Providing deep sea transportation of cargo to or from foreign ports are classified in U.S. Industry 483111, Deep Sea Freight Transportation; and
- Providing inland water transportation of cargo on lakes, rivers, or intracoastal waterways (except on the Great Lakes System) are classified in U.S. Industry 483211, Inland Water Freight Transportation.

483114 Coastal and Great Lakes Passenger Transportation US

This U.S. industry comprises establishments primarily engaged in providing water transportation of passengers in coastal waters, the Great Lakes System, or deep seas between ports of the United States, Puerto Rico, and United States island possessions and protectorates. Marine transportation establishments using the facilities of the St. Lawrence Seaway Authority Commission are considered to be using the Great Lakes Water Transportation System.

- Providing inland water transportation of passengers on lakes, rivers or intracoastal waterways (except on the Great Lakes System) are classified in U.S. industry 483212, Inland Water Passenger Transportation;
- Providing scenic and sightseeing water transportation, such as harbor cruises, are classified in Industry 487210, Scenic and Sightseeing Transportation, Water; and
- Operating floating casinos (i.e., gambling cruises) are classified in Industry 713210, Casinos (except Casino Hotels).

4832 Inland Water Transportation

48321 Inland Water Transportation

This industry comprises establishments primarily engaged in providing inland water transportation of passengers and/or cargo on lakes, rivers, or intracoastal waterways (except on the Great Lakes System).

- Providing water transportation in deep sea, coastal, or on the Great Lakes System are classified in Industry Group 4831, Deep Sea, Coastal, and Great Lakes Water Transportation;
- Providing scenic and sightseeing water transportation, such as harbor cruises, are classified in Industry 48721, Scenic and Sightseeing Transportation, Water; and
- Operating floating casinos (i.e., gambling cruises, riverboat gambling casinos) are classified in Industry 71321, Casinos (except Casino Hotels).

Sector
48-49
Transportation
and Warehousing

■ = Cross-References

US—United States industry only. CAN—United States and Canadian industries are comparable. When neither US nor CAN appears, Canadian, Mexican, and United States industries are comparable.

www.harrisinfo.com

487

483211 Inland Water Freight Transportation US

This U.S. industry comprises establishments primarily engaged in providing inland water transportation of cargo on lakes, rivers, or intracoastal waterways (except on the Great Lakes System).

- Providing deep sea transportation of cargo to and from foreign ports are classified in U.S. Industry 483111, Deep Sea Freight Transportation; and
- Providing water transportation of cargo in coastal waters or on the Great Lakes System are classified in U.S. Industry 483113, Coastal and Great Lakes Freight Transportation.

483212 Inland Water Passenger Transportation US

This U.S. industry comprises establishments primarily engaged in providing inland water transportation of passengers on lakes, rivers, or intracoastal waterways (except on the Great Lakes System).

- Providing deep sea transportation of passengers to and from foreign ports are classified in U.S. Industry 483112, Deep Sea Passenger Transportation;
- Operating cruise ships or ferries in coastal waters or on the Great Lakes System are classified in U.S. Industry 483114, Coastal and Great Lakes Passenger Transportation; and
- Providing scenic and sightseeing water transportation, such as harbor cruises, are classified in Industry 487210, Scenic and Sightseeing Transportation, Water.

►484 TRUCK TRANSPORTATION

Industries in the Truck Transportation subsector provide over-the-road transportation of cargo using motor vehicles, such as trucks and tractor trailers. The subsector is subdivided into general freight trucking and specialized freight trucking. This distinction reflects differences in equipment used, type of load carried, scheduling, terminal, and other networking services. General freight transportation establishments handle a wide variety of general commodities, generally palletized, and transported in a container or van trailer. Specialized freight transportation is the transportation of cargo that, because of size, weight, shape, or other inherent characteristics require specialized equipment for transportation.

Each of these industry groups is further subdivided based on distance traveled. Local trucking establishments primarily carry goods within a single metropolitan area and its adjacent nonurban areas. Long distance trucking establishments carry goods between metropolitan areas.

The Specialized Freight Trucking industry group includes a separate industry for Used Household and Office Goods Moving. The household and office goods movers are separated because of the substantial network of establishments that has developed to deal with local and long-distance moving and the associated storage. In this area, the same establishment provides both local and long-distance services, while other specialized freight establishments generally limit their services to either local or long-distance hauling.

4841 General Freight Trucking

This industry group comprises establishments primarily engaged in providing general freight trucking. General freight establishments handle a wide variety of commodities, generally palletized, and transported in a container or van trailer. The establishments of this industry group provide a combination of the following network activities: local pickup, local sorting and terminal operations, line-haul, destination sorting and terminal operations, and local delivery.

48411 General Freight Trucking, Local

See industry description for 484110 below.

484110 General Freight Trucking, Local

This industry comprises establishments primarily engaged in providing local general freight trucking. General freight establishments handle a wide variety of commodities, generally palletized and transported in a container or van trailer. Local general freight trucking establishments usually provide trucking within a metropolitan area, which may cross state lines. Generally the trips are same-day return.

- Operating independent trucking terminals are classified in Industry 488490, Other Support Activities for Road Transportation; and
- Providing general freight long-distance trucking including all North American international travel are classified in Industry 48412, General Freight Trucking, Long-distance.

US—United States industry only. CAN—United States and Canadian industries are comparable. When neither US nor CAN appears, Canadian, Mexican, and United States industries are comparable.

48412 General Freight Trucking, Long-distance

This industry comprises establishments primarily engaged in providing long-distance general freight trucking. General freight establishments handle a wide variety of commodities, generally palletized and transported in a container or van trailer. Long-distance general freight trucking establishments usually provide trucking between metropolitan areas which may cross North American country borders. Included in this industry are establishments operating as truckload (TL) or less than truckload (LTL) carriers.

- Providing courier services are classified in Industry 49211, Couriers;
- Providing warehousing services of general freight are classified in Industry 49311, General Warehousing and Storage;
- Providing specialized freight trucking are classified in Industry Group 4842, Specialized Freight Trucking;
- Operating independent trucking terminals are classified in Industry 48849, Other Support Activities for Road Transportation; and
- Providing local general freight trucking services are classified in Industry 48411, General Freight Trucking, Local.

484121 General Freight Trucking, Long-distance, Truckload ^{CAN}

This U.S. industry comprises establishments primarily engaged in providing long-distance general freight truckload (TL) trucking. These long-distance general freight truckload carrier establishments provide full truck movement of freight from origin to destination. The shipment of freight on a truck is characterized as a full single load not combined with other shipments.

- Providing general freight long-distance, less than truckload trucking are classified in U.S. Industry 484122, General Freight Trucking, Long-distance, Less Than Truckload;
- Providing specialized freight trucking are classified in Industry Group 4842, Specialized Freight Trucking;
- Operating independent trucking terminals are classified in Industry 488490, Other Support Activities for Road Transportation; and
- Providing local general freight trucking services are classified in Industry 484110, General Freight Trucking, Local.

484122 General Freight Trucking, Long-distance, Less Than Truckload ^{CAN}

This U.S. industry comprises establishments primarily engaged in providing long-distance, general freight, less than truckload (LTL) trucking. LTL carriage is characterized as multiple shipments combined onto a single truck for multiple deliveries within a network. These establishments are generally characterized by the following network activities: local pickup, local sorting and terminal operations, line-haul, destination sorting and terminal operations, and local delivery.

- Providing courier services are classified in Industry 492110, Couriers;
- Providing warehousing services of general freight are classified in Industry 493110, General Warehousing and Storage;
- Providing specialized freight trucking are classified in Industry Group 4842, Specialized Freight Trucking;
- Operating independent trucking terminals are classified in Industry 488490, Other Support Activities for Road Transportation;
- Providing general freight long-distance truckload trucking are classified in U.S. Industry 484121, General Freight Trucking, Long-distance, Truckload; and
- Providing local general freight trucking services are classified in Industry 484110, General Freight Trucking, Local.

4842 Specialized Freight Trucking

This industry group comprises establishments primarily engaged in providing local or long-distance specialized freight trucking. The establishments of this industry are primarily engaged in the transportation of freight that, because of size, weight, shape, or other inherent characteristics, requires specialized equipment, such as flatbeds, tankers, or refrigerated trailers. This industry includes the transportation of used household, institutional, and commercial furniture and equipment.

48421 Used Household and Office Goods Moving

See industry description for 484210 below.

484210 Used Household and Office Goods Moving

This industry comprises establishments primarily engaged in providing local or long-distance trucking of used household, used institutional, or used commercial furniture and equipment. Incidental packing and storage activities are often provided by these establishments.

48422 Specialized Freight (except Used Goods) Trucking, Local

See industry description for 484220 below.

Sector

48-49

Transportation and Warehousing

■ = Cross-References

US—United States industry only. CAN—United States and Canadian industries are comparable. When neither US nor CAN appears, Canadian, Mexican, and United States industries are comparable.

www.harrisinfo.com

489

484220 Specialized Freight (except Used Goods) Trucking, Local

This industry comprises establishments primarily engaged in providing local, specialized trucking. Local trucking establishments provide trucking within a metropolitan area that may cross state lines. Generally the trips are same-day return.

- Providing long-distance specialized freight (except used goods) trucking including all North American international travel are classified in Industry 48423, Specialized Freight (except Used Goods) Trucking, Long-distance;
- Providing local general freight trucking are classified in U.S. Industry 484110, General Freight Trucking, Local;
- Providing trucking of used household and office goods are classified in Industry 484210, Used Household and Office Goods Moving; and
- Providing waste collection are classified in Industry Group 5621, Waste Collection.

48423 Specialized Freight (except Used Goods) Trucking, Long-distance

See industry description for 484230 below.

484230 Specialized Freight (except Used Goods) Trucking, Long-distance

This industry comprises establishments primarily engaged in providing long-distance specialized trucking. These establishments provide trucking between metropolitan areas that may cross North American country borders.

- Providing local specialized freight trucking (except used goods) are classified in Industry 484220, Specialized Freight (except Used Goods) Trucking, Local;
- Providing long-distance general freight trucking including all North American international travel are classified in Industry 48412, General Freight Trucking, Long-distance; and
- Providing trucking of used household and office goods are classified in Industry 484210, Used Household and Office Goods Moving.

▶485 TRANSIT AND GROUND PASSENGER TRANSPORTATION

Industries in the Transit and Ground Passenger Transportation subsector include a variety of passenger transportation activities, such as urban transit systems; chartered bus, school bus, and interurban bus transportation; and taxis. These activities are distinguished based primarily on such production process factors as vehicle types, routes, and schedules.

In this subsector, the principal splits identify scheduled transportation as separate from nonscheduled transportation. The scheduled transportation industry groups are Urban Transit Systems, Interurban and Rural Bus Transportation, and School and Employee Bus Transportation. The nonscheduled industry groups are the Charter Bus Industry and Taxi and Limousine Service. The Other Transit and Ground Passenger Transportation Industry group includes both scheduled and nonscheduled transportation.

Scenic and sightseeing ground transportation services are not included in this subsector but are included in Subsector 487, Scenic and Sightseeing Transportation. Sightseeing does not usually involve place-to-place transportation; the passenger's trip starts and ends at the same location.

4851 Urban Transit Systems

48511 Urban Transit Systems

This industry comprises establishments primarily engaged in operating local and suburban passenger transit systems over regular routes and on regular schedules within a metropolitan area and its adjacent nonurban areas. Such transportation systems involve the use of one or more modes of transport including light rail, commuter rail, subways, streetcars, as well as buses and other motor vehicles.

- Operating local and suburban passenger transit systems using only one mode of transportation are classified according to the mode of transport;
- Providing scenic and sightseeing transportation are classified in Industry 48711, Scenic and Sightseeing Transportation, Land;
- Providing support services to transit and ground transportation are classified in Industry Group 4884, Support Activities for Road Transportation; and
- Providing interurban and rural bus transportation are classified in Industry 48521, Interurban and Rural Bus Transportation.

485111 Mixed Mode Transit Systems ᵁˢ

This U.S. industry comprises establishments primarily engaged in operating local and suburban

Sector

48-49

Transportation
and Warehousing

■ = Cross-References

US—United States industry only. CAN—United States and Canadian industries are comparable. When neither US nor CAN appears, Canadian, Mexican, and United States industries are comparable.

490

Harris InfoSource

ground passenger transit systems using more than one mode of transport over regular routes and on regular schedules within a metropolitan area and its adjacent nonurban areas.

- Operating local and suburban passenger transit systems using only one mode of transportation are classified according to the mode of transport; and
- Providing support services to transit and ground passenger transportation are classified in Industry Group 4884, Support Activities for Road Transportation.

485112 Commuter Rail Systems ᵁˢ

This U.S. industry comprises establishments primarily engaged in operating local and suburban commuter rail systems over regular routes and on a regular schedule within a metropolitan area and its adjacent nonurban areas. Commuter rail is usually characterized by reduced fares, multiple ride, and commutation tickets and mostly used by passengers during the morning and evening peak periods.

- Operating local and suburban mass passenger transit systems using both commuter rail and another mode of transport are classified in U.S. Industry 485111, Mixed Mode Transit Systems;
- Operating a subway system are classified in U.S. Industry 485119, Other Urban Transit Systems; and
- Providing scenic and sightseeing transportation on land are classified in Industry 487110, Scenic and Sightseeing Transportation, Land.

485113 Bus and Other Motor Vehicle Transit Systems

This U.S. industry comprises establishments primarily engaged in operating local and suburban passenger transportation systems using buses or other motor vehicles over regular routes and on regular schedules within a metropolitan area and its adjacent nonurban areas.

- Operating local and suburban passenger transportation systems using both a bus or other motor vehicle and another mode of transport are classified in U.S. Industry 485111, Mixed Mode Transit Systems;
- Providing interurban and rural bus transportation are classified in Industry 485210, Interurban and Rural Bus Transportation; and
- Providing scenic and sightseeing transportation using buses or other motor vehicles are classified in Industry 487110, Scenic and Sightseeing Transportation, Land.

485119 Other Urban Transit Systems ᵁˢ

This U.S. industry comprises establishments primarily engaged in operating local and suburban ground passenger transit systems (except mixed mode transit systems, commuter rail systems, and buses and other motor vehicles) over regular routes and on regular schedules within a metropolitan area and its adjacent nonurban areas.

- Operating local and suburban ground passenger transit systems using more than one mode of transport are classified in U.S. Industry 485111, Mixed Mode Transit Systems;
- Providing local and suburban passenger transportation using commuter rail systems are classified in U.S. Industry 485112, Commuter Rail Systems; and
- Operating local and suburban bus transit systems are classified in U.S. Industry 485113, Bus and Other Motor Vehicle Transit Systems.

4852 Interurban and Rural Bus Transportation

48521 Interurban and Rural Bus Transportation
See industry description for 485210 below.

485210 Interurban and Rural Bus Transportation

This industry comprises establishments primarily engaged in providing bus passenger transportation over regular routes and on regular schedules, principally outside a single metropolitan area and its adjacent nonurban areas.

- Providing scenic and sightseeing transportation using buses are classified in Industry 487110, Scenic and Sightseeing Transportation, Land;
- Providing buses for charter are classified in Industry 485510, Charter Bus Industry;
- Operating local and suburban bus transit systems are classified in U.S. Industry 485113, Bus and Other Motor Vehicle Transit Systems; and
- Operating independent bus terminals are classified in Industry 488490, Other Support Activities for Road Transportation.

Sector
48-49

Transportation
and Warehousing

■ = Cross-References

US—United States industry only. CAN—United States and Canadian industries are comparable. When neither US nor CAN appears, Canadian, Mexican, and United States industries are comparable.

www.harrisinfo.com

491

4853 Taxi and Limousine Service

48531 Taxi Service
See industry description for 485310 below.

485310 Taxi Service
This industry comprises establishments primarily engaged in providing passenger transportation by automobile or van, not operated over regular routes and on regular schedules. Establishments of taxi-cab owner/operator, taxicab fleet operators, or taxicab organizations are included in this industry.

- Providing special needs transportation services (except to and from school or work) for the infirm, elderly, or handicapped are classified in U.S. Industry 485991, Special Needs Transportation;
- Providing limousine services are classified in Industry 485320, Limousine Service; and
- Providing scheduled shuttle services between hotels, airports, or other destination points are classified in U.S. Industry 485999, All Other Transit and Ground Passenger Transportation.

48532 Limousine Service
See industry description for 485320 below.

485320 Limousine Service
This industry comprises establishments primarily engaged in providing an array of specialty and luxury passenger transportation services via limousine or luxury sedans generally on a reserved basis. These establishments do not operate over regular routes and on regular schedules.

- Providing taxi services are classified in Industry 485310, Taxi Service; and
- Providing scheduled shuttle services between hotels, airports, or other destination points are classified in U.S. Industry 485999, All Other Transit and Ground Passenger Transportation.

4854 School and Employee Bus Transportation

48541 School and Employee Bus Transportation
See industry description for 485410 below.

485410 School and Employee Bus Transportation
This industry comprises establishments primarily engaged in providing buses and other motor vehicles to transport pupils to and from school or employees to and from work.

- Operating local and suburban bus transit systems are classified in U.S. Industry, 485113 Bus and Other Motor Vehicle Transit Systems;
- Providing interurban and rural bus transportation are classified in Industry 485210, Interurban and Rural Bus Transportation; and
- Providing buses for charter are classified in Industry 485510, Charter Bus Industry.

4855 Charter Bus Industry

48551 Charter Bus Industry
See industry description for 485510 below.

485510 Charter Bus Industry
This industry comprises establishments primarily engaged in providing buses for charter. These establishments provide bus services to meet customers' road transportation needs and generally do not operate over fixed routes and on regular schedules.

- Providing scenic and local sightseeing transportation using buses are classified in Industry 487110, Scenic and Sightseeing Transportation, Land; and
- Providing interurban and rural bus transportation are classified in Industry 485210, Interurban and Rural Bus Transportation.

4859 Other Transit and Ground Passenger Transportation

Sector
48-49

Transportation and Warehousing

■ = Cross-References

US—United States industry only. CAN—United States and Canadian industries are comparable. When neither US nor CAN appears, Canadian, Mexican, and United States industries are comparable.

48599 Other Transit and Ground Passenger Transportation

This industry comprises establishments primarily engaged in providing other transit and ground passenger transportation—except urban transit systems, interurban and rural bus transportation, taxi services, school and employee bus transportation, charter bus services, and limousine services (except shuttle services). Shuttle services (except employee bus) and special needs transportation services are included in this industry. Shuttle services establishments generally travel within a metropolitan area and its adjacent nonurban areas on regular routes, on regular schedules and provide services between hotels, airports, or other destination points. Special needs transportation establishments provide passenger transportation to the infirm, elderly, or handicapped. These establishments may use specially equipped vehicles to provide passenger transportation.

- Providing school or employee bus transportation for the infirm, elderly, or handicapped are classified in Industry 48541, School and Employee Bus Transportation;
- Providing ambulance services for emergency and medical purposes are classified in Industry 62191, Ambulance Services;
- Operating urban transit systems are classified in Industry Group 4851, Urban Transit Systems;
- Providing interurban and rural bus transportation are classified in Industry 48521, Interurban and Rural Bus Transportation;
- Providing taxi services and/or limousine services (except shuttle services) are classified in Industry Group 4853; Taxi and Limousine Service; and
- Providing buses for charter are classified in Industry 48551, Charter Bus Industry.

485991 Special Needs Transportation [US]

This U.S. industry comprises establishments primarily engaged in providing special needs transportation (except to and from school or work) to the infirm, elderly, or handicapped. These establishments may use specially equipped vehicles to provide passenger transportation.

- Providing school or employee bus transportation for the infirm, elderly, or handicapped are classified in Industry 485410, School and Employee Bus Transportation; and
- Providing ambulance services for emergency and medical purposes are classified in Industry 62191, Ambulance Services.

485999 All Other Transit and Ground Passenger Transportation [US]

This U.S. industry comprises establishments primarily engaged in providing ground passenger transportation (except urban transit systems; interurban and rural bus transportation, taxi and/or limousine services (except shuttle services), school and employee bus transportation, charter bus services, and special needs transportation). Establishments primarily engaged in operating shuttle services and vanpools are included in this industry. Shuttle services establishments generally provide travel on regular routes and on regular schedules between hotels, airports, or other destination points.

- Providing urban transit systems are classified in Industry Group 4851, Urban Transit Systems;
- Providing interurban and rural bus transportation are classified in Industry 485210, Interurban and Rural Bus Transportation;
- Providing taxi and/or limousine services (except shuttle services) are classified in Industry Group 4853, Taxi and Limousine Service;
- Providing school and employee bus transportation (including for the infirm, elderly, or handicapped) are classified in Industry 485410, School and Employee Bus Transportation;
- Providing buses for charter are classified in Industry 485510, Charter Bus Industry;
- Providing special needs transportation (except to and from school or work) for the infirm, elderly, or handicapped are classified in Industry 485991, Special Needs Transportation; and
- Providing ambulance services for emergency and medical purposes are classified in Industry 621910, Ambulance Services.

486 PIPELINE TRANSPORTATION

Industries in the Pipeline Transportation subsector use transmission pipelines to transport products, such as crude oil, natural gas, refined petroleum products, and slurry. Industries are identified based on the products transported (i.e., pipeline transportation of crude oil, natural gas, refined petroleum products, and other products).

The Pipeline Transportation of Natural Gas industry includes the storage of natural gas because the storage is usually done by the pipeline establishment and because a pipeline is inherently a network in which all the nodes are interdependent.

4861 Pipeline Transportation of Crude Oil

48611 Pipeline Transportation of Crude Oil

See industry description for 486110 below.

Transportation and Warehousing

■ = Cross-References

486110 Pipeline Transportation of Crude Oil

This industry comprises establishments primarily engaged in the pipeline transportation of crude oil.

- Providing the pipeline transportation of natural gas are classified in Industry 486210, Pipeline Transportation of Natural Gas; and
- Providing the pipeline transportation of refined petroleum products are classified in Industry 486910, Pipeline Transportation of Refined Petroleum Products.

4862 Pipeline Transportation of Natural Gas

48621 Pipeline Transportation of Natural Gas

See industry description for 486210 below.

486210 Pipeline Transportation of Natural Gas

This industry comprises establishments primarily engaged in the pipeline transportation of natural gas from processing plants to local distribution systems.

- Establishments primarily engaged in providing natural gas to the end consumer are classified in Industry 221210, Natural Gas Distribution.

4869 Other Pipeline Transportation

This industry group comprises establishments primarily engaged in the pipeline transportation of products (except crude oil and natural gas).

48691 Pipeline Transportation of Refined Petroleum Products

See industry description for 486910 below.

486910 Pipeline Transportation of Refined Petroleum Products

This industry comprises establishments primarily engaged in the pipeline transportation of refined petroleum products.

48699 All Other Pipeline Transportation

See industry description for 486990 below.

486990 All Other Pipeline Transportation

This industry comprises establishments primarily engaged in the pipeline transportation of products except crude oil, natural gas, and refined petroleum products.

- Providing pipeline transportation of crude oil are classified in Industry 486110, Pipeline Transportation of Crude Oil;
- Providing pipeline transportation of natural gas are classified in Industry 486210, Pipeline Transportation of Natural Gas;
- Providing pipeline transportation of refined petroleum products are classified in Industry 486910, Pipeline Transportation of Refined Petroleum Products; and
- Providing pipeline transportation of water are classified in Industry 221310, Water Supply and Irrigation Systems.

▶487 SCENIC AND SIGHTSEEING TRANSPORTATION

Industries in the Scenic and Sightseeing Transportation subsector utilize transportation equipment to provide recreation and entertainment. These activities have a production process distinct from passenger transportation carried out for the purpose of other types of for-hire transportation. This process does not emphasize efficient transportation; in fact, such activities often use obsolete vehicles, such as steam trains, to provide some extra ambience. The activity is local in nature, usually involving a same-day return to the point of departure.

The Scenic and Sightseeing Transportation subsector is separated into three industries based on the mode: land, water, and other.

Activities that are recreational in nature and involve participation by the customer, such as whitewater rafting, are generally excluded from this subsector, unless they impose an impact on part of the

Sector 48-49

Transportation and Warehousing

■ = Cross-References

US—United States industry only. CAN—United States and Canadian industries are comparable. When neither US nor CAN appears, Canadian, Mexican, and United States industries are comparable.

494 Harris InfoSource

transportation system. Charter boat fishing, for example, is included in the Scenic and Sightseeing Transportation, Water industry.

4871 Scenic and Sightseeing Transportation, Land

48711 Scenic and Sightseeing Transportation, Land
See industry description for 487110 below.

487110 Scenic and Sightseeing Transportation, Land
This industry comprises establishments primarily engaged in providing scenic and sightseeing transportation on land, such as sightseeing buses and trolleys, steam train excursions, and horse-drawn sightseeing rides. The services provided are usually local and involve same-day return to place of origin.

- Operating aerial trams or aerial cable cars are classified in Industry 487990, Scenic and Sightseeing Transportation, Other;
- Providing sporting services, such as pack trains, are classified in Industry 713990, All Other Recreation and Amusement Industries;
- Providing inner-city and rural bus transportation are classified in Industry 485210, Interurban and Rural Bus Transportation;
- Providing buses for charter are classified in Industry 485510, Charter Bus Industry;
- Operating local and suburban passenger transit systems are classified in Industry 48511, Urban Transit Systems; and
- Providing passenger travel arrangements and tours are classified in Industry Group 5615, Travel Arrangement and Reservation Services.

4872 Scenic and Sightseeing Transportation, Water

48721 Scenic and Sightseeing Transportation, Water
See industry description for 487210 below.

487210 Scenic and Sightseeing Transportation, Water
This industry comprises establishments primarily engaged in providing scenic and sightseeing transportation on water. The services provided are usually local and involve same-day return to place of origin.

- Providing recreation services, such as fishing guides, whitewater rafting, parasailing, and water skiing are classified in Industry 713990, All Other Amusement and Recreation Industries;
- Providing water taxi services are classified in Industry 48321, Inland Water Transportation;
- Providing water transportation of passengers are classified in Subsector 483, Water Transportation;
- Operating floating casinos (i.e., gambling cruises or riverboat casinos) are classified in Industry 713210, Casinos (except Casino Hotels); and
- Providing boat rental without operators are classified in U.S. Industry 532292, Recreational Goods Rental.

4879 Scenic and Sightseeing Transportation, Other

48799 Scenic and Sightseeing Transportation, Other
See industry description for 487990 below.

487990 Scenic and Sightseeing Transportation, Other
This industry comprises establishments primarily engaged in providing scenic and sightseeing transportation (except on land and water). The services provided are usually local and involve same-day return to place of departure.

- Providing recreational activities, such as hang gliding, are classified in Industry 713990, All Other Amusement and Recreation Industries; and
- Providing scheduled or nonscheduled air transportation of passengers or specialty flying services are classified in Subsector 481, Air Transportation.

➡ 488 SUPPORT ACTIVITIES FOR TRANSPORTATION
Industries in the Support Activities for Transportation subsector provide services that support transportation. These services may be provided to transportation carrier establishments or to the general public. This subsector includes a wide array of establishments, including air traffic control services, marine cargo handling, and motor vehicle towing.

Sector
48-49

**Transportation
and Warehousing**

■ = Cross-References

US—United States industry only. CAN—United States and Canadian industries are comparable. When neither US nor CAN appears, Canadian, Mexican, and United States industries are comparable.

The Support Activities for Transportation subsector includes services to transportation but is separated by type of mode serviced. The Support Activities for Rail Transportation industry includes services to the rail industry (e.g., railroad switching and terminal establishments).

Ship repair and maintenance not done in a shipyard are included in Other Support Activities for Water Transportation. An example would be a floating dry-dock services in a harbor.

Excluded from this subsector are establishments primarily engaged in providing factory conversion and overhaul of transportation equipment, which are classified in Subsector 336, Transportation Equipment Manufacturing. Also, establishments primarily engaged in providing rental and leasing of transportation equipment without operator are classified in Subsector 532, Rental and Leasing Services.

4881 Support Activities for Air Transportation

This industry group comprises establishments primarily engaged in providing services to the air transportation industry. These services include airport operation, servicing, repairing (except factory conversion and overhaul of aircraft), maintaining and storing aircraft, and ferrying aircraft.

48811 Airport Operations

This industry comprises establishments primarily engaged in (1) operating international, national, or civil airports or public flying field or (2) supporting airport operations (except special food services contractors), such as rental of hangar space, air traffic control services, baggage handling services, and cargo handling services.

- Providing factory conversion, overhaul, and rebuilding of aircraft are classified in Industry 33641, Aerospace Product and Parts Manufacturing;
- Wholesaling fuel at airports are classified in Industry 42272, Petroleum and Petroleum Products Wholesalers (except Bulk Stations and Terminals);
- Providing airport janitorial services are classified in Industry 56172, Janitorial Services; and
- Providing food services at airports on a contractual arrangement (i.e., food service contractors) are classified in Industry 72231, Food Service Contractors.

488111 Air Traffic Control CAN

This U.S. industry comprises establishments primarily engaged in providing air traffic control services to regulate the flow of air traffic.

488119 Other Airport Operations CAN

This U.S. industry comprises establishments primarily engaged in (1) operating international, national, or civil airports, or public flying field or (2) supporting airport operations, such as rental of hangar space, and providing baggage handling and/or cargo handling services.

- Providing air traffic control services are classified in U.S. Industry 488111, Air Traffic Control;
- Providing factory conversion, overhaul, and rebuilding of aircraft are classified in Industry 33641, Aerospace Product and Parts Manufacturing;
- Wholesaling fuel at airports are classified in Industry 422720, Petroleum and Petroleum Products Wholesalers (except Bulk Stations and Terminals);
- Providing airport janitorial services are classified in Industry 561720, Janitorial Services; and
- Providing food services at airports on a contractual arrangement are classified in Industry 722310, Food Service Contractors.

48819 Other Support Activities for Air Transportation

See industry description for 488190 below.

488190 Other Support Activities for Air Transportation

This industry comprises establishments primarily engaged in providing specialized services for air transportation (except air traffic control and other airport operations).

- Wholesaling fuel at airports are classified in Industry 422720, Petroleum and Petroleum Products Wholesalers (except Bulk Stations and Terminals);
- Providing aircraft janitorial services are classified in Industry 561720, Janitorial Services;
- Providing air traffic control services are classified in U.S. Industry 488111, Air Traffic Control;

Sector
48-49

**Transportation
and Warehousing**

■ = Cross-References

US—United States industry only. CAN—United States and Canadian industries are comparable. When neither US nor CAN appears, Canadian, Mexican, and United States industries are comparable.

496

Harris InfoSource

■ Providing airport operations (except air traffic control) are classified in U.S. Industry 488119, Other Airport Operations (except Air Traffic Control);
■ Providing factory conversion, overhaul, and rebuilding of aircraft are classified in Industry 33641, Aerospace Product and Parts Manufacturing; and
■ Providing food services to airlines on a contractual arrangement are classified in Industry 722310, Food Service Contractors.

4882 Support Activities for Rail Transportation

48821 Support Activities for Rail Transportation
See industry description for 488210 below.

488210 Support Activities for Rail Transportation
This industry comprises establishments primarily engaged in providing specialized services for railroad transportation including servicing, routine repairing (except factory conversion, overhaul or rebuilding of rolling stock), and maintaining rail cars; loading and unloading rail cars; and operating independent terminals.

■ Providing railroad car rental are classified in U.S. Industry 532411, Commercial Air, Rail, and Water Transportation Equipment Rental and Leasing;
■ Factory conversion, overhaul, or rebuilding of railroad rolling stock are classified in Industry 336510, Railroad Rolling Stock Manufacturing;
■ Providing rail car janitorial services are classified in Industry 561720, Janitorial Services; and
■ Providing dredging services are classified in Industry 234990, All Other Heavy Construction.

4883 Support Activities for Water Transportation

48831 Port and Harbor Operations
See industry description for 488310 below.

488310 Port and Harbor Operations
This industry comprises establishments primarily engaged in operating ports, harbors (including docking and pier facilities), or canals.

■ Providing stevedoring and other marine cargo handling services are classified in Industry 488320, Marine Cargo Handling;
■ Providing navigational services to shipping are classified in Industry 488330, Navigational Services to Shipping; and
■ Operating docking and/or storage facilities and commonly known as marinas are classified in Industry 713930, Marinas.

48832 Marine Cargo Handling
See industry description for 488320 below.

488320 Marine Cargo Handling
This industry comprises establishments primarily engaged in providing stevedoring and other marine cargo handling services (except warehousing).

■ Preparing freight for transportation are classified in U.S. Industry 488991, Packing and Crating;
■ Operating general merchandise, refrigerated, or other warehousing and storage facilities are classified in Subsector 493, Warehousing and Storage; and
■ Operating docking and pier facilities are classified in Industry 488310, Port and Harbor Operations.

48833 Navigational Services to Shipping
See industry description for 488330 below.

488330 Navigational Services to Shipping
This industry comprises establishments primarily engaged in providing navigational services to shipping. Marine salvage establishments are included in this industry.

■ Providing water transportation of barges (except coastal or Great Lake barge transportation services) are classified in U.S. Industry 483211, Inland Water Freight Transportation; and
■ Providing coastal and/or Great Lakes barge transportation services are classified in U.S. Industry 483113, Coastal and Great Lakes Freight Transportation.

Sector

48-49

Transportation and Warehousing

■ = Cross-References

US—United States industry only. CAN—United States and Canadian industries are comparable. When neither US nor CAN appears, Canadian, Mexican, and United States industries are comparable.

www.harrisinfo.com

497

48839 Other Support Activities for Water Transportation
See industry description for 488390 below.

488390 Other Support Activities for Water Transportation
This industry comprises establishments primarily engaged in providing services to water transportation (except port and harbor operations; marine cargo handling services; and navigational services to shipping).

- Ship painting are classified in Industry 235210, Painting and Wall Covering Contractors;
- Providing ship janitorial services are classified in Industry 561720, Janitorial Services;
- Operating port, harbor, or canal facilities are classified in Industry 488310, Port and Harbor Operations;
- Providing stevedoring and other marine cargo handling services are classified in Industry 488320, Marine Cargo Handling;
- Providing navigational services to shipping are classified in Industry 488330, Navigational Services to Shipping; and
- Providing ship overhauling or repairs in a shipyard are classified in U.S. Industry 336611, Ship Building and Repairing.

4884 Support Activities for Road Transportation

48841 Motor Vehicle Towing
See industry description for 488410 below.

488410 Motor Vehicle Towing
This industry comprises establishments primarily engaged in towing light or heavy motor vehicles, both local and long distance. These establishments may provide incidental services, such as storage and emergency road repair services.

- Operating gasoline stations are classified in Industry Group 4471, Gasoline Stations;
- Providing automotive repair and maintenance are classified in Industry Group 8111, Automotive Repair and Maintenance; and
- Both retailing automotive parts and accessories, and repairing automobiles and known as automotive supply stores are classified Industry 441310, Automotive Parts and Accessories Stores.

48849 Other Support Activities for Road Transportation
See industry description for 488490 below.

488490 Other Support Activities for Road Transportation
This industry comprises establishments primarily engaged in providing services (except motor vehicle towing) to road network users.

- Providing automotive repair and maintenance are classified in Industry Group 8111, Automotive Repair and Maintenance;
- Providing towing services to motor vehicles are classified in Industry 488410, Motor Vehicle Towing;
- Providing a network for busing in combination with providing terminal services are classified in Industry 485210, Interurban and Rural Bus Transportation; and
- Providing a network for trucking in combination with providing terminal services are classified in Subsector 484, Truck Transportation.

4885 Freight Transportation Arrangement

48851 Freight Transportation Arrangement
See industry description for 488510 below.

488510 Freight Transportation Arrangement
This industry comprises establishments primarily engaged in arranging transportation of freight between shippers and carriers. These establishments are usually known as freight forwarders, marine shipping agents, or customs brokers and offer a combination of services spanning transportation modes.

- Establishments primarily engaged in tariff and freight rate consulting services are classified in U.S. Industry 541614, Process, Physical Distribution, and Logistics Consulting Services.

4889 Other Support Activities for Transportation

Sector 48-49

Transportation and Warehousing

■ = Cross-References

US—United States industry only. CAN—United States and Canadian industries are comparable. When neither US nor CAN appears, Canadian, Mexican, and United States industries are comparable.

498

Harris InfoSource

48899 Other Support Activities for Transportation

This industry comprises establishments primarily engaged in providing support activities to transportation (except for air transportation, rail transportation, water transportation, road transportation, and freight transportation arrangement).

- Providing support activities for air transportation are classified in Industry Group 4881, Support Activities for Air Transportation;
- Providing support activities for rail transportation are classified in Industry Group 4882, Support Activities for Rail Transportation;
- Providing support activities for water transportation are classified in Industry Group 4883, Support Activities for Water Transportation;
- Providing support activities for road transportation are classified in Industry Group 4884, Support Activities for Road Transportation;
- Arranging transportation of freight between shippers and carriers are classified in Industry 48851, Freight Transportation Arrangement;
- Providing tariff and freight rate consulting services are classified in Industry 54161, Management Consulting Services;
- Operating stockyards for fattening livestock are classified in Subsector 112, Animal Production; and
- Providing packaging and labeling services are classified in Industry 56191, Packaging and Labeling Services.

488991 Packing and Crating ᵁˢ

This U.S. industry comprises establishments primarily engaged in packing, crating, and otherwise preparing goods for transportation.

- Establishments primarily engaged in providing packaging and labeling services are classified in Industry 561910, Packaging and Labeling Services.

488999 All Other Support Activities for Transportation ᵁˢ

This U.S. industry comprises establishments primarily engaged in providing support activities to transportation (except for air transportation, rail transportation, water transportation, road transportation, freight transportation arrangement, and packing and crating).

- Operating stockyards for fattening livestock are classified in Subsector 112, Animal Production;
- Providing tariff and freight rate consulting services are classified in U.S. Industry 541614, Process, Physical Distribution, and Logistics Consulting Services;
- Providing packing and crating services for transportation are classified in U.S. Industry 488991, Packing and Crating;
- Providing support activities for air transportation are classified in Industry Group 4881, Support Activities for Air Transportation;
- Providing support activities for rail transportation are classified in Industry 488210, Support Activities for Rail Transportation;
- Providing support activities for water transportation are classified in Industry Group 4883, Support Activities for Water Transportation;
- Providing support activities for road transportation are classified in Industry Group 4884, Support Activities for Road Transportation; and
- Arranging transportation of freight between shippers and carriers are classified in Industry 488510, Freight Transportation Arrangement.

➡491 POSTAL SERVICE

The Postal Service subsector includes the activities of the National Post Office and its subcontractors in delivering letters and small parcels, normally without pick-up at the senders' location. These articles can be described as those that can be handled by one person without using special equipment. This allows the collection, pick up, and delivery operations to be done with limited labor costs and minimal equipment. Sorting and transportation activities, where necessary, are generally mechanized. The restriction to small parcels distinguishes these establishments from those in the transportation industries.

The traditional activity of the National Postal Service is described in this subsector. Subcontractors include rural Post Offices on contract to the Postal Service.

Bulk transportation of mail on contract to the Postal Service is not included here, because it is usually done by transportation establishments that carry other customers' cargo as well.

4911 Postal Service

49111 Postal Service

See industry description for 491110 below.

Sector
48-49

Transportation
and Warehousing

■ = Cross-References

US—United States industry only. CAN—United States and Canadian industries are comparable. When neither US nor CAN appears, Canadian, Mexican, and United States industries are comparable.

www.harrisinfo.com

499

491110 Postal Service

This industry comprises establishments primarily engaged in operating the National Postal Service. Establishments primarily engaged in performing one or more postal service, such as sorting, routing, and/or delivery, on a contract basis (except the bulk transportation of mail) are included in this industry.

- Providing bulk transportation of mail on a contract basis to and from postal service establishments are classified in Industry Group 4841, General Freight Trucking;
- Providing courier services are classified in Industry 492110, Couriers;
- Providing mailbox services along with other business services are classified in U.S. Industry 561431, Private Mail Centers; and
- Providing local messenger and delivery services are classified in Industry 492210, Local Messengers and Local Delivery.

▶492 COURIERS AND MESSENGERS

Industries in the Couriers and Messengers subsector provide inner-city and/or local delivery of parcels. These articles can be described as those that may be handled by one person without using special equipment. This allows the collection, pick-up, and delivery operations to be done with limited labor costs and minimal equipment. Sorting and transportation activities, where necessary, are generally mechanized. The restriction to small parcels partly distinguishes these establishments from those in the transportation industries. The complete network of courier services establishments also distinguishes these transportation services from local messenger and delivery establishments in this subsector. This includes the establishments that perform inner-city transportation as well as establishments that, under contract to them, perform local pick-up and delivery. Messengers, which usually deliver within a metropolitan or single urban area, may use bicycle, foot, small truck, or van.

4921 Couriers

49211 Couriers
See industry description for 492110 below.

492110 Couriers
This industry comprises establishments primarily engaged in providing air, surface, or combined courier delivery services of parcels generally between metropolitan areas or urban centers. The establishments of this industry form a network including courier local pick-up and delivery to serve their customers' needs.

- Providing messenger and delivery services within a metropolitan area or within an urban center are classified in Industry 492210, Local Messengers and Local Delivery; and
- Providing the truck transportation of palletized general freight are classified in Industry Group 4841, General Freight Trucking.

4922 Local Messengers and Local Delivery

49221 Local Messengers and Local Delivery
See industry description for 492210 below.

492210 Local Messengers and Local Delivery
This industry comprises establishments primarily engaged in providing local messenger and delivery services of small items within a single metropolitan or within an urban center. These establishments generally provide point-to-point pickup and delivery and do not operate as part of an inner-city courier network.

- Providing local letter and parcel delivery services as part of an inner-city courier network are classified in Industry 492110, Couriers;
- Operating the National Postal Service or providing postal services on a contract basis (except the bulk transportation of mail) are classified in Industry 491110, Postal Service; and
- Providing the bulk transportation of mail on a contract basis to and from Postal Service establishments are classified in Industry Group 4841, General Freight Trucking.

Sector
48-49

Transportation and Warehousing

■ = Cross-References

US—United States industry only. CAN—United States and Canadian industries are comparable. When neither US nor CAN appears, Canadian, Mexican, and United States industries are comparable.

►493 WAREHOUSING AND STORAGE

Industries in the Warehousing and Storage subsector are primarily engaged in operating warehousing and storage facilities for general merchandise, refrigerated goods, and other warehouse products. These establishments provide facilities to store goods. They do not sell the goods they handle. These establishments take responsibility for storing the goods and keeping them secure. They may also provide a range of services, often referred to as logistics services, related to the distribution of goods. Logistics services can include labeling, breaking bulk, inventory control and management, light assembly, order entry and fulfillment, packaging, pick and pack, price marking and ticketing, and transportation arrangement. However, establishments in this industry group always provide warehousing or storage services in addition to any logistic services. Furthermore, the warehousing or storage of goods must be more than incidental to the performance of services, such as price marking.

Bonded warehousing and storage services and warehouses located in free trade zones are included in the industries of this subsector.

4931 Warehousing and Storage

49311 General Warehousing and Storage
See industry description for 493110 below.

493110 General Warehousing and Storage
This industry comprises establishments primarily engaged in operating merchandise warehousing and storage facilities. These establishments generally handle goods in containers, such as boxes, barrels, and/or drums, using equipment, such as forklifts, pallets, and racks. They are not specialized in handling bulk products of any particular type, size, or quantity of goods or products.

- Renting or leasing space for self storage are classified in Industry 531130, Lessors of Miniwarehouses and Self-storage Units; and
- Selling in combination with handling and/or distributing goods to other wholesale or retail establishments are classified in Sector 42, Wholesale Trade.

49312 Refrigerated Warehousing and Storage
See industry description for 493120 below.

493120 Refrigerated Warehousing and Storage
This industry comprises establishments primarily engaged in operating refrigerated warehousing and storage facilities. Establishments primarily engaged in the storage of furs for the trade are included in this industry. The services provided by these establishments include blast freezing, tempering, and modified atmosphere storage services.

- Establishments primarily engaged in storing furs (except for the trade) and garments are classified in Industry 812320, Dry-cleaning and Laundry Services (except Coin-operated).

49313 Farm Product Warehousing and Storage
See industry description for 493130 below.

493130 Farm Product Warehousing and Storage
This industry comprises establishments primarily engaged in operating bulk farm product warehousing and storage facilities (except refrigerated). Grain elevators primarily engaged in storage are included in this industry.

- Operating refrigerated warehousing and storage facilities are classified in Industry 493120, Refrigerated Warehousing and Storage; and
- Storing grains and field beans (i.e., grain elevators) as an incidental activity to sales are classified in Industry 42251, Grain and Field Bean Wholesalers.

49319 Other Warehousing and Storage
See industry description for 493190 below.

Sector 48-49

Transportation and Warehousing

■ = Cross-References

US—United States industry only. CAN—United States and Canadian industries are comparable. When neither US nor CAN appears, Canadian, Mexican, and United States industries are comparable.

www.harrisinfo.com

501

493190 Other Warehousing and Storage

This industry comprises establishments primarily engaged in operating warehousing and storage facilities (except general merchandise, refrigerated, and farm product warehousing and storage).

- Renting or leasing space for self storage are classified in Industry 531130, Lessors of Miniwarehouses and Self-storage Units;
- Storing hazardous materials for treatment and disposal are classified in U.S. Industry 562211, Hazardous Waste Treatment and Disposal;

- Operating general warehousing and storage facilities are classified in Industry 493110, General Warehousing and Storage;
- Operating refrigerated warehousing and storage facilities are classified in Industry 493120, Refrigerated Warehousing and Storage; and
- Operating farm product warehousing and storage facilities are classified in Industry 493130, Farm Product Warehousing and Storage.

Sector

48-49

Transportation and Warehousing

■ = Cross-References

US—United States industry only. CAN—United States and Canadian industries are comparable. When neither US nor CAN appears, Canadian, Mexican, and United States industries are comparable.

502

Harris InfoSource

Sector 5 | Information

The Sector as a Whole

THE INFORMATION sector comprises establishments engaged in the following processes: (a) producing and distributing information and cultural products, (b) providing the means to transmit or distribute these products as well as data or communications, and (c) processing data.

The main components of this sector are the publishing industries, including software publishing, the motion picture and sound recording industries, the broadcasting and telecommunications industries, and the information services and data processing industries.

The expressions "information age" and "global information economy" are used with considerable frequency today. The general idea of an "information economy" includes both the notion of industries primarily producing, processing, and distributing information, as well as the idea that every industry is using available information and information technology to reorganize and make themselves more productive.

For the purpose of developing NAICS, it is the transformation of information into a commodity that is produced and distributed by a number of growing industries that is at issue. The Information sector groups three types of establishments: (1) those engaged in producing and distributing information and cultural products; (2) those that provide the means to transmit or distribute these products as well as data or communications; and (3) those that process data. Cultural products are those that directly express attitudes, opinions, ideas, values, and artistic creativity; provide entertainment; or offer information and analysis concerning the past and present. Included in this definition are popular, mass-produced, products as well as cultural products that normally have a more limited audience, such as poetry books, literary magazines, or classical records. These activities were formerly classified throughout the existing national classifications. Traditional publishing is in manufacturing; broadcasting in communications; software production in business services; film production in amusement services; and so forth.

Discover the highlights of this new sector on page 17.

The unique characteristics of information and cultural products, and of the processes involved in their production and distribution, distinguish the Information sector from the goods-producing and service-producing sectors. Some of these characteristics are:

1. Unlike traditional goods, an "information or cultural product," such as a newspaper online or television program, does not necessarily have tangible qualities, nor is it necessarily associated with a particular form. A movie can be shown at a movie theater, on a television broadcast, through video-on-demand or rented at a local video store. A sound recording can be aired on radio, embedded in multimedia products, or sold at a record store.

2. Unlike traditional services, the delivery of these products does not require direct contact between the supplier and the consumer.

3. The value of these products to the consumer lies in their informational, educational, cultural, or entertainment content, not in the format in which they are distributed. Most of these products are protected from unlawful reproduction by copyright laws.

4. The intangible property aspect of information and cultural products makes the processes involved in their production and distribution very different from goods and services. Only those possessing the rights to these works are authorized to reproduce, alter, improve, and distribute them. Acquiring and using these rights

Sector 5
Information

often involves significant costs. In addition, technology is revolutionizing the distribution of these products. It is possible to distribute them in a physical form, via broadcast, or online.

5. Distributors of information and cultural products can easily add value to the products they distribute. For instance, broadcasters add advertising not contained in the original product. This capacity means that unlike traditional distributors, they derive revenue not from sale of the distributed product to the final consumer, but from those who pay for the privilege of adding information to the original product. Similarly, a database publisher can acquire the rights to thousands of previously published newspaper and periodical articles and add new value by providing search and software and organizing the information in a way that facilitates research and retrieval. These products often command a much higher price than the original information.

The distribution modes for information commodities may either eliminate the necessity for traditional manufacture, or reverse the conventional order of manufacture-distribute: A newspaper distributed online, for example, can be printed locally or by the final consumer. Similarly, it is anticipated that packaged software, which today is mainly bought through the traditional retail channels, will soon be available mainly online. The NAICS Information sector is designed to make such economic changes transparent as they occur, or to facilitate designing surveys that will monitor the new phenomena and provide data to analyze the changes.

Many of the industries in the NAICS Information sector are engaged in producing products protected by copyright law, or in distributing them (other than distribution by traditional wholesale and retail methods). Examples are traditional publishing industries, software and database publishing industries, and film and sound industries. Broadcasting and telecommunications industries and information providers and processors are also included in the Information sector, because their technologies are so closely linked to other industries in the Information sector.

▶511 PUBLISHING INDUSTRIES

Industries in the Publishing Industries subsector group establishments engaged in the publishing of newspapers, magazines, other periodicals, and books, as well as database and software publishing. In general, these establishments, which are known as publishers, issue copies of works for which they usually possess copyright. Works may be in one or more formats including traditional print form, CD-ROM, or online. Publishers may publish works originally created by others for which they have obtained the rights and/or works that they have created in-house. Software publishing is included here because the activity, creation of a copyrighted product and bringing it to market, is equivalent to the creation process for other types of intellectual products.

In NAICS, publishing, the reporting, writing, editing, and other processes that are required to create an edition of a newspaper, is treated as a major economic activity in its own right, rather than as a subsidiary activity to a manufacturing activity, printing. Thus, publishing is classified in the Information sector; whereas, printing remains in the NAICS Manufacturing sector. In part, the NAICS classification reflects the fact that publishing increasingly takes place in establishments that are physically separate from the associated printing establishments. More crucially, the NAICS classification of book and newspaper publishing is intended to portray their roles in a modern economy, in which they do not resemble manufacturing activities.

Music publishers are not included in the Publishing Industries subsector, but are included in the Motion Picture and Sound Recording Industries subsector. Reproduction of prepackaged software is treated in NAICS as a manufacturing activity; online distribution of software products is in the Information sector, and custom design of software to client specifications is included in the Professional, Scientific, and Technical Services sector. These distinctions arise because of the different ways that software is created, reproduced, and distributed.

The Information sector does not include products, such as manifold business forms. Information is not the essential component of these items. Establishments producing these items are included in Subsector 323, Printing and Related Support Activities.

Sector **51**

Information

■ = Cross-References

US—United States industry only. CAN—United States and Canadian industries are comparable. When neither US nor CAN appears, Canadian, Mexican, and United States industries are comparable.

504 Harris InfoSource

5111 Newspaper, Periodical, Book, and Database Publishers

This industry group comprises establishments primarily engaged in publishing newspapers, magazines, other periodicals, books, databases, and other works, such as calendars, greeting cards, and maps. These works are characterized by the intellectual creativity required in their development and are usually protected by copyright. Publishers distribute or arrange for the distribution of these works.

Publishing establishments may create the works in-house, contract for, purchase, or compile works that were originally created by others. These works may be published in one or more formats, such as print and/or electronic form, including online. Establishments in this industry may print, reproduce, or offer direct access to the works themselves or may arrange with others to carry out such functions.

- Establishments that both print and publish may fill excess capacity with commercial or job printing. However, the publishing activity is still considered to be the primary activity of these establishments.

51111 Newspaper Publishers
See industry description for 511110 below.

511110 Newspaper Publishers
This industry comprises establishments known as newspaper publishers. Establishments in this industry carry out operations necessary for producing and distributing newspapers, including gathering news; writing news columns, feature stories, and editorials; and selling and preparing advertisements. These establishments may publish newspapers in print or electronic form.

- Establishments primarily engaged in printing newspapers without publishing are classified in Industry 32311, Printing;
- Establishments, such as trade associations, schools and universities, and social welfare organizations that publish newsletters for distribution to their membership, but that are not commonly known as newspaper publishers, are classified according to their primary activity designation;
- Establishments primarily engaged in supplying the news media with information, such as news, reports, and pictures, are classified in Industry 514110, News Syndicates; and
- Establishments of independent representatives primarily engaged in selling advertising space are classified in Industry 541840, Media Representatives.

51112 Periodical Publishers
See industry description for 511120 below.

511120 Periodical Publishers
This industry comprises establishments known as magazine or periodical publishers. These establishments carry out the operations necessary for producing and distributing magazines and other periodicals, such as gathering, writing, and editing articles, and selling and preparing advertisements. These establishments may publish magazines and other periodicals in print or electronic form.

- Establishments primarily engaged in printing periodicals without publishing are classified in Industry 32311, Printing;
- Establishments, such as trade associations, schools and universities, and social welfare organizations, that publish magazines and periodicals for distribution to their membership, but that are not commonly known as periodical publishers, are classified according to their primary activity designation;
- Establishments primarily engaged in publishing databases and directories are classified in Industry 511140, Database and Directory Publishers; and
- Establishments of independent representatives primarily engaged in selling advertising space are classified in Industry 541840, Media Representatives.

51113 Book Publishers
See industry description for 511130 below.

511130 Book Publishers
This industry comprises establishments known as book publishers. Establishments in this industry carry out design, editing, and marketing activities necessary for producing and distributing books. These establishments may publish books in print, electronic, or audio form.

- Establishments primarily engaged in printing books without publishing are classified in Industry 32311, Printing;
- Establishments known as music publishers are classified in Industry 512230, Music Publishers;
- Establishments, such as trade associations, schools and universities, and social welfare organizations, that publish books for distribution to their membership, that are not commonly known as book publishers, are classified according to their primary activity designation; and
- Book clubs primarily engaged in direct sales activities without publishing are classified in Industry 454390, Other Direct Selling Establishments.

Discover the highlights of this new sector on page 17.

Sector 51

Information

■ = Cross-References

US—United States industry only. CAN—United States and Canadian industries are comparable. When neither US nor CAN appears, Canadian, Mexican, and United States industries are comparable.

51114 Database and Directory Publishers
See industry description for 511140 below.

511140 Database and Directory Publishers
This industry comprises establishments primarily engaged in publishing compilations and collections of information or facts that are logically organized to facilitate their use. These collections may be published in print or electronic form. Electronic versions may be provided directly to customers by the establishment or offered through online services or third-party vendors.

- Printing without publishing databases and directories are classified in Industry 32311, Printing;
- Publishing encyclopedias are classified in Industry 511130, Book Publishers;
- Direct access to databases developed by others are classified in U.S. Industry 514191, online Information Services; and
- Publishing computer software are classified in Industry 511210, Software Publishers.

51119 Other Publishers
This industry comprises establishments known as publishers (except newspaper, magazine, book, directory, database, and music publishers). These establishments may publish works in print or electronic form.

- Establishments known as newspaper publishers are classified in Industry 51111, Newspaper Publishers;
- Establishments known as magazine and other periodical publishers are classified in Industry 51112, Periodical Publishers;
- Establishments known as book publishers are classified in Industry 51113, Book Publishers;
- Establishments primarily engaged in directory and database publishing are classified in Industry 51114, Database and Directory Publishers;
- Establishments known as music publishers are classified in Industry 51223, Music Publishers; and
- Establishments primarily engaged in manufacturing manifold business forms are classified in Industry 32311, Printing.

511191 Greeting Card Publishers [US]
This U.S. industry comprises establishments primarily engaged in publishing greeting cards.

- Establishments primarily engaged in printing greeting cards without publishing are classified in Industry 32311, Printing.

511199 All Other Publishers [US]
This U.S. industry comprises establishments generally known as publishers (except newspaper, magazine, book, directory, database, music, and greeting card publishers). These establishment may publish works in print or electronic form.

- Establishments known as newspaper publishers are classified in Industry 511110, Newspaper Publishers;
- Establishments known as magazine or other periodical publishers are classified in Industry 511120, Magazine Publishers;
- Establishments known as book publishers are classified in Industry 511130, Book Publishers;
- Establishments primarily engaged in directory and database publishing are classified Industry 511140, Database and Directory Publishers;
- Establishments primarily engaged in greeting card publishing are classified in U.S. Industry 511191, Greeting Card Publishers;
- Establishments known as music publishers are classified in Industry 512230, Music Publishers;
- Establishments primarily engaged in manufacturing manifold business forms are classified in U.S. Industry 323116, Manifold Business Forms Printing; and
- Establishments primarily engaged in manufacturing day schedulers are classified in U.S. Industry 323118, Blankbooks, Looseleaf Binders and Devices Manufacturing.

5112 Software Publishers

51121 Software Publishers
See industry description for 511210 below.

511210 Software Publishers
This industry comprises establishments primarily engaged in computer software publishing or publishing and reproduction. Establishments in this industry carry out operations necessary for producing and distributing computer software, such as designing, providing documentation, assisting in installation, and providing support services to software purchasers. These establishments may design, develop, and publish, or publish only.

- Reselling packaged software are classified in Sector 42, Wholesale Trade or Sector 44-45, Retail Trade;
- Designing software to meet the needs of specific users are classified in U.S. Industry 541511, Custom Computer Programming Services; and
- Mass duplication of software are classified in U.S. Industry 334611, Software Reproducing.

Sector **51**

Information

■ = Cross-References

US—United States industry only. CAN—United States and Canadian industries are comparable. When neither US nor CAN appears, Canadian, Mexican, and United States industries are comparable.

506   Harris InfoSource

➡️512 MOTION PICTURE AND SOUND RECORDING INDUSTRIES

Industries in the Motion Picture and Sound Recording Industries subsector group establishments involved in the production and distribution of motion pictures and sound recordings. While producers and distributors of motion pictures and sound recordings issue works for sale as traditional publishers do, the processes are sufficiently different to warrant placing establishments engaged in these activities in a separate subsector. Production is typically a complex process that involves several distinct types of establishments that are engaged in activities, such as contracting with performers, creating the film or sound content, and providing technical postproduction services. Film distribution is often to exhibitors, such as theaters and broadcasters, rather than through the wholesale and retail distribution chain. When the product is in a mass-produced form, NAICS treats production and distribution as the major economic activity as it does in the Publishing Industries subsector, rather than as a subsidiary activity to the manufacture of such products.

This subsector does not include establishments primarily engaged in the wholesale distribution of video cassettes and sound recordings, such as compact discs and audio tapes; these establishments are included in the Wholesale Trade sector. Reproduction of video cassettes and sound recordings that is carried out separately from establishments engaged in production and distribution is treated in NAICS as a manufacturing activity.

Discover the highlights of this new sector on page 17.

5121 Motion Picture and Video Industries

This industry group comprises establishments primarily engaged in the production and/or distribution of motion pictures, videos, television programs, or commercials; in the exhibition of motion pictures; or in the provision of postproduction and related services.

51211 Motion Picture and Video Production

See industry description for 512110 below.

512110 Motion Picture and Video Production

This industry comprises establishments primarily engaged in producing, or producing and distributing motion pictures, videos, television programs, or television and video commercials.

- Producing motion pictures and videos on contract as independent producers are classified in Industry 711510, Independent Artists, Writers, and Performers;
- Providing teleproduction and other postproduction services are classified in U.S. Industry 512191, Teleproduction and Other Postproduction Services;
- Providing video taping of weddings, special events, and/or business inventories are classified in Industry 54192, Photographic Services;
- Providing motion picture laboratory services are classified in U.S. Industry 512199, Other Motion Picture and Video Industries;
- Providing mass duplication and packaging of video tapes are classified in U.S. Industry 334612, Prerecorded Compact Disc (except Software), Tape, and Record Reproducing; and
- Acquiring distribution rights and distributing motion pictures and videos are classified in Industry 512120, Motion Picture and Video Distribution.

51212 Motion Picture and Video Distribution

See industry description for 512120 below.

512120 Motion Picture and Video Distribution

This industry comprises establishments primarily engaged in acquiring distribution rights and distributing film and video productions to motion picture theaters, television networks and stations, and exhibitors.

- Producing and distributing motion pictures and videos are classified in Industry 512110, Motion Picture and Video Production;
- Wholesaling video cassette tapes and discs are classified in Industry 421690, Other Electronic Parts and Equipment Wholesalers;
- Providing mass duplication and packaging of video tapes are classified in U.S. Industry 334612, Prerecorded Compact Disc (except Software), Tape, and Record Reproducing;
- Providing motion picture footage (via film libraries) to producers are classified in U.S. Industry 512199, Other Motion Picture and Video Industries;
- Renting video tapes and discs to the general public are classified in Industry 532230, Video Tape and Disc Rental; and
- Selling video cassettes and discs to the general public are classified in Industry 451220, Prerecorded Tape, Compact Disc and Record Stores.

Sector **51**

Information

■ = Cross-References

US—United States industry only. CAN—United States and Canadian industries are comparable. When neither US nor CAN appears, Canadian, Mexican, and United States industries are comparable.

51213 Motion Picture and Video Exhibition

This industry comprises establishments primarily engaged in operating motion picture theaters and/or exhibiting motion pictures or videos at film festivals, and so forth.

512131 Motion Picture Theaters (except Drive-ins)ᵁˢ

This U.S. industry comprises establishments primarily engaged in operating motion picture theaters (except drive-ins) and/or exhibiting motion pictures or videos at film festivals, and so forth.

512132 Drive-in Motion Picture Theaters ᵁˢ

This U.S. industry comprises establishments primarily engaged in operating drive-in motion picture theaters.

51219 Postproduction Services and Other Motion Picture and Video Industries

This industry comprises establishments primarily engaged in providing postproduction services and other services to the motion picture industry, including specialized motion picture or video postproduction services, such as editing, film/tape transfers, subtitling, credits, closed captioning, and computer-produced graphics, animation and special effects, as well as developing and processing motion picture film.

- Mass duplicating video tapes and film are classified in Industry 33461, Manufacturing and Reproducing Magnetic and Optical Media;
- Providing audio services for film, television, and video productions are classified in Industry 51224, Sound Recording Studios;
- Renting wardrobes and costumes for motion picture production are classified in Industry 53222, Formal Wear and Costume Rental;
- Renting studio equipment are classified in Industry 53249, Other Commercial and Industrial Machinery and Equipment Rental and Leasing; and
- Casting actors and actresses with production companies are classified in Industry 56131, Employment Placement Agencies.

512191 Teleproduction and Other Postproduction Services ᵁˢ

This U.S. industry comprises establishments primarily engaged in providing specialized motion picture or video postproduction services, such as editing, film/tape transfers, subtitling, credits, closed captioning, and animation and special effects.

- Mass duplicating video tapes and film are classified in Industry 33461, Manufacturing and Reproducing Magnetic and Optical Media;
- Developing and processing motion picture film are classified in U.S. Industry 512199, Other Motion Picture and Video Industries;
- Providing audio services for film, television, and video productions are classified in Industry 512240, Sound Recording Studios; and
- Acquiring distribution rights and distributing film and video productions to motion picture theaters, television networks and stations, and exhibitors are classified in Industry 512120, Motion Picture and Video Distribution.

512199 Other Motion Picture and Video Industries ᵁˢ

This U.S. industry comprises establishments primarily engaged in providing motion picture and video services (except motion picture and video production, distribution, exhibition, and teleproduction and other postproduction services).

- Renting wardrobes and costumes for motion picture production are classified in Industry 532220, Formal Wear and Costume Rental;
- Renting studio equipment are classified in Industry 532490, Other Commercial and Industrial Machinery and Equipment Rental and Leasing;
- Casting actors and actresses with production companies are classified in Industry 561310, Employment Placement Agencies;
- Motion picture and video production are classified in Industry 512110, Motion Picture and Video Production;
- Motion picture and video distribution are classified in Industry 512120, Motion Picture and Video Distribution;
- Teleproduction and other postproduction services are classified in U.S. Industry 512191, Teleproduction and Other Postproduction Services; and
- Motion picture and video exhibition are classified in Industry 51213, Motion Picture and Video Exhibition.

5122 Sound Recording Industries

This industry group comprises establishments primarily engaged in producing and distributing musical recordings, in publishing music, or in providing sound recording and related services.

■ = Cross-References

Sector **51**

Information

US—United States industry only. CAN—United States and Canadian industries are comparable. When neither US nor CAN appears, Canadian, Mexican, and United States industries are comparable.

508

Harris InfoSource

51221 Record Production
See industry description for 512210 below.

512210 Record Production
This industry comprises establishments primarily engaged in record production (e.g., tapes, CDs). These establishments contract with artists and arrange and finance the production of original master recordings. Establishments in this industry hold the copyright to the master recording and derive most of their revenues from the sales, leasing, and licensing of master recordings. Establishments in this industry do not have their own duplication or distribution capabilities.

- Releasing, promoting, and distributing recordings are classified in Industry 512220, Integrated Record Production/Distribution;
- Promoting and authorizing the use of musical works in various media are classified in Industry 512230, Music Publishers;
- Mass duplication services are classified in U.S. Industry 334612, Prerecorded Compact Disc (except Software), Tape, and Record Reproducing;
- Wholesaling music recordings are classified in Industry 421690, Other Electronic Parts and Equipment Wholesalers;
- Managing the careers of artists are classified in Industry 711410, Agents and Managers for Artists, Athletes, Entertainers and Other Public Figures;
- Providing facilities and technical expertise for recording musical performances are classified in Industry 512240, Sound Recording Studios; and
- Producing albums on contract as independent producers are classified in Industry 711510, Independent Artists, Writers, and Performers.

51222 Integrated Record Production/Distribution
See industry description for 512220 below.

512220 Integrated Record Production/Distribution
This industry comprises establishments primarily engaged in releasing, promoting, and distributing sound recordings. These establishments manufacture or arrange for the manufacture of recordings, such as audio tapes/cassettes and compact discs, and promote and distribute these products to whole-salers, retailers, or directly to the public. Establishments in this industry produce master recordings themselves, or obtain reproduction and distribution rights to master recordings produced by record production companies or other integrated record companies.

- Contracting with musical artists, arranging for the production of master recordings, and marketing the reproduction rights are classified in Industry 512210, Record Production;
- Providing facilities and technical expertise for recording musical performances are classified in Industry 512240, Sound Recording Studios;
- Mass duplication of recorded products are classified in U.S. Industry 334612, Prerecorded Compact Disc (except Software), Tape, and Record Reproducing;
- Wholesaling records, tapes, and compact discs without producing recordings are classified in Sector 42, Wholesale Trade; and
- Retailing records, tapes, and compact discs without producing recordings are classified in Sector 44-45, Retail Trade.

51223 Music Publishers
See industry description for 512230 below.

512230 Music Publishers
This industry comprises establishments primarily engaged in acquiring and registering copyrights for musical compositions in accordance with law and promoting and authorizing the use of these compositions in recordings, radio, television, motion pictures, live performances, print, or other media. Establishments in this industry represent the interests of the songwriter or other owners of musical compositions to produce revenues from the use of such works, generally through licensing agreements. These establishments may own the copyright or act as administrator of the music copyrights on behalf of copyright owners.

- Establishments primarily engaged as independent songwriters who act as their own publishers are classified in Industry 711510, Independent Artists, Writers, and Performers.

51224 Sound Recording Studios
See industry description for 512240 below.

Discover the high-lights of this new sector on page 17.

Sector 51

Information

■ = Cross-References

US—United States industry only. CAN—United States and Canadian industries are comparable. When neither US nor CAN appears, Canadian, Mexican, and United States industries are comparable.

www.harrisinfo.com

509

512240 Sound Recording Studios

This industry comprises establishments primarily engaged in providing the facilities and technical expertise for sound recording in a studio. Establishments in this industry may provide audio production or postproduction services for producing master recordings, and may provide audio services for film, television, and video productions.

- Releasing, promoting, and distributing sound recordings are classified in Industry 512220, Integrated Record Production/Distribution;
- Providing mass duplication of recorded products are classified in U.S. Industry 334612, Prerecorded Compact Disc (except Software), Tape, and Record Reproducing; and
- Contracting with musical artists, arranging for the production of master recordings, and marketing the reproduction rights are classified in Industry 512210, Record Production.

51229 Other Sound Recording Industries

See industry description for 512290 below.

512290 Other Sound Recording Industries

This industry comprises establishments primarily engaged in providing sound recording services (except record production, distribution, music publishing, and sound recording in a studio). Establishments in this industry provide services, such as the audio recording of meetings and conferences.

- Producing records, including contracting with musical artists, arranging and financing the production of master recordings, and marketing the reproduction rights are classified in Industry 512210, Record Production;
- Releasing, promoting, and distributing sound recordings are classified in Industry 512220, Integrated Record Production/Distribution;
- Promoting and authorizing the use of musical works in various media are classified in Industry 512230, Music Publishers;
- Providing facilities and expertise for recording musical performance are classified in Industry 512240, Sound Recording Studios;
- Providing mass duplication of recorded products are classified in U.S. Industry 334612, Prerecorded Compact Disc (except Software), Tape, and Record Reproducing; and
- Organizing and promoting the presentation of performing arts productions are classified in Industry Group 7113, Promoters of Performing Arts, Sports and Similar Events.

▶ 513 BROADCASTING AND TELECOMMUNICATIONS

Industries in the Broadcasting and Telecommunications subsector include establishments providing point-to-point communications and the services related to that activity. The industry groups (Radio and Television Broadcasting, Cable Networks and Program Distribution, and Telecommunications) are based on differences in the methods of communication and in the nature of services provided. The Radio and Television Broadcasting industry group includes establishments that operate broadcasting studios and facilities for over the air or satellite delivery of radio and television programs of entertainment, news, talk, and the like. These establishments are often engaged in the production and purchase of programs and generating revenues from the sale of air time to advertisers and from donations, subsidies, and/or the sale of programs. The Cable Networks and Program Distribution industry group includes two types of establishments. Those in the Cable Networks industry operate studios and facilities for the broadcasting of programs that are typically narrowcast in nature (limited format, such as news, sports, education, and youth-oriented programming). The services of these establishments are typically sold on a subscription or fee basis. Delivery of the programs to customers is handled by other establishments, in the Cable and Other Program Distribution industry, that operate cable systems, direct-to-home satellite systems, or other similar systems. The Telecommunications industry group is primarily engaged in operating, maintaining, and/or providing access to facilities for the transmission of voice, data, text, sound, and full motion picture video between network termination points. A transmission facility may be based on a single technology or a combination of technologies. Establishments primarily engaged as independent contractors in the maintenance and installation of broadcasting and telecommunications systems are classified in Sector 23, Construction.

5131 Radio and Television Broadcasting

This industry group comprises establishments primarily engaged in operating broadcast studios and facilities for over-the-air or satellite delivery of radio and television programs. These establishments are often engaged in the production or purchase of programs or generate revenues from the sale of air time to advertisers, from donations and subsidies, or from the sale of programs.

Sector **51**

Information

■ = Cross-References

US—United States industry only. CAN—United States and Canadian industries are comparable. When neither US nor CAN appears, Canadian, Mexican, and United States industries are comparable.

510 Harris InfoSource

51311 Radio Broadcasting

This industry comprises establishments primarily engaged in broadcasting audio signals. These establishments operate radio broadcasting studios and facilities for the transmission of aural programming by radio to the public, to affiliates, or to subscribers. The radio programs may include entertainment, news, talk shows, business data, or religious services.

■ Establishments primarily engaged in producing taped radio programming are classified in Industry 51229, Other Sound Recording Industries.

513111 Radio Networks ᵁˢ

This U.S. industry comprises establishments primarily engaged in assembling and transmitting aural programming to their affiliates or subscribers via over-the-air broadcasts, cable, or satellite. The programming covers a wide variety of material, such as news services, religious programming, weather, sports, or music.

■ Establishments primarily engaged in producing taped radio programming are classified in Industry 512290, Other Sound Recording Industries.

513112 Radio Stations ᵁˢ

This U.S. industry comprises establishments primarily engaged in broadcasting aural programs by radio to the public. Programming may originate in their own studios, from an affiliated network, or from external sources.

51312 Television Broadcasting

See industry description for 513120 below.

513120 Television Broadcasting

This industry comprises establishments primarily engaged in broadcasting images together with sound. These establishments operate television broadcasting studios and facilities for the programming and transmission of programs to the public. These establishments also produce or transmit visual programming to affiliated broadcast television stations, which in turn broadcast the programs to the public on a predetermined schedule. Programming may originate in their own studios, from an affiliated network, or from external sources.

■ Producing taped television program materials are classified in Industry 512110, Motion Picture and Video Production;
■ Furnishing cable and other pay television services are classified in Industry 513220, Cable and Other Program Distribution; and
■ Producing and broadcasting television programs for cable and satellite television systems are classified in Industry 513210, Cable Networks.

5132 Cable Networks and Program Distribution

This industry group comprises establishments that primarily assemble program material and transmit television programs for cable and satellite systems, or that operate these systems.

51321 Cable Networks

See industry description for 513210 below.

513210 Cable Networks

This industry comprises establishments primarily engaged in operating studios and facilities for the broadcasting of programs on a subscription or fee basis. The broadcast programming is typically narrowcast in nature (e.g., limited format, such as news, sports, education, or youth-oriented). These establishments produce programming in their own facilities or acquire programming from external sources. The programming material is usually delivered to a third party, such as cable systems or direct-to-home satellite systems, for transmission to viewers.

■ Producing taped television program material are classified in Industry 512110, Motion Picture and Video Production;
■ Producing and transmitting television programs to affiliated stations are classified in Industry 513120, Television Broadcasting;
■ Furnishing cable and other pay television services are classified in Industry 513220, Cable and Other Program Distribution; and
■ Retailing merchandise by electronic media, such as television, are classified in Industry 454110, Electronic Shopping and Mail-order Houses.

Discover the highlights of this new sector on page 17.

Sector 51

Information

■ = Cross-References

US—United States industry only. CAN—United States and Canadian industries are comparable. When neither US nor CAN appears, Canadian, Mexican, and United States industries are comparable.

www.harrisinfo.com

511

51322 Cable and Other Program Distribution
See industry description for 513220 below.

513220 Cable and Other Program Distribution
This industry comprises establishments primarily engaged as third-party distribution systems for broadcast programming. The establishments of this industry deliver visual, aural, or textual programming received from cable networks, local television stations, or radio networks to consumers via cable or direct-to-home satellite systems on a subscription or fee basis. These establishments do not generally originate programming material.

■ Producing and broadcasting television programs for cable and satellite television systems are classified in Industry 513210, Cable Networks; and
■ Maintenance and installation of cable systems as independent contractors are classified in Sector 23, Construction.

5133 Telecommunications
This industry group comprises establishments primarily engaged in operating, maintaining or providing access to facilities for the transmission of voice, data, text, and full motion picture video between network termination points and telecommunications reselling. Transmission facilities may be based on a single technology or a combination of technologies.

51331 Wired Telecommunications Carriers
See industry description for 513310 below.

513310 Wired Telecommunications Carriers
This industry comprises establishments engaged in (1) operating and maintaining switching and transmission facilities to provide direct communications via landlines, microwave, or a combination of landlines and satellite linkups or (2) furnishing telegraph and other nonvocal communications using their own facilities.

■ Broadcasting scheduled television programs via cable or satellite facilities on a subscription or fee basis are classified in Industry 513220, Cable and Other Program Distribution;
■ Providing coin-operated pay telephones are classified in Industry 812990, All Other Personal Services;
■ Operating and maintaining wireless networks are classified in Industry 51332, Wireless Telecommunications Carriers (except Satellite);
■ Reselling telecommunications, without operating a network are classified in Industry 513330, Telecommunications Resellers;
■ Publishing telephone directories are classified in Industry 511140, Database and Directory Publishers; and
■ Maintaining and installing wired telecommunication systems as independent contractors are classified in Sector 23, Construction.

51332 Wireless Telecommunications Carriers (except Satellite)
This industry comprises establishments primarily engaged in operating and maintaining switching and transmission facilities that provide direct communications via airwaves. Included in this industry are establishments providing wireless telecommunications network services, such as cellular telephone or paging services.

■ Establishments primarily engaged in providing telephone answering services using pagers are classified in Industry 56142, Telephone Call Centers.

513321 Paging US
This U.S. industry comprises establishments primarily engaged in operating paging networks. The establishments of this industry may also supply and maintain equipment used to receive signals.

■ Establishments primarily engaged in providing telephone answering services using pagers are classified in U.S. Industry 561421, Telephone Answering Services.

513322 Cellular and Other Wireless Telecommunications US
This U.S. industry comprises establishments primarily engaged in operating cellular telecommunications and other wireless telecommunications networks (except paging).

■ Establishments primarily engaged in operating paging networks are classified in U.S. Industry 513321, Paging.

Sector **51**

Information

■ = Cross-References

US—United States industry only. CAN—United States and Canadian industries are comparable. When neither US nor CAN appears, Canadian, Mexican, and United States industries are comparable.

512

Harris InfoSource

51333 Telecommunications Resellers
See industry description for 513330 below.

513330 Telecommunications Resellers
This industry comprises establishments primarily engaged in purchasing access and network capacity from owners and operators of the networks and reselling wired and wireless telecommunications services to businesses and households. Establishments in this industry resell telecommunications; they do not operate and maintain telecommunications switching and transmission facilities.

- Operating and maintaining wired telecommunications networks are classified in Industry 513310, Wired Telecommunications Carriers;
- Reselling satellite telecommunications services are classified in Industry 513340, Satellite Telecommunications; and
- Operating and maintaining wireless telecommunications are classified in Industry 51332, Wireless Telecommunications Carriers (except Satellite).

51334 Satellite Telecommunications
See industry description for 513340 below.

513340 Satellite Telecommunications
This industry comprises establishments primarily engaged in providing point-to-point telecommunications services to other establishments in the telecommunications and broadcasting industries by forwarding and receiving communications signals via a system of satellites or reselling satellite telecommunications.

- Establishments primarily engaged in providing direct-to-home satellite television systems to individual households or consumers are classified in Industry 513220, Cable and Other Program Distribution.

51339 Other Telecommunications
See industry description for 513390 below.

513390 Other Telecommunications
This industry comprises establishments primarily engaged in (1) providing specialized telecommunications applications, such as satellite tracking, communications telemetry, and radar station operations or (2) providing satellite terminal stations and associated facilities operationally connected with one or more terrestrial communications systems and capable of transmitting telecommunications to or receiving telecommunications from satellite systems.

- Providing satellite telecommunications are classified in Industry 513340, Satellite Telecommunications; and
- Providing custom design, programming, or facilities management services for integrated computer and telecommunications systems or operations are classified in Industry 54151, Computer Systems Design and Related Services.

▶514 INFORMATION SERVICES AND DATA PROCESSING SERVICES
Industries in the Information Services and Data Processing Services subsector group establishments providing information, storing information, providing access to information, and processing information. The main components of the subsector are news syndicates, libraries, archives, online information service providers, and data processors.

5141 Information Services
This industry group comprises establishments primarily engaged in providing information, storing information, and/or providing access to information.

51411 News Syndicates
See industry description for 514110 below.

514110 News Syndicates
This industry comprises establishments primarily engaged in supplying information, such as news reports, articles, pictures, and features, to the news media.

- Independent writers and journalists (including photojournalists) are classified in Industry 711510, Independent Artists, Writers, and Performers.

Discover the highlights of this new sector on page 17.

Sector 51

Information

■ = Cross-References

US—United States industry only. CAN—United States and Canadian industries are comparable. When neither US nor CAN appears, Canadian, Mexican, and United States industries are comparable.

51412 Libraries and Archives
See industry description for 514120 below.

514120 Libraries and Archives
This industry comprises establishments primarily engaged in providing library or archive services. These establishments are engaged in maintaining collections of documents (e.g., books, journals, newspapers, and music) and facilitating the use of such documents (recorded information regardless of its physical form and characteristics) as are required to meet the informational, research, educational, or recreational needs of their user. These establishments may also acquire, research, store, preserve, and generally make accessible to the public historical documents, photographs, maps, audio material, audiovisual material, and other archival material of historical interest. All or portions of these collections may be accessible electronically.

■ Providing stock footage (via motion picture and video tape libraries) to the media, multimedia, and advertising industries are classified in Industry 512199, Other Motion Picture and Video Industries; and
■ Distributing film and video productions to motion picture theaters, television networks and stations, and exhibitors are classified in Industry 512120, Motion Picture and Video Distribution.

51419 Other Information Services
This industry comprises establishments primarily engaged in providing information services (except news syndicates, libraries, and archives). Included in this industry are Internet service providers, online information access services, and telephone-based (i.e., toll call) information services. Online information services establishments are engaged in the provision of direct access to computer-held information published by others via telecommunications networks. These establishments often provide electronic mail services, bulletin boards, browsers, and search routines.

■ Publishing or compiling and offer direct online access to information that they publish or compile are classified in Subsector 511, Publishing Industries, according to activity;
■ Supplying information to the news media are classified in Industry 514110, News Syndicates; and
■ Operating libraries and archives are classified in Industry 514120, Libraries and Archives.

514191 online Information Services ^{CAN}
This U.S. industry comprises Internet access providers, Internet service providers, and similar establishments primarily engaged in providing direct access through telecommunications networks to computer-held information compiled or published by others.

■ Establishments primarily engaged in publishing or compiling information and offering direct online access to the information that they publish or compile are classified in Subsector 511, Publishing Industries, according to activity.

514199 All Other Information Services ^{CAN}
This U.S. industry comprises establishments primarily engaged in providing information services (except news syndicates, libraries, archives, and online information access). Activities performed by establishments in this industry include telephone-based information recordings and information search services on a contract basis.

■ Publishing or compiling and offer direct online access to information that they publish or compile are classified in Subsector 511, Publishing Industries, according to activity;
■ Supplying information to the news media are classified in Industry 514110, News Syndicates;
■ Operating libraries and archives are classified in Industry 514120, Libraries and Archives; and
■ Providing online information services are classified in U.S. Industry 514191, Online Information Services.

5142 Data Processing Services

51421 Data Processing Services
See industry description for 514210 below.

514210 Data Processing Services
This industry comprises establishments primarily engaged in providing electronic data processing services. These establishments may provide complete processing and preparation of reports from data supplied by customers; specialized services, such as automated data entry services; or may make data processing resources available to clients on an hourly or timesharing basis.

Sector **51**

Information

■ = Cross-References

■ Providing text processing and desktop publishing services are classified in Industry 561410, Document Preparation Services;

■ Providing on-site management and operation of a client's data-processing facilities are classified in U.S. Industry 541513, Computer Facilities Management Services;

■ Providing online access to information and services developed by others are classified in U.S. Industry 514191, Online Information Services;

■ Providing access to microcomputers and office equipment, as well as other office support services are classified in Industry 56143, Business Service Centers;

■ Processing financial transactions, such as credit card transactions, are classified in Industry 522320, Financial Transactions Processing, Reserve, and Clearinghouse Activities; and

■ Providing payroll processing services using data processing techniques are classified in U.S. Industry 541214, Payroll Services.

Sector 51

Information

■ = Cross-References

US—United States industry only. CAN—United States and Canadian industries are comparable. When neither US nor CAN appears, Canadian, Mexican, and United States industries are comparable.

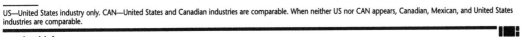

www.harrisinfo.com

515

NAICS United States Structure

Sector	Name	Sub-sectors	Industry groups	NAICS 5-digit industries	U.S. 6-digit industries	TOTAL U.S. industries	New industries
11	Agriculture, Forestry, Fishing and, Hunting	5	19	42	32	64	20
21	Mining	3	5	10	28	29	—
22	Utilities	1	3	6	6	10	6
23	Construction	3	14	28	—	28	3
31–33	Manufacturing	21	84	184	408	474	79
42	Wholesale Trade	2	18	69	—	69	—
44–45	Retail Trade	12	27	61	18	72	17
48-49	Transportation and Warehousing	11	29	42	25	57	28
51	Information	4	9	28	12	34	20
52	Finance and Insurance	5	11	32	15	42	23
53	Real Estate and Rental and Leasing	3	8	19	9	24	15
54	Professional, Scientific, and Technical Services	1	9	35	17	47	28
55	Management of Companies and Enterprises	1	1	1	3	3	1
56	Administrative and Support and Waste Management and Remediation Services	2	11	29	23	43	29
61	Educational Services	1	7	12	7	17	12
62	Health Care and Social Assistance	4	18	30	16	39	27
71	Arts, Entertainment, and Recreation	3	9	23	3	25	19
72	Accommodation and Food Services	2	7	11	7	15	10
81	Other Services (except Public Administration)	4	14	30	30	49	19
92	Public Administration	8	8	29	—	29	2
	TOTAL	96	311	721	659	1170	358

To learn more about the changes by sector go to pages 15-18.

Sector 51

Information

Sector 52 Finance and Insurance

The Sector as a Whole

THE FINANCE AND INSURANCE sector comprises establishments primarily engaged in financial transactions (transactions involving the creation, liquidation, or change in ownership of financial assets) and/or in facilitating financial transactions. Three principal types of activities are identified:

1. Raising funds by taking deposits and/or issuing securities and, in the process, incurring liabilities. Establishments engaged in this activity use raised funds to acquire financial assets by making loans and/or purchasing securities. Putting themselves at risk, they channel funds from lenders to borrowers and transform or repackage the funds with respect to maturity, scale, and risk. This activity is known as financial intermediation.

2. Pooling of risk by underwriting insurance and annuities. Establishments engaged in this activity collect fees, insurance premiums, or annuity considerations; build up reserves; invest those reserves; and make contractual payments. Fees are based on the expected incidence of the insured risk and the expected return on investment.

3. Providing specialized services facilitating or supporting financial intermediation, insurance, and employee benefit programs.

In addition, monetary authorities charged with monetary control are included in this sector.

The subsectors, industry groups, and industries within the NAICS sector are defined on the basis of their unique production processes. As with all industries, the production processes are distinguished by their use of specialized human resources and specialized physical capital. In addition, the way in which these establishments acquire and allocate financial capital, their source of funds, and the use of those funds provides a third basis for distinguishing characteristics of the production process. For instance, the production process in raising funds through deposit-taking is different from the process of raising funds in bond or money markets. The process of making loans to individuals also requires different production processes than does the creation of investment pools or the underwriting of securities.

Most of the subsectors contain one or more industry groups of (1) intermediaries with similar patterns of raising and using funds and (2) establishments engaged in activities that facilitate, or are otherwise related to, that type of financial or insurance intermediation.

Industries within this sector are defined in terms of activities for which a production process can be specified, and many of these activities are not exclusive to a particular type of financial institution. To deal with the varied activities taking place within existing financial institutions, the approach is to split these institutions into components performing specialized services. This requires defining the units engaged in providing those services and developing procedures that allow for their delineation. These units are the equivalents for of the establishments defined for other industries.

The output of many financial services, as well as the inputs and the processes by which they are combined, cannot be observed at a single location and can only be defined at a higher level of the organizational structure of the enterprise. Additionally, a number of independent activities that represent separate and distinct production processes may take place at a single location belonging to a multilocation financial firm. Activities are more likely to be homogeneous with respect to production characteristics than are locations, at least in financial

Visit page 16 to learn more about this sector.

Visit page 16 to learn more about this sector.

Sector 52

Finance and Insurance

services. The classification defines activities broadly enough that it can be used both by those classifying by location and by those employing a more top-down approach to the delineation of the establishment.

Establishments engaged in activities that facilitate, or are otherwise related to, the various types of intermediation have been included in individual subsectors, rather than in a separate subsector dedicated to services alone because these services are performed by intermediaries as well as by specialist establishments and the extent to which the activity of the intermediaries can be separately identified is not clear.

The sector has been defined to encompass establishments primarily engaged in financial transactions; that is, transactions involving the creation, liquidation, or change in ownership of financial assets or in facilitating financial transactions. Financial industries are extensive users of electronic means for facilitating the verification of financial balances, authorizing transactions, transferring funds to and from transactors' accounts, notifying banks (or credit card issuers) of the individual transactions, and providing daily summaries. Since these transaction processing activities are integral to the production of services, establishments that principally provide a financial transaction processing service are classified to this sector, rather than to the data processing industry in the Information sector.

Legal entities that hold portfolios of assets on behalf of others are significant and data on them are required for a variety of purposes. Thus for NAICS, these funds, trusts, and other financial vehicles are the fifth subsector of the sector. These entities earn interest, dividends, and other property income, but have little or no employment and no revenue from the sale of services. Separate establishments and employees devoted to the management of funds are classified in Industry Group 5239, Other Financial Investment Activities.

▶521 MONETARY AUTHORITIES—CENTRAL BANK

The Monetary Authorities—Central Bank subsector groups establishments that engage in performing central banking functions, such as issuing currency, managing the Nation's money supply and international reserves, holding deposits that represent the reserves of other banks and other central banks, and acting as fiscal agent for the central government.

5211 Monetary Authorities—Central Bank

52111 Monetary Authorities—Central Bank ^{CAN}
See industry description for 521110 below.

521110 Monetary Authorities—Central Bank ^{CAN}
This industry comprises establishments primarily engaged in performing central banking functions, such as issuing currency, managing the Nation's money supply and international reserves, holding deposits that represent the reserves of other banks and other central banks, and acting as fiscal agent for the central government.

■ Establishments of the Board of Governors of the Federal Reserve System are classified in Industry 921130, Public Finance Activities.

▶522 CREDIT INTERMEDIATION AND RELATED ACTIVITIES

Industries in the Credit Intermediation and Related Activities subsector group establishments that (1) lend funds raised from depositors; (2) lend funds raised from credit market borrowing; or (3) facilitate the lending of funds or issuance of credit by engaging in such activities as mortgage and loan brokerage, clearinghouse and reserve services, and check cashing services.

5221 Depository Credit Intermediation ^{CAN}
This industry group comprises establishments primarily engaged in accepting deposits (or share deposits) and in lending funds from these deposits. Within this group, industries are defined on the basis of differences in the types of deposit liabilities assumed and in the nature of the credit extended.

Sector 52

Finance and Insurance

■ = Cross-References

US—United States industry only. CAN—United States and Canadian industries are comparable. When neither US nor CAN appears, Canadian, Mexican, and United States industries are comparable.

52211 Commercial Banking CAN
See industry description for 522110 below.

522110 Commercial Banking CAN
This industry comprises establishments primarily engaged in accepting demand and other deposits and making commercial, industrial, and consumer loans. Commercial banks and branches of foreign banks are included in this industry.

- Establishments primarily engaged in credit card banking are classified in Industry 522210, Credit Card Issuing;
- Establishments known as industrial banks and primarily engaged in accepting deposits are classified in Industry 522190, Other Depository Credit Intermediation; and Establishments of depository institutions primarily engaged in trust activities are classified in U.S. Industry 523991, Trust, Fiduciary, and Custody Activities.

52212 Savings Institutions US
See industry description for 522120 below.

522120 Savings Institutions US
This industry comprises establishments primarily engaged in accepting time deposits, making mortgage and real estate loans, and investing in high-grade securities. Savings and loan associations and savings banks are included in this industry.

- Establishments primarily engaged in accepting demand and other deposits and making all types of loans are classified in Industry 522110, Commercial Banking.

52213 Credit Unions CAN
See industry description for 522130 below.

Visit page 16 to learn more about this sector.

522130 Credit Unions CAN
This industry comprises establishments primarily engaged in accepting members' share deposits in cooperatives that are organized to offer consumer loans to their members.

52219 Other Depository Credit Intermediation CAN
See industry description for 522190 below.

522190 Other Depository Credit Intermediation CAN
This industry comprises establishments primarily engaged in accepting deposits and lending funds (except commercial banking, savings institutions, and credit unions). Establishments known as industrial banks or Morris Plans and primarily engaged in accepting deposits, and private banks (i.e., unincorporated banks) are included in this industry.

- Establishments primarily engaged in accepting demand and other deposits and making all types of loans are classified in Industry 522110, Commercial Banking;
- Establishments primarily engaged in accepting time deposits are classified in Industry 522120, Savings Institutions;
- Establishments primarily engaged in accepting members' share deposits in cooperatives are classified in Industry 522130, Credit Unions; and
- Establishments known as industrial banks and Morris Plans and are primarily engaged in providing nondepository credit are classified in U.S. Industry 52229, All Other Nondepository Credit Intermediation.

5222 Nondepository Credit Intermediation CAN
This industry group comprises establishments, both public (government-sponsored enterprises) and private, primarily engaged in extending credit or lending funds raised by credit market borrowing, such as issuing commercial paper or other debt instruments or by borrowing from other financial intermediaries. Within this group, industries are defined on the basis of the type of credit being extended.

52221 Credit Card Issuing CAN
See industry description for 522210 below.

Sector **52**

Finance and Insurance

■ = Cross-References

US—United States industry only. CAN—United States and Canadian industries are comparable. When neither US nor CAN appears, Canadian, Mexican, and United States industries are comparable.

522210 Credit Card Issuing ^{CAN}

This industry comprises establishments primarily engaged in providing credit by issuing credit cards. Credit card issuance provides the funds required to purchase goods and services in return for payment of the full balance or payments on an installment basis. Credit card banks are included in this industry.

- Establishments primarily engaged in issuing cards that contain a stored prepaid value are classified with the industry providing the service represented by the cards, such as transit fare cards, in Subsector 482, Rail Transportation, and long-distance telephone cards in Subsector 513, Broadcasting and Telecommunications, respectively.

52222 Sales Financing ^{CAN}

See industry description for 522220 below.

522220 Sales Financing ^{CAN}

This industry comprises establishments primarily engaged in sales financing or sales financing in combination with leasing. Sales financing establishments are primarily engaged in lending money for the purpose of providing collateralized goods through a contractual installment sales agreement, either directly from or through arrangements with dealers.

- Establishments not engaged in sales financing, but primarily engaged in providing leases for equipment and other assets are classified in Subsector 532, Rental and Leasing Services.

52229 Other Nondepository Credit Intermediation ^{CAN}

This industry comprises establishments primarily engaged in making cash loans or extending credit through credit instruments (except credit cards and sales finance agreements).

- Establishments primarily engaged in providing credit sales by issuing credit cards are classified in Industry 52221, Credit Card Issuing;
- Establishments primarily engaged in providing leases for equipment and other assets without sales financing are classified in Subsector 532, Rental and Leasing Services;
- Establishments primarily engaged in accepting deposits and lending funds from these deposits are classified in Industry Group 5221, Depository Credit Intermediation;
- Establishments primarily engaged in arranging loans for others on a commission or fee basis are classified Industry 52231, Mortgage and Nonmortgage Loan Brokers; and
- Establishments primarily engaged in guaranteeing international trade loans are classified in Industry 52412, Direct Insurance (except Life, Health, and Medical) Carriers.

522291 Consumer Lending ^{CAN}

This U.S. industry comprises establishments primarily engaged in making unsecured cash loans to consumers.

- Accepting deposits and lending funds from these deposits are classified in Industry Group 5221, Depository Credit Intermediation; and
- Arranging loans for others on a commission or fee basis are classified Industry 522310, Mortgage and Nonmortgage Loan Brokers.

522292 Real Estate Credit ^{US}

This U.S. industry comprises establishments primarily engaged in lending funds with real estate as collateral.

- Servicing loans are classified in Industry 522390, Other Activities Related to Credit Intermediation;
- Arranging loans for others on a commission or fee basis are classified in Industry 522310, Mortgage and Nonmortgage Loan Brokers; and
- Accepting deposits and lending funds secured by real estate are classified in Industry Group 5221, Depository Credit Intermediation.

522293 International Trade Financing ^{US}

This U.S. industry comprises establishments primarily engaged in providing one or more of the following: (1) working capital funds to U.S. exporters; (2) lending funds to foreign buyers of U.S. goods; and (3) lending funds to domestic buyers of imported goods.

- Guaranteeing international trade loans are classified in U.S. Industry 524126, Direct Property and Casualty Insurance Carriers;
- Brokering international trade loans are classified in Industry 522310, Mortgage and Nonmortgage Loan Brokers; and
- Accepting deposits and lending funds from these deposits are classified in Industry Group 5221, Depository Credit Intermediation.

522294 Secondary Market Financing ^{US}

This U.S. industry comprises establishments primarily engaged in buying, pooling, and repackaging loans for sale to others on the secondary market.

Sector 52

Finance and Insurance

US—United States industry only. CAN—United States and Canadian industries are comparable. When neither US nor CAN appears, Canadian, Mexican, and United States industries are comparable.

520

Harris InfoSource

522298 All Other Nondepository Credit Intermediation ^{US}

This U.S. industry comprises establishments primarily engaged in providing nondepository credit (except credit card issuing, sales financing, consumer lending, real estate credit, international trade financing, and secondary market financing). Examples of types of lending in this industry are: short-term inventory credit, agricultural lending (except real estate and sales financing) and consumer cash lending secured by personal property.

- Establishments primarily engaged in providing credit sales funding are classified in Industry 522210, Credit Card Issuing;
- Establishments primarily engaged in sales financing or sales financing in combination with leasing are classified in Industry 522220, Sales Financing;
- Establishments primarily engaged in making unsecured cash loans to consumers are classified in U.S. Industry 522291, Consumer Lending;
- Establishments primarily engaged in lending funds with real estate as collateral are classified in U.S. Industry 522292, Real Estate Credit;
- Establishments primarily engaged in international trade financing are classified in U.S. Industry 522293, International Trade Financing;
- Establishments primarily engaged in buying, pooling, and repackaging loans for sale to others on the secondary market are classified in U.S. Industry 522294, Secondary Market Financing; and
- Establishments known as industrial banks or Morris Plans and are primarily engaged in accepting deposits are classified in Industry 522190, Other Depository Credit Intermediation.

5223 Activities Related to Credit Intermediation

This industry group comprises establishments primarily engaged in facilitating credit intermediation by performing activities, such as arranging loans by bringing borrowers and lenders together and clearing checks and credit card transactions.

52231 Mortgage and Nonmortgage Loan Brokers ^{CAN}

See industry description for 522310 below.

522310 Mortgage and Nonmortgage Loan Brokers ^{CAN}

This industry comprises establishments primarily engaged in arranging loans by bringing borrowers and lenders together on a commission or fee basis.

- Lending funds with real estate as collateral are classified in U.S. Industry 522292, Real Estate Credit; and
- Servicing loan are classified in Industry 522390, Other Activities Related to Credit Intermediation.

52232 Financial Transactions Processing, Reserve, and Clearinghouse Activities ^{CAN}

See industry description for 522320 below.

522320 Financial Transactions Processing, Reserve, and Clearinghouse Activities ^{CAN}

This industry comprises establishments primarily engaged in providing one or more of the following: (1) financial transaction processing (except central banks); (2) reserve and liquidity services (except central banks); and (3) check or other financial instrument clearinghouse services (except central banks).

- Establishments primarily engaged in nonfinancial data and electronic transaction processing are classified in Industry Group 5142, Data Processing Services; and
- Establishments of the central bank primarily engaged in check clearing and other financial transaction processing are classified in Industry 521110, Monetary Authorities—Central Bank.

52239 Other Activities Related to Credit Intermediation ^{CAN}

See industry description for 522390 below.

522390 Other Activities Related to Credit Intermediation ^{CAN}

This industry comprises establishments primarily engaged in facilitating credit intermediation (except mortgage and loan brokerage; and financial transactions processing, reserve, and clearing-house activities).

- Arranging loans for others on a commission or fee basis are classified in Industry 522310, Mortgage and Nonmortgage Loan Brokers;
- Providing financial transactions processing, reserve, and clearinghouse activities are classified in Industry 522320, Financial Transactions Processing, Reserve, and Clearinghouse Activities;
- Foreign currency exchange dealing are classified in Industry 523130, Commodity Contracts Dealing; and
- Providing escrow services (except real estate) are classified in U.S. Industry 523991, Trust, Fiduciary, and Custody Activities.

Visit page 16 to learn more about this sector.

Sector **52**

Finance and Insurance

■ = Cross-References

US—United States industry only. CAN—United States and Canadian industries are comparable. When neither US nor CAN appears, Canadian, Mexican, and United States industries are comparable.

www.harrisinfo.com

521

▶523 SECURITIES, COMMODITY CONTRACTS, AND OTHER FINANCIAL INVESTMENTS AND RELATED ACTIVITIES

Industries in the Securities, Commodity Contracts, and Other Financial Investments and Related Activities subsector group establishments that are primarily engaged in one of the following: (1)underwriting securities issues and/or making markets for securities and commodities; (2) acting as agents (i.e., brokers) between buyers and sellers of securities and commodities; (3) providing securities and commodity exchange services; and (4) providing other services, such as managing portfolios of assets; providing investment advice; and trust, fiduciary, and custody services.

5231 Securities and Commodity Contracts Intermediation and Brokerage

This industry group comprises establishments primarily engaged in putting capital at risk in the process of underwriting securities issues or in making markets for securities and commodities; and those acting as agents and/or brokers between buyers and sellers of securities and commodities, usually charging a commission.

52311 Investment Banking and Securities Dealing CAN

See industry description for 523110 below.

523110 Investment Banking and Securities Dealing CAN

This industry comprises establishments primarily engaged in underwriting, originating, and/or maintaining markets for issues of securities. Investment bankers act as principals (i.e., investors who buy or sell on their own account) in firm commitment transactions or act as agents in best effort and standby commitments. This industry also includes establishments acting as principals in buying or selling securities generally on a spread basis, such as securities dealers or stock option dealers.

- Establishments primarily engaged in acting as agents (i.e., brokers) in buying or selling securities on a commission or transaction fee basis are classified in Industry 523120, Securities Brokerage; and
- Investment clubs or individual investors primarily engaged in buying or selling financial contracts (e.g., securities) on their own account are classified in Industry 523910, Miscellaneous Intermediation.

52312 Securities Brokerage CAN

See industry description for 523120 below.

523120 Securities Brokerage CAN

This industry comprises establishments primarily engaged in acting as agents (i.e., brokers) between buyers and sellers in buying or selling securities on a commission or transaction fee basis.

- Establishments primarily engaged in investment banking and securities dealing (i.e., buying or selling securities on their own account) are classified in Industry 523110, Investment Banking and Securities Dealing.

52313 Commodity Contracts Dealing CAN

See industry description for 523130 below.

523130 Commodity Contracts Dealing CAN

This U.S. industry comprises establishments primarily engaged in acting as principals (i.e., investors who buy or sell for their own account) in buying or selling spot or futures commodity contracts or options, such as precious metals, foreign currency, oil, or agricultural products, generally on a spread basis.

- Acting as agents (i.e., brokers) in buying or selling spot or future commodity contracts on a commission or transaction fee basis are classified in Industry 523140, Commodity Contracts Brokerage; and
- Buying and selling physical commodities for resale to other than the general public are classified in Subsector 421, Wholesale Trade, Durable Goods.

52314 Commodity Contracts Brokerage CAN

See industry description for 523140 below.

523140 Commodity Contracts Brokerage CAN

This industry comprises establishments primarily engaged in acting as agents (i.e., brokers) in buying or selling spot or future commodity contracts or options on a commission or transaction fee basis.

Sector 52

Finance and
Insurance

■ = Cross-References

US—United States industry only. CAN—United States and Canadian industries are comparable. When neither US nor CAN appears, Canadian, Mexican, and United States industries are comparable.

522

Harris InfoSource

- Acting as principals in buying or selling spot or futures commodity contracts generally on a spread basis are classified in Industry 523130, Commodity Contracts Dealing; and
- Buying and selling physical commodities for resale to other than the general public are classified in Sector 421, Wholesale Trade, Durable Goods.

5232 Securities and Commodity Exchanges

52321 Securities and Commodity Exchanges
See industry description for 523210 below.

523210 Securities and Commodity Exchanges
This industry comprises establishments primarily engaged in furnishing physical or electronic market-places for the purpose of facilitating the buying and selling of stocks, stock options, bonds, or commodity contracts.

- Establishments primarily engaged in investment banking, and securities dealing, securities brokering commodity contracts dealing, or commodity contracts brokering are classified in Industry Group 5231, Securities and Commodity Contracts Intermediation and Brokerage.

5239 Other Financial Investment Activities
This industry group comprises establishments primarily engaged in one of the following: (1) acting as principals in buying or selling financial contracts (except investment bankers, securities dealers, and commodity contracts dealers); (2) acting as agents (i.e., brokers) (except securities brokerages and commodity contracts brokerages) in buying or selling financial contracts; or (3) providing other investment services (except securities and commodity exchanges), such as portfolio management; investment advice; and trust, fiduciary, and custody services.

52391 Miscellaneous Intermediation ^{CAN}
See industry description for 523910 below.

523910 Miscellaneous Intermediation
This industry comprises establishments primarily engaged in acting as principals (except investment bankers, securities dealers, and commodity contracts dealers) in buying or selling of financial contracts generally on a spread basis. Principals are investors that buy or sell for their own account.

- Establishments primarily engaged in investment banking, securities dealing, securities brokering, commodity contracts dealing, or commodity contracts brokering are classified in Industry Group 5231, Securities and Commodity Contracts Intermediation and Brokerage.

52392 Portfolio Management
See industry description for 523920 below.

523920 Portfolio Management
This industry comprises establishments primarily engaged in managing the portfolio assets (i.e., funds) of others on a fee or commission basis. Establishments in this industry have the authority to make investment decisions, and they derive fees based on the size and/or overall performance of the portfolio.

- Establishments primarily engaged in investment banking and securities dealing, commodity contracts dealing, or commodity contracts brokering are classified in Industry Group 5231, Securities and Commodity Contracts Intermediation and Brokerage.

52393 Investment Advice ^{CAN}
See industry description for 523930 below.

523930 Investment Advice ^{CAN}
This industry comprises establishments primarily engaged in providing customized investment advice to clients on a fee basis, but do not have the authority to execute trades. Primary activities performed by establishments in this industry are providing financial planning advice and investment counseling to meet the goals and needs of specific clients.

Visit page 16 to learn more about this sector.

Sector **52**

Finance and Insurance

■ = Cross-References

US—United States industry only. CAN—United States and Canadian industries are comparable. When neither US nor CAN appears, Canadian, Mexican, and United States industries are comparable.

■ Establishments providing investment advice in conjunction with their primary activity, such as portfolio management, or the sale of stocks, bonds, annuities, and real estate, are classified according to their primary activity; and

■ Establishments known as publishers providing generalized investment information to subscribers are classified in Subsector 511, Publishing Industries.

52399 All Other Financial Investment Activities CAN

This industry comprises establishments primarily engaged in acting as agents or brokers (except securities brokerages and commodity contracts brokerages) in buying and selling financial contracts providing financial investment activities (except securities and commodity exchanges, portfolio management, and investment advice).

■ Investment banking and securities dealing, securities brokering commodity contracts dealing, or commodity contracts brokering are classified in Industry Group 5231, Securities and Commodity Contracts Intermediation and Brokerage;

■ Acting as principals (except investment bankers, securities dealers, and commodity contracts dealers) in buying or selling financial contracts (except securities or commodity contracts) are classified in Industry 52391, Miscellaneous Intermediation;

■ Furnishing physical or electronic marketplaces for the purpose of facilitating the buying and selling of securities and commodities are classified in Industry 52321, Securities and Commodity Exchanges;

■ Managing the portfolio assets (i.e., funds) of others are classified in Industry 52392, Portfolio Management;

■ Providing customized investment advice are classified in Industry 52393, Investment Advice;

■ Awarding grants from trust funds are classified in Industry 81321, Grant making and Giving Services;

■ Performing real estate escrow or real estate fiduciary activities are classified in Industry 53139, Other Activities Related to Real Estate; and

■ Financial transactions processing, reserve, and clearinghouse activities are classified in Industry 52232, Financial Transactions Processing, Reserve, and Clearinghouse Activities.

523991 Trust, Fiduciary, and Custody Activities US

This U.S. industry comprises establishments primarily engaged in providing trust, fiduciary, and custody services to others, as instructed, on a fee or contract basis, such as bank trust offices and escrow agencies (except real estate).

■ Managing the portfolio assets (i.e., funds) of others are classified in Industry 523920, Portfolio Management;

■ Performing real estate escrow or real estate fiduciary activities are classified in Industry 531390, All Other Activities Related to Real Estate; and

■ Awarding grants from trust funds are classified in Industry 81321, Grant making and Giving Services.

523999 Miscellaneous Financial Investment Activities US

This U.S. industry comprises establishments primarily engaged in acting as agents and/or brokers (except securities brokerages and commodity contracts brokerages) in buying or selling financial contracts and those providing financial investment services (except securities and commodity exchanges; portfolio management; investment advice; and trust, fiduciary, and custody services) on a fee or commission basis.

■ Investment banking and securities dealing, commodity contracts dealing, or commodity contracts brokering are classified in Industry Group 5231, Securities and Commodity Contracts Intermediation and Brokerage;

■ Acting as principals (except investment bankers, securities dealers, and commodity contracts dealers) in buying or selling financial contracts are classified in Industry 523910, Miscellaneous Intermediation;

■ Furnishing physical or electrical marketplaces for the purpose of facilitating the buying and selling of securities and commodities are classified in Industry 523210, Securities and Commodity Exchanges;

■ Managing the portfolio assets (i.e., funds) of others are classified in Industry 523920, Portfolio Management;

■ Providing customized investment advice are classified in Industry 523930, Investment Advice;

■ Providing trust, fiduciary, and custody services to others are classified in U.S. Industry 523991, Trust, Fiduciary, and Custody Activities; and

■ Financial transactions processing, reserve, and clearinghouse activities are classified in Industry 522320, Financial Transactions Processing, Reserve, and Clearinghouse Activities.

▶524 INSURANCE CARRIERS AND RELATED ACTIVITIES

Industries in the Insurance Carriers and Related Activities subsector group establishments that are primarily engaged in one of the following (1) underwriting (assuming the risk, assigning premiums, and so forth) annuities and insurance policies or (2) facilitating such underwriting by selling insurance policies, and by providing other insurance and employee-benefit related services.

5241 Insurance Carriers

This industry group comprises establishments primarily engaged in underwriting (assuming the risk, assigning premiums, and so forth) annuities and insurance policies and investing premiums to build up a portfolio of

US—United States industry only. CAN—United States and Canadian industries are comparable. When neither US nor CAN appears, Canadian, Mexican, and United States industries are comparable.

Sector 52

Finance and Insurance

■ = Cross-References

financial assets to be used against future claims. Direct insurance carriers are establishments that are primarily engaged in initially underwriting and assuming the risk of annuities and insurance policies. Reinsurance carriers are establishments that are primarily engaged in assuming all or part of the risk associated with an existing insurance policy (or set of policies) originally underwritten by another insurance carrier. Industries are defined in terms of the type of risk being insured against, such as death, loss of employment because of age or disability, and property damage. Contributions and premiums are set on the basis of actuarial calculations of probable payoffs based on risk factors from experience tables and expected investment returns on reserves.

52411 Direct Life, Health, and Medical Insurance Carriers CAN

This industry comprises establishments primarily engaged in initially underwriting (i.e., assuming the risk and assigning premiums) annuities and life insurance policies, disability income insurance policies, accidental death and dismemberment insurance policies, and health and medical insurance policies.

- Establishments primarily engaged in reinsuring life insurance policies are classified in Industry 52413, Reinsurance Carriers;
- Legal entities (i.e., funds, plans, and/or programs) organized to provide insurance and employee benefits exclusively for the sponsor, firm, or its employees or members are classified in Industry Group 5251, Insurance and Employee Benefit Funds; and
- HMO establishments providing health care services are classified in Industry 62149, Other Outpatient Care Centers.

524113 Direct Life Insurance Carriers US

This U.S. industry comprises establishments primarily engaged in initially underwriting (i.e., assuming the risk and assigning premiums) annuities and life insurance policies, disability income insurance policies, and accidental death and dismemberment insurance policies.

- Establishments primarily engaged in reinsuring life insurance policies, disability income insurance policies, and accidental death and dismemberment insurance policies are classified in Industry 524130, Reinsurance Carriers; and
- Legal entities (i.e., funds, plans, and/or programs) organized to provide insurance and employee benefits exclusively for the sponsor, firm, or its employees or members are classified in Industry Group 5251, Insurance and Employee Benefit Funds.

Visit page 16 to learn more about this sector.

524114 Direct Health and Medical Insurance Carriers US

This U.S. industry comprises establishments primarily engaged in initially underwriting (i.e., assuming the risk and assigning premiums) health and medical insurance policies. Group hospitalization plans and HMO establishments (except those providing health care services) that provide health and medical insurance policies without providing health care services are included in this industry.

- HMO establishments that provide both health care services and underwrite health and medical insurance are classified in U.S. Industry 621491, HMO Medical Centers;
- Establishments primarily engaged in reinsuring health insurance policies are classified in Industry 524130, Reinsurance Carriers; and
- Legal entities (i.e., funds, plans, and/or programs) organized to provide health- and welfare-related employee benefits exclusively for the sponsor's employees or members are classified in Industry 525120, Health and Welfare Funds.

52412 Direct Insurance (except Life, Health, and Medical) Carriers CAN

This industry comprises establishments primarily engaged in initially underwriting (i.e., assuming the risk and assigning premiums) various types of insurance policies (except life, disability income, accidental death and dismemberment, and health and medical insurance policies).

- Establishments primarily engaged in reinsuring insurance policies are classified in Industry 524130, Reinsurance Carriers;
- Legal entities (i.e., funds, plans, and/or programs) organized to provide insurance and employee benefits exclusively for the sponsor, firm, or its employees or members are classified in Industry Group 5251, Insurance and Employee Benefit Funds; and
- Establishments primarily engaged in initially underwriting annuities and life insurance policies, disability income insurance policies, accidental death and dismemberment insurance policies, and health and medical insurance policies are classified in Industry 52411, Direct Life, Health, and Medical Insurance Carriers.

524126 Direct Property and Casualty Insurance Carriers US

This U.S. industry comprises establishments primarily engaged in initially underwriting (i.e., assuming the risk and assigning premiums) insurance policies that protect policyholders against losses that may occur as a result of property damage or liability.

- Establishments primarily engaged in reinsuring property and casualty insurance policies are classified in Industry 524130, Reinsurance Carriers.

Sector 52

Finance and Insurance

■ = Cross-References

US—United States industry only. CAN—United States and Canadian industries are comparable. When neither US nor CAN appears, Canadian, Mexican, and United States industries are comparable.

524127 Direct Title Insurance Carriers ^{US}

This U.S. industry comprises establishments primarily engaged in initially underwriting (i.e., assuming the risk and assigning premiums) insurance policies to protect the owners of real estate or real estate creditors against loss sustained by reason of any title defect to real property.

■ Establishments primarily engaged in reinsuring title insurance policies are classified in Industry 524130, Reinsurance Carriers.

524128 Other Direct Insurance (except Life, Health, and Medical) Carriers ^{US}

This U.S. industry comprises establishments primarily engaged in initially underwriting (e.g., assuming the risk, assigning premiums) insurance policies (except life, disability income, accidental death and dismemberment, health and medical, property and casualty, and title insurance policies).

■ Reinsuring insurance policies are classified in Industry 524130, Reinsurance Carriers;
■ Initially underwriting annuities and life insurance policies, disability income insurance policies, and accidental death and dismemberment insurance policies are classified in U.S. Industry 524113, Direct Life Insurance Carriers;
■ Initially underwriting health and medical insurance policies are classified in U.S. Industry 524114, Direct Health and Medical Insurance Carriers;
■ Initially underwriting property and casualty insurance policies are classified in U.S. Industry 524126, Direct Property and Casualty Insurance Carriers; and
■ Initially underwriting title insurance policies are classified in U.S. Industry 524127, Direct Title Insurance Carriers.

52413 Reinsurance Carriers ^{CAN}

See industry description for 524130 below.

524130 Reinsurance Carriers ^{CAN}

This industry comprises establishments primarily engaged in assuming all or part of the risk associated with existing insurance policies originally underwritten by other insurance carriers.

■ Initially underwriting annuities and life insurance policies, disability income insurance policies, accidental death and dismemberment insurance policies, and health and medical insurance policies are classified in Industry 52411, Direct Life, Health, and Medical Insurance Carriers; and
■ Initially underwriting various types of insurance policies (except life, disability income, accidental death and dismemberment, and health and medical insurance policies) are classified in Industry 52412, Direct Insurance (except Life, Health, and Medical) Carriers.

5242 Agencies, Brokerages, and Other Insurance Related Activities

This industry group comprises establishments primarily engaged in (1) acting as agents (i.e., brokers) in selling annuities and insurance policies or (2) providing other employee benefits and insurance related services, such as claims adjustment and third party administration.

52421 Insurance Agencies and Brokerages ^{CAN}

See industry description for 524210 below.

524210 Insurance Agencies and Brokerages ^{CAN}

This industry comprises establishments primarily engaged in acting as agents (i.e., brokers) in selling annuities and insurance policies.

■ Establishments primarily engaged in underwriting annuities and insurance policies are classified in Industry Group 5241, Insurance Carriers.

52429 Other Insurance Related Activities ^{CAN}

This industry comprises establishments primarily engaged in providing services related to insurance (except insurance agencies and brokerages).

■ Managing the portfolio assets (i.e., funds) of others are classified in Industry 52392, Portfolio Management;
■ Acting as agents (i.e., brokers) in selling annuities and insurance policies are classified in Industry 52421, Insurance Agencies and Brokerages; and
■ Providing actuarial consulting services are classified in Industry 54161, Management Consulting Services.

524291 Claims Adjusting ^{CAN}

This U.S. industry comprises establishments primarily engaged in investigating, appraising, and settling insurance claims.

Sector 52

Finance and
Insurance

■ = Cross-References

US—United States industry only. CAN—United States and Canadian industries are comparable. When neither US nor CAN appears, Canadian, Mexican, and United States industries are comparable.

526

Harris InfoSource

524292 Third Party Administration of Insurance and Pension Funds ᵁˢ

This U.S. industry comprises establishments primarily engaged in providing third party administration services of insurance and pension funds, such as claims processing and other administrative services to insurance carriers, employee-benefit plans, and self-insurance funds.

- Managing the portfolio assets (i.e., funds) of others are classified in Industry 523920, Portfolio Management; and
- Providing actuarial consulting services are classified in U.S. Industry 541612, Human Resources Management and Executive Search Consulting Services.

524298 All Other Insurance Related Activities ᵁˢ

This U.S. industry comprises establishments primarily engaged in providing insurance services on a contract or fee basis (except insurance agencies and brokerages, claims adjusting, and third party administration). Insurance advisory services and insurance rate-making services are included in this industry.

- Providing actuarial consulting services are classified in U.S. Industry 541612, Human Resources Management and Executive Search Consulting Services;
- Acting as agents (i.e., brokers) in selling annuities and insurance policies are classified in Industry 524210, Insurance Agencies and Brokerages;
- Insurance claims adjusting are classified in U.S. Industry 524291, Claims Adjusting; and
- Third party administration services of insurance and pension funds are classified in U.S. Industry 524292, Third Party Administration of Insurance and Pension Funds.

▶525 FUNDS, TRUSTS, AND OTHER FINANCIAL VEHICLES ᵁˢ

Industries in the Funds, Trusts, and Other Financial Vehicles subsector are comprised of legal entities (i.e., funds, plans, and/or programs) organized to pool securities or other assets on behalf of shareholders or beneficiaries of employee benefit or other trust funds. The portfolios are customized to achieve specific investment characteristics, such as diversification, risk, rate of return, and price volatility. These entities earn interest, dividends, and other property income, but have little or no employment and no revenue from the sale of services. Establishments with employees devoted to the management of funds are classified in Industry Group 5239, Other Financial Investment Activities.

Establishments primarily engaged in holding the securities of (or other equity interests in) other firms are classified in Sector 55, Management of Companies and Enterprises.

Visit page 16 to learn more about this sector.

5251 Insurance and Employee Benefit Funds ᵁˢ

This industry group comprises legal entities (i.e., funds, plans, and/or programs) organized to provide insurance and employee benefits exclusively for the sponsor, firm, or its employees or members.

52511 Pension Funds ᵁˢ

See industry description for 525110 below.

525110 Pension Funds ᵁˢ

This industry comprises legal entities (i.e., funds, plans, and/or programs) organized to provide retirement income benefits exclusively for the sponsor's employees or members.

- Managing portfolios of pension funds are classified in Industry 523920, Portfolio Management; and
- Initially underwriting annuities are classified in U.S. Industry 524113, Direct Life Insurance Carriers.

52512 Health and Welfare Funds ᵁˢ

See industry description for 525120 below.

525120 Health and Welfare Funds ᵁˢ

This industry comprises legal entities (i.e., funds, plans, and/or programs) organized to provide medical, surgical, hospital, vacation, training, and other health-and welfare-related employee benefits exclusively for the sponsor's employees or members.

- Managing portfolios of health and welfare funds are classified in Industry 523920, Portfolio Management; and
- Third party claims administration of health and welfare plans are classified in U.S. Industry 524292, Third Party Administration of Insurance and Pension Funds.

Sector **52**

Finance and Insurance

■ = Cross-References

US—United States industry only. CAN—United States and Canadian industries are comparable. When neither US nor CAN appears, Canadian, Mexican, and United States industries are comparable.

52519 Other Insurance Funds US
See industry description for 525190 below.

525190 Other Insurance Funds US
This industry comprises legal entities (i.e., funds—except pension, and health-and welfare-related employee benefit funds) organized to provide insurance exclusively for the sponsor, firm, or its employees or members. Self-insurance funds (except employee benefit funds) and workers' compensation insurance funds are included in this industry.

- Legal entities (i.e., funds, plans, and/or programs) organized to provide retirement income benefits exclusively for the sponsor's employees or members are classified in Industry 525110, Pension Funds;
- Legal entities (i.e., funds, plans, and/or programs) organized to provide health-and welfare-related employee benefits exclusively for the sponsor's employees or members are classified in Industry 525120, Health and Welfare Related Funds;
- Establishments primarily engaged in managing portfolios of insurance funds are classified in Industry 523920, Portfolio Management;
- Establishments primarily engaged in third party claims administration of insurance, and other employee benefit funds are classified in U.S. Industry 524292, Third Party Administration of Insurance and Pension Funds; and
- Establishments primarily engaged in providing insurance on a fee or contract basis are classified in Industry Group 5241, Insurance Carriers.

5259 Other Investment Pools and Funds US
This industry group comprises legal entities (i.e., investment pools and/or funds) organized to pool securities or other assets (except insurance and employee-benefit funds) on behalf of shareholders, unit holders, or beneficiaries.

52591 Open-end Investment Funds US
See industry description for 525910 below.

525910 Open-end Investment Funds US
This industry comprises legal entities (i.e., open-end investment funds) organized to pool assets that consist of securities or other financial instruments. Shares in these pools are offered to the public in an initial offering with additional shares offered continuously and perpetually and redeemed at a specific price determined by the net asset value.

52592 Trusts, Estates, and Agency Accounts US
See industry description for 525920 below.

525920 Trusts, Estates, and Agency Accounts US
This industry comprises legal entities, trusts, estates, or agency accounts, administered on behalf of the beneficiaries under the terms of a trust agreement, will, or agency agreement.

- Managing portfolios of trusts are classified in Industry 523920, Portfolio Management;
- Administering personal estates are classified in U.S. Industry 523991, Trust, Fiduciary, and Custody Services; and
- Operating businesses of trusts and bankruptcy estates are classified according to the kind of business operated.

52593 Real Estate Investment Trusts US
See industry description for 525930 below.

525930 Real Estate Investment Trusts US
This industry comprises legal entities that are Real Estate Investment Trusts (REITs).

- Legal entities of mortgage-backed investment funds that are not REITs are classified elsewhere in the Funds, Trusts, and Other Financial Vehicles subsector based on the types of funds; and
- Legal entities of investments in real estate that are not REITs are classified in Industry Group 5311, Lessors of Real Estate.

52599 Other Financial Vehicles US
See industry description for 525990 below.

Sector 52

Finance and Insurance

■ = Cross-References

US—United States industry only. CAN—United States and Canadian industries are comparable. When neither US nor CAN appears, Canadian, Mexican, and United States industries are comparable.

528

Harris InfoSource

525990 Other Financial Vehicles US

This industry comprises legal entities (i.e., funds—except insurance and employee benefit funds; open-end investment funds; trusts, estates, and agency accounts; and Real Estate Investment Trusts (REITs).

- Legal entities (i.e., funds, plans, and programs) that provide insurance and employee benefits exclusively for the sponsor, firm, or its employees or members are classified in Industry Group 5251, Insurance and Employee Benefit Funds;
- Legal entities (i.e., open-end investment funds) organized to pool assets that consist of securities or other financial instruments, where the pools are offered to the public in an initial offering with additional shares offered continuously and perpetually at a specific price determined by the net asset value, are classified in Industry 525910, Open-End Investment Funds;
- Legal entities (i.e., trusts, estates, or agency accounts) administered on behalf of the beneficiaries under the terms of a trust agreement, will, or agency agreement are classified in Industry 525920, Trusts, Estates, and Agency Accounts; and
- Legal entities that are Real Estate Investment Trusts (REITs) are classified in Industry 525930, Real Estate Investment Trusts.

Sector **52**

Finance and
Insurance

■ = Cross-References

US—United States industry only. CAN—United States and Canadian industries are comparable. When neither US nor CAN appears, Canadian, Mexican, and United States industries are comparable.

NAICS United States Structure

Sector	Name	Sub-sectors	Industry groups	NAICS 5-digit industries	U.S. 6-digit industries	TOTAL U.S. industries	New industries
11	Agriculture, Forestry, Fishing and, Hunting	5	19	42	32	64	20
21	Mining	3	5	10	28	29	—
22	Utilities	1	3	6	6	10	6
23	Construction	3	14	28	—	28	3
31–33	Manufacturing	21	84	184	408	474	79
42	Wholesale Trade	2	18	69	—	69	—
44–45	Retail Trade	12	27	61	18	72	17
48-49	Transportation and Warehousing	11	29	42	25	57	28
51	Information	4	9	28	12	34	20
52	Finance and Insurance	5	11	32	15	42	23
53	Real Estate and Rental and Leasing	3	8	19	9	24	15
54	Professional, Scientific, and Technical Services	1	9	35	17	47	28
55	Management of Companies and Enterprises	1	1	1	3	3	1
56	Administrative and Support and Waste Management and Remediation Services	2	11	29	23	43	29
61	Educational Services	1	7	12	7	17	12
62	Health Care and Social Assistance	4	18	30	16	39	27
71	Arts, Entertainment, and Recreation	3	9	23	3	25	19
72	Accommodation and Food Services	2	7	11	7	15	10
81	Other Services (except Public Administration)	4	14	30	30	49	19
92	Public Administration	8	8	29	—	29	2
	TOTAL	96	311	721	659	1170	358

To learn more about the changes by sector go to pages 15-18.

Sector **52**

Finance and Insurance

Sector 53
Real Estate and Rental and Leasing

The Sector as a Whole

THE REAL ESTATE AND RENTAL AND LEASING sector comprises establishments primarily engaged in renting, leasing, or otherwise allowing the use of tangible or intangible assets, and establishments providing related services. The major portion of this sector comprises establishments that rent, lease, or otherwise allow the use of their own assets by others. The assets may be tangible, as is the case of real estate and equipment, or intangible, as is the case with patents and trademarks.

This sector also includes establishments primarily engaged in managing real estate for others, selling, renting and/or buying real estate for others, and appraising real estate. These activities are closely related to this sector's main activity, and it was felt that from a production basis they would best be included here. In addition, a substantial proportion of property management is self-performed by lessors.

The main components of this sector are the real estate lessors industries; equipment lessors industries (including motor vehicles, computers, and consumer goods); and lessors of nonfinancial intangible assets (except copyrighted works).

Excluded from this sector are real estate investment trusts (REITS) and establishments primarily engaged in renting or leasing equipment with operators. REITS are classified in Subsector 525, Funds, Trusts, and Other Financial Vehicles because they are considered investment vehicles. Establishments renting or leasing equipment with operators are classified in various subsectors of NAICS depending on the nature of the services provided (e.g, transportation, construction, agriculture). These activities are excluded from this sector because the client is paying for the expertise and knowledge of the equipment operator, in addition to the rental of the equipment. In many cases, such as the rental of heavy construction equipment, the operator is essential to operate the equipment.

➡531 REAL ESTATE

Industries in the Real Estate subsector group establishments that are primarily engaged in renting or leasing real estate to others; managing real estate for others; selling, buying, or renting real estate for others; and providing other real estate related services, such as appraisal services.

Establishments primarily engaged in subdividing and developing unimproved real estate and constructing buildings for sale are classified in Subsector 233, Building, Developing, and General Contracting.

Real Estate Investment Trusts (REITS) are classified in Subsector 525, Funds, Trusts, and Other Financial Vehicles because they are considered investment vehicles.

5311 Lessors of Real Estate

53111 Lessors of Residential Buildings and Dwellings ^{CAN}
See industry description for 531110 below.

Sector 53
Real Estate and Rental and Leasing

US—United States industry only. CAN—United States and Canadian industries are comparable. When neither US nor CAN appears, Canadian, Mexican, and United States industries are comparable.

531110 Lessors of Residential Buildings and Dwellings ^{CAN}

This industry comprises establishments primarily engaged in acting as lessors of buildings used as residences or dwellings, such as single-family homes, apartment buildings, and town homes. Included in this industry are owner-lessors and establishments renting real estate and then acting as lessors in subleasing it to others. The establishments in this industry may manage the property themselves or have another establishment manage it for them.

■ Establishments primarily engaged in managing residential real estate for others are classified in U.S. Industry 531311, Residential Property Managers.

53112 Lessors of Nonresidential Buildings (except Miniwarehouses)^{CAN}

See industry description for 531120 below.

531120 Lessors of Nonresidential Buildings (except Miniwarehouses)^{CAN}

This industry comprises establishments primarily engaged in acting as lessors of buildings (except miniwarehouses and self-storage units) that are not used as residences or dwellings. Included in this industry are owner-lessors and establishments renting real estate and then acting as lessors in sub-leasing it to others. The establishments in this industry may manage the property themselves or have another establishment manage it for them.

■ Acting as lessors of buildings used as residences or dwellings are classified in Industry 531110, Lessors of Residential Buildings and Dwellings;
■ Renting or leasing space for self-storage are classified in Industry 531130, Lessors of Miniwarehouses and Self-storage Units;
■ Managing nonresidential real estate for others are classified in U.S. Industry 531312, Nonresidential Property Managers;
■ Managing and operating arenas, stadiums, theaters, or other related facilities and promoting and organizing performing arts productions, sports events, and similar events at those facilities are classified in Industry 711310, Promoters of Performing Arts, Sports, and Similar Events with Facilities; and
■ Operating public and contract general merchandise warehousing and storage facilities are classified in Industry 493110, General Warehousing and Storage.

53113 Lessors of Miniwarehouses and Self-storage Units ^{CAN}

See industry description for 531130 below.

531130 Lessors of Miniwarehouses and Self-storage Units ^{CAN}

This industry comprises establishments primarily engaged in renting or leasing space for self-storage. These establishments provide secure space (i.e., rooms, compartments, lockers, containers, or outdoor space) where clients can store and retrieve their goods.

■ Operating public and contract general merchandise warehousing and storage facilities are classified in Industry 493110, General Warehousing and Storage; and
■ Operating coin-operated lockers are classified in Industry 812990, All Other Personal Services.

53119 Lessors of Other Real Estate Property ^{CAN}

See industry description for 531190 below.

531190 Lessors of Other Real Estate Property ^{CAN}

This industry comprises establishments primarily engaged in acting as lessors of real estate (except buildings), such as manufactured home (i.e., mobile home) sites, vacant lots, and grazing land.

■ Acting as lessors of buildings used as residences or dwellings including manufactured (mobile) homes on-site are classified in Industry 531110, Lessors of Residential Buildings and Dwellings;
■ Acting as lessors of buildings (except miniwarehouses and self-storage units) that are not used as residences or dwellings—are classified in Industry 531120, Lessors of Nonresidential Buildings (except Miniwarehouses); and
■ Renting or leasing space for self-storage are classified in Industry 531130, Lessors of Miniwarehouses and Self-storage Units.

5312 Offices of Real Estate Agents and Brokers

53121 Offices of Real Estate Agents and Brokers

See industry description for 531210 below.

Sector **53**

Real Estate and
Rental and Leasing

■ = Cross-References

US—United States industry only. CAN—United States and Canadian industries are comparable. When neither US nor CAN appears, Canadian, Mexican, and United States industries are comparable.

532   Harris InfoSource

531210 Offices of Real Estate Agents and Brokers

This industry comprises establishments primarily engaged in acting as agents and/or brokers in one or more of the following: (1) selling real estate for others; (2) buying real estate for others; and (3) renting real estate for others.

5313 Activities Related to Real Estate

This industry group comprises establishments primarily engaged in providing real estate services (except lessors of real estate and offices of real estate agents and brokers). Included in this industry group are establishments primarily engaged in activities, such as, managing real estate for others and appraising real estate.

53131 Real Estate Property Managers CAN

This industry comprises establishments primarily engaged in managing real property for others. Management includes ensuring that various activities associated with the overall operation of the property are performed, such as collecting rents, and overseeing other services (e.g., maintenance, security, trash removal.)

- Establishments primarily engaged in acting as lessors of real estate are classified in Industry Group 5311, Lessors of Real Estate; and
- Establishments formed on behalf of individual condominium owners or homeowners are classified in Industry 81399, Other Similar Organizations (except Business, Professional, Labor, and Political Organizations).

531311 Residential Property Managers US

This U.S. industry comprises establishments primarily engaged in managing residential real estate for others.

- Establishments primarily engaged in managing nonresidential real estate for others are classified in U.S. Industry 531312, Nonresidential Property Managers;
- Establishments primarily engaged in acting as lessors of buildings used as residences or dwellings are classified in Industry 531110, Lessors of Residential Buildings and Dwellings; and
- Establishments formed on behalf of individual residential condominium owners or homeowners are classified in Industry 81399, Other Similar Organizations (except Business, Professional, Labor, and Political Organizations).

531312 Nonresidential Property Managers US

This U.S. industry comprises establishments primarily engaged in managing nonresidential real estate for others.

- Establishments primarily engaged in managing residential real estate for others are classified in U.S. Industry 531311, Residential Property Managers;
- Establishments primarily engaged in acting as lessors of buildings (except miniwarehouses and self storage units) that are not used as residences or dwellings are classified in Industry 531120, Lessors of Nonresidential Buildings (except Miniwarehouses);
- Establishments primarily engaged in renting or leasing space for self-storage are classified in Industry 531130, Lessors of Miniwarehouses and Self-storage Units; and
- Establishments formed on behalf of individual nonresidential condominium owner are classified in Industry 81399, Other Similar Organizations (except Business, Professional, Labor, and Political Organizations).

53132 Offices of Real Estate Appraisers CAN

See industry description for 531320 below.

531320 Offices of Real Estate Appraisers CAN

This industry comprises establishments primarily engaged in estimating the fair market value of real estate.

53139 Other Activities Related to Real Estate CAN

531390 Other Activities Related to Real Estate CAN

This industry comprises establishments primarily engaged in performing real estate related services (except lessors of real estate, offices of real estate agents and brokers, real estate property managers, and offices of real estate appraisers).

- Acting as lessors of real estate are classified in Industry Group 5311, Lessors of Real Estate;
- Selling, buying, and/or renting real estate for others are classified in Industry 531210, Offices of Real Estate Agents and Brokers;
- Managing real estate for others are classified in Industry 53131, Real Estate Property Managers;
- Estimating fair market value of real estate are classified in Industry 531320, Offices of Real Estate Appraisers; and
- Researching public land records for ownership of titles and/or conveying real estate titles are classified in U.S. Industry 541191, Title Abstract and Settlement Offices.

Sector **53**

Real Estate and Rental and Leasing

■ = Cross-References

US—United States industry only. CAN—United States and Canadian industries are comparable. When neither US nor CAN appears, Canadian, Mexican, and United States industries are comparable.

▶532 RENTAL AND LEASING SERVICES

Industries in the Rental and Leasing Services subsector include establishments that provide a wide array of tangible goods, such as automobiles, computers, consumer goods, and industrial machinery and equipment, to customers in return for a periodic rental or lease payment.

The subsector includes two main types of establishments: (1) those that are engaged in renting consumer goods and equipment and (2) those that are engaged in leasing machinery and equipment of the kind often used for business operations. The first type typically operates from a retail-like or store-front facility and maintains inventories of goods that are rented for short periods of time. The latter type typically does not operate from retail-like locations or maintain inventories, and offers longer term leases. These establishments work directly with clients to enable them to acquire the use of equipment on a lease basis, or they work with equipment vendors or dealers to support the marketing of equipment to their customers under lease arrangements. Equipment lessors generally structure lease contracts to meet the specialized needs of their clients and use their remarketing expertise to find other users for previously leased equipment. Establishments that provide operating and capital (i.e., finance) leases are included in this subsector. Establishments primarily engaged in leasing in combination with providing loans are classified in Sector 52, Finance and Insurance.

Establishments primarily engaged in leasing real property are classified in Subsector 531, Real Estate. Those establishments primarily engaged in renting or leasing equipment with operators are classified in various subsectors of NAICS depending on the nature of the services provided (e.g., Transportation, Construction, Agriculture). These activities are excluded from this subsector since the client is paying for the expertise and knowledge of the equipment operator, in addition to the rental of the equipment. In many cases, such as the rental of heavy construction equipment, the operator is essential to operate the equipment. Likewise, since the provision of crop harvesting services includes both the equipment and operator, it is included in the agriculture subsector. The rental or leasing of copyrighted works is classified in Sector 51, Information, and the rental or leasing of assets, such as patents, trademarks, and/or licensing agreements is classified in Subsector 533, Lessors of Nonfinancial Intangible Assets (except Copyrighted Works).

5321 Automotive Equipment Rental and Leasing

This industry group comprises establishments primarily engaged in renting or leasing the following types of vehicles: passenger cars and trucks without drivers, and utility trailers. These establishments generally operate from a retail-like facility. Some establishments offer only short-term rental, others only longer term leases, and some provide both type of services.

53211 Passenger Car Rental and Leasing

This industry comprises establishments primarily engaged in renting or leasing passenger cars without drivers.

- Renting or leasing passenger cars with drivers (e.g., limousines, hearses, taxis) are classified in Industry Group 4853, Taxi and Limousine Service;
- Retailing passenger cars through sales or lease arrangements are classified in Industry Group 4411, Automobile Dealers; and
- Leasing passenger cars in combination with providing loans to buyers of such vehicles are classified in Sector 52, Finance and Insurance.

532111 Passenger Car Rental ᶜᴬᴺ

This U.S. industry comprises establishments primarily engaged in renting passenger cars without drivers, generally for short periods of time.

- Leasing passenger cars without drivers, generally for long periods of time are classified in U.S. Industry 532112, Passenger Car Leasing; and
- Renting or leasing passenger cars with drivers (e.g., limousines, hearses, taxis) are classified in Industry Group 4853, Taxi and Limousine Service.

532112 Passenger Car Leasing ᶜᴬᴺ

This U.S. industry comprises establishments primarily engaged in leasing passenger cars without drivers, generally for long periods of time.

- Renting passenger cars without drivers, generally for short periods of time are classified in U.S. Industry 532111, Passenger Car Rental;
- Renting or leasing passenger cars with drivers (e.g., limousines, hearses, taxis) are classified in Industry Group 4853, Taxi and Limousine Service;

Sector **53**

Real Estate and
Rental and Leasing

■ = Cross-References

US—United States industry only. CAN—United States and Canadian industries are comparable. When neither US nor CAN appears, Canadian, Mexican, and United States industries are comparable.

534

Harris InfoSource

- Retailing passenger cars through sales or lease arrangements are classified in Industry Group 4411, Automobile Dealers; and
- Leasing passenger cars in combination with providing loans to buyers of such vehicles are classified in Sector 52, Finance and Insurance.

53212 Truck, Utility Trailer, and RV (Recreational Vehicle) Rental and Leasing
See industry description for 532120 below.

532120 Truck, Utility Trailer, and RV (Recreational Vehicle) Rental and Leasing
This industry comprises establishments primarily engaged in renting or leasing, without drivers, one or more of the following: trucks, truck tractors or buses: semitrailers, utility trailers, or RVs (recreational vehicles).

- Renting recreational goods, such as pleasure boats, canoes, motorcycles, mopeds, or bicycles, are classified in Industry 53229, Other Consumer Goods Rental;
- Renting or leasing farm tractors, industrial equipment, and industrial trucks, such as forklifts and other materials handling equipment, are classified in Industry 532490, Other Commercial and Industrial Machinery Equipment Rental and Leasing;
- Renting or leasing mobile home sites are classified in Industry 53119, Lessors of Other Real Estate Property;
- Retailing vehicles commonly referred to as RVs through sales or lease arrangements are classified in Industry 44121, Recreational Vehicle Dealers; and
- Leasing trucks, utility trailers, and RVs in combination with providing loans to buyers of such vehicles are classified in Sector 52, Finance and Insurance.

5322 Consumer Goods Rental

This industry group comprises establishments primarily engaged in renting personal and household-type goods. Establishments classified in this industry group generally provide short-term rental although in some instances, the goods may be leased for longer periods of time. These establishments often operate from a retail-like or store-front facility.

53221 Consumer Electronics and Appliances Rental
See industry description for 532210 below.

532210 Consumer Electronics and Appliances Rental
This industry comprises establishments primarily engaged in renting consumer electronics equipment and appliances, such as televisions, stereos, and refrigerators. Included in this industry are appliance rental centers.

- Renting or leasing computers are classified in Industry 532420, Office Machinery and Equipment Rental and Leasing; and
- Renting a range of consumer, commercial, and industrial equipment, such as lawn and garden equipment, home repair tools, and party and banquet equipment, are classified in Industry 532310, General Rental Centers.

53222 Formal Wear and Costume Rental
See industry description for 532220 below.

532220 Formal Wear and Costume Rental
This industry comprises establishments primarily engaged in renting clothing, such as formal wear, costumes (e.g., theatrical), or other clothing (except laundered uniforms and work apparel).

- Establishments primarily engaged in laundering and supplying uniforms and other work apparel are classified in Industry 81233, Linen and Uniform Supply.

53223 Video Tape and Disc Rental
See industry description for 532230 below.

532230 Video Tape and Disc Rental
This industry comprises establishments primarily engaged in renting prerecorded video tapes and discs for home electronic equipment.

- Theatrical distribution of motion pictures and videos are classified in Subsector 512, Motion Picture and Sound Recording Industries;
- Renting video recorders and players are classified in Industry 532210, Consumer Electronics and Appliances Rental; and
- Retailing prerecorded video tapes and discs are classified in Industry 451220, Prerecorded Tape, Compact Disc, and Record Stores.

Sector 53

Real Estate and
Rental and Leasing

■ = Cross-References

US—United States industry only. CAN—United States and Canadian industries are comparable. When neither US nor CAN appears, Canadian, Mexican, and United States industries are comparable.

www.harrisinfo.com

535

53229 Other Consumer Goods Rental
This industry comprises establishments primarily engaged in renting consumer goods (except consumer electronics and appliances, formal wear and costumes, and prerecorded video tapes).

- Renting consumer electronics and appliances are classified in Industry 53221, Consumer Electronics and Appliances Rental;
- Renting formal wear and costumes are classified in Industry 53222, Formal Wear and Costume Rental;
- Renting prerecorded video tapes are classified in Industry 53223, Video Tape and Disc Rental;
- Renting a general line of products, such as lawn and garden equipment, home repair tools, and party and banquet equipment, are classified in Industry 53231, General Rental Centers;
- Renting medical equipment (except home health equipment), such as electromedical and electrotherapeutic apparatus, are classified in Industry 53249, Other Commercial and Industrial Machinery and Equipment Rental and Leasing;
- Providing home health care services and home health equipment are classified in Industry 62161, Home Health Care Services; and
- Retailing and renting musical instruments are classified in Industry 45114, Musical Instrument and Supplies Stores.

532291 Home Health Equipment Rental ^{US}
This U.S. industry comprises establishments primarily engaged in renting home-type health and invalid equipment, such as wheel chairs, hospital beds, oxygen tanks, walkers, and crutches.

- Renting medical equipment (except home health equipment), such as electromedical and electrotherapeutic apparatus, are classified in Industry 532490, Other Commercial and Industrial Machinery and Equipment Rental and Leasing; and
- Providing home health care services and home health equipment are classified in Industry 62161, Home Health Care Services.

532292 Recreational Goods Rental ^{US}
This U.S. industry comprises establishments primarily engaged in renting recreational goods, such as bicycles, canoes, motorcycles, skis, sailboats, beach chairs, and beach umbrellas.

532299 All Other Consumer Goods Rental ^{US}
This U.S. industry comprises establishments primarily engaged in renting consumer goods and products (except consumer electronics and appliances; formal wear and costumes; prerecorded video tapes and discs for home electronic equipment; home health furniture and equipment; and recreational goods). Included in this industry are furniture rental centers and party rental supply centers.

- Renting consumer electronics and appliances are classified in Industry 532210, Consumer Electronics and Appliances Rental;
- Renting formal wear and costumes are classified in Industry 532220, Formal Wear and Costume Rental;
- Renting video tapes are classified in Industry 532230, Video Tape and Disc Rental;
- Renting home health furniture and equipment are classified in U.S. Industry 532291, Home Health Equipment Rental;
- Renting recreational goods are classified in U.S. Industry 532292, Recreational Goods Rental;
- Retailing and renting musical instruments are classified in Industry 451140, Musical Instrument and Supplies Stores; and
- Renting a range of consumer, commercial, and industrial equipment, such as lawn and garden equipment, home repair tools, and party and banquet equipment, are classified in Industry 532310, General Rental Centers.

5323 General Rental Centers

53231 General Rental Centers
See industry description for 532310 below.

532310 General Rental Centers
This industry comprises establishments primarily engaged in renting a range of consumer, commercial, and industrial equipment. Establishments in this industry typically operate from conveniently located facilities where they maintain inventories of goods and equipment that they rent for short periods of time. The type of equipment that establishments in this industry provide often includes, but is not limited to: audio-visual equipment, contractors and builders tools and equipment, home repair tools, lawn and garden equipment, moving equipment and supplies, and party and banquet equipment and supplies.

- Renting trucks and trailers without drivers are classified in Industry 532120, Truck, Utility Trailer, and RV (Recreational Vehicle) Rental and Leasing;
- Renting party and banquet equipment are classified in Industry 53229, Other Consumer Goods Rental;
- Renting heavy construction equipment without operators are classified in U.S. Industry 532412, Construction, Mining, and Forestry Machinery and Equipment Rental and Leasing; and
- Renting specialized types of commercial and industrial equipment, such as garden tractors or public address systems, are classified in Industry 532490, Other Commercial and Industrial Machinery and Equipment Rental and Leasing.

Sector 53

Real Estate and
Rental and Leasing

■ = Cross-References

US—United States industry only. CAN—United States and Canadian industries are comparable. When neither US nor CAN appears, Canadian, Mexican, and United States industries are comparable.

536

Harris InfoSource

5324 Commercial and Industrial Machinery and Equipment Rental and Leasing

This industry group comprises establishments primarily engaged in renting or leasing commercial-type and industrial-type machinery and equipment. The types of establishments included in this industry group are generally involved in providing capital or investment-type equipment that clients use in their business operations. These establishments typically cater to a business clientele and do not generally operate a retail-like or store-front facility.

53241 Construction, Transportation, Mining, and Forestry Machinery and Equipment Rental and Leasing

This industry comprises establishments primarily engaged in renting or leasing one or more of the following without operators: heavy construction, off-highway transportation, mining, and forestry machinery and equipment. Establishments in this industry may rent or lease products, such as aircraft, railroad cars, steamships, tugboats, bulldozers, earthmoving equipment, well-drilling machinery and equipment, or cranes.

- Renting or leasing automobiles or trucks without operators are classified in Industry Group 5321, Automotive Equipment Rental and Leasing;
- Renting or leasing air, rail, highway, and water transportation equipment with operators are classified in Sector 48-49, Transportation and Warehousing, based on their primary activity;
- Renting or leasing heavy construction equipment with operators are classified in Industry 23499, All Other Heavy Construction;
- Renting or leasing heavy equipment for mining with operators are classified in Industry 21311, Support Activities for Mining;
- Renting or leasing heavy equipment for forestry with operators are classified in Industry Group 1153, Support Activities for Forestry; and
- Leasing heavy equipment in combination with providing loans to buyers of such equipment are classified in Sector 52, Finance and Insurance.

532411 Commercial Air, Rail, and Water Transportation Equipment Rental and Leasing US

This U.S. industry comprises establishments primarily engaged in renting or leasing off-highway transportation equipment without operators, such as aircraft, railroad cars, steamships, or tugboats.

- Renting or leasing air, rail, highway, and water transportation equipment with operators are classified in Sector 48-49, Transportation and Warehousing, based on their primary activity;
- Renting pleasure boats are classified in U.S. Industry 532292, Recreational Goods Rental; and
- Renting or leasing automobiles or trucks without drivers are classified in Industry Group 5321, Automotive Equipment Rental and Leasing.

532412 Construction, Mining, and Forestry Machinery and Equipment Rental and Leasing US

This U.S. industry comprises establishments primarily engaged in renting or leasing heavy equipment without operators that may be used for construction, mining, or forestry, such as bulldozers, earth-moving equipment, well-drilling machinery and equipment, or cranes.

- Renting or leasing heavy construction equipment with operators are classified in Industry 23499, All Other Heavy Construction;
- Renting or leasing heavy equipment for mining with operators are classified in Industry 21311, Support Activities for Mining;
- Renting or leasing heavy equipment for forestry with operators are classified in Industry Group 1153, Support Activities for Forestry; and
- Leasing heavy equipment in combination with providing loans to buyers of such equipment are classified in Sector 52, Finance and Insurance.

53242 Office Machinery and Equipment Rental and Leasing

See industry description for 532420 below.

532420 Office Machinery and Equipment Rental and Leasing

This industry comprises establishments primarily engaged in renting or leasing office machinery and equipment, such as computers, office furniture, duplicating machines (i.e., copiers), or facsimile machines.

- Renting or leasing residential furniture are classified in Industry 53229, Other Consumer Goods Rental; and
- Leasing office machinery and equipment in combination with providing loans to buyers of such equipment are classified in Sector 52, Finance and Insurance.

53249 Other Commercial and Industrial Machinery and Equipment Rental and Leasing

See industry description for 532490 below.

Sector **53**

Real Estate and
Rental and Leasing

■ = Cross-References

US—United States industry only. CAN—United States and Canadian industries are comparable. When neither US nor CAN appears, Canadian, Mexican, and United States industries are comparable.

www.harrisinfo.com

537

532490 Other Commercial and Industrial Machinery and Equipment Rental and Leasing

This industry comprises establishments primarily engaged in renting or leasing nonconsumer-type machinery and equipment (except heavy construction, transportation, mining, and forestry machinery and equipment without operators; and office machinery and equipment). Establishments in this industry rent or lease products, such as, manufacturing equipment; metalworking, telecommunications, motion picture, or theatrical machinery and equipment; institutional (i.e., public building) furniture, such as furniture for schools, theaters, or buildings; or agricultural equipment without operators.

- Renting or leasing heavy equipment without operators are classified in Industry 53241, Construction, Transportation, Mining, and Forestry Machinery and Equipment Rental and Leasing;
- Renting or leasing office machinery and equipment are classified in Industry 532420, Office Machinery and Equipment Rental and Leasing;
- Renting or leasing agricultural machinery and equipment with operators are classified in Subsector 115, Support Activities for Agriculture and Forestry;
- Renting home furniture or medical equipment for home use are classified in Industry 53229, Other Consumer Goods Rental and Leasing; and
- Leasing nonconsumer machinery and equipment in combination with providing loans to buyers of such equipment are classified in Sector 52, Finance and Insurance.

▶533 LESSORS OF NONFINANCIAL INTANGIBLE ASSETS (EXCEPT COPYRIGHTED WORKS)

Industries in the Lessors of Nonfinancial Intangible Assets (except Copyrighted Works) subsector include establishments that are primarily engaged in assigning rights to assets, such as patents, trademarks, brand names, and/or franchise agreements for which a royalty payment or licensing fee is paid to the asset holder. Establishments in this subsector own the patents, trademarks, and/or franchise agreements that they allow others to use or reproduce for a fee and may or may not have created those assets.

Establishments that allow franchisees the use of the franchise name, contingent on the franchisee buying products or services from the franchisor, are classified elsewhere.

Excluded from this subsector are establishments primarily engaged in leasing real property and establishments primarily engaged in leasing tangible assets, such as automobiles, computers, consumer goods, and industrial machinery and equipment. These establishments are classified in Subsector 531, Real Estate and Subsector 532, Rental and Leasing Services, respectively.

5331 Lessors of Nonfinancial Intangible Assets (Except Copyrighted Works)

53311 Lessors of Nonfinancial Intangible Assets (Except Copyrighted Works)
See industry description for 533110 below.

533110 Lessors of Nonfinancial Intangible Assets (Except Copyrighted Works)
This industry comprises establishments primarily engaged in assigning rights to assets, such as patents, trademarks, brand names, and/or franchise agreements for which a royalty payment or licensing fee is paid to the asset holder.

- Establishments primarily engaged in producing, reproducing, and/or distributing copyrighted works are classified in Sector 51, Information;
- Independent artists, writers, and performers primarily engaged in creating copyrighted works are classified in Industry 711510, Independent Artists, Writers, and Performers;
- Establishments primarily engaged in leasing real property are classified in Subsector 531, Real Estate;
- Establishments primarily engaged in leasing tangible assets, such as automobiles, computers, consumer goods, and industrial machinery and equipment, are classified in Subsector 532, Rental and Leasing Services; and
- Establishments that allow franchisees the use of the franchise name, contingent on the franchisee buying products or services from the franchisor are classified elsewhere.

Sector 53

Real Estate and Rental and Leasing

■ = Cross-References

US—United States industry only. CAN—United States and Canadian industries are comparable. When neither US nor CAN appears, Canadian, Mexican, and United States industries are comparable.

538

Harris InfoSource

Sector 54
Professional, Scientific, and Technical Services

The Sector as a Whole

THE PROFESSIONAL, SCIENTIFIC, AND TECHNICAL SERVICES sector comprises establishments that specialize in performing professional, scientific, and technical activities for others. These activities require a high degree of expertise and training. The establishments in this sector specialize according to expertise and provide these services to clients in a variety of industries and, in some cases, to households. Activities performed include: legal advice and representation; accounting, bookkeeping, and payroll services; architectural, engineering, and specialized design services; computer services; consulting services; research services; advertising services; photographic services; translation and interpretation services; veterinary services; and other professional, scientific, and technical services.

This sector excludes establishments primarily engaged in providing a range of day-to-day office administrative services, such as financial planning, billing and recordkeeping, personnel, and physical distribution and logistics. These establishments are classified in Sector 56, Administrative and Support and Waste Management and Remediation Services.

Visit page 18 to learn more about this sector.

▶541 PROFESSIONAL, SCIENTIFIC, AND TECHNICAL SERVICES

Industries in the Professional, Scientific, and Technical Services subsector group establishments engaged in processes where human capital is the major input. These establishments make available the knowledge and skills of their employees, often on an assignment basis, where an individual or team is responsible for the delivery of services to the client. The individual industries of this subsector are defined on the basis of the particular expertise and training of the services provider.

The distinguishing feature of the Professional, Scientific, and Technical Services subsector is the fact that most of the industries grouped in it have production processes that are almost wholly dependent on worker skills. In most of these industries, equipment and materials are not of major importance, unlike health care, for example, where "high-tech" machines and materials are important collaborating inputs to labor skills in the production of health care. Thus, the establishments classified in this subsector sell expertise. Much of the expertise requires degrees, though not in every case.

5411 Legal Services

54111 Offices of Lawyers
See industry description for 541110 below.

541110 Offices of Lawyers
This industry comprises offices of legal practitioners known as lawyers or attorneys (i.e., counselors-at-law) primarily engaged in the practice of law. Establishments in this industry may provide expertise in a range or in specific areas of law, such as criminal law, corporate law, family and estate law, patent law, real estate law, or tax law.

■ Establishments of legal practitioners (except lawyers or attorneys) primarily engaged in providing specialized legal or para-legal services are classified in Industry 54119, Other Legal Services.

Sector 54
Professional, Scientific, and Technical Services

■ = Cross-References

54112 Offices of Notaries
See industry description for 541120 below.

541120 Offices of Notaries
This industry comprises establishments (except offices of lawyers and attorneys) primarily engaged in drafting, approving, and executing legal documents, such as real estate transactions, wills, and contracts; and in receiving, indexing, and storing such documents.

- Establishments of lawyers and attorneys primarily engaged in the practice of law are classified in Industry 541110, Offices of Lawyers; and
- Establishments of notaries public engaged in activities, such as administering oaths and taking affidavits and depositions, witnessing and certifying signatures on documents, but not empowered to draw and approve legal documents and contracts, are classified in U.S. Industry 541199, All Other Legal Services.

54119 Other Legal Services
This industry comprises establishments of legal practitioners (except lawyers and attorneys) primarily engaged in providing specialized legal or paralegal services.

- Establishments of lawyers and attorneys primarily engaged in the practice of law are classified in Industry 54111, Offices of Lawyers; and
- Establishments (except offices of lawyers, attorneys, and paralegals) primarily engaged in providing arbitration and conciliation services are classified in Industry 54199, All Other Professional, Scientific, and Technical Services.

541191 Title Abstract and Settlement Offices ᵁˢ
This U.S. industry comprises establishments (except offices of lawyers and attorneys) primarily engaged in one or more of the following activities: (1) researching public land records to gather information relating to real estate titles; (2) preparing documents necessary for the transfer of the title, financing, and settlement; (3) conducting final real estate settlements and closings; and (4) filing legal and other documents relating to the sale of real estate. Real estate settlement offices, title abstract companies, and title search companies are included in this industry.

- Establishments of lawyers and attorneys primarily engaged in the practice of law are classified in Industry 541110, Offices of Lawyers.

541199 All Other Legal Services ᵁˢ
This U.S. industry comprises establishments of legal practitioners (except offices of lawyers and attorneys, settlement offices, and title abstract offices). These establishments are primarily engaged in providing specialized legal or paralegal services.

- Establishments of lawyers and attorneys primarily engaged in the practice of law are classified in Industry 541110, Offices of Lawyers;
- Establishments (except offices of lawyers and attorneys) primarily engaged in researching public land records for ownership or title; preparing documents necessary for the transfer of the title, financing, and settlement; conducting final real estate settlements and closings; and/or filing legal and other documents relating to the sale of real estate are classified in U.S. Industry 541191, Title Abstract and Settlement Offices; and
- Establishments (except offices of lawyers, attorneys, and paralegals) primarily engaged in providing arbitration and conciliation services are classified in Industry 541990, All Other Professional, Scientific, and Technical Services.

5412 Accounting, Tax Preparation, Bookkeeping, and Payroll Services

54121 Accounting, Tax Preparation, Bookkeeping, and Payroll Services
This industry comprises establishments primarily engaged in providing services, such as auditing of accounting records, designing accounting systems, preparing financial statements, developing budgets, preparing tax returns, processing payrolls, bookkeeping, and billing.

541211 Offices of Certified Public Accountants ᵁˢ
This U.S. industry comprises establishments of accountants that are certified to audit the accounting records of public and private organizations and to attest to compliance with generally accepted accounting practices. Offices of certified public accountants (CPAs) may provide one or more of the following accounting services: (1) auditing financial statements; (2) designing accounting systems; (3) preparing financial statements; (4) developing budgets; and (5) providing advice on matters related to accounting. These establishments may also provide related services, such as bookkeeping, tax return preparation, and payroll processing.

Sector **54**

Professional,
Scientific, and
Technical Services

■ = Cross-References

US—United States industry only. CAN—United States and Canadian industries are comparable. When neither US nor CAN appears, Canadian, Mexican, and United States industries are comparable.

540

Harris InfoSource

- Providing tax return preparation services only are classified in U.S. Industry 541213, Tax Preparation Services;
- Providing payroll processing services only are classified in U.S. Industry 541214, Payroll Services; and
- Providing accounting, bookkeeping, and billing services are classified in U.S. Industry 541219, Other Accounting Services.

541213 Tax Preparation Services CAN
This U.S. industry comprises establishments (except offices of CPAs) engaged in providing tax return preparation services without also providing accounting, bookkeeping, billing, or payroll processing services. Basic knowledge of tax law and filing requirements is required.

- Establishments of CPAs are classified in U.S. Industry 541211, Offices of Certified Public Accountants;
- Establishments of non-CPAs providing payroll services along with tax return preparation services are classified in U.S. Industry 541214, Payroll Services;
- Establishments of non-CPAs providing accounting, bookkeeping, or billing services along with tax return preparation services are classified in U.S. Industry 541219, Other Accounting Services; and
- Establishments providing computer data processing services at their own facility for others are classified in Industry 514210, Data Processing Services.

541214 Payroll Services US
This U.S. industry comprises establishments (except offices of CPAs) engaged in the following without also providing accounting, bookkeeping, or billing services: (1) collecting information on hours worked, pay rates, deductions, and other payroll-related data from their clients and (2) using that information to generate paychecks, payroll reports, and tax filings. These establishments may use data processing and tabulating techniques as part of providing their services.

541219 Other Accounting Services US
This U.S. industry comprises establishments (except offices of CPAs) engaged in providing accounting services (except tax return preparation services only or payroll services only). These establishments may also provide tax return preparation or payroll services. Accountant (except CPA) offices, bookkeeper offices, and billing offices are included in this industry.

- Establishments of CPAs are classified in U.S. Industry 541211, Offices of Certified Public Accountants;
- Establishments of non-CPAs engaged in providing tax return preparation services only are classified in U.S. Industry 541213, Tax Preparation Services; and
- Establishments of non-CPAs engaged in providing payroll services only are classified in U.S. Industry 541214, Payroll Services.

5413 Architectural, Engineering, and Related Services

54131 Architectural Services
See industry description for 541310 below.

541310 Architectural Services
This industry comprises establishments primarily engaged in planning and designing residential, institutional, leisure, commercial, and industrial buildings and structures by applying knowledge of design, construction procedures, zoning regulations, building codes, and building materials.

- Planning and designing the development of land areas are classified in Industry 541320, Landscape Architectural Services; and
- Both the design and construction of buildings, highways, or other structures or in managing construction projects are classified Sector 23, Construction, according to the type of project.

54132 Landscape Architectural Services
See industry description for 541320 below.

541320 Landscape Architectural Services
This industry comprises establishments primarily engaged in planning and designing the development of land areas for projects, such as parks and other recreational areas; airports; highways; hospitals; schools; land subdivisions; and commercial, industrial, and residential areas, by applying knowledge of land characteristics, location of buildings and structures, use of land areas, and design of landscape projects.

- Establishments primarily engaged in providing landscape care and maintenance services and/or installing trees, shrubs, plants, lawns, or gardens along with the design of landscape plans are classified in Industry 561730, Landscaping Services.

Visit page 18 to learn more about this sector.

Sector 54

Professional, Scientific, and Technical Services

■ = Cross-References

US—United States industry only. CAN—United States and Canadian industries are comparable. When neither US nor CAN appears, Canadian, Mexican, and United States industries are comparable.

www.harrisinfo.com

541

54133 Engineering Services
See industry description for 541330 below.

541330 Engineering Services
This industry comprises establishments primarily engaged in applying physical laws and principles of engineering in the design, development, and utilization of machines, materials, instruments, structures, processes, and systems. The assignments undertaken by these establishments may involve any of the following activities: provision of advice, preparation of feasibility studies, preparation of preliminary and final plans and designs, provision of technical services during the construction or installation phase, inspection and evaluation of engineering projects, and related services.

- ■ Planning and designing computer systems that integrate computer hardware, software, and communication technologies are classified in U.S. Industry 541512, Computer Systems Design Services;
- ■ Performing surveying and mapping services of the surface of the earth, including the sea floor, are classified in Industry 541370, Surveying and Mapping (except Geophysical) Services;
- ■ Gathering, interpreting, and mapping geophysical data are classified in Industry 541360, Geophysical Surveying and Mapping Services;
- ■ Creating and developing designs and specifications that optimize the use, value, and appearance of products are classified in Industry 541420, Industrial Design Services;
- ■ Providing advice and assistance to others on environmental issues, such as the control of environmental contamination from pollutants, toxic substances, and hazardous materials are classified in Industry 541620, Environmental Consulting Services; and
- ■ Both the design and construction of buildings, highways, and other structures or in managing construction projects are classified in Sector 23, Construction, according to the type of project.

54134 Drafting Services
See industry description for 541340 below.

541340 Drafting Services
This industry comprises establishments primarily engaged in drawing detailed layouts, plans, and illustrations of buildings, structures, systems, or components from engineering and architectural specifications.

54135 Building Inspection Services
See industry description for 541350 below.

541350 Building Inspection Services
This industry comprises establishments primarily engaged in providing building inspection services. These establishments typically evaluate all aspects of the building structure and component systems and prepare a report on the physical condition of the property, generally for buyers or others involved in real estate transactions. Building inspection bureaus and establishments providing home inspection services are included in this industry.

- ■ Inspecting buildings for termites and other pests are classified in Industry 561710, Exterminating and Pest Control Services;
- ■ Inspecting buildings for hazardous materials are classified in Industry 541620, Environmental Consulting Services; and
- ■ Conducting inspections and enforcing public building codes and standards are classified in Industry 925110, Administration of Housing Programs.

54136 Geophysical Surveying and Mapping Services
See industry description for 541360 below.

Sector 54

Professional, Scientific, and Technical Services

541360 Geophysical Surveying and Mapping Services
This industry comprises establishments primarily engaged in gathering, interpreting, and mapping geophysical data. Establishments in this industry often specialize in locating and measuring the extent of subsurface resources, such as oil, gas, and minerals, but they may also conduct surveys for engineering purposes. Establishments in this industry use a variety of surveying techniques depending on the purpose of the survey, including magnetic surveys, gravity surveys, seismic surveys, or electrical and electromagnetic surveys.

- ■ Establishments primarily engaged in taking core samples, drilling test wells, or other mine development activities (except geophysical surveying and mapping) on a contract basis for others are classified in Industry 21311, Support Activities for Mining.

■ = Cross-References

US—United States industry only. CAN—United States and Canadian industries are comparable. When neither US nor CAN appears, Canadian, Mexican, and United States industries are comparable.

542

Harris InfoSource

54137 Surveying and Mapping (except Geophysical) Services
See industry description for 541370 below.

541370 Surveying and Mapping (except Geophysical) Services
This industry comprises establishments primarily engaged in performing surveying and mapping services of the surface of the earth, including the sea floor. These services may include surveying and mapping of areas above or below the surface of the earth, such as the creation of view easements or segregating rights in parcels of land by creating underground utility easements.

- Providing geophysical surveying and mapping services are classified in Industry 541360, Geophysical Surveying and Mapping Services; and
- Publishing atlases and maps are classified in U.S. Industry 511199, All Other Publishers.

54138 Testing Laboratories
See industry description for 541380 below.

541380 Testing Laboratories
This industry comprises establishments primarily engaged in performing physical, chemical, and other analytical testing services, such as acoustics or vibration testing, assaying, biological testing (except medical and veterinary), calibration testing, electrical and electronic testing, geotechnical testing, mechanical testing, nondestructive testing, or thermal testing. The testing may occur in a laboratory or on-site.

- Laboratory testing for the medical profession are classified in Industry 62151, Medical and Diagnostic Laboratories;
- Veterinary testing services are classified in Industry 541940, Veterinary Services; and
- Auto-emissions testing are classified in U.S. Industry 811198, All Other Automotive Repair and Maintenance.

5414 Specialized Design Services
This industry group comprises establishments providing specialized design services (except architectural, engineering, and computer systems design).

54141 Interior Design Services
See industry description for 541410 below.

541410 Interior Design Services
This industry comprises establishments primarily engaged in planning, designing, and administering projects in interior spaces to meet the physical and aesthetic needs of people using them, taking into consideration building codes, health and safety regulations, traffic patterns and floor planning, mechanical and electrical needs, and interior fittings and furniture. Interior designers and interior design consultants work in areas, such as hospitality design, health care design, institutional design, commercial and corporate design, and residential design. This industry also includes interior decorating consultants engaged exclusively in providing aesthetic services associated with interior spaces.

54142 Industrial Design Services
See industry description for 541420 below.

541420 Industrial Design Services
This industry comprises establishments primarily engaged in creating and developing designs and specifications that optimize the use, value, and appearance of their products. These services can include the determination of the materials, construction, mechanisms, shape, color, and surface finishes of the product, taking into consideration human characteristics and needs, safety, market appeal, and efficiency in production, distribution, use, and maintenance. Establishments providing automobile or furniture industrial design services or industrial design consulting services are included in this industry.

- Applying physical laws and principles of engineering in the design, development, and utilization of machines, materials, instruments, structures, processes, and systems are classified in Industry 541330, Engineering Services; and
- Designing clothing, shoes, or jewelry are classified in Industry 541490, Other Specialized Design Services.

Visit page 18 to learn more about this sector.

Sector 54

Professional, Scientific, and Technical Services

■ = Cross-References

US—United States industry only. CAN—United States and Canadian industries are comparable. When neither US nor CAN appears, Canadian, Mexican, and United States industries are comparable.

www.harrisinfo.com

543

54143 Graphic Design Services
See industry description for 541430 below.

541430 Graphic Design Services
This industry comprises establishments primarily engaged in planning, designing, and managing the production of visual communication in order to convey specific messages or concepts, clarify complex information, or project visual identities. These services can include the design of printed materials, packaging, advertising, signage systems, and corporate identification (logos). This industry also includes commercial artists engaged exclusively in generating drawings and illustrations requiring technical accuracy or interpretative skills.

- Establishments primarily engaged in creating and/or placing public display advertising material are classified in Industry 541850, Display Advertising; and
- Independent artists primarily engaged in creating and selling visual artwork for noncommercial use and independent cartoonists are classified in Industry 711510, Independent Artists, Writers, and Performers.

54149 Other Specialized Design Services
See industry description for 541490 below.

541490 Other Specialized Design Services
This industry comprises establishments primarily engaged in providing professional design services (except architectural, landscape architecture, engineering, interior, industrial, graphic, and computer system design).

- Providing architectural design services are classified in Industry 541310, Architectural Services;
- Providing landscape architecture design services are classified in Industry 541320, Landscape Architectural Services;
- Providing engineering design services are classified in Industry 541330, Engineering Services;
- Providing interior design services are classified in Industry 541410, Interior Design Services;
- Providing industrial design services are classified in Industry 541420, Industrial Design Services;
- Providing graphic design services are classified in Industry 541430, Graphic Design Services;
- Providing computer systems design services are classified in U.S. Industry 541512, Computer Systems Design Services; and
- Operating as independent theatrical designers are classified in Industry 711510, Independent Artists, Writers, and Performers.

5415 Computer Systems Design and Related Services
See industry description for 54151 below.

54151 Computer Systems Design and Related Services
This industry comprises establishments primarily engaged in providing expertise in the field of information technologies through one or more of the following activities: (1) writing, modifying, testing, and supporting software to meet the needs of a particular customer; (2) planning and designing computer systems that integrate computer hardware, software, and communication technologies; (3) on-site management and operation of clients' computer systems and/or data processing facilities; and (4) other professional and technical computer-related advice and services.

- Selling computer hardware or software products from retail-like locations and providing supporting services, such as customized assembly of personal computers, are classified in Industry 44312, Computer and Software Stores;
- Wholesaling computer hardware or software products and providing supporting services, such as customized assembly of personal computers, are classified in Industry 42143, Computer and Computer Peripheral Equipment and Software Wholesalers;
- Publishing packaged software are classified in Industry 51121, Software Publishers; and
- Providing computer data processing services at their own facility for others are classified in Industry 51421, Data Processing Services.

541511 Custom Computer Programming Services ᵁˢ
This U.S. industry comprises establishments primarily engaged in writing, modifying, testing, and supporting software to meet the needs of a particular customer.

- Publishing packaged software are classified in Industry 511210, Software Publishers; and
- Planning and designing computer systems that integrate computer hardware, software, and communication technologies, even though such establishments may provide custom software as an integral part of their services, are classified in U.S. Industry 541512, Computer Systems Design Services.

■ = Cross-References

US—United States industry only. CAN—United States and Canadian industries are comparable. When neither US nor CAN appears, Canadian, Mexican, and United States industries are comparable.

Sector 54

Professional, Scientific, and Technical Services

541512 Computer Systems Design Services [US]

This U.S. industry comprises establishments primarily engaged in planning and designing computer systems that integrate computer hardware, software, and communication technologies. The hardware and software components of the system may be provided by this establishment or company as part of integrated services or may be provided by third parties or vendors. These establishments often install the system and train and support users of the system.

- Selling computer hardware or software products and systems from retail-like locations, and providing supporting services, such as customized assembly of personal computers are classified in Industry 443120, Computer and Software Stores; and
- Wholesaling computer hardware or software products and providing supporting services, such as customized assembly of personal computers, are classified in Industry 421430, Computer and Computer Peripheral Equipment and Software Wholesalers.

541513 Computer Facilities Management Services [US]

This U.S. industry comprises establishments primarily engaged in providing on-site management and operation of clients' computer systems and/or data processing facilities. Establishments providing computer systems or data processing facilities support services are included in this industry.

- Establishments primarily engaged in providing computer data processing services at their own facility for others are classified in Industry 514210, Data Processing Services.

541519 Other Computer Related Services [US]

This U.S. industry comprises establishments primarily engaged in providing computer related services (except custom programming, systems integration design, and facilities management services). Establishments providing computer disaster recovery services or software installation services are included in this industry.

- Providing custom computer programming services are classified in U.S. Industry 541511, Custom Computer Programming Services;
- Providing computer systems integration design services are classified in U.S. Industry 541512, Computer Systems Design Services; and
- Providing computer systems and/or data processing facilities management services are classified in U.S. Industry 541513, Computer Facilities Management Services.

Visit page 18 to learn more about this sector.

5416 Management, Scientific, and Technical Consulting Services

54161 Management Consulting Services

This industry comprises establishments primarily engaged in providing advice and assistance to businesses and other organizations on management issues, such as strategic and organizational planning; financial planning and budgeting; marketing objectives and policies; human resource policies, practices, and planning; production scheduling; and control planning.

- Establishments primarily engaged in providing a range of day-to-day office administrative services, such as financial planning, billing and recordkeeping, personnel, and physical distribution and logistics, are classified in Industry 56111, Office Administrative Services;
- Establishments primarily engaged in administering, overseeing, and managing other establishments of the company or enterprise (except government establishments) are classified in Industry 55111, Management of Companies and Enterprises;
- Government establishments primarily engaged in administering, overseeing, and managing governmental programs are classified in Sector 92, Public Administration;
- Establishments primarily engaged in professional and management development training are classified in Industry 61143 Professional and Management Development Training;
- Establishments primarily engaged in listing employment vacancies and in selecting, referring, and placing applicants in employment are classified in Industry 56131, Employment Placement Agencies;
- Establishments primarily engaged in developing and implementing public relations plans are classified in Industry 54182, Public Relations Agencies;
- Establishments primarily engaged in developing and conducting marketing research or public opinion polling are classified in Industry 54191, Market Research and Public Opinion Polling;
- Establishments primarily engaged in planning and designing industrial processes and systems are classified in Industry 54133, Engineering Services;
- Establishments primarily engaged in planning and designing computer systems are classified in Industry 54151, Computer Systems Design and Related Services; and
- Establishments primarily engaged in providing financial investment advice services are classified in Industry 52393, Investment Advice.

Sector **54**

Professional, Scientific, and Technical Services

■ = Cross-References

US—United States industry only. CAN—United States and Canadian industries are comparable. When neither US nor CAN appears, Canadian, Mexican, and United States industries are comparable.

541611 Administrative Management and General Management Consulting Services ^{CAN}

This U.S. industry comprises establishments primarily engaged in providing operating advice and assistance to businesses and other organizations on administrative management issues, such as financial planning and budgeting, equity and asset management, records management, office planning, strategic and organizational planning, site selection, new business startup, and business process improvement. This industry also includes establishments of general management consultants that provide a full range of administrative; human resource; marketing; process, physical distribution, and logistics; or other management consulting services to clients.

- Establishments primarily engaged in providing a range of day-to-day office administrative services, such as financial planning, billing and recordkeeping, personnel, and physical distribution and logistics, are classified in Industry 561110, Office Administrative Services;
- Establishments primarily engaged in administering, overseeing, and managing other establishments of the company or enterprise (except government establishments) are classified in U.S. Industry 551114, Corporate, Subsidiary, and Regional Managing Offices;
- Government establishments primarily engaged in administering, overseeing, and managing governmental programs are classified in Sector 92, Public Administration; and
- Establishments primarily engaged in providing investment advice are classified in Industry 523930, Investment Advice.

541612 Human Resources and Executive Search Consulting Services ^{CAN}

This U.S. industry comprises establishments primarily engaged in providing advice and assistance to businesses and other organizations in one or more of the following areas: (1) human resource and personnel policies, practices, and procedures; (2) employee benefits planning, communication, and administration; (3) compensation systems planning; (4) wage and salary administration; and (5) executive search and recruitment.

- Professional and management development training are classified in Industry 611430, Professional and Management Development Training; and
- Listing employment vacancies and in selecting, referring, and placing applicants in employment are classified in Industry 561310, Employment Placement Agencies.

541613 Marketing Consulting Services ^{US}

This U.S. industry comprises establishments primarily engaged in providing operating advice and assistance to businesses and other organizations on marketing issues, such as developing marketing objectives and policies, sales forecasting, new product developing and pricing, licensing and franchise planning, and marketing planning and strategy.

- Developing and implementing public relations plans are classified in Industry 541820, Public Relations Agencies; and
- Developing and conducting marketing research or public opinion polling are classified in Industry 541910, Marketing Research and Public Opinion Polling.

541614 Process, Physical Distribution, and Logistics Consulting Services ^{US}

This U.S. industry comprises establishments primarily engaged in providing operating advice and assistance to businesses and other organizations in areas, such as: (1) manufacturing operations improvement; (2) productivity improvement; (3) production planning and control; (4) quality assurance and quality control; (5) inventory management; (6) distribution networks; (7) warehouse use, operations, and utilization; (8) transportation and shipment of goods and materials; and (9) materials management and handling.

- Planning and designing industrial processes and systems are classified in Industry 541330, Engineering Services; and
- Providing computer systems integration design services are classified in U.S. Industry 541512, Computer Systems Design Services.

541618 Other Management Consulting Services ^{US}

This U.S. industry comprises establishments primarily engaged in providing management consulting services (except administrative and general management consulting; human resources consulting; marketing consulting; or process, physical distribution, and logistics consulting). Establishments providing telecommunications or utilities management consulting services are included in this industry.

- Providing administrative and general management consulting services are classified in U.S. Industry 541611, Administrative Management and General Management Consulting Services;
- Providing human resources and executive search consulting services are classified in U.S. Industry 541612, Human Resources and Executive Search Consulting Services;
- Providing marketing consulting services are classified in U.S. Industry 541613, Marketing Consulting Services; and
- Providing process, physical distribution, and logistics consulting services are classified in U.S. Industry 541614, Process, Physical Distribution, and Logistics Consulting Services.

Sector **54**

Professional, Scientific, and Technical Services

■ = Cross-References

US—United States industry only. CAN—United States and Canadian industries are comparable. When neither US nor CAN appears, Canadian, Mexican, and United States industries are comparable.

546

Harris InfoSource

54162 Environmental Consulting Services
See industry description for 541620 below.

541620 Environmental Consulting Services
This industry comprises establishments primarily engaged in providing advice and assistance to businesses and other organizations on environmental issues, such as the control of environmental contamination from pollutants, toxic substances, and hazardous materials. These establishments identify problems (e.g., inspect buildings for hazardous materials), measure and evaluate risks, and recommend solutions. They employ a multidisciplined staff of scientists, engineers, and other technicians with expertise in areas, such as air and water quality, asbestos contamination, remediation, and environmental law. Establishments providing sanitation or site remediation consulting services are included in this industry.

- Environmental remediation are classified in Industry 562910, Remediation Services; and
- Providing environmental engineering services are classified in Industry 541330, Engineering Services.

54169 Other Scientific and Technical Consulting Services
See industry description for 541690 below.

541690 Other Scientific and Technical Consulting Services
This industry comprises establishments primarily engaged in providing advice and assistance to businesses and other organizations on scientific and technical issues (except environmental).

- Establishments primarily engaged in environmental consulting are classified in Industry 541620, Environmental Consulting Services.

5417 Scientific Research and Development Services
This industry group comprises establishments engaged in conducting original investigation undertaken on a systematic basis to gain new knowledge (research) and/or the application of research findings or other scientific knowledge for the creation of new or significantly improved products or processes (experimental development). The industries within this industry group are defined on the basis of the domain of research; that is, on the scientific expertise of the establishment.

54171 Research and Development in the Physical, Engineering, and Life Sciences
See industry description for 541710 below.

541710 Research and Development in the Physical, Engineering, and Life Sciences
This industry comprises establishments primarily engaged in conducting research and experimental development in the physical, engineering, or life sciences, such as agriculture, electronics, environmental, biology, botany, biotechnology, computers, chemistry, food, fisheries, forests, geology, health, mathematics, medicine, oceanography, pharmacy, physics, veterinary, and other allied subjects.

- Providing physical, chemical, or other analytical testing services (except medical or veterinary) are classified in Industry 541380, Testing Laboratories;
- Providing medical laboratory testing for humans are classified in U.S. Industry 621511, Medical Laboratories; and
- Providing veterinary testing services are classified in Industry 541940, Veterinary Services.

54172 Research and Development in the Social Sciences and Humanities
See industry description for 541720 below.

541720 Research and Development in the Social Sciences and Humanities
This industry comprises establishments primarily engaged in conducting research and analysis in cognitive development, sociology, psychology, language, behavior, economic, and other social science and humanities research.

- Establishments primarily engaged in marketing research are classified in Industry 541910, Marketing Research and Public Opinion Polling.

Visit page 18 to learn more about this sector.

Sector **54**

Professional, Scientific, and Technical Services

■ = Cross-References

US—United States industry only. CAN—United States and Canadian industries are comparable. When neither US nor CAN appears, Canadian, Mexican, and United States industries are comparable.

www.harrisinfo.com

547

5418 Advertising and Related Services

54181 Advertising Agencies
See industry description for 541810 below.

541810 Advertising Agencies
This industry comprises establishments primarily engaged in creating advertising campaigns and placing such advertising in periodicals, newspapers, radio and television, or other media. These establishments are organized to provide a full range of services (i.e., through in-house capabilities or subcontracting), including advice, creative services, account management, production of advertising material, media planning, and buying (i.e., placing advertising).

- Purchasing advertising space from media outlets and reselling it directly to advertising agencies or individual companies are classified in Industry 541830, Media Buying Agencies;
- Conceptualizing and producing artwork or graphic designs without providing other advertising agency services are classified in Industry 541430, Graphic Design Services;
- Creating direct mail advertising campaigns are classified in Industry 541860, Direct Mail Advertising;
- Providing marketing consulting services are classified in U.S. Industry 541613, Marketing Consulting Services; and
- Selling media time or space for media owners as independent representatives are classified in Industry 541840, Media Representatives.

54182 Public Relations Agencies
See industry description for 541820 below.

541820 Public Relations Agencies
This industry comprises establishments primarily engaged in designing and implementing public relations campaigns. These campaigns are designed to promote the interests and image of their clients. Establishments providing lobbying, political consulting, or public relations consulting are included in this industry.

54183 Media Buying Agencies
See industry description for 541830 below.

541830 Media Buying Agencies
This industry comprises establishments primarily engaged in purchasing advertising time or space from media outlets and reselling it to advertising agencies or individual companies directly.

- Selling time and space to advertisers for media owners as independent representatives are classified in Industry 541840, Media Representatives; and
- Creating advertising campaigns and placing such advertising in media are classified in Industry 541810, Advertising Agencies.

54184 Media Representatives
See industry description for 541840 below.

541840 Media Representatives
This industry comprises establishments of independent representatives primarily engaged in selling media time or space for media owners.

- Purchasing advertising time or space from media outlets and reselling it directly to advertising agencies or individual companies are classified in Industry 541830, Media Buying Agencies; and
- Creating advertising campaigns and placing such advertising in media are classified in Industry 541810, Advertising Agencies.

54185 Display Advertising
See industry description for 541850 below.

541850 Display Advertising
This industry comprises establishments primarily engaged in creating and designing public display advertising, campaign materials, such as printed, painted, or electronic displays, and/or placing such

Sector **54**

Professional,
Scientific, and
Technical Services

■ = Cross-References

US—United States industry only. CAN—United States and Canadian industries are comparable. When neither US nor CAN appears, Canadian, Mexican, and United States industries are comparable.

548

Harris InfoSource

displays on indoor or outdoor billboards and panels, or on or within transit vehicles or facilities, shopping malls, retail (in-store) displays, and other display structures or sites.

- Providing sign lettering and painting services are classified in Industry 541890 , Other Services Related to Advertising;
- Printing paper on paperboard signs are classified in Industry 32311, Printing;
- Erecting display boards are classified in Sector 23, Construction; and
- Manufacturing electrical, mechanical, or plate signs and point-of-sale advertising displays are classified in Industry 339950, Sign Manufacturing.

54186 Direct Mail Advertising
See industry description for 541860 below.

541860 Direct Mail Advertising
This industry comprises establishments primarily engaged in (1) creating and designing advertising campaigns for the purpose of distributing advertising materials (e.g., coupons, flyers, samples) or specialties (e.g., key chains, magnets, pens with customized messages imprinted) by mail or other direct distribution; and/or (2) preparing advertising materials or specialties for mailing or other direct distribution. These establishments may also compile, maintain, sell, and rent mailing lists.

- The direct distribution or delivery (e.g., door-to-door, windshield placement) of advertisements or samples are classified in Industry 541870, Advertising Material Distribution Services;
- Distributing advertising specialties for clients who wish to use such materials for promotional purposes are classified in Industry 541890, Other Services Related to Advertising;
- Creating advertising campaigns and placing such advertising in media are classified in Industry 541810, Advertising Agencies; and
- Compiling and selling mailing lists without providing direct mail advertising services are classified in Industry 511140, Database and Directory Publishing.

54187 Advertising Material Distribution Services
See industry description for 541870 below.

541870 Advertising Material Distribution Services
This industry comprises establishments primarily engaged in the direct distribution or delivery of advertisements (e.g., circulars, coupons, handbills) or samples. Establishments in this industry use methods, such as delivering advertisements or samples door-to-door, placing flyers or coupons on car windshields in parking lots, or handing out samples in retail stores.

- Creating and designing advertising campaigns for the purpose of distributing advertising materials or samples through the mail or by other direct distribution are classified in Industry 541860, Direct Mail Advertising;
- Publishing newspapers or operating television stations or on-line information services are classified in Sector 51, Information; and
- Distributing advertising specialties (e.g., key chains, magnets, or pens with customized messages imprinted) to clients who wish to use such materials for promotional purposes are classified in Industry 541890, Other Services Related to Advertising.

54189 Other Services Related to Advertising
See industry description for 541890 below.

541890 Other Services Related to Advertising
This industry comprises establishments primarily engaged in providing advertising services (except advertising agency services, public relations agency services, media buying agency services, media representative services, display advertising services, direct mail advertising services, advertising material distribution services, and marketing consulting services).

- Creating advertising campaigns and placing such advertising in newspapers, television, or other media are classified in Industry 541810, Advertising Agencies;
- Designing and implementing public relations campaigns are classified in Industry 541820, Public Relations Agencies;
- Purchasing advertising time or space from media outlets and reselling it directly to advertising agencies or individual companies are classified in Industry 541830, Media Buying Agencies;
- Selling media time or space for media owners as independent representatives are classified in Industry 541840, Media Representatives;
- Providing display advertising services (except aerial) are classified in Industry 541850, Display Advertising;
- Providing direct distribution or delivery (e.g., door-to-door, windshield placement) of advertisements or samples are classified in Industry 541870, Advertising Material Distribution Services;
- Providing direct mail advertising services are classified in Industry 541860, Direct Mail Advertising;

Visit page 18 to learn more about this sector.

Sector 54

Professional, Scientific, and Technical Services

■ = Cross-References

US—United States industry only. CAN—United States and Canadian industries are comparable. When neither US nor CAN appears, Canadian, Mexican, and United States industries are comparable.

www.harrisinfo.com

 549

- Publishing newspapers or operating television stations or on-line information services are classified in Sector 51, Information; and
- Providing marketing consulting services are classified in U.S. Industry 541613, Marketing Consulting Services.

5419 Other Professional, Scientific, and Technical Services

This industry group comprises establishments engaged in professional, scientific, and technical services (except legal services; accounting, tax preparation, bookkeeping, and related services; architectural, engineering, and related services; specialized design services; computer systems design and related services; management, scientific, and technical consulting services; scientific research and development services; and advertising and related services).

54191 Marketing Research and Public Opinion Polling

See industry description for 541910 below.

541910 Marketing Research and Public Opinion Polling

This industry comprises establishments primarily engaged in systematically gathering, recording, tabulating, and presenting marketing and public opinion data.

- Providing research and analysis in economics, sociology, and related fields are classified in Industry 541720, Research and Development in the Social Sciences and Humanities; and
- Providing advice and counsel on marketing strategies are classified in U.S. Industry 541613, Marketing Consulting Services.

54192 Photographic Services

This industry comprises establishments primarily engaged in providing still, video, or digital photography services. These establishments may specialize in a particular field of photography, such as commercial and industrial photography, portrait photography, and special events photography. Commercial or portrait photography studios are included in this industry.

- Producing film and videotape for commercial exhibition or sale are classified in Industry 51211, Motion Picture and Video Production;
- Developing still photographs are classified in Industry 81292, Photofinishing;
- Developing motion picture film are classified in Industry 51219, Postproduction and Other Motion Picture and Video Industries;
- Taking, developing, and selling artistic, news or other types of photographs on a freelance basis, such as photojournalists, are classified in Industry 71151, Independent Artists, Writers, and Performers; and
- Supplying and servicing automatic photography machines in places of business operated by others are classified in Industry 81299, All Other Personal Services.

541921 Photography Studios, Portrait US

This U.S. industry comprises establishments known as portrait studios primarily engaged in providing still, video, or digital portrait photography services.

- Producing film and videotape for commercial exhibition or sale are classified in Industry 512110, Motion Picture and Video Production;
- Developing still photographs are classified in Industry 81292, Photofinishing;
- Developing motion picture film are classified in U.S. Industry 512199, Other Motion Picture and Video Industries;
- Taking, developing, and selling artistic, news or other types of photographs on a freelance basis, such as photojournalists, are classified in Industry 711510, Independent Artists, Writers, and Performers; and
- Supplying and servicing automatic photography machines in places of business operated by others are classified in Industry 812990, All Other Personal Services.

541922 Commercial Photography US

This U.S. industry comprises establishments primarily engaged in providing commercial photography services, generally for advertising agencies, publishers, and other business and industrial users.

- Producing film and videotape for commercial exhibition or sale are classified in Industry 512110, Motion Picture and Video Production;
- Developing still photographs are classified in Industry 81292, Photofinishing;
- Developing motion picture film are classified in U.S. Industry 512199, Other Motion Picture and Video Industries;
- Taking, developing, and selling artistic, news, or other types of photographs on a freelance basis, such as photojournalists, are classified in Industry 711510, Independent Artists, Writers, and Performers; and
- Supplying and servicing coin-operated photography machines in places of business operated by others are classified in Industry 812990, All Other Personal Services.

54193 Translation and Interpretation Services

See industry description for 541930 below.

Sector 54

Professional,
Scientific, and
Technical Services

■ = Cross-References

US—United States industry only. CAN—United States and Canadian industries are comparable. When neither US nor CAN appears, Canadian, Mexican, and United States industries are comparable.

550

Harris InfoSource

541930 Translation and Interpretation Services

This industry comprises establishments primarily engaged in translating written material and interpreting speech from one language to another and establishments primarily engaged in providing sign language services.

- Providing transcription services are classified in Industry 561410, Document Preparation Services;
- Providing real-time (i.e., simultaneous) closed captioning services for live television performances, at meetings and conferences are classified in U.S. Industry 561492, Court Reporting and Stenotype Services;
- Providing film or tape closed captioning services are classified in U.S. Industry 512191, Teleproduction and Other Postproduction Services; and
- Analyzing handwriting are classified in Industry 541990, All Other Professional, Scientific, and Technical Services.

54194 Veterinary Services

See industry description for industry 541940 below.

541940 Veterinary Services

This industry comprises establishments of licensed veterinary practitioners primarily engaged in the practice of veterinary medicine, dentistry, or surgery for animals; and establishments primarily engaged in providing testing services for licensed veterinary practitioners.

- Providing veterinary research and development services are classified in Industry 541710, Research and Development in the Physical, Engineering, and Life Sciences;
- Providing nonveterinary pet care services, such as boarding or grooming pets, are classified in Industry 812910, Pet Care (except Veterinary) Services;
- Providing animal breeding services or boarding horses are classified in Industry 115210, Support Activities for Animal Production; and
- Transporting pets are classified in U.S. Industry 485991, Special Needs Transportation.

54199 All Other Professional, Scientific, and Technical Services

See industry description for 541990 below.

541990 All Other Professional, Scientific, and Technical Services

This industry comprises establishments primarily engaged in the provision of professional, scientific, or technical services (except legal services; accounting, tax preparation, bookkeeping, and related services; architectural, engineering, and related services; specialized design services; computer systems design and related services; management, scientific, and technical consulting services; scientific research and development services; advertising and related services; market research and public opinion polling; photographic services; translation and interpretation services; and veterinary services).

- Providing legal services are classified in Industry Group 5411, Legal Services;
- Providing accounting, tax preparation, bookkeeping, and payroll services are classified in Industry Group 5412, Accounting, Tax Preparation, Bookkeeping, and Payroll Services;
- Providing architectural, engineering, and related services are classified in Industry Group 5413, Architectural, Engineering, and Related Services;
- Providing specialized design services are classified in Industry Group 5414, Specialized Design Services;
- Providing computer systems design and related services are classified in Industry Group 5415, Computer Systems Design and Related Services;
- Providing management, scientific, and technical consulting services are classified in Industry Group 5416, Management, Scientific, and Technical Consulting Services;
- Providing scientific research and development services are classified in Industry Group 5417, Scientific Research and Development Services;
- Providing advertising and related services are classified in Industry Group 5418, Advertising and Related Services;
- Providing marketing research and public opinion polling are classified in Industry 541910, Marketing Research and Public Opinion Polling;
- Providing photographic services are classified in Industry 54192, Photographic Services;
- Providing translation and interpretation services are classified in Industry 541930, Translation and Interpretation Services;
- Providing veterinary services are classified in Industry 541940, Veterinary Services; and
- Providing real estate appraisal services are classified in Industry 531320, Offices of Real Estate Appraisers.

Visit page 18 to learn more about this sector.

Sector **54**

Professional, Scientific, and Technical Services

■ = Cross-References

US—United States industry only. CAN—United States and Canadian industries are comparable. When neither US nor CAN appears, Canadian, Mexican, and United States industries are comparable.

www.harrisinfo.com

551

NAICS United States Structure

Sector	Name	Sub-sectors	Industry groups	NAICS 5-digit industries	U.S. 6-digit industries	TOTAL U.S. industries	New industries
11	Agriculture, Forestry, Fishing and, Hunting	5	19	42	32	64	20
21	Mining	3	5	10	28	29	—
22	Utilities	1	3	6	6	10	6
23	Construction	3	14	28	—	28	3
31–33	Manufacturing	21	84	184	408	474	79
42	Wholesale Trade	2	18	69	—	69	—
44–45	Retail Trade	12	27	61	18	72	17
48-49	Transportation and Warehousing	11	29	42	25	57	28
51	Information	4	9	28	12	34	20
52	Finance and Insurance	5	11	32	15	42	23
53	Real Estate and Rental and Leasing	3	8	19	9	24	15
54	Professional, Scientific, and Technical Services	1	9	35	17	47	28
55	Management of Companies and Enterprises	1	1	1	3	3	1
56	Administrative and Support and Waste Management and Remediation Services	2	11	29	23	43	29
61	Educational Services	1	7	12	7	17	12
62	Health Care and Social Assistance	4	18	30	16	39	27
71	Arts, Entertainment, and Recreation	3	9	23	3	25	19
72	Accommodation and Food Services	2	7	11	7	15	10
81	Other Services (except Public Administration)	4	14	30	30	49	19
92	Public Administration	8	8	29	—	29	2
	TOTAL	96	311	721	659	1170	358

To learn more about the changes by sector go to pages 15-18.

Sector **54**

Professional,
Scientific, and
Technical Services

Sector 55

Management of Companies and Enterprises

The Sector as a Whole

THE MANAGEMENT OF COMPANIES AND ENTERPRISES sector comprises (1) establishments that hold the securities of (or other equity interests in) companies and enterprises for the purpose of owning a controlling interest or influencing management decisions or (2) establishments (except government establishments) that administer, oversee, and manage establishments of the company or enterprise and that normally undertake the strategic or organizational planning and decision making role of the company or enterprise. Establishments that administer, oversee, and manage may hold the securities of the company or enterprise.

Establishments in this sector perform essential activities that are often undertaken, in-house, by establishments in many sectors of the economy. By consolidating the performance of these activities of the enterprise at one establishment, economies of scale are achieved.

Government establishments primarily engaged in administering, overseeing, and managing governmental programs are classified in Sector 92, Public Administration. Establishments primarily engaged in providing a range of day-to-day office administrative services, such as financial planning, billing and recordkeeping, personnel, and physical distribution and logistics are classified in Industry 56111, Office Administrative Services.

Go to page 17 to find out how changes to this sector impact employment statistics.

➡551 MANAGEMENT OF COMPANIES AND ENTERPRISES

Industries in the Management of Companies and Enterprises subsector include three main types of establishments: (1) those that hold the securities of (or other equity interests in) companies and enterprises; (2) those (except government establishments) that administer, oversee, and manage other establishments of the company or enterprise but do not hold the securities of these establishments; and (3) those that both administer, oversee, and manage other establishments of the company or enterprise and hold the securities of (or other equity interests in) these establishments. Those establishments that administer, oversee, and manage normally undertake the strategic or organizational planning and decision making role of the company or enterprise.

5511 Management of Companies and Enterprises

55111 Management of Companies and Enterprises
This industry comprises (1) establishments primarily engaged in holding the securities of (or other equity interests in) companies and enterprises for the purpose of owning a controlling interest or influencing the management decisions or (2) establishments (except government establishments) that administer, oversee, and manage other establishments of the company or enterprise and that normally undertake the strategic or organizational planning and decision making role of the company or enterprise. Establishments that administer, oversee, and manage may hold the securities of the company or enterprise.

- Establishments primarily engaged in holding the securities of companies or enterprises and operating these entities are classified according to the business operated;
- Establishments primarily engaged in holding the securities of depository banks and operating these entities are classified in Industry Group 5221, Depository Credit Intermediation;

Sector 55

Management of Companies and Enterprises

■ = Cross-References

US—United States industry only. CAN—United States and Canadian industries are comparable. When neither US nor CAN appears, Canadian, Mexican, and United States industries are comparable.

■ Establishments primarily engaged in providing a single service to other establishments of the company or enterprise, such as trucking, warehousing, research and development, and data processing are classified according to the service provided; and
■ Government establishments primarily engaged in administering, overseeing, and managing governmental programs are classified in Sector 92, Public Administration.

551111 Offices of Bank Holding Companies ᵁˢ

This U.S. industry comprises legal entities known as bank holding companies primarily engaged in holding the securities of (or other equity interests in) companies and enterprises for the purpose of owning a controlling interest or influencing the management decisions of these firms. The holding companies in this industry do not administer, oversee, and manage other establishments of the company or enterprise whose securities they hold.

■ Holding the securities of (or other equity interests in) a company or enterprise and administering, overseeing, and managing establishments of the company or enterprise whose securities they hold are classified in U.S. Industry 551114, Corporate, Subsidiary, and Regional Managing Offices; and
■ Holding the securities of depository banks and operating these entities are classified in Industry Group 5221, Depository Credit Intermediation.

551112 Offices of Other Holding Companies ᵁˢ

This U.S. industry comprises legal entities known as holding companies (except bank holding) primarily engaged in holding the securities of (or other equity interests in) companies and enterprises for the purpose of owning a controlling interest or influencing the management decisions of these firms. The holding companies in this industry do not administer, oversee, and manage other establishments of the company or enterprise whose securities they hold.

■ Holding the securities of (or other equity interests in) depository banks for the purpose of owning a controlling interest or influencing the management decisions of these firms are classified in U.S. Industry 551111, Offices of Bank Holding Companies;
■ Holding the securities of (or other equity interests in) a company or enterprise and administering, overseeing, and managing establishments of the company or enterprise whose securities they hol are classified in U.S. Industry 551114, Corporate, Subsidiary, and Regional Managing Offices; and
■ Holding the securities of companies or enterprises and operating these entities are classified according to the business operated.

551114 Corporate, Subsidiary, and Regional Managing Offices ᶜᴬᴺ

This U.S. industry comprises establishments (except government establishments) primarily engaged in administering, overseeing, and managing other establishments of the company or enterprise. These establishments normally undertake the strategic or organizational planning and decision making role of the company or enterprise. Establishments in this industry may hold the securities of the company or enterprise.

■ Government establishments primarily engaged in administering, overseeing, and managing governmental programs are classified in Sector 92, Public Administration;
■ Legal entities known as bank holding companies that do not administer, oversee, and manage other establishments of the companies or enterprises whose securities they hold are classified in U.S. Industry 551111, Offices of Bank Holding Companies; and
■ Legal entities known as holding companies(except bank holding) that do not administer, oversee, and manage other establishments of the companies or enterprises whose securities they hold are classified in U.S. Industry 551112, Offices of Other Holding Companies.

Sector **55**

Management of Companies and Enterprises

■ = Cross-References

US—United States industry only. CAN—United States and Canadian industries are comparable. When neither US nor CAN appears, Canadian, Mexican, and United States industries are comparable.

554

Harris InfoSource

Sector 56

Administrative and Support and Waste Management and Remediation Services

The Sector as a Whole

THE ADMINISTRATIVE AND SUPPORT AND WASTE MANAGEMENT AND REMEDIATION SERVICES sector comprises establishments performing routine support activities for the day-to-day operations of other organizations. These essential activities are often undertaken in-house by establishments in many sectors of the economy. The establishments in this sector specialize in one or more of these support activities and provide these services to clients in a variety of industries and, in some cases, to households. Activities performed include: office administration, hiring and placing of personnel, document preparation and similar clerical services, solicitation, collection, security and surveillance services, cleaning, and waste disposal services.

The administrative and management activities performed by establishments in this sector are typically on a contract or fee basis. These activities may also be performed by establishments that are part of the company or enterprise. However, establishments involved in administering, overseeing, and managing other establishments of the company or enterprise, are classified in Sector 55, Management of Companies and Enterprises. These establishments normally undertake the strategic and organizational planning and decision-making role of the company or enterprise. Government establishments engaged in administering, overseeing, and managing governmental programs are classified in Sector 92, Public Administration.

➡561 ADMINISTRATIVE AND SUPPORT SERVICES

Industries in the Administrative and Support Services subsector group establishments engaged in activities that support the day-to-day operations of other organizations. The processes employed in this sector (e.g., general management, personnel administration, clerical activities, cleaning activities) are often integral parts of the activities of establishments found in all sectors of the economy. The establishments classified in this subsector have specialized in one or more of these activities and can, therefore, provide services to clients in a variety of industries and, in some cases, to households. The individual industries of this subsector are defined on the basis of the particular process that they are engaged in and the particular services they provide

Many of the activities performed in this subsector are ongoing routine support functions that all businesses and organizations must do and that they have traditionally done for themselves. Recent trends, however, are to contract or purchase such services from businesses that specialize in such activities and can, therefore, provide the services more efficiently.

The industries in this subsector cannot be viewed as strictly "support." The Travel Arrangement and Reservation Services industry group, includes travel agents, tour operators, and providers of other travel arrangement services, such as hotel and restaurant reservations and arranging the purchase of tickets, serves many types of clients, including individual consumers. This group was placed in this subsector because the services are often of the "support" nature (e.g., travel arrangement) and businesses and other organizations are increasingly the ones purchasing such services.

Sector 56

Administrative and Support and Waste Management and Remediation Services

The administrative and management activities performed by establishments in this sector are typically on a contract or fee basis. These activities may also be performed by establishments that are part of the company or enterprise. However, establishments involved in administering, overseeing, and managing other establishments of the company or enterprise, are classified in Sector 55, Management of Companies and Enterprises. These establishments normally undertake the strategic and organizational planning and decision-making role of the company or enterprise. Government establishments engaged in administering, overseeing and managing governmental programs are classified in Sector 92, Public Administration.

5611 Office Administrative Services

56111 Office Administrative Services
See industry description for 561110 below.

561110 Office Administrative Services
This industry comprises establishments primarily engaged in providing a range of day-to-day office administrative services, such as financial planning; billing and record-keeping; personnel; and physical distribution and logistics. These establishments do not provide operating staff to carry out the complete operations of a business.

- Holding the securities or financial assets of companies and enterprises for the purpose of controlling them and influencing their management decisions are classified in U.S. Industry 551111, Offices of Bank Holding Companies or U.S. Industry 551112, Offices of Other Holding Companies;
- Administering, overseeing, and managing other establishments of the company or enterprise (except government establishments) are classified in U.S. Industry 551114, Corporate, Subsidiary, and Regional Managing Offices;
- Government establishments primarily engaged in administering, overseeing, and managing governmental programs are classified in Sector 92, Public Administration;
- Providing computer facilities management are classified in U.S. Industry 541513, Computer Facilities Management Services;
- Providing construction management are classified in Sector 23, Construction, by type of construction project managed;
- Providing farm management are classified in U.S. Industry 115116, Farm Management Services;
- Managing real property for others are classified in Industry 53131, Real Estate Property Managers;
- Providing food services management at institutional, governmental, commercial, or industrial locations are classified in Industry 722310, Food Service Contractors;
- Providing management advice without day-to-day management are classified in Industry 54161, Management Consulting Services;
- Providing both management and operating staff for the complete operation of a client's business, such as a hotel, restaurant, mine site, or hospital are classified according to the industry of the establishment operated; and
- Providing only one of the support services (e.g., accounting services) that establishments in this industry provide are classified in the appropriate industry according to the service provided.

5612 Facilities Support Services

56121 Facilities Support Services
See industry description for 561210 below.

561210 Facilities Support Services
This industry comprises establishments primarily engaged in providing operating staff to perform a combination of support services within a client's facilities. Establishments in this industry typically provide a combination of services, such as janitorial; maintenance; trash disposal; guard and security; mail routing reception; laundry; and related services to support operations within facilities. These establishments provide operating staff to carry out these support activities; but, are not involved with or responsible for the core business or activities of the client. Establishments providing facilities (except computer and/or data processing) operation support services and establishments operating correctional facilities (i.e., jails) on a contract or fee basis are included in this industry.

- Establishments primarily engaged in providing only one of the support services (e.g., janitorial services) that establishments in this industry provide are classified in the appropriate industry according to the service provided;
- Establishments primarily engaged in providing management and operating staff for the complete operation of a client's establishment, such as a hotel, restaurant, mine, or hospital, are classified according to the industry of the establishment operated;
- Establishments primarily engaged in providing on-site management and operation of a client's computer systems and/or data processing facilities are classified in U.S. Industry 541513, Computer Facilities Management Services; and
- Government correctional institutions are classified in Industry 922140, Correctional Institutions.

Sector 56

Administrative and Support and Waste Management and Remediation Services

■ = Cross-References

US—United States industry only. CAN—United States and Canadian industries are comparable. When neither US nor CAN appears, Canadian, Mexican, and United States industries are comparable.

556

Harris InfoSource

5613 Employment Services

56131 Employment Placement Agencies
See industry description for 561310 below.

561310 Employment Placement Agencies
This industry comprises establishments primarily engaged in listing employment vacancies and in referring or placing applicants for employment. The individuals referred or placed are not employees of the employment agencies.

- Providing executive search consulting services are classified in U.S. Industry 541612, Human Resources and Executive Search Consulting Services;
- Supplying their own employees for limited periods of time to supplement the working force of a client's business are classified in Industry 561320, Temporary Help Services;
- Providing human resources and human resource management services to clients are classified in Industry 561330, Employee Leasing Services; and
- Representing models, entertainers, athletes, and other public figures in the capacity as their agent or manager are classified in Industry 711410, Agents and Managers for Artists, Athletes, Entertainers, and Other Public Figures.

56132 Temporary Help Services
See industry description for 561320 below.

561320 Temporary Help Services
This industry comprises establishments primarily engaged in supplying workers to clients' businesses for limited periods of time to supplement the working force of the client. The individuals provided are employees of the temporary help service establishment. However, these establishments do not provide direct supervision of their employees at the clients' work sites.

- Providing human resources and human resource management services to clients are classified in Industry 561330, Employee Leasing Services;
- Supplying farm labor are classified in U.S. Industry 115115, Farm Labor Contractors and Crew Leaders;
- Providing operating staff to perform a combination of services to support operations within a client's facilities are classified in Industry 561210, Facilities Support Services;
- Listing employment vacancies and in referring or placing applicants for employment are classified in Industry 561310, Employment Placement Agencies; and
- Representing models, entertainers, athletes, and other public figures in the capacity as their agent or manager are classified in Industry 711410, Agents and Managers for Artists, Athletes, Entertainers, and Other Public Figures.

56133 Employee Leasing Services
See industry description for 561330 below.

561330 Employee Leasing Services
This industry comprises establishments primarily engaged in providing human resources and human resource management services to staff client businesses. Establishments in this industry operate in a coemployment relationship with client businesses or organizations and are specialized in performing a wide range of human resource and personnel management duties, such as payroll accounting, payroll tax return preparation, benefits administration, recruiting, and managing labor relations. Employee leasing establishments typically acquire and lease back some or all of the employees of their clients and serve as the employer of the leased employees for payroll, benefits, and related purposes. Employee leasing establishments exercise varying degrees of decision making relating to their human resource or personnel management role, but do not have management accountability for the work of their clients' operations with regard to strategic planning, output, or profitability. Professional employer organizations (PEO) and establishments providing labor or staff leasing services are included in this industry.

- Supplying their own employees for limited periods of time to supplement the working force of a client's business are classified in Industry 561320, Temporary Help Services; and
- Listing employment vacancies and in referring or placing applicants for employment are classified in Industry 561310, Employment Placement Agencies.

Sector **56**

Administrative and Support and Waste Management and Remediation Services

■ = Cross-References

US—United States industry only. CAN—United States and Canadian industries are comparable. When neither US nor CAN appears, Canadian, Mexican, and United States industries are comparable.

www.harrisinfo.com

557

5614 Business Support Services

This industry group comprises establishments engaged in performing activities that are ongoing routine business support functions that businesses and organizations traditionally do for themselves.

56141 Document Preparation Services

See industry description for 561410 below.

561410 Document Preparation Services

This industry comprises establishments primarily engaged in one or more of the following: (1) letter or resume writing; (2) document editing or proofreading; (3) typing, word processing, or desktop publishing; and (4) stenographic (except court reporting or stenotype recording), transcription, and other secretarial services.

- Providing verbatim reporting and steno recording of live legal proceedings and transcribing subsequent recorded materials are classified in U.S. Industry 561492, Court Reporting and Stenotype Services;
- Performing prepress and postpress services in support of printing activities are classified in Industry 32312, Support Activities for Printing;
- Providing document translation services are classified in Industry 541930, Translation and Interpretation Services;
- Photocopying, duplicating, and other document copying services, with or without a range of other office support services (except printing) are classified in U.S. Industry 561439, Other Business Service Centers (including Copy Shops); and
- Providing document copying services in combination with printing services, with or without a range of other office support services, and establishments known as quick or digital printers are classified in Industry 32311, Printing.

56142 Telephone Call Centers

This industry comprises (1) establishments primarily engaged in answering telephone calls and relaying messages to clients and (2) establishments primarily engaged in providing telemarketing services on a contract or fee basis for others, such as promoting clients' products or services by telephone; taking orders for clients by telephone; and soliciting contributions or providing information for clients by telephone. Telemarketing establishments never own the product or provide the service that they are representing and generally can originate and/or receive calls for others.

- Providing paging and beeper transmission services are classified in Industry 51332, Wireless Telecommunications Carriers (except Satellite);
- Organizing and conducting fundraising campaigns on a contract or fee basis, that may include telephone solicitation services are classified in Industry 56149, Other Business Support Services; and
- Gathering, recording, tabulating, and presenting marketing and public opinion data, that may include telephone canvassing services are classified in Industry 54191, Marketing Research and Public Opinion Polling.

561421 Telephone Answering Services US

This U.S. industry comprises establishments primarily engaged in answering telephone calls and relaying messages to clients.

- Establishments primarily engaged in providing paging or beeper transmission services are classified in Industry 51332, Wireless Telecommunications Carriers (except Satellite).

561422 Telemarketing Bureaus US

This U.S. industry comprises establishments primarily engaged in providing telemarketing services on a contract or fee basis for others, such as: (1) promoting clients' products or services by telephone, (2) taking orders for clients by telephone, and (3) soliciting contributions or providing information for clients by telephone. These establishments never own the product or provide the services they are representing and generally can originate and/or receive calls for others.

- Organizing and conducting fundraising campaigns on a contract or fee basis, that may include telephone solicitation services are classified in U.S. Industry 561499, All Other Business Support Services; and
- Gathering, recording, tabulating, and presenting marketing and public opinion data, that may include telephone canvassing services are classified in Industry 541910, Marketing Research and Public Opinion Polling.

56143 Business Service Centers

This industry comprises (1) establishments primarily engaged in providing mailbox rental and other postal and mailing services (except direct mail advertising); (2) establishments, generally known as copy centers or shops, primarily engaged in providing photocopying, duplicating, blueprinting, and other document copying services without also providing printing services (i.e., offset printing, quick printing,

Sector 56

Administrative and Support and Waste Management and Remediation Services

■ = Cross-References

US—United States industry only. CAN—United States and Canadian industries are comparable. When neither US nor CAN appears, Canadian, Mexican, and United States industries are comparable.

digital printing, prepress services); and (3) establishments that provide a range of office support services (except printing services), such as mailing services, document copying services, facsimile services, word processing services, on-site PC rental services, and office product sales.

- Operating contract post offices are classified in Industry 49111, Postal Service;
- Delivering letters and parcels are classified in Subsector 492, Couriers and Messengers;
- Providing voice mailbox services are classified in Industry 56142, Telephone Call Centers;
- Providing direct mail advertising services are classified in Industry 54186, Direct Mail Advertising;
- Providing document copying services in combination with printing services, with or without a range of other office support services, and establishments known as quick or digital printers are classified in Industry 32311, Printing; and
- Providing only one of the support services (e.g., word processing services) that establishments in this industry provide are classified in the appropriate industry according to the service provided.

561431 Private Mail Centers [US]

This U.S. industry comprises (1) establishments primarily engaged in providing mailbox rental and other postal and mailing (except direct mail advertising) services or (2) establishments engaged in providing these mailing services along with one or more other office support services, such as facsimile services, word processing services, on-site PC rental services, and office product sales.

- Operating contract post offices are classified in Industry 491110, Postal Service;
- Delivering letters and parcels are classified in Subsector 492, Couriers and Messengers;
- Providing voice mailbox services are classified in U.S. Industry 561421, Telephone Answering Services;
- Providing direct mail advertising services are classified in Industry 541860, Direct Mail Advertising; and
- Providing only one of the support services (e.g., word processing services) that establishments in this industry provide are classified in the appropriate industry according to the service provided.

561439 Other Business Service Centers (including Copy Shops) [US]

This U.S. industry comprises (1) establishments generally known as copy centers or shops primarily engaged in providing photocopying, duplicating, blueprinting, and other document copying services, without also providing printing services (e.g., offset printing, quick printing, digital printing, prepress services) and (2) establishments (except private mail centers) engaged in providing a range of office support services (except printing services), such as document copying services, facsimile services, word processing services, on-site PC rental services, and office product sales.

- Establishments engaged in providing document copying services in combination with printing services, with or without a range of other office support services, and establishments known as quick or digital printers are classified in Industry 32311, Printing;
- Establishments engaged in providing mailbox rental and other postal and mailing services with or without one or more other office support services (except printing) are classified in U.S. Industry 561431, Private Mail Centers; and
- Establishments exclusively engaged in providing a single office support service (except document copying) to clients, but not the range of office support services that establishments in this industry may provide, are classified according to the service provided.

56144 Collection Agencies
See industry description for 561440 below.

561440 Collection Agencies
This industry comprises establishments primarily engaged in collecting payments for claims and remitting payments collected to their clients.

- Repossessing tangible assets are classified in U.S. Industry 561491, Repossession Services; and
- Providing financing to others by factoring accounts receivables (i.e., assuming the risk of collection and credit losses) are classified in U.S. Industry 522298, All Other Nondepository Credit Intermediation.

56145 Credit Bureaus
See industry description for 561450 below.

561450 Credit Bureaus
This industry comprises establishments primarily engaged in compiling information, such as credit and employment histories on individuals and credit histories on businesses, and providing the information to financial institutions, retailers, and others who have a need to evaluate the credit worthiness of these persons and businesses.

Sector 56

Administrative and Support and Waste Management and Remediation Services

■ = Cross-References

US—United States industry only. CAN—United States and Canadian industries are comparable. When neither US nor CAN appears, Canadian, Mexican, and United States industries are comparable.

www.harrisinfo.com

559

56149 Other Business Support Services

This industry comprises establishments primarily engaged in providing business support services (except secretarial and other document preparation services; telephone answering or telemarketing services; private mail services or document copying services conducted as separate activities or in conjunction with other office support services; monetary debt collection services; and credit reporting services).

- Providing secretarial and other document preparation services are classified in Industry 56141, Document Preparation Services;
- Providing telephone answering or telemarketing services are classified in Industry 56142, Telephone Call Centers;
- Providing private mail services; document copying services (except printing services); and/or a range of office support services (except printing) are classified in Industry 56143, Business Service Centers;
- Providing document copying services in combination with printing services, with or without a range of other office support services, and establishments known as quick or digital printers are classified in Industry 32311, Printing;
- Providing monetary debt collection services are classified in Industry 56144, Collection Agencies;
- Providing credit reporting services are classified in Industry 56145, Credit Bureaus; and
- Providing film or tape captioning or subtitling services are classified in Industry 51219, Postproduction and Other Motion Picture and Video Industries.

561491 Repossession Services ᵁˢ

This U.S. industry comprises establishments primarily engaged in repossessing tangible assets (e.g., automobiles, boats, equipment, planes, furniture, appliances) for the creditor as a result of delinquent debts.

- Establishments primarily engaged in providing monetary debt collection services are classified in Industry 561440, Collection Agencies.

561492 Court Reporting and Stenotype Services ᵁˢ

This U.S. industry comprises establishments primarily engaged in providing verbatim reporting and stenotype recording of live legal proceedings and transcribing subsequent recorded materials.

- Providing stenotype recording of correspondence, reports, and other documents or in providing document transcription services are classified in Industry 561410, Document Preparation Services; and
- Providing film or tape captioning or subtitling services are classified in U.S. Industry 512191, Teleproduction and Other Postproduction Services.

561499 All Other Business Support Services ᵁˢ

This U.S. industry comprises establishments primarily engaged in providing business support services (except secretarial and other document preparation services; telephone answering and telemarketing services; private mail services or document copying services conducted as separate activities or in conjunction with other office support services; monetary debt collection services; credit reporting services; repossession services; and court reporting and stenotype recording services).

- Providing secretarial and other document preparation services are classified in Industry 561410, Document Preparation Services;
- Providing telephone answering or telemarketing services are classified in Industry 56142, Telephone Call Centers;
- Providing private mail services, document copying services without printing services and/or a range of office support services are classified in Industry 56143, Business Service Centers;
- Providing document copying services in combination with printing services (with or without one or more other office support services) and establishments known as quick or digital printers are classified in Industry 32311, Printing;
- Providing monetary debt collection services are classified in Industry 561440, Collection Agencies;
- Providing credit reporting services are classified in Industry 561450, Credit Bureaus;
- Providing repossession services are classified in U.S. Industry 561491, Repossession Services; and
- Providing court reporting and stenotype services are classified in U.S. Industry 561492, Court Reporting and Stenotype Services.

5615 Travel Arrangement and Reservation Services

56151 Travel Agencies

See industry description for 561510 below.

561510 Travel Agencies

This industry comprises establishments primarily engaged in acting as agents in selling travel, tour, and accommodation services to the general public and commercial clients.

- Arranging and assembling tours that they generally sell through travel agencies or on their own account are classified in Industry 561520, Tour Operators;
- Providing guide services, such as archeological, museum, tourist, hunting, or fishing, are classified in Industry 713990, All Other Amusement and Recreation Industries; and

Sector**56**

Administrative and Support and Waste Management and Remediation Services

■ = Cross-References

US—United States industry only. CAN—United States and Canadian industries are comparable. When neither US nor CAN appears, Canadian, Mexican, and United States industries are comparable.

560

Harris InfoSource

- Providing reservation services (e.g., accommodations, entertainment events, travel) are classified in U.S. Industry 561599, All Other Travel Arrangement and Reservation Services.

56152 Tour Operators
See industry description for 561520 below.

561520 Tour Operators
This industry comprises establishments primarily engaged in arranging and assembling tours. The tours are sold through travel agencies or tour operators. Travel or wholesale tour operators are included in this industry.

- Acting as agents in selling travel, tour, and accommodation services to the general public and commercial clients are classified in Industry 561510, Travel Agencies;
- Conducting scenic and sightseeing tours are classified in Subsector 487, Scenic and Sightseeing Transportation; and
- Providing guide services, such as archeological, museum, tourist, hunting, or fishing are classified in Industry 713990, All Other Amusement and Recreation Industries.

56159 Other Travel Arrangement and Reservation Services
This industry comprises establishments (except travel agencies and tour operators) primarily engaged in providing travel arrangement and reservation services.

- Establishments primarily engaged in arranging the rental of vacation properties are classified in Industry 53121, Offices of Real Estate Agents and Brokers;
- Travel agencies are classified in Industry 56151, Travel Agencies;
- Tour operators are classified in Industry 56152, Tour Operators;
- Automobile clubs (i.e., enthusiasts' clubs) (except road and travel services) are classified in Industry 81341, Civic and Social Organizations; and
- Establishments primarily engaged in organizing, promoting, and/or managing events, such as business and trade shows, conventions, conferences, and meetings (whether or not they manage and provide the staff to operate the facilities in which these events take place), are classified in Industry 56192, Convention and Trade Show Organizers.

561591 Convention and Visitors Bureaus ᵁˢ
This U.S. industry comprises establishments primarily engaged in marketing and promoting communities and facilities to businesses and leisure travelers through a range of activities, such as assisting organizations in locating meeting and convention sites; providing travel information on area attractions, lodging accommodations, restaurants; providing maps; and organizing group tours of local historical, recreational, and cultural attractions.

- Establishments primarily engaged in organizing, promoting, and/or managing events, such as business and trade shows, conventions, conferences, and meetings (whether or not they manage and provide the staff to operate the facilities in which these events take place), are classified in Industry 561920, Convention and Trade Show Organizers.

561599 All Other Travel Arrangement and Reservation Services ᵁˢ
This U.S. industry comprises establishments (except travel agencies, tour operators, and convention and visitors bureaus) primarily engaged in providing travel arrangement and reservation services.

- Establishments primarily engaged in arranging the rental of vacation properties are classified in Industry 531210, Offices of Real Estate Agents and Brokers;
- Travel agencies are classified in Industry 561510, Travel Agencies;
- Tour operators are classified in Industry 561520, Tour Operators;
- Convention and visitors bureaus are classified in U.S. Industry 561591, Convention and Visitors Bureaus;
- Establishments primarily engaged in organizing, promoting, and/or managing events, such as business and trade shows, conventions, conferences, and meetings (whether or not they manage and provide the staff to operate the facilities in which these events take place), are classified in Industry 561920, Convention and Trade Show Organizers; and
- Automobile clubs (i.e., enthusiasts' clubs) (except road and travel services) are classified in Industry 813410, Civic and Social Organizations.

5616 Investigation and Security Services

56161 Investigation, Guard, and Armored Car Services
This industry comprises establishments primarily engaged in providing one or more of the following: (1) investigation and detective services; (2) guard and patrol services; and (3) picking up and delivering money, receipts, or other valuable items with personnel and equipment to protect such properties while in transit.

Sector **56**

Administrative and Support and Waste Management and Remediation Services

■ = Cross-References

US—United States industry only. CAN—United States and Canadian industries are comparable. When neither US nor CAN appears, Canadian, Mexican, and United States industries are comparable.

www.harrisinfo.com

561

- Providing credit checks are classified in Industry 56145, Credit Bureaus; and
- Selling, installing, monitoring, and maintaining security systems and devices (e.g., burglar and fire alarm systems) are classified in Industry 56162, Security Systems Services.

561611 Investigation Services ^{CAN}
This U.S. industry comprises establishments primarily engaged in providing investigation and detective services.

- Establishments primarily engaged in providing credit checks are classified in Industry 561450, Credit Bureaus.

561612 Security Guards and Patrol Services ^{CAN}
This U.S. industry comprises establishments primarily engaged in providing guard and patrol services, such as bodyguard, guard dog, and parking security services.

- Establishments primarily engaged in selling, installing, monitoring, and maintaining security systems and devices, such as burglar and fire alarms and locking devices, are classified in Industry 56162, Security Systems Services.

561613 Armored Car Services ^{CAN}
This U.S. industry comprises establishments primarily engaged in picking up and delivering money, receipts, or other valuable items. These establishments maintain personnel and equipment to protect such properties while in transit.

56162 Security Systems Services
This industry comprises establishments engaged in (1) selling security systems, such as burglar and fire alarms and locking devices, along with installation, repair, or monitoring services or (2) remote monitoring of electronic security alarm systems.

- Selling security systems for buildings without installation, repair, or monitoring services are classified in Sector 42, Wholesale Trade or Sector 44-45, Retail Trade;
- Retailing motor vehicle security systems with or without installation or repair services are classified in Industry 44131, Automotive Parts and Accessories Stores; and
- Providing key duplication services are classified in Industry 81149, Other Personal and Household Goods Repair and Maintenance.

561621 Security Systems Services (except Locksmiths)^{CAN}
This U.S. industry comprises establishments primarily engaged in (1) selling security alarm systems, such as burglar and fire alarms, along with installation, repair, or monitoring services or (2) remote monitoring of electronic security alarm systems.

- Selling security alarm systems for buildings, without installation, repair, or monitoring services, are classified in Sector 42, Wholesale Trade or Sector 44-45, Retail Trade; and
- Retailing motor vehicle security systems with or without installation or repair services are classified in Industry 441310, Automotive Parts and Accessories Stores.

561622 Locksmiths ^{CAN}
This U.S. industry comprises establishments primarily engaged in (1) selling mechanical or electronic locking devices, safes, and security vaults, along with installation, repair, rebuilding, or adjusting services or (2) installing, repairing, rebuilding, and adjusting mechanical or electronic locking devices, safes, and security vaults.

- Selling security systems, such as locking devices, safes, and vaults, without installation or maintenance services are classified in Sector 42, Wholesale Trade or Sector 44-45, Retail Trade; and
- Providing key duplication services are classified in Industry 811490, Other Personal and Household Goods Repair and Maintenance.

5617 Services to Buildings and Dwellings

56171 Exterminating and Pest Control Services
See industry description for 561710 below.

561710 Exterminating and Pest Control Services
This industry comprises establishments primarily engaged in exterminating and controlling birds,

---

Sector **56**

Administrative and
Support and Waste
Management and
Remediation Services

■ = Cross-References

US—United States industry only. CAN—United States and Canadian industries are comparable. When neither US nor CAN appears, Canadian, Mexican, and United States industries are comparable.

562

Harris InfoSource

mosquitoes, rodents, termites, and other insects and pests (except for crop production and forestry production). Establishments providing fumigation services are included in this industry.

- Establishments primarily engaged in providing pest control for crop or forestry production are classified in Subsector 115, Support Activities for Agriculture and Forestry.

56172 Janitorial Services
See industry description for 561720 below.

561720 Janitorial Services
This industry comprises establishments primarily engaged in cleaning building interiors, interiors of transportation equipment (e.g., aircraft, rail cars, ships) and/or windows.

- Cleaning building exteriors (except sandblasting and window cleaning) or chimneys are classified in Industry 561790, Other Services to Buildings and Dwellings; and
- Sandblasting building exteriors are classified in Industry 235990, All Other Special Trade Contractors.

56173 Landscaping Services
See industry description for 561730 below.

561730 Landscaping Services
This industry comprises (1) establishments primarily engaged in providing landscape care and maintenance services and/or installing trees, shrubs, plants, lawns, or gardens and (2) establishments primarily engaged in providing these services along with the design of landscape plans and/or the construction (i.e., installation) of walkways, retaining walls, decks, fences, ponds, and similar structures.

- Installing artificial turf or in constructing (i.e., installing) walkways, retaining walls, decks, fences, ponds, or similar structures are classified in Sector 23, Construction;
- Planning and designing the development of land areas for projects, such as parks and other recreational areas; airports; highways; hospitals; schools; land subdivisions; and commercial, industrial, and residential areas (without also installing trees, shrubs, plants, lawns/gardens, walkways, retaining walls, decks, and similar items or structures), are classified in Industry 541320, Landscape Architectural Services; and
- Retailing landscaping materials and providing the installation and maintenance of these materials are classified in Industry 444220, Nursery and Garden Centers.

56174 Carpet and Upholstery Cleaning Services
See industry description for 561740 below.

561740 Carpet and Upholstery Cleaning Services
This industry comprises establishments primarily engaged in cleaning and dyeing used rugs, carpets, and upholstery.

- Rug repair not associated with rug cleaning are classified in Industry 811490, Other Personal and Household Goods Repair and Maintenance; and
- Reupholstering and repairing furniture are classified in Industry 811420, Reupholstery and Furniture Repair.

56179 Other Services to Buildings and Dwellings
See Industry description for 561790 below.

561790 Other Services to Buildings and Dwellings
This industry comprises establishments primarily engaged in providing services to buildings and dwellings (except exterminating and pest control; janitorial; landscaping care and maintenance; and carpet and upholstery cleaning).

- Providing exterminating and pest control services are classified in Industry 561710, Exterminating and Pest Control Services;
- Providing janitorial services are classified in Industry 561720, Janitorial Services;
- Providing landscaping care and maintenance are classified in Industry 561730, Landscaping Services;
- Providing carpet and upholstery cleaning services are classified in Industry 561740, Carpet and Upholstery Cleaning Services; and
- Sandblasting building exteriors are classified in Industry 235990, All Other Special Trade Contractors.

Sector **56**

Administrative and
Support and Waste
Management and
Remediation Services

■ = Cross-References

US—United States industry only. CAN—United States and Canadian industries are comparable. When neither US nor CAN appears, Canadian, Mexican, and United States industries are comparable.

www.harrisinfo.com 563

5619 Other Support Services

This industry group comprises establishments primarily engaged in providing day-to-day business and other organizational support services (except office administrative services; facilities support services; employment services; business support services; travel arrangement and reservation services; security and investigation services; and services to buildings and dwellings).

56191 Packaging and Labeling Services

See industry description for 561910 below.

561910 Packaging and Labeling Services

This industry comprises establishments primarily engaged in packaging client owned materials. The services may include labeling and/or imprinting the package.

- Processing clients' owned materials into a different product, such as mixing water and concentrate to produce soft drinks, are classified in Sector 31-33, Manufacturing;
- Providing aerosol packaging services are classified in U.S. Industry 325998, All Other Miscellaneous Chemical Product and Preparation Manufacturing;
- Providing packing and crating services incidental to transportation are classified in U.S. Industry 488991, Packing and Crating;
- Providing warehousing services, as well as packaging or other logistics services are classified in Industry Group 4931, Warehousing and Storage; and
- Providing packing and crating services for agricultural products are classified in U.S. Industry 115114, Postharvest Crop Activities (except Cotton Ginning).

56192 Convention and Trade Show Organizers

See industry description for 561920 below.

561920 Convention and Trade Show Organizers

This industry comprises establishments primarily engaged in organizing, promoting, and/or managing events, such as business and trade shows, conventions, conferences, and meetings (whether or not they manage and provide the staff to operate the facilities in which these events take place).

- Establishments primarily engaged in organizing, promoting, and/or managing live performing arts productions, sports events, and similar events, such as festivals (whether or not they manage and provide the staff to operate the facilities in which that these events take place), are classified in Industry Group 7113, Promoters of Performing Arts, Sports, and Similar Events.

56199 All Other Support Services

See industry description for 561990 below.

561990 All Other Support Services

This industry comprises establishments primarily engaged in providing day-to-day business and other organizational support services (except office administrative services, facilities support services, employment services, business support services, travel arrangement and reservation services, security and investigation services, services to buildings and other structures, packaging and labeling services, and convention and trade show organizing services).

- Providing office administrative services are classified in Industry 561110, Office Administrative Services;
- Providing facilities support services are classified in Industry 561210, Facilities Support Services;
- Providing employment services are classified in Industry Group 5613, Employment Services;
- Providing business support services are classified in Industry Group 5614, Business Support Services;
- Providing travel arrangement and reservation services are classified in Industry Group 5615, Travel Arrangement and Reservation Services;
- Providing security and investigation services are classified in Industry Group 5616, Investigation and Security Services;
- Providing services to buildings and other structures are classified in Industry Group 5617, Services to Buildings and Dwellings;
- Providing packaging and labeling services are classified in Industry 561910, Packaging and Labeling Services; and
- Organizing, promoting, and/or managing conferences, conventions, and trade shows (whether or not they manage and provide the staff to operate the facilities in which these events take place) are classified in Industry 561920, Convention and Trade Show Organizers.

Sector 56

Administrative and
Support and Waste
Management and
Remediation Services

■ = Cross-References

US—United States industry only. CAN—United States and Canadian industries are comparable. When neither US nor CAN appears, Canadian, Mexican, and United States industries are comparable.

564

Harris InfoSource

➡️562 WASTE MANAGEMENT AND REMEDIATION SERVICES

Industries in the Waste Management and Remediation Services subsector group establishments engaged in the collection, treatment, and disposal of waste materials. This includes establishments engaged in local hauling of waste materials; operating materials recovery facilities (i.e., those that sort recyclable materials from the trash stream); providing remediation services (i.e., those that provide for the cleanup of contaminated buildings, mine sites, soil, or ground water); and providing septic pumping and other miscellaneous waste management services. There are three industry groups within the subsector that separate these activities into waste collection, waste treatment and disposal, and remediation and other waste management.

Excluded from this subsector are establishments primarily engaged in collecting, treating, and disposing waste through sewer systems or sewage treatment facilities that are classified in Industry 22132, Sewage Treatment Facilities and establishments primarily engaged in long-distance hauling of waste materials that are classified in Industry 48423, Specialized Freight (except Used Goods) Trucking, Long-distance. Also, there are some activities that appear to be related to waste management, but that are not included in this subsector. For example, establishments primarily engaged in providing waste management consulting services are classified in Industry 54162,Environmental Consulting Services.

5621 Waste Collection ^{CAN}

56211 Waste Collection ^{CAN}

This industry comprises establishments primarily engaged in (1) collecting and/or hauling hazardous waste, nonhazardous waste, and/or recyclable materials within a local area and/or (2) operating hazardous or nonhazardous waste transfer stations. Hazardous waste collection establishments may be responsible for the identification, treatment, packaging, and labeling of wastes for the purposes of transport.

- ■ Long-distance trucking of waste are classified in Industry 48423, Specialized Freight (except Used Goods) Trucking, Long-distance;
- ■ Operating facilities for separating and sorting recyclable materials from nonhazardous waste streams (i.e., garbage) and/or for sorting commingled recyclable materials, such as paper, plastics, and metal cans, into distinct categories are classified in Industry 56292, Materials Recovery Facilities; and
- ■ Collecting and/or hauling in combination with disposal of waste materials are classified in Industry 56221, Waste Treatment and Disposal.

562111 Solid Waste Collection ^{US}

This U.S. industry comprises establishments primarily engaged in one or more of the following: (1) collecting and/or hauling nonhazardous solid waste (i.e., garbage) within a local area; (2) operating nonhazardous solid waste transfer stations; and (3) collecting and/or hauling mixed recyclable materials within a local area.

- ■ Long-distance trucking of waste are classified in Industry 484230, Specialized Freight (except Used Goods) Trucking, Long-distance;
- ■ Collecting and/or hauling in combination with disposal of nonhazardous waste materials are classified in Industry 56221, Waste Treatment and Disposal;
- ■ Collecting and/or hauling hazardous waste within a local area and/or operating hazardous waste transfer station are classified in U.S. Industry 562112, Hazardous Waste Collection;
- ■ Collecting and removing debris, such as brush or rubble, within a local area are classified in U.S. Industry 562119, Other Waste Collection; and
- ■ Operating facilities for separating and sorting recyclable materials from nonhazardous waste streams (i.e., garbage) and/or for sorting commingled recyclable materials, such as paper, plastics, and metal cans, into distinct categories are classified in Industry 562920, Materials Recovery Facilities.

562112 Hazardous Waste Collection ^{US}

This U.S. industry comprises establishments primarily engaged in collecting and/or hauling hazardous waste within a local area and/or operating hazardous waste transfer stations. Hazardous waste collection establishments may be responsible for the identification, treatment, packaging, and labeling of wastes for the purposes of transport.

- ■ Long-distance trucking of waste-are classified in Industry 484230, Specialized Freight (except Used Goods) Trucking, Long-distance;
- ■ Collecting and/or hauling in combination with disposal of hazardous waste materials are classified in U.S. Industry 562211, Hazardous Waste Treatment and Disposal;
- ■ Collecting and/or hauling nonhazardous solid waste (i.e., garbage) and/or recyclable materials within a local area and/or operating nonhazardous solid waste transfer stations are classified in U.S. Industry 562111, Solid Waste Collection; and
- ■ Collecting and removing debris, such as brush or rubble, within a local area are classified in U.S. Industry 562119, Other Waste Collection.

Sector **56**

Administrative and Support and Waste Management and Remediation Services

■ = Cross-References

US—United States industry only. CAN—United States and Canadian industries are comparable. When neither US nor CAN appears, Canadian, Mexican, and United States industries are comparable.

www.harrisinfo.com

565

562119 Other Waste Collection ^{US}

This U.S. industry comprises establishments primarily engaged in collecting and/or hauling waste (except nonhazardous solid waste and hazardous waste) within a local area. Establishments engaged in brush or rubble removal services are included in this industry.

- Long-distance trucking of waste are classified in Industry 484230, Specialized Freight (except Used Goods) Trucking, Long-distance;
- Collecting and/or hauling in combination with disposal of waste material are classified in Industry Group 5622, Waste Treatment and Disposal;
- Collecting and/or hauling nonhazardous solid waste (i.e., garbage) or mixed recyclable materials within a local area or operating nonhazardous solid waste transfer stations are classified in U.S. Industry 562111, Solid Waste Collection;
- Collecting and/or hauling hazardous waste within a local area or operating hazardous waste transfer stations are classified in U.S. Industry 562112, Hazardous Waste Collection; and
- Operating facilities for separating and sorting recyclable materials from nonhazardous waste streams (i.e., garbage) and/or for sorting commingled recyclable materials, such as paper, plastics, and metal cans, into distinct categories are classified in Industry 562920, Materials Recovery Facilities.

5622 Waste Treatment and Disposal ^{CAN}

56221 Waste Treatment and Disposal ^{CAN}

This industry comprises establishments primarily engaged in (1) operating waste treatment or disposal facilities (except sewer systems or sewage treatment facilities) or (2) the combined activity of collecting and/or hauling of waste materials within a local area and operating waste treatment or disposal facilities. Waste combusters or incinerators (including those that may produce byproducts such as electricity), solid waste landfills, and compost dumps are included in this industry.

- Collecting, treating, and disposing waste through sewer systems or sewage treatment facilities are classified in Industry 22132, Sewage Treatment Facilities; and
- Manufacturing compost are classified in Industry 32531, Fertilizer Manufacturing.

562211 Hazardous Waste Treatment and Disposal ^{US}

This U.S. industry comprises establishments primarily engaged in (1) operating treatment and/or disposal facilities for hazardous waste or (2) the combined activity of collecting and/or hauling of hazardous waste materials within a local area and operating treatment or disposal facilities for hazardous waste.

- Operating landfills for the disposal of nonhazardous solid waste are classified in U.S. Industry 562212, Solid Waste Landfill;
- Operating combustors and incinerators for the disposal of nonhazardous solid waste are classified in U.S. Industry 562213, Solid Waste Combustors and Incinerators;
- Collecting, treating, and disposing waste through sewer systems or sewage treatment facilities are classified in Industry 221320, Sewage Treatment Facilities; and
- Operating nonhazardous waste treatment and disposal facilities (except landfills, combustors, incinerators, and sewer systems or sewage treatment facilities) are classified in U.S. Industry 562219, Other Nonhazardous Waste Treatment and Disposal.

562212 Solid Waste Landfill ^{US}

This U.S. industry comprises establishments primarily engaged in (1) operating landfills for the disposal of nonhazardous solid waste or (2) the combined activity of collecting and/or hauling nonhazardous waste materials within a local area and operating landfills for the disposal of nonhazardous solid waste.

- Operating treatment and/or disposal facilities for hazardous waste are classified in U.S. Industry 562211, Hazardous Waste Treatment and Disposal;
- Operating combustors and incinerators for the disposal of nonhazardous solid waste are classified in U.S. Industry 562213, Solid Waste Combustors and Incinerators;
- Collecting, treating, and disposing waste through sewer systems or sewage treatment facilities are classified in Industry 221320, Sewage Treatment Facilities;
- Operating nonhazardous waste treatment and disposal facilities (except landfills, combustors, incinerators, and sewer systems or sewage treatment facilities) are classified in U.S. Industry 562219, Other Nonhazardous Waste Treatment and Disposal; and
- Manufacturing compost are classified in U.S. Industry 325314, Fertilizer (Mixing Only) Manufacturing.

562213 Solid Waste Combustors and Incinerators ^{US}

This U.S. industry comprises establishments primarily engaged in operating combustors and incinerators for the disposal of nonhazardous solid waste. These establishments may produce byproducts, such as electricity and steam.

- Operating treatment and/or disposal facilities for hazardous waste are classified in U.S. Industry 562211, Hazardous Waste Treatment and Disposal;

Sector 56

Administrative and Support and Waste Management and Remediation Services

■ = Cross-References

- Operating landfills for the disposal of nonhazardous solid waste are classified in U.S. Industry 562212, Solid Waste Landfill;
- Collecting, treating, and disposing waste through sewer systems or sewage treatment facilities are classified in Industry 221320, Sewage Treatment Facilities; and
- Operating nonhazardous waste treatment and disposal facilities (except landfills, combustors, incinerators, and sewer systems or sewage treatment facilities) are classified in U.S. Industry 562219, Other Nonhazardous Waste Treatment and Disposal.

562219 Other Nonhazardous Waste Treatment and Disposal ᵁˢ

This U.S. industry comprises establishments primarily engaged in (1) operating nonhazardous waste treatment and disposal facilities (except landfills, combustors, incinerators and sewer systems or sewage treatment facilities) or (2) the combined activity of collecting and/or hauling of nonhazardous waste materials within a local area and operating waste treatment or disposal facilities (except landfills, combustors, incinerators and sewer systems, or sewage treatment facilities). Compost dumps are included in this industry.

- Operating landfills for the disposal of nonhazardous solid waste are classified in U.S. Industry 562212, Solid Waste Landfill;
- Operating combustors and incinerators for the disposal of nonhazardous solid waste are classified in U.S. Industry 562213, Solid Waste Combustors and Incinerators;
- Collecting, treating, and disposing waste through sewer systems or sewage treatment facilities are classified in Industry 221320, Sewage Treatment Facilities; and
- Manufacturing compost are classified in U.S. Industry 325314, Fertilizer (Mixing Only) Manufacturing.

5629 Remediation and Other Waste Management Services ᶜᴬᴺ

This industry group comprises establishments primarily engaged in remediation and other waste management services (except waste collection, waste treatment and disposal, and waste management consulting services).

56291 Remediation Services ᶜᴬᴺ

See industry description for 562910 below.

562910 Remediation Services ᶜᴬᴺ

This industry comprises establishments primarily engaged in one or more of the following: (1) remediation and cleanup of contaminated buildings, mine sites, soil, or ground water; (2) integrated mine reclamation activities, including demolition, soil remediation, waste water treatment, hazardous material removal, contouring land, and revegetation; and (3) asbestos, lead paint, and other toxic material abatement.

- Developing remedial action plans are classified in Industry 541620, Environmental Consulting Services;
- Excavating soil are classified in Industry 235930, Excavation Contractors;
- Individual activities as part of a reclamation or remediation project are classified according to the primary activity;
- Building modifications to alleviate radon gas are classified in Sector 23, Construction; and
- Collecting, treating, and disposing waste water through sewer systems or sewage treatment facilities are classified in Industry 221320, Sewage Treatment Facilities.

56292 Materials Recovery Facilities ᶜᴬᴺ

See industry description for 562920 below.

562920 Materials Recovery Facilities ᶜᴬᴺ

This industry comprises establishments primarily engaged in (1) operating facilities for separating and sorting recyclable materials from nonhazardous waste streams (i.e., garbage) and/or (2) operating facilities where commingled recyclable materials, such as paper, plastics, used beverage cans, and metals, are sorted into distinct categories.

- Establishments primarily engaged in wholesaling automotive, industrial, and other recyclable materials are classified in Industry 421930, Recyclable Material Wholesalers.

56299 All Other Waste Management Services ᶜᴬᴺ

This industry comprises establishments primarily engaged in waste management services (except waste collection, waste treatment and disposal, remediation, operation of materials recovery facilities, and waste management consulting services).

- Collecting and/or hauling waste within a local area are classified in Industry 56211, Waste Collection;
- Long-distance trucking of waste are classified in Industry 48423, Specialized Freight (except Used Goods) Trucking, Long-distance;

Sector **56**

Administrative and Support and Waste Management and Remediation Services

■ = Cross-References

US—United States industry only. CAN—United States and Canadian industries are comparable. When neither US nor CAN appears, Canadian, Mexican, and United States industries are comparable.

■ Operating treatment or disposal facilities (except sewer systems or sewage treatment facilities) for wastes are classified in Industry 56221, Waste Treatment and Disposal;

■ Collecting, treating, and disposing waste through sewer systems or sewage treatment facilities are classified in Industry 22132, Sewage Treatment Facilities;

■ Remediation and cleanup of contaminated buildings, mine sites, soil, or ground water are classified in Industry 56291, Remediation Services;

■ Operating facilities for separating and sorting recyclable materials from nonhazardous waste streams (i.e., garbage) or where commingled recyclable materials, such as paper, plastics, and metal cans, are sorted into distinct categories are classified in Industry 56292, Materials Recovery Facilities;

■ Installing septic tanks are classified in Industry 23511, Plumbing, Heating, and Air-conditioning Contractors; and

■ Providing waste management consulting services, such as developing remedial action plans, are classified in Industry 54162, Environmental Consulting Services.

562991 Septic Tank and Related Services ᵁˢ

This U.S. industry comprises establishments primarily engaged in (1) pumping (i.e., cleaning) septic tanks and cesspools and/or (2) renting and/or servicing portable toilets.

■ Installing septic tanks are classified in Industry 235110, Plumbing, Heating, and Air-conditioning Contractors; and

■ Cleaning and rodding sewers and catch basins are classified in U.S. Industry 562998, All Other Miscellaneous Waste Management Services.

562998 All Other Miscellaneous Waste Management Services ᵁˢ

This U.S. industry comprises establishments primarily engaged in providing waste management services (except waste collection, waste treatment and disposal, remediation, operation of materials recovery facilities, septic tank pumping and related services, and waste management consulting services).

■ Collecting and/or hauling waste within a local area are classified in Industry 56211, Waste Collection;

■ Long-distance trucking of waste are classified in Industry 484230, Specialized Freight (except Used Goods) Trucking, Long-distance;

■ Operating treatment or disposal facilities (except sewer systems or sewage treatment facilities) for wastes-are classified in Industry 56221 Waste Treatment and Disposal;

■ Collecting, treating, and disposing waste through sewer systems or sewage treatment facilities are classified in Industry 221320, Sewage Treatment Facilities;

■ The remediation and cleanup of contaminated buildings, mine sites, soil, or ground water are classified in Industry 562910, Remediation Services;

■ Operating facilities for separating and sorting recyclable materials from nonhazardous waste streams (i.e., garbage) or for sorting commingled recyclable materials, such as paper, plastics, and metal cans, into distinct categories are classified in Industry 562920, Materials Recovery Facilities;

■ Pumping (i.e., cleaning) cesspools, portable toilets, and septic tanks or renting portable toilets are classified in U.S. Industry 562991, Septic Tank and Related Services; and

■ Providing waste management consulting services, such as developing remedial action plans, are classified in Industry 541620, Environmental Consulting Services.

Sector 56

Administrative and Support and Waste Management and Remediation Services

■ = Cross-References

US—United States industry only. CAN—United States and Canadian industries are comparable. When neither US nor CAN appears, Canadian, Mexican, and United States industries are comparable.

568

Harris InfoSource

Sector 6| Educational Services

The Sector as a Whole

The Educational Services sector comprises establishments that provide instruction and training in a wide variety of subjects. This instruction and training is provided by specialized establishments, such as schools, colleges, universities, and training centers. These establishments may be privately owned and operated for profit or not for profit, or they may be publicly owned and operated. They may also offer food and accommodation services to their students.

Educational services are usually delivered by teachers or instructors that explain, tell, demonstrate, supervise, and direct learning. Instruction is imparted in diverse settings, such as educational institutions, the workplace, or the home through correspondence, television, or other means. It can be adapted to the particular needs of the students, for example sign language can replace verbal language for teaching students with hearing impairments. All industries in the sector share this commonality of process, namely, labor inputs of instructors with the requisite subject matter expertise and teaching ability.

▶611 EDUCATIONAL SERVICES

Industries in the Educational Services subsector provide instruction and training in a wide variety of subjects. The instruction and training is provided by specialized establishments, such as schools, colleges, universities, and training centers.

The subsector is structured according to level and type of educational services. Elementary and secondary schools, junior colleges and colleges, universities, and professional schools correspond to a recognized series of formal levels of education designated by diplomas, associate degrees (including equivalent certificates) and degrees. The remaining industry groups are based more on the type of instruction or training offered and the levels are not always as formally defined. The establishments are often highly specialized, many offering instruction in a very limited subject matter, for example ski lessons or one specific computer software package. Within the sector, the level and types of training that are required of the instructors and teachers vary depending on the industry.

Establishments that manage schools and other educational establishments on a contractual basis are classified in this subsector if they both manage the operation and provide the operating staff. Such establishments are classified in the educational services subsector based on the type of facility managed and operated.

Sector 6|
Educational Services

6111 Elementary and Secondary Schools

61111 Elementary and Secondary Schools ^{CAN}
See industry description for 611110 below.

611110 Elementary and Secondary Schools ^{CAN}
This industry comprises establishments primarily engaged in furnishing academic courses and associated course work that comprise a basic preparatory education. A basic preparatory education

ordinarily constitutes kindergarten through 12th grade. This industry includes school boards and school districts.

- ■ Establishments primarily engaged in providing preschool or prekindergarten education are classified in Industry 624410, Child Day Care Services; and
- ■ Military academies, college level are classified in Industry 61131, Colleges, Universities, and Professional Schools.

6112 Junior Colleges

61121 Junior Colleges
See industry description for 611210 below.

611210 Junior Colleges
This industry comprises establishments primarily engaged in furnishing academic, or academic and technical, courses and granting associate degrees, certificates, or diplomas below the baccalaureate level. The requirement for admission to an associate or equivalent degree program is at least a high school diploma or equivalent general academic training.

6113 Colleges, Universities, and Professional Schools

61131 Colleges, Universities, and Professional Schools
See industry description for 611310 below.

611310 Colleges, Universities, and Professional Schools
This industry comprises establishments primarily engaged in furnishing academic courses and granting degrees at baccalaureate or graduate levels. The requirement for admission is at least a high school diploma or equivalent general academic training.

- ■ Establishments primarily engaged in furnishing academic, or academic and technical, courses and granting associate degrees, certificates, or diplomas below the baccalaureate level are classified in Industry 611210, Junior Colleges.

6114 Business Schools and Computer and Management Training

61141 Business and Secretarial Schools
See industry description for 611410 below.

611410 Business and Secretarial Schools
This industry comprises establishments primarily engaged in offering courses in office procedures and secretarial and stenographic skills and may offer courses in basic office skills, such as word processing. In addition, these establishments may offer such classes as office machine operation, reception, communications, and other skills designed for individuals pursuing a clerical or secretarial career.

- ■ Offering computer training (except computer repair) are classified in Industry 611420, Computer Training;
- ■ Offering academic degrees (e.g., baccalaureate, graduate level) in business education are classified in Industry 611310, Colleges, Universities, and Professional Schools; and
- ■ Offering training in the maintenance and repair of computers are classified in Industry 611519, Other Technical and Trade Schools.

61142 Computer Training
See industry description for 611420 below.

611420 Computer Training
This industry comprises establishments primarily engaged in conducting computer training (except computer repair), such as computer programming, software packages, computerized business systems, computer electronics technology, computer operations, and local area network management. Instruction may be provided at the establishment's facilities or at an off-site location, including the client's own facilities.

- ■ Offering training in the maintenance and repair of computers are classified in Industry 61151, Technical and Trade Schools; and
- ■ Computer retailing, wholesaling, or computer system designing that may also provide computer training are classified in their appropriate industries.

Sector **61**
Educational Services

■ = Cross-References

US—United States industry only. CAN—United States and Canadian industries are comparable. When neither US nor CAN appears, Canadian, Mexican, and United States industries are comparable.

570

Harris InfoSource

61143 Professional and Management Development Training
See industry description for 611430 below.

611430 Professional and Management Development Training
This industry comprises establishments primarily engaged in offering an array of short duration courses and seminars for management and professional development. Training for career development may be provided directly to individuals or through employers' training programs; and courses may be customized or modified to meet the special needs of customers. Instruction may be provided at the establishment's facilities or at an off-site location, including the client's own facilities.

- Advising clients on human resource and training issues without providing the training are classified in U.S. Industry 541612, Human Resources and Executive Search Consulting Services; and
- Offering academic degrees (e.g., baccalaureate, graduate level) are classified in Industry 611310, Colleges, Universities and Professional Schools.

6115 Technical and Trade Schools

61151 Technical and Trade Schools
This industry comprises establishments primarily engaged in offering vocational and technical training in a variety of technical subjects and trades. The training often leads to job-specific certification.

- Offering courses in office procedures and secretarial and stenographic skills are classified in Industry 61141, Business and Secretarial Schools;
- Offering computer training (except computer repair) are classified in Industry 61142, Computer Training;
Offering professional and management development training are classified in Industry 61143, Professional and Management Development Training;
- Offering academic courses that may also offer technical and trade courses are classified according to the type of school;
- Specialty air transportation services which may also provide flight training are classified in Industry 48121, Nonscheduled Air Transportation; and
- Offering registered nursing training are classified in Industry 61121, Junior Colleges or Industry 61131, Colleges, Universities, and Professional Schools.

611511 Cosmetology and Barber Schools ᵁˢ
This U.S. industry comprises establishments primarily engaged in offering training in barbering, hair styling, or the cosmetic arts, such as makeup or skin care. These schools provide job-specific certification.

611512 Flight Training ᵁˢ
This U.S. industry comprises establishments primarily engaged in offering aviation and flight training. These establishments may offer vocational training, recreational training, or both.

- Establishments primarily engaged in specialty air transportation services which may also provide flight training are classified in U.S. Industry 481219, Other Nonscheduled Air Transportation.

611513 Apprenticeship Training ᵁˢ
This U.S. industry comprises establishments primarily engaged in offering apprenticeship training programs. These programs involve applied training as well as course work.

611519 Other Technical and Trade Schools ᵁˢ
This U.S. industry comprises establishments primarily engaged in offering job or career vocational or technical courses (except cosmetology and barber training, aviation and flight training, and apprenticeship training). The curriculums offered by these schools are highly structured and specialized and lead to job-specific certification.

- Offering courses in office procedures and secretarial and stenographic skills are classified in Industry 611410, Business and Secretarial Schools;
- Offering computer training (except computer repair) are classified in Industry 611420, Computer Training;
- Professional and management development training are classified in Industry 611430, Professional and Management Development Training;
- Offering registered nursing training with academic degrees (e.g., associate baccalaureate) are classified in Industry 611210, Junior Colleges or Industry 611310, Colleges, Universities and Professional Schools;
- Offering aviation and flight training are classified in U.S. Industry 611512, Flight Training;
- Offering cosmetology and barber training are classified in U.S. Industry 611511, Cosmetology and Barber Schools;
- Offering academic courses that may also offer technical and trade courses are classified according to the type of school; and
- Offering apprenticeship training programs are classified in U.S. Industry 611513, Apprenticeship Training.

Sector **61**

Educational Services

■ = Cross-References

US—United States industry only. CAN—United States and Canadian industries are comparable. When neither US nor CAN appears, Canadian, Mexican, and United States industries are comparable.

www.harrisinfo.com

571

6116 Other Schools and Instruction

This industry group comprises establishments primarily engaged in offering or providing instruction (except academic schools, colleges, and universities; and business, computer, management, technical, or trade instruction).

61161 Fine Arts Schools

See industry description for 611610 below.

611610 Fine Arts Schools

This industry comprises establishments primarily engaged in offering instruction in the arts, including dance, art, drama, and music.

- Establishments offering high school diplomas or academic degrees (i.e., even if they specialize in fine arts) are classified elsewhere in this subsector according to the type of school; and
- Establishments primarily engaged in offering courses in commercial and graphic arts and commercial photography are classified in U.S. Industry 611519, Other Technical and Trade Schools.

61162 Sports and Recreation Instruction

See industry description for 611620 below.

611620 Sports and Recreation Instruction

This industry comprises establishments, such as camps and schools, primarily engaged in offering instruction in athletic activities to groups of individuals. Overnight and day sports instruction camps are included in this industry.

- Establishments primarily engaged in operating overnight recreational camps that may offer some athletic instruction in addition to other activities are classified in U.S. Industry 721214, Recreation and Vacation Camps (except campgrounds);
- Establishments primarily engaged in operating sports and recreation establishments that also offer athletic instruction are classified in Sector 71, Arts, Entertainment, and Recreation;
- Independent (i.e., freelance) athletes engaged in providing sports instruction and participating in spectator sporting events are classified in U.S. Industry 711219, Other Spectator Sports; and
- Offering academic courses that may also offer athletic instruction are classified according to the type of school.

61163 Language Schools

See industry description for 611630 below.

611630 Language Schools

This industry comprises establishments primarily engaged in offering foreign language instruction (including sign language). These establishments are designed to offer language instruction ranging from conversational skills for personal enrichment to intensive training courses for career or educational opportunities.

- Offering academic courses that may also offer language instruction are classified according to type of school; and
- Providing translation and interpretation services are classified in Industry 541930, Translation and Interpretation Services.

61169 All Other Schools and Instruction

This industry comprises establishments primarily engaged in offering instruction (except business, computer, management, technical, trade, fine arts, athletic, and language instruction). Also excluded from this industry are academic schools, colleges, and universities.

- Offering elementary and secondary school instruction are classified in Industry 61111, Elementary and Secondary Schools;
- Offering junior college instruction are classified in Industry 61121, Junior Colleges;
- Offering college, university, and professional school instruction with academic degrees (e.g., baccalaureate, graduate) are classified in Industry 61131, Colleges, Universities and Professional Schools;
- Offering business, computer (except computer repair), and management training are classified in Industry Group 6114, Business Schools and Computer and Management Training;
- Offering technical and trade school instruction (e.g., computer repair and maintenance) are classified in Industry 61151, Technical and Trade Schools;
- Offering fine arts instruction are classified in Industry 61161, Fine Arts Schools;
- Offering sports and recreation instruction are classified in Industry 61162, Sports and Recreation Instruction; and
- Offering language instruction are classified in Industry 61163, Language Schools.

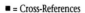

■ = Cross-References

Sector **61**

Educational Services

US—United States industry only. CAN—United States and Canadian industries are comparable. When neither US nor CAN appears, Canadian, Mexican, and United States industries are comparable.

572

Harris InfoSource

611691 Exam Preparation and Tutoring us

This U.S. industry comprises establishments primarily engaged in offering preparation for standardized examinations and/or academic tutoring services.

- Establishments primarily engaged in offering truck and bus driving instruction are classified in U.S. Industry 611519, Other Technical and Trade Schools.

611699 All Other Miscellaneous Schools and Instruction us

This U.S. industry comprises establishments primarily engaged in offering instruction (except business, computer, management, technical, trade, fine arts, athletic, language instruction, tutoring, and automobile driving instruction). Also excluded from this industry are academic schools, colleges, and universities.

- Offering elementary and secondary school instruction are classified in Industry 611110, Elementary and Secondary Schools;
- Offering junior college instruction are classified in Industry 611210, Junior Colleges;
- Offering college, university, and professional school instruction with academic degrees (e.g., baccalaureate, graduate) are classified in Industry 611310, Colleges, Universities and Professional Schools;
- Offering business, computer (except computer repair), and management training are classified in Industry Group 6114, Business Schools and Computer and Management Training;
- Offering technical and trade school instruction (e.g., computer repair and maintenance) are classified in Industry 61151, Technical and Trade Schools;
- Offering fine arts instruction are classified in Industry 611610, Fine Arts Schools;
- Offering sports and recreation instruction are classified in Industry 611620, Sports and Recreation Instruction;
- Offering language instruction are classified in Industry 611630, Language Schools;
- Offering exam preparation and tutoring services are classified in U.S. Industry 611691, Exam Preparation and Tutoring; and
- Offering automobile driving instruction are classified in U.S. Industry 611692, Automobile Driving Schools.

6117 Educational Support Services

61171 Educational Support Services

See industry description for 611710 below.

611710 Educational Support Services

This industry comprises establishments primarily engaged in providing noninstructional services that support educational processes or systems.

- Providing job training for the unemployed, underemployed, physically disabled, and persons who have a job market disadvantage because of lack of education or job skills are classified in Industry 624310, Vocational Rehabilitation Services; and
- Conducting research and analysis in cognitive development are classified in Industry 541720, Research and Development in the Social Sciences and Humanities.

Sector 61

Educational Services

■ = Cross-References

US—United States industry only. CAN—United States and Canadian industries are comparable. When neither US nor CAN appears, Canadian, Mexican, and United States industries are comparable.

NAICS United States Structure

Sector	Name	Sub-sectors	Industry groups	NAICS 5-digit industries	U.S. 6-digit industries	TOTAL U.S. industries	New industries
11	Agriculture, Forestry, Fishing and, Hunting	5	19	42	32	64	20
21	Mining	3	5	10	28	29	—
22	Utilities	1	3	6	6	10	6
23	Construction	3	14	28	—	28	3
31–33	Manufacturing	21	84	184	408	474	79
42	Wholesale Trade	2	18	69	—	69	—
44–45	Retail Trade	12	27	61	18	72	17
48-49	Transportation and Warehousing	11	29	42	25	57	28
51	Information	4	9	28	12	34	20
52	Finance and Insurance	5	11	32	15	42	23
53	Real Estate and Rental and Leasing	3	8	19	9	24	15
54	Professional, Scientific, and Technical Services	1	9	35	17	47	28
55	Management of Companies and Enterprises	1	1	1	3	3	1
56	Administrative and Support and Waste Management and Remediation Services	2	11	29	23	43	29
61	Educational Services	1	7	12	7	17	12
62	Health Care and Social Assistance	4	18	30	16	39	27
71	Arts, Entertainment, and Recreation	3	9	23	3	25	19
72	Accommodation and Food Services	2	7	11	7	15	10
81	Other Services (except Public Administration)	4	14	30	30	49	19
92	Public Administration	8	8	29	—	29	2
	TOTAL	96	311	721	659	1170	358

To learn more about the changes by sector go to pages 15-18.

Sector **61**

Educational Services

Sector 62
Health Care and Social Assistance

The Sector as a Whole

THE HEALTH CARE AND SOCIAL ASSISTANCE sector comprises establishments providing health care and social assistance for individuals. The sector includes both health care and social assistance because it is sometimes difficult to distinguish between the boundaries of these two activities. The industries in this sector are arranged on a continuum starting with those establishments providing medical care exclusively, continuing with those providing health care and social assistance, and finally finishing with those providing only social assistance. The services provided by establishments in this sector are delivered by trained professionals. All industries in the sector share this commonality of process, namely, labor inputs of health practitioners or social workers with the requisite expertise. Many of the industries in the sector are defined based on the educational degree held by the practitioners included in the industry.

Excluded from this sector are aerobic classes in Subsector 713, Amusement, Gambling, and Recreation Industries and nonmedical diet and weight reducing centers in Subsector 812, Personal and Laundry Services. Although these can be viewed as health services, these services are not typically delivered by health practitioners.

Visit page 16 to learn more about this sector.

▶621 AMBULATORY HEALTH CARE SERVICES

Industries in the Ambulatory Health Care Services subsector provide health care services directly or indirectly to ambulatory patients and do not usually provide inpatient services. Health practitioners in this subsector provide outpatient services, with the facilities and equipment not usually being the most significant part of the production process.

6211 Offices of Physicians

62111 Offices of Physicians
This industry comprises establishments of health practitioners having the degree of M.D. (Doctor of medicine) or D.O. (Doctor of osteopathy) primarily engaged in the independent practice of general or specialized medicine (e.g., anesthesiology, oncology, ophthalmology, psychiatry) or surgery. These practitioners operate private or group practices in their own offices (e.g., centers, clinics) or in the facilities of others, such as hospitals or HMO medical centers.

- Medical centers primarily engaged in providing emergency medical care for accident or trauma victims and ambulatory surgical centers primarily engaged in providing surgery on an outpatient basis are classified in Industry 62149, Other Outpatient Care Centers;
- Establishments of oral pathologists are classified in Industry 62121, Offices of Dentists; and
- Establishments of speech or voice pathologists are classified in Industry 62134, Offices of Physical, Occupational and Speech Therapists, and Audiologists.

621111 Offices of Physicians (except Mental Health Specialists) US
This U.S. industry comprises establishments of health practitioners having the degree of M.D. (Doctor of medicine) or D.O. (Doctor of osteopathy) primarily engaged in the independent practice of general or specialized medicine (except psychiatry or psychoanalysis) or surgery. These practitioners operate private or group practices in their own offices (e.g., centers, clinics) or in the facilities of others, such as hospitals or HMO medical centers.

Sector 62
Health Care and Social Assistance

■ = Cross-References

US—United States industry only. CAN—United States and Canadian industries are comparable. When neither US nor CAN appears, Canadian, Mexican, and United States industries are comparable.

575

■ Establishments of physicians primarily engaged in the independent practice of psychiatry or psychoanalysis are classified in U.S. Industry 621112, Offices of Physicians, Mental Health Specialists;
■ Freestanding medical centers primarily engaged in providing emergency medical care for accident or catastrophe victims and freestanding ambulatory surgical centers primarily engaged in providing surgery on an outpatient basis are classified in U.S. Industry 621493, Freestanding Ambulatory Surgical and Emergency Centers;
■ Establishments of oral pathologists are classified in Industry 621210, Offices of Dentists; and
■ Establishments of speech or voice pathologists are classified in Industry 621340, Offices of Physical, Occupational and Speech Therapists, and Audiologists.

621112 Offices of Physicians, Mental Health Specialists ^{US}

This U.S. industry comprises establishments of health practitioners having the degree of M.D. (Doctor of medicine) or D.O. (Doctor of osteopathy) primarily engaged in the independent practice of psychiatry or psychoanalysis. These practitioners operate private or group practices in their own offices (e.g., centers, clinics) or in the facilities of others, such as hospitals or HMO medical centers.

6212 Offices of Dentists

62121 Offices of Dentists

See industry description for 621210 below.

621210 Offices of Dentists

This industry comprises establishments of health practitioners having the degree of D.M.D. (Doctor of dental medicine), D.D.S. (Doctor of dental surgery), or D.D.Sc. (Doctor of dental science) primarily engaged in the independent practice of general or specialized dentistry or dental surgery. These practitioners operate private or group practices in their own offices (e.g., centers, clinics) or in the facilities of others, such as hospitals or HMO medical centers. They can provide either comprehensive preventive, cosmetic, or emergency care, or specialize in a single field of dentistry.

■ Establishments known as dental laboratories primarily engaged in making dentures, artificial teeth, and orthodontic appliances to order for dentists are classified U.S. Industry 339116, Dental Laboratories; and
■ Establishments of dental hygienists primarily engaged in cleaning teeth and gums or establishments of denturists primarily engaged in taking impressions for and fitting dentures are classified in U.S. Industry 621399, Offices of All Other Miscellaneous Health Practitioners.

6213 Offices of Other Health Practitioners

This industry group comprises establishments of independent health practitioners (except physicians and dentists).

62131 Offices of Chiropractors

See industry description for 621310 below.

621310 Offices of Chiropractors

This industry comprises establishments of health practitioners having the degree of D.C. (Doctor of chiropractic) primarily engaged in the independent practice of chiropractic. These practitioners provide diagnostic and therapeutic treatment of neuromusculoskeletal and related disorders through the manipulation and adjustment of the spinal column and extremities, and operate private or group practices in their own offices (e.g., centers, clinics) or in the facilities of others, such as hospitals or HMO medical centers.

62132 Offices of Optometrists

See industry description for 621320 below.

621320 Offices of Optometrists

This industry comprises establishments of health practitioners having the degree of O.D. (Doctor of optometry) primarily engaged in the independent practice of optometry. These practitioners provide eye examinations to determine visual acuity or the presence of vision problems and to prescribe eyeglasses, contact lenses, and eye exercises. They operate private or group practices in their own offices (e.g., centers, clinics) or in the facilities of others, such as hospitals or HMO medical centers, and may also provide the same service as opticians, such as selling and fitting prescription eyeglasses and contact lenses.

Sector 62

Health Care and
Social Assistance

■ = Cross-References

US—United States industry only. CAN—United States and Canadian industries are comparable. When neither US nor CAN appears, Canadian, Mexican, and United States industries are comparable.

576

Harris InfoSource

■ Opticians primarily engaged in selling and fitting prescription eyeglasses and contact lenses are classified in Industry 446130, Optical Goods Stores; and

■ Physicians primarily engaged in the independent practice of ophthalmology are classified in U.S. Industry 621111, Offices of Physicians (except Mental Health Specialists).

62133 Offices of Mental Health Practitioners (except Physicians)
See industry description for 621330 below.

621330 Offices of Mental Health Practitioners (except Physicians)
This industry comprises establishments of independent mental health practitioners (except physicians) primarily engaged in (1) the diagnosis and treatment of mental, emotional, and behavioral disorders and/or (2) the diagnosis and treatment of individual or group social dysfunction brought about by such causes as mental illness, alcohol and substance abuse, physical and emotional trauma, or stress. These practitioners operate private or group practices in their own offices (e.g., centers, clinics) or in the facilities of others, such as hospitals or HMO medical centers.

■ Establishments of psychiatrists, psychoanalysts, and psychotherapists having the degree of M.D. (Doctor of medicine) or D.O. (Doctor of osteopathy) are classified in U.S. Industry 621112, Offices of Physicians, Mental Health Specialists.

62134 Offices of Physical, Occupational and Speech Therapists, and Audiologists
See industry description for 621340 below.

621340 Offices of Physical, Occupational and Speech Therapists, and Audiologists
This industry comprises establishments of independent health practitioners primarily engaged in one of the following: (1) administering medically prescribed physical therapy treatment for patients suffering from injuries or muscle, nerve, joint, and bone disease; (2) planning and administering educational, recreational, and social activities designed to help patients or individuals with disabilities, regain physical or mental functioning or to adapt to their disabilities; and (3) diagnosing and treating speech, language, or hearing problems. These practitioners operate private or group practices in their own offices (e.g., centers, clinics) or in the facilities of others, such as hospitals or HMO medical centers.

62139 Offices of All Other Health Practitioners
This industry comprises establishments of independent health practitioners (except physicians; dentists; chiropractors; optometrists; mental health specialists; physical, occupational, and speech therapists; and audiologists). These practitioners operate private or group practices in their own offices (e.g., centers, clinics) or in the facilities of others, such as hospitals or HMO medical centers.

■ The independent practice of medicine (i.e., physicians) are classified in Industry 62111, Offices of Physicians;
■ The independent practice of dentistry are classified in Industry 62121, Offices of Dentists;
■ The independent practice of chiropractic are classified in Industry 62131, Offices of Chiropractors;
■ The independent practice of optometry are classified in Industry 62132, Offices of Optometrists;
■ The independent practice of mental health (except physicians) are classified in Industry 62133,
Offices of Mental Health Practitioners (except Physicians); and
■ The independent practice of physical, occupational, and speech therapy and audiology are classified in
Industry 62134, Offices of Physical, Occupational and Speech Therapists, and Audiologists.

621391 Offices of Podiatrists
This U.S. industry comprises establishments of health practitioners having the degree of D.P. (Doctor of podiatry) primarily engaged in the independent practice of podiatry. These practitioners diagnose and treat diseases and deformities of the foot and operate private or group practices in their own offices (e.g., centers, clinics) or in the facilities of others, such as hospitals or HMO medical centers.

621399 Offices of All Other Miscellaneous Health Practitioners ᵁˢ
This U.S. industry comprises establishments of independent health practitioners (except physicians; dentists; chiropractors; optometrists; mental health specialists; physical, occupational, and speech therapists; audiologists; and podiatrists). These practitioners operate private or group practices in their own offices (e.g., centers, clinics) or in the facilities of others, such as hospitals or HMO medical centers.

■ The independent practice of medicine (i.e., physicians) are classified in Industry 62111, Offices of Physicians;
■ The independent practice of dentistry are classified in Industry 621210, Offices of Dentists;
■ The independent practice of chiropractic are classified in Industry 621310, Offices of Chiropractors;
■ The independent practice of optometry are classified in Industry 621320, Offices of Optometrists;

Visit page 16 to learn more about this sector.

Sector **62**

Health Care and Social Assistance

■ = Cross-References

US—United States industry only. CAN—United States and Canadian industries are comparable. When neither US nor CAN appears, Canadian, Mexican, and United States industries are comparable.

www.harrisinfo.com

577

■ The independent practice of mental health (except physicians) are classified in Industry 621330, Offices of Mental Health Practitioners (except Physicians);
■ The independent practice of physical, occupational, and speech therapy, and audiology are classified in Industry 621340, Offices of Physical, Occupational and Speech Therapists, and Audiologists; and
■ The independent practice of podiatry are classified in U.S. Industry 621391, Offices of Podiatrists.

6214 Outpatient Care Centers

62141 Family Planning Centers
See industry description for 621410 below.

621410 Family Planning Centers
This industry comprises establishments with medical staff primarily engaged in providing a range of family planning services on an outpatient basis, such as contraceptive services, genetic and prenatal counseling, voluntary sterilization, and therapeutic and medically indicated termination of pregnancy.

62142 Outpatient Mental Health and Substance Abuse Centers
See industry description for 621420 below.

621420 Outpatient Mental Health and Substance Abuse Centers
This industry comprises establishments with medical staff primarily engaged in providing outpatient services related to the diagnosis and treatment of mental health disorders and alcohol and other substance abuse. These establishments generally treat patients who do not require inpatient treatment. They may provide a counseling staff and information regarding a wide range of mental health and substance abuse issues and/or refer patients to more extensive treatment programs, if necessary.

■ Establishments known and licensed as hospitals primarily engaged in the inpatient treatment of mental health and substance abuse illnesses with an emphasis on medical treatment and monitoring are classified in Industry 622210, Psychiatric and Substance Abuse Hospitals; and
■ Establishments primarily engaged in the inpatient treatment of mental health and substance abuse illness with an emphasis on residential care and counseling rather than medical treatment are classified in Industry 623220, Residential Mental Health and Substance Abuse Facilities.

62149 Other Outpatient Care Centers
This industry comprises establishments with medical staff primarily engaged in providing general or specialized outpatient care (except family planning centers and outpatient mental health and substance abuse centers). Centers or clinics of health practitioners with different degrees from more than one industry practicing within the same establishment (i.e., Doctor of medicine and Doctor of dental medicine) are included in this industry.

■ Physician walk-in centers are classified in Industry 62111, Offices of Physicians;
■ Centers and clinics of health practitioners from the same industry primarily engaged in the independent practice of their profession are classified in Industry 62111, Offices of Physicians; Industry 62121, Offices of Dentists; and Industry Group 6213, Offices of Other Health Practitioners;
■ Family planning centers are classified in Industry 62141, Family Planning Centers;
■ Outpatient mental health and substance abuse centers are classified in Industry 62142, Outpatient Mental Health and Substance Abuse Centers;
■ HMO establishments (except those providing health care services) primarily engaged in underwriting health and medical insurance policies are classified in Industry 52411, Direct Life, Health, and Medical Insurance Carriers; and
■ Establishments known and licensed as hospitals that also perform ambulatory surgery and emergency room services are classified in Subsector 622, Hospitals.

621491 HMO Medical Centers US
This U.S. industry comprises establishments with physicians and other medical staff primarily engaged in providing a range of outpatient medical services to the health maintenance organization (HMO) subscribers with a focus generally on primary health care. These establishments are owned by the HMO. Included in this industry are HMO establishments that both provide health care services and underwrite health and medical insurance policies.

■ Health practitioners or health practitioner groups contracting to provide their services to subscribers of prepaid health plans are classified in Industry 62111, Offices of Physicians;
■ Industry 621210, Offices of Dentists; and Industry Group 6213, Offices of Other Health Practitioners; and
■ HMO establishments (except those providing health care services) primarily engaged in underwriting and administering health and medical insurance policies are classified in U.S. Industry 524114, Direct Health and Medical Insurance Carriers.

Sector **62**

Health Care and
Social Assistance

■ = Cross-References

US—United States industry only. CAN—United States and Canadian industries are comparable. When neither US nor CAN appears, Canadian, Mexican, and United States industries are comparable.

621492 Kidney Dialysis Centers [US]

This U.S. industry comprises establishments with medical staff primarily engaged in providing outpatient kidney or renal dialysis services.

621493 Freestanding Ambulatory Surgical and Emergency Centers [US]

This U.S. industry comprises establishments with physicians and other medical staff primarily engaged in (1) providing surgical services (e.g., orthoscopic and cataract surgery) on an outpatient basis or (2) providing emergency care services (e.g., setting broken bones, treating lacerations, or tending to patients suffering injuries as a result of accidents, trauma, or medical conditions necessitating immediate medical care) on an outpatient basis. Outpatient surgical establishments have specialized facilities, such as operating and recovery rooms, and specialized equipment, such as anesthetic or X-ray equipment.

- Physician walk-in centers are classified in U.S. Industry 621111, Offices of Physicians (except Mental Health Specialists); and
- Establishments known and licensed as hospitals that also perform ambulatory surgery and emergency room services are classified in Subsector 622, Hospitals.

621498 All Other Outpatient Care Centers [US]

This U.S. industry comprises establishments with medical staff primarily engaged in providing general or specialized outpatient care (except family planning centers, outpatient mental health and substance abuse centers, HMO medical centers, kidney dialysis centers, and freestanding ambulatory surgical and emergency centers). Centers or clinics of health practitioners with different degrees from more than one industry practicing within the same establishment (i.e., Doctor of medicine and Doctor of dental medicine) are included in this industry.

Visit page 16 to learn more about this sector.

- Physician walk-in centers are classified in U.S. Industry 621111, Offices of Physicians (except Mental Health Specialists);
- Centers and clinics of health practitioners from the same industry primarily engaged in the independent practice of their profession are classified in Industry 62111, Offices of Physicians; Industry 621210, Offices of Dentists; and Industry Group 6213, Offices of Other Health Practitioners;
- Family planning centers are classified in Industry 621410, Family Planning Centers;
- Outpatient mental health and substance abuse centers are classified in Industry 621420, Outpatient Mental Health and Substance Abuse Centers;
- HMO medical centers are classified in U.S. Industry 621491, HMO Medical Centers;
- Dialysis centers are classified in U.S. Industry 621492, Kidney Dialysis Centers; and
- Freestanding ambulatory surgical and emergency centers are classified in U.S. Industry 621493, Freestanding Ambulatory Surgical and Emergency Centers.

6215 Medical and Diagnostic Laboratories

62151 Medical and Diagnostic Laboratories

This industry comprises establishments known as medical and diagnostic laboratories primarily engaged in providing analytic or diagnostic services, including body fluid analysis and diagnostic imaging, generally to the medical profession or to the patient on referral from a health practitioner.

- Establishments, such as dental, optical, and orthopedic laboratories, primarily engaged in providing the following activities to the medical profession, respectively: making dentures, artificial teeth, and orthodontic appliances to prescription; grinding of lenses to prescription; and making orthopedic or prosthetic appliances to prescription are classified in Industry 33911, Medical Equipment and Supplies Manufacturing.

621511 Medical Laboratories [US]

This U.S. industry comprises establishments known as medical laboratories primarily engaged in providing analytic or diagnostic services, including body fluid analysis, generally to the medical profession or to the patient on referral from a health practitioner.

- Establishments known as dental laboratories primarily engaged in making dentures, artificial teeth, and orthodontic appliances to prescription are classified in U.S. Industry 339116, Dental Laboratories;
- Establishments known as optical laboratories primarily engaged in grinding of lenses to prescription are classified in U.S. Industry 339115, Ophthalmic Goods Manufacturing; and Establishments known as orthopedic laboratories primarily engaged in making orthopedic or prosthetic appliances to prescription are classified in U.S. Industry 339113, Surgical Appliance and Supplies Manufacturing.

Sector **62**

Health Care and Social Assistance

■ = Cross-References

US—United States industry only. CAN—United States and Canadian industries are comparable. When neither US nor CAN appears, Canadian, Mexican, and United States industries are comparable.

www.harrisinfo.com

579

621512 Diagnostic Imaging Centers ᵁˢ

This U.S. industry comprises establishments known as diagnostic imaging centers primarily engaged in producing images of the patient generally on referral from a health practitioner.

6216 Home Health Care Services

62161 Home Health Care Services

See industry description for 621610 below.

621610 Home Health Care Services

This industry comprises establishments primarily engaged in providing skilled nursing services in the home, along with a range of the following: personal care services; homemaker and companion services; physical therapy; medical social services; medications; medical equipment and supplies; counseling; 24-hour home care; occupation and vocational therapy; dietary and nutritional services; speech therapy; audiology; and high-tech care, such as intravenous therapy.

- In-home health services provided by establishments of health practitioners and others primarily engaged in the independent practice of their profession are classified in Industry 62111, Offices of Physicians; Industry 621210, Offices of Dentists; and Industry Group 6213, Offices of Other Health Practitioners; and U.S. Industry 621999, All Other Miscellaneous Ambulatory Health Care Services; and
- Establishments primarily engaged in renting or leasing products for home health care are classified in U.S. Industry 532291, Home Health Equipment Rental.

6219 Other Ambulatory Health Care Services

This industry group comprises establishments primarily engaged in providing ambulatory health care services (except offices of physicians, dentists, and other health practitioners; outpatient care centers; medical laboratories and diagnostic imaging centers; and home health care providers).

62191 Ambulance Services

See industry description for 621910 below.

621910 Ambulance Services

This industry comprises establishments primarily engaged in providing transportation of patients by ground or air, along with medical care. These services are often provided during a medical emergency but are not restricted to emergencies. The vehicles are equipped with lifesaving equipment operated by medically trained personnel.

- Establishments primarily engaged in providing transportation of the disabled or elderly (without medical care) are classified in U.S. Industry 485991, Special Needs Transportation.

62199 All Other Ambulatory Health Care Services

This industry comprises establishments primarily engaged in providing ambulatory health care services (except office physicians, dentists, and other health practitioners; outpatient care centers; medical and diagnostic laboratories; home health care providers; and ambulances).

- Establishments primarily engaged in the independent practice of medicine are classified in Industry 62111, Offices of Physicians;
- Establishments primarily engaged in the independent practice of dentistry are classified in Industry 62121, Offices of Dentists;
- Establishments primarily engaged in the independent practice of health care (except offices of physicians and dentists) are classified in Industry Group 6213, Offices of Other Health Practitioners;
- Establishments primarily engaged in providing general or specialized outpatient care services are classified in Industry Group 6214, Outpatient Care Centers;
- Establishments primarily engaged in providing home health care services are classified in Industry 62161, Home Health Care Services;
- Establishments primarily engaged in transportation of patients by ground or air, along with medical care are classified in Industry 62191, Ambulance Services; and
- Establishments known as medical and diagnostic laboratories primarily engaged in providing analytic or diagnostic services are classified in Industry 62151, Medical and Diagnostic Laboratories.

621991 Blood and Organ Banks ᵁˢ

This U.S. industry comprises establishments primarily engaged in collecting, storing, and distributing blood and blood products and storing and distributing body organs.

Sector 62

Health Care and
Social Assistance

■ = Cross-References

US—United States industry only. CAN—United States and Canadian industries are comparable. When neither US nor CAN appears, Canadian, Mexican, and United States industries are comparable.

580

Harris InfoSource

621999 All Other Miscellaneous Ambulatory Health Care Services US

This U.S. industry comprises establishments primarily engaged in providing ambulatory health care services (except offices of physicians, dentists, and other health practitioners; outpatient care centers; medical and diagnostic laboratories; home health care providers; ambulances; and blood and organ banks).

- Establishments primarily engaged in the independent practice of medicine are classified in Industry 62111, Offices of Physicians;
- Establishments primarily engaged in the independent practice of dentistry are classified in Industry 621210, Offices of Dentists;
- Establishments primarily engaged in the independent practice of health care (except offices of physicians and dentists) are classified in Industry Group 6213, Offices of Other Health Practitioners;
- Establishments primarily engaged in providing general or specialized outpatient care services are classified in Industry Group 6214, Outpatient Care Centers;
- Establishments primarily engaged in providing home health care services are classified in Industry 621610, Home Health Care Services;
- Establishments primarily engaged in the transportation of patients by ground or air, along with medical care are classified in Industry 621910, Ambulance Services;
- Establishments known as medical and diagnostic laboratories primarily engaged in providing analytic or diagnostic services are classified in Industry 62151, Medical and Diagnostic Laboratories; and
- Blood and organ banks are classified in U.S. Industry 621991, Blood and Organ Banks.

▶ 622 HOSPITALS

Industries in the Hospitals subsector provide medical, diagnostic, and treatment services that include physician, nursing, and other health services to inpatients and the specialized accommodation services required by inpatients. Hospitals may also provide outpatient services as a secondary activity. Establishments in the Hospitals subsector provide inpatient health services, many of which can only be provided using the specialized facilities and equipment that form a significant and integral part of the production process.

6221 General Medical and Surgical Hospitals

62211 General Medical and Surgical Hospitals

See industry description for 622110 below.

622110 General Medical and Surgical Hospitals

This industry comprises establishments known and licensed as general medical and surgical hospitals primarily engaged in providing diagnostic and medical treatment (both surgical and nonsurgical) to inpatients with any of a wide variety of medical conditions. These establishments maintain inpatient beds and provide patients with food services that meet their nutritional requirements. These hospitals have an organized staff of physicians and other medical staff to provide patient care services. These establishments usually provide other services, such as outpatient services, anatomical pathology services, diagnostic X-ray services, clinical laboratory services, operating room services for a variety of procedures, and pharmacy services.

6222 Psychiatric and Substance Abuse Hospitals

62221 Psychiatric and Substance Abuse Hospitals

See industry description for 622210 below.

622210 Psychiatric and Substance Abuse Hospitals

This industry comprises establishments known and licensed as psychiatric and substance abuse hospitals primarily engaged in providing diagnostic, medical treatment, and monitoring services for inpatients who suffer from mental illness or substance abuse disorders. The treatment often requires an extended stay in the hospital. These establishments maintain inpatient beds and provide patients with food services that meet their nutritional requirements. They have an organized staff of physicians and other medical staff to provide patient care services. Psychiatric, psychological, and social work services are available at the facility. These hospitals usually provide other services, such as outpatient services, clinical laboratory services, diagnostic X-ray services, and electron-cephalograph services.

- Establishments primarily engaged in providing treatment of mental health and substance abuse illnesses on an exclusively outpatient basis are classified in Industry 621420, Outpatient Mental Health and Substance Abuse Centers;

Visit page 16 to learn more about this sector.

Sector **62**

Health Care and Social Assistance

■ = Cross-References

US—United States industry only. CAN—United States and Canadian industries are comparable. When neither US nor CAN appears, Canadian, Mexican, and United States industries are comparable.

■ Establishments referred to as hospitals but are primarily engaged in providing inpatient treatment of mental health and substance abuse illness with the emphasis on counseling rather than medical treatment are classified in Industry 623220, Residential Mental Health and Substance Abuse Facilities; and

■ Establishments referred to as hospitals but are primarily engaged in providing residential care for persons diagnosed with mental retardation are classified in Industry 623210, Residential Mental Retardation Facilities.

6223 Specialty (except Psychiatric and Substance Abuse) Hospitals

62231 Specialty (except Psychiatric and Substance Abuse) Hospitals
See industry description for 622310 below.

622310 Specialty (except Psychiatric and Substance Abuse) Hospitals
This industry consists of establishments known and licensed as specialty hospitals primarily engaged in providing diagnostic and medical treatment to inpatients with a specific type of disease or medical condition (except psychiatric or substance abuse). Hospitals providing long-term care for the chronically ill and hospitals providing rehabilitation, restorative, and adjustive services to physically challenged or disabled people are included in this industry. These establishments maintain inpatient beds and provide patients with food services that meet their nutritional requirements. They have an organized staff of physicians and other medical staff to provide patient care services. These hospitals may provide other services, such as outpatient services, diagnostic X-ray services, clinical laboratory services, operating room services, physical therapy services, educational and vocational services, and psychological and social work services.

■ Establishments known and licensed as hospitals primarily engaged in providing diagnostic and therapeutic inpatient services for a variety of medical conditions, both surgical and nonsurgical, are classified in Industry 622110, General Medical and Surgical Hospitals; and

■ Establishments known and licensed as hospitals primarily engaged in providing diagnostic and treatment services for inpatients with psychiatric or substance abuse illnesses are classified in Industry 622210, Psychiatric and Substance Abuse Hospitals.

■ Establishments referred to as hospitals but are primarily engaged in providing inpatient nursing and rehabilitative services to persons requiring convalescence are classified in Industry 623110, Nursing Care Facilities;

■ Establishments referred to as hospitals but are primarily engaged in providing residential care of persons diagnosed with mental retardation are classified in Industry 623210, Residential Mental Retardation Facilities; and

■ Establishments referred to as hospitals but are primarily engaged in providing inpatient treatment for mental health and substance abuse illnesses with the emphasis on counseling rather than medical treatment are classified in Industry 623220, Residential Mental Health and Substance Abuse Facilities.

▶623 NURSING AND RESIDENTIAL CARE FACILITIES
Industries in the Nursing and Residential Care Facilities subsector provide residential care combined with either nursing, supervisory, or other types of care as required by the residents. In this subsector, the facilities are a significant part of the production process and the care provided is a mix of health and social services with the health services being largely some level of nursing services.

6231 Nursing Care Facilities

62311 Nursing Care Facilities
See industry description for 623110 below.

623110 Nursing Care Facilities
This industry comprises establishments primarily engaged in providing inpatient nursing and rehabilitative services. The care is generally provided for an extended period of time to individuals requiring nursing care. These establishments have a permanent core staff of registered or licensed practical nurses who, along with other staff, provide nursing and continuous personal care services.

■ Assisted-living facilities with on-site nursing care facilities are classified in U.S. Industry 623311, Continuing Care Retirement Communities; and

■ Psychiatric convalescent homes are classified in Industry 623220, Residential Mental Health and Substance Abuse Facilities.

6232 Residential Mental Retardation, Mental Health, and Substance Abuse Facilities
This industry group comprises establishments primarily engaged in providing residential care (but not licensed hospital care) to people with mental retardation, mental illness, or substance abuse problems.

Sector **62**

Health Care and
Social Assistance

US—United States industry only. CAN—United States and Canadian industries are comparable. When neither US nor CAN appears, Canadian, Mexican, and United States industries are comparable.

582

Harris InfoSource

62321 Residential Mental Retardation Facilities

See industry description for 623210 below.

623210 Residential Mental Retardation Facilities

This industry comprises establishments (e.g., group homes, hospitals, intermediate care facilities) primarily engaged in providing residential care services for persons diagnosed with mental retardation. These facilities may provide some health care, though the focus is room, board, protective supervision, and counseling.

- Establishments primarily engaged in providing inpatient treatment of mental health and substance abuse illnesses with an emphasis on counseling rather than medical treatment are classified in Industry 623220, Residential Mental Health and Substance Abuse Facilities;
- Establishments primarily engaged in providing treatment of mental health and substance abuse illnesses on an exclusively outpatient basis are classified in Industry 621420, Outpatient Mental Health and Substance Abuse Centers; and
- Establishments known and licensed as hospitals primarily engaged in providing inpatient treatment of mental health and substance abuse illnesses with an emphasis on medical treatment and monitoring are classified in Industry 622210, Psychiatric and Substance Abuse Hospitals.

62322 Residential Mental Health and Substance Abuse Facilities

See industry description for 623220 below.

623220 Residential Mental Health and Substance Abuse Facilities

This industry comprises establishments primarily engaged in providing residential care and treatment for patients with mental health and substance abuse illnesses. These establishments provide room, board, supervision, and counseling services. Although medical services may be available at these establishments, they are incidental to the counseling, mental rehabilitation, and support services offered. These establishments generally provide a wide range of social services in addition to counseling.

- Establishments primarily engaged in providing treatment of mental health and substance abuse illnesses on an exclusively outpatient basis are classified in Industry 621420, Outpatient Mental Health and Substance Abuse Centers;
- Establishments primarily engaged in providing residential care for persons diagnosed with mental retardation are classified in Industry 623210, Residential Mental Retardation Facilities; and
- Establishments known and licensed as hospitals primarily engaged in providing inpatient treatment of mental health and substance abuse illnesses with an emphasis on medical treatment and monitoring are classified in Industry 622210, Psychiatric and Substance Abuse Hospitals.

Visit page 16 to learn more about this sector.

6233 Community Care Facilities for the Elderly

62331 Community Care Facilities for the Elderly

This industry comprises establishments primarily engaged in providing residential and personal care services for (1) the elderly and other persons who are unable to fully care for themselves and/or (2) the elderly and other persons who do not desire to live independently. The care typically includes room, board, supervision, and assistance in daily living, such as housekeeping services. In some instances these establishments provide skilled nursing care for residents in separate on-site facilities.

- Establishments primarily engaged in providing inpatient nursing and rehabilitative services are classified in Industry 62311, Nursing Care Facilities; and
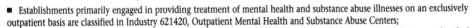
- Apartment or condominium complexes where people live independently in rented housing units are classified in Industry 53111, Lessors of Residential Buildings and Dwellings.

623311 Continuing Care Retirement Communities ᵁˢ

This U.S. industry comprises establishments primarily engaged in providing a range of residential and personal care services with on-site nursing care facilities for (1) the elderly and other persons who are unable to fully care for themselves and/or (2) the elderly and other persons who do not desire to live independently. Individuals live in a variety of residential settings with meals, housekeeping, social, leisure, and other services available to assist residents in daily living. Assisted-living facilities with on-site nursing care facilities are included in this industry.

- Establishments primarily engaged in providing inpatient nursing and rehabilitative services are classified in Industry 623110, Nursing Care Facilities;
- Assisted-living facilities without on-site nursing care facilities are classified in U.S. Industry 623312, Homes for the Elderly; and
- Apartment or condominium complexes where people live independently in rented housing units are classified in Industry 531110, Lessors of Residential Buildings and Dwellings.

Sector **62**

Health Care and Social Assistance

■ = Cross-References

US—United States industry only. CAN—United States and Canadian industries are comparable. When neither US nor CAN appears, Canadian, Mexican, and United States industries are comparable.

www.harrisinfo.com

583

623312 Homes for the Elderly ^{us}

This U.S. industry comprises establishments primarily engaged in providing residential and personal care services (i.e., without on-site nursing care facilities) for (1) the elderly or other persons who are unable to fully care for themselves and/or (2) the elderly or other persons who do not desire to live independently. The care typically includes room, board, supervision, and assistance in daily living, such as housekeeping services.

- Assisted-living facilities with on-site nursing care facilities are classified in U.S. Industry 623311, Continuing Care Retirement Communities;
- Homes for the elderly with nursing care or rest homes with nursing care are classified in Industry 623110, Nursing Care Facilities; and
- Apartment or condominium complexes where people live independently in rented or owned housing units are classified in Industry 53111, Lessors of Residential Buildings and Dwellings.

6239 Other Residential Care Facilities

This industry group comprises establishments of residential care facilities (except residential mental retardation, mental health, and substance abuse facilities and community care facilities for the elderly).

62399 Other Residential Care Facilities

See industry description for 623990 below.

623990 Other Residential Care Facilities

This industry comprises establishments primarily engaged in providing residential care (except residential mental retardation facilities, residential health and substance abuse facilities, continuing care retirement communities, and homes for the elderly). These establishments also provide supervision and personal care services.

- Residential mental retardation facilities are classified in Industry 623210, Residential Mental Retardation Facilities;
- Continuing care retirement communities are classified in U.S. Industry 623311, Continuing Care Retirement Communities;
- Residential mental health and substance abuse facilities are classified in 623220, Residential Mental Health and Substance Abuse Facilities;
- Homes for the elderly without nursing care are classified in U.S. Industry 623312, Homes for the Elderly;
- Establishments primarily engaged in providing inpatient nursing and rehabilitative services are classified in Industry 623110, Nursing Care Facilities;
- Establishments primarily engaged in providing temporary shelter are classified in U.S. Industry 624221, Temporary Shelters; and
- Correctional camps are classified in Industry 922140, Correctional Institutions.

▶624 SOCIAL ASSISTANCE

Industries in the Social Assistance subsector provide a wide variety of social assistance services directly to their clients. These services do not include residential or accommodation services, except on a short stay basis.

6241 Individual and Family Services

62411 Child and Youth Services

See industry description for 624110 below.

624110 Child and Youth Services

This industry comprises establishments primarily engaged in providing nonresidential social assistance services for children and youth. These establishments provide for the welfare of children in such areas as adoption and foster care, drug prevention, life skills training, and positive social development.

- Youth recreational centers are classified in Industry 713940, Fitness and Recreational Sports Centers;
- Youth recreational sports teams and leagues are classified in Industry 713990, All Other Amusement and Recreation Industries;
- Scouting organizations are classified in Industry 813410, Civic and Social Organizations; and
- Establishments primarily engaged in providing day care services for children are classified in Industry 624410, Child Day Care Services.

62412 Services for the Elderly and Persons with Disabilities

See industry description for 624120 below.

Sector 62

Health Care and Social Assistance

■ = Cross-References

US—United States industry only. CAN—United States and Canadian industries are comparable. When neither US nor CAN appears, Canadian, Mexican, and United States industries are comparable.

584

Harris InfoSource

624120 Services for the Elderly and Persons with Disabilities

This industry comprises establishments primarily engaged in providing nonresidential social assistance services to improve the quality of life for the elderly, persons diagnosed with mental retardation, or persons with disabilities. These establishments provide for the welfare of these of individuals in such areas as day care, nonmedical home care or homemaker services, social activities, group support, and companionship.

- Providing job training for persons diagnosed with mental retardation or persons with disabilities are classified in Industry 624310, Vocational Rehabilitation Services;
- Providing residential care for the elderly, persons diagnosed with mental retardation, or persons with disabilities are classified in Subsector 633, Nursing and Residential Care Facilities; and
- Providing in-home health care services are classified in Subsector 621, Ambulatory Health Care Services.

62419 Other Individual and Family Services

See industry description for 624190 below.

624190 Other Individual and Family Services

This industry comprises establishments primarily engaged in providing nonresidential individual and family social assistance services (except those specifically directed toward children, the elderly, persons diagnosed with mental retardation, or persons with disabilities).

- Providing clinical psychological and psychiatric social counseling services are classified in Industry 621330, Offices of Mental Health Practitioners (except Physicians);
- Providing child and youth social assistance services (except day care) are classified in Industry 624110, Child and Youth Services;
- Providing child day care services are classified in Industry 624410, Child Day Care Services;
- Providing social assistance services for the elderly, persons diagnosed with mental retardation, and persons with disabilities are classified in Industry 624120, Services for the Elderly and Persons with Disabilities;
- Community action advocacy are classified in U.S. Industry 813319, Other Social Advocacy Organizations; and
- Providing in-home health care services are classified in Subsector 621, Ambulatory Health Care Services.

6242 Community Food and Housing, and Emergency and Other Relief Services

62421 Community Food Services

See industry description for 624210 below.

624210 Community Food Services

This industry comprises establishments primarily engaged in the collection, preparation, and delivery of food for the needy. Establishments in this industry may also distribute clothing and blankets to the poor. These establishments may prepare and deliver meals to persons who by reason of age, disability, or illness are unable to prepare meals for themselves; collect and distribute salvageable or donated food; or prepare and provide meals at fixed or mobile locations. Food banks, meal delivery programs, and soup kitchens are included in this industry.

62422 Community Housing Services

This industry comprises establishments primarily engaged in providing one or more of the following community housing services: (1) short term emergency shelter for victims of domestic violence, sexual assault, or child abuse; (2) temporary residential shelter for the homeless, runaway youths, and patients and families caught in medical crises; (3) transitional housing for low-income individuals and families; (4) volunteer construction or repair of low cost housing, in partnership with the homeowner who may assist in construction or repair work; and (5) repair of homes for elderly or disabled homeowners. These establishments may operate their own shelter; or may subsidize housing using existing homes, apartments, hotels, or motels; or may require a low-cost mortgage or work (sweat) equity.

- Central offices of government housing programs are classified in Industry 92511, Administration of Housing Programs.

624221 Temporary Shelters US

This U.S. industry comprises establishments primarily engaged in providing (1) short term emergency shelter for victims of domestic violence, sexual assault, or child abuse and/or (2) temporary residential shelter for homeless individuals or families, runaway youth, and patients and families caught in medical crises. These establishments may operate their own shelters or may subsidize housing using existing homes, apartments, hotels, or motels.

Visit page 16 to learn more about this sector.

Sector **62**

Health Care and Social Assistance

■ = Cross-References

US—United States industry only. CAN—United States and Canadian industries are comparable. When neither US nor CAN appears, Canadian, Mexican, and United States industries are comparable.

www.harrisinfo.com

585

■ Establishments primarily engaged in providing emergency shelter for victims of domestic or international disasters or conflicts are classified in Industry 624230, Emergency and Other Relief Services.

624229 Other Community Housing Services ᵁˢ

This U.S. industry comprises establishments primarily engaged in providing one or more of the following community housing services: (1) transitional housing to low-income individuals and families; (2) volunteer construction or repair of low-cost housing, in partnership with the homeowner who may assist in the construction or repair work; and (3) the repair of homes for elderly or disabled homeowners. These establishments may subsidize housing using existing homes, apartments, hotels, or motels or may require a low-cost mortgage or sweat equity. These establishments may also provide low-income families with furniture and household supplies.

■ Central offices of government housing programs are classified in Industry 925110, Administration of Housing Programs.

62423 Emergency and Other Relief Services

See industry description for 624230 below.

624230 Emergency and Other Relief Services

This industry comprises establishments primarily engaged in providing food, shelter, clothing, medical relief, resettlement, and counseling to victims of domestic or international disasters or conflicts (e.g., wars).

6243 Vocational Rehabilitation Services

62431 Vocational Rehabilitation Services

See industry description for 624310 below.

624310 Vocational Rehabilitation Services

This industry comprises (1) establishments primarily engaged in providing vocational rehabilitation or habilitation services, such as job counseling, job training, and work experience, to unemployed and underemployed persons, persons with disabilities, and persons who have a job market disadvantage because of lack of education, job skill, or experience and (2) establishments primarily engaged in providing training and employment to persons with disabilities. Vocational rehabilitation job training facilities (except schools) and sheltered workshops (i.e., work experience centers) are included in this industry.

■ Schools (except high schools) primarily engaged in providing vocational training are classified in Industry 61151, Technical and Trade Schools;
■ Vocational high schools are classified in Industry 611110, Elementary and Secondary Schools; and
■ Establishments primarily engaged in providing career and vocational counseling (except rehabilitative) are classified in Industry 611710, Educational Support Services.

6244 Child Day Care Services

62441 Child Day Care Services

See industry description for 624410 below.

624410 Child Day Care Services

This industry comprises establishments primarily engaged in providing day care of infants or children. These establishments generally care for preschool children, but may care for older children when they are not in school and may also offer prekindergarten educational programs.

■ Establishments primarily engaged in offering kindergarten educational programs are classified in Industry 611110, Elementary and Secondary Schools.

Sector **62**

Health Care and
Social Assistance

■ = Cross-References

US—United States industry only. CAN—United States and Canadian industries are comparable. When neither US nor CAN appears, Canadian, Mexican, and United States industries are comparable.

586

Harris InfoSource

Sector 71
Arts, Entertainment, and Recreation

The Sector as a Whole

THE ARTS, ENTERTAINMENT, AND RECREATION sector includes a wide range of establishments that operate facilities or provide services to meet varied cultural, entertainment, and recreational interests of their patrons. This sector comprises (1) establishments that are involved in producing, promoting, or participating in live performances, events, or exhibits intended for public viewing; (2) establishments that preserve and exhibit objects and sites of historical, cultural, or educational interest; and (3) establishments that operate facilities or provide services that enable patrons to participate in recreational activities or pursue amusement, hobby, and leisure time interests.

Some establishments that provide cultural, entertainment, or recreational facilities and services are classified in other sectors. Excluded from this sector are: (1) establishments that provide both accommodations and recreational facilities, such as hunting and fishing camps and resort and casino hotels are classified in Subsector 721, Accommodation; (2) restaurants and night clubs that provide live entertainment in addition to the sale of food and beverages are classified in Subsector 722, Food Services and Drinking Places; (3) motion picture theaters, libraries and archives, and publishers of newspapers, magazines, books, periodicals, and computer software are classified in Sector 51, Information; and (4) establishments using transportation equipment to provide recreational and entertainment services, such as those operating sightseeing buses, dinner cruises, or helicopter rides are classified in Subsector 487, Scenic and Sightseeing Transportation.

Visit page 16 to learn more about this sector.

➡711 PERFORMING ARTS, SPECTATOR SPORTS, AND RELATED INDUSTRIES

Industries in the Performing Arts, Spectator Sports, and Related Industries subsector group establishments that produce or organize and promote live presentations involving the performances of actors and actresses, singers, dancers, musical groups and artists, athletes, and other entertainers, including independent (i.e., freelance) entertainers and the establishments that manage their careers. The classification recognizes four basic processes: (1) producing (i.e., presenting) events; (2) organizing, managing, and/or promoting events; (3) managing and representing entertainers; and (4) providing the artistic, creative and technical skills necessary to the production of these live events. Also, this subsector contains four industries for performing arts companies. Each is defined on the basis of the particular skills of the entertainers involved in the presentations.

The industry structure for this subsector makes a clear distinction between performing arts companies and performing artists (i.e., independent or freelance). Although not unique to arts and entertainment, freelancing is a particularly important phenomenon in this Performing Arts, Spectator Sports, and Related Industries subsector. Distinguishing this activity from the production activity is a meaningful process differentiation. This approach, however, is difficult to implement in the case of musical groups (i.e., companies) and artists, especially pop groups. These establishments tend to be more loosely organized and it can be difficult to distinguish companies from freelancers. For this reason, NAICS includes one industry that covers both musical groups and musical artists.

This subsector contains two industries for Industry Group 7113, Promoters of Performing Arts, Sports, and Similar Events, one for those that operate facilities and another for those that do not. This is because there

Sector 71
Arts, Entertainment, and Recreation

US—United States industry only. CAN—United States and Canadian industries are comparable. When neither US nor CAN appears, Canadian, Mexican, and United States industries are comparable.

are significant differences in cost structures between those promoters that manage and provide the staff to operate facilities and those that do not. In addition to promoters without facilities other industries in this subsector include establishments that may operate without permanent facilities. These types of establishments include: performing arts companies, musical groups and artists, spectator sports, and independent (i.e., freelance) artists, writers, and performers.

Excluded from this subsector are nightclubs. Some nightclubs promote live entertainment on a regular basis and it can be argued that they could be classified in Industry Group 7113, Promoters of Performing Arts, Sports, and Similar Events with Facilities. However, since most of these establishments function as any other drinking place when they do not promote entertainment and because most of their revenue is derived from sale of food and beverages, they are classified in Subsector 722, Food Services and Drinking Places.

7111 Performing Arts Companies

This industry group comprises establishments primarily engaged in producing live presentations involving the performances of actors and actresses, singers, dancers, musical groups and artists, and other performing artists.

71111 Theater Companies and Dinner Theaters

See industry description for 711110 below.

711110 Theater Companies and Dinner Theaters

This industry comprises (1) companies, groups, or theaters primarily engaged in producing the following live theatrical presentations: musicals; operas; plays; and comedy, improvisational, mime, and puppet shows and (2) establishments, commonly known as dinner theaters, engaged in producing live theatrical productions and in providing food and beverages for consumption on the premises. Theater groups or companies may or may not operate their own theater or other facility for staging their shows.

- Establishments, such as nightclubs, primarily engaged in providing food and beverages for consumption on the premises and that also present live nontheatrical entertainment, are classified in Subsector 722, Food Services and Drinking Places;
- Establishments primarily engaged in organizing, managing, and/or promoting performing arts productions without producing their own shows are classified in Industry Group 7113, Promoters of Performing Arts, Sports, and Similar Events;
- Companies, groups, or theaters primarily engaged in producing all types of live theatrical dance presentations are classified in Industry 711120, Dance Companies;
- Freelance producers and performing artists (except musicians and vocalists) primarily engaged in theatrical activities independent of a company or group are classified in Industry 711510, Independent Artists, Writers, and Performers; and
- Musicians and vocalists are classified in Industry 711130, Musical Groups and Artists.

71112 Dance Companies

See industry description for 711120 below.

711120 Dance Companies

This industry comprises companies, groups, or theaters primarily engaged in producing all types of live theatrical dance (e.g., ballet, contemporary dance, folk dance) presentations. Dance companies or groups may or may not operate their own theater or other facility for staging their shows.

- Establishments, such as exotic dance clubs, primarily engaged in providing food and beverages for consumption on the premises and that also present live dance entertainment, are classified in Subsector 722, Food Services and Drinking Places;
- Establishments primarily engaged in organizing, promoting, and/or managing dance productions without producing their own shows are classified in Industry Group 7113, Promoters of Performing Arts, Sports, and Similar Events; and
- Freelance producers and dancers primarily engaged in theatrical activities independent of a company or group are classified in Industry 711510, Independent Artists, Writers, and Performers.

71113 Musical Groups and Artists

See industry description for 711130 below.

711130 Musical Groups and Artists

This industry comprises (1) groups primarily engaged in producing live musical entertainment (except theatrical musical or opera productions) and (2) independent (i.e., freelance) artists primarily engaged in providing live musical entertainment. Musical groups and artists may perform in front of a live audience or in a studio, and may or may not operate their own facilities for staging their shows.

Sector 71

Arts, Entertainment, and Recreation

■ = Cross-References

US—United States industry only. CAN—United States and Canadian industries are comparable. When neither US nor CAN appears, Canadian, Mexican, and United States industries are comparable.

588

Harris InfoSource

■ Establishments primarily engaged in organizing, promoting, and/or managing concerts and other musical performances without producing their own shows are classified in Industry Group 7113, Promoters of Performing Arts, Sports, and Similar Events;

■ Companies, groups, or theaters primarily engaged in producing theatrical musicals and opera productions are classified in Industry 711110, Theater Companies and Dinner Theaters; and

■ Freelance producers (except musical groups and artists) primarily engaged in musical activities independent of a company or group are classified in Industry 711510, Independent Artists, Writers, and Performers.

71119 Other Performing Arts Companies
See industry description for 711190 below.

711190 Other Performing Arts Companies
This industry comprises companies or groups (except theater companies, dance companies, musical groups, and artists) primarily engaged in producing live theatrical presentations.

■ Establishments, such as comedy clubs or nightclubs, primarily engaged in providing food and beverages for consumption on the premises and that also present live nontheatrical entertainment are classified in Subsector 722, Food Services and Drinking Places;

■ Establishments primarily engaged in organizing, promoting, and/or managing ice skating shows, circuses, and other live performing arts presentations without producing their own shows are classified in Industry Group 7113, Promoters of Performing Arts, Sports, and Similar Events;

■ Theater companies and groups (except dance) or dinner theaters engaged in producing musicals; plays; operas; and comedy, improvisational, mime, and puppet shows are classified in Industry 711110, Theater Companies and Dinner Theaters;

■ Dance companies or groups are classified in Industry 711120, Dance Companies;

■ Freelance producers and performing artists (except musicians and vocalists) are classified in Industry 711510, Independent Artists, Writers, and Performers; and

■ Musical groups and independent musicians and vocalists are classified in Industry 711130, Musical Groups and Artists.

Visit page 16 to learn more about this sector.

7112 Spectator Sports

71121 Spectator Sports
This industry comprises (1) sports teams or clubs primarily participating in live sporting events before a paying audience; (2) establishments primarily engaged in operating racetracks; (3) independent athletes engaged in participating in live sporting or racing events before a paying audience; (4) owners of racing participants, such as cars, dogs, and horses, primarily engaged in entering them in racing events or other spectator sports events; and (5) establishments, such as sports trainers, primarily engaged in providing specialized services to support participants in sports events or competitions. The sports teams and clubs included in this industry may or may not operate their own arena, stadium, or other facility for presenting their games or other spectator sports events.

■ Establishments primarily engaged in promoting sporting events without participating in sporting events are classified in Industry Group 7113, Promoters of Performing Arts, Sports, and Similar Events;

■ Establishments, such as youth league baseball teams, primarily engaged in participating in sporting events for recreational purposes without playing before a paying audience are classified in Industry 71399, All Other Amusement and Recreation Industries;

■ Amateur, semiprofessional, or professional athletic associations or leagues are classified in Industry 81399, Other Similar Organizations (except Business, Professional, Labor, and Political Organizations);

■ Establishments primarily engaged in representing or managing the careers of sports figures are classified in Industry 71141 Agents and Managers for Artists, Athletes, Entertainers, and Other Public Figures;

■ Independent athletes engaged in providing sports instruction without participating in sporting events before a paying audience are classified in Industry 61162, Sports and Recreation Instruction;

■ Independent athletes exclusively engaged in endorsing products or making speeches are classified in Industry 71151, Independent Artists, Writers, and Performers; and

■ Establishments primarily engaged in raising horses, mules, donkeys, and other equines are classified in Industry 112920, Horse and Other Equine Production.

711211 Sports Teams and Clubs CAN
This U.S. industry comprises professional or semiprofessional sports teams or clubs primarily engaged in participating in live sporting events, such as baseball, basketball, football, hockey, soccer, and jai alai games, before a paying audience. These establishments may or may not operate their own arena, stadium, or other facility for presenting these events.

■ Establishments primarily engaged in promoting sporting events without participating in sporting events are classified in Industry Group 7113, Promoters of Performing Arts, Sports, and Similar Events;

Sector **71**

Arts, Entertainment, and Recreation

■ = Cross-References

US—United States industry only. CAN—United States and Canadian industries are comparable. When neither US nor CAN appears, Canadian, Mexican, and United States industries are comparable.

www.harrisinfo.com

589

■ Establishments, such as youth league baseball teams, primarily engaged in participating in sporting events for recreational purposes without playing before a paying audience are classified in Industry 713990, All Other Amusement and Recreation Industries; and

■ Amateur, semiprofessional, or professional athletic associations or leagues are classified in Industry 813990, Other Similar Organizations (except Business, Professional, Labor, and Political Organizations).

711212 Racetracks ^{US}

This U.S. industry comprises establishments primarily engaged in operating racetracks. These establishments may also present and /or promote the events, such as auto, dog, and horse races, held in these facilities.

■ Owners of racing participants, such as cars, dogs, and horses, primarily engaged in entering them in racing events; trainers of racing participants; and independent athletes, such as jockeys and race car drivers, primarily engaged in participating in racing events are classified in U.S. Industry 711219, Other Spectator Sports.

711219 Other Spectator Sports ^{US}

This U.S. industry comprises (1) independent athletes, such as professional or semiprofessional golfers, boxers, and race car drivers, primarily engaged in participating in live sporting or racing events before a paying audience; (2) owners of racing participants, such as cars, dogs, and horses, primarily engaged in entering them in racing events or other spectator sports events; and (3) establishments, such as sports trainers, primarily engaged in providing specialized services required to support participants in sports events or competitions.

■ Establishments primarily engaged in operating racetracks are classified in U.S. Industry 711212, Racetracks;

■ Establishments primarily engaged in representing or managing the careers of sports figures are classified in Industry 711410, Agents and Managers for Artists, Athletes, Entertainers, and Other Public Figures;

■ Independent athletes engaged in providing sports instruction without participating in sporting events before a paying audience are classified in Industry 611620, Sports and Recreation Instruction;

■ Independent athletes exclusively engaged in endorsing products or making speeches are classified in Industry 711510, Independent Artists, Writers, and Performers; and

■ Establishments primarily engaged in raising horses, mules, donkeys, and other equines are classified in Industry 112920, Horse and Other Equine Production.

7113 Promoters of Performing Arts, Sports, and Similar Events

71131 Promoters of Performing Arts, Sports, and Similar Events with Facilities
See industry description for 711310 below.

711310 Promoters of Performing Arts, Sports, and Similar Events with Facilities

This industry comprises establishments primarily engaged in (1) organizing, promoting, and/or managing live performing arts productions, sports events, and similar events, such as State fairs, county fairs, agricultural fairs, concerts, and festivals, held in facilities that they manage and operate and/or (2) managing and providing the staff to operate arenas, stadiums, theaters, or other related facilities for rent to other promoters.

■ Producing live performances and that may also promote the performances and/or operate the facilities where the performances take place are classified in Industry Group 7111, Performing Arts Companies;

■ Operating racetracks and that may also promote the events held in these facilities are classified in U.S. Industry 711212, Race Tracks;

■ Presenting sporting events and that may also promote these sporting events and/or operate the stadiums or arenas where the sporting events take place are classified in U.S. Industry 711211, Sports Teams and Clubs;

■ Organizing, promoting, and/or managing conventions, conferences, and trade shows and that may also operate the facilities where these events take place are classified in Industry 561920, Convention and Trade Show Organizers;

■ Organizing, promoting, and/or managing performing arts productions, sports events, and similar events in facilities managed and operated by others are classified in Industry 711320 Promoters of Performing Arts, Sports, and Similar Events without Facilities; and

■ Leasing stadiums, arenas, theaters, and other related facilities to others without operating the facilities are classified in Industry 531120, Lessors of Nonresidential Buildings (except Miniwarehouses).

71132 Promoters of Performing Arts, Sports, and Similar Events without Facilities
See industry description for 711320 below.

711320 Promoters of Performing Arts, Sports, and Similar Events without Facilities

This industry comprises promoters primarily engaged in organizing, promoting, and/or managing

Sector 71

Arts, Entertainment, and Recreation

■ = Cross-References

US—United States industry only. CAN—United States and Canadian industries are comparable. When neither US nor CAN appears, Canadian, Mexican, and United States industries are comparable.

590

Harris InfoSource

live performing arts productions, sports events, and similar events, such as state fairs, county fairs, agricultural fairs, concerts, and festivals, in facilities that are managed and operated by others. Theatrical (except motion picture) booking agencies are included in this industry.

- Booking motion pictures or videos are classified in U.S. Industry 512199, Other Motion Picture and Video Industries;
- Producing live performances and that may also promote the performances are classified in Industry Group 7111, Performing Arts Companies;
- Operating racetracks and that may also promote the events held in these facilities are classified in U.S. Industry 711212, Racetracks;
- Presenting sporting events and that may also promote these events are classified in U.S. Industry 711211, Sports Teams and Clubs;
- Organizing, promoting, and/or managing conventions, conferences, and trade shows and that may also operate the facilities where these events take place are classified in Industry 561920, Convention and Trade Show Organizers;
- Organizing, promoting, and/or managing performing arts, sports, and similar events in facilities they manage or operate are classified in Industry 711310, Promoters of Performing Arts, Sports, and Similar Events with Facilities; and
- Operating amateur, semiprofessional, or professional athletic associations or leagues are classified in Industry 813990, Other Similar Organizations (except Business, Professional, Labor, and Political Organizations).

7114 Agents and Managers for Artists, Athletes, Entertainers, and Other Public Figures

71141 Agents and Managers for Artists, Athletes, Entertainers, and Other Public Figures
See industry description for 711410 below.

711410 Agents and Managers for Artists, Athletes, Entertainers, and Other Public Figures
This industry comprises establishments of agents and managers primarily engaged in representing and/or managing creative and performing artists, sports figures, entertainers, and other public figures. The representation and management includes activities, such as representing clients in contract negotiations; managing or organizing client's financial affairs; and generally promoting the careers of their clients.

Visit page 16 to learn more about this sector.

- Establishments primarily engaged in supplying models to clients are classified in Industry 561320, Temporary Help Services; and
- Establishments known as model registries primarily engaged in recruiting and placing models for clients are classified in Industry 561310, Employment Placement Agencies.

7115 Independent Artists, Writers, and Performers

71151 Independent Artists, Writers, and Performers
See industry description for 711510 below.

711510 Independent Artists, Writers, and Performers
This industry comprises independent (i.e., freelance) individuals primarily engaged in performing in artistic productions, in creating artistic and cultural works or productions, or in providing technical expertise necessary for these productions. This industry also includes athletes and other celebrities exclusively engaged in endorsing products and making speeches or public appearances for which they receive a fee.

- Freelance musicians and vocalists are classified in Industry 711130, Musical Groups and Artists;
- Independent commercial artists and graphic designers are classified in Industry 541430, Graphic Design Services; and
- Artisans and craftspersons are classified in the Sector 31-33, Manufacturing.

➡712 MUSEUMS, HISTORICAL SITES, AND SIMILAR INSTITUTIONS
Industries in the Museums, Historical Sites, and Similar Institutions subsector engage in the preservation and exhibition of objects, sites, and natural wonders of historical, cultural, and/or educational value.

7121 Museums, Historical Sites, and Similar Institutions

71211 Museums
See industry description for 712110 below.

Sector 71

Arts, Entertainment, and Recreation

■ = Cross-References

US—United States industry only. CAN—United States and Canadian industries are comparable. When neither US nor CAN appears, Canadian, Mexican, and United States industries are comparable.

712110 Museums

This industry comprises establishments primarily engaged in the preservation and exhibition of objects of historical, cultural, and/or educational value.

- Commercial art galleries primarily engaged in selling art objects are classified in Industry 453920, Art Dealers.

71212 Historical Sites

See industry description for 712120 below.

712120 Historical Sites

This industry comprises establishments primarily engaged in the preservation and exhibition of sites, buildings, forts, or communities that describe events or persons of particular historical interest. Archeological sites, battlefields, historical ships, and pioneer villages are included in this industry.

71213 Zoos and Botanical Gardens

See industry description for 712130 below.

712130 Zoos and Botanical Gardens

This industry comprises establishments primarily engaged in the preservation and exhibition of live plant and animal life displays.

71219 Nature Parks and Other Similar Institutions

See industry description for 712190 below.

712190 Nature Parks and Other Similar Institutions

This industry comprises establishments primarily engaged in the preservation and exhibition of natural areas or settings.

- Establishments primarily engaged in operating commercial hunting or fishing preserves (e.g., game farms) are classified in Industry 114210, Hunting and Trapping.

►713 AMUSEMENT, GAMBLING, AND RECREATION INDUSTRIES

Industries in the Amusement, Gambling, and Recreation Industries subsector (1) operate facilities where patrons can primarily engage in sports, recreation, amusement, or gambling activities and/or (2) provide other amusement and recreation services, such as supplying and servicing amusement devices in places of business operated by others; operating sports teams, clubs, or leagues engaged in playing games for recreational purposes; and guiding tours without using transportation equipment.

This subsector does not cover all establishments providing recreational services. Other sectors of NAICS also provide recreational services. Providers of recreational services are often engaged in processes classified in other sectors of NAICS. For example, operators of resorts and hunting and fishing camps provide both accommodation and recreational facilities and services. These establishments are classified in Subsector 721, Accommodation, partly to reflect the significant costs associated with the provision of accommodation services and partly to ensure consistency with international standards. Likewise, establishments using transportation equipment to provide recreational and entertainment services, such as those operating sightseeing buses, dinner cruises, or helicopter rides, are classified in Subsector 48-49, Transportation and Warehousing. The industry groups in this subsector highlight particular types of activities: amusement parks and arcades, gambling industries, and other amusement and recreation industries. The groups, however, are not all inclusive of the activity. The Gambling Industries industry group does not provide for full coverage of gambling activities. For example, casino hotels are classified in Subsector 721, Accommodation; and horse and dog racing tracks are classified in Industry Group 7112, Spectator Sports.

7131 Amusement Parks and Arcades

This industry group comprises establishments primarily engaged in operating amusement parks and amusement arcades and parlors.

71311 Amusement and Theme Parks

See industry description for 713110 below.

Sector **71**

Arts, Entertainment, and Recreation

■ = Cross-References

US—United States industry only. CAN—United States and Canadian industries are comparable. When neither US nor CAN appears, Canadian, Mexican, and United States industries are comparable.

592

Harris InfoSource

713110 Amusement and Theme Parks

This industry comprises establishments, known as amusement or theme parks, primarily engaged in operating a variety of attractions, such as mechanical rides, water rides, games, shows, theme exhibits, refreshment stands, and picnic grounds. These establishments may lease space to others on a concession basis.

- Operating mechanical or water rides on a concession basis in amusement parks, fairs, and carnivals or in operating a single attraction, such as a waterslide, are classified in Industry 713990, All Other Amusement and Recreation Industries;
- Operating refreshment stands on a concession basis are classified in Industry Group 7222, Limited-service Eating Places;
- Supplying and servicing coin-operated amusement (except gambling) devices in other's facilities are classified in Industry 713990, All Other Amusement and Recreation Industries;
- Supplying and servicing coin-operated gambling devices (e.g., slot machines) in places of business operated by others are classified in Industry 713290, Other Gambling Industries; and
- Organizing, promoting, and/or managing events, such as carnivals and fairs, with or without facilities are classified in Industry Group 7113, Promoters of Performing Arts, Sports, and Similar Events.

71312 Amusement Arcades

See industry description for 713120 below.

713120 Amusement Arcades

This industry comprises establishments primarily engaged in operating amusement (except gambling, billiard, or pool) arcades and parlors.

- Supplying and servicing coin-operated amusement (except gambling) devices in places of business operated by others or in operating billiard or pool parlors are classified in Industry 713990, All Other Amusement and Recreation Industries;
- Operating bingo, off-track betting, or slot machine parlors or in supplying and servicing coin-operated gambling devices (e.g., slot machines or video gambling terminals) in places of business operated by others are classified in Industry 713290, Other Gambling Industries;
- Operating casinos (except casino hotels) are classified in Industry 713210, Casinos (except Casino Hotels); and
- Operating casino hotels are classified in Industry 721120, Casino Hotels.

Visit page 16 to learn more about this sector.

7132 Gambling Industries

This industry group comprises establishments (except casino hotels) primarily engaged in operating gambling facilities, such as casinos, bingo halls, and video gaming terminals, or in the provision of gambling services, such as lotteries and off-track betting. Casino hotels are classified in Industry 72112.

71321 Casinos (except Casino Hotels)

See industry description for 713210 below.

713210 Casinos (except Casino Hotels)

This industry comprises establishments primarily engaged in operating gambling facilities that offer table wagering games along with other gambling activities, such as slot machines and sports betting. These establishments often provide food and beverage services. Included in this industry are floating casinos (i.e., gambling cruises, riverboat casinos).

- Operating bingo, off-track betting, or slot machine parlors or in supplying and servicing coin-operated gambling devices, such as slot machines and video gaming terminals in places of business operated by others, are classified in Industry 713290, Other Gambling Industries; and
- Operating casino hotels are classified in Industry 721120, Casino Hotels.

71329 Other Gambling Industries

See industry description for 713290 below.

713290 Other Gambling Industries

This industry comprises establishments primarily engaged in operating gambling facilities (except casinos or casino hotels) or providing gambling services.

- Operating casinos are classified in Industry 713210, Casinos (except Casino Hotels);
- Operating casino hotels are classified in Industry 721120, Casino Hotels;
- Operating facilities with coin-operated nongambling amusement devices are classified in Industry 713120, Amusement Arcades;
- Supplying and servicing coin-operated nongambling amusement devices in places of business operated by others are classified in Industry 713990, All Other Amusement and Recreation Industries; and
- Operating racetracks or presenting live racing or sporting events are classified in Industry 71121, Spectator Sports.

Sector **71**

Arts, Entertainment, and Recreation

■ = Cross-References

US—United States industry only. CAN—United States and Canadian industries are comparable. When neither US nor CAN appears, Canadian, Mexican, and United States industries are comparable.

www.harrisinfo.com 593

7139 Other Amusement and Recreation Industries

71391 Golf Courses and Country Clubs
See industry description for 713910 below.

713910 Golf Courses and Country Clubs
This industry comprises (1) establishments primarily engaged in operating golf courses (except miniature) and (2) establishments primarily engaged in operating golf courses, along with dining facilities and other recreational facilities that are known as country clubs. These establishments often provide food and beverage services, equipment rental services, and golf instruction services.

- Operating driving ranges and miniature golf courses are classified in Industry 713990, All Other Amusement and Recreation Industries; and
- Operating resorts where golf facilities are combined with accommodations are classified in Industry Group 7211, Traveler Accommodation.

71392 Skiing Facilities
See industry description for 713920 below.

713920 Skiing Facilities
This industry comprises establishments engaged in (1) operating downhill, cross-country, or related skiing areas and/or (2) operating equipment, such as ski lifts and tows. These establishments often provide food and beverage services, equipment rental services, and ski instruction services. Four season resorts without accommodations are included in this industry.

- Establishments primarily engaged in operating resorts where skiing facilities are combined with accommodations are classified in Industry Group 7211, Traveler Accommodation.

71393 Marinas
See industry description for 713930 below.

713930 Marinas
This industry comprises establishments, commonly known as marinas, engaged in operating docking and/or storage facilities for pleasure craft owners, with or without one or more related activities, such as retailing fuel and marine supplies; and repairing, maintaining, or renting pleasure boats.

- Renting pleasure boats are classified in U.S. Industry 532292, Recreational Goods Rental;
- Repairing pleasure boats are classified in Industry 811490, Other Personal and Household Goods Repair and Maintenance;
- Retailing marine supplies are classified in U.S. Industry 441222, Boat Dealers; and
- Retailing fuel for boats are classified in Industry 447190, Other Gasoline Stations.

71394 Fitness and Recreational Sports Centers
See industry description for 713940 below.

713940 Fitness and Recreational Sports Centers
This industry comprises establishments primarily engaged in operating fitness and recreational sports facilities featuring exercise and other active physical fitness conditioning or recreational sports activities, such as swimming, skating, or racquet sports.

- Establishments primarily engaged in providing nonmedical services to assist clients in attaining or maintaining a desired weight are classified in U.S. Industry 812191, Diet and Weight Reducing Centers;
- Establishments primarily engaged in operating health resorts and spas where recreational facilities are combined with accommodations are classified in Industry 721110, Hotels (except Casino Hotels) and Motels; and
- Recreational sports clubs (i.e., sports teams) not operating sports facilities are classified in Industry 713990, All Other Amusement and Recreation Industries.

71395 Bowling Centers
See industry description for 713950 below.

713950 Bowling Centers
This industry comprises establishments engaged in operating bowling centers. These establishments often provide food and beverage services.

Sector **71**

Arts, Entertainment, and Recreation

■ = Cross-References

US—United States industry only. CAN—United States and Canadian industries are comparable. When neither US nor CAN appears, Canadian, Mexican, and United States industries are comparable.

594

Harris InfoSource

71399 All Other Amusement and Recreation Industries
See industry description for 713990 below.

713990 All Other Amusement and Recreation Industries
This industry comprises establishments (except amusement parks and arcades; gambling industries; golf courses and country clubs; skiing facilities; marinas; fitness and recreational sports centers; and bowling centers) primarily engaged in providing recreational and amusement services.

■ Establishments primarily engaged in operating amusement parks and arcades are classified in Industry Group 7131, Amusement Parks and Arcades;

■ Establishments primarily engaged in operating gambling facilities (except casino hotels) or providing gambling services are classified in Industry Group 7132, Gambling Industries;

■ Establishments primarily engaged in operating casino hotels are classified in Industry 721120, Casino Hotels;

■ Establishments primarily engaged in operating golf courses (except miniature) and country clubs are classified in Industry 713910, Golf Courses and Country Clubs;

■ Establishments primarily engaged in operating skiing facilities without hotel accommodation are classified in Industry 713920, Skiing Facilities;

■ Establishments primarily engaged in operating resorts where recreational facilities are combined with lodging are classified in Industry Group 7211, Traveler Accommodation;

■ Establishments primarily engaged in operating marinas are classified in Industry 713930, Marinas;

■ Establishments primarily engaged in operating fitness and recreational sports centers are classified in Industry 713940, Fitness and Recreational Sports Centers;

■ Establishments primarily engaged in operating bowling centers are classified in Industry 713950, Bowling Centers;

■ Establishments primarily engaged in operating instructional camps, such as sports camps, fine arts camps, and computer camps, are classified in Sector 61, Educational Services, based on the nature of instruction;

■ Independent athletes engaged in participating in sporting events before a paying audience are classified in U.S. Industry 711219, Other Spectator Sports;

■ Independent athletes engaged in providing sports instruction without participating in sporting events before a paying audience are classified in Industry 611620, Sports and Recreation Instruction;

■ Independent athletes exclusively engaged in endorsing products or making speeches are classified in Industry 71151, Independent Artists, Writers, and Performers;

■ Establishments primarily engaged in providing scenic and sightseeing transportation are classified in Subsector 487, Scenic and Sightseeing Transportation;

■ Aviation clubs primarily engaged in providing specialty air and flying services are classified in U.S. Industry 481219, Other Nonscheduled Air Transportation;

■ Aviation clubs primarily engaged in advocating social and political causes are classified in U.S. Industry 813319, Other Social Advocacy Organizations; and

■ Amateur, semiprofessional, or professional athletic associations or leagues are classified in Industry 813990, Other Similar Organizations (except Business, Professional, Labor, and Political Organizations).

Visit page 16 to learn more about this sector.

Sector 71

Arts, Entertainment, and Recreation

■ = Cross-References

US—United States industry only. CAN—United States and Canadian industries are comparable. When neither US nor CAN appears, Canadian, Mexican, and United States industries are comparable.

www.harrisinfo.com

595

NAICS United States Structure

Sector	Name	Sub-sectors	Industry groups	NAICS 5-digit industries	U.S. 6-digit industries	TOTAL U.S. industries	New industries
11	Agriculture, Forestry, Fishing and, Hunting	5	19	42	32	64	20
21	Mining	3	5	10	28	29	—
22	Utilities	1	3	6	6	10	6
23	Construction	3	14	28	—	28	3
31–33	Manufacturing	21	84	184	408	474	79
42	Wholesale Trade	2	18	69	—	69	—
44–45	Retail Trade	12	27	61	18	72	17
48-49	Transportation and Warehousing	11	29	42	25	57	28
51	Information	4	9	28	12	34	20
52	Finance and Insurance	5	11	32	15	42	23
53	Real Estate and Rental and Leasing	3	8	19	9	24	15
54	Professional, Scientific, and Technical Services	1	9	35	17	47	28
55	Management of Companies and Enterprises	1	1	1	3	3	1
56	Administrative and Support and Waste Management and Remediation Services	2	11	29	23	43	29
61	Educational Services	1	7	12	7	17	12
62	Health Care and Social Assistance	4	18	30	16	39	27
71	Arts, Entertainment, and Recreation	3	9	23	3	25	19
72	Accommodation and Food Services	2	7	11	7	15	10
81	Other Services (except Public Administration)	4	14	30	30	49	19
92	Public Administration	8	8	29	—	29	2
	TOTAL	96	311	721	659	1170	358

To learn more about the changes by sector go to pages 15-18.

Sector 71

Arts, Entertainment, and Recreation

Sector 72

Accommodation and Food Services

The Sector as a Whole

THE ACCOMMODATION AND FOOD SERVICES sector comprises establishments providing customers with lodging and/or preparing meals, snacks, and beverages for immediate consumption. The sector includes both accommodation and food services establishments because the two activities are often combined at the same establishment.

Excluded from this sector are civic and social organizations; amusement and recreation parks; theaters; and other recreation or entertainment facilities providing food and beverage services.

▶721 ACCOMMODATION

Industries in the Accommodation subsector provide lodging or short-term accommodations for travelers, vacationers, and others. There is a wide range of establishments in these industries. Some provide lodging only; while others provide meals, laundry, and recreational facilities, as well as lodging. Lodging establishments are classified in this subsector even if the provision of complementary services generates more revenue. The type of complementary services provided vary from establishment to establishment.

The subsector is organized into three industry groups: (1) traveler accommodation, (2) recreational accommodation, and (3) rooming and boarding houses. The Traveler Accommodation industry group includes establishments that primarily provide traditional types of lodging services. This group includes hotels, motels, and bed and breakfast inns. In addition to lodging, these establishments may provide a range of other services to their guests. The RV (Recreational Vehicle) Parks and Recreational Camps industry group includes establishments that operate lodging facilities primarily designed to accommodate outdoor enthusiasts. Included are travel trailer campsites, recreation vehicle parks, and outdoor adventure retreats. The Rooming and Boarding Houses industry group includes establishments providing temporary or longer-term accommodations that for the period of occupancy may serve as a principal residence. Board (i.e., meals) may be provided but is not essential.

Establishments that manage short-stay accommodation establishments (e.g., hotels and motels) on a contractual basis are classified in this subsector if they both manage the operation and provide the operating staff. Such establishments are classified based on the type of facility managed and operated.

7211 Traveler Accommodation

72111 Hotels (except Casino Hotels) and Motels
See industry description for 721110 below.

721110 Hotels (except Casino Hotels) and Motels
This industry comprises establishments primarily engaged in providing short-term lodging in facilities known as hotels, motor hotels, resort hotels, and motels. The establishments in this industry may offer services, such as food and beverage services, recreational services, conference rooms and convention services, laundry services, parking, and other services.

Go to page 16 to find out how changes to this sector impact economic statistics.

Sector 72

Accommodation and Food Services

■ = Cross-References

US—United States industry only. CAN—United States and Canadian industries are comparable. When neither US nor CAN appears, Canadian, Mexican, and United States industries are comparable.

www.harrisinfo.com

597

- Providing short-term lodging with a casino on the premises—are classified in Industry 721120, Casino Hotels; and
- Providing short-term lodging in facilities known as bed-and-breakfast inns, youth hostels, housekeeping cabins and cottages, and tourist homes are classified in Industry 72119, Other Traveler Accommodation.

72112 Casino Hotels
See industry description for 721120 below.

721120 Casino Hotels
This industry comprises establishments primarily engaged in providing short-term lodging in hotel facilities with a casino on the premises. The casino on premises includes table wagering games and may include other gambling activities, such as slot machines and sports betting. These establishments generally offer a range of services and amenities, such as food and beverage services, entertainment, valet parking, swimming pools, and conference and convention facilities.

- Providing short-term lodging in facilities known as hotels and motels that provide limited gambling activities, such as slot machines, without a casino on the premises are classified in Industry 721110, Hotels (except Casino Hotels) and Motels; and
- Operating as stand-alone casinos are classified in Industry 713210, Casinos (except Casino Hotels).

72119 Other Traveler Accommodation
This industry comprises establishments primarily engaged in providing short-term lodging (except hotels, motels, and casino hotels).

- Providing short-term lodging in facilities known as hotels without a casino on the premises are classified in Industry 72111, Hotels (except Casino Hotels) and Motels; and
- Providing short-term lodging in facilities known as hotels with a casino on the premises are classified in Industry 72112, Casino Hotels.

721191 Bed-and-Breakfast Inns CAN
This U.S. industry comprises establishments primarily engaged in providing short-term lodging in facilities known as bed-and-breakfast inns. These establishments provide short-term lodging in private homes or small buildings converted for this purpose. Bed-and-breakfast inns are characterized by a highly personalized service and inclusion of a full breakfast in a room rate.

721199 All Other Traveler Accommodation US
This U.S. industry comprises establishments primarily engaged in providing short-term lodging (except hotels, motels, casino hotels, and bed-and-breakfast inns).

- Providing short-term lodging in facilities known as hotels without a casino on the premises are classified in Industry 721110, Hotels (except Casino Hotels) and Motels;
- Providing short-term lodging in facilities known as hotels with a casino on the premises are classified in Industry 721120, Casino Hotels; and
- Providing short-term lodging in establishments known as bed-and-breakfast inns are classified in U.S. Industry 721191, Bed-and-Breakfast Inns.

7212 RV (Recreational Vehicle) Parks and Recreational Camps

72121 RV (Recreational Vehicle) Parks and Recreational Camps
This industry comprises establishments primarily engaged in operating recreational vehicle parks and campgrounds and recreational and vacation camps. These establishments cater to outdoor enthusiasts and are characterized by the type of accommodation and by the nature and the range of recreational facilities and activities provided to their clients.

- Operating recreational facilities without accommodations are classified in Subsector 713, Amusement, Gambling and Recreation Industries;
- Operating instructional camps, such as sports camps, fine arts camps, and computer camps, are classified in Sector 61, Educational Services, based on the nature of instruction;
- Operating children's day camps (except instructional) are classified in Industry 71399, All Other Amusement and Recreation Industries; and
- Acting as lessors of residential mobile home sites (i.e., trailer parks) are classified in Industry 53119, Lessors of Other Real Estate Property.

Sector **72**
Accommodation and Food Services

■ = Cross-References

US—United States industry only. CAN—United States and Canadian industries are comparable. When neither US nor CAN appears, Canadian, Mexican, and United States industries are comparable.

721211 RV (Recreational Vehicle) Parks and Campgrounds ᶜᴬᴺ

This U.S. industry comprises establishments primarily engaged in operating sites to accommodate campers and their equipment, including tents, tent trailers, travel trailers, and RVs (recreational vehicles). These establishments may provide access to facilities, such as washrooms, laundry rooms, recreation halls and playgrounds, stores, and snack bars.

- Operating recreational facilities without accommodations are classified in Subsector 713, Amusement, Gambling, and Recreation Industries; and
- Acting as lessors of residential mobile home sites (i.e., trailer parks) are classified in Industry 531190, Lessors of Other Real Estate Property.

721214 Recreational and Vacation Camps (except Campgrounds)ᵁˢ

This U.S. industry comprises establishments primarily engaged in operating overnight recreational camps, such as children's camps, family vacation camps, hunting and fishing camps, and outdoor adventure retreats that offer trail riding, whitewater rafting, hiking, and similar activities. These establishments provide accommodation facilities, such as cabins and fixed camp sites, and other amenities, such as food services, recreational facilities and equipment, and organized recreational activities.

- Operating instructional camps, such as sports camps, fine arts camps, and computer camps, are classified in the Sector 61, Educational Services, based on the nature of instruction; and
- Operating children's day camps (except instructional) are classified in Industry 713990, All Other Amusement and Recreation Industries.

7213 Rooming and Boarding Houses

72131 Rooming and Boarding Houses

See industry description for 721310 below.

721310 Rooming and Boarding Houses

This industry comprises establishments primarily engaged in operating rooming and boarding houses and similar facilities, such as fraternity houses, sorority houses, off-campus dormitories, residential clubs, and workers' camps. These establishments provide temporary or longer-term accommodations which, for the period of occupancy, may serve as a principal residence. These establishments also may provide complementary services, such as housekeeping, meals, and laundry services.

➡722 FOOD SERVICES AND DRINKING PLACES

Industries in the Food Services and Drinking Places subsector prepare meals, snacks, and beverages to customer order for immediate on-premises and off-premises consumption. There is a wide range of establishments in these industries. Some provide food and drink only; while others provide various combinations of seating space, waiter/waitress services and incidental amenities, such as limited entertainment. The industries in the subsector are grouped based on the type and level of services provided. The industry groups are full-service restaurants; limited-service eating places; special food services, such as food service contractors, caterers, and mobile food services, and drinking places.

Food services and drink activities at hotels and motels; amusement parks, theaters, casinos, country clubs, and similar recreational facilities; and civic and social organizations are included in this subsector only if these services are provided by a separate establishment primarily engaged in providing food and beverage services.

Excluded from this subsector are establishments operating dinner cruises. These establishments are classified in Subsector 487, Scenic and Sightseeing Transportation because those establishments utilize transportation equipment to provide scenic recreational entertainment.

7221 Full-service Restaurants

This industry group comprises establishments primarily engaged in providing food services to patrons who order and are served while seated (i.e., waiter/waitress service) and pay after eating. Establishments that provide these type of food services to patrons with any combination of other services, such as carryout services are classified in this industry.

Go to page 16 to find out how changes to this sector impact economic statistics.

Sector 72

Accommodation and Food Services

■ = Cross-References

US—United States industry only. CAN—United States and Canadian industries are comparable. When neither US nor CAN appears, Canadian, Mexican, and United States industries are comparable.

72211 Full-service Restaurants
See industry description for 722110 below.

722110 Full-service Restaurants
This industry comprises establishments primarily engaged in providing food services to patrons who order and are served while seated (i.e. waiter/waitress service) and pay after eating. These establishments may provide this type of food services to patrons in combination with selling alcoholic beverages, providing takeout services, or presenting live nontheatrical entertainment.

- Providing food services where patrons generally order or select items and pay before eating are classified in U.S. Industry 722211, Limited-service Restaurants;
- Selling a specialty snack or nonalcoholic beverage for consumption on or near the premises are classified in U.S. Industry 722213, Snack and Nonalcoholic Beverage Bars;
- Preparing and serving alcoholic beverages known as bars, taverns, or nightclubs are classified in Industry 722410, Drinking Places (Alcoholic Beverages); and
- Presenting live theatrical productions and providing food and beverages for consumption on the premises are classified in Industry 711110, Theater Companies and Dinner Theaters.

7222 Limited-service Eating Places
This industry group comprises establishments primarily engaged in providing food services where patrons generally order or select items and pay before eating. Most establishments do not have waiter/waitress service, but some provide limited service, such as cooking to order (i.e., per special request), bringing food to seated customers, or providing off-site delivery.

72221 Limited-service Eating Places
This industry comprises establishments primarily engaged in (1) providing food services where patrons generally order or select items and pay before eating or (2) selling a specialty snack or nonalcoholic beverage for consumption on or near the premises. Food and drink may be consumed on the premises, taken out, or delivered to customers' location. Some establishments in this industry may provide these food services (except snack and nonalcoholic beverage bars) in combination with selling alcoholic beverages.

- Providing food services to patrons who order and are served while seated and pay after eating in combination with providing takeout service are classified in Industry 72211, Full-service Restaurants;
- Retailing confectionery goods and nuts not packaged for immediate consumption are classified in Industry 44529, Other Specialty Food Stores;
- Retailing baked goods (e.g., pretzels, doughnuts, cookies, and bagels) not baked on the premises and not for immediate consumption are classified in Industry 44529, Other Specialty Food Stores;
- Retailing baked goods (e.g., doughnuts and bagels) and providing food services to patrons who order and are served while seated and pay after eating are classified in Industry 72211, Full-service Restaurants;
- Selling snacks and nonalcoholic beverages from mobile vehicles are classified in Industry 72233, Mobile Food Services; and
- Preparing and serving alcoholic beverages, known as bars, taverns, or nightclubs, are classified in Industry 72241, Drinking Places (Alcoholic Beverages).

722211 Limited-service Restaurants ᵁˢ
This U.S. industry comprises establishments primarily engaged in providing food services (except snack and nonalcoholic beverage bars) where patrons generally order or select items and pay before eating. Food and drink may be consumed on premises, taken out, or delivered to customers' location. Some establishments in this industry may provide these food services in combination with selling alcoholic beverages.

- Preparing and serving meals for immediate consumption using cafeteria-style serving equipment that are known as cafeterias are classified in U.S. Industry 722212, Cafeterias;
- Providing food services to patrons who order and are served while seated and they pay after eating are classified in Industry 722110, Full-service Restaurants;
- Selling a specialty snack (e.g., ice cream, frozen yogurt, candy, cookies) or nonalcoholic beverages, for consumption on or near the premises are classified in U.S. Industry 722213, Snack and Nonalcoholic Beverage Bars;
- Retailing confectionery goods and nuts not packaged for immediate consumption are classified in U.S. Industry 445292, Confectionery and Nut Stores;
- Retailing baked goods (e.g., pretzels, doughnuts, cookies, and bagels) not baked on the premises and not for immediate consumption are classified in U.S. Industry 445291, Baked Goods Stores;
- Preparing and serving alcoholic beverages known as bars, taverns, or nightclubs, are classified in Industry 722410, Drinking Places (Alcoholic Beverages); and
- Selling baked goods, (e.g., doughnuts and bagels) and providing food services to patrons who order and are served while seated and pay after eating, are classified in Industry 722110, Full-service Restaurants.

Sector 72
Accommodation and Food Services

■ = Cross-References

US—United States industry only. CAN—United States and Canadian industries are comparable. When neither US nor CAN appears, Canadian, Mexican, and United States industries are comparable.

600

Harris InfoSource

722212 Cafeterias ᵁˢ

This U.S. industry comprises establishments, known as cafeterias, primarily engaged in preparing and serving meals for immediate consumption using cafeteria-style serving equipment, such as steam tables, a refrigerated area, and self-service nonalcoholic beverage dispensing equipment. Patrons select from food and drink items on display in a continuous cafeteria line.

- Providing food services to patrons who order and are served while seated and pay after eating are classified in Industry 722110, Full-service Restaurants; and
- Providing food services where patrons generally order or select items and pay before eating are classified in U.S. Industry 722211, Limited-service Restaurants.

722213 Snack and Nonalcoholic Beverage Bars ᵁˢ

This U.S. industry comprises establishments primarily engaged in (1) preparing and/or serving a specialty snack, such as ice cream, frozen yogurt, cookies, or popcorn or (2) serving nonalcoholic beverages, such as coffee, juices, or sodas for consumption on or near the premises. These establishments may carry and sell a combination of snack, nonalcoholic beverage, and other related products (e.g., coffee beans, mugs, coffee makers) but generally promote and sell a unique snack or nonalcoholic beverage.

- Selling one or more of the following food specialties: hamburgers, hot dogs, pizza, chicken, specialty cuisines are classified in U.S. Industry 722211, Limited-service Restaurants or Industry 722110, Full-service Restaurants, based on type of food services provided to patrons;
- Preparing and serving snacks and nonalcoholic beverages from mobile vehicles are classified in Industry 722330 Mobile Food Services;
- Retailing confectionery goods and nuts not packaged for immediate consumption are classified in U.S. Industry 445292, Confectionery and Nut Stores;
- Retailing baked goods (e.g., pretzels, doughnuts, cookies, and bagels) not baked on the premises and not for immediate consumption, are classified in U.S. Industry 445291, Baked Goods Stores; and
- Retailing baked goods (e.g., doughnuts and bagels) and providing food services to patrons who order and are served while seated and pay after eating are classified in Industry 722110, Full-service Restaurants.

Go to page 16 to find out how changes to this sector impact economic statistics.

7223 Special Food Services

This industry group comprises establishments primarily engaged in providing one of the following food services: (1) at the customers' location; (2) a location designated by the customer; or (3) from motorized vehicles or nonmotorized carts.

72231 Food Service Contractors

See industry description for 722310 below.

722310 Food Service Contractors

This industry comprises establishments primarily engaged in providing food services at institutional, governmental, commercial, or industrial locations of others based on contractual arrangements with these type of organizations for a specified period of time. The establishments of this industry provide food services for the convenience of the contracting organization or the contracting organization's customers. The contractual arrangement of these establishments with contracting organizations may vary from type of facility operated (e.g., cafeteria, restaurant, fast-food eating place), revenue sharing, cost structure, to providing personnel. Management staff is always provided by the food services contractor.

- Providing food services on a single event basis are classified in Industry 722320, Caterers; and
- Supplying and servicing food vending machines are classified in Industry 454210, Vending Machine Operators.

72232 Caterers

See industry description for 722320 below.

722320 Caterers

This industry comprises establishments primarily engaged in providing single event-based food services. These establishments generally have equipment and vehicles to transport meals and snacks to events and/or prepare food at an off-premise site. Banquet halls with catering staff are included in this industry. Examples of events catered by establishments in this industry are graduation parties, wedding receptions, business or retirement luncheons, and trade shows.

- Preparing and serving meals and snacks for immediate consumption from motorized vehicles or nonmotorized carts are classified in Industry 722330, Mobile Caterers;

Sector 72

Accommodation and Food Services

■ = Cross-References

US—United States industry only. CAN—United States and Canadian industries are comparable. When neither US nor CAN appears, Canadian, Mexican, and United States industries are comparable.

■ Providing food services at institutional, governmental, commercial, or industrial locations of others or providing food services (e.g., airline contractors, industrial caterers) based on contractual arrangements for a specified period of time are classified in Industry 722310, Food Service Contractors; and
■ Renting facilities without their own catering staff are classified in Industry 531120, Lessors of Nonresidential Buildings (except Miniwarehouses).

72233 Mobile Food Services
See industry description for 722330 below.

722330 Mobile Food Services
This industry comprises establishments primarily engaged in preparing and serving meals and snacks for immediate consumption from motorized vehicles or nonmotorized carts. The establishment is the central location from which the caterer route is serviced, not each vehicle, or cart. Included in this industry are establishments primarily engaged in providing food services from vehicles, such as hot dog cart, and ice cream truck.

■ Providing food services where patrons generally order or select items and pay before eating are classified in U.S. Industry 722211, Limited-service Restaurants;
■ Selling unprepared foods, such as vegetables, melons, and nuts or fruit from carts are classified in Industry 454390, Other Direct Selling Establishments;
■ Selling and promoting specialty snacks (e.g.. ice cream, frozen yogurt, cookies, popcorn) or nonalcoholic beverages in nonmobile facilities for consumption on or near the premises, are classified in U.S. Industry 722213, Snack and Nonalcoholic Beverage Bars;
■ Selling food specialties, such as hamburgers, hot dogs, chicken, pizza, or specialty cuisines from nonmobile facilities, are classified in U.S. Industry 722211, Limited-service Restaurants or Industry 722110, Full-service Restaurants based on type of food services provided to patrons; and
■ Operating as street vendors (except food) are classified in Industry 454390, Other Direct Selling Establishments.

7224 Drinking Places (Alcoholic Beverages)
This industry group comprises establishments primarily engaged in preparing and serving alcoholic beverages for immediate consumption.

72241 Drinking Places (Alcoholic Beverages)
See industry description for 722410 below.

722410 Drinking Places (Alcoholic Beverages)
This industry comprises establishments known as bars, taverns, nightclubs or drinking places primarily engaged in preparing and serving alcoholic beverages for immediate consumption. These establishments may also provide limited food services.

■ Preparing and serving alcoholic beverages (i.e., not known as bars or taverns) and providing food services to patrons who order and are served while seated and pay after eating are classified in Industry 722110, Full-service Restaurants
■ Preparing and serving alcoholic beverages (i.e., known as bars or taverns) and providing food services to patrons who order and are served while seated and pay after eating are classified in Industry 722211, Limited-service Restaurants;
■ Operating a civic or social association with a bar for their members are classified in Industry 81341, Civic and Social Organizations;
■ Retailing packaged alcoholic beverages not for immediate consumption on the premises are classified in Industry 445310, Beer, Wine, and Liquor Stores; and
■ Operating discotheques or dance clubs without selling alcoholic beverages are classified in Industry 713990, All Other Amusement and Recreation Industries.

Sector **72**

Accommodation and
Food Services

■ = Cross-References

US—United States industry only. CAN—United States and Canadian industries are comparable. When neither US nor CAN appears, Canadian, Mexican, and United States industries are comparable.

602

Harris InfoSource

Sector 81
Other Services
(Except Public Administration)

The Sector as a Whole

THE OTHER SERVICES (EXCEPT PUBLIC ADMINISTRATION) sector comprises establishments engaged in providing services not specifically provided for elsewhere in the classification system. Establishments in this sector are primarily engaged in activities, such as equipment and machinery repairing, promoting or administering religious activities, grantmaking, advocacy, and providing drycleaning and laundry services, personal care services, death care services, pet care services, photofinishing services, temporary parking services, and dating services. Private households that engage in employing workers on or about the premises in activities primarily concerned with the operation of the household are included in this sector. Excluded from this sector are establishments primarily engaged in retailing new equipment and also performing repairs and general maintenance on equipment. These establishments are classified in Sector 44-45, Retail Trade.

▶811 REPAIR AND MAINTENANCE

Industries in the Repair and Maintenance subsector restore machinery, equipment, and other products to working order. These establishments also typically provide general or routine maintenance (i.e., servicing) on such products to ensure they work efficiently and to prevent breakdown and unnecessary repairs.

The NAICS structure for this subsector brings together most types of repair and maintenance establishments and categorizes them based on production processes (i.e., on the type of repair and maintenance activity performed, and the necessary skills, expertise, and processes that are found in different repair and maintenance establishments). This NAICS classification does not delineate between repair services provided to businesses versus those that serve households. Although some industries primarily serve either businesses or households, separation by class of customer is limited by the fact that many establishments serve both. Establishments repairing computers and consumer electronics products are two examples of such overlap.

The Repair and Maintenance subsector does not include all establishments that do repair and maintenance. For example, a substantial amount of repair is done by establishments that also manufacture machinery, equipment, and other goods. These establishments are included in the Manufacturing sector in NAICS. In addition, repair of transportation equipment is often provided by or based at transportation facilities, such as airports, seaports, and these activities are included in the Transportation and Warehousing sector. A particularly unique situation exists with repair of buildings. Plumbing, electrical installation and repair, painting and decorating, and other construction-related establishments are often involved in performing installation or other work on new construction as well as providing repair services on existing structures. While some specialize in repair, it is difficult to distinguish between the two types and all have been included in the Construction sector.

Excluded from this subsector are establishments primarily engaged in rebuilding or remanufacturing machinery and equipment. These are classified in Sector 31-33, Manufacturing. Also excluded are retail establishments that provide after-sale services and repair. These are classified in Sector 44-45, Retail Trade.

Sector 81

Other Services (Except Public Administration)

US—United States industry only. CAN—United States and Canadian industries are comparable. When neither US nor CAN appears, Canadian, Mexican, and United States industries are comparable.

8111 Automotive Repair and Maintenance

This industry group comprises establishments involved in providing repair and maintenance services for automotive vehicles, such as passenger cars, trucks, and vans, and all trailers. Establishments in this industry group employ mechanics with specialized technical skills to diagnose and repair the mechanical and electrical systems for automotive vehicles, repair automotive interiors, and paint or repair automotive exteriors.

81111 Automotive Mechanical and Electrical Repair and Maintenance

This industry comprises establishments primarily engaged in providing mechanical or electrical repair and maintenance services for automotive vehicles, such as passenger cars, trucks and vans, and all trailers. These establishments specialize in or may provide a wide range of these services.

- Retailing automotive vehicles and automotive parts and accessories and also providing automotive repair services are classified in Subsector 441, Motor Vehicle and Parts Dealers;
- Retailing motor fuels and also providing automotive vehicle repair services are classified in Industry Group 4471, Gasoline Stations;
- Changing motor oil and lubricating the chassis of automotive vehicles are classified in Industry 81119, Other Automotive Repair and Maintenance;
- Providing automotive vehicle air-conditioning repair are classified in Industry 81119, Other Automotive Repair and Maintenance; and
- Motorcycle repair and maintenance services are classified in Industry 81149, Other Personal and Household Goods Repair and Maintenance.

811111 General Automotive Repair ^{CAN}

This U.S. industry comprises establishments primarily engaged in providing (1) a wide range of mechanical and electrical repair and maintenance services for automotive vehicles, such as passenger cars, trucks, and vans, and all trailers or (2) engine repair and replacement.

- Retailing new automotive parts and accessories and also providing automotive repair services are classified in Industry 441310, Automotive Parts and Accessories Stores;
- Changing motor oil and lubricating the chassis of automotive vehicles are classified in U.S. Industry 811191, Automotive Oil Change and Lubrication Shops;
- Replacing and repairing automotive vehicle exhaust systems are classified in U.S. Industry 811112, Automotive Exhaust System Repair;
- Replacing and repairing automotive vehicle transmissions are classified in U.S. Industry 811113, Automotive Transmission Repair;
- Retailing motor fuels and also providing automotive vehicle repair services are classified in Industry Group 4471, Gasoline Stations;
- Retailing automobiles and light trucks for highway use and also providing automotive repair services are classified in Industry Group 4411, Automobile Dealers; and
- Motorcycle repair and maintenance services are classified in Industry 811490, Other Personal and Household Goods Repair and Maintenance.

811112 Automotive Exhaust System Repair ^{CAN}

This U.S. industry comprises establishments primarily engaged in replacing or repairing exhaust systems of automotive vehicles, such as passenger cars, trucks, and vans.

- Establishments primarily engaged in motorcycle repair and maintenance services are classified in Industry 811490, Other Personal and Household Goods Repair and Maintenance.

811113 Automotive Transmission Repair ^{US}

This U.S. industry comprises establishments primarily engaged in replacing or repairing transmissions of automotive vehicles, such as passenger cars, trucks, and vans.

- Establishments primarily engaged in motorcycle repair and maintenance services are classified in Industry 811490, Other Personal and Household Goods Repair and Maintenance.

811118 Other Automotive Mechanical and Electrical Repair and Maintenance ^{US}

This U.S. industry comprises establishments primarily engaged in providing specialized mechanical or electrical repair and maintenance services (except engine repair and replacement, exhaust systems repair, and transmission repair) for automotive vehicles, such as passenger cars, trucks, and vans, and all trailers.

- Providing a wide range of mechanical and electrical automotive vehicle repair or specializing in engine repair or replacement are classified in U.S. Industry 811111, General Automotive Repair;
- Replacing and repairing automotive vehicle exhaust systems are classified in U.S. Industry 811112, Automotive Exhaust System Repair;
- Replacing and repairing automotive vehicle transmissions are classified in U.S. Industry 811113, Automotive Transmission Repair;

Sector 81

Other Services (Except Public Administration)

■ = Cross-References

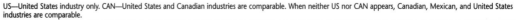

US—United States industry only. CAN—United States and Canadian industries are comparable. When neither US nor CAN appears, Canadian, Mexican, and United States industries are comparable.

604

Harris InfoSource

- Providing automotive vehicle air-conditioning repair are classified in U.S. Industry 811198, All Other Automotive Repair and Maintenance; and
- Motorcycle repair and maintenance services are classified in Industry 811490, Other Personal and Household Goods Repair and Maintenance.

81112 Automotive Body, Paint, Interior, and Glass Repair
This industry comprises establishments primarily engaged in providing one or more of the following: (1) repairing or customizing automotive vehicles, such as passenger cars, trucks, and vans, and all trailer bodies and interiors; (2) painting automotive vehicle and trailer bodies; (3) replacing, repairing, and/or tinting automotive vehicle glass; and (4) customizing automobile, truck, and van interiors for the physically disabled or other customers with special requirements.

- Manufacturing automotive vehicles and trailers or customizing these vehicles on an assembly-line basis are classified in Subsector 336, Transportation Equipment Manufacturing;
- Motorcycle repair and maintenance services are classified in Industry 81149, Other Personal and Household Goods Repair and Maintenance.

811121 Automotive Body, Paint, and Interior Repair and Maintenance CAN
This U.S. industry comprises establishments primarily engaged in repairing or customizing automotive vehicles, such as passenger cars, trucks, and vans, and all trailer bodies and interiors; and/or painting automotive vehicles and trailer bodies.

- Automotive glass replacement, repair and/or tinting are classified in U.S. Industry 811122, Automotive Glass Replacement Shops;
- Manufacturing automotive vehicles and trailers or customizing these vehicles on an assembly-line basis are classified in Subsector 336, Transportation Equipment Manufacturing; and
- Motorcycle repair and maintenance services are classified in Industry 811490, Other Personal and Household Goods Repair and Maintenance.

811122 Automotive Glass Replacement Shops CAN
This U.S. industry comprises establishments primarily engaged in replacing, repairing, and/or tinting automotive vehicle, such as passenger car, truck, and van, glass.

- Establishments primarily engaged in motorcycle repair and maintenance service are classified in Industry 811490, Other Personal and Household Goods Repair and Maintenance.

81119 Other Automotive Repair and Maintenance
This industry comprises establishments primarily engaged in providing automotive repair and maintenance services (except mechanical and electrical repair and maintenance; transmission repair; and body, paint, interior, and glass repair) for automotive vehicles, such as passenger cars, trucks, and vans, and all trailers.

- Tire retreading or recapping are classified in Industry 32621, Tire Manufacturing;
- Automotive vehicle mechanical and electrical repair and maintenance are classified in Industry 81111, Automotive Mechanical and Electrical Repair and Maintenance;
- Automotive body, paint, interior, and glass repair are classified in Industry 81112, Automotive Body, Paint, Interior, and Glass Repair; and
- Motorcycle repair and maintenance services are classified in Industry 81149, Other Personal and Household Goods Repair and Maintenance.

811191 Automotive Oil Change and Lubrication Shops US
This U.S. industry comprises establishments primarily engaged in changing motor oil and lubricating the chassis of automotive vehicles, such as passenger cars, trucks, and vans.

- Establishments primarily engaged in motorcycle repair and maintenance services are classified in Industry 811490, Other Personal and Household Goods Repair and Maintenance.

811192 Car Washes CAN
This U.S. industry comprises establishments primarily engaged in cleaning, washing, and/or waxing automotive vehicles, such as passenger cars, trucks, and vans, and trailers.

811198 All Other Automotive Repair and Maintenance US
This U.S. industry comprises establishments primarily engaged in providing automotive repair and maintenance services (except mechanical and electrical repair and maintenance; body, paint, interior, and glass repair; motor oil change and lubrication; and car washing) for automotive vehicles, such as passenger cars, trucks, and vans, and all trailers.

Sector **81**

Other Services (Except Public Administration)

■ = Cross-References

US—United States industry only. CAN—United States and Canadian industries are comparable. When neither US nor CAN appears, Canadian, Mexican, and United States industries are comparable.

www.harrisinfo.com

605

- Tire retreading or recapping are classified in Industry 32621, Tire Manufacturing;
- Providing a range of mechanical and electrical automotive vehicle repair or specializing in engine repair or replacement are classified in U.S. Industry 811111, General Automotive Repair;
- Replacing and repairing automotive vehicle exhaust systems are classified in U.S. Industry 811112, Automotive Exhaust System Repair;
- Replacing and repairing automotive vehicle transmissions are classified in U.S. Industry 811113, Automotive Transmission Repair;
- Repairing or customizing automotive vehicle bodies and interiors are classified in U.S. Industry 811121, Automotive Body, Paint, and Interior Repair and Maintenance;
- Replacing, repairing, and/or tinting automotive glass are classified in U.S. Industry 811122, Automotive Glass Replacement Shops;
- Changing motor oil and lubricating the chassis of automotive vehicles are classified in U.S. Industry 811191, Automotive Oil Change and Lubrication Shops;
- Cleaning, washing, and/or waxing automotive vehicles and trailers are classified in U.S. Industry 811192, Car Washes;
- Motorcycle repair and maintenance services are classified in Industry 811490, Other Personal and Household Goods Repair and Maintenance; and
- Retailing and installing audio equipment are classified in Industry 441310, Automotive Parts and Accessories Stores.

8112 Electronic and Precision Equipment Repair and Maintenance

This industry group comprises establishments primarily engaged in repairing electronic equipment, such as computers and communications equipment, and highly specialized precision instruments. Establishments in this industry group typically have staff skilled in repairing items having complex, electronic components.

81121 Electronic and Precision Equipment Repair and Maintenance

This industry comprises establishments primarily engaged in repairing and maintaining one or more of the following: (1) consumer electronic equipment; (2) computers; (3) office machines; (4) communication equipment; and (5) other electronic and precision equipment and instruments, without retailing these products as new. Establishments in this industry repair items, such as microscopes, radar and sonar equipment, televisions, stereos, video recorders, computers, fax machines, photocopying machines, two-way radios and other communications equipment, scientific instruments, and medical equipment.

- Installing or maintaining home security systems are classified in Industry 56162, Security Systems Services;
- Retailing new radios, televisions, and other consumer electronics and also providing repair services are classified in Industry 44311, Appliance, Television, and Other Electronics Stores;
- Retailing new computers and computer peripherals and also providing repair services are classified in Industry 44312, Computer and Software Stores; and
- Rewinding armatures and rebuilding electric motors on a factory basis are classified in Industry 33531, Electrical Equipment Manufacturing.

811211 Consumer Electronics Repair and Maintenance us

This U.S. industry comprises establishments primarily engaged in repairing and maintaining consumer electronics, such as televisions, stereos, speakers, video recorders, CD players, radios, and cameras, without retailing new consumer electronics.

- Repairing computers and peripheral equipment are classified in U.S. Industry 811212, Computer and Office Machine Repair and Maintenance;
- Installing or maintaining home security systems are classified in U.S. Industry 561621, Security Systems Services (except Locksmiths);
- Retailing new radios, televisions, and other consumer electronics and also providing repair services are classified in U.S. Industry 443112, Radio, Television, and Other Electronics Stores; and
- Repairing two-way radios are classified in U.S. Industry 811213, Communication Equipment Repair and Maintenance.

811212 Computer and Office Machine Repair and Maintenance us

This U.S. industry comprises establishments primarily engaged in repairing and maintaining computers and office machines without retailing new computers and office machines, such as photocopying machines; and computer terminals, storage devices, printers; and CD-ROM drives.

- Retailing new computers and computer peripherals and also providing repair services are classified in Industry 443120, Computer and Software Stores; and
- Repairing and servicing fax machines are classified in Industry 811213, Communication Equipment Repair and Maintenance.

811213 Communication Equipment Repair and Maintenance us

This U.S. industry comprises establishments primarily engaged in repairing and maintaining communications equipment without retailing new communication equipment, such as telephones, fax machines, communications transmission equipment, and two-way radios.

- Retailing new telephones and also providing repair services are classified in U.S. Industry 443112, Radio, Television, and Other Electronics Stores; and

Sector **81**

Other Services (Except **Public Administration**)

■ = Cross-References

US—United States industry only. CAN—United States and Canadian industries are comparable. When neither US nor CAN appears, Canadian, Mexican, and United States industries are comparable.

606

Harris InfoSource

■ Repairing stereo and other consumer electronic equipment are classified in U.S. Industry 811211, Consumer Electronics Repair and Maintenance.

811219 Other Electronic and Precision Equipment Repair and Maintenance ᵘˢ

This U.S. industry comprises establishments primarily engaged in repairing and maintaining (without retailing) electronic and precision equipment (except consumer electronics, computers and office machines, and communications equipment). Establishments in this industry repair and maintain equipment, such as medical diagnostic imaging equipment, measuring and surveying instruments, laboratory instruments, and radar and sonar equipment.

■ Rewinding armatures and rebuilding electric motors on a factory basis are classified in U.S. Industry 335312, Motor and Generator Manufacturing;
■ Repairing stereo and other consumer electronic equipment are classified in U.S. Industry 811211, Consumer Electronics Repair and Maintenance;
■ Repairing computers and office machines are classified in U.S. Industry 811212, Computer and Office Machine Repair and Maintenance; and
■ Repairing communications equipment are classified in U.S. Industry 811213, Communication Equipment Repair and Maintenance.

8113 Commercial and Industrial Machinery and Equipment (except Automotive and Electronic) Repair and Maintenance

81131 Commercial and Industrial Machinery and Equipment (except Automotive and Electronic) Repair and Maintenance
See industry description for 811310 below.

811310 Commercial and Industrial Machinery and Equipment (except Automotive and Electronic) Repair and Maintenance

This industry comprises establishments primarily engaged in the repair and maintenance of commercial and industrial machinery and equipment. Establishments in this industry either sharpen/install commercial and industrial machinery blades and saws or provide welding (e.g., automotive, general) repair services; or repair agricultural and other heavy and industrial machinery and equipment (e.g., forklifts and other materials handling equipment, machine tools, commercial refrigeration equipment, construction equipment, and mining machinery).

■ Automotive repair (except welding) and maintenance are classified in Industry Group 8111, Automotive Repair and Maintenance;
■ Repairing and maintaining electronic and precision equipment are classified in Industry 81121, Electronic and Precision Equipment Repair and Maintenance;
■ Repairing and servicing aircraft are classified in Industry 488190, Other Support Activities for Air Transportation;
■ Converting, rebuilding, and overhauling aircraft are classified in Industry 336410, Aerospace Product and Parts Manufacturing;
■ Repairing and servicing railroad cars and engines are classified in Industry 488210, Support Activities for Rail Transportation;
■ Rebuilding or remanufacturing railroad engines and cars are classified in Industry 336510, Railroad Rolling Stock Manufacturing;
■ Repairing and overhauling ships at floating dry docks are classified in Industry 4883, Support Activities for Water Transportation;
■ Repairing and overhauling ships at shipyards are classified in Industry 33661, Ship and Boat Building;
■ Rewinding armatures or rebuilding electric motors on a factory basis are classified in U.S. Industry 335312, Motor and Generator Manufacturing; and
■ Repairing and maintaining home and garden equipment (e.g., sharpening or installing blades and saws) are classified in Industry 81111, Home and Garden Equipment and Appliance Repair and Maintenance.

8114 Personal and Household Goods Repair and Maintenance

81141 Home and Garden Equipment and Appliance Repair and Maintenance

This industry comprises establishments primarily engaged in repairing and servicing home and garden equipment and/or household-type appliances without retailing new equipment or appliances. Establishments in this industry repair and maintain items, such as lawnmowers, edgers, snow and leaf blowers, washing machines, clothes dryers, and refrigerators.

■ Retailing outdoor power equipment and also providing repair services are classified in Industry 44421, Outdoor Power Equipment Stores;
■ Retailing an array of new appliances and also providing repair services are classified in Industry 44311, Appliance, Television, and Other Electronics Stores;
■ Repairing, servicing, or installing central heating and air-conditioning equipment are classified in Subsector 23, Construction; and

Sector **81**

Other Services (Except Public Administration)

■ = Cross-References

US—United States industry only. CAN—United States and Canadian industries are comparable. When neither US nor CAN appears, Canadian, Mexican, and United States industries are comparable.

www.harrisinfo.com

607

■ Repairing commercial refrigeration equipment are classified in Industry 81131, Commercial and Industrial Machinery and Equipment (except Automotive and Electronic) Repair and Maintenance.

811411 Home and Garden Equipment Repair and Maintenance ^{CAN}

This U.S. industry comprises establishments primarily engaged in repairing and servicing home and garden equipment without retailing new home and garden equipment, such as lawnmowers, handheld power tools, edgers, snow and leaf blowers, and trimmers.

■ Establishments primarily engaged in retailing new outdoor power equipment and also providing repair services are classified in Industry 444210, Outdoor Power Equipment Stores.

811412 Appliance Repair and Maintenance ^{CAN}

This U.S. industry comprises establishments primarily engaged in repairing and servicing household appliances without retailing new appliances, such as refrigerators, stoves, washing machines, clothes dryers, and room air-conditioners.

■ Installing central heating and air-conditioning equipment are classified in Industry 235110, Plumbing, Heating, and Air-conditioning Contractors;
■ Repairing commercial refrigeration equipment are classified in Industry 811310, Commercial and Industrial Machinery and Equipment (except Automotive and Electronic) Repair and Maintenance; and
■ Retailing an array of new appliances and also providing repair services are classified in U.S. Industry 443111, Household Appliance Stores.

81142 Reupholstery and Furniture Repair

See industry description for 811420 below.

811420 Reupholstery and Furniture Repair

This industry comprises establishments primarily engaged in one or more of the following: (1) reupholstering furniture; (2) refinishing furniture; (3) repairing furniture; and (4) repairing and restoring furniture.

■ Automotive vehicle and trailer upholstery repair are classified in U.S. Industry 811121, Automotive Body, Paint, and Interior Repair and Maintenance; and
■ The restoration of museum pieces are classified in Industry 711510, Independent Artists, Writers, and Performers.

81143 Footwear and Leather Goods Repair

See industry description for 811430 below.

811430 Footwear and Leather Goods Repair

This industry comprises establishments primarily engaged in repairing footwear and/or repairing other leather or leather-like goods without retailing new footwear and leather or leather-like goods, such as handbags and briefcases.

■ Retailing new luggage and leather goods and also providing repair services are classified in Industry 448320, Luggage and Leather Goods Stores;
■ Shining shoes are classified in Industry 812990, All Other Personal Services; and
■ Repairing leather clothing are classified in Industry 811490, Other Personal and Household Goods Repair and Maintenance.

81149 Other Personal and Household Goods Repair and Maintenance

See industry description for 811490 below.

811490 Other Personal and Household Goods Repair and Maintenance

This industry comprises establishments primarily engaged in repairing and servicing personal or household-type goods without retailing new personal and household-type goods (except home and garden equipment, appliances, furniture, and footwear and leather goods). Establishments in this industry repair items, such as garments; watches; jewelry; musical instruments; bicycles and motorcycles; motorboats, canoes, sailboats, and other recreational boats.

■ Repairing home and garden equipment are classified in U.S. Industry 811411, Home and Garden Equipment Repair and Maintenance;
■ Repairing appliances are classified in U.S. Industry 811412, Appliance Repair and Maintenance;
■ Reupholstering and repairing furniture are classified in Industry 811420, Reupholstery and Furniture Repair;
■ Repairing footwear and leather goods are classified in Industry 811430, Footwear and Leather Goods Repair;
■ Operating marinas and providing a range of other services including boat cleaning and repair are classified in Industry 713930, Marinas; and
■ Drycleaning garments are classified in Industry Group 8123, Drycleaning and Laundry Services.

Sector **81**

Other Services (Except Public Administration)

■ = Cross-References

US—United States industry only. CAN—United States and Canadian industries are comparable. When neither US nor CAN appears, Canadian, Mexican, and United States industries are comparable.

➡812 PERSONAL AND LAUNDRY SERVICES

Industries in the Personal and Laundry Services subsector group establishments that provide personal and laundry services to individuals, households, and businesses. Services performed include: personal care services; death care services; laundry and drycleaning services; and a wide range of other personal services, such as pet care (except veterinary) services, photofinishing services, temporary parking services, and dating services.

The Personal and Laundry Services subsector is by no means all-inclusive of the services that could be termed personal services (i.e., those provided to individuals rather than businesses). There are many other subsectors, as well as sectors, that provide services to persons. Establishments providing legal, accounting, tax preparation, architectural, portrait photography, and similar professional services are classified in Sector 54, Professional, Scientific, and Technical Services; those providing job placement, travel arrangement, home security, interior and exterior house cleaning, exterminating, lawn and garden care, and similar support services are classified in Sector 56, Administrative and Support, Waste Management and Remediation Services; those providing health and social services are classified in Sector 62, Health Care and Social Assistance; those providing amusement and recreation services are classified in Sector 71, Arts, Entertainment, and Recreation; those providing educational instruction are classified in Sector 61, Educational Services; those providing repair services are classified in Subsector 811, Repair and Maintenance; and those providing spiritual, civic, and advocacy services are classified in Subsector 813, Religious, Grantmaking, Civic, Professional, and Similar Organizations.

8121 Personal Care Services CAN

This industry group comprises establishments, such as barber and beauty shops, that provide appearance care services to individual consumers.

81211 Hair, Nail, and Skin Care Services CAN

This industry comprises establishments primarily engaged in one or more of the following: (1) providing hair care services; (2) providing nail care services; and (3) providing facials or applying makeup (except permanent makeup).

- Offering training in barbering, hair styling, or the cosmetic arts are classified in Industry 61151, Technical and Trade Schools;
- Providing massage, electrolysis (i.e., hair removal), permanent makeup, or tanning services are classified in Industry 81219, Other Personal Care Services; and
- Providing medical skin care services (e.g., cosmetic surgery, dermatology) are classified in Sector 62, Health Care and Social Assistance.

812111 Barber Shops US

This U.S. industry comprises establishments known as barber shops or men's hair stylist shops primarily engaged in cutting, trimming, and styling boys' and men's hair; and/or shaving and trimming men's beards.

- Offering training in barbering are classified in U.S. Industry 611511, Cosmetology and Barber Schools; and
- Providing hair care services (except establishments known as barber shops or men's hair stylists) are classified in U.S. Industry 812112, Beauty Salons.

812112 Beauty Salons US

This U.S. industry comprises establishments (except those known as barber shops or men's hair stylist shops) primarily engaged in one or more of the following: (1) cutting, trimming, shampooing, weaving, coloring, waving, or styling hair; (2) providing facials; and (3) applying makeup (except permanent makeup).

- Cutting, trimming, and styling men's and boys' hair (known as barber shops or men's hair stylist shops) are classified in U.S. Industry 812111, Barber Shops;
- Offering training in hair styling or the cosmetic arts are classified in U.S. Industry 611511, Cosmetology and Barber Schools;
- Providing nail care services are classified in U.S. Industry 812113, Nail Salons;
- Providing massage, electrolysis (i.e., hair removal), permanent makeup, or tanning services are classified in U.S. Industry 812199, All Other Personal Care Services; and
- Providing medical skin care services (e.g., cosmetic surgery, dermatology) are classified in Sector 62, Health Care and Social Assistance.

812113 Nail Salons US

This U.S. industry comprises establishments primarily engaged in providing nail care services, such as manicures, pedicures, and nail extensions.

Sector **81**

Other Services (Except Public Administration)

■ = Cross-References

US—United States industry only. CAN—United States and Canadian industries are comparable. When neither US nor CAN appears, Canadian, Mexican, and United States industries are comparable.

www.harrisinfo.com

609

81219 Other Personal Care Services ^{CAN}

This industry comprises establishments primarily engaged in providing personal care services (except hair, nail, facial, or nonpermanent makeup services).

- Providing hair, nail, facial, or nonpermanent makeup services are classified in Industry 81211, Hair, Nail, and Skin Care Services;
- Operating physical fitness facilities are classified in Industry 71394, Fitness and Recreational Sports Centers;
- Operating health resorts and spas that provide lodging are classified in Industry 72111, Hotels (except Casino Hotels) and Motels; and
- Providing medical or surgical hair replacement or weight reduction are classified in Sector 62, Health Care and Social Assistance.

812191 Diet and Weight Reducing Centers ^{US}

This U.S. industry comprises establishments primarily engaged in providing nonmedical services to assist clients in attaining or maintaining a desired weight. The sale of weight reduction products, such as food supplements, may be an integral component of the program. These services typically include individual or group counseling, menu and exercise planning, and weight and body measurement monitoring.

- Operating physical fitness facilities are classified in Industry 713940, Fitness and Recreational Sports Centers;
- Operating health resorts and spas that provide lodging are classified in Industry 721110, Hotels (except Casino Hotels) and Motels; and
- Providing medical or surgical weight reduction are classified in Sector 62, Health Care and Social Assistance.

812199 Other Personal Care Services ^{US}

This U.S. industry comprises establishments primarily engaged in providing personal care services (except hair, nail, facial, nonpermanent makeup, or nonmedical diet and weight reducing services).

- Cutting, trimming, and styling men's and boys' hair (known as barber shops or men's hair stylist shops) are classified in U. S. Industry 812111, Barber Shops;
- Providing hair, facial, or nonpermanent makeup services (except establishments known as barber shops or men's hair stylist shops) are classified in U.S. Industry 812112, Beauty Shops;
- Nail care services are classified in U.S. Industry 812113, Nail Salons;
- Providing nonmedical diet and weight reducing services are classified in U.S. Industry 812191, Diet and Weight Reducing Centers; and
- Providing medical or surgical hair replacement or weight reduction services are classified in Sector 62, Health Care and Social Assistance.

8122 Death Care Services ^{CAN}

81221 Funeral Homes and Funeral Services ^{CAN}
See industry description for 812210 below.

812210 Funeral Homes and Funeral Services ^{CAN}

This industry comprises establishments primarily engaged in preparing the dead for burial or interment and conducting funerals (i.e., providing facilities for wakes, arranging transportation for the dead, selling caskets and related merchandise). Funeral homes combined with crematories are included in this industry.

- Establishments (except funeral homes) primarily engaged in cremating the dead are classified in Industry 812220, Cemeteries and Crematories.

81222 Cemeteries and Crematories ^{CAN}
See industry description for 812220 below.

812220 Cemeteries and Crematories ^{CAN}

This industry comprises establishments primarily engaged in operating sites or structures reserved for the interment of human or animal remains and/or cremating the dead.

- Crematories combined with funeral homes are classified in Industry 812210, Funeral Homes and Funeral Services.

8123 Drycleaning and Laundry Services ^{CAN}

81231 Coin-operated Laundries and Drycleaners ^{CAN}
See industry description for 812310 below.

US—United States industry only. CAN—United States and Canadian industries are comparable. When neither US nor CAN appears, Canadian, Mexican, and United States industries are comparable.

812310 Coin-operated Laundries and Drycleaners CAN

This industry comprises (1) establishments primarily engaged in operating facilities with coin-operated or similar self-service laundry and drycleaning equipment for customer use on the premises and (2) establishments primarily engaged in supplying and servicing coin-operated or similar self-service laundry and drycleaning equipment for customer use in places of business operated by others, such as apartments and dormitories.

81232 Drycleaning and Laundry Services (except Coin-operated)CAN

See industry description for 812320 below.

812320 Drycleaning and Laundry Services (except Coin-operated)CAN

This industry comprises establishments primarily engaged in one or more of the following: (1) providing drycleaning services (except coin-operated); (2) providing laundering services (except linen and uniform supply or coin-operated); (3) providing drop off and pickup sites for laundries and/or drycleaners; and (4) providing specialty cleaning services for specific types of garments and other textile items (except carpets and upholstery), such as fur, leather, or suede garments; wedding gowns; hats; draperies; and pillows. These establishments may provide all, a combination of, or none of the cleaning services on the premises.

- Supplying laundered linens and uniforms on a rental or contract basis are classified in Industry 81233, Linen and Uniform Supply;
- Operating coin-operated or similar self-service laundry or drycleaning facilities are classified in Industry 812310, Coin-operated Laundries and Drycleaners; and
- Cleaning used carpets and upholstery are classified in Industry 561740, Carpet and Upholstery Cleaning Services.

81233 Linen and Uniform Supply CAN

This industry comprises establishments primarily engaged in supplying, on a rental or contract basis, laundered items, such as uniforms, gowns and coats, table linens, bed linens, towels, clean room apparel, and treated mops or shop towels.

812331 Linen Supply US

This U.S. industry comprises establishments primarily engaged in supplying, on a rental or contract basis, laundered items, such as table and bed linens; towels; diapers; and uniforms, gowns, or coats of the type used by doctors, nurses, barbers, beauticians, and waitresses.

- Establishments primarily engaged in supplying, on a rental or contract basis, laundered industrial work uniforms and related work clothing are classified in U.S. Industry 812332, Industrial Launderers.

812332 Industrial Launderers US

This U.S. industry comprises establishments primarily engaged in supplying, on a rental or contract basis, laundered industrial work uniforms and related work clothing, such as protective apparel (flame and heat resistant) and clean room apparel; dust control items, such as treated mops, rugs, mats, dust tool covers, cloths, and shop or wiping towels.

- Establishments primarily engaged in supplying, on a rental or contract basis, laundered uniforms, gowns or coats of the type used by doctors, nurses, barbers, beauticians, and waitresses are classified in U.S. Industry 812331, Linen Supply.

8129 Other Personal Services CAN

The industry group comprises establishments primarily engaged in providing personal services (except personal care services, death care services, or drycleaning and laundry services).

81291 Pet Care (except Veterinary) Services CAN

See industry description for 812910 below.

812910 Pet Care (except Veterinary) Services CAN

This industry comprises establishments primarily engaged in providing pet care services (except veterinary), such as boarding, grooming, sitting, and training pets.

- Practicing veterinary medicine are classified in Industry 541940, Veterinary Services;
- Boarding horses are classified in Industry 115210, Support Activities for Animal Production; and
- Transporting pets are classified in U.S. Industry 485991, Special Needs Transportation.

Sector **81**

Other Services (Except Public Administration)

■ = Cross-References

US—United States industry only. CAN—United States and Canadian industries are comparable. When neither US nor CAN appears, Canadian, Mexican, and United States industries are comparable.

www.harrisinfo.com

611

81292 Photofinishing ^{CAN}

This industry comprises establishments primarily engaged in developing film and/or making photographic slides, prints, and enlargements.

- Establishments primarily engaged in processing motion picture film for the motion picture and television industries are classified in Industry 51219, Postproduction and Other Motion Picture and Video Industries.

812921 Photofinishing Laboratories (except One-hour)^{CAN}

This U.S. industry comprises establishments (except those known as "one-hour" photofinishing labs) primarily engaged in developing film and/or making photographic slides, prints, and enlargements.

- Establishments primarily engaged in processing motion picture film for the motion picture and television industries are classified in U.S. Industry 512199, Other Motion Picture and Video Industries; and
- Establishments known as "one-hour" photofinishing labs are classified in U.S. Industry 812922, One-hour Photofinishing.

812922 One-hour Photofinishing ^{CAN}

This U.S. industry comprises establishments known as "one-hour" photofinishing labs primarily engaged in developing film and/or making photographic slides, prints, and enlargements on a short turnaround or while-you-wait basis.

- Photofinishing laboratories (except those known as "one-hour" photofinishing labs) are classified in U.S. Industry 812921, Photofinishing Laboratories (except One-hour).

81293 Parking Lots and Garages ^{CAN}

See industry description for 812930 below.

812930 Parking Lots and Garages ^{CAN}

This industry comprises establishments primarily engaged in providing parking space for motor vehicles, usually on an hourly, daily, or monthly basis and/or valet parking services.

- Establishments primarily engaged in providing extended or dead storage of motor vehicles are classified in Industry 493190, Other Warehousing and Storage .

81299 All Other Personal Services ^{CAN}

See industry description for 812990 below.

812990 All Other Personal Services ^{CAN}

This industry comprises establishments primarily engaged in providing personal services (except personal care services, death care services, drycleaning and laundry services, pet care services, photofinishing services, or parking space and/or valet parking services).

- Providing personal care services are classified in Industry Group 8121, Personal Care Services;
- Providing death care services are classified in Industry Group 8122, Death Care Services;
- Providing drycleaning and laundry services are classified in Industry Group 8123, Drycleaning and Laundry Services;
- Providing pet care (except veterinary) services are classified in Industry 812910, Pet Care (except Veterinary) Services;
- Practicing veterinary medicine are classified in Industry 541940, Veterinary Services;
- Providing photofinishing services are classified in Industry 81292, Photofinishing; and
- Providing parking space for motor vehicles and/or valet parking services are classified in Industry 812930, Parking Lots and Garages.

▶813 RELIGIOUS, GRANTMAKING, CIVIC, PROFESSIONAL, AND SIMILAR ORGANIZATIONS

Industries in the Religious, Grantmaking, Civic, Professional, and Similar Organizations subsector group establishments that organize and promote religious activities; support various causes through grantmaking; advocate various social and political causes; and promote and defend the interests of their members.

The industry groups within the subsector are defined in terms of their activities, such as establishments that provide funding for specific causes or for a variety of charitable causes; establishments that advocate and actively promote causes and beliefs for the public good; and establishments that have an active membership structure to promote causes and represent the interests of their members. Establishments in this subsector may publish newsletters, books, and periodicals, for distribution to their membership.

Sector 81

Other Services (Except Public Administration)

■ = Cross-References

US—United States industry only. CAN—United States and Canadian industries are comparable. When neither US nor CAN appears, Canadian, Mexican, and United States industries are comparable.

612

Harris InfoSource

8131 Religious Organizations ^{CAN}

81311 Religious Organizations ^{CAN}
See industry description for 813110 below.

813110 Religious Organizations ^{CAN}
This industry comprises (1) establishments primarily engaged in operating religious organizations, such as churches, religious temples, and monasteries and/or (2) establishments primarily engaged in administering an organized religion or promoting religious activities.

- Schools, colleges, or universities operated by religious organizations are classified in Sector 61, Educational Services;
- Radio and television stations operated by religious organizations are classified in Subsector 513, Broadcasting and Telecommunications;
- Publishing houses operated by religious organizations are classified in Subsector 511, Publishing Industries;
- Establishments operated by religious organizations primarily engaged in health and social assistance for individuals are classified in Sector 62, Health Care and Social Assistance; and
- Used merchandise stores operated by religious organizations are classified in Industry 453310, Used Merchandise Stores.

8132 Grantmaking and Giving Services ^{CAN}

81321 Grantmaking and Giving Services ^{CAN}
This industry comprises (1) establishment known as grantmaking foundations or charitable trusts and (2) establishments primarily engaged in raising funds for a wide range of social welfare activities, such as health, educational, scientific, and cultural activities.

- Providing trust management services for others are classified in Industry 52392, Portfolio Management;
- Organizing and conducting fundraising campaigns on a contract or fee basis are classified in Industry 56149, Other Business Support Services;
- Providing telemarketing services for others are classified in Industry 56142, Telephone Call Centers;
- Raising funds for political purposes are classified in Industry 81394, Political Organizations;
- Advocating social causes or issues are classified in Industry 81331, Social Advocacy Organizations; and
- Conducting health research are classified in Industry 54171, Research and Development in the Physical, Engineering, and Life Sciences.

813211 Grantmaking Foundations ^{US}
This U.S. industry comprises establishments known as grantmaking foundations or charitable trusts. Establishments in this industry award grants from trust funds based on a competitive selection process or the preferences of the foundation managers and grantors; or fund a single entity, such as a museum or university.

- Establishments primarily engaged in providing trust management services for others are classified in Industry 523920, Portfolio Management.

813212 Voluntary Health Organizations ^{US}
This U.S. industry comprises establishments primarily engaged in raising funds for health related research, such as disease (e.g., heart, cancer, diabetes) prevention, health education, and patient services.

- Establishments primarily engaged in raising funds for a wide range of social welfare activities, such as educational, scientific, cultural, and health, are classified in U.S. Industry 813219, Other Grantmaking and Giving Services;
- Establishments primarily engaged in organizing and conducting fundraising campaigns on a contract or fee basis are classified in U.S. Industry 561499, All Other Business Support Services;
- Establishments primarily engaged in providing telemarketing services for others are classified in U.S. Industry 561422, Telemarketing Bureaus;
- Establishments known as grantmaking foundations or charitable trusts are classified in U.S. Industry 813211, Grantmaking Foundations; and
- Establishments primarily engaged in conducting health research are classified in Industry 541710, Research and Development in the Physical, Engineering, and Life Sciences.

813219 Other Grantmaking and Giving Services ^{US}
This U.S. industry comprises establishments (except voluntary health organizations) primarily engaged in raising funds for a wide range of social welfare activities, such as educational, scientific, cultural, and health.

- Establishments primarily engaged in raising funds for health related research are classified in U.S. Industry 813212, Voluntary Health Organizations;

Sector **81**

Other Services (Except Public Administration)

 = Cross-References

US—United States industry only. CAN—United States and Canadian industries are comparable. When neither US nor CAN appears, Canadian, Mexican, and United States industries are comparable.

www.harrisinfo.com

613

- Establishments known as grantmaking foundations or charitable trusts are classified in U.S. Industry 813211, Grantmaking Foundations;
- Establishments primarily engaged in organizing and conducting fundraising campaigns on a contract or fee basis are classified in U.S. Industry 561499, All Other Business Support Services;
- Establishments primarily engaged in providing telemarketing services for others are classified in U.S. Industry 561422, Telemarketing Bureaus;
- Establishments primarily engaged in raising funds for political purposes are classified in Industry 813940, Political Organizations; and
- Establishments primarily engaged in advocating social causes or issues are classified in Industry 81331, Social Advocacy Organizations.

8133 Social Advocacy Organizations ^{CAN}

81331 Social Advocacy Organizations ^{CAN}

This industry comprises establishments primarily engaged in promoting a particular cause or working for the realization of a specific social or political goal to benefit a broad or specific constituency. These organizations may solicit contributions and offer memberships to support these goals.

- Promoting the civic and social interests of their members are classified in Industry 81341, Civic and Social Organizations;
- Promoting the interests of the organized labor and union employees are classified in Industry 81393, Labor Unions and Similar Labor Organizations; and
- Providing legal services for social advocacy organizations are classified in Industry Group 5411, Legal Services.

813311 Human Rights Organizations

This U.S. industry comprises establishments primarily engaged in promoting causes associated with human rights either for a broad or specific constituency. Establishments in this industry address issues, such as protecting and promoting the broad constitutional rights and civil liberties of individuals and those suffering from neglect, abuse, or exploitation; promoting the interests of specific groups, such as children, women, senior citizens, or persons with disabilities; improving relations between racial, ethnic, and cultural groups; and promoting voter education and registration. These organizations may solicit contributions and offer memberships to support these causes.

- Promoting the interests of organized labor and union employees are classified in Industry 813930, Labor Unions and Similar Labor Organizations; and
- Providing legal services for human rights organizations are classified in Industry Group 5411, Legal Services.

813312 Environment, Conservation, and Wildlife Organizations ^{US}

This U.S. industry comprises establishments primarily engaged in promoting the preservation and protection of the environment and wildlife. Establishments in this industry address issues, such as clean air and water; global warming; conserving and developing natural resources, including land, plant, water, and energy resources; and protecting and preserving wildlife and endangered species. These organizations may solicit contributions and offer memberships to support these causes.

- Establishments primarily engaged in providing legal services for environment, conservation, and wildlife organizations are classified in Industry Group 5411, Legal Services.

813319 Other Social Advocacy Organizations ^{US}

This U.S. industry comprises establishments primarily engaged in social advocacy (except human rights and environmental protection, conservation, and wildlife preservation). Establishments in this industry address issues, such as peace and international understanding; community action (excluding civic organizations); or advancing social causes, such as firearms safety, drunk driving prevention, drug abuse awareness. These organizations may solicit contributions and offer memberships to support these causes.

- Advocating human rights issues are classified in U.S. Industry 813311, Human Rights Organizations;
- Promoting the preservation and protection of the environment and wildlife are classified in U.S. Industry 813312, Environment, Conservation, and Wildlife Organizations;
- Promoting the civic and social interests of their members are classified in Industry 813410, Civic and Social Organizations;
- Providing legal services for social advocacy organizations are classified in Industry Group 5411, Legal Services; and
- Providing community action services, such as community action services agencies, are classified in Industry 624190, Other Individual and Family Services.

Sector **81**

Other Services (Except Public Administration)

■ = Cross-References

US—United States industry only. CAN—United States and Canadian industries are comparable. When neither US nor CAN appears, Canadian, Mexican, and United States industries are comparable.

8134 Civic and Social Organizations ^{CAN}

81341 Civic and Social Organizations ^{CAN}
See industry description for 813410 below.

813410 Civic and Social Organizations ^{CAN}
This industry comprises establishments primarily engaged in promoting the civic and social interests of their members. Establishments in this industry may operate bars and restaurants for their members.

- Establishments of insurance offices operated by fraternal benefit organizations are classified in Subsector 524, Insurance Carriers and Related Activities;
- Establishments primarily engaged in operating residential fraternity and sorority houses are classified in Industry 721310, Rooming and Boarding Houses; and
- Establishments primarily engaged in providing travel arrangements and reservation services, such as automobile travel clubs or motor travel clubs are classified in U.S. Industry 561599, All Other Travel Arrangement and Reservation Services.

8139 Business, Professional, Labor, Political, and Similar Organizations ^{CAN}
This industry group comprises establishments primarily engaged in promoting the interests of their members (except religious organizations, social advocacy organizations, and civic and social organizations). Examples of establishments in this industry are business associations, professional organizations, labor unions, and political organizations.

81391 Business Associations ^{CAN}
See industry description for 813910 below.

813910 Business Associations ^{CAN}
This industry comprises establishments primarily engaged in promoting the business interests of their members. These establishments may conduct research on new products and services; develop market statistics; sponsor quality and certification standards; lobby public officials; or publish newsletters, books, or periodicals for distribution to their members.

- Establishments owned by their members but organized to perform a specific business function, such as common marketing of crops, joint advertising, or buying cooperatives, are classified according to their primary activity;
- Establishments primarily engaged in promoting the professional interests of their members and the profession as a whole are classified in Industry 813920, Professional Organizations;
- Establishments primarily engaged in promoting the interests of organized labor and union employees, such as trade unions, are classified in Industry 813930, Labor Unions and Similar Labor Organizations; and
- Establishments primarily engaged in lobbying public officials (i.e., lobbyists) are classified in Industry 541820, Public Relations Agencies.

81392 Professional Organizations ^{CAN}
See industry description for 813920 below.

813920 Professional Organizations ^{CAN}
This industry comprises establishments primarily engaged in promoting the professional interests of their members and the profession as a whole. These establishments may conduct research; develop statistics; sponsor quality and certification standards; lobby public officials; or publish newsletters, books, or periodicals, for distribution to their members.

- Promoting the business interests of their members are classified in Industry 813910, Business Associations; and
- Lobbying public officials (i.e., lobbyists) are classified in Industry 541820, Public Relations Agencies.

81393 Labor Unions and Similar Labor Organizations ^{CAN}
See industry description for 813930 below.

813930 Labor Unions and Similar Labor Organizations ^{CAN}
This industry comprises establishments primarily engaged in promoting the interests of organized labor and union employees.

Sector **81**

Other Services (Except Public Administration)

■ = Cross-References

US—United States industry only. CAN—United States and Canadian industries are comparable. When neither US nor CAN appears, Canadian, Mexican, and United States industries are comparable.

www.harrisinfo.com 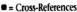 615

81394 Political Organizations CAN
See industry description for 813940 below.

813940 Political Organizations CAN
This industry comprises establishments primarily engaged in promoting the interests of national, state, or local political parties or candidates. Included are political groups organized to raise funds for a political party or individual candidates.

- Organizing and conducting fundraising campaigns on a contract or fee basis are classified in U.S. Industry 561499, All Other Business Support Services; and
- Providing telemarketing services for others are classified in U.S. Industry 561422, Telemarketing Bureaus.

81399 Other Similar Organizations (except Business, Professional, Labor, and Political Organizations)CAN
See industry description for 813990 below.

813990 Other Similar Organizations (except Business, Professional, Labor, and Political Organizations)CAN
This industry comprises establishments (except religious organizations, social advocacy organizations, civic and social organizations, business associations, professional organizations, labor unions, and political organizations) primarily engaged in promoting the interest of their members.

- Operating religious organizations, such as churches, religious temples, and monasteries, are classified in Industry 813110, Religious Organizations;
- Raising funds for a wide range of social welfare activities and establishments known as grantmaking foundations or charitable trusts are classified in Industry 81321, Grantmaking and Giving Services;
- Advocating social causes or issues are classified in Industry 81331, Social Advocacy Organizations;
- Promoting the civic and social interests of their members are classified in Industry 813410, Civic and Social Organizations;
- Promoting the business interests of their members are classified in Industry 813910, Business Associations;
- Promoting the professional interests of their members and the profession as a whole are classified in Industry 813920, Professional Organizations;
- Promoting the interests of organized labor and union employees are classified in Industry 813930, Labor Unions and Similar Labor Organizations;
- Promoting the interests of national, state, or local political parties or candidates are classified in Industry 813940, Political Organizations; and
- Providing recreational and amusement services, such as recreational or youth sports teams and leagues, are classified in Industry 713990, All Other Amusement and Recreation Industries.

▶814 PRIVATE HOUSEHOLDS
Industries in the Private Households subsector include private households that engage in employing workers on or about the premises in activities primarily concerned with the operation of the household. These private households may employ individuals, such as cooks, maids, and butlers, and outside workers, such as gardeners, caretakers, and other maintenance workers.

8141 Private Households

81411 Private Households
See industry description for 814110 below.

814110 Private Households
This industry comprises private households primarily engaged in employing workers on or about the premises in activities primarily concerned with the operation of the household. These private households may employ individuals, such as cooks, maids, nannies, and butlers, and outside workers, such as gardeners, caretakers, and other maintenance workers.

Sector **81**

Other Services (Except **Public Administration**)

■ = Cross-References

US—United States industry only. CAN—United States and Canadian industries are comparable. When neither US nor CAN appears, Canadian, Mexican, and United States industries are comparable.

616

Harris InfoSource

Sector 92 Public Administration

The Sector as a Whole

THE PUBLIC ADMINISTRATION sector consists of establishments of federal, state, and local government agencies that administer, oversee, and manage public programs and have executive, legislative, or judicial authority over other institutions within a given area. These agencies also set policy, create laws, adjudicate civil and criminal legal cases, provide for public safety and for national defense. In general, government establishments in the Public Administration sector oversee governmental programs and activities that are not performed by private establishments. Establishments in this sector typically are engaged in the organization and financing of the production of public goods and services, most of which are provided for free or at prices that are not economically significant.

Government establishments also engage in a wide range of productive activities covering not only public goods and services but also individual goods and services similar to those produced in sectors typically identified with private-sector establishments. In general, ownership is not a criterion for classification in NAICS. Therefore, government establishments engaged in the production of private-sector-like goods and services should be classified in the same industry as private-sector establishments engaged in similar activities.

As a practical matter, it is difficult to identify separate establishment detail for many government agencies. To the extent that separate establishment records are available, the administration of governmental programs is classified in Sector 92, Public Administration, while the operation of that same governmental program is classified elsewhere in NAICS based on the activities performed. For example, the governmental administrative authority for an airport is classified in Industry 92612, Regulation and Administration of Transportation Programs, while operating the airport is classified in Industry 48811, Airport Operations. When separate records are not available to distinguish between the administration of a governmental program and the operation of it, the establishment is classified in Sector 92, Public Administration.

Examples of government-provided goods and services that are classified in sectors other than Public Administration include: schools, classified in Sector 61, Educational Services; hospitals, classified in Subsector 622, Hospitals; establishments operating transportation facilities, classified in Sector 48-49, Transportation and Warehousing; the operation of utilities, classified in Sector 22, Utilities; and the Government Printing Office, classified in Subsector 323, Printing and Related Support Activities.

Sector 92
Public Administration

▶921 EXECUTIVE, LEGISLATIVE, AND OTHER GENERAL GOVERNMENT SUPPORT US

The Executive, Legislative, and Other General Government Support subsector groups offices of government executives, legislative bodies, public finance and general government support.

9211 Executive, Legislative, and Other General Government Support US

92111 Executive Offices US
See industry description for 921110 below.

921110 Executive Offices ^{us}

This industry comprises government establishments serving as offices of chief executives and their advisory committees and commissions. This industry includes offices of the president, governors, and mayors, in addition to executive advisory commissions.

92112 Legislative Bodies ^{us}

See industry description for 921120 below.

921120 Legislative Bodies ^{us}

This industry comprises government establishments serving as legislative bodies and their advisory committees and commissions. Included in this industry are legislative bodies, such as Congress, state legislatures, and advisory and study legislative commissions.

92113 Public Finance Activities ^{us}

See industry description for 921130 below.

921130 Public Finance Activities ^{us}

This industry comprises government establishments primarily engaged in public finance, taxation and monetary policy. Included are financial administration activities, such as monetary policy; tax administration and collection; custody and disbursement of funds; debt and investment administration; auditing activities; and government employee retirement trust fund administration.

■ Administering income maintenance programs are classified in Industry 923130, Administration of Human Resource Programs (except Education, Public Health, and Veterans' Affairs Programs);
■ Regulating insurance and banking institutions are classified in Industry 926150, Regulation, Licensing, and Inspection of Miscellaneous Commercial Sectors; and
■ Performing central banking functions, such as issuing currency and acting as the fiscal agent for the central government are classified in Industry 521110, Monetary Authorities-Central Bank.

92114 Executive and Legislative Offices, Combined ^{us}

See industry description for 921140 below.

921140 Executive and Legislative Offices, Combined ^{us}

This industry comprises government establishments serving as councils and boards of commissioners or supervisors and such bodies where the chief executive (e.g., county executive or city mayor) is a member of the legislative body (e.g., county or city council) itself.

■ Serving as offices of chief executives are classified in Industry 921110, Executive Offices; and
■ Serving as legislative bodies are classified in Industry 921120, Legislative Bodies.

92115 American Indian and Alaska Native Tribal Governments ^{us}

See industry description for 921150 below.

921150 American Indian and Alaska Native Tribal Governments ^{us}

This industry comprises American Indian and Alaska Native governing bodies. Establishments in this industry perform legislative, judicial, and administrative functions for their American Indian and Alaska Native lands. Included in this industry are American Indian and Alaska Native councils, courts, and law enforcement bodies.

■ Establishments primarily engaged in providing funding for American Indian and Alaska Native tribal programs through commercial activities, such as gaming, are classified in the industry of the commercial activity; and
■ Government establishments providing public administration of American Indian and Alaska Native affairs are classified in Industry 923130, Administration of Human Resource Programs (except Education, Public Health, and Veterans' Affairs Programs).

92119 Other General Government Support ^{us}

See industry description for 921190 below.

921190 Other General Government Support ^{us}

This industry comprises government establishments primarily engaged in providing general support for government. Such support services include personnel services, election boards, and other general government support establishments that are not classified elsewhere in public administration.

Sector **92**

Public Administration

■ = Cross-References

US—United States industry only. CAN—United States and Canadian industries are comparable. When neither US nor CAN appears, Canadian, Mexican, and United States industries are comparable.

- Government establishments primarily engaged in serving as offices of chief executives and their advisory committees and commissions are classified in Industry 921110, Executive Offices;
- Government establishments primarily engaged in serving as legislative bodies and their advisory committees and commissions are classified in Industry 921120, Legislative bodies;
- Government establishments primarily engaged in providing administration of public finance, tax collection, and monetary policy programs are classified in Industry 921130, Public Finance Activities;
- Government establishments primarily engaged in serving as combined executive and legislative offices are classified in Industry 921140, Executive and Legislative Offices, Combined; and
- Establishments primarily engaged in serving as American Indian or Alaska Native tribal leadership are classified in Industry 921150, American Indian and Alaska Native Tribal Governments.

▶922 JUSTICE, PUBLIC ORDER, AND SAFETY ACTIVITIES ᵁˢ

The Justice, Public Order, and Safety Activities subsector groups government establishments engaged in the administration of justice, public order, and safety programs.

9221 Justice, Public Order, and Safety Activities ᵁˢ

92211 Courts ᵁˢ
See industry description for 922110 below.

922110 Courts ᵁˢ
This industry comprises civilian courts of law (except Indian tribal and Alaska Native courts). Included in this industry are civilian courts, courts of law, and sheriffs' offices conducting court functions only.

- Government establishments primarily engaged in operating military courts are classified in Industry 928110, National Security; and
- Establishments primarily engaged in operating Indian tribal or Alaska Native courts are classified in Industry 921150, American Indian and Alaska Native Tribal Governments.

92212 Police Protection ᵁˢ
See industry description for 922120 below.

922120 Police Protection ᵁˢ
This industry comprises government establishments primarily engaged in criminal and civil law enforcement, police, traffic safety, and other activities related to the enforcement of the law and preservation of order. Combined police and fire departments are included in this industry.

- Government establishments primarily engaged in prosecution are classified in Industry 922130, Legal Counsel and Prosecution;
- Government establishments primarily engaged in collection of law enforcement statistics are classified in Industry 922190, Other Justice, Public Order, and Safety Activities;
- Government establishments primarily engaged in providing police service for the military or National Guard are classified in Industry 928110, National Security;
- Government establishments primarily engaged in providing police service for tribal governments are classified in Industry 921150, American Indian and Alaska Native Tribal Governments;
- Government establishments primarily engaged in enforcing immigration laws are classified in Industry 928120, International Affairs;
- Sheriffs' offices conducting court functions only are classified in Industry 922110, Courts; and
- Private establishments primarily engaged in providing security and investigation services are classified in Industry 56161, Investigation, Guard, and Armored Car Services.

92213 Legal Counsel and Prosecution ᵁˢ
See industry description for 922130 below.

922130 Legal Counsel and Prosecution ᵁˢ
This industry comprises government establishments primarily engaged in providing legal counsel or prosecution services for the government.

- Government establishments primarily engaged in collecting criminal justice statistics are classified in Industry 922190, Other Justice, Public Order, and Safety Activities.

92214 Correctional Institutions ᵁˢ
See industry description for 922140 below.

Sector **92**

Public Administration

■ = Cross-References

US—United States industry only. CAN—United States and Canadian industries are comparable. When neither US nor CAN appears, Canadian, Mexican, and United States industries are comparable.

www.harrisinfo.com

619

922140 Correctional Institutions ᵁˢ

This industry comprises government establishments primarily engaged in managing and operating correctional institutions. The facility is generally designed for the confinement, correction, and rehabilitation of adult and/or juvenile offenders sentenced by a court.

- Government establishments primarily engaged in operating half-way houses for ex-criminal offenders and delinquent youths are classified in Industry 623990, Other Residential Care Facilities; and
- Establishments primarily engaged in managing or operating correctional facilities owned by others are classified in Industry 561210, Facilities Support Services.

92215 Parole Offices and Probation Offices ᵁˢ

See industry description for 922150 below.

922150 Parole Offices and Probation Offices ᵁˢ

This industry comprises government establishments primarily engaged in judicially administering probation offices, parole offices and boards, and pardon boards.

- Government establishments primarily engaged in providing probation, parole, and pardon activities as an integral part of a central administrative corrections' office are classified in Industry 922140, Correctional Institutions.

92216 Fire Protection ᵁˢ

See industry description for 922160 below.

922160 Fire Protection ᵁˢ

This industry comprises government establishments primarily engaged in fire fighting and other related fire protection activities. Government establishments providing combined fire protection and ambulance or rescue services are classified in this industry.

- Forest fire fighting are classified in Industry 115310, Support Activities for Forestry;
- Providing combined police and fire protection services are classified in Industry 922120, Police Protection;
- Providing fire fighting services as a commercial activity are classified in Industry 561990, All Other Support Services; and
- Providing ambulance services without fire protection service are classified in Industry 621910, Ambulance Services.

92219 Other Justice, Public Order, and Safety Activities ᵁˢ

See industry description for 922190 below.

922190 Other Justice, Public Order, and Safety Activities ᵁˢ

This industry comprises government establishments primarily engaged in public order and safety (except courts, police protection, legal counsel and prosecution, correctional institutions, parole offices, probation offices, pardon boards, and fire protection). These establishments include the general administration of public order and safety programs. Government establishments responsible for the collection of statistics on public safety are included in this industry.

- Serving as civilian courts of law (except Indian tribal and Alaska Native) are classified in Industry 922110, Courts;
- Criminal and civil law enforcement, police, traffic safety and similar activities related to the enforcement of law are classified in Industry 922120, Police Protection;
- Providing legal counsel to or prosecution services for their governments are classified in Industry 922130, Legal Counsel and Prosecution;
- The confinement, correction, and rehabilitation of adult and juvenile offenders sentenced by a court are classified in Industry 922140, Correctional Institutions;
- Judicially administering probation offices, parole offices and boards, and pardon boards are classified in Industry 922150, Parole Offices and Probation Offices; and
- Fire fighting and other related fire protection activities are classified in Industry 922160, Fire Protection.

➤923 ADMINISTRATION OF HUMAN RESOURCE PROGRAMS ᵁˢ

The Administration of Human Resources Programs subsector groups government establishments primarily engaged in the administration of human resource programs.

9231 Administration of Human Resource Programs ᵁˢ

92311 Administration of Education Programs ᵁˢ

See industry description for 923110 below.

Sector **92**

Public Administration

■ = Cross-References

US—United States industry only. CAN—United States and Canadian industries are comparable. When neither US nor CAN appears, Canadian, Mexican, and United States industries are comparable.

620

Harris InfoSource

923110 Administration of Education Programs ᵁˢ

This industry comprises government establishments primarily engaged in the central coordination, planning, supervision and administration of funds, policies, intergovernmental activities, statistical reports and data collection, and centralized programs for educational administration. Government scholarship programs are included in this industry.

- Schools and local school boards are classified in Subsector 611, Educational Services.

92312 Administration of Public Health Programs ᵁˢ

See industry description for 923120 below.

923120 Administration of Public Health Programs ᵁˢ

This industry comprises government establishments primarily engaged in the planning, administration, and coordination of public health programs and services, including environmental health activities, mental health, categorical health programs, health statistics, and immunization services. Government establishments primarily engaged in conducting public health-related inspections are included in this industry.

- Operating hospitals (i.e., government or military) are classified in Subsector 622, Hospitals;
- Providing health care in a clinical setting (i.e., military or government clinics) are classified in Subsector 621, Ambulatory Health Care Services; and
- Inspecting food, plants, animals, and other agriculture products are classified in Industry 926140, Regulation of Agricultural Marketing and Commodities.

92313 Administration of Human Resource Programs (except Education, Public Health, and Veterans' Affairs Programs)ᵁˢ

See industry description for 923130 below.

923130 Administration of Human Resource Programs (except Education, Public Health, and Veterans' Affairs Programs)ᵁˢ

This industry comprises government establishments primarily engaged in the planning, administration, and coordination of programs for public assistance, social work, and welfare activities. The administration of Social Security, disability insurance, Medicare, unemployment insurance, and workers' compensation programs are included in this industry.

- Administering veterans' programs are classified in Industry 923140, Administration of Veterans' Affairs;
- Operating state employment job service offices are classified in Industry 561310, Employment Placement Agencies; and
- Operating programs for public assistance, social work, and welfare are classified in Subsector 624, Social Assistance.

92314 Administration of Veterans' Affairs ᵁˢ

See industry description for 923140 below.

923140 Administration of Veterans' Affairs ᵁˢ

This industry comprises government establishments primarily engaged in the administration of programs of assistance, training, counseling, and other services to veterans and their dependents, heirs or survivors. Included in this industry are Veterans' Affairs offices that maintain liaison and coordinate activities with other service organizations and governmental agencies.

- Government establishments operating veterans' hospitals are classified in Subsector 622, Hospitals;
- providing veterans' insurance are classified in Subsector 524, Insurance Carriers and Related Activities; and
- Establishments operating civic and social organizations for veterans are classified in Industry 813410, Civic and Social Organizations.

➧924 ADMINISTRATION OF ENVIRONMENTAL QUALITY PROGRAMS ᵁˢ

The Administration of Environmental Quality Programs subsector groups government establishments primarily engaged in the administration of environmental quality.

9241 Administration of Environmental Quality Programs ᵁˢ

92411 Administration of Air and Water Resource and Solid Waste Management Programs ᵁˢ

See industry description for 924110 below.

Sector 92

Public Administration

■ = Cross-References

US—United States industry only. CAN—United States and Canadian industries are comparable. When neither US nor CAN appears, Canadian, Mexican, and United States industries are comparable.

924110 Administration of Air and Water Resource and Solid Waste Management Programs US

This industry comprises government establishments primarily engaged in one or more of the following: (1) the administration, regulation, and enforcement of air and water resource programs; (2) the administration and regulation of solid waste management programs; (3) the administration and regulation of water and air pollution control and prevention programs; (4) the administration and regulation of flood control programs; (5) the administration and regulation of drainage development and water resource consumption programs; (6) the administration and regulation of toxic waste removal and cleanup programs; and (7) coordination of these activities at intergovernmental levels.

- Operating water and irrigation systems are classified in Industry 221310, Water Supply and Irrigation Systems;
- Administering sanitation districts are classified in Industry 926130, Regulation and Administration of Communications, Electric, Gas, and Other Utilities;
- Operating sewage treatment facilities are classified in Industry 221320, Sewage Treatment Facilities; and
- Providing waste collection, treatment, disposal, and/or remediation are classified in Subsector 562, Waste Management and Remediation Services.

92412 Administration of Conservation Programs US

See industry description for 924120 below.

924120 Administration of Conservation Programs US

This industry comprises government establishments primarily engaged in the administration, regulation, supervision and control of land use, including recreational areas; conservation and preservation of natural resources; erosion control; geological survey program administration; weather forecasting program administration; and the administration and protection of publicly and privately owned forest lands. Government establishments responsible for planning, management, regulation and conservation of game, fish, and wildlife populations, including wildlife management areas and field stations; and other administrative matters relating to the protection of fish, game, and wildlife are included in this industry.

- Operating parks are classified in Industry 712190, Nature Parks and Other Similar Institutions;
- Operating forest property are classified in Subsector 113, Forestry and Logging;
- Geophysical surveying and/or mapping are classified in Industry 541360, Geophysical Surveying and Mapping Services;
- Surveying and/or mapping (except geophysical) are classified in Industry 541370, Surveying and Mapping (except Geophysical) Services;
- Weather forecasting are classified in Industry 541990, All Other Professional, Scientific and Technical Services;
- Operating fish and game preserves are classified in Industry 712130, Zoos and Botanical Gardens; and
- Serving as urban planning commissions are classified in Industry 925120, Administration of Urban Planning and Community and Rural Development.

➤925 ADMINISTRATION OF HOUSING PROGRAMS, URBAN PLANNING, AND COMMUNITY DEVELOPMENT US

The Administration of Housing Programs, Urban Planning, and Community Development subsector groups government establishments primarily engaged in the administration of housing, urban planning, and community development.

9251 Administration of Housing Programs, Urban Planning, and Community Development US

92511 Administration of Housing Programs US

See industry description for 925110 below.

925110 Administration of Housing Programs US

This industry comprises government establishments primarily engaged in the administration and planning of housing programs.

- Operating government rental housing are classified in Subsector 531, Real Estate;
- Conducting building inspections and enforcing building codes and standards are classified in Industry 926150, Regulation, Licensing, and Inspection of Miscellaneous Commercial Sectors; and
- Buying, pooling, and repackaging mortgages or home loans for sale to others on the secondary market are classified in U.S. Industry 522294, Secondary Market Financing.

■ = Cross-References

Sector 92
Public Administration

US—United States industry only. CAN—United States and Canadian industries are comparable. When neither US nor CAN appears, Canadian, Mexican, and United States industries are comparable.

622

Harris InfoSource

92512 Administration of Urban Planning and Community and Rural Development ^{US}
See industry description for 925120 below.

925120 Administration of Urban Planning and Community and Rural Development ^{US}
This industry comprises government establishments primarily engaged in the administration and planning of the development of urban and rural areas. Included in this industry are government zoning boards and commissions.

➡926 ADMINISTRATION OF ECONOMIC PROGRAMS ^{US}
This subsector comprises government establishments primarily engaged in the administration of economic programs.

9261 Administration of Economic Programs ^{US}

92611 Administration of General Economic Programs ^{US}
See industry description for 926110 below.

926110 Administration of General Economic Programs ^{US}
This industry comprises government establishments primarily engaged in the administration, promotion and development of economic resources, including business, industry, and tourism. Included in this industry are government establishments responsible for the development of general statistical data and analysis and promotion of the general economic well being of the governed area.

92612 Regulation and Administration of Transportation Programs ^{US}
See industry description for 926120 below.

926120 Regulation and Administration of Transportation Programs ^{US}
This industry comprises government establishments primarily engaged in the administration, regulation, licensing, planning, inspection, and investigation of transportation services and facilities. Included in this industry are government establishments responsible for motor vehicle and operator licensing, the Coast Guard (except the Coast Guard Academy), and parking authorities.

- Operating airports, railroads, depots, ports, toll roads and bridges, and other transportation facilities are classified in Sector 48-49, Transportation and Warehousing;
- Operating parking lots and parking garages are classified in Industry 812930, Parking Lots and Garages;
- Operating automobile safety inspection and emission testing facilities are classified in Industry Group 8111, Automotive Repair and Maintenance;
- Building and/or maintaining roads and highways are classified in Industry 234110, Highway and Street Construction;
- Providing air traffic control services are classified in U.S. Industry 488111, Air Traffic Control; and
- Operating weigh stations are classified in Industry 488490, Other Support Activities for Road Transportation.

92613 Regulation and Administration of Communications, Electric, Gas, and Other Utilities ^{US}
See industry description for 926130 below.

926130 Regulation and Administration of Communications, Electric, Gas, and Other Utilities ^{US}
This industry comprises government establishments primarily engaged in the administration, regulation, licensing and inspection of utilities, such as communications, electric power (including fossil, nuclear, solar, water, and wind), gas and water supply, and sewerage..

- Government establishments primarily engaged in operating utilities are classified in Subsector 221, Utilities.

92614 Regulation of Agricultural Marketing and Commodities ^{US}
See industry description for 926140 below.

926140 Regulation of Agricultural Marketing and Commodities ^{US}
This industry comprises government establishments primarily engaged in the planning, administration, and coordination of agricultural programs for production, marketing, and utilization, including

Sector **92**
Public Administration

■ = Cross-References

US—United States industry only. CAN—United States and Canadian industries are comparable. When neither US nor CAN appears, Canadian, Mexican, and United States industries are comparable.

www.harrisinfo.com 623

educational and promotional activities. Included in this industry are government establishments responsible for regulating and controlling the grading and inspection of food, plants, animals, and other agricultural products.

- Administering programs for developing economic data about agricultural and trade in agricultural products are classified in Industry 926110, Administration of General Economic Programs;
- Administering programs for the conservation of natural resources are classified in Industry Group 9241, Administration of Environmental Quality Programs; and
- Administering food stamp programs are classified in Industry 923130, Administration Human Resource Programs (except Education, Public Health, and Veterans' Affairs Programs).

92615 Regulation, Licensing, and Inspection of Miscellaneous Commercial Sectors ^{US}
See industry description for 926150 below.

926150 Regulation, Licensing, and Inspection of Miscellaneous Commercial Sectors ^{US}
This industry comprises government establishments primarily engaged in the regulation, licensing, and inspection of commercial sectors, such as retail trade, professional occupations, manufacturing, mining, construction and services. Included in this industry are government establishments maintaining physical standards, regulating hazardous conditions not elsewhere classified, and enforcing alcoholic beverage control regulations.

- Regulating, administering, and inspecting transportation services and facilities are classified in Industry 926120, Regulation and Administration of Transportation Programs; and
- Regulating, administering, and inspecting communications, electric, gas, and other utilities are classified in Industry 926130, Regulation and Administration of Communications, Electric, Gas, and Other Utilities.

➡️927 SPACE RESEARCH AND TECHNOLOGY ^{US}
This subsector group comprises government establishments that conduct space research.

9271 Space Research and Technology ^{US}

92711 Space Research and Technology ^{US}
See industry description for 927110 below.

927110 Space Research and Technology ^{US}
This industry comprises government establishments primarily engaged in the administration and operations of space flights, space research, and space exploration. Included in this industry are government establishments operating space flight centers.

- Private establishments primarily engaged in providing space freight transportation are classified in U.S. Industry 481212, Nonscheduled Chartered Freight Air Transportation;
- Government establishments primarily engaged in manufacturing aerospace vehicles and parts are classified in Industry 33641, Aerospace Product and Parts Manufacturing; and
- Government establishments primarily engaged in manufacturing space satellites are classified in Industry 334220, Radio and Television Broadcasting and Wireless Communications Equipment Manufacturing.

➡️928 NATIONAL SECURITY AND INTERNATIONAL AFFAIRS ^{US}
This subsector comprises government establishments primarily engaged in national security and international affairs.

9281 National Security and International Affairs ^{US}

92811 National Security ^{US}
See industry description for 928110 below.

928110 National Security ^{US}
This industry comprises government establishments of the Armed Forces, including the National Guard, primarily engaged in national security and related activities.

- Operating military service academies are classified in Industry 611310, Colleges, Universities, and Professional Schools; and
- Regulating and administering water transportation, such as the U.S. Coast Guard and the Merchant Marine, are classified in Industry 926120, Regulation and Administration of Transportation Programs.

Sector **92**
Public Administration

■ = Cross-References

US—United States industry only. CAN—United States and Canadian industries are comparable. When neither US nor CAN appears, Canadian, Mexican, and United States industries are comparable.

92812 International Affairs ᵁˢ
See industry description for 928120 below.

928120 International Affairs ᵁˢ
This industry comprises establishments of U.S. and foreign governments primarily engaged in international affairs and programs relating to other nations and peoples.

- Private sector trade associations and councils are classified in Industry 813910, Business Associations; and
- Government establishments administering international trade, such as trade commissions and councils are classified in Industry 926110, Administration of General Economic Programs.

Sector 92
Public Administration

■ = Cross-References

US—United States industry only. CAN—United States and Canadian industries are comparable. When neither US nor CAN appears, Canadian, Mexican, and United States industries are comparable.

www.harrisinfo.com

625

NAICS United States Structure

Sector	Name	Sub-sectors	Industry groups	NAICS 5-digit industries	U.S. 6-digit industries	TOTAL U.S. industries	New industries
11	Agriculture, Forestry, Fishing and, Hunting	5	19	42	32	64	20
21	Mining	3	5	10	28	29	—
22	Utilities	1	3	6	6	10	6
23	Construction	3	14	28	—	28	3
31–33	Manufacturing	21	84	184	408	474	79
42	Wholesale Trade	2	18	69	—	69	—
44–45	Retail Trade	12	27	61	18	72	17
48-49	Transportation and Warehousing	11	29	42	25	57	28
51	Information	4	9	28	12	34	20
52	Finance and Insurance	5	11	32	15	42	23
53	Real Estate and Rental and Leasing	3	8	19	9	24	15
54	Professional, Scientific, and Technical Services	1	9	35	17	47	28
55	Management of Companies and Enterprises	1	1	1	3	3	1
56	Administrative and Support and Waste Management and Remediation Services	2	11	29	23	43	29
61	Educational Services	1	7	12	7	17	12
62	Health Care and Social Assistance	4	18	30	16	39	27
71	Arts, Entertainment, and Recreation	3	9	23	3	25	19
72	Accommodation and Food Services	2	7	11	7	15	10
81	Other Services (except Public Administration)	4	14	30	30	49	19
92	Public Administration	8	8	29	—	29	2
	TOTAL	96	311	721	659	1170	358

To learn more about the changes by sector go to pages 15-18.

Sector **92**

Public Administration

HOW TO USE THIS SECTION:

This section shows you all NAICS codes, alphabetized by the first word of their six-digit national industry description. You'll find the layout of this section to be similar to the way your phonebook is set up, with the first word of the page and the last word of the page listed in the upper margin.

Once you have found the code for the industry relevant to your needs, refer to the NAICS Titles & Descriptions of Industries section which begins on page 273 for in-depth NAICS code descriptions.

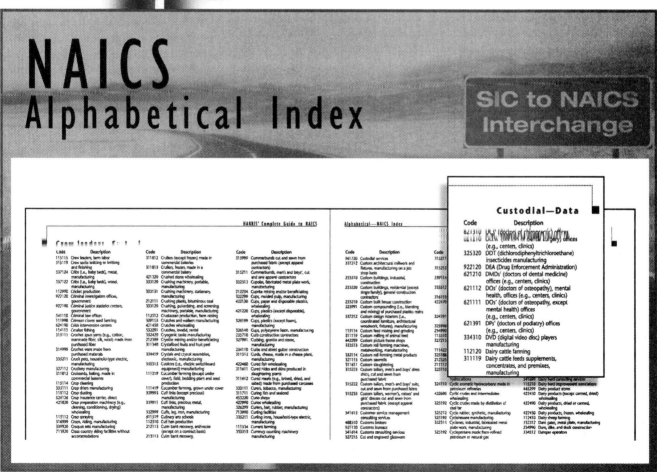

NAICS
Alphabetical Index

SIC to NAICS Interchange

Code	Description
513112	AM radio stations
334119	ATMs (automatic teller machines) manufacturing
311611	Abattoirs
621410	Abortion clinics
334519	Abrasion testing machines manufacturing
339114	Abrasive points, wheels, and disks, dental, manufacturing
327910	Abrasive products manufacturing
212322	Abrasive sand quarrying and/or beneficiating
212399	Abrasive stones (e.g., emery, grindstones, hones, pumice) mining and/or beneficiating
421840	Abrasives wholesaling
212399	Abrasives, natural, mining and/or beneficiating
322121	Absorbent paper stock manufacturing
332420	Absorbers, gas, manufacturing
334513	Absorption analyzers, industrial process type (e.g., infrared), manufacturing
234120	Abutment construction
611691	Academic tutoring services
611310	Academies, college or university
611110	Academies, elementary or secondary
611210	Academies, junior college
611310	Academies, military service (college)
611620	Academies, riding instruction
334511	Acceleration indicators and systems components, aerospace type, manufacturing
325199	Accelerators (i.e., basic synthetic chemical) manufacturing
334519	Accelerometers (except aerospace type) manufacturing
813319	Accident prevention associations
524130	Accidental and health reinsurance carriers
524113	Accidental death and dismemberment insurance carriers, direct
524113	Accidental death and dismemberment insurance underwriting, direct
339992	Accordions and parts manufacturing
561440	Account collection services
541219	Accountants' (except CPAs) offices
541219	Accountants' (except CPAs) private practices
541211	Accountants' (i.e., CPAs) offices, certified public
541211	Accountants' (i.e., CPAs) private practices, certified public
813920	Accountants' associations
541211	Accounting (i.e., CPAs) services, certified public
421420	Accounting machines wholesaling
541219	Accounting services (except CPAs)
332420	Accumulators, industrial pressure vessels, manufacturing
325211	Acetal resins manufacturing
325199	Acetaldehyde manufacturing
325221	Acetate fibers and filaments manufacturing
325191	Acetate of lime, natural, made by distillation of wood
313111	Acetate spun yarns made from purchased fiber
325199	Acetates, not specified elsewhere by process, manufacturing
325199	Acetic acid manufacturing
325199	Acetic anhydride manufacturing
325199	Acetin manufacturing
325191	Acetone, natural, manufacturing
325199	Acetone, synthetic, manufacturing

Code	Description
332420	Acetylene cylinders manufacturing
325120	Acetylene manufacturing
325411	Acetylsalicylic acid manufacturing
325132	Acid dyes, synthetic organic, manufacturing
325199	Acid esters, not specified elsewhere by process, manufacturing
324110	Acid oils made in petroleum refineries
562211	Acid waste disposal facilities
562211	Acid waste treatment facilities
334513	Acidity (i.e., pH) instruments, industrial process type, manufacturing
334516	Acidity (i.e., pH) measuring equipment, laboratory analysis-type, manufacturing
213112	Acidizing oil and gas field wells on a contract basis
311511	Acidophilus milk manufacturing
422690	Acids wholesaling
325199	Acids, organic, not specified elsewhere by process, manufacturing
111219	Acorn squash farming, field, bedding plant and seed production
541330	Acoustical engineering consulting services
235420	Acoustical paneling construction contractors
332323	Acoustical suspension systems, metal, manufacturing
541330	Acoustical system engineering design services
541380	Acoustics testing laboratories or services
325199	Acrolein manufacturing
325212	Acrylate rubber manufacturing
325212	Acrylate-butadiene rubber manufacturing
313112	Acrylic and modacrylic filament yarn throwing, twisting, texturizing, or winding purchased yarn
325222	Acrylic fibers and filaments manufacturing
326113	Acrylic film and unlaminated sheet (except packaging) manufacturing
325211	Acrylic resins manufacturing
325212	Acrylic rubber manufacturing
313111	Acrylic spun yarns made from purchased fiber
325222	Acrylonitrile fibers and filaments manufacturing
325199	Acrylonitrile manufacturing
325211	Acrylonitrile-butadiene-styrene (ABS) resins manufacturing
334519	Actinometers, meteorological, manufacturing
339931	Action figures manufacturing
325998	Activated carbon or charcoal manufacturing
624120	Activity centers for disabled persons, the elderly, and persons diagnosed with mental retardation
711510	Actors, independent
711510	Actresses, independent
541612	Actuarial consulting services
333995	Actuators, fluid power, manufacturing
621111	Acupuncturists' (MDs or DOs) offices (e.g., centers, clinics)
621399	Acupuncturists' (except MDs or DOs) offices (e.g., centers, clinics)
325110	Acyclic hydrocarbons (e.g., butene, ethylene, propene) (except acetylene) made from refined petroleum or liquid hydrocarbons
332993	Adapters, bombcluster, manufacturing
333313	Adding machines manufacturing

Code	Description
325998	Additive preparations for gasoline (e.g., antiknock preparations, detergents, gum inhibitors) manufacturing
561499	Address bar coding services
511140	Address list compilers
511140	Address list publishers
511140	Address list publishers and printing combined
511140	Address list publishing (i.e., establishments known as publishers)
323112	Address lists flexographic printing without publishing
323111	Address lists gravure printing without publishing
323110	Address lists lithographic (offset) printing without publishing
323119	Address lists printing (except flexographic, gravure, lithographic, screen) without publishing
323113	Address lists screen printing without publishing
421420	Addressing machines wholesaling
322222	Adhesive tape (except medical) made from purchased materials
339113	Adhesive tape, medical, manufacturing
325520	Adhesives (except asphalt, dental, gypsum base) manufacturing
422690	Adhesives and sealants wholesaling
325199	Adipic acid esters or amines manufacturing
325199	Adipic acid manufacturing
325199	Adiponitrile manufacturing
233320	Administration building construction
922110	Administrative courts
541611	Administrative management consulting services
561110	Administrative management services
523991	Administrators of private estates
327123	Adobe bricks manufacturing
624110	Adoption agencies
624110	Adoption services, child
325411	Adrenal derivatives, uncompounded, manufacturing
325412	Adrenal medicinal preparations manufacturing
611691	Adult literacy instruction
541810	Advertising agencies
541810	Advertising agency consulting services
541870	Advertising material (e.g., coupons, flyers, samples) direct distribution services
541860	Advertising material preparation services for mailing or other direct distribution
323110	Advertising materials (e.g., coupons, flyers) lithographic (offset) printing without publishing
541840	Advertising media representatives (i.e., independent of media owners)
511120	Advertising periodical publishers
511120	Advertising periodical publishers and printing combined
511120	Advertising periodical publishing (i.e., establishments known as publishers)
541850	Advertising services, indoor or outdoor display
541890	Advertising specialty (e.g., keychain, magnet, pen) distribution services
541850	Advertising, aerial
921110	Advisory commissions, executive government
921120	Advisory commissions, legislative
487990	Aerial cable car, scenic and sightseeing, operation
333315	Aerial cameras manufacturing

Aerial dusting—Aircraft

Code	Description
115112	Aerial dusting or spraying (i.e., using specialized or dedicated aircraft)
541360	Aerial geophysical surveying services
541370	Aerial surveying (except geophysical) services
487990	Aerial tramway, scenic and sightseeing, operation
333923	Aerial work platforms manufacturing
713940	Aerobic dance and exercise centers
421860	Aeronautical equipment and supplies wholesaling
334511	Aeronautical systems and instruments manufacturing
325998	Aerosol can filling on a job order or contract basis
332431	Aerosol cans manufacturing
325998	Aerosol packaging services
332919	Aerosol valves manufacturing
325620	After-shave preparations manufacturing
332410	Aftercoolers (i.e., heat exchangers) manufacturing
325414	Agar culture media manufacturing
325411	Agar-agar grinding manufacturing
212399	Agate mining and/or beneficiating
111998	Agave farming
522293	Agencies of foreign banks (i.e., trade financing)
524210	Agencies, insurance
522310	Agencies, loan
531210	Agencies, real estate
531390	Agencies, real estate escrow
531390	Agents' offices, real estate escrow
711410	Agents, artists'
711410	Agents, authors'
711410	Agents, celebrities'
711410	Agents, entertainers'
812320	Agents, laundry and drycleaning
711410	Agents, modeling
711410	Agents, public figures'
531210	Agents, real estate
488510	Agents, shipping
711410	Agents, sports figures'
711410	Agents, talent
711410	Agents, theatrical talent
212210	Agglomerates, iron ore, beneficiating
333120	Aggregate spreaders manufacturing
325414	Aggressins (except in-vitro) manufacturing
551112	Agreement corporation (except international trade financing)
522293	Agreement corporations (i.e., international trade financing)
524126	Agricultural (i.e., crop, livestock) insurance carriers, direct
422910	Agricultural chemicals wholesaling
541690	Agricultural consulting services
926140	Agricultural cooperative extension program administration
522298	Agricultural credit institutions, making loans or extending credit (except real estate, sales financing)
711320	Agricultural fair managers without facilities
711320	Agricultural fair organizers without facilities
711320	Agricultural fair promoters without facilities
332212	Agricultural handtools (e.g., hay forks, hoes, rakes, spades), nonpowered, manufacturing
421820	Agricultural implements wholesaling
522298	Agricultural lending (except real estate, sales financing)
327410	Agricultural lime manufacturing

Code	Description
212312	Agricultural limestone mining and/or beneficiating
422910	Agricultural limestone wholesaling
532490	Agricultural machinery and equipment rental or leasing
811310	Agricultural machinery and equipment repair and maintenance services
421820	Agricultural machinery and equipment wholesaling
511120	Agricultural magazine and periodical publishers
511120	Agricultural magazine and periodical publishers and printing combined
511120	Agricultural magazine and periodical publishing (i.e., establishments known as publishers)
323112	Agricultural magazines and periodicals flexographic printing without publishing
323111	Agricultural magazines and periodicals gravure printing without publishing
323110	Agricultural magazines and periodicals lithographic (offset) printing without publishing
323119	Agricultural magazines and periodicals printing (except flexographic, gravure, lithographic, screen) without publishing
323113	Agricultural magazines and periodicals screen printing without publishing
926140	Agricultural marketing services government
926140	Agricultural pest and weed regulation, government
484220	Agricultural products trucking, local
531190	Agricultural property rental leasing
926140	Agriculture fair boards administration
115115	Agriculture production or harvesting crews
541710	Agriculture research and development laboratories or services
541690	Agrology consulting services
541690	Agronomy consulting services
624110	Aid to families with dependent children (AFDC)
928110	Air Force
621910	Air ambulance services
336399	Air bag assemblies manufacturing
336612	Air boat building
336340	Air brake systems and parts, automotive, truck, and bus, manufacturing
481212	Air cargo carriers (except air couriers), nonscheduled
481112	Air cargo carriers (except air couriers), scheduled
332439	Air cargo containers, metal, manufacturing
335313	Air circuit breakers manufacturing
481111	Air commuter carriers, scheduled
333912	Air compressors manufacturing
492110	Air courier services
332322	Air cowls, sheet metal, manufacturing
336399	Air filters, automotive, truck, and bus, manufacturing
334512	Air flow controllers (except valves), air-conditioning and refrigeration, manufacturing
313230	Air laid nonwoven fabrics manufacturing
481211	Air passenger carriers, nonscheduled
481111	Air passenger carriers, scheduled
421730	Air pollution control equipment and supplies wholesaling
335211	Air purification equipment, portable, manufacturing
333411	Air purification equipment, stationary, manufacturing

Code	Description
332420	Air receiver tanks, heavy gauge metal, manufacturing
333411	Air scrubbing systems manufacturing
711310	Air show managers with facilities
711320	Air show managers without facilities
711310	Air show organizers with facilities
711320	Air show organizers without facilities
711310	Air show promoters with facilities
711320	Air show promoters without facilities
235110	Air system balancing and testing contractors
481211	Air taxi services
334511	Air traffic control radar systems and equipment manufacturing
611519	Air traffic control schools
488111	Air traffic control services (except military)
928110	Air traffic control, military
333411	Air washers (i.e., air scrubbers) manufacturing
532210	Air-conditioner rental
811412	Air-conditioner, window, repair and maintenance services
336391	Air-conditioners, motor vehicle, manufacturing
421620	Air-conditioners, room, wholesaling
333415	Air-conditioners, unit (e.g., motor home, travel trailer, window), manufacturing
333415	Air-conditioning and warm air heating combination units manufacturing
333415	Air-conditioning compressors (except motor vehicle) manufacturing
333415	Air-conditioning condensers and condensing units manufacturing
333415	Air-conditioning equipment (except motor vehicle) manufacturing
421730	Air-conditioning equipment (except room units) wholesaling
235110	Air-conditioning installation contractors
221330	Air-conditioning supply
487210	Airboat (i.e., swamp buggy) operation
334511	Airborne navigational systems manufacturing
334220	Airborne radio communications equipment manufacturing
331491	Aircraft and automotive wire and cable (except aluminum, copper) made from purchased nonferrous metals (except aluminum copper) in wire drawing plants
331422	Aircraft and automotive wire or cable made from purchased copper in wire drawing plants
332995	Aircraft artillery manufacturing
336413	Aircraft assemblies, subassemblies, and parts (except engines) manufacturing
336413	Aircraft auxiliary parts (e.g., crop dusting, external fuel tanks, inflight refueling equipment) manufacturing
333999	Aircraft carrier catapults manufacturing
481219	Aircraft charter services (i.e., general purpose aircraft used for a variety of specialty air and flying services)
481211	Aircraft charter services, passenger
336413	Aircraft control surface assemblies manufacturing
336411	Aircraft conversions (i.e., major modifications to system)
441229	Aircraft dealers
336412	Aircraft engine and engine parts (except carburetors, pistons, piston rings, valves) manufacturing
333924	Aircraft engine cradles manufacturing

Code	Description
334519	Aircraft engine instruments manufacturing
336412	Aircraft engine overhauling
336412	Aircraft engine rebuilding
421860	Aircraft engines and parts wholesaling
421860	Aircraft equipment and supplies wholesaling
488190	Aircraft ferrying services
334511	Aircraft flight instruments (except engine instruments) manufacturing
336413	Aircraft fuselage wing tail and similar assemblies manufacturing
488119	Aircraft hangar rental
332510	Aircraft hardware, metal, manufacturing
488190	Aircraft inspection services
926120	Aircraft inspection, government
561720	Aircraft janitorial services
336321	Aircraft lighting fixtures manufacturing
333924	Aircraft loading hoists manufacturing
488190	Aircraft maintenance and repair services (except factory conversion, factory overhaul, factory rebuilding)
336411	Aircraft manufacturing
336411	Aircraft overhauling
488119	Aircraft parking service
336413	Aircraft propellers and parts manufacturing
336411	Aircraft rebuilding (i.e., restoration to original design specifications)
532411	Aircraft rental and leasing
336360	Aircraft seats manufacturing
488190	Aircraft testing services
314999	Aircraft tie down strap assemblies (except leather) manufacturing
326211	Aircraft tire manufacturing
336412	Aircraft turbines manufacturing
811420	Aircraft upholstery repair
421860	Aircraft wholesaling
333412	Aircurtains manufacturing
336413	Airframe assemblies (except for guided missiles) manufacturing
336419	Airframe assemblies for guided missiles manufacturing
334511	Airframe equipment instruments manufacturing
325612	Airfreshners manufacturing
722310	Airline food service contractors
561599	Airline reservation services
561599	Airline ticket offices
332313	Airlocks, fabricated metal plate work, manufacturing
481112	Airmail carriers, scheduled
532411	Airplane rental or leasing
488119	Airport baggage handling services
488119	Airport cargo handling services
531190	Airport leasing, not operating airport, rental or leasing
335311	Airport lighting transformers manufacturing
485999	Airport limousine services (i.e., shuttle)
488119	Airport operators (e.g., civil, international, national)
234110	Airport runway construction
488119	Airport runway maintenance services
485999	Airport shuttle services
488119	Airports, civil, operation and maintenance
334511	Airspeed instruments (aeronautical) manufacturing
212399	Alabaster mining and/or beneficiating
421610	Alarm apparatus, electric, wholesaling
334518	Alarm clocks manufacturing
561621	Alarm system monitoring services

Code	Description
334290	Alarm systems and equipment manufacturing
561621	Alarm systems sales combined with installation, maintenance, or monitoring services
323118	Albums (e.g., photo, scrap) manufacturing
422120	Albums, photo, wholesaling
422690	Alcohol, industrial, wholesaling
922120	Alcohol, tobacco, and firearms control
926150	Alcoholic beverage control boards
492210	Alcoholic beverage delivery service
722410	Alcoholic beverage drinking places
312140	Alcoholic beverages (except brandy) distilling
422810	Alcoholic beverages (except distilled spirits, wine) wholesaling
312130	Alcoholic beverages, brandy, distilling
422820	Alcoholic beverages, wine and distilled spirits wholesaling
624190	Alcoholism and drug addiction self-help organizations
624190	Alcoholism counseling (except medical treatment), nonresidential
623220	Alcoholism rehabilitation facilities (except licensed hospitals), residential
622210	Alcoholism rehabilitation hospitals
624190	Alcoholism self-help organizations
621420	Alcoholism treatment centers and clinics (except hospitals), outpatient
325199	Aldehydes manufacturing
312120	Ale brewing
422810	Ale wholesaling
111940	Alfalfa hay farming
311119	Alfalfa meal, dehydrated, manufacturing
311119	Alfalfa prepared as feed for animals
111998	Alfalfa seed farming
111419	Alfalfa sprout farming, grown under cover
422910	Alfalfa wholesaling
311119	Alfalfa, cubed, manufacturing
111998	Algae farming
325199	Alginates (e.g., calcium, potassium, sodium) manufacturing
325199	Alginic acid manufacturing
334519	Alidades, surveying, manufacturing
333319	Alignment equipment, motor vehicle, manufacturing
325110	Aliphatic (e.g., hydrocarbons) (except acetylene) made from refined petroleum or liquid hydrocarbons
324110	Aliphatic chemicals (i.e., acyclic) made in petroleum refineries
325181	Alkalies manufacturing
422690	Alkalies wholesaling
335912	Alkaline cell primary batteries manufacturing
335911	Alkaline cell storage batteries (i.e., nickel-cadmium, nickel-iron, silver oxide-zinc) manufacturing
335912	Alkaline manganese primary batteries manufacturing
325211	Alkyd resins manufacturing
324110	Alkylates made in petroleum refineries
421110	All terrain vehicles (ATV's) wholesaling
336999	All terrain vehicles (ATV's), wheeled or tracked, manufacturing
441221	All-terrain vehicle (ATV) dealers
325414	Allergenic extracts (except diagnostic substances) manufacturing
325414	Allergens manufacturing
621111	Allergists' offices (e.g., centers, clinics)
234110	Alley construction
112519	Alligator production, farm raising

Code	Description
331513	Alloy steel castings (except investment), unfinished, manufacturing
331314	Alloying purchased aluminum metals
331423	Alloying purchased copper
331423	Alloying purchased copper metals
331492	Alloying purchased nonferrous metals (except aluminum, copper)
325211	Allyl resins manufacturing
323121	Almanac binding without printing
511130	Almanac publishers
511130	Almanac publishers and printing combined
511130	Almanac publishing (i.e., establishments known as publishers)
323117	Almanacs printing and binding without publishing
323117	Almanacs printing without publishing
111335	Almond farming
115114	Almond hulling and shelling
311999	Almond pastes manufacturing
111998	Aloe farming
112990	Alpaca production
721110	Alpine skiing facilities with accommodations (i.e., ski resort)
713920	Alpine skiing facilities without accommodations
334515	Alternator and generator testers manufacturing
336322	Alternators and generators for internal combustion engines manufacturing
334511	Altimeters, aeronautical, manufacturing
212391	Alum, natural, mining and/or beneficiating
327125	Alumina fused refractories manufacturing
327113	Alumina porcelain insulators manufacturing
331311	Alumina refining
327125	Aluminous refractory cement manufacturing
331312	Aluminum alloys made from bauxite or alumina producing primary aluminum and manufacturing
331314	Aluminum alloys made from scrap or dross
331316	Aluminum bar made by extruding purchased aluminum
331316	Aluminum bar made in integrated secondary smelting and extruding mills
331314	Aluminum billet made from purchased aluminum
331314	Aluminum billet made in integrated secondary smelting and rolling mills
332431	Aluminum cans manufacturing
331524	Aluminum castings (except die-castings), unfinished, manufacturing
325188	Aluminum chloride manufacturing
332812	Aluminum coating of metal products for the trade
325188	Aluminum compounds, not specified elsewhere by process, manufacturing
331521	Aluminum die-casting foundries
331521	Aluminum die-castings, unfinished, manufacturing
331314	Aluminum extrusion ingot (i.e., billet), secondary
331314	Aluminum flakes made from purchased aluminum
331315	Aluminum foil made by flat rolling purchased aluminum
331315	Aluminum foil made in integrated secondary smelting and flat rolling mills
332112	Aluminum forgings made from purchased metals, unfinished

Aluminum foundries—Animal feeds

Code	Description
331524	Aluminum foundries (except die-casting)
332999	Aluminum freezer foil not made in rolling mills
325188	Aluminum hydroxide (i.e., alumina trihydrate) manufacturing
331312	Aluminum ingot and other primary aluminum production shapes made from bauxite or alumina
331314	Aluminum ingot made from purchased aluminum
331314	Aluminum ingot, secondary smelting of aluminum and manufacturing
331314	Aluminum ingot, secondary, manufacturing
332999	Aluminum ladders manufacturing
327910	Aluminum oxide (fused) abrasives manufacturing
331311	Aluminum oxide refining
331316	Aluminum pipe made by extruding purchased aluminum
331316	Aluminum pipe made in integrated secondary smelting and extruding mills
233310	Aluminum plant construction, general construction contractors
331315	Aluminum plate made by continuous casting purchased aluminum
331315	Aluminum plate made by flat rolling purchased aluminum
331315	Aluminum plate made in integrated secondary smelting and continuous casting mills
331315	Aluminum plate made in integrated secondary smelting and flat rolling mills
331312	Aluminum producing from alumina
331314	Aluminum recovering from scrap and making ingot and billet (except by rolling)
331316	Aluminum rod made by extruding purchased aluminum
331316	Aluminum rod made in integrated secondary smelting and extruding mills
331312	Aluminum shapes (e.g., bar, ingot, rod, sheet) made by producing primary aluminum and manufacturing
331315	Aluminum sheet made by flat rolling purchased aluminum
331315	Aluminum sheet made in integrated secondary smelting and flat rolling mills
331314	Aluminum smelting, secondary, and making ingot and billet (except by rolling)
325188	Aluminum sulfate manufacturing
331316	Aluminum tube blooms made by extruding purchased aluminum
331316	Aluminum tube blooms made in integrated secondary smelting and extruding mills
331316	Aluminum tube made by drawing or extruding purchased aluminum
331316	Aluminum tube made in integrated secondary smelting and drawing plants
331316	Aluminum tube made in integrated secondary smelting and extruding mills
331315	Aluminum welded tube made by flat rolling purchased aluminum
331315	Aluminum welded tube made in integrated secondary smelting and flat rolling mills
813410	Alumni associations
813410	Alumni clubs
325188	Alums (e.g., aluminum ammonium sulfate, aluminum potassium sulfate) manufacturing
212393	Alunite mining and/or beneficiating
333131	Amalgamators (i.e., metallurgical and mining machinery) manufacturing
339114	Amalgams, dental, manufacturing
111998	Amaranth farming
713990	Amateur sports teams, recreational
325920	Amatols manufacturing
212393	Amblygonite mining and/or beneficiating
922160	Ambulance and fire service combined
336213	Ambulance bodies manufacturing
621910	Ambulance services, air or ground
336211	Ambulances assembling on purchased chassis
421110	Ambulances wholesaling
621493	Ambulatory surgical centers and clinics, freestanding
921150	American Indian or Alaska Native tribal councils
921150	American Indian or Alaska Native tribal courts
921150	American Indian or Alaska Native, tribal chief's or chairman's office
212399	Amethyst mining and/or beneficiating
334516	Amino acid analyzers, laboratory-type, manufacturing
325211	Amino resins manufacturing
325211	Amino-aldehyde resins manufacturing
325192	Aminoanthraquinone manufacturing
325192	Aminoazobenzene manufacturing
325192	Aminoazotoluene manufacturing
325192	Aminophenol manufacturing
422690	Ammonia (except fertilizer material) wholesaling
325311	Ammonia, anhydrous and aqueous, manufacturing
422910	Ammonia, fertilizer material, wholesaling
325612	Ammonia, household-type, manufacturing
325188	Ammonium chloride manufacturing
325188	Ammonium compounds, not specified elsewhere by process, manufacturing
325188	Ammonium hydroxide manufacturing
325188	Ammonium molybdate manufacturing
325311	Ammonium nitrate manufacturing
325188	Ammonium perchlorate manufacturing
325312	Ammonium phosphates manufacturing
325311	Ammonium sulfate manufacturing
325188	Ammonium thiosulfate manufacturing
421990	Ammunition (except sporting) wholesaling
332993	Ammunition (i.e., more than 30 mm., more than 1.18 inch) manufacturing
332439	Ammunition boxes, metal, manufacturing
321920	Ammunition boxes, wood, manufacturing
332994	Ammunition carts (i.e., 30 mm or less, 1.18 inch or less) manufacturing
332995	Ammunition carts (i.e., more than 30 mm., more than 1.18 inch) manufacturing
332993	Ammunition loading and assembling plants
332992	Ammunition, small arms (i.e., 30 mm. or less, 1.18 inch or less), manufacturing
334515	Ampere-hour meters manufacturing
325411	Amphetamines, uncompounded, manufacturing
334310	Amplifiers (e.g., auto, home, musical instrument, public address) manufacturing
334220	Amplifiers, (e.g., RF power and IF), broadcast and studio equipment, manufacturing
335999	Amplifiers, magnetic, pulse, and maser, manufacturing
713120	Amusement arcades
233320	Amusement building construction
713990	Amusement device (except gambling) concession operators (i.e., supplying and servicing in others' facilities)
713120	Amusement device (except gambling) parlors, coin-operated
713120	Amusement devices (except gambling) operated in own facilities
339999	Amusement machines, coin-operated, manufacturing
421850	Amusement park equipment wholesaling
713110	Amusement parks (e.g., theme, water)
713990	Amusement ride concession operators (i.e., supplying and servicing in others' facilities)
325199	Amyl acetate manufacturing
325412	Analgesic preparations manufacturing
334111	Analog computers manufacturing
421490	Analytical instruments (e.g., chromatographic, photometers, spectrographs) wholesaling
334515	Analyzers for testing electrical characteristics manufacturing
334513	Analyzers, industrial process control type, manufacturing
235990	Anchored earth retention construction contractors
114111	Anchovy fishing
212325	Andalusite mining and/or beneficiating
332999	Andirons manufacturing
339112	Anesthesia apparatus manufacturing
621111	Anesthesiologists' offices (e.g., centers, clinics)
325412	Anesthetic preparations manufacturing
325411	Anesthetics, uncompounded, manufacturing
325412	Angiourographic diagnostic preparations manufacturing
333515	Angle rings (i.e., a machine tool accessory) manufacturing
332911	Angle valves, industrial-type, manufacturing
332999	Angle, irons metal, manufacturing
334511	Angle-of-attack instrumentation manufacturing
334511	Angle-of-yaw instrumentation manufacturing
112420	Angora goat farming
325311	Anhydrous ammonia manufacturing
311512	Anhydrous butterfat manufacturing
325222	Anidex fibers and filaments manufacturing
325192	Aniline manufacturing
112519	Animal aquaculture (except finfish, shellfish)
325182	Animal black manufacturing
813910	Animal breeders' associations
812220	Animal cemeteries
712130	Animal exhibits, live
311611	Animal fats (except poultry and small game) produced in slaughtering plants
311613	Animal fats rendering
311119	Animal feed mills (except dog and cat) manufacturing
311111	Animal feed mills, dog and cat, manufacturing
422910	Animal feeds (except pet food) wholesaling
311119	Animal feeds, prepared (except dog and cat), manufacturing

Code	Description
311111	Animal feeds, prepared, dog and cat, manufacturing
313112	Animal fiber yarn twisting or winding of purchased yarn
812910	Animal grooming services
422590	Animal hair wholesaling
541940	Animal hospitals
311613	Animal oil rendering
926140	Animal quarantine service, government
813312	Animal rights organizations
712130	Animal safari parks
115210	Animal semen banks
233320	Animal shelter/clinic construction
812910	Animal shelters
114210	Animal trapping, commercial
332999	Animal traps, metal (except wire), manufacturing
813312	Animal welfare associations or leagues
336999	Animal-drawn vehicles and parts manufacturing
711510	Animated cartoon artists, independent
512120	Animated cartoon distribution
512110	Animated cartoon production
512110	Animated cartoon production and distribution
325998	Anise oil manufacturing
315119	Anklets, sheer hosiery or socks, knitting or knitting and finishing
325191	Annato extract manufacturing
332811	Annealing metals for the trade
332420	Annealing vats manufacturing
711510	Announcers, independent radio and television
524113	Annuities underwriting
332991	Annular ball bearings manufacturing
334513	Annunciators, relay and solid-state types, industrial display, manufacturing
333298	Anodizing equipment manufacturing
332813	Anodizing metals and metal products for the trade
421620	Answering machines, telephone, wholesaling
561421	Answering services, telephone
325320	Ant poisons manufacturing
325412	Antacid preparations manufacturing
235990	Antenna installation construction contractors
421690	Antennas wholesaling
334220	Antennas, satellite, manufacturing
334220	Antennas, transmitting and receiving, manufacturing
325412	Anthelmintic preparations manufacturing
325192	Anthracene manufacturing
212113	Anthracite beneficiating (e.g., crushing, screening, washing, cleaning, sizing)
213113	Anthracite mine tunneling on a contract basis
212113	Anthracite mining and/or beneficiating
213113	Anthracite mining services on a contract basis
325132	Anthraquinone dyes manufacturing
332995	Antiaircraft artillery manufacturing
325412	Antibacterial preparations manufacturing
325412	Antibiotic preparations manufacturing
422210	Antibiotics wholesaling
325411	Antibiotics, uncompounded, manufacturing
325411	Anticholinergics, uncompounded, manufacturing
325411	Anticonvulsants, uncompounded, manufacturing
325412	Antidepressant preparations manufacturing

Code	Description
325411	Antidepressants, uncompounded, manufacturing
325998	Antifreeze preparations manufacturing
422690	Antifreeze wholesaling
325414	Antigens manufacturing
325412	Antihistamine preparations manufacturing
325131	Antimony based pigments manufacturing
212299	Antimony concentrates mining and/or beneficiating
212299	Antimony ores mining and/or beneficiating
325188	Antimony oxide (except pigments) manufacturing
331419	Antimony refining, primary
325412	Antineoplastic preparations manufacturing
325620	Antiperspirants, personal, manufacturing
813319	Antipoverty advocacy organizations
325412	Antipyretic preparations manufacturing
811121	Antique and classic automotive restoration
441120	Antique auto dealers
422920	Antique book wholesaling
811420	Antique furniture repair and restoration shops
421210	Antique furniture wholesaling
421220	Antique homefurnishing wholesaling
421220	Antique houseware wholesaling
421940	Antique jewelry wholesaling
453310	Antique shops
332913	Antiscald bath and shower valves manufacturing
325998	Antiscaling compounds manufacturing
325412	Antiseptic preparations manufacturing
422210	Antiseptics wholesaling
325414	Antiserums manufacturing
325412	Antispasmodic preparations manufacturing
332995	Antisubmarine projectors manufacturing
332995	Antitank rocket launchers manufacturing
325414	Antitoxins manufacturing
325414	Antivenoms manufacturing
531110	Apartment building rental or leasing
531110	Apartment hotel rental or leasing
531311	Apartment managers' offices
531110	Apartment rental or leasing
233220	Apartments (e.g., garden, high-rise) construction
212392	Apatite mining and/or beneficiating
212325	Aplite mining and/or beneficiating
446110	Apothecaries
331491	Apparatus wire and cord (except aluminum, copper) made from purchased nonferrous metals (except aluminum, copper) in wire drawing plants
331422	Apparatus wire or cord made from purchased copper in wire drawing plants
331319	Apparatus wire or cord made in aluminum wire drawing plants
448150	Apparel accessory stores
314999	Apparel fillings (e.g., cotton mill waste, kapok) manufacturing
315999	Apparel findings and trimmings cut and sewn from purchased fabric (except apparel contractors)
561910	Apparel folding and packaging services
812320	Apparel pressing services
448130	Apparel stores, children's and infants' clothing
448110	Apparel stores, men's and boys' clothing

Code	Description
453310	Apparel stores, used clothing
448120	Apparel stores, women's and girls' clothing
315211	Apparel trimmings and findings, men's and boys', cut and sew apparel contractors
315212	Apparel trimmings and findings, women's, girls', and infants', cut and sew apparel contractors
422310	Apparel trimmings wholesaling
313221	Apparel webbings manufacturing
315292	Apparel, fur (except apparel contractors), manufacturing
315211	Apparel, fur, men's and boys', cut and sew apparel contractors
315212	Apparel, fur, women's, girls', and infants', cut and sew apparel contractors
315211	Apparel, men's and boys', cut and sew apparel contractors
315212	Apparel, women's, girls', and infants', cut and sew contractors
111331	Apple orchards
312130	Applejack distilling
334512	Appliance controls manufacturing
335999	Appliance cords made from purchased insulated wire
332510	Appliance hardware, metal, manufacturing
334512	Appliance regulators (except switches) manufacturing
532210	Appliance rental
443111	Appliance stores, household-type
453310	Appliance stores, household-type, used
334518	Appliance timers manufacturing
811412	Appliance, household-type, repair and maintenance services without retailing new appliances
421720	Appliances, gas (except dryers, freezers, refrigerators), wholesaling
421620	Appliances, household-type (except gas ranges, gas water heaters), wholesaling
421450	Appliances, surgical, wholesaling
541511	Applications software programming services, custom computer
511210	Applications software, computer, packaged
321999	Applicators, wood, manufacturing
315211	Appliqueing on men's and boys' apparel
314999	Appliqueing on textile products (except apparel)
315212	Appliqueing on women's, girls', and infants' apparel
323118	Appointment books and refills manufacturing
541990	Appraisal (except real estate) services
531320	Appraisal services, real estate
531320	Appraisers' offices, real estate
611513	Apprenticeship training programs
111339	Apricot farming
812331	Apron supply services
316999	Aprons for textile machinery, leather, manufacturing
316999	Aprons, leather (e.g., blacksmith's, welder's), manufacturing
315999	Aprons, waterproof (e.g., plastics, rubberized fabric), rubberizing fabric and manufacturing aprons
315212	Aprons, waterproof (including plastics, rubberized fabric), woman's, girls', and infants', cut and sew apparel contractors
315999	Aprons, waterproof (including rubberized fabric, plastics), cut and sewn from purchased fabric (except apparel contractors)

Aprons—Arts

Code	Description
315211	Aprons, waterproof (including rubberized fabric, plastics), men's and boys', cut and sew apparel contractors
315211	Aprons, work (except leather), men's and boys, cut and sew apparel contractors
315212	Aprons, work (except leather), women's, girls', and infants', cut and sew apparel contractors
315225	Aprons, work (except leather, waterproof), men's and boys', cut and sewn from purchased fabric (except apparel contractors)
315239	Aprons, work (except waterproof, leather), women's, misses', and girls', cut and sewn from purchased fabric (except apparel contractors)
332999	Aquarium accessories, metal, manufacturing
712130	Aquariums
327215	Aquariums made from purchased glass
234910	Aqueduct construction
541990	Arbitration and conciliation services (except by attorney, paralegal)
333513	Arbor presses, metalworking, manufacturing
712130	Arboreta
561730	Arborist services
333515	Arbors (i.e., a machine tool accessory) manufacturing
334510	Arc lamp units, electrotherapeutic (except infrared, ultraviolet), manufacturing
335129	Arc lighting fixtures (except electrotherapeutic), electric, manufacturing
333992	Arc welding equipment manufacturing
335311	Arc-welding transformers, separate solid-state, manufacturing
713120	Arcades, amusement
339113	Arch supports, orthopedic, manufacturing
541720	Archeological research and development services
712120	Archeological sites (i.e., public display)
339920	Archery equipment manufacturing
421910	Archery equipment wholesaling
713990	Archery ranges
321213	Arches, glue laminated or pre-engineered wood, manufacturing
421490	Architect's equipment and supplies wholesaling
541310	Architects' (except landscape) offices
541310	Architects' (except landscape) private practices
813920	Architects' associations
541320	Architects' offices, landscape
541320	Architects' private practices, landscape
541310	Architectural (except landscape) consultants' offices
541310	Architectural (except landscape) design services
541310	Architectural (except landscape) services
327331	Architectural block, concrete (e.g., fluted, ground face, screen, slump, split), manufacturing
325510	Architectural coatings (i.e., paint) manufacturing
332323	Architectural metalwork manufacturing
421390	Architectural metalwork wholesaling
327112	Architectural sculptures, clay, manufacturing
327991	Architectural sculptures, stone, manufacturing
541320	Architectural services, landscape
235610	Architectural sheet metal construction contractors
327123	Architectural terra cotta manufacturing
327390	Architectural wall panels, precast concrete, manufacturing
337212	Architectural woodwork and fixtures (i.e., custom designed interiors) manufacturing
514120	Archives
316211	Arctics, plastics or plastics soled fabric upper, manufacturing
316211	Arctics, rubber or rubber soled fabric, manufacturing
335129	Area and sports luminaries (e.g., stadium lighting fixtures), electric, manufacturing
711310	Arena operators
531120	Arena, no promotion of events, rental or leasing
212311	Argillite mining or quarrying
325120	Argon manufacturing
315999	Arm bands, elastic, cut and sewn from purchased fabric (except apparel contractors)
315211	Arm bands, elastic, men's and boys', cut and sew apparel contractors
315212	Arm bands, elastic, women's, girls', and infants', cut and sew apparel contractors
335314	Armature relays manufacturing
335312	Armature rewinding on a factory basis
811310	Armature rewinding services (except on an assembly line or factory basis)
335312	Armatures, industrial, manufacturing
928110	Armed forces
332993	Arming and fusing devices, missile, manufacturing
331111	Armor plate made in steel mills
331422	Armored cable made from purchased copper in wire drawing plants
331422	Armored cable, copper, made in integrated secondary smelting and drawing plants
561613	Armored car services
336992	Armored military vehicles and parts manufacturing
928110	Army
422690	Aromatic chemicals wholesaling
113210	Aromatic wood gathering
488999	Arrangement of car pools and vanpools
335931	Arrestors and coils, lighting, manufacturing
325320	Arsenate insecticides manufacturing
325188	Arsenates (except insecticides) manufacturing
325131	Arsenic based pigments manufacturing
325188	Arsenic compounds, not specified elsewhere by process, manufacturing
212393	Arsenic mineral mining and/or beneficiating
325320	Arsenite insecticides manufacturing
325188	Arsenites manufacturing
611610	Art (except commercial or graphic) instruction
453920	Art auctions
453920	Art dealers
712110	Art galleries (except retail)
453920	Art galleries retailing art
327420	Art goods (e.g., gypsum, plaster of paris) manufacturing
422990	Art goods wholesaling
712110	Art museums
315211	Art needlework contractors on men's and boys' apparel
315212	Art needlework contractors on women's, girls', and infants' apparel
314999	Art needlework on clothing for the trade
323111	Art print gravure printing without publishing
511199	Art print publishers
511199	Art print publishers and printing combined
511199	Art print publishing (i.e., establishment known as publishers)
323112	Art prints flexographic printing without publishing
323110	Art prints lithographic (offset) printing without publishing
323119	Art prints printing (except flexographic, gravure, lithographic, screen) without publishing
323113	Art prints screen printing without publishing
511199	Art publishers
511199	Art publishing (i.e., establishments known as publishers)
711510	Art restorers, independent
611610	Art schools (except academic), fine
611519	Art schools, commercial or graphic
541430	Art services, commercial
541430	Art services, graphic
541430	Art studios, commercial
453998	Art supply stores
621340	Art therapists' offices (e.g., centers, clinics)
111219	Artichoke farming, field, bedding plant and seed production
311421	Artichokes, canned, manufacturing
422990	Artificial Christmas trees wholesaling
339999	Artificial flower arrangements assembled from purchased components
422930	Artificial flowers wholesaling
334511	Artificial horizon instrumentation manufacturing
115210	Artificial insemination services for livestock
115210	Artificial insemination services for pets
339113	Artificial limbs manufacturing
235990	Artificial turf construction contractors
312111	Artificially carbonated waters manufacturing
332993	Artillery (i.e., more than 30 mm., more than 1.18 inch) manufacturing
339942	Artist's paint manufacturing
339942	Artist's supplies (except paper) manufacturing
711510	Artists (except commercial, musical), independent
711510	Artists (i.e., painters), independent
711410	Artists' agents or managers
422990	Artists' supplies wholesaling
541430	Artists, independent commercial
541430	Artists, independent graphic
541430	Artists, independent medical
926110	Arts and cultural program administration, government
711310	Arts event managers with facilities
711320	Arts event managers without facilities
711310	Arts event organizers with facilities
711320	Arts event organizers without facilities
711310	Arts event promoters with facilities
711320	Arts event promoters without facilities
711310	Arts festival managers with facilities
711320	Arts festival managers without facilities
711310	Arts festival organizers with facilities
711320	Arts festival organizers without facilities
711310	Arts festival promoters with facilities
711320	Arts festival promoters without facilities

Code	Description
562910	Asbestos abatement services
212399	Asbestos mining and/or beneficiating
562910	Asbestos removal contractors
325411	Ascorbic acid (i.e., vitamin C), uncompounded, manufacturing
315211	Ascots, men's and boys', cut and sew apparel contractors
315993	Ascots, men's and boys', cut and sewn from purchased fabric (except apparel contractors)
562111	Ash collection services
562111	Ash hauling, local
212399	Ash, volcanic, mining and/or beneficiating
327215	Ashtrays made from purchased glass
327212	Ashtrays, glass, made in glass making plants
327112	Ashtrays, pottery, manufacturing
111219	Asparagus farming, field, bedding plant and seed production
324110	Asphalt and asphaltic materials made in petroleum refineries
322121	Asphalt paper made in paper mills
234110	Asphalt paving (e.g., public sidewalks, roads, streets) contractors
324121	Asphalt paving blocks made from purchased asphaltic materials
324121	Asphalt paving mixtures made from purchased asphaltic materials
324110	Asphalt paving mixtures made in petroleum refineries
324121	Asphalt road compounds made from purchased asphaltic materials
212399	Asphalt rock mining and/or beneficiating
324122	Asphalt roofing cements made from purchased asphaltic materials
324122	Asphalt roofing coatings made from purchased asphaltic materials
333120	Asphalt roofing construction machinery manufacturing
421330	Asphalt roofing shingles wholesaling
324122	Asphalt saturated boards made from purchased asphaltic materials
324122	Asphalt saturated mats and felts made from purchased asphaltic materials and paper
235710	Asphalt seal coating construction contractors
324122	Asphalt shingles made from purchased asphaltic materials
235520	Asphalt tile construction contractors
212399	Asphalt, native, mining and/or beneficiating
235710	Asphalting of private driveways and parking areas construction contractors
541380	Assaying services
336213	Assembly line conversions of purchased vans and mini-vans
336312	Assembly line rebuilding of automotive and truck gasoline engines
336350	Assembly line rebuilding of automotive, truck, and bus transmissions
333518	Assembly machines manufacturing
233310	Assembly plant construction
336120	Assembly plants, heavy trucks, and buses on chassis of own manufacture
336112	Assembly plants, light trucks on chassis of own manufacture
336112	Assembly plants, mini-vans on chassis of own manufacture
336111	Assembly plants, passenger car, on chassis of own manufacture
336112	Assembly plants, sport utility vehicles on chassis of own manufacture

Code	Description
921130	Assessor's offices, tax
325613	Assistants, textile and leather finishing, manufacturing
623311	Assisted-living facilities with on-site nursing facilities
623312	Assisted-living facilities without on-site nursing care facilities
813311	Associations for retired persons, advocacy
325412	Astringent preparations manufacturing
812990	Astrology services
711219	Athletes, amateur, independent
711219	Athletes, independent (i.e., participating in live sports events)
813990	Athletic associations, regulatory
315228	Athletic clothing (except team athletic uniforms), men's, boys' and unisex (i.e., sized without regard to gender), cut and sewn from purchased fabric (except apparel contractors)
315239	Athletic clothing (except team athletic uniforms), women's, misses', and girls', cut and sewn from purchased fabric (except apparel contractors)
315191	Athletic clothing made in apparel knitting mills
315211	Athletic clothing, men's and boys', cut and sew apparel contractors
315212	Athletic clothing, women's, girls', and infants', cut and sew apparel contractors
713940	Athletic club facilities, physical fitness
713990	Athletic clubs (i.e., sports teams) not operating sports facilities, recreational
451110	Athletic equipment and supply stores (including uniforms)
234990	Athletic field construction
422340	Athletic footwear wholesaling
339920	Athletic goods (except ammunition, clothing, footwear, small arms) manufacturing
421910	Athletic goods (except apparel, footwear, nonspecialty) wholesaling
813990	Athletic leagues (i.e., regulating bodies)
448210	Athletic shoe (except bowling, golf, spiked) stores
316219	Athletic shoes (except rubber or plastics soled with fabric upper) manufacturing
316211	Athletic shoes, plastics or plastics soled fabric upper (except cleated), manufacturing
316211	Athletic shoes, rubber or rubber soled fabric uppers (except cleated), manufacturing
315119	Athletic socks, knitting or knitting and finishing
421910	Athletic uniforms wholesaling
315299	Athletic uniforms, team, cut and sewn from purchased fabric (except apparel contractors)
315211	Athletic uniforms, team, men's and boys', cut and sew apparel contractors
315212	Athletic uniforms, team, women's, girls', and infants, cut and sew apparel contractors
511199	Atlas publishers
511199	Atlas publishers and printing combined
511199	Atlas publishing (i.e., establishments known as publishers)
323112	Atlases flexographic printing without publishing
323111	Atlases gravure printing without publishing
323110	Atlases lithographic (offset) printing without publishing

Code	Description
323119	Atlases printing (except flexographic, gravure, lithographic, screen) without publishing
323113	Atlases screen printing without publishing
335999	Atom smashers (i.e., particle accelerators) manufacturing
339999	Atomizers (e.g., perfumes) manufacturing
325411	Atropine and derivatives manufacturing
316991	Attache cases, all materials, manufacturing
333112	Attachments, powered lawn and garden equipment, manufacturing
333412	Attic fans manufacturing
922130	Attorney generals' offices
541110	Attorneys' offices
541110	Attorneys' private practices
453998	Auction houses (general merchandise)
422590	Auction markets, horses and mules
422520	Auction markets, livestock (except horses, mules)
422590	Auction markets, tobacco
561990	Auctioneers, independent
421990	Audio and video tapes and disks, prerecorded, wholesaling
337129	Audio cabinets (i.e., housings), wood, manufacturing
443112	Audio equipment stores (except automotive)
421620	Audio equipment, household-type, wholesaling
512290	Audio recording of meetings or conferences
512240	Audio recording post-production services
532490	Audio visual equipment rental or leasing
334515	Audiofrequency oscillators manufacturing
334510	Audiological equipment, electromedical, manufacturing
621340	Audiologists' offices (e.g., centers, clinics)
334515	Audiometers (except medical) manufacturing
334613	Audiotape, blank, manufacturing
421690	Audiotapes, blank, wholesaling
541211	Auditing accountants' (i.e., CPAs) offices
541211	Auditing accountants' (i.e., CPAs) private practices
541211	Auditing services (i.e., CPA services), accounts
921190	Auditor's offices, government
233320	Auditorium construction
531120	Auditorium rental or leasing
541211	Auditors' (i.e., CPAs) offices, accounts
541211	Auditors' (i.e., CPAs) private practices, accounts
213113	Auger coal mining services on a contract basis
333120	Augers (except mining-type) manufacturing
333131	Augers, mining-type, manufacturing
332212	Augers, nonpowered, manufacturing
711410	Authors' agents or managers
711510	Authors, independent
421120	Auto body shop supplies wholesaling
721110	Auto courts, lodging
441310	Auto supply stores
339114	Autoclaves, dental, manufacturing
332420	Autoclaves, industrial-type, manufacturing
339111	Autoclaves, laboratory-type (except dental), manufacturing

Autogiros—Bacteriological

Code	Description
336411	Autogiros manufacturing
235950	Automated and revolving door construction contractors
334510	Automated blood and body fluid analyzers (except laboratory) manufacturing
522320	Automated clearinghouses, bank or check (except central bank)
514210	Automated data processing services
332911	Automatic (i.e., controlling-type, regulating) valves, industrial-type, manufacturing
334516	Automatic chemical analyzers, laboratory-type, manufacturing
812310	Automatic laundries, coin-operated
454210	Automatic merchandising machine operators
333512	Automatic screw machines manufacturing
334119	Automatic teller machines (ATM) manufacturing
421420	Automatic teller machines (ATM) wholesaling
336350	Automatic transmissions, automotive, truck, and bus, manufacturing
421120	Automobile accessories (except tires, tubes) wholesaling
334220	Automobile antennas manufacturing
421110	Automobile auctions
336211	Automobile bodies, passenger car, manufacturing
484220	Automobile carrier trucking, local
484230	Automobile carrier trucking, long-distance
813410	Automobile clubs (except road and travel services)
561599	Automobile clubs, road and travel services
721110	Automobile courts, lodging
493190	Automobile dead storage
441110	Automobile dealers, new only or new and used
441120	Automobile dealers, used only
611692	Automobile driving schools
522220	Automobile finance leasing companies
522220	Automobile financing
421120	Automobile glass wholesaling
332510	Automobile hardware, metal, manufacturing
541420	Automobile industrial design services
524126	Automobile insurance carriers, direct
532112	Automobile leasing
333921	Automobile lifts (i.e., garage-type, service station) manufacturing
812930	Automobile parking garages or lots
441310	Automobile parts dealers
325612	Automobile polishes and cleaners manufacturing
541380	Automobile proving and testing grounds
711212	Automobile racetracks
611620	Automobile racing schools
711219	Automobile racing teams
334310	Automobile radio receivers manufacturing
532111	Automobile rental
485320	Automobile rental with driver (except shuttle service, taxis)
561491	Automobile repossession services
336360	Automobile seat covers manufacturing
332999	Automobile seat frames, metal, manufacturing
421120	Automobile service station equipment wholesaling
561920	Automobile show managers
561920	Automobile show organizers
561920	Automobile show promoters
332618	Automobile skid chains made from purchased wire
335911	Automobile storage batteries manufacturing
332611	Automobile suspension springs manufacturing
336212	Automobile transporter trailers, multi-car, manufacturing
336214	Automobile transporter trailers, single car, manufacturing
336360	Automobile trimmings, textile, manufacturing
333923	Automobile wrecker (i.e., tow truck) hoists manufacturing
336211	Automobile wrecker truck bodies manufacturing
336211	Automobile wreckers assembling on purchased chassis
336111	Automobiles assembling on chassis of own manufacture
421110	Automobiles wholesaling
339932	Automobiles, children's, manufacturing
421730	Automotive air-conditioners wholesaling
811198	Automotive air-conditioning repair shops
441310	Automotive audio equipment stores
811121	Automotive body shops
811118	Automotive brake repair shops
422690	Automotive chemicals (except lubrication greases, lubrication oils) wholesaling
811192	Automotive detailing services (i.e., cleaning, polishing)
334515	Automotive electrical engine diagnostic equipment manufacturing
811118	Automotive electrical repair shops
335931	Automotive electrical switches manufacturing
334519	Automotive emissions testing equipment manufacturing
811198	Automotive emissions testing services
811111	Automotive engine repair and replacement shops
811112	Automotive exhaust system repair and replacement shops
811118	Automotive front end alignment shops
811122	Automotive glass shops
336322	Automotive harness and ignition sets manufacturing
335110	Automotive light bulbs manufacturing
336321	Automotive lighting fixtures manufacturing
811191	Automotive oil change and lubrication shops
331319	Automotive or aircraft wire and cable made in aluminum wire drawing plants
811121	Automotive paint shops
441310	Automotive parts and supply stores
441310	Automotive parts dealers, used
421120	Automotive parts, new, wholesaling
811118	Automotive radiator repair shops
421620	Automotive radios wholesaling
811111	Automotive repair and replacement shops, general
811198	Automotive rustproofing and undercoating shops
334290	Automotive theft alarm systems manufacturing
441320	Automotive tire dealers
811198	Automotive tire repair (except retreading) shops
811113	Automotive transmission repair shops
811118	Automotive tune-up shops
811121	Automotive upholstery shops
811192	Automotive washing and polishing
336330	Automotive, truck and bus steering assemblies and parts manufacturing
336330	Automotive, truck and bus suspension assemblies and parts (except springs) manufacturing
339992	Autophones (organs with perforated music rolls) manufacturing
335311	Autotransformers for switchboards (except telephone switchboards) manufacturing
335311	Autotransformers manufacturing
712130	Aviaries
112990	Aviaries (i.e., raising birds for sale)
813319	Aviation advocacy organizations
481219	Aviation clubs providing a variety of air transportation activities to the general public
488119	Aviation clubs, primarily providing flying field services to the general public
713990	Aviation clubs, recreational
324110	Aviation fuels manufacturing
611512	Aviation schools
111339	Avocado farming
332212	Awls manufacturing
235990	Awning construction contractors
421390	Awnings (except canvas) wholesaling
314912	Awnings and canopies, outdoor, made from purchased fabrics
422990	Awnings, canvas, wholesaling
326199	Awnings, rigid plastics or fiberglass, manufacturing
332322	Awnings, sheet metal, manufacturing
332212	Axes manufacturing
336350	Axle bearings, automotive, truck, and bus, manufacturing
331111	Axles, rolled or forged, made in steel mills
111421	Azalea farming
325920	Azides explosive materials manufacturing
325132	Azine dyes manufacturing
325132	Azo dyes manufacturing
325192	Azobenzene manufacturing
332994	BB guns manufacturing
332992	BB shot manufacturing
448130	Baby clothing shops
422330	Baby clothing wholesaling
311422	Baby foods (including meats) canning
422490	Baby foods, canned, wholesaling
311514	Baby formula, fresh, processed, and bottled, manufacturing
421210	Baby furniture wholesaling
325620	Baby powder and baby oil manufacturing
333997	Baby scales manufacturing
812990	Baby shoe bronzing services
561310	Babysitting bureaus (i.e., registries)
624410	Babysitting services in provider's own home, child day care
624410	Babysitting services, child day care
332913	Backflow preventors, plumbing, manufacturing
112111	Backgrounding, cattle
333120	Backhoes manufacturing
311612	Bacon, slab and sliced, made from purchased carcasses
311611	Bacon, slab and sliced, produced in slaughtering plants
325414	Bacterial vaccines manufacturing
325414	Bacterins (i.e., bacterial vaccines) manufacturing
621511	Bacteriological laboratories, diagnostic

Code	Description
621511	Bacteriological laboratories, medical
541710	Bacteriological research and development laboratories or services
314999	Badges, fabric, manufacturing
332999	Badges, metal, manufacturing
326199	Badges, plastics, manufacturing
339920	Badminton equipment manufacturing
332313	Baffles, fabricated metal plate work, manufacturing
316110	Bag leather manufacturing
332993	Bag loading plants, ammunition, manufacturing
333993	Bag opening, filling, and closing machines manufacturing
722110	Bagel shops, full service
722213	Bagel shops, on premise baking and carryout service
311812	Bagels made in commercial bakeries
322223	Bags (except plastics only) made by laminating or coating combinations of purchased plastics, foil and paper
316991	Bags (i.e., luggage), all materials, manufacturing
313249	Bags and bagging fabric made in warp knitting mills
313241	Bags and bagging fabrics made in weft knitting mills
316991	Bags, athletic, manufacturing
322223	Bags, coated paper, made from purchased paper
322223	Bags, foil, made from purchased foil
339920	Bags, golf, manufacturing
313111	Bags, hemp, made from purchased fiber
322224	Bags, multiwall, made from purchased uncoated paper
422130	Bags, paper and disposable plastics, wholesaling
322224	Bags, paper, uncoated, made from purchased paper
314911	Bags, plastic, made from purchased woven plastics
326111	Bags, plastics film, single wall or multiwall, manufacturing
339920	Bags, punching, manufacturing
314911	Bags, rubberized fabric, manufacturing
314999	Bags, sleeping, manufacturing
314911	Bags, textile, made from purchased woven or knitted materials
422990	Bags, textile, wholesaling
322224	Bags, uncoated paper, made from purchased paper
812990	Bail bonding services
339920	Bait, artificial, fishing, manufacturing
421910	Bait, artificial, wholesaling
422990	Bait, live, wholesaling
112511	Baitfish production, farm raising
311422	Baked beans canning
311813	Baked goods (except bread, bread-type rolls), frozen, manufacturing
445210	Baked ham stores
311811	Bakeries with baking from flour on the premises, retailing not for immediate consumption
315211	Bakers' service apparel, washable, men's and boys', cut and sew apparel contractors
315225	Bakers' service apparel, washable, men's and boys', cut and sewn from purchased fabric (except apparel contractors)
315212	Bakers' service apparel, washable, women's, cut and sew apparel contractors

Code	Description
315239	Bakers' service apparel, washable, women's, misses', and girls, cut and sewn from purchased fabric (except apparel contractors)
333294	Bakery machinery and equipment manufacturing
421830	Bakery machinery and equipment wholesaling
333294	Bakery ovens manufacturing
422490	Bakery products (except frozen) wholesaling
311821	Bakery products, dry (e.g., biscuits, cookies, crackers), manufacturing
311812	Bakery products, fresh (i.e., bread, cakes, doughnuts, pastries), made in commercial bakeries
422420	Bakery products, frozen, wholesaling
445291	Bakery stores, retailing only (except immediate consumption)
311320	Baking chocolate made from cacao beans
311330	Baking chocolate made from purchased chocolate
311999	Baking powder manufacturing
333997	Balances (except laboratory-type) manufacturing
421440	Balances and scales (except laboratory) wholesaling
421490	Balances and scales, laboratory, wholesaling
339111	Balances and scales, laboratory-type, manufacturing
333319	Balancing equipment, motor vehicle, manufacturing
332323	Balcony railings, metal, manufacturing
333111	Bale throwers manufacturing
332618	Bale ties made from purchased wire
333111	Balers, farm-type (e.g., cotton, hay, straw), manufacturing
333999	Baling machinery (e.g., paper, scrap metal) manufacturing
332991	Ball bearings manufacturing
212324	Ball clay mining and/or beneficiating
333613	Ball joints (except aircraft, motor vehicle) manufacturing
339941	Ball point pens manufacturing
332911	Ball valves, industrial-type, manufacturing
335311	Ballasts (i.e., transformers) manufacturing
711120	Ballet companies
711510	Ballet dancers, independent
711120	Ballet productions, live theatrical
611610	Ballet schools (except academic)
316219	Ballet slippers manufacturing
453220	Balloon shops
812990	Balloon-o-gram services
326199	Balloons, plastics, manufacturing
326299	Balloons, rubber, manufacturing
713990	Ballrooms
339920	Balls, baseball, basketball, football, golf, tennis, pool, and bowling, manufacturing
339932	Balls, rubber (except athletic equipment), manufacturing
331111	Balls, steel, made in steel mills
113210	Balsam needles gathering
111339	Banana farming
115114	Banana ripening
315299	Band uniforms cut and sewn from purchased fabric (except apparel contractors)
315211	Band uniforms, men's and boys', cut and sew apparel contractors

Code	Description
315212	Band uniforms, women's, girls', and infants', cut and sew apparel contractors
339113	Bandages and dressings, surgical and orthopedic, manufacturing
422210	Bandages wholesaling
315212	Bandeaux, women's and girls', cut and sew apparel contractors
315231	Bandeaux, women's, misses', and girls', cut and sewn from purchased fabric (except apparel contractors)
711130	Bands
711130	Bands, dance
711130	Bands, musical
333210	Bandsaws, woodworking-type, manufacturing
339992	Banjos and parts manufacturing
334511	Bank and turn indicators and components (aeronautical instruments) manufacturing
233320	Bank building construction
531120	Bank building rental or leasing
332999	Bank chests, metal, manufacturing
522320	Bank clearinghouse associations
524128	Bank deposit insurance carriers, direct
332323	Bank fixtures, ornamental metal, manufacturing
551111	Bank holding companies (except managing)
523991	Bank trust offices
813910	Bankers' associations
926150	Banking regulatory agencies
611519	Banking schools (training in banking)
523110	Banking, investment
525920	Bankruptcy estates
521110	Banks, Federal Reserve
522110	Banks, commercial
522210	Banks, credit card
522190	Banks, private (i.e., unincorporated)
522120	Banks, savings
522293	Banks, trade (i.e., international trade financing)
314999	Banners made from purchased fabrics
332323	Bannisters, metal, manufacturing
531120	Banquet hall rental or leasing
722320	Banquet halls with catering staff
327991	Baptismal fonts, cut stone, manufacturing
813920	Bar associations
561499	Bar code imprinting services
331316	Bar made by extruding purchased aluminum
331319	Bar made by rolling purchased aluminum
333516	Bar mill machinery, metalworking, manufacturing
325611	Bar soaps manufacturing
331316	Bar, aluminum, made in integrated secondary smelting and extruding mills
331319	Bar, aluminum, made in integrated secondary smelting and rolling mills
331421	Bar, copper and copper alloy, made from purchased copper or in integrated secondary smelting and rolling, drawing or extruding plants
331491	Bar, nonferrous metals (except aluminum, copper), made from purchased metals in wire drawing plants or in integrated secondary smelting and rolling, drawing, or extruding plants
311421	Barbecue sauce manufacturing
335221	Barbecues, grills, and braziers manufacturing
331222	Barbed and twisted wire made in wire drawing plants

Barbed wire—Beach umbrellas

Code	Description
332618	Barbed wire made from purchased wire
611511	Barber colleges
421850	Barber shop equipment and supplies wholesaling
812111	Barber shops
332211	Barber's scissors, manufacturing
315211	Barbers' service apparel, washable, men's and boys', cut and sew apparel contractors
315225	Barbers' service apparel, washable, men's and boys', cut and sewn from purchased fabric (except apparel contractors)
325412	Barbiturate preparations manufacturing
325411	Barbiturates, uncompounded, manufacturing
325411	Barbituric acid manufacturing
336611	Barge building
532411	Barge rental or leasing
332312	Barge sections, prefabricated metal, manufacturing
483211	Barge transportation, canal
483113	Barge transportation, coastal or Great Lakes
212393	Barite mining and/or beneficiating
327992	Barite processing beyond beneficiation
325188	Barium compounds, not specified elsewhere by process, manufacturing
325188	Barium hydroxide manufacturing
325412	Barium in-vivo diagnostic substances manufacturing
212393	Barium ores mining and/or beneficiating
327992	Barium processing beyond beneficiation
113210	Bark gathering
111199	Barley farming, field and seed production
311119	Barley feed, chopped, crushed or ground, manufacturing
311211	Barley flour manufacturing
311213	Barley, malt, manufacturing
332323	Barn stanchions and standards manufacturing
334519	Barographs manufacturing
334519	Barometers manufacturing
332410	Barometric condensers manufacturing
233320	Barrack construction
321920	Barrel heading and staves manufacturing
332994	Barrels, gun (i.e., 30 mm. or less, 1.18 inch or less), manufacturing
332995	Barrels, gun (i.e., more than 30 mm., more than 1.18 inch), manufacturing
332439	Barrels, metal, manufacturing
421840	Barrels, new and reconditioned, wholesaling
321920	Barrels, wood, coopered, manufacturing
332999	Barricades, metal, manufacturing
541110	Barristers' offices
541110	Barristers' private practices
722410	Bars (i.e., drinking places), alcoholic beverage
331411	Bars made in primary copper smelting and refining mills
332312	Bars, concrete reinforcing, manufacturing
331111	Bars, iron, made in steel mills
421510	Bars, metal (except precious), wholesaling
331221	Bars, steel, made in cold rolling mills
331111	Bars, steel, made in steel mills
611519	Bartending schools
561990	Bartering services
325131	Barytes based pigments manufacturing
212393	Barytes mining and/or beneficiating

Code	Description
212319	Basalt crushed and broken stone mining and/or beneficiating
212311	Basalt mining or quarrying
561210	Base facilities operation support services
315211	Baseball caps (except plastics), men's and boys', cut and sew apparel contractors
315212	Baseball caps (except plastics), women's, girls', and infants', cut and sew apparel contractors
315991	Baseball caps cut and sewn from purchased fabric (except apparel contractors)
711211	Baseball clubs, professional or semiprofessional
713990	Baseball clubs, recreational
339920	Baseball equipment and supplies (except footwear, uniforms) manufacturing
421910	Baseball equipment and supplies wholesaling
611620	Baseball instruction, camps, or schools
711211	Baseball teams, professional or semiprofessional
315299	Baseball uniforms cut and sewn from purchased fabric (except apparel contractors)
315211	Baseball uniforms, men's and boys', cut and sew apparel contractors
315212	Baseball uniforms, women's and girls', cut and sew apparel contractors
421730	Baseboard heaters, electric, non-portable, wholesaling
333414	Baseboard heating equipment manufacturing
321918	Baseboards, floor, wood, manufacturing
332321	Baseboards, metal, manufacturing
711211	Basketball clubs, professional or semiprofessional
713990	Basketball clubs, recreational
339920	Basketball equipment and supplies (except footwear, uniforms) manufacturing
611620	Basketball instruction, camps, or schools
711211	Basketball teams, professional or semiprofessional
315299	Basketball uniforms cut and sewn from purchased fabric (except apparel contractors)
315211	Basketball uniforms, men's and boys', cut and sew apparel contractors
315212	Basketball uniforms, women's and girls', cut and sew apparel contractors
422990	Baskets wholesaling
331222	Baskets, iron or steel, made in wire drawing plants
332618	Baskets, metal, made from purchased wire
321920	Baskets, wood (e.g., round stave, veneer), manufacturing
337125	Bassinets, reed and rattan, manufacturing
339992	Bassoons manufacturing
212299	Bastnaesite mining and/or beneficiating
335211	Bath fans with integral lighting fixture, residential, manufacturing
335211	Bath fans, residential, manufacturing
314110	Bath mats and bath sets made in carpet mills
326299	Bath mats, rubber, manufacturing
325620	Bath salts manufacturing
442299	Bath shops
713990	Bathing beaches
315999	Bathing caps, rubber, manufacturing

Code	Description
315191	Bathing suits made in apparel knitting mills
315291	Bathing suits, infants', cut and sewn from purchased fabric (except apparel contractors)
315211	Bathing suits, men's and boys', cut and sew apparel contractors
315228	Bathing suits, men's and boys', cut and sewn from purchased fabric (except apparel contractors)
315212	Bathing suits, women's, girls', and infants', cut and sew apparel contractors
315239	Bathing suits, women's, misses', and girls', cut and sewn from purchased fabric (except apparel contractors)
315192	Bathrobes made in apparel knitting mills
315291	Bathrobes, infants', cut and sewn from purchased fabric (except apparel contractors)
315211	Bathrobes, men's and boys', cut and sew apparel contractors
315221	Bathrobes, men's and boys', cut and sewn from purchased fabric (except apparel contractors)
315212	Bathrobes, women's, girls', and infants', cut and sew apparel contractors
315231	Bathrobes, women's, misses', and girls', cut and sewn from purchased fabric (except apparel contractors)
421220	Bathroom accessories wholesaling
327111	Bathroom accessories, vitreous china and earthenware, manufacturing
326199	Bathroom and toilet accessories, plastics, manufacturing
332998	Bathroom fixtures manufacturing
333997	Bathroom scales manufacturing
337110	Bathroom vanities (except freestanding), stock or custom wood, manufacturing
812199	Baths, steam or turkish
235990	Bathtub refinishing construction contractors
332998	Bathtubs, metal, manufacturing
326191	Bathtubs, plastics, manufacturing
611620	Baton instruction
624221	Battered women's shelters
421610	Batteries (except automotive) wholesaling
421120	Batteries, automotive, wholesaling
335912	Batteries, primary, dry or wet, manufacturing
335911	Batteries, rechargeable, manufacturing
335911	Batteries, storage, manufacturing
311822	Batters, prepared, made from purchased flour
311211	Batters, prepared, made in flour mills
335999	Battery chargers, solid-state, manufacturing
334515	Battery testers, electrical, manufacturing
712120	Battlefields
314999	Batts and batting (except nonwoven fabrics) manufacturing
327125	Bauxite brick manufacturing
212299	Bauxite mining and/or beneficiating
325998	Bay oil manufacturing
454390	Bazaars (i.e., temporary stands)
532292	Beach chair rental
713990	Beach clubs, recreational
562998	Beach maintenance and cleaning services
316211	Beach sandals, plastics or plastics soled fabric upper, manufacturing
316211	Beach sandals, rubber or rubber soled fabric upper, manufacturing
532292	Beach umbrella rental

Code	Description
339999	Beach umbrellas manufacturing
713990	Beaches, bathing
315191	Beachwear made in apparel knitting mills
315291	Beachwear, infants', cut and sewn from purchased fabric (except apparel contractors)
315211	Beachwear, men's and boys', cut and sew apparel contractors
315228	Beachwear, men's and boys', cut and sewn from purchased fabric (except apparel contractors)
315212	Beachwear, women's, girls', and infants', cut and sew apparel contractors
315239	Beachwear, women's, misses', and girls', cut and sewn from purchased fabric (except apparel contractors)
333513	Beader machines, metalworking, manufacturing
314999	Beading on textile products (except apparel) for the trade
333292	Beaming machinery for yarn manufacturing
313112	Beaming yarn
321113	Beams, wood, made from logs or bolts
111219	Bean (except dry) farming, field and seed production
115114	Bean cleaning
111130	Bean farming, dry, field and seed production
111419	Bean sprout farming, grown under cover
311422	Beans, baked, canning
422510	Beans, dry, wholesaling
332212	Bearing pullers, handtools, manufacturing
336312	Bearings (e.g., camshaft, crankshaft, connecting rod), automotive and truck gasoline engine, manufacturing
421840	Bearings wholesaling
332991	Bearings, ball and roller, manufacturing
333613	Bearings, plain (except internal combustion engine), manufacturing
812112	Beautician services
611511	Beauty schools
812112	Beauty and barber shops, combined
711310	Beauty pageant managers with facilities
711320	Beauty pageant managers without facilities
711310	Beauty pageant organizers with facilities
711320	Beauty pageant organizers without facilities
711310	Beauty pageant promoters with facilities
711320	Beauty pageant promoters without facilities
421850	Beauty parlor equipment and supplies wholesaling
812112	Beauty parlors
422210	Beauty preparations wholesaling
812112	Beauty salons
812112	Beauty shops
422210	Beauty supplies wholesaling
446120	Beauty supply stores
721191	Bed and breakfast inns
337122	Bed frames, wood household-type, manufacturing
812331	Bed linen supply services
335211	Bedcoverings, electric, manufacturing
111422	Bedding plant growing (except vegetable and melon bedding plants)
315212	Bedjackets, women's, girls' and infants', cut and sew apparel contractors

Code	Description
315231	Bedjackets, women's, misses', juniors', and girls', cut and sewn from purchased fabric (except apparel contractors)
337122	Bedroom furniture (except upholstered), wood household-type, manufacturing
337122	Beds (except hospital), wood household-type, manufacturing
337124	Beds (including cabinet and folding), metal household-type (except hospital), manufacturing
339111	Beds, hospital, manufacturing
421450	Beds, hospital, wholesaling
337910	Beds, sleep-system ensembles (i.e., flotation, adjustable), manufacturing
337122	Beds, wood dormitory-type, manufacturing
337122	Beds, wood hotel-type, manufacturing
314129	Bedspreads and bed sets made from purchased fabrics
313249	Bedspreads and bed sets made in lace mills
313249	Bedspreads and bed sets made in warp knitting mills
313241	Bedspreads and bed sets made in weft knitting mills
112910	Bee production (i.e., apiculture)
311611	Beef carcasses, half carcasses, primal and sub-primal cuts, produced in slaughtering plants
112112	Beef cattle feedlots (except stockyards for transportation)
112111	Beef cattle ranching or farming
311611	Beef produced in slaughtering plants
311612	Beef stew made from purchased carcasses
311612	Beef, primal and sub-primal cuts, made from purchased carcasses
422910	Beekeeping supplies wholesaling
513321	Beeper (i.e., radio pager) communication carriers
327213	Beer bottles, glass, manufacturing
312120	Beer brewing
332431	Beer cans manufacturing
333415	Beer cooling and dispensing equipment manufacturing
332439	Beer kegs, light gauge metal, manufacturing
445310	Beer stores, packaged
422810	Beer wholesaling
325612	Beeswax polishes and waxes manufacturing
112910	Beeswax production
111219	Beet farming (except sugar beets), field, including plant and seed production
311313	Beet pulp, dried, manufacturing
311313	Beet sugar refining
541720	Behavioral research and development services
325412	Belladonna preparations manufacturing
332999	Bellows, hand, manufacturing
333999	Bellows, industrial type, manufacturing
339992	Bells (musical instruments) manufacturing
335999	Bells, electric, manufacturing
422310	Belt and buckle assembly kits wholesaling
333922	Belt conveyor systems manufacturing
316999	Belt laces, leather, manufacturing
316110	Belting butts, curried or rough, manufacturing
313221	Belting fabrics, narrow woven
316999	Belting for machinery, leather, manufacturing
316110	Belting leather, manufacturing

Code	Description
314999	Belting made from purchased fabrics
421840	Belting, industrial, wholesaling
326220	Belting, rubber (e.g., conveyor, elevator, transmission), manufacturing
482112	Beltline railroads
315999	Belts, apparel (e.g., fabric, leather, vinyl), cut and sewn from purchased fabric (except apparel contractors)
315211	Belts, apparel (e.g., fabric, leather, vinyl), men's and boys', cut and sew apparel contractors
315212	Belts, apparel (e.g., fabric, leather, vinyl), women's, girls', and infants', cut and sew apparel contractors
332618	Belts, conveyor, made from purchased wire
332618	Belts, drying, made from purchased wire
316999	Belts, leather safety, manufacturing
332994	Belts, machine gun (i.e., 30 mm. or less, 1.18 inch or less), manufacturing
332995	Belts, machine gun (i.e., more than 30 mm., more than 1.18 inch), manufacturing
315999	Belts, money, any material, cut and sewn from purchased fabric (except apparel contractors)
315211	Belts, money, any material, men's and boys', cut and sew apparel contractors
315212	Belts, money, any material, women's and girls', cut and sew apparel contractors
339111	Benches, laboratory-type, manufacturing
337127	Benches, park-type (except concrete, stone), manufacturing
337127	Benches, public building-type, manufacturing
337127	Benches, work, manufacturing
333513	Bending and forming machines, metalworking, manufacturing
332996	Bends, pipe, made from purchased metal pipe
541612	Benefit consulting services
111998	Bentgrass seed farming
212325	Bentonite mining and/or beneficiating
321999	Bentwood (steam bent) products (except furniture) manufacturing
325192	Benzaldehyde manufacturing
325320	Benzene hexachloride (BHC) insecticides manufacturing
325110	Benzene made from refined petroleum or liquid hydrocarbons
324110	Benzene made in petroleum refineries
325192	Benzoic acid manufacturing
311421	Berries, canned, manufacturing
422480	Berries, fresh, wholesaling
115113	Berries, machine harvesting
111334	Berry (except strawberry) farming
321920	Berry crates, wood, wirebound, manufacturing
321920	Berry cups, veneer and splint, manufacturing
333111	Berry harvesting machines manufacturing
212299	Beryl mining and/or beneficiating
327113	Beryllia porcelain insulators manufacturing
331528	Beryllium castings (except die-castings), unfinished manufacturing
212299	Beryllium concentrates beneficiating
331522	Beryllium die-castings, unfinished, manufacturing
212299	Beryllium ores mining and/or beneficiating
325188	Beryllium oxide manufacturing

Beryllium refining—Blankets

Code	Description
331419	Beryllium refining, primary
334517	Beta-ray irradiation equipment manufacturing
335999	Betatrons manufacturing
813910	Better business bureaus
722213	Beverage (e.g., coffee, juice, soft drink) bars, nonalcoholic, fixed location
311930	Beverage bases manufacturing
422490	Beverage bases wholesaling
421830	Beverage bottling machinery wholesaling
422490	Beverage concentrates wholesaling
327213	Beverage containers, glass, manufacturing
421740	Beverage coolers, mechanical, wholesaling
311930	Beverage flavorings (except coffee based) manufacturing
722330	Beverage stands, nonalcoholic, mobile
311930	Beverage syrups (except coffee based) manufacturing
422810	Beverages, alcoholic (except distilled spirits, wine), wholesaling
312120	Beverages, beer, ale, and malt liquors, manufacturing
311514	Beverages, dietary, dairy and nondairy based
312111	Beverages, fruit and vegetable drinks, cocktails, and ades, manufacturing
311421	Beverages, fruit and vegetable juice, manufacturing
312140	Beverages, liquors (except brandies), manufacturing
311511	Beverages, milk based (except dietary), manufacturing
312112	Beverages, naturally carbonated bottled water, manufacturing
312111	Beverages, soft drink (including artificially carbonated waters), manufacturing
422820	Beverages, wine and distilled spirits, wholesaling
312130	Beverages, wines and brandies, manufacturing
314999	Bias bindings made from purchased fabrics
313221	Bias bindings, woven, manufacturing
611699	Bible schools (except degree granting)
813110	Bible societies
315999	Bibs and aprons, waterproof (e.g., plastics, rubber, similar materials), cut and sewn from purchased fabric (except apparel contractors)
315211	Bibs and aprons, waterproof (e.g., plastics, rubber, similar materials), men's and boys', cut and sew apparel contractors
315999	Bibs and aprons, waterproof (e.g., plastics, rubber, similar materials), rubberizing fabric and manufacturing bibs and aprons
315212	Bibs and aprons, waterproof (e.g., plastics, rubber, similar materials), women's, girls', and infants', cut and sew apparel contractors
315212	Bibs, waterproof, cut and sew apparel contractors
451110	Bicycle (except motorized) shops
453310	Bicycle (except motorized) shops, used
492210	Bicycle courier
333912	Bicycle pumps manufacturing
532292	Bicycle rental
811490	Bicycle repair and maintenance shops without retailing new bicycles

Code	Description
441221	Bicycle shops, motorized
421910	Bicycles (except motorized) wholesaling
336991	Bicycles and parts manufacturing
421110	Bicycles, motorized, wholesaling
327111	Bidets, vitreous china, manufacturing
561440	Bill collection services
541850	Billboard display advertising services
339950	Billboards manufacturing
333516	Billet mill machinery, metalworking, manufacturing
331111	Billets, steel, made in steel mills
316993	Billfolds, all materials, manufacturing
339920	Billiard equipment and supplies manufacturing
421910	Billiard equipment and supplies wholesaling
713990	Billiard parlors
713990	Billiard rooms
541219	Billing services
322130	Binder's board manufacturing
422120	Binders, looseleaf, wholesaling
333293	Bindery machinery manufacturing
314999	Binding carpets and rugs for the trade
333313	Binding equipment (i.e., plastics or tape binding), office-type, manufacturing
422310	Binding, textile, wholesaling
314999	Bindings, bias, made from purchased fabrics
313221	Bindings, narrow woven, manufacturing
713290	Bingo halls
713290	Bingo parlors
316991	Binocular cases manufacturing
333314	Binoculars manufacturing
421460	Binoculars wholesaling
332313	Bins, fabricated metal plate work, manufacturing
332439	Bins, metal, manufacturing
421390	Bins, storage, wholesaling
621498	Biofeedback centers and clinics, outpatient
339113	Biohazard protective clothing and accessories manufacturing
541380	Biological (except medical, veterinary) testing laboratories or services
541690	Biological consulting services
621511	Biological laboratories, diagnostic
422210	Biologicals and allied products wholesaling
541710	Biology research and development laboratories or services
541710	Biotechnology research and development laboratories or services
311119	Bird feed, prepared, manufacturing
112990	Bird production (e.g., canaries, love birds, parakeets, parrots)
561710	Bird proofing services
712190	Bird sanctuaries
621410	Birth control clinics
326299	Birth control devices (i.e., diaphragms, prophylactics) manufacturing
325412	Birth control pills manufacturing
311812	Biscuits, bread-type, made in commercial bakeries
331419	Bismuth refining, primary
112990	Bison production
333515	Bits and knives for metalworking lathes, planers, and shapers manufacturing
333515	Bits, drill, metalworking, manufacturing
332212	Bits, edge tool, woodworking, manufacturing
333120	Bits, rock drill, construction and surface mining-type, manufacturing

Code	Description
333132	Bits, rock drill, oil and gas field-type, manufacturing
333131	Bits, rock drill, underground mining-type, manufacturing
212399	Bitumens, native, mining and/or beneficiating
212111	Bituminous coal and lignite surface mine site development for own account
212111	Bituminous coal cleaning plants
212111	Bituminous coal crushing
213113	Bituminous coal mining services on a contract basis
212111	Bituminous coal or lignite beneficiating (e.g., cleaning, crushing, screening, washing)
213113	Bituminous coal or lignite surface mine site development on a contract basis
212111	Bituminous coal screening plants
212111	Bituminous coal stripping (except on a contract, fee, or other basis)
213113	Bituminous coal stripping service on a contract basis
212111	Bituminous coal surface mining and/or beneficiating
212112	Bituminous coal underground mine site development for own account
212112	Bituminous coal underground mining or mining and beneficiating
212111	Bituminous coal washeries
212319	Bituminous limestone mining and/or beneficiating
213113	Bituminous or lignite auger mining service on a contract basis
212319	Bituminous sandstone mining and/or beneficiating
325131	Black pigments (except carbon black, bone black, lamp black) manufacturing
421510	Black plate wholesaling
111334	Blackberry farming
421490	Blackboards wholesaling
339942	Blackboards, framed, manufacturing
327991	Blackboards, unframed, slate, manufacturing
331111	Blackplate made in steel mills
316999	Blacksmith's aprons, leather, manufacturing
311312	Blackstrap invert made from purchased raw cane sugar
311311	Blackstrap molasses made in sugarcane mill
235710	Blacktop, private driveways and parking areas, construction contractors
811310	Blade sharpening, commercial and industrial machinery and equipment
421710	Blades (e.g., knife, saw) wholesaling
333120	Blades for graders, scrapers, bulldozers, and snowplows manufacturing
332211	Blades, knife and razor, manufacturing
422210	Blades, razor, wholesaling
332213	Blades, saw, all types, manufacturing
325131	Blanc fixe (i.e., barium sulfate, precipitated) manufacturing
332992	Blank cartridges (i.e., 30 mm. or less, 1.18 inch or less) manufacturing
334613	Blank tapes, audio and video, manufacturing
421690	Blank tapes, audio and video, wholesaling
323118	Blankbooks and refills manufacturing
422120	Blankbooks wholesaling
314911	Blanket bags manufacturing
314129	Blankets (except electric) made from purchased fabrics or felts

Code	Description
421220	Blankets (except electric) wholesaling
313210	Blankets and bedspreads made in broadwoven fabric mills
335211	Blankets, electric, manufacturing
421620	Blankets, electric, wholesaling
313230	Blankets, nonwoven fabric, manufacturing
327212	Blanks for electric light bulbs, glass, made in glass making plants
333515	Blanks, cutting tool, manufacturing
327215	Blanks, ophthalmic lens and optical glass, made from purchased glass
327212	Blanks, ophthalmic lens and optical glass, made in glass making plants
321912	Blanks, wood (e.g., bowling pins, handles, textile machinery accessories), manufacturing
311411	Blast freezing on a contract basis
327992	Blast furnace slag processing
331111	Blast furnaces
212322	Blast sand quarrying and/or beneficiating
234990	Blasting (except building demolition)
325920	Blasting accessories (e.g., caps, fuses, ignitors, squibbs) manufacturing
325920	Blasting powders manufacturing
213113	Blasting services, coal mining, on a contract basis
213114	Blasting services, metal mining, on a contract basis
213115	Blasting services, nonmetallic minerals mining (except fuels) on a contract basis
337127	Bleacher seating manufacturing
422690	Bleaches wholesaling
325612	Bleaches, formulated for household use, manufacturing
325188	Bleaching agents, inorganic, manufacturing
325199	Bleaching agents, organic, manufacturing
313311	Bleaching broadwoven fabrics
212325	Bleaching clay mining and/or beneficiating
333292	Bleaching machinery for textiles manufacturing
313312	Bleaching textile products, apparel, and fabrics (except broadwoven)
212231	Blende (zinc) mining and/or beneficiating
311211	Blended flour made in flour mills
335211	Blenders, household-type electric, manufacturing
325620	Blending and compounding perfume bases
311119	Blending animal feed
312130	Blending brandy
312140	Blending distilled beverages (except brandy)
312130	Blending wines
336411	Blimps (i.e., aircraft) manufacturing
337920	Blinds (e.g., mini, venetian, vertical), all materials, manufacturing
421220	Blinds and shades, window, wholesaling
331411	Blister copper manufacturing
561910	Blister packaging services
333923	Block and tackle manufacturing
312113	Block ice manufacturing
324121	Blocks, asphalt paving, made from purchased asphaltic materials
327331	Blocks, concrete and cinder, manufacturing
327124	Blocks, fire clay, manufacturing

Code	Description
327212	Blocks, glass, made in glass making plants
321999	Blocks, tackle, wood, manufacturing
321999	Blocks, tailors' pressing wood, manufacturing
621511	Blood analysis laboratories
334516	Blood bank process equipment manufacturing
621991	Blood banks
325413	Blood derivative in-vitro diagnostic substances manufacturing
325414	Blood derivatives manufacturing
422210	Blood derivatives wholesaling
621991	Blood donor stations
325414	Blood fractions manufacturing
325413	Blood glucose test kits manufacturing
422210	Blood plasma wholesaling
339112	Blood pressure apparatus manufacturing
621991	Blood pressure screening facilities
621999	Blood pressure screening services
812990	Blood pressure testing machine concession operators, coin-operated
339111	Blood testing apparatus, laboratory-type, manufacturing
339112	Blood transfusion equipment manufacturing
333516	Blooming and slabbing mill machinery, metalworking, manufacturing
331111	Blooms, steel, made in steel mills
315191	Blouses made in apparel knitting mills
315291	Blouses, infants', manufacturing
315212	Blouses, women's, girls', and infants', cut and sew apparel contractors
315232	Blouses, women's, misses', and girls', cut and sewn from purchased fabric (except apparel contractors)
335211	Blow dryers, household-type electric, manufacturing
333220	Blow molding machinery for plastics manufacturing
332212	Blow torches manufacturing
333412	Blower filter units manufacturing
333111	Blowers, forage, manufacturing
421830	Blowers, industrial, wholesaling
333112	Blowers, leaf, manufacturing
221210	Blue gas, carbureted, production and distribution
111334	Blueberry farming
114111	Bluefish fishing
111998	Bluegrass-Kentucky seed farming
541340	Blueprint drafting services
333315	Blueprint equipment manufacturing
421420	Blueprinting equipment wholesaling
561439	Blueprinting services
212311	Bluestone mining or quarrying
325620	Blushes, face, manufacturing
921130	Board of Governors, Federal Reserve
321219	Board, bagasse, manufacturing
327420	Board, gypsum, manufacturing
321219	Board, particle, manufacturing
115210	Boarding horses
721310	Boarding houses
611110	Boarding schools, elementary or secondary
812910	Boarding services, pet
921120	Boards of supervisors, county and local
813910	Boards of trade
324122	Boards, asphalt saturated, made from purchased asphaltic materials
321999	Boards, bulletin, wood and cork, manufacturing
321999	Boards, wood (e.g., clip, ironing, meat, pastry), manufacturing
321113	Boards, wood, made from logs or bolts

Code	Description
321912	Boards, wood, resawing purchased lumber
336321	Boat and ship lighting fixtures manufacturing
441222	Boat dealers, new and used
541330	Boat engineering design services
484220	Boat hauling, truck, local
484230	Boat hauling, truck, long-distance
333923	Boat lifts manufacturing
532411	Boat rental (except pleasure)
532411	Boat rental or leasing, commercial
532292	Boat rental, pleasure
332312	Boat sections, prefabricated metal, manufacturing
441222	Boat trailer dealers
336212	Boat transporter trailers, multi-unit, manufacturing
336214	Boat transporter trailers, single-unit, manufacturing
336612	Boat yards (i.e., boat manufacturing facilities)
487210	Boat, fishing charter, operation
811490	Boat, pleasure, repair and maintenance services without retailing new boats
713930	Boating clubs with marinas
713990	Boating clubs without marinas
421860	Boats (except pleasure) wholesaling
336612	Boats (i.e., suitable or intended for personal use) manufacturing
326199	Boats, inflatable plastics, manufacturing
421910	Boats, pleasure (e.g., canoes, motorboats, sailboats), wholesaling
321912	Bobbin blocks and blanks, wood, manufacturing
322214	Bobbins, fiber, made from purchased paperboard
333292	Bobbins, textile machinery, manufacturing
339920	Bobsleds manufacturing
812320	Bobtailers, laundry and drycleaning
713990	Boccie ball courts
421110	Bodies, motor vehicle, wholesaling
713940	Body building studios, physical fitness
561612	Body guard services
811121	Body shops, automotive
315191	Body stockings made in apparel knitting mills
315212	Body stockings, women's, girls', and infants', cut and sew apparel contractors
315239	Body stockings, women's, misses', and girls', cut and sewn from purchased fabric (except apparel contractors)
332995	Bofors guns manufacturing
332410	Boiler casings manufacturing
235110	Boiler chipping, scaling, cleaning
235110	Boiler cleaning
235110	Boiler contractors
334513	Boiler controls, industrial, power, and marine-type, manufacturing
332919	Boiler couplings and drains, plumbing and heating-type, manufacturing
332911	Boiler gauge cocks, industrial-type, manufacturing
811310	Boiler repair and maintenance shops (except manufacturing)
331210	Boiler tubes, wrought, made from purchased iron
421720	Boilers (e.g., heating, hot water, power, steam) wholesaling
333414	Boilers, heating, manufacturing
332410	Boilers, power, manufacturing
311612	Bologna made from purchased carcasses
332722	Bolts, metal, manufacturing

Bolts—Bows

Code	Description	Code	Description	Code	Description
326199	Bolts, nuts, and rivets, plastics, manufacturing	421420	Bookkeeping machines wholesaling	212391	Boron compounds prepared at beneficiating plants
333924	Bomb lifts manufacturing	541219	Bookkeeping services	325188	Boron compounds, not specified
332993	Bomb loading and assembling plants	713290	Bookmakers		elsewhere by process, manufacturing
332993	Bombcluster adapters manufacturing	514120	Bookmobiles	212391	Boron mineral mining and/or beneficiating
332993	Bombs manufacturing	323117	Books printing and binding without publishing	325188	Borosilicate manufacturing
523120	Bond brokerages	323117	Books printing without publishing	325412	Botanical extract preparations (except in-vitro diagnostics) manufacturing
523110	Bond dealing (i.e., acting as a principal in dealing securities to investors)	422920	Books wholesaling	712130	Botanical gardens
322233	Bond paper made from purchased paper	427120	Books, sales or receipt, wholesaling	325320	Botanical insecticides manufacturing
322121	Bond paper made in paper mills	323116	Books, sales, manifold, printing	422210	Botanicals wholesaling
493190	Bonded warehousing (except farm products, general merchandise, refrigerated)	339920	Boomerangs manufacturing	541710	Botany research and development laboratories or services
		813410	Booster clubs	326199	Bottle caps and lids, plastics, manufacturing
493130	Bonded warehousing, farm products (except refrigerated)	486990	Booster pumping station (except natural gas, petroleum)	332115	Bottle caps and tops, metal, stamping
493110	Bonded warehousing, general merchandise	486110	Booster pumping station, crude oil transportation	321999	Bottle corks manufacturing
493120	Bonded warehousing, refrigerated	486210	Booster pumping station, natural gas transportation	321999	Bottle covers, willow, rattan, and reed, manufacturing
313230	Bonded-fiber fabrics manufacturing			561990	Bottle exchanges
332812	Bonderizing metal and metal products for the trade	486910	Booster pumping station, refined petroleum products transportation	335211	Bottle warmers, household-type electric, manufacturing
524126	Bonding, fidelity or surety insurance, direct	332993	Boosters and bursters, artillery, manufacturing	333993	Bottle washers, packaging machinery, manufacturing
812990	Bondsperson services	335311	Boosters, feeder voltage (i.e., electrical transformers), manufacturing	454312	Bottled gas dealers, direct selling
325182	Bone black manufacturing	421850	Boot and shoe cut stock and findings wholesaling	422490	Bottled water (except water treating) wholesaling
327112	Bone china manufacturing			454390	Bottled water providers, direct selling
339112	Bone drills manufacturing	316999	Boot and shoe cut stock and findings, leather, manufacturing	421840	Bottles (except waste) wholesaling
311119	Bone meal prepared as feed for animals and fowls	321999	Boot and shoe lasts, all materials, manufacturing	327213	Bottles (i.e., bottling, canning, packaging), glass, manufacturing
339999	Bone novelties manufacturing	623990	Boot camps for delinquent youth	326160	Bottles, plastics, manufacturing
339112	Bone plates and screws manufacturing	333298	Boot making and repairing machinery manufacturing	332439	Bottles, vacuum, manufacturing
339112	Bone rongeurs manufacturing			421930	Bottles, waste, wholesaling
311613	Bones, fat, rendering	812990	Bootblack parlors	312111	Bottling flavored water
323121	Book binding shops	422340	Boots (e.g., hiking, western, work) wholesaling	333993	Bottling machinery (e.g., capping, filling, labeling, sterilizing, washing) manufacturing
323121	Book binding without printing	316219	Boots, dress and casual (except plastics, rubber), children's and infants', manufacturing	
454110	Book clubs, not publishing, mail-order			
813410	Book discussion clubs			421830	Bottling machinery and equipment wholesaling
332999	Book ends, metal, manufacturing	316213	Boots, dress and casual (except plastics, rubber), men's, manufacturing	335121	Boudoir lamp fixtures manufacturing
322222	Book paper made by coating purchased paper	316214	Boots, dress and casual (except plastics, rubber), women's, manufacturing	311422	Bouillon canning
				311423	Bouillon made in dehydration plants
322222	Book paper, coated, made from purchased paper	316219	Boots, hiking (except rubber, plastics), children's and infants', manufacturing	212319	Boulder crushed and broken mining and/or beneficiating
322121	Book paper, coated, made in paper mills	316213	Boots, hiking (except rubber, plastics), men's, manufacturing	324199	Boulets (i.e., fuel bricks) made from refined petroleum
511130	Book publishers (e.g., hardback, paperback, tape)	316214	Boots, hiking (except rubber, plastics), women's, manufacturing	422590	Bovine semen wholesaling
511130	Book publishers and printing combined	316211	Boots, plastics or plastics soled fabric upper, manufacturing	315211	Bow ties, men's and boys', cut and sew apparel contractors
511130	Book publishers publishing all formats			
511130	Book publishers, university press	316211	Boots, rubber or rubber soled fabric upper, manufacturing	315993	Bow ties, men's and boys', cut and sewn from purchased fabric (except apparel contractors)
511130	Book publishing (i.e., establishments known as publishers)	212391	Borate, natural, mining and/or beneficiating	
451211	Book stores	325188	Borax (i.e., sodium borate) manufacturing	235990	Bowling alley installation and service construction contractors
453310	Book stores, used			713950	Bowling alleys
316110	Bookbinder's leather manufacturing	212391	Borax, crude, ground or pulverized, mining and/or beneficiating	337127	Bowling center furniture manufacturing
333293	Bookbinding machines manufacturing	325320	Bordeaux mixture insecticides manufacturing	713950	Bowling centers
323121	Bookbinding without printing			421910	Bowling equipment and supplies wholesaling
337125	Bookcases (except wood and metal), household-type, manufacturing	325188	Boric acid manufacturing	
		235930	Boring contractors, building construction	451110	Bowling equipment and supply stores
337214	Bookcases (except wood), office-type, manufacturing	333512	Boring machines, metalworking, manufacturing	611620	Bowling instruction
				713990	Bowling leagues or teams, recreational
337124	Bookcases, metal household-type, manufacturing	213114	Boring test holes for metal mining on a contract basis	321912	Bowling pin blanks manufacturing
337122	Bookcases, wood household-type, manufacturing	213115	Boring test holes for nonmetallic minerals mining (except fuels) on a contract basis	339920	Bowling pin machines, automatic, manufacturing
337211	Bookcases, wood office-type, manufacturing			326199	Bowls and bowl covers, plastics, manufacturing
713290	Bookies	333512	Boring, drilling, and milling machine combinations, metalworking, manufacturing	321999	Bowls, wood, turned and shaped, manufacturing
512199	Booking agencies, motion picture			314999	Bows made from purchased fabrics
512199	Booking agencies, motion picture or video productions			339920	Bows, archery, manufacturing
711320	Booking agencies, theatrical (except motion picture)			316999	Bows, shoe, leather, manufacturing
541219	Bookkeepers' offices			
541219	Bookkeepers' private practices			

Code	Description
321920	Box cleats, wood, manufacturing
321920	Box lumber manufacturing
311991	Box lunches (for sale off premises) manufacturing
321920	Box shook manufacturing
337910	Box springs, assembled, made from purchased spring
316999	Box toes (i.e., shoe cut stock), leather, manufacturing
311612	Boxed beef made from purchased carcasses
311611	Boxed beef produced in slaughtering plants
311612	Boxed meat produced from purchased carcasses
311611	Boxed meats produced in slaughtering plants
711219	Boxers, independent professional
421840	Boxes and crates, industrial (except disposable plastics, paperboard, waste), wholesaling
321920	Boxes, cigar, wood and part wood, manufacturing
322211	Boxes, corrugated and solid fiber, made from purchased paper or paperboard
335932	Boxes, electrical wiring (e.g., junction, outlet, switch), manufacturing
322212	Boxes, folding (except corrugated), made from purchased paperboard
316991	Boxes, hat (except paper or paperboard), manufacturing
321920	Boxes, jewelry, wood or part wood, manufacturing
316999	Boxes, leather, manufacturing
332439	Boxes, light gauge metal, manufacturing
422130	Boxes, paperboard and disposable plastics, wholesaling
322215	Boxes, sanitary food (except folding), made from purchased paper or paperboard
322213	Boxes, setup (i.e., not shipped flat), made from purchased paperboard
322211	Boxes, shipping, laminated paper and paperboard, made from purchased paperboard
336211	Boxes, truck (e.g., cargo, dump, utility, van), assembled on purchased chassis
421930	Boxes, waste, wholesaling
321920	Boxes, wood, manufacturing
321920	Boxes, wood, plain or fabric covered, nailed or lock corner, manufacturing
711211	Boxing clubs, professional or semiprofessional
713990	Boxing clubs, recreational
339920	Boxing equipment manufacturing
711310	Boxing event managers with facilities
711320	Boxing event managers without facilities
711310	Boxing event organizers with facilities
711320	Boxing event organizers without facilities
711310	Boxing event promoters with facilities
711320	Boxing event promoters without facilities
337215	Boxspring frames manufacturing
813410	Boy guiding organizations
623990	Boys' and girls' residential facilities (e.g., homes, ranches, villages)
721214	Boys' camps (except day, instructional)
611620	Boys' camps, sports instruction
611620	Boys' camps, sports instructor
713990	Boys' day camps (except instructional)
315119	Boys' socks manufacturing
111334	Boysenberry farming
315212	Bra-slips, women's and girls', cut and sew apparel contractors

Code	Description
315231	Bra-slips, women's, misses', and juniors', cut and sewn from purchased fabric (except apparel contractors)
339911	Bracelets, precious metal, manufacturing
115112	Bracing of orchard trees and vines
332510	Brackets (i.e., builder's hardware-type), metal, manufacturing
332618	Brackets made from purchased wire
321918	Brackets, wood, manufacturing
421710	Brads wholesaling
331222	Brads, iron or steel, wire or cut, made in wire drawing plants
332618	Brads, metal, made from purchased wire
333292	Braiding machinery for textiles manufacturing
313221	Braiding narrow fabrics
336340	Brake and brake parts, automotive, truck, and bus, manufacturing
336340	Brake caliper assemblies, automotive, truck, and bus, manufacturing
336340	Brake cylinders, master and wheel, automotive, truck, and bus, manufacturing
336340	Brake discs (rotor), automotive, truck, and bus, manufacturing
336340	Brake drums, automotive, truck, and bus, manufacturing
325998	Brake fluid, synthetic, manufacturing
324191	Brake fluids, petroleum, made from refined petroleum
336340	Brake hose assemblies manufacturing
336340	Brake lining, automotive, truck, and bus, manufacturing
336340	Brake pads and shoes, automotive, truck, and bus, manufacturing
811118	Brake repair shops, automotive
333319	Brake service equipment (except mechanic's hand tools), motor vehicle, manufacturing
333613	Brakes and clutches (except electromagnetic industrial controls, motor vehicle) manufacturing
335314	Brakes and clutches, electromagnetic, manufacturing
336510	Brakes and parts for railroad rolling stock manufacturing
335314	Brakes, electromagnetic, manufacturing
333513	Brakes, press, metalworking, manufacturing
311212	Bran and other residues of milling rice
522110	Branches of foreign banks
521110	Branches, Federal Reserve Bank
533110	Brand name licensing
115210	Branding
339943	Branding irons (i.e., marking irons) manufacturing
422820	Brandy and brandy spirits wholesaling
312130	Brandy distilling
331522	Brass die-castings, unfinished, manufacturing
331525	Brass foundries (except die-casting)
421720	Brass goods, plumbers', wholesaling
325612	Brass polishes manufacturing
331421	Brass products, rolling, drawing, or extruding, made from purchased copper or in integrated secondary smelting and rolling, drawing or extruding plants
315212	Brassieres cut and sew apparel contractors
315231	Brassieres cut and sewn from purchased fabric (except apparel contractors)
332323	Brasswork, ornamental, manufacturing
335221	Braziers, barbecue, manufacturing
111335	Brazil nut farming

Code	Description
325191	Brazilwood extract manufacturing
332811	Brazing (i.e., hardening) metals and metal products for the trade
311822	Bread and bread-type roll mixes made from purchased flour
311812	Bread and bread-type rolls made in commercial bakeries
311999	Bread crumbs not made in bakeries
335211	Bread machines, household-type electric, manufacturing
333294	Bread slicing machinery manufacturing
333993	Bread wrapping machines manufacturing
212113	Breakers, anthracite mining and/or beneficiating
333131	Breakers, coal, manufacturing
332919	Breakers, vacuum, plumbing, manufacturing
311340	Breakfast bars, nonchocolate covered, manufacturing
311230	Breakfast cereals manufacturing
422490	Breakfast cereals wholesaling
234990	Breakwater construction
332313	Breechings, fabricated metal plate work, manufacturing
112990	Breeding of pets (e.g., birds, cats, dogs)
115210	Breeding, animal, services
312120	Breweries
311211	Brewers' and distillers' flakes and grits, corn, manufacturing
311213	Brewers' malt manufacturing
325191	Brewers' pitch made by distillation of wood
311212	Brewers' rice manufacturing
422490	Brewers' yeast wholesaling
333294	Brewery machinery manufacturing
235410	Bricklaying construction contractors
421320	Bricks (except refractory) wholesaling
327121	Bricks (i.e., common, face, glazed, hollow, vitrified), clay, manufacturing
327123	Bricks, adobe, manufacturing
327124	Bricks, clay refractory, manufacturing
327331	Bricks, concrete, manufacturing
327215	Bricks, glass, made from purchased glass
327212	Bricks, glass, made in glass making plants
327125	Bricks, nonclay refractory, manufacturing
315233	Bridal dresses or gowns, custom made
315233	Bridal dresses or gowns, women's, misses', and girls', cut and sewn from purchased fabric (except apparel contractors)
315212	Bridal dresses or gowns, women's, misses', and juniors', apparel contractors
448190	Bridal gown shops (except custom)
532220	Bridal wear rental
333999	Bridge and gate lifting machinery manufacturing
611699	Bridge and other card game instruction
321114	Bridge and trestle parts, wood, treating
234120	Bridge and tunnel construction management firms
713990	Bridge clubs, recreational
234120	Bridge construction
234120	Bridge decking construction
235210	Bridge painting construction contractors
332312	Bridge sections, prefabricated metal, manufacturing
488490	Bridge, tunnel, and highway operations
339116	Bridges, custom made in dental laboratories
334515	Bridges, electrical (e.g., Kelvin, megohm, vacuum tube, Wheatstone), manufacturing

Bridle—Bulk mail

Code	Description
316110	Bridle leather manufacturing
234990	Bridle path construction
316991	Briefcases, all materials, manufacturing
315291	Briefs, infants', cut and sewn from purchased fabric (except apparel contractors)
315192	Briefs, underwear, made in apparel knitting mills
315211	Briefs, underwear, men's and boys', cut and sew apparel contractors
315221	Briefs, underwear, men's and boys', cut and sewn from purchased fabric (except apparel contractors)
315231	Briefs, underwear, women's, misses', and girls', cut and sewn from purchased fabric (except apparel contractors)
315212	Briefs, women's, girls', and infants', cut and sew apparel contractors
212393	Brimstone mining and/or beneficiating
311421	Brining of fruits and vegetables
212210	Briquets, iron, mining and/or beneficiating
324199	Briquettes, petroleum, made from refined petroleum
422590	Bristles wholesaling
322130	Bristols board stock manufacturing
322121	Bristols paper stock manufacturing
333515	Broaches (i.e., a machine tool accessory) manufacturing
333512	Broaching machines, metalworking, manufacturing
334220	Broadcast equipment (including studio), for radio and television, manufacturing
541910	Broadcast media rating services
421690	Broadcasting equipment wholesaling
513111	Broadcasting networks, radio
513120	Broadcasting networks, television
611519	Broadcasting schools
513112	Broadcasting stations, radio
513120	Broadcasting stations, television
513112	Broadcasting studio, radio station
711110	Broadway theaters
313210	Broadwoven fabrics (except rugs, tire fabrics) weaving
313311	Broadwoven fabrics finishing
313210	Brocades weaving
111219	Broccoli farming, field, bedding plant and seed production
112320	Broiler chicken production
523140	Brokerages, commodity contracts
524210	Brokerages, insurance
522310	Brokerages, loan
522310	Brokerages, mortgage
531210	Brokerages, real estate
523120	Brokerages, securities
524210	Brokers' offices, insurance
522310	Brokers' offices, loan
522310	Brokers' offices, mortgage
531210	Brokers' offices, real estate
325188	Bromine manufacturing
325199	Bromochloromethane manufacturing
339112	Bronchoscopes (except electromedical) manufacturing
334510	Bronchoscopes, electromedical, manufacturing
331522	Bronze die-castings, unfinished, manufacturing
331525	Bronze foundries (except die-casting)
325910	Bronze printing inks manufacturing
331421	Bronze products, rolling, drawing, or extruding, made from purchased copper or in integrated secondary smelting and rolling, drawing or extruding plants
111199	Broomcorn farming

Code	Description
422590	Broomcorn wholesaling
421220	Brooms and brushes, household-type, wholesaling
339994	Brooms, hand and machine, manufacturing
311422	Broth (except seafood) canning
311313	Brown beet sugar refining
212111	Brown coal mining and/or beneficiating
212210	Brown ore mining and/or beneficiating
311313	Brown sugar made from beet sugar
311312	Brown sugar made from purchased raw cane sugar
311311	Brown sugar made in sugarcane mill
325411	Brucine manufacturing
212325	Brucite mining and/or beneficiating
335991	Brush blocks, carbon or molded graphite, manufacturing
321912	Brush blocks, wood, turned and shaped
234990	Brush clearing or cutting
562119	Brush collection services
562119	Brush hauling, local
562119	Brush removal services
335991	Brushes and brush stock contacts, electric, carbon and graphite, manufacturing
339942	Brushes, artists', manufacturing
339994	Brushes, household-type and industrial, manufacturing
339994	Brushes, paint (except artists'), manufacturing
326299	Brushes, rubber, manufacturing
333512	Brushing machines, metalworking, manufacturing
335991	Brushplates, carbon or graphite, manufacturing
111219	Brussel sprout farming, field, bedding plant and seed production
325620	Bubble bath preparations manufacturing
326199	Bubble packaging materials, plastics, manufacturing
333120	Bucket and scarifier teeth manufacturing
333922	Buckets, elevator or conveyor, manufacturing
333120	Buckets, excavating (e.g., clamshell, concrete, drag scraper, dragline, shovel), manufacturing
321920	Buckets, wood, coopered, manufacturing
339993	Buckles and buckle parts (including shoe) manufacturing
111199	Buckwheat farming
311211	Buckwheat flour manufacturing
921130	Budget agencies, government
112990	Buffalo production
722212	Buffet eating places
337122	Buffets (furniture), wood, manufacturing
333512	Buffing and polishing machines, metalworking, manufacturing
327910	Buffing and polishing wheels, abrasive and nonabrasive, manufacturing
325612	Buffing compounds manufacturing
333991	Buffing machines, handheld power-driven, manufacturing
332813	Buffing metals and metal products for the trade
316110	Buffings, russet, manufacturing
332510	Builder's hardware, metal, manufacturing
233310	Building alterations, industrial, general construction contractors
233320	Building alterations, nonresidential, commercial and institutional buildings, general construction contractors

Code	Description
233220	Building alterations, residential (except single family), general construction contractors
233210	Building alterations, single family, general construction contractors
541310	Building architectural design services
421320	Building blocks (e.g., cinder, concrete) wholesaling
421310	Building board (e.g., fiber, flake, particle) wholesaling
561720	Building cleaning services, interior
561720	Building cleaning services, janitorial
233310	Building components manufacturing plant construction, general construction contractors
233310	Building construction, industrial, general construction contractors
233220	Building construction, residential (except single family), general construction contractors
233210	Building construction, single family, general construction contractors
561790	Building exterior cleaning services (except sand blasting, window cleaning)
235910	Building front metal, construction contractors
541350	Building inspection bureaus
541350	Building inspection services
926150	Building inspections, government
326199	Building materials (e.g., fascia, panels, siding, soffit), plastics, manufacturing
444190	Building materials supply dealers
421390	Building materials, fiberglass (except insulation, roofing, siding), wholesaling
213112	Building oil and gas well foundations on a contract basis
326199	Building panels, corrugated and flat, plastics, manufacturing
322121	Building paper stock manufacturing
421390	Building paper wholesaling
334512	Building services monitoring controls, automatic, manufacturing
925110	Building standards agencies, government
421320	Building stone wholesaling
327121	Building tile, clay, manufacturing
531110	Building, apartment, rental or leasing
213112	Building, erecting, repairing, and dismantling oil and gas field rigs and derricks on a contract basis
531120	Building, nonresidential (except miniwarehouse), rental or leasing
531110	Building, residential, rental or leasing
321991	Buildings, mobile, commercial use, manufacturing
321992	Buildings, prefabricated and portable, wood, manufacturing
332311	Buildings, prefabricated metal, manufacturing
421390	Buildings, prefabricated nonwood, wholesaling
421310	Buildings, prefabricated wood, wholesaling
327999	Built-up mica manufacturing
335110	Bulbs, electric light, complete, manufacturing
311211	Bulgur (flour) manufacturing
422710	Bulk gasoline stations
484220	Bulk liquids trucking, local
484230	Bulk liquids trucking, long-distance
484110	Bulk mail truck transportation, contract, local
484121	Bulk mail truck transportation, contract, long-distance

Code	Description
493190	Bulk petroleum storage
422710	Bulk stations, petroleum
332420	Bulk storage tanks, heavy gauge metal, manufacturing
115210	Bull testing stations
532412	Bulldozer rental or leasing without operator
333120	Bulldozers manufacturing
332992	Bullet jackets and cores (i.e., 30 mm. or less, 1.18 inch or less) manufacturing
321999	Bulletin boards, wood and cork, manufacturing
339113	Bulletproof vests manufacturing
212221	Bullion, gold, produced at the mine
212222	Bullion, silver, produced at the mine
336399	Bumpers and bumperettes assembled, automotive, truck, and bus, manufacturing
333313	Bundling machinery (e.g., box strapping, mail, newspaper) manufacturing
321999	Bungs, wood, manufacturing
339111	Bunsen burners manufacturing
315291	Buntings, infants', cut and sewn from purchased fabric (except apparel contractors)
315212	Buntings, infants', cut and ew apparel contractors
334513	Buoyancy instruments, industrial process-type, manufacturing
321999	Buoys, cork, manufacturing
332313	Buoys, fabricated plate work metal, manufacturing
561621	Burglar alarm monitoring services
561621	Burglar alarm sales combined with installation, maintenance, or monitoring services
334290	Burglar alarm systems and equipment manufacturing
524126	Burglary and theft insurance carriers, direct
339995	Burial caskets and cases manufacturing
421850	Burial caskets wholesaling
315299	Burial garments cut and sewn from purchased fabric (except apparel contractors)
315211	Burial garments, men's and boys', cut and sew apparel contractors
315212	Burial garments, women's, girls' and infants', cut and sew apparel contractors
524128	Burial insurance carriers, direct
339995	Burial vaults (except concrete, stone) manufacturing
327390	Burial vaults, concrete and precast terrazzo, manufacturing
327991	Burial vaults, stone, manufacturing
422990	Burlap wholesaling
711110	Burlesque companies
212325	Burley mining and/or beneficiating
313311	Burling and mending broadwoven fabrics
313312	Burling and mending fabrics (except broadwoven)
335311	Burner ignition transformers manufacturing
421720	Burners, fuel oil and distillate oil, wholesaling
333414	Burners, heating, manufacturing
332811	Burning metals and metal products for the trade
333512	Burnishing machines, metalworking, manufacturing
321999	Burnt wood articles manufacturing
314999	Burnt-out laces manufacturing

Code	Description
112920	Burro production
212399	Burrstones, natural, mining and/or beneficiating
335313	Bus bar structures, switchgear-type, manufacturing
335931	Bus bars, electrical conductors (except switchgear-type), manufacturing
336211	Bus bodies assembling on purchased chassis
336211	Bus bodies manufacturing
541850	Bus card advertising services
485510	Bus charter services (except scenic, sightseeing)
541850	Bus display advertising services
611519	Bus driver training
485210	Bus line operation, inter-city
485113	Bus line, local (except mixed mode)
485410	Bus operation, school and employee
532120	Bus rental or leasing
485113	Bus services, urban and suburban (except mixed mode)
488490	Bus terminal operation, independent
561599	Bus ticket offices
485113	Bus transit systems (except mixed mode)
336120	Buses (except trackless trolley) assembling on chassis of own manufacture
421110	Buses wholesaling
487110	Buses, scenic and sightseeing operation
336510	Buses, trackless trolley, manufacturing
333613	Bushings, plain (except internal combustion engine), manufacturing
326199	Bushings, plastics, manufacturing
321999	Bushings, wood, manufacturing
813910	Business associations
611410	Business colleges or schools not offering academic degrees
611310	Business colleges or schools offering baccalaureate or graduate degrees
323112	Business directories flexographic printing without publishing
323111	Business directories gravure printing without publishing
323110	Business directories lithographic (offset) printing without publishing
323119	Business directories printing (except flexographic, gravure, lithographic, screen) without publishing
323113	Business directories screen printing without publishing
511140	Business directory publishers
511140	Business directory publishers and printing combined
511140	Business directory publishing (i.e., establishments known as publishers)
323112	Business forms (except manifold) flexographic printing without publishing
323111	Business forms (except manifold) gravure printing without publishing
323110	Business forms (except manifold) lithographic printing
323119	Business forms (except manifold) printing (except flexographic, gravure, lithographic, screen) without publishing
323113	Business forms (except manifold) screen printing without publishing
323116	Business forms, manifold, printing
421420	Business machines and equipment (except computers) wholesaling
541611	Business management consulting services
561110	Business management services
541720	Business research and development services

Code	Description
611410	Business schools not offering academic degrees
561439	Business service centers (except private mail centers)
561439	Business service centers (except private mail centers) providing range of office support services (except printing)
541611	Business start-up consulting services
325211	Butadiene copolymers containing less than 50 percent butadiene manufacturing
325212	Butadiene copolymers containing more than 50 percent butadiene manufacturing
325199	Butadiene made from alcohol
325110	Butadiene made from refined petroleum or liquid hydrocarbons
325212	Butadiene rubber (i.e., polybutadiene) manufacturing
325110	Butane made from refined petroleum or liquid hydrocarbons
211112	Butane, natural, mining
445210	Butcher shops
332211	Butcher's knives manufacturing
311512	Butter manufacturing
333294	Butter processing machinery manufacturing
422430	Butter wholesaling
311512	Butter, creamery and whey, manufacturing
332911	Butterfly valves, industrial-type, manufacturing
311511	Buttermilk manufacturing
111219	Butternut squash farming, field, bedding plant and seed production
335912	Button cells, primary batteries, manufacturing
333298	Buttonhole and eyelet machinery manufacturing
315211	Buttonhole making apparel contractors, men's and boys'
315212	Buttonhole making apparel contractors, women's, misses', girls', and infants' (except fur)
315212	Buttonhole making, fur goods, women's, girls', and infants', cut and sew apparel contractors
315211	Buttonholing and button covering apparel contractors, men's and boys'
315212	Buttonholing and button covering apparel contractors, women's, misses', and girls'
339993	Buttons (except precious metal, precious stones, semiprecious stones) manufacturing
339911	Buttons, precious metal, precious stones, semiprecious stones, manufacturing
325199	Butyl acetate manufacturing
325212	Butyl rubber manufacturing
324110	Butylene (i.e., butene) made in petroleum refineries
325110	Butylene made from refined petroleum or liquid hydrocarbons
531210	Buyers' agents, real estate, offices
531210	Buying agencies, real estate
531210	Buying real estate for others (i.e., agents, brokers)
332212	C-clamps manufacturing
541512	CAD (computer-aided design) systems integration design services
541512	CAE (computer-aided engineering) systems integration design services
541512	CAM (computer-aided manufacturing) systems integration design services

CAT scanner—Camp furniture

Code	Description	Code	Description	Code	Description
621512	CAT (computerized axial tomography) scanner centers	331222	Cable, iron or steel, insulated or armored, made in wire drawing plants	325188	Calcium inorganic compounds, not specified elsewhere by process, manufacturing
334220	CB (citizens band) radios manufacturing	335929	Cable, nonferrous, insulated, or armored, made from purchased nonferrous wire	325199	Calcium organic compounds, not specified elsewhere by process, manufacturing
334112	CD-ROM drives manufacturing				
334611	CD-ROM, software, mass reproducing	332618	Cable, noninsulated wire, made from purchased wire	325199	Calcium oxalate manufacturing
525990	CMOs (collateralized mortgage obligations)	421510	Cable, wire (except insulated), wholesaling	327410	Calcium oxide (i.e., quicklime) manufacturing
541211	CPAs' (certified public accountants) offices	333111	Cabs for agricultural machinery manufacturing	421420	Calculators and calculating machines wholesaling
611699	CPR (cardiac pulmonary resusitation) training and certification	333120	Cabs for construction machinery manufacturing	333313	Calculators manufacturing
334411	CRT (cathode ray tube) manufacturing			511199	Calendar publishers
621512	CT-SCAN (computer tomography) centers	333924	Cabs for industrial trucks manufacturing	511199	Calendar publishers and printing combined
334517	CT/CAT (computerized axial tomography) scanners manufacturing	111339	Cactus fruit farming	511199	Calendar publishing (i.e., establishments known as publishers)
		541370	Cadastral surveying services		
485310	Cab (i.e., taxi) services	339920	Caddy carts manufacturing	453998	Calendar shops
336112	Cab and chassis, light trucks and vans, manufacturing	331419	Cadmium refining, primary	323112	Calendars flexographic printing without publishing
		337215	Cafeteria fixtures manufacturing		
111219	Cabbage farming, field, bedding plant and seed production	722310	Cafeteria food service contractors (e.g., government office cafeterias, hospital cafeterias, school cafeterias)	323111	Calendars gravure printing without publishing
233210	Cabin construction			323110	Calendars lithographic (offset) printing without publishing
336612	Cabin cruiser	337127	Cafeteria furniture manufacturing		
334511	Cabin environment indicators, transmitters, and sensors manufacturing	337127	Cafeteria tables and benches manufacturing	323119	Calendars printing (except flexographic, lithographic, gravure, screen) without publishing
332510	Cabinet hardware, metal, manufacturing	722212	Cafeterias		
444190	Cabinet stores, kitchen (except custom), to be installed	325411	Caffeine and derivatives (i.e., basic chemicals) manufacturing	323113	Calendars screen printing without publishing
		315291	Caftans, infants', cut and sewn from purchased fabric (except apparel contractors)	313311	Calendering broadwoven fabrics
235510	Cabinet work on site construction contractors			333220	Calendering machinery for plastics manufacturing
337214	Cabinets (except wood), office-type, freestanding, manufacturing	315211	Caftans, men's and boys', cut and sew apparel contractors	333292	Calendering machinery for textiles manufacturing
337129	Cabinets (i.e., housings), wood (e.g., sewing machines, stereo, television), manufacturing	315223	Caftans, men's and boys', cut and sewn from purchased fabric (except apparel contractors)	313312	Calendering textile products, apparel, and fabrics (except broadwoven)
337110	Cabinets, kitchen (except freestanding), stock or custom wood, manufacturing	315212	Caftans, women's, girls', and infants', cut and sew apparel contractors	112111	Calf (e.g., feeder, stocker, veal) production
421310	Cabinets, kitchen, built in, wholesaling	315231	Caftans, women's, misses' and girls', cut and sewn from purchased fabric (except apparel contractors)	315119	Calf high sheer hosiery knitting or knitting and finishing
421210	Cabinets, kitchen, free standing, wholesaling			541380	Calibration and certification testing laboratories or services
337124	Cabinets, metal (i.e., bathroom, kitchen) (except freestanding), manufacturing	332618	Cages made from purchased wire		
		235930	Caisson contractors, building construction	332212	Calipers and dividers, machinists' precision tools, manufacturing
337124	Cabinets, metal household-type, freestanding, manufacturing	234990	Caisson drilling	336340	Calipers, brake, automotive, truck, and bus, manufacturing
337124	Cabinets, metal, radio and television, manufacturing	332420	Caissons, underwater work, manufacturing	339992	Calliopes (steam organs) manufacturing
337122	Cabinets, wood household-type, freestanding, manufacturing	311999	Cake frosting manufacturing	532210	Camcorder rental
		311999	Cake frosting mixes manufacturing	334310	Camcorders manufacturing
337211	Cabinets, wood office-type, freestanding, manufacturing	311822	Cake mixes made from purchased flour	326211	Camelback (i.e., retreading material) manufacturing
721199	Cabins, housekeeping	311340	Cake ornaments, confectionery, manufacturing	333220	Camelback (i.e., retreading materials) machinery manufacturing
513220	Cable TV providers (except networks)	311813	Cake, frozen, manufacturing		
513210	Cable broadcasting networks	311812	Cakes, baking (except frozen), made in commercial bakeries	316991	Camera carrying bags, all materials, manufacturing
485119	Cable car systems (except mixed mode), commuter			421410	Camera equipment and supplies, photographic, wholesaling
487110	Cable car, land, scenic and sightseeing operation	212231	Calamine mining and/or beneficiating		
		212221	Calaverite mining and/or beneficiating	333314	Camera lenses manufacturing
334220	Cable decoders manufacturing	212312	Calcareous tufa crushed and broken stone mining and/or beneficiating	811211	Camera repair shops without retailing new cameras
234920	Cable laying				
513220	Cable program distribution operators	212311	Calcareous tufa mining or quarrying	443130	Camera shops, photographic
235310	Cable splicing, electrical, construction contractors	325510	Calcimines manufacturing	711510	Cameramen, independent (freelance)
		422950	Calcimines, wholesaling	333315	Cameras (except digital, television, video) manufacturing
235310	Cable television hookup construction contractors	212392	Calcined phosphate rock mining and/or beneficiating		
		324199	Calcining petroleum coke from refined petroleum	334220	Cameras, television, manufacturing
234920	Cable television line construction			315212	Camisoles, women's and girls', cut and sew apparel contractors
513210	Cable television networks	212399	Calcite mining and/or beneficiating		
334220	Cable television transmission and receiving equipment manufacturing	325188	Calcium carbide, chloride, and hypochlorite manufacturing	315231	Camisoles, women's, misses' and girls', cut and sewn from purchased fabric (except apparel contractors)
331422	Cable, copper (e.g., armored, bare, insulated), made from purchased copper in wire drawing plants	325199	Calcium citrate manufacturing		
		327410	Calcium hydroxide (i.e., hydrated lime) manufacturing	337124	Camp furniture, metal, manufacturing
331422	Cable, copper (e.g., armored, bare, insulated), made in integrated secondary smelting and drawing plants			337125	Camp furniture, reed and rattan, manufacturing
		325188	Calcium hypochlorite manufacturing	337122	Camp furniture, wood, manufacturing

Code	Description
813940	Campaign organizations, political
441210	Camper dealers, recreational
532120	Camper rental
336214	Camper units, slide-in, for pick-up trucks, manufacturing
721211	Campgrounds
325191	Camphor, natural, manufacturing
325199	Camphor, synthetic, manufacturing
421910	Camping equipment and supplies wholesaling
336214	Camping trailers and chassis manufacturing
421110	Camping trailers wholesaling
721214	Camps (except day, instructional)
713990	Camps (except instructional), day
623990	Camps, boot or disciplinary (except correctional), for delinquent youth
611620	Camps, sports instruction
333515	Cams (i.e., a machine tool accessory) manufacturing
333513	Can forming machines, metalworking, manufacturing
332618	Can keys made from purchased wire
332431	Can lids and ends, metal, manufacturing
332212	Can openers (except electric) manufacturing
335211	Can openers, household-type electric, manufacturing
483211	Canal barge transportation
234990	Canal construction
488310	Canal maintenance services (except dredging)
488310	Canal operation
483212	Canal passenger transportation
221310	Canal, irrigation
333313	Canceling machinery, postal office-type, manufacturing
923120	Cancer detection program administration
622310	Cancer hospitals
541710	Cancer research laboratories or services
311340	Candied fruits and fruit peel manufacturing
713950	Candle pin bowling alleys
713950	Candle pin bowling centers
453998	Candle shops
339999	Candles manufacturing
422990	Candles wholesaling
311320	Candy bars, chocolate (including chocolate covered), made from cacao beans
311340	Candy bars, nonchocolate, manufacturing
311330	Candy stores, chocolate, candy made on premises not for immediate consumption
311340	Candy stores, nonchocolate, candy made on premises, not for immediate consumption
445292	Candy stores, packaged, retailing only
422450	Candy wholesaling
311320	Candy, chocolate, made from cacao beans
111930	Cane farming, sugar, field production
311312	Cane sugar made from purchased raw cane sugar
311311	Cane sugar made in sugarcane mill
422490	Cane sugar, refined, wholesaling
311312	Cane syrup made from purchased raw cane sugar
311311	Cane syrup made in sugarcane mill
339999	Canes (except orthopedic) manufacturing
332999	Canes, metal, manufacturing

Code	Description
332993	Canisters, ammunition, manufacturing
422490	Canned foods (e.g., fish, meat, seafood, soups) wholesaling
311611	Canned meats (except poultry) produced in slaughtering plants
311911	Canned nuts manufacturing
233310	Cannery construction
311711	Cannery, fish
311711	Cannery, shellfish
311421	Canning fruits and vegetables
311421	Canning jams and jellies
333993	Canning machinery manufacturing
311615	Canning poultry (except baby and pet food)
311422	Canning soups (except seafood)
421840	Canning supplies wholesaling
311711	Canning, fish, crustacea, and mollusks
332995	Cannons manufacturing
339112	Cannulae manufacturing
532292	Canoe rental
713990	Canoeing, recreational
311225	Canola (rapeseed) oil, cake and meal, made from purchased oils
311223	Canola (rapeseed) oil, cake and meal, made in crushing mills
111120	Canola farming, field and seed production
332322	Canopies, sheet metal, manufacturing
332431	Cans, aluminum, manufacturing
332431	Cans, metal, manufacturing
332431	Cans, steel, manufacturing
111219	Cantaloupe farming, field, bedding plant and seed production
722213	Canteens, fixed location
722330	Canteens, mobile
321912	Cants, resawed (lumber), manufacturing
314911	Canvas bags manufacturing
339942	Canvas board, artist's, manufacturing
314912	Canvas products (except bags) made from purchased canvas or canvas substitutes
422990	Canvas products wholesaling
316211	Canvas shoes, plastics soled fabric upper, manufacturing
316211	Canvas shoes, rubber soled fabric upper, manufacturing
339942	Canvas, artist's, prepared on frames, manufacturing
313210	Canvases weaving
454390	Canvassers (door-to-door), headquarters for retail sale of merchandise, direct selling
335999	Capacitors (except electronic), fixed and variable, manufacturing
334414	Capacitors, electronic, fixed and variable, manufacturing
421690	Capacitors, electronic, wholesaling
315212	Capes (except fur), women's, girls' and infants', cut and sew apparel contractors
315234	Capes (except fur, waterproof), women's, misses', and girls', cut and sewn from purchased fabric (except apparel contractors)
315292	Capes, fur (except apparel contractors), manufacturing
315212	Capes, fur, women's, girls', and infants', cut and sew apparel contractors
315299	Capes, waterproof (e.g., plastics, rubber, similar materials), cut and sewn from purchased fabric (except apparel contractors)
235810	Capping of water wells construction contractors

Code	Description
333993	Capping, sealing, and lidding packaging machinery manufacturing
325199	Caprolactam manufacturing
315991	Caps (except fur, leather) cut and sewn from purchased fabric (except apparel contractors)
315991	Caps (i.e., apparel accessory) cut and sewn from purchased fabric (except fur, leather, apparel contractors)
315211	Caps (i.e., apparel accessory), men's and boys', cut and sew apparel contractors
315212	Caps (i.e., apparel accessory), women's, girls', and infants', cut and sew apparel contractors
315299	Caps and gowns, academic, cut and sewn from purchased fabric (except apparel contractors)
315211	Caps and gowns, academic, men's and boys', cut and sew apparel contractors
315212	Caps and gowns, academic, women's and girls', cut and sew apparel contractors
335931	Caps and plugs, attachment, electric, manufacturing
332115	Caps and tops, bottle, metal, stamping
336214	Caps for pick-up trucks manufacturing
325998	Caps for toy pistols manufacturing
315191	Caps made in apparel knitting mills
325920	Caps, blasting and detonating, manufacturing
332993	Caps, bomb, manufacturing
315292	Caps, fur (except apparel contractors), manufacturing
316999	Caps, heel and toe, leather, manufacturing
315292	Caps, leather (except apparel contractors), manufacturing
315991	Caps, textiles, straw, fur-felt, and wool-felt, cut and sewn from purchased fabric (except apparel contractors)
315211	Caps, textiles, straw, fur-felt, and wool-felt, men's and boys', cut and sew apparel contractors
315212	Caps, textiles, straw, fur-felt, and wool-felt, women's, girls', and infants', cut and sew apparel contractors
325998	Capsules, gelatin, empty, manufacturing
334290	Car alarm manufacturing
336211	Car bodies, kit, manufacturing
811192	Car detailers
532112	Car leasing
483212	Car lighters (i.e., ferries), inland waters (except on Great Lakes system)
485999	Car pool operation
488999	Car pools, arrangement of
532111	Car rental
532111	Car rental agencies
561599	Car rental reservation services
811111	Car repair shops, general
332999	Car seals, metal, manufacturing
337125	Car seats, infant (except metal), manufacturing
334310	Car stereos manufacturing
421850	Car wash equipment and supplies wholesaling
811192	Car washes
331111	Car wheels, rolled steel, made in steel mills
325188	Carbides (e.g., boron, calcium, silicon, tungsten) manufacturing
332994	Carbines manufacturing
325199	Carbinol manufacturing
325211	Carbohydrate plastics manufacturing

Carbon—Casings

Code	Description
334510	Carbon arc lamp units, electrotherapeutic (except infrared and ultraviolet), manufacturing
325182	Carbon black manufacturing
422690	Carbon black wholesaling
327125	Carbon brick manufacturing
325120	Carbon dioxide manufacturing
325188	Carbon disulfide manufacturing
335991	Carbon electrodes and contacts, electric, manufacturing
325188	Carbon inorganic compounds manufacturing
334290	Carbon monoxide detectors manufacturing
421690	Carbon monoxide detectors, electronic, wholesaling
325199	Carbon organic compounds, not specified elsewhere by process, manufacturing
339944	Carbon paper manufacturing
335991	Carbon specialties for aerospace use (except gaskets) manufacturing
335991	Carbon specialties for electrical use manufacturing
335991	Carbon specialties for mechanical use (except gaskets) manufacturing
325199	Carbon tetrachloride manufacturing
325998	Carbon, activated, manufacturing
312111	Carbonated soda manufacturing
312111	Carbonated soft drinks manufacturing
325188	Carbonic acid manufacturing
333292	Carbonizing equipment for processing wool manufacturing
313312	Carbonizing textile fibers
335991	Carbons, electric, manufacturing
335991	Carbons, lighting, manufacturing
325998	Carburetor cleaners manufacturing
336311	Carburetors, all types, manufacturing
316993	Card cases (except metal) manufacturing
339911	Card cases, precious metal, manufacturing
713290	Card rooms (e.g., poker rooms)
453220	Card shops, greeting
337122	Card table sets (furniture), wood, manufacturing
337124	Card table sets, metal, manufacturing
422130	Cardboard products wholesaling
322130	Cardboard stock manufacturing
322226	Cardboard, laminated or surface coated, made from purchased paperboard
313230	Carded nonwoven fabrics manufacturing
313111	Carded yarn manufacturing
325412	Cardiac preparations manufacturing
333292	Carding machinery for textiles manufacturing
313312	Carding textile fibers
334510	Cardiodynameter manufacturing
334510	Cardiographs manufacturing
621111	Cardiologists' offices (e.g., centers, clinics)
334510	Cardiophone, electric, manufacturing
334510	Cardioscope manufacturing
334510	Cardiotachometer manufacturing
323112	Cards (e.g., business, greeting, playing, postcards, trading) flexographic printing without publishing
323111	Cards (e.g., business, greeting, playing, postcards, trading) gravure printing without publishing
323110	Cards (e.g., business, greeting, playing, postcards, trading) lithographic (offset) printing without publishing

Code	Description
323119	Cards (e.g., business, greeting, playing, postcards, trading) printing (except flexographic, gravure, lithographic, screen) without publishing
323113	Cards (e.g., business, greeting, playing, postcards, trading) screen printing without publishing
322299	Cards, die-cut (except office supply) made from purchased paper or paperboard
322231	Cards, die-cut office supply (e.g., index, library, time recording), made from purchased paper or paperboard
422120	Cards, greeting, wholesaling
******	Cards, publishing — see specific product
481112	Cargo carriers, air, scheduled
488390	Cargo checkers, marine
488330	Cargo salvaging, marine
336611	Cargo ship building
488390	Cargo surveyors, marine
488490	Cargo surveyors, truck transportation
333319	Carnival and amusement park rides manufacturing
333319	Carnival and amusement park shooting gallery machinery manufacturing
421850	Carnival equipment wholersaling
713990	Carnival ride concession operators (i.e., supplying and servicing in others' facilities)
711190	Carnival traveling shows
212291	Carnotite mining and/or beneficiating
333922	Carousel conveyors (e.g., luggage) manufacturing
333319	Carousels (i.e., merry-go-rounds) manufacturing
332212	Carpenter's handtools, nonelectric (except saws), manufacturing
611513	Carpenters' apprenticeship training
235510	Carpentry (rough and framing) construction contractors
235510	Carpentry (trim and finish) construction contractors
532490	Carpentry equipment rental or leasing
333319	Carpet and floor cleaning equipment, electric commercial-type, manufacturing
335212	Carpet and floor cleaning equipment, household-type electric, manufacturing
532490	Carpet and rug cleaning equipment rental or leasing
313111	Carpet and rug yarn spinning
532299	Carpet and rug, residential, rental
561740	Carpet cleaning on customers' premises
561740	Carpet cleaning plants
561740	Carpet cleaning services
314999	Carpet cutting and binding
235520	Carpet laying or removal construction contractors
313210	Carpet linings (except felt) weaving
313230	Carpet paddings, nonwoven, manufacturing
442210	Carpet stores
333319	Carpet sweepers, mechanical, manufacturing
421220	Carpet wholesaling
314110	Carpets and rugs made from textile materials
321999	Carpets, cork, manufacturing
332311	Carports, prefabricated metal, manufacturing
487110	Carriage, horse-drawn, operation
339932	Carriages, baby, manufacturing
339932	Carriages, doll, manufacturing
334210	Carrier equipment (i.e., analog, digital), telephone, manufacturing

Code	Description
111219	Carrot farming, field, bedding plant and seed production
311991	Carrots, cut, peeled or sliced fresh, manufacturing
722211	Carryout restaurants
336111	Cars, electric, for highway use, assembling on chassis of own manufacture
333131	Cars, mining, manufacturing
541370	Cartographic surveying services
333993	Carton filling machinery manufacturing
322299	Cartons, egg, molded pulp manufacturing
322212	Cartons, folding (except milk), made from purchased paperboard
322215	Cartons, milk, made from purchased paper or paperboard
422130	Cartons, paper and paperboard, wholesaling
711510	Cartoonists, independent
333991	Cartridge (i.e., powder) handheld power-driven tools manufacturing
332992	Cartridge cases for ammunition (i.e., 30 mm.or less, 1.18 inch or less) manufacturing
331421	Cartridge cups, discs, and sheets, copper and copper alloy, made from purchased copper or in integrated secondary smelting and rolling, drawing or extruding plants
422120	Cartridge toner wholesaling
332992	Cartridges (i.e., 30 mm. or less, 1.18 inch or less) manufacturing
339920	Carts, caddy, manufacturing
333924	Carts, grocery, made from purchased wire
333112	Carts, lawn and garden-type, manufacturing
332211	Carving sets manufacturing
333319	Car washing machinery manufacturing
111219	Casaba melon farming, field, bedding plant and seed production
316110	Case leather manufacturing
325222	Casein fibers and filaments manufacturing
325211	Casein plastics manufacturing
311514	Casein, dry and wet, manufacturing
332321	Casements, metal, manufacturing
316993	Cases, jewelry (except metal), manufacturing
339911	Cases, jewelry, precious metal, manufacturing
316991	Cases, luggage, manufacturing
316991	Cases, musical instrument, manufacturing
321920	Cases, shipping, wood, wirebound, manufacturing
321920	Cases, wood packing, nailed or lock corner, manufacturing
321920	Cases, wood shipping, nailed or lock corner, manufacturing
332439	Cash boxes, light gauge metal, manufacturing
532420	Cash register rental or leasing
333313	Cash registers (i.e., point of sales terminals) manufacturing
421420	Cash registers wholesaling
111335	Cashew farming
211112	Casing-head butane and propane production
326121	Casings, sausage, nonrigid plastics, manufacturing
332313	Casings, scroll, fabricated metal plate work, manufacturing

Code	Description
332322	Casings, sheet metal, manufacturing
233320	Casino construction
721120	Casino hotels
713210	Casinos (except casino hotels)
332510	Casket hardware, metal, manufacturing
339995	Caskets, burial, manufacturing
421850	Caskets, burial, wholesaling
321920	Casks, wood, coopered, manufacturing
111219	Cassava farming, field and seed casava production
335211	Casseroles, household-type electric, manufacturing
334612	Cassette tapes, pre-recorded audio, mass reproducing
532230	Cassette, prerecorded video, rental
421990	Cassettes, prerecorded audio and video, wholesaling
331511	Cast iron brake shoes, railroad, manufacturing
331511	Cast iron pipe and pipe fittings manufacturing
421510	Cast iron pipe wholesaling
331511	Cast iron railroad car wheels manufacturing
331513	Cast steel railroad car wheels, unfinished, manufacturing
327390	Cast stone, concrete (except structural), manufacturing
327124	Castable refractories, clay, manufacturing
327125	Castable refractories, nonclay, manufacturing
332510	Casters, furniture, manufacturing
332510	Casters, industrial, manufacturing
561310	Casting agencies (i.e., motion picture, theatrical, video)
561310	Casting agencies, motion picture or video
561310	Casting agencies, theatrical
561310	Casting bureaus (e.g., motion picture, theatrical, video)
561310	Casting bureaus, motion picture or video
561310	Casting bureaus, theatrical
331528	Castings (except die-castings), nonferrous metals (except aluminum, copper), unfinished manufacturing
331524	Castings (except die-castings), unfinished, aluminum, manufacturing
331525	Castings (except die-castings), unfinished, copper, manufacturing
331511	Castings, compacted graphite iron, unfinished, manufacturing
331511	Castings, malleable iron, unfinished, manufacturing
331513	Castings, steel (except investment), unfinished, manufacturing
331511	Castings, unfinished iron (e.g., ductile, gray, malleable, semisteel), manufacturing
311223	Castor oil and pomace made in crushing mills
316213	Casual shoes (except athletic, plastic, rubber), men's, manufacturing
316214	Casual shoes (except athletic, rubber, plastic), women's, manufacturing
316219	Casual shoes (except rubber, plastics), children's and infants', manufacturing
524126	Casualty insurance carriers, direct
311111	Cat food manufacturing
325998	Cat litter manufacturing
112990	Cat production
511199	Catalog (i.e., mail order, store merchandise) publishers

Code	Description
511199	Catalog (i.e., mail order, store merchandise) publishers and printing combined
511199	Catalog (i.e., mail order, store merchandise) publishing (i.e., establishments known as publishers)
454110	Catalog (i.e., order taking) offices of mail-order houses
511140	Catalog of collections publishers
511140	Catalog of collections publishers and printing combined
511140	Catalog of collections publishing (i.e., establishments known as publishers)
452990	Catalog showrooms, general merchandise (except catalog mail-order)
323112	Catalogs flexographic printing without publishing
323111	Catalogs gravure printing without publishing
323110	Catalogs lithographic (offset) printing without publishing
323112	Catalogs of collections flexographic printing without publishing
323111	Catalogs of collections gravure printing without publishing
323110	Catalogs of collections lithographic (offset) printing without publishing
323119	Catalogs of collections printing (except flexographic, gravure, lithographic, screen) without publishing
323113	Catalogs of collections screen printing without publishing
323119	Catalogs printing (except flexographic, gravure, lithographic, screen) without publishing
323113	Catalogs screen printing without publishing
336399	Catalytic converters, engine exhaust, automotive, truck, and bus, manufacturing
332995	Catapult guns manufacturing
562998	Catch basin cleaning services
722320	Caterers
722320	Catering services, social
112511	Catfish production, farm raising
325412	Cathartic preparations manufacturing
339112	Catheters manufacturing
334411	Cathode ray tubes (CRT) manufacturing
335999	Cathodic protection equipment manufacturing
212399	Catlinite mining and/or beneficiating
422990	Cats wholesaling
311421	Catsup manufacturing
112111	Cattle conditioning operations
112111	Cattle farming or ranching
333111	Cattle feeding and watering equipment manufacturing
112112	Cattle feedlots (except stockyards for transportation)
311119	Cattle feeds, supplements, concentrates, and premixes, manufacturing
115210	Cattle spraying
422520	Cattle wholesaling
111219	Cauliflower farming, field, bedding plant and seed production
325520	Caulking compounds (except gypsum base) manufacturing
332212	Caulking guns, nonpowered, manufacturing
422690	Caulking materials wholesaling
234120	Causeway construction
325181	Caustic potash manufacturing
325181	Caustic soda (i.e., sodium hydroxide) manufacturing

Code	Description
422690	Caustic soda wholesaling
712190	Caverns (i.e., natural wonder tourist attractions)
337122	Cedar chests manufacturing
325998	Cedar oil manufacturing
235420	Ceiling construction contractors
444190	Ceiling fan stores
335211	Ceiling fans with integral lighting fixture, residential, manufacturing
335211	Ceiling fans, residential, manufacturing
335122	Ceiling lighting fixtures, commercial, industrial, and institutional, manufacturing
335121	Ceiling lighting fixtures, residential, manufacturing
321912	Ceiling lumber, dressed, resawing purchased lumber
321113	Ceiling lumber, made from logs or bolts
235610	Ceiling metal construction contractors
334519	Ceilometers manufacturing
711410	Celebrities' agents or managers
711510	Celebrity spokespersons, independent
111219	Celery farming, field, bedding plant and seed production
212393	Celestite mining and/or beneficiating
325221	Cellophane film or sheet manufacturing
422120	Cellophane tape wholesaling
339992	Cellos and parts manufacturing
513322	Cellular telephone communication carriers
513322	Cellular telephone services
443112	Cellular telephone stores
334220	Cellular telephones manufacturing
421690	Cellular telephones wholesaling
325199	Cellulose acetate (except resins) manufacturing
325211	Cellulose acetate resins manufacturing
325211	Cellulose nitrate resins manufacturing
325211	Cellulose propionate resins manufacturing
325211	Cellulose resins manufacturing
325211	Cellulose xanthate (viscose) manufacturing
325221	Cellulosic fibers and filaments manufacturing
325221	Cellulosic filament yarn manufacturing
326113	Cellulosic plastics film and unlaminated sheet (except packaging) manufacturing
325221	Cellulosic staple fibers manufacturing
327310	Cement (e.g., hydraulic, masonry, portland, pozzolana) manufacturing
327310	Cement clinker manufacturing
327310	Cement kiln manufacturing
234930	Cement plant construction
212312	Cement rock crushed and broken stone mining and/or beneficiating
421320	Cement wholesaling
327420	Cement, Keene's (i.e., tiling plaster), manufacturing
327124	Cement, clay refractory, manufacturing
325520	Cement, rubber, manufacturing
421830	Cement-making machinery wholesaling
213112	Cementing oil and gas well casings on a contract basis
324122	Cements, asphalt roofing, made from purchased asphaltic materials
339114	Cements, dental, manufacturing
812220	Cematary management services
812220	Cemeteries
812220	Cemetery associations (i.e., operators)
453998	Cemetery memorial dealers (e.g., headstones, markers, vaults)
561730	Cemetery plot care services

Centering machines—Chemical

Code	Description
333512	Centering machines, metalworking, manufacturing
514120	Centers for documentation (i.e., archives)
624120	Centers, senior citizens'
421730	Central heating equipment, warm-air, wholesaling
325412	Central nervous system stimulant preparations manufacturing
334210	Central office and switching equipment, telephone, manufacturing
333319	Central vacuuming systems, commercial-type, manufacturing
335212	Central vacuuming systems, household-type, manufacturing
327320	Central-mixed concrete manufacturing
551114	Centralized administrative offices
333911	Centrifugal pumps manufacturing
333999	Centrifuges, industrial-type, manufacturing
325411	Cephalosporin, uncompounded, manufacturing
325131	Ceramic colors manufacturing
421320	Ceramic construction materials (except refractory) wholesaling
327999	Ceramic fiber manufacturing
333994	Ceramic kilns and furnaces manufacturing
444190	Ceramic tile stores
327122	Ceramic tiles, floor and wall, manufacturing
611610	Ceramics instruction
311211	Cereal grain flour manufacturing
311211	Cereal grain germ manufacturing
422490	Cereal products wholesaling
541710	Cerebral palsy research laboratories or services
212299	Cerium concentrates mining and/or beneficiating
212299	Cerium ores mining and/or beneficiating
325188	Cerium salts manufacturing
523120	Certificate of deposit (CD) brokers' offices
923110	Certification of schools and teachers
541211	Certified accountants' offices
523930	Certified financial planners, customized, fees paid by client
541211	Certified public accountants' (CPAs) offices
212231	Cerussite mining and/or beneficiating
339113	Cervical collars manufacturing
325188	Cesium and cesium compounds, not specified elsewhere by process, manufacturing
562991	Cesspool cleaning services
325199	Cetyl alcohol manufacturing
335211	Chafing dishes, household-type electric, manufacturing
332999	Chain fittings manufacturing
333923	Chain hoists manufacturing
332323	Chain ladders, metal, manufacturing
332618	Chain link fencing and fence gates made from purchased wire
331222	Chain link fencing, iron or steel, made in wire drawing plants
332618	Chain made from purchased wire
332213	Chain saw blades manufacturing
333991	Chain saws, handheld power-driven, manufacturing
332618	Chain, welded, made from purchased wire
339911	Chains or necklace, precious metal, manufacturing

Code	Description
333613	Chains, power transmission, manufacturing
334519	Chains, surveyor's, manufacturing
421830	Chain saws wholesaling
337121	Chair and couch springs, assembled, manufacturing
337215	Chair glides manufacturing
337215	Chair seats for furniture manufacturing
337122	Chairs (except upholstered), wood household-type, manufacturing
337214	Chairs (except wood), office-type, manufacturing
337127	Chairs, barber and beauty (i.e., hydraulic), manufacturing
337127	Chairs, barber, beauty shop (i.e., hydraulic), manufacturing
337125	Chairs, cane, wood household-type, manufacturing
339114	Chairs, dentist's, manufacturing
337124	Chairs, metal household-type (except upholstered), manufacturing
337127	Chairs, portable folding, auditorium-type, manufacturing
337127	Chairs, stacking, auditorium-type, manufacturing
337121	Chairs, upholstered household-type (except dining room, kitchen), manufacturing
337211	Chairs, wood office-type, manufacturing
212234	Chalcocite mining and/or beneficiating
212234	Chalcopyrite mining and/or beneficiating
339942	Chalk (e.g., artist's, blackboard, carpenter's, marking, tailor's), manufacturing
212312	Chalk crushed and broken stone mining and/or beneficiating
212312	Chalk, ground or otherwise treated, mining and/or beneficiating
339942	Chalkboards, framed, manufacturing
711130	Chamber musical groups
711130	Chamber orchestras
813910	Chambers of commerce
313210	Chambrays weaving
333512	Chamfering machines, metalworking, manufacturing
316110	Chamois leather manufacturing
422990	Chamois, leather, wholesaling
312130	Champagne method sparkling wine, manufacturing
335122	Chandeliers, commercial, industrial, and institutional electric, manufacturing
335121	Chandeliers, residential, manufacturing
333311	Change making machines manufacturing
325182	Channel black manufacturing
234990	Channel construction
234990	Channel cutoff construction, general construction contractors
332323	Channels, furring metal, manufacturing
325191	Charcoal (except activated) manufacturing
325191	Charcoal briquettes, wood, manufacturing
422990	Charcoal wholesaling
325998	Charcoal, activated, manufacturing
522210	Charge card issuing
813211	Charitable trusts, awarding grants
611699	Charm schools
481212	Charter air freight services
481211	Charter air passenger services
485510	Charter bus services (except scenic, sightseeing)
487210	Charter fishing boat operation

Code	Description
333515	Chasers (i.e., a machine tool accessory) manufacturing
212399	Chasers mining and/or beneficiating
332812	Chasing metals and metal products for the trade
336111	Chassis, automobile, manufacturing
336120	Chassis, heavy truck, with or without cabs, manufacturing
336112	Chassis, light truck and utility, manufacturing
421110	Chassis, motor vehicle, wholesaling
561310	Chauffeur registries
611519	Chauffeur training
315991	Chauffeurs' hats and caps cut and sewn from purchased fabric (except apparel contractors)
315211	Chauffeurs' hats and caps, men's, cut and sew apparel contractors
315212	Chauffeurs' hats and caps, women's, cut and sew apparel contractors
522390	Check cashing services
521110	Check clearing activities of the central bank
522320	Check clearing services (except central banks)
522320	Check clearinghouse services (except central banks)
421420	Check handling machines wholesaling
812990	Check room services
522320	Check validation services
332911	Check valves, industrial-type, manufacturing
333313	Check writing machines manufacturing
316993	Checkbook covers, (except metal), manufacturing
339911	Checkbook covers, precious metal, manufacturing
323116	Checkbooks and refills printing
339932	Checkers and checkerboards manufacturing
611620	Cheerleading instruction, camps, or schools
311513	Cheese (except cottage cheese) manufacturing
311513	Cheese analogs manufacturing
311941	Cheese based salad dressing manufacturing
422450	Cheese confections (e.g., curls, puffs) wholesaling
311919	Cheese curls and puffs manufacturing
333294	Cheese processing machinery manufacturing
311513	Cheese products, imitation or substitute, manufacturing
311513	Cheese spreads manufacturing
422430	Cheese wholesaling
311511	Cheese, cottage, manufacturing
311513	Cheese, imitation or substitute, manufacturing
311513	Cheese, natural (except cottage cheese), manufacturing
313210	Cheesecloths weaving
422690	Chemical additives (e.g., concrete, food, fuel, oil) wholesaling
234930	Chemical complexes or facility construction
541690	Chemical consulting services
541330	Chemical engineering services
313311	Chemical finishing (e.g., fire, mildew, water resistance) broadwoven fabrics
313312	Chemical finishing (e.g., fire, mildew, water resistance) fabrics (except broadwoven and textile products)
422690	Chemical gases wholesaling

Code	Description
421830	Chemical industries machinery and equipment wholesaling
333298	Chemical kilns manufacturing
332710	Chemical milling job shops
333512	Chemical milling machines, metalworking, manufacturing
333298	Chemical processing machinery and equipment manufacturing
541710	Chemical research and development laboratories or services
327112	Chemical stoneware (i.e., pottery products) manufacturing
326191	Chemical toilets, plastics, manufacturing
115112	Chemical treatment of soil for crops
213112	Chemically treating oil and gas wells (e.g., acidizing, bailing, swabbing) on a contract basis
422690	Chemicals (except agriculture) (e.g., automotive, household, industrial, photographic) wholesaling
422910	Chemicals, agricultural, wholesaling
315191	Chemises made in apparel knitting mills
315212	Chemises, women's and girls', cut and sew apparel contractors
315231	Chemises, women's, misses' and girls', cut and sewn from purchased fabric (except apparel contractors)
111339	Cherry farming
113210	Cherry gum, gathering
339932	Chessmen and chessboards manufacturing
325191	Chestnut extract manufacturing
113210	Chestnut gum, gathering
321920	Chests for tools, wood, manufacturing
332999	Chests, fire or burglary resistive, metal, manufacturing
332999	Chests, money, metal, manufacturing
332999	Chests, safe deposit, metal, manufacturing
311340	Chewing gum base manufacturing
333294	Chewing gum machinery manufacturing
311340	Chewing gum manufacturing
422450	Chewing gum wholesaling
312229	Chewing tobacco manufacturing
422940	Chewing tobacco wholesaling
422440	Chicken and chicken products (except packaged frozen) wholesaling
333111	Chicken brooders manufacturing
321920	Chicken coops (i.e., crates), wood, wirebound for shipping poultry, manufacturing
321992	Chicken coops, prefabricated, wood, manufacturing
112310	Chicken egg production
333111	Chicken feeders manufacturing
311119	Chicken feeds, prepared, manufacturing
112340	Chicken hatcheries
332618	Chicken netting made from purchased wire
112320	Chicken production (except egg laying)
311615	Chickens, processing, fresh, frozen, canned, or cooked (except baby and pet food)
311615	Chickens, slaughtering and dressing
422590	Chicks wholesaling
111998	Chicory farming
624410	Child day care centers
624410	Child day care services
624410	Child day care services in provider's own home
624410	Child day care, before or after school, separate from schools
623990	Child group foster homes
624110	Child guidance agencies

Code	Description
624110	Child welfare services
621410	Childbirth preparation classes
622210	Children's hospitals, psychiatric or substance abuse
622310	Children's hospitals, specialty (except psychiatric, substance abuse)
721214	Children's camps (except day, instructional)
422330	Children's clothing wholesaling
511199	Children's coloring book publishers
622110	Children's hospitals, general
316219	Children's shoes (except orthopedic extension, plastics, rubber) manufacturing
315119	Children's socks manufacturing
421920	Children's vehicles (except bicycles) wholesaling
623990	Children's villages
311422	Chili con carne canning
311942	Chili pepper or powder manufacturing
311421	Chili sauce manufacturing
339992	Chimes and parts (musical instruments) manufacturing
335999	Chimes, electric, manufacturing
327390	Chimney caps, concrete, manufacturing
561790	Chimney cleaning services
235410	Chimney construction contractors
561790	Chimney sweep (i.e., cleaning) services
212324	China clay mining and/or beneficiating
337122	China closets, wood, manufacturing
327112	China cooking ware manufacturing
811490	China repair services
327112	China tableware, vitreous, manufacturing
442299	Chinaware stores
421440	Chinaware, commercial, wholesaling
421220	Chinaware, household-type, wholesaling
112930	Chinchilla production
311422	Chinese foods canning
311999	Chinese noodles, fried, manufacturing
111219	Chinese pea farming, bedding plant and seed production
313210	Chintzes weaving
333298	Chip placement machinery manufacturing
322130	Chipboard (i.e., paperboard) stock manufacturing
321219	Chipboard manufacturing
322226	Chipboard, laminated or surface coated, made from purchased paperboard
321113	Chipper mills (except portable)
333112	Chippers (i.e., shredders), lawn and garden-type, manufacturing
333120	Chippers, portable, commercial (e.g., brush, limb, log), manufacturing
333291	Chippers, stationary (e.g., log), manufacturing
422450	Chips (e.g., corn, potato) wholesaling
621310	Chiropractors' offices (e.g., centers, clinics)
332212	Chisels manufacturing
333991	Chisels, handheld power-driven, manufacturing
111219	Chive farming, field, bedding plant and seed production
325199	Chloral manufacturing
325320	Chlordane insecticides manufacturing
325188	Chloride of lime manufacturing
325212	Chlorinated rubber, synthetic, manufacturing
325188	Chlorine compounds, not specified elsewhere by process, manufacturing
325188	Chlorine dioxide manufacturing
325181	Chlorine manufacturing

Code	Description
325199	Chloroacetic acid manufacturing
325192	Chlorobenzene manufacturing
325120	Chlorodifluoromethane manufacturing
325120	Chlorofluorocarbon gases manufacturing
325199	Chloroform manufacturing
325192	Chloronaphthalene manufacturing
325192	Chlorophenol manufacturing
325199	Chloropicrin manufacturing
325212	Chloroprene rubber manufacturing
325212	Chlorosulfonated polyethylenes manufacturing
325188	Chlorosulfonic acid manufacturing
325192	Chlorotoluene manufacturing
311330	Chocolate (coating, instant, liquor, syrups) made from purchased chocolate
311320	Chocolate (e.g., coatings, instant, liquor, syrups) made from cacao beans
422490	Chocolate (except candy) wholesaling
311320	Chocolate bars made from cocoa beans
422450	Chocolate candy wholesaling
311330	Chocolate coatings and syrups made from purchased chocolate
311330	Chocolate covered candy bars made from purchased chocolate
311330	Chocolate covered granola bars made from purchased chocolate
311511	Chocolate drink (milk based) manufacturing
311511	Chocolate milk manufacturing
333294	Chocolate processing machinery manufacturing
311320	Chocolate, confectionery, made from cacao beans
711130	Choirs
334416	Chokes for electronic circuitry manufacturing
325414	Cholera serums manufacturing
325320	Cholinesterse inhibitors used as insecticides manufacturing
311412	Chop suey, frozen, manufacturing
115113	Chopping and silo filling
711510	Choreographers, independent
311412	Chow mein, frozen, manufacturing
311711	Chowders, fish and seafood, canning
311712	Chowders, frozen fish and seafood, manufacturing
621399	Christian Science practitioners' offices (e.g., centers, clinics)
422990	Christmas ornaments wholesaling
453220	Christmas stores
333132	Christmas tree assemblies, oil and gas field-type, manufacturing
111421	Christmas tree growing
335129	Christmas tree lighting sets, electric, manufacturing
339999	Christmas tree ornaments (except electric, glass) manufacturing
327215	Christmas tree ornaments made from purchased glass
327212	Christmas tree ornaments, glass, made in glass making plants
422990	Christmas trees (e.g., artificial, cut) wholesaling
339999	Christmas trees, artificial, manufacturing
454390	Christmas trees, cut, direct selling
334516	Chromatographic instruments, laboratory-type, manufacturing
334513	Chromatographs, industrial process-type, manufacturing
325131	Chrome pigments (e.g., chrome green, chrome orange, chrome yellow) manufacturing
332813	Chrome plating metals and metal products for the trade

Chromic acid—Clinic construction

Code	Description	Code	Description	Code	Description
325188	Chromic acid manufacturing	333298	Circuit board making machinery manufacturing	333298	Clayworking and tempering machinery manufacturing
212299	Chromite mining and/or beneficiating				
325188	Chromium compounds, not specified elsewhere by process, manufacturing	421690	Circuit boards wholesaling	812332	Clean room apparel supply services
		334412	Circuit boards, printed, bare, manufacturing	233310	Clean room construction, general construction contractors
212299	Chromium concentrates beneficiating				
212299	Chromium ore mining and/or beneficiating	421610	Circuit breakers wholesaling	339113	Clean room suits and accessories manufacturing
		335313	Circuit breakers, air, manufacturing		
325188	Chromium oxide manufacturing	335313	Circuit breakers, power, manufacturing	812320	Cleaners, drycleaning and laundry service (except coin-operated)
331419	Chromium refining, primary	922110	Circuit courts		
325188	Chromium salts manufacturing	334515	Circuit testers manufacturing	335212	Cleaners, household-type electric vacuum, manufacturing
622310	Chronic disease hospitals	421690	Circuits, integrated, wholesaling		
334518	Chronographs manufacturing	313241	Circular (i.e., weft) fabrics knitting	561790	Cleaning (e.g., power sweeping, washing) driveways and parking lots
334518	Chronometers manufacturing	541870	Circular direct distribution services		
334516	Chronoscopes manufacturing	333292	Circular knitting machinery manufacturing	332813	Cleaning and descaling metals and metal products for the trade
333512	Chucking machines, automatic, metalworking, manufacturing				
		333991	Circular saws, handheld power-driven, manufacturing	812320	Cleaning and dyeing plants (except rug cleaning plants)
333515	Chucks (i.e., a machine tool accessory) manufacturing				
		333210	Circular saws, woodworking-type, stationary, manufacturing	311212	Cleaning and polishing rice
337127	Church furniture (except concrete, stone) manufacturing			561790	Cleaning building exteriors (except sand blasting, window cleaning)
		514120	Circulating libraries		
421490	Church supplies (except plated ware, silverware) wholesaling	711190	Circus companies	235990	Cleaning building exteriors construction contractors
		711190	Circuses		
233320	Church, synagogue, mosque, temple, and related building construction	334220	Citizens band (CB) radios manufacturing	561740	Cleaning carpets
		325199	Citral manufacturing	422690	Cleaning compounds and preparations wholesaling
813110	Churches	325199	Citrates, not specified elsewhere by process, manufacturing		
332313	Chutes, fabricated metal plate work, manufacturing			335999	Cleaning equipment, ultrasonic (except dental, medical), manufacturing
		325199	Citric acid manufacturing		
333294	Cider presses manufacturing	325998	Citronella oil manufacturing	561720	Cleaning homes
311941	Cider vinegar manufacturing	325199	Citronellal manufacturing	333131	Cleaning machinery, mining-type, manufacturing
312130	Cider, alcoholic, manufacturing	115112	Citrus grove cultivation services		
311941	Cider, nonalcoholic, manufacturing	111320	Citrus groves (except orange)	561720	Cleaning new building interiors after construction
326199	Cigar and cigarette holders, plastics, manufacturing	311119	Citrus pulp, cattle feed, manufacturing		
		311411	Citrus pulp, frozen, manufacturing	235990	Cleaning new buildings after construction contractors
321920	Cigar boxes, wood and part wood, manufacturing	921120	City and town councils		
		921110	City and town managers' offices	561720	Cleaning offices
316993	Cigar cases (except metal) manufacturing	485113	City bus services (except mixed mode)	213112	Cleaning oil and gas field lease tanks on a contract basis
		922110	City or county courts		
339911	Cigar cases, precious metal, manufacturing	541320	City planning services	213112	Cleaning out (e.g., bailing out, steam cleaning, swabbing) wells on a contract basis
		813410	Civic associations		
312229	Cigar manufacturing	233320	Civic center construction		
453991	Cigar stores	541330	Civil engineering services	212113	Cleaning plants, anthracite coal
316993	Cigarette cases (except metal) manufacturing	813311	Civil liberties organizations	212111	Cleaning plants, bituminous coal
		921190	Civil rights commissions	561740	Cleaning plants, carpet and rug
339911	Cigarette cases, precious metal, manufacturing	921190	Civil service commissions	115210	Cleaning poultry houses
		524291	Claims adjusting, insurance	561740	Cleaning rugs
339999	Cigarette holders manufacturing	524292	Claims processing services, insurance, third-party	561740	Cleaning services, carpet and rug
339999	Cigarette lighter flints manufacturing			561720	Cleaning shopping centers
339999	Cigarette lighters (except precious metal) manufacturing	114112	Clam digging	561790	Cleaning swimming pools
		112512	Clam production, farm raising	213112	Cleaning wells on a contract basis
422990	Cigarette lighters wholesaling	333515	Clamps (i.e., a machine tool accessory) manufacturing	213112	Cleaning, repairing, and dismantling oil and gas field lease tanks on a contract basis
333298	Cigarette making machinery manufacturing				
		339112	Clamps, surgical, manufacturing		
322299	Cigarette paper made from purchased paper	339992	Clarinets and parts manufacturing	321918	Clear and finger joint wood moldings manufacturing
		316999	Clasps, shoe (leather), manufacturing		
322121	Cigarette paper made in paper mills	813410	Classic car clubs	522320	Clearinghouses, bank or check
322299	Cigarette paper, book, made from purchased paper	711120	Classical dance companies	523999	Clearinghouses, commodity exchange or securities exchange
		711130	Classical musical artists, independent		
453991	Cigarette stands, permanent	711130	Classical musical groups	316219	Cleated athletic shoes manufacturing
454390	Cigarette stands, temporary	212325	Clay (except kaolin, ball) mining and/or beneficiating	332211	Cleavers manufacturing
325221	Cigarette tow, cellulosic fiber, manufacturing			315299	Clerical vestments cut and sewn from purchased fabric (except apparel contractors)
		327112	Clay and ceramic statuary manufacturing		
333311	Cigarette vending machines manufacturing				
		212325	Clay bleaching	315191	Clerical vestments made in apparel knitting mills
312221	Cigarettes manufacturing	421320	Clay construction materials (except refractory) wholesaling		
422940	Cigarettes wholesaling			315211	Clerical vestments, men's and boys, cut and sew apparel contractors
422940	Cigars wholesaling	327124	Clay refractories (e.g., mortar, brick, tile, block) manufacturing		
325411	Cinchona and derivatives (i.e., basic chemicals) manufacturing			315212	Clerical vestments, women's and girls', cut and sew apparel contractors
		212324	Clay, ball, mining and/or beneficiating		
327331	Cinder (clinker) block, concrete, manufacturing	212325	Clay, ceramic and refractory minerals, mining and/or beneficiating	316211	Climbing shoes, plastics or plastics soled fabric upper, manufacturing
		212325	Clay, fire, mining and/or beneficiating		
233320	Cinema construction	339942	Clay, modeling, manufacturing	316211	Climbing shoes, rubber or rubber soled fabric upper, manufacturing
512131	Cinemas	212324	Clay, natural, mining and/or beneficiating		
711510	Cinematographers, independent			233320	Clinic construction
212299	Cinnabar mining and/or beneficiating				

Code	Description
621111	Clinical pathologists' offices (e.g., centers, clinics)
621330	Clinical psychologists' offices (e.g., centers, clinics)
******	Clinics, medical — see type
621498	Clinics/centers of health practitioners from more than one industry practicing within the same establishment
621498	Clinics/centers of health practitioners with multi-industry degrees
321999	Clipboards, wood, manufacturing
332212	Clippers for animal use, nonelectric, manufacturing
332211	Clippers, fingernail and toenail, manufacturing
514199	Clipping services, news
332994	Clips, gun (i.e., 30 mm. or less, 1.18 inch or less), manufacturing
332995	Clips, gun (i.e., more than 30 mm., more than 1.18 inch), manufacturing
334518	Clock materials and parts (except crystals) manufacturing
334518	Clock or watch springs, precision, made from purchased wire
334310	Clock radios manufacturing
811490	Clock repair shops without retailing new clocks
448310	Clock shops
334518	Clocks assembling
334518	Clocks assembling from purchased components
421940	Clocks wholesaling
561492	Closed captioning services, real-time (i.e., simultaneous)
512191	Closed captioning services, taped material
513220	Closed circuit television (CCTV)
334220	Closed circuit television equipment manufacturing
525990	Closed-end investment funds (except REITs)
332115	Closures, metal, stamping
422130	Closures, paper and disposable plastics, wholesaling
327910	Cloth (e.g., aluminum oxide, garnet, emery, silicon carbide) coated manufacturing
561990	Cloth cutting, bolting, or winding for the trade
333292	Cloth spreading machinery manufacturing
321999	Cloth winding reels, wood
332618	Cloth, woven wire, made from purchased wire
334512	Clothes dryer controls, including dryness controls, manufacturing
811412	Clothes dryer, household-type, repair and maintenance services without retailing new clothes dryers
321999	Clothes dryers (clothes horses), wood manufacturing
422990	Clothes hangers wholesaling
326199	Clothes hangers, plastics, manufacturing
321999	Clothes poles, wood, manufacturing
326199	Clothespins, plastics, manufacturing
321999	Clothespins, wood, manufacturing
448150	Clothing accessories stores
422330	Clothing accessories, women's, children's, and infants', wholesaling
541490	Clothing design services
532220	Clothing rental (except industrial launderer, linen supply)
811490	Clothing repair shops, alterations only
448130	Clothing stores, children's and infants'

Code	Description
448140	Clothing stores, family
448110	Clothing stores, men's and boys'
453310	Clothing stores, used
448120	Clothing stores, women's and girls'
339931	Clothing, doll, manufacturing
315292	Clothing, fur (except apparel contractors), manufacturing
315211	Clothing, fur, men's and boys', cut and sew apparel contractors
315212	Clothing, fur, women's, girls', and infants', cut and sew apparel contractors
315292	Clothing, leather or sheep-lined (except apparel contractors), manufacturing
315211	Clothing, leather or sheep-lined, men's and boys', cut and sew apparel contractors
315212	Clothing, leather or sheep-lined, women's, girls', and infants', cut and sew apparel contractors
422320	Clothing, men's and boys', wholesaling
315291	Clothing, water resistant, infants', cut and sewn from purchased fabric (except apparel contractors)
315211	Clothing, water resistant, men's and boy's, cut and sew apparel contractors
315228	Clothing, water resistant, not specified elsewhere, men's and boys', cut and sewn from purchased fabric (except apparel contractors)
315239	Clothing, water resistant, not specified elsewhere, women's, misses', and girls', cut and sewn from purchased fabric (except apparel contractors)
315212	Clothing, water resistant, women's, girls' and infants', cut and sew apparel contractors
315291	Clothing, water-repellent, infants', cut and sewn from purchased fabric (except apparel contractors)
315211	Clothing, water-repellent, men's and boys', cut and sew apparel contractors
315228	Clothing, water-repellent, not specified elsewhere, men's and boys', cut and sewn from purchased fabric (except apparel contractors)
315239	Clothing, water-repellent, not specified elsewhere, women's, misses', and girls', cut and sewn from purchased fabric (except apparel contractors)
315212	Clothing, water-repellent, women's, girls', and infants', cut and sew apparel contractors
315299	Clothing, waterproof, cut and sewn from purchased fabric (except apparel contractors)
315211	Clothing, waterproof, men's and boys', cut and sew apparel contractors
315212	Clothing, waterproof, women's, girls', and infants', cut and sew apparel contractors
422330	Clothing, women's, children's, and infants', wholesaling
339994	Cloths (except chemically treated), dusting and polishing, manufacturing
325612	Cloths, dusting and polishing, chemically treated, manufacturing
325998	Clove oil manufacturing
111940	Clover hay farming
111998	Clover seed farming
721310	Clubs, residential
339920	Clubs, sporting goods (e.g., golf, Indian), manufacturing

Code	Description
333613	Clutches and brakes (except electromagnetic industrial controls, motor vehicle) manufacturing
234930	Co-generation plant construction
325413	Coagulation in-vitro diagnostic substances manufacturing
325412	Coagulation in-vivo diagnostic substances manufacturing
333922	Coal and ore conveyors manufacturing
212113	Coal beneficiating plants, anthracite
212111	Coal beneficiating plants, bituminous or lignite (surface or underground)
333131	Coal breakers, cutters, and pulverizers manufacturing
332322	Coal chutes, sheet metal, manufacturing
454319	Coal dealers, direct selling
211111	Coal gasification at mine site
484220	Coal hauling, truck, local
211111	Coal liquefaction at mine site
213113	Coal mining services
213113	Coal mining support services (tunneling, blasting, training, overburden removal)
486990	Coal pipeline transportation
211111	Coal pyrolysis
325192	Coal tar distillates manufacturing
324121	Coal tar paving materials made from purchased coal tar
422690	Coal tar products, primary and intermediate, wholesaling
325211	Coal tar resins manufacturing
421520	Coal wholesaling
212113	Coal, anthracite, mining and/or beneficiating
212111	Coal, bituminous, beneficiating
212112	Coal, bituminous, underground mining or mining and beneficiating
212111	Coal, brown, mining and/or beneficiating
926120	Coast Guard (except academy)
483113	Coastal freight transportation to and from domestic ports
483114	Coastal passenger transportation to and from domestic ports
483113	Coastal shipping of freight to and from domestic ports
812331	Coat (e.g., barber's, beautician's, doctor's, nurse's) supply services
332618	Coat hangers made from purchased wire
315292	Coat linings, fur (except apparel contractors), manufacturing
315211	Coat linings, fur, men's and boys', cut and sew apparel contractors
315212	Coat linings, fur, women's, girls', and infants', cut and sew apparel contractors
448190	Coat stores
315999	Coat trimmings fabric cut and sewn from purchased fabric (except apparel contractors)
315211	Coat trimmings, fabric, men's and boys', cut and sew apparel contractors
315212	Coat trimmings, fabric, women's, girls', and infants', cut and sew apparel contractors
322226	Coated board made from purchased paperboard
322130	Coated board made in paperboard mills
235990	Coating and glazing of concrete surfaces construction contractors
324122	Coating compounds, tar, made from purchased asphaltic materials
332812	Coating metals and metal products for the trade
235990	Coating of concrete structures with plastics, construction contractors

Coating of metal—Coin-operated

Code	Description	Code	Description	Code	Description
332812	Coating of metal and metal products with plastics for the trade	315234	Coats, tailored (except fur, leather), women's, misses', and girls', cut and sewn from purchased fabric	325411	Cod liver oil, medicinal, uncompounded, manufacturing
335110	Coating purchased light bulbs	315999	Coats, waterproof (e.g., plastics, rubberized fabric, similar materials) rubberizing fabric and manufacturing coats	325411	Codeine and derivatives (i.e., basic chemicals) manufacturing
322222	Coating purchased papers for nonpackaging applications (except photosensitive paper)			333993	Coding, dating, and imprinting packaging machinery manufacturing
322221	Coating purchased papers for packaging applications	315211	Coats, waterproof (i.e., plastic, rubberized fabric, similar materials), men's and boy's, cut and sew apparel contractors	445299	Coffee and tea (i.e., packaged) stores
311320	Coatings, chocolate, made from cacao beans			722330	Coffee carts, mobile
315239	Coats (except fur, leather, tailored, waterproof), women's, misses', and girls', cut and sewn from purchased fabric (except apparel contractors)	315212	Coats, waterproof (i.e., plastics, rubberized fabric, similar materials), women's, girls', and infants', cut and sew apparel contractors	311920	Coffee concentrates (i.e., instant coffee) manufacturing
				311920	Coffee extracts manufacturing
				111339	Coffee farming
315228	Coats (except fur, leather, tailored, waterproof, work), men's and boys', cut and sewn from purchased fabric (except apparel contractors)	315999	Coats, waterproof, (e.g., plastics, rubberized fabric, similar materials) cut and sewn from purchased fabric (except apparel contractors)	322299	Coffee filters made from purchased paper
				311920	Coffee flavoring and syrups (i.e., made from coffee) manufacturing
		315212	Coats, women's, girls', and infants', cut and sew apparel contractors	333319	Coffee makers and urns, commercial-type, manufacturing
315292	Coats (including tailored), leather or sheep-lined (except apparel contractors), manufacturing	331319	Coaxial cable made in aluminum wire drawing plants	335211	Coffee makers, household-type electric, manufacturing
315212	Coats (including tailored, leather, or sheep-lined), women's, girls', and infants', cut and sew apparel contractors	421610	Coaxial cable wholesaling	311920	Coffee roasting
		331422	Coaxial cable, copper, made from purchased copper in wire drawing plants	333294	Coffee roasting and grinding machinery (i.e., food manufacturing-type) manufacturing
315292	Coats, artificial leather, cut and sewn from purchased fabric (except apparel contractors)	331491	Coaxial cable, nonferrous metals (except aluminum, copper), made from purchased nonferrous metals (except aluminum, copper) in wire drawing plants	722213	Coffee shops, on premise brewing
				311920	Coffee substitute manufacturing
315211	Coats, artificial leather, men's and boys', cut and sew apparel contractors			337122	Coffee tables, wood, manufacturing
				422490	Coffee wholesaling
315212	Coats, artificial leather, women's, girls', and infants', cut and sew apparel contractors			311920	Coffee, blended, manufacturing
		335929	Coaxial cable, nonferrous, made from purchased nonferrous wire	312111	Coffee, iced, manufacturing
		334417	Coaxial connectors manufacturing	311920	Coffee, instant and freeze dried, manufacturing
315292	Coats, fur (except apparel contractors), manufacturing	325188	Cobalt 60 (i.e., radioactive cobalt) manufacturing	454390	Coffee-break service providers, direct selling
315211	Coats, fur, men's and boys', cut and sew apparel contractors	325188	Cobalt chloride manufacturing	234990	Cofferdam construction
		325188	Cobalt compounds, not specified elsewhere by process, manufacturing	487110	Cog railway, scenic and sightseeing, operation
315212	Coats, fur, women's, girls', and infants', cut and sew apparel contractors	212299	Cobalt concentrates beneficiating	541720	Cognitive research and development services
315291	Coats, infants' (except waterproof), cut and sewn from purchased fabric (except apparel contractors)	212299	Cobalt ores mining and/or beneficiating	333518	Coil winding and cutting machinery, metalworking, manufacturing
		331419	Cobalt refining, primary		
		325188	Cobalt sulfate manufacturing	332612	Coiled springs (except clock, watch), light gauge, manufacturing
315292	Coats, leather, (except apparel contractors)	325411	Cocaine and derivatives (i.e., basic chemicals) manufacturing	332611	Coiled springs, heavy gauge, manufacturing
315211	Coats, leather, men's and boys', cut and sew apparel contractors	332913	Cocks, drain, plumbing, manufacturing	335312	Coils for motors and generators manufacturing
		722410	Cocktail lounges		
315212	Coats, leather, women's, girls', and infants', cut and sew apparel contractors	311999	Cocktail mixes, dry, manufacturing	336322	Coils, ignition, internal combustion engines, manufacturing
		422820	Cocktails, alcoholic, premixed, wholesaling	332996	Coils, pipe, made from purchased metal pipe
315211	Coats, men's and boys', cut and sew apparel contractors	311320	Cocoa (e.g., instant, mix, mixed with other ingredients, powder drink, powdered) made from cacao beans	333313	Coin counting machinery manufacturing
315211	Coats, nontailored service apparel (e.g., laboratory, mechanics', medical), men's and boys', cut and sew apparel contractors			561990	Coin pick-up services, parking meter
		422590	Cocoa beans wholesaling	316993	Coin purses (except metal) manufacturing
		311320	Cocoa butter made from cocoa beans		
		311330	Cocoa, powdered drink, prepared, made from purchased chocolate	339911	Coin purses, precious metal, manufacturing
315228	Coats, nontailored service apparel (e.g., laboratory, mechanics', medical), men's and boys', cut and sewn from purchased fabric (except apparel contractors)	311330	Cocoa, powdered, made from purchased chocolate	421420	Coin sorting machines wholesaling
				333313	Coin wrapping machines manufacturing
		311330	Cocoa, powdered, mixed with other ingredients, made from purchased chocolate	339999	Coin-operated amusement machines (except jukebox) manufacturing
315212	Coats, nontailored service apparel (e.g., laboratory, medical, mechanics'), women's and girls', cut and sew apparel contractors	311225	Coconut oil made from purchased oils	812310	Coin-operated drycleaners and laundries
		311223	Coconut oil made in crushing mills	713290	Coin-operated gambling device concession operators (i.e., supplying and servicing in others' facilities)
		111339	Coconut tree farming		
315239	Coats, nontailored service apparel (e.g., laboratory, medical, mechanics'), women's, misses', and girls', cut and sewn from purchased fabric (except apparel contractors)	311999	Coconut, desiccated and shredded, manufacturing	339999	Coin-operated gambling devices manufacturing
		114111	Cod catching	421990	Coin-operated game machines wholesaling
		114111	Cod fishing		
		311711	Cod liver oil extraction, crude, produced in a cannery	334310	Coin-operated jukebox manufacturing
315222	Coats, tailored (except fur, leather), men's and boys', cut and sewn from purchased fabric (except apparel contractors)	311712	Cod liver oil extraction, crude, produced in a fresh and frozen seafood plant	812310	Coin-operated laundry and drycleaning routes (i.e., concession operators)

Code	Description
713990	Coin-operated nongambling amusement device concession operators (i.e., supplying and servicing in others' facilities)
812990	Coin-operated personal service machine (e.g., blood pressure, locker, photographic, scale, shoeshine) concession operators
421440	Coin-operated phonographs and vending machines wholesaling
333311	Coin-operated vending machines manufacturing
339911	Coins minting
421940	Coins wholesaling
221210	Coke oven gas, production and distribution
324199	Coke oven products (e.g., coke, gases, tars) made in coke oven establishments
331111	Coke oven products made in steel mills
421520	Coke wholesaling
324110	Coke, petroleum, made in petroleum refineries
335110	Cold cathode fluorescent lamp tubes manufacturing
332111	Cold forgings made from purchased iron or steel, unfinished
332112	Cold forgings made from purchased nonferrous metals, unfinished
325412	Cold remedies manufacturing
333516	Cold rolling mill machinery, metalworking, manufacturing
331221	Cold rolling steel shapes (e.g., bar, plate, rod, sheet, strip) made from purchased steel
493120	Cold storage locker services
421740	Cold storage machinery wholesaling
233310	Cold storage plant construction
493120	Cold storage warehousing
311991	Cole slaw, fresh, manufacturing
212391	Colemanite mining and/or beneficiating
311612	Collagen sausage casings made from purchased hides
332439	Collapsible tubes (e.g., toothpaste, glue), metal, manufacturing
315191	Collar and cuff sets made in apparel knitting mills
315212	Collar and cuff sets, women's, girls' and infants', cut and sew apparel contractors
315239	Collar and cuff sets, women's, misses' and girls', cut and sewn from purchased fabric (except apparel contractors)
316110	Collar leather, manufacturing
111219	Collard farming, field, bedding plant and seed production
333515	Collars (i.e., a machine tool accessory) manufacturing
316999	Collars and collar pads (i.e., harness) manufacturing
316999	Collars, dog, manufacturing
333613	Collars, shaft for power transmission equipment, manufacturing
525990	Collateralized mortgage obligations (CMOs)
333293	Collating machinery for printing and bookbinding manufacturing
333313	Collating machinery, office-type, manufacturing
453220	Collectible gift shops (e.g., crystal, pewter, porcelain)
812320	Collecting and distributing agents, laundry and drycleaning
561440	Collection agencies
561440	Collection agencies, accounts

Code	Description
221320	Collection, treatment, and disposal of waste through a sewer system
335312	Collector rings for motors and generators manufacturing
453998	Collector's items shops (e.g., autograph, card, coin, stamp)
454110	Collector's items, mail-order houses
611691	College board preparation centers
611691	College entrance exam preparation instruction
611710	College selection services
611310	Colleges (except junior colleges)
611511	Colleges, barber and beauty
611210	Colleges, community
611210	Colleges, junior
333515	Collets (i.e., a machine tool accessory) manufacturing
325620	Colognes manufacturing
422210	Colognes wholesaling
334510	Colon scopes, electromedical, manufacturing
812199	Color consulting services (i.e., personal care services)
325131	Color pigments, inorganic (except bone black, carbon black, lamp black), manufacturing
325132	Color pigments, organic (except animal black, bone black), manufacturing
323122	Color separation services, for the printing trade
334516	Colorimeters, laboratory-type, manufacturing
511199	Coloring book publishing (i.e., establishments known as publishers)
421920	Coloring books wholesaling
316110	Coloring leather
332813	Coloring metals and metal products (except coating) for the trade
339113	Colostomy appliances manufacturing
212299	Columbite mining and/or beneficiating
212299	Columbium ores mining and/or beneficiating
327420	Columns, architectural or ornamental plaster work, manufacturing
332420	Columns, fractionating, manufacturing
321918	Columns, porch, wood, manufacturing
316993	Comb cases (except metal) manufacturing
339911	Comb cases, precious metal, manufacturing
334512	Combination limit and fan controls manufacturing
112990	Combination livestock farming (except dairy, poultry)
334512	Combination oil and hydronic controls manufacturing
333111	Combines (i.e., harvester-threshers) manufacturing
313312	Combing and converting top
333292	Combing machinery for textiles manufacturing
313312	Combing textile fibers
115113	Combining, agricultural
332999	Combs, metal, manufacturing
326199	Combs, plastics, manufacturing
326299	Combs, rubber, manufacturing
334513	Combustion control instruments (except commercial, household furnace-type) manufacturing
541330	Combustion engineering consulting services
562211	Combustors, hazardous waste
562213	Combustors, nonhazardous solid waste
711510	Comedians, independent

Code	Description
711110	Comedy troupes
812990	Comfort station operation
314129	Comforters made from purchased fabrics
511120	Comic book publishers
511120	Comic book publishers and printing combined
511120	Comic book publishing (i.e., establishments known as publishers)
323112	Comic books flexographic printing without publishing
323111	Comic books gravure printing without publishing
323110	Comic books lithographic (offset) printing without publishing
323119	Comic books printing (except flexographic, gravure, lithographic, screen) without publishing
323113	Comic books screen printing without publishing
811310	Commercial and industrial machinery repair and maintenance services
233320	Commercial and institutional building construction management firms
541430	Commercial art services
541430	Commercial artists, independent
311812	Commercial bakeries
522110	Commercial banking
522110	Commercial banks
233320	Commercial building construction
531120	Commercial building rental or leasing
561450	Commercial credit reporting bureaus
541430	Commercial illustration services
541430	Commercial illustrators, independent
335122	Commercial lighting fixtures, electric, manufacturing
523120	Commercial note brokers' offices
523110	Commercial paper dealing (i.e., acting as a principal in dealing securities to investors)
541922	Commercial photography services
531312	Commercial property managing
531210	Commercial real estate agencies
531210	Commercial real estate agents' offices
531312	Commercial real estate property managers' offices
811310	Commercial refrigeration equipment repair and maintenance services
422120	Commercial stationery suppliers wholesaling
334518	Commercial timing mechanisms manufacturing
233320	Commercial warehouse construction, general construction contractors
512110	Commercials, television, production
445110	Commissaries, primarily groceries
522298	Commodity Credit Corporation
523130	Commodity contract trading companies
523140	Commodity contracts brokerages
523140	Commodity contracts brokers' offices
523130	Commodity contracts dealing (i.e., acting as a principal in dealing commodities to investors)
523210	Commodity contracts exchanges
523140	Commodity contracts floor brokers
523130	Commodity contracts floor traders (i.e., acting as a principal in dealing commodities to investors)
523130	Commodity contracts floor trading (i.e., acting as a principal in dealing commodities to investors)
523140	Commodity contracts options brokerages

Commodity—Computer-aided

Code	Description
523130	Commodity contracts options dealing (i.e., acting as a principal in dealing commodities to investors)
523130	Commodity contracts traders (i.e., acting as a principal in dealing commodities to investors)
523140	Commodity futures brokerages
541990	Commodity inspection services
212325	Common clay mining and/or beneficiating
212321	Common sand quarrying and/or beneficiating
212325	Common shale mining and/or beneficiating
923120	Communicable disease program administration
541430	Communication design services, visual
235310	Communication equipment construction contractors
811213	Communication equipment repair and maintenance services
234920	Communication transmission and power line construction management firms
926130	Communications commissions
421690	Communications equipment wholesaling
334220	Communications equipment, mobile and microwave, manufacturing
334210	Communications headgear, telephone, manufacturing
926130	Communications licensing commissions and agencies
335929	Communications wire and cable, nonferrous, made from purchased nonferrous wire
331319	Communications wire or cable made in aluminum wire drawing plants
331422	Communications wire or cable, copper, made from purchased copper in wire drawing plants
331491	Communications wire or cable, nonferrous metals (except aluminum, copper), made from purchased nonferrous metals (except aluminum, copper) in wire drawing plants
311812	Communion wafer manufacturing
813319	Community action advocacy organizations
624190	Community action service agencies
624120	Community centers (except recreational only), adult
624110	Community centers (except recreational only), youth
813219	Community chests
611210	Community colleges
611210	Community colleges offering a wide variety of academic and technical training
925120	Community development agencies, government
813211	Community foundations
621498	Community health centers and clinics, outpatient
923120	Community health programs administration
624210	Community meals, social services
712110	Community museums
924120	Community recreation programs, government
923130	Community social service program administration
711110	Community theaters
335312	Commutators, electric motor, manufacturing
481111	Commuter air carriers, scheduled

Code	Description
485113	Commuter bus operation (except mixed mode)
485112	Commuter rail systems (except mixed mode)
485111	Commuter transit systems, mixed mode (e.g., bus, commuter rail, subway combination)
334310	Compact disc players (e.g., automotive, household-type) manufacturing
421990	Compact discs (CDs), prerecorded, wholesaling
334611	Compact discs (i.e., CD-ROM), software, mass reproducing
334612	Compact discs, prerecorded audio, mass reproducing
334613	Compact discs, recordable or rewritable, blank, manufacturing
335110	Compact fluorescent light bulbs manufacturing
339911	Compacts, precious metal, manufacturing
316993	Compacts, solid leather, manufacturing
112990	Companion animals production (e.g., cats, dogs, parakeets, parrots)
624120	Companion services for disabled persons, the elderly, and persons diagnosed with mental retardation
333314	Comparators, optical, manufacturing
334511	Compasses, gyroscopic and magnetic (except portable), manufacturing
334519	Compasses, portable magnetic-type, manufacturing
541612	Compensation consulting services
541612	Compensation planning services
511140	Compiling mailing lists
311119	Complete feed, livestock, manufacturing
711510	Composers, independent
322214	Composite cans (i.e., foil-fiber and other combinations) manufacturing
562219	Compost dumps
325314	Compost manufacturing
325120	Compressed and liquefied industrial gas manufacturing
332911	Compressed gas cylinder valves manufacturing
422690	Compressed gases (except LP gas) wholesaling
321219	Compression modified wood manufacturing
333220	Compression molding machinery for plastics manufacturing
339991	Compression packings manufacturing
532490	Compressor, air and gas, rental or leasing
421830	Compressors (except air-conditioning, refrigeration) wholesaling
333912	Compressors, air and gas, general purpose-type, manufacturing
421730	Compressors, air-conditioning, wholesaling
336391	Compressors, motor vehicle air-conditioning, manufacturing
421740	Compressors, refrigeration, wholesaling
541710	Computer and related hardware research and development laboratories or services
421430	Computer boards, loaded, wholesaling
421690	Computer boards, unloaded, wholesaling
235310	Computer cable construction contractors
421690	Computer chips wholesaling
541519	Computer disaster recovery services
813410	Computer enthusiasts clubs

Code	Description
811212	Computer equipment repair and maintenance services without retailing new computers
443120	Computer equipment stores
323116	Computer forms (manifold or continuous) printing
337124	Computer furniture, metal household-type, manufacturing
337122	Computer furniture, wood household-type, manufacturing
514210	Computer input preparation services
334119	Computer input/output equipment (except terminals) manufacturing
611420	Computer operator training
422120	Computer paper supplies wholesaling
322231	Computer paper, single layered continuous, die-cut, made from purchased paper
532420	Computer peripheral equipment rental or leasing
421430	Computer peripheral equipment wholesaling
325992	Computer printer toner cartridges manufacturing
421430	Computer printers wholesaling
541511	Computer program or software development, custom
611420	Computer programming schools
541511	Computer programming services, custom
532420	Computer rental or leasing
611519	Computer repair training
334111	Computer servers manufacturing
514210	Computer service bureaus
541511	Computer software analysis and design services, custom
541511	Computer software programming services, custom
511210	Computer software publishers, packaged
511210	Computer software publishing and reproduction
511210	Computer software publishing including design and development, packaged (i.e., establishments known as publishers)
541511	Computer software support services, custom
334613	Computer software tapes and disks, blank, rigid and floppy, manufacturing
611420	Computer software training
454110	Computer software, mail-order houses
421430	Computer software, packaged, wholesaling
443120	Computer stores
541513	Computer systems facilities (i.e., clients' facilities) management and operation services
541512	Computer systems integration analysis and design services
541512	Computer systems integration design consulting services
541512	Computer systems integrator services
334119	Computer terminals manufacturing
514210	Computer time leasing
514210	Computer time rental
514210	Computer time sharing services
621512	Computer tomography (CT-SCAN) centers
611420	Computer training (except repair)
532230	Computer video game rental
541512	Computer-aided design (CAD) systems integration design services
541512	Computer-aided engineering (CAE) systems integration design services

Code	Description
541512	Computer-aided manufacturing (CAM) systems integration design services
334517	Computerized axial tomography (CT/CAT) scanners manufacturing
334512	Computerized environmental control systems for buildings manufacturing
334111	Computers manufacturing
421430	Computers wholesaling
325411	Concentrated medicinal chemicals, uncompounded, manufacturing
311930	Concentrates, drink (except frozen fruit juice), manufacturing
311930	Concentrates, flavoring (except coffee based), manufacturing
311411	Concentrates, frozen fruit juice, manufacturing
421520	Concentrates, metallic, wholesaling
333131	Concentration machinery, mining-type, manufacturing
711130	Concert artists, independent
711320	Concert booking agencies
711310	Concert hall operators
531120	Concert hall, no promotion of events, rental or leasing
711310	Concert managers with facilities
711320	Concert managers without facilities
711310	Concert organizers with facilities
711320	Concert organizers without facilities
711310	Concert promoters with facilities
711320	Concert promoters without facilities
713990	Concession operators, amusement device (except gambling) and ride
722330	Concession stands, mobile
812990	Concierge services
926150	Conciliation and mediation services, government
234110	Concrete (e.g., roads, highways, public sidewalks, streets) construction contractors
325998	Concrete additive preparations (e.g., curing, hardening) manufacturing
422690	Concrete additives wholesaling
327320	Concrete batch plants (including temporary)
235410	Concrete block laying construction contractors
235940	Concrete breaking and cutting construction contractors
421320	Concrete building products wholesaling
235710	Concrete construction contractors (i.e., parking areas, private driveways, sidewalks)
235710	Concrete finishing construction contractors
333120	Concrete finishing machinery manufacturing
235990	Concrete form construction contractors
332322	Concrete forms, sheet metal, manufacturing
327390	Concrete furniture (e.g., benches, tables) manufacturing
333120	Concrete gunning equipment manufacturing
333120	Concrete mixing machinery, portable, manufacturing
421810	Concrete processing equipment wholesaling
235910	Concrete products (e.g., structural precast or prestressed), placement, construction contractors
333298	Concrete products forming machinery manufacturing
327390	Concrete products, precast (except block, brick and pipe), manufacturing

Code	Description
235710	Concrete pumping construction contractors
235910	Concrete reinforcement placement, construction contractors
332312	Concrete reinforcing bars manufacturing
421510	Concrete reinforcing bars wholesaling
332618	Concrete reinforcing mesh made from purchased wire
327390	Concrete tanks manufacturing
327999	Concrete, dry mixture, manufacturing
211112	Condensate, cycle, natural gas production
333294	Condensed and evaporated milk machinery manufacturing
311514	Condensed milk manufacturing
311514	Condensed, evaporated or powdered whey, manufacturing
332410	Condenser boxes, metal, manufacturing
335999	Condensers (except electronic), fixed and variable, manufacturing
334414	Condensers, electronic, manufacturing
421690	Condensers, electronic, wholesaling
332410	Condensers, steam, manufacturing
335312	Condensers, synchronous, electric, manufacturing
421830	Condensing units (except air-conditioning, refrigeration) wholesaling
421730	Condensing units, air-conditioning, wholesaling
421740	Condensing units, refrigeration, wholesaling
326299	Condom manufacturing
813990	Condominium corporations
531312	Condominium managers' offices, commercial
531311	Condominium managers' offices, residential
813990	Condominium owners' associations
561599	Condominium time share exchange services
233220	Condominiums, multifamily, construction
335931	Conductor connectors, solderless connectors, sleeves, or soldering lugs, manufacturing
234920	Conduit construction
327123	Conduit, vitrified clay, manufacturing
331210	Conduit, welded and lock joint, made from purchased iron or steel
335932	Conduits and fittings, electrical, manufacturing
327332	Conduits, concrete, manufacturing
322214	Cones (e.g., winding yarn, string, ribbon, cloth), fiber, made from purchased paperboard
311821	Cones, ice cream, manufacturing
327112	Cones, pyrometric, earthenware, manufacturing
311313	Confectioner's beet sugar manufacturing
311312	Confectioner's powdered sugar made from purchased raw cane sugar
311320	Confectionery chocolate made from cacao beans
333294	Confectionery machinery manufacturing
722213	Confectionery snack shops, made on premises with carryout services
445292	Confectionery stores, packaged, retailing only
422450	Confectionery wholesaling
311340	Confectionery, nonchocolate, manufacturing
531120	Conference center, no promotion of events, rental or leasing
322299	Confetti made from purchased paper

Code	Description
921120	Congress of the United States
336312	Connecting rods, automotive and truck gasoline engine, manufacturing
335931	Connectors and terminals for electrical devices manufacturing
335931	Connectors, electric cord, manufacturing
334417	Connectors, electronic (e.g., coaxial, cylindrical, printed circuit, rack and panel), manufacturing
421690	Connectors, electronic, wholesaling
335313	Connectors, power, manufacturing
335931	Connectors, solderless (wiring devices), manufacturing
335931	Connectors, twist on wire (i.e., nuts), manufacturing
813312	Conservation advocacy organizations
234990	Conservation and development construction
924120	Conservation and reclamation agencies
712190	Conservation areas
611310	Conservatories of music (colleges or universities)
712130	Conservatories, botanical
711510	Conservators, independent
611610	Conservatory of music (except academic)
453310	Consignment shops, used
336350	Constant velocity joints, automotive, truck, and bus, manufacturing
813940	Constituencies' associations, political party
325520	Construction adhesives (except asphalt, gypsum base) manufacturing
813910	Construction associations
541330	Construction engineering services
532412	Construction form rental
522292	Construction lending
532412	Construction machinery and equipment rental or leasing without operator
811310	Construction machinery and equipment repair and maintenance services
421810	Construction machinery and equipment wholesaling
333120	Construction machinery manufacturing
234120	Construction management firms, bridge and tunnel
233320	Construction management firms, commercial and institutional building firms
234110	Construction management firms, highway and street
234930	Construction management firms, industrial nonbuilding
233310	Construction management firms, manufacturing and industrial building
233220	Construction management firms, multifamily
234990	Construction management firms, nonbuilding (except industrial)
234920	Construction management firms, power and communication transmission line
233210	Construction management firms, single family
234910	Construction management firms, water, sewer and pipeline
421610	Construction materials, electrical, wholesaling
322233	Construction paper, school and art, made from purchased paper
322121	Construction paper, school and art, made in paper mills
212321	Construction sand and gravel beneficiating (e.g., grinding, screening, washing)

Construction—Copper foil

Code	Description
212321	Construction sand or gravel dredging
333120	Construction-type tractors and attachments manufacturing
928120	Consulates
******	Consultants — see specific activity
813920	Consultants' associations
531390	Consultants', real estate (except appraisers), offices
541330	Consulting engineers' offices
541330	Consulting engineers' private practices
812990	Consumer buying services
541990	Consumer credit counseling services
561450	Consumer credit reporting bureaus
532210	Consumer electronics rental
811211	Consumer electronics repair and maintenance services without retailing new consumer electronics
421620	Consumer electronics wholesaling
522291	Consumer finance companies (i.e., unsecured cash loans)
922190	Consumer product safety commissions
926110	Consumer protection offices
443112	Consumer-type electronic stores (e.g., radio, television, video camera)
334514	Consumption meters (e.g., gas, water) manufacturing
524128	Contact lens insurance, direct
339115	Contact lenses manufacturing
421460	Contact lenses wholesaling
335931	Contacts, electrical (except carbon and graphite), manufacturing
335991	Contacts, electrical, carbon and graphite, manufacturing
322130	Container board stock manufacturing
336611	Container ship building
484110	Container trucking services, local
484121	Container trucking services, long-distance
327213	Containers for packaging, bottling, and canning, glass, manufacturing
332439	Containers, air cargo, metal, manufacturing
332999	Containers, foil (except bags), manufacturing
421840	Containers, industrial, wholesaling
332439	Containers, light gauge metal (except cans), manufacturing
422130	Containers, paper and disposable plastics, wholesaling
321920	Containers, wood, manufacturing
712110	Contemporary art museums
711120	Contemporary dance companies
623311	Continuing care retirement communities
325412	Contraceptive preparations manufacturing
213112	Contract services for oil and gas fields
******	Contractors — see specific activity
813910	Contractors' associations
315211	Contractors, men's and boys', cut and sew apparel
315212	Contractors, women's, girls' and infants', cut and sew apparel
325412	Contrast media in-vivo diagnostic substances (e.g., iodine, barium) manufacturing
335314	Control circuit devices, magnet and solid-state, manufacturing
335314	Control circuit relays, industrial, manufacturing
335314	Control equipment, electric, manufacturing
335313	Control panels, electric power distribution, manufacturing
335311	Control transformers manufacturing
332912	Control valves, fluid power, manufacturing
332911	Control valves, industrial-type, manufacturing
921130	Controller's and comptrollers' offices, government
334513	Controllers for process variables (e.g., electric, electronic, mechanical, pneumatic operation) manufacturing
334290	Controlling equipment, street light, manufacturing
335314	Controls and control accessories, industrial, manufacturing
335314	Controls for adjustable speed drives manufacturing
334514	Controls, revolution and timing instruments, manufacturing
623110	Convalescent homes or convalescent hospitals (except psychiatric)
623220	Convalescent homes or hospitals for psychiatric patients
446199	Convalescent supply stores
335221	Convection ovens (including portable), household-type, manufacturing
445120	Convenience food stores
447110	Convenience food with gasoline stations
335931	Convenience outlets, electric, manufacturing
561591	Convention and visitors bureaus
561591	Convention bureaus
531120	Convention center, no promotion of events, rental or leasing
561920	Convention managers
561920	Convention organizers
561920	Convention promoters
561920	Convention services
813110	Convents (except schools)
313311	Converters, broadwoven piece goods
335312	Converters, phase and rotary, electrical equipment, manufacturing
337121	Convertible sofas (except futons) manufacturing
336399	Convertible tops for automotive, truck, and bus, manufacturing
313311	Converting textiles, broadwoven
313312	Converting textiles, narrow woven
316110	Convertors, leather
313312	Convertors, narrow woven piece goods
421830	Conveying equipment (except farm) wholesaling
421820	Conveying equipment, farm, wholesaling
326220	Conveyor belts, rubber, manufacturing
235950	Conveyor system construction contractors
333922	Conveyors, farm-type, manufacturing
311612	Cooked meats made from purchased carcasses
311822	Cookie dough made from purchased flour
722213	Cookie shops, on premise baking and carryout service
311821	Cookies manufacturing
422490	Cookies wholesaling
311821	Cookies, filled, manufacturing
335211	Cooking appliances (except convection, microwave ovens), household-type electric portable, manufacturing
311320	Cooking chocolate made from cacao beans
333319	Cooking equipment (i.e., fryers, microwave ovens, ovens, ranges), commercial-type, manufacturing
421440	Cooking equipment, commercial, wholesaling
421620	Cooking equipment, electric household-type, wholesaling
421720	Cooking equipment, gas, household-type, wholesaling
422490	Cooking oils wholesaling
611519	Cooking schools
331511	Cooking utensils, cast iron, manufacturing
332214	Cooking utensils, fabricated metal, manufacturing
327212	Cooking utensils, glass and glass ceramic, made in glass making plants
421220	Cooking utensils, household-type, wholesaling
327112	Cooking ware (e.g., stoneware, coarse earthenware, pottery), manufacturing
327215	Cooking ware made from purchased glass
327212	Cooking ware made in glass making plants
327112	Cooking ware, china, manufacturing
327112	Cooking ware, fine earthenware, manufacturing
221330	Cooled air distribution
326199	Coolers or ice chests, plastics (except foam), manufacturing
326140	Coolers or ice chests, polystyrene foam, manufacturing
333415	Coolers, refrigeration, manufacturing
333415	Coolers, water, manufacturing
235910	Cooling tower construction contractors
333415	Cooling towers manufacturing
321920	Cooperage manufacturing
321920	Cooperage stock (e.g., heading, hoops, staves) manufacturing
321920	Cooperage stock mills
421840	Cooperage stock wholesaling
531311	Cooperative apartment managers' offices
233220	Cooperative construction
812331	Cooperative hospital laundries (i.e., linen supply services)
524113	Cooperative life insurance organizations
813990	Cooperative owners' associations
321920	Coopered tubs manufacturing
332212	Coordinate and contour measuring machines, machinists' precision tools, manufacturing
532420	Copier rental or leasing
327123	Coping, wall, clay, manufacturing
327390	Copings, concrete, manufacturing
331525	Copper alloy castings (except die-castings), unfinished, manufacturing
331423	Copper alloys (e.g., brass, bronze) made from purchased metal or scrap
331411	Copper alloys made in primary copper smelting and refining mills
331423	Copper and copper-based shapes (e.g., cake, ingot, slag, wire bar) made from purchased metal or scrap
325131	Copper base pigments manufacturing
212234	Copper beneficiating plants
325188	Copper chloride manufacturing
325612	Copper cleaners manufacturing
325188	Copper compounds, not specified elsewhere by process, manufacturing
331411	Copper concentrate refining
331522	Copper die-casting foundries
331522	Copper die-castings, unfinished, manufacturing
331421	Copper foil made from purchased metal or scrap

Code	Description	Code	Description	Code	Description
332999	Copper foil not made in rolling mills	333131	Core drills, underground mining-type, manufacturing	922140	Correctional boot camps
332112	Copper forgings made from purchased metals, unfinished	322214	Cores (i.e., all-fiber, nonfiber ends of any material), fiber, made from purchased paperboard	561210	Correctional facility operation on a contract or fee basis
331525	Copper foundries (except die-casting)			922140	Correctional institutions
325188	Copper iodide manufacturing			322211	Corrugated and solid fiber boxes made from purchased paper or paperboard
212234	Copper ore concentrates recovery	332992	Cores, bullet (i.e., 30 mm. or less, 1.18 inch or less), manufacturing	322211	Corrugated and solid fiberboard pads made from purchased paper or paperboard
212234	Copper ore mine site development for own account	332997	Cores, sand foundry, manufacturing		
212234	Copper ores mining and/or beneficiating	321999	Cork products (except gaskets) manufacturing	322211	Corrugated paper made from purchased paper or paperboard
331423	Copper powder, flakes, and paste made from purchased copper	421840	Cork wholesaling	331221	Corrugating iron or steel in cold rolling mills
331421	Copper products (except communication wire, energy wire) made by drawing purchased copper	321999	Corks, bottle, manufacturing	315212	Corselets cut and sew apparel contractors
		111421	Corms farming		
		311230	Corn breakfast foods manufacturing	315231	Corselets, women's, misses', and girls', cut and sewn from purchased fabric (except apparel contractors)
331421	Copper products (except communication wire, energy wire) made by rolling, drawing, or extruding purchased copper	311919	Corn chips and related corn snacks manufacturing		
		422450	Corn chips and related corn snacks wholesaling	315212	Corsets and allied garments (except surgical), women's, cut and sew apparel contractors
331421	Copper products (except communication wire, energy wire) made in integrated secondary smelting and extruding mills	311340	Corn confections manufacturing		
		321992	Corn cribs, prefabricated, wood, manufacturing	315231	Corsets and allied garments (except surgical), women's, misses', and girls', cut and sewn from purchased fabric (except apparel contractors)
331421	Copper products (except communication wire, energy wire) made in integrated secondary smelting mills and drawing plants	311221	Corn dextrin manufacturing		
		115114	Corn drying		
		111150	Corn farming (except sweet corn), field and seed production	339113	Corsets, surgical, manufacturing
				325411	Cortisone, uncompounded ,manufacturing
331423	Copper secondary smelting and alloying	311211	Corn flour manufacturing		
331423	Copper secondary smelting and refining from purchased metal or scrap	311221	Corn gluten feed manufacturing	212399	Corundum mining and/or beneficiating
		311221	Corn gluten meal manufacturing	316993	Cosmetic bags (except metal) manufacturing
331411	Copper shapes (e.g., bar, billet, ingot, plate, sheet) made in primary copper smelting and refining mills	333111	Corn heads for combines manufacturing		
		311211	Corn meal made in flour mills	339911	Cosmetic bags, precious metal, manufacturing
		311221	Corn oil cake and meal manufacturing		
331411	Copper smelting and refining, primary	311225	Corn oil made from purchased oils	325620	Cosmetic creams, lotions, and oils manufacturing
235610	Copper smithing contractors, in connection with construction work	311221	Corn oil mills		
		311221	Corn oil, crude and refined, made by wet milling corn	561910	Cosmetic kit assembling and packaging services
325188	Copper sulfate manufacturing			446120	Cosmetics stores
212234	Copper-water precipitates	333111	Corn pickers and shellers manufacturing	422210	Cosmetics wholesaling
561439	Copy centers (except combined with printing services)	335211	Corn poppers, household-type electric, manufacturing	812112	Cosmetology salons or shops
				611511	Cosmetology schools
561439	Copy shops (except combined with printing services)	333294	Corn popping machinery (i.e., food manufacturing-type) manufacturing	541490	Costume design services (except independent theatrical costume designers)
421420	Copying machines wholesaling	333319	Corn popping machines, commercial-type, manufacturing		
314991	Cord (except tire, wire) manufacturing				
335931	Cord connectors, electric, manufacturing	339113	Corn remover and bunion pad manufacturing	711510	Costume designers, independent theatrical
314992	Cord for reinforcing rubber tires, industrial belting, and fuel cells manufacturing	115114	Corn shelling	339914	Costume jewelry manufacturing
		311221	Corn starch manufacturing	448150	Costume jewelry stores
		311221	Corn sweeteners (e.g., dextrose, fructose, glucose) made by wet milling corn	421940	Costume jewelry wholesaling
331422	Cord sets, flexible, made from purchased copper in wire drawing plants			532220	Costume rental
				448190	Costume shops (including theatrical)
331319	Cord sets, flexible, made in aluminum wire drawing plants	311999	Corn syrups made from purchased sweeteners	315299	Costumes (e.g., lodge, masquerade, theatrical) cut and sewn from purchased fabric (except apparel contractors)
331491	Cord sets, flexible, nonferrous metals (except aluminum, copper), made from purchased nonferrous metals (except aluminum, copper) in wire drawing plants	311213	Corn, malt, manufacturing		
		339112	Corneal microscopes manufacturing		
		311612	Corned meats made from purchased carcasses	315212	Costumes (e.g., lodge, masquerade, theatrical) women's, girls' and infants', cut and sew apparel contractors
		316999	Corners, luggage, leather, manufacturing		
314991	Cordage (except wire) manufacturing	339992	Cornets and parts manufacturing	315211	Costumes (e.g., lodge, masquerade, theatrical), men's and boys', cut and sew apparel contractors
333292	Cordage and rope (except wire) making machines manufacturing	332322	Cornices, sheet metal, manufacturing		
		321918	Cornices, wood, manufacturing		
421840	Cordage wholesaling	112320	Cornish hen production	337121	Cot springs, assembled, manufacturing
325920	Cordite explosive materials manufacturing	422490	Cornmeal, edible, wholesaling	337124	Cots, metal household-type, manufacturing
		212325	Cornwall stone mining and/or beneficiating		
334210	Cordless telephones (except cellular) manufacturing	923120	Coroners' offices	337122	Cots, wood household-type, manufacturing
		813211	Corporate foundations, awarding grants		
313221	Cords and braids, narrow woven, manufacturing	541430	Corporate identification (i.e., logo) design services	311511	Cottage cheese manufacturing
				531110	Cottage rental or leasing
313210	Corduroys weaving	541110	Corporate law offices	721199	Cottages, housekeeping
333994	Core baking and mold drying ovens manufacturing	551114	Corporate offices	332722	Cotter pins, metal, manufacturing
		115210	Corralling, drovers	422990	Cotton (except raw) wholesaling
213112	Core cutting in oil and gas wells, on a contract basis	332323	Corrals, metal, manufacturing	339113	Cotton and cotton balls, absorbent, manufacturing
		325998	Correction fluids (i.e., typewriter) manufacturing		
213112	Core drilling, exploration services, oil and gas field			333111	Cotton balers and presses manufacturing

Cotton battings—Cresols

Code	Description
314999	Cotton battings (except nonwoven batting) manufacturing
313111	Cotton cordage spun yarns made from purchased fiber
313210	Cotton fabrics, broadwoven, weaving
313221	Cotton fabrics, narrow woven weaving
111920	Cotton farming, field and seed production
322121	Cotton fiber paper stock manufacturing
115111	Cotton ginning
333111	Cotton ginning machinery manufacturing
333111	Cotton picker and stripper harvesting machinery manufacturing
313111	Cotton spun yarns made from purchased fiber
313113	Cotton thread manufacturing
339113	Cotton tipped applicators manufacturing
115113	Cotton, machine harvesting
422590	Cotton, raw, wholesaling
111920	Cottonseed farming
311225	Cottonseed oil made from purchased oils
311223	Cottonseed oil, cake and meal, made in crushing mills
337121	Couch springs, assembled, manufacturing
337121	Couches, upholstered, manufacturing
311340	Cough drops (except medicated) manufacturing
325412	Cough drops, medicated, manufacturing
325412	Cough medicines manufacturing
334513	Coulometric analyzers, industrial process-type, manufacturing
334516	Coulometric analyzers, laboratory-type, manufacturing
325199	Coumarin manufacturing
325211	Coumarone-indene resins manufacturing
926110	Councils of Economic Advisers
624190	Counseling services
621410	Counseling services, family planning
541110	Counselors' at law offices
541110	Counselors' at law private practices
334519	Count rate meters, nuclear radiation, manufacturing
235990	Counter top construction contractors
334514	Counter type registers manufacturing
337215	Counter units (except refrigerated) manufacturing
333515	Counterbores (i.e., a machine tool accessory), metalworking, manufacturing
332212	Counterbores and countersinking bits, woodworking, manufacturing
334511	Countermeasure sets (e.g., active countermeasures, jamming equipment) manufacturing
334514	Counters (e.g., electrical, electronic, mechanical), totalizing, manufacturing
316999	Counters (i.e., shoe cut stock), leather, manufacturing
333415	Counters and display cases, refrigerated, manufacturing
334514	Counters, revolution, manufacturing
333515	Countersinks (i.e., a machine tool accessory) manufacturing
337215	Countertops (except kitchen and bathroom), wood or plastics laminated on wood, manufacturing
337110	Countertops (i.e., kitchen, bathroom), wood or plastics laminated on wood, manufacturing
326199	Countertops, plastics, manufacturing
327991	Countertops, stone, manufacturing
337110	Countertops, wood, manufacturing
334514	Counting devices manufacturing
713910	Country clubs
711130	Country musical artists, independent
711130	Country musical groups
921120	County commissioners
925120	County development agencies
923110	County supervisors of education (except school boards)
921110	County supervisors' and executives' offices
332919	Couplings, hose, metal (except fluid power), manufacturing
333613	Couplings, mechanical power transmission, manufacturing
332996	Couplings, pipe, made from purchased metal pipe
541870	Coupon direct distribution services
561990	Coupon redemption services (i.e., clearinghouse)
492110	Courier services (i.e., inter-city network)
611410	Court reporting schools
561492	Court reporting services
922110	Courts of law, civilian (except American Indian or Alaska Native)
921150	Courts, American Indian or Alaska Native
922110	Courts, civilian (except American Indian or Alaska Native)
928110	Courts, military
922110	Courts, small claims
315211	Coveralls, work, men's and boys', cut and sew apparel contractors
315225	Coveralls, work, men's and boys', cut and sewn from purchased fabric (except apparel contractors)
315212	Coveralls, work, women's, girls', and infants', cut and sew apparel contractors
315239	Coveralls, work, women's, misses', and girls', cut and sewn from purchased fabric (except apparel contractors)
314912	Covers (e.g., boat, swimming pool, truck) made from purchased fabrics
332313	Covers, annealing, fabricated metal plate work, manufacturing
321999	Covers, bottle and demijohn, willow, rattan, and reed, manufacturing
332313	Covers, floating, fabricated metal plate work, manufacturing
111219	Cow pea (except dry) farming, field and seed production
332322	Cowls, sheet metal, manufacturing
111130	Cowpea farming, dry, field and seed production
332618	Crab traps made from purchased wire
114112	Crabbing
333294	Cracker making machinery manufacturing
311821	Crackers (e.g., graham, soda) manufacturing
333518	Cradle assembly machinery (i.e., wire making equipment) manufacturing
337122	Cradles, wood, manufacturing
339932	Craft and hobby kits and sets manufacturing
561920	Craft fair managers
561920	Craft fair organizers
561920	Craft fair promoters
421920	Craft kits wholesaling
451120	Craft supply stores (except needlecraft)
611513	Craft union apprenticeship training programs
111334	Cranberry farming
335314	Crane and hoist controls, including metal mill, manufacturing
532412	Crane rental or leasing without operator
421810	Cranes (except industrial) wholesaling
333120	Cranes, construction-type, manufacturing
333924	Cranes, industrial truck, manufacturing
421830	Cranes, industrial, wholesaling
421810	Cranes, mining, wholesaling
333923	Cranes, overhead traveling, manufacturing
325998	Crankcase additive preparations manufacturing
336312	Crankshaft assemblies, automotive and truck gasoline engine, manufacturing
333512	Crankshaft grinding machines manufacturing
321920	Crates (e.g., berry, butter, fruit, vegetable) made of wood, wirebound, manufacturing
488991	Crating goods for shipping
112512	Crawfish production, farm raising
114112	Crayfish fishing
339942	Crayons manufacturing
311511	Cream manufacturing
325199	Cream of tartar manufacturing
333111	Cream separators, farm-type, manufacturing
333294	Cream separators, industrial, manufacturing
422430	Cream stations wholesaling
422430	Cream wholesaling
311514	Cream, dried and powdered, manufacturing
311512	Creamery butter manufacturing
422430	Creamery products (except canned) wholesaling
422490	Creamery products, canned, wholesaling
313311	Crease resistant finishing of broadwoven fabric
313312	Crease resistant finishing of fabrics (except broadwoven)
561450	Credit agencies
323119	Credit and identification card imprinting, embossing, and encoding
326199	Credit and identification card stock, plastics, manufacturing
524126	Credit and other financial responsibility insurance carriers, direct
561450	Credit bureaus
522210	Credit card banks
522210	Credit card issuing
812990	Credit card notification services (i.e., lost or stolen card reporting)
522320	Credit card processing services
561450	Credit investigation services
524113	Credit life insurance carriers, direct
561450	Credit rating services
541990	Credit repair (i.e., counseling) services, consumer
561450	Credit reporting bureaus
522130	Credit unions
333999	Cremating ovens manufacturing
812220	Crematories (except combined with funeral homes)
111219	Crenshaw melon farming, field, bedding plant and seed production
325192	Creosote made by distillation of coal tar
325191	Creosote made by distillation of wood tar
321114	Creosoting of wood
322299	Crepe paper made from purchased paper
325211	Cresol resins manufacturing
325211	Cresol-furfural resins manufacturing
325192	Cresols made by distillation of coal tar

Code	Description
325192	Cresylic acids made from refined petroleum or natural gas
115115	Crew leaders, farm labor
315119	Crew socks knitting or knitting and finishing
337124	Cribs (i.e., baby beds), metal, manufacturing
337122	Cribs (i.e., baby beds), wood, manufacturing
112990	Cricket production
922120	Criminal investigation offices, government
922190	Criminal justice statistics centers, government
541110	Criminal law offices
111998	Crimson cloves seed farming
624190	Crisis intervention centers
114111	Croaker fishing
313111	Crochet spun yarns (e.g., cotton, manmade fiber, silk, wool) made from purchased fiber
314999	Crochet ware made from purchased materials
335211	Crock pots, household-type electric, manufacturing
327112	Crockery manufacturing
311812	Croissants, baking, made in commercial bakeries
115114	Crop cleaning
333111	Crop driers manufacturing
115112	Crop dusting
524126	Crop insurance carrier, direct
421820	Crop preparation machinery (e.g., cleaning, conditioning, drying) wholesaling
115112	Crop spraying
316999	Crops, riding, manufacturing
339920	Croquet sets manufacturing
713920	Cross country skiing facilities without accommodations
332911	Cross valves, industrial-type, manufacturing
321114	Crossties, treating
311812	Croutons and bread crumbs made in commercial bakeries
421840	Crowns and closures, metal, wholesaling
332115	Crowns, metal (e.g., bottle, can), stamping
327124	Crucibles, fire clay, manufacturing
327125	Crucibles, graphite, magnesite, chrome, silica, or other nonclay materials, manufacturing
311221	Crude corn oil manufacturing
486110	Crude oil pipeline transportation
324110	Crude oil refining
422710	Crude oil terminals
422720	Crude oil wholesaling (except bulk stations, terminals)
211111	Crude petroleum from oil sand
211111	Crude petroleum from oil shale
211111	Crude petroleum production
324110	Crude petroleum refineries
422990	Crude rubber wholesaling
336322	Cruise control mechanisms, electronic, automotive, truck, and bus, manufacturing
483114	Cruise lines (i.e., deep sea passenger transportation to and from domestic ports)
483112	Cruise lines (i.e., deep sea passenger transportation to or from foreign ports)
561599	Cruise ship ticket offices
713210	Cruises, gambling
115310	Cruising timber

Code	Description
311812	Crullers (except frozen) made in commercial bakeries
311813	Crullers, frozen, made in a commercial bakery
421320	Crushed stone wholesaling
333120	Crushing machinery, portable, manufacturing
333131	Crushing machinery, stationary, manufacturing
212111	Crushing plants, bituminous coal
333120	Crushing, pulverizing, and screening machinery, portable, manufacturing
112512	Crustacean production, farm raising
339113	Crutches and walkers manufacturing
421450	Crutches wholesaling
532291	Crutches, invalid, rental
332420	Cryogenic tanks manufacturing
212399	Cryolite mining and/or beneficiating
311340	Crystallized fruits and fruit peel manufacturing
334419	Crystals and crystal assemblies, electronic, manufacturing
335313	Cubicles (i.e., electric switchboard equipment) manufacturing
111219	Cucumber farming (except under cover), field, bedding plant and seed production
111419	Cucumber farming, grown under cover
339993	Cuff links (except precious) manufacturing
339911	Cuff links, precious metal, manufacturing
332999	Cuffs, leg, iron, manufacturing
611519	Culinary arts schools
112310	Cull hen production
212113	Culm bank recovery, anthracite (except on a contract basis)
213113	Culm bank recovery, anthracite, on a contract basis
212111	Culm bank recovery, bituminous coal or lignite (except on a contract basis)
213113	Culm bank recovery, coal, on a contract basis
315212	Culottes, women's, girls' and infants', cut and sew apparel contractors
315239	Culottes, women's, misses', and girls', cut and sewn from purchased fabric (except apparel contractors)
111422	Cultivated florist greens growing
421820	Cultivating machinery and equipment wholesaling
115112	Cultivation services
333111	Cultivators, farm-type, manufacturing
333112	Cultivators, powered, lawn and garden-type, manufacturing
926110	Cultural and arts development support program administration
325414	Culture media manufacturing
326191	Cultured marble plumbing fixtures manufacturing
326199	Cultured marble products (except plumbing fixtures) manufacturing
112512	Cultured pearl production, farm raising
326199	Cultured stone products (except plumbing fixtures) manufacturing
234910	Culvert construction
235710	Culvert construction contractors
327332	Culvert pipe, concrete, manufacturing
332313	Culverts, fabricated metal plate work, manufacturing
332322	Culverts, sheet metal, manufacturing
325110	Cumene made from refined petroleum or liquid hydrocarbons
324110	Cumene made in petroleum refineries

Code	Description
315999	Cummerbunds cut and sewn from purchased fabric (except apparel contractors)
315211	Cummerbunds, men's and boys', cut and sew apparel contractors
332313	Cupolas, fabricated metal plate work, manufacturing
212234	Cuprite mining and/or beneficiating
322299	Cups, molded pulp, manufacturing
422130	Cups, paper and disposable plastics, wholesaling
421220	Cups, plastics (except disposable), wholesaling
326199	Cups, plastics (except foam), manufacturing
326140	Cups, polystyrene foam, manufacturing
235710	Curb construction contractors
327991	Curbing, granite and stone, manufacturing
234110	Curbs and street gutter construction
311513	Curds, cheese, made in a cheese plant, manufacturing
422460	Cured fish wholesaling
311611	Cured hides and skins produced in slaughtering plants
311612	Cured meats (e.g., brined, dried, and salted) made from purchased carcasses
333111	Curers, tobacco, manufacturing
311711	Curing fish and seafood
453220	Curio shops
422990	Curios wholesaling
326299	Curlers, hair, rubber, manufacturing
713990	Curling facilities
335211	Curling irons, household-type electric, manufacturing
111334	Currant farming
333313	Currency counting machinery manufacturing
421420	Currency handling machines wholesaling
335311	Current limiting reactors, electrical, manufacturing
334515	Current measuring equipment manufacturing
335931	Current taps, attachment plug and screw shell types, manufacturing
421610	Current-carrying wiring devices wholesaling
316110	Currying furs
316110	Currying leather
442291	Curtain and drapery stores, packaged
812320	Curtain cleaning services
337920	Curtain or drapery fixtures (e.g., poles, rods, rollers) manufacturing
337920	Curtain rods and fittings manufacturing
321999	Curtain stretchers, wood, manufacturing
235910	Curtain wall construction contractors
332321	Curtain wall, metal, manufacturing
313210	Curtains and draperies made in broadwoven fabric mills
314121	Curtains and draperies, window, made from purchased fabrics
313249	Curtains made in lace mills
313249	Curtains made in warp knitting mills
313241	Curtains made in weft knitting mills
421220	Curtains wholesaling
337121	Cushion springs, assembled, manufacturing
314129	Cushions (except carpet, springs) made from purchased fabrics
326150	Cushions, carpet and rug, urethane and other foam plastics (except polystrene), manufacturing
311520	Custard, frozen, manufacturing

Custodial services—Data entry

Code	Description
561720	Custodial services
337212	Custom architectural millwork and fixtures, manufacturing on a job shop basis
233310	Custom buildings, industrial, construction
233220	Custom buildings, residential (except single family), general construction contractors
233210	Custom built house construction
325991	Custom compounding (i.e., blending and mixing) of purchased plastics resins
337212	Custom design interiors (i.e., coordinated furniture, architectural woodwork, fixtures), manufacturing
115114	Custom feed mixing and grinding
311119	Custom milling of animal feed
442299	Custom picture frame shops
333513	Custom roll forming machines, metalworking, manufacturing
332114	Custom roll forming metal products
321113	Custom sawmills
311611	Custom slaughtering
315223	Custom tailors, men's and boys' dress shirts, cut and sewn from purchased fabric
315222	Custom tailors, men's and boys' suits, cut and sewn from purchased fabric
315233	Custom tailors, women's, misses' and girls' dresses cut and sewn from purchased fabric (except apparel contractors)
541613	Customer service management consulting services
488510	Customs brokers
921130	Customs bureaus
541614	Customs consulting services
327215	Cut and engraved glassware made from purchased glass
315211	Cut and sew apparel contractors, men's and boys'
315212	Cut and sew apparel contractors, women's, girls', and infants'
111422	Cut flower growing
111422	Cut rose growing
316999	Cut stock for boots and shoes manufacturing
321912	Cut stock manufacturing
327991	Cut stone bases (e.g., desk sets pedestals, lamps, plaques and similar small particles) manufacturing
327991	Cut stone products (e.g., blocks, statuary) manufacturing
333512	Cut-off machines, metalworking, manufacturing
811490	Cutlery (e.g., knives, scissors) sharpening, household-type
421710	Cutlery wholesaling
332211	Cutlery, nonprecious and precious plated metal, manufacturing
339912	Cutlery, precious (except precious plated) metal, manufacturing
335931	Cutouts, switch and fuse, manufacturing
333131	Cutters, coal, manufacturing
332212	Cutters, glass, manufacturing
333515	Cutters, metal milling, manufacturing
113310	Cutting and transporting timber
213112	Cutting cores in oil and gas wells on a contract basis
332212	Cutting dies (e.g., paper, leather, textile) manufacturing
332212	Cutting dies (except metal cutting) manufacturing

Code	Description
333514	Cutting dies, metalworking, manufacturing
315211	Cutting fabric owned by others for men's and boys' apparel
315212	Cutting fabric owned by others for women's, girls', and infants' apparel
339114	Cutting instruments, dental, manufacturing
333512	Cutting machines, metalworking, manufacturing
316110	Cutting of leather
422470	Cutting of purchased carcasses (except boxed meat cut on an assembly-line basis) wholesaling
324191	Cutting oils made from refined petroleum
325998	Cutting oils, synthetic, manufacturing
234990	Cutting right-of-way
113310	Cutting timber
327215	Cutting, engraving, etching, painting or polishing purchased glass
111422	Cuttings farming
325188	Cyanides manufacturing
212325	Cyanite mining and/or beneficiating
211112	Cycle condensate production
325110	Cyclic aromatic hydrocarbons made from refined petroleum or liquid hydrocarbons
324110	Cyclic aromatic hydrocarbons made in petroleum refineries
422690	Cyclic crudes and intermediates wholesaling
325192	Cyclic crudes made by distillation of coal tar
325212	Cyclo rubber, synthetic, manufacturing
325192	Cyclohexane manufacturing
332313	Cyclones, industrial, fabricated metal plate work, manufacturing
325192	Cyclopentane made from refined petroleum or natural gas
325192	Cyclopropane made from refined petroleum or natural gas
325412	Cyclopropane medicinal preparations manufacturing
325191	Cycloterpenes manufacturing
335999	Cyclotrons manufacturing
333512	Cylinder boring machines manufacturing
336312	Cylinder heads, automotive and truck gasoline engine, manufacturing
327332	Cylinder pipe, prestressed concrete, manufacturing
332618	Cylinder wire cloth made from purchased wire
332994	Cylinders and clips, gun (i.e., 30 mm. or less, 1.18 inch or less), manufacturing
332995	Cylinders and clips, gun (i.e., more than 30 mm., more than 1.18 inch), manufacturing
333995	Cylinders, fluid power, manufacturing
336340	Cylinders, master brake (new and rebuilt), manufacturing
332420	Cylinders, pressure, manufacturing
334417	Cylindrical connectors, electronic, manufacturing
332991	Cylindrical roller bearings manufacturing
339992	Cymbals and parts manufacturing
339112	Cystoscopes (except electromedical) manufacturing
334510	Cystoscopes, electromedical, manufacturing
325413	Cytology and histology in-vitro diagnostic substances manufacturing
621511	Cytology health laboratories

Code	Description
621310	DCs' (doctors of chiropractic) offices (e.g., centers, clinics)
621210	DDSs' (doctors of dental surgery) offices (e.g., centers, clinics)
325320	DDT (dichlorodiphenyltrichloroethane) insecticides manufacturing
922120	DEA (Drug Enforcement Administration)
621210	DMDs' (doctors of dental medicine) offices (e.g., centers, clinics)
621112	DOs' (doctors of osteopathy), mental health, offices (e.g., centers, clinics)
621111	DOs' (doctors of osteopathy, except mental health) offices (e.g., centers, clinics)
621391	DPs' (doctors of podiatry) offices (e.g., centers, clinics)
334310	DVD (digital video disc) players manufacturing
112120	Dairy cattle farming
311119	Dairy cattle feeds supplements, concentrates, and premixes, manufacturing
422430	Dairy depots wholesaling
311514	Dairy food canning
112420	Dairy goat farming
112111	Dairy heifer replacement production
541690	Dairy herd consulting services
115210	Dairy herd improvement associations
445299	Dairy product stores
422430	Dairy products (except canned, dried) wholesaling
422490	Dairy products, dried or canned, wholesaling
422430	Dairy products, frozen, wholesaling
112410	Dairy sheep farming
332312	Dam gates, metal plate, manufacturing
234990	Dam, dike, and dock construction
334512	Damper operators (e.g., electric, pneumatic, thermostatic) manufacturing
332322	Dampers, sheet metal, manufacturing
235990	Dampproofing, building, construction contractors
711130	Dance bands
713940	Dance centers, aerobic
711120	Dance companies
711310	Dance festival managers with facilities
711320	Dance festival managers without facilities
711310	Dance festival organizers with facilities
711320	Dance festival organizers without facilities
711310	Dance festival promoters with facilities
711320	Dance festival promoters without facilities
531120	Dance hall rental or leasing
713990	Dance halls
611610	Dance instruction
711120	Dance productions, live theatrical
611610	Dance schools
611610	Dance studios
711120	Dance theaters
621340	Dance therapists' offices (e.g., centers, clinics)
711120	Dance troupes
711510	Dancers, independent
313113	Darning thread (e.g., cotton, manmade fibers, silk, wool) manufacturing
332994	Dart guns manufacturing
339932	Darts and dart games manufacturing
334210	Data communications equipment (e.g., bridges, gateways, routers) manufacturing
514210	Data entry services

Code	Description
334513	Data loggers, industrial process-type, manufacturing
514210	Data processing computer services
541513	Data processing facilities (i.e., clients' facilities) management and operation services
421430	Data processing machines, computer, wholesaling
514210	Data processing services (except payroll services, financial transition processing services)
511140	Database and directory publishers
511140	Database and directory publishers and printing combined
511140	Database and directory publishing (i.e., establishments known as publishers)
511140	Database publishers
511140	Database publishers and printing combined
511140	Database publishing (i.e., establishments known as publishers)
323112	Databases flexographic printing without publishing
323111	Databases gravure printing without publishing
323110	Databases lithographic (offset) printing without publishing
323119	Databases printing (except flexographic, gravure, lithographic, screen) without publishing
323113	Databases screen printing without publishing
111339	Date farming
339943	Date stamps, hand operated, manufacturing
311423	Dates, dried, made in dehydration plant
311340	Dates, sugared and stuffed, manufacturing
334518	Dating devices and machines (except rubber stamps) manufacturing
812990	Dating services
333923	Davits manufacturing
******	Day camps, instructional — see type of instruction
624120	Day care centers for disabled persons, the elderly, and persons diagnosed with mental retardation
624120	Day care centers, adult
624410	Day care centers, child or infant
624410	Day care services, child or infant
332510	Dead bolts manufacturing
******	Dealers — see type
561440	Debt collection services
333512	Deburring machines, metalworking, manufacturing
334515	Decade boxes (i.e., capacitance, inductance, resistance) manufacturing
325199	Decahydronaphthalene manufacturing
327112	Decalcomania on china and glass for the trade
339999	Decalcomania work (except on china, glass)
327215	Decorated glassware made from purchased glass
327112	Decorating china (e.g., encrusting gold, silver, other metal on china) for the trade
541410	Decorating consulting services, interior
335129	Decorative area lighting fixtures (except residential) manufacturing
335121	Decorative area lighting fixtures, residential, manufacturing
712110	Decorative art museums

Code	Description
327212	Decorative glassware made in glass making plants
335110	Decorative lamp bulbs manufacturing
315211	Decorative stitching contractors on men's and boys' apparel
315212	Decorative stitching contractors on women's, misses', girls', and infants' apparel
314999	Decorative stitching on textile articles and apparel
321918	Decorative wood moldings (e.g., base, chair rail, crown, shoe) manufacturing
115114	Decorticating flax
483113	Deep sea freight transportation to or from domestic ports
483111	Deep sea freight transportation to or from foreign ports
483114	Deep sea passenger transportation to and from domestic ports
483112	Deep sea passenger transportation to or from foreign ports
333319	Deep-fat fryers, commercial-type, manufacturing
335211	Deep-fat fryers, household-type electric, manufacturing
112990	Deer production
334510	Defibrilators manufacturing
325312	Defluorinated phosphates manufacturing
325998	Defoamers and antifoaming agents manufacturing
325320	Defoliants manufacturing
325998	Degreasing preparations for machinery parts manufacturing
325612	Degreasing preparations, household-type, manufacturing
333415	Dehumidifiers (except portable electric) manufacturing
335211	Dehumidifiers, portable electric, manufacturing
311514	Dehydrated milk manufacturing
311423	Dehydrating fruits and vegetables
311423	Dehydrating potato products (e.g., flakes, granules)
325998	Deicing preparations manufacturing
322110	Deinking plants
322110	Deinking recovered paper
722211	Delicatessen restaurants
333997	Delicatessen scales manufacturing
445210	Delicatessens (except grocery store, restaurants)
445110	Delicatessens primarily retailing a range of grocery items and meats
561440	Delinquent account collection services
623990	Delinquent youth halfway group homes
115114	Delinting cottonseed
332618	Delivery cases made from purchased wire
492210	Delivery service (except as part of inter-city carrier network, U.S. Postal Service)
334515	Demand meters, electric, manufacturing
541720	Demographic research and development services
235940	Demolition of buildings or other structures construction contractors
541890	Demonstration services, merchandise
336212	Demountable cargo containers manufacturing
325193	Denatured alcohol manufacturing
313210	Denims weaving
321219	Densified wood manufacturing
333315	Densitometers (except laboratory analytical) manufacturing

Code	Description
334516	Densitometers, laboratory analytical, manufacturing
334513	Density and specific gravity instruments, industrial process-type, manufacturing
621512	Dental X-ray laboratories
339114	Dental alloys for amalgams manufacturing
339114	Dental chairs manufacturing
421450	Dental chairs wholesaling
339114	Dental equipment and instruments manufacturing
421450	Dental equipment and supplies wholesaling
811219	Dental equipment repair and maintenance services
325620	Dental floss manufacturing
339114	Dental glues and cements manufacturing
339114	Dental hand instruments (e.g., forceps) manufacturing
611519	Dental hygienist schools
621399	Dental hygienists' offices (e.g., centers, clinics)
339114	Dental impression materials manufacturing
339114	Dental instrument delivery systems manufacturing
524114	Dental insurance carriers, direct
339116	Dental laboratories
339114	Dental laboratory equipment manufacturing
541710	Dental research and development laboratories or services
611310	Dental schools
621210	Dental surgeons' offices (e.g., centers, clinics)
611519	Dental technician schools
339114	Dental wax manufacturing
325611	Dentifrices manufacturing
422210	Dentifrices wholesaling
813920	Dentists' associations
621210	Dentists' offices (e.g., centers, clinics)
421450	Dentists' professional supplies wholesaling
325620	Denture adhesives manufacturing
325620	Denture cleaners, effervescent, manufacturing
339114	Denture materials manufacturing
339116	Dentures, custom made in dental laboratories
621399	Denturists' offices (e.g., centers, clinics)
561720	Deodorant servicing of rest rooms
325612	Deodorants (except personal) manufacturing
422690	Deodorants (except personal) wholesaling
325620	Deodorants, personal, manufacturing
422210	Deodorants, personal, wholesaling
561720	Deodorizing services
452110	Department stores
812199	Depilatory (i.e., hair removal) salons
325620	Depilatory preparations manufacturing
332813	Depolishing metals and metal products for the trade
524128	Deposit or share insurance carriers, direct
522110	Depository trust companies
339113	Depressors, tongue, manufacturing
332995	Depth charge projectors manufacturing
332993	Depth charges manufacturing
325412	Dermatological preparations manufacturing
621111	Dermatologists' offices (e.g., centers, clinics)

Derrick building—Differential

Code	Description
213112	Derrick building, repairing, and dismantling at oil and gas fields on a contract basis
333132	Derricks, oil and gas field-type, manufacturing
325998	Desalination kits manufacturing
327992	Desiccants, activated clay, manufacturing
233320	Designing and erecting combined, commercial, general construction contractors
233310	Designing and erecting combined, industrial, general construction contractors
233220	Designing and erecting combined, residential (except single family housing), general construction contractors
233210	Designing and erecting combined, single family housing, general construction contractors
335211	Desk fans, electric, manufacturing
335122	Desk lamps, commercial, electric, manufacturing
335121	Desk lamps, residential, electric, manufacturing
316999	Desk sets, leather, manufacturing
337214	Desks (except wood), office-type, manufacturing
337122	Desks, wood household-type, manufacturing
337211	Desks, wood office-type, manufacturing
561410	Desktop publishing services
422430	Desserts, dairy, wholesaling
311520	Desserts, frozen (except bakery), manufacturing
311813	Desserts, frozen bakery, manufacturing
811192	Detailing services (i.e., cleaning and polishing), automotive
115112	Detasseling corn
561611	Detective agencies
334519	Detectors, scintillation, manufacturing
922140	Detention centers
325611	Detergents (e.g., dishwashing, industrial, laundry) manufacturing
422690	Detergents wholesaling
331492	Detinning scrap (e.g., cans)
325920	Detonating caps, cord, fuses, and primers manufacturing
325920	Detonators (except ammunition) manufacturing
332993	Detonators, ammunition (i.e., more than 30 mm., more than 1.18 inch), manufacturing
621420	Detoxification centers and clinics (except hospitals), outpatient
622210	Detoxification hospitals
325188	Deuterium oxide (i.e., heavy water) manufacturing
325992	Developers, prepared photographic, manufacturing
336411	Developing and producing prototypes for aircraft
336412	Developing and producing prototypes for aircraft engines and engine parts
336413	Developing and producing prototypes for aircraft parts (except engines) and auxiliary equipment
336414	Developing and producing prototypes for complete guided missiles and space vehicles
336419	Developing and producing prototypes for guided missile and space vehicle components
336415	Developing and producing prototypes for guided missile and space vehicle engines
333315	Developing equipment, film, manufacturing
926110	Development assistance program administration
813311	Developmentally disabled advocacy organizations
235990	Dewatering construction contractors
111334	Dewberry farming
325520	Dextrin glues manufacturing
311221	Dextrin made by wet milling corn
212319	Diabase crushed and broken stone mining and/or beneficiating
212311	Diabase mining or quarrying
325412	Diagnostic biological preparations (except in-vitro) manufacturing
811198	Diagnostic centers without repair, automotive
334510	Diagnostic equipment, MRI (magnetic resonance imaging), manufacturing
334510	Diagnostic equipment, electromedical, manufacturing
421450	Diagnostic equipment, medical, wholesaling
621512	Diagnostic imaging centers (medical)
811219	Diagnostic imaging equipment repair and maintenance services
422210	Diagnostic reagents wholesaling
325413	Diagnostic substances, in-vitro, manufacturing
422210	Diagnostics, in-vitro and in-vivo, wholesaling
332212	Dial indicators, machinists' precision tools, manufacturing
621492	Dialysis centers and clinics
334510	Dialysis equipment, electromedical, manufacturing
325312	Diammonium phosphates manufacturing
332618	Diamond cloths made from purchased wire
339913	Diamond cutting and polishing
333514	Diamond dies, metalworking, manufacturing
327910	Diamond dressing wheels manufacturing
421940	Diamonds (except industrial) wholesaling
212399	Diamonds, industrial, mining and/or beneficiating
421840	Diamonds, industrial, wholesaling
315212	Diaper covers, water resistant and waterproof, cut and sew apparel contractors
315291	Diaper covers, waterproof, infants', cut and sewn from purchased fabric (except apparel contractors)
812331	Diaper supply services
314999	Diapers (except disposable) made from purchased fabrics
422330	Diapers (except paper) wholesaling
322291	Diapers, disposable, made from purchased paper or textile fiber
322121	Diapers, disposable, made in paper mills
422130	Diapers, paper, wholesaling
326299	Diaphragms (i.e., birth control device), rubber, manufacturing
323118	Diaries manufacturing
511199	Diary and time scheduler publishers
212325	Diaspore mining and/or beneficiating
334510	Diathermy apparatus, electromedical, manufacturing
334510	Diathermy units manufacturing
212399	Diatomaceous earth mining and/or beneficitating
327992	Diatomaceous earth processing beyond beneficiation
212399	Diatomite mining and/or beneficiating
325992	Diazo (i.e., whiteprint) paper and cloth, sensitized, manufacturing
325120	Dichlorodifluoromethane manufacturing
325188	Dichromates manufacturing
315212	Dickeys, women's, girls', and Infants', cut and sew apparel contractors
315239	Dickeys, women's, misses' and girls', cut and sewn from purchased fabric (except apparel contractors)
333313	Dictating machines manufacturing
421420	Dictating machines wholesaling
561410	Dictation services
323117	Dictionaries printing and binding without publishing
323117	Dictionaries printing without publishing
323121	Dictionary binding without printing
511130	Dictionary publishers
511130	Dictionary publishers and printing combined
511130	Dictionary publishing (i.e., establishments known as publishers)
325211	Dicyandiamine resins manufacturing
333514	Die sets for metal stamping presses manufacturing
333512	Die sinking machines, metalworking, manufacturing
333511	Die-casting dies manufacturing
333513	Die-casting machines, metalworking, manufacturing
331521	Die-castings, aluminum, unfinished, manufacturing
331522	Die-castings, nonferrous metals (except aluminum), unfinished, manufacturing
322299	Die-cut paper products (except for office use) made from purchased paper or paperboard
322231	Die-cut paper products for office use made from purchased paper or paperboard
333994	Dielectric industrial heating equipment manufacturing
333514	Dies and die holders for metal cutting and forming (except threading) manufacturing
333515	Dies and taps (i.e., a machine tool accessory) manufacturing
332212	Dies, cutting (except metal cutting), manufacturing
333514	Dies, metalworking (except threading), manufacturing
333514	Dies, plastics forming, manufacturing
332212	Dies, steel rule (except metal cutting), manufacturing
333514	Dies, steel rule, metal cutting, manufacturing
333618	Diesel and semidiesel engines manufacturing
324110	Diesel fuels manufacturing
812191	Diet centers, non-medical
812191	Diet workshops
311514	Dietary drinks, dairy and nondairy based, manufacturing
325192	Diethylcyclohexane manufacturing
325199	Diethylene glycol manufacturing
621399	Dieticians' offices (e.g., centers, clinics)
813920	Dietitians' associations
336350	Differential and rear axle assemblies, automotive, truck, and bus, manufacturing

Code	Description
334513	Differential pressure instruments, industrial process-type, manufacturing
334516	Differential thermal analysis instruments, laboratory-type, manufacturing
332420	Digesters, industrial-type, manufacturing
325412	Digestive system preparations manufacturing
334119	Digital cameras manufacturing
334111	Digital computers manufacturing
334513	Digital displays of process variables manufacturing
334515	Digital panel meters, electricity measuring, manufacturing
323115	Digital printing (e.g., billboards, other large format graphic materials)
323115	Digital printing (e.g., graphics, high resolution)
333293	Digital printing presses manufacturing
334515	Digital test equipment (e.g., electronic and electrical circuits and equipment testing) manufacturing
334310	Digital video disc players manufacturing
325412	Digitalis medicinal preparations manufacturing
325411	Digitoxin, uncompounded, manufacturing
325211	Diisocyanate resins manufacturing
111219	Dill farming, field and seed production
321113	Dimension lumber, hardwood, made from logs or bolts
321912	Dimension lumber, hardwood, resawing purchased lumber
321113	Dimension lumber, made from logs or bolts
321912	Dimension lumber, resawing purchased lumber
321113	Dimension lumber, softwood, made from logs or bolts
321912	Dimension lumber, softwood, resawing purchased lumber
321912	Dimension stock, hardwood, manufacturing
321912	Dimension stock, softwood, manufacturing
321912	Dimension stock, wood, manufacturing
327991	Dimension stone dressing and manufacturing
327991	Dimension stone for buildings manufacturing
212311	Dimension stone mining or quarrying
325199	Dimethyl divinyl acetylene (di-isopropenyl acetylene) manufacturing
325199	Dimethylhydrazine manufacturing
335931	Dimmer switches, outlet box mounting-type, manufacturing
722110	Diners, full service
337124	Dinette sets, metal household-type, manufacturing
326299	Dinghies, inflatable rubber, manufacturing
336612	Dinghy (except inflatable rubber) manufacturing
337124	Dining room chairs (including upholstered), metal, manufacturing
337125	Dining room chairs (including upholstered), plastics manufacturing
337122	Dining room chairs (including upholstered), wood, manufacturing
337124	Dining room furniture, metal household-type, manufacturing
337122	Dining room furniture, wood household-type, manufacturing
487210	Dinner cruises

Code	Description
711110	Dinner theaters
311412	Dinners, frozen (except seafood-based), manufacturing
311712	Dinners, frozen seafood, manufacturing
422420	Dinners, frozen, wholesaling
326199	Dinnerware, plastics (except polystyrene foam), manufacturing
326140	Dinnerware, polystyrene foam, manufacturing
334515	Diode and transistor testers manufacturing
421690	Diodes wholesaling
334413	Diodes, solid-state (e.g., germanium, silicon), manufacturing
212313	Diorite crushed and broken stone mining and/or beneficiating
212311	Diorite mining or quarrying
325192	Diphenylamine manufacturing
928120	Diplomatic services
311941	Dips (except cheese and sour cream based) manufacturing
325320	Dips (i.e., pesticides), cattle and sheep, manufacturing
311513	Dips, cheese based, manufacturing
311511	Dips, sour cream based, manufacturing
334112	Direct access storage devices manufacturing
513220	Direct broadcast satellite (DBS)
325132	Direct dyes manufacturing
541860	Direct mail advertising services
541860	Direct mail or other direct distribution advertising campaign services
454110	Direct mailers (i.e., selling own merchandise)
331111	Direct reduction of iron ore
454390	Direct selling of merchandise (door-to-door)
513220	Direct-to-home satellite systems
213111	Directional drilling of oil and gas wells on a contract basis
812210	Director services, funeral
323112	Directories flexographic printing without publishing
323111	Directories gravure printing without publishing
323110	Directories lithographic (offset) printing without publishing
323119	Directories printing (except flexographic, gravure, lithographic, screen) without publishing
323113	Directories screen printing without publishing
711510	Directors (i.e., film, motion picture, music, theatrical), independent
711510	Directors, independent motion picture
711510	Directors, independent music
511140	Directory and database publishers
511140	Directory compilers
511140	Directory publishers
511140	Directory publishers and printing combined
511140	Directory publishing (i.e., establishments known as publishers)
541870	Directory, telephone, distribution on a contract basis
524113	Disability insurance carriers, direct
524113	Disability insurance underwriting, direct
624120	Disability support groups
623990	Disabled group homes without nursing care
922190	Disaster preparedness and management offices, government
624230	Disaster relief services
711510	Disc jockeys, independent

Code	Description
623990	Disciplinary camps for delinquent youth
713990	Discotheques (except those serving alcoholic beverages)
812990	Discount buying services
511199	Discount coupon book publishers
511199	Discount coupon book publishers and printing combined
511199	Discount coupon book publishing (i.e., establishments known as publishers)
323112	Discount coupon books flexographic printing without publishing
323111	Discount coupon books gravure printing without publishing
323110	Discount coupon books lithographic (offset) printing without publishing
323119	Discount coupon books printing (except flexographic, gravure, lithographic, screen) without publishing
323113	Discount coupon books screen printing without publishing
452110	Discount department stores
813212	Disease awareness fundraising organizations
115112	Disease control for crops
813212	Disease research (e.g., cancer, heart) fundraising organizations
541940	Disease testing services, veterinary
313249	Dishcloths made in warp knitting mills
313241	Dishcloths made in weft knitting mills
421220	Dishes, household-type (except disposable plastics, paper), wholesaling
422130	Dishes, paper and disposable plastics, wholesaling
327112	Dishes, pottery, manufacturing
339932	Dishes, toy, manufacturing
321999	Dishes, wood, manufacturing
325611	Dishwasher detergents manufacturing
335228	Dishwashers, household-type, manufacturing
421620	Dishwashers, household-type, wholesaling
421440	Dishwashing equipment, commercial-type, wholesaling
333319	Dishwashing machines, commercial-type, manufacturing
335228	Dishwashing machines, household-type, manufacturing
325612	Disinfectants, household-type and industrial, manufacturing
514210	Disk and diskette conversion services
514210	Disk and diskette recertification services
332611	Disk and ring springs, heavy gauge, manufacturing
334112	Disk drives, computer, manufacturing
421430	Disk drives, computer, wholesaling
334613	Diskettes, blank, manufacturing
421690	Diskettes, blank, wholesaling
235950	Dismantling of machinery and other industrial equipment construction contractors
213112	Dismantling of oil well rigs on a contract basis
235940	Dismantling steel oil tanks (except oil field work) construction contractors
333913	Dispensing and measuring pumps (e.g., gasoline, lubricants) manufacturing
325132	Disperse dyes manufacturing
325510	Dispersions, pigment, manufacturing
541850	Display advertising services
421440	Display cases (except refrigerated) wholesaling
337215	Display cases and fixtures (except refrigerated) manufacturing

Display cases—Drag strips

Code	Description
333415	Display cases, refrigerated, manufacturing
421740	Display cases, refrigerated, wholesaling
321999	Display forms for boots and shoes, all materials, manufacturing
334513	Display instruments, industrial process control-type, manufacturing
541890	Display lettering services
339950	Displays (e.g., counter, floor, point-of-purchase) manufacturing
335912	Disposable flashlight batteries manufacturing
422130	Disposable plastics products (e.g., boxes, cups, cutlery, dishes, sanitary food containers) wholesaling
334511	Distance measuring equipment (DME), aeronautical, manufacturing
325191	Distillates, wood, manufacturing
333994	Distillation ovens, charcoal and coke, manufacturing
422820	Distilled alcoholic beverages wholesaling
325998	Distilled water manufacturing
311213	Distiller's malt manufacturing
312140	Distilleries
421830	Distillery machinery wholesaling
312140	Distilling alcoholic beverages (except brandy)
312130	Distilling brandy
333298	Distilling equipment (except beverage) manufacturing
333294	Distilling equipment, beverage, manufacturing
312140	Distilling potable liquor (except brandy)
334515	Distortion meters and analyzers manufacturing
335313	Distribution boards, electric, manufacturing
335313	Distribution cutouts manufacturing
421610	Distribution equipment, electrical, wholesaling
234910	Distribution line construction, oil and gas fields
221330	Distribution of cooled air
221122	Distribution of electric power
221330	Distribution of heated air
221210	Distribution of manufactured gas
221210	Distribution of natural gas
221330	Distribution of steam heat
335311	Distribution transformers, electric, manufacturing
336322	Distributor cap and rotor for internal combustion engines manufacturing
336322	Distributors for internal combustion engines manufacturing
813910	Distributors' associations
551114	District and regional offices
922130	District attorneys' offices
333120	Ditchers and trenchers, self-propelled, manufacturing
325412	Diuretic preparations manufacturing
332212	Dividers, machinists' precision tools, manufacturing
451110	Diving equipment stores
561990	Diving services on a contract or fee basis
531120	Dock and associated building rental or leasing
488330	Docking and undocking marine vessel services
488310	Docking facility operations
621310	Doctors of chiropractic (DCs) offices (e.g., centers, clinics)
621210	Doctors of dental medicine (DMDs) offices (e.g., centers, clinics)

Code	Description
621210	Doctors of dental surgery (DDSs) offices (e.g., centers, clinics)
621320	Doctors of optometry (ODs) offices (e.g., centers, clinics)
621112	Doctors of osteopathy (DOs), mental health, offices (e.g., centers, clinics)
621111	Doctors of osteopathy (DOs, except mental health) offices (e.g., centers, clinics)
621391	Doctors of podiatry (DPs) offices (e.g., centers, clinics)
621330	Doctors of psychology offices (e.g., centers, clinics)
561439	Document copying services (except combined with printing services)
561439	Document duplicating services (except combined with printing services)
561410	Document preparation services
561410	Document transcription services
325110	Dodecene made from refined petroleum or liquid hydrocarbons
311111	Dog and cat food (e.g., canned, dry, frozen, semimoist), manufacturing
311111	Dog food manufacturing
316999	Dog furnishings (e.g., collars, harnesses, leashes, muzzles), manufacturing
711219	Dog owners, race (i.e., racing dogs)
812910	Dog pounds
112990	Dog production
711212	Dog racetracks
711219	Dog racing kennels
422990	Dogs wholesaling
322299	Doilies, paper, made from purchased paper
339932	Doll carriages and carts manufacturing
339931	Doll clothing manufacturing
452990	Dollar stores
333924	Dollies manufacturing
421920	Dolls wholesaling
339931	Dolls, doll parts, and doll clothing (except wigs) manufacturing
212312	Dolomite crushed and broken stone mining and/or beneficiating
212311	Dolomite mining or quarrying
327410	Dolomite, dead-burned, manufacturing
327410	Dolomitic lime manufacturing
212319	Dolomitic marble crushed and broken stone mining and/or beneficiating
212311	Dolomitic marble mining or quarrying
114111	Dolphin fishing
233320	Dome construction
112920	Donkey production
332321	Door and jamb assemblies, metal, manufacturing
235510	Door and window construction contractors
332321	Door frames and sash, metal, manufacturing
321911	Door frames and sash, wood and covered wood, manufacturing
332322	Door hoods, sheet metal, manufacturing
321911	Door jambs, wood, manufacturing
332510	Door locks manufacturing
332510	Door opening and closing devices (except electrical) manufacturing
335999	Door opening and closing devices, electrical, manufacturing
321918	Door shutters, wood, manufacturing
444190	Door stores
321918	Door trim, wood molding, manufacturing
321911	Door units, prehung, wood and covered wood, manufacturing

Code	Description
541870	Door-to-door distribution of advertising materials (e.g., coupons, flyers, samples)
454390	Door-to-door retailing of merchandise, direct selling
314110	Doormats, all materials (except entirely of rubber or plastics), manufacturing
326199	Doormats, plastics, manufacturing
326299	Doormats, rubber, manufacturing
421310	Doors and door frames wholesaling
326199	Doors and door frames, plastics, manufacturing
321911	Doors, combination screen-storm, wood, manufacturing
332321	Doors, metal, manufacturing
332999	Doors, safe and vault, metal, manufacturing
327215	Doors, unframed glass, made from purchased glass
321911	Doors, wood and covered wood, manufacturing
325510	Dopes, paint, and laquer, manufacturing
336612	Dories building
721310	Dormitories
233320	Dormitory construction
233220	Dormitory construction, general construction contractors
334519	Dosimetry devices manufacturing
333294	Dough mixing machinery (i.e., food manufacturing-type) manufacturing
722110	Doughnut shops, full service
722213	Doughnut shops, on premise baking and carryout service
311812	Doughnuts (except frozen) made in commercial bakeries
311813	Doughnuts, frozen, manufacturing
422420	Doughs, frozen, wholesaling
311211	Doughs, prepared, made in flour mills
311822	Doughs, refrigerated or frozen, made from purchased flour
333210	Dovetailing machines, woodworking-type, manufacturing
332722	Dowel pins, metal, manufacturing
321999	Dowels, wood, manufacturing
315291	Down-filled clothing, infants', cut and sewn from purchased fabric (except apparel contractors)
315211	Down-filled clothing, men's and boys', cut and sew apparel contractors
315228	Down-filled clothing, men's and boys', cut and sewn from purchased fabric (except apparel contractors)
315212	Down-filled clothing, women's, girls' and infants' cut and sew apparel contractors
315239	Down-filled clothing, women's, misses', and girls', cut and sewn from purchased fabric (except apparel contractors)
713920	Downhill skiing facilities without accommodations
235610	Downspout construction contractors
332322	Downspouts, sheet metal, manufacturing
334513	Draft gauges, industrial process-type, manufacturing
334519	Drafting instruments manufacturing
421490	Drafting instruments wholesaling
339942	Drafting materials (except instruments and tables) manufacturing
541340	Drafting services
337127	Drafting tables and boards manufacturing
421490	Drafting tables wholesaling
541340	Draftsmen's offices
711212	Drag strips

Code	Description
333120	Draglines, crawler, manufacturing
325191	Dragon's blood manufacturing
333111	Drags, farm-type equipment, manufacturing
333120	Drags, road construction and road maintenance equipment, manufacturing
212399	Dragstones mining and/or beneficiating
561790	Drain cleaning services
332913	Drain cocks, plumbing, manufacturing
325612	Drain pipe cleaners manufacturing
332999	Drain plugs, magnetic, metal, manufacturing
327123	Drain tile, clay, manufacturing
234990	Drainage project construction
235110	Drainage system installation (e.g., cesspool, septic tank) construction contractors
337110	Drainboards, wood or plastics laminated on wood, manufacturing
213113	Draining or pumping coal mines on a contract basis
213114	Draining or pumping of metal mines on a contract basis
213115	Draining or pumping of nonmetallic mineral mines (except fuels) on a contract basis
611610	Drama schools (except academic)
314121	Draperies made from purchased fabrics or sheet goods
421220	Draperies wholesaling
812320	Drapery cleaning services
339113	Drapes, surgical, disposable, manufacturing
333518	Draw bench machines manufacturing
315192	Drawers, apparel, made in apparel knitting mills
315211	Drawers, men's and boys', cut and sew apparel contractors
315221	Drawers, men's and boys', cut and sewn from purchased fabric (except apparel contractors)
315212	Drawers, women's, girls', and infants', cut and sew apparel contractors
315231	Drawers, women's, misses', and girls', cut and sewn from purchased fabric (except apparel contractors)
325998	Drawing inks manufacturing
331222	Drawing iron or steel wire from purchased iron or steel
331222	Drawing iron or steel wire from purchased iron or steel and fabricating wire products
333292	Drawing machinery for textiles manufacturing
337127	Drawing tables and boards, artist's, manufacturing
332212	Drawknives manufacturing
336611	Dredge building
333120	Dredging machinery manufacturing
234990	Dredging, general construction contractors
315992	Dress and semidress gloves cut and sewn from purchased fabric (except apparel contractors)
315191	Dress and semidress gloves made in apparel knitting mills
315211	Dress and semidress gloves, men's and boys', cut and sew apparel contractors
315212	Dress and semidress gloves, women's, girls', and infants', cut and sew apparel contractors
316219	Dress shoes, children's and infants', manufacturing
316213	Dress shoes, men's, manufacturing

Code	Description
316214	Dress shoes, women's, manufacturing
448190	Dress shops
532220	Dress suit rental
315999	Dress trimmings cut and sewn from purchased fabric (except apparel contractors)
315212	Dress trimmings, women's, girls', and infants', cut and sew apparel contractors
422990	Dressed furs and skins wholesaling
337124	Dressers, metal, manufacturing
337122	Dressers, wood, manufacturing
315191	Dresses made in apparel knitting mills
422330	Dresses wholesaling
315191	Dresses, hand-knit, manufacturing
315291	Dresses, infants', cut and sewn from purchased fabric (except apparel contractors)
315233	Dresses, women's, misses', and girls', cut and sewn from purchased fabric (except apparel contractors)
315212	Dresses, women's, misses', girls', and infants', cut and sew apparel contractors
316110	Dressing (i.e., bleaching, blending, currying, scraping, tanning) furs
315212	Dressing gowns, women's, girls', and infants', cut and sew apparel contractors
315231	Dressing gowns, women's, misses', and girls', cut and sewn from purchased fabric (except apparel contractors)
316110	Dressing hides
311615	Dressing small game
337124	Dressing tables, metal, manufacturing
337122	Dressing tables, wood, manufacturing
421450	Dressings, medical, wholesaling
339113	Dressings, surgical, manufacturing
422490	Dried foods (e.g., fruits, milk, vegetables) wholesaling
311612	Dried meats made from purchased carcasses
212392	Dried phosphate rock mining and/or beneficiating
325510	Driers, paint, and varnish, manufacturing
325992	Driers, photographic chemical, manufacturing
333315	Driers, photographic, manufacturing
334511	Driftmeters, aeronautical, manufacturing
333515	Drill bits, metalworking, manufacturing
332212	Drill bits, woodworking, manufacturing
333512	Drill presses, metalworking, manufacturing
333210	Drill presses, woodworking-type, manufacturing
332999	Drill stands, metal, manufacturing
213112	Drill-stem testing in oil, gas, dry, and service well drilling on a contract basis
235930	Drilled pier construction contractors
235930	Drilled shaft construction contractors
339913	Drilling pearls
336611	Drilling and production platforms, floating, oil and gas, building
213111	Drilling directional oil and gas field wells on a contract basis
333132	Drilling equipment, oil and gas field-type, manufacturing
333131	Drilling equipment, underground mining-type, manufacturing
213111	Drilling for gas on a contract basis
213111	Drilling for oil on a contract basis
213111	Drilling gas and oil field wells on a contract basis
333512	Drilling machines, metalworking, manufacturing

Code	Description
325998	Drilling mud compounds, conditioners, and additives (except bentonites) manufacturing
422690	Drilling muds wholesaling
213111	Drilling oil and gas field service wells on a contract basis
213112	Drilling rat holes and mouse holes at oil and gas fields on a contract basis
333132	Drilling rigs, oil and gas field-type, manufacturing
213113	Drilling services for coal mining on a contract basis
213114	Drilling services for metal mining on a contract basis
213115	Drilling services for nonmetallic mineral (except fuels) mining on a contract basis
213112	Drilling shot holes at oil and gas fields on a contract basis
213112	Drilling site preparation at oil and gas fields on a contract basis
213111	Drilling water intake wells, oil and gas field on a contract basis
235810	Drilling water wells construction contractors
313210	Drills weaving
333131	Drills, core, underground mining-type, manufacturing
339114	Drills, dental, manufacturing
332212	Drills, hand held, nonelectric, manufacturing
333991	Drills, handheld power-driven (except heavy construction and mining type), manufacturing
333131	Drills, rock, underground mining-type, manufacturing
311999	Drink powder mixes (except chocolate, coffee, milk based, tea) manufacturing
311320	Drink powdered mixes, cocoa, made from cacao
311330	Drink powdered mixes, cocoa, made from purchased cocoa
311511	Drink, chocolate milk, manufacturing
332998	Drinking fountains (except mechanically refrigerated), metal, manufacturing
326191	Drinking fountains (except mechanically refrigerated), plastics, manufacturing
333415	Drinking fountains, refrigerated, manufacturing
327111	Drinking fountains, vitreous china, non-refrigerated, manufacturing
722410	Drinking places (i.e., bars, lounges, taverns), alcoholic
312111	Drinks, fruit (except juice), manufacturing
333613	Drive chains, bicycle and motorcycle, manufacturing
336350	Drive shafts and half shafts, automotive, truck, and bus, manufacturing
512132	Drive-in motion picture theaters
722211	Drive-in restaurants
611692	Driver education
611692	Driver training schools (except bus, heavy equipment, truck)
711219	Drivers, harness or race car
333612	Drives, high-speed industrial (except hydrostatic), manufacturing
561790	Driveway cleaning (e.g., power sweeping, washing) services
235710	Driveway construction contractors
713990	Driving ranges, golf
488490	Driving services (e.g., automobile, truck delivery)
332111	Drop forgings made from purchased iron or steel, unfinished

Drop hammers—Earthenware

Code	Description
333513	Drop hammers, metal forging and shaping, manufacturing
812320	Drop-off and pick-up sites for laundries and drycleaners
813319	Drug abuse prevention advocacy organizations
623220	Drug addiction rehabilitation facilities (except licensed hospitals), residential
622210	Drug addiction rehabilitation hospitals
624190	Drug addiction self-help organizations
621420	Drug addiction treatment centers and clinics (except hospitals), outpatient
922120	Drug enforcement agencies and offices
422210	Drug proprietaries wholesaling
446110	Drug stores
422210	Druggists' sundries wholesaling
422210	Drugs wholesaling
711130	Drum and bugle corps (i.e., drill teams)
333924	Drum cradles manufacturing
339992	Drums (musical instruments), parts, and accessories manufacturing
332439	Drums, light gauge metal, manufacturing
421840	Drums, new and reconditioned, wholesaling
326199	Drums, plastics (i.e., containers), manufacturing
321920	Drums, plywood, manufacturing
321920	Drums, shipping, wood, wirebound, manufacturing
813319	Drunk driving prevention advocacy organizations
311422	Dry beans canning
422510	Dry beans wholesaling
484230	Dry bulk carrier, truck, long-distance
484220	Dry bulk trucking (except garbage collection, garbage hauling), local
335912	Dry cell primary batteries, single and multiple cell, manufacturing
335912	Dry cells, primary (e.g., AAA, AA, C, D, 9V), manufacturing
233310	Dry cleaning plant construction
325120	Dry ice (i.e., solid carbon dioxide) manufacturing
422690	Dry ice wholesaling
311514	Dry milk manufacturing
333294	Dry milk processing machinery manufacturing
311514	Dry milk products and mixture manufacturing
311514	Dry milk products for animal feed manufacturing
327999	Dry mix concrete manufacturing
311822	Dry mixes made from purchased flour
311823	Dry pasta manufacturing
311823	Dry pasta packaged with other ingredients made in dry pasta plants
335211	Dry shavers (i.e., electric razors) manufacturing
235110	Dry well construction contractors
812320	Drycleaner drop-off and pick-up sites
812320	Drycleaners (except coin-operated)
335224	Drycleaning and laundry machines, household-type, manufacturing
333312	Drycleaning equipment and machinery manufacturing
421850	Drycleaning equipment and supplies wholesaling
812310	Drycleaning machine routes (i.e., concession operators), coin-operated or similar self-service
812320	Drycleaning plants (except rug cleaning plants)
325612	Drycleaning preparations manufacturing

Code	Description
812320	Drycleaning services (except coin-operated)
812310	Drycleaning services, coin-operated or similar self-service
336611	Drydock, floating, building
488390	Drydocks, floating (i.e., routine repair and maintenance of ships and boats)
532210	Dryer, clothes, rental
335224	Dryers, clothes, household-type, gas and electric, manufacturing
421620	Dryers, hair, wholesaling
335224	Dryers, household-type laundry, manufacturing
339111	Dryers, laboratory-type, manufacturing
333312	Dryers, laundry (except household-type), manufacturing
311711	Drying fish and seafood
333298	Drying kilns, lumber, manufacturing
333292	Drying machinery for textiles manufacturing
235420	Drywall construction contractors
421320	Drywall supplies wholesaling
713950	Duck pin bowling alleys
713950	Duck pin bowling centers
112390	Duck production
313210	Ducks weaving
311615	Ducks, processing, fresh, frozen, canned, or cooked
311615	Ducks, slaughtering and dressing
561790	Duct cleaning services
322222	Duct tape made from purchased materials
235610	Duct work, sheet metal, construction contractors
331511	Ductile iron castings, unfinished, manufacturing
331511	Ductile iron foundries
332313	Ducting, fabricated metal plate work, manufacturing
335313	Ducts for electrical switchboard apparatus manufacturing
332322	Ducts, sheet metal, manufacturing
721214	Dude ranches
339920	Dumbbells manufacturing
235950	Dumbwaiter construction contractors
333921	Dumbwaiters manufacturing
212325	Dumortierite mining and/or beneficiating
336212	Dump trailer manufacturing
484220	Dump trucking (e.g., gravel, sand, top soil)
562119	Dump trucking of rubble or brush with collection or disposal
336211	Dump-truck lifting mechanisms manufacturing
333131	Dumpers, mining car, manufacturing
562219	Dumps, compost
562212	Dumps, nonhazardous solid waste (e.g., trash)
315291	Dungarees, infants', cut and sewn from purchased fabric (except apparel contractors)
315211	Dungarees, men's and boys', cut and sew apparel contractors
315224	Dungarees, men's and boys', cut and sewn from purchased fabric (except apparel contractors)
315212	Dungarees, women's girls' and infants', cut and sew apparel contractors
315239	Dungarees, women's, misses', and girls', cut and sewn from purchased fabric (except apparel contractors)
531110	Duplex houses (i.e., single family) rental or leasing

Code	Description
335931	Duplex receptacles, electrical, manufacturing
233220	Duplexes, double (i.e., one unit above the other) multifamily, construction
233210	Duplexes, single family, construction
325910	Duplicating inks manufacturing
532420	Duplicating machine (e.g., copier) rental or leasing
333512	Duplicating machines (e.g., key cutting), metalworking, manufacturing
311211	Durum flour manufacturing
333411	Dust and fume collecting equipment manufacturing
314999	Dust cloths made from purchased fabrics
235950	Dust collecting equipment construction contractors
421730	Dust collection equipment wholesaling
812332	Dust control textile item (e.g., cloths, mats, mops, rugs, shop towels) supply services
315212	Dusters (i.e., apparel), women's and girls', cut and sew apparel contractors
315231	Dusters (i.e., apparel), women's, misses', and girls', cut and sewn from purchased fabric (except apparel contractors)
333111	Dusters, farm-type, manufacturing
115112	Dusting crops
445310	Duty free liquor shops
531110	Dwelling rental or leasing
332311	Dwellings, prefabricated metal, manufacturing
325998	Dye preparations, clothing, household-type, manufacturing
313311	Dyeing broadwoven fabrics
316110	Dyeing furs
313312	Dyeing gloves, woven or knit, for the trade
316110	Dyeing leather
333292	Dyeing machinery for textiles manufacturing
313312	Dyeing textile products and fabrics (except broadwoven fabrics)
422690	Dyes, industrial, wholesaling
325131	Dyes, inorganic, manufacturing
325191	Dyes, natural, manufacturing
325132	Dyes, synthetic organic, manufacturing
422690	Dyestuffs wholesaling
325920	Dynamite manufacturing
334519	Dynamometers manufacturing
335312	Dynamos, electric (except automotive), manufacturing
335312	Dynamotors manufacturing
335932	EMTs (electrical metallic tube) manufacturing
812199	Ear piercing services
532412	Earth moving equipment rental or leasing without operator
234990	Earth moving not connected with building construction
334220	Earth station communications equipment manufacturing
513390	Earth stations (except satellite telecommunication carriers)
513340	Earth stations for satellite communication carriers
212399	Earth, diatomaceous, mining and/or beneficiating
212325	Earth, fuller's (e.g., all natural bleaching clays), mining and/or beneficiating
327112	Earthenware table and kitchen articles, coarse, manufacturing
327112	Earthenware, commercial and household, semivitreous, manufacturing

Code	Description
311119	Earthworm food and bedding manufacturing
112990	Earthworm hatcheries
339942	Easels, artists', manufacturing
422130	Eating utensils, disposable plastics, wholesaling
332322	Eaves, sheet metal, manufacturing
327112	Ecclesiastical statuary, clay, manufacturing
327420	Ecclesiastical statuary, gypsum, manufacturing
327999	Ecclesiastical statuary, paper mache, manufacturing
327991	Ecclesiastical statuary, stone, manufacturing
332999	Ecclesiastical ware, precious plated metal, manufacturing
541690	Economic consulting services
926110	Economic development agencies, government
928120	Economic development assistance (i.e., international), government
541720	Economic research and development services
332410	Economizers (i.e., power boiler accessory) manufacturing
522298	Edge Act corporations (except international trade financing)
522293	Edge Act corporations (i.e., international trade financing)
332212	Edge tools, woodworking (e.g., augers, bits, countersinks), manufacturing
333315	Editing equipment, motion picture (e.g., rewinders, splicers, titlers, viewers), manufacturing
561410	Editing services
923110	Education offices, nonoperating
923110	Education program administration
923110	Education statistics centers, government
611710	Educational consultants
611710	Educational guidance counseling services
611710	Educational testing evaluation services
611710	Educational testing services
813211	Educational trusts, awarding grants
813920	Educators' associations
114111	Eel fishing
325412	Effervescent salts manufacturing
541614	Efficiency management (i.e., efficiency expert) consulting services
321920	Egg cases, wood, manufacturing
335211	Egg cookers, household-type electric, manufacturing
112340	Egg hatcheries, poultry
311823	Egg noodles, dry, manufacturing
311991	Egg noodles, fresh, manufacturing
112310	Egg production, chicken
112330	Egg production, turkey
311999	Egg substitutes manufacturing
312140	Eggnog, alcoholic, manufacturing
311514	Eggnog, canned, nonalcoholic, manufacturing
311511	Eggnog, fresh, nonalcoholic, manufacturing
311511	Eggnog, nonalcoholic (except canned), manufacturing
111219	Eggplant farming (except under cover), field, bedding plant and seed production
111419	Eggplant farming, grown under cover
422440	Eggs wholesaling
311999	Eggs, processed, manufacturing
334515	Elapsed time meters, electronic, manufacturing

Code	Description
313210	Elastic fabrics, more than 12 inches in width, weaving
313221	Elastic fabrics, narrow woven, manufacturing
339113	Elastic hosiery, orthopedic, manufacturing
325222	Elastomeric fibers and filaments manufacturing
325211	Elastomers (except synthetic rubber) manufacturing
325212	Elastomers, synthetic rubber, manufacturing
332322	Elbows for conductor pipe, hot air ducts, and stovepipe, sheet metal, manufacturing
332919	Elbows, pipe, metal (except made from purchased pipe), manufacturing
921190	Election boards
334512	Electric air cleaner controls, automatic, manufacturing
334513	Electric and electronic controllers, industrial process-type, manufacturing
336111	Electric automobiles for highway use manufacturing
335999	Electric bells manufacturing
335211	Electric blankets manufacturing
421620	Electric blankets wholesaling
335211	Electric comfort heating equipment, portable, manufacturing
335999	Electric fence chargers manufacturing
335311	Electric furnace transformers manufacturing
334512	Electric heat proportioning controls, modulating controls, manufacturing
335110	Electric lamp bulb parts (except glass blanks) manufacturing
335110	Electric lamps (i.e., light bulbs) manufacturing
335110	Electric light bulbs, complete, manufacturing
811310	Electric motor repair and maintenance services, commercial or industrial
421610	Electric motors, wiring supplies, and lighting fixtures wholesaling
339992	Electric musical instruments manufacturing
333618	Electric outboard motors manufacturing
221122	Electric power brokers
221121	Electric power control
221122	Electric power distribution systems
221119	Electric power generation, (except fossil fuel, hydroelectric, nuclear)
221112	Electric power generation, fossil fuel (e.g., coal, oil, gas)
221111	Electric power generation, hydroelectric
221113	Electric power generation, nuclear
221119	Electric power generation, solar
221119	Electric power generation, tidal
221119	Electric power generation, wind
234920	Electric power transmission line and tower construction
221121	Electric power transmission systems
334512	Electric space heater controls, automatic, manufacturing
335211	Electric space heaters, portable, manufacturing
333415	Electric warm air (i.e., forced air) furnaces manufacturing
235310	Electrical construction contractors
541330	Electrical engineering services
811310	Electrical generating and transmission equipment repair and maintenance services
541360	Electrical geophysical surveying services

Code	Description
336322	Electrical ignition cable sets for internal combustion engines manufacturing
335932	Electrical metallic tube (EMTs) manufacturing
561990	Electrical meter reading services, contract
334515	Electrical network analyzers manufacturing
334515	Electrical power measuring equipment manufacturing
235310	Electrical repair construction contractors
811118	Electrical repair shops, automotive
339950	Electrical signs manufacturing
421440	Electrical signs wholesaling
444190	Electrical supply stores
541380	Electrical testing laboratories or services
335211	Electrically heated bed coverings manufacturing
611513	Electricians' apprenticeship training
334515	Electricity and electrical signal measuring instruments manufacturing
334515	Electricity and electrical signal testing equipment manufacturing
334510	Electrocardiographs manufacturing
335999	Electrochemical generators (i.e., fuel cells) manufacturing
333512	Electrochemical milling machines, metalworking, manufacturing
333512	Electrode discharge metal cutting machines manufacturing
333992	Electrode holders, welding, manufacturing
335991	Electrodes for thermal and electrolytic uses, carbon and graphite, manufacturing
334513	Electrodes used in industrial process measurement manufacturing
335110	Electrodes, cold cathode fluorescent lamp, manufacturing
333992	Electrodes, welding, manufacturing
334510	Electroencephalographs manufacturing
334510	Electrogastrograph manufacturing
332912	Electrohydraulic servo valves, fluid power, manufacturing
812199	Electrolysis (i.e., hair removal) salons
325412	Electrolyte in-vivo diagnostic substances manufacturing
334513	Electrolytic conductivity instruments, industrial process-type, manufacturing
334516	Electrolytic conductivity instruments, laboratory-type, manufacturing
333512	Electrolytic metal cutting machines manufacturing
334513	Electromagnetic flowmeters manufacturing
541360	Electromagnetic geophysical surveying services
334514	Electromechanical counters manufacturing
334510	Electromedical diagnostic equipment manufacturing
334510	Electromedical equipment manufacturing
421450	Electromedical equipment wholesaling
334510	Electromedical therapy equipment manufacturing
331112	Electrometallurical ferroalloy manufacturing
334510	Electromyographs manufacturing
333992	Electron beam welding equipment manufacturing
335999	Electron linear accelerators manufacturing

Electron microprobes—Engineers'

Code	Description
334516	Electron microprobes, laboratory-type, manufacturing
334516	Electron microscopes manufacturing
334516	Electron paramagnetic spin-type apparatus manufacturing
333298	Electron tube machinery manufacturing
334411	Electron tube parts (e.g., bases, getters, guns) (except glass blanks) manufacturing
327215	Electron tube parts, glass blanks, made from purchased glass
327212	Electron tube parts, glass blanks, made in glass making plants
334515	Electron tube test equipment manufacturing
334411	Electron tubes manufacturing
333512	Electron-discharge metal cutting machines manufacturing
235310	Electronic control system construction contractors
514210	Electronic data processing services
511140	Electronic database publishers
511140	Electronic database publishing (i.e., establishments known as publishers)
611519	Electronic equipment repair training
522320	Electronic financial payment services
522320	Electronic funds transfer services
713120	Electronic game arcades
421920	Electronic games wholesaling
334511	Electronic guidance systems and equipment manufacturing
421690	Electronic parts (e.g., condensers, connectors, switches) wholesaling
323122	Electronic prepress services for the printing trade
541710	Electronic research and development laboratories or services
334515	Electronic test equipment for testing electrical characteristics manufacturing
541380	Electronic testing laboratories or services
334514	Electronic totalizing counters manufacturing
339932	Electronic toys and games manufacturing
421690	Electronic tubes (e.g., industrial, receiving, transmitting) wholesaling
334516	Electrophoresis instruments manufacturing
333298	Electroplating machinery and equipment manufacturing
332813	Electroplating metals and formed products for the trade
235210	Electrostatic painting construction contractors
335999	Electrostatic particle accelerators manufacturing
333411	Electrostatic precipitation equipment manufacturing
334510	Electrotherapeutic apparatus manufacturing
335110	Electrotherapeutic lamp bulbs for ultraviolet and infrared radiation manufacturing
334510	Electrotherapy units manufacturing
323122	Electrotype plate preparation services
333293	Electrotyping machinery manufacturing
334516	Elemental analyzers manufacturing
611110	Elementary schools
332323	Elevator guide rails, metal, manufacturing
235950	Elevator installation contractors
421830	Elevators wholesaling
333921	Elevators, passenger and freight, manufacturing

Code	Description
112990	Elk production
325998	Embalming fluids manufacturing
812210	Embalming services
928120	Embassies
313311	Embossing broadwoven fabrics
316110	Embossing leather
323122	Embossing plate preparation services
339943	Embossing stamps manufacturing
313312	Embossing textile products and fabrics (except broadwoven)
313222	Embroideries, Schiffli machine, manufacturing
315211	Embroidering contractors on men's and boys' apparel
315212	Embroidering contractors on women's, misses', girls', and infants' apparel
314999	Embroidering on textile products (except apparel) for the trade
339932	Embroidery kits manufacturing
333292	Embroidery machinery manufacturing
422310	Embroidery products wholesaling
313111	Embroidery spun yarns (e.g., cotton, manmade fiber, silk, wool) made from purchased fiber
313113	Embroidery thread (e.g., cotton, manmade fibers, silk, wool) manufacturing
335122	Emergency lighting (i.e., battery backup) manufacturing
621493	Emergency medical centers and clinics, freestanding
621910	Emergency medical transportation services, air or ground
922190	Emergency planning and management offices, government
624230	Emergency relief services
488410	Emergency road services (i.e., tow service)
624221	Emergency shelters (except for victims of domestic or international disasters or conflicts)
624230	Emergency shelters for victims of domestic or international disasters or conflicts
212399	Emery mining and/or beneficiating
811198	Emissions testing without repair, automotive
541612	Employee assessment consulting services
541612	Employee benefit consulting services
525110	Employee benefit pension plans
525120	Employee benefit plans (except pension)
524292	Employee benefit plans, third-party administrative processing services
485410	Employee bus services
541612	Employee compensation consulting services
561330	Employee leasing services
813930	Employees' associations for improvement of wages and working conditions
561310	Employment agencies
561310	Employment agencies, motion picture or video
561310	Employment agencies, radio or television
561310	Employment agencies, theatrical
561310	Employment placement agencies or services
561310	Employment referral agencies or services
561310	Employment registries
112390	Emu production
325613	Emulsifiers (i.e., surface-active agents) manufacturing
325510	Enamel paints manufacturing

Code	Description
212322	Enamel sand quarrying and/or beneficiating
332214	Enameled metal cutting utensils
332812	Enameling metals and metal products for the trade
333994	Enameling ovens manufacturing
422950	Enamels wholesaling
339114	Enamels, dental, manufacturing
323121	Encyclopedia binding without printing
511130	Encyclopedia publishers
511130	Encyclopedia publishers and printing combined
511130	Encyclopedia publishing (i.e., establishments known as publishers)
323117	Encyclopedias printing and binding without publishing
323117	Encyclopedias printing without publishing
337124	End tables, metal, manufacturing
337122	End tables, wood, manufacturing
111219	Endive farming (except under cover), field, bedding plant and seed production
111419	Endive farming, grown under cover
325411	Endocrine products, uncompounded, manufacturing
422210	Endocrine substances wholesaling
621210	Endodontists' offices (e.g., centers, clinics)
334510	Endoscopic equipment, electromedical (e.g., bronchoscopes, colonoscopes, cystoscopes), manufacturing
325320	Endrin insecticides manufacturing
541690	Energy consulting services
334512	Energy cutoff controls, residential and commercial types, manufacturing
926110	Energy development and conservation agencies, nonoperating
926130	Energy development and conservation programs, government
334515	Energy measuring equipment, electrical, manufacturing
926110	Energy program administration
331319	Energy wire or cable made in aluminum wire drawing plants
331422	Energy wire or cable, copper, made from purchased copper in wire drawing plants
331491	Energy wire or cable, nonferrous metals (except aluminum, copper), made from purchased nonferrous metals (except aluminum, copper) in wire drawing plants
924110	Enforcement of environmental and pollution control regulations
336312	Engine block assemblies, automotive and truck gasoline, manufacturing
325998	Engine degreasers manufacturing
336311	Engine intake and exhaust valves manufacturing
811310	Engine repair (except automotive, small engine)
811111	Engine repair and replacement shops, automotive
811411	Engine repair, small engine
325998	Engine starting fluids manufacturing
421120	Engine testing equipment, motor vehicle, wholesaling
541330	Engineering consulting services
541330	Engineering design services
541710	Engineering research and development laboratories or services
541330	Engineering services
813920	Engineers' associations

Code	Description
421490	Engineers' equipment and supplies wholesaling
541330	Engineers' offices
541330	Engineers' private practices
336412	Engines and engine parts, aircraft (except carburetors, pistons, piston rings, valves), manufacturing
336312	Engines and parts (except diesel), automotive and truck, manufacturing
421860	Engines and parts, aircraft, wholesaling
421120	Engines and parts, automotive, new, wholesaling
421860	Engines and turbines, marine, wholesaling
333618	Engines, diesel and semidiesel, manufacturing
333618	Engines, diesel locomotive, manufacturing
421830	Engines, internal combustion (except aircraft, automotive), wholesaling
333618	Engines, internal combustion (except aircraft, nondiesel automotive), manufacturing
333618	Engines, natural gas, manufacturing
111219	English pea farming (except under cover), field, bedding plant and seed production
111419	English pea farming, grown under cover
332212	Engraver's handtools, nonpowered, manufacturing
339911	Engraving and etching precious (except precious plated) metal jewelry and flatware
339912	Engraving and etching precious metal flatware
421830	Engraving machinery wholesaling
332812	Engraving metals and metal products (except printing plates) for the trade
323122	Engraving printing plate, for the printing trade
333315	Enlargers, photographic, manufacturing
315191	Ensemble dresses made in apparel knitting mills
315212	Ensemble dresses, women's, girls', and infants', cut and sew apparel contractors
315233	Ensemble dresses, women's, misses', and girls', cut and sewn from purchased fabric (except apparel contractors)
711130	Ensembles, musical
926110	Enterprise development program administration
711410	Entertainers' agents or managers
711510	Entertainers, independent
541710	Entomological research and development laboratories or services
115112	Entomological service, agricultural
541690	Entomology consulting services
333291	Envelope making machinery manufacturing
422110	Envelope paper, bulk, wholesaling
333313	Envelope stuffing, sealing, and addressing machinery manufacturing
322232	Envelopes (i.e., mailing, stationery) made from any material
422120	Envelopes wholesaling
813312	Environmental advocacy organizations
541620	Environmental consulting services
235110	Environmental control construction contractors
541330	Environmental engineering services
923120	Environmental health program administration
924110	Environmental protection program administration

Code	Description
562910	Environmental remediation services
541710	Environmental research and development laboratories or services
541380	Environmental testing laboratories or services
325413	Enzyme and isoenzyme in-vitro diagnostic substances manufacturing
325199	Enzyme proteins (i.e., basic synthetic chemicals) (except pharmaceutical use) manufacturing
325411	Enzyme proteins (i.e., basic synthetic chemicals), pharmaceutical use, manufacturing
325132	Eosin dyes manufacturing
325411	Ephedrine and derivatives (i.e., basic chemicals) manufacturing
325211	Epichlorohydrin bisphenol manufacturing
325211	Epichlorohydrin diphenol manufacturing
325212	Epichlorohydrin elastomers manufacturing
325520	Epoxy adhesives manufacturing
325510	Epoxy coatings made from purchased resins
325211	Epoxy resins manufacturing
923130	Equal employment opportunity offices
115210	Equine boarding
522220	Equipment finance leasing
326299	Erasers, rubber or rubber and abrasive combined, manufacturing
213112	Erecting oil and gas field lease tanks on a contract basis
325411	Ergot alkaloids (i.e., basic chemicals) manufacturing
541330	Erosion control engineering services
235950	Escalator installation contractors
333921	Escalators manufacturing
421830	Escalators wholesaling
111219	Escarole farming (except under cover), field, bedding plant and seed production
111419	Escarole farming, grown under cover
812990	Escort services, social
523991	Escrow agencies (except real estate)
531390	Escrow agencies, real estate
325998	Essential oils manufacturing
422690	Essential oils wholesaling
325199	Essential oils, synthetic, manufacturing
541990	Estate assessment (i.e., appraisal) services
541110	Estate law offices
325211	Ester gum manufacturing
325199	Esters, not specified elsewhere by process, manufacturing
812112	Esthetician (i.e., skin care) services
115310	Estimating timber
333295	Etching equipment, semiconductor, manufacturing
332812	Etching metals and metal products (except printing plates) for the trade
325110	Ethane made from refined petroleum or liquid hydrocarbons
211112	Ethane recovered from oil and gas field gases
325193	Ethanol, nonpotable, manufacturing
813410	Ethnic associations
711510	Ethnic dancers, independent
711320	Ethnic festival managers without facilities
711320	Ethnic festival organizers without facilities
711310	Ethnic festival promoters with facilities
711320	Ethnic festival promoters without facilities
325191	Ethyl acetate, natural, manufacturing

Code	Description
325199	Ethyl acetate, synthetic, manufacturing
422820	Ethyl alcohol wholesaling
325193	Ethyl alcohol, nonpotable, manufacturing
312140	Ethyl alcohol, potable, manufacturing
325199	Ethyl butyrate manufacturing
325199	Ethyl cellulose (except resins) manufacturing
325199	Ethyl chloride manufacturing
325199	Ethyl ether manufacturing
325199	Ethyl formate manufacturing
325199	Ethyl nitrite manufacturing
325199	Ethyl perhydrophenanthrene manufacturing
325110	Ethylbenzene made from refined petroleum or liquid hydrocarbons
325211	Ethylcellulose plastics manufacturing
325199	Ethylene glycol ether manufacturing
325199	Ethylene glycol manufacturing
325110	Ethylene made from refined petroleum or liquid hydrocarbons
324110	Ethylene made in petroleum refineries
325199	Ethylene oxide manufacturing
325212	Ethylene-propylene rubber manufacturing
325212	Ethylene-propylene-nonconjugated diene (EPDM) rubber manufacturing
325211	Ethylene-vinyl acetate resins manufacturing
325998	Eucalyptus oil manufacturing
311514	Evaporated milk manufacturing
334519	Evaporation meters manufacturing
333415	Evaporative condensers (i.e., heat transfer equipment) manufacturing
611691	Exam preparation services
421810	Excavating machinery and equipment wholesaling
213112	Excavating mud pits, slush pits, and cellars at oil and gas fields on a contract basis
235930	Excavation construction contractors
333120	Excavators (e.g., power shovels) manufacturing
321999	Excelsior (e.g., pads, wrappers) manufacturing
523999	Exchange clearinghouses, commodities or securities
332410	Exchangers, heat, manufacturing
523210	Exchanges, commodity contracts
523210	Exchanges, securities
335312	Exciter assemblies, motor and generator, manufacturing
531210	Exclusive buyers' agencies
531210	Exclusive buyers' agents, offices of
487210	Excursion boat operation
921140	Executive and legislative office combinations
561110	Executive management services
921110	Executive offices, federal, state, and local (e.g., governor, mayor, president)
541612	Executive placement consulting services
541612	Executive search consulting services
713940	Exercise centers
532292	Exercise equipment rental
451110	Exercise equipment stores
339920	Exercise machines manufacturing
621340	Exercise physiologists' offices (e.g., centers, clinics)
336399	Exhaust and tail pipes, automotive, truck, and bus, manufacturing
333412	Exhaust fans, industrial and commercial-type, manufacturing
811112	Exhaust system repair and replacement shops, automotive

Exhaust systems—Farm product

Code	Description
336399	Exhaust systems and parts, automotive, truck, and bus, manufacturing
531120	Exhibition hall, no promotion of events, rental or leasing
624190	Ex-offender rehabilitation agencies
624190	Ex-offender self-help organizations
316110	Exotic leathers manufacturing
332312	Expansion joints, metal, manufacturing
541710	Experimental farms
213113	Exploration services for coal (except geophysical surveying and mapping) on a contract basis
213114	Exploration services for metal (except geophysical surveying and mapping) on a contract basis
213115	Exploration services for nonmetallic minerals (except geophysical surveying and mapping) on a contract basis
213112	Exploration services for oil and gas (except geophysical surveying and mapping) on a contract basis
422690	Explosives (except ammunition, fireworks) wholesaling
325920	Explosives manufacturing
522293	Export trading companies (i.e., international trade financing)
522293	Export-Import banks
333315	Exposure meters, photographic, manufacturing
622310	Extended care hospitals (except mental, substance abuse)
335999	Extension cords made from purchased insulated wire
321999	Extension ladders, wood, manufacturing
321999	Extension planks, wood, manufacturing
235420	Exterior insulation finishing system construction contractors
321918	Exterior wood shutters manufacturing
325320	Exterminating chemical products (e.g., fungicides, insecticides, pesticides) manufacturing
561710	Exterminating services
421990	Extinguishers, fire, wholesaling
333120	Extractors, piling, manufacturing
311920	Extracts, essences and preparations, coffee, manufacturing
311920	Extracts, essences and preparations, tea, manufacturing
311942	Extracts, food (except coffee, meat), manufacturing
311942	Extracts, malt, manufacturing
325191	Extracts, natural dyeing and tanning, manufacturing
326291	Extruded, molded or lathe-cut rubber goods manufacturing
333220	Extruding machinery for plastics and rubber manufacturing
333292	Extruding machinery for yarn manufacturing
333513	Extruding machines, metalworking, manufacturing
331319	Extrusion billet made by rolling purchased aluminum
331319	Extrusion billet, aluminum, made in integrated secondary smelting and rolling mills
333514	Extrusion dies for use with all materials manufacturing
331319	Extrusion ingot made by rolling purchased aluminum
331319	Extrusion ingot, aluminum, made in integrated secondary smelting and rolling mills
331312	Extrusion ingot, primary aluminium, manufacturing
325412	Eye and ear preparations manufacturing
621991	Eye banks
339112	Eye examining instruments and apparatus manufacturing
325620	Eye make-up (e.g., eye shadow, eyebrow pencil, mascara) manufacturing
622310	Eye, ear, nose, and throat hospitals
316993	Eyeglass cases, all materials, manufacturing
339115	Eyeglass frames (i.e., fronts and temples), ophthalmic, manufacturing
421460	Eyeglasses wholesaling
315211	Eyelet making contractors on men's and boys' apparel
315212	Eyelet making contractors on women's, misses', girls', and infants' apparel
339993	Eyelets, metal, manufacturing
339115	Eyes, glass and plastics, manufacturing
522294	FHLMC (Federal Home Loan Mortgage Corporation)
513112	FM radio stations
522294	FNMA (Federal National Mortgage Association)
313312	Fabric (except broadwoven) finishing
451130	Fabric shops
325612	Fabric softeners manufacturing
332312	Fabricated bar joists manufacturing
332996	Fabricated pipe and pipe fittings made from purchased pipe
332313	Fabricated plate work manufacturing
314991	Fabricated rope products (e.g., nets, slings) made in cordage or twine mills
332312	Fabricated structural metal manufacturing
321213	Fabricated structural wood members (except trusses) manufacturing
313210	Fabrics (except rug, tire fabrics), broadwoven, weaving
314992	Fabrics for reinforcing rubber tires, industrial belting, and fuel cells manufacturing
313311	Fabrics, broadwoven, finishing
313311	Fabrics, broadwoven, mercerizing
313249	Fabrics, knit, made in warp knit fabric mills
313241	Fabrics, knit, made in weft knit fabric mills
313249	Fabrics, lace, made in lace mills
313221	Fabrics, narrow woven, weaving
313230	Fabrics, nonwoven, manufacturing
422310	Fabrics, textile (except burlap, felt), wholesaling
332618	Fabrics, woven wire, made from purchased wire
325620	Face creams (e.g., cleansing, moisturizing) manufacturing
335932	Face plates (i.e., outlet or switch covers) manufacturing
525990	Face-amount certificate funds
812112	Facial salons
422130	Facial tissue wholesaling
322291	Facial tissues made from purchased paper
322121	Facial tissues made in paper mills
561210	Facilities (except computer operation) support services
541513	Facilities (i.e., clients' facilities) management and operation services, computer systems or data processing
541513	Facilities (i.e., clients' facilities) support services, computer systems or data processing
513310	Facilities-based telecommunication carriers (except wireless)
333512	Facing machines, metalworking, manufacturing
334210	Facsimile equipment, standalone, manufacturing
532420	Facsimile machine rental or leasing
811213	Facsimile machine repair and maintenance services
421690	Facsimile machines wholesaling
325992	Facsimile toner cartridges manufacturing
522298	Factoring accounts receivable
233310	Factory construction
711310	Fair managers with facilities, agricultural
711320	Fair managers without facilities, agricultural
711310	Fair organizers with facilities, agricultural
711320	Fair organizers without facilities, agricultural
711310	Fair promoters with facilities, agricultural
711320	Fair promoters without facilities, agricultural
448140	Family clothing stores
621210	Family dentists' offices (e.g., centers, clinics)
713120	Family fun centers
541110	Family law offices
621111	Family physicians' offices (e.g., centers, clinics)
621410	Family planning centers
621410	Family planning counseling services
722110	Family restaurants, full service
722211	Family restaurants, limited service
624190	Family social service agencies
624190	Family welfare services
326220	Fan belts, rubber or plastics, manufacturing
334512	Fan controls, temperature responsive, manufacturing
316110	Fancy leathers manufacturing
335211	Fans (except attic), household-type electric, manufacturing
336322	Fans, electric cooling, automotive, truck, and bus, manufacturing
335211	Fans, household-type kitchen, manufacturing
421620	Fans, household-type, wholesaling
333412	Fans, industrial and commercial-type, manufacturing
421830	Fans, industrial, wholesaling
334514	Fare collection equipment manufacturing
311211	Farina (except breakfast food) made in flour mills
311230	Farina, breakfast cereal, manufacturing
233320	Farm building construction
332311	Farm buildings, prefabricated metal, manufacturing
321992	Farm buildings, prefabricated or portable, wood, manufacturing
813910	Farm bureaus
532490	Farm equipment rental or leasing
813410	Farm granges
115115	Farm labor contractors
811310	Farm machinery and equipment repair and maintenance services
421820	Farm machinery and equipment wholesaling
115116	Farm management services
522292	Farm mortgage lending
493130	Farm product warehousing and storage (except refrigerated)
493120	Farm product warehousing and storage, refrigerated

Code	Description
484220	Farm products hauling, local
484230	Farm products trucking, long-distance
332420	Farm storage tanks, heavy gauge metal, manufacturing
422910	Farm supplies wholesaling
532490	Farm tractor rental or leasing
333111	Farm tractors and attachments manufacturing
333111	Farm wagons manufacturing
333922	Farm-type conveyers manufacturing
813910	Farmers' associations
813910	Farmers' unions
******	Farming — see type
531190	Farmland rental or leasing
115210	Farriers
112210	Farrow-to-finish operations
541490	Fashion design services
541490	Fashion designer services
722211	Fast food restaurants
421710	Fasteners (e.g., bolts, nuts, rivets, screws) wholesaling
339993	Fasteners (e.g., glove, hook-and-eye, slide, snap) manufacturing
334511	Fathometers manufacturing
334519	Fatigue testing machines, industrial, mechanical, manufacturing
311611	Fats, animal (except poultry, small game), produced in slaughtering plants
311613	Fats, animal, rendering
112112	Fattening cattle
325199	Fatty acid esters and amines manufacturing
325199	Fatty acids (e.g., margaric, oleic, stearic) manufacturing
325199	Fatty alcohols manufacturing
327111	Faucet handles, vitreous china and earthenware, manufacturing
332913	Faucets, plumbing, manufacturing
532420	Fax machine rental or leasing
811213	Fax machine repair and maintenance services
339999	Feather dusters manufacturing
315291	Feather-filled clothing, infants', cut and sewn from purchased fabric (except apparel contractors)
315239	Feather-filled clothing, jackets, and vests, women's, misses', and juniors', cut and sewn from purchased fabric (except apparel contractors)
315211	Feather-filled clothing, men's and boys', cut and sew apparel contractors
315228	Feather-filled clothing, men's and boys', cut and sewn from purchased fabric (except apparel contractors)
315212	Feather-filled clothing, women's, girls', and infants', cut and sew apparel contractors
422590	Feathers wholesaling
339999	Feathers, preparing (i.e., for use in apparel and textile products)
514110	Feature syndicates (i.e., advice columns, comic, news)
522294	Federal Agricultural Mortgage Corporation
926120	Federal Aviation Administration (except air traffic control)
922120	Federal Bureau of Investigation (FBI)
926130	Federal Communications Commission (FCC)
522298	Federal Home Loan Banks (FHLB)
522294	Federal Home Loan Mortgage Corporation (FHLMC)
522294	Federal Intermediate Credit Bank
522292	Federal Land Banks

Code	Description
522294	Federal National Mortgage Association (FNMA)
521110	Federal Reserve Banks or Branches
921130	Federal Reserve Board of Governors
522130	Federal credit unions
922120	Federal police services
522120	Federal savings and loan associations (S&L)
522120	Federal savings banks
813219	Federated charities
813930	Federation of workers, labor organizations
813930	Federations of labor
422910	Feed additives wholesaling
316999	Feed bags for horses manufacturing
314911	Feed bags made from purchased woven or knitted materials
311119	Feed concentrates, animal, manufacturing
311514	Feed grade dry milk products manufacturing
311119	Feed premixes, animal, manufacturing
333111	Feed processing equipment, farm-type, manufacturing
444220	Feed stores (except pet)
453910	Feed stores, pet
311119	Feed supplements, animal (except cat, dog), manufacturing
311111	Feed supplements, dog and cat, manufacturing
112112	Feed yards (except stockyards for transportation), cattle
112111	Feeder calf production
112210	Feeder pig farming
335311	Feeder voltage regulators and boosters (i.e., electrical transformers) manufacturing
421820	Feeders, animal, wholesaling
333131	Feeders, mineral beneficiating-type, manufacturing
112112	Feedlots (except stockyards for transportation), cattle
112210	Feedlots (except stockyards for transportation), hog
112410	Feedlots (except stockyards for transportation), lamb
422910	Feeds (except pet) wholesaling
311111	Feeds, prepared for dog and cat, manufacturing
311119	Feeds, prepared, for animals (except cat, dog) manufacturing
311119	Feeds, specialty (e.g., guinea pig, mice, mink), manufacturing
212299	Feldspar mining and/or beneficiating
327992	Feldspar processing beyond beneficiation
339941	Felt tip markers manufacturing
422990	Felt wholesaling
322121	Felts, asphalt, made in paper mills
313210	Felts, broadwoven, weaving
313230	Felts, nonwoven, manufacturing
235990	Fence construction contractors
331222	Fence gates, posts, and fittings, iron or steel, made in wire drawing plants
331111	Fence posts, iron or steel, made in steel mills
332323	Fences and gates (except wire), metal, manufacturing
421390	Fencing (except wood) wholesaling
332618	Fencing and fence gates made from purchased wire
421390	Fencing and fencing accessories, wire, wholesaling
444190	Fencing dealers

Code	Description
339920	Fencing equipment (sporting goods) manufacturing
321999	Fencing, prefabricated sections, wood, manufacturing
321999	Fencing, wood (except rough pickets, poles, and rails), manufacturing
421310	Fencing, wood, wholesaling
212299	Ferberite ores and concentrates mining and/or beneficiating
333298	Fermentation equipment, chemical, manufacturing
422810	Fermented malt beverages wholesaling
332420	Fermention tanks, heavy gauge metal tanks, manufacturing
212299	Ferralloy ores (except vanadium) (e.g., chromium, columbium, molybdenum, tungsten) mining and/or beneficiating
325188	Ferric chloride manufacturing
325188	Ferric oxide manufacturing
325131	Ferric oxide pigments manufacturing
333319	Ferris wheels manufacturing
331112	Ferroalloys manufacturing
421510	Ferroalloys wholesaling
331112	Ferrochromium manufacturing
325188	Ferrocyanides manufacturing
331112	Ferromanganese manufacturing
331112	Ferromolybdenum manufacturing
331112	Ferrophosphorus manufacturing
331112	Ferrosilicon manufacturing
331112	Ferrotitanium manufacturing
331112	Ferrotungsten manufacturing
332111	Ferrous forgings made from purchased iron or steel, unfinished
421510	Ferrous metals wholesaling
331112	Ferrovanadium manufacturing
483114	Ferry passenger transportation, Great Lakes
336611	Ferryboat building
621410	Fertility clinics
422910	Fertilizer and fertilizer materials wholesaling
115112	Fertilizer application for crops
212393	Fertilizer minerals, natural, mining and/or beneficiating
325314	Fertilizers, mixed, made in plants not manufacturing fertilizer materials
325311	Fertilizers, mixed, made in plants producing nitrogenous fertilizer materials
325312	Fertilizers, mixed, made in plants producing phosphatic fertilizer materials
325311	Fertilizers, natural organic (except compost), manufacturing
325311	Fertilizers, of animal waste origin, manufacturing
325311	Fertilizers, of sewage origin, manufacturing
561730	Fertilizing lawns
333111	Fertilizing machinery, farm-type, manufacturing
111998	Fescue seed farming
711310	Festival managers with facilities
711320	Festival managers without facilities
711310	Festival of arts managers with facilities
711320	Festival of arts managers without facilities
711310	Festival of arts organizers with facilities
711320	Festival of arts organizers without facilities
711310	Festival of arts promoters with facilities
711320	Festival of arts promoters without facilities
711310	Festival organizers with facilities
711320	Festival organizers without facilities

Festival promotors—Fire escapes

Code	Description
711310	Festival promoters with facilities
711320	Festival promoters without facilities
325412	Fever remedy preparations manufacturing
322214	Fiber cans and drums (i.e., all-fiber, nonfiber ends of any material) made from purchased paperboard
422130	Fiber cans and drums wholesaling
322214	Fiber drums made from purchased paperboard
337125	Fiber furniture (except upholstered), household-type, manufacturing
313221	Fiber glasses, narrow woven, weaving
235310	Fiber optic cable construction contractors
335921	Fiber optic cable manufacturing
334417	Fiber optic connectors manufacturing
322214	Fiber spools, reels, blocks made from purchased paperboard
322214	Fiber tubes made from purchased paperboard
314999	Fiber, textile recovery from textile mill waste and rags
321219	Fiberboard manufacturing
421310	Fiberboard wholesaling
421390	Fiberglass building materials (except insulation, roofing, siding) wholesaling
313210	Fiberglass fabrics weaving
422310	Fiberglass fabrics wholesaling
327993	Fiberglass insulation products manufacturing
325221	Fibers and filaments, cellulosic, manufacturing and texturizing
325222	Fibers and filaments, noncellulosic, manufacturing and texturizing
335991	Fibers, carbon and graphite, manufacturing
327212	Fibers, glass, textile, made in glass making plants
422690	Fibers, manmade, wholesaling
422590	Fibers, vegetable, wholesaling
323121	Fiction book binding without printing
511130	Fiction book publishers
511130	Fiction book publishers and printing combined
511130	Fiction book publishing (i.e., establishments known as publishers)
323117	Fiction books printing and binding without publishing
323117	Fiction books printing without publishing
524126	Fidelity insurance carriers, direct
531390	Fiduciaries', real estate, offices
523991	Fiduciary agencies (except real estate)
332995	Field artillery manufacturing
315211	Field jackets, military, cut and sew apparel contractors
315228	Field jackets, military, men's and boys', cut and sewn from purchased fabric (except apparel contractors)
111421	Field nurseries (i.e., growing of flowers and shrubbery)
334515	Field strength and intensity measuring equipment, electrical, manufacturing
336211	Fifth wheel assemblies manufacturing
111339	Fig farming
711219	Figure skaters, independent
335110	Filaments for electric lamp bulbs manufacturing
111335	Filbert farming
115114	Filbert hulling and shelling
422120	File cards and folders wholesaling
322231	File folders (e.g., accordion, expanding, hanging, manila) made from purchased paper and paperboard
333515	Files (i.e., a machine tool accessory) manufacturing
332212	Files, handheld, manufacturing
337214	Filing cabinets (except wood), office-type, manufacturing
337211	Filing cabinets, wood, office type, manufacturing
333512	Filing machines, metalworking, manufacturing
212399	Fill dirt pits mining and/or beneficiating
325510	Fillers, wood (e.g., dry, liquid, paste), manufacturing
314999	Filling (except nonwoven textile), upholstery, manufacturing
311999	Fillings, cake or pie (except fruits, meat, vegetables), manufacturing
711510	Film actors, independent
514120	Film archives
541380	Film badge testing (i.e., radiation testing) laboratories or services
333315	Film developing equipment manufacturing
421410	Film developing equipment wholesaling
512120	Film distribution agencies
512120	Film distribution, motion picture and video
512131	Film festivals exhibitors
512120	Film libraries, commercial distribution
512199	Film libraries, motion picture or video, stock footage
512191	Film or tape closed captioning
512191	Film or video transfer services
512199	Film processing laboratories, motion picture
711510	Film producers, independent
512110	Film studios producing films
421410	Film, photographic, wholesaling
326113	Film, plastics (except packaging), manufacturing
326112	Film, plastics, packaging, manufacturing
325992	Film, sensitized (e.g., camera, motion picture, X-ray), manufacturing
512110	Films, motion picture production
512110	Films, motion picture production and distribution
422130	Filter papers wholesaling
327112	Filtering media, pottery, manufacturing
336399	Filters (e.g., air, engine oil, fuel) automotive, truck, and bus, manufacturing
333411	Filters, air-conditioner, manufacturing
334419	Filters, electronic component-type, manufacturing
333411	Filters, furnace, manufacturing
333999	Filters, industrial and general line (except internal combustion engine, warm air furnace), manufacturing
322299	Filters, paper, made from purchased paper
221310	Filtration plant, water
212322	Filtration sand quarrying and/or beneficiating
332993	Fin assemblies, mortar, manufacturing
332993	Fin assemblies, torpedo and bomb, manufacturing
522291	Finance companies (i.e., unsecured cash loans)
523140	Financial futures brokerages
523930	Financial investment advice services, customized, fees paid by client
511120	Financial magazine and periodical publishers
511120	Financial magazine and periodical publishers and printing combined
511120	Financial magazine and periodical publishing (i.e., establishments known as publishers)
323112	Financial magazines and periodicals flexographic printing without publishing
323111	Financial magazines and periodicals gravure printing without publishing
323110	Financial magazines and periodicals lithographic (offset) printing without publishing
323119	Financial magazines and periodicals printing (except flexographic, gravure, lithographic, screen) without publishing
323113	Financial magazines and periodicals screen printing without publishing
541611	Financial management consulting (except investment advice) services
523930	Financial planning services, customized, fees paid by client
522320	Financial transactions processing (except central bank)
521110	Financial transactions processing of the central bank
316999	Findings, boot and shoe, manufacturing
339913	Findings, jeweler's, manufacturing
315212	Findings, suit and coat (e.g., coat fromts, pockets), women's, girls', and infants', cut and sew apparel contractors
315999	Findings, suit and coat (e.g., coat fronts, pockets), cut and sewn from purchased fabric (except apparel contractors)
315211	Findings, suit and coat (e.g., coat fronts, pockets), men's and boys', cut and sew apparel contractors
712110	Fine arts museums
611610	Fine arts schools (except academic)
722110	Fine dining restaurants, full service
422110	Fine paper, bulk, wholesaling
114111	Finfish fishing (e.g., flounder, salmon, trout)
112511	Finfish production, farm raising
112511	Finfish, hatcheries
321213	Finger joint lumber manufacturing
561611	Fingerprint services
314110	Finishing (e.g., dyeing) rugs and carpets
325613	Finishing agents, textile and leather, manufacturing
316110	Finishing hides and skins on a contract basis
316110	Finishing leather
333292	Finishing machinery for textile manufacturing
313311	Finishing plants, broadwoven fabric
611110	Finishing schools, secondary
561621	Fire alarm monitoring services
561621	Fire alarm sales combined with installation, maintenance, or monitoring services
922160	Fire and rescue service
212325	Fire clay mining and/or beneficiating
922160	Fire departments (e.g., government, volunteer)
334290	Fire detection and alarm systems manufacturing
334519	Fire detector systems, nonelectric, manufacturing
332321	Fire doors, metal, manufacturing
235990	Fire escape construction contractors
332323	Fire escapes, metal, manufacturing

Code	Description
325998	Fire extinguisher chemical preparations manufacturing
422690	Fire extinguisher preparations wholesaling
421990	Fire extinguishers wholesaling
339999	Fire extinguishers, portable, manufacturing
611519	Fire fighter training schools
561990	Fire fighting services as a commercial activity
314999	Fire hose, textile, made from purchased materials
332911	Fire hydrant valves manufacturing
332911	Fire hydrants, complete, manufacturing
524126	Fire insurance carriers, direct
541380	Fire insurance underwriters' laboratories
922160	Fire investigation service, government
922160	Fire marshals' offices
922160	Fire prevention offices, government
115310	Fire prevention, forest
325998	Fire retardant chemical preparations manufacturing
233320	Fire station construction
421990	Firearms (except sporting) wholesaling
813319	Firearms advocacy organizations
332994	Firearms manufacturing
421910	Firearms, sporting, wholesaling
336611	Fireboat building
327124	Firebrick, clay refractories, manufacturing
315211	Firefighters' dress uniforms, men's, cut and sew apparel contractors
315222	Firefighters' dress uniforms, men's, cut and sewn from purchased fabric (except apparel contractors)
315212	Firefighters' dress uniforms, women's, cut and sew apparel contractors
315234	Firefighters' dress uniforms, women's, cut and sewn from purchased fabric (except apparel contractors)
922160	Firefighting (except forest), volunteer and government
421850	Firefighting equipment and supplies wholesaling
922160	Firefighting services (including volunteer)
339113	Firefighting suits and accessories manufacturing
115310	Firefighting, forest
332999	Fireplace fixtures and equipment manufacturing
333414	Fireplace inserts (i.e., heat directing) manufacturing
326120	Fireplace logs, plastics, manufacturing
421720	Fireplaces, gas, wholesaling
235990	Fireproofing buildings construction contractors
321999	Firewood and fuel wood containing fuel binder manufacturing
454319	Firewood dealers, direct selling
421990	Firewood wholesaling
713990	Fireworks display services
325998	Fireworks manufacturing
453998	Fireworks shops (i.e., permanent location)
421920	Fireworks wholesaling
327112	Firing china for the trade
321920	Firkins and kits, wood, coopered, manufacturing
611699	First aid instruction
339113	First aid, snake bite, or burn kits manufacturing
421450	First-aid kits wholesaling
422210	First-aid supplies wholesaling

Code	Description
422460	Fish (except canned, packaged frozen) wholesaling
924120	Fish and game agencies
311711	Fish and marine animal oils produced in a cannery
311712	Fish and marine animal oils produced in a fresh and frozen seafood plant
311711	Fish and seafood chowder canning
924120	Fish and wildlife conservation program administration
311711	Fish egg bait canning
112511	Fish farms, finfish
112512	Fish farms, shellfish
334511	Fish finders (i.e., sonar) manufacturing
311119	Fish food for feeding fish manufacturing
311712	Fish freezing (e.g., blocks, fillets, ready-to-serve products)
325411	Fish liver oils, medicinal, uncompounded, manufacturing
445220	Fish markets
311711	Fish meal produced in a cannery
311712	Fish meal produced in a fresh and frozen seafood plant
332212	Fish wire (i.e., electrical wiring tool) manufacturing
311711	Fish, canned and cured, manufacturing
422490	Fish, canned, wholesaling
311711	Fish, curing, drying, pickling, salting, and smoking
311712	Fish, fresh or frozen, manufacturing
311712	Fish, fresh prepared, manufacturing
422420	Fish, packaged frozen, wholesaling
422990	Fish, tropical, wholesaling
541710	Fisheries research and development laboratories or services
114111	Fisheries, finfish
114112	Fisheries, shellfish
487210	Fishing boat charter operation
336611	Fishing boat, commercial, building
721214	Fishing camps with accommodation facilities
713990	Fishing clubs, recreational
421910	Fishing equipment and supplies (except commercial) wholesaling
213112	Fishing for tools at oil and gas fields on a contract basis
713990	Fishing guide services
332211	Fishing knives manufacturing
314999	Fishing nets made from purchased materials
713990	Fishing piers
114210	Fishing preserves
451110	Fishing supply stores (e.g., bait)
339920	Fishing tackle and equipment (except lines, nets, seines) manufacturing
713940	Fitness centers
421910	Fitness equipment and supplies wholesaling
713940	Fitness salons
713940	Fitness spas without accommodations
326122	Fittings and unions, rigid plastics pipe, manufacturing
421720	Fittings and valves, plumber's, wholesaling
326122	Fittings, rigid plastics pipe, manufacturing
331511	Fittings, soil and pressure pipe, cast iron, manufacturing
713950	Five pin bowling centers
722213	Fixed location refreshment stands
325992	Fixers, prepared photographic, manufacturing
337920	Fixtures (e.g., poles, rods, rollers), curtain and drapery, manufacturing

Code	Description
421610	Fixtures, electric lighting, wholesaling
421440	Fixtures, store (except refrigerated), wholesaling
337215	Fixtures, store display, manufacturing
453998	Flag and banner shops
561990	Flagging (i.e., traffic control) services
332323	Flagpoles, metal, manufacturing
321999	Flagpoles, wood, manufacturing
314999	Flags, textile (e.g., banners, bunting, emblems, pennants), made from purchased fabrics
212311	Flagstone mining or quarrying
327991	Flagstones cutting
321219	Flakeboard manufacturing
331221	Flakes made from purchased iron or steel
331314	Flakes, aluminum, made from purchased aluminum
331111	Flakes, iron or steel, made in steel mills
334516	Flame photometers manufacturing
812332	Flame resistant clothing supply services
334512	Flame safety controls for furnaces and boilers manufacturing
332995	Flame throwers manufacturing
333512	Flange facing machines, metalworking, manufacturing
332991	Flange units, ball or roller bearing, manufacturing
332919	Flanges and flange unions, pipe, metal, manufacturing
315223	Flannel shirts (except work shirts), men's and boys', cut and sewn from purchased fabric (except apparel contractors)
315291	Flannel shirts, infants', cut and sewn from purchased fabric (except apparel contractors)
315211	Flannel shirts, men's and boys', cut and sew apparel contractors
315212	Flannel shirts, women's, girls', and infants', cut and sew apparel contractors
315232	Flannel shirts, women's, misses', and girls', cut and sewn from purchased fabric (except apparel contractors)
315225	Flannel shirts, work, men's and boys', cut and sewn from purchased fabric (except apparel contractors)
313210	Flannels, broadwoven, weaving
325998	Flares manufacturing
333315	Flash apparatus, photographic, manufacturing
335110	Flash bulbs, photographic, manufacturing
233810	Flashing construction contractors
335912	Flashlight batteries manufacturing
335110	Flashlight bulb manufacturing
335129	Flashlights manufacturing
421610	Flashlights wholesaling
313249	Flat (i.e., warp) fabrics knitting
331221	Flat bright steel strip made in cold rolling mills
327211	Flat glass (e.g., float, plate) manufacturing
421390	Flat glass wholesaling
334119	Flat panel displays (i.e., complete units), computer peripheral equipment, manufacturing
332612	Flat springs (except clock, watch), light gauge, manufacturing
332611	Flat springs, heavy gauge, manufacturing
336212	Flatbed trailers, commercial, manufacturing
484220	Flatbed trucking, local

Flatbed trucking—Fluorocarbon

Code	Description
484230	Flatbed trucking, long-distance
331111	Flats, iron or steel, made in steel mills
321920	Flats, wood, greenhouse, manufacturing
421220	Flatware (except plated, precious) wholesaling
332211	Flatware, nonprecious and precious plated metal, manufacturing
421940	Flatware, precious and plated, wholesaling
311942	Flavor extracts (except coffee) manufacturing
311511	Flavored milk drinks manufacturing
311930	Flavoring concentrates (except coffee based) manufacturing
422490	Flavoring extracts (except for fountain use) wholesaling
325199	Flavoring materials (i.e., basic synthetic chemicals such as coumarin) manufacturing
311930	Flavoring pastes, powders, and syrups for soft drink manufacturing
313111	Flax spun yarns made from purchased fiber
111120	Flaxseed farming, field and seed production
311225	Flaxseed oil made from purchased oils
311223	Flaxseed oil made in crushing mills
531190	Flea market space (except under roof) rental or leasing
531120	Flea market space, under roof, rental or leasing
454390	Flea markets, temporary location, direct selling
453310	Flea markets, used merchandise, permanent
325320	Flea powders or sprays manufacturing
532112	Fleet leasing, passenger vehicle
316110	Fleshers, leather (i.e., flesh side of split leather), manufacturing
334112	Flexible (i.e., floppy) magnetic disk drives manufacturing
332999	Flexible metal hose and tubing manufacturing
322221	Flexible packaging sheet materials (except foil-paper laminates) made by coating or laminating purchased paper
322225	Flexible packaging sheet materials made by laminating purchased foil
334412	Flexible wiring boards, bare, manufacturing
325910	Flexographic inks manufacturing
323122	Flexographic plate preparation services
323112	Flexographic printing (except books, manifold business forms, printing grey goods)
333293	Flexographic printing presses manufacturing
339920	Flies, artificial fishing, manufacturing
334511	Flight and navigation sensors, transmitters, and displays manufacturing
611519	Flight attendant schools
334511	Flight recorders (i.e., black boxes) manufacturing
333319	Flight simulation machinery manufacturing
611512	Flight training schools
212325	Flint clay mining and/or beneficiating
327992	Flint processing beyond beneficiation
339999	Flints, lighter, manufacturing
321113	Flitches (i.e., veneer stock) made in sawmills
334512	Float controls, residential and commercial types, manufacturing
561990	Float decorating services
541490	Float design services
327124	Floaters, glasshouse, clay, manufacturing
713210	Floating casinos (i.e., gambling cruises, riverboat casinos)
332313	Floating covers, fabricated metal plate work, manufacturing
311711	Floating factory ships seafood processing
332812	Flocking metals and metal products for the trade
234990	Flood control project construction
332312	Flood gates, metal plate, manufacturing
335129	Floodlights (i.e., lighting fixtures) manufacturing
321918	Floor baseboards, wood, manufacturing
442210	Floor covering stores (except wood or ceramic tile only)
444190	Floor covering stores, wood or ceramic tile only
421220	Floor coverings wholesaling
326192	Floor coverings, linoleum, manufacturing
326192	Floor coverings, resilient, manufacturing
326192	Floor coverings, rubber, manufacturing
326192	Floor coverings, vinyl, manufacturing
332312	Floor jacks, metal, manufacturing
335121	Floor lamps (i.e., lighting fixtures), residential, manufacturing
235520	Floor laying, finishing, or refinishing construction contractors
421850	Floor maintenance equipment wholesaling
326299	Floor mats (e.g., bath, door), rubber, manufacturing
325612	Floor polishes and waxes manufacturing
332312	Floor posts, adjustable metal, manufacturing
532490	Floor sanding machine rental or leasing
333319	Floor sanding, washing, and polishing machines, commercial-type, manufacturing
335212	Floor scrubbing and shampooing machines, household-type electric, manufacturing
335211	Floor standing fans, household-type electric, manufacturing
327122	Floor tile, ceramic, manufacturing
321214	Floor trusses, wood, manufacturing
335212	Floor waxers and polishers, household-type electric, manufacturing
532490	Floor waxing equipment rental or leasing
332323	Flooring, open steel (i.e., grating), manufacturing
332322	Flooring, sheet metal, manufacturing
321114	Flooring, wood block, treating
321918	Flooring, wood, manufacturing
421310	Flooring, wood, wholesaling
334112	Floppy disk drives manufacturing
561422	Floral wire services (i.e., telemarketing services)
422930	Florist's supplies wholesaling
453110	Florists
327112	Florists' articles, red earthenware, manufacturing
333131	Flotation machinery, mining-type, manufacturing
114111	Flounder fishing
314911	Flour bags made from purchased woven or knitted materials
333294	Flour milling machinery manufacturing
311230	Flour mills, breakfast cereal, manufacturing
311211	Flour mills, cereals grains (except breakfast cereals, rice)
311211	Flour mixes made in flour mills
422490	Flour wholesaling
311822	Flour, blended or self-rising, made from purchased flour
311211	Flour, blended, prepared, or self-rising (except rice), made in flour mills
311213	Flour, malt, manufacturing
311212	Flour, rice, manufacturing
321999	Flour, wood, manufacturing
335314	Flow actuated electrical switches manufacturing
334513	Flow instruments, industrial process-type, manufacturing
327420	Flower boxes, plaster of paris, manufacturing
111421	Flower bulb growing
422910	Flower bulbs wholesaling
111422	Flower growing
327112	Flower pots, red earthenware, manufacturing
111422	Flower seed production
453998	Flower shops, artificial or dried
453110	Flower shops, fresh
561920	Flower show managers
561920	Flower show organizers
561920	Flower show promoters
422930	Flowers wholesaling
339999	Flowers, artificial (except glass, plastics), manufacturing
327123	Flue lining, clay, manufacturing
421320	Flue pipe and linings wholesaling
332322	Flues, stove and furnace, sheet metal, manufacturing
332439	Fluid milk shipping containers, light gauge metal, manufacturing
311511	Fluid milk substitutes processing
333995	Fluid power actuators manufacturing
332912	Fluid power aircraft subassemblies manufacturing
333995	Fluid power cylinders manufacturing
332912	Fluid power hose assemblies manufacturing
333996	Fluid power motors manufacturing
333996	Fluid power pumps manufacturing
332912	Fluid power valves and hose fittings manufacturing
421830	Fluid-power transmission equipment wholesaling
334513	Fluidic devices, circuits, and systems for process control, manufacturing
332313	Flumes, fabricated metal plate work, manufacturing
332322	Flumes, sheet metal, manufacturing
325188	Fluoboric acid manufacturing
335311	Fluorescent ballasts (i.e., transformers) manufacturing
325132	Fluorescent dyes manufacturing
335110	Fluorescent lamp tubes, electric, manufacturing
335122	Fluorescent lighting fixtures, commercial, institutional, and industrial electric, manufacturing
335121	Fluorescent lighting fixtures, residential, manufacturing
335311	Fluorescent lighting transformers manufacturing
325120	Fluorinated hydrocarbon gases manufacturing
325188	Fluorine manufacturing
212393	Fluorite mining and/or beneficiating
325212	Fluoro rubbers manufacturing
325211	Fluoro-polymer resins manufacturing
325212	Fluorocarbon derivative rubbers manufacturing

Code	Description
325222	Fluorocarbon fibers and filaments manufacturing
325120	Fluorocarbon gases manufacturing
325211	Fluorohydrocarbon resins manufacturing
334517	Fluoroscopes manufacturing
334517	Fluoroscopic X-ray apparatus and tubes manufacturing
212393	Fluorspar mining and/or beneficiating
335110	Fluroescent lamp electrodes, cold cathode, manufacturing
332998	Flush tanks, metal, manufacturing
332913	Flush valves, plumbing, manufacturing
339992	Flutes and parts manufacturing
325998	Fluxes (e.g., brazing, galvanizing, soldering, welding) manufacturing
325320	Fly sprays manufacturing
332999	Fly swatters, metal, manufacturing
541870	Flyer direct distribution (except direct mail) services
713990	Flying clubs, recreational
488119	Flying field operators
611512	Flying instruction
335129	Flytraps, electrical, manufacturing
336312	Flywheels and ring gears, automotive and truck gasoline engine, manufacturing
326150	Foam plastics products (except polystrene) manufacturing
326140	Foam polystyrene products manufacturing
422990	Foam rubber wholesaling
422610	Foam, plastics, wholesaling
322223	Foil bags made from purchased foil
332999	Foil containers (except bags) manufacturing
332999	Foil not made in rolling mills
322225	Foil sheet, laminating purchased foil sheets for packaging applications
331315	Foil, aluminum, made by flat rolling purchased aluminum
331315	Foil, aluminum, made in integrated secondary smelting and flat rolling mills
331421	Foil, copper, made from purchased metal or scrap
331491	Foil, gold, made by rolling purchased metals or scrap
331491	Foil, nickel, made by rolling purchased metals or scrap
331491	Foil, silver, made by rolling purchased metals or scrap
422120	Folders, file, wholesaling
561910	Folding and packaging services, textile and apparel
322130	Folding boxboard stock manufacturing
322212	Folding boxes (except corrugated) made from purchased paperboard
322212	Folding paper and paperboard containers (except corrugated) made from purchased paperboard
111422	Foliage growing
711120	Folk dance companies
711510	Folk dancers, independent
445110	Food (i.e., groceries) stores
446191	Food (i.e., health) supplement stores
336999	Food (vendor) carts on wheels manufacturing
624210	Food banks
722330	Food carts, mobile
333294	Food choppers, grinders, mixers, and slicers (i.e., food manufacturing-type) manufacturing
325132	Food coloring, synthetic, manufacturing
311942	Food colorings, natural, manufacturing

Code	Description
722310	Food concession contractors (e.g., convention facilities, entertainment facilities, sporting facilities)
322299	Food containers made from molded pulp
326140	Food containers, polystyrene foam, manufacturing
322215	Food containers, sanitary (except folding), made from purchased paper or paperboard
322212	Food containers, sanitary, folding, made from purchased paperboard
333294	Food dehydrating equipment (except household-type) manufacturing
923130	Food distribution program administration, government
311942	Food extracts (except coffee, meat) manufacturing
926140	Food inspection agencies
811310	Food machinery repair and maintenance services
335211	Food mixers, household-type electric, manufacturing
333993	Food packaging machinery manufacturing
327213	Food packaging, glass, manufacturing
421830	Food processing machinery and equipment wholesaling
233310	Food products manufacturing or packaging plant construction
541710	Food research and development laboratories or services
722310	Food service contractors, airline
722310	Food service contractors, cafeteria
722310	Food service contractors, concession operator (e.g., convention facilities, entertainment facilities, sporting facilities)
421440	Food service equipment (except refrigerated), commercial, wholesaling
923120	Food service health inspections
326111	Food storage bags, plastics film, single wall or multiwall, manufacturing
541380	Food testing laboratories or services
322299	Food trays, molded pulp, manufacturing
333319	Food warming equipment, commercial-type, manufacturing
335228	Food waste disposal units, household-type, manufacturing
311991	Food, prepared, perishable, packaged for individual resale
339113	Foot appliances, orthopedic, manufacturing
621391	Foot specialists (podiatry) offices (e.g., centers, clinics)
711211	Football clubs, professional or semiprofessional
713990	Football clubs, recreational
339920	Football equipment and supplies (except footwear, uniforms) manufacturing
421910	Football equipment and supplies wholesaling
611620	Football instruction, camps, or schools
711211	Football teams, professional or semiprofessional
316211	Footholds, plastics or plastics soled fabric upper, manufacturing
316211	Footholds, rubber or rubber soled fabric upper, manufacturing
315119	Footies, sheer, knitting or knitting and finishing
451110	Footwear (e.g., bowling, golf, spiked), specialty sports, stores

Code	Description
316211	Footwear (except house slippers), plastics or plastics soled fabric uppers, manufacturing
333298	Footwear making or repairing machinery manufacturing
326199	Footwear parts (e.g., heels, soles), plastics, manufacturing
326299	Footwear parts (e.g., heels, soles, soling strips), rubber, manufacturing
422340	Footwear wholesaling
316219	Footwear, athletic (except rubber or plastics soled with fabric upper), manufacturing
316219	Footwear, children's (except house slippers, orthopedic extension, plastics, rubber), manufacturing
316219	Footwear, children's, leather or vinyl upper with rubber or plastics soles, manufacturing
316213	Footwear, men's (except house slippers, athletic, orthopedic extension, plastics, rubber), manufacturing
316213	Footwear, men's leather or vinyl upper with rubber or plastics soles, manufacturing
316214	Footwear, women's (except house slippers, athletic, orthopedic extension, plastics, rubber) manufacturing
316214	Footwear, women's leather or vinyl upper with rubber or plastics soles, manufacturing
339112	Forceps, surgical, manufacturing
523130	Foreign currency exchange dealing (i.e., acting as a principal in dealing commodities to investors)
523130	Foreign currency exchange services (i.e., selling to the public)
928120	Foreign economic and social development services, government
928120	Foreign government service
611630	Foreign language schools
928120	Foreign missions
541380	Forensic (except medical) laboratories or services
621511	Forensic laboratories, medical
621111	Forensic pathologists' offices (e.g., centers, clinics)
531190	Forest land rental or leasing
115310	Forest management plans preparation
113210	Forest nurseries for reforestation, growing trees
421990	Forest products (except lumber) wholesaling
484230	Forest products trucking, long-distance
532412	Forestry machinery and equipment rental or leasing
811310	Forestry machinery and equipment repair and maintenance services
421810	Forestry machinery and equipment wholesaling
541710	Forestry research and development laboratories or services
115310	Forestry services
333513	Forging machinery and hammers manufacturing
332111	Forgings made from purchased iron or steel, unfinished
331111	Forgings, iron or steel, made in steel mills
811310	Forklift repair and maintenance services
421830	Forklift trucks (except log) wholesaling
333924	Forklifts manufacturing
332212	Forks, handtools (e.g., garden, hay, manure), manufacturing

Forks—Frozen

Code	Description	Code	Description	Code	Description
332211	Forks, table, nonprecious and precious plated metal, manufacturing	332999	Fountains (except drinking), metal, manufacturing	541614	Freight rate consulting services
331222	Form ties made in wire drawing plants	332998	Fountains, drinking (except mechanically refrigerated), manufacturing	483113	Freight shipping on the Great Lakes system (including the St Lawrence Seaway)
315211	Formal jackets, men's and boys', cut and sew apparel contractors	421720	Fountains, drinking (except refrigerated), wholesaling	541614	Freight traffic consulting services
315222	Formal jackets, men's and boys', cut and sewn from purchased fabric (except apparel contractors)	421740	Fountains, drinking, refrigerated, wholesaling	481212	Freight transportation, air, charter services
532220	Formal wear rental	327420	Fountains, plaster of paris, manufacturing	481212	Freight transportation, air, nonscheduled
325199	Formaldehyde manufacturing			483113	Freight transportation, deep sea, to and from domestic ports
325199	Formalin manufacturing	333415	Fountains, refrigerated drinking, manufacturing	483111	Freight transportation, deep sea, to or from foreign ports
325199	Formic acid manufacturing	713920	Four season ski resorts without accommodations	483211	Freight transportation, inland waters (except on Great Lakes system)
333513	Forming machines (except drawing), metalworking, manufacturing	333291	Fourdrinier machinery manufacturing	311411	French fries, frozen, pre-cooked, manufacturing
327112	Forms for dipped rubber products, pottery, manufacturing	332618	Fourdrinier wire cloth made from purchased wire	311412	French toast, frozen, manufacturing
235990	Forms for poured concrete construction contractors	112930	Fox production	335312	Frequency converters (i.e., electric generators) manufacturing
421420	Forms handling machines wholesaling	335312	Fractional horsepower electric motors manufacturing	334515	Frequency meters (e.g., electrical, electronic, mechanical) manufacturing
332322	Forms, concrete, sheet metal, manufacturing	333298	Fractionating equipment, chemical, manufacturing	334515	Frequency synthesizers manufacturing
321999	Forms, display, boot and shoe, all materials, manufacturing	211112	Fractionating natural gas liquids	235420	Fresco construction contractors
422120	Forms, paper (e.g., business, office, sales), wholesaling	333319	Frame and body alignment equipment, motor vehicle, manufacturing	422460	Fresh fish wholesaling
312130	Fortified wines manufacturing	332999	Frames and handles, handbag and luggage, metal, manufacturing	422480	Fresh fruits, vegetables and berries wholesaling
812990	Fortune-telling services	421220	Frames and pictures wholesaling	422470	Fresh meats wholesaling
624110	Foster care placement agencies	339942	Frames for artist's canvases (i.e., stretchers) manufacturing	422440	Fresh poultry wholesaling
624110	Foster home placement services			422460	Fresh seafood wholesaling
235410	Foundation (e.g., block, brick, stone) construction contractors	333292	Frames for textile making machinery manufacturing	339992	Fretted instruments and parts manufacturing
235930	Foundation digging (i.e., excavation) construction contractors	332321	Frames, door and window, metal, manufacturing	313221	Fringes weaving
235930	Foundation drilling construction contractors	321911	Frames, door and window, wood, manufacturing	325510	Frit manufacturing
				114119	Frog fishing
315212	Foundation garments, women's and girls', cut and sew apparel contractors	332999	Frames, metal, lamp shade, manufacturing	112519	Frog production, farm raising
315231	Foundation garments, women's, misses', and girls', cut and sewn from purchased fabric (except apparel contractors)	332999	Frames, metal, umbrella and parasol, manufacturing	331111	Frogs, iron or steel, made in steel mills
				811118	Front end alignment shops, automotive
		339999	Frames, mirror and picture, all materials, manufacturing	421820	Frost protection machinery wholesaling
325620	Foundations (i.e., make-up) manufacturing	421460	Frames, ophthalmic, wholesaling	311999	Frosting, prepared, manufacturing
235710	Foundations of buildings, poured concrete, construction contractors	533110	Franchise agreements, leasing, selling or licensing, without providing other services	311411	Frozen ades, drinks and cocktail mixes, manufacturing
331528	Foundries (except die-casting), nonferrous metals (except aluminum, copper)	813410	Fraternal associations or lodges, social or civic	311812	Frozen bread and bread-type rolls, made in commercial bakeries
		524113	Fraternal life insurance organizations	311813	Frozen cake manufacturing
		813410	Fraternal lodges	311411	Frozen citrus pulp manufacturing
331524	Foundries, aluminum (except die-casting)	813410	Fraternal organizations	311520	Frozen custard manufacturing
331525	Foundries, brass, bronze, and copper (except die-casting) manufacturing	813410	Fraternities (except residential)	722213	Frozen custard stands, fixed location
		721310	Fraternity houses	311520	Frozen desserts (except bakery) manufacturing
331525	Foundries, copper (except die-casting)	621493	Freestanding ambulatory surgical centers and clinics		
331521	Foundries, die-casting, aluminum			311412	Frozen dinners (except seafood-based) manufacturing
331522	Foundries, die-casting, nonferrous metals (except aluminum)	621493	Freestanding emergency medical centers and clinics	311822	Frozen doughs made from purchased flour
331511	Foundries, iron (i.e., ductile, gray, malleable, semisteel)	311423	Freeze-dried, food processing, fruits and vegetables	422460	Frozen fish (except packaged) wholesaling
331513	Foundries, steel (except investment)	335222	Freezers, chest and upright household-type, manufacturing	454390	Frozen food and freezer plan providers, direct selling
331512	Foundries, steel investment	421620	Freezers, household-type, wholesaling	326111	Frozen food bags, plastics film, single wall or multiwall, manufacturing
333511	Foundry casting molds manufacturing	333415	Freezing equipment, industrial and commercial-type, manufacturing	311412	Frozen food entrees (except seafood based), packaged, manufacturing
325998	Foundry core oil, wash, and wax manufacturing	311712	Freezing fish (e.g., blocks, fillets, ready-to-serve products)	422420	Frozen foods, packaged (except dairy products), wholesaling
332997	Foundry cores manufacturing	488210	Freight car cleaning services	311411	Frozen fruit and vegetable processing
811310	Foundry machinery and equipment repair and maintenance services	481112	Freight carriers (except air couriers), air, scheduled	311411	Frozen fruits, fruit juices, and vegetables, manufacturing
421830	Foundry machinery and equipment wholesaling	481212	Freight charter services, air	311612	Frozen meat pies (i.e., tourtires) made from purchased carcasses
332997	Foundry pattern making	488510	Freight forwarding	445210	Frozen meat stores
421510	Foundry products wholesaling	482111	Freight railways, line-haul	422470	Frozen meats (except packaged) wholesaling
212322	Foundry sand quarrying and/or beneficiating	482112	Freight railways, short-line or beltline	311412	Frozen pizza manufacturing
422450	Fountain fruits and syrups wholesaling	541614	Freight rate auditor services	311412	Frozen pot pies manufacturing
335129	Fountain lighting fixtures manufacturing				
339941	Fountain pens manufacturing				

Code	Description
422440	Frozen poultry (except packaged) wholesaling
311412	Frozen rice dishes manufacturing
422460	Frozen seafood (except packaged) wholesaling
311412	Frozen side dishes manufacturing
311412	Frozen soups (except seafood) manufacturing
311412	Frozen waffles manufacturing
111336	Fruit and tree nut combination farming
445230	Fruit and vegetable stands, permanent
311423	Fruit and vegetables, dehydrating, manufacturing
321920	Fruit baskets, veneer and splint, manufacturing
311421	Fruit brining
311421	Fruit butters manufacturing
321920	Fruit crates, wood, wirebound, manufacturing
312111	Fruit drinks (except juice), manufacturing
311942	Fruit extracts (except coffee) manufacturing
111419	Fruit farming, grown under cover
311211	Fruit flour, meal, and powders, manufacturing
333111	Fruit harvesting machines manufacturing
311421	Fruit juice canning
311411	Fruit juice concentrates, frozen, manufacturing
311421	Fruit juices, fresh, manufacturing
445230	Fruit markets
311340	Fruit peel products (e.g., candied, crystallized, glace, glazed) manufacturing
311421	Fruit pickling
311421	Fruit pie fillings, canned
311421	Fruit pie fillings, canning
311520	Fruit pops, frozen, manufacturing
115114	Fruit precooling
115114	Fruit sorting, grading, and packing
445230	Fruit stands, permanent
454390	Fruit stands, temporary
111421	Fruit stock (e.g., plants, seedlings, trees) growing
311930	Fruit syrups, flavoring, manufacturing
115113	Fruit, machine harvesting
115114	Fruit, sun drying
115114	Fruit, vacuum cooling
311340	Fruits (e.g., candied, crystallized, glazed) manufacturing
326199	Fruits and vegetables, artificial, plastics, manufacturing
311423	Fruits dehydrating (except sun drying)
311421	Fruits pickling
339999	Fruits, artificial (except glass, plastics), manufacturing
327215	Fruits, artificial, made from purchased glass
327212	Fruits, artificial, made in glass making plants
311421	Fruits, canned, manufacturing
422490	Fruits, canned, wholesaling
422480	Fruits, fresh, wholesaling
311411	Fruits, frozen, manufacturing
422420	Fruits, frozen, wholesaling
112320	Fryer chicken production
335211	Fryers, household-type electric, manufacturing
311320	Fudge, chocolate, made from cacao beans
311330	Fudge, chocolate, made from purchased chocolate
311340	Fudge, nonchocolate, manufacturing

Code	Description
326299	Fuel bladders, rubber, manufacturing
324199	Fuel briquettes or boulets made from refined petroleum
335999	Fuel cells, electrochemical generators, manufacturing
334413	Fuel cells, solid-state, manufacturing
334519	Fuel densitometers, aircraft engine, manufacturing
336312	Fuel injection systems and parts, automotive and truck gasoline engine, manufacturing
334519	Fuel mixture indicators, aircraft engine, manufacturing
454311	Fuel oil (i.e., heating) dealers, direct selling
422710	Fuel oil bulk stations and terminals
235110	Fuel oil burner construction contractors
422720	Fuel oil truck jobbers
422720	Fuel oil wholesaling (except bulk stations, terminals)
324110	Fuel oils manufacturing
325188	Fuel propellants, solid inorganic, not specified elsewhere by process, manufacturing
325199	Fuel propellants, solid organic, not specified elsewhere by process, manufacturing
336322	Fuel pumps, electric, automotive, truck, and bus, manufacturing
336312	Fuel pumps, mechanical, automotive and truck gasoline engine, manufacturing
334519	Fuel system instruments, aircraft, manufacturing
334519	Fuel totalizers, aircraft engine, manufacturing
421520	Fuel, coal and coke, wholesaling
422720	Fueling aircraft (except on contract basis)
488190	Fueling aircraft on a contract or fee basis
324110	Fuels, jet, manufacturing
321113	Fuel wood made from sawmill waste
722110	Full service restaurants
212325	Fuller's earth mining and/or beneficiating
327992	Fuller's earth processing beyond beneficiating
332313	Fumigating chambers, fabricated metal plate work, manufacturing
115114	Fumigating grain
561710	Fumigating services
334515	Function generators manufacturing
561499	Fundraising campaign organization services on a contract or fee basis
334119	Funds transfer devices manufacturing
525110	Funds, employee benefit pension
525120	Funds, health and welfare
525990	Funds, mutual, closed-end
525910	Funds, mutual, open-ended
525110	Funds, pension
525190	Funds, self-insurance (except employee benefit funds)
812210	Funeral director services
812210	Funeral homes
812210	Funeral homes combined with crematories
524128	Funeral insurance carriers, direct
812210	Funeral parlors
325320	Fungicides manufacturing
315292	Fur accessories and trimings (except apparel contractors) manufacturing
315211	Fur accessories and trimings, men's and boys', cut and sew apparel contractors

Code	Description
315212	Fur accessories and trimings, women's, girls', and infants', cut and sew apparel contractors
315292	Fur apparel (e.g., capes, coats, hats, jackets, neckpieces) (except apparel contractors) manufacturing
315211	Fur apparel (e.g., capes, coats, hats, jackets, neckpieces), men's and boys', cut and sew apparel contractors
315212	Fur apparel (e.g., capes, coats, hats, jackets, neckpieces), women's, girls', and infants', cut and sew apparel contractors
448190	Fur apparel stores
112930	Fur bearing animal production
315292	Fur clothing (except apparel contractors) manufacturing
422330	Fur clothing wholesaling
315211	Fur clothing, men's and boys', cut and sew apparel contractors
315212	Fur clothing, women's, girls', and infants', cut and sew apparel contractors
421930	Fur cuttings and scraps wholesaling
541490	Fur design services
315211	Fur finishers, liners, and buttonhole makers, men's and boys', cut and sew apparel contractors
315212	Fur finishers, liners, and buttonhole makers, women's, girls', and infants', cut and sew apparel contractors
812320	Fur garment cleaning services
811490	Fur garment repair shops without retailing new fur garments
315292	Fur plates and trimmings (except apparel contractors) manufacturing
315211	Fur plates and trimmings, men's and boys', cut and sew apparel contractors
315212	Fur plates and trimmings, women's, girls', and infants', cut and sew apparel contractors
532220	Fur rental
493120	Fur storage warehousing for the trade
316110	Fur stripping
325182	Furnace black manufacturing
332322	Furnace casings, sheet metal, manufacturing
235110	Furnace construction contractors
333411	Furnace filters manufacturing
332322	Furnace flues, sheet metal, manufacturing
234930	Furnace for industrial plant construction
333414	Furnaces (except forced air), heating, manufacturing
333994	Furnaces and ovens, semiconductor wafer, manufacturing
421720	Furnaces, (except forced air), heating, wholesaling
339114	Furnaces, dental laboratory, manufacturing
333414	Furnaces, floor and wall, manufacturing
421830	Furnaces, industrial process, wholesaling
333994	Furnaces, industrial-type, manufacturing
339111	Furnaces, laboratory-type (except dental), manufacturing
333415	Furnaces, warm air (i.e., forced air), manufacturing
421730	Furnaces, warm air (i.e., forced air), wholesaling
333994	Furnances and ovens for drying and redrying, industrial process-type, manufacturing
422320	Furnishings (except shoes), men's and boys', wholesaling

Furnishings—Garbage

Code	Description
422330	Furnishings (except shoes), women's, girls' and infants', wholesaling
448150	Furnishings stores, men's and boys'
448150	Furnishings stores, women's and girls'
421210	Furniture (except drafting tables, hospital beds, medical furniture) wholesaling
337124	Furniture (except upholstered), metal household-type, manufacturing
337214	Furniture (except wood), office-type, padded, upholstered, or plain, manufacturing
337125	Furniture (except wood, metal, upholstered) indoor and outdoor household-type, manufacturing
532299	Furniture (i.e., residential) rental centers
442110	Furniture and appliance stores (i.e., primarily retailing furniture)
561740	Furniture cleaning on customers' premises
561740	Furniture cleaning services
541420	Furniture design services
321912	Furniture dimension stock, hardwood, unfinished, manufacturing
321912	Furniture dimension stock, softwood, unfinished, manufacturing
321912	Furniture dimension stock, unfinished wood, manufacturing
337215	Furniture frames and parts, metal, manufacturing
337215	Furniture frames, wood, manufacturing
332510	Furniture hardware, metal, manufacturing
321999	Furniture inlays manufacturing
484210	Furniture moving, used
421210	Furniture parts wholesaling
337215	Furniture parts, finished metal, manufacturing
337215	Furniture parts, finished plastics, manufacturing
337215	Furniture parts, finished wood, manufacturing
325612	Furniture polishes and waxes manufacturing
811420	Furniture refinishing shops
811420	Furniture repair shops
811420	Furniture reupholstering shops
332612	Furniture springs, unassembled, made from purchased wire
321912	Furniture squares, unfinished hardwood, manufacturing
442110	Furniture stores (e.g., household, office, outdoor)
453310	Furniture stores, used
327215	Furniture tops, glass (e.g., beveled, cut, polished), made from purchased glass
314999	Furniture trimmings made from purchased fabrics
327991	Furniture, cut stone (i.e., benches, tables, church)
337127	Furniture, factory-type (e.g., cabinets, stools, tool stands, work benches), manufacturing
532291	Furniture, home health, rental
339111	Furniture, hospital (e.g., hospital beds, operating room furniture), manufacturing
337121	Furniture, household-type, upholstered on frames of any material, manufacturing
532490	Furniture, institutional (i.e. public building), rental or leasing
337127	Furniture, institutional, manufacturing
339111	Furniture, laboratory-type (e.g., benches, cabinets, stools, tables), manufacturing
532420	Furniture, office, rental or leasing
337211	Furniture, office-type, padded, upholstered, or plain wood, manufacturing
337124	Furniture, outdoor metal household-type (e.g., beach, garden, lawn, porch), manufacturing
337122	Furniture, outdoor wood household-type (e.g., beach, garden, lawn, porch), manufacturing
337127	Furniture, public building (e.g., church, library, school, theater), manufacturing
532299	Furniture, residential, rental or leasing
337127	Furniture, restaurant-type, manufacturing
337122	Furniture, unassembled or knock-down wood household-type, manufacturing
337122	Furniture, unfinished wood household-type, manufacturing
337122	Furniture, wood household-type, not upholstered (except TV and radio housings, and sewing machine cabinets), manufacturing
448190	Furriers
332323	Furring channels, sheet metal, manufacturing
316110	Furs, dressed (e.g., bleached, curried, dyed, scraped, tanned), manufacturing
422990	Furs, dressed, wholesaling
422590	Furs, raw, wholesaling
335313	Fuse clips and blocks, electric, manufacturing
335931	Fuse cutouts, manufacturing
335313	Fuse mountings, electric power, manufacturing
332993	Fuses ammunition (i.e., more than 30 mm., more than 1.18 inch) manufacturing
421610	Fuses, electric, wholesaling
335313	Fuses, electrical, manufacturing
325191	Fustic wood extract manufacturing
337122	Futon frames manufacturing
523140	Futures commodity contracts brokerages
523140	Futures commodity contracts brokers' offices
523130	Futures commodity contracts dealing (i.e., acting as a principal in dealing commodities to investors)
523210	Futures commodity contracts exchanges
335931	GFCI (ground fault circuit interrupters) manufacturing
522294	GNMA (Government National Mortgage Association)
334220	GPS (global positioning system) equipment manufacturing
212319	Gabbro crushed and broken stone mining and/or beneficiating
212311	Gabbro mining or quarrying
316211	Gaitors, plastics or plastics soled fabric upper, manufacturing
316211	Gaitors, rubber or rubber soled fabric upper, manufacturing
212231	Galena mining and/or beneficiating
712110	Galleries, art (except retail)
453920	Galleries, art, retail
713990	Galleries, shooting
316211	Galoshes, plastics or plastics soled fabric upper, manufacturing
316211	Galoshes, rubber, or rubber soled fabric upper, manufacturing
333516	Galvanizing machinery manufacturing
331111	Galvanizing metals and metal formed products made in steel mills
332812	Galvanizing metals and metal products for the trade
334515	Galvanometers (except geophysical) manufacturing
334519	Galvanometers, geophysical, manufacturing
325191	Gambier extract manufacturing
921130	Gambling control boards, nonoperating
713290	Gambling control boards, operating gambling activities
713210	Gambling cruises
713290	Gambling device arcades or parlors, coin-operated
713290	Gambling device concession operators (i.e., supplying and servicing in others' facilities), coin-operated
924120	Game and inland fish agencies
334611	Game cartridge software, mass reproducing
114210	Game preserves, commercial
114210	Game propagation
114210	Game retreats
421430	Game software wholesaling
451120	Game stores (including electronic)
924120	Game wardens
339932	Games (except coin operated), children's and adult, manufacturing
421920	Games (except coin-operated) wholesaling
339999	Games, coin-operated, manufacturing
421990	Games, coin-operated, wholesaling
334611	Games, computer software, mass reproducing
511210	Games, computer software, publishing
334517	Gamma ray irradiation equipment manufacturing
212319	Ganister crushed and broken stone mining and/or beneficiating
235510	Garage door construction contractors
335999	Garage door openers manufacturing
332321	Garage doors, metal, manufacturing
321911	Garage doors, wood, manufacturing
233320	Garage, commercial or institutional, construction contractors
812930	Garages, automobile parking
811198	Garages, do-it-yourself automotive repair
811111	Garages, general automotive repair (except gasoline service stations)
332311	Garages, prefabricated metal, manufacturing
321992	Garages, prefabricated wood, manufacturing
332439	Garbage cans, light gauge metal, manufacturing
562111	Garbage collection services
562213	Garbage disposal combustors or incinerators
562212	Garbage disposal landfills
421440	Garbage disposal unites, commercial-type, wholesaling
333319	Garbage disposal units, commercial-type, manufacturing
335228	Garbage disposal units, household-type, manufacturing
421620	Garbage disposal units, household-type, wholesaling
562212	Garbage dumps
562111	Garbage hauling, local
333994	Garbage incinerators (except precast concrete) manufacturing
327390	Garbage incinerators, precast concrete, manufacturing

Code	Description
562111	Garbage pick-up services
336211	Garbage truck bodies manufacturing
336120	Garbage trucks assembling on chassis of own manufacture
336211	Garbage trucks assembling on purchased chassis
111130	Garbanzo farming, dry, field and seed production
444220	Garden centers
813410	Garden clubs
811411	Garden equipment repair and maintenance services without retailing new garden equipment
327390	Garden furniture, precast concrete, manufacturing
327991	Garden furniture, stone, manufacturing
337122	Garden furniture, wood, manufacturing
326220	Garden hose, rubber or plastics, manufacturing
421820	Garden machinery and equipment wholesaling
333112	Garden machinery and equipment, powered, manufacturing
561730	Garden maintenance services
541320	Garden planning services
327112	Garden pottery manufacturing
444210	Garden power equipment stores
422910	Garden supplies (e.g., fertilizers, pesticides) wholesaling
811411	Garden tool sharpening and repair services
532490	Garden tractor rental or leasing
339999	Garden umbrellas manufacturing
712130	Gardens, zoological or botanical
111219	Garlic farming (except under cover), field, bedding plant and seed production
111419	Garlic farming under cover
811490	Garment alteration and/or repair shops without retailing new garments
812320	Garment cleaning (e.g., fur, leather, suede) services
321999	Garment hangers, wood, manufacturing
316110	Garment leather manufacturing
314911	Garment storage bags manufacturing
315292	Garments, leather or sheep-lined (except apparel contractors), manufacturing
315211	Garments, leather or sheep-lined, men's and boys', cut and sew apparel contractors
315212	Garments, leather or sheep-lined, women's, girls', and infants', cut and sew apparel contractors
313320	Garments, oiling (i.e., waterproofing)
212399	Garnet mining and/or beneficiating
333292	Garnetting machinery for textiles manufacturing
314999	Garnetting of textile waste and rags
315212	Garter belts cut and sew apparel contractors
315231	Garter belts cut and sewn from purchased fabric (except apparel contractors)
315212	Garters, women's, cut and sew apparel contractors
315231	Garters, women's, misses', and girls', cut and sewn from purchased fabric (except apparel contractors)
334513	Gas analyzers, industrial process-type, manufacturing
334516	Gas analyzers, laboratory-type, manufacturing
334513	Gas and liquid analysis instruments, industrial process-type, manufacturing

Code	Description
334512	Gas burner automatic controls (except valves) manufacturing
333414	Gas burners, heating, manufacturing
334513	Gas chromatographic instruments, industrial process-type, manufacturing
334516	Gas chromatographic instruments, laboratory-type, manufacturing
333414	Gas fireplaces manufacturing
421720	Gas fireplaces wholesaling
334513	Gas flow instrumentation, industrial process-type, manufacturing
333999	Gas generating machinery, general purpose-type, manufacturing
421720	Gas hot water heaters wholesaling
334519	Gas leak detectors manufacturing
235990	Gas leakage detection contractors
523999	Gas lease brokers' offices
335129	Gas lighting fixtures manufacturing
421990	Gas lighting fixtures wholesaling
235110	Gas line hookup construction contractors
333298	Gas liquefying machinery manufacturing
234910	Gas main construction
339113	Gas masks manufacturing
561990	Gas meter reading services, contract
421720	Gas ranges wholesaling
333319	Gas ranges, commercial-type, manufacturing
335221	Gas ranges, household-type, manufacturing
333999	Gas separating machinery manufacturing
333414	Gas space heaters manufacturing
332420	Gas storage tanks, heavy gauge metal, manufacturing
336399	Gas tanks assembled, automotive, truck, and bus, manufacturing
333611	Gas turbine generator set units manufacturing
333611	Gas turbines (except aircraft) manufacturing
336412	Gas turbines, aircraft, manufacturing
332911	Gas valves, industrial-type, manufacturing
333992	Gas welding equipment manufacturing
333992	Gas welding rods, coated or cored, manufacturing
213111	Gas well drilling on a contract basis
333132	Gas well machinery and equipment manufacturing
213112	Gas well rig building, repairing, and dismantling on a contract basis
213112	Gas, compressing natural, in the field on a contract basis
221210	Gas, manufactured, production and distribution
221210	Gas, mixed natural and manufactured, production and distribution
211112	Gas, natural liquefied petroleum, extraction
221210	Gas, natural, distribution
211111	Gas, natural, extraction
211112	Gas, natural, liquids, extraction
486210	Gas, natural, pipeline operation
211112	Gas, residue, extraction
333414	Gas-oil burners, combination, manufacturing
422690	Gases, compressed and liquefied (except liquefied petroleum gas), wholesaling
325120	Gases, industrial (i.e., compressed, liquefied, solid), manufacturing
211112	Gases, petroleum, liquefied, extraction
339991	Gasket, packing, and sealing devices manufacturing

Code	Description
339991	Gaskets manufacturing
421840	Gaskets wholesaling
334514	Gasmeters, consumption registering, manufacturing
334514	Gasmeters, large capacity, domestic and industrial, manufacturing
422710	Gasoline bulk stations and terminals
334514	Gasoline dispensing meters (except pumps) manufacturing
336412	Gasoline engine parts (except carburetors, pistons, piston rings, valves), aircraft, manufacturing
336312	Gasoline engine parts (except carburetors, pistons, piston rings, valves), automotive and truck, manufacturing
333618	Gasoline engines (except aircraft, automotive, truck) manufacturing
336412	Gasoline engines, aircraft, manufacturing
336312	Gasoline engines, automotive and truck, manufacturing
324110	Gasoline made in petroleum refineries
421120	Gasoline marketing equipment wholesaling
333913	Gasoline measuring and dispensing pumps manufacturing
486910	Gasoline pipeline transportation
235990	Gasoline pump construction contractors
421120	Gasoline service station equipment wholesaling
447110	Gasoline stations with convenience stores
447190	Gasoline stations without convenience stores
422720	Gasoline wholesaling (except bulk stations, terminals)
447110	Gasoline with convenience stores
211112	Gasoline, natural, production
313312	Gassing yarn (i.e., singeing)
621111	Gastroenterologists' offices (e.g., centers, clinics)
339112	Gastroscopes (except electromedical) manufacturing
334510	Gastroscopes, electromedical, manufacturing
333999	Gate and bridge lifting machinery manufacturing
332911	Gate valves, industrial-type, manufacturing
332323	Gates, holding, sheet metal, manufacturing
332323	Gates, metal (except wire), manufacturing
113210	Gathering of forest products (e.g., barks, gums, needles, seeds)
113210	Gathering, extracting, and selling tree seeds
332212	Gauge blocks, machinists' precision tools, manufacturing
334514	Gauges (e.g., oil pressure, water temperature, speedometer, tachometer), motor vehicle, manufacturing
334513	Gauges (i.e., analog, digital), industrial process-type, manufacturing
334514	Gauges for computing pressure-temperature corrections manufacturing
333314	Gauges, machinist's precision tool, optical, manufacturing
332212	Gauges, machinists' precision tools (except optical), manufacturing
422210	Gauze wholesaling
339113	Gauze, surgical, made from purchased fabric

Gauzes—Glass

Code	Description	Code	Description	Code	Description
313210	Gauzes, surgical, made in broadwoven fabric mills	532490	Generator rental or leasing	115111	Ginning cotton
321999	Gavels, wood, manufacturing	335312	Generator sets, prime mover (except turbine generator sets), manufacturing	111219	Ginseng farming (except under cover), field, bedding plant and seed production
333512	Gear cutting and finishing machines, metalworking, manufacturing	333611	Generator sets, turbine (e.g., gas, hydraulic, steam), manufacturing	111419	Ginseng farming under cover
332212	Gear pullers, handtools, manufacturing	335311	Generator voltage regulators, electric induction and step-type (except engine electrical equipment), manufacturing	113210	Ginseng gathering
333513	Gear rolling machines, metalworking, manufacturing			327390	Girders and beams, prestressed concrete, manufacturing
333612	Gearmotors (i.e., power transmission equipment) manufacturing	335312	Generators and sets, electric (except internal combustion engine, welding, turbine generator sets), manufacturing	327390	Girders, prestressed concrete, manufacturing
336350	Gears (e.g., crown, pinion, spider), automotive, truck, and bus, manufacturing	335312	Generators for gas-electric and oil-electric vehicles, manufacturing	315192	Girdles and other foundation garments made in apparel knitting mills
333612	Gears, power transmission (except aircraft, motor vehicle), manufacturing	336322	Generators for internal combustion engines manufacturing	315212	Girdles, women's, cut and sew apparel contractors
112390	Geese production	335312	Generators for storage battery chargers (except internal combustion engine and aircraft), manufacturing	315231	Girdles, women's, misses', and girls', cut and sewn from purchased fabric (except apparel contractors)
311615	Geese, processing, fresh, frozen, canned, or cooked			813410	Girl guiding organizations
311615	Geese, slaughtering and dressing	334517	Generators, X-ray, manufacturing	721214	Girls' camps (except day, instructional)
334519	Geiger counters manufacturing	421610	Generators, electrical (except motor vehicle), wholesaling	611620	Girls' camps, sports instruction
325998	Gelatin capsules, empty, manufacturing	421120	Generators, motor vehicle electrical, new, wholesaling	713990	Girls' day camps (except instructional)
311999	Gelatin dessert preparations manufacturing	421140	Generators, motor vehicle electrical, used, wholesaling	315111	Girls' hosiery, sheer, full length or knee length, knitting and finishing
311999	Gelatin for cooking manufacturing	332995	Generators, smoke, manufacturing	315119	Girls' socks manufacturing
422490	Gelatin, edible, wholesaling	621511	Genetic testing laboratories	325411	Glandular derivatives, uncompounded, manufacturing
422690	Gelatin, inedible, wholesaling	541710	Genetics research and development laboratories or services	325412	Glandular medicinal preparations manufacturing
212399	Gem stone (e.g., amethyst, garnet, agate, ruby, sapphire, jade) mining and/or beneficiating	541690	Geochemical consulting services	325612	Glass and tile cleaning preparations manufacturing
421940	Gem stones wholesaling	321992	Geodesic domes, prefabricated, wood, manufacturing	327215	Glass blanks for electric light bulbs made from purchased glass
333298	Gemstone processing machinery manufacturing	541370	Geodetic surveying services	327212	Glass blanks for electric light bulbs made in glass making plants
812990	Genealogical investigation services	541370	Geographic information system (GIS) base mapping services	235410	Glass block laying construction contractors
921190	General accounting offices, government	541330	Geological engineering services	313210	Glass broadwoven fabrics weaving
811111	General automotive repair shops	213112	Geological exploration (except surveying) for oil and gas on a contract basis	313221	Glass fabrics, narrow woven weaving
112990	General combination animal farming			327212	Glass fiber, textile type, made in glass making plants
111998	General combination crop farming (except fruit and nut combinations, oilseed and grain, vegetable)	541710	Geological research and development laboratories or services	327212	Glass fiber, unsheathed, made in glass making plants
926110	General economics statistical agencies	924120	Geological research program administration	235920	Glass installation (except automotive) construction contractors
484110	General freight trucking, local	541360	Geological surveying services	811122	Glass installation, automotive repair
484122	General freight trucking, long-distance, less-than-truckload (LTL)	541330	Geophysical engineering services	327212	Glass making and blowing by hand
484121	General freight trucking, long-distance, truckload	213112	Geophysical exploration (except surveying) for oil and gas on a contract basis	333298	Glass making machinery (e.g., blowing, forming, molding) manufacturing
541611	General management consulting services	334519	Geophysical instruments manufacturing	327213	Glass packaging containers manufacturing
622110	General medical and surgical hospitals	541360	Geophysical mapping services	327215	Glass products (except packaging containers) made from purchased glass
421990	General merchandise, durable goods, wholesaling	541360	Geophysical surveying services		
422990	General merchandise, nondurable goods, wholesaling	541370	Geospatial mapping services	327212	Glass products (except packaging containers) made in a glass making plants
921190	General public administration	541380	Geotechnical testing laboratories or services		
532310	General rental centers	235810	Geothermal drilling construction contractors	212322	Glass sand quarrying and/or beneficiating
921190	General services departments, government	221330	Geothermal steam production	421930	Glass scrap wholesaling
452990	General stores	325199	Geraniol manufacturing	811122	Glass shops, automotive
493110	General warehousing and storage	331492	Germanium recovering from scrap and/or alloying purchased metals	444190	Glass stores
422210	General-line drugs wholesaling			235920	Glass tinting (except automotive) construction contractors
422410	General-line groceries wholesaling	331419	Germanium refining, primary	811122	Glass tinting, automotive
421840	General-line industrial supplies wholesaling	711510	Ghost writers, independent	235920	Glass work (except automotive) construction contractors
421930	General-line scrap wholesaling	453220	Gift shops		
421830	General-purpose industrial machinery and equipment wholesaling	322222	Gift wrap, laminated foil, made from purchased foil	811122	Glass work, automotive
		322222	Gift wrap, laminated, made from purchased paper	327215	Glass, automotive, made from purchased glass
336322	Generating apparatus and parts for internal combustion engines manufacturing	422120	Gift wrapping paper wholesaling	327212	Glass, automotive, made in glass making plants
		561910	Gift wrapping services		
335312	Generating apparatus and parts, electrical (except internal combustion engine and welding), manufacturing	212399	Gilsonite mining and/or beneficiating	421120	Glass, automotive, wholesaling
		111219	Ginger root farming (except under cover), field, bedding plant and seed production	327211	Glass, plate, made in glass making plants
333992	Generating apparatus and parts, welding, electrical, manufacturing				
335313	Generator control and metering panels, switchgear-type, manufacturing	111419	Ginger root farming under cover	421390	Glass, plate, wholesaling

Code	Description
333314	Glasses, field or opera, manufacturing
327124	Glasshouse refractories manufacturing
322299	Glassine wrapping paper made from purchased paper
322121	Glassine wrapping paper made in paper mills
327215	Glassware for industrial, scientific, and technical use made from purchased glass
327212	Glassware for industrial, scientific, and technical use made in glass making plants
327215	Glassware for lighting fixtures made from purchased glass
327212	Glassware for lighting fixtures made in glass making plants
442299	Glassware stores
327215	Glassware, art decorative and novelty, made from purchased glass
327212	Glassware, art, decorative, and novelty made in glass making plants
327215	Glassware, cutting and engraving, made from purchased glass
421220	Glassware, household-type, wholesaling
421450	Glassware, medical, wholesaling
325188	Glauber's salt manufacturing
212391	Glauber's salt mining and/or beneficiating
325510	Glaziers' putty manufacturing
235990	Glazing concrete surfaces, construction contractors
235920	Glazing construction contractors
315292	Glazing furs
332812	Glazing metals and metal products for the trade
334511	Glide slope instrumentation manufacturing
487990	Glider excursions
336411	Gliders (i.e., aircraft) manufacturing
334220	Global positioning system (GPS) equipment manufacturing
511199	Globe cover and map publishers
511199	Globe cover and map publishers and printing combined
511199	Globe cover and map publishing (i.e., establishments known as publishers)
323112	Globe covers and maps flexographic printing without publishing
323111	Globe covers and maps gravure printing without publishing
323110	Globe covers and maps lithographic (offset) printing without publishing
323119	Globe covers and maps printing (except flexographic, gravure, lithographic, screen) without publishing
323113	Globe covers and maps screen printing without publishing
332911	Globe valves, industrial-type, manufacturing
339999	Globes, geographical, manufacturing
316110	Glove leather manufacturing
315992	Glove linings (except fur), manufacturing
315292	Glove linings, fur (except apparel contractors), manufacturing
315211	Glove linings, fur, men's and boys', cut and sew apparel contractors
315212	Glove linings, fur, women's, girls', and infants', cut and sew apparel contractors
315992	Gloves and mittens (except athletic), leather, fabric, fur, or combinations, cut and sewn from purchased fabric (except apparel contractors)

Code	Description
315211	Gloves and mittens (except athletic), leather, fabric, fur, or combinations, men's and boys', cut and sew apparel contractors
315212	Gloves and mittens (except athletic), leather, fabric, fur, or combinations, women's, girls', and infants', cut and sew apparel contractors
315992	Gloves and mittens, woven or knit, cut and sewn from purchased fabric (except apparel contractors), manufacturing
315212	Gloves and mittens, woven or knit, women's, girls', and infants', cut and sew apparel contractors
315191	Gloves, knit, made in apparel knitting mills
315211	Gloves, leather (except athletic), men's and boys', cut and sew apparel contractors
315212	Gloves, leather (except athletic), women's, girls', and infants', cut and sew apparel contractors
315992	Gloves, leather (except athletic, cut and sewn apparel contractors), manufacturing
422320	Gloves, men's and boys', wholesaling
326199	Gloves, plastics, manufacturing
339113	Gloves, rubber (e.g., electrician's, examination, household-type, surgeon's), manufacturing
339920	Gloves, sport and athletic (e.g., baseball, boxing, racketball, handball), manufacturing
422330	Gloves, women's, children's, and infants', wholesaling
335110	Glow lamp bulbs manufacturing
339114	Glue, dental, manufacturing
325520	Glues (except dental) manufacturing
422690	Glues wholesaling
311221	Gluten feed, flour, and meal, made by wet milling corn
311221	Gluten manufacturing
325611	Glycerin (i.e., glycerol), natural, manufacturing
325199	Glycerin (i.e., glycerol), synthetic, manufacturing
325411	Glycosides, uncompounded, manufacturing
212313	Gneiss crushed and broken stone mining and/or beneficiating
212311	Gneiss mining or quarrying
112420	Goat farming (e.g., meat, milk, mohair production)
422590	Grain wholesaling
713990	Gocart raceways (i.e., amusement rides)
713990	Gocart tracks (i.e., amusement rides)
336999	Gocarts (except children's) manufacturing
421910	Gocarts wholesaling
339932	Gocarts, children's, manufacturing
339115	Goggles (e.g., industrial, safety, sun, underwater) manufacturing
331491	Gold and gold alloy bar, sheet, strip, and tubing made from purchased metals or scrap
332813	Gold and silver plating metals and metal products for the trade
332999	Gold beating (i.e., foil, leaf)
331419	Gold bullion or dore bar produced at primary metal refineries
332999	Gold foil and leaf not made in rolling mills
331491	Gold foil made by rolling purchased metals or scrap

Code	Description
212221	Gold lode mining and/or beneficiating
212221	Gold ore mine site development for own account
212221	Gold ore mining and/or beneficiating plants
212221	Gold ores, concentrates, bullion, and/or precipitates mining and/or beneficiating
212221	Gold placer mining and/or beneficiating
325910	Gold printing inks manufacturing
331492	Gold recovering from scrap and/or alloying purchased metals
331419	Gold refining, primary
331491	Gold rolling and drawing purchased metals or scrap
323121	Gold stamping books for the trade
813410	Golden age clubs
112511	Goldfish production, farm raising
713910	Golf and country clubs
441229	Golf cart dealers, powered
532292	Golf cart rental
421910	Golf carts (except motorized passenger) wholesaling
336999	Golf carts and similar motorized passenger carriers manufacturing
421860	Golf carts, motorized passenger, wholesaling
336999	Golf carts, powered, manufacturing
234990	Golf course construction
541320	Golf course design services
713910	Golf courses (except miniature, pitch-n-putt)
713990	Golf courses, miniature
713990	Golf courses, pitch-n-putt
713990	Golf driving ranges
421910	Golf equipment and supplies wholesaling
611620	Golf instruction, camps, or schools
713990	Golf practice ranges
451110	Golf pro shops
316219	Golf shoes, men's cleated, manufacturing
316219	Golf shoes, women's cleated, manufacturing
711219	Golfers, independent professional (i.e., participating in sports events)
339920	Golfing equipment (e.g., bags, balls, caddy carts, clubs, tees) manufacturing
335999	Gongs, electric, manufacturing
111334	Gooseberry farming
332212	Gouges, woodworking, manufacturing
445299	Gourmet food stores
522294	Government National Mortgage Association (GNMA)
561210	Government base facilities operation support services
522294	Government-sponsored enterprises providing secondary market financing
336312	Governors for automotive gasoline engines manufacturing
921110	Governors' offices
333618	Governors, diesel engine, manufacturing
333618	Governors, gasoline engine (except automotive), manufacturing
333611	Governors, steam, manufacturing
532220	Gown rental
315299	Gowns (e.g., academic, choir, clerical) cut and sewn from purchased fabric (except apparel contractors)
315211	Gowns (e.g., academic, choir, clerical), men's and boys', cut and sew apparel contractors
315212	Gowns (e.g., academic, choir, clerical), women's, and girls', cut and sew apparel contractors

Gowns—Grinding

Code	Description
315212	Gowns, formal, women's and girls', cut and sew apparel contractors
315233	Gowns, formal, women's, misses', and girls', cut and sewn from purchased fabric (except apparel contractors)
315299	Gowns, hospital, surgical and patient, cut and sewn from purchased fabric (except apparel contractors)
315211	Gowns, hospital, surgical and patient, men's and boys', cut and sew apparel contractors
315212	Gowns, hospital, surgical and patient, women's, girls', and infants', cut and sew apparel contractors
315212	Gowns, wedding, women's, cut and sew apparel contractors
315233	Gowns, wedding, women's, misses', and girls', cut and sewn from purchased fabric (except apparel contractors)
333120	Grader attachments manufacturing
333120	Graders, road, manufacturing
234110	Grading construction contractors for highway and street construction
235930	Grading for buildings, construction contractors
333294	Grading, cleaning, and sorting machinery (i.e., food manufacturing-type) manufacturing
333111	Grading, cleaning, and sorting machinery, farm-type, manufacturing
334512	Gradual switches, pneumatic, manufacturing
532220	Graduation cap and gown rental
315299	Graduation caps and gowns cut and sewn from purchased fabric (except apparel contractors)
315211	Graduation caps and gowns, men's and boys', cut and sew apparel contractors
315212	Graduation caps and gowns, women's and girls', cut and sew apparel contractors
311211	Graham flour manufacturing
311821	Graham wafers manufacturing
212399	Grahamite mining and/or beneficiating
312140	Grain alcohol, beverage, manufacturing
325193	Grain alcohol, nonpotable, manufacturing
115114	Grain cleaning
333111	Grain drills manufacturing
115114	Grain drying
233310	Grain elevator construction
422510	Grain elevators wholesaling grain
493130	Grain elevators, storage only
115114	Grain fumigation
115114	Grain grinding (except custom grinding for animal feed)
311119	Grain grinding, custom, for animal feed
484220	Grain hauling, local
484230	Grain hauling, long-distance
488210	Grain leveling and trimming in railroad cars
321999	Grain measures, wood, turned and shaped, manufacturing
333294	Grain milling machinery manufacturing
311211	Grain mills (except animal feed, breakfast cereal, rice)
311119	Grain mills, animal feed
311230	Grain mills, breakfast cereal
311212	Grain mills, rice
333111	Grain stackers manufacturing
422510	Grain wholesaling
311230	Grain, breakfast cereal, manufacturing
312120	Grain, brewers' spent, manufacturing
115113	Grain, machine harvesting

Code	Description
327910	Grains, abrasive, natural and artificial, manufacturing
813410	Granges
235410	Granite (i.e., exterior stonework) construction contractors
212313	Granite beneficiating plants (e.g., grinding or pulverizing)
212313	Granite crushed and broken stone mining and/or beneficiating
212311	Granite mining or quarrying
311320	Granola bars and clusters, chocolate, made from cacao beans
311330	Granola bars and clusters, chocolate, made from purchased chocolate
311340	Granola bars and clusters, nonchocolate, manufacturing
311230	Granola, cereal (except bars and clusters), manufacturing
813211	Grantmaking foundations
311313	Granulated beet sugar manufacturing
311312	Granulated cane sugar made from purchased raw cane sugar
311311	Granulated cane sugar made from sugar cane
333220	Granulator and pelletizer machinery for plastics manufacturing
212319	Granules, slate, mining and/or beneficiating
312130	Grape farming and making wine
111332	Grape farming without making wine
111320	Grapefruit groves
325998	Grapefruit oil manufacturing
311423	Grapes, artificially drying
541430	Graphic art and related design services
541430	Graphic artists, independent
325992	Graphic arts plates, sensitized, manufacturing
611519	Graphic arts schools
541430	Graphic design services
334515	Graphic recording meters, electric, manufacturing
335991	Graphite electrodes and contacts, electric, manufacturing
212399	Graphite mining and/or beneficiating
335991	Graphite specialties for aerospace use (except gaskets) manufacturing
335991	Graphite specialties for electrical use manufacturing
335991	Graphite specialties for mechanical use (except gaskets) manufacturing
327992	Graphite, natural (e.g., ground, pulverized, refined, blended), manufacturing
111940	Grass hay farming
333111	Grass mowing equipment (except lawn and garden) manufacturing
332212	Grass mowing equipment, nonpowered lawn and garden, manufacturing
333112	Grass mowing equipment, powered lawn and garden, manufacturing
111998	Grass seed farming
332323	Gratings (i.e., open steel flooring) manufacturing
333314	Gratings, diffraction, manufacturing
484220	Gravel hauling, local
484230	Gravel hauling, long-distance
212321	Gravel quarrying and/or beneficiating
235710	Gravel walk and driveway construction contractors
541360	Gravity geophysical surveying services
325910	Gravure inks manufacturing
323122	Gravure plate and cylinder preparation services

Code	Description
323111	Gravure printing (except books, manifold business forms, printing grey goods)
333293	Gravure printing presses manufacturing
311422	Gravy canning
311942	Gravy mixes, dry, manufacturing
331511	Gray iron foundries
531190	Grazing land rental or leasing
311613	Grease rendering
339991	Grease seals manufacturing
311225	Grease, inedible, animal and vegetable, refining and blending purchased oils
422990	Greases, inedible animal and vegetable, wholesaling
324191	Greases, petroleum lubricating, made from refined petroleum
325998	Greases, synthetic lubricating, manufacturing
483113	Great Lakes freight transportation
483114	Great Lakes passenger transportation
111219	Green bean farming, field and seed production
111219	Green cowpea farming, field and seed production
111219	Green lima bean farming, field and seed production
111219	Green pea farming, field and seed production
332311	Greenhouses, prefabricated metal, manufacturing
212399	Greensand mining and/or beneficiating
212311	Greenstone mining or quarrying
511191	Greeting card publishers
511191	Greeting card publishers and printing combined
511191	Greeting card publishing (i.e., establishments known as publishers)
453220	Greeting card shops
323112	Greeting cards (e.g., birthday, holiday, sympathy) flexographic printing without publishing
323111	Greeting cards (e.g., birthday, holiday, sympathy) gravure printing without publishing
323110	Greeting cards (e.g., birthday, holiday, sympathy) lithographic (offset) printing without publishing
323119	Greeting cards (e.g., birthday, holiday, sympathy) printing (except flexographic, gravure, lithographic, screen) without publishing
323113	Greeting cards (e.g., birthday, holiday, sympathy) screen printing without publishing
422120	Greeting cards wholesaling
332994	Grenade launchers manufacturing
332993	Grenades, hand or projectile, manufacturing
711212	Greyhound dog racetracks
335211	Griddles and grills, household-type portable electric, manufacturing
332618	Grilles and grillwork made from purchased wire
332323	Grills and grillwork, sheet metal, manufacturing
332323	Grillwork, ornamental metal, manufacturing
333991	Grinders, handheld power-driven, manufacturing
325411	Grinding and milling botanicals (i.e., for medicinal use)
327910	Grinding balls, ceramic, manufacturing
333512	Grinding machines, metalworking, manufacturing

Code	Description
332813	Grinding metal castings for the trade
324191	Grinding oils, petroleum, made from refined petroleum
212399	Grinding pebbles mining and/or beneficiating
212322	Grinding sand quarrying and/or beneficiating
311942	Grinding spices
327910	Grinding wheels manufacturing
212399	Grindstones mining and/or beneficiating
326299	Grips and handles, rubber, manufacturing
311211	Grits and flakes, corn brewer's, manufacturing
212319	Grits crushed and broken stone mining and/or beneficiating
422410	Groceries, general-line, wholesaling
322224	Grocers' bags and sacks made from purchased uncoated paper
326111	Grocery bags, plastics film, single wall or multiwall, manufacturing
333924	Grocery carts made from purchased wire
492210	Grocery delivery services (i.e., independent service from grocery store)
445110	Grocery stores
421840	Grommets wholesaling
326299	Grommets, rubber, manufacturing
812910	Grooming services, animal
335931	Ground clamps (i.e., electric wiring devices) manufacturing
335931	Ground fault circuit interrupters (GFCI) manufacturing
235810	Ground source heat pump construction contractors
322122	Ground wood paper products (e.g., publication and printing paper, tablet stock, wallpaper base) made in newsprint mills
422110	Groundwood paper, bulk, wholesaling
322121	Groundwood paper, coated, laminated, or treated in paper mills
322222	Groundwood paper, coated, made from purchased paper
322121	Groundwood paper, coated, made in paper mills
322122	Groundwood paper, newsprint, made in paper mills
322110	Groundwood pulp manufacturing
624410	Group day care centers, child or infant
623990	Group foster homes for children
623110	Group homes for the disabled with nursing care
623990	Group homes for the disabled without nursing care
623990	Group homes for the hearing impaired
623990	Group homes for the visually impaired
623210	Group homes, mental retardation
621491	Group hospitalization plans providing health care services
524114	Group hospitalization plans without providing health care services
114111	Grouper fishing
235710	Grout construction contractors
335122	Grow light fixtures (except residential) manufacturing
335121	Grow light fixtures, residential, electric, manufacturing
813910	Growers' associations
212393	Guano mining and/or beneficiating
111998	Guar farming
524127	Guaranteeing titles
561612	Guard dog services
812910	Guard dog training services
561612	Guard services

Code	Description
234110	Guardrail construction
332322	Guardrails, sheet metal highway, manufacturing
332323	Guards, bannisters, and railings, sheet metal, manufacturing
332618	Guards, wire, made from purchased wire
111339	Guavas farming
721199	Guest houses
721214	Guest ranches with accommodation facilities
812910	Guide dog training services
713990	Guide services (i.e., fishing, hunting, tourist)
713990	Guide services, fishing
713990	Guide services, hunting
713990	Guide services, tourist
511199	Guide, street map, publishers
511199	Guide, street map, publishers and printing combined
511199	Guide, street map, publishing (i.e., establishments known as publishers)
336415	Guided missile and space vehicle engine manufacturing
541710	Guided missile and space vehicle engine research and development
336414	Guided missile and space vehicle manufacturing
336419	Guided missile and space vehicle parts (except engines) manufacturing
541710	Guided missile and space vehicle parts (except engines) research and development
421860	Guided missiles and space vehicles wholesaling
336414	Guided missiles, complete, assembling
323112	Guides, street map, flexographic printing without publishing
323111	Guides, street map, gravure printing without publishing
323110	Guides, street map, lithographic (offset) printing without publishing
323119	Guides, street map, printing (except flexographic, gravure, lithographic, screen) without publishing
323113	Guides, street map, screen printing without publishing
339992	Guitars and parts, electric and nonelectric, manufacturing
113210	Gum (i.e., forest product) gathering
325191	Gum and wood chemicals manufacturing
422690	Gum and wood chemicals wholesaling
311340	Gum, chewing, manufacturing
422450	Gum, chewing, wholesaling
322222	Gummed paper products (e.g., labels, sheets, tapes) made from purchased paper
422130	Gummed tapes (except cellophane) wholesaling
422120	Gummed tapes, cellophane, wholesaling
332994	Gun barrels (i.e., 30 mm. or less, 1.18 inch or less) manufacturing
332995	Gun barrels (i.e., more than 30 mm., more than 1.18 inch) manufacturing
713990	Gun clubs, recreational
813319	Gun control organizations
334413	Gun effect devices manufacturing
332111	Gun forgings made from purchased iron or steel, unfinished
331111	Gun forgings made in steel mills
332994	Gun magazines (i.e., 30 mm. or less, 1.18 inch or less) manufacturing
332995	Gun magazines (i.e., more than 30 mm., more than 1.18 inch) manufacturing

Code	Description
451110	Gun shops
333314	Gun sighting and fire control equipment and instruments, optical, manufacturing
333314	Gun sights, optical, manufacturing
332612	Gun springs manufacturing
321912	Gun stocks, wood, manufacturing
332510	Gun trigger locks manufacturing
332995	Gun turrets (i.e., more than 30 mm., more than 1.18 inch) manufacturing
325920	Gunpowder manufacturing
421990	Guns (except sporting) wholesaling
332994	Guns (i.e., 30 mm. or less, 1.18 inch or less) manufacturing
332995	Guns (i.e., more than 30 mm., more than 1.18 inch) manufacturing
332994	Guns, BB and pellet, manufacturing
332212	Guns, caulking, nonpowered, manufacturing
421910	Guns, sporting equipment, wholesaling
451110	Gunsmith shops retailing new guns
811490	Gunsmith shops without retailing new guns
235610	Gutter and down spout construction contractors
561790	Gutter cleaning services
332114	Gutters and down spouts sheet metal, custom roll formed, manufacturing
421330	Gutters and down spouts wholesaling
326199	Gutters and down spouts, plastics, manufacturing
234110	Gutters, concrete, street and highway construction
332322	Gutters, sheet metal (except custom roll formed), manufacturing
339920	Gymnasium and playground equipment, manufacturing
713940	Gymnasiums
611620	Gymnastics instruction, camps, or schools
339113	Gynecological supplies and appliances manufacturing
621111	Gynecologists' offices (e.g., centers, clinics)
212399	Gypsite mining and/or beneficiating
327420	Gypsum building products manufacturing
421390	Gypsum building products wholesaling
212399	Gypsum mining and/or beneficiating
327420	Gypsum products (e.g., block, board, plaster, lath, rock, tile) manufacturing
334511	Gyrocompasses manufacturing
334511	Gyrogimbals manufacturing
334511	Gyroscopes manufacturing
311221	HFCS (high fructose corn syrup) manufacturing
325413	HIV test kits manufacturing
621491	HMO (health maintenance organization) medical centers and clinics
334511	HUD (heads-up display) systems, aeronautical, manufacturing
624310	Habilitation job counseling and training, vocational
114111	Haddock fishing
212299	Hafnium mining and/or beneficiating
422310	Hair accessories wholesaling
326299	Hair care products (e.g., combs, curlers), rubber, manufacturing
333111	Hair clippers for animal use, electric, manufacturing
332212	Hair clippers for animal use, nonelectric, manufacturing
335211	Hair clippers for human use, electric, manufacturing

Hair clippers—Hardening

Code	Description
332211	Hair clippers for human use, nonelectric, manufacturing
325620	Hair coloring preparations manufacturing
335211	Hair curlers, household-type electric, manufacturing
332999	Hair curlers, metal, manufacturing
335211	Hair driers, electric (except equipment designed for beauty parlor use), manufacturing
421620	Hair dryers wholesaling
333319	Hair dryers, beauty parlor-type, manufacturing
339999	Hair nets, made from purchased netting
325620	Hair preparations (e.g., conditioners, dyes, rinses, shampoos) manufacturing
422210	Hair preparations (except professional) wholesaling
421850	Hair preparations, professional, wholesaling
812199	Hair removal (i.e., dipilatory, electrolysis) services
812199	Hair replacement services (except by offices of physicians)
325620	Hair sprays manufacturing
812112	Hair stylist salons or shops, unisex or women's
812111	Hair stylist services, men's
812112	Hair stylist services, unisex or women's
812111	Hair stylist shops, men's
812199	Hair weaving services
339994	Hairbrushes manufacturing
422990	Hairbrushes wholesaling
812112	Hairdresser services
812112	Hairdressing salons or shops, unisex or women's
339999	Hairpieces (e.g., toupees, wigs, wiglets) manufacturing
422990	Hairpieces (e.g., toupees, wigs, wiglets) wholesaling
339993	Hairpins (except rubber) manufacturing
326299	Hairpins, rubber, manufacturing
332612	Hairsprings (except clock, watch) manufacturing
114111	Hake fishing
623990	Halfway group homes for delinquents and exoffenders
623220	Halfway houses for patients with mental health illnesses
623220	Halfway houses, substance abuse (e.g., alcoholism, drug addiction)
114111	Halibut fishing
531120	Hall and banquet room, nonresidential, rental or leasing
334413	Hall effect devices manufacturing
531120	Hall, nonresidential, rental or leasing
339912	Hollowware, precious metal, manufacturing
712110	Halls of fame
335110	Halogen light bulbs manufacturing
325192	Halogenated aromatic hydrocarbon derivatives manufacturing
325199	Halogenated hydrocarbon derivatives (except aromatic) manufacturing
311340	Halvah manufacturing
332111	Hammer forgings made from purchased iron or steel, unfinished
332112	Hammer forgings made from purchased nonferrous metals, unfinished
333120	Hammer mill machinery (i.e., rock and ore crushing machines), portable, manufacturing
333131	Hammer mill machinery (i.e., rock and ore crushing machines), stationary, manufacturing
332212	Hammers, handtools, manufacturing
339992	Hammers, piano, manufacturing
321999	Hammers, wood, meat, manufacturing
314999	Hammocks, fabric, manufacturing
337124	Hammocks, metal framed, manufacturing
337122	Hammocks, wood framed, manufacturing
326199	Hampers, laundry, plastics, manufacturing
337125	Hampers, laundry, reed, wicker, rattan, manufacturing
332322	Hampers, laundry, sheet metal, manufacturing
311611	Hams (except poultry) produced in slaughtering plants
311612	Hams, canned, made from purchased carcasses
311615	Hams, poultry, manufacturing
311612	Hams, preserved (except poultry), made from purchased carcasses
327215	Hand blowing purchased glass
333319	Hand dryers, commercial-type, manufacturing
334111	Hand held computers (e.g., PDAs) manufacturing
313249	Hand knitting lace or warp fabric products
812320	Hand laundries
325620	Hand lotions manufacturing
339943	Hand operated stamps (e.g., canceling, postmark, shoe, textile marking), manufacturing
325611	Hand soaps (e.g., hard, liquid, soft) manufacturing
334518	Hand stamps (e.g., date, time), timing mechanism operated, manufacturing
333924	Hand trucks manufacturing
313221	Hand weaving fabric, 12 inches or less (30cm)
313210	Hand weaving fabrics, more than 12 inches (30 cm) in width
316110	Handbag leather manufacturing
448150	Handbag stores
316993	Handbags (except metal), men's, manufacturing
422330	Handbags wholesaling
339911	Handbags, precious metal, manufacturing
316992	Handbags, women's, all materials (except precious metal), manufacturing
713940	Handball club facilities
541870	Handbill direct distribution services
332999	Handcuffs manufacturing
332212	Handheld edge tools (except saws, scissors-type), nonelectric, manufacturing
485991	Handicapped passenger transportation services
611110	Handicapped, schools for, elementary or secondary
611610	Handicrafts instruction
315999	Handkerchiefs (except paper) cut and sewn from purchased fabric
315211	Handkerchiefs (except paper), men's and boys', cut and sew apparel contractors
315212	Handkerchiefs (except paper), women's, girls', and infants', cut and sew apparel contractors
322291	Handkerchiefs, paper, made from purchased paper
321912	Handle blanks, wood, manufacturing
321912	Handle stock, sawed or planed, manufacturing
321999	Handles (e.g., broom, mop, hand tool), wood, manufacturing
422990	Handles (e.g., broom, mop, paint) wholesaling
326199	Handles (e.g., brush, tool, umbrella), plastics, manufacturing
316999	Handles (e.g., luggage, whip), leather, manufacturing
332999	Handles (e.g., parasol, umbrella), metal, manufacturing
327111	Handles, faucet, vitreous china and earthenware, manufacturing
541420	Handtool industrial design services
332212	Handtool metal blades (e.g., putty knives, scrapers, screw drivers) manufacturing
421710	Handtools (except motor vehicle mechanics', machinists' precision) wholesaling
332212	Handtools, machinists' precision, manufacturing
421830	Handtools, machinists' precision, wholesaling
332212	Handtools, motor vehicle mechanics', manufacturing
421120	Handtools, motor vehicle mechanics', wholesaling
333991	Handtools, power-driven, manufacturing
444130	Handtools, power-driven, repair and maintenance services retailing new power-driven handtools
811411	Handtools, power-driven, repair and maintenance services without retailing new power-driven handtools
541990	Handwriting analysis services
541990	Handwriting expert services
336411	Hang gliders manufacturing
233320	Hangar (i.e., aircraft storage buildings) construction
332321	Hangar doors, metal, manufacturing
488119	Hangar rental, aircraft
321999	Hangers, wooden, garment, manufacturing
111422	Hanging basket plant growing
234990	Harbor construction
234990	Harbor dredging construction contractors
488310	Harbor maintenance services (except dredging)
488310	Harbor operation
487210	Harbor sightseeing tours
488330	Harbor tugboat services
213112	Hard banding oil and gas field service on a contract basis
311340	Hard candies manufacturing
212111	Hard coal (except Pennsylvania anthracite) surface mining and/or beneficiating
212113	Hard coal surface mining
212113	Hard coal underground mining
334112	Hard disk drives manufacturing
334613	Hard drive media manufacturing
313210	Hard fiber fabrics, broadwoven, weaving
313111	Hard fiber spun yarns made from purchased fiber
313113	Hard fiber thread manufacturing
313221	Hard fiber, narrow woven, weaving
339113	Hard hats manufacturing
321219	Hardboard manufacturing
332811	Hardening (i.e., heat treating) metals and metal products for the trade

Code	Description
334519	Hardness testing equipment manufacturing
421710	Hardware (except motor vehicle) wholesaling
332618	Hardware cloth, woven wire, made from purchased wire
444130	Hardware stores
421120	Hardware, motor vehicle, wholesaling
326199	Hardware, plastics, manufacturing
335932	Hardware, transmission pole and line, manufacturing
421610	Hardware, transmission pole and line, wholesaling
321912	Hardwood dimension lumber and stock, resawing purchased lumber
325191	Hardwood distillates manufacturing
321211	Hardwood plywood composites manufacturing
321211	Hardwood veneer or plywood manufacturing
339992	Harmonicas manufacturing
334419	Harness assemblies for electronic use manufacturing
711219	Harness drivers
422910	Harness equipment wholesaling
316110	Harness leather manufacturing
332999	Harness parts, metal, manufacturing
711212	Harness racetracks
316999	Harnesses and harness parts, leather, manufacturing
316999	Harnesses, dog, manufacturing
339992	Harps and parts manufacturing
339992	Harpsichords manufacturing
333111	Harrows (e.g., disc, spring, tine) manufacturing
315991	Harvest hats, straw, manufacturing
113210	Harvesting berries or nuts from native and non-cultivated plants
333111	Harvesting machinery and equipment, agriculture, manufacturing
421820	Harvesting machinery and equipment, agriculture, wholesaling
335211	Hassock fans, electric, manufacturing
448150	Hat and cap stores
339999	Hat blocks manufacturing
315991	Hat bodies (e.g., fur-felt, straw, wool-felt) cut and sewn from purchased fabric (except apparel contractors)
315211	Hat bodies (e.g., fur-felt, straw, wool-felt), men's and boys', cut and sew apparel contractors
315212	Hat bodies (e.g., fur-felt, straw, wool-felt), women's, girls', and infants', cut and sew apparel contractors
812320	Hat cleaning services
315999	Hat findings cut and sewn from purchased fabric (except apparel contractors)
315211	Hat findings, men's and boys', cut and sew apparel contractors
315212	Hat findings, women's, girls', and infants', cut and sew apparel contractors
315999	Hat linings and trimmings cut and sewn from purchased fabric (except apparel contractors)
315211	Hat linings and trimmings, men's and boys', cut and sew apparel contractors
315212	Hat linings and trimmings, women's, girls', and infants', cut and sew apparel contractors
112511	Hatcheries, finfish
112340	Hatcheries, poultry
112512	Hatcheries, shellfish
332212	Hatchets manufacturing

Code	Description
315991	Hats (except fur, knitting mill products, leather) cut and sewn from purchased fabric (except apparel contractors)
422320	Hats and caps, men's and boys', wholesaling
422330	Hats and caps, women's, girls' and infants', wholesaling
322299	Hats made from purchased paper
315191	Hats made in apparel knitting mills
315991	Hats, cloth, cut and sewn from purchased fabric (except apparel contractors)
315211	Hats, cloth, men's and boys', cut and sew apparel contractors
315212	Hats, cloth, women's, girls', and infants', cut and sew apparel contractors
315292	Hats, fur (except apparel contractors), manufacturing
315211	Hats, fur, men's and boys', cut and sew apparel contractors
315212	Hats, fur, women's, girls', and infants', cut and sew apparel contractors
315991	Hats, fur-felt, straw, and wool-felt, cut and sewn from purchased fabric (except apparel contractors)
315211	Hats, fur-felt, straw, and wool-felt, men's and boys', cut and sew apparel contractors
315212	Hats, fur-felt, straw, and wool-felt, women's, girls', and infants', cut and sew apparel contractors
315292	Hats, leather (except apparel contractors), manufacturing
315211	Hats, leather, men's and boys', cut and sew apparel contractors
315212	Hats, leather, women's, girls', and infants', cut and sew apparel contractors
315211	Hats, men's and boys', cut and sew apparel contractors
315991	Hats, trimmed, cut and sewn from purchased fabric (except apparel contractors)
315211	Hats, trimmed, men's and boys', cut and sew apparel contractors
315212	Hats, trimmed, women's, girls', and infants', cut and sew apparel contractors
315212	Hats, women's, girls', and infants', cut and sew apparel contractors
333111	Hay balers and presses manufacturing
111940	Hay farming (e.g., alfalfa hay, clover hay, grass hay)
115113	Hay mowing, raking, baling, and chopping
111998	Hay seed farming
422910	Hay wholesaling
311119	Hay, cubed, manufacturing
333111	Haying machines manufacturing
421820	Haying machines wholesaling
562112	Hazardous waste collection services
562211	Hazardous waste disposal facilities
562211	Hazardous waste disposal facilities combined with collection and/or local hauling of hazardous waste
562211	Hazardous waste material disposal facilities
562211	Hazardous waste material treatment facilities
562211	Hazardous waste treatment facilities
562211	Hazardous waste treatment facilities combined with collection and/or local hauling of hazardous waste
111335	Hazelnut farming
551114	Head offices
311212	Head rice manufacturing

Code	Description
624410	Head start programs, separate from schools
315999	Headbands, women's and girls', cut and sewn from purchased fabric (except apparel contractors)
315212	Headbands, women's, girls', and infants', cut and sew apparel contractors
337122	Headboards, wood, manufacturing
321920	Heading, barrel (i.e., cooperage stock), wood, manufacturing
334419	Heads (e.g., recording, read/write), manufacturing
334511	Heads-up display (HUD) systems, aeronautical, manufacturing
446110	Health and beauty aids stores
525120	Health and welfare funds
713940	Health club facilities, physical fitness
422490	Health foods (except fresh fruits, vegetables) wholesaling
422480	Health foods, fresh fruits and vegetables, wholesaling
524114	Health insurance carriers, direct
335110	Health lamp bulbs, infrared and ultraviolet radiation, manufacturing
621491	Health maintenance organization (HMO) medical centers and clinics
233320	Health or athletic club construction
923120	Health planning and development agencies, government
813920	Health professionals' associations
926150	Health professions licensure agencies
923120	Health program administration
541710	Health research and development laboratories or services
813212	Health research fundraising organizations
621999	Health screening services (except by offices of health practitioners)
621111	Health screening services in physicians' offices
721110	Health spas (i.e., physical fitness facilities) with accommodations
713940	Health spas without accommodations, physical fitness
923120	Health statistics centers, government
713940	Health studios, physical fitness
446199	Hearing aid stores
421450	Hearing aids wholesaling
334510	Hearing aids, electronic, manufacturing
621999	Hearing testing services (except by offices of audiologists)
621340	Hearing testing services by offices of audiologists
336211	Hearse bodies manufacturing
532111	Hearse rental
485320	Hearse rental with driver
336111	Hearses assembling on chassis of own manufacture
336211	Hearses assembling on purchased chassis
334510	Heart-lung machine, manufacturing
332410	Heat exchangers manufacturing
235110	Heat pump construction contractors
333415	Heat pumps manufacturing
421730	Heat pumps wholesaling
325992	Heat sensitized (i.e., thermal) paper made from purchased paper
335991	Heat shields, carbon or graphite, manufacturing
332811	Heat treating metals and metal products for the trade
333994	Heat treating ovens, industrial process-type, manufacturing
221330	Heat, steam, distribution
221330	Heated air distribution

Heaters—Holsters

Code	Description
335211	Heaters, portable electric space, manufacturing
421620	Heaters, portable electric, wholesaling
333414	Heaters, space (except portable electric), manufacturing
333414	Heaters, swimming pool, manufacturing
335211	Heaters, tape, manufacturing
333415	Heating and air conditioning combination units manufacturing
334512	Heating and cooling system controls, residential and commercial, manufacturing
421720	Heating boilers, steam and hot water, wholesaling
235110	Heating construction contractors
541330	Heating engineering consulting services
333414	Heating equipment, hot water (except hot water heaters), manufacturing
421720	Heating equipment, hot water, wholesaling
421730	Heating equipment, warm air (i.e. forced air), wholesaling
333415	Heating equipment, warm air (i.e., forced air), manufacturing
454311	Heating oil dealers, direct selling
324110	Heating oils made in petroleum refineries
335211	Heating pads, electric, manufacturing
334512	Heating regulators manufacturing
221330	Heating steam (suppliers of heat) providers
335211	Heating units for electric appliances manufacturing
333414	Heating units, baseboard, manufacturing
234990	Heavy construction equipment rental with operator
532412	Heavy construction equipment rental without operator
611519	Heavy equipment operation schools
611519	Heavy equipment repair training
811310	Heavy machinery and equipment repair and maintenance services
336120	Heavy trucks assembling on chassis of own manufacture
336211	Heavy trucks assembling on purchased chassis
325188	Heavy water (i.e., deuterium oxide) manufacturing
332212	Hedge shears and trimmers, nonelectric, manufacturing
333112	Hedge trimmers, powered, manufacturing
316999	Heel caps, leather or metal, manufacturing
316999	Heel lifts, leather, manufacturing
321999	Heels, boot and shoe, finished wood, manufacturing
316999	Heels, boot and shoe, leather, manufacturing
332611	Helical springs, hot wound heavy gauge, manufacturing
332612	Helical springs, light gauge, manufacturing
481212	Helicopter carriers, freight, nonscheduled
481112	Helicopter freight carriers, scheduled
481211	Helicopter passenger carriers (except scenic, sightseeing), nonscheduled
481111	Helicopter passenger carriers, scheduled
487990	Helicopter ride, scenic and sightseeing, operation
336411	Helicopters manufacturing
325120	Helium manufacturing
325120	Helium recovery from natural gas

Code	Description
339113	Helmets (except athletic), safety (e.g., motorized vehicle crash helmets, space helmets), manufacturing
339920	Helmets, athletic (except motorized vehicle crash helmets), manufacturing
561320	Help supply services
212210	Hematite mining and/or beneficiating
325413	Hematology in-vitro diagnostic substances manufacturing
325412	Hematology in-vivo diagnostic substances manufacturing
334516	Hematology instruments manufacturing
325414	Hematology products (except diagnostic substances) manufacturing
325191	Hemlock extract manufacturing
113210	Hemlock gum gathering
621492	Hemodialysis centers and clinics
313111	Hemp bags made from purchased fiber
313111	Hemp ropes made from purchased fiber
313111	Hemp spun yarns made from purchased fiber
315211	Hemstitching apparel contractors on men's and boys' apparel
315212	Hemstitching apparel contractors on women's, girls', and infants' apparel
325110	Heptanes made from refined petroleum or liquid hydrocarbons
325110	Heptenes made from refined petroleum or liquid hydrocarbons
111419	Herb farming, grown under cover
111998	Herb farming, open field
111421	Herbaceous perennial growing
621399	Herbalists' offices (e.g., centers, clinics)
712110	Herbariums
325320	Herbicides manufacturing
711310	Heritage festival managers with facilities
711320	Heritage festival managers without facilities
711310	Heritage festival organizers with facilities
711320	Heritage festival organizers without facilities
711310	Heritage festival promoters with facilities
711320	Heritage festival promoters without facilities
712120	Heritage villages
114111	Herring fishing
325199	Heterocyclic chemicals, not specified elsewhere by process, manufacturing
325199	Hexadecanol manufacturing
325199	Hexamethylenediamine manufacturing
325199	Hexamethylenetetramine manufacturing
325199	Hexanol manufacturing
311611	Hides and skins produced in slaughtering plants
316110	Hides and skins, finishing on a contract basis
422590	Hides wholesaling
316110	Hides, tanning, currying, dressing, and finishing
337122	High chairs, wood, children's, manufacturing
311221	High fructose corn syrup (HFCS) manufacturing
335110	High intensity lamp bulbs manufacturing
331112	High percentage nonferrous alloying elements (i.e., ferroalloys) manufacturing
611110	High schools
611110	High schools offering both academic and technical courses
611110	High schools offering both academic and vocational courses
234110	Highway and street construction management firms

Code	Description
332312	Highway bridge sections, prefabricated metal, manufacturing
234110	Highway construction (except elevated)
234120	Highway construction, elevated
234110	Highway guardrail construction contractors
332322	Highway guardrails, sheet metal, manufacturing
235310	Highway lighting and electrical signal construction contractors
333120	Highway line marking machinery manufacturing
235210	Highway line painting construction contractors
922120	Highway patrols, police
336120	Highway tractors assembled on chassis of own manufacture
336211	Highway tractors assembling on purchased chassis
332510	Hinges, metal, manufacturing
813410	Historical clubs
712120	Historical forts
712110	Historical museums
712120	Historical ships
712120	Historical sites
336399	Hitches, trailer, automotive, truck, and bus, manufacturing
451120	Hobby shops
339932	Hobbyhorses manufacturing
421920	Hobbyists' supplies wholesaling
333515	Hobs (i.e., metal gear cutting tool) manufacturing
711211	Hockey clubs, professional or semiprofessional
713990	Hockey clubs, recreational
339920	Hockey equipment (except apparel) manufacturing
421910	Hockey equipment and supplies wholesaling
611620	Hockey instruction, camps, or schools
339920	Hockey skates manufacturing
711211	Hockey teams, professional or semiprofessional
713990	Hockey teams, recreational
115112	Hoeing
332212	Hoes, garden and mason's handtools, manufacturing
112210	Hog and pig (including breeding, farrowing, nursery, and finishing activities) farming
333111	Hog feeding and watering equipment manufacturing
112210	Hog feedlots (except stockyards for transportation)
422520	Hogs wholesaling
321920	Hogsheads, coopered wood, manufacturing
333923	Hoists (except aircraft loading) manufacturing
421830	Hoists (except automotive) wholesaling
333924	Hoists, aircraft loading, manufacturing
421120	Hoists, automotive, wholesaling
551112	Holding companies (except bank, managing)
551114	Holding companies that manage
551111	Holding companies, bank (except managing)
333313	Holepunchers (except hand operated), office-type, manufacturing
339942	Holepunchers, hand operated, manufacturing
332999	Hollowware, precious plated metal, manufacturing
316999	Holsters, leather, manufacturing

Code	Description
452990	Home and auto supply stores
532310	Home and garden equipment rental centers
235310	Home automation system construction contractors
332115	Home canning lids and rings, metal stamping
621610	Home care of elderly, medical
624120	Home care of elderly, non-medical
444110	Home centers, building materials
624229	Home construction organizations, work (sweat) equity
454390	Home delivery newspaper routes, direct selling
337124	Home entertainment centers, metal, manufacturing
337122	Home entertainment centers, wood, manufacturing
522292	Home equity credit lending
621610	Home health agencies
611519	Home health aid schools
621610	Home health care agencies
532291	Home health furniture and equipment rental
444110	Home improvement centers
233220	Home improvements, residential (except single family), construction
233210	Home improvements, residential single-family, construction
541350	Home inspection services
621610	Home nursing services (except private practices)
621399	Home nursing services, private practice
453998	Home security equipment stores
561920	Home show managers
561920	Home show organizers
561920	Home show promoters
334310	Home stereo systems manufacturing
334310	Home tape recorders and players (e.g., cartridge, cassette, reel) manufacturing
334310	Home theater audio and video equipment manufacturing
333512	Home workshop metal cutting machine tools (except handtools, welding equipment) manufacturing
442299	Homefurnishings stores
421220	Homefurnishings wholesaling
624221	Homeless shelters
624120	Homemaker's service for elderly or disabled persons, non-medical
621399	Homeopaths' offices (e.g., centers, clinics)
813990	Homeowners' associations
813990	Homeowners' associations, condominium
524126	Homeowners' insurance carriers, direct
524128	Homeowners' warranty insurance carriers, direct
623990	Homes for children with health care incidental
623220	Homes for emotionally disturbed adults or children
623110	Homes for the aged with nursing care
623312	Homes for the aged without nursing care
623110	Homes for the elderly with nursing care
623312	Homes for the elderly without nursing care
623990	Homes for unwed mothers
623210	Homes with or without health care, mental retardation
623220	Homes, psychiatric convalescent
311211	Hominy grits (except breakfast food), manufacturing

Code	Description
311230	Hominy grits, prepared as cereal breakfast food, manufacturing
311421	Hominy, canned, manufacturing
333294	Homogenizing machinery, food, manufacturing
311511	Homogenizing milk
212399	Hones mining and/or beneficiating
112910	Honey bee production
311999	Honey processing
422490	Honey wholesaling
111219	Honeydew melon farming, field, bedding plant and seed production
333512	Honing and lapping machines manufacturing
333515	Honing heads (i.e., a machine tool accessory) manufacturing
922140	Honor camps
332313	Hoods, industrial, fabricated metal plate work, manufacturing
332322	Hoods, range (except household-type), sheet metal, manufacturing
335211	Hoods, range, household-type, manufacturing
115210	Hoof trimming
339993	Hook and eye fasteners (i.e., sewing accessories) manufacturing
332722	Hook and eye latches manufacturing
313221	Hook and loop fastener fabric manufacturing
332722	Hooks (i.e., general purpose fasteners), metal, manufacturing
339920	Hooks, fishing, manufacturing
332212	Hooks, handtools (e.g., baling, bush, grass, husking), manufacturing
332722	Hooks, metal screw, manufacturing
331111	Hoops made in steel mills
331111	Hoops, galvanized, made in steel mills
332999	Hoops, metal (except wire), fabricated from purchased metal
321920	Hoops, sawed or split wood for tight or slack cooperage, manufacturing
311942	Hop extract manufacturing
422490	Hop extract wholesaling
111998	Hop farming
333515	Hopper feed devices (i.e., a machine tool accessory) manufacturing
332313	Hoppers, fabricated metal plate work, manufacturing
332439	Hoppers, light gauge metal, manufacturing
422590	Hops wholesaling
334511	Horizon situation instrumentation manufacturing
325413	Hormone in vitro diagnostic substances manufacturing
325412	Hormone preparations (except in-vitro diagnostics) manufacturing
325411	Hormones and derivatives, uncompounded, manufacturing
112920	Horse (including thoroughbreds) production
332999	Horse bits manufacturing
316999	Horse boots and muzzles manufacturing
711212	Horse racetracks
711219	Horse racing stables
713990	Horse rental services, recreational saddle
711310	Horse show managers with facilities
711320	Horse show managers without facilities
711310	Horse show organizers with facilities
711320	Horse show organizers without facilities
711310	Horse show promoters with facilities
711320	Horse show promoters without facilities
336214	Horse trailers (except fifth-wheel-type) manufacturing

Code	Description
336212	Horse trailers, fifth-wheel-type, manufacturing
487110	Horse-drawn carriage operation
713990	Horseback riding, recreational
311611	Horsemeat produced in slaughtering plants
311111	Horsemeat, processing, for dog and cat food
311421	Horseradish (except sauce) canning
311941	Horseradish, prepared sauce, manufacturing
115210	Horses (except racehorses), boarding
422590	Horses wholesaling
115210	Horses, training (except racehorses)
331222	Horseshoe nails, iron or steel, made in wire drawing plants
115210	Horseshoeing
332111	Horseshoes, ferrous forged, made from purchased iron or steel
541690	Horticultural consulting services
332722	Hose clamps, metal, manufacturing
332912	Hose couplings and fittings, fluid power, manufacturing
332919	Hose couplings, metal (except fluid power), manufacturing
313221	Hose fabrics, tubular, weaving
332999	Hose, flexible metal, manufacturing
421840	Hose, industrial, wholesaling
326220	Hoses, reinforced, made from purchased rubber or plastics manufacturing
326220	Hoses, rubberized fabric, manufacturing
315119	Hosiery (except sheer), women's, girls' and infants', manufacturing
333292	Hosiery machines manufacturing
448190	Hosiery stores
422320	Hosiery, men's and boys', wholesaling
339113	Hosiery, orthopedic support, manufacturing
315111	Hosiery, sheer, women's, misses', and girls' full-length and knee-length, knitting or knitting and finishing
422330	Hosiery, women's and girls', wholesaling
422330	Hosiery, women's, children's, and infants', wholesaling
621610	Hospice care services, in home
623110	Hospices, inpatient care
813920	Hospital administrators' associations
524114	Hospital and medical service plans, direct, without providing health care services
813910	Hospital associations
532291	Hospital bed rental and leasing (i.e. home use)
339111	Hospital beds manufacturing
421450	Hospital beds wholesaling
233320	Hospital construction
421450	Hospital equipment and supplies wholesaling
532291	Hospital equipment rental (i.e. home use)
339111	Hospital furniture (e.g., hospital beds, operating room furniture) manufacturing
532291	Hospital furniture and equipment rental (i.e. home use)
421450	Hospital furniture wholesaling
926150	Hospital licensure agencies
611519	Hospital management schools (except academic)
611310	Hospital management schools offering baccalaureate or graduate degrees
315211	Hospital service apparel, washable, men's and boys', cut and sew apparel contractors

Hospital—Hunting

Code	Description
315225	Hospital service apparel, washable, men's and boys', cut and sewn from purchased fabric (except apparel contractors)
315212	Hospital service apparel, washable, women's and girls', cut and sew apparel contractors
315239	Hospital service apparel, washable, women's, misses', and girls', cut and sewn from purchased fabric (except apparel contractors)
611519	Hospitality management schools (except academic)
611310	Hospitality management schools offering baccalaureate or graduate degrees
524114	Hospitalization insurance carriers, direct, without providing health care services
62****	Hospitals (see type)
622210	Hospitals for alcoholics
622210	Hospitals, addiction
541940	Hospitals, animal
622110	Hospitals, general medical and surgical
622110	Hospitals, general pediatric
622210	Hospitals, mental (except mental retardation)
623210	Hospitals, mental retardation
622210	Hospitals, psychiatric (except convalescent)
623220	Hospitals, psychiatric convalescent
622210	Hospitals, psychiatric pediatric
622310	Hospitals, specialty (except psychiatric, substance abuse)
622210	Hospitals, substance abuse
721199	Hostels
487990	Hot air balloon ride, scenic and sightseeing, operation
333311	Hot beverage vending machines manufacturing
332812	Hot dip galvanizing metals and metal products for the trade
311612	Hot dogs (except poultry) made from purchased carcasses
311611	Hot dogs (except poultry) produced in slaughtering plants
311615	Hot dogs, poultry, manufacturing
332111	Hot forgings made from purchased iron or steel, unfinished
332112	Hot forgings made from purchased nonferrous metals, unfinished
213112	Hot oil treating of oil field tanks on a contract basis
213112	Hot shot service on a contract basis
333516	Hot strip mill machinery, metalworking, manufacturing
453998	Hot tub stores
421910	Hot tubs wholesaling
321920	Hot tubs, coopered, manufacturing
326191	Hot tubs, plastics or fiberglass, manufacturing
326299	Hot water bottles, rubber, manufacturing
335228	Hot water heaters (including nonelectric), household-type, manufacturing
331111	Hot-rolling iron or steel products in steel mills
333516	Hot-rolling mill machinery, metalworking, manufacturing
331221	Hot-rolling purchased steel
531120	Hotel building, not operating hotel, rental or leasing
531110	Hotel building, residential, rental or leasing
233320	Hotel construction

Code	Description
421440	Hotel equipment and supplies (except furniture) wholesaling
421210	Hotel furniture wholesaling
561110	Hotel management services (except complete operation of client's business)
721110	Hotel management services (i.e., providing management and operating staff to run hotel)
561599	Hotel reservation services
327112	Hotel tableware and kitchen articles, vitreous china, manufacturing
721110	Hotels (except casino hotels)
721110	Hotels with golf courses, tennis courts, and/or other health spa facilities (i.e., resorts)
721120	Hotels, casino
721110	Hotels, membership
721120	Hotels, resort, with casinos
721110	Hotels, resort, without casinos
721120	Hotels, seasonal, with casinos
721110	Hotels, seasonal, without casinos
624190	Hotline centers
333319	Hotplates, commercial-type, manufacturing
335211	Hotplates, household-type electric, manufacturing
235990	House moving construction contractors
235210	House painting construction contractors
111422	House plant growing
812990	House sitting services
316212	House slippers manufacturing
316212	House slippers, plastics or plastics soled fabric upper, manufacturing
316212	House slippers, rubber or rubber soled fabric upper, manufacturing
454390	House-to-house direct selling
532292	Houseboat rental
315191	Housecoats made in apparel knitting mills
315291	Housecoats, infants', cut and sewn from purchased fabric (except apparel contractors)
315212	Housecoats, women's, girls', and infants', cut and sew apparel contractors
315231	Housecoats, women's, misses', and girls', cut and sewn from purchased fabric (except apparel contractors)
315212	Housedresses, women's and girls', cut and sew apparel contractors
315233	Housedresses, women's, misses', and girls', cut and sewn from purchased fabric (except apparel contractors)
443111	Household-type appliance stores
421620	Household-type appliances, electrical, wholesaling
327112	Household-type earthenware, semivitreous, manufacturing
421210	Household-type furniture wholesaling
337121	Household-type furniture, upholstered, manufacturing
337122	Household-type furniture, wood, not upholstered (except TV and radio housings and sewing machine cabinets), manufacturing
325320	Household-type insecticides manufacturing
421620	Household-type laundry equipment (e.g., dryers, washers) wholesaling
327112	Household-type tableware and kitchen articles, vitreous china, manufacturing
334518	Household-type timing mechanisms manufacturing
321999	Household-type woodenware manufacturing

Code	Description
814110	Households, private, employing (e.g., cooks, maids, chauffeurs, gardeners)
814110	Households, private, employing domestic personnel
721199	Housekeeping cabins
721199	Housekeeping cottages
561720	Housekeeping services (i.e., cleaning services)
922140	Houses of correction
531110	Houses rental or leasing
332311	Houses, prefabricated metal, manufacturing
321991	Houses, prefabricated mobile homes, manufacturing
321992	Houses, prefabricated, wood (except mobile homes), manufacturing
233210	Houses, single family attached, construction
233210	Houses, single family detached, construction
233210	Houses, single family semi-detached construction
421220	Housewares (except electric) wholesaling
442299	Housewares stores
421620	Housewares, electric, wholesaling
624229	Housing assistance agencies
531110	Housing authorities operating residential buildings
925110	Housing authorities, nonoperating
233220	Housing construction, multifamily
233210	Housing construction, single family
922120	Housing police, government
925110	Housing programs, planning and development, government
624229	Housing repair organizations, volunteer
336612	Hovercraft building
487120	Hovercraft sightseeing operation
332995	Howitzers manufacturing
321999	Hubs, wood, manufacturing
111334	Huckleberry farming
113210	Huckleberry greens, gathering of
212299	Huebnerite mining and/or beneficiating
115114	Hulling and shelling of nuts
333111	Hulling machinery, farm-type, manufacturing
712110	Human history museums
541612	Human resource consulting services
813311	Human rights advocacy organizations
921190	Human rights commissions, government
813312	Humane societies
541720	Humanities research and development services
421730	Humidifiers and dehumidifiers (except portable) wholesaling
421620	Humidifiers and dehumidifiers, portable, wholesaling
335211	Humidifiers, portable electric, manufacturing
333415	Humidifying equipment (except portable) manufacturing
334512	Humidistats (e.g., duct, skeleton, wall) manufacturing
334512	Humidity controls, air-conditioning-type, manufacturing
334519	Humidity instruments (except industrial process and air-conditioning type) manufacturing
334513	Humidity instruments, industrial process-type, manufacturing
212399	Humus, peat, mining and/or beneficiating
721214	Hunting camps with accommodation facilities
713990	Hunting clubs, recreational

Code	Description
315211	Hunting coats and vests, men's and boys', cut and sew apparel contractors
315228	Hunting coats and vests, men's and boys', cut and sewn from purchased fabric (except apparel contractors)
421910	Hunting equipment and supplies wholesaling
713990	Hunting guide services
332211	Hunting knives manufacturing
114210	Hunting preserves
334111	Hybrid computers manufacturing
334413	Hybrid integrated circuits manufacturing
112511	Hybrid striped bass production
327410	Hydrated lime (i.e., calcium hydroxide), manufacturing
332912	Hydraulic aircraft subassemblies manufacturing
333995	Hydraulic cylinders, fluid power, manufacturing
811310	Hydraulic equipment repair and maintenance services
324110	Hydraulic fluids made in petroleum refineries
324191	Hydraulic fluids, petroleum, made from refined petroleum
325998	Hydraulic fluids, synthetic, manufacturing
213112	Hydraulic fracturing wells on a contract basis
332912	Hydraulic hose fittings, fluid power, manufacturing
326220	Hydraulic hoses (without fitting), rubber or plastics, manufacturing
421830	Hydraulic power transmission equipment wholesaling
421830	Hydraulic pumps and parts wholesaling
333996	Hydraulic pumps, fluid power, manufacturing
336340	Hydraulic slave cylinders, automotive, truck, and bus clutch, manufacturing
333611	Hydraulic turbine generator set units manufacturing
333611	Hydraulic turbines manufacturing
332912	Hydraulic valves, fluid power, manufacturing
325188	Hydrazine manufacturing
325188	Hydrochloric acid manufacturing
325188	Hydrocyanic acid manufacturing
234990	Hydroelectric plant construction
325188	Hydrofluoric acid manufacturing
325188	Hydrofluosilicic acid manufacturing
336611	Hydrofoil vessel building and repairing in shipyard
325120	Hydrogen manufacturing
325188	Hydrogen peroxide manufacturing
325188	Hydrogen sulfide manufacturing
311225	Hydrogenating purchased oil
541370	Hydrographic mapping services
541370	Hydrographic surveying services
541690	Hydrology consulting services
334519	Hydrometers (except industrial process-type) manufacturing
334513	Hydrometers, industrial process-type, manufacturing
334512	Hydronic circulator control, automatic, manufacturing
421720	Hydronic heating equipment and supplies wholesaling
333414	Hydronic heating equipment manufacturing
334512	Hydronic limit control manufacturing
334512	Hydronic limit, pressure, and temperature controls, manufacturing
334511	Hydrophones manufacturing

Code	Description
111419	Hydroponic crop farming
325192	Hydroquinone manufacturing
333996	Hydrostatic drives manufacturing
541380	Hydrostatic testing laboratories or services
333996	Hydrostatic transmissions manufacturing
325188	Hydrosulfites manufacturing
339113	Hydrotherapy equipment manufacturing
334519	Hygrometers (except industrial process-type) manufacturing
334513	Hygrometers, industrial process-type, manufacturing
334519	Hygrothermographs manufacturing
621399	Hypnotherapists' offices (e.g., centers, clinics)
325411	Hypnotic drugs, uncompounded, manufacturing
325188	Hypochlorites manufacturing
339112	Hypodermic needles and syringes manufacturing
325188	Hypophosphites manufacturing
321213	I-joists, wood, fabricating
514191	ISP (internet service providers)
339112	IV apparatus manufacturing
312113	Ice (except dry ice) manufacturing
422990	Ice (except dry ice) wholesaling
334512	Ice bank controls manufacturing
335222	Ice boxes, household-type, manufacturing
326199	Ice buckets, plastics (except foam), manufacturing
326140	Ice buckets, polystyrene foam, manufacturing
326150	Ice buckets, urethane or other plastics foam (except polystyrene), manufacturing
332439	Ice chests or coolers, metal, manufacturing
326199	Ice chests or coolers, plastics (except plastics foam) manufacturing
326140	Ice chests or coolers, polystyrene foam, manufacturing
326150	Ice chests or coolers, urethane or other plastics foam (except polystyrene) manufacturing
445299	Ice cream (i.e., packaged) stores
422430	Ice cream and ices wholesaling
311821	Ice cream cones manufacturing
422490	Ice cream cones wholesaling
333294	Ice cream making machinery manufacturing
311520	Ice cream manufacturing
311514	Ice cream mix manufacturing
722213	Ice cream parlors
311520	Ice cream specialties manufacturing
722330	Ice cream truck vendors
333311	Ice cream vending machines manufacturing
422430	Ice cream wholesaling
335211	Ice crushers, household-type electric, manufacturing
333999	Ice crushers, industrial and commercial-type, manufacturing
711211	Ice hockey clubs, professional or semiprofessional
713990	Ice hockey clubs, recreational
334512	Ice maker controls manufacturing
333415	Ice making machinery manufacturing
421740	Ice making machines wholesaling
311520	Ice milk manufacturing
311514	Ice milk mix manufacturing
311520	Ice milk specialties manufacturing
339920	Ice skates manufacturing
711190	Ice skating companies

Code	Description
713940	Ice skating rinks
711190	Ice skating shows
312130	Ice wine
325120	Ice, dry, manufacturing
422690	Ice, dry, wholesaling
312111	Iced coffee manufacturing
312111	Iced tea manufacturing
212399	Iceland spar (i.e., optical grade calcite), mining and/or beneficiating
311520	Ices, flavored sherbets, manufacturing
332999	Identification plates, metal, manufacturing
421410	Identity recorders wholesaling
332993	Igniters, ammunition tracer (i.e., more than 30 mm., more than 1.18 inch), manufacturing
334512	Ignition controls for gas appliances and furnaces, automatic, manufacturing
336322	Ignition points and condensers for internal combustion engines manufacturing
334515	Ignition testing instruments manufacturing
336322	Ignition wiring harness for internal combustion engines manufacturing
335122	Illuminated indoor lighting fixtures (e.g., directional, exit) manufacturing
541430	Illustrators, independent commercial
212299	Ilmenite ores mining and/or beneficiating
327420	Images, small gypsum, manufacturing
327999	Images, small papier-mache, manufacturing
323122	Imagesetting services, prepress
312221	Imitation tobacco cigarettes, manufacturing
335211	Immersion heaters, household-type electric, manufacturing
624230	Immigrant resettlement services
928120	Immigration services
923120	Immunization program administration
621111	Immunologists' offices (e.g., centers, clinics)
334516	Immunology instruments, laboratory, manufacturing
333991	Impact wrenches, handheld power-driven, manufacturing
334515	Impedance measuring equipment manufacturing
334514	Impeller and counter driven flow meters manufacturing
339113	Implants, surgical, manufacturing
213112	Impounding and storing salt water in connection with petroleum production
221310	Impounding reservoirs, irrigation
339114	Impression material, dental, manufacturing
711110	Improvisational theaters
334512	In-built thermostats, filled system and bimetal types, manufacturing
454390	In-home sales of merchandise, direct selling
325413	In-vitro diagnostic substances manufacturing
325412	In-vivo diagnostic substances manufacturing
335110	Incandescent filament lamp bulbs, complete, manufacturing
325998	Incense manufacturing
334512	Incinerator control systems, residential and commercial-type, manufacturing
333994	Incinerators (except precast concrete) manufacturing
562211	Incinerators, hazardous waste, operating

Incinerators—Inks

Code	Description
562213	Incinerators, nonhazardous solid waste
327390	Incinerators, precast concrete, manufacturing
235950	Incinerators, small, construction contractors
541213	Income tax compilation services
541213	Income tax return preparation services
333313	Incoming mail handling equipment (e.g., opening, scanning, sorting) manufacturing
339113	Incubators, infant, manufacturing
339111	Incubators, laboratory-type, manufacturing
333111	Incubators, poultry, manufacturing
325998	Indelible inks manufacturing
488190	Independent pilot, air (except owner-operators)
488490	Independent truck driver (except owner-operators)
333515	Indexing, rotary tables (i.e., a machine tool accessory) manufacturing
325998	India inks manufacturing
921190	Indian affairs programs, government
334515	Indicating instruments, electric, manufacturing
334519	Indicator testers, turntable, manufacturing
334513	Indicators, industrial process control-type, manufacturing
325188	Indium chloride manufacturing
624190	Individual and family social services, multi-purpose
523910	Individuals investing in financial contracts on own account
541850	Indoor display advertising services
713120	Indoor play areas
333994	Induction heating equipment, industrial process-type, manufacturing
334416	Inductors, electronic component-type (e.g., chokes, coils, transformers), manufacturing
233310	Industrial and manufacturing building construction contractors
233310	Industrial and manufacturing building construction management firms
813910	Industrial associations
522190	Industrial banks (i.e., known as), depository
522298	Industrial banks (i.e., known as), nondepository
314992	Industrial belting reinforcement, cord and fabric, manufacturing
233310	Industrial building construction, general construction contractors
531120	Industrial building rental or leasing
722310	Industrial caters (i.e., providing food services on a contractual arrangement (except single event base))
422690	Industrial chemicals wholesaling
421840	Industrial containers wholesaling
335314	Industrial controls (e.g., push button, selector, and pilot switches, manufacturing
421610	Industrial controls, electrical, wholesaling
541420	Industrial design consulting services
533110	Industrial design licensing
541420	Industrial design services
926110	Industrial development program administration
541330	Industrial engineering services
811310	Industrial equipment and machinery repair and maintenance services
315211	Industrial garments, men's and boys', cut and sew apparel contractors
315225	Industrial garments, men's and boys', cut and sewn from purchased fabric (except apparel contractors)
315212	Industrial garments, women's and girls', cut and sew apparel contractors
315239	Industrial garments, women's, misses', and girls', cut and sewn from purchased fabric (except apparel contractors)
325120	Industrial gases manufacturing
422690	Industrial gases wholesaling
327212	Industrial glassware and glass products, pressed or blown, made in glass making plants
327215	Industrial glassware made from purchased glass
234930	Industrial incinerator construction contractors
813930	Industrial labor unions
541320	Industrial land use planning services
812332	Industrial launderers
335122	Industrial lighting fixtures, electric, manufacturing
522298	Industrial loan companies, nondepository
336510	Industrial locomotives and parts manufacturing
421830	Industrial machinery and equipment (except electrical) wholesaling
335122	Industrial mercury lighting fixtures, electric, manufacturing
333511	Industrial molds (except steel ingot) manufacturing
331511	Industrial molds, steel ingot, manufacturing
234930	Industrial nonbuilding construction management firms
332997	Industrial pattern manufacturing
234930	Industrial plant appurtenance construction
233310	Industrial plant construction, general construction contractors
334513	Industrial process control instruments manufacturing
325510	Industrial product finishes and coatings (i.e., paint) manufacturing
541710	Industrial research and development laboratories or services
421450	Industrial safety devices (e.g., eye shields, face shields, first-aid kits) wholesaling
325998	Industrial salt manufacturing
422690	Industrial salt wholesaling
212322	Industrial sand beneficiating (e.g., screening, washing)
212322	Industrial sand sandpits and dredging
333997	Industrial scales manufacturing
234930	Industrial structures, construction (except building)
421840	Industrial supplies (except disposable plastics, paper) wholesaling
422130	Industrial supplies, disposable plastics, paper, wholesaling
541380	Industrial testing laboratories or services
621340	Industrial therapists' offices (e.g., centers, clinics)
811310	Industrial truck (e.g., forklifts) repair and maintenance services
532490	Industrial truck rental or leasing
333924	Industrial trucks and tractors manufacturing
421830	Industrial trucks, tractors, or trailers wholesaling
812332	Industrial uniform supply services
421930	Industrial wastes to be reclaimed wholesaling
311611	Inedible products (e.g., hides, skins, pulled wool, wool grease) produced in slaughtering plants
334511	Inertial navigation systems, aeronautical, manufacturing
311422	Infant and junior food canning
311230	Infant cereals, dry, manufacturing
624410	Infant day care centers
624410	Infant day care services
339113	Infant incubators manufacturing
311514	Infant's formulas manufacturing
316219	Infant's shoes (except plastics, rubber), manufacturing
315291	Infants water resistant outerwear cut and sewn from purchased fabric (except apparel contractors)
315291	Infants' apparel cut and sewn from purchased fabric (except apparel contractors)
422330	Infants' clothing wholesaling
315212	Infants' cut and sew apparel contractors
514191	Information access services, on-line
541512	Information management computer systems integration design services
514199	Information search services, on a contract or fee basis
334516	Infrared analytical instruments, laboratory-type, manufacturing
334511	Infrared homing systems, aeronautical, manufacturing
334513	Infrared instruments, industrial process-type, manufacturing
335110	Infrared lamp bulbs manufacturing
335129	Infrared lamp fixtures manufacturing
333994	Infrared ovens, industrial, manufacturing
334413	Infrared sensors, solid-state, manufacturing
621498	Infusion therapy centers and clinics, outpatient
331319	Ingot made by rolling purchased aluminum
331111	Ingot made in steel mills
331319	Ingot, aluminum, made in integrated secondary smelting and rolling mills
331492	Ingot, nonferrous metals (except aluminum, copper), secondary smelting and refining
331312	Ingot, primary aluminium, manufacturing
331419	Ingot, primary, nonferrous metals (except aluminum, copper), manufacturing
421510	Ingots (except precious) wholesaling
421940	Ingots, precious, wholesaling
621399	Inhalation therapists' offices (e.g., centers, clinics)
339112	Inhalation therapy equipment manufacturing
339112	Inhalators, surgical and medical, manufacturing
325998	Inhibitors (e.g., corrosion, oxidation, polymerization) manufacturing
333220	Injection molding machinery for plastics manufacturing
325612	Ink eradicators manufacturing
422120	Ink, writing, wholesaling
339944	Inked ribbons manufacturing
422120	Inked ribbons wholesaling
325910	Inkjet cartridges manufacturing
325910	Inkjet inks manufacturing
325910	Inks, printing, manufacturing
421840	Inks, printing, wholesaling

Code	Description
325998	Inks, writing, manufacturing
316999	Inner soles, leather, manufacturing
326211	Inner tubes manufacturing
337910	Innerspring cushions manufacturing
721191	Inns, bed and breakfast
422690	Inorganic chemicals wholesaling
325131	Inorganic pigments (except bone black, carbon black, lamp black) manufacturing
334119	Input/output equipment, computer (except terminals), manufacturing
115112	Insect control for crops
335129	Insect lamps, electric, manufacturing
332618	Insect screening made from purchased wire
325320	Insecticides manufacturing
333515	Inserts, cutting tool, manufacturing
541350	Inspection bureaus, building
926150	Inspection for labor standards
488490	Inspection or weighing services, truck transportation
488190	Inspection services, aircraft
541350	Inspection services, building or home
235950	Installation of machinery and other industrial equipment construction contractors
213112	Installing production equipment at the oil or gas field on a contract basis
522220	Installment sales financing
311920	Instant coffee manufacturing
311230	Instant hot cereals manufacturing
323114	Instant printing (i.e., quick printing)
311920	Instant tea manufacturing
233320	Institutional and commercial building construction management firms
233320	Institutional building construction
337127	Institutional furniture manufacturing
335122	Institutional lighting fixtures, electric, manufacturing
******	Instruction — see type of training
512110	Instructional video production
336322	Instrument control panels (i.e., assembling purchased gauges), automotive, truck, and bus, manufacturing
334511	Instrument landing system instrumentation, airborne or airport, manufacturing
333314	Instrument lenses manufacturing
334514	Instrument panels, assembling gauges made in the same establishment
334515	Instrument shunts manufacturing
332612	Instrument springs, precision (except clock, watch), manufacturing
335311	Instrument transformers (except complete instruments) for metering or protective relaying use manufacturing
334519	Instrumentation for reactor controls, auxiliary, manufacturing
421830	Instruments (except electrical) (e.g., controlling, indicating, recording) wholesaling
334513	Instruments for industrial process control manufacturing
334515	Instruments for measuring electrical quantities manufacturing
334511	Instruments, aeronautical, manufacturing
334515	Instruments, electric (i.e., testing electrical characteristics), manufacturing
339112	Instruments, mechanical microsurgical, manufacturing
339992	Instruments, musical, manufacturing
421990	Instruments, musical, wholesaling

Code	Description
421490	Instruments, professional and scientific, wholesaling
331422	Insulated wire or cable made from purchased copper in wire drawing plants
331319	Insulated wire or cable made in aluminum wire drawing plants
421610	Insulated wire or cable wholesaling
331422	Insulated wire or cable, copper, made in integrated secondary smelting and drawing plants
322299	Insulating batts, fills, or blankets made from purchased paper
327993	Insulating batts, fills, or blankets, fiberglass, manufacturing
327124	Insulating firebrick and shapes, clay, manufacturing
327215	Insulating glass, sealed units, made from purchased glass
327211	Insulating glass, sealed units, made in glass making plants
321999	Insulating materials, cork, manufacturing
325998	Insulating oils manufacturing
235990	Insulating pipes and boilers construction contractors
335929	Insulating purchased wire
326150	Insulation and cushioning, foam plastics (except polystrene), manufacturing
326140	Insulation and cushioning, polystyrene foam plastics, manufacturing
321219	Insulation board, cellular fiber or hard pressed wood, manufacturing
235420	Insulation construction contractors
421330	Insulation materials wholesaling
235990	Insulation of pipes and boilers construction contractors
335932	Insulators, electrical (except glass, porcelain), manufacturing
327113	Insulators, electrical porcelain, manufacturing
327215	Insulators, electrical, glass, made from purchased glass
327212	Insulators, electrical, glass, made in glass making plants
421610	Insulators, electrical, wholesaling
325412	Insulin preparations manufacturing
325411	Insulin, uncompounded, manufacturing
524298	Insurance advisory services
524210	Insurance agencies
524210	Insurance brokerages
531120	Insurance building rental or leasing
524113	Insurance carriers, disability, direct
524126	Insurance carriers, fidelity, direct
524114	Insurance carriers, health, direct
524113	Insurance carriers, life, direct
524126	Insurance carriers, property and casualty, direct
524126	Insurance carriers, surety, direct
524127	Insurance carriers, title, direct
524291	Insurance claims adjusting
524291	Insurance claims investigation services
524292	Insurance claims processing services, third party
926150	Insurance commissions, government
524298	Insurance coverage consulting services
524292	Insurance fund, third party administrative services (except claims adjusting only)
524298	Insurance investigation services (except claims investigation)
524298	Insurance loss prevention services
524292	Insurance plan administrative services (except claims adjusting only), third-party

Code	Description
524298	Insurance rate making services
524298	Insurance reporting services
524291	Insurance settlement offices
524298	Insurance underwriters laboratories and standards services
524113	Insurance underwriting, disability, direct
524114	Insurance underwriting, health and medical, direct
524113	Insurance underwriting, life, direct
524126	Insurance underwriting, property and casualty, direct
524127	Insurance underwriting, title, direct
813910	Insurers' associations
323111	Intaglio printing
335312	Integral horsepower electric motors manufacturing
421690	Integrated circuits wholesaling
334413	Integrated microcircuits manufacturing
512220	Integrated record companies (i.e., releasing, promoting, distributing)
512220	Integrated record production and distribution
334515	Integrated-circuit testers manufacturing
334515	Integrating electricity meters manufacturing
334514	Integrating meters, nonelectric, manufacturing
712110	Interactive museums
234910	Interceptor construction
485210	Inter-city bus line operation
483113	Intercoastal freight transportation to and from domestic ports
334290	Intercom systems and equipment manufacturing
332410	Intercooler shells manufacturing
483114	Intercostal transportation of passengers to and from domestic ports
333314	Interferometers manufacturing
541410	Interior decorating consultant services
541410	Interior decorating consulting services
541410	Interior design consulting services
541410	Interior design services
541410	Interior designer services
315211	Interlinings (e.g., belt loops, pockets) for suits, coats, and trousers, men's and boys', cut and sew apparel contractors
315212	Interlinings (e.g., belt loops, pockets) for suits, coats, skirts, and dresses, women's, girls' and infants', cut and sew apparel contractors
623210	Intermediate care facilities, mental retardation
921130	Internal Revenue Service
334515	Internal combustion engine analyzers (i.e., testing electrical characteristics) manufacturing
333618	Internal combustion engines (except aircraft, nondiesel automotive, nondiesel truck) manufacturing
421830	Internal combustion engines (except aircraft, nondiesel automotive, nondiesel truck) wholesaling
336412	Internal combustion engines, aircraft, manufacturing
336312	Internal combustion engines, automotive and truck gasoline, manufacturing
928120	International Monetary Fund
522293	International trade financing
514191	Internet access providers
514191	Internet service providers (ISP)
621111	Internists' offices (e.g., centers, clinics)
541940	Internists' offices, veterinary
541930	Interpretation services, language

Interpretive—Jai alai

Code	Description
712190	Interpretive centers, nature
711120	Interpretive dance companies
711510	Interpretive dancers, independent
485210	Interstate bus line operation
485210	Interurban bus line operation
339113	Intraocular lenses manufacturing
483211	Intracoastal transportation of freight
483212	Intracoastal transportation of passengers
339113	Intrauterine devices manufacturing
325412	Intravenous (IV) solution preparations manufacturing
812990	Introduction services, social
532291	Invalid equipment rental (i.e. home use)
561990	Inventory computing services
541614	Inventory planning and control management consulting services
561990	Inventory taking services
311312	Invert sugar made from purchased raw cane sugar
335312	Inverters, rotating electrical, manufacturing
335999	Inverters, solid-state, manufacturing
561611	Investigation services (except credit), private
561450	Investigation services, credit
561611	Investigators, private
523930	Investment advice consulting services, customized, fees paid by client
523930	Investment advice counseling services, customized, fees paid by client
523930	Investment advisory services, customized, fees paid by client
523110	Investment banking
331524	Investment castings, aluminum, unfinished, manufacturing
331525	Investment castings, copper (except die-castings), unfinished manufacturing
331528	Investment castings, nonferrous metal (except aluminum, copper), unfinished, manufacturing
331512	Investment castings, steel, unfinished, manufacturing
523910	Investment clubs
525990	Investment funds, closed-end
525910	Investment funds, open-ended
325188	Iodides manufacturing
325412	Iodinated in-vivo diagnostic substances manufacturing
325188	Iodine, crude or resublimed, manufacturing
334519	Ion chambers manufacturing
325211	Ion exchange resins manufacturing
325211	Ionomer resins manufacturing
325199	Ionone manufacturing
331491	Iridium bar, rod, sheet, strip and tubing made from purchased metals or scrap
212299	Iridium mining and/or beneficiating
331492	Iridium recovering from scrap and/or alloying purchased metals
331419	Iridium refining, primary
421390	Iron and steel architectural shapes wholesaling
325131	Iron based pigments manufacturing
331511	Iron castings, unfinished, manufacturing
325188	Iron compounds, not specified elsewhere by process, manufacturing
332111	Iron forgings made from purchased iron, unfinished
331511	Iron foundries
339113	Iron lungs manufacturing
212210	Iron ore (e.g., hematite, magnetite, siderite, taconite) mining and/or beneficiating

Code	Description
212210	Iron ore agglomerates mining and/or beneficiating
212210	Iron ore beneficiating plants (e.g., agglomeration, sintering)
212210	Iron ore mine site development for own account
331111	Iron ore recovery from open hearth slag
212210	Iron ore, blocked, mining and/or beneficiating
331111	Iron sinter made in steel mills
325188	Iron sulphate manufacturing
235910	Iron work structural, construction contractors
331111	Iron, pig, manufacturing
335224	Ironers and mangles, household-type (except portable irons), manufacturing
332999	Ironing boards, metal, manufacturing
321999	Ironing boards, wood, manufacturing
335211	Irons, household-type electric, manufacturing
334517	Irradiation apparatus and tubes (e.g., industrial, medical diagnostic, medical therapeutic, research, scientific), manufacturing
334517	Irradiation equipment manufacturing
115114	Irradiation of fruits and vegetables
926130	Irrigation districts, nonoperating
421820	Irrigation equipment wholesaling
333111	Irrigation equipment, agriculture, manufacturing
327332	Irrigation pipe, concrete, manufacturing
332322	Irrigation pipe, sheet metal, manufacturing
234990	Irrigation project construction
221310	Irrigation system operation
325110	Isobutane made from refined petroleum or liquid hydrocarbons
211112	Isobutane recovered from oil and gas field gases
325110	Isobutene made from refined petroleum or liquid hydrocarbons
325211	Isobutylene polymer resins manufacturing
325212	Isobutylene-isoprene rubber manufacturing
325212	Isocyanate rubber manufacturing
325192	Isocyanates manufacturing
335311	Isolation transformers manufacturing
211112	Isopentane recovered from oil and gas field gases
325110	Isoprene made from refined petroleum or liquid hydrocarbons
325199	Isopropyl alcohol manufacturing
311422	Italian foods canning
333120	Jack hammers manufacturing
315191	Jackets made in apparel knitting mills
332992	Jackets, bullet (i.e., 30 mm. or less, 1.18 inch or less), manufacturing
315292	Jackets, fur (except apparel contractors), manufacturing
315211	Jackets, fur, men's and boys', cut and sew apparel contractors
315212	Jackets, fur, women's, girls', and infants', cut and sew apparel contractors
332313	Jackets, industrial, fabricated metal plate work, manufacturing
315291	Jackets, infants', cut and sewn from purchased fabric (except apparel contractors)
315292	Jackets, leather (except welders') or sheep-lined (except apparel contractors), manufacturing

Code	Description
315211	Jackets, leather (except welders') or sheep-lined, men's and boys', cut and sew apparel contractors
315212	Jackets, leather (except welders') or sheep-lined, women's, girls', and infants', cut and sew apparel contractors
315211	Jackets, men's and boys', cut and sew apparel contractors
315225	Jackets, nontailored work, men's and boys', cut and sewn from purchased fabric (except apparel contractors)
315239	Jackets, nontailored work, women's, misses', and girls', cut and sewn from purchased fabric (except apparel contractors)
315239	Jackets, nontailored, women's, misses', and girls', cut and sewn from purchased fabric (except apparel contractors)
315228	Jackets, not tailored (except work), men's and boys', cut and sewn from purchased fabric (except apparel contractors)
315211	Jackets, service apparel (e.g., laboratory, medical), men's and boys', cut and sew apparel contractors
315225	Jackets, service apparel (e.g., laboratory, medical), men's and boys', cut and sewn from purchased fabric (except apparel contractors)
315212	Jackets, service apparel (e.g., laboratory, medical), women's and girls', cut and sew apparel contractors
315239	Jackets, service apparel (e.g., laboratory, medical), women's, misses', and girls', cut and sewn from purchased fabric (except apparel contractors)
315291	Jackets, ski, infants', cut and sewn from purchased fabric (except apparel contractors)
315211	Jackets, ski, men's and boys', cut and sew apparel contractors
315228	Jackets, ski, men's and boys', cut and sewn from purchased fabric (except apparel contractors)
315212	Jackets, ski, women's, girls', and infants', cut and sew apparel contractors
315239	Jackets, ski, women's, misses', and girls', cut and sewn from purchased fabric (except apparel contractors)
315222	Jackets, tailored (except fur, leather, sheep-lined), men's and boys', cut and sewn from purchased fabric (except apparel contractors)
315234	Jackets, tailored (except fur, sheep-lined), women's, misses', and girls', cut and sewn from purchased fabric (except apparel contractors)
315211	Jackets, tailored, men's and boys', cut and sew apparel contractors
315212	Jackets, tailored, women's, girls', and infants', cut and sew apparel contractors
316999	Jackets, welder's, leather, manufacturing
315212	Jackets, women's, girls', and infants', cut and sew apparel contractors
332212	Jacks (except hydraulic, pneumatic) manufacturing
333999	Jacks, hydraulic and pneumatic, manufacturing
333292	Jacquard card cutting machinery manufacturing
313210	Jacquard woven fabrics weaving
212399	Jade mining and/or beneficiating
611620	Jai alai instruction, camps, or schools

Code	Description
711211	Jai alai teams, professional or semiprofessional
561210	Jail operation on a contract or fee basis
922140	Jails
332321	Jalousies, metal, manufacturing
422690	Janitorial chemicals wholesaling
421850	Janitorial equipment and supplies wholesaling
561720	Janitorial services
561720	Janitorial services, aircraft
332812	Japanning metals and metal products for the trade
316110	Japanning of leather
333994	Japanning ovens manufacturing
325510	Japans manufacturing
327213	Jars for packaging, bottling, and canning, glass, manufacturing
326199	Jars, plastics, manufacturing
711120	Jazz dance companies
711510	Jazz dancers, independent
711510	Jazz musical artists, independent
711130	Jazz musical groups
315211	Jean-cut casual slacks, men's and boys', cut and sew apparel contractors
315224	Jean-cut casual slacks, men's and boys', cut and sewn from purchased fabric (except apparel contractors)
315212	Jean-cut casual slacks, women's, girls, and infants', cut and sew apparel contractors
315239	Jean-cut casual slacks, women's, misses', and girls', cut and sewn from purchased fabric (except apparel contractors)
315291	Jeans, infants', cut and sewn from purchased fabric (except apparel contractors)
315211	Jeans, men's and boys', cut and sew apparel contractors
315239	Jeans, women's, misses', and girls', cut and sewn from purchased fabric (except apparel contractors)
315212	Jeans, women's, misses', girls', and infants', cut and sew apparel contractors
311421	Jellies and jams manufacturing
422490	Jellies and jams wholesaling
311340	Jelly candies manufacturing
315191	Jerseys made in apparel knitting mills
315211	Jerseys, men's and boys', cut and sew apparel contractors
315223	Jerseys, men's and boys', cut and sewn from purchased fabric (except apparel contractors)
315212	Jerseys, women's, girls', and infants', cut and sew apparel contractors
315232	Jerseys, women's, misses', and girls', cut and sewn from purchased fabric (except apparel contractors)
324110	Jet fuels manufacturing
336412	Jet propulsion and internal combustion engines and parts, aircraft, manufacturing
332993	Jet propulsion projectiles (except guided missiles) manufacturing
234990	Jetty construction
339911	Jewel settings and mountings, precious metal, manufacturing
339913	Jeweler's findings and materials manufacturing
332212	Jeweler's handtools, nonelectric, manufacturing
421940	Jewelers' findings wholesaling
422990	Jewelry boxes wholesaling
541490	Jewelry design services

Code	Description
811490	Jewelry repair shops without retailing new jewelry
448150	Jewelry stores, costume
448310	Jewelry stores, precious
421940	Jewelry wholesaling
339914	Jewelry, costume, manufacturing
339911	Jewelry, natural or cultured pearls, manufacturing
339911	Jewelry, precious metal, manufacturing
333514	Jigs (e.g., checking, gauging, inspection) manufacturing
333514	Jigs and fixtures for use with machine tools manufacturing
333991	Jigsaws, handheld power-driven, manufacturing
333210	Jigsaws, woodworking-type, stationary, manufacturing
624310	Job counseling, vocational rehabilitation or habilitation
323119	Job printing (except flexographic, gravure, lithographic, screen)
323112	Job printing, flexographic
323111	Job printing, gravure
323119	Job printing, letterpress
323110	Job printing, lithographic
323110	Job printing, offset
323113	Job printing, screen
336370	Job stampings, automotive, metal, manufacturing
624310	Job training, vocational rehabilitation or habilitation
711219	Jockeys, horse racing
339920	Jogging machines, manufacturing
315191	Jogging suits made in apparel knitting mills
315291	Jogging suits, infants', cut and sewn from purchased fabric (except apparel contractors)
315211	Jogging suits, men's and boys', cut and sew apparel contractors
315228	Jogging suits, men's and boys', cut and sewn from purchased fabric (except apparel contractors)
315212	Jogging suits, women's, girls', and infants', cut and sew apparel contractors
315239	Jogging suits, women's, misses', and girls', cut and sewn from purchased fabric (except apparel contractors)
325520	Joint compounds (except gypsum base) manufacturing
327420	Joint compounds, gypsum based, manufacturing
333210	Jointers, woodworking-type, manufacturing
333613	Joints, swivel (except aircraft, motor vehicle), manufacturing
333613	Joints, universal (except aircraft, motor vehicle), manufacturing
336413	Joints, universal, aircraft, manufacturing
336350	Joints, universal, automotive, truck, and bus, manufacturing
332312	Joists, fabricated bar, manufacturing
332322	Joists, sheet metal, manufacturing
111998	Jojoba farming
711510	Journalists, independent (freelance)
334119	Joystick devices manufacturing
611620	Judo instruction, camps, or schools
326150	Jugs, vacuum, foam plastics (except polystyrene), manufacturing
332439	Jugs, vacuum, light gauge metal, manufacturing
326140	Jugs, vacuum, polystyrene foam plastics, manufacturing

Code	Description
333294	Juice extractors (i.e., food manufacturing-type) manufacturing
335211	Juice extractors, household-type electric, manufacturing
311520	Juice pops, frozen, manufacturing
422490	Juices, canned or fresh, wholesaling
422420	Juices, frozen, wholesaling
311411	Juices, fruit or vegetable concentrates, frozen, manufacturing
311421	Juices, fruit or vegetable, canned manufacturing
311421	Juices, fruit or vegetable, fresh, manufacturing
311411	Juices, fruit or vegetable, frozen, manufacturing
713990	Jukebox concession operators (i.e., supplying and servicing in others' facilities)
334310	Jukeboxes manufacturing
315212	Jumpsuits, women's, girls', and infants', cut and sew apparel contractors
315234	Jumpsuits, women's, misses', and girls', cut and sewn from purchased fabric (except apparel contractors)
335932	Junction boxes, electrical wiring, manufacturing
813910	Junior chambers of commerce
611210	Junior colleges
611210	Junior colleges offering a wide variety of academic and technical training
611110	Junior high schools
313210	Jute bags made in broadwoven mills
422310	Jute piece goods (except burlap) wholesaling
337124	Juvenile furniture (except upholstered), metal manufacturing
337122	Juvenile furniture (except upholstered), wood, manufacturing
337125	Juvenile furniture, rattan and reed, manufacturing
337121	Juvenile furniture, upholstered, manufacturing
623990	Juvenile halfway group homes
511120	Juvenile magazine and periodical publishers
511120	Juvenile magazine and periodical publishers and printing combined
511120	Juvenile magazine and periodical publishing (i.e., establishments known as publishers)
323112	Juvenile magazines and periodicals flexographic printing without publishing
323111	Juvenile magazines and periodicals gravure printing without publishing
323110	Juvenile magazines and periodicals lithographic (offset) printing without publishing
323119	Juvenile magazines and periodicals printing (except flexographic, gravure, lithographic, screen) without publishing
323113	Juvenile magazines and periodicals screen printing without publishing
111219	Kale farming, field, bedding plant and seed production
212324	Kaolin mining and/or beneficiating
327992	Kaolin, processing beyond beneficiation
713990	Kayaking, recreational
327420	Keene's cement manufacturing
321920	Kegs, wood, coopered, manufacturing
311119	Kelp meal and pellets, animal feed manufacturing
334515	Kelvin bridges (i.e., electrical measuring instruments) manufacturing
111998	Kenaf farming

Kennels—Laboratory

Code	Description
112990	Kennels, breeding and raising stock for sale
711219	Kennels, dog racing
812910	Kennels, pet boarding
212391	Kernite mining and/or beneficiating
211111	Kerogen processing
324110	Kerosene manufacturing
333414	Kerosene space heaters manufacturing
311421	Ketchup manufacturing
325199	Ketone compounds, not specified elsewhere by process, manufacturing
332420	Kettles, heavy gauge metal, manufacturing
332510	Key blanks manufacturing
316993	Key cases (except metal) manufacturing
339911	Key cases, precious metal, manufacturing
333512	Key cutting machines manufacturing
811490	Key duplicating shops
332618	Key rings made from purchased wire
334119	Keyboards, computer peripheral equipment, manufacturing
339992	Keyboards, piano or organ, manufacturing
336322	Keyless entry systems, automotive, truck, and bus, manufacturing
421710	Keys and locks wholesaling
334210	Keysets, telephone, manufacturing
621492	Kidney dialysis centers and clinics
234930	Kiln construction
321999	Kiln drying lumber
327124	Kiln furniture, clay, manufacturing
333994	Kilns (except cement, chemical, wood) manufacturing
333298	Kilns (i.e., cement, chemical, wood) manufacturing
421830	Kilns, industrial, wholesaling
611110	Kindergartens
334519	Kinematic test and measuring equipment manufacturing
561910	Kit assembling and packaging services
336211	Kit car bodies manufacturing
421620	Kitchen appliances, household-type, electric, wholesaling
327112	Kitchen articles, coarse earthenware, manufacturing
444190	Kitchen cabinet (except custom) stores
337110	Kitchen cabinets (except freestanding), stock or custom wood, manufacturing
421310	Kitchen cabinets, built in, wholesaling
337122	Kitchen chairs (e.g., upholstered), wood, manufacturing
337124	Kitchen chairs (including upholstered), metal, manufacturing
337125	Kitchen chairs (including upholstered), plastics manufacturing
332211	Kitchen cutlery, nonprecious and precious plated metal, manufacturing
325612	Kitchen degreasing and cleaning preparations manufacturing
337124	Kitchen furniture, household-type, metal, manufacturing
337124	Kitchen furniture, metal household-type, manufacturing
337122	Kitchen furniture, wood household-type, manufacturing
421440	Kitchen utensils, commercial, wholesaling
332214	Kitchen utensils, fabricated metal (e.g., colanders, garlic presses, ice scream scoops, spatulas), manufacturing
421220	Kitchen utensils, household-type, wholesaling
326199	Kitchen utensils, plastics, manufacturing

Code	Description
442299	Kitchenware stores
327112	Kitchenware, commercial and household-type, vitreous china, manufacturing
327112	Kitchenware, semivitreous earthenware, manufacturing
321999	Kitchenware, wood, manufacturing
339932	Kites manufacturing
111339	Kiwi fruit farming
334411	Klystron tubes manufacturing
314911	Knapsacks (e.g., backpacks, book bags) manufacturing
314911	Knapsacks, made from purchased woven or knitted materials
315211	Knickers, dress, men's and boys', cut and sew apparel contractors
315291	Knickers, infants', cut and sewn from purchased fabric (except apparel contractors)
315228	Knickers, men's and boys', cut and sewn from purchased fabric (except apparel contractors)
315212	Knickers, women's, girls', and infants', cut and sew apparel contractors
315239	Knickers, women's, misses', and girls', cut and sewn from purchased fabric (except apparel contractors)
337122	Knickknack shelves, wood, manufacturing
332211	Knife blades manufacturing
332211	Knife blanks manufacturing
335313	Knife switches, electric power switchgear-type, manufacturing
311812	Knishes (except frozen) made in commercial bakeries
311813	Knishes, frozen, manufacturing
315992	Knit gloves cut and sewn from purchased fabric (except apparel contractors)
315191	Knit gloves made in apparel knitting mills
315211	Knit gloves, men's and boys', cut and sew apparel contractors
315212	Knit gloves, women's, girls', and infants', cut and sew apparel contractors
313113	Knitting and crocheting thread manufacturing
313249	Knitting and finishing lace
313249	Knitting and finishing warp fabric
313241	Knitting and finishing weft fabric
313249	Knitting lace
333292	Knitting machinery manufacturing
313111	Knitting spun yarns (e.g., cotton, manmade fiber, silk, wool) made from purchased fiber
313249	Knitting warp fabric
313241	Knitting weft fabric
332211	Knives (e.g., hunting, pocket, table nonprecious, table precious plated) manufacturing
421710	Knives (except disposable plastics) wholesaling
333515	Knives and bits for metalworking lathes, planers, and shapers manufacturing
332212	Knives and bits for woodworking lathes, planers, and shapers manufacturing
422130	Knives, disposable plastics, wholesaling
335211	Knives, household-type electric carving, manufacturing
339112	Knives, surgical, manufacturing
339992	Knobs, organ, manufacturing
321999	Knobs, wood, manufacturing
333292	Knot tying machinery for textiles manufacturing

Code	Description
333513	Knurling machines, metalworking, manufacturing
322130	Kraft liner board manufacturing
322121	Kraft paper stock manufacturing
212325	Kyanite mining and/or beneficiating
334419	LCD (liquid crystal display) screen units manufacturing
334413	LED (light emitting diode) manufacturing
621399	LPNs' (licensed practical nurses) offices (e.g., centers, clinics)
484122	LTL (less-than-truckload) long-distance freight trucking
321213	LVL (laminated veneer lumber) manufacturing
339942	Label making equipment, handheld, manufacturing
333993	Labeling (i.e., packaging) machinery manufacturing
561910	Labeling services
323110	Labels lithographic (offset) printing on a job-order basis
313221	Labels weaving
422310	Labels, textile, wholesaling
561320	Labor (except farm) contractors (i.e., personnel suppliers)
561320	Labor (except farm) pools
115115	Labor contractors, farm
813930	Labor federations
561330	Labor leasing services
926150	Labor management negotiations boards, government
541612	Labor relations consulting services
926110	Labor statistics agencies
813930	Labor unions (except apprenticeship programs)
54	Laboratories (see specific type)
621512	Laboratories, dental X-ray
233310	Laboratories, manufacturing, construction
621511	Laboratories, medical (except radiological, X-ray)
621512	Laboratories, medical radiological or X-ray
334516	Laboratory analytical instruments (except optical) manufacturing
333314	Laboratory analytical optical instruments (e.g., microscopes) manufacturing
311119	Laboratory animal feed manufacturing
112990	Laboratory animal production (e.g., guinea pigs, mice, rats)
315211	Laboratory coats, men's and boys', cut and sew apparel contractors
315225	Laboratory coats, men's and boys', cut and sewn from purchased fabric (except apparel contractors)
315212	Laboratory coats, women's, cut and sew apparel contractors
315239	Laboratory coats, women's, misses', and girls', cut and sewn from purchased fabric (except apparel contractors)
421490	Laboratory equipment (except dental, medical, ophthalmic) wholesaling
421450	Laboratory equipment, dental and medical, wholesaling
327215	Laboratory glassware (e.g., beakers, test tubes, vials) made from purchased glass
327212	Laboratory glassware (e.g., beakers, test tubes, vials) made in glass making plants
811219	Laboratory instrument repair and maintenance services
512199	Laboratory services, motion picture

Code	Description
334515	Laboratory standards testing instruments (e.g., capacitance, electrical resistance, inductance) manufacturing
541380	Laboratory testing (except medical, veterinary) services
621511	Laboratory testing services, medical (except radiological, X-ray)
621512	Laboratory testing services, medical radiological or X-ray
541940	Laboratory testing services, veterinary
233320	Laboratory, commercial and educational, construction
339111	Laboratory-type centrifuges manufacturing
339111	Laboratory-type distilling apparatus manufacturing
339111	Laboratory-type equipment (e.g., balances, centrifuges, furnaces) manufacturing
339111	Laboratory-type evaporation apparatus manufacturing
339111	Laboratory-type freezers manufacturing
339111	Laboratory-type furniture (e.g., benches, cabinets, stools, tables) (except dental) manufacturing
339111	Laboratory-type sample preparation apparatus manufacturing
333292	Lace and net making machinery manufacturing
316110	Lace leather manufacturing
313249	Lace manufacturing
313249	Lace products (except apparel) made in lace mills
314999	Lace, burnt-out, manufacturing
313221	Laces (e.g. shoe), textile, manufacturing
316999	Laces (e.g., shoe), leather, manufacturing
332812	Lacquering metals and metal products for the trade
333994	Lacquering ovens manufacturing
325510	Lacquers manufacturing
422950	Lacquers wholesaling
325199	Lactic acid manufacturing
311514	Lactose manufacturing
332999	Ladder jacks, metal, manufacturing
321999	Ladder jacks, wood, manufacturing
321912	Ladder rounds or rungs, hardwood, manufacturing
421830	Ladders wholesaling
321999	Ladders, extension, wood, manufacturing
326199	Ladders, fiberglass, manufacturing
332323	Ladders, metal chain, manufacturing
332323	Ladders, permanently installed, metal, manufacturing
332999	Ladders, portable metal, manufacturing
332313	Ladle bails, fabricated metal plate work, manufacturing
332313	Ladles, fabricated metal plate work, manufacturing
312120	Lager brewing
483211	Lake freight transportation (except on Great Lakes system)
483113	Lake freight transportation, Great Lakes
483212	Lake passenger transportation (except on Great Lakes system)
483114	Lake passenger transportation, Great Lakes
325132	Lakes (i.e., organic pigments) manufacturing
311611	Lamb carcasses, half carcasses, primal and sub-primal cuts, produced in slaughtering plants

Code	Description
112410	Lamb feedlots (except stockyards for transportation)
311612	Lamb, primal and sub-primal cuts, made from purchased carcasses
332999	Laminated aluminum foil (except bags, liners) manufacturing
327215	Laminated glass made from purchased glass
327211	Laminated glass made in glass making plants
326130	Laminated plastics plate, rod, and sheet, manufacturing
321213	Laminated structural wood members (except trusses) manufacturing
321213	Laminated veneer lumber (LVL) manufacturing
322225	Laminating foil for flexible packaging applications
332813	Laminating metals and metal formed products without fabricating
322222	Laminating purchased foil sheets for nonpackaging applications
322226	Laminating purchased paperboard
322222	Laminating purchased papers for nonpackaging applications
322221	Laminating purchased papers for packaging applications
313320	Laminating purchased textiles
335311	Lamp ballasts manufacturing
327112	Lamp bases, pottery, manufacturing
325182	Lamp black manufacturing
335110	Lamp bulb parts (except glass blanks), electric, manufacturing
335110	Lamp bulbs and tubes, electric (i.e., fluorescent, incandescent filament, vapor), manufacturing
335110	Lamp bulbs and tubes, health, infrared and ultraviolet radiation, manufacturing
332618	Lamp frames, wire, made from purchased wire
335931	Lamp holders manufacturing
332999	Lamp shade frames, metal, manufacturing
335121	Lamp shades (except glass, plastics), residential, manufacturing
327215	Lamp shades made from purchased glass
327212	Lamp shades made in glass making plants
326199	Lamp shades, plastics, manufacturing
442299	Lamp shops, electric
335931	Lamp sockets and receptacles (i.e., electric wiring devices) manufacturing
421220	Lamps (i.e., lighting fixtures) wholesaling
335122	Lamps (i.e., lighting fixtures), commercial, industrial, and institutional, manufacturing
335121	Lamps (i.e., lighting fixtures), residential, electric, manufacturing
334517	Lamps, X-ray, manufacturing
335129	Lamps, insect, electric fixture, manufacturing
234990	Land clearing
234990	Land drainage construction contractors
234990	Land leveling, irrigation, construction contractors
924120	Land management program administration
421820	Land preparation machinery, agricultural, wholesaling
333120	Land preparation machinery, construction, manufacturing

Code	Description
421810	Land preparation machinery, construction, wholesaling
234990	Land reclamation
925120	Land redevelopment agencies, government
531190	Land rental or leasing
233110	Land subdividers and developers (except cemeteries)
541370	Land surveying services
335312	Land transportation motors and generators manufacturing
541320	Land use design services
541320	Land use planning services
562212	Landfills
332312	Landing mats, aircraft, metal, manufacturing
541320	Landscape architects' offices
541320	Landscape architects' private practices
541320	Landscape architectural services
561730	Landscape care and maintenance services
541320	Landscape consulting services
561730	Landscape contractors (except construction)
541320	Landscape design services
561730	Landscape installation services
541320	Landscape planning services
561730	Landscaping services (except planning)
541930	Language interpretation services
541720	Language research and development services
611630	Language schools
541930	Language services (e.g., interpretation, sign, translation)
541930	Language translation services
335129	Lanterns (e.g., carbide, electric, gas, gasoline, kerosene) manufacturing
339913	Lapidary work manufacturing
334111	Laptop computers manufacturing
311613	Lard made from purchased fat
311611	Lard produced in slaughtering plants
422470	Lard wholesaling
333512	Laser boring, drilling, and cutting machines, metalworking, manufacturing
334413	Laser diodes manufacturing
532230	Laser disc, video, rental
334612	Laser disks, prerecorded video, mass reproducing
334510	Laser equipment, electromedical, manufacturing
334510	Laser systems and equipment, medical, manufacturing
333992	Laser welding equipment manufacturing
316999	Lashes (i.e., whips) manufacturing
321999	Last sole patterns, all materials, manufacturing
212325	Laterite mining and/or beneficiating
326299	Latex foam rubber manufacturing
325510	Latex paint (i.e., water based) manufacturing
325212	Latex rubber, synthetic, manufacturing
332312	Lath, expanded metal, manufacturing
321219	Lath, fiber, manufacturing
327420	Lath, gypsum, manufacturing
321912	Lath, wood, manufacturing
333512	Lathes, metalworking, manufacturing
333210	Lathes, woodworking-type, manufacturing
235420	Lathing construction contractors
321912	Lathmills, wood
316110	Latigo leather manufacturing
812332	Laundered mat and rug supply services
812332	Launderers, industrial
812310	Launderettes

Laundries—Leather

Code	Description
812320	Laundries (except coin-operated, linen supply, uniform supply)
812310	Laundries, coin-operated or similar self-service
812331	Laundries, linen and uniform supply
812310	Laundromats
812320	Laundry and drycleaning agents
314911	Laundry bags made from purchased woven or knitted materials
325612	Laundry bluing manufacturing
812320	Laundry drop-off and pick-up sites
335224	Laundry equipment (e.g., dryers, washers), household-type, manufacturing
333312	Laundry extractors manufacturing
332439	Laundry hampers, light gauge metal, manufacturing
337125	Laundry hampers, rattan, reed, wicker or willow, manufacturing
812310	Laundry machine routes (i.e., concession operators), coin-operated or similar self-service
333312	Laundry machinery and equipment (except household-type) manufacturing
421620	Laundry machinery and equipment, household-type (e.g., dryers, washers), wholesaling
421850	Laundry machinery, equipment, and supplies, commercial, wholesaling
314999	Laundry nets made from purchased materials
333312	Laundry pressing machines (except household-type) manufacturing
812320	Laundry services (except coin-operated, linen supply, uniform supply)
812310	Laundry services, coin-operated or similar self-service
812332	Laundry services, industrial
812331	Laundry services, linen supply
325611	Laundry soap, chips, and powder manufacturing
422690	Laundry soap, chips, and powder, wholesaling
332998	Laundry tubs, metal, manufacturing
326191	Laundry tubs, plastics, manufacturing
325199	Lauric acid esters and amines manufacturing
332998	Lavatories, metal, manufacturing
327111	Lavatories, vitreous china, manufacturing
922190	Law enforcement statistics centers, government
541110	Law firms
541110	Law offices
541110	Law practices
611310	Law schools
333112	Lawn and garden equipment manufacturing
811411	Lawn and garden equipment repair and maintenance services without retailing new lawn and garden equipment
713990	Lawn bowling clubs
561730	Lawn care services (e.g., fertilizing, mowing, seeding, spraying)
422910	Lawn care supplies (e.g., chemicals, fertilizers, pesticides) wholesaling
332212	Lawn edgers, nonpowered, manufacturing
333112	Lawn edgers, powered, manufacturing
561730	Lawn fertilizing services
337125	Lawn furniture (except concrete, metal, stone, wood) manufacturing
337124	Lawn furniture, metal, manufacturing
337122	Lawn furniture, wood, manufacturing
332919	Lawn hose nozzles and lawn sprinklers manufacturing
421820	Lawn maintenance machinery and equipment wholesaling
561730	Lawn maintenance services
811411	Lawn mower repair and maintenance shops without retailing new lawn mowers
421820	Lawn mowers wholesaling
561730	Lawn mowing services
444210	Lawn power equipment stores
561730	Lawn seeding services
561730	Lawn spraying services
444220	Lawn supply stores
532490	Lawnmower rental or leasing
333112	Lawnmowers (except agricultural-type), powered, manufacturing
333111	Lawnmowers, agricultural-type, powered, manufacturing
332212	Lawnmowers, nonpowered, manufacturing
541110	Lawyers' offices
541110	Lawyers' private practices
325412	Laxative preparations manufacturing
112310	Layer-type chicken production
212291	Leaching of uranium, radium, or vanadium ores
335911	Lead acid storage batteries manufacturing
331491	Lead and lead alloy bar, pipe, plate, rod, sheet, strip, and tubing made from purchased metals or scrap
325131	Lead based pigments manufacturing
235990	Lead burning construction contractors
331528	Lead castings (except die-castings), unfinished, manufacturing
331522	Lead die-castings, unfinished, manufacturing
332999	Lead foil not made in rolling mills
212231	Lead ore mine site development for own account
212231	Lead ore mining and/or beneficiating
325188	Lead oxides (except pigments) manufacturing
562910	Lead paint abatement services
562910	Lead paint removal contractors
325131	Lead pigments manufacturing
331492	Lead recovering from scrap and/or alloying purchased metals
331491	Lead rolling, drawing, or extruding purchased metals or scrap
325188	Lead silicate manufacturing
331419	Lead smelting and refining, primary
327992	Lead, black (i.e., natural graphite), ground, refined, or blended, manufacturing
335110	Lead-in wires, electric lamp, made from purchased wire
212231	Lead-zinc ore mining and/or beneficiating
333112	Leaf blowers manufacturing
332212	Leaf skimmers and rakes, nonpowered swimming pool, manufacturing
332611	Leaf springs manufacturing
422590	Leaf tobacco wholesaling
332999	Leaf, metal, manufacturing
334519	Leak detectors, water, manufacturing
813920	Learned societies
611691	Learning centers offering remedial courses
541720	Learning disabilities research and development services
211111	Lease condensate production
213112	Lease tank, erecting, cleaning, and repairing on a contract basis
316999	Leashes, dog, manufacturing
******	Leasing — see type of property or article being leased
522220	Leasing in combination with sales financing
315292	Leather apparel (e.g., capes, coats, hats, jackets) (except apparel contractors) manufacturing
315211	Leather apparel (e.g., capes, coats, hats, jackets), men's and boys', cut and sew apparel contractors
315212	Leather apparel (e.g., capes, coats, hats, jackets), women's, girls', and infants', cut and sew apparel contractors
316999	Leather belting manufacturing
315292	Leather clothing (except apparel contractors) manufacturing
315212	Leather clothing manufacturing, women's, girls', and infants', cut and sew apparel contractors
315211	Leather clothing, men's and boys', cut and sew apparel contractors
448190	Leather coat stores
316110	Leather coloring, cutting, embossing, and japanning
316110	Leather converters
422990	Leather cut stock (except boot, shoe) wholesaling
316999	Leather cut stock for shoe and boot manufacturing
422340	Leather cut stock for shoe and boot wholesaling
316219	Leather footwear (except house slippers, men's, women's) manufacturing
316213	Leather footwear, men's (except athletic, slippers), manufacturing
316212	Leather footwear, slippers, manufacturing
316214	Leather footwear, women's (except athletic, slippers), manufacturing
812320	Leather garment cleaning services
315211	Leather gloves or mittens (except athletic), men's and boys', cut and sew apparel contractors
315212	Leather gloves or mittens (except athletic), women's, girls', and infants', cut and sew apparel contractors
315992	Leather gloves or mittens (except athletic, cut and sewn apparel contractors) manufacturing
339920	Leather gloves, athletic, manufacturing
422990	Leather goods (except belting, footwear, handbags, gloves, luggage) wholesaling
811430	Leather goods repair shops without retailing new leather goods
448320	Leather goods stores
316993	Leather goods, small personal (e.g., coin purses, eyeglass cases, key cases), manufacturing
316992	Leather handbags and purses manufacturing
316212	Leather house slippers manufacturing
316991	Leather luggage manufacturing
316110	Leather tanning, currying, and finishing
316219	Leather upper athletic footwear manufacturing
316999	Leather welting manufacturing
333298	Leather working machinery manufacturing
313320	Leather, artificial, made from purchased fabric

Code	Description	Code	Description	Code	Description
322226	Leatherboard (i.e., paperboard based) made from purchased paperboard	333515	Letter pins (e.g., gauging, measuring) manufacturing	334511	Light reconnaissance and surveillance systems and equipment manufacturing
322130	Leatherboard (i.e., paperboard based) made in paperboard mills	561410	Letter writing services	334512	Light responsive appliance controls manufacturing
311225	Lecithin made from purchased oils	325910	Letterpress inks manufacturing	441110	Light utility truck dealers, new only or new and used
311223	Lecithin, cottonseed, made in crushing mills	323122	Letterpress plate preparation services	441120	Light utility truck dealers, used only
311222	Lecithin, soybean, made in crushing mills	333293	Letterpress printing presses manufacturing	336112	Light utility trucks assembling on chassis of own manufacture
111219	Leek farming, field, bedding plant and seed production	339950	Letters for signs manufacturing	325998	Lighter fluids (e.g., charcoal, cigarette) manufacturing
541110	Legal aid services	322231	Letters, die-cut, made from purchased cardboard	483211	Lighterage (i.e., freight transportation except vessel supply services)
922130	Legal counsel offices, government	111219	Lettuce farming, field, bedding plant and seed production	339999	Lighters, cigar and cigarette (except motor vehicle, precious metal), manufacturing
315119	Leggings knitting or knitting and finishing	234990	Levee construction	339911	Lighters, cigar and cigarette, clad with precious metal, manufacturing
315291	Leggings, infants', cut and sewn from purchased fabric (except apparel contractors)	334513	Level and bulk measuring instruments, industrial process-type, manufacturing	422990	Lighters, cigar and cigarette, wholesaling
316999	Leggings, welder's, leather, manufacturing	334519	Level gauges, radiation-type, manufacturing	488310	Lighthouse operation
315212	Leggings, women's, girls', and infants', cut and sew apparel contractors	334519	Levels and tapes, surveying, manufacturing	335991	Lighting carbons manufacturing
315239	Leggings, women's, misses' and girls', cut and sewn from purchased fabric (except apparel contractors)	332212	Levels, carpenter's, manufacturing	421990	Lighting equipment, gas, wholesaling
315239	Leggins, women's, misses', and girls', cut and sewn from purchased fabric (except apparel contractors)	524126	Liability insurance carriers, direct	444190	Lighting fixture stores
921140	Legislative and executive office combinations	514120	Libraries (except motion picture stock footage, motion picture commercial distribution)	335129	Lighting fixtures, airport (e.g., approach, ramp, runway, taxi), manufacturing
921120	Legislative assemblies	512199	Libraries, motion picture stock footage film	335122	Lighting fixtures, commercial electric, manufacturing
921120	Legislative bodies (e.g., federal, local, and state)	512199	Libraries, videotape, stock footage	421610	Lighting fixtures, electric, wholesaling
921120	Legislative commissions	233320	Library construction	335122	Lighting fixtures, industrial electric, manufacturing
111320	Lemon groves	561990	License issuing services (except government), motor vehicle	335122	Lighting fixtures, institutional electric, manufacturing
325998	Lemon oil manufacturing	621399	Licensed practical nurses' (LPNs) offices (e.g., centers, clinics)	335129	Lighting fixtures, nonelectric (e.g., propane, kerosene, carbide), manufacturing
514120	Lending libraries	926130	Licensing and inspecting of utilities	335121	Lighting fixtures, residential electric, manufacturing
421460	Lens blanks, ophthalmic, wholesaling	926150	Licensing and permit issuance for business operations, government	561790	Lighting maintenance services (e.g., bulb and fuse replacement and cleaning)
327215	Lens blanks, optical and ophthalmic, made from purchased glass	926150	Licensing and permit issuance for professional occupations, government	235310	Lighting system construction contractors
327212	Lens blanks, optical and ophthalmic, made in glass making plants	926120	Licensing of transportation equipment, facilities, and services	711510	Lighting technicians, theatrical, independent
326199	Lens blanks, plastics ophthalmic or optical, manufacturing	311340	Licorice candy manufacturing	335311	Lighting transformers manufacturing
333314	Lens coating (except ophthalmic)	332431	Lids and ends, can, metal, manufacturing	335311	Lighting transformers, street and airport, manufacturing
339115	Lens coating, ophthalmic	332115	Lids, jar, metal, stamping	335931	Lightning arrestors and coils manufacturing
333314	Lens grinding (except ophthalmic)	561611	Lie detection services	235990	Lightning conductor construction contractors
339115	Lens grinding, ophthalmic (except in retail stores)	334519	Lie detectors manufacturing	335931	Lightning protection equipment manufacturing
446130	Lens grinding, ophthalmic, in retail stores	611699	Life guard training	326211	Lignin plastics manufacturing
333315	Lens hoods, camera, manufacturing	524210	Life insurance agencies	213113	Lignite mining services on a contract basis
333314	Lens mounting (except ophthalmic)	524113	Life insurance carriers, direct	212111	Lignite surface mining and/or beneficiating
339115	Lens mounts, ophthalmic, manufacturing	339113	Life preservers manufacturing	111130	Lima bean farming, dry, field and seed production
333314	Lens polishing (except ophthalmic)	326199	Life rafts, inflatable plastics, manufacturing	339113	Limbs, artificial, manufacturing
339115	Lens polishing, ophthalmic	326299	Life rafts, inflatable rubberized fabric, manufacturing	421320	Lime (except agricultural) wholesaling
333314	Lenses (except ophthalmic) manufacturing	524130	Life reinsurance carriers	111320	Lime groves
339115	Lenses, ophthalmic, manufacturing	541710	Life sciences research and development laboratories or services	325998	Lime oil manufacturing
111130	Lentil farming, dry, field and seed production	561320	Lifeguard supply services	327410	Lime production
315191	Leotards made in apparel knitting mills	421830	Lift trucks, industrial, wholesaling	212312	Lime rock, ground, mining and/or beneficiating
315212	Leotards, women's, girls', and infants', cut and sew apparel contractors	316999	Lifts, heel, leather, manufacturing	422910	Lime, agricultural, wholesaling
315239	Leotards, women's, misses', and girls', cut and sewn from purchased fabric (except apparel contractors)	333298	Light bulb and tube (i.e., electric lamp) machinery manufacturing	325320	Lime-sulfur fungicides manufacturing
212393	Lepidolite mining and/or beneficiating	335110	Light bulbs manufacturing	212312	Limestone (except bituminous) crushed and broken stone mining and/or beneficiating
622310	Leprosy hospitals	421610	Light bulbs wholesaling		
******	Lessors — see specific type of asset or property being rented or leased	335110	Light bulbs, sealed beam automotive, manufacturing	212312	Limestone beneficiating plants (e.g., grinding or pulverizing)
333313	Letter folding, stuffing, and sealing machinery manufacturing	334413	Light emitting diodes (LED) manufacturing		
		333315	Light meters, photographic, manufacturing		
		336510	Light rail cars and equipment manufacturing		
		485119	Light rail systems (except mixed mode), commuter		

Limestone—Locker

Code	Description
212311	Limestone mining or quarrying
212319	Limestone, bituminous, mining and/or beneficiating
334512	Limit controls (e.g., air-conditioning, appliance, heating) manufacturing
511199	Limited editions art print publishers
452990	Limited price variety stores
212210	Limonite mining and/or beneficiating
532111	Limousine rental without driver
485320	Limousine services (except shuttle services)
485320	Limousines for hire with driver (except taxis)
325320	Lindane pesticides manufacturing
334512	Line or limit control for electric heat manufacturing
561730	Line slash (i.e., rights of way) maintenance services
335311	Line voltage regulators (i.e., electric transformers) manufacturing
335999	Linear accelerators manufacturing
332991	Linear ball bearings manufacturing
334514	Linear counters manufacturing
325222	Linear esters fibers and filaments manufacturing
332991	Linear roller bearings manufacturing
442299	Linen stores
812331	Linen supply services
421220	Linens (e.g., bath, bed, table) wholesaling
314129	Linens made from purchased materials
327123	Liner brick and plates, vitrified clay, manufacturing
332313	Liners, industrial, fabricated metal plate work, manufacturing
114111	Lingcod fishing
448190	Lingerie stores
422330	Lingerie wholesaling
315212	Lingerie, women's, cut and sew apparel contractors
315231	Lingerie, women's, misses', and girls', cut and sewn from purchased fabric (except apparel contractors)
316110	Lining leather manufacturing
316999	Linings, boot and shoe, leather, manufacturing
314999	Linings, casket, manufacturing
315211	Linings, hat, men's, cut and sew apparel contractors
315999	Linings, hat, men's, cut and sewn from purchased fabric (except apparel contractors)
314999	Linings, luggage, manufacturing
332999	Linings, metal safe and vault, manufacturing
332994	Links, ammunition (i.e., 30 mm. or less, 1.18 inch or less), manufacturing
332995	Links, ammunition (i.e., more than 30 mm., more than 1.18 inch), manufacturing
325199	Linoleic acid esters and amines manufacturing
235520	Linoleum construction contractors
326192	Linoleum floor coverings manufacturing
333293	Linotype machines manufacturing
311225	Linseed oil made from purchased oils
311223	Linseed oil, cake and meal, made in crushing mills
327390	Lintels, concrete, manufacturing
325412	Lip balms manufacturing
325620	Lipsticks manufacturing
422690	Liquefied gases (except LP) wholesaling
422710	Liquefied petroleum gas (LPG) bulk stations and terminals

Code	Description
332420	Liquefied petroleum gas (LPG) cylinders manufacturing
454312	Liquefied petroleum gas (LPG) dealers, direct selling
221210	Liquefied petroleum gas (LPG) distribution through mains
324110	Liquefied petroleum gas (LPG) made in refineries
422720	Liquefied petroleum gas (LPG) wholesaling (except bulk stations, terminals)
211112	Liquefied petroleum gases (LPG), natural
325120	Liquid air manufacturing
334513	Liquid analysis instruments, industrial process-type, manufacturing
311313	Liquid beet syrup manufacturing
334516	Liquid chromatographic instruments, laboratory-type, manufacturing
334513	Liquid concentration instruments, industrial process-type, manufacturing
334514	Liquid flow meters manufacturing
211112	Liquid hydrocarbons recovered from oil and gas field gases
334512	Liquid level controls, residential and commercial heating-type, manufacturing
334513	Liquid level instruments, industrial process-type, manufacturing
332420	Liquid oxygen tanks manufacturing
311313	Liquid sugar made from beet sugar
311312	Liquid sugar made from purchased raw cane sugar
311311	Liquid sugar made in sugarcane mill
211112	Liquids, natural gas (e.g., ethane, isobutane, natural gasoline, propane) recovered from oil and gas field gases
445310	Liquor stores, package
311320	Liquor, chocolate, made from cacao beans
311330	Liquor, chocolate, made from purchased chocolate
422820	Liquors wholesaling
312130	Liquors, brandy, distilling and blending
422820	Liquors, distilled, wholesaling
312140	Liquors, distilling and blending (except brandy)
339942	List finders and roledex address files manufacturing
531390	Listing services, real estate
711410	Literary agents
325131	Litharge manufacturing
335912	Lithium batteries, primary, manufacturing
325188	Lithium compounds, not specified elsewhere by process, manufacturing
212393	Lithium mineral mining and/or beneficiating
325910	Lithographic inks manufacturing
323122	Lithographic plate preparation services
323110	Lithographic printing (except books, manifold business forms, printing grey goods, quick printing)
333293	Lithographic printing presses manufacturing
325131	Lithopone manufacturing
334510	Lithotripters manufacturing
711310	Live arts center operators
422990	Live bait wholesaling
711310	Live theater operators
332995	Livens projectors (i.e., ordnance) manufacturing
422520	Livestock (except horses, mules) wholesaling

Code	Description
422520	Livestock auction markets (except horses, mules)
422590	Livestock auction markets, horses and mules
541690	Livestock breeding consulting services
115210	Livestock breeding services (except consulting)
422910	Livestock feeds wholesaling
311119	Livestock feeds, supplements, concentrates and premixes, manufacturing
541940	Livestock inspecting and testing services, veterinary
115210	Livestock spraying
484220	Livestock trucking, local
484230	Livestock trucking, long-distance
541940	Livestock veterinary services
422590	Livestock, horses and mules, wholesaling
337124	Living room furniture (except upholstered), metal, manufacturing
337122	Living room furniture (except upholstered), wood, manufacturing
337121	Living room furniture, upholstered, manufacturing
112990	Llama production
334418	Loaded computer boards manufacturing
421430	Loaded computer boards wholesaling
333120	Loaders, shovel, manufacturing
332993	Loading and assembling bombs
488490	Loading and unloading at truck terminals
488320	Loading and unloading services at ports and harbors
488210	Loading and unloading services at rail terminals
333131	Loading machines, underground mining, manufacturing
334418	Loading printed circuit boards
234990	Loading station construction, mine, general construction contractor
522310	Loan brokerages
522310	Loan brokers' or agents' offices (i.e., independent)
522291	Loan companies (i.e., consumer, personal, small, student)
522292	Loan correspondents (i.e., lending funds with real estate as collateral)
522390	Loan servicing
541820	Lobbying services
541820	Lobbyists' offices
114112	Lobster fishing
334210	Local area network (LAN) communications equipment (e.g., bridges, gateways, routers) manufacturing
541512	Local area network (LAN) computer systems integration design services
611420	Local area network (LAN) management training
485113	Local bus services (except mixed mode)
492210	Local letter and parcel delivery services (except as part of inter-city carrier network, U.S. Postal Service)
492110	Local letter and parcel delivery services as part of inter-city courier network
485112	Local passenger rail systems (except mixed mode)
813940	Local political organizations
513310	Local telephone carriers (except wireless)
485111	Local transit systems, mixed mode (e.g., bus, commuter rail, subway combinations)
332722	Lock washers, metal, manufacturing
454390	Locker meat provisioners, direct selling

Code	Description
337215	Lockers (except refrigerated) manufacturing
421440	Lockers (except refrigerated) wholesaling
812990	Lockers, coin operated, rental
333415	Lockers, refrigerated, manufacturing
421740	Lockers, refrigerated, wholesaling
332510	Locks (except coin-operated, time locks) manufacturing
234990	Locks and waterway construction
333311	Locks, coin-operated, manufacturing
421710	Locks, security, wholesaling
421850	Locksmith equipment and supplies wholesaling
561622	Locksmith services
561622	Locksmith services with or without sales of locking devices, safes, and security vaults
561622	Locksmith shops
488210	Locomotive and rail car repair (except factory conversion, factory overhaul, factory rebuilding)
336321	Locomotive and railroad car light fixtures manufacturing
333923	Locomotive cranes manufacturing
333618	Locomotive diesel engines manufacturing
336510	Locomotives manufacturing
336510	Locomotives rebuilding
421860	Locomotives wholesaling
212221	Lode gold mining and/or beneficiating
321992	Log cabins, prefabricated wood, manufacturing
333120	Log debarking machinery, portable, manufacturing
333291	Log debarking machinery, stationary, manufacturing
113310	Log harvesting
484220	Log hauling, local
484230	Log hauling, long-distance
333120	Log splitters, portable, manufacturing
333291	Log splitters, stationary, manufacturing
111334	Loganberry farming
113310	Logging
541330	Logging engineering services
532412	Logging equipment rental or leasing without operator
421810	Logging equipment wholesaling
482112	Logging railroads
336212	Logging trailers manufacturing
213112	Logging wells on a contract basis
334515	Logic circuit testers manufacturing
541614	Logistics management consulting services
333414	Logs, gas fireplace, manufacturing
325191	Log wood extract manufacturing
513310	Long-distance telephone carriers (except wireless)
513330	Long-distance telephone resellers (except satellite)
513340	Long-distance telephone satellite communication carriers
488320	Longshoremen services
333292	Loom bobbins manufacturing
333292	Loom reeds manufacturing
333292	Looms for textiles manufacturing
333292	Loopers for textiles manufacturing
323118	Looseleaf binders and devices manufacturing
422120	Looseleaf binders wholesaling
322233	Looseleaf fillers and paper made from purchased paper
322121	Looseleaf fillers and paper made in paper mills

Code	Description
325620	Lotions (e.g., body, face, hand) manufacturing
713290	Lottery control boards (i.e., operating lotteries)
921130	Lottery control boards, nonoperating
713290	Lottery corporations
713290	Lottery ticket sales agents (except retail stores)
713290	Lottery ticket vendors (except retail stores)
334310	Loudspeakers manufacturing
722410	Lounges, cocktail
315192	Lounging robes and dressing gowns made in apparel knitting mills
315291	Lounging robes and dressing gowns, infants', cut and sewn from purchased fabric (except apparel contractors)
315211	Lounging robes and dressing gowns, men's and boys', cut and sew apparel contractors
315221	Lounging robes and dressing gowns, men's and boys', cut and sewn from purchased fabric (except apparel contractors)
315212	Lounging robes and dressing gowns, women's, girls', and infants', cut and sew apparel contractors
315231	Lounging robes and dressing gowns, women's, misses', and girls', cut and sewn from purchased fabric (except apparel contractors)
333314	Loupes (e.g., jewelers) manufacturing
321911	Louver windows and doors, made from purchased glass with wood frame
332321	Louver windows, metal, manufacturing
332322	Louvers, sheet metal, manufacturing
335121	Low voltage lighting equipment, residential, electric, manufacturing
311340	Lozenges, nonmedicated, candy, manufacturing
422710	Lubricating oils and greases bulk stations and terminals
324110	Lubricating oils and greases made in petroleum refineries
422720	Lubricating oils and greases wholesaling (except bulk stations, terminals)
324191	Lubricating oils and greases, petroleum, made from refined petroleum
325998	Lubricating oils and greases, synthetic, manufacturing
336510	Lubrication systems, locomotive (except pumps), manufacturing
332510	Luggage hardware, metal, manufacturing
314999	Luggage linings manufacturing
336399	Luggage racks, car top, automotive, truck, and bus, manufacturing
811430	Luggage repair shops without retailing new luggage
448320	Luggage stores
421990	Luggage wholesaling
316991	Luggage, all materials, manufacturing
335931	Lugs and connectors, electrical, manufacturing
421610	Lugs and connectors, electrical, wholesaling
421310	Lumber (e.g., dressed, finished, rough) wholesaling
321113	Lumber (i.e., rough, dressed) made from logs or bolts
561990	Lumber grading services
444190	Lumber retailing yards
321113	Lumber stacking or sticking, made from logs or bolts

Code	Description
321912	Lumber stacking or sticking, resawing purchased lumber
493190	Lumber storage terminals
321113	Lumber, hardwood dimension, made from logs or bolts
321912	Lumber, hardwood dimension, resawing purchased lumber
321999	Lumber, kiln drying
321213	Lumber, parallel strand, manufacturing
321113	Lumber, softwood dimension, made from logs or bolts
321912	Lumber, softwood dimension, resawing purchased lumber
335122	Luminous panel ceilings, electric, manufacturing
335311	Luminous tube transformers manufacturing
332439	Lunch boxes, light gauge metal, manufacturing
722330	Lunch wagons
311612	Luncheon meat (except poultry) made from purchased carcasses
311611	Luncheon meat (except poultry) produced in slaughtering plants
311615	Luncheon meat, poultry, manufacturing
532111	Luxury automobile rental
485320	Luxury automobiles for hire with driver (except taxis)
325612	Lye, household-type, manufacturing
321219	MDF (medium density fiberboard) manufacturing
621112	MDs' (medical doctors), mental health, offices (e.g., centers, clinics)
621111	MDs' (medical doctors, except mental health) offices (e.g., centers, clinics)
334413	MOS (metal oxide silicon) devices manufacturing
562920	MRF (materials recovery facilities)
621512	MRI (magnetic resonance imaging) centers
334510	MRI (magnetic resonance imaging) medical diagnostic equipment manufacturing
111335	Macadamia farming
422490	Macaroni wholesaling
311823	Macaroni, dry, manufacturing
311991	Macaroni, fresh, manufacturing
332212	Machetes manufacturing
332999	Machine bases, metal, manufacturing
332322	Machine guards, sheet metal, manufacturing
332994	Machine gun belts (i.e., 30 mm. or less, 1.18 inch or less) manufacturing
332995	Machine gun belts (i.e., more than 30 mm., more than 1.18 inch) manufacturing
332994	Machine guns (i.e., 30 mm. or less, 1.18 inch or less) manufacturing
332995	Machine guns (i.e., more than 30 mm., more than 1.18 inch) manufacturing
332722	Machine keys manufacturing
332212	Machine knives (except metal cutting) manufacturing
333515	Machine knives, metal cutting, manufacturing
235950	Machine rigging construction contractors
332710	Machine shops
333515	Machine tool attachments and accessories manufacturing
335311	Machine tool transformers manufacturing
421830	Machine tools and accessories wholesaling

Machine tools—Managers'

Code	Description
811310	Machine tools repair and maintenance services
333512	Machine tools, metal cutting, manufacturing
333513	Machine tools, metal forming, manufacturing
522220	Machinery finance leasing
421420	Machines, office, wholesaling
332212	Machinist's precision measuring tools (except optical) manufacturing
421830	Machinists' precision measuring tools wholesaling
334511	Machmeters manufacturing
114111	Mackerel fishing
315291	Mackinaws, infants', cut and sewn from purchased fabric (except apparel contractors)
315211	Mackinaws, men's and boys', cut and sew apparel contractors
315228	Mackinaws, men's and boys', cut and sewn from purchased fabric (except apparel contractors)
315212	Mackinaws, women's, girls', and infants', cut and sew apparel contractors
315239	Mackinaws, women's, misses', and girls', cut and sewn from purchased fabric (except apparel contractors)
541840	Magazine advertising representatives (i.e., independent of media owners)
511120	Magazine publishers
511120	Magazine publishers and printing combined
511120	Magazine publishers, publishing only
511120	Magazine publishing (i.e., establishments known as publishers)
337122	Magazine racks, wood, manufacturing
451212	Magazine stands (i.e., permanent)
323112	Magazines and periodicals flexographic printing without publishing
323111	Magazines and periodicals gravure printing without publishing
323110	Magazines and periodicals lithographic (offset) printing without publishing
323119	Magazines and periodicals printing (except flexographic, gravure, lithographic, screen) without publishing
323113	Magazines and periodicals screen printing without publishing
422920	Magazines wholesaling
711190	Magic shows
451120	Magic supply stores
711510	Magicians, independent
327125	Magnesia refractory cement manufacturing
325411	Magnesia, medicinal, uncompounded, manufacturing
212325	Magnesite mining and/or beneficiating
327992	Magnesite, crude (e.g., calcined, dead-burned, ground), manufacturing
331491	Magnesium and magnesium alloy bar, rod, shape, sheet, strip, and tubing made from purchased metals or scrap
325188	Magnesium carbonate manufacturing
331528	Magnesium castings (except die-castings), unfinished, manufacturing
325188	Magnesium chloride manufacturing
325188	Magnesium compounds, not specified elsewhere by process, manufacturing
331522	Magnesium die-castings, unfinished, manufacturing
331491	Magnesium foil made by rolling purchased metals or scrap
332999	Magnesium foil not made in rolling mills

Code	Description
331492	Magnesium recovering from scrap and/or alloying purchased metals
331419	Magnesium refining, primary
331491	Magnesium rolling, drawing, or extruding purchased metals or scrap
331422	Magnet wire, insulated, made from purchased copper in wire drawing plants
331319	Magnet wire, insulated, made in aluminum wire drawing plants
331491	Magnet wire, nonferrous metals (except aluminum, copper), made from purchased nonferrous metals (except aluminum, copper) in wire drawing plants
334613	Magnetic and optical media, blank, manufacturing
334514	Magnetic counters manufacturing
334513	Magnetic flow meters, industrial process-type, manufacturing
333513	Magnetic forming machines, metalworking, manufacturing
541360	Magnetic geophysical surveying services
334119	Magnetic ink recognition devices, computer peripheral equipment, manufacturing
334613	Magnetic recording media for tapes, cassettes, and disks, manufacturing
621512	Magnetic resonance imaging (MRI) centers
334510	Magnetic resonance imaging (MRI) medical diagnostic equipment manufacturing
334516	Magnetic resonance imaging (MRI) type apparatus (except medical diagnostic) manufacturing
334613	Magnetic tapes, cassettes and disks, blank, manufacturing
421690	Magnetic tapes, cassettes, and disks, blank, wholesaling
334112	Magnetic/optical combination storage units for computers manufacturing
334519	Magnetometers manufacturing
334411	Magnetron tubes manufacturing
327113	Magnets, permanent, ceramic or ferrite, manufacturing
332999	Magnets, permanent, metallic, manufacturing
339115	Magnifiers, corrective vision-type, manufacturing
333314	Magnifying glasses (except corrective vision-type) manufacturing
333314	Magnifying instruments, optical, manufacturing
114111	Mahimahi fishing
561310	Maid registries
561720	Maid services (i.e., cleaning services)
337215	Mail carrier cases and tables, wood, manufacturing
332322	Mail chutes, sheet metal, manufacturing
333313	Mail handling machinery, post office-type, manufacturing
561499	Mail presorting services
454110	Mail-order houses
561431	Mailbox rental centers, private
561431	Mailbox rental services combined with one or more other office support services, private
332439	Mailboxes, light gauge metal, manufacturing
322214	Mailing cases and tubes, paper fiber (i.e., all-fiber, nonfiber ends of any material), made from purchased paperboard

Code	Description
532420	Mailing equipment rental or leasing
511140	Mailing list compiling services
511140	Mailing list publishers
421420	Mailing machines wholesaling
334111	Mainframe computers manufacturing
488190	Maintenance and repair services, aircraft (except factory conversion, factory overhaul, factory rebuilding)
561730	Maintenance of plants and shrubs in buildings
488210	Maintenance of rights-of-way and structures, railway
488119	Maintenance services, runway
488310	Maintenance services, waterfront terminal (except dredging)
711211	Major league baseball clubs
812112	Make-up (except permanent) salons
325620	Make-up (i.e., cosmetics) manufacturing
812199	Make-up salons, permanent
523110	Making markets for securities
337125	Malacca furniture (except upholstered), household-type, manufacturing
325320	Malathion insecticides manufacturing
325192	Maleic anhydride manufacturing
531120	Mall property operation (i.e., not operating contained businesses) rental or leasing
331511	Malleable iron foundries
332212	Mallets (e.g., rubber, wood) manufacturing
321999	Mallets, wood, manufacturing
325199	Malonic dinitrile manufacturing
524126	Malpractice insurance carriers, direct
311942	Malt extract and syrups manufacturing
422490	Malt extract wholesaling
311213	Malt flour manufacturing
312120	Malt liquor brewing
311213	Malt manufacturing
333294	Malt milling machinery manufacturing
311213	Malt sprouts manufacturing
422490	Malt wholesaling
311514	Malted milk manufacturing
311213	Malting (germinating and drying grains)
311221	Maltodextrins manufacturing
621512	Mammogram (i.e., breast imaging) centers
422690	Man-made fibers wholesaling
711410	Management agencies for artists, entertainers, and other public figures
611430	Management development training
561110	Management services (except complete operation of client's business)
115116	Management services, farm
711310	Managers of agricultural fairs with facilities
711320	Managers of agricultural fairs without facilities
711310	Managers of arts events with facilities
711320	Managers of arts events without facilities
711310	Managers of festivals with facilities
711320	Managers of festivals without facilities
711310	Managers of live performing arts productions (e.g., concerts) with facilities
711320	Managers of live performing arts productions (e.g., concerts) without facilities
711310	Managers of sports events with facilities
711320	Managers of sports events without facilities
531312	Managers' offices, commercial condominium
531312	Managers' offices, commercial real estate

Code	Description
531312	Managers' offices, nonresidential real estate
531311	Managers' offices, residential condominium
531311	Managers' offices, residential real estate
711410	Managers, authors'
711410	Managers, celebrities'
561920	Managers, convention
711410	Managers, entertainers'
711410	Managers, pubic figures'
711410	Managers, sports figures'
561920	Managers, trade fair or show
531312	Managing commercial condominiums
531312	Managing commercial real estate
531311	Managing cooperative apartments
523920	Managing investment funds
523920	Managing mutual funds
561110	Managing offices of dentists
561110	Managing offices of physicians and surgeons
561110	Managing offices of professionals (e.g., dentists, physicians, surgeons)
523920	Managing personal investment trusts
531311	Managing residential condominiums
531311	Managing residential real estate
523920	Managing trusts
111320	Mandarin groves
339992	Mandolins manufacturing
333515	Mandrels (i.e., a machine tool accessory) manufacturing
212299	Manganese concentrates beneficiating
325188	Manganese dioxide manufacturing
331112	Manganese metal ferroalloys manufacturing
212299	Manganese ores mining and/or beneficiating
212210	Manganiferous ores valued for iron content, mining and/or beneficiating
212299	Manganiferousares ores (not valued for iron content) mining and/or beneficiating
212299	Manganite mining and/or beneficiating
111339	Mango farming
325191	Mangrove extract manufacturing
234920	Manhole construction contractors
331511	Manhole covers, cast iron, manufacturing
812113	Manicure and pedicure salons
611511	Manicure and pedicure schools
325620	Manicure preparations manufacturing
812113	Manicurist services
323116	Manifold business forms printing
336312	Manifolds (i.e., intake and exhaust), automotive and truck gasoline engine, manufacturing
332996	Manifolds, pipe, made from purchased metal pipe
322231	Manila folders, die-cut, made from purchased paper or paperboard
325221	Manmade cellulosic fibers manufacturing
313221	Manmade fabric, narrow woven, weaving
313210	Manmade fabrics, broadwoven, weaving
313113	Manmade fiber thread manufacturing
325222	Manmade fibers and filaments (except cellulosic) manufacturing
313111	Manmade staple spun yarns made from purchased fiber
541890	Mannequin decorating services
339999	Mannequins manufacturing
421440	Mannequins wholesaling
325920	Mannitol hexanitrate explosive materials manufacturing

Code	Description
334513	Manometers, industrial process-type, manufacturing
561320	Manpower pools
235430	Mantel construction contractors
621399	Manual-arts therapists' offices (e.g., centers, clinics)
421390	Manufactured (i.e., mobile) homes wholesaling
321991	Manufactured (mobile) buildings for commercial use (e.g., banks, offices) manufacturing
321991	Manufactured (mobile) classrooms manufacturing
453930	Manufactured (mobile) home dealers
531190	Manufactured (mobile) home parks
453930	Manufactured (mobile) home parts and accessory dealers
531190	Manufactured (mobile) home sites rental or leasing
321991	Manufactured (mobile) homes manufacturing
221210	Manufactured gas production and distribution
813910	Manufacturers' associations
233310	Manufacturing and industrial building construction management firms
531120	Manufacturing building rental or leasing
532490	Manufacturing machinery and equipment rental or leasing
541614	Manufacturing management consulting services
541614	Manufacturing operations improvement consulting services
511199	Map publishers
511199	Map publishers and printing combined
511199	Map publishing (i.e., establishments known as publishers)
111998	Maple sap concentrating (i.e., producing pure maple syrup in the field)
111998	Maple sap gathering
111998	Maple syrup (i.e., maple sap reducing)
311999	Maple syrup mixing into other products
541370	Mapping (except geophysical) services
541360	Mapping services, geophysical
422920	Maps (except globe, school, wall) wholesaling
323112	Maps flexographic printing without publishing
323111	Maps gravure printing without publishing
323110	Maps lithographic (offset) printing without publishing
323119	Maps printing (except flexographic, gravure, lithographic, screen) without publishing
323113	Maps screen printing without publishing
212319	Marble crushed and broken stone mining and/or beneficiating
212311	Marble mining or quarrying
235430	Marble, granite, and slate work (interior) construction contractors
235410	Marble, granite, and slatework (i.e., exterior) construction contractors
339932	Marbles manufacturing
212393	Marcasite mining and/or beneficiating
325199	Margaric acid manufacturing
311221	Margarine and other corn oils made by wet milling corn
422490	Margarine wholesaling
311225	Margarine-butter blend made from purchased fats and oils
311225	Margarines (including imitation) made from purchased fats and oils
713930	Marinas

Code	Description
928110	Marine Corps
335314	Marine and navy auxiliary controls, manufacturing
488390	Marine cargo checkers and surveyors
488320	Marine cargo handling services
234990	Marine construction
541330	Marine engineering services
333618	Marine engines manufacturing
332510	Marine hardware, metal, manufacturing
332999	Marine horns, compressed air or steam, metal, manufacturing
524126	Marine insurance carriers, direct
712110	Marine museums
611519	Marine navigational schools
325510	Marine paints manufacturing
332410	Marine power boilers manufacturing
334220	Marine radio communications equipment manufacturing
524130	Marine reinsurance carriers
488330	Marine salvaging services
447190	Marine service stations
488510	Marine shipping agency
335911	Marine storage batteries manufacturing
421860	Marine supplies (except pleasure) wholesaling
421910	Marine supplies, pleasure, wholesaling
441222	Marine supply dealers
541990	Marine surveyor (i.e., ship appraiser) services
488330	Marine vessel traffic reporting services
339999	Marionettes (i.e., puppets) manufacturing
339942	Marker boards (i.e., whiteboards) manufacturing
541910	Marketing analysis services
541613	Marketing consulting services
541613	Marketing management consulting services
541910	Marketing research services
339943	Marking devices manufacturing
422120	Marking devices wholesaling
333518	Marking machines, metal, manufacturing
212312	Marl crushed and broken stone mining and/or beneficiating
311421	Marmalade manufacturing
321999	Marquetry, wood, manufacturing
624190	Marriage counseling services (except by offices of mental health practitioners)
922120	Marshals' offices
311340	Marshmallow creme manufacturing
311340	Marshmallows manufacturing
611620	Martial arts instruction, camps, or schools
311340	Marzipan (i.e., candy) manufacturing
335999	Maser (i.e., microwave amplification by stimulated emission of radiation) amplifiers manufacturing
321999	Mashers, wood potato, manufacturing
322222	Masking tape made from purchased paper
332212	Mason's handtools manufacturing
421320	Mason's materials wholesaling
444190	Masonry (e.g., block, brick, stone) dealers
235410	Masonry construction contractors
334516	Mass spectrometers manufacturing
334516	Mass spectroscopy instrumentation manufacturing
234990	Mass transit construction
335211	Massage machines, electric (except designed for beauty and barber shop use), manufacturing
812199	Massage parlors

Massage—Medical

Code	Description
611519	Massage therapist instruction
512210	Master recording leasing and licensing
422690	Mastics (except construction) wholesaling
321999	Masts, wood, manufacturing
812332	Mat and rug supply services
325998	Matches and match books manufacturing
422990	Matches and match books wholesaling
811310	Materials handling equipment repair and maintenance services
532490	Materials handling machinery and equipment rental or leasing
421830	Materials handling machinery and equipment wholesaling
541614	Materials management consulting services
562920	Materials recovery facilities (MRF)
923120	Maternity and child health program administration
315212	Maternity bras and corsets, women's, cut and sew apparel contractors
315231	Maternity bras and corsets, women's, misses', and girls', cut and sewn from purchased fabric (except apparel contractors)
622310	Maternity hospitals
448120	Maternity shops
541710	Mathematics research and development laboratories or services
332618	Mats and matting made from purchased wire
332212	Mattocks (i.e., handtools) manufacturing
326299	Mattress protectors, rubber, manufacturing
332612	Mattress springs and spring units made from purchased wire
442110	Mattress stores (including waterbeds)
337910	Mattresses (i.e., box spring, innerspring, noninnerspring) manufacturing
337910	Mattresses made from felt, foam rubber, urethane and similar materials
421210	Mattresses wholesaling
326199	Mattresses, air, plastics, manufacturing
326299	Mattresses, air, rubber, manufacturing
311812	Matzo baking made in commercial bakeries
332212	Mauls, metal, manufacturing
321999	Mauls, wood, manufacturing
233320	Mausoleum construction
812220	Mausoleums
311941	Mayonnaise manufacturing
921110	Mayor's offices
624210	Meal delivery programs
311119	Meal, alfalfa, manufacturing
311119	Meal, bone, prepared as feed for animals and fowls, manufacturing
311211	Meal, corn, for human consumption made in flour mills
421830	Measuring and testing equipment (except automotive) wholesaling
333515	Measuring attachments (e.g., sine bars) for machine tool manufacturing
334515	Measuring equipment for electronic and electrical circuits and equipment manufacturing
811219	Measuring instrument repair and maintenance services
334515	Measuring instruments and meters, electric, manufacturing
334513	Measuring instruments, industrial process control-type, manufacturing
332212	Measuring tools, machinist's (except optical), manufacturing

Code	Description
334514	Measuring wheels manufacturing
311613	Meat and bone meal and tankage, produced in rendering plant
311612	Meat canning (except baby, pet food, poultry), made from purchased carcasses
311611	Meat canning (except poultry) produced in slaughtering plants
311422	Meat canning, baby food, manufacturing
311111	Meat canning, dog and cat, pet food, made from purchased carcasses
311615	Meat canning, poultry (except baby and pet food), manufacturing
311612	Meat extracts made from purchased carcasses
333294	Meat grinders, food-type, manufacturing
445210	Meat markets
311615	Meat products (e.g., hot dogs, luncheon meats, sausages) made from a combination of poultry and other meats
311612	Meat products canning (except baby, pet food, poultry) made from purchased carcasses
311111	Meat products, dog and cat, pet food, canning, made from purchased carcasses
311612	Meats (except poultry), cured or smoked, made from purchased carcasses
422470	Meats and meat products (except canned, packaged frozen) wholesaling
311611	Meats fresh, chilled or frozen (except poultry and small game), produced in slaughtering plants
422490	Meats, canned, wholesaling
311611	Meats, cured or smoked, produced in slaughtering plants
422470	Meats, cured or smoked, wholesaling
311612	Meats, fresh or chilled (except poultry and small game), frozen, made from purchased carcasses
422470	Meats, fresh, wholesaling
422470	Meats, frozen (except packaged), wholesaling
422420	Meats, packaged frozen, wholesaling
611513	Mechanic's apprenticeship training
333924	Mechanic's creepers manufacturing
325611	Mechanic's hand soaps and pastes manufacturing
332212	Mechanic's handtools, nonpowered, manufacturing
611519	Mechanic's schools (except apprenticeship)
421120	Mechanic's tools wholesaling
235110	Mechanical construction contractors
541330	Mechanical engineering services
313311	Mechanical finishing of broadwoven fabrics
316110	Mechanical leather manufacturing
334513	Mechanical measuring instruments, industrial process-type, manufacturing
339942	Mechanical pencil refills manufacturing
339941	Mechanical pencils manufacturing
811310	Mechanical power transmission equipment repair and maintenance services
421840	Mechanical power transmission supplies (e.g., gears, pulleys, sprockets) wholesaling
326291	Mechanical rubber goods (i.e., extruded, lathe-cut, molded) manufacturing
421840	Mechanical rubber goods wholesaling
541380	Mechanical testing laboratories or services

Code	Description
333311	Mechanisms for coin-operated machines manufacturing
334518	Mechanisms, clockwork operated device, manufacturing
541840	Media advertising representatives (i.e., independent of media owners)
541830	Media buying agencies
541830	Media buying services
541840	Media representatives (i.e., independent of media owners)
926150	Mediation and conciliation services, government
624190	Mediation, social service, family, agencies
621512	Medical X-ray laboratories
811219	Medical and surgical equipment repair and maintenance services
541430	Medical art services
541430	Medical artists, independent
923130	Medical assistance programs administration, government
531120	Medical building rental or leasing
334510	Medical cleaning equipment, ultrasonic, manufacturing
524298	Medical cost evaluation services
621112	Medical doctors' (MDs), mental health, offices (e.g. centers, clinics)
621111	Medical doctors' (MDs, except mental health) offices (e.g., centers, clinics)
532490	Medical equipment (except home health furniture and equipment) rental or leasing
421450	Medical equipment wholesaling
421450	Medical furniture wholesaling
327215	Medical glassware made from purchased glass
327212	Medical glassware made in glass making plants
421450	Medical glassware wholesaling
541430	Medical illustration services
541430	Medical illustrators, independent
421450	Medical instruments wholesaling
524114	Medical insurance carriers, direct
621511	Medical laboratories (except radiological, X-ray)
621512	Medical laboratories, radiological or X-ray
621511	Medical pathology laboratories
541922	Medical photography services
334517	Medical radiation therapy equipment manufacturing
621512	Medical radiological laboratories
524130	Medical reinsurance carriers
541710	Medical research and development laboratories or services
611310	Medical schools
315211	Medical service apparel, men's and boys', cut and sew apparel contractors
315225	Medical service apparel, men's and boys', cut and sewn from purchased fabric (except apparel contractors)
315212	Medical service apparel, women's, cut and sew apparel contractors
315239	Medical service apparel, women's, misses', and girls', cut and sewn from purchased fabric (except apparel contractors)
524114	Medical service plans without providing health care services
422210	Medical sundries, rubber, wholesaling
421450	Medical supplies wholesaling
611519	Medical technician schools
339112	Medical thermometers manufacturing

Code	Description
334510	Medical ultrasound equipment manufacturing
923130	Medicare and Medicaid administration
325411	Medicinal chemicals, uncompounded, manufacturing
337110	Medicine cabinets (except freestanding), wood household-type, manufacturing
337124	Medicine cabinets, metal household-type, manufacturing
321219	Medium density fiberboard (MDF) manufacturing
212399	Meerschaum mining and/or beneficiating
531120	Meeting hall and room rental or leasing
325211	Melamine resins manufacturing
111219	Melon farming (e.g., cantaloupe, casaba, honeydew, watermelon), field, bedding plant and seed production
111419	Melon farming, grown under cover
313230	Melt blown nonwoven fabrics manufacturing
315291	Melton jackets, infants', cut and sewn from purchased fabric (except apparel contractors)
315211	Melton jackets, men's and boys', cut and sew apparel contractors
315228	Melton jackets, men's and boys', cut and sewn from purchased fabric (except apparel contractors)
315212	Melton jackets, women's, girls', and infants', cut and sew apparel contractors
315239	Melton jackets, women's, misses', and girls', cut and sewn from purchased fabric (except apparel contractors)
813410	Membership associations, civic or social
721110	Membership hotels
812220	Memorial gardens (i.e., burial places)
334418	Memory boards manufacturing
422320	Men's and boys' clothing wholesaling
422320	Men's and boys' furnishings (except shoes) wholesaling
315119	Men's socks knitting or knitting and finishing
114111	Menhaden fishing
623210	Mental retardation intermediate care facilities
622210	Mental (except mental retardation) hospitals
621420	Mental health centers and clinics (except hospitals), outpatient
623220	Mental health facilities, residential
623220	Mental health halfway houses
622210	Mental health hospitals
621112	Mental health physicians' offices (e.g., centers, clinics)
923120	Mental health program administration
623210	Mental retardation facilities (e.g., homes, hospitals, intermediate care facilities), residential
623210	Mental retardation homes
623210	Mental retardation hospitals
561450	Mercantile credit reporting bureaus
313311	Mercerizing broadwoven fabrics
333292	Mercerizing machinery manufacturing
313312	Mercerizing narrow woven textile products and fabrics (except broadwoven)
326111	Merchandise bags, plastics film, single wall or multiwall, manufacturing
421440	Merchandising machines, coin-operated, wholesaling
926120	Merchant Marine (except academy)
813910	Merchants' associations
335912	Mercuric oxide batteries manufacturing

Code	Description
212299	Mercury (quicksilver) mining and/or beneficiating
335999	Mercury arc rectifiers (i.e., electrical apparatus) manufacturing
325188	Mercury chloride manufacturing
325188	Mercury compounds, not specified elsewhere by process, manufacturing
325920	Mercury fulminate explosive materials manufacturing
335110	Mercury halide lamp bulbs manufacturing
212299	Mercury ores mining and/or beneficiating
325188	Mercury oxide manufacturing
332618	Mesh made from purchased wire
331422	Mesh, wire, made from purchased copper in wire drawing plants
331319	Mesh, wire, made in aluminum wire drawing plants
331111	Mesh, wire, made in steel mills
331222	Mesh, wire, made in wire drawing mills
331491	Mesh, wire, nonferrous metals (except aluminum, copper), made from purchased nonferrous metals (except aluminum, copper) in wire drawing plants
561421	Message services, telephone answering
492210	Messenger service
325412	Metabolite in-vivo diagnostic substances manufacturing
332431	Metal cans manufacturing
333298	Metal casting machinery and equipment manufacturing
235610	Metal ceiling construction contractors
333512	Metal cutting machine tools
332213	Metal cutting saw blades manufacturing
422690	Metal cyanides wholesaling
333513	Metal deposit forming machines manufacturing
334519	Metal detectors manufacturing
339113	Metal fabric and mesh safety gloves manufacturing
332999	Metal foil containers (except bags) manufacturing
333513	Metal forming machine tools manufacturing
337121	Metal framed furniture, household-type, upholstered, manufacturing
235910	Metal furring contractors
339943	Metal hand stamps manufacturing
333994	Metal melting furnaces, industrial, manufacturing
213114	Metal mining support services (shaft sinking, tunneling, blasting)
336370	Metal motor vehicle body parts stamping
334413	Metal oxide silicon (MOS) devices manufacturing
325612	Metal polishes (i.e., tarnish removers) manufacturing
331314	Metal powder and flake made from purchased aluminum
331423	Metal powder and flake made from purchased copper
331221	Metal powder and flake made from purchased iron or steel
331492	Metal powder and flake nonferrous (except aluminum, copper) made from purchased metal
331111	Metal powder and flake, iron or steel, manufacturing
421510	Metal products (e.g., bars, ingots, plates, rods, shapes, sheets) wholesaling

Code	Description
421930	Metal scrap and waste wholesaling
332116	Metal stampings (except automotive, cans, cooking, closures, crowns), unfinished, manufacturing
421520	Metallic concentrates wholesaling
325131	Metallic pigments, inorganic, manufacturing
325199	Metallic soap manufacturing
313320	Metallizing purchased textiles
541380	Metallurgical testing laboratories or services
421510	Metals sales offices
421510	Metals service centers
421510	Metals, ferrous and nonferrous, wholesaling
421940	Metals, precious, wholesaling
333512	Metalworking lathes manufacturing
532490	Metalworking machinery and equipment rental or leasing
421830	Metalworking machinery and equipment wholesaling
334519	Meteorologic tracking systems manufacturing
811219	Meteorological instrument repair and maintenance services
334519	Meteorological instruments manufacturing
541990	Meteorological services
561990	Meter reading services, contract
334514	Metering devices (except electrical and industrial process control) manufacturing
335313	Metering panels, electric, manufacturing
334514	Meters (except electrical and industrial process control) manufacturing
421830	Meters (except electrical, parking) wholesaling
334515	Meters, electrical (i.e., graphic recording, panelboard, pocket, portable), manufacturing
421610	Meters, electrical, wholesaling
334513	Meters, industrial process control-type, manufacturing
334514	Meters, parking, manufacturing
421850	Meters, parking, wholesaling
334515	Meters, power factor and phase angle, manufacturing
325320	Methoxychlor insecticides manufacturing
325191	Methyl acetone manufacturing
325211	Methyl acrylate resins manufacturing
325199	Methyl alcohol (i.e., methanol), synthetic, manufacturing
325193	Methyl alcohol (methanol), natural, manufacturing
325211	Methyl cellulose resins manufacturing
325199	Methyl chloride manufacturing
325211	Methyl methacrylate resins manufacturing
325199	Methyl perhydrofluorine manufacturing
325199	Methyl salicylate manufacturing
325132	Methyl violet toners manufacturing
325199	Methylamine manufacturing
325199	Methylene chloride manufacturing
311422	Mexican foods canning
311412	Mexican foods, frozen, manufacturing
212399	Mica mining and/or beneficiating
327992	Mica processing beyond benefication
327999	Mica products manufacturing
212319	Mica schist crushed and broken stone mining and/or beneficiating
212311	Mica schist mining or quarrying
311119	Micro and macro premixes, livestock, manufacturing

Micro-lithography—Mink

Code	Description
333295	Micro-lithography equipment, semiconductor, manufacturing
334516	Microbiology instruments manufacturing
325413	Microbiology, virology, and serology in-vitro diagnostic substances manufacturing
334111	Microcomputers manufacturing
334413	Microcontroller chip manufacturing
333315	Microfiche equipment (e.g., cameras, projectors, readers) manufacturing
333315	Microfilm equipment (e.g., cameras, projectors, readers) manufacturing
421420	Microfilm equipment and supplies wholesaling
514210	Microfilm recording and imaging services
212299	Microlite mining and/or beneficiating
332212	Micrometers, machinist's precision tools, manufacturing
334310	Microphones manufacturing
334516	Microprobes (e.g., electron, ion, laser, X-ray) manufacturing
334413	Microprocessor chip manufacturing
333314	Microscopes (except electron, proton) manufacturing
334516	Microscopes, electron and proton, manufacturing
334220	Microwave communications equipment manufacturing
334419	Microwave components manufacturing
335221	Microwave ovens (including portable), household-type, manufacturing
333319	Microwave ovens, commercial-type, manufacturing
513330	Microwave telecommunication resellers
334515	Microwave test equipment manufacturing
326199	Microwaveware, plastics, manufacturing
315291	Middies, infants', cut and sewn from purchased fabric (except apparel contractors)
315212	Middies, women's, girls' and infants', cut and sew apparel contractors
315232	Middies, women's, misses', and girls', cut and sewn from purchased fabric (except apparel contractors)
611110	Middle schools
621399	Midwives' offices (e.g., centers, clinics)
721310	Migrant workers' camps
611310	Military academies, college level
611110	Military academies, elementary or secondary
928110	Military bases and camps
315211	Military dress uniforms, men's and boys', cut and sew apparel contractors
315222	Military dress uniforms, men's and boys', cut and sewn from purchased fabric (except apparel contractors)
315234	Military dress uniforms, tailored, women's, misses' and girls', cut and sewn from purchased fabric (except apparel contractors)
315212	Military dress uniforms, women's, cut and sew apparel contractors
332999	Military insignia, metal, manufacturing
314999	Military insignia, textile, manufacturing
712110	Military museums
928110	Military police
928110	Military reserve armories and bases
611310	Military service academies (college)
928110	Military training schools (except academies)
421860	Military vehicles (except trucks) wholesaling

Code	Description
311511	Milk based drinks (except dietary) manufacturing
311514	Milk based drinks, dietary, manufacturing
322130	Milk carton board made in paperboard mills
322226	Milk carton board stock made from purchased paperboard
311511	Milk drink, chocolate, manufacturing
484220	Milk hauling, local
311511	Milk pasteurizing
311511	Milk processing (e.g., bottling, homogenizing, pasteurizing, vitaminizing) manufacturing
333294	Milk processing (except farm-type) machinery manufacturing
112120	Milk production, dairy cattle
311511	Milk substitutes manufacturing
115210	Milk testing for butterfat and milk solids
311511	Milk, acidophilus, manufacturing
422490	Milk, canned or dried, wholesaling
311514	Milk, concentrated, condensed, dried, evaporated, and powdered, manufacturing
311511	Milk, fluid (except canned), manufacturing
422430	Milk, fluid (except canned), wholesaling
311514	Milk, malted, manufacturing
311514	Milk, powdered, manufacturing
311514	Milk, ultra-high temperature, manufacturing
112120	Milking dairy cattle
112420	Milking dairy goat
112410	Milking dairy sheep
421820	Milking machinery and equipment wholesaling
333111	Milking machines manufacturing
311514	Milkshake mixes manufacturing
314999	Mill menders, contract, woven fabrics
316999	Mill strapping for textile mills, leather, manufacturing
421840	Mill supplies wholesaling
315991	Millinery cut and sewn from purchased fabric (except apparel contractors)
422310	Millinery supplies wholesaling
315999	Millinery trimmings cut and sewn from purchased fabric (except apparel contractors)
315211	Millinery trimmings, men's and boys', cut and sew apparel contractors
315212	Millinery trimmings, women's, girls', and infants', cut and sew apparel contractors
422330	Millinery wholesaling
315211	Millinery, men's and boys', cut and sew apparel contractors
315212	Millinery, women's, girls', and infants', cut and sew apparel contractors
333512	Milling machines, metalworking, manufacturing
311212	Milling rice
212399	Millstones mining and/or beneficiating
421310	Millwork wholesaling
337212	Millwork, custom architectural, manufacturing
321114	Millwork, treating
235950	Millwrights
111199	Milo farming, field and seed production
711110	Mime theaters
333922	Mine conveyors manufacturing
213114	Mine development for metal mining on a contract basis
213115	Mine development for nonmetallic minerals mining (except fuels) on a contract basis

Code	Description
234930	Mine loading and discharging station construction
321114	Mine props, treating
562910	Mine reclamation services, integrated (e.g., demolition, hazardous material removal, soil remediation)
213113	Mine shaft sinking services for coal mining on a contract basis
213114	Mine shaft sinking services for metal mining on a contract basis
213115	Mine shaft sinking services for nonmetallic minerals (except fuels) on a contract basis
321114	Mine ties, wood, treated, manufacturing
213113	Mine tunneling services for coal mining on a contract basis
213114	Mine tunneling services for metal mining on a contract basis
213115	Mine tunneling services for nonmetallic minerals (except fuels) on a contract basis
335129	Miner's lamps manufacturing
325131	Mineral colors and pigments manufacturing
311119	Mineral feed supplements (except cat, dog) manufacturing
311111	Mineral feed supplements, dog and cat, manufacturing
212393	Mineral pigments, natural, mining and/or beneficiating
333131	Mineral processing and beneficiating machinery manufacturing
523910	Mineral royalties or leases dealing (i.e., acting as a principal in dealing royalties or leases to investors)
311119	Mineral supplements, animal (except cat, dog), manufacturing
422910	Mineral supplements, animal, wholesaling
311111	Mineral supplements, dog and cat, manufacturing
327993	Mineral wool insulation materials manufacturing
327993	Mineral wool products (e.g., board, insulation, tile) manufacturing
421520	Minerals (except construction materials, petroleum) wholesaling
332993	Mines, ammunition, manufacturing
331111	Mini-mills, steel
713990	Miniature golf courses
337920	Miniblinds manufacturing
334111	Minicomputers manufacturing
926150	Minimum wage program administration
******	Mining — see type
234930	Mining appurtenance construction contractors
813910	Mining associations
333131	Mining cars manufacturing
541330	Mining engineering services
336510	Mining locomotives and parts manufacturing
421810	Mining machinery and equipment (except petroleum) wholesaling
532412	Mining machinery and equipment rental or leasing
811310	Mining machinery and equipment repair and maintenance services
421830	Mining machinery and equipment, petroleum, wholesaling
531190	Mining property leasing
336112	Minivans assembling on chassis of own manufacture
531130	Miniwarehouse rental or leasing
112930	Mink production

Code	Description
112511	Minnow production, farm raising
711211	Minor league baseball clubs
111998	Mint farming
421220	Mirrors (except automotive) wholesaling
421120	Mirrors, automotive, wholesaling
327215	Mirrors, framed or unframed, made from purchased glass
333314	Mirrors, optical, manufacturing
234990	Missile facility construction
332993	Missile warheads manufacturing
561611	Missing person tracing services
813110	Missions, religious organization
332212	Miter boxes manufacturing
315992	Mittens cut and sewn from purchased fabric (except apparel contractors)
315191	Mittens, knit, made in apparel knitting mills
315992	Mittens, leather (except apparel contractors), manufacturing
315211	Mittens, leather, men's and boys', cut and sew apparel contractors
315212	Mittens, leather, women's, girls', and infants', cut and sew apparel contractors
315211	Mittens, men's and boys', cut and sew apparel contractors
315212	Mittens, women's, girls', and infants', cut and sew apparel contractors
315992	Mittens, woven or knit, cut and sewn from purchased fabric (except apparel contractors)
315211	Mittens, woven or knit, men's and boys', cut and sew apparel contractors
315212	Mittens, woven or knit, women's, girls', and infants', cut and sew apparel contractors
311230	Mix grain breakfast manufacturing
311514	Mix, ice cream, manufacturing
312140	Mixed drinks, alcoholic, manufacturing
111940	Mixed hay farming
485111	Mixed mode transit systems (e.g., bus, commuter rail, subway combinations)
333120	Mixers, concrete, portable, manufacturing
422490	Mixes (e.g., cake, dessert, pie) wholesaling
311211	Mixes, flour (e.g., biscuit, cake, doughnut, pancake) made in flour mills
311822	Mixes, flour (e.g., biscuit, cake, doughnut, pancake), made from purchased flour
325314	Mixing purchased fertilizer materials
531190	Mobile (manufactured) home parks
531190	Mobile (manufactured) home site rental or leasing
531110	Mobile (manufactured) home, on site, rental or leasing
321991	Mobile (manufactured) homes, manufacturing
621512	Mobile X-ray facilities (medical)
621512	Mobile breast imaging centers
811192	Mobile car and truck washes
334220	Mobile communications equipment manufacturing
311119	Mobile feed mill
722330	Mobile food stands
453930	Mobile home dealers, manufactured
321991	Mobile home manufacturing
532120	Mobile home rental (except on site)
235990	Mobile home site setup and tie down construction contractors
484220	Mobile home towing services, local
484230	Mobile home towing services, long-distance
624210	Mobile soup kitchens

Code	Description
333924	Mobile straddle carriers manufacturing
513322	Mobile telephone communication carriers
316219	Moccasins manufacturing
325222	Modacrylic fibers and filaments manufacturing
313111	Modacrylic spun yarns made from purchased fiber
339932	Model kits manufacturing
421920	Model kits wholesaling
339932	Model railroad manufacturing
561310	Model registries
561320	Model supply services
711410	Modeling agents
339942	Modeling clay manufacturing
611519	Modeling schools
711410	Models' agents or managers
339999	Models, anatomical, manufacturing
711510	Models, independent
339932	Models, toy and hobby (e.g., airplane, boat, ship), manufacturing
421690	Modems wholesaling
334210	Modems, carrier equipment, manufacturing
711120	Modern dance companies
337214	Modular furniture systems (except wood frame), office-type, manufacturing
337211	Modular furniture systems, wood frame office-type, manufacturing
233210	Modular house assembly and installation on site, construction
233210	Modular house construction
334518	Modules for clocks and watches manufacturing
112420	Mohair farming
313112	Mohair yarn twisting or winding of purchased yarn
422590	Mohair, raw, wholesaling
334516	Moisture analyzers, laboratory-type, manufacturing
334513	Moisture meters, industrial process-type, manufacturing
311312	Molasses made from purchased raw cane sugar
311313	Molasses made from sugar beets
311311	Molasses made in sugarcane mill
422490	Molasses wholesaling
311312	Molasses, blackstrap, made from purchased raw cane sugar
311311	Molasses, blackstrap, made in sugarcane mill
339991	Molded packings and seals manufacturing
322299	Molded pulp products (e.g., egg cartons, food containers, food trays) manufacturing
421310	Molding (e.g., sheet metal, wood) wholesaling
332321	Molding and trim (except motor vehicle), metal, manufacturing
212322	Molding sand quarrying and/or beneficiating
336370	Moldings and trim, motor vehicle, stamping
321918	Moldings, clear and finger joint wood, manufacturing
321918	Moldings, wood and covered wood, manufacturing
333511	Molds (except steel ingot), industrial, manufacturing
331511	Molds for casting steel ingots manufacturing
333511	Molds for forming materials (e.g., glass, plastics, rubber) manufacturing

Code	Description
333511	Molds for metal casting (except steel ingot) manufacturing
333511	Molds for plastics and rubber working machinery manufacturing
331511	Molds, steel ingot, industrial, manufacturing
112512	Mollusk production, farm raising
212299	Molybdenite mining and/or beneficiating
331491	Molybdenum and molybdenum alloy bar, plate, pipe, rod, sheet, tubing, and wire made from purchased metals or scrap
212299	Molybdenum ores mining and/or beneficiating
331491	Molybdenum rolling, drawing, or extruding purchased metals or scrap
331112	Molybdenum silicon ferroalloys manufacturing
212299	Molybdite mining and/or beneficiating
813110	Monasteries (except schools)
212299	Monazite mining and/or beneficiating
332999	Money chests, metal, manufacturing
525990	Money market mutual funds, closed-end
525910	Money market mutual funds, open-ended
522390	Money order issuance services
334119	Monitors, computer peripheral equipment, manufacturing
325120	Monochlorodifluoromethane manufacturing
334516	Monochrometers, laboratory-type, manufacturing
334413	Monolithic integrated circuits (solid-state) manufacturing
325199	Monomethylparaminophenol sulfate manufacturing
333923	Monorail systems (except passenger-type) manufacturing
485119	Monorail transit systems (except mixed mode), commuter
487110	Monorail, scenic and sightseeing, operation
325199	Monosodium glutamate manufacturing
611110	Montessori schools, elementary or secondary
453998	Monument (i.e., burial marker) dealers
421990	Monuments and grave markers wholesaling
327991	Monuments and tombstone, cut stone (except finishing or lettering to order only), manufacturing
333319	Mop wringers manufacturing
441221	Moped dealers
532292	Moped rental
336991	Mopeds and parts manufacturing
421110	Mopeds wholesaling
339994	Mops, floor and dust, manufacturing
325132	Mordant dyes manufacturing
325613	Mordants manufacturing
325411	Morphine and derivatives (i.e., basic chemicals) manufacturing
522190	Morris Plans (i.e., known as), depository
522298	Morris Plans (i.e., known as), nondepository
333120	Mortar mixers, portable, manufacturing
332993	Mortar shells manufacturing
327125	Mortar, nonclay refractory, manufacturing
332995	Mortars manufacturing
327124	Mortars, clay refractory, manufacturing
522292	Mortgage banking (i.e., nondepository mortgage lending)
522310	Mortgage brokerages

Mortgage—Mule

Code	Description
522310	Mortgage brokers' or agents' offices (i.e., independent)
522292	Mortgage companies
524126	Mortgage guaranty insurance carriers, direct
812210	Mortician services
333210	Mortisers, woodworking-type, manufacturing
812210	Mortuaries
235430	Mosaic construction contractors (except fresco)
327122	Mosaic tile, ceramic, manufacturing
813110	Mosques, religious
926130	Mosquito eradication districts
561710	Mosquito eradication services
113210	Moss gathering
531120	Motel building, not operating motel, rental or leasing
233320	Motel construction
561110	Motel management services (except complete operation of client's business)
721110	Motels
325320	Moth repellants manufacturing
421430	Mother boards wholesaling
512110	Motion picture and video production
512110	Motion picture and video production and distribution
512191	Motion picture animation, post-production
512199	Motion picture booking agencies
333315	Motion picture cameras manufacturing
421410	Motion picture cameras, equipment, and supplies wholesaling
541690	Motion picture consulting services
711510	Motion picture directors, independent
512120	Motion picture distribution exclusive of production
532490	Motion picture equipment rental or leasing
512131	Motion picture exhibition
512131	Motion picture exhibitors for airlines
512131	Motion picture exhibitors, itinerant
512120	Motion picture film distributors
512199	Motion picture film laboratories
512120	Motion picture film libraries
514120	Motion picture film libraries, archives
512199	Motion picture film libraries, stock footage
325992	Motion picture film manufacturing
512199	Motion picture film reproduction for theatrical distribution
512199	Motion picture laboratories
512191	Motion picture or video editing services
512191	Motion picture or video post-production services
512191	Motion picture or video titling
711510	Motion picture producers, independent
512110	Motion picture production
512110	Motion picture production and distribution
512191	Motion picture production special effects, post-production
333315	Motion picture projectors manufacturing
512110	Motion picture studios, producing motion pictures
512132	Motion picture theaters, drive-in
512131	Motion picture theaters, indoor
532220	Motion picture wardrobe and costume rental
441221	Motor bike dealers
926120	Motor carrier licensing and inspection offices
485210	Motor coach operation, interurban and rural

Code	Description
335314	Motor control accessories (including overload relays) manufacturing
335314	Motor control centers, manufacturing
335314	Motor controls, electric, manufacturing
421610	Motor controls, electric, wholesaling
721110	Motor courts
484110	Motor freight carrier, general, local
484122	Motor freight carrier, general, long-distance, less-than-truckload (LTL)
484121	Motor freight carrier, general, long-distance, truckload
484210	Motor freight carrier, used household goods
335312	Motor generator sets (except automotive, turbine generator sets) manufacturing
333611	Motor generator sets, turbo generators, manufacturing
441210	Motor home dealers
532120	Motor home rental (except on site)
531190	Motor home rental on site
421110	Motor homes wholesaling
336213	Motor homes, self-contained, assembling on purchased chassis
336120	Motor homes, self-contained, mounted on heavy truck chassis of own manufacture
336112	Motor homes, self-contained, mounted on light duty truck chassis of own manufacture
721110	Motor hotels
721110	Motor inns
721110	Motor lodges
324191	Motor oils, petroleum, made from refined petroleum
325998	Motor oils, synthetic, manufacturing
811310	Motor repair and maintenance services, commercial or industrial
441221	Motor scooters dealers
336991	Motor scooters manufacturing
335314	Motor starters, contractors, and controllers, industrial, manufacturing
561599	Motor travel clubs
333997	Motor truck scales manufacturing
326220	Motor vehicle belts, rubber or plastics, manufacturing
332510	Motor vehicle hardware, metal, manufacturing
326220	Motor vehicle hoses, rubber or plastics, manufacturing
334514	Motor vehicle instruments (e.g., fuel level gauges, oil pressure, speedometers, tachometers, water temperature) manufacturing
421120	Motor vehicle instruments, electric, wholesaling
336360	Motor vehicle interior systems (e.g., headliners, panels, seats, trims) manufacturing
561990	Motor vehicle license issuing services, private franchise
926120	Motor vehicle licensing offices, government
336370	Motor vehicle metal bumper stampings
336370	Motor vehicle metal parts stamping
336370	Motor vehicle metal stampings (e.g., body parts, fenders, hub caps, tops, trim) manufacturing
326199	Motor vehicle moldings and extrusions, plastics, manufacturing
325510	Motor vehicle paints manufacturing
421120	Motor vehicle parts and accessories, new, wholesaling
421140	Motor vehicle parts, used, wholesaling

Code	Description
336360	Motor vehicle seat frames, metal, manufacturing
336360	Motor vehicle seats manufacturing
421130	Motor vehicle tires and tubes wholesaling
326211	Motor vehicle tires manufacturing
488410	Motor vehicle towing services
336360	Motor vehicle trimmings manufacturing
421110	Motor vehicles wholesaling
811490	Motorboat (i.e., inboard and outboard) repair and maintenance services
336612	Motorboat, inboard or outboard, building
441221	Motorcycle dealers
441221	Motorcycle parts and accessories dealers
421120	Motorcycle parts, new, wholesaling
711212	Motorcycle racetracks
711219	Motorcycle racing teams
532292	Motorcycle rental
811490	Motorcycle repair shops without retailing new motorcycles
336991	Motorcycles and parts manufacturing
421110	Motorcycles wholesaling
335312	Motors, electric (except engine starting motors, gearmotors, outboard), manufacturing
421610	Motors, electric, wholesaling
333996	Motors, fluid power, manufacturing
333612	Motors, gear, manufacturing
333618	Motors, outboard, manufacturing
421910	Motors, outboard, wholesaling
336322	Motors, starter, for internal combustion engines, manufacturing
713990	Mountain hiking, recreational
561910	Mounting merchandise on cards
334119	Mouse devices, computer peripheral equipment, manufacturing
213112	Mouse hole and rat hole drilling at oil and gas fields on a contract basis
339992	Mouthpieces for musical instruments manufacturing
325620	Mouthwashes (except medicinal) manufacturing
325412	Mouthwashes, medicated, manufacturing
334518	Movements, watch or clock, manufacturing
512110	Movie production and distribution
512131	Movie theaters (except drive-in)
512132	Movie theaters, drive-in
561730	Mowing services (e.g., highway, lawn, road strip)
325520	Mucilage adhesives manufacturing
213112	Mud service for oil field drilling on a contract basis
811112	Muffler repair and replacement shops
336399	Mufflers and resonators, automotive, truck, and buses manufacturing
315191	Mufflers made in apparel knitting mills
421120	Mufflers, exhaust, wholesaling
315211	Mufflers, men's and boys', cut and sew apparel contractors
315993	Mufflers, men's and boys', cut and sewn from purchased fabric (except apparel contractors)
315999	Mufflers, women's and girls', cut and sewn from purchased fabric (except apparel contractors)
315212	Mufflers, women's, girls', and infants', cut and sew apparel contractors
422910	Mulch wholesaling
333112	Mulchers, lawn and garden-type, manufacturing
112920	Mule production

Code	Description
422590	Mules wholesaling
114111	Mullet fishing
712110	Multidisciplinary museums
233220	Multifamily construction management firms
334515	Multimeters manufacturing
334210	Multiplex equipment, telephone, manufacturing
624190	Multiservice centers, neighborhood
233320	Municipal building construction
212391	Muriate of potash, mining
325412	Muscle relaxant preparations manufacturing
212399	Muscovite mining and/or beneficiating
233320	Museum construction
712110	Museums
111411	Mushroom farming
111411	Mushroom spawn farming
311421	Mushrooms canning
514120	Music archives
711510	Music arrangers, independent
512230	Music book (i.e., bound sheet music) publishers
512230	Music book (i.e., bound sheet music) publishers and printing combined
512230	Music book (i.e., bound sheet music) publishing (i.e., establishments known as publishers)
323117	Music books printing or printing and binding without publishing
339999	Music boxes manufacturing
512230	Music copyright authorizing use
512230	Music copyright buying and licensing
711310	Music festival managers with facilities
711320	Music festival managers without facilities
711310	Music festival organizers with facilities
711320	Music festival organizers without facilities
711310	Music festival promoters with facilities
711320	Music festival promoters without facilities
611610	Music instruction (e.g., guitar, piano)
512230	Music publishers
339992	Music rolls, perforated, manufacturing
611610	Music schools (except academic)
451220	Music stores (e.g., cassette, compact disc, record, tape)
453310	Music stores (e.g., cassette, instrument, record, tape), used
451140	Music stores (i.e., instrument)
621340	Music therapists' offices (e.g., centers, clinics)
512110	Music video production
512110	Music video production and distribution
323112	Music, sheet, flexographic printing without publishing
323111	Music, sheet, gravure printing without publishing
323110	Music, sheet, lithographic (offset) printing without publishing
323119	Music, sheet, printing (except flexographic, gravure, lithographic, screen) without publishing
512230	Music, sheet, publishers and printing combined
512230	Music, sheet, publishing (i.e., establishment known as publishers)
323113	Music, sheet, screen printing without publishing
422990	Music, sheet, wholesaling
711130	Musical artists, independent
711130	Musical groups (except musical theater groups)
339992	Musical instrument accessories (e.g., mouthpieces, reeds, stands, traps) manufacturing
421990	Musical instrument accessories and supplies wholesaling
316991	Musical instrument cases, all materials, manufacturing
532299	Musical instrument rental
811490	Musical instrument repair shops without retailing new musical instruments
339992	Musical instruments (except toy) manufacturing
421990	Musical instruments wholesaling
339932	Musical instruments, toy, manufacturing
711130	Musical productions (except musical theater productions), live
512220	Musical recording, releasing, promoting, and distributing
421990	Musical recordings (e.g., compact discs, records, tapes) wholesaling
711110	Musical theater companies or groups
711110	Musical theater productions, live
711130	Musicians, independent
111219	Muskmelon farming, field, bedding plant and seed production
114112	Mussel fishing
112512	Mussel production, farm raising
111120	Mustard seed farming, field and seed production
311941	Mustard, prepared, manufacturing
523120	Mutual fund agencies (i.e., brokerages)
523120	Mutual fund agents' (i.e., brokers') offices
523920	Mutual fund managing
525990	Mutual funds, closed-end
525910	Mutual funds, open-ended
522120	Mutual savings banks
621511	Mycology health laboratories
325191	Myrobalans extract manufacturing
325411	N-methylpiperazine manufacturing
325212	N-type rubber manufacturing
924110	NOAA (National Oceanic and Atmospheric Administration)
333991	Nail guns, handheld power-driven, manufacturing
333513	Nail heading machines manufacturing
325620	Nail polish remover manufacturing
325620	Nail polishes manufacturing
812113	Nail salons
333991	Nailers and staplers, handheld power-driven, manufacturing
421510	Nails wholesaling
331319	Nails, aluminum, made in wire drawing plants
332618	Nails, brads, and staples made from purchased wire
331222	Nails, iron or steel, made in wire drawing plants
331491	Nails, nonferrous metals (except aluminum, copper), made from purchased nonferrous metals (except aluminum, copper) in wire drawing plants
339950	Name plate blanks manufacturing
332999	Name plate blanks, metal, manufacturing
325998	Napalm manufacturing
325192	Naphtha made by distillation of coal tar
324110	Naphtha made in petroleum refineries
325192	Naphtha, solvent, made by distillation of coal tar
325192	Naphthalene made from refined petroleum or natural gas
325192	Naphthalenesulfonic acid manufacturing
325199	Naphthenic acid soaps manufacturing
325192	Naphthenic acids made from refined petroleum or natural gas
324110	Naphthenic acids made in petroleum refineries
325192	Naphthol, alpha and beta, manufacturing
325192	Naphtholsulfonic acids manufacturing
421220	Napkins (except paper) wholesaling
314129	Napkins made from purchased fabrics
422130	Napkins, paper, wholesaling
322291	Napkins, table, made from purchased paper
322121	Napkins, table, made in paper mills
313311	Napping broadwoven fabrics
333292	Napping machinery for textiles manufacturing
313312	Napping textile products and fabrics (except broadwoven fabrics)
313221	Narrow fabrics weaving
927110	National Aeronautics and Space Administration
522298	National Credit Union Administration (NCUA)
928110	National Guard
926120	National Transportation Safety Board
522110	National commercial banks
712190	National parks
311422	Nationality specialty foods canning
311412	Nationality specialty foods, frozen, manufacturing
212399	Native asphalt mining and/or beneficiating
327310	Natural (i.e., calcined earth) cement manufacturing
212399	Natural abrasives (e.g., emery, grindstones, hones, pumice) (except sand) mining and/or beneficiating
313113	Natural fiber (i.e., hemp, linen, ramie) thread manufacturing
313210	Natural fiber fabrics (i.e., jute, linen, hemp, ramie), broadwoven, weaving
313221	Natural fiber fabrics (i.e., jute, linen, hemp, ramie), narrow woven, weaving
313111	Natural fiber spun yarns (i.e., hemp, jute, ramie, flax) made from purchased fiber
221210	Natural gas brokers
234910	Natural gas compressing station construction
221210	Natural gas distribution systems
333618	Natural gas engines manufacturing
211112	Natural gas liquids (e.g., ethane, isobutane, natural gasoline, propane) recovered from oil and gas field gases
486910	Natural gas liquids pipeline transportation
221210	Natural gas marketers
486210	Natural gas pipeline transportation
211111	Natural gas production
486210	Natural gas transmission (i.e., processing plants to local distribution systems)
211111	Natural gas, offshore production
211112	Natural gasoline recovered from oil and gas field gases
712110	Natural history museums
325199	Natural nonfood coloring, manufacturing
813312	Natural resource preservation organizations
712110	Natural science museums
712190	Natural wonder tourist attractions (e.g., caverns, waterfalls)

Naturally carbonated water—Nightshirts

Code	Description
312112	Naturally carbonated water, purifying and bottling
712190	Nature centers
712190	Nature parks
712190	Nature preserves
712190	Nature reserves
621399	Naturopaths' offices (e.g., centers, clinics)
334511	Nautical systems and instruments manufacturing
332995	Naval artillery manufacturing
336611	Naval ship building
325191	Naval stores, gum or wood, manufacturing
811219	Navigational instruments (e.g., radar, sonar) repair and maintenance services
421860	Navigational instruments (except electronic) wholesaling
334511	Navigational instruments manufacturing
421690	Navigational instruments, electronic (e.g., radar, sonar), wholesaling
928110	Navy
312120	Near beer brewing
311613	Neatsfoot oil rendering
315292	Neckpieces, fur (except apparel contractors), manufacturing
315211	Neckpieces, fur, men's and boys', cut and sew apparel contractors
315212	Neckpieces, fur, women's, girls', and infants', cut and sew apparel contractors
315191	Neckties made in apparel knitting mills
315211	Neckties, men's and boys', cut and sew apparel contractors
315993	Neckties, men's and boys', cut and sewn from purchased fabric (except apparel contractors)
422320	Neckties, men's and boys', wholesaling
315999	Neckties, women's and girls', cut and sewn from purchased fabric (except apparel contractors)
315212	Neckties, women's, girls', and infants', cut and sew apparel contractors
315191	Neckwear made in a apparel knitting mills
448150	Neckwear stores
315993	Neckwear, men's and boys', cut and sewn from purchased fabric (except apparel contractors)
315211	Neckwear, men's and boys', cut and sew apparel contractors
315212	Neckwear, women's, girls' and infants', cut and sew apparel contractors
111339	Nectarine farming
332991	Needle roller bearings manufacturing
451130	Needlecraft sewing supply stores
339993	Needles (except hypodermic, phonograph, styli) manufacturing
333292	Needles for knitting machinery manufacturing
339112	Needles, hypodermic and suture, manufacturing
334419	Needles, phonograph and styli, manufacturing
422310	Needles, sewing, wholesaling
315211	Needlework art contractors on men's and boys' apparel
315212	Needlework art contractors on women's, girls', and infants' apparel
315192	Negligees made in apparel knitting mills
315212	Negligees, women's, cut and sew apparel contractors
315231	Negligees, women's, misses', and girls', cut and sewn from purchased fabric (except apparel contractors)

Code	Description
813319	Neighborhood development advocacy organizations
325120	Neon manufacturing
339950	Neon signs manufacturing
325212	Neoprene manufacturing
212325	Nepheline syenite mining and/or beneficiating
334516	Nephelometers (except meteorological) manufacturing
334519	Nephoscopes manufacturing
333292	Net and lace making machinery manufacturing
422310	Net goods wholesaling
313210	Nets and nettings, more than 12 inches in width, weaving
313249	Netting made in warp knitting mills
313241	Netting made in weft knitting mills
313249	Netting made on a lace or net machine
326199	Netting, plastics, manufacturing
332618	Netting, woven, made from purchased wire
513111	Network broadcasting service, radio
513111	Network radio broadcasting
541512	Network systems integration design services, computer
513120	Network television broadcasting
513210	Networks, cable television
622310	Neurological hospitals
621111	Neurologists' offices (e.g., centers, clinics)
621111	Neuropathologists' offices (e.g., centers, clinics)
312140	Neutral spirit, beverages (except fruit), manufacturing
422820	Neutral spirits wholesaling
334516	Neutron activation analysis instruments manufacturing
441110	New car dealers
541613	New product development consulting services
321918	Newel posts, wood, manufacturing
451212	News dealers
514110	News picture gathering and distributing services
514110	News reporting services
514110	News service syndicates
514110	News ticker services
511120	Newsletter publishers
511120	Newsletter publishers and printing combined
511120	Newsletter publishing (i.e., establishments known as publishers)
323112	Newsletters flexographic printing without publishing
323111	Newsletters gravure printing without publishing
323110	Newsletters lithographic (offset) printing without publishing
323119	Newsletters printing (except flexographic, gravure, lithographic, screen) without publishing
323113	Newsletters screen printing without publishing
541840	Newspaper advertising representatives (i.e., independent of media owners)
422920	Newspaper agencies wholesaling
511110	Newspaper branch offices
711510	Newspaper columnists, independent (freelance)
514110	Newspaper feature syndicates
333293	Newspaper inserting equipment manufacturing
511110	Newspaper publishers

Code	Description
511110	Newspaper publishers and printing combined
511110	Newspaper publishing (i.e., establishments known as publishers)
323112	Newspapers flexographic printing without publishing
323111	Newspapers gravure printing without publishing
323110	Newspapers lithographic (offset) printing without publishing
323119	Newspapers printing (except flexographic, gravure, lithographic, screen) without publishing
323113	Newspapers screen printing without publishing
422920	Newspapers wholesaling
322122	Newsprint mills
322122	Newsprint paper, manufacturing
422110	Newsprint wholesaling
451212	Newsstands (i.e., permanent)
339941	Nibs (i.e., pen points) manufacturing
331522	Nickel alloy die-castings, unfinished, manufacturing
325188	Nickel ammonium sulfate manufacturing
331491	Nickel and nickel alloy pipe, plate, sheet, strip, and tubing made from purchased metals or scrap
335911	Nickel cadmium storage batteries manufacturing
325188	Nickel carbonate manufacturing
331528	Nickel castings (except die-castings), unfinished, manufacturing
325188	Nickel compounds, not specified elsewhere by process, manufacturing
212234	Nickel concentrates recovery
331522	Nickel die-castings, unfinished, manufacturing
332999	Nickel foil not made in rolling mills
212234	Nickel ore beneficiating plants
212234	Nickel ore mine site development for own account
212234	Nickel ores mining and/or beneficiating
331492	Nickel recovering from scrap and/or alloying purchased metals
331419	Nickel refining, primary
331491	Nickel rolling, drawing, or extruding purchased metals or scrap
325188	Nickel sulfate manufacturing
325411	Nicotine and derivatives (i.e., basic chemicals) manufacturing
325320	Nicotine insecticides manufacturing
713990	Night clubs without alcoholic beverages
722410	Night clubs, alcoholic beverage
337122	Night stands, wood, manufacturing
315192	Nightgowns made in apparel knitting mills
315291	Nightgowns, infants', cut and sewn from purchased fabric (except apparel contractors)
315211	Nightgowns, men's and boys', cut and sew apparel contractors
315221	Nightgowns, men's and boys', cut and sewn from purchased fabric (except apparel contractors)
315212	Nightgowns, women's, girls', and infants', cut and sew apparel contractors
315231	Nightgowns, women's, misses', and girls', cut and sewn from purchased fabric (except apparel contractors)
315192	Nightshirts made in apparel knitting mills
315291	Nightshirts, infants', cut and sewn from purchased fabric (except apparel contractors)

Code	Description
315211	Nightshirts, men's and boys', cut and sew apparel contractors
315221	Nightshirts, men's and boys', cut and sewn from purchased fabric (except apparel contractors)
315212	Nightshirts, women's, girls', and infants', cut and sew apparel contractors
315231	Nightshirts, women's, misses', and girls', cut and sewn from purchased fabric (except contractors)
315192	Nightwear made in apparel knitting mills
315291	Nightwear, infants', cut and sewn from purchased fabric (except apparel contractors)
315211	Nightwear, men's and boys', cut and sew apparel contractors
315221	Nightwear, men's and boys', cut and sewn from purchased fabric (except apparel contractors)
422320	Nightwear, men's and boys', wholesaling
315212	Nightwear, women's, girls', and infants', cut and sew apparel contractors
315231	Nightwear, women's, misses', and girls', cut and sewn from purchased fabric (except apparel contractors)
331419	Niobium refining, primary
326299	Nipples and teething rings, rubber, manufacturing
332996	Nipples, metal, made from purchased pipe
325192	Nitrated hydrocarbon derivatives manufacturing
325311	Nitric acid manufacturing
325212	Nitrile rubber manufacturing
325212	Nitrile-butadiene rubber manufacturing
325212	Nitrile-chloroprene rubbers manufacturing
325192	Nitroaniline manufacturing
325192	Nitrobenzene manufacturing
325211	Nitrocellulose (i.e., pyroxylin) resins manufacturing
325920	Nitrocellulose explosive materials manufacturing
325221	Nitrocellulose fibers manufacturing
325120	Nitrogen manufacturing
325311	Nitrogenous fertilizer materials manufacturing
325314	Nitrogenous fertilizers made by mixing purchased materials
325920	Nitroglycerin explosive materials manufacturing
325192	Nitrophenol manufacturing
325192	Nitrosated hydrocarbon derivatives manufacturing
325132	Nitroso dyes manufacturing
325920	Nitrostarch explosive materials manufacturing
325199	Nitrous ether manufacturing
325120	Nitrous oxide manufacturing
339113	Noise protectors, personal, manufacturing
541380	Non-destructive testing laboratories or services
312120	Nonalcoholic beer brewing
312130	Nonalcoholic wines manufacturing
551112	Nonbank holding companies (except managing)
234990	Nonbuilding structures (except industrial) contractor
234930	Nonbuilding structures, industrial construction

Code	Description
325222	Noncellulosic fibers and filaments manufacturing
325222	Noncellulosic filament yarn manufacturing
325222	Noncellulosic staple fibers and filaments manufacturing
111339	Noncitrus fruit farming
327125	Nonclay refractories (e.g., block, brick, mortar, tile) manufacturing
311514	Nondairy creamers, dry, manufacturing
311511	Nondairy creamers, liquid, manufacturing
325110	Nonene made from refined petroleum or liquid hydrocarbons
311514	Nonfat dry milk manufacturing
331522	Nonferrous (except aluminum) die-casting foundries
331492	Nonferrous alloys (except aluminum, copper) made from purchased nonferrous metals
331492	Nonferrous alloys (except aluminum, copper) made in integrated secondary smelting and alloying plants
331419	Nonferrous metal (except aluminum, copper) shapes made in primary nonferrous metal smelting and refining mills
331491	Nonferrous metal shapes (except aluminum, copper) made by rolling, drawing, or extruding purchased nonferrous metal
331491	Nonferrous metal shapes (except aluminum, copper) made in integrated secondary smelting and extruding mills
331491	Nonferrous metal shapes (except aluminum, copper) made in integrated secondary smelting and rolling mills
331491	Nonferrous metal shapes (except aluminum, copper) made in integrated secondary smelting mills and wire drawing plants
331528	Nonferrous metals (except aluminum, copper) foundries (except die-casting)
331419	Nonferrous metals (except aluminum, copper) made in primary nonferrous metal smelting and refining mills
331492	Nonferrous metals (except aluminum, copper) secondary smelting and refining
331419	Nonferrous metals (except aluminum, copper) smelting and refining, primary
331528	Nonferrous metals (except aluminum, copper) unfinished castings (except die-castings) manufacturing
421510	Nonferrous metals (except precious) wholesaling
331491	Nonferrous wire (except aluminum, copper) made from purchased nonferrous metals (except aluminum, copper) in wire drawing plants
331491	Nonferrous wire (except aluminum, copper) made in integrated secondary smelting mills and wire drawing plants
323121	Nonfiction book binding without printing
511130	Nonfiction book publishers
511130	Nonfiction book publishers and printing combined
511130	Nonfiction book publishing (i.e., establishments known as publishers)
323117	Nonfiction books printing and binding without publishing
323117	Nonfiction books printing without publishing

Code	Description
562219	Nonhazardous waste treatment and disposal facilities (except combustors, incinerators, landfills, sewer systems, sewage treatment facilities)
213115	Nonmetallic minerals mining support services (e.g., blasting, shaft sinking, tunneling) on a contract basis
325412	Nonprescription drug preparations manufacturing
422210	Nonprescription drugs wholesaling
531312	Nonresidential property managing
531120	Nonresidential building (except miniwarehouse) rental or leasing
481212	Nonscheduled air freight transportation
481211	Nonscheduled air passenger transportation
332214	Nonstick metal cooking utensils
337122	Nonupholstered, household-type, custom wood furniture, manufacturing
313230	Nonwoven fabric tapes manufacturing
313230	Nonwoven fabrics manufacturing
313230	Nonwoven felts manufacturing
311999	Noodle mixes made from purchased dry ingredients
311423	Noodle mixes made in dehydration plants
311823	Noodle mixes made in dry pasta plants
311823	Noodles, dry, manufacturing
311991	Noodles, fresh, manufacturing
311999	Noodles, fried, manufacturing
339113	Nose and ear plugs manufacturing
541199	Notary public services
541199	Notary publics' private practices
334111	Notebook computers manufacturing
322233	Notebooks (including mechanically bound by wire, or plastics) made from purchased paper
422120	Notebooks wholesaling
332999	Novelties and specialties, nonprecious metal and precious plated, manufacturing
422990	Novelties wholesaling
316999	Novelties, leather (e.g., cigarette lighter covers, key fobs), manufacturing
339999	Novelties, not specified elsewhere, manufacturing
339911	Novelties, precious metal (except precious plated), manufacturing
321999	Novelties, wood fiber, manufacturing
453220	Novelty shops
315211	Novelty stitching contractors on men's and boys' apparel
315212	Novelty stitching contractors on women's, girls', and infants' apparel
326199	Nozzles, aerosol spray, plastics, manufacturing
332919	Nozzles, fire fighting, manufacturing
332919	Nozzles, lawn hose, manufacturing
332911	Nuclear application valves manufacturing
541690	Nuclear energy consulting services
926130	Nuclear energy inspection and regulation offices
325188	Nuclear fuel scrap reprocessing
325188	Nuclear fuels, inorganic, manufacturing
334519	Nuclear instrument modules manufacturing
334517	Nuclear irradiation equipment manufacturing
325412	Nuclear medicine (e.g., radioactive isotopes) preparations manufacturing
234930	Nuclear reactor containment structure construction

Nuclear reactor—Oil well

Code	Description
332410	Nuclear reactor steam supply systems manufacturing
332410	Nuclear reactors control rod drive mechanisms manufacturing
332410	Nuclear reactors manufacturing
332313	Nuclear shielding, fabricated metal plate work, manufacturing
332420	Nuclear waste casks, heavy gauge metal, manufacturing
721214	Nudist camps with accommodation facilities
713990	Nudist camps without accommodations
335314	Numerical controls, manufacturing
333512	Numerically controlled metal cutting machine tools manufacturing
812990	Numerology services
621610	Nurse associations, visiting
561310	Nurse registries
611519	Nurse's aides schools
113210	Nurseries for reforestation growing trees
444220	Nursery and garden centers without tree production
337122	Nursery furniture (except upholstered), wood, manufacturing
337124	Nursery furniture, metal, manufacturing
624410	Nursery schools
422930	Nursery stock (except plant bulbs, seeds) wholesaling
111421	Nursery stock growing
111421	Nursery with tree production (except for reforestation)
813920	Nurses' associations
621399	Nurses', licensed practical or registered, offices (e.g., centers, clinics)
621610	Nursing agencies, primarily providing home nursing services
623110	Nursing care facilities
623110	Nursing homes
611519	Nursing schools (except academic)
445292	Nut (i.e., packaged) stores
115114	Nut hulling and shelling
331221	Nut rods, iron or steel, made in cold rolling mills
331111	Nut rods, iron or steel, made in steel mills
333111	Nut shellers, farm-type, manufacturing
446191	Nutrition (i.e., food supplement) stores
621399	Nutritionists' offices (e.g., centers, clinics)
422450	Nuts (e.g., canned, roasted, salted) wholesaling
311320	Nuts, chocolate covered, made from cacao beans
311330	Nuts, chocolate covered, made from purchased chocolate
311340	Nuts, covered (except chocolate covered), manufacturing
311911	Nuts, kernels and seeds, roasting and processing
115113	Nuts, machine harvesting
332722	Nuts, metal, manufacturing
311911	Nuts, salted, roasted, cooked, canned, manufacturing
422590	Nuts, unprocessed or shelled only, wholesaling
325222	Nylon fibers and filaments manufacturing
315111	Nylon hosiery, sheer, women's, misses', and girls' full-length and knee-length, knitting or knitting and finishing
325211	Nylon resins manufacturing
313111	Nylon spun yarns made from purchased fiber
313113	Nylon thread manufacturing

Code	Description
313112	Nylon yarn twisting or winding of purchased yarn
315111	Nylons, sheer, women's, misses', and girls' full-length and knee-length, knitting or knitting and finishing
621320	ODs' (doctors of optometry) offices (e.g., centers, clinics)
321219	OSB (oriented strandboard) manufacturing
325191	Oak extract manufacturing
321999	Oars, wood, manufacturing
111199	Oat farming, field and seed production
311211	Oat flour manufacturing
311230	Oatmeal (i.e., cereal breakfast food) manufacturing
311230	Oats, breakfast cereal, manufacturing
311230	Oats, rolled (i.e., cereal breakfast food), manufacturing
812910	Obedience training services, pet
339992	Oboes manufacturing
713990	Observation towers
622310	Obstetrical hospital
621111	Obstetricians' offices (e.g., centers, clinics)
339992	Ocarinas manufacturing
926150	Occupational safety and health administration
926150	Occupational safety and health standards agencies
813920	Occupational therapists' associations
621340	Occupational therapists' offices (e.g., centers, clinics)
541710	Oceanographic research and development laboratories or services
212393	Ocher mining and/or beneficiating
325131	Ocher pigments manufacturing
339992	Octophones manufacturing
114112	Octopus fishing
332995	Oerlikon guns manufacturing
721310	Off campus dormitories
336999	Off-highway tracked vehicles (except construction, armored military) manufacturing
333120	Off-highway trucks manufacturing
336999	Off-road all terrain vehicles (ATV's), wheeled or tracked, manufacturing
441221	Off-road all-terrain vehicles (ATV), wheeled or tracked, dealers
713290	Off-track betting parlors
624190	Offender self-help organizations
561110	Office administration services
541512	Office automation computer systems integration design services
233320	Office building construction
531120	Office building rental or leasing
561720	Office cleaning services
421420	Office equipment wholesaling
337214	Office furniture (except wood), padded, upholstered, or plain (except wood), manufacturing
532420	Office furniture rental or leasing
442110	Office furniture stores
421210	Office furniture wholesaling
337211	Office furniture, padded, upholstered, or plain wood, manufacturing
561320	Office help supply services
811212	Office machine repair and maintenance services (except communication equipment)
532420	Office machinery and equipment rental or leasing
421420	Office machines wholesaling
561110	Office management services

Code	Description
322121	Office paper (e.g., computer printer, photocopy, plain paper) made in paper mills
322233	Office paper (e.g., computer printer, photocopy, plain paper), cut sheet, made from purchased paper
422120	Office supplies (except furniture, machines) wholesaling
322231	Office supplies, die-cut paper, made from purchased paper or paperboard
561320	Office supply pools
453210	Office supply stores
325910	Offset inks manufacturing
323122	Offset plate preparation services
323110	Offset printing (except books, manifold business forms, printing grey goods)
333293	Offset printing presses manufacturing
211111	Offshore crude petroleum production
211111	Offshore natural gas production
334515	Ohmmeters manufacturing
324110	Oil (i.e., petroleum) refineries
325998	Oil additive preparations manufacturing
324110	Oil additives made in petroleum refineries
422690	Oil additives wholesaling
211111	Oil and gas field development for own account
211111	Oil and gas field exploration for own account
213112	Oil and gas field services (except contract drilling) on a contract basis
333132	Oil and gas field-type drilling machinery and equipment (except offshore floating platforms) manufacturing
336611	Oil and gas offshore floating platforms manufacturing
213111	Oil and gas well drilling services (redrilling, spudding, tailing) on a contract basis
333414	Oil burners, heating, manufacturing
421720	Oil burners, heating, wholesaling
811191	Oil change and lubrication shops, automotive
422690	Oil drilling muds wholesaling
213112	Oil field exploration (except surveying) on a contract basis
532412	Oil field machinery and equipment rental or leasing
336399	Oil filters, automotive, truck, and bus, manufacturing
421120	Oil filters, automotive, wholesaling
422590	Oil kernels wholesaling
523999	Oil lease brokers' offices
211112	Oil line drip, natural gas liquid
333913	Oil measuring and dispensing pumps manufacturing
422590	Oil nuts wholesaling
234930	Oil refinery construction
533110	Oil royalty companies
523910	Oil royalty dealing (i.e., acting as a principal in dealing royalties to investors)
533110	Oil royalty leasing
213112	Oil sampling services on a contract basis
339991	Oil seals manufacturing
211111	Oil shale mining and/or beneficiating
562910	Oil spill cleanup services
332420	Oil storage tanks, heavy gauge metal, manufacturing
532412	Oil well drilling machinery and equipment rental or leasing
213111	Oil well drilling on a contract basis
213112	Oil well logging on a contract basis

Code	Description
421830	Oil well machinery and equipment wholesaling
213112	Oil well rig building, repairing, and dismantling, on a contract basis
421830	Oil well supply houses wholesaling
311613	Oil, animal, rendering
311221	Oil, corn crude and refined, made by wet milling corn
311225	Oil, olive, made from purchased oils
422710	Oil, petroleum, bulk stations and terminals
422720	Oil, petroleum, wholesaling (except bulk stations, terminals)
311225	Oil, vegetable stearin, made from purchased oils
421930	Oil, waste, wholesaling
324199	Oil-based additives made from refined petroleum
333911	Oil-well and oil-field pumps manufacturing
313320	Oilcloth manufacturing
313320	Oiling of purchased textiles and apparel
325998	Oils (e.g., cutting, lubricating), synthetic, manufacturing
325192	Oils made by distillation of coal tar
422490	Oils, cooking and salad, wholesaling
324110	Oils, fuel, manufacturing
422990	Oils, inedible, animal or vegetable, wholesaling
324191	Oils, lubricating petroleum, made from refined petroleum
325998	Oils, lubricating, synthetic, manufacturing
324191	Oils, petroleum lubricating, re-refining used
325613	Oils, soluble (i.e., textile finishing assistants), manufacturing
325411	Oils, vegetable and animal, medicinal, uncompounded, manufacturing
325191	Oils, wood, made by distillation of wood
111191	Oilseed and grain combination farming, field and seed production
422990	Oilseed cake and meal wholesaling
333294	Oilseed crushing and extracting machinery manufacturing
111120	Oilseed farming (except soybean), field and seed production
422590	Oilseeds wholesaling
212399	Oilstones mining and/or beneficiating
111219	Okra farming, field, bedding plant and seed production
623312	Old age homes without nursing care
923130	Old age survivors and disability programs
623312	Old soldiers' homes without nursing care
325222	Olefin fibers and filaments manufacturing
325110	Olefins made from refined petroleum or liquid hydrocarbons
325199	Oleic acid (i.e., red oil) manufacturing
325199	Oleic acid esters manufacturing
325188	Oleum (i.e., fuming sulfuric acid) manufacturing
111339	Olive farming
311225	Olive oil made from purchased oils
311223	Olive oil made in crushing mills
311421	Olives brined
311423	Olives, dried, made in dehydration plant
212325	Olivine, non-gem, mining and/or beneficiating
334511	Omnibearing instrumentation manufacturing
514191	On-line access service providers

Code	Description
233210	On-site mobile home repair construction
233210	On-site modular homes assembly construction
233210	On-site prefabricated homes assembly construction
621111	Oncologists' offices (e.g., centers, clinics)
233210	One family house construction—general construction contractors
812922	One-hour photofinishing services
111219	Onion farming, field, bedding plant and seed production
311421	Onions pickled
212319	Onyx marble crushed and broken stone mining and/or beneficiating
212311	Onyx marble mining or quarrying
512132	Open air motion picture theaters
711110	Opera companies
315991	Opera hats cut and sewn from purchased fabric (except apparel contractors)
315211	Opera hats, men's and boys', cut and sew apparel contractors
315212	Opera hats, women's, girls', and infants', cut and sew apparel contractors
711130	Opera singers, independent
927110	Operating and launching government satellites
339111	Operating room tables manufacturing
511210	Operating systems software, computer, packaged
541614	Operations research consulting services
233320	Operative builders of commercial and institutional buildings
233310	Operative builders of manufacturing and industrial buildings
233220	Operative builders of multifamily housing
233210	Operative builders of single family housing
325411	Ophthalmic agents, uncompounded, manufacturing
421460	Ophthalmic goods (except cameras) wholesaling
339112	Ophthalmic instruments and apparatus (except laser surgical) manufacturing
621111	Ophthalmologists' offices (e.g., centers, clinics)
339112	Ophthalmometers and ophthalmoscopes manufacturing
541910	Opinion research services
325411	Opium and opium derivatives (i.e., basic chemicals) manufacturing
333314	Optical alignment and display instruments (except photographic) manufacturing
334112	Optical disk drives manufacturing
421460	Optical goods (except cameras) wholesaling
446130	Optical goods stores (except offices of optometrists)
212399	Optical grade calcite mining and/or beneficiating
333314	Optical gun sighting and fire control equipment and instruments manufacturing
811219	Optical instrument repair and maintenance services
333298	Optical lens making and grinding machinery manufacturing
334119	Optical readers and scanners manufacturing
514210	Optical scanning services

Code	Description
333314	Optical test and inspection equipment manufacturing
334413	Optoelectronic devices manufacturing
339112	Optometers manufacturing
421460	Optometric equipment and supplies wholesaling
813920	Optometrists' associations
621320	Optometrists' offices (e.g., centers, clinics)
621210	Oral and maxillofacial surgeons' offices (e.g., centers, clinics)
325412	Oral contraceptive preparations manufacturing
621210	Oral pathologists' offices (e.g., centers, clinics)
111310	Orange groves
325998	Orange oil manufacturing
115112	Orchard cultivation services (e.g., bracing, planting, pruning, removal, spraying, surgery)
111998	Orchard grass seed farming
711510	Orchestra conductors, independent
711130	Orchestras
454110	Order taking offices of mail-order houses
421990	Ordnance and accessories wholesaling
421520	Ore concentrates wholesaling
333131	Ore crushing, washing, screening, and loading machinery manufacturing
421520	Ores (e.g., gold, iron, lead, silver, zinc) wholesaling
621991	Organ banks, body
621991	Organ donor centers, body
422690	Organic chemicals wholesaling
325222	Organic fibers and filaments (except cellulosic) manufacturing
325132	Organic pigments, dyes, lakes, and toners manufacturing
541612	Organization development consulting services
928120	Organization for Economic Cooperation and Development
928120	Organization of American States
326199	Organizers for closets, drawers, and shelves, plastics, manufacturing
711310	Organizers of agricultural fairs with facilities
711320	Organizers of agricultural fairs without facilities
711310	Organizers of arts events with facilities
711320	Organizers of arts events without facilities
711310	Organizers of festivals with facilities
711320	Organizers of festivals without facilities
711310	Organizers of live performing arts productions (e.g., concerts) with facilities
711320	Organizers of live performing arts productions (e.g., concerts) without facilities
711310	Organizers of sports events with facilities
711320	Organizers of sports events without facilities
325199	Organo-inorganic compound manufacturing
325320	Organo-phosphate based insecticides manufacturing
321219	Oriented strandboard (OSB) manufacturing
327420	Ornamental and architectural plaster work (e.g., columns, mantels, molding) manufacturing
112511	Ornamental fish production, farm raising
421390	Ornamental ironwork wholesaling

Ornamental metalwork—Packing materials

Code	Description
235990	Ornamental metalwork construction contractors
332323	Ornamental metalwork manufacturing
111422	Ornamental plant growing
561730	Ornamental tree and shrub services
321918	Ornamental woodwork (e.g., cornices, mantels) manufacturing
339999	Ornaments, Christmas tree (except electric, glass), manufacturing
335129	Ornaments, Christmas tree, electric, manufacturing
327212	Ornaments, Christmas tree, glass, made in glass making plants
327215	Ornaments, Christmas tree, made from purchased glass
623990	Orphanages
325998	Orris oil manufacturing
325192	Orthodichlorobenzene manufacturing
339116	Orthodontic appliance, custom made in dental laboratories
339114	Orthodontic appliances manufacturing
621210	Orthodontists' offices (e.g., centers, clinics)
339113	Orthopedic canes manufacturing
339113	Orthopedic devices manufacturing
421450	Orthopedic equipment and supplies wholesaling
339113	Orthopedic extension shoes manufacturing
339113	Orthopedic hosiery, elastic, manufacturing
622310	Orthopedic hospitals
621111	Orthopedic physicians' offices (e.g., centers, clinics)
327420	Orthopedic plaster, gypsum, manufacturing
316219	Orthopedic shoes (except extension shoes), children's, manufacturing
316213	Orthopedic shoes (except extension shoes), men's, manufacturing
316214	Orthopedic shoes (except extension shoes), women's, manufacturing
448210	Orthopedic shoes stores
621111	Orthopedic surgeons' offices (e.g., centers, clinics)
334515	Oscillators (e.g., instrument type audiofrequency and radiofrequency) manufacturing
334515	Oscilloscopes manufacturing
212299	Osmium mining and/or beneficiating
334516	Osmometers manufacturing
325998	Ossein manufacturing
622110	Osteopathic hospitals
621111	Osteopathic physicians' (except mental health) offices (e.g., centers, clinics)
112390	Ostrich production
621111	Otolaryngologists' offices (e.g., centers, clinics)
334510	Otoscopes, electromedical, manufacturing
337121	Ottomans, upholstered, manufacturing
541850	Out-of-home media (i.e., display) advertising services
441222	Outboard motor dealers
811490	Outboard motor repair shops
333618	Outboard motors manufacturing
421910	Outboard motors wholesaling
713990	Outdoor adventure operations (e.g., white water rafting) without accommodations
721214	Outdoor adventure retreats with accommodation facilities
541850	Outdoor display advertising services
421210	Outdoor furniture wholesaling

Code	Description
451110	Outdoor sporting equipment stores
315191	Outerwear hand-knitted for the trade
422320	Outerwear, men's and boys', wholesaling
422330	Outerwear, women's, children's, and infants', wholesaling
335932	Outlet boxes, electrical wiring, manufacturing
335931	Outlets (i.e., receptacles), electrical, manufacturing
335931	Outlets, convenience, electric, manufacturing
621420	Outpatient mental health centers and clinics (except hospitals)
621420	Outpatient treatment centers and clinics (except hospitals) for substance abuse (i.e., alcoholism, drug addiction)
621420	Outpatient treatment centers and clinics for alcoholism
621420	Outpatient treatment centers and clinics for drug addiction
541990	Outplacement services
325612	Oven cleaners manufacturing
334512	Oven temperature controls, nonindustrial, manufacturing
811412	Oven, household-type, repair and maintenance services without retailing new ovens
421720	Ovens (except electric), household-type, wholesaling
234930	Ovens construction, industrial
234930	Ovens, baker's, construction
333294	Ovens, bakery, manufacturing
234930	Ovens, coke, construction
333319	Ovens, commercial-type, manufacturing
421440	Ovens, commercial-type, wholesaling
421620	Ovens, electric household-type, wholesaling
335221	Ovens, freestanding household-type, manufacturing
333994	Ovens, industrial process-type, manufacturing
421830	Ovens, industrial, wholesaling
339111	Ovens, laboratory-type, manufacturing
335211	Ovens, portable household-type (except microwave and convection ovens), manufacturing
335221	Ovens, portable household-type convention and microwave, manufacturing
327215	Ovenware made from purchased glass
327212	Ovenware, glass, made in glass making plants
315211	Overall jackets, work, men's and boys', cut and sew apparel contractors
315225	Overall jackets, work, men's and boys', cut and sewn from purchased fabric (except apparel contractors)
315211	Overalls, work, men's and boys', cut and sew apparel contractors
315225	Overalls, work, men's and boys', cut and sewn from purchased fabric (except apparel contractors)
213113	Overburden removal for coal mining on a contract basis
213114	Overburden removal for metal mining on a contract basis
213115	Overburden removal for nonmetallic minerals mining (except fuels) on a contract basis
315211	Overcoats, men's and boys', cut and sew apparel contractors

Code	Description
315222	Overcoats, men's and boys', cut and sewn from purchased fabric (except apparel contractors)
315212	Overcoats, women's, girls', and infants', cut and sew apparel contractors
315234	Overcoats, women's, misses', and girls', cut and sewn from purchased fabric (except apparel contractors)
333922	Overhead conveyors manufacturing
333315	Overhead projectors (except computer peripheral) manufacturing
334119	Overhead projectors, computer peripheral-type, manufacturing
333923	Overhead traveling cranes manufacturing
234120	Overpass construction
316211	Overshoes, plastics or plastics soled fabric upper, manufacturing
316211	Overshoes, rubber, or rubber soled fabric, manufacturing
325199	Oxalates (e.g., ammonium oxalate, ethyl oxalate, sodium oxalate) manufacturing
325199	Oxalic acid manufacturing
339991	Oxial mechanical face seals manufacturing
532291	Oxygen equipment rental (i.e. home use)
325120	Oxygen manufacturing
339112	Oxygen tents manufacturing
114112	Oyster dredging
112512	Oyster production, farm raising
212399	Ozokerite mining and/or beneficiating
333319	Ozone machines for water purification manufacturing
813940	PACs (Political Action Committees)
334210	PBX (private branch exchange) equipment manufacturing
561330	PEO (professional employer organizations)
334510	PET (position emission tomography) scanners manufacturing
326122	PVC pipe manufacturing
621999	Pacemaker monitoring services
334510	Pacemakers manufacturing
326299	Pacifiers, rubber, manufacturing
713990	Pack trains (i.e., trail riding), recreational
445310	Package stores (i.e., liquor)
511210	Packaged computer software publishers
511210	Packaged computer software publishing (i.e., establishments known as publishers)
326112	Packaging film, plastics, single-web or multiweb, manufacturing
115114	Packaging fresh or farm-dried fruits and vegetables
541420	Packaging industrial design services
333993	Packaging machinery manufacturing
421840	Packaging material wholesaling
561910	Packaging services (except packing and crating for transportation)
326150	Packaging, foam plastics (except polystyrene), manufacturing
326199	Packaging, plastics (e.g., blister, bubble), manufacturing
325998	Packer's fluids manufacturing
488991	Packing and preparing goods for shipping
321920	Packing cases, wood, nailed or lock corner, manufacturing
321920	Packing crates, wood, manufacturing
115114	Packing fruits and vegetables
421830	Packing machinery and equipment wholesaling
421840	Packing materials wholesaling

Code	Description
316211	Pacs, plastics or plastics soled fabric upper, manufacturing
316211	Pacs, rubber or rubber soled fabric upper, manufacturing
322232	Padded envelopes manufacturing
314999	Padding and wadding (except nonwoven fabric) manufacturing
422310	Paddings, apparel, wholesaling
321999	Paddles, wood, manufacturing
332510	Padlocks manufacturing
314129	Pads and protectors (e.g., ironing board, mattress, table), textile, made from purchased fabrics or felts
313230	Pads and wadding, nonwoven, manufacturing
322211	Pads, corrugated and solid fiberboard, made from purchased paper or paperboard
322233	Pads, desk, made from purchased paper
321999	Pads, excelsior, wood, manufacturing
322291	Pads, incontinent and bed, manufacturing
332999	Pads, soap impregnated scouring, manufacturing
321999	Pads, table, rattan, reed, and willow, manufacturing
334220	Pagers manufacturing
513321	Paging services
321920	Pails, coopered wood, manufacturing
326199	Pails, plastics, manufacturing
321920	Pails, plywood, manufacturing
321920	Pails, wood, manufacturing
621498	Pain therapy centers and clinics, outpatient
325510	Paint and varnish removers manufacturing
333994	Paint baking and drying ovens manufacturing
339994	Paint rollers manufacturing
422950	Paint rollers wholesaling
811121	Paint shops, automotive
333991	Paint spray guns, handheld pneumatic, manufacturing
333912	Paint sprayers (i.e., compressor and spray gun unit) manufacturing
332999	Paint sticks, metal, manufacturing
326199	Paint sticks, plastics, manufacturing
321999	Paint sticks, wood, manufacturing
444120	Paint stores
325510	Paint thinner and reducer preparations manufacturing
325510	Paintbrush cleaners manufacturing
339994	Paintbrushes manufacturing
422950	Paintbrushes wholesaling
422950	Painter's supplies (except artist's, turpentine) wholesaling
711510	Painters (i.e., artists), independent
332812	Painting metals and metal products for the trade
711510	Painting restorers, independent
235210	Painting, exterior (except roof) and interior, construction contractors
235610	Painting, roof, construction contractors
325510	Paints (except artist's) manufacturing
422950	Paints (except artist's) wholesaling
339942	Paints, artist's, manufacturing
422990	Paints, artist's, wholesaling
325510	Paints, emulsion (i.e., latex paint), manufacturing
325510	Paints, oil and alkyd vehicle, manufacturing
315192	Pajamas made in apparel knitting mills

Code	Description
315291	Pajamas, infants', cut and sewn from purchased fabric (except apparel contractors)
315211	Pajamas, men's and boys', cut and sew apparel contractors
315221	Pajamas, men's and boys', cut and sewn from purchased fabric (except apparel contractors)
315231	Pajamas, women's and girls', cut and sewn from purchased fabric (except apparel contractors)
315212	Pajamas, women's, girls', and infants', cut and sew apparel contractors
339942	Palettes, artist's, manufacturing
212299	Palladium mining and/or beneficiating
321920	Pallet containers, wood or wood and metal combination, manufacturing
333924	Pallet movers manufacturing
333924	Pallet or skid jacks manufacturing
332999	Pallet parts, metal, manufacturing
321920	Pallet parts, wood, manufacturing
532490	Pallet rental or leasing
421830	Pallets and skids wholesaling
322211	Pallets, corrugated and solid fiber, made from purchased paper or paperboard
332999	Pallets, metal, manufacturing
321920	Pallets, wood or wood and metal combination, manufacturing
812990	Palm reading services
311225	Palm-kernel oil made from purchased oils
311223	Palm-kernel oil, cake, and meal made in crushing mills
325199	Palmitic acid esters and amines manufacturing
323121	Pamphlet binding without printing
511130	Pamphlet publishers
511130	Pamphlet publishers and printing combined
511130	Pamphlet publishing (i.e., establishments known as publishers)
323117	Pamphlets printing and binding without publishing
323117	Pamphlets printing without publishing
422920	Pamphlets wholesaling
315991	Panama hats cut and sewn from purchased fabric (except apparel contractors)
315211	Panama hats, men's and boys', cut and sew apparel contractors
315212	Panama hats, women's, girls', and infants', cut and sew apparel contractors
311822	Pancake mixes made from purchased flour
311999	Pancake syrups (except pure maple) manufacturing
311412	Pancakes, frozen, manufacturing
321918	Panel work, wood millwork, manufacturing
334513	Panelboard indicators, recorders, and controllers, receiver industrial process-type, manufacturing
335313	Panelboards, electric power distribution, manufacturing
421610	Panelboards, electric power distribution, wholesaling
235510	Paneling construction contractors
421310	Paneling wholesaling
335313	Panels, generator control and metering, manufacturing
321211	Panels, hardwood plywood, manufacturing
332311	Panels, prefabricated metal building, manufacturing

Code	Description
321992	Panels, prefabricated wood building, manufacturing
321212	Panels, softwood plywood, manufacturing
315192	Panties made in apparel knitting mills
315291	Panties, infants', cut and sewn from purchased fabric (except apparel contractors)
315212	Panties, women's and girls', cut and sew apparel contractors
315231	Panties, women's, misses', and girls', cut and sewn from purchased fabric (except apparel contractors)
315239	Pants outfits (except pantsuits), women's, misses', and girls', cut and sewn from purchased fabric (except apparel contractors)
315212	Pants outfits, women's, girls', and infants', cut and sew apparel contractors
315211	Pants, athletic, men's and boys', cut and sew apparel contractors
315291	Pants, athletic, infants', cut and sewn from purchased fabric (except apparel contractors)
315191	Pants, athletic, made in apparel knitting mills
315228	Pants, athletic, men's and boys' (e.g., gymnastic, ski), cut and sewn from purchased fabric (except apparel contractors)
315212	Pants, athletic, women's, girls', and infants', cut and sew apparel contractors
315239	Pants, athletic, women's, misses', and girls', cut and sewn from purchased fabric (except apparel contractors)
315211	Pants, dress, men's and boys', cut and sew apparel contractors
315224	Pants, dress, men's and boys', cut and sewn from purchased fabric (except apparel contractors)
315291	Pants, infants' waterproof, cut and sewn from purchased fabric (except apparel contractors)
315212	Pants, infants', cut and sew apparel contractors
315291	Pants, infants', cut and sewn from purchased fabric (except apparel contractors)
315292	Pants, leather (except apparel contractors), manufacturing
315211	Pants, leather, men's and boys', cut and sew apparel contractors
315211	Pants, men's and boys', cut and sew apparel contractors
315191	Pants, outerwear, made in apparel knitting mills
315299	Pants, rubber and rubberized fabric, made in the same establishment as the basic material
315291	Pants, sweat, infant's, cut and sewn from purchased fabric (except apparel contractors)
315228	Pants, sweat, men's and boys', cut and sewn from purchased fabric (except apparel contractors)
315212	Pants, sweat, women's, girls', and infants', cut and sew apparel contractors
315239	Pants, sweat, women's, misses', and girls', cut and sewn from purchased fabric (except apparel contractors)
315211	Pants, unisex sweat, cut and sew apparel contractors

Pants—Parsnip

Code	Description
315228	Pants, unisex sweat, cut and sewn from purchased fabric (except apparel contractors)
315299	Pants, vulcanized rubber, manufacturing
315299	Pants, waterproof outerwear (except infants'), cut and sewn from purchased fabric (except apparel contractors)
315211	Pants, waterproof outerwear, men's and boys', cut and sew apparel contractors
315212	Pants, waterproof outerwear, women's, girls', and infants', cut and sew apparel contractors
315212	Pants, women's, girls', and infants', cut and sew apparel contractors
315239	Pants, women's, misses', and girls', cut and sewn from purchased fabric (except apparel contractors)
315211	Pants, work (except dungarees, jeans), men's and boys', cut and sew apparel contractors
315225	Pants, work (except dungarees, jeans), men's and boys', cut and sewn from purchased fabric (except apparel contractors)
315291	Pantsuits, infants', cut and sewn from purchased fabric (except apparel contractors)
315212	Pantsuits, women's, girls', and infants', cut and sew apparel contractors
315234	Pantsuits, women's, misses', and girls', cut and sewn from purchased fabric (except apparel contractors)
315212	Panty girdles cut and sew apparel contractors
315231	Panty girdles, women's, misses', and girls', cut and sewn from purchased fabric (except apparel contractors)
315111	Panty hose, women's and girls', knitting or knitting and finishing
111339	Papaya farming
327910	Paper (e.g., aluminum oxide, emery, garnet, silicon carbide), abrasive coated, made from purchased paper
422110	Paper (e.g., fine, printing, writing), bulk, wholesaling
322121	Paper (except newsprint, uncoated groundwood) manufacturing
322121	Paper (except newsprint, uncoated groundwood) products made in paper mills
322121	Paper (except newsprint, uncoated groundwood), coated, laminated or treated, made in paper mills
422130	Paper (except office supplies, printing paper, stationery, writing paper) wholesaling
333291	Paper and paperboard coating and finishing machinery manufacturing
333291	Paper and paperboard converting machinery manufacturing
333291	Paper and paperboard corrugating machinery manufacturing
333291	Paper and paperboard cutting and folding machinery manufacturing
333291	Paper and paperboard die-cutting and stamping machinery manufacturing
421830	Paper and pulp industries manufacturing machinery wholesaling
333291	Paper bag making machinery manufacturing
422130	Paper bags wholesaling
322223	Paper bags, coated, made from purchased paper
322224	Paper bags, uncoated, made from purchased paper
212324	Paper clay mining and/or beneficiating
332618	Paper clips made from purchased wire
331222	Paper clips, iron or steel, made in wire drawing plants
322215	Paper cups made from purchased paper or paperboard
339942	Paper cutters, office-type, manufacturing
322299	Paper dishes (e.g., cups, plates) made from purchased molded pulp
322215	Paper dishes (e.g., cups, plates) made from purchased paper or paperboard
315212	Paper dresses, women's, girls', and infants', cut and sew apparel contractors
315233	Paper dresses, women's, misses', and girls', cut and sewn from purchased fabric (except apparel contractors)
313221	Paper fabric, narrow woven, weaving
313210	Paper fabrics, broadwoven, weaving
235210	Paper hanging or removal construction contractors
332618	Paper machine wire cloth made from purchased wire
333291	Paper making machinery manufacturing
811310	Paper making machinery repair and maintenance services
322121	Paper mills (except newsprint, uncoated groundwood paper mills)
322122	Paper mills, newsprint
322122	Paper mills, uncoated groundwood
322291	Paper napkins and tablecloths made from purchased paper
322299	Paper novelties made from purchased paper
322215	Paper plates made from purchased paper or paperboard
322299	Paper products (except office supply), die-cut, made from purchased paper or paperboard
322231	Paper products, die-cut office supply, made from purchased paper or paperboard
233310	Paper pulp mill construction
332992	Paper shells (i.e., 30 mm. or less, 1.18 inch or less) manufacturing
322121	Paper stock for conversion into paper products (e.g., bag and sack stock, envelope stock, tissue stock, wallpaper stock) manufacturing
322291	Paper towels made from purchased paper
322121	Paper towels made in paper mills
313111	Paper yarn manufacturing
322121	Paper, asphalt, made in paper mills
421390	Paper, building, wholesaling
339944	Paper, carbon, manufacturing
322211	Paper, corrugated, made from purchased paper or paperboard
322122	Paper, newsprint and uncoated groundwood, manufacturing
422120	Paper, office (e.g., carbon, computer, copier, typewriter), wholesaling
325992	Paper, photographic sensitized, manufacturing
421930	Paper, scrap, wholesaling
339944	Paper, stencil, manufacturing
322130	Paperboard (e.g., can/drum stock, container board, corrugating medium, folding carton stock, linerboard, tube) manufacturing
422130	Paperboard and paperboard products (except office supplies) wholesaling
333291	Paperboard box making machinery manufacturing
322130	Paperboard coating, laminating, or treating in paperboard mills
333291	Paperboard making machinery manufacturing
322130	Paperboard mills
322130	Paperboard products (e.g., containers) made in paperboard mills
322226	Paperboard, pasted, lined, laminated, or surface coated, made from purchased paperboard
327999	Papier-mache statuary and related art goods (e.g., urns, vases) manufacturing
713990	Para sailing, recreational
314999	Parachutes manufacturing
213112	Paraffin services, oil and gas field, on a contract basis
324110	Paraffin waxes made in petroleum refineries
325110	Paraffins made from refined petroleum or liquid hydrocarbons
541199	Paralegal services
321213	Parallel strand lumber manufacturing
621399	Paramedics' offices (e.g., centers, clinics)
325132	Pararosaniline dyes manufacturing
621511	Parasitology health laboratories
339999	Parasols manufacturing
325320	Parathion insecticides manufacturing
485991	Paratransit transportation services
561431	Parcel mailing services combined with one or more other office support services, private
561431	Parcel mailing services, private
333997	Parcel post scales manufacturing
316110	Parchment leather manufacturing
922150	Pardon boards and offices
813410	Parent-teachers' associations
624190	Parenting support services
325320	Paris green insecticides manufacturing
234990	Park construction
922120	Park police
332812	Parkerizing metals and metal products for the trade
812930	Parking garages, automobile
561790	Parking lot cleaning (e.g., power sweeping, washing) services
235710	Parking lot construction contractors
812930	Parking lots, automobile
334514	Parking meters manufacturing
561612	Parking security services
488119	Parking services, aircraft
812930	Parking services, valet
233320	Parking structure construction
713110	Parks (e.g., theme, water), amusement
924120	Parks and recreation commission, government
712190	Parks, national
712190	Parks, nature
712130	Parks, wild animal
234110	Parkway construction
611310	Parochial schools, college level
611110	Parochial schools, elementary or secondary
922150	Parole offices
321918	Parquet flooring, hardwood, manufacturing
321918	Parquetry, hardwood, manufacturing
111219	Parsley farming, field, bedding plant and seed production
111219	Parsnip farming, field, bedding plant and seed production

Code	Description
335999	Particle accelerators, high voltage, manufacturing
334516	Particle beam excitation instruments, laboratory-type, manufacturing
334516	Particle size analyzers manufacturing
321219	Particleboard manufacturing
421310	Particleboard wholesaling
337215	Partitions for floor attachment, prefabricated, manufacturing
421440	Partitions wholesaling
322211	Partitions, corrugated and solid fiber, made from purchased paper or paperboard
337215	Partitions, freestanding, prefabricated, manufacturing
332323	Partitions, ornamental metal, manufacturing
441310	Parts and accessories dealers, automotive
421120	Parts, new, motor vehicle, wholesaling
421140	Parts, used, motor vehicle, wholesaling
532299	Party (i.e., banquet) equipment rental
454390	Party plan merchandisers, direct selling
812990	Party planning services
532299	Party rental supply centers
481211	Passenger air transportation, nonscheduled
481111	Passenger air transportation, scheduled
233320	Passenger and freight terminal building construction
333922	Passenger baggage belt loaders (except industrial truck) manufacturing
532112	Passenger car leasing
532111	Passenger car rental
481211	Passenger carriers, air, nonscheduled
481111	Passenger carriers, air, scheduled
485320	Passenger limousine rental with driver (except shuttle service, taxi)
482111	Passenger railways, line-haul
336611	Passenger ship building
483114	Passenger transportation, coastal or Great Lakes
483114	Passenger transportation, deep sea, to and from domestic ports
483112	Passenger transportation, deep sea, to or from foreign ports
483212	Passenger transportation, inland waters (except on Great Lakes system)
532112	Passenger van leasing
532111	Passenger van rental
532111	Passenger van rental agencies
485320	Passenger van rental with driver (except shuttle service, taxi)
532112	Passenger vehicle fleet leasing
111339	Passion fruit farming
928120	Passport issuing services
541921	Passport photography services
311422	Pasta based products canning
333294	Pasta making machinery (i.e., food manufacturing-type) manufacturing
311999	Pasta mixes made from purchased dry ingredients
311823	Pasta, dry, manufacturing
311991	Pasta, fresh, manufacturing
331314	Paste made from purchased aluminum
331423	Paste made from purchased copper
331221	Paste made from purchased iron or steel
331111	Paste, iron or steel, made in steel mills
331492	Paste, nonferrous metals (except aluminum, copper), made from purchased metal
325520	Pastes, adhesive, manufacturing
311421	Pastes, fruit and vegetable, canning

Code	Description
333294	Pasteurizing equipment, food, manufacturing
311511	Pasteurizing milk
311612	Pastrami made from purchased carcasses
311812	Pastries (e.g., Danish, French), fresh, made in commercial bakeries
311813	Pastries (e.g., Danish, French), frozen, manufacturing
311822	Pastries, uncooked, manufacturing
321999	Pastry boards, wood, manufacturing
541199	Patent agent services (i.e., patent filing and searching services)
541110	Patent attorneys' offices
541110	Patent attorneys' private practices
541990	Patent broker services (i.e., patent marketing services)
533110	Patent buying and licensing
533110	Patent leasing
316110	Patent leather manufacturing
325412	Patent medicine preparations manufacturing
621511	Pathological analysis laboratories
621111	Pathologists' (except oral, speech, voice) offices (e.g., centers, clinics)
621111	Pathologists', forensic, offices (e.g., centers, clinics)
621111	Pathologists', neuropathological, offices (e.g., centers, clinics)
621210	Pathologists', oral, offices (e.g., centers, clinics)
621340	Pathologists', speech or voice, offices (e.g., centers, clinics)
621111	Pathologists', surgical, offices (e.g., centers, clinics)
621511	Pathology laboratories, medical
334510	Patient monitoring equipment (e.g., intensive care, coronary care unit) manufacturing
421450	Patient monitoring equipment wholesaling
327331	Patio block, concrete, manufacturing
235710	Patio construction contractors
336611	Patrol boat building
561612	Patrol services, security
541990	Patrolling (i.e., visual inspection) of electric transmission or gas lines
511199	Pattern and plan (e.g., clothing patterns) publishers
511199	Pattern and plan (e.g., clothing patterns) publishers and printing combined
332997	Patterns (except shoe), industrial, manufacturing
421830	Patterns (except shoe), industrial, wholesaling
323112	Patterns and plans (e.g., clothing patterns) flexographic printing without publishing
323111	Patterns and plans (e.g., clothing patterns) gravure printing without publishing
323110	Patterns and plans (e.g., clothing patterns) lithographic (offset) printing without publishing
323119	Patterns and plans (e.g., clothing patterns) printing (except flexographic, gravure, lithographic, screen) without publishing
511199	Patterns and plans (e.g., clothing patterns) publishing (i.e., establishments known as publishers)
323113	Patterns and plans (e.g., clothing patterns) screen printing without publishing

Code	Description
339999	Patterns, shoe, manufacturing
421850	Patterns, shoe, wholesaling
212399	Pavers mining and/or beneficiating
324121	Paving blocks and mixtures made from purchased asphaltic materials
327331	Paving blocks, concrete, manufacturing
327121	Paving brick, clay, manufacturing
234110	Paving construction contractors
333120	Paving machinery manufacturing
522298	Pawnshops
812990	Pay telephone equipment concession operators
513210	Pay television networks
541214	Payroll processing services
111219	Pea (except dry) farming, field and seed production
111130	Pea farming, dry, field and seed production
928120	Peace Corps
813319	Peace advocacy organizations
111339	Peach farming
325132	Peacock blue lake manufacturing
311911	Peanut butter blended with jelly manufacturing
311911	Peanut butter manufacturing
311223	Peanut cake, meal, and oil made in crushing mills
333111	Peanut combines (i.e., diggers, packers, threshers) manufacturing
111992	Peanut farming
311225	Peanut oil made from purchased oils
333294	Peanut roasting machines (i.e., food manufacturing-type) manufacturing
115114	Peanut shelling
115113	Peanut, machine harvesting
111339	Pear farming
339913	Pearl drilling, peeling, or sawing
325131	Pearl essence pigment, synthetic, manufacturing
331511	Pearlitic castings, malleable iron, unfinished, manufacturing
421940	Pearls wholesaling
339914	Pearls, costume, manufacturing
212399	Peat grinding
212399	Peat humus mining and/or beneficiating
212399	Peat mining and/or beneficiating
327999	Peat pots, molded pulp, manufacturing
212321	Pebbles (except grinding) mining and/or beneficiating
212399	Pebbles grinding
111335	Pecan farming
115114	Pecan hulling and shelling
311942	Pectin manufacturing
621111	Pediatricians' (except mental health) offices (e.g., centers, clinics)
621112	Pediatricians', mental health, offices (e.g., centers, clinics)
812113	Pedicure and manicure salons
812113	Pedicurist services
115210	Pedigree (i.e., livestock, pets, poultry) record services
334514	Pedometers manufacturing
813920	Peer review boards
212325	Pegmatite, feldspar, mining and/or beneficiating
316999	Pegs, leather shoe, manufacturing
332994	Pellet guns manufacturing
333131	Pellet mills machinery, mining-type, manufacturing
332992	Pellets, air rifle and pistol, manufacturing
316110	Pelts bleaching, currying, dyeing, scraping, and tanning
422590	Pelts, raw, wholesaling
339112	Pelvimeters manufacturing

Pen—Pharmacies

Code	Description
339941	Pen refills and cartridges manufacturing
339942	Pencil leads manufacturing
339942	Pencil sharpeners manufacturing
321999	Pencil slats, wood, manufacturing
339942	Pencils (except mechanical) manufacturing
422120	Pencils wholesaling
339941	Pencils, mechanical, manufacturing
335122	Pendant lamps (except residential), electric, manufacturing
335121	Pendant lamps fixtures, residential electric, manufacturing
325613	Penetrants manufacturing
325998	Penetrating fluids, synthetic, manufacturing
325412	Penicillin preparations manufacturing
325411	Penicillin, uncompounded, manufacturing
922140	Penitentiaries
212113	Pennsylvania anthracite mining and/or beneficiating
339941	Pens manufacturing
422120	Pens, writing, wholesaling
523920	Pension fund managing
524292	Pension fund, third party administrative services
525110	Pension funds
525110	Pension plans (e.g., employee benefit, retirement)
332313	Penstocks, fabricated metal plate, manufacturing
325192	Pentachlorophenol manufacturing
325199	Pentaerythritol manufacturing
325110	Pentanes made from refined petroleum or liquid hydrocarbons
325110	Pentenes made from refined petroleum or liquid hydrocarbons
325920	Pentolite explosive materials manufacturing
111219	Pepper (e.g., bell, chili, green, hot, red, sweet) farming
311942	Pepper (i.e., spice) manufacturing
325998	Peppermint oil manufacturing
313210	Percales weaving
114111	Perch fishing
325188	Perchloric acid manufacturing
325199	Perchloroethylene manufacturing
335211	Percolators, household-type electric, manufacturing
332992	Percussion caps (i.e., 30 mm. or less, 1.18 inch or less), ammunition, manufacturing
339992	Percussion musical instruments manufacturing
213112	Perforating oil and gas well casings on a contract basis
711510	Performers (i.e., entertainers), independent
711510	Performing artists, independent
711310	Performing arts center operators
611610	Performing arts schools (except academic)
325199	Perfume materials (i.e., basic synthetic chemicals, such as terpineol) manufacturing
446120	Perfume stores
325620	Perfumes manufacturing
422210	Perfumes wholesaling
511120	Periodical publishers
511120	Periodical publishers and printing combined
511120	Periodical publishing (i.e., establishments known as publishers)

Code	Description
323112	Periodicals flexographic printing without publishing
323111	Periodicals gravure printing without publishing
323110	Periodicals lithographic (offset) printing without publishing
323119	Periodicals printing (except flexographic, gravure, lithographic, screen) without publishing
323113	Periodicals screen printing without publishing
422920	Periodicals wholesaling
621210	Periodontists' offices (e.g., centers, clinics)
334418	Peripheral controller boards manufacturing
421430	Peripheral equipment, computer, wholesaling
333314	Periscopes manufacturing
327992	Perlite aggregates manufacturing
212399	Perlite mining and/or beneficiating
327992	Perlite, expanded, manufacturing
331524	Permanent mold castings, aluminum, unfinished, manufacturing
331525	Permanent mold castings, copper, unfinished, manufacturing
331528	Permanent mold castings, nonferrous metal (except aluminum, copper), unfinished, manufacturing
325620	Permanent wave preparations manufacturing
325188	Peroxides, inorganic, manufacturing
325199	Peroxides, organic, manufacturing
325132	Persian orange lake manufacturing
111339	Persimmon farming
513322	Personal communication services (PCS) (i.e., communication carriers)
334418	Personal computer modems manufacturing
334111	Personal computers manufacturing
522291	Personal credit institutions (i.e., unsecured cash loans)
525920	Personal estates (i.e., managing assets)
522291	Personal finance companies (i.e., unsecured cash loans)
551112	Personal holding companies
525920	Personal investment trusts
523991	Personal investments trust administration
523920	Personal investments trusts, managing
316993	Personal leather goods (e.g., coin purses, eyeglass cases, key cases), small, manufacturing
561612	Personal protection services (except security systems services)
339113	Personal safety devices, not specified elsewhere, manufacturing
422130	Personal sanitary paper products wholesaling
812990	Personal shopping services
525920	Personal trusts
441221	Personal watercraft dealers
336999	Personal watercraft manufacturing
532292	Personal watercraft rental
561320	Personnel (e.g., industrial, office) suppliers
813990	Personnel management associations
541612	Personnel management consulting services
921190	Personnel offices, government
325320	Pest (e.g., ant, rat, roach, rodent) control poison manufacturing
561710	Pest control (except agricultural, forestry) services

Code	Description
926140	Pest control programs, agriculture, government
115112	Pest control services, agricultural
115310	Pest control services, forestry
422690	Pesticides (except agricultural) wholesaling
325320	Pesticides manufacturing
422910	Pesticides, agricultural, wholesaling
812910	Pet boarding services
812220	Pet cemeteries
311119	Pet food (except cat, dog) manufacturing
422490	Pet food wholesaling
311111	Pet food, dog and cat, manufacturing
812910	Pet grooming services
524128	Pet health insurance carriers, direct
541940	Pet hospitals
926150	Pet licensing
453910	Pet shops
812910	Pet sitting services
422990	Pet supplies (except pet food) wholesaling
453910	Pet supply stores
812910	Pet training services
324110	Petrochemical feedstocks made in petroleum refineries
234930	Petrochemical plant construction
324110	Petrochemicals made in petroleum refineries
422710	Petroleum and petroleum products bulk stations and terminals
422720	Petroleum and petroleum products wholesaling (except bulk stations, terminals)
422720	Petroleum brokers
324110	Petroleum coke made in petroleum refineries
324110	Petroleum cracking and reforming
324110	Petroleum distillation
541330	Petroleum engineering services
211112	Petroleum gases, liquefied, recovering from oil and gas field gases
324199	Petroleum jelly made from refined petroleum
324110	Petroleum jelly made in petroleum refineries
324191	Petroleum lubricating oils made from refined petroleum
324110	Petroleum lubricating oils made in petroleum refineries
486110	Petroleum pipelines, crude
486910	Petroleum pipelines, refined
325211	Petroleum polymer resins manufacturing
324110	Petroleum refineries
234930	Petroleum refinery construction
333298	Petroleum refining machinery manufacturing
332420	Petroleum storage tanks, heavy gauge metal, manufacturing
324199	Petroleum waxes made from refined petroleum
211111	Petroleum, crude, production (i.e., extraction)
422990	Pets wholesaling
712130	Petting zoos
337127	Pews, church, manufacturing
339912	Pewter ware manufacturing
233310	Pharmaceutical manufacturing plant construction
325412	Pharmaceutical preparations (e.g., capsules, liniments, ointments, tablets) manufacturing
422210	Pharmaceuticals wholesaling
446110	Pharmacies

Code	Description
813920	Pharmacists' associations
334515	Phase angle meters manufacturing
335312	Phase converters (i.e., electrical equipment) manufacturing
112390	Pheasant production
325192	Phenol manufacturing
325211	Phenol-formaldehyde resins manufacturing
325211	Phenol-furfural resins manufacturing
325211	Phenolic resins manufacturing
325211	Phenoxy resins manufacturing
813211	Philanthropic trusts, awarding grants
212399	Phlogopite mining and/or beneficiating
334510	Phonocardiographs manufacturing
334612	Phonograph records manufacturing
421990	Phonograph records wholesaling
421440	Phonographs, coin-operated, wholesaling
325199	Phosgene manufacturing
212392	Phosphate rock mining and/or beneficiating
325312	Phosphatic fertilizer materials manufacturing
325314	Phosphatic fertilizers made by mixing purchased materials
325132	Phosphomolybdic acid lakes and toners manufacturing
325199	Phosphoric acid esters manufacturing
325312	Phosphoric acid manufacturing
325188	Phosphorus compounds, not specified elsewhere by process, manufacturing
325188	Phosphorus oxychloride manufacturing
325132	Phosphotungstic acid lakes and toners manufacturing
323118	Photo albums and refills manufacturing
422120	Photo albums wholesaling
421410	Photo finishing equipment wholesaling
711510	Photo journalists, independent (freelance)
323122	Photocomposition services, for the printing trade
422120	Photocopy supplies wholesaling
811212	Photocopying machine repair and maintenance services without retailing new photocopy machines
333315	Photocopying machines manufacturing
561439	Photocopying services (except combined with printing services)
325992	Photocopying toner cartridges manufacturing
334413	Photoelectric cells, solid-state (e.g., electronic eye), manufacturing
333293	Photoengraving machinery manufacturing
323122	Photoengraving plate preparation services
812921	Photofinishing labs (except one-hour)
812922	Photofinishing labs, one-hour
812921	Photofinishing services (except one-hour)
812922	Photofinishing services, one-hour
335110	Photoflash and photoflood lamp bulbs and tubes manufacturing
333315	Photoflash equipment manufacturing
541370	Photogrammetric mapping services
322299	Photograph folders, mats, and mounts manufacturing
541922	Photographers specializing in aerial photography
711510	Photographers, independent artistic
325992	Photographic chemicals manufacturing
333315	Photographic equipment (except lenses) manufacturing

Code	Description
421410	Photographic equipment and supplies wholesaling
532210	Photographic equipment rental
811211	Photographic equipment repair shops without retailing new photographic equipment
325992	Photographic film, cloth, paper, and plate, sensitized, manufacturing
333314	Photographic lenses manufacturing
812990	Photographic machine concession operators, coin-operated
443130	Photographic supply stores
326113	Photographic, micrographic, and X-ray plastics, sheet, and film (except sensitized), manufacturing
611610	Photography schools, art
611519	Photography schools, commercial
541922	Photography services, commercial
541921	Photography services, portrait (e.g., still, video)
541922	Photography studios, commercial
541921	Photography studios, portrait
327212	Photomask blanks, glass, made in glass making plants
325992	Photomasks manufacturing
334516	Photometers (except photographic exposure meters) manufacturing
334516	Photonexcitation analyzers manufacturing
325992	Photosensitized paper manufacturing
323122	Phototypesetting services
334413	Photovoltaic devices, solid-state, manufacturing
812990	Phrenology services
325199	Phthalate acid manufacturing
325211	Phthalic alkyd resins manufacturing
325192	Phthalic anhydride manufacturing
325211	Phthalic anhydride resins manufacturing
325132	Phthalocyanine pigments manufacturing
541614	Physical distribution consulting services
621340	Physical equestrian therapeutists' offices (e.g., centers, clinics)
713940	Physical fitness centers
621999	Physical fitness evaluation services (except by offices of health practitioners)
713940	Physical fitness facilities
713940	Physical fitness studios
334519	Physical properties testing and inspection equipment manufacturing
622310	Physical rehabilitation hospitals
541710	Physical science research and development laboratories or services
621340	Physical therapists' offices (e.g., centers, clinics)
621340	Physical therapy offices (e.g., centers, clinics)
621340	Physical-integration practitioners' offices (e.g., centers, clinics)
621111	Physicians' (except mental health) offices (e.g., centers, clinics)
621399	Physicians' assistants' offices (e.g., centers, clinics)
621112	Physicians', mental health, offices (e.g., centers, clinics)
541690	Physics consulting services
541710	Physics research and development laboratories or services
621340	Physiotherapists' offices (e.g., centers, clinics)
339112	Physiotherapy equipment (except electrotherapeutic) manufacturing
325411	Physostigmine and derivatives (i.e., basic chemicals) manufacturing

Code	Description
332510	Piano hardware, metal, manufacturing
339992	Piano parts and materials (except piano hardware) manufacturing
532299	Piano rental
451140	Piano stores
339992	Piccolos and parts manufacturing
336112	Pick-up trucks, light duty, assembling on chassis of own manufacture
333292	Picker machinery for textiles manufacturing
333292	Picker sticks for looms manufacturing
311712	Picking crab meat
333516	Picklers and pickling machinery, metalworking, manufacturing
311421	Pickles manufacturing
311421	Pickling fruits and vegetables
332813	Pickling metals and metal products for the trade
332212	Picks (i.e., handtools) manufacturing
812320	Pickup and drop-off sites for drycleaners and laundries
336214	Pickup canopies, caps, or covers manufacturing
713990	Picnic grounds
326199	Picnic jugs, plastics (except foam), manufacturing
325920	Picric acid explosive materials manufacturing
334511	Pictorial situation instrumentation manufacturing
442299	Picture frame shops, custom
311822	Pie crust shells, uncooked, made from purchased flour
422310	Piece goods (except burlap, felt) wholesaling
451130	Piece goods stores
422990	Piece goods, burlap and felt, wholesaling
234990	Pier construction
531120	Piers and associated building rental or leasing
713110	Piers, amusement
422420	Pies (e.g., fruit, meat, poultry), frozen, wholesaling
311812	Pies, fresh, made in commercial bakeries
311812	Pies, frozen, manufacturing
334419	Piezoelectric crystals manufacturing
334419	Piezoelectric devices manufacturing
112210	Pig farming
331111	Pig iron manufacturing
421510	Pig iron wholesaling
311612	Pig's feet, cooked and pickled, made from purchased carcasses
325132	Pigment, scarlet lake, manufacturing
325132	Pigments (except animal black, bone black), organic, manufacturing
325131	Pigments (except bone black, carbon black, lamp black), inorganic, manufacturing
212393	Pigments, natural, mineral, mining and/or beneficiating
422950	Pigments, paint, wholesaling
114111	Pilchard fishing
313249	Pile fabrics made in warp knitting mills
313241	Pile fabrics made in weft knitting mills
332313	Pile shells, fabricated metal plate, manufacturing
332322	Pile shells, sheet metal, manufacturing
333120	Pile-driving equipment manufacturing
235930	Piling (i.e., bored, cast-in-place, drilled) construction contractors
321114	Pilings, foundation and marine construction, treating

Pilings—Plastics

Code	Description
331111	Pilings, iron or steel plain sheet, made in steel mills
321114	Pilings, round wood, cutting and treating
321114	Pilings, wood, treating
332991	Pillow blocks with ball or roller bearings manufacturing
812320	Pillow cleaning services
314129	Pillowcases, bed, made from purchased fabrics
314129	Pillows, bed, made from purchased materials
488490	Pilot car services (i.e., wide load warning services)
488330	Piloting services, water transportation
713120	Pinball arcades
713990	Pinball machine concession operators (i.e., supplying and servicing in others' facilities)
339999	Pinball machines, coin-operated, manufacturing
113210	Pine gum extracting
325191	Pine oil manufacturing
111339	Pineapple farming
325191	Pinene manufacturing
713990	Ping pong parlors
212325	Pinite mining and/or beneficiating
339993	Pins (except precious) manufacturing
339911	Pins and broaches, precious metal, manufacturing
712120	Pioneer villages
331210	Pipe (e.g., heavy riveted, lock joint, seamless, welded) made from purchased iron or steel
332996	Pipe and pipe fittings made from purchased metal pipe
331511	Pipe and pipe fittings, cast iron, manufacturing
333516	Pipe and tube rolling mill machinery, metalworking, manufacturing
332323	Pipe bannisters, metal, manufacturing
326299	Pipe bits and stems, tobacco, hard rubber, manufacturing
339999	Pipe cleaners manufacturing
332996	Pipe couplings made from purchased metal pipe
331511	Pipe couplings, cast iron, manufacturing
333512	Pipe cutting and threading machines, metalworking, manufacturing
332996	Pipe fabricating (i.e., bending, cutting, threading) made from purchased metal pipe
326122	Pipe fittings, rigid plastics, manufacturing
332323	Pipe guards, metal, manufacturing
332999	Pipe hangers and supports, metal, manufacturing
332996	Pipe headers made from purchased metal pipe
331316	Pipe made by extruding purchased aluminum
332323	Pipe railings, metal, manufacturing
325520	Pipe sealing compounds manufacturing
213112	Pipe testing services, oil and gas field, on a contract basis
422940	Pipe tobacco wholesaling
312229	Pipe tobacco, prepared, manufacturing
331316	Pipe, aluminum, made in integrated secondary smelting and extruding mills
327332	Pipe, concrete, manufacturing

Code	Description
331421	Pipe, extruded and drawn, brass, bronze, and copper, made from purchased copper or in integrated secondary smelting and rolling, drawing or extruding plants
332313	Pipe, fabricated metal plate, manufacturing
331111	Pipe, iron or steel, made in steel mills
421510	Pipe, metal, wholesaling
331491	Pipe, nonferrous metals (except aluminum, copper), made from purchased metals or scrap
326122	Pipe, rigid plastics, manufacturing
332322	Pipe, sheet metal, manufacturing
513112	Piped-in music services, radio transmitted
234920	Pipelaying construction contractors
234910	Pipeline (e.g., gas, oil, sewer, water) construction
234910	Pipeline (e.g., gas, oil, water, sewer) construction management
213112	Pipeline construction on oil and gas lease gathering lines to point of distribution on a contract basis
541990	Pipeline inspection (i.e., visual) services
421830	Pipeline machinery and equipment wholesaling
234910	Pipeline rehabilitation construction contractors
488999	Pipeline terminal facilities, independently operated
486990	Pipeline transportation (except crude oil, natural gas, refined petroleum products)
486110	Pipeline transportation, crude oil
486910	Pipeline transportation, gasoline and other refined petroleum products
486210	Pipeline transportation, natural gas
234910	Pipeline wrapping construction contractors
339992	Pipes, organ, manufacturing
339999	Pipes, smoker's, manufacturing
212399	Pipestones mining and/or beneficiating
111335	Pistachio farming
332994	Pistols manufacturing
336311	Pistons and piston rings manufacturing
421830	Pistons, hydraulic and pneumatic, wholesaling
325192	Pitch made by distillation of coal tar
324122	Pitch, roofing, made from purchased asphaltic materials
325191	Pitch, wood, manufacturing
212291	Pitchblende mining and/or beneficiating
334519	Pitometers manufacturing
325411	Pituitary gland derivatives, uncompounded, manufacturing
325412	Pituitary gland preparations manufacturing
722211	Pizza delivery shops
311822	Pizza doughs made from purchased flour
722110	Pizza parlors, full service
722211	Pizza parlors, limited service
422490	Pizzas (except frozen) wholesaling
311991	Pizzas, fresh, manufacturing
311412	Pizzas, frozen, manufacturing
422420	Pizzas, frozen, wholesaling
722110	Pizzerias, full service
722211	Pizzerias, limited-service (e.g., take-out)
314129	Placemats, all materials, made from purchased materials
561310	Placement agencies or services, employment
621991	Placenta banks
212221	Placer gold mining and/or beneficiating
212222	Placer silver mining and/or beneficiating

Code	Description
813110	Places of worship
334417	Planar cable connectors manufacturing
333210	Planers woodworking-type, stationary, manufacturing
333120	Planers, bituminous, manufacturing
333991	Planers, handheld power-driven, manufacturing
333512	Planers, metalworking, manufacturing
332212	Planes, handheld, nonpowered, manufacturing
712110	Planetariums
321912	Planing mills (except millwork)
321918	Planing mills, millwork
321912	Planing purchased lumber
525120	Plans, health and welfare related employee benefit
525110	Plans, pension
561730	Plant and shrub maintenance in buildings
422990	Plant food wholesaling
325311	Plant foods, mixed, made in plants producing nitrogenous fertilizer materials
325312	Plant foods, mixed, made in plants producing phosphatic fertilizer materials
325320	Plant growth regulants manufacturing
561730	Plant maintenance services
111422	Plant, ornamental, growing
111422	Plant, potted flower and foliage, growing
111339	Plantain farming
115112	Planting crops
421820	Planting machinery and equipment, farm-type, wholesaling
333111	Planting machines, farm-type, manufacturing
333513	Plasma jet spray metal forming machines manufacturing
333512	Plasma process metal cutting machines (except welding equipment) manufacturing
333992	Plasma welding equipment manufacturing
621991	Plasmapheresis centers
325414	Plasmas manufacturing
422210	Plasmas, blood, wholesaling
327420	Plaster and plasterboard, gypsum, manufacturing
327420	Plaster of paris manufacturing
327420	Plaster of paris products (e.g., columns, statuary, urns) manufacturing
421320	Plaster wholesaling
327420	Plaster, gypsum, manufacturing
235420	Plastering (i.e., ornamental, plain) construction contractors
212325	Plastic fire clay mining and/or beneficiating
621111	Plastic surgeons' offices (e.g., centers, clinics)
325510	Plastic wood fillers manufacturing
325199	Plasticizers (i.e., basic synthetic chemicals) manufacturing
422610	Plasticizers wholesaling
337125	Plastics (including fiberglass) furniture (except upholstered), household-type, manufacturing
326220	Plastics and rubber belts and hoses (without fittings) manufacturing
325211	Plastics and synthetic resins regenerating, precipitating, and coagulating
422130	Plastics bags wholesaling
422610	Plastics basic shapes wholesaling
313320	Plastics coating of textiles and apparel

Code	Description
326113	Plastics film and unlaminated sheet (except packaging) manufacturing
422990	Plastics foam (except disposable) wholesaling
421840	Plastics foam packing and packaging materials wholesaling
422130	Plastics foam products, disposable (except packaging, packing), wholesaling
315299	Plastics gowns (except infants') cut and sewn from purchased fabric (except apparel contractors)
315291	Plastics gowns, infants', cut and sewn from purchased fabric (except apparel contractors)
315211	Plastics gowns, men's and boys', cut and sew apparel contractors
315212	Plastics gowns, women's, girls', and infants, cut and sew apparel contractors
421830	Plastics industries machinery, equipment, and supplies wholesaling
337110	Plastics laminated over particleboard (e.g., fixture tops) manufacturing
422610	Plastics materials (e.g., film, rod, shape, sheet, tubing) wholesaling
315299	Plastics rainwear cut and sewn from purchased fabric (except apparel contractors)
315211	Plastics rainwear, men's and boys', cut and sewn apparel contractors
315212	Plastics rainwear, women's, girls', and infants', cut and sew apparel contractors
325991	Plastics resins compounding from recycled materials
422610	Plastics resins wholesaling
325991	Plastics resins, custom compounding of purchased
421930	Plastics scrap wholesaling
333220	Plastics working machinery manufacturing
325510	Plastisol coating compounds manufacturing
524126	Plate glass insurance carriers, direct
421390	Plate glass wholesaling
333516	Plate rolling mill machinery, metalworking, manufacturing
332313	Plate work (e.g., bending, cutting, punching, shaping, welding), fabricated metal, manufacturing
331315	Plate, aluminum, made by continuous casting purchased aluminum
331315	Plate, aluminum, made by flat rolling purchased aluminum
331315	Plate, aluminum, made in integrated secondary smelting and continuous casting mills
331315	Plate, aluminum, made in integrated secondary smelting and flat rolling mills
331421	Plate, copper and copper alloy, made from purchased copper or in integrated secondary smelting and rolling, drawing or extruding plants
331111	Plate, iron or steel, made in steel mills
326130	Plate, laminated plastics, manufacturing
331491	Plate, nonferrous metals (except aluminum, copper), made from purchased metals or scrap
332211	Plated metal cutlery manufacturing
421940	Plated metal cutlery or flatware wholesaling
332211	Plated metal flatware manufacturing
332999	Plated ware (e.g., ecclesiastical ware, hollowware, toilet ware) manufacturing

Code	Description
335932	Plates (i.e., outlet or switch covers), face, manufacturing
322299	Plates, molded pulp, manufacturing
326140	Plates, polystyrene foam, manufacturing
332813	Plating metals and metal products for the trade
331491	Platinum and platinum alloy rolling, drawing, or extruding from purchased metals or scrap
331491	Platinum and platinum alloy sheet and tubing made from purchased metals or scrap
332999	Platinum foil and leaf not made in rolling mills
212299	Platinum mining and/or beneficiating
331492	Platinum recovering from scrap and/or alloying purchased metals
331419	Platinum refining, primary
421910	Playground equipment and supplies wholesaling
421920	Playing cards wholesaling
337124	Playpens, children's metal, manufacturing
337122	Playpens, children's wood, manufacturing
315291	Playsuits, infants', cut and sewn from purchased fabric (except apparel contractors)
315212	Playsuits, women's, girls', and infants', cut and sew apparel contractors
315239	Playsuits, women's, misses', and girls', cut and sewn from purchased fabric (except apparel contractors)
711510	Playwrights, independent
532292	Pleasure boat rental
336612	Pleasure boats manufacturing
421910	Pleasure boats wholesaling
315211	Pleating contractors on men's and boys' apparel
315212	Pleating contractors on women's, girls', and infants' apparel
332212	Pliers, handtools, manufacturing
327331	Plinth blocks, precast terrazzo, manufacturing
334119	Plotters, computer, manufacturing
115112	Plowing
333120	Plows, construction (e.g., excavating, grading), manufacturing
421820	Plows, farm, wholesaling
333111	Plows, farm-type, manufacturing
111422	Plug (i.e., floriculture products) growing
332911	Plug valves, industrial-type, manufacturing
213112	Plugging and abandoning wells on a contract basis
335931	Plugs, electric cord, manufacturing
332999	Plugs, magnetic metal drain, manufacturing
321999	Plugs, wood, manufacturing
111339	Plum farming
421720	Plumber's brass goods wholesaling
332212	Plumber's handtools, nonpowered, manufacturing
325520	Plumber's putty manufacturing
611513	Plumbers' apprenticeship training
332919	Plumbing and heating inline valves (e.g., check, cutoffs, stop) manufacturing
421720	Plumbing and heating valves wholesaling
235110	Plumbing construction contractors
532490	Plumbing equipment rental or leasing
421720	Plumbing equipment wholesaling

Code	Description
332913	Plumbing fittings and couplings (e.g., compression fittings, metal elbows, metal unions) manufacturing
332913	Plumbing fixture fittings and trim, all materials, manufacturing
326191	Plumbing fixtures (e.g., shower stalls, toilets, urinals), plastics or fiberglass, manufacturing
421720	Plumbing fixtures wholesaling
332998	Plumbing fixtures, metal, manufacturing
327111	Plumbing fixtures, vitreous china, manufacturing
421720	Plumbing supplies wholesaling
444190	Plumbing supply stores
421310	Plywood wholesaling
321211	Plywood, faced with nonwood materials, hardwood, manufacturing
321212	Plywood, faced with nonwood materials, softwood, manufacturing
321211	Plywood, hardwood faced, manufacturing
321211	Plywood, hardwood, manufacturing
321212	Plywood, softwood faced, manufacturing
321212	Plywood, softwood, manufacturing
332912	Pneumatic aircraft subassemblies manufacturing
334513	Pneumatic controllers, industrial process type, manufacturing
333995	Pneumatic cylinders, fluid power, manufacturing
326220	Pneumatic hose (without fittings), rubber or plastics, manufacturing
332912	Pneumatic hose fittings, fluid power, manufacturing
421830	Pneumatic pumps and parts wholesaling
333996	Pneumatic pumps, fluid power, manufacturing
334512	Pneumatic relays, air-conditioning-type, manufacturing
333922	Pneumatic tube conveyors manufacturing
235950	Pneumatic tube system construction contractors
332912	Pneumatic valves, fluid power, manufacturing
322231	Pocket folders made from purchased paper or paperboard
332211	Pocket knives manufacturing
339911	Pocketbooks, precious metal, manufacturing
339911	Pocketbooks, precious metal, men's, manufacturing
339911	Pocketbooks, precious metal, women's, manufacturing
315211	Pockets (e.g., coat, suit), men's and boys', cut and sew apparel contractors
315212	Pockets (e.g., coat, suit), women's, girls', and infants', cut and sew apparel contractors
621391	Podiatrists' offices (e.g., centers, clinics)
813410	Poetry clubs
711510	Poets, independent
334119	Point of sale terminals manufacturing
421420	Point of sale terminals wholesaling
334119	Pointing devices, computer peripheral equipment, manufacturing
315292	Pointing furs
339114	Points, abrasive dental, manufacturing
334516	Polariscopes manufacturing
334516	Polarizers manufacturing
334516	Polarographic equipment manufacturing
234920	Pole line construction contractors
421610	Pole line hardware wholesaling

Poles—Portable toilet

Code	Description
327390	Poles, concrete, manufacturing
421510	Poles, metal, wholesaling
321114	Poles, round wood, cutting and treating
321113	Poles, wood, made from from log or bolts
321114	Poles, wood, treating
922120	Police academies
922120	Police and fire departments, combined
315991	Police caps and hats (except protective head gear) cut and sewn from purchased fabric (except apparel contractors)
315211	Police caps and hats (except protective head gear), men's, cut and sew apparel contractors
315212	Police caps and hats (except protective head gear), women's, cut and sew apparel contractors
922120	Police departments (except American Indian or Alaska Native)
315222	Police dress uniforms, men's, cut and sewn from purchased fabric (except apparel contractors)
315234	Police dress uniforms, women's, cut and sewn from purchased fabric (except apparel contractors)
453998	Police supply stores
611519	Police training schools
315211	Police uniforms, men's, cut and sew apparel contractors
315212	Police uniforms, women's, cut and sew apparel contractors
921150	Police, American Indian or Alaska Native tribal
311212	Polished rice manufacturing
333991	Polishers, handheld power-driven, manufacturing
325612	Polishes (e.g., automobile, furniture, metal, shoe) manufacturing
422690	Polishes (e.g., automobile, furniture, metal, shoe, stove) wholesaling
333512	Polishing and buffing machines, metalworking, manufacturing
332813	Polishing metals and metal products for the trade
325612	Polishing preparations manufacturing
327910	Polishing wheels manufacturing
813940	Political action committees (PACs)
813940	Political campaign organizations
711510	Political cartoonists, independent
541820	Political consulting services
541910	Political opinion polling services
813940	Political organizations or clubs
813940	Political parties
115112	Pollinating
114111	Pollock fishing
421830	Pollution control equipment (except air) wholesaling
421730	Pollution control equipment, air, wholesaling
924110	Pollution control program administration
541380	Pollution testing (except automotive emissions testing) services
315191	Polo shirts made in apparel knitting mills
315211	Polo shirts, men's and boys', cut and sew apparel contractors
315223	Polo shirts, men's and boys', cut and sewn from purchased fabric (except apparel contractors)
315212	Polo shirts, women's, girls', and infants', cut and sew apparel contractors
315232	Polo shirts, women's, misses', and girls', cut and sewn from purchased fabric (except apparel contractors)

Code	Description
325211	Polyacrylonitrile resins manufacturing
325211	Polyamide resins manufacturing
325211	Polycarbonate resins manufacturing
325222	Polyester fibers and filaments manufacturing
313112	Polyester filament yarn throwing, twisting, texturizing, or winding of purchased yarn
326113	Polyester film and unlaminated sheet (except packaging) manufacturing
325211	Polyester resins manufacturing
313111	Polyester spun yarns made from purchased fiber
313113	Polyester thread manufacturing
326113	Polyethylene film and unlaminated sheet (except packaging) manufacturing
325211	Polyethylene resins manufacturing
325212	Polyethylene rubber manufacturing
325211	Polyethylene terephathalate (PET) resins manufacturing
325222	Polyethylene terephthalate (PET) fibers and filaments manufacturing
334519	Polygraph machines manufacturing
561611	Polygraph services
325211	Polyhexamethylenediamine adipamide resins manufacturing
325199	Polyhydric alcohol esters and amines manufacturing
325199	Polyhydric alcohols manufacturing
325211	Polyisobutylene resins manufacturing
325212	Polyisobutylene rubber manufacturing
325212	Polyisobutylene-isoprene rubber manufacturing
325211	Polymethacrylate resins manufacturing
325212	Polymethylene rubber manufacturing
325222	Polyolefin fibers and filaments manufacturing
313112	Polypropylene filament yarn throwing, twisting, texturizing, or winding of purchased yarn
326113	Polypropylene film and unlaminated sheet (except packaging) manufacturing
325211	Polypropylene resins manufacturing
313111	Polypropylene spun yarns made from purchased fiber
326140	Polystyrene foam packaging manufacturing
325211	Polystyrene resins manufacturing
325212	Polysulfide rubber manufacturing
325211	Polytetrafluoroethylene resins manufacturing
325510	Polyurethane coatings manufacturing
326150	Polyurethane foam products manufacturing
325211	Polyurethane resins manufacturing
325211	Polyvinyl alcohol resins manufacturing
325211	Polyvinyl chloride (PVC) resins manufacturing
325222	Polyvinyl ester fibers and filaments manufacturing
326113	Polyvinyl film and unlaminated sheet (except packaging) manufacturing
325211	Polyvinyl halide resins manufacturing
325211	Polyvinyl resins manufacturing
325222	Polyvinylidene chloride (i.e., saran) fibers and filaments manufacturing
111339	Pomegranate farming
315299	Ponchos and similar waterproof raincoats (except infants') cut and sewn from purchased fabric (except apparel contractors)

Code	Description
315291	Ponchos and similar waterproof raincoats, infants', cut and sewn from purchased fabric (except apparel contractors)
315211	Ponchos and similar waterproof raincoats, men's and boys', cut and sew apparel contractors
315212	Ponchos and similar waterproof raincoats, women's, girls', and infants', cut and sew apparel contractors
234990	Pond construction
112920	Pony production
713990	Pool halls
713990	Pool parlors
713990	Pool rooms
312111	Pop, soda, manufacturing
311919	Popcorn (except candy covered), popped, manufacturing
311999	Popcorn (except popped) manufacturing
311340	Popcorn balls manufacturing
111150	Popcorn farming, field and seed production
335211	Popcorn poppers, household-type electric, manufacturing
422450	Popcorn wholesaling
311340	Popcorn, candy covered popped, manufacturing
313210	Poplins weaving
621391	Popopediatricians' offices (e.g., centers, clinics)
711130	Popular musical artists, independent
711130	Popular musical groups
532120	Popup camper rental
327113	Porcelain parts, electrical and electronic device, molded, manufacturing
327112	Porcelain, chemical, manufacturing
337122	Porch furniture (except upholstered), wood, manufacturing
337920	Porch shades, wood slat, manufacturing
337124	Porch swings, metal, manufacturing
321918	Porch work (e.g., columns, newels, rails, trellises), wood, manufacturing
114111	Porgy fishing
311422	Pork and beans canning
311611	Pork carcasses, half carcasses, and primal and sub-primal cuts produced in slaughtering plants
311919	Pork rinds manufacturing
311612	Pork, primal and sub-primal cuts, made from purchased carcasses
926120	Port authorities and districts, nonoperating
488310	Port facility operation
332311	Portable buildings, prefabricated metal, manufacturing
321992	Portable buildings, prefabricated wood, manufacturing
332998	Portable chemical toilets, metal, manufacturing
334111	Portable computers manufacturing
335211	Portable cooking appliances (except convection, microwave ovens), household-type electric, manufacturing
335211	Portable electric space heaters manufacturing
335211	Portable hair dryers, electric, manufacturing
335211	Portable humidifiers and dehumidifiers manufacturing
334310	Portable stereo systems manufacturing
334515	Portable test meters manufacturing
562991	Portable toilet pumping (i.e., cleaning) services

Code	Description
562991	Portable toilet renting and/or servicing
326191	Portable toilets, plastics, manufacturing
312120	Porter brewing
812990	Porter services
422810	Porter wholesaling
523920	Portfolio fund managing
541921	Portrait photography services
541921	Portrait photography studios
621512	Position emission tomography (PET) scanner centers
334510	Position emission tomography (PET) scanners manufacturing
334511	Position indicators (e.g., for landing gear, stabilizers), airframe equipment, manufacturing
336312	Positive crankcase ventilation (PCV) valves, engine, manufacturing
334514	Positive displacement meters manufacturing
235510	Post frame construction contractors
332212	Post hole diggers, nonpowered, manufacturing
333120	Post hole diggers, powered, manufacturing
233320	Post office construction
333997	Post office-type scales manufacturing
512191	Post-production facilities, motion picture or video
512191	Post-synchronization sound dubbing
333313	Postage meters manufacturing
421420	Postage meters wholesaling
333311	Postage stamp vending machines manufacturing
491110	Postal delivery services, local, operated by U.S. Postal Service
491110	Postal delivery services, local, operated on a contract basis
337215	Postal service lock boxes manufacturing
491110	Postal services operated by U.S. Postal Service
491110	Postal stations operated by U.S. Postal Service
491110	Postal stations operated on a contract basis
511199	Postcard publishers
511199	Postcard publishers and printing combined
511199	Postcard publishing (i.e., establishments known as publishers)
323112	Postcards flexographic printing without publishing
323111	Postcards gravure printing without publishing
323110	Postcards lithographic (offset) printing without publishing
323119	Postcards printing (except flexographic, gravure, lithographic, screen) without publishing
323113	Postcards screen printing without publishing
422120	Postcards wholesaling
511199	Poster publishers
511199	Poster publishers and printing combined
511199	Poster publishing (i.e., establishments known as publishers)
323112	Posters flexographic printing without publishing
323111	Posters gravure printing without publishing
323110	Posters lithographic (offset) printing without publishing
323119	Posters printing (except flexographic, gravure, lithographic, screen) without publishing

Code	Description
323113	Posters screen printing without publishing
235990	Posthole digging construction contractors
323121	Postpress services (e.g., beveling, bronzing, edging, foil stamping, gilding, tradebinding) on printed materials
327390	Posts, concrete, manufacturing
321114	Posts, round wood, cutting and treating
321114	Posts, wood, treating
311412	Pot pies, frozen, manufacturing
212391	Potash mining and/or beneficiating
325314	Potassic fertilizers made by mixing purchased materials
325188	Potassium aluminum sulfate manufacturing
325188	Potassium bichromate and chromate manufacturing
325199	Potassium bitartrate manufacturing
325188	Potassium bromide manufacturing
212391	Potassium bromide, natural, mining and/or beneficiating
325181	Potassium carbonate manufacturing
325188	Potassium chlorate manufacturing
325188	Potassium chloride manufacturing
212391	Potassium chloride mining and/or beneficiating
212391	Potassium compounds prepared at beneficiating plants
212391	Potassium compounds, natural, mining and/or beneficiating
325188	Potassium cyanide manufacturing
325181	Potassium hydroxide manufacturing
325188	Potassium hypochlorate manufacturing
325188	Potassium inorganic compounds, not specified elsewhere by process, manufacturing
325188	Potassium iodide manufacturing
325188	Potassium nitrate manufacturing
325199	Potassium organic compounds, not specified elsewhere by process, manufacturing
325188	Potassium permanganate manufacturing
325188	Potassium salts manufacturing
212391	Potassium salts, natural, mining and/or beneficiating
325188	Potassium sulfate manufacturing
422450	Potato chips and related snacks wholesaling
311919	Potato chips manufacturing
115114	Potato curing
333111	Potato diggers, harvesters, and planters manufacturing
111211	Potato farming, field and seed potato production
311211	Potato flour manufacturing
332214	Potato mashers manufacturing
311999	Potato mixes made from purchased dry ingredients
311423	Potato products (e.g., flakes, granules) dehydrating
311221	Potato starches manufacturing
311919	Potato sticks manufacturing
311991	Potatoes, peeled or cut, manufacturing
334513	Potentiometric instruments (except X-Y recorders), industrial process-type, manufacturing
334515	Potentiometric instruments (except industrial process-type) manufacturing
339999	Potpourri manufacturing
332420	Pots (e.g., annealing, melting, smelting), heavy gauge metal, manufacturing
332214	Pots and pans, fabricated metal, manufacturing

Code	Description
327124	Pots, glass-house, clay refractory, manufacturing
311612	Potted meats made from purchased carcasses
327112	Pottery products (except plumbing fixtures and porcelain) manufacturing
325314	Potting soil manufacturing
311615	Poultry (e.g., canned, cooked, fresh, frozen) manufacturing
311615	Poultry (e.g., canned, cooked, fresh, frozen) processing
422440	Poultry and poultry products (except canned, packaged frozen) wholesaling
333111	Poultry brooders, feeders, and waterers manufacturing
311615	Poultry canning (except baby, pet food)
115210	Poultry catching services
445210	Poultry dealers
421820	Poultry equipment wholesaling
311119	Poultry feeds, supplements, and concentrates manufacturing
112340	Poultry hatcheries
332618	Poultry netting made from purchased wire
311615	Poultry slaughtering, dressing, and packing
422490	Poultry, canned, wholesaling
422440	Poultry, live and dressed, wholesaling
422420	Poultry, packaged frozen, wholesaling
333991	Powder actuated handheld power tools manufacturing
332812	Powder coating metals and metal products for the trade
325510	Powder coatings manufacturing
331221	Powder made from purchased iron or steel
331314	Powder made from purchased aluminum
331423	Powder made from purchased copper
333513	Powder metal forming presses manufacturing
332117	Powder metallurgy products manufactured on a job or order basis
314999	Powder puffs and mitts manufacturing
331111	Powder, iron or steel, made in steel mills
331492	Powder, nonferrous metals (except aluminum, copper), made from purchased metal
311999	Powdered drink mixes (except chocolate, coffee, tea, milk based) manufacturing
311514	Powdered milk manufacturing
325620	Powders (e.g., baby, body, face, talcum, toilet) manufacturing
311999	Powders, baking, manufacturing
333912	Power (i.e., pressure) washer units manufacturing
234920	Power and communication transmission line construction management services
441222	Power boat dealers
332410	Power boilers manufacturing
335313	Power circuit breakers manufacturing
335313	Power connectors manufacturing
335999	Power converter units (i.e., AC to DC), static, manufacturing
444210	Power equipment stores, outdoor
334515	Power factor meters manufacturing
335313	Power fuses (i.e., 600 volts and over) manufacturing
235950	Power generating equipment construction contractors
221119	Power generation, electric (except fossil fuel, hydroelectric, nonhazardous solid waste, nuclear)

Power generation—Prestressed

Code	Description
221112	Power generation, fossil fuel (e.g., coal, gas, oil), electric
221111	Power generation, hydroelectric
562213	Power generation, nonhazardous solid waste combustor or incinerator electric
221113	Power generation, nuclear electric
221119	Power generation, solar electric
221119	Power generation, tidal electric
221119	Power generation, wind electric
335312	Power generators manufacturing
421710	Power handtools (e.g., drills, sanders, saws) wholesaling
812320	Power laundries, commercial and family
234920	Power line construction
541990	Power line inspection (i.e., visual) services
334515	Power measuring equipment, electrical, manufacturing
234930	Power plant (except hydroelectric) construction
234990	Power plant, hydroelectric, construction
336330	Power steering hose assemblies manufacturing
336330	Power steering pumps manufacturing
335999	Power supplies, regulated and unregulated, manufacturing
335313	Power switchboards manufacturing
335313	Power switching equipment manufacturing
335311	Power transformers, electric, manufacturing
421610	Power transmission equipment, electrical, wholesaling
421840	Power transmission supplies (e.g., gears, pulleys, sprockets), mechanical, wholesaling
333319	Power washer cleaning equipment manufacturing
532490	Power washer rental or leasing
561790	Power washing building exteriors
336322	Power window and door lock systems, automotive, truck, and bus, manufacturing
333991	Power-driven handtools manufacturing
212399	Pozzolana mining and/or beneficiating
621399	Practical nurses' offices (e.g., centers, clinics), licensed
315299	Prayer shawls cut and sewn from purchased fabric (except apparel contractors)
315191	Prayer shawls made in apparel knitting mills
315211	Prayer shawls, men's and boys', cut and sew apparel contractors
315212	Prayer shawls, women's, girls', and infants', cut and sew apparel contractors
624410	Pre-kindergarten centers (except part of elementary school system)
334612	Pre-recorded magnetic audio tapes and cassettes mass reproducing
327331	Precast concrete block and brick manufacturing
327332	Precast concrete pipe manufacturing
235910	Precast concrete product placement construction contractors
327390	Precast concrete products (except brick, block, pipe) manufacturing
331491	Precious metal bar, rod, sheet, strip, and tubing made from purchased metals or scrap
331492	Precious metals recovering from scrap and/or alloying purchased metals
331419	Precious metals refining, primary
421940	Precious metals wholesaling

Code	Description
212399	Precious stones mining and/or beneficiating
421940	Precious stones wholesaling
811219	Precision equipment calibration
332212	Precision tools, machinist's (except optical), manufacturing
332721	Precision turned products manufacturers (i.e., known as)
334514	Predetermined counters manufacturing
233220	Prefabricated apartment construction
233220	Prefabricated apartment erection
233220	Prefabricated building (except house) erection, residential
444190	Prefabricated building dealers
233310	Prefabricated building erection, industrial
421390	Prefabricated buildings (except wood) wholesaling
332311	Prefabricated buildings, metal, manufacturing
421310	Prefabricated buildings, wood, wholesaling
321992	Prefabricated homes (except mobile homes), wood, manufacturing
332311	Prefabricated homes, metal, manufacturing
233210	Prefabricated house construction
233210	Prefabricated house erection
233320	Prefabricated nonresidential building (except industrial) erection
321992	Prefabricated wood buildings manufacturing
321211	Prefinished hardwood plywood manufacturing
321212	Prefinished softwood plywood manufacturing
621410	Pregnancy counseling centers
325413	Pregnancy test kits manufacturing
233220	Premanufactured housing (except single family) erection
233210	Premanufactured housing erection, single family
334611	Prepackaged software, mass reproducing
213112	Preparation of oil and gas field drilling sites on a contract basis
212113	Preparation plants, anthracite
611110	Preparatory schools, elementary or secondary
311822	Prepared flour mixes made from purchased flour
311211	Prepared flour mixes made in flour mills
422490	Prepared foods (except frozen) wholesaling
422420	Prepared foods, frozen (except dairy products), wholesaling
422430	Prepared foods, frozen dairy, wholesaling
311991	Prepared meals, perishable, packaged for individual resale
311941	Prepared sauces (except gravy, tomato based) manufacturing
488991	Preparing goods for transportation (i.e., crating, packing)
323122	Prepress printing services (e.g., color separation, imagesetting, photocomposition, typesetting)
541350	Prepurchase home inspection services
421990	Prerecorded audio and video tapes and discs wholesaling
512220	Prerecorded audio tapes and compact discs integrated manufacture, release, and distribution
454110	Prerecorded tape, compact disc, and record mail-order houses

Code	Description
624410	Preschool centers
422210	Prescription drugs wholesaling
111421	Preseeded mat farming
311421	Preserves (e.g., imitation) canning
321114	Preserving purchased wood and wood products
313311	Preshrinking broadwoven fabrics
313312	Preshrinking textile products and fabrics (except broadwoven)
921110	President's office, United States
325611	Presoaks manufacturing
333513	Press brakes, metalworking, manufacturing
514199	Press clipping services
332111	Press forgings made from purchased iron or steel, unfinished
332112	Press forgings made from purchased nonferrous metals, unfinished
422130	Pressed and molded pulp goods (e.g., egg cartons, shipping supplies) wholesaling
313230	Pressed felts manufacturing
321999	Pressed logs of sawdust and other wood particles, nonpetroleum binder, manufacturing
333513	Presses (e.g., bending, punching, shearing, stamping), metal forming, manufacturing
333294	Presses (i.e., food manufacturing-type) manufacturing
333210	Presses for making composite woods (e.g., hardboard, medium density fiberboard (MDF), particleboard, plywood) manufacturing
333111	Presses, farm-type, manufacturing
333999	Presses, metal baling, manufacturing
333293	Presses, printing (except textile), manufacturing
321999	Pressing blocks, wood, tailor's, manufacturing
336350	Pressure and clutch plate assemblies, automotive, truck, and bus, manufacturing
334519	Pressure and vacuum indicators, aircraft engine, manufacturing
332911	Pressure control valves (except fluid power), industrial-type, manufacturing
332912	Pressure control valves, fluid power, manufacturing
334512	Pressure controllers, air-conditioning system-type, manufacturing
332214	Pressure cookers, household-type, manufacturing
334513	Pressure gauges (e.g., dial, digital), industrial process-type, manufacturing
334513	Pressure instruments, industrial process-type, manufacturing
327332	Pressure pipe, reinforced concrete, manufacturing
322222	Pressure sensitive paper and tape (except medical) made from purchased materials
334519	Pressure transducers manufacturing
321113	Pressure treated lumber made from logs or bolts and treated
321114	Pressure treated lumber made from purchased lumber
334512	Pressurestats manufacturing
327331	Prestressed concrete blocks or bricks manufacturing
327332	Prestressed concrete pipes manufacturing
327390	Prestressed concrete products (except blocks, bricks, pipes) manufacturing

Code	Description
722213	Pretzel shops, on premise baking and carryout service
422490	Pretzels (except frozen) wholesaling
311919	Pretzels (except soft) manufacturing
422420	Pretzels, frozen, wholesaling
311812	Pretzels, soft, manufacturing
335129	Prewired poles, brackets, and accessories for electric lighting, manufacturing
926150	Price control agencies
111339	Prickly pear farming
331312	Primary aluminum production and manufacturing aluminum alloys
331312	Primary aluminum production and manufacturing aluminum shapes (e.g., bar, ingot, rod, sheet)
335912	Primary batteries manufacturing
334513	Primary elements for process flow measurement (i.e., orifice plates) manufacturing
334512	Primary oil burner controls (e.g., cadmium cells, stack controls) manufacturing
334513	Primary process temperature sensors manufacturing
331312	Primary refining of aluminum
331411	Primary refining of copper
331419	Primary refining of nonferrous metals (except aluminum, copper)
611110	Primary schools
331312	Primary smelting of aluminum
331411	Primary smelting of copper
331419	Primary smelting of nonferrous metals (except aluminum, copper)
335312	Prime mover generator sets (except turbine generator sets) manufacturing
332993	Primers (i.e., more than 30 mm., more than 1.18 inch), ammunition, manufacturing
325510	Primers, paint, manufacturing
323115	Print shops, digital
323119	Print shops, engraving
323112	Print shops, flexographic
323111	Print shops, gravure
323119	Print shops, letterpress
323110	Print shops, lithographic (offset) (except grey goods, manifold business forms, printing books, quick printing)
323114	Print shops, quick
323113	Print shops, screen
334418	Printed circuit assemblies manufacturing
334418	Printed circuit boards loading
421690	Printed circuit boards wholesaling
334412	Printed circuit boards, bare, manufacturing
334419	Printed circuit laminates manufacturing
334119	Printers, computer, manufacturing
421430	Printers, computer, wholesaling
323117	Printing books without publishing
313311	Printing broadwoven fabrics grey goods
313312	Printing fabric grey goods (except broadwoven)
325910	Printing inks manufacturing
421840	Printing inks wholesaling
333292	Printing machinery for textiles manufacturing
323116	Printing manifold business forms
422120	Printing paper (except bulk) wholesaling
422110	Printing paper, bulk, wholesaling
333293	Printing plate engraving machinery manufacturing
323122	Printing plate preparation services
333293	Printing plates, blank (except photosentive), manufacturing

Code	Description
323121	Printing postpress services (e.g., beveling, bronzing, edging, foil stamping) to printed products (e.g., books, cards, paper)
323122	Printing prepress services (e.g., color separation, imagesetting, photocomposition, typesetting)
333293	Printing press rollers manufacturing
333293	Printing presses (except textile) manufacturing
313312	Printing textile products (except apparel)
811310	Printing trade machinery repair and maintenance services
421830	Printing trade machinery, equipment, and supplies wholesaling
323115	Printing, digital (e.g., billboards, other large format graphical materials)
323115	Printing, digital (e.g., graphics, high resolution)
323119	Printing, engraving, on paper products
323112	Printing, flexographic (except books, grey goods, manifold business forms)
323111	Printing, gravure (except books, grey goods, manifold business forms)
323119	Printing, letterpress (except books, grey goods, manifold business forms)
323110	Printing, lithographic (except books, grey goods, manifold business forms, quick printing)
323110	Printing, photo-offset (except books, grey goods, manifold business forms, printing books)
323114	Printing, quick
323113	Printing, screen (except books, manifold business forms, printing grey goods)
233310	Printing/publishing plant construction
333314	Prisms, optical, manufacturing
337127	Prison bed manufacturing
233320	Prison construction
922140	Prison farms
922140	Prisons
522190	Private banks (i.e., unincorporated)
334210	Private branch exchange (PBX) equipment manufacturing
611310	Private colleges (except community or junior college)
561611	Private detective services
525920	Private estates (i.e., administering on behalf of beneficiaries)
814110	Private households employing domestic personnel
814110	Private households with employees
561611	Private investigation services (except credit)
561431	Private mail centers
561431	Private mailbox rental centers
611110	Private schools, elementary or secondary
493190	Private warehousing and storage (except farm products, general merchandise, refrigerated)
493130	Private warehousing and storage, farm products (except refrigerated)
493110	Private warehousing and storage, general merchandise
493120	Private warehousing and storage, refrigerated
451110	Pro shops (e.g., golf, skiing, tennis)
922150	Probation offices
212391	Probertite mining and/or quarrying
334510	Probes, electric medical, manufacturing
339112	Probes, surgical, manufacturing
325411	Procaine and derivatives (i.e., basic chemicals) manufacturing

Code	Description
334513	Process control instruments, industrial, manufacturing
541199	Process server services
541199	Process serving services
311513	Processed cheeses manufacturing
422470	Processed meats (e.g., luncheon, sausage) wholesaling
311612	Processed meats manufacturing
422440	Processed poultry (e.g., luncheon) wholesaling
311615	Processed poultry manufacturing
314999	Processing of textile mill waste and recovering fibers
621111	Proctologists' offices (e.g., centers, clinics)
422910	Produce containers wholesaling
445230	Produce markets
445230	Produce stands, permanent
454390	Produce stands, temporary
422480	Produce, fresh, wholesaling
813910	Producers' associations
711510	Producers, independent
561910	Product sterilization and packaging services
541380	Product testing laboratories or services
524128	Product warranty insurance carriers, direct
334514	Production counters manufacturing
541614	Production planning and control consulting services
541614	Productivity improvement consulting services
813920	Professional associations
711219	Professional athletes, independent (i.e., participating in sports events)
711211	Professional baseball clubs
323121	Professional book binding without printing
511130	Professional book publishers
511130	Professional book publishers and printing combined
511130	Professional book publishing (i.e., establishments known as publishers)
323117	Professional books printing and binding without publishing
323117	Professional books printing without publishing
611430	Professional development training
561330	Professional employer organizations (PEO)
421490	Professional equipment and supplies (except dental, medical, ophthalmic) wholesaling
611691	Professional examination review instructions
711211	Professional football clubs
421490	Professional instruments wholesaling
511120	Professional magazine and periodical publishers
511120	Professional magazine and periodical publishers and printing combined
511120	Professional magazine and periodical publishing (i.e., establishments known as publishers)
323112	Professional magazines and periodicals flexographic printing without publishing
323111	Professional magazines and periodicals gravure printing without publishing
323110	Professional magazines and periodicals lithographic (offset) printing without publishing
323119	Professional magazines and periodicals printing (except flexographic, gravure, lithographic, screen) without publishing

Professional magazines—Public relations

Code	Description
323113	Professional magazines and periodicals screen printing without publishing
813920	Professional membership associations
531120	Professional office building rental or leasing
611310	Professional schools (e.g., business administration, dental, law, medical)
315211	Professional service apparel, washable, men's and boys', cut and sew apparel contractors
315225	Professional service apparel, washable, men's and boys', cut and sewn from purchased fabric (except apparel contractors)
315212	Professional service apparel, washable, women's, cut and sew apparel contractors
315239	Professional service apparel, washable, women's, misses', and girls', cut and sewn from purchased fabric (except apparel contractors)
611620	Professional sports (e.g., golf, skiing, swimming, tennis) instructors (i.e., not participating in sporting events)
711211	Professional sports clubs
711310	Professional sports promoters with facilities
711320	Professional sports promoters without facilities
813920	Professional standards review boards
326130	Profile shapes (e.g., plate, rod, sheet), laminated plastics, manufacturing
326121	Profile shapes (e.g., rod, tube), nonrigid plastics, manufacturing
525990	Profit-sharing funds
512110	Program producing, television
334513	Programmers, process-type, manufacturing
511210	Programming language and compiler software publishers, packaged
541511	Programming services, custom computer
332993	Projectiles (except guided missile), jet propulsion, manufacturing
333315	Projection equipment (e.g., motion picture, slide), photographic, manufacturing
421410	Projection equipment (e.g., motion picture, slide), photographic, wholesaling
532490	Projection equipment rental or leasing, motion picture
333314	Projection lenses manufacturing
333315	Projection screens (i.e., motion picture, overhead, slide) manufacturing
334310	Projection television manufacturing
332995	Projectors (e.g., antisub, depth charge release, grenade, livens, rocket), ordnance, manufacturing
711310	Promoters of agricultural fairs with facilities
711320	Promoters of agricultural fairs without facilities
711310	Promoters of arts events with facilities
711320	Promoters of arts events without facilities
561920	Promoters of conventions with or without facilities
711310	Promoters of festivals with facilities
711320	Promoters of festivals without facilities
711310	Promoters of live performing arts productions (e.g., concerts) with facilities

Code	Description
711320	Promoters of live performing arts productions (e.g., concerts) without facilities
711310	Promoters of sports events with facilities
711320	Promoters of sports events without facilities
561920	Promoters of trade fairs or shows with or without facilities
561410	Proofreading services
111421	Propagation material farming
422710	Propane bulk stations and terminals
324110	Propane gases made in petroleum refineries
211112	Propane recovered from oil and gas field gases
333518	Propeller straightening presses manufacturing
334514	Propeller type meters with registers manufacturing
332999	Propellers, ship and boat, made from purchased metal
524126	Property and casualty insurance carriers, direct
524130	Property and casualty reinsurance carriers
524126	Property damage insurance carriers, direct
531312	Property managers' offices, commercial real estate
531312	Property managers' offices, nonresidential real estate
531311	Property managers' offices, residential real estate
531312	Property managing, commercial real estate
531312	Property managing, nonresidential real estate
531311	Property managing, residential real estate
813990	Property owners' associations
561612	Property protection services (except armored car, security systems)
921130	Property tax assessors' offices
326299	Prophylactics manufacturing
112910	Propolis production, bees
336415	Propulsion units and parts, guided missile and space vehicle, manufacturing
325199	Propylcarbinol manufacturing
324110	Propylene (i.e., propene) made in petroleum refineries
325199	Propylene glycol manufacturing
325110	Propylene made from refined petroleum or liquid hydrocarbons
325211	Propylene resins manufacturing
213113	Prospect and test drilling services for coal mining on contract basis
213114	Prospect and test drilling services for metal mining on contract basis
213115	Prospect and test drilling services for nonmetallic mineral mining (except fuels) on a contract basis
339113	Prosthetic appliances and supplies manufacturing
421450	Prosthetic appliances and supplies wholesaling
446199	Prosthetic stores
621210	Prosthodontists' offices (e.g., centers, clinics)
561612	Protection services (except armored car, security systems), personal or property
812332	Protective apparel supply services
523999	Protective committees, security holders

Code	Description
316211	Protective footwear, plastics or plastics-soled fabric upper, manufacturing
316211	Protective footwear, rubber or rubber-soled fabric upper, manufacturing
561612	Protective guard services
339920	Protectors, sports (e.g., baseball, basketball, hockey), manufacturing
334516	Protein analyzers, laboratory-type, manufacturing
325222	Protein fibers and filaments manufacturing
325211	Protein plastics manufacturing
712190	Provincial parks
334511	Proximity warning (i.e., collision avoidance) equipment manufacturing
111339	Prune farming
332212	Pruners manufacturing
311423	Prunes, dried, made in dehydration plants
115112	Pruning of orchard trees and vines
561730	Pruning services, ornamental tree and shrub
325131	Prussian blue pigments manufacturing
332212	Pry (i.e., crow) bars manufacturing
212299	Psilomelane mining and/or beneficiating
621420	Psychiatric centers and clinics (except hospitals), outpatient
623220	Psychiatric convalescent homes or hospitals
622210	Psychiatric hospitals (except convalescent)
621112	Psychiatrists' offices (e.g., centers, clinics)
812990	Psychic services
621112	Psychoanalysts' (MDs or DOs) offices (e.g., centers, clinics)
621330	Psychoanalysts' (except MDs or DOs) offices (e.g., centers, clinics)
813920	Psychologists' associations
621330	Psychologists' offices (e.g., centers, clinics), clinical
541720	Psychology research and development services
621112	Psychotherapists' (MDs or DOs) offices (e.g., centers, clinics)
621330	Psychotherapists' (except MDs or DOs) offices (e.g., centers, clinics)
541211	Public accountants' (CPAs) offices, certified
541211	Public accountants' (CPAs) private practices, certified
541219	Public accountants' (except CPAs) offices
541219	Public accountants' (except CPAs) private practices
532490	Public address system rental or leasing
811213	Public address system repair and maintenance services
334310	Public address systems and equipment manufacturing
421690	Public address systems and equipment wholesaling
421210	Public building furniture wholesaling
922130	Public defenders' offices
711410	Public figures' agents or managers
923120	Public health program administration, nonoperating
541910	Public opinion polling services
541910	Public opinion research services
921190	Public property management services, government
922130	Public prosecutors' offices
541820	Public relations agencies
541820	Public relations consulting services
541820	Public relations services

Code	Description
813319	Public safety advocacy organizations
922190	Public safety bureaus and statistics centers, government
922190	Public safety statistics centers, government
926130	Public service (except transportation) commissions, nonoperating
813410	Public speaking improvement clubs
611699	Public speaking training
561492	Public stenography services
926120	Public transportation commissions, nonoperating
926130	Public utility (except transportation) commissions, nonoperating
813910	Public utility associations
551112	Public utility holding companies
233320	Public warehouse construction
493190	Public warehousing and storage (except farm products, general merchandise, refrigerated, self storage)
493110	Public warehousing and storage (except self storage), general merchandise
493130	Public warehousing and storage, farm products (except refrigerated)
493120	Public warehousing and storage, refrigerated
51	Publishers (see specific type)
51	Publishers and printing combined (see specific type of publisher)
51	Publishers or publishing (see specific type)
541840	Publishers' advertising representatives (i.e., independent of media owners)
511130	Publishers, book
511130	Publishers, book, combined with printing
511140	Publishers, database
511140	Publishers, directory
511191	Publishers, greeting card
511191	Publishers, greeting card, combined with printing
511120	Publishers, magazine
511120	Publishers, magazine, combined with printing
511199	Publishers, map
512230	Publishers, music
511110	Publishers, newspaper
511110	Publishers, newspaper, combined with printing
511210	Publishers, packaged computer software
511120	Publishers, periodical
511120	Publishers, periodical, combined with printing
511199	Publishers, racing form
511110	Publishing and printing or publishing only, newspaper (i.e., establishments known as publishers)
511191	Publishing, greeting card, (i.e., establishments known as publishers)
311520	Pudding pops, frozen, manufacturing
311999	Puddings, canned dessert, manufacturing
311999	Puddings, dessert, manufacturing
333923	Pulleys (except power transmission), metal, manufacturing
333613	Pulleys, power transmission, manufacturing
321999	Pulleys, wood, manufacturing
213112	Pulling oil and gas field casings, tubes, or rods on a contract basis
621111	Pulmonary specialists' offices (e.g., centers, clinics)
322122	Pulp and newsprint combined manufacturing
322121	Pulp and paper (except groundwood, newsprint) combined manufacturing
322130	Pulp and paperboard combined manufacturing
333291	Pulp making machinery manufacturing
322110	Pulp manufacturing (i.e., chemical, mechanical, or semichemical processes) without making paper
322110	Pulp manufacturing (made from bagasse, linters, rags, straw, wastepaper, or wood) without making paper
322122	Pulp mills and groundwood paper, uncoated and untreated, manufacturing
322110	Pulp mills not making paper or paperboard
322122	Pulp mills producing newsprint paper
322121	Pulp mills producing paper (except groundwood, newsprint)
322130	Pulp mills producing paperboard
322299	Pulp products, molded, manufacturing
333291	Pulp, paper, and paperboard molding machinery manufacturing
212399	Pulpstones, natural, mining and/or beneficiating
113310	Pulpwood logging camps
421990	Pulpwood wholesaling
334515	Pulse (i.e., signal) generators manufacturing
334519	Pulse analyzers, nuclear monitoring, manufacturing
327992	Pumice (except abrasives) processing beyond beneficiation
327910	Pumice and pumicite abrasives manufacturing
212399	Pumice mining and/or beneficiating
212399	Pumicite mining and/or beneficiating
562991	Pumping (i.e., cleaning) cesspools and septic tanks
562991	Pumping (i.e., cleaning) portable toilets
213112	Pumping oil and gas wells on a contract basis
213113	Pumping or draining coal mines on a contract basis
213114	Pumping or draining metal mines on a contract basis
213115	Pumping or draining nonmetallic mineral mines (except fuel) on a contract basis
234910	Pumping station construction
111219	Pumpkin farming, field and seed production
421120	Pumps (e.g., fuel, oil, power steering, water), automotive, wholesaling
336312	Pumps (e.g., fuel, oil, water), mechanical, automotive and truck gasoline engine (except power steering), manufacturing
333911	Pumps (except fluid power), general purpose, manufacturing
316214	Pumps (i.e., dress shoes) manufacturing
421830	Pumps and pumping equipment, industrial-type, wholesaling
333911	Pumps for railroad equipment lubrication systems manufacturing
333996	Pumps, fluid power, manufacturing
333911	Pumps, industrial and commercial-type, general purpose, manufacturing
333913	Pumps, measuring and dispensing (e.g., gasoline), manufacturing
333911	Pumps, oil field or well, manufacturing
333911	Pumps, sump or water, residential-type, manufacturing
313230	Punched felts manufacturing
332212	Punches (except paper), nonpowered handtool, manufacturing
333514	Punches for use with machine tools manufacturing
333513	Punching machines, metalworking, manufacturing
711110	Puppet theaters
339999	Puppets manufacturing
921190	Purchasing and supply agencies, government
522298	Purchasing of accounts receivable
332323	Purlins, metal, manufacturing
316993	Purses (except precious metal), men's, manufacturing
316992	Purses (except precious metal), women's, manufacturing
339911	Purses, precious metal or clad with precious metal, manufacturing
333515	Pushers (i.e., a machine tool accessory) manufacturing
332212	Putty knives manufacturing
421920	Puzzles wholesaling
325320	Pyrethrin insecticides manufacturing
334519	Pyrheliometers manufacturing
212393	Pyrite concentrates mining and/or beneficiating
212393	Pyrite mining and/or beneficiating
325191	Pyroligneous acids manufacturing
212299	Pyrolusite mining and/or beneficiating
327112	Pyrometer tubes manufacturing
334513	Pyrometers, industrial process-type, manufacturing
327112	Pyrometric cones, earthenware, manufacturing
212399	Pyrophyllite mining and/or beneficiating
327992	Pyrophyllite processing beyond beneficiation
332994	Pyrotechnic pistols and projectors manufacturing
325998	Pyrotechnics (e.g., flares, flashlight bombs, signals) manufacturing
325211	Pyroxylin (i.e., nitrocellulose) resins manufacturing
212393	Pyrrhotite mining and/or beneficiating
112390	Quail production
611430	Quality assurance training
541990	Quantity surveyor services
327122	Quarry tiles, clay, manufacturing
333131	Quarrying machinery and equipment manufacturing
421810	Quarrying machinery and equipment wholesaling
316999	Quarters (i.e., shoe cut stock), leather, manufacturing
212399	Quartz crystal, pure, mining and/or beneficiating
334419	Quartz crystals, electronic application, manufacturing
212319	Quartzite crushed and broken stone mining and/or beneficiating
212311	Quartzite dimension stone mining or quarrying
325191	Quebracho extracts manufacturing
112910	Queen bee production
325191	Quercitron extracts manufacturing
323114	Quick printing
811191	Quick-lube shops
327410	Quicklime (i.e., calcium oxide) manufacturing
212299	Quicksilver ores and metal mining and/or beneficiating
314999	Quilting of textiles
314129	Quilts made from purchased materials
111339	Quince farming

Quinine—Radium

Code	Description
325411	Quinine and derivatives (i.e., basic chemicals) manufacturing
523999	Quotation services, securities
523999	Quotation services, stock
334519	RADIAC (radioactivity detection, identification, and computation) equipment manufacturing
525930	REITs (real estate investment trusts)
525990	REMICs (real estate mortgage investment conduits)
522294	REMICs (real estate mortgage investment conduits) issuing, private
621399	RNs' (registered nurses) offices (e.g., centers, clinics)
721211	RV (recreational vehicle) parks
532120	RV (recreational vehicle) rental or leasing
441210	RV dealers
311119	Rabbit food manufacturing
112930	Rabbit production
311615	Rabbits processing (i.e., canned, cooked, fresh, frozen)
311615	Rabbits slaughtering and dressing
711219	Race car drivers
711219	Race car owners (i.e., racing cars)
336999	Race cars manufacturing
711219	Race dog owners (i.e., racing dogs)
711219	Racehorse owners (i.e., racing horses)
711219	Racehorse trainers
711219	Racehorse training
332991	Races, ball or roller bearing, manufacturing
511199	Racetrack program publishers
511199	Racetrack program publishers and printing combined
323112	Racetrack programs flexographic printing without publishing
323111	Racetrack programs gravure printing without publishing
323110	Racetrack programs lithographic (offset) printing without publishing
323119	Racetrack programs printing (except flexographic, gravure, lithographic, screen) without publishing
511199	Racetrack programs publishing (i.e., establishments known as publishers)
323113	Racetrack programs screen printing without publishing
711212	Racetracks (e.g., automobile, dog, horse)
713990	Racetracks, slot car (i.e., amusement devices)
335932	Raceways manufacturing
713990	Raceways, gocart (i.e., amusement rides)
511199	Racing form publishers
511199	Racing form publishers and printing combined
323112	Racing forms flexographic printing without publishing
323111	Racing forms gravure printing without publishing
323110	Racing forms lithographic (offset) printing without publishing
323119	Racing forms printing (except flexographic, gravure, lithographic, screen) without publishing
511199	Racing forms publishing (i.e., establishments known as publishers)
323113	Racing forms screen printing without publishing
711219	Racing stables, horse
711219	Racing teams (e.g., automobile, motorcycle, snowmobile)
334417	Rack and panel connectors manufacturing
336330	Rack and pinion steering assemblies manufacturing
336399	Racks (e.g., bicycle, luggage, ski, tire), automotive, truck, and buses manufacturing
332313	Racks (e.g., trash), fabricated metal plate, manufacturing
332618	Racks, household-type, made from purchased wire
713940	Racquetball club facilities
811219	Radar and sonar equipment repair and maintenance services
334511	Radar detectors manufacturing
421690	Radar equipment wholesaling
513390	Radar station operations
334511	Radar systems and equipment manufacturing
334515	Radar testing instruments, electric, manufacturing
334519	Radiation detection and monitoring instruments manufacturing
541380	Radiation dosimetry (i.e., radiation testing) laboratories or services
812332	Radiation protection garment supply services
339113	Radiation shielding aprons, gloves, and sheeting manufacturing
541380	Radiation testing laboratories or services
325998	Radiator additive preparations manufacturing
326220	Radiator and heater hoses, rubber or plastics, manufacturing
811118	Radiator repair shops, automotive
332322	Radiator shields and enclosures, sheet metal, manufacturing
333414	Radiators (except motor vehicle, portable electric) manufacturing
336399	Radiators and cores manufacturing
421120	Radiators, motor vehicle, wholesaling
335211	Radiators, portable electric, manufacturing
541840	Radio advertising representatives (i.e., independent of media owners)
443112	Radio and television stores
332312	Radio and television tower sections, fabricated structural metal, manufacturing
488330	Radio beacon (i.e., ship navigation) services
513111	Radio broadcasting network services
513111	Radio broadcasting networks
513112	Radio broadcasting stations (e.g., AM, FM, shortwave)
513111	Radio broadcasting syndicates
711510	Radio commentators, independent
541690	Radio consulting services
511120	Radio guide publishers
511120	Radio guide publishers and printing combined
511120	Radio guide publishing (i.e., establishments known as publishers)
323112	Radio guides flexographic printing without publishing
323111	Radio guides gravure printing without publishing
323110	Radio guides lithographic (offset) printing without publishing
323119	Radio guides printing (except flexographic, gravure, lithographic, screen) without publishing
323113	Radio guides screen printing without publishing
334310	Radio headphones manufacturing
326199	Radio housings, plastics, manufacturing
334511	Radio magnetic instrumentation (RMI) manufacturing
513321	Radio paging services communication carriers
421690	Radio parts and accessories (e.g., transitors, tubes) wholesaling
512290	Radio program tape production (except independent producers)
334310	Radio receiving sets manufacturing
811211	Radio repair and maintenance services without retailing new radios
323111	Radio schedule gravure printing without publishing
511120	Radio schedule publishers
511120	Radio schedule publishers and printing combined
511120	Radio schedule publishing (i.e., establishments known as publishers)
323112	Radio schedules flexographic printing without publishing
323110	Radio schedules lithographic (offset) printing without publishing
323119	Radio schedules printing (except flexographic, gravure, lithographic, screen) without publishing
323113	Radio schedules screen printing without publishing
513112	Radio stations (e.g., AM, FM, shortwave)
561410	Radio transcription services
334220	Radio transmitting antennas and ground equipment manufacturing
325188	Radioactive elements manufacturing
541360	Radioactive geophysical surveying services
325412	Radioactive in-vivo diagnostic substances manufacturing
325188	Radioactive isotopes manufacturing
422210	Radioactive pharmaceutical isotopes wholesaling
562112	Radioactive waste collecting and/or local hauling
562211	Radioactive waste collecting and/or local hauling in combination with disposal and/or treatment facilities
562211	Radioactive waste disposal facilities
484230	Radioactive waste hauling, long-distance
562211	Radioactive waste treatment facilities
334519	Radioactivity detection, identification, and computation (RADIAC) equipment manufacturing
334515	Radiofrequency measuring equipment manufacturing
334515	Radiofrequency oscillators manufacturing
541380	Radiographic testing laboratories or services
541380	Radiographing welded joints on pipes and fittings
541380	Radiography inspection services
621512	Radiological laboratories, medical
621512	Radiological laboratory services, medical
621111	Radiologists' offices (e.g., centers, clinics)
421690	Radios (except household-type) wholesaling
421620	Radios, household-type, wholesaling
111219	Radish farming, field and seed production
325188	Radium chloride manufacturing
334517	Radium equipment manufacturing
325188	Radium luminous compounds manufacturing
212291	Radium ores mining and/or beneficiating

Code	Description
235990	Radon remediation construction contractors
541380	Radon testing laboratories or services
326299	Rafts, rubber inflatable, manufacturing
421930	Rags wholesaling
335931	Rail bonds, propulsion and signal circuit electric, manufacturing
331111	Rail joints and fastenings made in steel mills
336510	Rail laying and tamping equipment manufacturing
485112	Rail transportation (except mixed mode), commuter
332323	Railings, metal, manufacturing
321918	Railings, wood stair, manufacturing
923130	Railroad Retirement Board
926120	Railroad and warehouse commissions, nonoperating
333613	Railroad car journal bearings, plain, manufacturing
532411	Railroad car rental and leasing
336510	Railroad cars and car equipment manufacturing
421860	Railroad cars wholesaling
336510	Railroad cars, self-propelled, manufacturing
234990	Railroad construction
331111	Railroad crossings, iron or steel, made in steel mills
421860	Railroad equipment and supplies wholesaling
336510	Railroad locomotives and parts (except diesel engines) manufacturing
339932	Railroad models, hobby and toy, manufacturing
531190	Railroad right of way leasing
336510	Railroad rolling stock manufacturing
336360	Railroad seating manufacturing
334290	Railroad signaling equipment manufacturing
488210	Railroad switching services
488210	Railroad terminals, independent operation
561599	Railroad ticket offices
321114	Railroad ties (i.e., bridge, cross, switch) treating
421990	Railroad ties, wood, wholesaling
333997	Railroad track scales manufacturing
482111	Railroad transportation, line-haul
487110	Railroad transportation, scenic and sightseeing
482112	Railroad transportation, short-line or beltline
487110	Railroad, scenic and sightseeing operation
482111	Railroads, line-haul
482112	Railroads, short-line or beltline
321999	Rails (except rough), wood fence, manufacturing
421510	Rails and accessories, metal, wholesaling
331319	Rails made by rolling or drawing purchased aluminum
331111	Rails rerolled or renewed in steel mills
331319	Rails, aluminum, made in integrated secondary smelting and drawing plants
331319	Rails, aluminum, made in integrated secondary smelting and rolling mills
331111	Rails, iron or steel, made in steel mills
113310	Rails, rough wood, manufacturing
332312	Railway bridge sections, prefabricated metal, manufacturing
335312	Railway motors and control equipment, electric, manufacturing
234990	Railway roadbed construction

Code	Description
485112	Railway systems (except mixed mode), commuter
488210	Railway terminals, independent operation
482111	Railway transportation, line-haul
487110	Railway transportation, scenic and sightseeing
482112	Railway transportation, short-line or beltline
334519	Rain gauges manufacturing
315211	Raincoats water resistant, men's and boys', cut and sew apparel contractors
313320	Raincoats waterproofing (i.e., oiling)
315299	Raincoats, rubber or rubberized fabric, manufacturing
315291	Raincoats, water resistant, infants', cut and sewn from purchased fabric (except apparel contractors)
315228	Raincoats, water resistant, nontailored, men's and boys', cut and sewn from purchased fabric (except apparel contractors)
315239	Raincoats, water resistant, nontailored, women's, misses', and girls', cut and sewn from purchased fabric (except apparel contractors)
315222	Raincoats, water resistant, tailored, men's and boys', cut and sewn from purchased fabric (except apparel contractors)
315234	Raincoats, water resistant, tailored, women's, misses', and girls', cut and sewn from purchased fabric (except apparel contractors)
315212	Raincoats, water resistant, women's, girls', and infants', cut and sew apparel contractors
315291	Raincoats, water-repellent, infants', cut and sewn from purchased fabric (except apparel contractors)
315211	Raincoats, water-repellent, men's and boys', cut and sew apparel contractors
315228	Raincoats, water-repellent, nontailored, men's and boys', cut and sewn from purchased fabric (except apparel contractors)
315239	Raincoats, water-repellent, nontailored, women's, misses', and girls', cut and sewn from purchased fabric (except apparel contractors)
315222	Raincoats, water-repellent, tailored, men's and boys', cut and sewn from purchased fabric (except apparel contractors)
315234	Raincoats, water-repellent, tailored, women's, misses', and girls', cut and sewn from purchased fabric (except apparel contractors)
315212	Raincoats, water-repellent, women's, girls', and infants', cut and sew apparel contractors
315299	Raincoats, waterproof (except infants'), cut and sewn from purchased fabric (except apparel contractors)
315299	Raincoats, waterproof, infants', cut and sewn from purchased fabric (except apparel contractors)
315211	Raincoats, waterproof, men's and boys', cut and sew apparel contractors
315212	Raincoats, waterproof, women's, girls', and infants', cut and sew apparel contractors
111332	Raisin farming

Code	Description
112990	Raising swans, peacocks, flamingos, or other adornment birds
311423	Raisins made in dehydration plants
333111	Rakes, hay, manufacturing
332212	Rakes, nonpowered handtool, manufacturing
313111	Ramie spun yarns made from purchased fiber
316999	Rands (i.e., shoe cut stock), leather, manufacturing
333315	Range finders, photographic, manufacturing
335211	Range hoods with integral lighting fixtures, household-type, manufacturing
335211	Range hoods, household-type, manufacturing
333319	Ranges, commercial-type, manufacturing
335221	Ranges, household-type cooking, manufacturing
624190	Rape crisis centers
311225	Rapeseed (i.e., canola) oil made from purchased oils
311223	Rapeseed (i.e., canola) oil made in crushing mills
111120	Rapeseed farming, field and seed production
336510	Rapid transit cars and equipment manufacturing
325188	Rare earth compounds, not specified elsewhere by process, manufacturing
212299	Rare earth metal concentrates beneficiating
212299	Rare earth metal ores mining and/or beneficiating
325188	Rare earth salts manufacturing
453310	Rare manuscript stores
111334	Raspberry farming
332212	Rasps, handheld, manufacturing
332212	Ratchets, nonpowered, manufacturing
524298	Rate making services, insurance
334511	Rate-of-climb instrumentation manufacturing
213112	Rathole and mousehole drilling at oil and gas fields on a contract basis
112390	Ratite production
337125	Rattan furniture, household-type, manufacturing
321999	Rattan ware (except furniture) manufacturing
112990	Rattlesnake production
311313	Raw beet sugar manufacturing
422590	Raw farm products (e.g., field beans, grains) wholesaling
316110	Rawhide manufacturing
114111	Ray fishing
325221	Rayon fibers and filaments manufacturing
313111	Rayon spun yarns made from purchased fiber
313113	Rayon thread manufacturing
313112	Rayon yarn throwing, twisting, texturizing, or winding purchased filament
331221	Razor blade strip steel made in cold rolling mills
332211	Razor blades manufacturing
422210	Razor blades wholesaling
316999	Razor strops manufacturing
332211	Razors (except electric) manufacturing
422210	Razors (except electric) wholesaling
335211	Razors, electric, manufacturing
421620	Razors, electric, wholesaling

Re-refining—Refining

Code	Description
324191	Re-refining used petroleum lubricating oils
332313	Reactor containment vessels, fabricated metal plate, manufacturing
332410	Reactors, nuclear, manufacturing
333315	Readers, microfilm or microfiche, manufacturing
336211	Ready-mix concrete trucks assembling on purchased chassis
327320	Ready-mixed concrete manufacturing and distributing
531190	Real estate (except building) rental or leasing
531210	Real estate agencies
531210	Real estate agents' offices
531320	Real estate appraisal services
531320	Real estate appraisers' offices
531390	Real estate asset management services (except property management)
813910	Real estate boards
531210	Real estate brokerages
531210	Real estate brokers' offices
531390	Real estate consultants' (except agents, appraisers) offices
522292	Real estate credit lending
531390	Real estate escrow agencies
531390	Real estate escrow agents' offices
531390	Real estate fiduciaries' offices
525930	Real estate investment trusts (REITs)
541110	Real estate law offices
531390	Real estate listing services
525990	Real estate mortgage investment conduits (REMICs)
522294	Real estate mortgage investment conduits (REMICs) issuing, private
531312	Real estate property managers' offices, commercial
531311	Real estate property managers' offices, residential
531130	Real estate rental or leasing of miniwarehouses and self-storage units
531120	Real estate rental or leasing of nonresidential building (except miniwarehouse)
531110	Real estate rental or leasing of residential building
611519	Real estate schools
524127	Real estate title insurance carriers, direct
233110	Real property (i.e., land, except cemetery lots) development or subdivision
561492	Real-time (i.e., simultaneous) closed captioning of live television performances, meetings, conferences, and so forth
333515	Reamers (i.e., a machine tool accessory) manufacturing
333512	Reaming machines, metalworking, manufacturing
235910	Rebar construction contractors
323121	Rebinding books, magazines, or pamphlets
513112	Rebroadcast radio stations
336312	Rebuilding automotive and truck gasoline engines
326212	Rebuilding tires
326212	Recapping tires
422120	Receipt books wholesaling
334220	Receiver-transmitter units (i.e., transceivers) manufacturing
335931	Receptacles (i.e., outlets), electrical, manufacturing
421610	Receptacles, electrical, wholesaling
531120	Reception hall rental or leasing

Code	Description
335122	Recessed lighting housings and trim (except residential), electric, manufacturing
335121	Recessed lighting housings and trim, residential electric, manufacturing
335911	Rechargeable battery packs made from purchased battery cells and housings
335911	Rechargeable nickel cadmium (NICAD) batteries manufacturing
314999	Reclaimed wool processing
326299	Reclaiming rubber from waste or scrap
234990	Reclamation projects construction
337121	Recliners, upholstered, manufacturing
332994	Recoil mechanisms (i.e., 30 mm. or less, 1.18 inch or less), gun, manufacturing
332995	Recoil mechanisms (i.e., more than 30 mm., more than 1.18 inch), gun, manufacturing
332995	Recoilless rifles manufacturing
421840	Reconditioned barrels and drums wholesaling
213111	Reconditioning oil and gas field wells on a contract basis
811310	Reconditioning shipping barrels and drums
321219	Reconstituted wood panels manufacturing
321219	Reconstituted wood sheets and boards manufacturing
312229	Reconstituting tobacco
512210	Record producers (except independent)
711510	Record producers, independent
512210	Record production (except independent record producers) without duplication or distribution
512220	Record releasing, promoting, and distributing combined with mass duplication
451220	Record stores, new
453310	Record stores, used
421620	Recorders (e.g., tape, video), household-type, wholesaling
334513	Recorders, industrial process control-type, manufacturing
334515	Recorders, oscillographic, manufacturing
512290	Recording books on tape or disc (except publishers)
512290	Recording seminars and conferences, audio
512240	Recording studios, sound, operating on a contract or fee basis
711510	Recording technicians, independent
541611	Records management consulting services
314999	Recovered fibers processing
331492	Recovering and refining of nonferrous metals (except aluminum, copper) from scrap
331492	Recovering silver from used photographic film or X-ray plates
621340	Recreational (e.g., art, dance, music) therapists' offices (e.g., centers, clinics)
233320	Recreational building construction
721214	Recreational camps with accommodation facilities (except campgrounds)
713990	Recreational camps without accommodations
713990	Recreational day camps (except instructional)
421910	Recreational equipment and supplies (except vehicles) wholesaling
532292	Recreational goods rental

Code	Description
924120	Recreational programs administration, government
713940	Recreational sports club facilities
713990	Recreational sports clubs (i.e., sports teams) not operating sports facilities
713990	Recreational sports teams and leagues
532120	Recreational trailer rental
441210	Recreational vehicle (RV) dealers
532120	Recreational vehicle (RV) rental or leasing
721211	Recreational vehicle parks
441210	Recreational vehicle parts and accessories stores
421110	Recreational vehicles wholesaling
335999	Rectifiers (except electronic component type, semiconductor) manufacturing
334419	Rectifiers, electronic component-type (except semiconductor), manufacturing
421690	Rectifiers, electronic, wholesaling
334413	Rectifiers, semiconductor, manufacturing
333298	Rectifying equipment, chemical, manufacturing
562111	Recyclable material collection services
562111	Recyclable material hauling, local
484230	Recyclable material hauling, long-distance
421930	Recyclable materials (e.g., glass, metal, paper) wholesaling
325612	Recycling drycleaning fluids
811212	Recycling inkjet cartridges
325998	Recycling services for degreasing solvents (e.g., engine, machinery) manufacturing
325199	Red oil (i.e., oleic acid) manufacturing
925120	Redevelopment land agencies, government
334516	Redox (i.e., oxidation-reduction potential) instruments manufacturing
333612	Reducers, speed, manufacturing
333612	Reduction gears and gear units (except aircraft power transmission equipment, automotive) manufacturing
337125	Reed furniture (except upholstered), household-type, manufacturing
212399	Reed peat mining and/or beneficiating
321999	Reed ware (except furniture) manufacturing
339992	Reeds, musical instrument, manufacturing
339920	Reels, fishing, manufacturing
332999	Reels, metal, manufacturing
326199	Reels, plastics, manufacturing
321999	Reels, plywood, manufacturing
321999	Reels, wood, manufacturing
514120	Reference libraries
561310	Referral agencies or services, employment
624190	Referral services for personal and social problems
486910	Refined petroleum products pipeline transportation
324110	Refineries, petroleum
324110	Refinery gases made in petroleum refineries
421830	Refinery machinery and equipment wholesaling
331312	Refining aluminum, primary
331314	Refining aluminum, secondary
331411	Refining copper, primary
331423	Refining copper, secondary
331419	Refining nonferrous metals and alloys (except aluminum, copper), primary
331492	Refining nonferrous metals and alloys (except aluminum, copper), secondary

Code	Description
335129	Reflectors for lighting equipment, metal, manufacturing
333314	Reflectors, optical, manufacturing
326199	Reflectors, plastics, manufacturing
115310	Reforestation
922140	Reformatories
325991	Reformulating plastics resins from recycled plastics products
334513	Refractometers, industrial process-type, manufacturing
334516	Refractometers, laboratory-type, manufacturing
421840	Refractories (e.g., block, brick, mortar, tile) wholesaling
327124	Refractories (e.g., block, brick, mortar, tile), clay, manufacturing
327125	Refractories (e.g., block, brick, mortar, tile), nonclay, manufacturing
235410	Refractory brick construction contractors
327125	Refractory cement, nonclay, manufacturing
212325	Refractory minerals mining and/or beneficiating
722330	Refreshment stands, mobile
311822	Refrigerated doughs made from purchased flour
333415	Refrigerated lockers manufacturing
484220	Refrigerated products trucking, local
484230	Refrigerated products trucking, long-distance
493120	Refrigerated warehousing
235110	Refrigeration and freezer installation contractors
333415	Refrigeration compressors manufacturing
334512	Refrigeration controls, residential and commercial-type, manufacturing
421740	Refrigeration equipment and supplies, commercial-type, wholesaling
811310	Refrigeration equipment repair and maintenance services, industrial and commercial-type
333415	Refrigeration equipment, industrial and commercial-type, manufacturing
334512	Refrigeration thermostats manufacturing
421740	Refrigeration units, motor vehicle, wholesaling
333415	Refrigeration units, truck-type, manufacturing
334512	Refrigeration/air-conditioning defrost controls manufacturing
532210	Refrigerator rental
811412	Refrigerator, household-type, repair and maintenance services without retailing new refrigerators
335222	Refrigerator/freezer combinations, household-type, manufacturing
335222	Refrigerators (e.g., absorption, mechanical), household-type, manufacturing
421740	Refrigerators (e.g., reach-in, walk-in), commercial-type, wholesaling
421620	Refrigerators, household-type, wholesaling
624230	Refugee settlement services
562212	Refuse collecting and operating solid waste landfills
562111	Refuse collection services
562213	Refuse disposal combustors or incinerators
562212	Refuse disposal landfills
562111	Refuse hauling, local
484230	Refuse hauling, long-distance
315299	Regalia cut and sewn from purchased fabric (except apparel contractors)
315211	Regalia, men's and boys', cut and sew apparel contractors
315212	Regalia, women's, girls', and infants', cut and sew apparel contractors
325221	Regenerated cellulosic fibers manufacturing
925120	Regional planning and development program administration
621399	Registered nurses' (RNs) offices (e.g., centers, clinics)
334514	Registers, linear tallying, manufacturing
332323	Registers, metal air, manufacturing
561310	Registries, employment
335311	Regulating transformers, power system-type, manufacturing
926140	Regulation and inspection of agricultural products
926130	Regulation of utilities
335311	Regulators (i.e., electric transformers), feeder voltage, manufacturing
336322	Regulators, motor vehicle voltage for internal combustion engines manufacturing
335313	Regulators, power, manufacturing
421610	Regulators, voltage (except motor vehicle), wholesaling
624190	Rehabilitation agencies for offenders
622310	Rehabilitation hospitals (except alcoholism, drug addiction)
622210	Rehabilitation hospitals, alcoholism and drug addiction
624310	Rehabilitation job counseling and training, vocational
922150	Rehabilitation services, correctional, government
332618	Reinforcing mesh, concrete, made from purchased wire
524130	Reinsurance carriers
334515	Relays (except electrical, electronic), instrument, manufacturing
421610	Relays wholesaling
335314	Relays, electrical and electronic, manufacturing
624230	Relief services, disaster
624230	Relief services, emergency
323121	Religious book binding without printing
511130	Religious book publishers
511130	Religious book publishers and printing combined
451211	Religious book stores
323117	Religious books printing and binding without publishing
323117	Religious books printing without publishing
511130	Religious books publishing (i.e., establishments known as publishers)
337127	Religious furniture manufacturing
421210	Religious furniture wholesaling
453998	Religious goods (except books) stores
511120	Religious magazine and periodical publishers
511120	Religious magazine and periodical publishers and printing combined
511120	Religious magazine and periodical publishing (i.e., establishments known as publishers)
323112	Religious magazines and periodicals flexographic printing without publishing
323111	Religious magazines and periodicals gravure printing without publishing
323110	Religious magazines and periodicals lithographic (offset) printing without publishing
323119	Religious magazines and periodicals printing (except flexographic, gravure, lithographic, screen) without publishing
323113	Religious magazines and periodicals screen printing without publishing
813110	Religious organizations
421490	Religious supplies wholesaling
311421	Relishes canning
562910	Remediation and clean up of contaminated buildings, mine sites, soil, or ground water
562910	Remediation services, environmental
422310	Remnants, piece goods, wholesaling
233310	Remodeling industrial buildings
233320	Remodeling nonresidential (except industrial) buildings
233220	Remodeling residential (except single family) buildings
233210	Remodeling single family buildings
334290	Remote control units (e.g., garage door, television) manufacturing
541360	Remote sensing geophysical surveying services
213112	Removal of condensate gasoline from field gathering lines on a contract basis
213113	Removal of overburden for coal mining on a contract basis
213114	Removal of overburden for metal mining on a contract basis
213115	Removal of overburden for nonmetallic minerals mining (except fuels) on a contract basis
562920	Removal of recyclable materials from a waste stream
621492	Renal dialysis centers and clinics
311613	Rendering animals (carrion) for feed
311613	Rendering fats
311613	Rendering plants
422990	Rennets wholesaling
233310	Renovating industrial buildings
233320	Renovating nonresidential (except industrial) buildings
233220	Renovating residential (except single family) buildings
233210	Renovating single family buildings
926150	Rent control agencies
532310	Rent-all centers
******	Rental — see type of article or property being rented
531210	Renting real estate for others (i.e. agents, brokers)
541611	Reorganizational consulting services
522294	Repackaging loans for sale to others (i.e., private conduits)
******	Repair — see type of article being repaired
323121	Repairing books
233310	Repairing industrial buildings
233320	Repairing nonresidential (except industrial) buildings
233220	Repairing residential (except single family) building
233210	Repairing single family buildings
334210	Repeater and transceiver equipment, carrier line, manufacturing
711110	Repertory companies, theatrical
322231	Report covers made from purchased paper or paperboard
711510	Reporters, independent (freelance)
561491	Repossession services

Reproduction—Riveting

Code	Description
512199	Reproduction of motion picture films for theatrical distribution
115210	Reproductive flushing services for animals
621410	Reproductive health services centers
561439	Reprographic services
712130	Reptile exhibits, live
321912	Resawing purchased lumber
621910	Rescue services, air
621910	Rescue services, medical
513340	Resellers, satellite telecommunication
513330	Resellers, telecommunication (except satellite)
325411	Reserplnes (i.e., basic chemicals) manufacturing
561599	Reservation (e.g., airline, car rental, hotel, restaurant) services
522320	Reserve and liquidity services (except central bank)
234990	Reservoir construction
721310	Residence clubs, organizational
531110	Residential building rental or leasing
561720	Residential cleaning services
721310	Residential clubs
233220	Residential construction (except single family)
233210	Residential construction, single family
623220	Residential group homes for the emotionally disturbed
531110	Residential hotel rental or leasing
531311	Residential property managing
531210	Residential real estate agencies
531210	Residential real estate agents' offices
531210	Residential real estate brokerages
531210	Residential real estate brokers' offices
531311	Residential real estate property managers' offices
531190	Residential trailer parks
211112	Residue gas production
326192	Resilient floor coverings (e.g., sheet, tile) manufacturing
235520	Resilient flooring construction contractors
325211	Resins, plastics (except custom compounding purchased resins), manufacturing
422610	Resins, plastics, wholesaling
422690	Resins, synthetic rubber, wholesaling
334515	Resistance measuring equipment manufacturing
334513	Resistance thermometers and bulbs, industrial process-type, manufacturing
333992	Resistance welding equipment manufacturing
334415	Resistors, electronic, manufacturing
421690	Resistors, electronic, wholesaling
335312	Resolvers manufacturing
334516	Resonance instruments (i.e., laboratory-type) manufacturing
334419	Resonant reed devices, electronic, manufacturing
325192	Resorcinol manufacturing
721120	Resort hotels with casinos
721110	Resort hotels without casinos
334510	Respiratory analysis equipment, electromedical, manufacturing
339113	Respiratory protection mask manufacturing
621399	Respiratory therapists' offices (e.g., centers, clinics)
623110	Rest homes with nursing care
623312	Rest homes without nursing care
561720	Rest room cleaning services
812990	Rest room operation

Code	Description
813910	Restaurant associations
233320	Restaurant construction
421440	Restaurant equipment (except furniture) wholesaling
337127	Restaurant furniture (e.g., carts, chairs, foodwagons, tables) manufacturing
421210	Restaurant furniture wholesaling
561720	Restaurant kitchen cleaning services
492210	Restaurant meals delivery services (i.e., independent delivery services)
722211	Restaurants, carryout
722211	Restaurants, fast food
722110	Restaurants, full service
811420	Restoration and repair of antique furniture
811121	Restoration shops, antique and classic automotive
339113	Restraints, patient, manufacturing
561410	Resume writing services
234110	Resurfacing streets and highways
******	Retail — see type of dealer, shop, or store
333997	Retail scales (e.g., butcher, delicatessen, produce) manufacturing
813910	Retailers' associations
235710	Retaining wall, concrete, construction contractors
235410	Retaining wall, masonary (i.e., brick, stone), construction contractors
325998	Retarders (e.g., flameproofing agents, mildewproofing agents) manufacturing
339112	Retinoscopes (except electromedical) manufacturing
334510	Retinoscopes, electromedical, manufacturing
813410	Retirement associations, social
623311	Retirement communities, continuing care
623110	Retirement homes with nursing care
623312	Retirement homes without nursing care
531110	Retirement hotel rental or leasing
525110	Retirement pension plans
332420	Retorts, heavy gauge metal, manufacturing
339112	Retractors, medical, manufacturing
326211	Retreading materials, tire, manufacturing
326212	Retreading tires
813110	Retreat houses, religious
115114	Retting flax
811420	Reupholstery shops, furniture
522292	Reverse mortgage lending
234990	Revetment construction
332994	Revolvers manufacturing
235950	Revolving door construction contractors
213111	Reworking oil and gas wells on a contract basis
331419	Rhenium refining, primary
335931	Rheostats (i.e., dimmer switches), current carrying wiring device, manufacturing
334419	Rheostats, electronic, manufacturing
335314	Rheostats, industrial control, manufacturing
212299	Rhodium mining and/or beneficiating
212299	Rhodochrosite mining and/or beneficiating
111219	Rhubarb farming, field and seed production
111419	Rhubarb, grown under cover
339944	Ribbons (e.g., cash register, printer, typewriter), inked, manufacturing
314999	Ribbons made from purchased fabrics
313221	Ribbons made in narrow woven fabric mills

Code	Description
313230	Ribbons made in nonwoven fabric mills
339944	Ribbons, inked, manufacturing
422120	Ribbons, inked, wholesaling
422310	Ribbons, textile, wholesaling
111160	Rice (except wild rice) farming, field and seed production
311212	Rice bran, flour, and meals, manufacturing
311230	Rice breakfast foods manufacturing
311212	Rice cleaning and polishing
115114	Rice drying
311212	Rice flour manufacturing
311213	Rice malt manufacturing
311212	Rice meal manufacturing
311212	Rice milling
311999	Rice mixes (i.e., uncooked and packaged with other ingredients) made from purchased rice and dry ingredients
311423	Rice mixes (i.e., uncooked and packaged with other ingredients) made in dehydration plants
311212	Rice mixes (i.e., uncooked and packaged with other ingredients) made in rice mills
311221	Rice starches manufacturing
311212	Rice, brewer's, manufacturing
311212	Rice, brown, manufacturing
422490	Rice, polished, wholesaling
422510	Rice, unpolished, wholesaling
315211	Riding clothes, men's and boys', cut and sew apparel contractors
315228	Riding clothes, men's and boys', cut and sewn from purchased fabric (except apparel contractors)
315212	Riding clothes, women's and girls', cut and sew apparel contractors
315239	Riding clothes, women's, misses', and girls', cut and sewn from purchased fabric (except apparel contractors)
713990	Riding clubs, recreational
316999	Riding crops manufacturing
611620	Riding instruction academies or schools
713990	Riding stables
713990	Rifle clubs, recreational
332994	Rifles (except recoilless, toy) manufacturing
332994	Rifles, BB and pellet, manufacturing
332994	Rifles, pneumatic, manufacturing
332995	Rifles, recoilless, manufacturing
339932	Rifles, toy, manufacturing
333512	Rifling machines, metalworking, manufacturing
213112	Rig skidding, oil and gas field, on a contract basis
336399	Rims, automotive, truck, and bus wheel, manufacturing
336311	Rings, piston, manufacturing
713940	Rinks, ice or roller skating
212319	Riprap (except granite, limestone) preparation plants
212319	Riprap (except limestone and granite) mining or quarrying
212313	Riprap, granite, mining or quarrying
212313	Riprap, granite, preparation plants
212312	Riprap, limestone, mining or quarrying
212312	Riprap, limestone, preparation plants
483211	River freight transportation
483212	River passenger transportation
713990	River rafting, recreational
713210	Riverboat casinos
333991	Riveting guns, handheld power-driven, manufacturing
333513	Riveting machines, metalworking, manufacturing

Code	Description
332722	Rivets, metal, manufacturing
325320	Roach poisons manufacturing
234110	Road (except elevated) construction
711110	Road companies, theatrical
421810	Road construction and maintenance machinery wholesaling
234120	Road elevated (e.g., bridges) construction
324199	Road oils made from refined petroleum
324110	Road oils made in petroleum refineries
311911	Roasted nuts and seeds manufacturing
112320	Roaster chicken production
335211	Roasters (i.e., cooking appliances), household-type electric, manufacturing
311920	Roasting coffee
333294	Roasting machinery manufacturing
315291	Robes, lounging, infants', cut and sewn from purchased fabric (except apparel contractors)
315192	Robes, lounging, made in apparel knitting mills
315211	Robes, lounging, men's and boys', cut and sew apparel contractors
315221	Robes, lounging, men's and boys', cut and sewn from purchased fabric (except apparel contractors)
315212	Robes, lounging, women's, girls', and infants', cut and sew apparel contractors
315231	Robes, lounging, women's, misses', and girls', cut and sewn from purchased fabric (except apparel contractors)
333120	Rock crushing machinery, portable, manufacturing
333131	Rock crushing machinery, stationary, manufacturing
333132	Rock drill bits, oil and gas field-type, manufacturing
333120	Rock drills, construction and surface mining-type, manufacturing
333131	Rock drills, underground mining-type, manufacturing
711130	Rock musical artists, independent
711130	Rock musical groups
234990	Rock removal, underwater, construction
212393	Rock salt mining and/or beneficiating
336312	Rocker arms and parts, automotive and truck gasoline engine, manufacturing
337122	Rockers (except upholstered), wood, manufacturing
337121	Rockers, upholstered, manufacturing
332313	Rocket casings, fabricated metal work, manufacturing
336412	Rocket engines, aircraft, manufacturing
336415	Rocket engines, guided missile, manufacturing
332995	Rocket launchers manufacturing
336414	Rockets (guided missiles), space and military, complete, manufacturing
332993	Rockets, ammunition (except guided missiles, pyrotechnic), manufacturing
114111	Rockfish fishing
339932	Rocking horses manufacturing
331316	Rod made by extruding purchased aluminum
331319	Rod made by rolling purchased aluminum
333516	Rod rolling mill machinery, metalworking, manufacturing
331316	Rod, aluminum, made in integrated secondary smelting and extruding mills
331319	Rod, aluminum, made in integrated secondary smelting and rolling mills

Code	Description
331421	Rod, copper and copper alloy, made from purchased copper or in integrated secondary smelting and rolling, drawing or extruding plants
326130	Rod, laminated plastics, manufacturing
331491	Rod, nonferrous metals (except aluminum, copper), made from purchased metals or scrap
326121	Rod, nonrigid plastics, manufacturing
325320	Rodent poisons manufacturing
325320	Rodenticides manufacturing
711310	Rodeo managers with facilities
711320	Rodeo managers without facilities
711310	Rodeo organizers with facilities
711320	Rodeo organizers without facilities
711310	Rodeo promoters with facilities
711320	Rodeo promoters without facilities
339920	Rods and rod parts, fishing, manufacturing
326299	Rods, hard rubber, manufacturing
331111	Rods, iron or steel, made in steel mills
421510	Rods, metal (except precious), wholesaling
334519	Rods, surveyor's, manufacturing
332991	Roller bearings manufacturing
711211	Roller hockey clubs, professional or semiprofessional
316110	Roller leather manufacturing
339920	Roller skates manufacturing
713940	Roller skating rinks
333120	Rollers, road construction and maintenance machinery, manufacturing
321999	Rollers, wood, manufacturing
332321	Rolling doors for industrial buildings and warehouses, metal, manufacturing
333516	Rolling mill machinery and equipment, metalworking, manufacturing
333516	Rolling mill roll machines manufacturing
331511	Rolling mill rolls, iron, manufacturing
331513	Rolling mill rolls, steel, manufacturing
321999	Rolling pins, wood, manufacturing
336510	Rolling stock, railroad, rebuilding
311812	Rolls and buns (including frozen) made in commercial bakeries
326299	Rolls and roll coverings, rubber (e.g., industrial, papermill, painters', steelmill) manufacturing
111219	Romaine lettuce farming, field and seed production
315291	Rompers, infants', cut and sewn from purchased fabric (except apparel contractors)
315212	Rompers, women's, girls', and infants', cut and sew apparel contractors
332322	Roof deck, sheet metal, manufacturing
235610	Roof spraying, painting or coating, construction contractors
321214	Roof trusses, wood, manufacturing
326299	Roofing (i.e., single ply rubber membrane) manufacturing
324122	Roofing cements, asphalt, made from purchased asphaltic materials
324122	Roofing coatings made from purchased asphaltic materials
235610	Roofing construction contractors
324122	Roofing felts made from purchased asphaltic materials
444190	Roofing material dealers
421330	Roofing materials (except wood) wholesaling
421310	Roofing materials, wood, wholesaling
327123	Roofing tile, clay, manufacturing
327390	Roofing tile, concrete, manufacturing
332322	Roofing, sheet metal, manufacturing

Code	Description
333415	Room air-conditioners manufacturing
421620	Room air-conditioners wholesaling
337122	Room dividers, wood household-type, manufacturing
333414	Room heaters (except portable electric) manufacturing
335211	Room heaters, portable electric, manufacturing
334512	Room thermostats manufacturing
721310	Rooming and boarding houses
325320	Root removing chemicals manufacturing
311221	Root starches manufacturing
332999	Rope fittings manufacturing
332618	Rope, wire, made from purchased wire
314991	Ropes (except wire rope) manufacturing
421840	Ropes (except wire rope) wholesaling
313111	Ropes, hemp, made from purchased fiber
421510	Ropes, wire (except insulated), wholesaling
339911	Rosaries and other small religious articles, precious metal, manufacturing
212291	Roscoelite (vanadium hydromica) mining and/or beneficiating
111421	Rose bush growing
325211	Rosins (i.e., modified resins) manufacturing
325191	Rosins made by distillation of pine gum or pine wood
422690	Rosins wholesaling
333111	Rotary hoes manufacturing
333111	Rotary tillers, farm-type, manufacturing
334514	Rotary type meters, consumption registering, manufacturing
325320	Rotenone insecticides manufacturing
323111	Rotogravure printing
323122	Rotogravure printing plates and cylinders preparation services
335312	Rotor retainers and housings manufacturing
335312	Rotors (i.e., for motors) manufacturing
325620	Rouge, cosmetic, manufacturing
321920	Round stave baskets (e.g., fruit, vegetable) manufacturing
321912	Rounds or rungs, furniture, hardwood, manufacturing
331111	Rounds, tube, steel, made in steel mills
421990	Roundwood wholesaling
213112	Roustabout mining services, on a contract basis
333991	Routers, handheld power-driven, manufacturing
333292	Roving machinery for textiles manufacturing
233210	Row house single family construction
532292	Rowboat rental
336612	Rowboats manufacturing
713990	Rowing clubs, recreational
112910	Royal jelly production, bees
326220	Rubber and plastics belts and hoses (without fittings) manufacturing
326299	Rubber bands manufacturing
325520	Rubber cements manufacturing
212324	Rubber clay mining and/or beneficiating
326192	Rubber floor coverings manufacturing
326291	Rubber goods, mechanical (i.e., extruded, lathe-cut, molded), manufacturing
421840	Rubber goods, mechanical (i.e., extruded, lathe-cut, molded), wholesaling
422210	Rubber goods, medical, wholesaling
325998	Rubber processing preparations (e.g., accelerators, stabilizers) manufacturing

Rubber scrap—Sandwiches

Code	Description
421930	Rubber scrap and scrap tires wholesaling
339943	Rubber stamps manufacturing
422120	Rubber stamps, wholesaling
313221	Rubber thread and yarns, fabric covered, manufacturing
333220	Rubber working machinery manufacturing
422990	Rubber, crude, wholesaling
325212	Rubber, synthetic, manufacturing
313320	Rubberizing purchased capes
313320	Rubberizing purchased cloaks
313320	Rubberizing purchased clothing
313320	Rubberizing purchased coats
313320	Rubberizing purchased textiles and apparel
212399	Rubbing stones mining and/or beneficiating
562111	Rubbish (i.e., nonhazardous solid waste) hauling, local
562111	Rubbish collection services
562213	Rubbish disposal combustors or incinerators
562212	Rubbish disposal landfills
484220	Rubbish hauling without collection or disposal, truck, local
484230	Rubbish hauling without collection or disposal, truck, long-distance
562119	Rubble hauling, local
562119	Rubble removal services
212399	Ruby mining and/or beneficiating
532299	Rug and carpet rental
561740	Rug cleaning plants
325612	Rug cleaning preparations manufacturing
561740	Rug cleaning services
442210	Rug stores
314110	Rugs and carpets made from textile materials
421220	Rugs wholesaling
321999	Rulers and rules (except slide), wood, manufacturing
332212	Rulers, metal, manufacturing
326199	Rulers, plastics, manufacturing
334519	Rules, slide, manufacturing
624221	Runaway youth shelters
488119	Runway maintenance services
485210	Rural bus services
324191	Rust arresting petroleum compounds made from refined petroleum
325998	Rust preventive preparations manufacturing
325612	Rust removers manufacturing
332812	Rustproofing metals and metal products for the trade
811198	Rustproofing shops, automotive
111219	Rutabaga farming, field and seed production
212299	Ruthenium ore mining and/or beneficiating
212299	Rutile mining and/or beneficiating
111199	Rye farming, field and seed production
311211	Rye flour manufacturing
311213	Rye malt manufacturing
111998	Ryegrass seed farming
325212	S-type rubber manufacturing
522294	SLMA (Student Loan Marketing Association)
114111	Sablefish fishing
325199	Saccharin manufacturing
325620	Sachet, scented, manufacturing
322224	Sacks, multiwall, made from purchased uncoated paper
422130	Sacks, paper, wholesaling
713990	Saddle horse rental services, recreational
325612	Saddle soaps manufacturing
321999	Saddle trees, wood, manufacturing
316110	Saddlery leather manufacturing
332999	Saddlery parts, metal, manufacturing
811430	Saddlery repair shops without retailing new saddlery
451110	Saddlery stores
422910	Saddlery wholesaling
316999	Saddles and parts, leather, manufacturing
332999	Safe deposit boxes and chests, metal, manufacturing
332999	Safe doors and linings, metal, manufacturing
332999	Safes, metal, manufacturing
421420	Safes, security, wholesaling
332911	Safety (i.e., pop-off) valves, industrial-type, manufacturing
316999	Safety belts, leather, manufacturing
541690	Safety consulting services
325920	Safety fuses, blasting, manufacturing
327215	Safety glass (including motor vehicle) made from purchased glass
339993	Safety pins manufacturing
332211	Safety razor blades manufacturing
332211	Safety razors manufacturing
111120	Safflower farming, field and seed production
311225	Safflower oil made from purchased oils
311223	Safflower oil made in crushing mills
441222	Sail boat dealers
339920	Sailboards manufacturing
336612	Sailboat building, not done in shipyards
532292	Sailboat rental
713930	Sailing clubs with marinas
713990	Sailing clubs without marinas
336611	Sailing ships, commercial, manufacturing
314912	Sails made from purchased fabrics
325181	Sal soda (i.e., washing soda) manufacturing
311423	Salad dressing mixes, dry, made in a dehydration plant
311942	Salad dressing mixes, dry, manufacturing
311941	Salad dressings manufacturing
422490	Salad dressings wholesaling
422490	Salad oils wholesaling
311991	Salads, fresh or refrigerated, manufacturing
422120	Sales books wholesaling
323116	Sales books, manifold, printing
522220	Sales financing
541613	Sales management consulting services
325199	Salicylic acid (except medicinal) manufacturing
325411	Salicylic acid, medicinal, uncompounded, manufacturing
212391	Salines (except common salt) mining and/or beneficiating
114111	Salmon fishing
233320	Salon construction
311421	Salsa canning
325998	Salt (except table) manufacturing
311942	Salt substitute manufacturing
213112	Salt water disposal systems, oil and gas field, on a contract basis
212393	Salt, common, mining and/or beneficiating
212393	Salt, rock, mining and/or beneficiating
311942	Salt, table, manufacturing
422490	Salt, table, wholesaling
311612	Salted meats made from purchased carcasses
311821	Saltines manufacturing
422210	Salts, bath, wholesaling
422690	Salts, industrial, wholesaling
334516	Sample analysis instruments (except medical) manufacturing
316991	Sample cases, all materials, manufacturing
334519	Sample changers, nuclear radiation, manufacturing
541870	Sample direct distribution services
323121	Samples and displays mounting
541910	Sampling services, statistical
421320	Sand (except industrial) wholesaling
212321	Sand and gravel quarrying (i.e., construction grade) and/or beneficiating
213112	Sand blasting pipelines on lease, oil and gas field on a contract basis
331524	Sand castings, aluminum, unfinished, manufacturing
331525	Sand castings, copper and copper-base alloy, unfinished, manufacturing
331528	Sand castings, nonferrous metals (except aluminum, copper), unfinished, manufacturing
484220	Sand hauling, local
484230	Sand hauling, long-distance
333120	Sand mixers manufacturing
212322	Sand, blast, quarrying and/or beneficiating
212321	Sand, construction grade, quarrying and/or beneficiating
212322	Sand, industrial (e.g., engine, filtration, glass grinding), quarrying and/or beneficiating
421840	Sand, industrial, wholesaling
316219	Sandals, children's (except rubber, plastics), manufacturing
316213	Sandals, men's footwear (except rubber, plastics), manufacturing
316211	Sandals, plastics or plastics soled fabric upper, manufacturing
316211	Sandals, rubber or rubber soled fabric upper, manufacturing
316214	Sandals, women's footwear (except rubber, plastics), manufacturing
332813	Sandblasting metals and metal products for the trade
235990	Sandblasting of building exteriors construction contractors
333991	Sanders, handheld power-driven, manufacturing
333319	Sanding machines, floor, manufacturing
333210	Sanding machines, woodworking-type, stationary, manufacturing
333291	Sandpaper making machines manufacturing
327910	Sandpaper manufacturing
212319	Sandstone crushed and broken stone mining
212311	Sandstone mining or quarrying
212399	Sandstone, bituminous, mining and/or beneficiating
722211	Sandwich shops, limited service
311612	Sandwich spreads, meat, made from purchased carcasses
311941	Sandwich spreads, salad dressing based, manufacturing
335211	Sandwich toasters and grills, household-type electric, manufacturing
422490	Sandwiches wholesaling
311991	Sandwiches, fresh (i.e., assembled and packaged for wholesale market), manufacturing

Code	Description
322212	Sanitary food container, folding, made from purchased paperboard
422130	Sanitary food containers (e.g., disposable plastics, paper, paperboard) wholesaling
322215	Sanitary food containers (except folding) made from purchased paper or paperboard
562212	Sanitary landfills
322291	Sanitary napkins and tampons made from purchased paper or textile fiber
322121	Sanitary napkins and tampons made in paper mills
322121	Sanitary paper products (except newsprint, uncoated groundwood) made in paper mills
422130	Sanitary paper products wholesaling
322121	Sanitary paper stock manufacturing
322291	Sanitary products made from purchased sanitary paper stock
322121	Sanitary products made in paper mills
332998	Sanitary ware (e.g., bathtubs, lavatories, sinks), metal, manufacturing
421720	Sanitary ware, china or enameled iron, wholesaling
541620	Sanitation consulting services
926130	Sanitation districts, nonoperating
924110	Sanitation engineering agencies, government
212399	Sapphire mining and/or beneficiating
325222	Saran (i.e., polyvinylidene chloride) fibers and filaments manufacturing
332612	Sash balance springs made from purchased wire
332321	Sash, door and window, metal, manufacturing
321911	Sash, door and window, wood and covered wood, manufacturing
316991	Satchels, all materials, manufacturing
334220	Satellite antennas manufacturing
334220	Satellite communications equipment manufacturing
513220	Satellite master antenna television service (SMATV)
513111	Satellite radio networks
513340	Satellite telecommunication carriers
513340	Satellite telecommunication resellers
513390	Satellite telemetry operations on a contract or fee basis
513220	Satellite television distribution systems
513210	Satellite television networks
513390	Satellite tracking stations on a contract or fee basis
325131	Satin white pigments manufacturing
335311	Saturable transformers manufacturing
324122	Saturated felts made from purchased paper
322121	Saturated felts made in paper mills
311423	Sauce mixes, dry, made in dehydration plants
311942	Sauce mixes, dry, manufacturing
311941	Sauces (except tomato based) manufacturing
311941	Sauces for meat (except tomato based) manufacturing
311941	Sauces for seafood (except tomato based) manufacturing
311941	Sauces for vegetable (except tomato based) manufacturing
311421	Sauces, tomato-based, canning
311421	Sauerkraut manufacturing
335211	Sauna heaters, electric, manufacturing
321992	Sauna rooms, prefabricated, wood, manufacturing

Code	Description
812199	Saunas
311612	Sausage and similar cased products made from purchased carcasses
422490	Sausage casings wholesaling
311612	Sausage casings, collagen, made from purchased hides
311611	Sausage casings, natural, produced in slaughtering plant
326121	Sausage casings, plastics, manufacturing
522120	Savings and loan associations (S&L)
524113	Savings bank life insurance carriers, direct
522120	Savings banks
332213	Saw blades, all types, manufacturing
811411	Saw repair and maintenance (except sawmills) without retailing new saws
321113	Sawdust and shavings (i.e., sawmill byproducts) manufacturing
422990	Sawdust wholesaling
321999	Sawdust, regrinding
321113	Sawed lumber made in sawmills
321912	Sawed lumber, resawing purchased lumber
333512	Sawing machines, metalworking, manufacturing
333210	Sawmill equipment manufacturing
532490	Sawmill machinery rental or leasing
421830	Sawmill machinery, equipment, and supplies wholesaling
321113	Sawmills
333210	Saws, bench and table, power-driven, woodworking-type, manufacturing
332213	Saws, hand, nonpowered, manufacturing
333991	Saws, handheld power-driven, manufacturing
339112	Saws, surgical, manufacturing
339992	Saxophones and parts manufacturing
235990	Scaffolding construction contractors
532490	Scaffolding rental or leasing
421810	Scaffolding wholesaling
332323	Scaffolds, metal, manufacturing
334519	Scalers, nuclear radiation, manufacturing
333997	Scales (except laboratory-type) manufacturing
339111	Scales and balances, laboratory-type, manufacturing
339111	Scales, laboratory, manufacturing
114112	Scallop fishing
812199	Scalp treating services
333210	Scarfing machines, woodworking-type, manufacturing
333516	Scarfing units, rolling mill machinery, metalworking, manufacturing
333120	Scarifiers, road, manufacturing
325132	Scarlet 2 R lake manufacturing
315191	Scarves made in apparel knitting mills
315211	Scarves, men's and boys', cut and sew apparel contractors
315993	Scarves, men's and boys', cut and sewn from purchased fabric (except apparel contractors)
315212	Scarves, women's, girls', and infants', cut and sew apparel contractors
315999	Scarves, women's, misses', and girls', cut and sewn from purchased fabric (except apparel contractors)
336350	Scattershield, engine, manufacturing
711510	Scenery designers, independent theatrical
532490	Scenery, theatrical, rental or leasing
487990	Scenic and sightseeing excursions, aerial
487110	Scenic and sightseeing excursions, land
487210	Scenic and sightseeing excursions, water

Code	Description
481112	Scheduled air freight carriers
481112	Scheduled air freight transportation
481111	Scheduled air passenger carriers
481111	Scheduled air passenger transportation
212299	Scheelite mining and/or beneficiating
313222	Schiffli machine embroideries manufacturing
333292	Schiffli machinery manufacturing
212319	Schist, mica, crushed and broken stone, mining and/or beneficiating
212311	Schist, mica, mining or quarrying
511120	Scholarly journal publishers
511120	Scholarly journal publishers and printing combined
511120	Scholarly journal publishing (i.e., establishments known as publishers)
323112	Scholarly journals flexographic printing without publishing
323111	Scholarly journals gravure printing without publishing
323110	Scholarly journals lithographic (offset) printing without publishing
323119	Scholarly journals printing (except flexographic, gravure, lithographic, screen) without publishing
323113	Scholarly journals screen printing without publishing
813211	Scholarship trusts (i.e., grantmaking, charitable trust foundations)
511120	Scholastic magazine and periodical publishers
511120	Scholastic magazine and periodical publishers and printing combined
511120	Scholastic magazine and periodical publishing (i.e., establishments known as publishers)
323112	Scholastic magazines and periodicals flexographic printing without publishing
323111	Scholastic magazines and periodicals gravure printing without publishing
323110	Scholastic magazines and periodicals lithographic (offset) printing without publishing
323119	Scholastic magazines and periodicals printing (except flexographic, gravure, lithographic, screen) without publishing
323113	Scholastic magazines and periodicals screen printing without publishing
611110	School boards, elementary and secondary
511130	School book publishers
511130	School book publishers and printing combined
511130	School book publishing (i.e., establishments known as publishers)
323117	School books printing and binding without publishing
323117	School books printing without publishing
233320	School building construction
532120	School bus rental or leasing
485410	School bus services
336211	School buses assembling on purchased chassis
421110	School buses wholesaling
611110	School districts, elementary or secondary
421490	School equipment and supplies (except books, furniture) wholesaling
337127	School furniture manufacturing
421210	School furniture wholesaling
541921	School photography (i.e., portrait photography) services
453210	School supply stores

School—Securities

Code	Description
323121	School text books binding without printing
511130	School textbook publishers
511130	School textbook publishers and printing combined
511130	School textbook publishing (i.e., establishments known as publishers)
323117	School textbooks printing and binding without publishing
323117	School textbooks printing without publishing
611110	Schools for the handicapped, elementary or secondary
611110	Schools for the mentally retarded (except preschool, job training, vocational rehabilitation)
611110	Schools for the physically disabled, elementary or secondary
611512	Schools, aviation
611511	Schools, barber
611511	Schools, beauty
611410	Schools, business, not offering academic degrees
611310	Schools, correspondence, college level
611511	Schools, cosmetology
611610	Schools, drama (except academic)
611110	Schools, elementary
611210	Schools, junior college
611210	Schools, junior college vocational
611630	Schools, language
611310	Schools, medical
611610	Schools, music (except academic)
611310	Schools, professional (colleges or universities)
611110	Schools, secondary
611620	Schools, sports instruction
712110	Science and technology museums
339932	Science kits (e.g., chemistry sets, microscopes, natural science sets), manufacturing
327215	Scientific apparatus glass made from purchased glass
813920	Scientific associations
327215	Scientific glassware made from purchased glass
327212	Scientific glassware, pressed or blown, made in glass making plants
421490	Scientific instruments wholesaling
421490	Scientific laboratory equipment wholesaling
334519	Scintillation detectors manufacturing
335211	Scissors, electric, manufacturing
332211	Scissors, nonelectric, manufacturing
332212	Scoops, metal (except kitchen-type), manufacturing
321999	Scoops, wood, manufacturing
339932	Scooters, children's, manufacturing
339950	Scoreboards manufacturing
212399	Scoria mining and/or beneficiating
313312	Scouring and combing textile fibers
325611	Scouring cleansers (e.g., pastes, powders) manufacturing
332999	Scouring pads, soap impregnated, manufacturing
813410	Scouting organizations
421930	Scrap materials wholesaling
323118	Scrapbooks and refills manufacturing
422120	Scrapbooks wholesaling
333131	Scraper loaders, underground mining-type, manufacturing
333120	Scrapers, construction-type, manufacturing
332321	Screen doors, metal frame, manufacturing

Code	Description
323122	Screen for printing, preparation services
323113	Screen printing (except manifold business forms, printing grey goods, printing books)
323113	Screen printing apparel and textile products (e.g. caps, napkins, placemats, T-shirts, towels)
313311	Screen printing broadwoven fabric grey goods
325910	Screen process inks manufacturing
333999	Screening and sifting machinery for general industrial use manufacturing
333120	Screening machinery, portable, manufacturing
333131	Screening machinery, stationary, manufacturing
212399	Screening peat
212113	Screening plants, anthracite
212111	Screening plants, bituminous coal or lignite
326199	Screening, window, plastics, manufacturing
711510	Screenplay writers, independent
313312	Screenprinting fabric grey goods (except broadwoven) and textile products (except apparel)
334419	Screens for liquid crystal display (LCD) manufacturing
332321	Screens, door and window, metal frame, manufacturing
321911	Screens, door and window, wood framed, manufacturing
333315	Screens, projection (i.e., motion picture, overhead, slide), manufacturing
421310	Screens, window and door, wholesaling
333512	Screw and nut slotting machines, metalworking, manufacturing
333922	Screw conveyors manufacturing
332212	Screw drivers, nonelectric, manufacturing
332722	Screw eyes, metal, manufacturing
333518	Screwdowns and boxes machinery, metal, manufacturing
333991	Screwdrivers and nut drivers, handheld power-driven, manufacturing
333518	Screwdriving machines manufacturing
332212	Screwjacks manufacturing
332722	Screws, metal, manufacturing
711510	Script writers, independent
339920	Scuba diving equipment manufacturing
611620	Scuba instruction, camps, or schools
711510	Sculptors, independent
611610	Sculpture instruction
327420	Sculptures (e.g., gypsum, plaster of paris) manufacturing
327112	Sculptures, architectural, clay, manufacturing
332212	Scythes manufacturing
212399	Scythestones mining and/or beneficiating
114111	Sea bass fishing
114111	Sea herring fishing
713990	Sea kayaking, recreational
111998	Sea plant agriculture
114111	Sea trout fishing
114112	Sea urchin fishing
422460	Seafood (except canned, packaged frozen) wholesaling
311711	Seafood and seafood products canning
311711	Seafood and seafood products curing
311712	Seafood dinners, frozen, manufacturing
445220	Seafood markets
311712	Seafood products, fresh prepared, manufacturing

Code	Description
311712	Seafood products, frozen, manufacturing
422490	Seafood, canned, wholesaling
311712	Seafood, fresh prepared, manufacturing
311712	Seafood, frozen, manufacturing
422420	Seafoods, packaged frozen, wholesaling
339943	Seal presses (e.g., notary), hand operated, manufacturing
422690	Sealants wholesaling
335110	Sealed beam automotive light bulbs manufacturing
325520	Sealing compounds for pipe threads and joints manufacturing
421840	Seals wholesaling
339991	Seals, grease or oil, manufacturing
333992	Seam welding equipment manufacturing
334511	Search and detection systems and instruments manufacturing
514199	Search services, information, on a contract or fee basis
335129	Searchlights, electric and nonelectric, manufacturing
453220	Seasonal and holiday decoration stores
721110	Seasonal hotels
561730	Seasonal property maintenance services (i.e., snow plowing in winter, landscaping during other seasons)
311942	Seasoning salt manufacturing
336360	Seat belts, motor vehicle and aircraft, manufacturing
421120	Seat covers, automotive, wholesaling
321999	Seat covers, rattan, manufacturing
326150	Seat cushions, foam plastics (except polystyrene), manufacturing
316999	Seatbelts, leather, manufacturing
336360	Seats for public conveyances, manufacturing
336360	Seats, railroad, manufacturing
321999	Seats, toilet, wood, manufacturing
488310	Seaway operation
111998	Seaweed farming
114119	Seaweed gathering
311711	Seaweed processing (e.g., dulse)
325199	Sebacic acid esters manufacturing
325199	Sebacic acid manufacturing
611630	Second language instruction
453310	Second-hand merchandise stores
522294	Secondary market financing (i.e., buying, pooling, repackaging loans for sale to others)
331492	Secondary refining of nonferrous metals (except aluminum, copper)
611110	Secondary schools offering both academic and technical courses
331492	Secondary smelting of nonferrous metals (except aluminum, copper)
611410	Secretarial schools
561410	Secretarial services
332311	Sections for prefabricated metal buildings manufacturing
321992	Sections, prefabricated wood building, manufacturing
523120	Securities brokerages
523120	Securities brokers' offices
523991	Securities custodians
523110	Securities dealers (i.e., acting as a principal in dealing securities to investors)
523110	Securities dealing (i.e., acting as a principal in dealing securities to investors)

Code	Description
523110	Securities distributing (i.e., acting as a principal in dealing securities to investors)
523210	Securities exchanges
523120	Securities floor brokers
523110	Securities floor traders (i.e., acting as a principal in dealing securities to investors)
523110	Securities flotation companies
523999	Securities holders' protective services
523110	Securities originating (i.e., acting as a principal in dealing securities to investors)
926150	Securities regulation commissions
523110	Securities trading (i.e., acting as a principal in dealing securities to investors)
523999	Securities transfer agencies
523110	Securities underwriting
561621	Security alarm systems sales combined with installation, maintenance, or monitoring services
541690	Security consulting services
561612	Security guard services
561612	Security patrol services
421420	Security safes wholesaling
561621	Security system monitoring services
421610	Security systems wholesaling
325412	Sedative preparations manufacturing
212399	Sedge peat mining and/or beneficiating
333131	Sedimentary mineral machinery manufacturing
314911	Seed bags made from purchased woven or knitted materials
115112	Seed bed preparing
115114	Seed cleaning
322232	Seed packets made from purchased paper
541380	Seed testing laboratories or services
325320	Seed treatment preparations manufacturing
333111	Seeders, farm-type, manufacturing
333112	Seeders, lawn and garden-type, manufacturing
115112	Seeding crops
561730	Seeding lawns
422450	Seeds (e.g., canned, roasted, salted) wholesaling
422910	Seeds (e.g., field, flower, garden) wholesaling
311911	Seeds, snack (e.g., canned, cooked, roasted, salted) manufacturing
541360	Seismic geophysical surveying services
213112	Seismograph exploration (except surveying) for oil and gas on a contract basis
334519	Seismographs manufacturing
334519	Seismometers manufacturing
334519	Seismoscopes manufacturing
212399	Selenite mining and/or beneficiating
331491	Selenium bar, rod, sheet, strip, and tubing made from purchased metals or scrap
325188	Selenium compounds, not specified elsewhere by process, manufacturing
325188	Selenium dioxide manufacturing
331492	Selenium recovering from scrap and/or alloying purchased metals
331419	Selenium refining, primary
624190	Self-help organizations (except for disabled persons, the elderly, persons diagnosed with mental retardation)

Code	Description
624120	Self-help organizations for disabled persons, the elderly, and persons diagnosed with mental retardation
624110	Self-help organizations, youth
525190	Self-insurance funds (except employee benefit funds)
811192	Self-service carwash
812310	Self-service drycleaners and laundries
531130	Self-storage unit rental or leasing
531130	Self-storage warehousing
531210	Selling real estate for others (i.e., agents, brokers)
115210	Semen collection
422590	Semen, bovine, wholesaling
421510	Semi-finished metal products wholesaling
336212	Semi-trailer manufacturing
532120	Semi-trailer rental or leasing
212111	Semianthracite surface mining and/or beneficiating
212112	Semianthracite underground mining or mining and beneficiating
212111	Semibituminous coal surface mining and/or beneficiating
212112	Semibituminous coal underground mining or mining and beneficiating
333295	Semiconductor assembly and packaging machinery manufacturing
335999	Semiconductor battery chargers manufacturing
334413	Semiconductor circuit networks (i.e., solid-state integrated circuits) manufacturing
334413	Semiconductor devices manufacturing
421690	Semiconductor devices wholesaling
334413	Semiconductor dice and wafers manufacturing
335999	Semiconductor high-voltage power supplies manufacturing
333295	Semiconductor making machinery manufacturing
334413	Semiconductor memory chips manufacturing
334515	Semiconductor test equipment manufacturing
333618	Semidiesel engines manufacturing
611110	Seminaries, below university grade
611310	Seminaries, theological, offering baccalaureate or graduate degrees
212399	Semiprecious stones mining and/or beneficiating
711211	Semiprofessional baseball clubs
711211	Semiprofessional football clubs
711211	Semiprofessional sports clubs
331511	Semisteel foundries
311211	Semolina flour manufacturing
624120	Senior citizens activity centers
813311	Senior citizens advocacy organizations
624120	Senior citizens centers
485991	Senior citizens transportation services
623312	Senior citizens' homes without nursing care
325992	Sensitized cloth or paper (e.g., blueprint, photographic) manufacturing
333315	Sensitometers, photographic, manufacturing
334510	Sentinel, cardiac, manufacturing
235110	Septic system construction contractors
562991	Septic tank cleaning services
562991	Septic tank pumping (i.e., cleaning) services
421390	Septic tanks (except concrete) wholesaling
421320	Septic tanks, concrete, wholesaling

Code	Description
332420	Septic tanks, heavy gauge metal, manufacturing
326199	Septic tanks, plastics or fiberglass, manufacturing
334512	Sequencing controls for electric heating equipment manufacturing
335999	Series capacitors (except electronic) manufacturing
212319	Serpentine crushed and broken stone mining and/or beneficiating
212311	Serpentine mining or quarrying
325414	Serums (except diagnostic substances) manufacturing
315211	Service apparel, washable, men's and boys', cut and sew apparel contractors
315225	Service apparel, washable, men's and boys', cut and sewn from purchased fabric (except apparel contractors)
315212	Service apparel, washable, women's, cut and sew apparel contractors
315239	Service apparel, washable, women's, misses' and girls', cut and sewn from purchased fabric (except apparel contractors)
421850	Service establishment equipment and supplies wholesaling
813910	Service industries associations
811310	Service machinery and equipment repair and maintenance services
561720	Service station cleaning and degreasing services
233320	Service station construction
447190	Service stations, gasoline
213111	Service well drilling on a contract basis
213112	Servicing oil and gas wells on a contract basis
337124	Serving carts, metal household-type, manufacturing
337122	Serving carts, wood household-type, manufacturing
335312	Servomotors manufacturing
111120	Sesame farming, field and seed production
711510	Set designers, independent theatrical
541191	Settlement offices, real estate
322213	Setup (i.e., not shipped flat) boxes made from purchased paperboard
322130	Setup boxboard stock manufacturing
234910	Sewage collection and disposal line construction
221320	Sewage disposal plants
333319	Sewage treatment equipment manufacturing
234910	Sewage treatment plant construction
221320	Sewage treatment plants or facilities
562998	Sewer cleaning and rodding services
562998	Sewer cleanout services
234910	Sewer construction
235110	Sewer hookup construction contractors
327123	Sewer pipe and fittings, clay, manufacturing
331511	Sewer pipe, cast iron, manufacturing
327332	Sewer pipe, concrete, manufacturing
221320	Sewer systems
234910	Sewer, water and pipeline construction management firms
422310	Sewing accessories wholesaling
339999	Sewing and mending kits assembling
316993	Sewing cases (except metal) manufacturing
339911	Sewing cases, precious metal, manufacturing
315211	Sewing fabric owned by others for men's and boys' apparel

Sewing fabrics—Shipping

Code	Description
315212	Sewing fabric owned by others for women's, girls' and infants' apparel
337129	Sewing machine cabinets, wood, manufacturing
443111	Sewing machine stores, household-type
811412	Sewing machine, household-type, repair shops without retailing new sewing machines
333298	Sewing machines (including household-type) manufacturing
421620	Sewing machines, household-type, wholesaling
421830	Sewing machines, industrial, wholesaling
451130	Sewing supply stores
313113	Sewing threads manufacturing
334511	Sextants (except surveying) manufacturing
334519	Sextants, surveying, manufacturing
337920	Shade pulls, window, manufacturing
335121	Shades, lamp (except glass, plastics), residential-type, manufacturing
337920	Shades, window (except outdoor canvas awnings), manufacturing
213113	Shaft sinking for coal mines on a contract basis
213114	Shaft sinking for metal mines on a contract basis
321113	Shakes (i.e., hand split shingles) manufacturing
212325	Shale (except oil shale) mining and/or beneficiating
327992	Shale, expanded, manufacturing
211111	Shale, oil, mining and/or beneficiating
111219	Shallot farming, field and seed production
325620	Shampoos and conditioners, hair, manufacturing
316999	Shanks, shoe, leather, manufacturing
333210	Shapers, woodworking-type, manufacturing
114111	Shark fishing
339994	Shaving brushes manufacturing
333512	Shaving machines, metalworking, manufacturing
325620	Shaving preparations (e.g., creams, gels, lotions, powders) manufacturing
422210	Shaving preparations wholesaling
333513	Shearing machines, metal forming, manufacturing
316110	Shearling (i.e., prepared sheepskin) manufacturing
333991	Shears and nibblers, handheld power-driven, manufacturing
332211	Shears, nonelectric, household-type (e.g., kitchen, barber, tailor) manufacturing
332212	Shears, nonelectric, tool-type (e.g., garden, pruners, tinsnip), manufacturing
333111	Shears, powered, for use on animals, manufacturing
322121	Sheathing paper (except newsprint, uncoated groundwood) made in paper mills
324122	Sheathing, asphalt saturated, made from refined petroleum
333613	Sheaves, mechanical power transmission, manufacturing
115210	Sheep dipping and shearing
112410	Sheep farming (e.g., meat, milk, wool production)
333111	Sheep shears, powered, manufacturing
422520	Sheep wholesaling
326140	Sheet (i.e., board), polystyrene foam insulation, manufacturing

Code	Description
333513	Sheet metal forming machines manufacturing
421330	Sheet metal roofing materials wholesaling
235610	Sheet metal work (except plumbing, heating, air-conditioning) construction contractors
332322	Sheet metal work (except stamped) manufacturing
611513	Sheet metal workers' apprenticeship training
323112	Sheet music flexographic printing without publishing
323111	Sheet music gravure printing without publishing
323110	Sheet music lithographic (offset) printing without publishing
323119	Sheet music printing (except flexographic, gravure, lithographic, screen) without publishing
512230	Sheet music publishers
512230	Sheet music publishers and printing combined
323113	Sheet music screen printing without publishing
451140	Sheet music stores
422990	Sheet music wholesaling
331111	Sheet pilings, plain, iron or steel, made in steel mills
331315	Sheet, aluminum, made by flat rolling purchased aluminum
331315	Sheet, aluminum, made in integrated secondary smelting and flat rolling mills
331421	Sheet, copper and copper alloy, made from purchased copper or in integrated secondary smelting and rolling, drawing or extruding plants
326130	Sheet, laminated plastics (except flexible packaging), manufacturing
326113	Sheet, plastics, unlaminated (except packaging), manufacturing
326299	Sheeting, rubber, manufacturing
314129	Sheets and pillowcases made from purchased fabrics
313210	Sheets and pillowcases made in broadwoven fabric mills
331111	Sheets, steel, made in steel mills
311119	Shell crushing and grinding for animal feed
311119	Shell crushing for feed
332993	Shell loading and assembly plants
212399	Shell mining and/or beneficiating
339999	Shell novelties
331111	Shell slugs, steel, made in steel mills
325510	Shellac manufacturing
422950	Shellac wholesaling
311711	Shellfish and shellfish products canning
311711	Shellfish curing
114112	Shellfish fishing (e.g., clam, crab, oyster, shrimp)
112512	Shellfish hatcheries
311712	Shellfish products, fresh prepared, manufacturing
311712	Shellfish products, frozen, manufacturing
311712	Shellfish, fresh prepared, manufacturing
311712	Shellfish, frozen, manufacturing
332993	Shells, artillery, manufacturing
332992	Shells, small arms (i.e., 30 mm. or less, 1.18 inch or less), manufacturing
624310	Sheltered workshops (i.e., work experience centers)

Code	Description
624221	Shelters (except for victims of domestic or international disasters or conflicts), emergency
624230	Shelters for victims of domestic or international disasters or conflicts, emergency
624221	Shelters, battered women's
624221	Shelters, homeless
624221	Shelters, runaway youth
624221	Shelters, temporary (e.g., battered women's, homeless, runaway youth)
337215	Shelving (except wire) manufacturing
421440	Shelving, commercial, wholesaling
332618	Shelving, wire, made from purchased wire
332812	Sherardizing of metals and metal products for the trade
311520	Sherbets manufacturing
922120	Sheriffs' offices (except court functions only)
922110	Sheriffs' offices, court functions only
332999	Shims, metal, manufacturing
321113	Shingle mills, wood
421330	Shingles (except wood) wholesaling
324122	Shingles made from purchased asphaltic materials
321113	Shingles, wood, sawed or hand split, manufacturing
421310	Shingles, wood, wholesaling
331525	Ship and boat propellers, cast brass, bronze and copper (except die-casting), unfinished, manufacturing
422990	Ship chandler wholesaling
483113	Ship chartering with crew, coastal or Great Lakes freight transportation
483114	Ship chartering with crew, coastal or Great Lakes passenger transportation
483111	Ship chartering with crew, deep sea freight transportation to or from foreign ports
483112	Ship chartering with crew, deep sea passenger transportation to or from foreign ports
483211	Ship chartering with crew, freight transportation, inland waters (except on Great Lakes system)
483212	Ship chartering with crew, passenger transportation, inland waters (except on Great Lakes system)
333923	Ship cranes and derricks manufacturing
561310	Ship crew employment agencies
561310	Ship crew registries
337127	Ship furniture manufacturing
488320	Ship hold cleaning services
235510	Ship joinery construction contractors
235210	Ship painting construction contractors
532411	Ship rental or leasing
336611	Ship repair done in a shipyard
336611	Ship scaling services done at a shipyard
488390	Ship scaling services not done at a shipyard
332312	Ship sections, prefabricated metal, manufacturing
513322	Ship-to-shore broadcasting communication carriers (except satellite)
331422	Shipboard cable made from purchased copper in wire drawing plants
331319	Shipboard cable made in aluminum wire drawing plants
488510	Shipping agents (freight forwarding)
314911	Shipping bags made from purchased woven or knitted materials
332439	Shipping barrels, drums, kegs, and pails, light gauge metal, manufacturing

Code	Description
321920	Shipping cases and drums, wood, wirebound, manufacturing
321920	Shipping cases, wood, nailed or lock corner, manufacturing
813910	Shipping companies' associations
421840	Shipping containers (except disposable plastics, paper) wholesaling
322211	Shipping containers made from purchased paperboard
322211	Shipping containers, corrugated, made from purchased paper or paperboard
321920	Shipping crates, wood, manufacturing
483113	Shipping freight to and from domestic ports (i.e., coastal, deep sea, Great Lakes system)
483111	Shipping freight to or from foreign ports, deep sea
483211	Shipping freight, inland waters (except on Great Lakes system)
326150	Shipping pads and shaped cushioning, foam plastics (except polystyrene), manufacturing
326140	Shipping pads and shaped cushioning, polystyrene foam, manufacturing
421840	Shipping pails, metal, wholesaling
511140	Shipping register publishers
511140	Shipping register publishers and printing combined
511140	Shipping register publishing (i.e., establishments known as publishers)
323112	Shipping registers flexographic printing without publishing
323111	Shipping registers gravure printing without publishing
323110	Shipping registers lithographic (offset) printing without publishing
323119	Shipping registers printing (except flexographic, gravure, lithographic, screen) without publishing
323113	Shipping registers screen printing without publishing
422130	Shipping supplies, paper and disposable plastics, wholesaling
336611	Ships (i.e., not suitable or intended for personal use) manufacturing
421860	Ships wholesaling
336611	Shipyard (i.e., facility capable of building ships)
315223	Shirts, outerwear (except work shirts), men's and boys', cut and sewn from purchased fabric (except apparel contractors)
315225	Shirts, outerwear work, men's and boys', cut and sewn from purchased fabric (except apparel contractors)
315291	Shirts, outerwear, infants', cut and sewn from purchased fabric (except apparel contractors)
315191	Shirts, outerwear, made in apparel knitting mills
315211	Shirts, outerwear, men's and boys', cut and sew apparel contractors
315223	Shirts, outerwear, unisex (i.e., sized without regard to gender), cut and sewn from purchased fabric (except apparel contractors)
315212	Shirts, outerwear, women's, girls', and infants', cut and sew apparel contractors
315232	Shirts, outerwear, women's, misses', and girls', cut and sewn from purchased fabric (except apparel contractors)
315291	Shirts, underwear, infants', cut and sewn from purchased fabric (except apparel contractors)

Code	Description
315192	Shirts, underwear, made in apparel knitting mills
315211	Shirts, underwear, men's and boys', cut and sew apparel contractors
315221	Shirts, underwear, men's and boys', cut and sewn from purchased fabric (except apparel contractors)
315212	Shirts, underwear, women's, girls', and infants', cut and sew apparel contractors
315231	Shirts, underwear, women's, misses', and girls', cut and sewn from purchased fabric (except apparel contractors)
111411	Shitake mushroom farming
111419	Shitake mushroom farming, grown under cover
336330	Shock absorbers, automotive, truck, and bus, manufacturing
448210	Shoe (except bowling, golf, spiked) stores
326299	Shoe and boot parts (e.g., heels, soles, soling strips), rubber, manufacturing
322212	Shoe boxes, folding, made from purchased paperboard
322213	Shoe boxes, setup, made from purchased paperboard
541490	Shoe design services
321999	Shoe display forms, all materials, manufacturing
316991	Shoe kits (i.e., cases), all materials, manufacturing
333298	Shoe making and repairing machinery manufacturing
421830	Shoe manufacturing and repairing machinery wholesaling
326199	Shoe parts (e.g., heels, soles), plastics, manufacturing
335211	Shoe polishers, household-type electric, manufacturing
325612	Shoe polishes and cleaners manufacturing
421850	Shoe repair materials wholesaling
811430	Shoe repair shops without retailing new shoes
316999	Shoe soles, leather, manufacturing
448210	Shoe stores, orthopedic
451110	Shoe stores, specialty sports footwear (e.g., bowling, golf, spiked)
321999	Shoe stretchers manufacturing
321999	Shoe trees manufacturing
422340	Shoes wholesaling
316219	Shoes, athletic (except rubber or plastics soled with fabric upper), manufacturing
316219	Shoes, ballet, manufacturing
316219	Shoes, children's and infant's (except house slippers, orthopedic extension, plastics, rubber), manufacturing
316219	Shoes, cleated or spiked, all materials, manufacturing
316213	Shoes, men's (except house slippers, athletic, rubber, extension shoes), manufacturing
339113	Shoes, orthopedic extension, manufacturing
316211	Shoes, plastics or plastics soled fabric upper (except cleated athletic shoes), manufacturing
316211	Shoes, rubber or rubber soled fabric upper (except cleated athletic), manufacturing
316219	Shoes, theatrical, manufacturing
316214	Shoes, women's (except house slippers, athletic, orthopedic extension, plastic, rubber), manufacturing
316219	Shoes, wooden, manufacturing

Code	Description
812990	Shoeshine parlors
812990	Shoeshine services
321920	Shook, box, manufacturing
713990	Shooting clubs, recreational
713990	Shooting galleries
713990	Shooting ranges
233320	Shop construction
421120	Shop equipment, service station, wholesaling
422130	Shopping bags, paper and plastics, wholesaling
531120	Shopping center (i.e., not operating contained businesses) rental or leasing
233320	Shopping center or mall construction
812990	Shopping services, personal
******	Shops — see type
235990	Shoring and underpinning construction contractors
111421	Short rotation woody tree growing (i.e., growing and harvesting cycle ten years or less)
482112	Short-line railroads
522298	Short-term inventory credit lending
311223	Shortening (except soybean) made in crushing mills
311222	Shortening , soybean, made in crushing mills
311225	Shortening made from purchased fats and oils
422490	Shortening, vegetable, wholesaling
315291	Shorts, outerwear, infants', cut and sewn from purchased fabric (except apparel contractors)
315191	Shorts, outerwear, made in apparel knitting mills
315211	Shorts, outerwear, men's and boys', cut and sew apparel contractors
315228	Shorts, outerwear, men's and boys', cut and sewn from purchased fabric (except apparel contractors)
315212	Shorts, outerwear, women's, girls', and infants', cut and sew apparel contractors
315239	Shorts, outerwear, women's, misses', and girls', cut and sewn from purchased fabric (except apparel contractors)
315192	Shorts, underwear, made in apparel knitting mills
315211	Shorts, underwear, men's and boys', cut and sew apparel contractors
315221	Shorts, underwear, men's and boys', cut and sewn from purchased fabric (except apparel contractors)
213112	Shot hole drilling, oil and gas field, on a contract basis
332813	Shot peening metal and metal products for the trade
332992	Shot, BB, manufacturing
332992	Shot, lead, manufacturing
332992	Shot, pellet, manufacturing
332992	Shot, steel, manufacturing
235710	Shotcrete construction contractors
332992	Shotgun shells manufacturing
332994	Shotguns manufacturing
333120	Shovel loaders manufacturing
332212	Shovels, handheld, manufacturing
333120	Shovels, power, manufacturing
337215	Showcases (except refrigerated) manufacturing
421440	Showcases (except refrigerated) wholesaling
333415	Showcases, refrigerated, manufacturing
314129	Shower and bath curtains, all materials, made from purchased fabric or sheet goods

Shower heads—Ski suits

Code	Description
332913	Shower heads, plumbing, manufacturing
332998	Shower receptors, metal, manufacturing
332999	Shower rods, metal, manufacturing
316211	Shower sandals or slippers, rubber, manufacturing
332998	Shower stalls, metal, manufacturing
326191	Shower stalls, plastics or fiberglass, manufacturing
115210	Showing of cattle, hogs, sheep, goats, and poultry
333111	Shredders, farm-type, manufacturing
212399	Shredding peat mining and/or beneficiating
114112	Shrimp fishing
112512	Shrimp production, farm raising
813110	Shrines, religious
561910	Shrink wrapping services
313311	Shrinking broadwoven fabrics
313312	Shrinking textile products and fabrics (except broadwoven)
561730	Shrub services (e.g., bracing, planting, pruning, removal, spraying, surgery, trimming)
111421	Shrubbery farming
311712	Shucking and packing fresh shellfish
488490	Shunting of trailers in truck terminals
488210	Shunting trailers in rail terminals
334515	Shunts, instrument, manufacturing
332321	Shutters, door and window, metal, manufacturing
321918	Shutters, door and window, wood and covered wood, manufacturing
326199	Shutters, plastics, manufacturing
321918	Shutters, wood, manufacturing
485999	Shuttle services (except employee bus)
333292	Shuttles for textile weaving machinery manufacturing
446199	Sick room supply stores
332212	Sickles manufacturing
212210	Siderite mining and/or beneficiating
234110	Sidewalk construction, public
235710	Sidewalk, private, construction contractors
421330	Siding (except wood) wholesaling
235610	Siding construction contractors
444190	Siding dealers
324122	Siding made from purchased asphaltic materials
321113	Siding mills, wood
321113	Siding, dressed lumber, manufacturing
326199	Siding, plastics, manufacturing
332322	Siding, sheet metal, manufacturing
421310	Siding, wood, wholesaling
212393	Sienna mining and/or beneficiating
325131	Sienna pigment manufacturing
333294	Sieves and screening equipment (i.e., food manufacturing-type) manufacturing
333298	Sieves and screening equipment, chemical preparation-type, manufacturing
333999	Sieves and screening equipment, general purpose-type, manufacturing
333131	Sieves and screening mineral beneficiating equipment manufacturing
332618	Sieves manufacturing
333294	Sifting machine (i.e., food manufacturing-type) manufacturing
333314	Sights, telescopic, manufacturing
487210	Sightseeing boat operation
487110	Sightseeing bus operation
487110	Sightseeing operation, human-drawn vehicle
235990	Sign contractors, installation (on buildings)
234110	Sign erection (i.e., highway, street) contractors
611630	Sign language instruction
611630	Sign language schools
541890	Sign language services
541890	Sign lettering and painting services
331422	Signal and control cable made from purchased copper in wire drawing plants
331319	Signal and control cable made in aluminum wire drawing plants
334515	Signal generators and averagers manufacturing
421610	Signal systems and devices wholesaling
335311	Signaling transformers, electric, manufacturing
334290	Signals (e.g., highway, pedestrian, railway, traffic) manufacturing
421990	Signs (except electrical) wholesaling
339950	Signs and signboards (except paper, paperboard) manufacturing
421440	Signs, electrical, wholesaling
325188	Silica gel manufacturing
212322	Silica mining and/or beneficiating
212322	Silica sand quarrying and/or beneficiating
325188	Silica, amorphous, manufacturing
325188	Silicofluorides manufacturing
331112	Silicomanganese ferroalloys manufacturing
327910	Silicon carbide abrasives manufacturing
334413	Silicon wafers, chemically doped, manufacturing
327992	Silicon, ultra high purity, manufacturing
325199	Silicone (except resins) manufacturing
325211	Silicone resins manufacturing
325212	Silicone rubber manufacturing
313210	Silk fabrics, broadwoven, weaving
541430	Silk screen design services
333292	Silk screens for textile fabrics manufacturing
313111	Silk spun yarns made from purchased fiber
313113	Silk thread manufacturing
313112	Silk throwing, spooling, twisting, or winding of purchased yarn
422590	Silk, raw, wholesaling
212325	Sillimanite mining and/or beneficiating
327390	Sills, concrete, manufacturing
233320	Silo construction
321918	Silo staves, wood, manufacturing
321912	Silo stock, wood, manufacturing
327390	Silos, prefabricated concrete, manufacturing
332311	Silos, prefabricated metal, manufacturing
331491	Silver and silver alloy bar, rod, sheet, strip, and tubing made from purchased metals or scrap
332999	Silver beating (i.e., foil, leaf)
325188	Silver bromide manufacturing
331419	Silver bullion or dore bar produced at primary metal refineries
325188	Silver chloride manufacturing
325188	Silver compounds, not specified elsewhere by process, manufacturing
332999	Silver foil and leaf not made in rolling mills
331491	Silver foil made by rolling purchased metals or scrap
325188	Silver nitrate manufacturing
212222	Silver ores mining and/or beneficiating
325612	Silver polishes manufacturing
331492	Silver recovering from scrap and/or alloying purchased metals
331492	Silver recovering from used photographic film or X-ray plates
331419	Silver refining, primary
331491	Silver rolling, drawing, or extruding purchased metals or scrap
532299	Silverware rental
421940	Silverware, precious and plated, wholesaling
333515	Sine bars (i.e., a machine tool accessory) manufacturing
711130	Singers, independent
813410	Singing societies
812990	Singing telegram services
233210	Single family construction management firms
531110	Single family house rental or leasing
621512	Single photon emission computerized tomography (SPECT) centers
213113	Sinking shafts for coal mining on a contract basis
213114	Sinking shafts for metal mining on a contract basis
332998	Sinks, metal, manufacturing
326191	Sinks, plastics, manufacturing
327111	Sinks, vitreous china, manufacturing
212210	Sintered iron ore produced at the mine
212392	Sintered phosphate rock mining and/or beneficiating
334290	Sirens (e.g., air raid, industrial, marine, vehicle) manufacturing
541611	Site location consulting services
541620	Site remediation consulting services
562910	Site remediation services
541611	Site selection consulting services
812990	Sitting services, house
812910	Sitting services, pet
313311	Sizing of broadwoven fabrics
313312	Sizing of fabric (except broadwoven)
339920	Skateboards manufacturing
339920	Skates and parts, ice and roller, manufacturing
713990	Skeet shooting facilities
331111	Skelp, iron or steel, made in steel mills
711510	Sketch artists, independent
321999	Skewers, wood, manufacturing
541320	Ski area design services
541320	Ski area planning services
532292	Ski equipment rental
713920	Ski lift and tow operators
721110	Ski lodges and resorts with accommodations
315191	Ski pants made in apparel knitting mills
315291	Ski pants, infants', cut and sewn from purchased fabric (except apparel contractors)
315211	Ski pants, men's and boys', cut and sew apparel contractors
315228	Ski pants, men's and boys', cut and sewn from purchased fabric (except apparel contractors)
315212	Ski pants, women's, girls', and infants', cut and sew apparel contractors
315239	Ski pants, women's, misses', and girls', cut and sewn from purchased fabric (except apparel contractors)
713920	Ski resorts without accommodations
315191	Ski suits made in apparel knitting mills
315291	Ski suits, infants', cut and sewn from purchased fabric (except apparel contractors)

Code	Description
315211	Ski suits, men's and boys', cut and sew apparel contractors
315228	Ski suits, men's and boys', cut and sewn from purchased fabric (except apparel contractors)
315212	Ski suits, women's, girls', and infants', cut and sew apparel contractors
315239	Ski suits, women's, misses', and girls', cut and sewn from purchased fabric (except apparel contractors)
234990	Ski tow construction
532490	Skid rental or leasing
213112	Skidding of rigs, oil and gas field, on a contract basis
321920	Skids and pallets, wood or wood and metal combination, manufacturing
332999	Skids, metal, manufacturing
711219	Skiers, independent (i.e., participating in sports events)
421910	Skiing equipment and supplies wholesaling
713920	Skiing facilities, cross country, without accommodations
713920	Skiing facilities, downhill, without accommodations
611620	Skiing instruction, camps, or schools
623110	Skilled nursing facilities
561910	Skin blister packaging services
611620	Skin diving instruction, camps, or schools
339112	Skin grafting equipment manufacturing
422990	Skins, dressed, wholesaling
422590	Skins, raw, wholesaling
316110	Skins, tanning, currying and finishing
561611	Skip tracing services
316110	Skirting leather manufacturing
315234	Skirts (except tennis skirts), women's, misses', and girls', cut and sewn from purchased fabric (except apparel contractors)
315191	Skirts made in apparel knitting mills
315291	Skirts, infants', cut and sewn from purchased fabric (except apparel contractors)
315239	Skirts, tennis, women's, misses', and girls', cut and sewn from purchased fabric (except apparel contractors)
315212	Skirts, women's, misses', girls', and infants', cut and sew apparel contractors
339920	Skis and skiing equipment (except apparel) manufacturing
316110	Skivers, leather, manufacturing
611620	Sky diving instruction, camps, or schools
235610	Skylight construction contractors
332322	Skylights, sheet metal, manufacturing
331419	Slab, nonferrous metals (except aluminum, copper), primary
331312	Slab, primary aluminum, manufacturing
331111	Slab, steel, made in steel mills
315191	Slacks made in apparel knitting mills
315291	Slacks, infants', cut and sewn from purchased fabric (except apparel contractors)
315291	Slacks, jean-cut casual, infants', cut and sewn from purchased fabric (except apparel contractors)
315191	Slacks, jean-cut casual, made in apparel knitting mills
315211	Slacks, jean-cut casual, men's and boys', cut and sew apparel contractors
315224	Slacks, jean-cut casual, men's and boys', cut and sewn from purchased fabric (except apparel contractors)

Code	Description
315212	Slacks, jean-cut casual, women's, girls', and infants', cut and sew apparel contractors
315239	Slacks, jean-cut casual, women's, misses', and girls', cut and sewn from purchased fabric (except apparel contractors)
315211	Slacks, men's and boys', cut and sew apparel contractors
315224	Slacks, men's and boys', cut and sewn from purchased fabric (except apparel contractors)
315212	Slacks, women's, girls', and infants', cut and sew apparel contractors
315239	Slacks, women's, misses', and girls', cut and sewn from purchased fabric (except apparel contractors)
333120	Slag mixers, portable, manufacturing
235410	Slate (i.e., exterior) construction contractors
212319	Slate crushed and broken stone mining and/or beneficiating
212311	Slate mining or quarrying
327991	Slate products manufacturing
311611	Slaughtering, custom
311991	Slaw, cole, fresh, manufacturing
332212	Sledgehammers manufacturing
339932	Sleds, children's, manufacturing
621498	Sleep disorder centers and clinics, outpatient
337215	Sleeper mechanisms, convertible bed, manufacturing
314999	Sleeping bags manufacturing
316999	Sleeves, welder's, leather, manufacturing
333294	Slicing machinery (i.e., food manufacturing-type) manufacturing
339993	Slide fasteners (i.e., zippers) manufacturing
332618	Slings, lifting, made from purchased wire
212324	Slip clay mining and/or beneficiating
335312	Slip rings for motors and generators manufacturing
421220	Slipcovers wholesaling
314129	Slipcovers, all materials, made from purchased materials
316212	Slipper socks made from purchased socks
315119	Slipper socks made in sock mills
422340	Slippers wholesaling
316219	Slippers, ballet, manufacturing
316212	Slippers, house, manufacturing
315192	Slips made in apparel knitting mills
315212	Slips, women's and girls', cut and sew apparel contractors
315231	Slips, women's, misses', and girls', cut and sewn from purchased fabric (except apparel contractors)
713990	Slot car racetracks (i.e., amusement devices)
713290	Slot machine concession operators (i.e., supplying and servicing in others' facilities)
713290	Slot machine parlors
339999	Slot machines manufacturing
333512	Slotting machines, metalworking, manufacturing
562212	Sludge disposal sites
333999	Sludge tables manufacturing
327331	Slumped brick manufacturing
486990	Slurry pipeline transportation
213112	Slush pits and cellars, excavation of, on a contract basis
541940	Small animal veterinary services

Code	Description
332992	Small arms ammunition (i.e., 30 mm. or less, 1.18 inch or less) manufacturing
926110	Small business development agencies
811411	Small engine repair and maintenance shops
311615	Small game, processing, fresh, frozen, canned or cooked
311615	Small game, slaughtering, dressing and packing
522291	Small loan companies (i.e., unsecured cash loans)
331492	Smelting and refining of nonferrous metals (except aluminum, copper), secondary
421830	Smelting machinery and equipment wholesaling
331492	Smelting nonferrous metals (except aluminum, copper), secondary
331419	Smelting of nonferrous metals (except aluminum, copper), primary
333994	Smelting ovens manufacturing
332420	Smelting pots and retorts manufacturing
212231	Smithsonite mining and/or beneficiating
334290	Smoke detectors manufacturing
421620	Smoke detectors, household-type, wholesaling
332995	Smoke generators manufacturing
311612	Smoked meats made from purchased carcasses
422990	Smokers' supplies wholesaling
453991	Smokers' supply stores
332313	Smokestacks, fabricated metal boiler plate, manufacturing
621999	Smoking cessation programs
312229	Smoking tobacco (e.g., cigarette, pipe) manufacturing
333311	Snack and confection vending machines manufacturing
722213	Snack bars (e.g., cookies, popcorn, pretzels), fixed location
722330	Snack stands, mobile
111219	Snap bean farming (i.e., bush and pole), field and seed production
335931	Snap switches (i.e., electric wiring devices) manufacturing
114111	Snapper fishing
488490	Snow clearing, highways and bridges, road transportation
321912	Snow fence lath manufacturing
321999	Snow fence, sections or rolls, manufacturing
333415	Snow making machinery manufacturing
111219	Snow pea farming, field and seed production
333120	Snow plow attachments (except lawn, garden-type) manufacturing
333112	Snow plow attachments, lawn and garden-type, manufacturing
561790	Snow plowing driveways and parking lots (i.e., not combined with any other service)
561730	Snow plowing services combined with landscaping services (i.e., seasonal property maintenance services)
421810	Snow plows wholesaling
488490	Snow removal, highway
532292	Snow ski equipment rental
421810	Snowblowers (except household-type) wholesaling
333112	Snowblowers and throwers, residential-type, manufacturing
421820	Snowblowers, household-type, wholesaling
441229	Snowmobile dealers

Snowmobile—Solenoid

Code	Description
711212	Snowmobile racetracks
711219	Snowmobile racing teams
336999	Snowmobiles and parts manufacturing
421110	Snowmobiles wholesaling
713990	Snowmobiling, recreational
339920	Snowshoes manufacturing
315191	Snowsuits made in apparel knitting mills
315291	Snowsuits, infants', cut and sewn from purchased fabric (except apparel contractors)
315211	Snowsuits, men's and boys', cut and sew apparel contractors
315228	Snowsuits, men's and boys', cut and sewn from purchased fabric (except apparel contractors)
315212	Snowsuits, women's, girls', and infants', cut and sew apparel contractors
315239	Snowsuits, women's, misses', and girls', cut and sewn from purchased fabric (except apparel contractors)
312229	Snuff manufacturing
422940	Snuff wholesaling
327111	Soap dishes, vitreous china and earthenware, manufacturing
332999	Soap dispensers, metal, manufacturing
325611	Soaps (e.g., bar, chip, powder) manufacturing
212399	Soapstone mining and/or beneficiating
711211	Soccer clubs, professional or semiprofessional
713990	Soccer clubs, recreational
611620	Soccer instruction, camps, or schools
711211	Soccer teams, professional or semiprofessional
923130	Social Security Administration, federal
923130	Social assistance cost-sharing, government
813319	Social change advocacy organizations
813410	Social clubs
812990	Social escort services
813410	Social organizations, civic and fraternal
541720	Social science research and development services
813319	Social service advocacy organizations
624190	Social service agencies, family
624190	Social service centers, multipurpose
422120	Social stationery wholesaling
813920	Social workers' associations
621330	Social workers' offices (e.g., centers, clinics)
541720	Sociological research and development services
541720	Sociology research and development services
332212	Sockets and socket sets manufacturing
335931	Sockets, electric, manufacturing
315119	Socks knitting or knitting and finishing
315119	Socks, men's and boy's, manufacturing
316212	Socks, slipper, made from purchased socks
315119	Socks, slipper, made in sock mills
111421	Sod farming
333111	Sod harvesting machines manufacturing
561730	Sod laying services
325181	Soda ash manufacturing
212391	Soda ash mining and/or beneficiating
212391	Soda ash, natural, mining and/or beneficiating
327213	Soda bottles, glass, manufacturing
312111	Soda carbonated, manufacturing
311821	Soda crackers manufacturing
333415	Soda fountain cooling and dispensing equipment manufacturing

Code	Description
421440	Soda fountain fixtures (except refrigerated) wholesaling
311930	Soda fountain syrups manufacturing
312111	Soda pop manufacturing
325199	Sodium acetate manufacturing
325199	Sodium alginate manufacturing
325188	Sodium aluminate manufacturing
325188	Sodium aluminum sulfate manufacturing
325188	Sodium antimoniate manufacturing
325320	Sodium arsenite insecticides manufacturing
325188	Sodium arsenite manufacturing
325199	Sodium benzoate manufacturing
325181	Sodium bicarbonate manufacturing
325188	Sodium bichromate and chromate manufacturing
325188	Sodium borate manufacturing
212391	Sodium borates, natural, mining and/or beneficiating
325188	Sodium borohydride manufacturing
325188	Sodium bromide manufacturing
325181	Sodium carbonate (i.e., soda ash) manufacturing
212391	Sodium carbonates, natural, mining and/or beneficiating
325188	Sodium chlorate manufacturing
325412	Sodium chloride pharmaceutical preparations manufacturing
212393	Sodium chloride, rock salt, mining and/or beneficiating
212391	Sodium compounds prepared at beneficiating plants
212391	Sodium compounds, natural (except common salt), mining and/or beneficiating
325188	Sodium cyanide manufacturing
325199	Sodium glutamate manufacturing
325188	Sodium hydrosulfite manufacturing
325181	Sodium hydroxide (i.e., caustic soda) manufacturing
325188	Sodium hypochlorite manufacturing
325188	Sodium inorganic compounds, not specified elsewhere by process, manufacturing
325188	Sodium molybdate manufacturing
325199	Sodium organic compounds, not specified elsewhere by process, manufacturing
325199	Sodium pentachlorophenate manufacturing
325188	Sodium perborate manufacturing
325188	Sodium peroxide manufacturing
325188	Sodium phosphate manufacturing
325188	Sodium polyphosphate manufacturing
325412	Sodium salicylate preparations manufacturing
325188	Sodium silicate (i.e., water glass) manufacturing
325188	Sodium silicofluoride manufacturing
325188	Sodium stannate manufacturing
325188	Sodium sulfate manufacturing
212391	Sodium sulfate, natural, mining and/or beneficiating
325199	Sodium sulfoxalate formaldehyde manufacturing
325188	Sodium tetraborate manufacturing
325188	Sodium thiosulfate manufacturing
325188	Sodium tungstate manufacturing
325188	Sodium uranate manufacturing
335110	Sodium vapor lamp bulbs manufacturing
337121	Sofa beds and chair beds, upholstered, manufacturing

Code	Description
337121	Sofas, convertible (except futons), manufacturing
337121	Sofas, upholstered, manufacturing
722213	Soft drink beverage bars, nonalcoholic, fixed location
332431	Soft drink cans manufacturing
311930	Soft drink concentrates (i.e., syrup) manufacturing
445299	Soft drink stores, bottled
333311	Soft drink vending machines manufacturing
312111	Soft drinks manufacturing
422490	Soft drinks wholesaling
311812	Soft pretzels made in a commercial bakery
325613	Softeners, leather or textile, manufacturing
541511	Software analysis and design services, custom computer
611420	Software application training
511210	Software computer, packaged, publishers
541519	Software installation services, computer
541511	Software programming services, custom computer
511210	Software publishers
511210	Software publishers, packaged
443120	Software stores, computer
421430	Software, computer, packaged, wholesaling
334611	Software, packaged, mass reproducing
321912	Softwood dimension lumber and stock, resawing purchased lumber
325191	Softwood distillates manufacturing
321212	Softwood plywood composites, manufacturing
321212	Softwood veneer or plywood, manufacturing
234990	Soil compacting service
924120	Soil conservation services, government
331511	Soil pipe, cast iron, manufacturing
562910	Soil remediation services
325998	Soil testing kits manufacturing
541380	Soil testing laboratories or services
334413	Solar cells manufacturing
421690	Solar cells wholesaling
926130	Solar energy regulation
333414	Solar energy heating equipment manufacturing
235110	Solar heating construction contractors
421720	Solar heating panels and equipment wholesaling
333414	Solar heating systems manufacturing
335122	Solar lighting fixtures (except residential), electric, manufacturing
335121	Solar lighting fixtures, residential, electric, manufacturing
421330	Solar reflective film wholesaling
334519	Solarimeters manufacturing
331491	Solder wire, nonferrous metals (except aluminum, copper), made from purchased metals or scrap
333992	Soldering equipment (except hand held) manufacturing
332212	Soldering guns and irons, handheld (including electric), manufacturing
332212	Soldering iron tips and tiplets manufacturing
335931	Solderless connectors (electric wiring devices) manufacturing
316110	Sole leather manufacturing
335314	Solenoid switches, industrial, manufacturing

Code	Description
332911	Solenoid valves (except fluid power), industrial-type, manufacturing
332912	Solenoid valves, fluid power, manufacturing
334419	Solenoids for electronic applications manufacturing
316999	Soles, boot and shoe, leather, manufacturing
541110	Solicitors' offices
922130	Solicitors' offices, government
541110	Solicitors' private practices
325188	Solid fuel propellants, inorganic, not specified elsewhere by process, manufacturing
562213	Solid waste combustors or incinerators, nonhazardous
562212	Solid waste landfills combined with collection and/or local hauling of nonhazardous waste materials
562212	Solid waste landfills, nonhazardous
711130	Soloists, independent musical
325132	Solvent dyes manufacturing
324110	Solvents made in petroleum refineries
334511	Sonabuoys manufacturing
421690	Sonar equipment wholesaling
334511	Sonar fish finders manufacturing
334511	Sonar systems and equipment manufacturing
512230	Song publishers
512230	Song publishers and printing combined
512230	Song publishing (i.e., establishment known as publishers)
711510	Song writers, independent
325612	Soot removing chemicals manufacturing
325199	Sorbitol manufacturing
111199	Sorghum farming, field and seed production
311211	Sorghum flour manufacturing
111998	Sorghum sudan seed farming
311999	Sorghum syrup manufacturing
813410	Sororities (except residential)
721310	Sorority houses
115114	Sorting, grading, cleaning, and packing of fruits and vegetables
532490	Sound and lighting equipment rental or leasing
234990	Sound barrier construction, highways
512191	Sound dubbing services, motion picture
235310	Sound equipment construction contractors
421330	Sound insulation wholesaling
235420	Sound proofing construction contractors
512240	Sound recording studios (except integrated record companies)
512220	Sound recording, integrated production, reproduction, release, and distribution
512220	Sound recording, releasing, promoting, and distributing
332431	Soup cans manufacturing
624210	Soup kitchens
311423	Soup mixes made in a dehydration plant
311999	Soup mixes, dry, made from purchased dry ingredients
422490	Soups (except frozen) wholesaling
311422	Soups (except seafood) canning
311711	Soups, fish and seafood, canning
311412	Soups, frozen (except seafood), manufacturing
311712	Soups, frozen fish and shellfish, manufacturing
422420	Soups, frozen, wholesaling
311511	Sour cream manufacturing
311511	Sour cream substitutes manufacturing
453220	Souvenir shops

Code	Description
311941	Soy sauce manufacturing
311222	Soybean cakes and meal manufacturing
311225	Soybean cooking oil made from purchased oils
111110	Soybean farming, field and seed production
325222	Soybean fibers and filaments manufacturing
311222	Soybean flour and grits manufacturing
311222	Soybean millfeed made in oil mills
311222	Soybean oil mills
311222	Soybean oil, cake, and meal, made in crushing mills
311222	Soybean oil, crude, manufacturing
311222	Soybean oil, deodorized, made in oil mills
311222	Soybean oil, refined, made in crushing mills
325211	Soybean plastics manufacturing
311222	Soybean protein concentrates manufacturing
311222	Soybean protein isolates made in crushing mills
422510	Soybeans wholesaling
336419	Space capsules manufacturing
927110	Space flight operations, government
333414	Space heaters (except portable electric) manufacturing
927110	Space research and development
334220	Space satellites, communications, manufacturing
332313	Space simulation chambers, fabricated metal plate work, manufacturing
339113	Space suits manufacturing
481212	Space transportation, freight, nonscheduled
334511	Space vehicle guidance systems and equipment manufacturing
336414	Space vehicles, complete, manufacturing
332212	Spades and shovels, handheld, manufacturing
311422	Spaghetti canning
311421	Spaghetti sauce canning
111219	Spaghetti squash farming, field, bedding plant and seed production
422490	Spaghetti wholesaling
311823	Spaghetti, dry, manufacturing
313210	Spandex broadwoven fabrics
325222	Spandex fiber, filaments, and yarn manufacturing
113210	Spanish moss gathering
212399	Spar, iceland, mining and/or beneficiating
327113	Spark plug insulators, porcelain, manufacturing
334515	Spark plug testing instruments, electric, manufacturing
336322	Spark plugs for internal combustion engines manufacturing
312130	Sparkling wine manufacturing
321999	Spars, wood, manufacturing
713940	Spas without accommodations, fitness
316999	Spats, leather, manufacturing
326299	Spatulas, rubber, manufacturing
337129	Speaker cabinets (i.e., housings), wood, manufacturing
813410	Speaker clubs
334310	Speaker systems manufacturing
711410	Speakers' bureaus
711510	Speakers, independent
325998	Spearmint oil manufacturing
711510	Special effect technicians, independent
512191	Special effects for motion picture production, post-production

Code	Description
485991	Special needs passenger transportation services
336211	Special purpose highway vehicle (e.g., firefighting vehicles) assembling on purchased chassis
336211	Special purpose highway vehicle (e.g., firefighting vehicles) bodies manufacturing
336120	Special purpose highway vehicles (e.g., firefighting vehicles) assembling on heavy chassis of own manufacture
421830	Special purpose industrial machinery and equipment wholesaling
525990	Special purpose vehicles
445299	Specialty food stores
316110	Specialty leathers manufacturing
513210	Specialty television (e.g., music, sports, news) cable networks
335311	Specialty transformers, electric, manufacturing
422210	Specialty-line pharmaceuticals wholesaling
334516	Specific ion measuring instruments, laboratory-type, manufacturing
235990	Spectator seating construction contractors
334516	Spectrofluorometers manufacturing
334516	Spectrographs manufacturing
334516	Spectrometers (e.g., electron diffraction, mass, NMR, Raman) manufacturing
334519	Spectrometers (e.g., liquid scintillation, nuclear) manufacturing
334516	Spectrophotometers (e.g., atomic absorption, atomic emission, flame, fluorescence, infrared, raman, visible) manufacturing
334515	Spectrum analyzers manufacturing
339112	Speculums manufacturing
541930	Speech (i.e., language) interpretation services
621340	Speech clinicians' offices (e.g., centers, clinics)
621340	Speech defect clinics
621340	Speech pathologists' offices (e.g., centers, clinics)
621340	Speech therapists' offices (e.g., centers, clinics)
333612	Speed changers (i.e., power transmission equipment) manufacturing
611699	Speed reading instruction
333612	Speed reducers (i.e., power transmission equipment) manufacturing
441310	Speed shops
334511	Speed, pitch, and roll navigational instruments and systems manufacturing
711212	Speedways
621991	Sperm banks, human
113210	Sphagnum moss gathering
212231	Sphalerite mining and/or beneficiating
339112	Sphygmomanometers manufacturing
111998	Spice farming
111419	Spice farming, grown under cover
311942	Spice grinding and blending
311942	Spice mixtures manufacturing
445299	Spice stores
311942	Spices and spice mix manufacturing
422490	Spices wholesaling
331112	Spiegeleisen ferroalloys manufacturing
332913	Spigots, plumbing fixture fitting, manufacturing
321999	Spigots, wood, manufacturing
331111	Spike rods made in steel mills
332618	Spikes made from purchased wire

Spikes—Stained glass

Code	Description
331222	Spikes, iron or steel, made in wire drawing plants
421510	Spikes, metal, wholesaling
111219	Spinach farming, field, bedding plant and seed production
333292	Spindles for textile machinery manufacturing
313111	Spinning carpet and rug yarn from purchased fiber
333292	Spinning machinery for textiles manufacturing
333513	Spinning machines, metalworking, manufacturing
332116	Spinning unfinished metal products
313111	Spinning yarn from purchased fiber
332618	Spiral cloth made from purchased wire
312140	Spirits, distilled (except brandy), manufacturing
422820	Spirits, distilled, wholesaling
333513	Spline rolling machines, metalworking, manufacturing
321920	Splint baskets for fruits and vegetables, manufacturing
339113	Splints manufacturing
316110	Splits, leather, manufacturing
212393	Spodumene mining and/or beneficiating
321999	Spokes, wood, manufacturing
114119	Sponge gathering
331111	Sponge iron
422990	Sponges wholesaling
332999	Sponges, metal scouring, manufacturing
326199	Sponges, plastics, manufacturing
326299	Sponges, rubber, manufacturing
313311	Sponging broadwoven fabrics
313312	Sponging textile products and fabrics (except broadwoven)
313112	Spooling of yarn
313112	Spooling of yarns for the trade
321999	Spools (except for textile machinery), wood, manufacturing
333292	Spools for textile machinery manufacturing
332211	Spoons, table, nonprecious and precious plated metal, manufacturing
315222	Sport coats (except fur, leather), men's and boys', cut and sewn from purchased fabric (except apparel contractors)
315292	Sport coats, fur (except apparel contractors), manufacturing
315211	Sport coats, fur, men's and boys', cut and sew apparel contractors
315292	Sport coats, leather (including artificial and tailored) (except apparel contractors), manufacturing
315211	Sport coats, leather (including artificial and tailored), men's and boys', cut and sew apparel contractors
315211	Sport coats, men's and boys', cut and sew apparel contractors
315211	Sport shirts, men's and boys', cut and sew apparel contractors
315223	Sport shirts, men's and boys', cut and sewn from purchased fabric (except apparel contractors)
532112	Sport utility vehicle leasing
532111	Sport utility vehicle rental
336112	Sport utility vehicles assembling on chassis of own manufacture
421110	Sport utility vehicles wholesaling
811490	Sporting equipment repair and maintenance without retailing new sports equipment

Code	Description
421910	Sporting firearms and ammunition wholesaling
339920	Sporting goods (except ammunition, clothing, footwear, small arms) manufacturing
421910	Sporting goods and supplies wholesaling
532292	Sporting goods rental
451110	Sporting goods stores
453310	Sporting goods stores, used
711310	Sports arena operators
611620	Sports camps (e.g., baseball, basketball, football), instructional
315228	Sports clothing (except team uniforms), men's and boys', cut and sewn from purchased fabric (except apparel contractors)
315239	Sports clothing (except team uniforms), women's, misses', and girls', cut and sewn from purchased fabric (except apparel contractors)
315191	Sports clothing made in apparel knitting mills
315211	Sports clothing, men's and boys', cut and sew apparel contractors
315299	Sports clothing, team uniforms, cut and sewn from purchased fabric (except apparel contractors)
315212	Sports clothing, women's and girls', cut and sew apparel contractors
713940	Sports club facilities, physical fitness
713990	Sports clubs (i.e., sports teams) not operating sports facilities, recreational
711211	Sports clubs, professional or semiprofessional
421910	Sports equipment and supplies wholesaling
532292	Sports equipment rental
711310	Sports event managers with facilities
711320	Sports event managers without facilities
711310	Sports event organizers with facilities
711320	Sports event organizers without facilities
711310	Sports event promoters with facilities
711320	Sports event promoters without facilities
711410	Sports figures' agents or managers
451110	Sports gear stores (e.g., outdoors, scuba, skiing)
712110	Sports halls of fame
611620	Sports instruction, camps, or schools
611620	Sports instructors, independent (i.e., not participating in sporting events)
711219	Sports professionals, independent (i.e., participating in sports events)
315191	Sports shirts made in apparel knitting mills
711310	Sports stadium operators
713990	Sports teams and leagues, recreational or youth
711211	Sports teams, professional or semiprofessional
621340	Sports therapists' offices (e.g., centers, clinics)
561599	Sports ticket offices
711219	Sports trainers, independent
422320	Sportswear, men's and boys', wholesaling
325612	Spot removers (except laundry presoaks) manufacturing
333992	Spot welding equipment manufacturing
335129	Spotlights (except vehicular) manufacturing
336321	Spotlights, vehicular, manufacturing
332322	Spouts, sheet metal, manufacturing
422950	Spray painting equipment (except industrial-type) wholesaling

Code	Description
421830	Spray painting equipment, industrial-type, wholesaling
333111	Sprayers and dusters, farm-type, manufacturing
421820	Sprayers, farm, wholesaling
333912	Sprayers, manual pump, general purpose-type, manufacturing
115112	Spraying crops
561730	Spraying lawns
333111	Spreaders, farm type, manufacturing
421820	Spreaders, fertilizer, wholesaling
333112	Spreaders, lawn and garden-type, manufacturing
115112	Spreading lime for crops
311513	Spreads, cheese, manufacturing
332722	Spring pins, metal, manufacturing
332722	Spring washers, metal, manufacturing
312112	Spring waters, purifying and bottling
333513	Spring winding and forming machines, metalworking, manufacturing
332612	Springs and spring units for seats made from purchased wire
337910	Springs, assembled bed and box, made from purchased spring
334518	Springs, clock and watch, made from purchased wire
332611	Springs, heavy gauge, manufacturing
332612	Springs, light gauge (except clock, watch), made from purchased wire
332612	Springs, precision (except clock, watch), manufacturing
421510	Springs, steel, wholesaling
235110	Sprinkler system construction contractors
333999	Sprinkler systems, automatic fire, manufacturing
421850	Sprinkler systems, fire, wholesaling
421820	Sprinklers, agricultural, wholesaling
332919	Sprinklers, lawn, manufacturing
333613	Sprockets, power transmission equipment, manufacturing
113210	Spruce gum gathering
213111	Spudding in oil and gas wells on a contract basis
313230	Spunbonded fabrics manufacturing
332212	Squares, carpenters', metal, manufacturing
713940	Squash club facilities
339920	Squash equipment (except apparel) manufacturing
111219	Squash farming, field, bedding plant and seed production
114112	Squid fishing
332999	Stabilizing bars, cargo, metal, manufacturing
711219	Stables, horse racing
713990	Stables, riding
333924	Stackers, industrial, truck-type, manufacturing
421830	Stackers, industrial, wholesaling
333924	Stackers, portable (except farm), manufacturing
233320	Stadium and arena construction
711310	Stadium operators
337127	Stadium seating manufacturing
531120	Stadium, no promotion of events, rental or leasing
561330	Staff leasing services
335129	Stage lighting equipment manufacturing
327211	Stained glass and stained glass products made in glass making plants
327215	Stained glass products made from purchased glass

Code	Description
331513	Stainless steel castings (except investment), unfinished, manufacturing
331111	Stainless steel made in steel mills
325510	Stains (except biological) manufacturing
422950	Stains wholesaling
325132	Stains, biological, manufacturing
332323	Stair railings, metal, manufacturing
321918	Stair railings, wood, manufacturing
332323	Stair treads, metal, manufacturing
326299	Stair treads, rubber, manufacturing
332323	Staircases, metal, manufacturing
332323	Stairs, metal, manufacturing
333921	Stairways, moving, manufacturing
321918	Stairwork (e.g., newel posts, railings, staircases, stairs), wood, manufacturing
321999	Stakes, surveyor's, wood, manufacturing
333111	Stalk choppers (i.e., shredders) manufacturing
332323	Stalls, metal, manufacturing
325998	Stamp pad ink manufacturing
339943	Stamp pads manufacturing
339911	Stamping coins
339943	Stamping devices, hand operated, manufacturing
333513	Stamping machines, metalworking, manufacturing
336370	Stamping metal motor vehicle body parts
336370	Stamping metal motor vehicle moldings and trims
332116	Stampings (except automotive, cans, cooking, closures, crowns), metal, unfinished, manufacturing
713210	Stand alone casinos (except slot machine parlors)
334515	Standards and calibration equipment for electrical measuring manufacturing
813920	Standards review committees, professional
926150	Standards, setting and management, agencies, government
334515	Standing wave ratio measuring equipment manufacturing
337215	Stands (except wire), merchandise display, manufacturing
711510	Standup comedians, independent
325188	Stannic and stannous chloride manufacturing
339942	Staple removers manufacturing
333991	Staplers and nailers, handheld power-driven, manufacturing
339942	Staplers manufacturing
332618	Staples made from purchased wire
421710	Staples wholesaling
331222	Staples, iron or steel, made in wire drawing plants
325520	Starch glues manufacturing
311221	Starches (except laundry) manufacturing
325612	Starches, laundry, manufacturing
112310	Started pullet production
336322	Starter and starter parts for internal combustion engines manufacturing
928120	State Department
522110	State commercial banks
522130	State credit unions
923110	State education departments
561310	State operated employment job services offices
922120	State police
522120	State savings banks
921130	State tax commissions
334413	Static converters, integrated circuits, manufacturing
334512	Static pressure regulators manufacturing
332410	Stationary power boilers manufacturing
327112	Stationery articles, pottery, manufacturing
323110	Stationery lithographic (offset) printing on a job-order basis
322233	Stationery made from purchased paper
453210	Stationery stores
422120	Stationery supplies wholesaling
335312	Stators for motors manufacturing
327420	Statuary (e.g., gypsum, plaster of paris) manufacturing
422990	Statuary (except religious) wholesaling
327112	Statuary, clay and ceramic, manufacturing
327991	Statuary, marble, manufacturing
327999	Statuary, vases, and urns, papier-mache, manufacturing
212399	Staurolite mining and/or beneficiating
321920	Staves, barrel, sawed or split, manufacturing
316999	Stays, shoe, leather, manufacturing
722110	Steak houses, full service
722211	Steak houses, limited service
812199	Steam baths
561790	Steam cleaning building exteriors
213112	Steam cleaning oil and gas wells on a contract basis
332410	Steam condensers manufacturing
333319	Steam cookers, commercial-type, manufacturing
335211	Steam cookers, household-type, manufacturing
611513	Steam fitters' apprenticeship training
235110	Steam fitting construction contractors
332919	Steam fittings, metal, manufacturing
221330	Steam heat distribution
333414	Steam heating equipment manufacturing
221330	Steam heating systems (i.e., suppliers of heat)
334512	Steam pressure controls, residential and commercial heating-type, manufacturing
221330	Steam production and distribution
333999	Steam separating machinery manufacturing
221330	Steam supply systems, including geothermal
333319	Steam tables manufacturing
487110	Steam train excursions
332911	Steam traps, industrial-type, manufacturing
333611	Steam turbine generator set units manufacturing
333611	Steam turbines manufacturing
532411	Steamship rental or leasing
325199	Stearic acid esters manufacturing
325199	Stearic acid manufacturing
325199	Stearic acid salts manufacturing
311613	Stearin, animal, rendering
212399	Steatite mining and/or beneficiating
327113	Steatite porcelain insulators manufacturing
331111	Steel balls made in steel mills
332431	Steel cans manufacturing
331513	Steel castings (except investment), unfinished, manufacturing
332111	Steel forgings made from purchased steel, unfinished
331513	Steel foundries (except investment)
235510	Steel framing construction contractors
331512	Steel investment castings, unfinished, manufacturing
331512	Steel investment foundries
332312	Steel joists manufacturing
331111	Steel manufacturing
331111	Steel mill products (e.g., bar, plate, rod, sheet, structural shapes) manufacturing
331111	Steel mills
332312	Steel railroad car racks manufacturing
327910	Steel shot abrasives manufacturing
421510	Steel wholesaling
332999	Steel wool manufacturing
421510	Steel wool wholesaling
235910	Steel work structural, construction contractors
235990	Steeplejacks
311221	Steepwater concentrate manufacturing
336330	Steering boxes, manual and power assist, manufacturing
336330	Steering columns, automotive, truck, and bus, manufacturing
336330	Steering wheels, automotive, truck, and bus, manufacturing
327215	Stemware made from purchased glass
327212	Stemware, glass, made in glass making plants
325910	Stencil inks manufacturing
339944	Stencil paper manufacturing
339943	Stencils for painting and marking (e.g., cardboard, metal) manufacturing
561410	Stenographic services (except court or stenographic reporting)
333313	Stenography machinery manufacturing
561492	Stenography services, public
561492	Stenotype recording services
332999	Stepladders, metal, manufacturing
321999	Stepladders, wood, manufacturing
337129	Stereo cabinets (i.e., housings), wood, manufacturing
532210	Stereo equipment rental
811211	Stereo equipment repair shops without retailing new stereo equipment
421620	Stereo equipment wholesaling
443112	Stereo stores (except automotive)
441310	Stereo stores, automotive
325212	Stereorubber manufacturing
339114	Sterilizers, dental, manufacturing
339113	Sterilizers, hospital and surgical, manufacturing
339111	Sterilizers, laboratory-type (except dental), manufacturing
332313	Sterilizing chambers, fabricated metal plate work, manufacturing
325411	Steriods, uncompounded, manufacturing
339112	Stethoscopes manufacturing
488320	Stevedoring services
339920	Sticks, sports (e.g., hockey, lacrosse), manufacturing
325132	Stilbene dyes manufacturing
324110	Still gases made in petroleum refineries
332420	Stills, heavy gauge metal, manufacturing
333293	Stitchers and trimmers book binding equipment manufacturing
315211	Stitching, decorative and novelty, contractors on men's and boys' apparel
315212	Stitching, decorative and novelty, contractors on women's, girls', and infants' apparel
314999	Stitching, decorative and novelty, on textile articles and apparel
523120	Stock brokerages
523120	Stock brokers' offices
711212	Stock car racetracks
711219	Stock car racing teams
711110	Stock companies, theatrical
523210	Stock exchanges

Stock footage—Structural

Code	Description
512199	Stock footage film libraries
512290	Stock music and other audio services
523120	Stock options brokerages
523110	Stock options dealing (i.e., acting as a principal in dealing securities to investors)
523210	Stock or commodity options exchanges
514199	Stock photo agencies
523999	Stock quotation services
523999	Stock transfer agencies
321912	Stock, chair, unfinished hardwood, manufacturing
112111	Stocker calf production
315111	Stockings (except socks), sheer, manufacturing
315111	Stockings, sheer, women's, misses', and girls', full-length and knee-length, knitting or knitting and finishing
488999	Stockyards (i.e., not for fattening or selling livestock), transportation
212319	Stone (except limestone and granite) beneficiating plants (e.g., grinding)
212311	Stone (except limestone and granite) mining or quarrying
333131	Stone beneficiating machinery manufacturing
332213	Stone cutting saw blades manufacturing
235410	Stone setting construction contractors
313311	Stone washing broadwoven fabrics
313312	Stone washing textile products, apparel, and fabrics (except broadwoven)
333298	Stone working machinery manufacturing
421320	Stone, building or crushed, wholesaling
212319	Stone, crushed and broken (except granite or limestone), mining and/or beneficiating
332212	Stonecutters' handtools, nonpowered, manufacturing
212399	Stones, abrasive (e.g., emery, grindstones, hones, pumice), mining and/or beneficiating
421940	Stones, precious and semiprecious, wholesaling
327999	Stones, synthetic, for gem stones and industrial use, manufacturing
327112	Stoneware (i.e., pottery products) manufacturing
212325	Stoneware clay mining and/or beneficiating
235410	Stonework construction contractors
337124	Stools, metal household-type (except upholstered), manufacturing
337122	Stools, wood household-type (except upholstered), manufacturing
621999	Stop smoking clinics
332911	Stop valves, industrial-type, manufacturing
332913	Stopcock drains, plumbing, manufacturing
321999	Stoppers, cork, manufacturing
326299	Stoppers, rubber, manufacturing
421610	Storage batteries (except automotive) wholesaling
335911	Storage batteries manufacturing
335312	Storage battery chargers (except internal combustion engine-type) manufacturing
421390	Storage bins wholesaling
334112	Storage devices, computer, manufacturing
486210	Storage of natural gas
332420	Storage tanks, heavy gauge metal, manufacturing
235910	Storage tanks, metal, construction contractors

Code	Description
421510	Storage tanks, metal, wholesaling
233320	Store construction
541850	Store display advertising services
337215	Store display fixtures manufacturing
421440	Store equipment (except furniture) wholesaling
235510	Store fixture construction contractors (i.e., built-in, on site)
421440	Store fixtures (except refrigerated) wholesaling
235910	Store front metal, installation, construction contractors
421210	Store furniture wholesaling
******	Stores — see type
562998	Storm basin cleanout services
332321	Storm doors and windows, metal, manufacturing
321911	Storm doors and windows, wood framed, manufacturing
711510	Storytellers, independent
312120	Stout brewing
332322	Stove boards, sheet metal, manufacturing
327123	Stove lining, clay, manufacturing
332322	Stove pipes and flues, sheet metal, manufacturing
811412	Stove, household-type, repair and maintenance services without retailing new stoves
335221	Stoves, ceramic disk element, household-type, manufacturing
333319	Stoves, commercial-type, manufacturing
421720	Stoves, cooking and heating (except electric), household-type, wholesaling
335221	Stoves, household-type cooking, manufacturing
333924	Straddle carriers, mobile, manufacturing
332211	Straight razors manufacturing
332911	Straightway (i.e., Y-type) valves, industrial-type, manufacturing
333999	Strainers, pipeline, manufacturing
321219	Strandboard, oriented, manufacturing
332618	Stranded wire, uninsulated, made from purchased wire
316110	Strap leather manufacturing
332999	Strappings, metal, manufacturing
316999	Straps (except watch), leather, manufacturing
316993	Straps, watch (except metal), manufacturing
339911	Straps, watch, precious metal, manufacturing
541611	Strategic planning consulting services
213112	Stratigraphic drilling, oil and gas field exploration on a contract basis
321999	Straw baskets manufacturing
315991	Straw hats manufacturing
422910	Straw wholesaling
111333	Strawberry farming
234110	Street and highway construction management firms
488490	Street cleaning service
234110	Street construction
335129	Street lighting fixtures (except traffic signals) manufacturing
234110	Street maintenance or repair
511199	Street map guide publishers
234110	Street paving
485119	Street railway systems (except mixed mode), commuter
421810	Street sweeping and cleaning equipment wholesaling
454390	Street vendors (except food)
722330	Street vendors, food

Code	Description
234990	Streetcar line construction
336510	Streetcars and car equipment, urban transit, manufacturing
713940	Strength development centers
336211	Stretch limousines assembling on purchased chassis
321999	Stretchers, curtain, wood, manufacturing
339113	Stretchers, medical, manufacturing
333513	Stretching machines, metalworking, manufacturing
111219	String bean farming, field and seed production
314991	Strings manufacturing
339992	Strings, musical instrument, manufacturing
212113	Strip mining, anthracite, on own account
212111	Strip mining, bituminous coal or lignite, on own account
212111	Strip mining, lignite, on own account
331421	Strip, copper and copper alloy, made from purchased copper or in integrated secondary smelting and rolling, drawing or extruding plants
331111	Strip, galvanized iron or steel, made in steel mills
331111	Strip, iron or steel, made in steel mills
331491	Strip, nonferrous metals (except aluminum, copper), made from purchased metals or scrap
211111	Stripper well production
213113	Stripping overburden services for coal mining on a contract basis
213114	Stripping overburden services for metal mining on a contract basis
213115	Stripping overburden services for nonmetallic minerals mining (except fuels) on a contract basis
334515	Stroboscopes manufacturing
335110	Strobotrons manufacturing
339932	Strollers, baby, manufacturing
212393	Strontianite mining and/or beneficiating
325188	Strontium carbonate manufacturing
325188	Strontium compounds, not specified elsewhere by process, manufacturing
212393	Strontium mineral mining and/or beneficiating
325188	Strontium nitrate manufacturing
421510	Structural assemblies, metal, wholesaling
421390	Structural assemblies, prefabricated (except wood), wholesaling
421310	Structural assemblies, prefabricated wood, wholesaling
421320	Structural clay tile (except refractory) wholesaling
327121	Structural clay tile manufacturing
321114	Structural lumber and timber, treating
321213	Structural members, glue laminated or pre-engineered wood, manufacturing
333516	Structural rolling mill machinery, metalworking, manufacturing
331319	Structural shapes made by rolling purchased aluminum
331319	Structural shapes, aluminum, made in integrated secondary smelting and rolling mills
331111	Structural shapes, iron or steel, made in steel mills
235910	Structural steel construction contractors
332312	Structural steel, fabricated, manufacturing
339932	Structural toy sets manufacturing

Code	Description
321213	Structural wood members (except trusses), fabricated, manufacturing
336330	Struts, automotive, truck, and bus, manufacturing
325411	Strychnine and derivatives (i.e., basic chemicals) manufacturing
327999	Stucco and stucco products manufacturing
235420	Stucco construction contractors
321113	Stud mills
115210	Stud services
522294	Student Loan Marketing Association (SLMA)
813410	Student clubs
611710	Student exchange programs
522291	Student loan companies
813410	Students' associations
813410	Students' unions
233320	Studio construction
334220	Studio equipment, radio and television broadcasting, manufacturing
541430	Studios, commercial art
321912	Studs, resawing purchased lumber
332322	Studs, sheet metal, manufacturing
921120	Study commissions, legislative
339931	Stuffed toys (including animals) manufacturing
333294	Stuffer, sausage machinery, manufacturing
113310	Stump removing in the field
325920	Styphnic acid explosive materials manufacturing
325110	Styrene made from refined petroleum or liquid hydrocarbons
324110	Styrene made in petroleum refineries
325211	Styrene resins manufacturing
325211	Styrene-acrylonitrile resins manufacturing
325212	Styrene-butadiene rubber containing less than 50 percent styrene manufacturing
325212	Styrene-chloroprene rubber manufacturing
325212	Styrene-isoprene rubber manufacturing
212111	Subbituminous coal surface mining and/or beneficiating
212112	Subbituminous coal underground mining or mining and beneficiating
332994	Submachine guns manufacturing
336611	Submarine building
333514	Subpresses, machine tool, manufacturing
334210	Subscriber loop equipment, telephone, manufacturing
513210	Subscription television networks
551114	Subsidiary management offices
623220	Substance abuse (i.e., alcoholism, drug addiction) halfway houses
623220	Substance abuse facilities, residential
813319	Substance abuse prevention advocacy organizations
621420	Substance abuse treatment centers and clinics (except hospitals), outpatient
335311	Substation transformers, electric power distribution, manufacturing
512191	Subtitling of motion picture film or video
485113	Suburban bus line services (except mixed mode)
485112	Suburban commuter rail systems (except mixed mode)
485111	Suburban transit systems, mixed mode (e.g., bus, commuter rail, subway combinations)
541850	Subway card display advertising services

Code	Description
336510	Subway cars manufacturing
421860	Subway cars wholesaling
234990	Subway construction
485119	Subway systems (except mixed mode), commuter
339112	Suction therapy apparatus manufacturing
812320	Suede garment cleaning services
313311	Sueding broadwoven fabrics
313312	Sueding textile products and fabrics (except broadwoven)
111991	Sugar beet farming
115113	Sugar beets, machine harvesting
311221	Sugar made by wet milling corn
333294	Sugar refining machinery manufacturing
325998	Sugar substitutes (i.e., synthetic sweeteners blended with other ingredients) made from purchased synthetic sweeteners
325199	Sugar substitutes (i.e., synthetic sweeteners blended with other ingredients) made in synthetic sweetener establishments
311312	Sugar, cane, made from purchased raw cane sugar
311311	Sugar, clarified, granulated, and raw, made in sugarcane mill
311312	Sugar, confectionery, made from purchased raw cane sugar
311313	Sugar, confectionery, made from sugar beets
311311	Sugar, confectionery, made in sugarcane mill
311312	Sugar, granulated, made from purchased raw cane sugar
311313	Sugar, granulated, made from sugar beets
311311	Sugar, granulated, made in sugarcane mill
311312	Sugar, invert, made from purchased raw cane sugar
311313	Sugar, invert, made from sugar beets
311311	Sugar, invert, made in sugarcane mill
311313	Sugar, liquid, made from sugar beets
311311	Sugar, raw, made in sugarcane mill
422590	Sugar, raw, wholesaling
311312	Sugar, refined, made from purchased raw cane sugar
422490	Sugar, refined, wholesaling
111930	Sugarcane farming, field production
311311	Sugarcane mills
311311	Sugarcane refining
115113	Sugarcane, machine harvesting
624190	Suicide crisis centers
532220	Suit rental
315999	Suit trimmings cut and sewn from purchased fabric (except apparel contractors)
315211	Suit trimmings, men's and boys', cut and sew apparel contractors
332510	Suitcase hardware, metal, manufacturing
316991	Suitcases, all materials, manufacturing
315211	Suits (i.e., nontailored, tailored, work), men's and boys', cut and sew apparel contractors
315212	Suits (i.e., nontailored, tailored, work), women's, misses', girls', and infants', cut and sew apparel contractors
315191	Suits made in apparel knitting mills
339113	Suits, firefighting, manufacturing
315291	Suits, infants' (e.g., warm-up, jogging, snowsuits), cut and sewn from purchased fabric (except apparel contractors)

Code	Description
422320	Suits, men's and boys', wholesaling
315239	Suits, nontailored (e.g., jogging, snow suit, warm-up), women's, misses', and girls', cut and sewn from purchased fabric (except apparel contractors)
315228	Suits, nontailored (e.g., jogging, snow, ski, warm-up), men's and boys', cut and sewn from purchased fabric (except apparel contractors)
339113	Suits, space, manufacturing
315222	Suits, tailored, men's and boys', cut and sewn from purchased fabric (except apparel contractors)
315234	Suits, tailored, women's, misses', and girls', cut and sewn from purchased fabric (except apparel contractors)
325411	Sulfa drugs, uncompounded, manufacturing
212391	Sulfate, sodium, mining and/or beneficiating
325188	Sulfides and sulfites manufacturing
325188	Sulfocyanides manufacturing
325411	Sulfonamides, uncompounded, manufacturing
325188	Sulfur and sulfur compounds, not specified elsewhere by process, manufacturing
325188	Sulfur chloride manufacturing
325188	Sulfur dioxide manufacturing
325188	Sulfur hexafluoride gas manufacturing
325320	Sulfur insecticides manufacturing
212393	Sulfur mining and/or beneficiating
211112	Sulfur recovered from natural gas
325188	Sulfur recovering or refining (except from sour natural gas)
212393	Sulfur, native, mining and/or beneficiating
325188	Sulfuric acid manufacturing
422690	Sulfuric acid wholesaling
325192	Sulphonated derivatives manufacturing
311423	Sulphured fruit and vegetables manufacturing
325191	Sumac extract manufacturing
721214	Summer camps (except day instructional)
713990	Summer day camps (except instructional)
721110	Summer resort hotels
711110	Summer theaters
235110	Sump pump construction contractors
333911	Sump pumps, residential-type, manufacturing
115114	Sun drying of dates, prunes, raisins, and olives
115114	Sun drying of fruits and vegetables
115114	Sun drying of tomatoes
812199	Sun tanning salons
111120	Sunflower farming, field and seed production
311223	Sunflower seed oil, cake and meal, made in crushing mills
446130	Sunglass stores
339115	Sunglasses and goggles manufacturing
421460	Sunglasses wholesaling
336399	Sunroofs and parts, automotive, truck, and bus, manufacturing
325620	Sunscreen lotions and oils manufacturing
315291	Sunsuits, infants', cut and sewn from purchased fabric (except apparel contractors)
325620	Suntan lotions and oils manufacturing
331111	Superalloys, iron or steel, manufacturing

Superalloys—Swimming pool

Code	Description
331492	Superalloys, nonferrous based, made from purchased metals or scrap
445110	Supermarkets
325312	Superphosphates manufacturing
452910	Superstores (i.e., food and general merchandise)
921190	Supply agencies, government
332913	Supply line assemblies, plumbing (i.e., flexible hose with fittings), manufacturing
624190	Support group services
339113	Supports, orthopedic (e.g., abdominal, ankle, arch, kneecap), manufacturing
325412	Suppositories manufacturing
524126	Surety insurance carriers, direct
325613	Surface active agents manufacturing
422690	Surface active agents wholesaling
334516	Surface area analyzers manufacturing
334512	Surface burner controls, temperature, manufacturing
322226	Surface coating purchased paperboard
333120	Surface mining machinery (except drilling) manufacturing
333295	Surface mount machinery for making printed circuit boards manufacturing
339920	Surfboards manufacturing
335999	Surge suppressors manufacturing
621111	Surgeons' (except dental) offices (e.g., centers, clinics)
541940	Surgeons' offices, veterinary
621210	Surgeons', dental, offices (e.g., centers, clinics)
115112	Surgery on trees and vines
541940	Surgery services, veterinary
421450	Surgical appliances wholesaling
339112	Surgical clamps manufacturing
339113	Surgical dressings manufacturing
339113	Surgical implants manufacturing
811219	Surgical instrument repair and maintenance services
421450	Surgical instruments and apparatus wholesaling
339112	Surgical knife blades and handles manufacturing
621111	Surgical pathologists' offices (e.g., centers, clinics)
339112	Surgical stapling devices manufacturing
339113	Surgical supplies (except medical instruments) manufacturing
421450	Surgical supplies wholesaling
334510	Surgical support systems (e.g., heart-lung machines) (except iron lungs) manufacturing
421450	Surgical towels wholesaling
311711	Surimi canning
311712	Surimi, fresh and frozen, manufacturing
213112	Surveying (except seismographic) oil or gas wells on a contract basis
541370	Surveying and mapping services (except geophysical)
421490	Surveying equipment and supplies wholesaling
811219	Surveying instrument repair and maintenance services
334519	Surveying instruments manufacturing
541360	Surveying services, geophysical
321999	Surveyor's stakes, wood, manufacturing
611699	Survival training instruction
315999	Suspenders cut and sewn from purchased fabric (except apparel contractors)
315211	Suspenders, men's and boys', cut and sew apparel contractors

Code	Description
315212	Suspenders, women's, girls', and infants', cut and sew apparel contractors
811118	Suspension repair shops, automotive
339113	Sutures, surgical, manufacturing
213112	Swabbing oil or gas wells on a contract basis
333513	Swaging machines, metalworking, manufacturing
487210	Swamp buggy operation
323121	Swatches and samples, mounting for the trade
332999	Swatters, fly metal, manufacturing
315299	Sweat bands cut and sewn from purchased fabric (except apparel contractors)
315191	Sweat bands made in apparel knitting mills
315211	Sweat bands, men's and boys', cut and sew apparel contractors
315212	Sweat bands, women's, girls', and infants', cut and sew apparel contractors
315191	Sweat pants made in apparel knitting mills
315291	Sweat pants, infants', cut and sewn from purchased fabric (except apparel contractors)
315228	Sweat pants, men's, boys', and unisex (i.e., sized without regard to gender), cut and sewn from purchased fabric (except apparel contractors)
315211	Sweat pants, men's, boys', and unisex, cut and sew apparel contractors
315212	Sweat pants, women's, girls', and infants', cut and sew apparel contractors
315239	Sweat pants, women's, misses', and girls', cut and sewn from purchased fabric (except apparel contractors)
315191	Sweat suits made in apparel knitting mills
315291	Sweat suits, infants', cut and sewn from purchased fabric (except apparel contractors)
315211	Sweat suits, men's and boys', cut and sew apparel contractors
315228	Sweat suits, men's and boys', cut and sewn from purchased fabric (except apparel contractors)
315212	Sweat suits, women's, girls', and infants', cut and sew apparel contractors
315239	Sweat suits, women's, misses', and girls', cut and sewn from purchased fabric (except apparel contractors)
316110	Sweatband leather manufacturing
315191	Sweater jackets made in apparel knitting mills
315291	Sweater jackets, infants', cut and sewn from purchased fabric (except apparel contractors)
315211	Sweater jackets, men's and boys', cut and sew apparel contractors
315228	Sweater jackets, men's and boys', cut and sewn from purchased fabric (except apparel contractors)
315212	Sweater jackets, women's, girls', and infants', cut and sew apparel contractors
315239	Sweater jackets, women's, misses', and girls', cut and sewn from purchased fabric (except apparel contractors)
315191	Sweater vests made in apparel knitting mills
315291	Sweater vests, infants', cut and sewn from purchased fabric (except apparel contractors)

Code	Description
315211	Sweater vests, men's and boys', cut and sew apparel contractors
315228	Sweater vests, men's and boys', cut and sewn from purchased fabric (except apparel contractors)
315212	Sweater vests, women's, girls', and infants', cut and sew apparel contractors
315239	Sweater vests, women's, misses', and girls', cut and sewn from purchased fabric (except apparel contractors)
315191	Sweaters made in apparel knitting mills
315291	Sweaters, infants', cut and sewn from purchased fabric (except apparel contractors)
315211	Sweaters, men's and boys', cut and sew apparel contractors
315228	Sweaters, men's and boys', cut and sewn from purchased fabric (except apparel contractors)
315212	Sweaters, women's, and girls', and infants', cut and sew apparel contractors
315239	Sweaters, women's, misses', and girls', cut and sewn from purchased fabric (except apparel contractors)
315191	Sweatshirts made in apparel knitting mills
315291	Sweatshirts, infants', cut and sewn from purchased fabric (except apparel contractors)
315211	Sweatshirts, men's and boys', cut and sew apparel contractors
315223	Sweatshirts, men's and boys', cut and sewn from purchased fabric (except apparel contractors)
315223	Sweatshirts, outerwear, unisex (sized without regard to gender), cut and sewn from purchased fabric (except apparel contractors)
315212	Sweatshirts, women's, girls', and infants', cut and sew apparel contractors
315232	Sweatshirts, women's, misses', and girls', cut and sewn from purchased fabric (except apparel contractors)
334515	Sweep generators manufacturing
334515	Sweep oscillators manufacturing
335212	Sweepers, household-type electric vacuum, manufacturing
325612	Sweeping compounds, absorbent, manufacturing
111219	Sweet corn farming, field and seed production
111219	Sweet pepper farming, field, bedding plant and seed production
115114	Sweet potato curing
111219	Sweet potato farming, field and seed potato production
311812	Sweet yeast goods (except frozen) manufacturing
311813	Sweet yeast goods, frozen, manufacturing
311999	Sweetening syrups (except pure maple) manufacturing
611620	Swimming instruction
325998	Swimming pool chemical preparations manufacturing
561790	Swimming pool cleaning and maintenance services
235990	Swimming pool construction contractors
326199	Swimming pool covers and liners, plastics, manufacturing
333319	Swimming pool filter systems manufacturing
333414	Swimming pool heaters manufacturing

Code	Description
335129	Swimming pool lighting fixtures manufacturing
453998	Swimming pool supply stores
713940	Swimming pools
421910	Swimming pools and equipment wholesaling
339920	Swimming pools, above ground, manufacturing
315191	Swimsuits made in apparel knitting mills
315291	Swimsuits, infants', cut and sewn from purchased fabric (except apparel contractors)
315211	Swimsuits, men's and boys', cut and sew apparel contractors
315228	Swimsuits, men's and boys', cut and sewn from purchased fabric (except apparel contractors)
315212	Swimsuits, women's, girls', and infants', cut and sew apparel contractors
315239	Swimsuits, women's, misses', and girls', cut and sewn from purchased fabric (except apparel contractors)
448190	Swimwear stores
422320	Swimwear, men's and boys', wholesaling
422330	Swimwear, women's, children's, and infants', wholesaling
311119	Swine feed, complete, manufacturing
311119	Swine feed, supplements, concentrates, and premixes, manufacturing
422520	Swine wholesaling
335932	Switch boxes, electrical wiring, manufacturing
335931	Switch cutouts manufacturing
335313	Switchboards and parts, power, manufacturing
421610	Switchboards, electrical distribution, wholesaling
335931	Switches for electrical wiring (e.g., pressure, pushbutton, snap, tumbler) manufacturing
334419	Switches for electronic applications manufacturing
335313	Switches, electric power (except pushbutton, snap, solenoid, tumbler), manufacturing
421610	Switches, electrical, wholesaling
421690	Switches, electronic, wholesaling
335931	Switches, outlet box mounting-type, manufacturing
334512	Switches, pneumatic positioning remote, manufacturing
334512	Switches, thermostatic, manufacturing
335313	Switchgear and switchgear accessories, manufacturing
335313	Switching equipment, power, manufacturing
334210	Switching equipment, telephone, manufacturing
488210	Switching services, railroad
114111	Swordfish fishing
332211	Swords, nonprecious and precious plated metal, manufacturing
212313	Syenite (except nepheline) crushed and broken stone mining and/or beneficiating
212311	Syenite (except nepheline) mining or quarrying
212325	Syenite, nepheline, mining and/or beneficiating
212221	Sylvanite mining and/or beneficiating
711130	Symphony orchestras
813110	Synagogues
335312	Synchronous condensers and timing motors, electric, manufacturing

Code	Description
335312	Synchronous motors manufacturing
334515	Synchroscopes manufacturing
514110	Syndicates, news
339992	Synthesizers, music, manufacturing
311340	Synthetic chocolate manufacturing
325212	Synthetic rubber (i.e., vulcanizable elastomers) manufacturing
422690	Synthetic rubber wholesaling
327999	Synthetic stones, for gem stones and industrial use, manufacturing
325199	Synthetic sweeteners (i.e., sweetening agents) manufacturing
339112	Syringes, hypodermic, manufacturing
422490	Syrup (except fountain) wholesaling
311313	Syrup made from sugar beets
311930	Syrup, beverage, manufacturing
311312	Syrup, cane, made from purchased raw cane sugar
311311	Syrup, cane, made in sugarcane mill
311320	Syrup, chocolate, made from cacao beans
311330	Syrup, chocolate, made from purchased chocolate
311999	Syrup, corn (except wet milled), manufacturing
311221	Syrup, corn, made by wet milling
311930	Syrup, flavoring (except coffee based), manufacturing
311920	Syrup, flavoring, coffee based, manufacturing
422450	Syrup, fountain, wholesaling
111998	Syrup, pure maple (i.e., maple syrup reducing)
311999	Syrup, sweetening (except pure maple), manufacturing
311999	Syrup, table, artificially flavored, manufacturing
541512	Systems integration design consulting services, computer
541512	Systems integration design services, computer
448190	T-shirt shops, custom printed
315291	T-shirts, outerwear, infants', cut and sewn from purchased fabric (except apparel contractors)
315191	T-shirts, outerwear, made in apparel knitting mills
315223	T-shirts, outerwear, men's and boys', cut and sewn from purchased fabric (except apparel contractors)
315211	T-shirts, outerwear, men's, boys' and unisex, cut and sew apparel contractors
315223	T-shirts, outerwear, unisex (i.e., sized without regard to gender), cut and sewn from purchased fabric (except apparel contractors)
315212	T-shirts, outerwear, women's, girls', and infants', cut and sew apparel contractors
315232	T-shirts, outerwear, women's, misses', and girls', cut and sewn from purchased fabric (except apparel contractors)
315291	T-shirts, underwear, infants', cut and sewn from purchased fabric (except apparel contractors)
315192	T-shirts, underwear, made in apparel knitting mills
315211	T-shirts, underwear, men's and boys', cut and sew apparel contractors
315221	T-shirts, underwear, men's and boys', cut and sewn from purchased fabric (except apparel contractors)
315231	T-shirts, underwear, women's, misses', and girls', cut and sewn from purchased fabric (except apparel contractors)

Code	Description
315212	T-shirts, underwear, women's, misses', girls', and infants', cut and sew apparel contractors
334519	T-squares (drafting) manufacturing
334510	TENS (transcutaneous electrical nerve stimulator) manufacturing
325920	TNT (trinitrotoluene) manufacturing
334310	TV (television) sets manufacturing
443112	TV (television) stores
532490	TV broadcasting and studio equipment rental or leasing
337124	TV stands and similar stands for consumer electronics, metal, manufacturing
337125	TV stands and similar stands for consumer electronics, plastics, manufacturing
337122	TV stands and similar stands for consumer electronics, wood, manufacturing
532299	Table and banquet accessory rental
327112	Table articles, coarse earthenware, manufacturing
327112	Table articles, earthenware, manufacturing
327112	Table articles, fine earthenware (i.e., whiteware), manufacturing
327112	Table articles, vitreous china, manufacturing
332211	Table cutlery, nonprecious and precious plated metal, manufacturing
339912	Table cutlery, precious metal, manufacturing
335121	Table lamps (i.e., lighting fixtures) manufacturing
812331	Table linen supply services
311225	Table oil made from purchased oils
311221	Table oil, corn, made by wet milling
311942	Table salt manufacturing
327991	Table tops, marble, manufacturing
337110	Table tops, wood, manufacturing
112310	Table-egg chicken production
314129	Tablecloths (except paper) made from purchased materials
313249	Tablecloths made in a lace mills
313249	Tablecloths made in a warp knitting mills
313210	Tablecloths made in broadwoven fabric mills
313241	Tablecloths made in weft knitting mills
322291	Tablecloths, paper, made from purchased paper
337214	Tables (except wood), office-type, manufacturing
337124	Tables, metal household-type, manufacturing
337122	Tables, wood household-type, manufacturing
337211	Tables, wood, office-type, manufacturing
322233	Tablets (e.g., memo, note, writing) made from purchased paper
322121	Tablets (e.g., memo, note, writing) made in paper mills
332999	Tablets, metal, manufacturing
421220	Tableware (except disposable, plated, precious) wholesaling
327215	Tableware made from purchased glass
327212	Tableware made in glass making plants
532299	Tableware rental
422130	Tableware, disposable, wholesaling
421940	Tableware, precious and plated, wholesaling
327112	Tableware, vitreous china, manufacturing

Tachometer—Teacher

Code	Description
334515	Tachometer generators manufacturing
451110	Tack shops
321999	Tackle blocks, wood, manufacturing
451110	Tackle shops (i.e., fishing)
339920	Tackle, fishing (except line, nets, seines), manufacturing
421710	Tacks wholesaling
331222	Tacks, iron or steel, made in wire drawing plants
332618	Tacks, metal, made from purchased wire
212210	Taconite concentrates or agglomerates beneficiating
212210	Taconite ores mining and/or beneficiating
334511	Taffrail logs manufacturing
213111	Tailing in oil and gas field wells on a contract basis
811490	Tailor shops, alterations only
332211	Tailor's scissors, nonelectric, manufacturing
315211	Tailored dress and sport coats, men's and boys', cut and sew apparel contractors
315222	Tailored dress and sport coats, men's and boys', cut and sewn from purchased fabric (except apparel contractors)
421850	Tailors' supplies wholesaling
722211	Take out eating places
212399	Talc mining and/or beneficiating
327992	Talc processing beyond beneficiation
325620	Talcum powders manufacturing
711410	Talent agencies
711410	Talent agents
541214	Talent payment services
325191	Tall oil (except skimmings) manufacturing
311611	Tallow produced in a slaughtering plant
311613	Tallow produced in rendering plant
334514	Tally counters manufacturing
334514	Tallying meters (except clocks, electrical instruments, watches) manufacturing
333120	Tampers, powered, manufacturing
332995	Tampions guns manufacturing
111320	Tangelo groves
111320	Tangerine groves
332995	Tank artillery manufacturing
336211	Tank bodies for trucks manufacturing
562998	Tank cleaning and disposal services, commercial or industrial
562991	Tank cleaning services, septic
315291	Tank tops, infants', cut and sewn from purchased fabric (except apparel contractors)
315211	Tank tops, men's and boys', cut and sew apparel contractors
315191	Tank tops, outerwear, made in apparel knitting mills
315223	Tank tops, outerwear, men's and boys', cut and sewn from purchased fabric (except apparel contractors)
315232	Tank tops, outerwear, women's, misses', and girls', cut and sewn from purchased fabric (except apparel contractors)
315192	Tank tops, underwear, made in apparel knitting mills
315221	Tank tops, underwear, men's and boys', cut and sewn from purchased fabric (except apparel contractors)
315231	Tank tops, underwear, women's, misses', and girls', cut and sewn from purchased fabric (except apparel contractors)
315212	Tank tops, women's, girls', and infants', cut and sew apparel contractors

Code	Description
336212	Tank trailer, liquid and dry bulk, manufacturing
334514	Tank truck meters manufacturing
336211	Tank trucks (e.g., fuel oil, milk, water) assembling on purchased chassis
532411	Tanker rental or leasing
484220	Tanker trucking (e.g., chemical, juice, milk, petroleum), local
484230	Tanker trucking (e.g., chemical, juice, milk, petroleum), long-distance
327390	Tanks, concrete, manufacturing
327111	Tanks, flush, vitreous china, manufacturing
332420	Tanks, heavy gauge metal, manufacturing
336992	Tanks, military (including factory rebuilding), manufacturing
333315	Tanks, photographic developing, fixing, and washing, manufacturing
421510	Tanks, storage metal, wholesaling
326199	Tanks, storage, plastics or fiberglass, manufacturing
321920	Tanks, wood, coopered, manufacturing
316110	Tannery leather manufacturing
333298	Tannery machinery manufacturing
325191	Tannic acid (i.e., tannins) manufacturing
325188	Tanning agents, inorganic, manufacturing
325199	Tanning agents, synthetic organic, manufacturing
316110	Tanning and currying furs
325191	Tanning extracts and materials, natural, manufacturing
812199	Tanning salons
212299	Tantalite mining and/or beneficiating
212299	Tantalum ores mining and/or beneficiating
331419	Tantalum refining, primary
711120	Tap dance companies
339942	Tape dispensers manufacturing
512120	Tape distribution for television
332212	Tape measures, metal, manufacturing
334310	Tape players and recorders, household-type, manufacturing
421620	Tape players and recorders, household-type, wholesaling
532210	Tape recorder rental
561990	Tape slitting (e.g., cutting plastic or leather into widths) for the trade
334112	Tape storage units (e.g., drive backups), computer peripheral equipment, manufacturing
512191	Tape transfer service
332991	Tapered roller bearings manufacturing
322231	Tapes (e.g., adding machine, calculator, cash register) made from purchased paper
322222	Tapes (e.g., cellophane, masking, pressure sensitive), gummed, made from purchased paper or other materials
313221	Tapes weaving
421690	Tapes, blank, audio and video, wholesaling
422120	Tapes, cellophane, wholesaling
334613	Tapes, magnetic recording (i.e., audio, data, video), blank, manufacturing
339113	Tapes, medical adhesive, manufacturing
421450	Tapes, medical and surgical, wholesaling
313230	Tapes, nonwoven fabric, manufacturing
421990	Tapes, prerecorded, audio or video, wholesaling
334519	Tapes, surveyor's, manufacturing
422310	Tapes, textile, wholesaling

Code	Description
313320	Tapes, varnished and coated (except magnetic), made from purchased fabric
235420	Taping and finishing drywall construction contractors
311221	Tapioca manufacturing
333512	Tapping machines, metalworking, manufacturing
333515	Taps and dies (i.e., a machine tool accessory) manufacturing
335931	Taps, current, attachment plug and screw shell types, manufacturing
316999	Taps, shoe, leather, manufacturing
325211	Tar acid resins manufacturing
324121	Tar and asphalt paving mixtures made from purchased asphaltic materials
325191	Tar and tar oils made by distillation of wood
325192	Tar made by distillation of coal tar
324110	Tar made in petroleum refineries
324122	Tar paper made from purchased asphaltic materials and paper
324122	Tar paper, building and roofing, made from purchased paper
322121	Tar paper, building and roofing, made in paper mills
324122	Tar roofing cements and coatings made from purchased asphaltic materials
211111	Tar sands mining
336411	Target drones, aircraft, manufacturing
336413	Targets, trailer type, aircraft, manufacturing
541614	Tariff rate consulting services
541614	Tariff rate information services
111219	Taro farming, field and seed production
314912	Tarpaulins made from purchased fabrics
421330	Tarred felts wholesaling
311941	Tartar sauce manufacturing
325199	Tartaric acid manufacturing
325199	Tartrates, not specified elsewhere by process, manufacturing
812199	Tattoo parlors
722410	Taverns (i.e., drinking places)
561440	Tax collection services on a contract or fee basis
541110	Tax law attorneys' offices
541110	Tax law attorneys' private practices
523910	Tax liens dealing (i.e., acting as a principal in dealing tax liens to investors)
541213	Tax return preparation services
921130	Taxation departments
541850	Taxicab card advertising services
485310	Taxicab dispatch services
485310	Taxicab fleet operators
485310	Taxicab organizations
485310	Taxicab owner-operators
485310	Taxicab services
421110	Taxicabs wholesaling
711510	Taxidermists, independent
421850	Taxidermy supplies wholesaling
334514	Taximeters manufacturing
813319	Taxpayers' advocacy organizations
311920	Tea (except herbal) manufacturing
445299	Tea and coffee (i.e., packaged) stores
311920	Tea blending
111998	Tea farming
327212	Tea kettles, glass and glass ceramic, made in glass making plants
422490	Tea wholesaling
311920	Tea, herbal, manufacturing
312111	Tea, iced, manufacturing
311920	Tea, instant, manufacturing
113210	Teaberries gathering
923110	Teacher certification bureaus

Code	Description
561310	Teacher registries
333319	Teaching machines (e.g., flight simulators) manufacturing
421490	Teaching machines (except computers), electronic, wholesaling
332214	Teakettles and coffee pots, fabricated metal (except electric, glass), manufacturing
335211	Teakettles, electric, manufacturing
327212	Teakettles, glass and glass ceramic, manufacturing
315299	Team athletic uniforms cut and sewn from purchased fabric (except apparel contractors)
315211	Team athletic uniforms, men's and boys', cut and sew apparel contractors
315212	Team athletic uniforms, women's and girls', cut and sew apparel contractors
325199	Tear gas manufacturing
313311	Teaseling broadwoven fabrics
313312	Teaseling fabrics (except broadwoven)
325412	Technetium medicinal preparations manufacturing
327212	Technical glassware and glass products, pressed or blown, made in glass making plants
327215	Technical glassware made from purchased glass
511120	Technical magazine and periodical publishers
511120	Technical magazine and periodical publishers and printing combined
511120	Technical magazine and periodical publishing (i.e., establishments known as publishers)
323112	Technical magazines and periodicals flexographic printing without publishing
323111	Technical magazines and periodicals gravure printing without publishing
323110	Technical magazines and periodicals lithographic (offset) printing without publishing
323119	Technical magazines and periodicals printing (except flexographic, gravure, lithographic, screen) without publishing
323113	Technical magazines and periodicals screen printing without publishing
511130	Technical manual and paperback book publishers
511130	Technical manual and paperback book publishers and printing combined
323121	Technical manual paper (books) binding without rebinding
511130	Technical manual publishers
511130	Technical manual publishing (i.e., establishments known as publishers)
323117	Technical manuals and papers (books) printing and binding without publishing
323117	Technical manuals and papers (books) printing without publishing
711510	Technical writers, independent
315212	Teddies, women's, cut and sew apparel contractors
315231	Teddies, women's, misses', and girls', cut and sewn from purchased fabric (except apparel contractors)
624110	Teen outreach services
339114	Teeth (except customized) manufacturing
339116	Teeth, custom made in dental laboratories
421450	Teeth, dental, wholesaling
513322	Telecommunications carriers, cellular telephone

Code	Description
513310	Telecommunications carriers, wired
532490	Telecommunications equipment rental or leasing
234920	Telecommunications line (e.g., telephone, telegraph) construction
541618	Telecommunications management consulting services
513310	Telecommunications networks, wired
513330	Telecommunications resellers
235310	Telecommunications wiring installation contractors
513310	Telegram services
812990	Telegram services, singing
421690	Telegraph equipment wholesaling
561422	Telemarketing bureaus
561422	Telemarketing services on a contract or fee basis
334513	Telemetering instruments, industrial process-type, manufacturing
513390	Telemetry and tracking system operations on a contract or fee basis
334416	Telephone and telegraph transformers, electronic component-type, manufacturing
334210	Telephone answering machines manufacturing
421620	Telephone answering machines wholesaling
561421	Telephone answering services
337215	Telephone booths manufacturing
561422	Telephone call centers
334210	Telephone carrier line equipment manufacturing
334210	Telephone carrier switching equipment manufacturing
513310	Telephone carriers, facilities-based (except wireless)
513340	Telephone communications carriers, satellite
513322	Telephone communications carriers, wireless (except satellite)
513330	Telephone communications resellers (except satellite)
624190	Telephone counseling services
323112	Telephone directories flexographic printing without publishing
323111	Telephone directories gravure printing without publishing
323110	Telephone directories lithographic (offset) printing without publishing
323119	Telephone directories printing (except flexographic, gravure, lithographic, screen) without publishing
323113	Telephone directories screen printing without publishing
541870	Telephone directory distribution services, door-to-door
511140	Telephone directory publishers
511140	Telephone directory publishers and printing combined
511140	Telephone directory publishing (i.e., establishments known as publishers)
811213	Telephone equipment repair and maintenance services without retailing new telephone equipment
421690	Telephone equipment wholesaling
234920	Telephone line construction
561422	Telephone solicitation services on a contract or fee basis
443112	Telephone stores (including cellular)
514199	Telephone-based recorded information services
334210	Telephones (except cellular telephone) manufacturing

Code	Description
421690	Telephones wholesaling
334220	Telephones, cellular, manufacturing
334210	Telephones, coin operated, manufacturing
334113	Teleprinters (i.e., computer terminals) manufacturing
512191	Teleproduction services
333314	Telescopes manufacturing
334310	Television (TV) sets manufacturing
541840	Television advertising representatives (i.e., independent of media owners)
443112	Television and radio stores
513120	Television broadcasting networks
513120	Television broadcasting stations
337129	Television cabinets (i.e., housings), wood, manufacturing
421410	Television cameras wholesaling
512110	Television commercial production
561310	Television employment agencies
511120	Television guide publishers
511120	Television guide publishers and printing combined
511120	Television guide publishing (i.e., establishments known as publishers)
323112	Television guides flexographic printing without publishing
323111	Television guides gravure printing without publishing
323110	Television guides lithographic (offset) printing without publishing
323119	Television guides printing (except flexographic, gravure, lithographic, screen) without publishing
323113	Television guides screen printing without publishing
326199	Television housings, plastics, manufacturing
513220	Television operations multichannel multipoint distribution services (MMDS)
513220	Television operations, closed circuit
513220	Television operations, multipoint distribution system
454110	Television order, home shopping
334411	Television picture tubes manufacturing
711510	Television producers, independent
532210	Television rental
811211	Television repair services without retailing new televisions
421620	Television sets wholesaling
512110	Television show production
512120	Television show syndicators
513210	Television subscription services
332312	Television tower sections, fabricated structural metal, manufacturing
334220	Television transmitting antennas and ground equipment manufacturing
234920	Television transmitting tower construction
334220	Television, closed-circuit equipment, manufacturing
212221	Telluride (gold) mining and/or beneficiating
331419	Tellurium refining, primary
813319	Temperance organizations
334512	Temperature controls, automatic, residential and commercial-types, manufacturing
334513	Temperature instruments, industrial process-type (except glass and bimetal thermometers), manufacturing
334512	Temperature sensors for motor windings manufacturing
327215	Tempered glass made from purchased glass

Tempering metals—Theatrical

Code	Description
332811	Tempering metals and metal products for the trade
334519	Templates, drafting, manufacturing
339115	Temples and fronts (i.e., eyeglass frames), ophthalmic, manufacturing
813110	Temples, religious
561320	Temporary employment services
561320	Temporary help services
624221	Temporary housing for families of medical patients
624221	Temporary shelters (e.g., battered women's, homeless, runaway youth)
561320	Temporary staffing services
713950	Ten pin bowling alleys
713950	Ten pin bowling centers
813319	Tenants' advocacy associations
813990	Tenants' associations (except advocacy)
813319	Tenants' associations, advocacy
713940	Tennis club facilities
234990	Tennis court construction
713940	Tennis courts
421910	Tennis equipment and supplies wholesaling
339920	Tennis goods (e.g., balls, frames, rackets) manufacturing
611620	Tennis instruction, camps, or schools
711219	Tennis professionals, independent (i.e., participating in sports events)
315191	Tennis shirts made in apparel knitting mills
315291	Tennis shirts, infants', cut and sewn from purchased fabric (except apparel contractors)
315211	Tennis shirts, men's and boys', cut and sew apparel contractors
315223	Tennis shirts, men's and boys', cut and sewn from purchased fabric (except apparel contractors)
315212	Tennis shirts, women's, girls', and infants', cut and sew apparel contractors
315239	Tennis shirts, women's, misses', and girls', cut and sewn from purchased fabric (except apparel contractors)
315191	Tennis skirts made in apparel knitting mills
315212	Tennis skirts, women's and girls', cut and sew apparel contractors
315239	Tennis skirts, women's, misses', and girls', cut and sewn from purchased fabric (except apparel contractors)
334519	Tensile strength testing equipment manufacturing
321999	Tent poles, wood, manufacturing
336214	Tent trailers (hard top and soft top) manufacturing
532292	Tent, camping, rental
532299	Tent, party, rental
314912	Tents made from purchased fabrics
335931	Terminals and connectors for electrical devices manufacturing
334113	Terminals, computer, manufacturing
422710	Terminals, petroleum
561710	Termite control services
325320	Termite poisons manufacturing
331111	Terneplate made in steel mills
421510	Terneplate wholesaling
331111	Ternes, iron or steel, long or short, made in steel mills
325199	Terpineol manufacturing
114119	Terrapin fishing
235430	Terrazzo construction contractors
327390	Terrazzo products, precast (except brick, block and pipe), manufacturing
313210	Terry broadwoven fabrics weaving

Code	Description
325199	Tert-butylated bis (p-phenoxyphenyl) ether fluid manufacturing
611710	Test development and evaluation services, educational
213114	Test drilling for metal mining on a contract basis
213115	Test drilling for nonmetallic minerals mining (except fuel) on a contract basis
334515	Test equipment for electronic and electrical circuits and equipment manufacturing
334515	Test sets, ignition harness, manufacturing
525920	Testamentary trusts
334519	Testers for checking hydraulic controls on aircraft manufacturing
421830	Testing and measuring equipment, electrical (except automotive), wholesaling
334519	Testing equipment (e.g., abrasion, shearing strength, tensile strength, torsion) manufacturing
541380	Testing laboratories (except medical, veterinary)
621511	Testing laboratories, medical
541940	Testing laboratories, veterinary
541940	Testing services for veterinarians
488190	Testing services, aircraft
611710	Testing services, educational
333993	Testing, weighing, inspecting, packaging machinery manufacturing
325199	Tetrachloroethylene manufacturing
325411	Tetracycline, uncompounded, manufacturing
325199	Tetraethyl lead manufacturing
325920	Tetryl explosive materials manufacturing
314911	Textile bags made from purchased woven or knitted materials
422990	Textile bags wholesaling
313210	Textile broadwoven fabrics mills
561990	Textile cutting services
541490	Textile design services
325613	Textile finishing assistants manufacturing
333292	Textile finishing machinery (e.g., bleaching, dyeing, mercerizing, printing) manufacturing
314999	Textile fire hose made from purchased material
561910	Textile folding and packaging services
327212	Textile glass fibers made in glass making plants
327112	Textile guides, porcelain, manufacturing
316999	Textile leathers (e.g., apron picker leather, mill strapping) manufacturing
421830	Textile machinery and equipment wholesaling
532490	Textile machinery rental or leasing
811310	Textile machinery repair and maintenance services
333292	Textile making machinery (except sewing machines) manufacturing
233310	Textile mill construction
313210	Textile mills, broadwoven fabrics
313221	Textile mills, narrow woven fabric
313221	Textile narrow woven fabric mills
325910	Textile printing inks manufacturing
333292	Textile printing machinery manufacturing
313210	Textile products (except apparel) made in broadwoven fabric mills
313249	Textile products (except apparel) made in lace mills
313221	Textile products (except apparel) made in narrow woven fabric mills

Code	Description
313249	Textile products (except apparel) made in warp knitting mills
313241	Textile products (except apparel) made in weft knitting mills
313312	Textile products finishing
325613	Textile scouring agents manufacturing
421930	Textile waste wholesaling
313320	Textile waterproofing
422310	Textiles (except burlap, felt) wholesaling
325221	Texturizing cellulosic yarn made in the same establishment
333292	Texturizing machinery for textiles manufacturing
325222	Texturizing noncellulosic yarn made in the same establishment
313112	Texturizing purchased yarn
212299	Thallium mining and/or beneficiating
711110	Theater companies (except dance)
711110	Theater companies (except dance), amateur
711120	Theater companies, dance
421410	Theater equipment (except seats) wholesaling
711310	Theater festival managers with facilities
711320	Theater festival managers without facilities
711310	Theater festival organizers with facilities
711320	Theater festival organizers without facilities
711310	Theater festival promoters with facilities
711320	Theater festival promoters without facilities
711310	Theater operators
611610	Theater schools
337127	Theater seating manufacturing
421510	Theater seats wholesaling
531120	Theater, property operation, rental or leasing
711120	Theaters, dance
711110	Theaters, dinner
711110	Theaters, live theatrical production (except dance)
512131	Theaters, motion picture (except drive-in)
512132	Theaters, motion picture, drive-in
512131	Theaters, motion picture, indoor
711110	Theaters, musical
512132	Theaters, outdoor motion picture
711320	Theatrical booking agencies (except motion picture)
315299	Theatrical costumes cut and sewn from purchased fabric (except apparel contractors)
315211	Theatrical costumes, men's and boys', cut and sew apparel contractors
315212	Theatrical costumes, women's, girls', and infants', cut and sew apparel contractors
711120	Theatrical dance productions, live
561310	Theatrical employment agencies
532490	Theatrical equipment (except costumes) rental or leasing
711310	Theatrical production managers with facilities
711320	Theatrical production managers without facilities
711310	Theatrical production organizers with facilities
711320	Theatrical production organizers without facilities
711310	Theatrical production promoters with facilities
711320	Theatrical production promoters without facilities

Code	Description
711110	Theatrical repertory companies
711110	Theatrical road companies
339999	Theatrical scenery manufacturing
711110	Theatrical stock companies
711410	Theatrical talent agents
561599	Theatrical ticket offices
532220	Theatrical wardrobe and costume rental
713110	Theme parks, amusement
325411	Theobromine and derivatives (i.e., basic chemicals) manufacturing
333314	Theodolites manufacturing
334519	Theodolites, surveying, manufacturing
611310	Theological seminaries offering baccalaureate or graduate degrees
334517	Therapeutic X-ray apparatus and tubes (e.g., medical, industrial, research) manufacturing
******	Therapists' offices — see type
421450	Therapy equipment wholesaling
334516	Thermal analysis instruments, laboratory-type, manufacturing
334516	Thermal conductivity instruments and sensors manufacturing
334513	Thermal conductivity instruments, industrial process-type, manufacturing
326140	Thermal insulation, polystyrene foam, manufacturing
541380	Thermal testing laboratories or services
334415	Thermistors (except industrial process-type) manufacturing
334513	Thermistors, industrial process-type, manufacturing
334519	Thermocouples (except industrial process, aircraft type, glass vacuum) manufacturing
334512	Thermocouples, glass vacuum, manufacturing
334513	Thermocouples, industrial process-type, manufacturing
335999	Thermoelectric generators manufacturing
333993	Thermoform, blister, and skin packaging machinery manufacturing
333220	Thermoforming machinery for plastics manufacturing
334516	Thermogravimetric analyzers manufacturing
334519	Thermometer, liquid-in-glass and bimetal types (except medical), manufacturing
421450	Thermometers wholesaling
334513	Thermometers, filled system industrial process type, manufacturing
339112	Thermometers, medical, manufacturing
325211	Thermoplastic resins and plastics materials manufacturing
325211	Thermosetting plastics resins manufacturing
325212	Thermosetting vulcanizable elastomers manufacturing
332911	Thermostatic traps, industrial-type, manufacturing
334512	Thermostats (e.g., air-conditioning, appliance, comfort heating, refrigeration) manufacturing
336399	Thermostats, automotive, truck, and bus, manufacturing
334519	Thickness gauging instruments, ultrasonic, manufacturing
332999	Thimbles for wire rope manufacturing
334413	Thin film integrated circuits manufacturing
333295	Thin layer deposition equipment, semiconductor, manufacturing

Code	Description
115112	Thinning of crops, mechanical and chemical
325188	Thiocyanate manufacturing
325199	Thioglycolic acid manufacturing
325212	Thiol rubber manufacturing
212299	Thorite mining and/or beneficiating
212299	Thorium ores mining and/or beneficiating
711212	Thoroughbred racetracks
422310	Thread (except industrial) wholesaling
333515	Thread cutting dies (i.e., a machine tool accessory) manufacturing
313312	Thread finishing
333292	Thread making machinery manufacturing
313113	Thread mills
333513	Thread rolling machines, metalworking, manufacturing
313113	Thread, all fibers, manufacturing
421840	Thread, industrial, wholesaling
326299	Thread, rubber (except fabric covered), manufacturing
333512	Threading machines, metalworking, manufacturing
115113	Threshing service
453310	Thrift shops, used merchandise
333298	Through-hole machinery, printed circuit board loading, manufacturing
325221	Throwing cellulosic yarn made in the same establishment
325222	Throwing noncellulosic yarn made in the same establishment
313112	Throwing purchased yarn
334519	Thrust power indicators, aircraft engine, manufacturing
332991	Thrust roller bearings manufacturing
334413	Thyristors manufacturing
325412	Thyroid preparations manufacturing
325320	Tick powders or sprays manufacturing
561599	Ticket (e.g., airline, bus, cruise ship, sports, theatrical) offices
561599	Ticket (e.g., airline, bus, cruise ship, sports, theatrical) sales offices
561599	Ticket (e.g., amusement, sports, theatrical) agencies
561599	Ticket (e.g., amusement, sports, theatrical) sales agencies
561599	Ticket agencies, amusement
561599	Ticket agencies, sports
561599	Ticket agencies, theatrical
561599	Ticket offices for foreign cruise ship companies
331111	Tie plates, iron or steel, made in steel mills
448150	Tie shops
331222	Tie wires made in wire drawing plants
315191	Ties made in apparel knitting mills
327390	Ties, concrete, railroad, manufacturing
315993	Ties, men's and boys' hand sewn (except apparel contractors), manufacturing
315211	Ties, men's and boys' hand sewn, cut and sew apparel contractors
321113	Ties, railroad, made from logs or bolts
321114	Ties, wood railroad bridge, cross, and switch, treating
321113	Ties, wood, made from logs or bolts
421990	Ties, wood, wholesaling
315119	Tights knitting or knitting and finishing
112511	Tilapia production
325520	Tile adhesives manufacturing
235430	Tile construction contractors
333298	Tile making machinery (except kilns) manufacturing

Code	Description
444190	Tile stores, ceramic
327122	Tile, ceramic wall and floor, manufacturing
327124	Tile, clay refractory, manufacturing
327121	Tile, clay, structural, manufacturing
321999	Tile, cork, manufacturing
327123	Tile, roofing and drain, clay, manufacturing
327123	Tile, sewer, clay, manufacturing
421320	Tile, structural clay (except refractory), wholesaling
114111	Tilefish fishing
333994	Tilemaking kilns manufacturing
326192	Tiles, floor (i.e., linoleum, rubber, vinyl), manufacturing
421820	Tillers, farm, wholesaling
333112	Tillers, lawn and garden-type, manufacturing
421990	Timber and timber products (except lumber) wholesaling
113310	Timber piling
113310	Timber pole cutting
234990	Timber removal, underwater
113110	Timber tracts operations
115310	Timber valuation
321114	Timber, structural, treating
321113	Timbers, made from logs or bolts
321213	Timbers, structural, glue laminated or pre-engineered wood, manufacturing
334518	Time clocks and time recording devices manufacturing
334513	Time cycle and program controllers, industrial process-type, manufacturing
334518	Time locks manufacturing
323118	Time planners/organizers and refills manufacturing
334512	Time program controls, air-conditioning systems, manufacturing
421420	Time recording machines wholesaling
561599	Time share exchange services, condominium
334518	Time stamps containing clock mechanisms manufacturing
335313	Time switches, electrical switchgear apparatus, manufacturing
334518	Timers for industrial use, clockwork mechanism, manufacturing
326220	Timing belt, rubber or plastics, manufacturing
335314	Timing devices, mechanical and solid-state (except clockwork), manufacturing
336312	Timing gears and chains, automotive and truck gasoline engine, manufacturing
334518	Timing mechanisms, clockwork, manufacturing
335312	Timing motors, synchronous, electric, manufacturing
331491	Tin and tin alloy bar, pipe, rod, sheet, strip, and tubing made from purchased metals or scrap
331419	Tin base alloys made in primary tin smelting and refining mills
325188	Tin chloride manufacturing
325188	Tin compounds, not specified elsewhere by process, manufacturing
332999	Tin foil not made in rolling mills
212299	Tin metal concentrates beneficiating
212299	Tin metal ores mining and/or beneficiating
325188	Tin oxide manufacturing
332431	Tin plate cans manufacturing
421510	Tin plate wholesaling

Tin recovering—Torsion

Code	Description
331492	Tin recovering from scrap and/or alloying purchased metals
331419	Tin refining, primary
331491	Tin rolling, drawing, or extruding purchased metals or scrap
325188	Tin salts manufacturing
235610	Tin smithing contractors, in connection with construction work
331111	Tin-free steel made in steel mills
325412	Tincture of iodine preparations manufacturing
332212	Tinner's snips manufacturing
331111	Tinplate made in steel mills
339999	Tinsel manufacturing
325998	Tint and dye preparations, household-type (except hair), manufacturing
325620	Tints, dyes, and rinses, hair, manufacturing
234930	Tipple construction
212111	Tipple operation, bituminous coal mining and/or beneficiating
316999	Tips, shoe, leather, manufacturing
421130	Tire and tube repair materials wholesaling
332618	Tire chains made from purchased wire
314992	Tire cord and fabric, all materials, manufacturing
336360	Tire covers made from purchased fabric
441320	Tire dealers, automotive
325998	Tire inflators, aerosol, manufacturing
333220	Tire making machinery manufacturing
333319	Tire mounting machines, motor vehicle, manufacturing
333220	Tire recapping machinery manufacturing
421830	Tire recapping machinery wholesaling
326211	Tire repair materials manufacturing
811198	Tire repair shops (except retreading), automotive
326212	Tire retreading, recapping or rebuilding
333320	Tire shredding machinery manufacturing
421130	Tire tubes, motor vehicle, wholesaling
326211	Tires (e.g., pneumatic, semi-pneumatic, solid rubber) manufacturing
421130	Tires, motor vehicle, wholesaling
326199	Tires, plastics, manufacturing
421930	Tires, scrap, wholesaling
421130	Tires, used (except scrap), wholesaling
111421	Tissue culture farming
322121	Tissue paper stock manufacturing
422130	Tissue paper, toilet and facial, wholesaling
327113	Titania porcelain insulators manufacturing
212299	Titaniferous-magnetite ores, valued chiefly for titanium content, mining and/or beneficiating
331491	Titanium and titanium alloy bar, billet, rod, sheet, strip, and tubing made from purchased metals or scrap
325131	Titanium based pigments manufacturing
331528	Titanium castings (except die-castings), unfinished, manufacturing
212299	Titanium concentrates beneficiating
331522	Titanium die-castings, unfinished, manufacturing
325188	Titanium dioxide manufacturing
332112	Titanium forgings made from purchased metals, unfinished
212299	Titanium ores mining and/or beneficiating
331419	Titanium refining, primary
331491	Titanium rolling, drawing, or extruding purchased metals or scrap
541191	Title abstract companies, real estate

Code	Description
541191	Title companies, real estate
524127	Title insurance carriers, real estate, direct
541191	Title search companies, real estate
512191	Titling of motion picture film or video
334516	Titrimeters manufacturing
335211	Toaster ovens, household-type electric, manufacturing
421620	Toasters, electric, wholesaling
335211	Toasters, household-type electric, manufacturing
422940	Tobacco (except leaf) wholesaling
422590	Tobacco auction markets
111910	Tobacco farming, field and seed production
115114	Tobacco grading
333111	Tobacco harvester machines manufacturing
321920	Tobacco hogshead stock, manufacturing
321920	Tobacco hogsheads, manufacturing
312210	Tobacco leaf processing and aging
339999	Tobacco pipes manufacturing
316993	Tobacco pouches (except metal) manufacturing
339911	Tobacco pouches, precious metal, manufacturing
333298	Tobacco processing machinery (except farm-type) manufacturing
312229	Tobacco products (e.g., chewing, smoking, snuff) manufacturing
422940	Tobacco products wholesaling
312229	Tobacco products, imitation (except cigarettes) manufacturing
312229	Tobacco sheeting services
312210	Tobacco stemming and redrying
453991	Tobacco stores
422590	Tobacco, leaf, wholesaling
339920	Toboggans manufacturing
316999	Toe caps, leather, manufacturing
311340	Toffee manufacturing
311991	Tofu (i.e., bean curd) (except frozen desserts) manufacturing
311520	Tofu frozen desserts manufacturing
332722	Toggle bolts, metal, manufacturing
325612	Toilet bowl cleaners manufacturing
332998	Toilet fixtures manufacturing
326191	Toilet fixtures, plastics, manufacturing
327111	Toilet fixtures, vitreous china, manufacturing
316993	Toilet kits and cases (except metal) manufacturing
339911	Toilet kits and cases, precious metal, manufacturing
322291	Toilet paper made from purchased paper
322121	Toilet paper made in paper mills
325620	Toilet preparations (e.g., cosmetics, deodorants, perfumes) manufacturing
422210	Toilet preparations wholesaling
562991	Toilet renting and/or servicing, portable
321999	Toilet seats, wood, manufacturing
422210	Toilet soaps wholesaling
422130	Toilet tissue wholesaling
332999	Toilet ware, precious plated metal, manufacturing
325620	Toilet water manufacturing
422210	Toiletries wholesaling
334210	Toll switching equipment, telephone, manufacturing
325110	Toluene made from refined petroleum or liquid hydrocarbons
324110	Toluene made in petroleum refineries
325192	Toluidines manufacturing
111219	Tomato farming (except under cover), field, bedding plant and seed production

Code	Description
111419	Tomato farming, grown under cover
333111	Tomato harvesting machines manufacturing
325992	Toner cartridges manufacturing
325992	Toner cartridges rebuilding
422120	Toner cartridges wholesaling
325132	Toners (except electrostatic, photographic) manufacturing
325992	Toners, electrostatic and photographic, manufacturing
339113	Tongue depressors manufacturing
316999	Tongues, boot and shoe, leather, manufacturing
339112	Tonometers, medical, manufacturing
332439	Tool boxes, light gauge metal, manufacturing
321920	Tool chests, wood, manufacturing
321999	Tool handles, wood, turned and shaped, manufacturing
541420	Tool industrial design services
337127	Tool stands, factory, manufacturing
331111	Tool steel made in steel mills
444130	Tool stores, power and hand (except outdoor)
333515	Toolholders (i.e., a machine tool accessory) manufacturing
333515	Tools and accessories for machine tools manufacturing
421120	Tools and equipment, motor vehicle, wholesaling
339114	Tools, dentist's, manufacturing
421710	Tools, hand (except motor vehicle, machinists' precision tools), wholesaling
332212	Tools, hand, metal blade (e.g., putty knives, scrapers, screw drivers)
333991	Tools, handheld power-driven, manufacturing
332212	Tools, handheld, nonpowered (except kitchen-type), manufacturing
421830	Tools, machinists' precision, wholesaling
332212	Tools, woodworking edge (e.g., augers, bits, countersinks), manufacturing
339994	Toothbrushes (except electric) manufacturing
422210	Toothbrushes (except electric) wholesaling
335211	Toothbrushes, electric, manufacturing
421620	Toothbrushes, electric, wholesaling
325611	Toothpastes, gels, and tooth powders manufacturing
321999	Toothpicks, wood, manufacturing
316999	Top lifts, boot and shoe, leather, manufacturing
484220	Top soil hauling, local
212325	Topaz, non-gem, mining and/or beneficiating
315211	Topcoats, men's and boys', cut and sew apparel contractors
315222	Topcoats, men's and boys', cut and sewn from purchased fabric (except apparel contractors)
541370	Topographic mapping services
541370	Topographic surveying services
422490	Toppings (except fountain) wholesaling
336399	Tops, convertible automotive, manufacturing
332995	Torpedo tubes manufacturing
332993	Torpedoes manufacturing
336350	Torque converters, automotive, truck, and bus, manufacturing
335312	Torque motors, electric, manufacturing
332611	Torsion bar manufacturing
334519	Torsion testing equipment manufacturing

Code	Description
311919	Tortilla chips manufacturing
311830	Tortillas manufacturing
334514	Totalizing fluid meters manufacturing
334514	Totalizing meters (except aircraft), consumption registering, manufacturing
339999	Toupees manufacturing
422990	Toupees wholesaling
487110	Tour bus, scenic and sightseeing, operation
561520	Tour operators (i.e., arranging and assembling tours)
561591	Tourism bureaus
926110	Tourism development offices, government
713990	Tourist guide services
721199	Tourist homes
561591	Tourist information bureaus
721110	Tourist lodges
336413	Tow targets, aircraft, manufacturing
488410	Tow truck services
336211	Tow trucks (including tilt and load) assembling on purchased chassis
336611	Towboat building and repairing
532411	Towboat rental or leasing
812331	Towel (except shop, wiping) supply services
327111	Towel bar holders, vitreous china and earthenware, manufacturing
812332	Towel supply services, shop or wiping
325620	Towelettes, premoistened, manufacturing
313210	Towels and washcloths made in broadwoven fabric mills
313249	Towels and washcloths made in warp knitting mills
313241	Towels and washcloths made in weft knitting mills
421220	Towels and washcloths wholesaling
314129	Towels or washcloths made from purchased fabrics
421840	Towels, industrial, wholesaling
322291	Towels, paper, made from purchased paper
322121	Towels, paper, made in paper mills
421450	Towels, surgical, wholesaling
234920	Tower construction, radio and television transmitting/receiving
336399	Towing bars and systems manufacturing
483211	Towing service, inland waters (except on Great Lakes system)
488410	Towing services, motor vehicle
233210	Town house construction
531110	Town house rental or leasing
233220	Town house-type apartment construction
541320	Town planners' offices
541320	Town planning services
562910	Toxic material abatement services
562910	Toxic material removal contractors
621511	Toxicology health laboratories
325414	Toxoids (e.g., diphtheria, tetanus) manufacturing
339932	Toy furniture and household-type equipment manufacturing
451120	Toy stores
339932	Toys (except dolls, stuffed toys) manufacturing
421920	Toys (including electronic) wholesaling
339931	Toys, doll, manufacturing
339931	Toys, stuffed, manufacturing
333515	Tracer and tapering machine tool attachments manufacturing
332993	Tracer igniters, ammunition (i.e., more than 30 mm., more than 1.18 inch), manufacturing
339920	Track and field athletic equipment (except apparel, footwear) manufacturing
335121	Track lighting fixtures and equipment, residential, electric, manufacturing
484220	Tracked vehicle freight transportation, local
484230	Tracked vehicle freight transportation, long-distance
487110	Tracked vehicle sightseeing operation
339113	Traction apparatus manufacturing
811310	Tractor, farm or construction equipment repair and maintenance services
532490	Tractor, farm, rental or leasing
532490	Tractor, garden, rental or leasing
333120	Tractors and attachments, construction-type, manufacturing
333111	Tractors and attachments, farm-type, manufacturing
333112	Tractors and attachments, lawn and garden-type, manufacturing
333120	Tractors, crawler, manufacturing
421820	Tractors, farm and garden, wholesaling
421110	Tractors, highway, wholesaling
333924	Tractors, industrial, manufacturing
421830	Tractors, industrial, wholesaling
811411	Tractors, lawn and garden repair and maintenance services without retailing new lawn and garden tractors
336120	Tractors, truck for highway use, assembled on chassis of own manufacture
813910	Trade associations
522293	Trade banks (i.e., international trade financing)
323121	Trade binding services
926110	Trade commissions, government
926110	Trade development program administration
561920	Trade fair managers
561920	Trade fair organizers
561920	Trade fair promoters
511120	Trade journal publishers
511120	Trade journal publishers and printing combined
511120	Trade journal publishing (i.e., establishments known as publishers)
323112	Trade journals flexographic printing without publishing
323111	Trade journals gravure printing without publishing
323110	Trade journals lithographic (offset) printing without publishing
323119	Trade journals printing (except flexographic, gravure, lithographic, screen) without publishing
323113	Trade journals screen printing without publishing
511120	Trade magazine and periodical publishers
511120	Trade magazine and periodical publishers and printing combined
511120	Trade magazine and periodical publishing (i.e., establishments known as publishers)
323112	Trade magazines and periodicals flexographic printing without publishing
323111	Trade magazines and periodicals gravure printing without publishing
323110	Trade magazines and periodicals lithographic (offset) printing without publishing
323119	Trade magazines and periodicals printing (except flexographic, gravure, lithographic, screen) without publishing
323113	Trade magazines and periodicals screen printing without publishing
561920	Trade show managers
561920	Trade show organizers
561920	Trade show promoters
611513	Trade union apprenticeship training programs
813930	Trade unions (except apprenticeship programs)
813930	Trade unions, locals
533110	Trademark licensing
523130	Trading companies, commodity contracts
452990	Trading posts, general merchandise
523110	Trading securities (i.e., acting as a principal in dealing securities to investors)
561990	Trading stamp promotion and sale to stores
561990	Trading stamp redemption services
334290	Traffic advisory and signalling systems manufacturing
922110	Traffic courts
541330	Traffic engineering consulting services
235210	Traffic lane painting construction contractors
514110	Traffic reporting services
334290	Traffic signals manufacturing
234990	Trail building
721214	Trail riding camps with accommodation facilities
713990	Trail riding, recreational
234990	Trailer camp construction
336399	Trailer hitches, motor vehicle, manufacturing
531190	Trailer park or court, residential
421120	Trailer parts, new, wholesaling
532120	Trailer rental or leasing
336214	Trailers for transporting horses (except fifth-wheel-type) manufacturing
336214	Trailers, camping, manufacturing
336212	Trailers, fifth-wheel type, for transporting horses, manufacturing
421830	Trailers, industrial, wholesaling
421110	Trailers, motor vehicle, wholesaling
115210	Training horses (except racehorses)
315212	Training pants (i.e., underwear), infants', cut and sew apparel contractors
315291	Training pants (i.e., underwear), infants', cut and sewn from purchased fabric (except apparel contractors)
711219	Training race dogs
711219	Training racehorses
339932	Trains and equipment, toy, electric or mechanical, manufacturing
713990	Trampoline facilities, recreational
485119	Tramway systems (except mixed mode), commuter
487990	Tramway, aerial, scenic and sightseeing operation
325412	Tranquilizer preparations manufacturing
336350	Transaxles, automotive, truck, and bus, manufacturing
334220	Transceivers (i.e., transmitter-receiver units) manufacturing
561410	Transcription services
334510	Transcutaneous electrical nerve stimulators (TENS) manufacturing

Transducers—Trolley

Code	Description
334419	Transducers (except pressure) manufacturing
334519	Transducers, pressure, manufacturing
484110	Transfer (trucking) services, general freight, local
523999	Transfer agencies, securities
421610	Transformers (except electronic) wholesaling
335311	Transformers, electric power, manufacturing
334416	Transformers, electronic component-types, manufacturing
421690	Transformers, electronic, wholesaling
335311	Transformers, ignition, for use on domestic fuel burners, manufacturing
335311	Transformers, reactor, manufacturing
335311	Transformers, separate solid-state arc-welding, manufacturing
335912	Transistor radio batteries manufacturing
334413	Transistors manufacturing
421690	Transistors wholesaling
541850	Transit advertising services
922120	Transit police
926120	Transit systems and authorities, nonoperating
485111	Transit systems, mixed mode (e.g., bus, commuter rail, subway combinations)
327320	Transit-mixed concrete manufacturing
624229	Transitional housing agencies
334519	Transits, surveying, manufacturing
541930	Translation services, language
234920	Transmission and distribution line construction
335311	Transmission and distribution voltage regulators manufacturing
316999	Transmission belting, leather, manufacturing
326220	Transmission belts, rubber, manufacturing
336399	Transmission coolers manufacturing
421610	Transmission equipment, electrical, wholesaling
324191	Transmission fluids, petroleum, made from refined petroleum
325998	Transmission fluids, synthetic, manufacturing
221121	Transmission of electric power
486210	Transmission of natural gas via pipeline (i.e., processing plants to local distribution systems)
335932	Transmission pole and line hardware manufacturing
811113	Transmission repair shops, automotive
332312	Transmission tower sections, fabricated structural metal, manufacturing
336350	Transmissions and parts, automotive, truck, and bus, manufacturing
421690	Transmitters wholesaling
334513	Transmitters, industrial process control-type, manufacturing
333111	Transplanters, farm-type, manufacturing
115112	Transplanting services
******	Transportation — see mode
481212	Transportation by spacecraft, freight
926120	Transportation departments, nonoperating
421860	Transportation equipment and supplies (except marine pleasure craft, motor vehicles) wholesaling
336360	Transportation equipment seating manufacturing
541614	Transportation management consulting services
926120	Transportation regulatory agencies

Code	Description
926120	Transportation safety programs, government
483111	Transporting freight to or from foreign ports, deep sea
483112	Transporting passengers to or from foreign ports, deep sea
212319	Trap rock crushed and broken stone mining and/or beneficiating
212311	Trap rock mining or quarrying
332618	Traps, animal and fish, made from purchased wire
332913	Traps, water, manufacturing
421910	Trapshooting equipment and supplies wholesaling
713990	Trapshooting facilities, recreational
333319	Trash and garbage compactors, commercial-type, manufacturing
335228	Trash and garbage compactors, household-type, manufacturing
326111	Trash bags, plastics film, single wall or multiwall, manufacturing
562111	Trash collection services
326199	Trash containers, plastics, manufacturing
562213	Trash disposal combustors or incinerators
562212	Trash disposal landfills
562111	Trash hauling, local
484230	Trash hauling, long-distance
332313	Trash racks, fabricated metal plate work, manufacturing
621493	Trauma centers (except hospitals), freestanding
561510	Travel agencies
511130	Travel guide book publishers
511130	Travel guide book publishers and printing combined
511130	Travel guide book publishing (i.e., establishments known as publishers)
323117	Travel guide books printing and binding without publishing
323117	Travel guide books printing without publishing
561520	Travel tour operators
721211	Travel trailer campsites
441210	Travel trailer dealers
421110	Travel trailers (e.g., tent trailers) wholesaling
336214	Travel trailers, recreational, manufacturing
624190	Travelers' aid centers
522390	Travelers' check issuance services
316991	Traveling bags, all materials, manufacturing
711190	Traveling shows, carnival
334411	Traveling wave tubes manufacturing
212312	Travertine crushed and broken stone mining and/or beneficiating
212311	Travertine mining or quarrying
337127	Tray trucks, restaurant, manufacturing
321920	Trays, carrier, wood, manufacturing
322299	Trays, food, molded pulp, manufacturing
333315	Trays, photographic printing and processing, manufacturing
332618	Trays, wire, made from purchased wire
321999	Trays, wood, wicker, and bagasse, manufacturing
326211	Tread rubber (i.e., camelback) manufacturing
332323	Treads, metal stair, manufacturing
921130	Treasurers offices', government
321114	Treating purchased wood and wood products

Code	Description
321114	Treating wood products with creosote or other preservatives
113310	Tree chipping in the field
111421	Tree crop farming (except forestry), short rotation growing and harvesting cycle
111335	Tree nut farming
311225	Tree nut oils (e.g., tung, walnut) made from purchased oils
311223	Tree nut oils (e.g., tung, walnut) made in crushing mill
561730	Tree pruning services
561730	Tree removal services
113210	Tree seed extracting
113210	Tree seed gathering
113210	Tree seed growing for reforestation
561730	Tree services (e.g., bracing, planting, pruning, removal, spraying, surgery, trimming)
333111	Tree shakers (e.g., citrus, nut, soft fruit) manufacturing
561730	Tree surgery services
561730	Tree trimming services
339999	Trees and plants, artificial, manufacturing
422930	Trees wholesaling
321918	Trellises, wood, manufacturing
234990	Trenching
333120	Trenching machines manufacturing
234120	Trestle construction
321114	Trestle parts, wood, treating
325221	Triacetate fibers and yarns manufacturing
921150	Tribal chief's or chairman's office, American Indian or Alaska Native
921150	Tribal councils, American Indian or Alaska Native
921150	Tribal courts, American Indian or Alaska Native
325199	Trichloroethylene manufacturing
325199	Trichlorophenoxyacetic acid manufacturing
325199	Tricresyl phosphate manufacturing
339932	Tricycles (except metal) manufacturing
336991	Tricycles, metal, adult and children's, manufacturing
325199	Tridecyl alcohol manufacturing
332321	Trim and molding (except motor vehicle), metal, manufacturing
332321	Trim, metal, manufacturing
321918	Trim, wood and covered wood, manufacturing
333112	Trimmers, hedge, electric, manufacturing
332212	Trimmers, hedge, nonelectric, manufacturing
333112	Trimmers, string, lawn and garden-type, manufacturing
315292	Trimmings, fur (except apparel contractors), manufacturing
315211	Trimmings, fur, men's and boys', cut and sew apparel contractors
315212	Trimmings, fur, women's, girls', and infants', cut and sew apparel contractos
316999	Trimmings, shoe, leather, manufacturing
325920	Trinitrotoluene (TNT) manufacturing
325199	Triphenyl phosphate manufacturing
333315	Tripods, camera and projector, manufacturing
212399	Tripoli mining and/or beneficiating
339112	Trocars manufacturing
485119	Trolley systems (except mixed mode), commuter
487110	Trolley, scenic and sightseeing, operation

Code	Description
339992	Trombones and parts manufacturing
212391	Trona mining and/or beneficiating
421940	Trophies wholesaling
332999	Trophies, nonprecious and precious plated metal, manufacturing
339912	Trophies, precious (except precious plated) metal, manufacturing
453998	Trophy (including awards and plaques) shops
321999	Trophy bases, wood, manufacturing
112511	Tropical fish production, farm raising
422990	Tropical fish wholesaling
561730	Tropical plant maintenance services
335129	Trouble lights manufacturing
332322	Troughs, elevator, sheet metal, manufacturing
332313	Troughs, industrial, fabricated metal plate work, manufacturing
335211	Trouser pressers, household-type electric, manufacturing
315191	Trousers made in apparel knitting mills
315211	Trousers, men's and boys', cut and sew apparel contractors
315224	Trousers, men's and boys', cut and sewn from purchased fabric (except apparel contractors)
114111	Trout fishing
112511	Trout production, farm raising
332212	Trowels manufacturing
532120	Truck (except industrial) rental or leasing
233310	Truck and automobile assembly plant construction
811192	Truck and bus washes
336211	Truck bodies and cabs manufacturing
336211	Truck bodies assembling on purchased chassis
336214	Truck campers (i.e., slide-in campers) manufacturing
441310	Truck cap stores
611519	Truck driving schools
111219	Truck farming, field, bedding plant and seed production
522220	Truck finance leasing
421120	Truck parts, new, wholesaling
811310	Truck refrigeration repair and maintenance services
811111	Truck repair shops, general
447190	Truck stops
532120	Truck tractor rental or leasing
336120	Truck tractors for highway use, assembling on chassis of own manufacture
336211	Truck tractors for highway use, assembling on purchased chassis
421110	Truck tractors, road, wholesaling
811121	Truck trailer body shops
421110	Truck trailers wholesaling
488490	Truck weighing station operation
532490	Truck, industrial, rental or leasing
327320	Truck-mixed concrete manufacturing
488490	Trucking terminals, independently operated
484210	Trucking used household, office, or institutional furniture and equipment
484110	Trucking, general freight, local
484122	Trucking, general freight, long-distance, less-than-truckload (LTL)
484121	Trucking, general freight, long-distance, truckload
484220	Trucking, specialized freight (except used goods), local
484230	Trucking, specialized freight (except used goods), long-distance

Code	Description
336120	Trucks, heavy, assembling on chassis of own manufacture
333924	Trucks, industrial, manufacturing
421830	Trucks, industrial, wholesaling
336112	Trucks, light duty, assembling on chassis of own manufacture
333120	Trucks, off-highway, manufacturing
421110	Trucks, road, wholesaling
111419	Truffles farming, grown under cover
339992	Trumpets and parts manufacturing
316991	Trunks (i.e., luggage), all materials, manufacturing
332313	Truss plates, metal, manufacturing
321214	Trusses, glue laminated or pre-engineered wood, manufacturing
321214	Trusses, wood roof or floor, manufacturing
321214	Trusses, wood, glue laminated or metal connected, manufacturing
523991	Trust administration, personal investment
523991	Trust companies, nondepository
813211	Trusts, charitable, awarding grants
813211	Trusts, educational, awarding grants
813211	Trusts, religious, awarding grants
325612	Tub and tile cleaning preparations manufacturing
331210	Tube (e.g., heavy riveted, lock joint, seamless, welded) made from purchased iron or steel
332912	Tube and hose fittings, fluid power, manufacturing
331316	Tube blooms made by extruding purchased aluminum
331316	Tube blooms, aluminum, made in integrated secondary smelting and extruding mills
331316	Tube made by drawing or extruding purchased aluminum
333516	Tube rolling mill machinery, metalworking, manufacturing
331111	Tube rounds, iron or steel, made in steel mills
331316	Tube, aluminum, made in integrated secondary smelting and drawing plants
331316	Tube, aluminum, made in integrated secondary smelting and extruding mills
331111	Tube, iron or steel, made in steel mills
326121	Tube, nonrigid plastics, manufacturing
331315	Tube, welded, aluminum, made by flat rolling purchased aluminum
331315	Tube, welded, aluminum, made in integrated secondary smelting and flat rolling mills
325414	Tuberculin (i.e., tuberculo-protein derived) manufacturing
622310	Tuberculosis and other respiratory illness hospitals
332996	Tubes made from purchased metal pipe
334517	Tubes, X-ray, manufacturing
334411	Tubes, cathode ray, manufacturing
334411	Tubes, electron, manufacturing
421690	Tubes, electronic (e.g., industrial, receiving, transmitting), wholesaling
334411	Tubes, klystron, manufacturing
331421	Tubing, copper and copper alloy, made from purchased copper or in integrated secondary smelting and rolling, drawing or extruding plants
332999	Tubing, flexible metal, manufacturing
331210	Tubing, mechanical and hypodermic sizes, cold-drawn stainless steel, made from purchased steel
421510	Tubing, metal, wholesaling

Code	Description
331491	Tubing, nonferrous metals (except aluminum, copper), made from purchased metals or scrap
326299	Tubing, rubber (except extruded, molded, lathe-cut), manufacturing
331111	Tubing, seamless steel, made in steel mills
331111	Tubing, wrought iron or steel, made in steel mills
332998	Tubs, laundry and bath, metal, manufacturing
235410	Tuck pointing construction contractors
212312	Tufa, calcareous, crushed and broken stone, mining and/or beneficiating
212311	Tufa, calcareous, mining or quarrying
333292	Tufting machinery for textiles manufacturing
336611	Tugboat building
532411	Tugboat rental or leasing
488330	Tugboat services, harbor operation
326199	Tumblers, plastics, manufacturing
332813	Tumbling (i.e., cleaning and polishing) metal and metal products for the trade
114111	Tuna fishing
811118	Tune-up shops, automotive
325188	Tungstates (e.g., ammonium tungstate, sodium tungstate) manufacturing
331491	Tungsten bar, rod, sheet, strip, and tubing made by rolling, drawing, or extruding purchased metals or scrap
331492	Tungsten carbide powder made by metallurgical process
325188	Tungsten compounds, not specified elsewhere by process, manufacturing
212299	Tungsten concentrates beneficiating
212299	Tungsten ores mining and/or beneficiating
811490	Tuning and repair of musical instruments
339992	Tuning forks manufacturing
234120	Tunnel and bridge construction management firms
234120	Tunnel construction
332313	Tunnel lining, fabricated metal plate work, manufacturing
213113	Tunneling services for coal mining on a contract basis
332313	Tunnels, wind, fabricated metal plate work, manufacturing
334513	Turbidity instruments, industrial process-type, manufacturing
334516	Turbidometers, laboratory-type, manufacturing
334513	Turbine flow meters, industrial process-type, manufacturing
333611	Turbine generator set units manufacturing
334514	Turbine meters, consumption registering, manufacturing
333611	Turbines (except aircraft) manufacturing
421830	Turbines (except transportation) wholesaling
421860	Turbines, transportation, wholesaling
561730	Turf (except artificial) installation services
422440	Turkey and turkey products (except packaged frozen) wholesaling
112330	Turkey egg production
311119	Turkey feeds, prepared, manufacturing
112340	Turkey hatcheries
112330	Turkey production
325613	Turkey red oil manufacturing
311615	Turkeys, processing, fresh, frozen, canned, or cooked
311615	Turkeys, slaughtering and dressing
812199	Turkish bathhouses

Turkish baths—Uniforms

Code	Description
812199	Turkish baths
332722	Turnbuckles manufacturing
333512	Turning machines (i.e., lathes), metalworking, manufacturing
321912	Turnings, furniture, unfinished wood, manufacturing
111219	Turnip farming, field, bedding plant and seed production
325191	Turpentine made by distillation of pine gum or pine wood
422690	Turpentine wholesaling
212399	Turquoise mining and/or beneficiating
333512	Turret lathes, metalworking, manufacturing
332995	Turrets, gun, manufacturing
114119	Turtle fishing
112519	Turtle production, farm raising
611691	Tutoring, academic
532220	Tuxedo rental
315211	Tuxedos cut and sew apparel contractors
315222	Tuxedos cut and sewn from purchased fabric (except apparel contractors)
313210	Twills weaving
421840	Twine wholesaling
314991	Twines manufacturing
421830	Twist drills wholesaling
513321	Two-way paging communication carriers
323122	Typesetting (i.e., computer controlled, hand, machine)
333293	Typesetting machinery manufacturing
422120	Typewriter paper wholesaling
811212	Typewriter repair and maintenance services
339944	Typewriter ribbons manufacturing
333313	Typewriters manufacturing
421420	Typewriters wholesaling
561410	Typing services
212291	Tyuyamunite mining and/or beneficiating
531130	U-lock storage
922130	U. S. attorneys' offices
311514	UHT (ultra high temperature) milk manufacturing
335999	UPS (uninterruptible power supplies) manufacturing
339992	Ukuleles and parts manufacturing
212391	Ulexite mining and/or beneficiating
336411	Ultra light aircraft manufacturing
325131	Ultramarine pigments manufacturing
333512	Ultrasonic boring, drilling, and cutting machines, metalworking, manufacturing
335999	Ultrasonic cleaning equipment (except dental, medical) manufacturing
339114	Ultrasonic dental equipment manufacturing
335999	Ultrasonic generators sold separately for inclusion in tools and equipment manufacturing
339113	Ultrasonic medical cleaning equipment manufacturing
334510	Ultrasonic medical equipment manufacturing
333513	Ultrasonic metal forming machines manufacturing
334510	Ultrasonic scanning devices, medical, manufacturing
334519	Ultrasonic testing equipment (except medical) manufacturing
333992	Ultrasonic welding equipment manufacturing
621512	Ultrasound imaging centers
335110	Ultraviolet lamp bulbs manufacturing
335129	Ultraviolet lamp fixtures manufacturing

Code	Description
334516	Ultraviolet-type analytical instruments manufacturing
325131	Umber manufacturing
212393	Umber mining and/or beneficiating
339999	Umbrellas manufacturing
422320	Umbrellas, men's and boys', wholesaling
322122	Uncoated groundwood paper mills
811198	Undercoating shops, automotive
333131	Underground mining machinery manufacturing
235940	Underground tank removal construction contractors
234120	Underpass construction contractors
812210	Undertaker services
421850	Undertakers' equipment and supplies wholesaling
335129	Underwater lighting fixtures manufacturing
334511	Underwater navigational systems manufacturing
234990	Underwater rock removal
315192	Underwear made in apparel knitting mills
315192	Underwear shirts made in apparel knitting mills
315291	Underwear shirts, infants', cut and sewn from purchased fabric (except apparel contractors)
315211	Underwear shirts, men's and boys', cut and sew apparel contractors
315221	Underwear shirts, men's and boys', cut and sewn from purchased fabric (except apparel contractors)
315212	Underwear shirts, women's, girls', and infants', cut and sew apparel contractors
315231	Underwear shirts, women's, misses', and girls', cut and sewn from purchased fabric (except apparel contractors)
315192	Underwear shorts made in apparel knitting mills
315291	Underwear shorts, infants', cut and sewn from purchased fabric (except apparel contractors)
315211	Underwear shorts, men's and boys', cut and sew apparel contractors
315221	Underwear shorts, men's and boys', cut and sewn from purchased fabric (except apparel contractors)
315212	Underwear shorts, women's, girls', and infants', cut and sew apparel contractors
315231	Underwear shorts, women's, misses', and girls', cut and sewn from purchased fabric (except apparel contractors)
315291	Underwear, infants', cut and sewn from purchased fabric (except apparel contractors)
315211	Underwear, men's and boys', cut and sew apparel contractors
315221	Underwear, men's and boys', cut and sewn from purchased fabric (except apparel contractors)
422320	Underwear, men's and boys', wholesaling
422330	Underwear, women's, children's, and infants', wholesaling
315231	Underwear, women's, misses', and girls', cut and sewn from purchased fabric (except apparel contractors)
315212	Underwear, women's, misses', girls', and infants', cut and sew apparel contractors
923130	Unemployment insurance program administration
812331	Uniform (except industrial) supply services

Code	Description
315991	Uniform hats and caps cut and sewn from purchased fabric (except apparel contractors)
315211	Uniform hats and caps, men's and boys', cut and sew apparel contractors
315212	Uniform hats and caps, women's, and girls', cut and sew apparel contractors
315232	Uniform shirts (except team athletic), women's, misses', and girls', cut and sewn from purchased fabric (except apparel contractors)
315223	Uniform shirts (except team athletic, work), men's and boys', cut and sewn from purchased fabric (except apparel contractors)
315211	Uniform shirts, men's and boys', cut and sew apparel contractors
315299	Uniform shirts, team athletic, cut and sewn from purchased fabric (except apparel contractors)
315212	Uniform shirts, women's and girls', cut and sew apparel contractors
315225	Uniform shirts, work, men's and boys', cut and sewn from purchased fabric (except apparel contractors)
448190	Uniform stores (except athletic)
451110	Uniform stores, athletic
812332	Uniform supply services, industrial
315299	Uniforms, band, cut and sewn from purchased fabric (except apparel contractors)
315211	Uniforms, band, men's and boys', cut and sew apparel contractors
315212	Uniforms, band, women's, girls', and infants', cut and sew apparel contractors
315211	Uniforms, dress (e.g., fire fighter, military, police), men's, cut and sew apparel contractors
315222	Uniforms, dress (e.g., fire fighter, military, police), men's, cut and sewn from purchased fabric (except apparel contractors)
315212	Uniforms, dress (e.g., military, police, fire fighter), women's, cut and sew apparel contractors
315234	Uniforms, dress, tailored (e.g., fire fighter, military, police), women's, misses', and girls', cut and sewn from purchased fabric (except apparel contractors)
315228	Uniforms, nontailored (except work), men's and boys', cut and sewn from purchased fabric (except apparel contractors)
315225	Uniforms, nontailored work, men's, cut and sewn from purchased fabric (except apparel contractors)
315191	Uniforms, nontailored, made in apparel knitting mills
315211	Uniforms, nontailored, men's and boys', cut and sew apparel contractors
315212	Uniforms, nontailored, women's and girls', cut and sew apparel contractors
315239	Uniforms, nontailored, women's, misses', and girls', cut and sewn from purchased fabric (except team athletic, apparel contractors)
315299	Uniforms, team athletic, cut and sewn from purchased fabric (except apparel contractors)
315211	Uniforms, team athletic, men's and boys', cut and sew apparel contractors
315212	Uniforms, team athletic, women's and girls', cut and sew apparel contractors

Code	Description
335999	Uninterruptible power supplies (UPS) manufacturing
525120	Union health and welfare funds
525110	Union pension funds
315192	Union suits made in apparel knitting mills
315291	Union suits, infants', cut and sewn from purchased fabric (except apparel contractors)
315211	Union suits, men's and boys', cut and sew apparel contractors
315221	Union suits, men's and boys', cut and sewn from purchased fabric (except apparel contractors)
315212	Union suits, women's, girls', and infants', cut and sew apparel contractors
315231	Union suits, women's, misses', and girls', cut and sewn from purchased fabric (except apparel contractors)
813930	Unions (except apprenticeship programs), labor
332919	Unions, pipe, metal (except made from purchased pipe), manufacturing
448140	Unisex clothing stores
422330	Unisex clothing wholesaling
812112	Unisex hair stylist shops
333414	Unit heaters (except portable electric) manufacturing
335211	Unit heaters, portable electric, manufacturing
525990	Unit investment trust funds
323116	Unit set forms (e.g., manifold credit card slips) printing
928120	United Nations
813219	United fund councils
813219	United funds for colleges
333613	Universal joints (except aircraft, motor vehicle) manufacturing
336413	Universal joints, aircraft, manufacturing
336350	Universal joints, automotive, truck, and bus, manufacturing
611310	Universities
813410	University clubs
511130	University press publishers
923110	University regents or boards, government
311812	Unleavened bread made in commercial bakeries
337121	Upholstered furniture, household-type, custom, manufacturing
337121	Upholstered furniture, household-type, on frames of any material, manufacturing
421850	Upholsterers' equipment and supplies (except fabrics) wholesaling
314999	Upholstering filling (except nonwoven fabric) manufacturing
811420	Upholstery (except motor vehicle) repair services
561740	Upholstery cleaning on customers' premises
561740	Upholstery cleaning services
316110	Upholstery leather manufacturing
451130	Upholstery materials stores
811121	Upholstery shops, automotive
332612	Upholstery springs and spring units made from purchased wire
316110	Upper leather manufacturing
316999	Uppers (i.e., shoe cut stock), leather, manufacturing
332111	Upset forgings made from purchased iron or steel, unfinished
332112	Upset forgings made from purchased nonferrous metals, unfinished

Code	Description
333513	Upsetters (i.e., forging machines) manufacturing
212291	Uraninite (pitchblende) mining and/or beneficiating
325188	Uranium compounds, not specified elsewhere by process, manufacturing
212291	Uranium ores mining and/or beneficiating
325188	Uranium oxide manufacturing
331419	Uranium refining, primary
325188	Uranium, enriched, manufacturing
212291	Uranium-radium-vanadium ore mine site development for own account
212291	Uranium-radium-vanadium ores mining and/or beneficiating
485113	Urban bus line services (except mixed mode)
485112	Urban commuter rail systems (except mixed mode)
541320	Urban planners' offices
925120	Urban planning commissions, government
541320	Urban planning services
485111	Urban transit systems, mixed mode (e.g., bus, commuter rail, subway combinations)
325311	Urea manufacturing
325211	Urea resins manufacturing
325211	Urea-formaldehyde resins manufacturing
326150	Urethane foam products manufacturing
325212	Urethane rubber manufacturing
621493	Urgent medical care centers and clinics (except hospitals), freestanding
332998	Urinals, metal, manufacturing
326191	Urinals, plastics, manufacturing
327111	Urinals, vitreous china, manufacturing
621511	Urinalysis laboratories
327420	Urns (e.g., gypsum, plaster of paris) manufacturing
335211	Urns, household-type electric, manufacturing
621111	Urologists' offices (e.g., centers, clinics)
441229	Used aircraft dealers
441310	Used automotive parts stores
441320	Used automotive tire dealers
453310	Used bicycle (except motorized) shops
441222	Used boat dealers
441120	Used car dealers
421110	Used cars wholesaling
484210	Used household and office goods moving
453930	Used manufactured (mobile) home dealers
453310	Used merchandise stores
441221	Used motorcycle dealers
421110	Used parts, motor vehicle, wholesaling
441210	Used recreational vehicle (RV) dealers
441320	Used tire dealers
421130	Used tires, motor vehicle, wholesaling
441229	Used utility trailer dealers
541618	Utilities management consulting services
332311	Utility buildings, prefabricated metal, manufacturing
326199	Utility containers (e.g., baskets, bins, boxes, buckets, dishpans, pails), plastics (except foam), manufacturing
511210	Utility software, computer, packaged
441229	Utility trailer dealers
532120	Utility trailer rental or leasing
336214	Utility trailers manufacturing
421110	Utility trailers wholesaling
326220	V-belts, rubber or plastics, manufacturing

Code	Description
334310	VCR (video cassette recorder) manufacturing
531190	Vacant lot rental or leasing
531190	Vacation and recreation land rental or leasing
721214	Vacation camps (except campgrounds, day instructional)
115210	Vaccinating livestock (except by veterinarians)
541940	Vaccination services, veterinary
325414	Vaccines (i.e., bacterial, virus) manufacturing
422210	Vaccines wholesaling
332439	Vacuum bottles and jugs manufacturing
336340	Vacuum brake booster, automotive, truck, and bus, manufacturing
326220	Vacuum cleaner belts, rubber or plastics, manufacturing
443111	Vacuum cleaner stores, household-type
335212	Vacuum cleaners (e.g., canister, handheld, upright) household-type electric, manufacturing
335212	Vacuum cleaners and sweepers, household-type electric, manufacturing
421620	Vacuum cleaners, household-type, wholesaling
333319	Vacuum cleaners, industrial and commercial-type, manufacturing
235950	Vacuum cleaning systems, built-in, construction contractors
333912	Vacuum pumps (except laboratory) manufacturing
339111	Vacuum pumps, laboratory-type, manufacturing
335314	Vacuum relays manufacturing
332420	Vacuum tanks, heavy gauge metal, manufacturing
327215	Vacuum tube blanks, glass, made from purchased glass
327212	Vacuum tube blanks, glass, made in glass making plants
334411	Vacuum tubes manufacturing
488119	Vacuuming of airport runways
333112	Vacuums, yard, manufacturing
812930	Valet parking services
316991	Valises, all materials, manufacturing
325191	Valonia extract manufacturing
333512	Valve grinding machines, metalworking, manufacturing
421840	Valves (except hydraulic, plumbing, pneumatic) wholesaling
332911	Valves for nuclear applications manufacturing
332911	Valves for water works and municipal water systems manufacturing
336311	Valves, engine, intake and exhaust, manufacturing
332912	Valves, hydraulic and pneumatic, fluid power, manufacturing
421830	Valves, hydraulic and pneumatic, wholesaling
332911	Valves, industrial-type (e.g., check, gate, globe, relief, safety), manufacturing
332919	Valves, inline plumbing and heating (e.g., cutoffs, stop), manufacturing
421720	Valves, plumbing and heating, wholesaling
316999	Vamps, leather, manufacturing
532120	Van (except passenger) rental or leasing without driver
532112	Van (passenger) leasing
532111	Van (passenger) rental
336213	Van and minivan conversions on purchased chassis

Van—Veterinary

Code	Description
811121	Van conversion shops (except on assembly line or factory basis)
484210	Van lines, moving and storage services
212291	Vanadium ores mining and/or beneficiating
325199	Vanillin, synthetic, manufacturing
337110	Vanities (except freestanding), stock or custom wood, manufacturing
337122	Vanities, freestanding, wood, manufacturing
337124	Vanities, metal household-type, manufacturing
316993	Vanity cases, leather, manufacturing
337110	Vanity tops, wood or plastics laminated on wood, manufacturing
485999	Vanpool operation
488999	Vanpools, arrangement of
336112	Vans, commercial and passenger light duty, assembling on chassis of own manufacture
334512	Vapor heating controls manufacturing
335110	Vapor lamps, electric, manufacturing
333999	Vapor separating machinery manufacturing
335211	Vaporizers, household-type electric, manufacturing
334513	Variable control instruments, industrial process-type, manufacturing
311612	Variety meats, edible organs, made from purchased meats
311611	Variety meats, edible organs, made in slaughtering plants
452990	Variety stores
334415	Varistors manufacturing
325510	Varnishes manufacturing
422950	Varnishes wholesaling
332812	Varnishing metals and metal products for the trade
313320	Varnishing purchased textiles and apparel
327420	Vases (e.g., gypsum, plaster of paris) manufacturing
327215	Vases, glass, made from purchased glass
327212	Vases, glass, made in glass making plants
327112	Vases, pottery (e.g., china, earthenware, stoneware), manufacturing
325132	Vat dyes, synthetic, manufacturing
332420	Vats, heavy gauge metal, manufacturing
332439	Vats, light gauge metal, manufacturing
711110	Vaudeville companies
332999	Vault doors and linings, metal, manufacturing
332999	Vaults (except burial), metal, manufacturing
339995	Vaults (except concrete) manufacturing
112111	Veal calf production
311611	Veal carcasses, half carcasses, primal and sub-primal cuts, produced in slaughtering plants
311612	Veal, primal and sub-primal cuts, made from purchased carcasses
325411	Vegetable alkaloids (i.e., basic chemicals) (e.g., caffeine, codeine, morphine, nicotine), manufacturing
111211	Vegetable and melon farming, potato dominant crop, field and seed production
111219	Vegetable and melon farming, vegetable (except potato) and melon dominant crops, field, bedding plants and seed production

Code	Description
111211	Vegetable and potato farming, potato dominant crop, field and seed potato production
111219	Vegetable and potato farming, vegetable (except potato) dominant crops, field, bedding plants and seed production
321920	Vegetable baskets, veneer and splint, manufacturing
311421	Vegetable brining
422990	Vegetable cake and meal wholesaling
311421	Vegetable canning
321920	Vegetable crates, wood, wirebound, manufacturing
422910	Vegetable dusts and sprays wholesaling
111419	Vegetable farming, grown under cover
311211	Vegetable flour manufacturing
311211	Vegetable flour, meal, and powders, made in flour mills
311411	Vegetable juice concentrates, frozen, manufacturing
311421	Vegetable juices canning
311421	Vegetable juices, fresh, manufacturing
445230	Vegetable markets
333294	Vegetable oil processing machinery manufacturing
311223	Vegetable oils (except soybean) made in crushing mills
311225	Vegetable oils made from purchased oils
115114	Vegetable precooling
115114	Vegetable sorting, grading, and packing
311221	Vegetable starches manufacturing
115114	Vegetable sun drying
115114	Vegetable vacuum cooling
311423	Vegetables dehydrating
311421	Vegetables pickling
422490	Vegetables, canned, wholesaling
311991	Vegetables, cut or peeled, fresh, manufacturing
422480	Vegetables, fresh, wholesaling
311411	Vegetables, frozen, manufacturing
422420	Vegetables, frozen, wholesaling
115113	Vegetables, machine harvesting
333997	Vehicle scales manufacturing
321912	Vehicle stock, hardwood, manufacturing
336991	Vehicle, children's, metal manufacturing
339932	Vehicles, children's (except bicycles and metal tricycles), manufacturing
421920	Vehicles, children's (except bicycles), wholesaling
421110	Vehicles, recreational, wholesaling
336321	Vehicular lighting fixtures manufacturing
316110	Vellum leather manufacturing
313210	Velvets, manmade fiber and silk, weaving
454210	Vending machine merchandisers, sale of products
333311	Vending machines manufacturing
421440	Vending machines wholesaling
333210	Veneer and plywood forming machinery manufacturing
321920	Veneer baskets, for fruits and vegetables, manufacturing
321211	Veneer mills, hardwood
321212	Veneer mills, softwood
321999	Veneer work, inlaid, manufacturing
811490	Venetian blind repair and maintenance shops without retailing new venetian blinds
321918	Venetian blind slats, wood, manufacturing
337920	Venetian blinds manufacturing
235110	Ventilating construction contractors

Code	Description
421730	Ventilating equipment and supplies (except household-type fans) wholesaling
333412	Ventilating fans, industrial and commercial-type, manufacturing
335211	Ventilating kitchen fans, household-type electric, manufacturing
335211	Ventilation and exhaust fans (except attic fans), household-type, manufacturing
561790	Ventilation duct cleaning services
332322	Ventilators, sheet metal, manufacturing
523910	Venture capital companies
212319	Verde' antique crushed and broken stone mining and/or beneficiating
212311	Verde' antique mining or quarrying
212399	Vermiculite mining and/or beneficiating
327992	Vermiculite, exfoliated, manufacturing
325412	Vermifuge preparations manufacturing
325131	Vermilion pigments manufacturing
312130	Vermouth manufacturing
337920	Vertical blinds manufacturing
488390	Vessel supply services
332420	Vessels, heavy gauge metal, manufacturing
315299	Vestments, academic and clerical, cut and sewn from purchased fabric (except apparel contractors)
315211	Vestments, academic and clerical, men's and boys', cut and sew apparel contractors
315212	Vestments, academic and clerical, women's and girls', cut and sew apparel contractors
315292	Vests, leather, fur, or sheep-lined (except apparel contractors), manufacturing
315211	Vests, leather, fur, or sheep-lined, men's and boys', cut and sew apparel contractors
315212	Vests, leather, fur, or sheep-lined, women's, girls', and infants', cut and sew apparel contractors
315211	Vests, men's and boys', cut and sew apparel contractors
315228	Vests, nontailored, men's and boys', cut and sewn from purchased fabric (except apparel contractors)
315239	Vests, nontailored, women's, misses', and girls', cut and sewn from purchased fabric (except apparel contractors)
315222	Vests, tailored, men's and boys', cut and sewn from purchased fabric (except apparel contractors)
315234	Vests, tailored, women's, misses', and girls', cut and sewn from purchased fabric
315212	Vests, women's, girls', and infants', cut and sew apparel contractors
813410	Veterans' membership organizations
923140	Veterans' affairs offices
923140	Veterans' benefits program administration, government
813311	Veterans' rights organizations
421490	Veterinarians' equipment and supplies wholesaling
339112	Veterinarians' instruments and apparatus manufacturing
422210	Veterinarians' medicines wholesaling
541940	Veterinarians' offices
541940	Veterinarians' practices
541940	Veterinary clinics
325412	Veterinary medicinal preparations manufacturing

Code	Description
541710	Veterinary research and development laboratories or services
541940	Veterinary services
541940	Veterinary services, livestock
541940	Veterinary services, pets and other animal specialties
541940	Veterinary testing laboratories
234120	Viaduct construction
523910	Viatical settlement companies
339992	Vibraphones manufacturing
334519	Vibration meters, analyzers, and calibrators, manufacturing
541380	Vibration testing laboratories or services
333120	Vibrators, concrete, manufacturing
421410	Video cameras (except household-type) wholesaling
334310	Video cameras, household-type, manufacturing
421620	Video cameras, household-type, wholesaling
811211	Video cassette recorder (VCR) repair services without retailing new video cassette recorders
532210	Video cassette recorder rental
334310	Video cassette recorders (VCR) manufacturing
334613	Video cassettes, blank, manufacturing
334612	Video cassettes, pre-recorded, mass reproducing
512191	Video conversion services (i.e., between formats)
532210	Video disc player rental
532230	Video disc rental for home electronic equipment (e.g., VCR)
713290	Video gambling device concession operators (i.e., supplying and servicing in others' facilities)
713120	Video game arcades (except gambling)
339932	Video game machines (except coin-operated) manufacturing
532230	Video game rental
713290	Video gaming device concession operators (i.e., supplying and servicing in others' facilities)
541921	Video photography services, portrait
512191	Video post-production services
512110	Video production
512110	Video production and distribution
512120	Video productions, distributing
532210	Video recorder rental
334612	Video tape or disk mass reproducing
532210	Video tape player rental
532230	Video tape rental for home electronic equipment (e.g., VCR)
532230	Video tape rental stores
451220	Video tape stores
334613	Video tapes, blank, manufacturing
421690	Video tapes, blank, wholesaling
421990	Video tapes, prerecorded, wholesaling
541921	Video taping services, special events (e.g., birthdays, weddings)
512199	Videotape libraries, stock footage
311941	Vinegar manufacturing
115112	Vineyard cultivation services
325199	Vinyl acetate (except resins) manufacturing
325211	Vinyl acetate resins manufacturing
326113	Vinyl and vinyl copolymer film and unlaminated sheet (except packaging) manufacturing
325211	Vinyl chloride resins manufacturing
313320	Vinyl coated fabrics manufacturing
325222	Vinyl fibers and filaments manufacturing
326192	Vinyl floor coverings manufacturing

Code	Description
235520	Vinyl flooring construction contractors
325211	Vinyl resins manufacturing
421330	Vinyl siding wholesaling
316219	Vinyl upper athletic footwear manufacturing
325222	Vinylidene chloride fiber and filament manufacturing
325211	Vinylidene resins manufacturing
339992	Violas and parts manufacturing
339992	Violins and parts manufacturing
325413	Viral in-vitro diagnostic test substances manufacturing
325414	Virus vaccines manufacturing
325221	Viscose fibers, bands, strips, and yarn manufacturing
334519	Viscosimeters (except industrial process-type) manufacturing
334513	Viscosity instruments, industrial process-type, manufacturing
332212	Vises (except machine tool attachments) manufacturing
621610	Visiting nurse associations
561591	Visitors bureaus
325412	Vitamin preparations manufacturing
446191	Vitamin stores
422210	Vitamins wholesaling
325411	Vitamins, uncompounded, manufacturing
711130	Vocalists, independent
611513	Vocational apprenticeship training
624310	Vocational habilitation job counseling
624310	Vocational habilitation job training facilities (except schools)
624310	Vocational rehabilitation agencies
624310	Vocational rehabilitation job counseling
624310	Vocational rehabilitation job training facilities (except schools)
624310	Vocational rehabilitation or habilitation services (e.g., job counseling, job training, work experience)
561421	Voice mailbox services
621340	Voice pathologists' offices (e.g., centers, clinics)
212399	Volcanic ash mining and/or beneficiating
212319	Volcanic rock crushed and broken stone mining and/or beneficiating
212319	Volcanic rock, mining or quarrying
335311	Voltage regulating transformers, electric power, manufacturing
421610	Voltage regulators (except motor vehicle) wholesaling
336322	Voltage regulators for internal combustion engines manufacturing
334413	Voltage regulators, integrated circuits, manufacturing
335311	Voltage regulators, transmission and distribution, manufacturing
334515	Voltmeters manufacturing
813212	Voluntary health organizations
624229	Volunteer housing repair organizations
333313	Voting machines manufacturing
421850	Voting machines wholesaling
322214	Vulcanized fiber products made from purchased paperboard
325212	Vulcanized oils manufacturing
333220	Vulcanizing machinery manufacturing
541511	WEB (i.e., internet) page design services, custom
332992	Wads, ammunition, manufacturing
333295	Wafer processing equipment, semiconductor, manufacturing
321219	Waferboard manufacturing
334413	Wafers (semiconductor devices) manufacturing

Code	Description
335211	Waffle irons, household-type electric, manufacturing
311412	Waffles, frozen, manufacturing
926150	Wage control agencies, government
339932	Wagons, children's (e.g., coaster, express, and play), manufacturing
333111	Wagons, farm-type, manufacturing
333112	Wagons, lawn and garden-type, manufacturing
321918	Wainscots, wood, manufacturing
561421	Wakeup call services
621111	Walk-in physicians' offices (e.g., centers, clinics)
532291	Walker, invalid, rental
339932	Walkers, baby (vehicles), manufacturing
333921	Walkways, moving, manufacturing
334518	Wall clocks manufacturing
235210	Wall covering or removal construction contractors
422950	Wall coverings (e.g., fabric, plastic) wholesaling
335122	Wall lamps (i.e., lighting fixtures), commercial, institutional, and industrial electric, manufacturing
335121	Wall lamps (i.e., lighting fixtures), residential electric, manufacturing
327122	Wall tile, ceramic, manufacturing
421310	Wallboard wholesaling
327420	Wallboard, gypsum, manufacturing
316993	Wallets (except metal) manufacturing
339911	Wallets, precious metal, manufacturing
444120	Wallpaper and wall coverings stores
325612	Wallpaper cleaners manufacturing
322222	Wallpaper made from purchased papers or other materials
422950	Wallpaper wholesaling
111335	Walnut farming
115114	Walnut hulling and shelling
712110	War museums
316991	Wardrobe bags (i.e., luggage) manufacturing
532220	Wardrobe rental
337124	Wardrobes, metal household-type, manufacturing
337122	Wardrobes, wood household-type, manufacturing
452910	Warehouse clubs (i.e., food and general merchandise)
332311	Warehouses, prefabricated metal, manufacturing
493190	Warehousing (except farm products, general merchandise, refrigerated)
493110	Warehousing (including foreign trade zones), general merchandise
493110	Warehousing and storage, general merchandise
813910	Warehousing associations
493130	Warehousing, farm products (except refrigerated)
493120	Warehousing, refrigerated
531130	Warehousing, self storage
334511	Warfare countermeasures equipment manufacturing
421730	Warm air heating equipment wholesaling
335211	Warming trays, electric, manufacturing
315191	Warmup suits made in apparel knitting mills
315291	Warmup suits, infants', cut and sewn from purchased fabric (except apparel contractors)
315211	Warmup suits, men's and boys', cut and sew apparel contractors

Warmup suits—Water

Code	Description
315228	Warmup suits, men's and boys', cut and sewn from purchased fabric (except apparel contractors)
315212	Warmup suits, women's, girls', and infants', cut and sew apparel contractors
315239	Warmup suits, women's, misses', and girls', cut and sewn from purchased fabric (except apparel contractors)
313249	Warp fabrics knitting
333292	Warping machinery manufacturing
524128	Warranty insurance carriers (e.g., appliance, automobile, homeowners, product), direct
315211	Washable service apparel (e.g., barbers', hospital, professional), men's and boys', cut and sew apparel contractors
315225	Washable service apparel (e.g., barbers', hospital, professional), men's and boys', cut and sewn from purchased fabric (except apparel contractors)
315212	Washable service apparel, women's and girls', cut and sew apparel contractors
315239	Washable service apparel, women's, misses', and girls', cut and sewn from purchased fabric (except apparel contractors)
321999	Washboards, wood and part wood, manufacturing
532210	Washer, clothes, rental
212113	Washeries, anthracite
212111	Washeries, bituminous coal or lignite
333131	Washers, aggregate and sand, stationary, manufacturing
332722	Washers, metal, manufacturing
234930	Washery, mining, construction
811412	Washing machine, household-type, repair and maintenance services without retailing new washing machine
335224	Washing machines, household-type, manufacturing
333312	Washing machines, laundry (except household-type), manufacturing
561720	Washroom sanitation services
562213	Waste (except sewage) treatment facilities, nonhazardous
562119	Waste (except solid and hazardous) collection services
562119	Waste (except solid and hazardous) hauling, local
562112	Waste collection services, hazardous
562111	Waste collection services, nonhazardous solid
221320	Waste collection, treatment, and disposal through a sewer system
562213	Waste disposal combustors or incinerators, nonhazardous solid
562211	Waste disposal facilities, hazardous
562212	Waste disposal landfills, nonhazardous solid
234990	Waste disposal plant construction
484220	Waste hauling, hazardous, local
484230	Waste hauling, hazardous, long-distance
562112	Waste hauling, local, hazardous
562111	Waste hauling, local, nonhazardous solid
484220	Waste hauling, nonhazardous, local
484230	Waste hauling, nonhazardous, long-distance
924110	Waste management program administration
421930	Waste materials wholesaling
562920	Waste recovery facilities
562112	Waste transfer stations, hazardous
562111	Waste transfer stations, nonhazardous solid

Code	Description
562211	Waste treatment facilities, hazardous
562211	Waste treatment plants, hazardous
322214	Wastebaskets, fiber made from purchased paperboard
316993	Watch bands (except metal) manufacturing
339914	Watch bands, metal (except precious), manufacturing
339911	Watch bands, precious metal, manufacturing
335912	Watch batteries manufacturing
327215	Watch crystals made from purchased glass
326199	Watch crystals, plastics, manufacturing
334518	Watch jewels manufacturing
811490	Watch repair shops without retailing new watches
448310	Watch shops
334518	Watchcase manufacturing
334518	Watches and parts (except crystals) manufacturing
421940	Watches and parts wholesaling
333415	Water (i.e., drinking) coolers, mechanical, manufacturing
325412	Water (i.e., drinking) decontamination or purification tablets manufacturing
337124	Water bed frames, metal, manufacturing
337122	Water bed frames, wood, manufacturing
337910	Water bed mattresses manufacturing
327111	Water closet bowls, vitreous china, manufacturing
332998	Water closets, metal, manufacturing
339942	Water colors, artist's, manufacturing
561990	Water conditioning services
924110	Water control and quality program administration
421740	Water coolers, mechanical, wholesaling
221310	Water distribution (except irrigation)
221310	Water distribution for irrigation
221310	Water filtration plant operation
334512	Water heater controls manufacturing
811412	Water heater repair and maintenance services without retailing new water heaters
333319	Water heaters (except boilers), commercial-type, manufacturing
421720	Water heaters (except electric) wholesaling
335228	Water heaters (including nonelectric), household-type, manufacturing
421620	Water heaters, electric, wholesaling
326220	Water hoses, rubber or plastics, manufacturing
213111	Water intake well drilling, oil and gas field on a contract basis
334519	Water leak detectors manufacturing
234910	Water main and line construction
713110	Water parks, amusement
331511	Water pipe, cast iron, manufacturing
234990	Water power project construction
335211	Water pulsating devices, household-type electric, manufacturing
235110	Water pump construction contractors
333319	Water purification equipment manufacturing
334513	Water quality monitoring and control systems manufacturing
325510	Water repellent coatings for wood, concrete and masonry manufacturing
315228	Water resistant jackets and windbreakers, nontailored, men's and boys', cut and sewn from purchased fabric (except apparel contractors)

Code	Description
315239	Water resistant jackets and windbreakers, not tailored, women's, misses' and girls', cut and sewn from purchased fabric (except apparel contractors)
315228	Water resistant outerwear (except overcoats), men's and boys', cut and sewn from purchased fabric (except apparel contractors)
315239	Water resistant outerwear (except overcoats), women's, misses', and girls', cut and sewn from purchased fabric (except apparel contractors)
315291	Water resistant outerwear infants', cut and sewn from purchased fabric (except apparel contractors)
315212	Water resistant outerwear, women's, girls', and infants', cut and sew apparel contractors
315222	Water resistant overcoats, men's and boys', cut and sewn from purchased fabric (except apparel contractors)
315234	Water resistant overcoats, women's, misses', and girls', cut and sewn from purchased fabric (except apparel contractors)
315211	Water resistant, men's and boys', cut and sew apparel contractors
316211	Water shoes, plastics or plastics soled fabric upper, manufacturing
316211	Water shoes, rubber or rubber soled fabric upper, manufacturing
532292	Water ski rental
454390	Water softener service providers, direct selling
421720	Water softening and conditioning equipment wholesaling
422690	Water softening compounds wholesaling
333319	Water softening equipment manufacturing
561990	Water softening services
445299	Water stores, bottled
221310	Water supply systems
235110	Water system balancing and testing construction contractors
332420	Water tanks, heavy gauge metal, manufacturing
483212	Water taxi services
332913	Water traps manufacturing
221310	Water treatment and distribution
333319	Water treatment equipment manufacturing
421830	Water treatment equipment, industrial, wholesaling
421850	Water treatment equipment, municipal, wholesaling
234990	Water treatment plant construction
221310	Water treatment plants
333611	Water turbines manufacturing
235810	Water well drilling (except oil or gas field water intake) construction contractors
333132	Water well drilling machinery manufacturing
312111	Water, artificially carbonated, manufacturing
422490	Water, bottled (except water treating), wholesaling
325998	Water, distilled, manufacturing
312111	Water, flavored, manufacturing
312112	Water, naturally carbonated, purifying and bottling
234910	Water, sewer, and pipeline construction management firms

Code	Description
315228	Water-repellent outerwear (except overcoats), men's and boys', cut and sewn from purchased fabric (except apparel contractors)
315239	Water-repellent outerwear (except overcoats), women's, misses', and girls', cut and sewn from purchased fabric (except apparel contractors)
315291	Water-repellent outerwear, infants', cut and sewn from purchased fabric (except apparel contractors)
315211	Water-repellent outerwear, men's and boys', cut and sew apparel contractors
315212	Water-repellent outerwear, women's, girls', and infants', cut and sew apparel contractors
315222	Water-repellent overcoats, men's and boys', cut and sewn from purchased fabric (except apparel contractors)
315234	Water-repellent overcoats, women's, misses', and girls', cut and sewn from purchased fabric (except apparel contractors)
712190	Waterfalls (i.e., natural wonder tourist attractions)
488310	Waterfront terminal operation (e.g., docks, piers, wharves)
326199	Watering cans, plastics, manufacturing
325611	Waterless hand soaps manufacturing
111219	Watermelon farming, field, bedding plant and seed production
334514	Watermeters, consumption registering, manufacturing
315999	Waterproof outerwear cut and sewn from purchased fabric (except apparel contractors)
315211	Waterproof outerwear, men's and boys', cut and sew apparel contractors
315999	Waterproof outerwear, rubberizing fabric and manufacturing outerwear
315212	Waterproof outerwear, women's, girls', and infants', cut and sew apparel contractors
313320	Waterproofing apparel, fabrics and textile products (e.g., oiling, rubberizing, waxing, varnishing)
235990	Waterproofing construction contractors
713990	Waterslides (i.e., amusement rides)
234990	Waterway construction
332911	Waterworks and municipal water system valves manufacturing
334515	Watt-hour and demand meters, combined, manufacturing
334515	Watt-hour and time switch meters, combined, manufacturing
334515	Watt-hour meters, electric, manufacturing
325191	Wattle extract manufacturing
334515	Wattmeters manufacturing
713940	Wave pools
334515	Waveform measuring and/or analyzing equipment manufacturing
339999	Wax figures (i.e., mannequins) manufacturing
712110	Wax museums
325612	Wax removers manufacturing
322222	Waxed paper for nonpackaging applications made from purchased paper
322221	Waxed paper for packaging applications made from purchased paper
422130	Waxed paper wholesaling
422690	Waxes (except petroleum) wholesaling

Code	Description
324199	Waxes, petroleum, made from refined petroleum
324110	Waxes, petroleum, made in petroleum refineries
325612	Waxes, polishing (e.g., floor, furniture), manufacturing
313320	Waxing purchased textiles and apparel
115114	Waxing, fruits or vegetables
112210	Weaning pig operations
336992	Weapons, self-propelled, manufacturing
541990	Weather forecasting services
924120	Weather research program administration
321918	Weather strip, wood, manufacturing
421330	Weather stripping wholesaling
334519	Weather tracking equipment manufacturing
333999	Weather vanes manufacturing
331422	Weatherproof wire or cable made from purchased copper in wire drawing plants
331319	Weatherproof wire or cable made in aluminum wire drawing plants
332321	Weatherstrip, metal, manufacturing
314999	Weatherstripping made from purchased textiles
313221	Weaving and finishing narrow fabrics
313210	Weaving and finishing of broadwoven fabrics (except rugs, tire fabric)
313210	Weaving broadwoven fabrics (except rugs, tire fabrics)
313210	Weaving broadwoven felts
313221	Weaving fabric less than 12 inches (30cm)
313210	Weaving fabrics more than 12 inches (30cm) in width
333292	Weaving machinery manufacturing
313221	Weaving narrow fabrics
314110	Weaving rugs, carpets, and mats
313221	Webbing weaving
321999	Webbing, cane, reed, and rattan, manufacturing
812990	Wedding chapels (except churches)
315212	Wedding dresses, women's, cut and sew apparel contractors
315233	Wedding dresses, women's, misses', and girls', cut and sewn from purchased fabric (except apparel contractors)
541921	Wedding photography services
812990	Wedding planning services
561730	Weed control and fertilizing services (except crop)
115112	Weed control services for crops
926140	Weed control, agriculture, government
333111	Weeding machines, farm-type, manufacturing
313241	Weft fabrics knitting
811219	Weighing equipment (e.g., balance, scales) repair and maintenance services
812191	Weight loss centers, non-medical
812191	Weight reducing centers, non-medical
713940	Weight training centers
541890	Welcoming services (i.e., advertising services)
331222	Welded iron or steel wire fabric made in wire drawing plants
339113	Welder's hoods manufacturing
316999	Welders' aprons, leather, manufacturing
316999	Welders' jackets, leggings, and sleeves, leather, manufacturing
333992	Welding equipment manufacturing
532412	Welding equipment rental or leasing
422690	Welding gases wholesaling

Code	Description
421830	Welding machinery and equipment wholesaling
333514	Welding positioners (i.e., jigs) manufacturing
811310	Welding repair services (e.g., automotive, general)
331491	Welding rod, uncoated, nonferrous metals (except aluminum, copper), made from purchased metals or scrap
421840	Welding supplies (except welding gases) wholesaling
333992	Welding wire or rods (i.e., coated, cored) manufacturing
235990	Welding, on site, construction contractors
332313	Weldments manufacturing
923130	Welfare administration, nonoperating
923130	Welfare programs administration
624190	Welfare service centers, multi-program
213112	Well casing running, cutting and pulling, oil and gas field on a contract basis
331210	Well casings (e.g., heavy riveted, lock joint, welded, wrought) made from purchased iron or steel
331111	Well casings, iron or steel, made in steel mills
213111	Well drilling (i.e., oil, gas, water intake wells) on a contract basis
532412	Well drilling machinery and equipment rental or leasing
333132	Well logging equipment manufacturing
213112	Well logging, oil and gas field, on a contract basis
213112	Well plugging, oil and gas field, on a contract basis
213112	Well pumping, oil and gas field, on a contract basis
213112	Well servicing, oil and gas field, on a contract basis
213112	Well surveying, oil and gas field, on a contract basis
332322	Wells, light, sheet metal, manufacturing
316110	Welting leather manufacturing
448140	Western wear stores
316110	Wet blues manufacturing
313230	Wet laid nonwoven fabrics manufacturing
322130	Wet machine board mills
311221	Wet milling corn and other vegetables
339920	Wet suits manufacturing
325613	Wetting agents manufacturing
487210	Whale watching excursions
234990	Wharf construction
100310	Wharf operation
311211	Wheat bran manufacturing
311230	Wheat breakfast cereal manufacturing
111140	Wheat farming, field and seed production
311211	Wheat flour manufacturing
311211	Wheat germ manufacturing
311213	Wheat malt manufacturing
334515	Wheatstone bridges (i.e., electrical measuring instruments) manufacturing
811118	Wheel alignment shops, automotive
532291	Wheel chair rental
334511	Wheel position indicators and transmitters, aircraft, manufacturing
332212	Wheel pullers, handtools, manufacturing
333924	Wheelbarrows manufacturing
339113	Wheelchairs manufacturing
421450	Wheelchairs wholesaling
336399	Wheels (i.e., rims), automotive, truck, and bus, manufacturing
327910	Wheels, abrasive, manufacturing

Wheels—Wire

Code	Description
331111	Wheels, car and locomotive, iron or steel, made in steel mills
421120	Wheels, motor vehicle, new, wholesaling
327910	Wheels, polishing and grinding, manufacturing
336330	Wheels, steering, automotive, truck, and bus, manufacturing
327910	Whetstones manufacturing
212399	Whetstones mining and/or beneficiating
311512	Whey butter manufacturing
311514	Whey, condensed, dried, evaporated, and powdered, manufacturing
311513	Whey, raw, liquid, manufacturing
311511	Whipped topping (except dry mix, frozen) manufacturing
311514	Whipped topping, dry mix, manufacturing
311412	Whipped topping, frozen, manufacturing
335211	Whippers, household-type electric, manufacturing
311511	Whipping cream manufacturing
316999	Whips, horse, manufacturing
316999	Whipstocks manufacturing
339113	Whirlpool baths (i.e., hydrotherapy equipment) manufacturing
421450	Whirlpool baths wholesaling
493190	Whiskey warehousing
325131	White extender pigments (e.g., barytes, blanc fixe, whiting) manufacturing
331528	White metal castings (except die-castings), unfinished, manufacturing
713990	White water rafting, recreational
235210	Whitewashing construction contractors
212312	Whiting crushed and broken stone, mining and/or beneficiating
114111	Whiting fishing
325131	Whiting manufacturing
334519	Whole body counters, nuclear, manufacturing
******	Wholesale — see type of product
561520	Wholesale tour operators
813910	Wholesalers' associations
337125	Wicker furniture (except upholstered), household-type, manufacturing
313221	Wicks manufacturing
334210	Wide area network communications equipment (e.g., bridges, gateways, routers) manufacturing
448150	Wig and hairpiece stores
422990	Wigs wholesaling
339999	Wigs, wiglets, toupees, hair pieces, manufacturing
712130	Wild animal parks
111199	Wild rice farming, field and seed production
721214	Wilderness camps
711510	Wildlife artists, independent
924120	Wildlife conservation agencies
813312	Wildlife preservation organizations
712190	Wildlife sanctuaries
212231	Willemite mining and/or beneficiating
337125	Willow furniture (except upholstered), household-type, manufacturing
321999	Willow ware (except furniture) manufacturing
333923	Winches manufacturing
421830	Winches wholesaling
924120	Wind and water erosion control agencies, government
334519	Wind direction indicators manufacturing
926130	Wind generated electrical power regulation

Code	Description
333611	Wind powered turbine generator sets manufacturing
333611	Wind turbines (i.e., windmill) manufacturing
315291	Windbreakers, infants', cut and sewn from purchased fabric (except apparel contractors)
315211	Windbreakers, men's and boys', cut and sew apparel contractors
315228	Windbreakers, men's and boys', cut and sewn from purchased fabric (except apparel contractors)
315212	Windbreakers, women's, girls', and infants', cut and sew apparel contractors
315239	Windbreakers, women's, misses', and girls', cut and sewn from purchased fabric (except apparel contractors)
333292	Winding machinery for textiles manufacturing
313112	Winding purchased yarn
313112	Winding, spooling, beaming and rewinding of purchased yarn
333611	Windmills, electric power, generation-type, manufacturing
333111	Windmills, farm-type, manufacturing
235510	Window and door construction contractors
325612	Window cleaning preparations manufacturing
561720	Window cleaning services
541890	Window dressing or trimming services, store
332321	Window frames and sash, metal, manufacturing
321911	Window frames and sash, wood and covered wood, manufacturing
332618	Window screening, woven, made from purchased wire
332321	Window screens, metal frame, manufacturing
321911	Window screens, wood framed, manufacturing
235990	Window shade installation construction contractors
811490	Window shade repair and maintenance shops
337920	Window shade rollers and fittings manufacturing
337920	Window shades (except awnings) manufacturing
421220	Window shades and blinds wholesaling
444190	Window stores
811122	Window tinting, automotive
442291	Window treatment stores
321918	Window trim, wood and covered wood moldings, manufacturing
321911	Window units, wood and covered wood, manufacturing
421310	Windows and window frames wholesaling
326199	Windows and window frames, plastics, manufacturing
321911	Windows, louver, wood, manufacturing
332321	Windows, metal, manufacturing
321911	Windows, wood and covered wood, manufacturing
336322	Windshield washer pumps, automotive, truck, and bus, manufacturing
336399	Windshield wiper blades and refills manufacturing
336322	Windshield wiper systems, automotive, truck, and bus, manufacturing
326199	Windshields, plastics, manufacturing
312130	Wine coolers manufacturing

Code	Description
422820	Wine coolers, alcoholic, wholesaling
445310	Wine shops, packaged
312130	Wineries
312130	Wines manufacturing
422820	Wines wholesaling
312130	Wines, cooking, manufacturing
325998	Wintergreen oil manufacturing
336399	Wipers, windshield, automotive, truck, and bus, manufacturing
313230	Wipes, nonwoven fabric, manufacturing
421840	Wiping cloths wholesaling
421510	Wire (except insulated) wholesaling
421510	Wire and cable (except electrical) wholesaling
333298	Wire and cable insulating machinery manufacturing
331222	Wire cages, iron or steel, made in wire drawing plants
331222	Wire carts (e.g., grocery, household, industrial), iron or steel, made in wire drawing plants
331422	Wire cloth made from purchased copper in wire drawing plants
331319	Wire cloth made in aluminum wire drawing plants
331422	Wire cloth, copper, made in integrated secondary smelting and drawing plants
331222	Wire cloth, iron or steel, made in wire drawing plants
331491	Wire cloth, nonferrous metals (except aluminum, copper), made from purchased metals or scrap
331222	Wire garment hangers, iron or steel, made in wire drawing plants
514110	Wire photo services
331111	Wire products, iron or steel, made in steel mills
331222	Wire products, iron or steel, made in wire drawing plants
421510	Wire rope (except insulated) wholesaling
333923	Wire rope hoists manufacturing
421510	Wire screening wholesaling
331319	Wire screening, aluminum, made in integrated secondary smelting and drawing plants
331491	Wire screening, nonferrous metals (except aluminum, copper), made from purchased nonferrous metals (except aluminum, copper) in wire drawing plants
561422	Wire services (i.e., telemarketing services), floral
514110	Wire services, news
331319	Wire, armored, made in aluminum wire drawing plants
331319	Wire, bare, made in aluminum wire drawing plants
331422	Wire, copper (except mechanical) (e.g., armored, bare, insulated), made from purchased copper in wire drawing plants
331422	Wire, copper (except mechanical) (e.g., armored, bare, insulated), made in integrated secondary smelting and drawing plants
331221	Wire, flat, rolled strip, made in cold rolling mills
331319	Wire, insulated, made in aluminum wire drawing plants
421610	Wire, insulated, wholesaling
331222	Wire, iron or steel (e.g., armored, bare, insulated), made in wire drawing plants

Code	Description
331421	Wire, mechanical, copper and copper alloy, made from purchased copper or in integrated secondary smelting and rolling, drawing or extruding plants
331491	Wire, nonferrous metals (except aluminum, copper), made from purchased nonferrous metals (except aluminum, copper) in wire drawing plants
331491	Wire, nonferrous metals (except aluminum, copper), made in integrated secondary smelting mills and wire drawing plants
513330	Wired telecommunication resellers
333518	Wiredrawing and fabricating machinery and equipment (except dies) manufacturing
333514	Wiredrawing and straightening dies manufacturing
513322	Wireless data communication carriers (except satellite)
513330	Wireless telecommunication resellers (except satellite)
513322	Wireless telephone communications carriers (except satellite)
213112	Wireline services, oil and gas field, on a contract basis
336322	Wiring harness and ignition sets for internal combustion engines manufacturing
421610	Wiring supplies wholesaling
325191	Witch hazel extract manufacturing
212299	Wolframite mining and/or beneficiating
212399	Wollastonite mining and/or beneficiating
422330	Women's and children's clothing accessories wholesaling
813410	Women's auxiliaries
923130	Women's bureaus
422330	Women's clothing wholesaling
813410	Women's clubs
624221	Women's shelters, battered
321213	Wood I-joists manufacturing
325191	Wood alcohol, natural, manufacturing
325199	Wood alcohol, synthetic, manufacturing
422990	Wood carvings wholesaling
113310	Wood chipping in the field
321113	Wood chips made in sawmills
332213	Wood cutting saw blades manufacturing
325191	Wood distillates manufacturing
321911	Wood door frames and sash manufacturing
333298	Wood drying kilns manufacturing
321114	Wood fence (i.e., pickets, poling, rails), treating
421310	Wood fencing wholesaling
325510	Wood fillers manufacturing
235520	Wood flooring construction contractors
321918	Wood flooring manufacturing
421310	Wood flooring wholesaling
321999	Wood flour manufacturing
337121	Wood framed furniture, upholstered, household-type, manufacturing
321999	Wood heel blocks manufacturing
321999	Wood heels, finished, manufacturing
321918	Wood moldings (e.g., pre-finished, unfinished), clear and finger joint, manufacturing
325191	Wood oils manufacturing
421990	Wood products (e.g., chips, posts, shavings, ties) wholesaling
321114	Wood products, creosoting purchased wood products
322110	Wood pulp manufacturing
422990	Wood pulp wholesaling

Code	Description
421310	Wood shingles wholesaling
321918	Wood shutters manufacturing
421310	Wood siding wholesaling
333414	Wood stoves manufacturing
422690	Wood treating preparations wholesaling
333210	Wood verneer laminating and gluing machines manufacturing
321911	Wood window frames and sash manufacturing
321999	Wood wool (excelsior) manufacturing
442299	Wood-burning stove stores
321999	Woodenware, kitchen and household, manufacturing
532412	Woodworking machinery and equipment rental or leasing
421830	Woodworking machinery wholesaling
333210	Woodworking machines (except handheld) manufacturing
333292	Wool and worsted finishing machinery manufacturing
313210	Wool fabrics, broadwoven, weaving
313221	Wool fabrics, narrow woven, weaving
313111	Wool spun yarn made from purchased fiber
313312	Wool tops and noils manufacturing
422590	Wool tops and noils wholesaling
314999	Wool waste processing
313112	Wool yarn, twisting or winding of purchased yarn
422590	Wool, raw, wholesaling
311941	Worcestershire sauce manufacturing
333313	Word processing equipment, dedicated, manufacturing
561410	Word processing services
624229	Work (sweat) equity home construction organizations
337127	Work benches manufacturing
812332	Work clothing and uniform supply services, industrial
422320	Work clothing, men's and boys', wholesaling
315211	Work coats and jackets, men's and boys', cut and sew apparel contractors
315225	Work coats and jackets, men's and boys', cut and sewn from purchased fabric (except apparel contractors)
624310	Work experience centers (i.e., sheltered workshops)
315191	Work gloves and mittens, knit, made in apparel knitting mills
315992	Work gloves, leather (except apparel contractors), manufacturing
315211	Work gloves, leather, men's and boys', cut and sew apparel contractors
315212	Work gloves, leather, women's and girls', cut and sew apparel contractors
315225	Work pants (except dungarees, jeans), men's and boys', cut and sewn from purchased fabric (except apparel contractors)
315211	Work pants, men's and boys', cut and sew apparel contractors
315211	Work shirts, men's and boys', cut and sew apparel contractors
315225	Work shirts, men's and boys', cut and sewn from purchased fabric (except apparel contractors)
316213	Work shoes, men's (except rubber or plastics protective footwear), manufacturing
721310	Workers' camps
525190	Workers' compensation insurance funds
923130	Workers' compensation program administration

Code	Description
721310	Workers' dormitories
213111	Workover of oil and gas wells on a contract basis
624310	Workshops for persons with disabilities
334111	Workstations, computer, manufacturing
928120	World Bank
813319	World peace and understanding advocacy organizations
112990	Worm production
422990	Worms wholesaling
313210	Worsted fabrics weaving
321999	Wrappers, excelsior, manufacturing
333993	Wrapping (i.e., packaging) machinery manufacturing
422130	Wrapping paper (except giftwrap) wholesaling
339999	Wreaths, artificial, manufacturing
488410	Wrecker services (i.e., towing services), motor vehicle
235940	Wrecking, buildings or other structures, construction contractors
332212	Wrenches, handtools, nonpowered, manufacturing
333991	Wrenches, impact, handheld power-driven, manufacturing
711219	Wrestlers, independent professional
711310	Wrestling event managers with facilities
711320	Wrestling event managers without facilities
711310	Wrestling event organizers with facilities
711320	Wrestling event organizers without facilities
711310	Wrestling event promoters with facilities
711320	Wrestling event promoters without facilities
711510	Writers of advertising copy, independent
711510	Writers, independent (freelance)
813410	Writing clubs
325998	Writing inks manufacturing
422120	Writing paper (except bulk) wholesaling
322233	Writing paper and envelopes, boxed sets, made from purchased paper
322121	Writing paper made in paper mills
322233	Writing paper, cut sheet, made from purchased paper
337124	Wrought iron furniture (except upholstered), household-type, manufacturing
332996	Wrought iron or steel pipe and tubing made from purchased metal pipe
331111	Wrought iron or steel pipe and tubing made in steel mills
212299	Wulfenite mining and/or beneficiating
212399	Wurtzite mining and/or beneficiating
334515	X-Y recorders (i.e., plotters (except computer peripheral equipment)) manufacturing
335110	X-mas tree light bulbs manufacturing
334517	X-ray apparatus and tubes (e.g., control, industrial, medical, research) manufacturing
325992	X-ray film and plates, sensitized, manufacturing
334517	X-ray generators manufacturing
541380	X-ray inspection services
334517	X-ray irradiation equipment manufacturing
621512	X-ray laboratories, medical or dental
421450	X-ray machines and parts, medical and dental, wholesaling
334517	X-ray tubes manufacturing
325320	Xanthone insecticides manufacturing
325110	Xylene made from refined petroleum or liquid hydrocarbons

Xylene—Zucchini

Code	Description
324110	Xylene made in petroleum refineries
339992	Xylophones and parts manufacturing
713930	Yacht basins
336612	Yacht building, not done in shipyards
713930	Yacht clubs with marinas
713990	Yacht clubs without marinas
532292	Yacht rental without crew
336611	Yachts built in shipyards
111219	Yam farming, field and seed production
335121	Yard Lights, residential electric, manufacturing
422310	Yard goods, textile (except burlap, felt), wholesaling
332212	Yardsticks, metal, manufacturing
321999	Yardsticks, wood, manufacturing
313111	Yarn spinning mills
313111	Yarn spun from purchased fiber
333292	Yarn texturizing machines manufacturing
313112	Yarn throwing, twisting, and winding of purchased yarn
313111	Yarn, carpet and rug, spun from purchased fiber
325221	Yarn, cellulosic filament, manufacturing
325221	Yarn, cellulosic filament, manufacturing and texturizing
327212	Yarn, fiberglass, made in glass making plants
325222	Yarn, noncellulosic fiber and filament, manufacturing
325222	Yarn, noncellulosic fiber and filament, manufacturing and texturizing
422990	Yarns wholesaling
511199	Yearbook publishers
511199	Yearbook publishers and printing combined
511199	Yearbook publishing (i.e., establishments known as publishers)
323112	Yearbooks flexographic printing without publishing
323111	Yearbooks gravure printing without publishing
323110	Yearbooks lithographic (offset) printing without publishing
323119	Yearbooks printing (except flexographic, gravure, lithographic, screen) without publishing
323113	Yearbooks screen printing without publishing
311999	Yeast manufacturing
422490	Yeast wholesaling
611699	Yoga instruction, camps, or schools
311511	Yogurt (except frozen) manufacturing
311514	Yogurt mix manufacturing
422430	Yogurt wholesaling
311520	Yogurt, frozen, manufacturing
111334	Youngberry farming
624110	Youth centers (except recreational only)
813410	Youth civic clubs
813410	Youth clubs (except recreational only)
813410	Youth farming organizations
624110	Youth guidance organizations
721199	Youth hostels
813410	Youth scouting organizations
624110	Youth self-help organizations
813410	Youth social clubs
713990	Youth sports leagues or teams
325222	Zein fibers and filaments manufacturing
325188	Zinc ammonium chloride manufacturing
331491	Zinc and zinc alloy bar, plate, pipe, rod, sheet, tubing, and wire made from purchased metals or scrap
325131	Zinc based pigments manufacturing
335912	Zinc carbon batteries manufacturing
331528	Zinc castings (except die-castings), unfinished, manufacturing
325188	Zinc chloride manufacturing
325188	Zinc compounds, not specified elsewhere by process, manufacturing
331522	Zinc die-castings, unfinished, manufacturing
331492	Zinc dust reclaiming
332999	Zinc foil and leaf not made in rolling mills
325188	Zinc hydrosulfite (i.e., zinc dithionite) manufacturing
212231	Zinc ore mine site development for own account
212231	Zinc ores mining and/or beneficiating
325188	Zinc oxide (except pigments) manufacturing
325412	Zinc oxide medicinal preparations manufacturing
331492	Zinc recovering from scrap and/or alloying purchased metals
331419	Zinc refining, primary
331491	Zinc rolling, drawing, or extruding purchased metals or scrap
325188	Zinc sulfide manufacturing
212231	Zinc-blende (sphalerite) mining and/or beneficiating
212231	Zincite mining and/or beneficiating
333298	Zipper making machinery manufacturing
313221	Zipper tape weaving
339993	Zippers (i.e., slide fasteners) manufacturing
422310	Zippers wholesaling
331491	Zirconium and zirconium alloy bar, rod, billet, sheet, strip, and tubing made from purchased metals or scrap
212299	Zirconium concentrates beneficiating
212299	Zirconium ores mining and/or beneficiating
331419	Zirconium refining, primary
331491	Zirconium rolling, drawing, or extruding purchased metals or scrap
339992	Zithers and parts manufacturing
925120	Zoning boards and commissions
712130	Zoological gardens
712130	Zoos
111219	Zucchini farming, field, bedding plant and seed production

HARRIS
INFOSOURCE™
Our Quality Enables Your Growth

About Using Business Information

w w w . h a r r i s i n f o . c o m

A Message from the CEO

For more than three decades, we have profiled American business establishments, enabling our customers to understand their best opportunities, reach the right companies and contact the appropriate decision-makers. When you think about it, the purpose of any information-based product is simply to help build your knowledge base and maximize your opportunity for making sales—enabling you to grow your top line, and enhance your return on investment.

Clearly, it all starts with the information. Tens of thousands of customers invest in our information products every year for one simple reason—because our accurate, in-depth and affordable data is the best overall value they've found anywhere, making us an essential part of their sales and marketing success.

It's our skill for matching the very best business information with state-of-the-art technology—across a wide variety of product options—that makes us truly unique in our industry. The entire Harris InfoSource product line has been engineered so you get the exact information you need in the medium you want, for the geographic area you are targeting.

Very often, finding the right information product for your specific needs becomes overly confusing because so many data providers sound the same. We have over 30 years of experience delivering business information to companies of every shape and size through a variety of easy-to-use technologies. Give us the opportunity to make a difference in your success, by fueling your sales and marketing machine with the very best information you'll find anywhere. We'll help you get to the right places and the right people—maximizing your top-line sales growth and your return on investment.

Our entire staff wishes you great success.

Dennis Abrahams, President/CEO

Business Info 101

Assessing the Value of Sales & Marketing Information

Knowing the source of the information you are going to be utilizing is the first step towards developing a successful sales and marketing campaign. Even the most creative, targeted direct mail piece won't work if it never reaches the right person.
It is important to know the answers to questions like:

- How accurate is the information?
- How often is it updated?
- Are you buying directly from the information source or from a reseller?

It is also important to have a clear idea of the type of information you need and to make sure that the information provider you choose can supply the appropriate data.

- Do you need the names of plant engineers or plant managers?
- Do you need to know how a company has changed over the last few years, or do you only need to know the company's current information?
- Do you need specific information, such as plant square footage, or do you just want basic mailing information?
- Do you need to build a detailed target customer profile?

About Harris

Harris InfoSource offers companies the opportunity to gain a competitive edge by making high-quality data available any time, anywhere. With our products, professionals can generate prospect lists, identify lucrative sales leads, analyze their markets accurately, and more.

We've been helping companies grow since 1971, providing the quality information companies need to fuel successful sales and marketing campaigns.

Our Information

Harris InfoSource is the nation's quality leader in researching, compiling, and providing business information for sales and marketing professionals. The Harris Core Database features more than 600,000 manufacturing and service establishments with multiple decision-makers for each company. This database is then segmented into an array of information products available on CD-ROM, online, and in print by geography and employment size.

The Harris Core Database is fueled by the high-quality information collected and updated by our three-tiered Editorial Department. The large Harris editorial team is responsible for researching and adding new listings to the database, calling existing company listings and updating the information already found in the core database.

Our Products

At Harris InfoSource, our understanding of how and why successful businesses use information allows us to provide data in a way that best fits the specific needs of our customers. Products range from Reference Directories for looking up customers one at a time to Selectory full-function databases that empower you with searching, sorting, printing, exporting, and customizing capabilities.

Selectory® Databases—available on CD-ROM and online—combine high-value information with powerful, yet easy-to-use technology. Users can search and sort by multiple fields of information, print and export data, hyperlink directly to company web sites and locate firms using MapBlast!® maps and more.

Reference Directories—available in print and on CD-ROM—are convenient, economical reference tools. Four cross-referenced sections allow users to easily find new customers in specific geographic areas or industries.

Custom Data Solutions is a service that allows users to receive the exact information they need in the format they prefer including Selectory CD-ROM databases, mailing labels, and ASCII telemarketing files. Immediate, free quotes are provided.

It's not about the Information Age, it's about the Age of your Information.

Your sales presentation may be perfect, but it also has to be delivered to the right person. Investments in sales and marketing campaigns rely on high quality information to make them worthwhile. Reaching the right decision-maker at the right time with the right pitch is instrumental to your success.

Strategic decisions based on penetration analysis will be compromised if the decision is based on an erroneous view of the market. A strategic plan based on an estimate of 10,000 potential customers will cost you dearly if the real number is closer to 3,000.

Some things to think about when trying to judge accuracy:

■ A database with many millions of records seems impressive, but may be littered with duplicates and inaccuracies.

■ Without stringent quality checks, duplicate records can abound. They can come as multiple company names for one address (Super Mart and SuperMart), divisions being listed as separate companies, a company being listed for both its shipping address and its billing address, etc.

■ Duplicates mean extra printing and postage costs for mail campaigns, wasted time by salespeople, and misguided strategic decisions.

At Harris InfoSource, we double and triple check records to eliminate duplicates. Our record count is within 95 percent of County Business Patterns as generated by the U.S. Census Bureau, ensuring our precision. Old information is often bad information.

And information gets old fast. In fact...

■ Over 25 percent of the decision-makers in a company change every year. If you use data that's two years old to do a mailing to 10,000 decision-makers in companies, you are likely to reach less than 5,500 of them.

■ Each year, about 40 percent of area codes, phone numbers and other basic company contact information changes.

■ In any given year, about 11 percent of all businesses have been added or have gone out of business that year.

At Harris InfoSource, we phone verify all new records. If we don't have phone verification, the information does not go into our product. We update our existing information continuously with phone and fax verification and put all our company profiles through a rigorous verification process.

Know Your Source

Compiler vs. Reseller—Are you buying company information from the people that collected it, or from a reseller? Many information providers are simply providers, not researchers.

Things to know about resellers:

■ They buy information from many sources, put it all together, and sell it. This may seem harmless, but it often results in a huge liability—old information.

■ Because the information comes from many different sources, there can be large inconsistencies between the depth and breadth of the information they provide.

■ Primary researchers usually won't release brand new information for resale, so the information you get from resellers is generally at least six months old, which often means many accuracy problems.

Harris InfoSource is a compiler. Because we don't rely on other companies to supply us with information, we are able to maintain strict control over the way the information is compiled and presented. This quality control allows you to be confident that you are getting the most up-to-date information available.

Information Breadth and Depth—How much can your source provide?

You probably have a good idea about the characteristics of your best customers and prospects. Make sure that the information provider you choose has deep enough information that you can really zoom in on your best prospects.

■ If you sell a highly specialized product, there's a good chance that your best customers are highly specialized as well. If your provider only has very basic company information, you may not be able to pinpoint those companies and end up buying information you don't need.

■ Think about the value of discovering 1,000 new prospects that have characteristics identical to your best customers. You can only do that if your information source has the necessary fields of information to compare them.

■ Who are you trying to reach? What is that person's title? Their name? Many information companies only have the CEO listed as a contact person. This is important information, but the CEO is often not the person who is going to make the initial decision to purchase your product or service. Make sure that the information you purchase contains the name of the person with whom you should be in contact.

We provide multiple contacts per company at no extra charge, listing the people you need to get to, from engineering, to sales, to purchasing, to IT. We also provide NAICS codes, Product Categories, Plant Square Footage, Employment Change percent, Fleet Size, and more.

With up to 35 fields of information per record, you'll find the criteria you need to target your market in the Harris Infosource company records. Experian credit scores are available for Selectory CD-ROM products.

What can you do with Business Information?

Business information is the lifeblood of growth and success. Acquiring good prospecting and marketplace information and putting it to good use is a necessity of all successful sales and marketing professionals.

Generate Leads
Give your inside or outside sales reps pre-qualified sales leads to enhance selling productivity.

Direct Mail
Compile a targeted list of prospects for a successful direct mail campaign.

Research
Estimate the size of the market using industry information. Determine the characteristics of your customers and put together a best-customer profile to use for future research. Find out how many companies you're competing against and get in-depth information about their businesses.

Motivate Independent Reps
Motivate and command the attention of your rep groups by providing them with leads of companies that are likely to buy or use your product or service.

Telemarketing
Directly feed your telemarketing system with qualified prospects.

Territory Management
Populate sales territories with prospects in order to get an accurate view of territory sales potential, and realign your territories based on complete market information.

Market Penetration Analysis
Compare current sales within an industry or in a region to the market potential of that industry to determine penetration.

All Leads Are Not Created Equal

It is important to trust your prospecting source and to be confident that the information you acquire is accurate and complete. In addition to increasing sales, good leads save time and money by allowing reps to spend more time selling and less time searching.

There are a number of indicators you should look for when trying to secure good leads.

A potentially good lead should be:

- **Pre-qualified**—There should be a strong likelihood of buying. This means the prospect conforms to your criteria for a good customer and has characteristics that make it a legitimate part of your target market.
- **Readily available**—A salesperson's talents lie in face-time, not research. Leads need to be found quickly so that reps can spend the majority of their time in front of customers.
- **Informative**—The lead should include the information necessary for effective knowledge-based selling. The lead should contain information on the appropriate decision-maker and product information needed for a personalized conversation.
- **Easily integrated**—A lead lacks value if it isn't in a salesperson's hands. A good lead needs to be quickly incorporated into the selling process (CRM or otherwise).

A quality source of business information will be able to address all of these issues. It will help you find pre-qualified leads, save time researching leads, and feed directly into your selling system—meaning more time in front of customers and more sales. It will allow your reps to track down top leads by NAICS or geographical location and provide them with the information they need for an effective sales conversation, including the appropriate decision-maker.

Business Info 101 Summary—
A Step-by-Step Approach

This is one example of a successful sales and marketing approach to the use of business information.

Step 1: Who are your customers?

Let's assume you have a customer database, but you don't know much about the characteristics of your customers. Where are they? What industries do they represent? What similarities do they have? What are their major differences? What is their demographic make-up?

In order to begin to discover the various similarities that exist within your customer base, you need to make sure that there's enough detailed information in your database to make an effective comparison. The first step is to match your customer records to a business information database and add key customer characteristics into your customer file, such as NAICS codes, product categories, number of employees.

A Harris InfoSource information consultant can help you do this with the Harris InfoSource business information database.

Once your customer file contains all this great information, you can build a profile of your best customers. A profile might be the combination of product categories, geographic locations, and company size categories of your most profitable or largest customer segment. Or it may be a unique characteristic that you discover by having comprehensive information about your customers.

Step 2: Where are the prospects that "look like" my best customers? How many are there?

You have identified the characteristics of companies that are interested in purchasing your products using the best source available...your own customer file. Using a Selectory Database, you can design a search to uncover prospects that have the same characteristics as your best customers (same industry, same size of company—whatever criteria you've established). You run your search, and you identify the "population of prospects"—the total pool of untapped potential. Classify the prospects by customer segment. For example, your number 1 segment might be manufacturers of blower fans and motors with less than 50 employees in Ohio, Wisconsin and Indiana. Your number 2 segment may be distributors of industrial equipment and machinery with 1-10 employees in Ohio.

Step 3: Determine your market penetration.

Market penetration works like this: You can use the sales information or employee size information from a business information database to derive an estimate of market size in dollars and develop market penetration statistics.

Scenario: If there are 2,000 manufacturers of blower fans and motors with less than 50 employees in Ohio, Wisconsin and Indiana (your #1 customer segment, as defined by you), and you sell 200 of them, then you have a 10 percent (200/2000) penetration into the segment.

The only way to know that 2,000 target prospects exist in your market area is to bump it up against a business information database.

Step 4: Develop a direct mail campaign to the 1,800 prospects in your #1 customer segment in your geographic market area.

Use the award-winning software features of Harris' Selectory Database products to easily create a direct marketing campaign. Use the mailing label feature to create your labels or to export the selected records to another software program that creates your labels.

Step 5: Provide your sales force with these targeted prospects.

Take the 1,800 prospects you have identified as your key target segment and provide leads to your sales people, either in printed form, or import the data into your contact management system such as ACT!™, Outlook® or Goldmine®. Selectory allows you to do this effortlessly.

Step 6: Use mapping software to examine the locations of your sales force in comparison to the target customer accounts, and realign your sales territories accordingly.

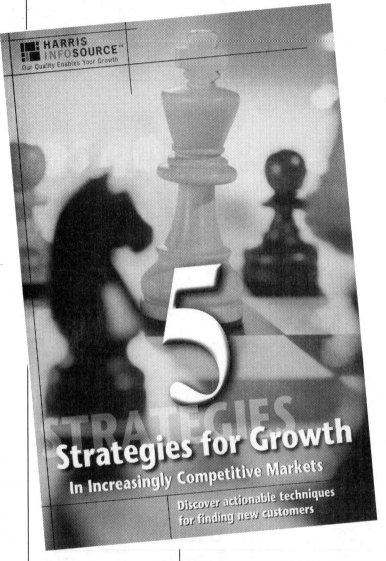